TimeOut

timeout.com/restaurants

GW00392613

)6

C

Features

EDITION **23**

RESTAURANTS

See page 28 for details of your 15% gastropub discount

CHEAP EATS

DRINKING

SHOPS & COURSES

MAPS & INDEXES

Unbiased reviews

The reviews in the *Time Out Eating & Drinking Guide* are based on the experiences of *Time Out* restaurant reviewers. Restaurants, bars and cafés are visited anonymously, and *Time Out* pays the bill. No payment of any kind has secured or influenced a review.

Oh, what a lovely year!

Guy Dimond takes a look at the openings, closings, movings and shakings in London's restaurant scene over the past 12 months.

Wizzy

The past year was a cracker, by all accounts. London has not merely been favourably compared to New York (the city most people consider to be the restaurant capital of the world), but was also described as 'the tastiest place on earth' by New York food connoisseurs. *Gourmet*, the world's leading food magazine (based in New York), ran a special issue on London in March 2005, summing up with: 'This is a city filled with chefs at the top of their powers… At this moment, London is the world's best place to eat.'

A few months later, that heady culinary optimism – not to mention the substantial number of culinary tourists that help keep our restaurant scene thriving – took a knock with the bomb attacks on London on 7 July. But the city carried on and braved the worst, just as it has always done. Tourist numbers dipped rather than dwindled, and restaurateurs can breathe a sigh of relief that Londoners still love eating out, more than ever before.

In fact, there has never been a better time to eat out, with quality rising across the board and value for money improving markedly in the mid-range. Here is our calendar of the year's most significant openings, as they happened.

2004

SEPTEMBER

Under starter's orders… and they're off! Gastropub the **Gun** (*see p112*), sister to the White Swan in the City, opens in a historic building overlooking the Thames on the Isle of Dogs. The critics are as impressed by the location and sensitive restoration of the building as they are by the straightforward British-oriented dishes. Local legend has it that Horatio Nelson used to raise his telescope to Lady Hamilton upstairs. Careful, madam, or you'll have his eye out.

OCTOBER

The Soho Hotel opens to a chorus of expense-account chip-and-pins in the media's heartland. Its **Refuel** bar/restaurant (*see p160*) instantly fills with well-groomed ad execs fresh off the production line. The restaurant side of things gets decent reviews, but it's the bar that, for a few moments at least, makes the Groucho Club seem so 1980s.

Oh, my, Amaya. We thought the height of Indian restaurant sophistication was chocolate samosas until Knightsbridge's **Amaya** (*see p131*) changed our minds. Here at last is a Modern Indian restaurant that's changed our preconceptions about Indian cooking, just as much as Nobu changed the way we felt about 'going for a Japanese'.

Those pioneering spirits of Borough Market, Spanish food stall Brindisa, open their first tapas bar next to the entrance to London's leading food market. It's packed from the first week. Hola, **Tapas Brindisa** (*see p260*).

NOVEMBER

With burgers, pizzas and potato crisps now available in gourmet versions, it had to happen – a gourmet fish and chip bar. Not the first of its type, granted, but we still think **Fish Club** (*see p308*) is the best. Little effort has been devoted to the interior or accoutrements; instead, all the love and care goes into the food: the freshest fish, the best chips, own-made pickled eggs. No fry-by-night operation, then.

DECEMBER

Conran's Bluebird project in Chelsea had always been been a mixed success. At last, Sir Terence gave up on trying to make the private room in the racing-car-themed behemoth pay its way, and opened the doors of the **Bluebird Dining Rooms** (*see p60*) to the public. He's also given his son Tom

Garden Café

Automat

The Ledbury

vroom to manouevre – well, sort of. It's still his dad's place, but Conran junior has done a great job, bringing in a talented chef (Mark Broadbent) and a menu of retro British dishes.

2005

JANUARY

The **Greyhound** (*see p109*) in Battersea didn't need to be rescued from the Dogs' Home, because it has pedigree written all over it. Sommelier Mark van der Goot has set up this gastropub with a fabulous wine list, and also had the sense to recruit a good chef, Tom Martinovic. A glass apart.

South African food might just be the next big thing. That's what they keep telling themselves in Cape Town, but it might also be true for London. **Chakalaka** (*see p121*), a modest and cheerful South African restaurant in Putney, certainly sets a good example with its easy-going mix of Afrikaner, Cape Malay and black African dishes. The rainbow nation's future is assured if they can mix as well as they can cook.

Not all the old banks and town halls turn into trendy wine bars. One former town hall has turned into **Shanghai Blues** (*see p70*), a trendy Chinese restaurant with an interior that gives a few nods to the influence that Alan Yau (Hakkasan, Yauatcha) has had on London's Chinese restaurants. Nice dim sum, and helpful staff too.

FEBRUARY

Turkish chain **Tas** is building an empire to rival the Ottomans. Among recent openings are a branch next to the British Museum (*see p272*), and a conversion of three railway arches into a bar, a restaurant and – our favourite – a deli specialising in Turkish produce, much of it organic.

Goodbye

We bid farewell to all the restaurants that have changed hands or turned in their lunch pail since the last edition. The following are just a small selection of the dearly departed.

Ashbells
A Notting Hill 'soul food' restaurant that was big on concept, but disappointing in the kitchen.

East@West
Celebrated Aussie chef and Christine Manfield packed up her tucker bag and headed back to Sydney.

Heartstone
A delightful organic brasserie in Camden. It breaks our heart to see it close.

Mandola
London's first, only, and last Sudanese restaurant; a Notting Hill institution.

C Notarianni & Sons
A charming Italian caff in Battersea. We'll miss the jukebox.

Osia
Brilliantly inventive and well-executed contemporary Australian food – but maybe Piccadilly Circus wasn't ready for the prices.

Otto Dining Lounge
Sleek modernism is out, and with it, restaurants designed like Scandinavian airport lounges. It's now French bar/restaurant **Graze** (*see p324*).

Putney Bridge
London's first purpose-built restaurant and bar for decades had a prime spot next to the Thames, but

Putney wouldn't pay the price for haute cuisine. It's now part of the **Thai Square** chain (*see p268*).

Santa Fe
When a wannabe chain restaurant brags about rolling out the concept, just see what happens.

Shumi
This pretentious Japanese-Italian turned Italian, then turned turtle. It still has the same Gstaad-set owners, and may reopen as Hush 2.

Southeast W9
Set up by revered cookery writer Vatcharin Bhumichitr, this pan-Asian restaurant finally ran out of steam.

Stanleys
No more S&M (sausage and mash) in this wonderfully designed space just north of Oxford Circus.

Thyme
The move from Clapham to Covent Garden wasn't a smart one for this Mod Euro restaurant: the exorbitant prices and lack of local loyalty discouraged repeat customers. Thyme, gentlemen, please.

Zilli 2
Aldo Zilli's chain has dramatic peaks and troughs (like his buddy Chris Evans' career). **Zilli Fish** (*see p87*) is still going strong.

Santa María del Buen Ayre

Zigni House

Amaya

MARCH

A parilla is an Argentinian-style barbecue, and **Santa María del Buen Ayre** (*see p43*) in Hackney is London's first. It's the real thing, complete with simple decor and chatty welcome. There's been a spate of new Ethiopean and Eritrean restaurants in the past few months, but **Zigni House** (*see p32*) in Islington deserves special mention for its buffet, budget prices and careful cooking.

APRIL

A low-key opening if ever there was one, Fitzrovia's little tapas bar/restaurant **Salt Yard** (*see p255*) was nonetheless quickly discovered by the critics, who all adored its high-quality Spanish and Italian-accented nibbles, plus its casual, friendly environment. Portuguese food gets a sudden awakening with the arrival of **Tugga** (*see p251*) in Chelsea, with 21st-century dishes created by a top chef from Oporto. It's an immediate hit with the locals.

Chef Christian Sandefeldt's long-awaited fish restaurant, **Deep** (*see p88*), opens to mixed reviews in Imperial Wharf, a new riverside development in Chelsea. Everyone loves the principled approach to using sustainable fish stocks; not everyone likes the location.

Park cafés have long been seen as one of the lowest forms of catering, but every now and then a new venue pops up to challenge the stereotype. This year it was the **Garden Café** (*see p298*) in Regent's Park; stylishly (re)designed, it offers great food, excellent drinks and friendly staff. No Wagon Wheels or 99s here, then.

It was the **Ledbury** (*see p97*) that really rocked the socks off the critics in spring. Run by the team behind the Square in Mayfair, it's brought a polish and professionalism that's never been seen before in Notting Hill. It's also brought Mayfair prices to a much less-salubrious neighbourhood –

but plenty of locals don't seem to mind paying for chef Brett Graham's outstanding Modern French dishes, or for the exemplary wine list and faultless service.

MAY

Thinking of changing Korea? So was chef Wizzy, when she left Nobu and Hakkasan, but she then decided to set up her own restaurant in Fulham – aptly called **Wizzy** (*see p202*). It's a little neighbourhood place, superficially nothing special, but the dishes she has reinvented from her native Korea are like nothing you'll have had before. Wizzy's definitely got Seoul.

There's been talk of a 'tea revival' for years, but no real evidence of it. **Tea Palace** (*see p301*) is therefore taking a chance, bringing fine teas to a beautiful, modern tearoom in Notting Hill. We love it – and wish them luck.

Borough Market is finally getting some good little restaurants nearby, including **Glas** (*see p121*), which serves traditional Swedish dishes in the form of a modern smörgåsbord. Simple, but good.

The national press were just getting over the media frenzy caused by the Ledbury when along comes another stunning restaurant to trump it. **Maze** (*see p128*) is run by Gordon Ramsay Holdings, but the Glasgwegian celebrity chef isn't there much. The chef is Jason Atherton, who has stamped his own style on the menu: lots of small plates, every one intriguing and extraordinary. The service is good, wine list superb and it's not as cheekily priced as you might expect from the Mayfair location.

JUNE

Alan Yau opened his third branch of **Busaba Eathai** (*see p265*) earlier in the year, close to Selfridges. But it was his sister Tina's restaurant that aroused more interest. Although her experience managing a Busaba outlet has clearly been ▶

It's your Wonderland

CANARY WHARF

More than 60 scrumptious cafés, tasty bars and delicious restaurants.
As sure as salmon is salmon... Oh the variety!   www.mycanarywharf.com

cafés & bars   arts & entertainment   events & offers   shops & restaurants

Hello

As the guide went to press, scores of new restaurant openings were planned. Dates are approximate, as are many other details.

SEPTEMBER 2005

Abingdon Road
11 Abingdon Road, W8.
The latest Modern British restaurant from Rebecca Mascarenhas, the creator of **Sonny's** (see p230) in Barnes.

Brew Wharf
Park Street, SE1.
Trevor Gulliver (of **St John** – see p55) is working with Alastair Hook (of Meantime Brewery) to create a spanking new microbrewery and pub on the edge of Borough Market.

Christopher's In The City
18 Creechurch Lane, EC3.
A second branch of the hugely successful Covent Garden **Christopher's** (see p36) is to open in the Square Mile. Expect refined Modern American dishes.

Comptoir Gascon
63 Charterhouse Street, EC1 (7608 0851).
The delicatessen associated with **Club Gascon** (see p92) will be adding 25 restaurant seats, while the deli itself is downsized.

Galvin
66 Baker Street, W1.
Talented chefs Chris Galvin (formerly of the Orrery and the Wolseley) and brother Jeff (former of L'Escargot) are setting up their own place, serving Modern French cooking.

The Glade
The former West Bar in the basement at **Sketch**

(see p129) is being converted into a daytime restaurant.

Icebar & Below Zero
29-33 Heddon Street, W1.
As part of its plan for global domination, Absolut Vodka is sponsoring a string of 'icebars' around the world, inspired by the Icehotel in Sweden. Yes, it really is lined with ice, and you'll need to wear a thermal suit to go in. Next door is Swedish-themed bar and restaurant, Below Zero.

Parlour at Sketch
What is currently the pâtisserie and tearoom (see p299) will turn into a bar, and only 'an element' of the pâtisserie will be kept during the day.

Le Relais de Venise
120 Marylebone Lane, W1.
A branch of a Parisian steakhouse with an ultra-basic menu: steak, frites, sauce.

Rhodes
The fine dining operation of Gary Rhodes's new British restaurant **Rhodes W1** (see p55) is set to open inside the Cumberland hotel.

The Terrace
Lincoln's Inn Fields, WC2.
Chef Patrick Williams, formerly of the Green in Cricklewood, is moving to the centre of town.

OCTOBER 2005

Awana
85 Sloane Avenue, SW3.
A branch of Victoria's Mango Tree, but with a Malaysian menu instead of a Thai one.

Bentley's
Swallow Street, W1.
Richard Corrigan of the **Lindsay House** (see p57) is the new proprietor of this long-established restaurant – which should blow some of the cobwebs out of the rafters when it reopens.

fish! kitchen
56-58 Coombe Road, Kingston upon Thames, Surrey.
Tony Allan, entrepreneur behind the **fish!** chain (see p89), has turned one of his wet fish shops into a posh chippie.

Imli
167 Wardour Street, W1.
A new Indian restaurant from the people behind upmarket **Tamarind** (see p133). Imli, incidentally, is Hindi for tamarind.

Ladurée
Harrods, Knightsbridge, SW1.
Famous for its fashionable macaroons in Paris (we're not making this up), a concession is opening inside Harrods.

Pied à Terre
34 Charlotte Street, W1 (7636 1178).
This highly regarded French haute cusine restaurant in Fitzrovia was devastated by a fire in 2004, but is to reopen after a complete rebuild.

3G
6 Little Portland Street, W1.
Not a type of mobile phone, but a predictably opulent new restaurant from that fun-loving threesome, **Les Trois Garçons** (see p101).

Veeraswamy
99 Regent Street, W1 (7734 1401).
This long-established Indian restaurant will reopen after

a two-month refurbishment, with a new look and menus.

NOVEMBER 2005

Brown's Hotel
Albemarle Street, W1 (7493 6020).
Not new, but extensively refurbished after Rocco Forte bought this Mayfair classic in 2003. The Grill will be the fine dining restaurant, but the hotel will also have a bar – and that legendary tearoom has been reinstated.

China Tang
The Dorchester, Park Lane, W1 (7629 8888).
Best-known for his Shanghai Tang clothes label, Hong Kong fashion designer David Tang is designing a new dim sum restaurant inside the Dorchester.

DECEMBER 2005

Yakitoria
A Japanese-themed restaurant in a new development next to Paddington.

2006

Gaia
Marlon Abela, the mystery millionaire behind a string of top restaurants including the **Greenhouse** (see p128) and **Umu** (see p186), plans to open a namesake of his Connecticut restaurant in Mayfair.

Scott's
20 Mount Street, W1.
This old-timer has changed hands more often than a grubby fiver, but its new owners are Caprice Holdings – **The Ivy** (see p223), **J Sheekey** (see p84), **Le Caprice** (see p227) and **Daphne's** (see p176) – so they're likely to reinvent it as a modern classic.

▶ incorporated into her own place – **Isarn** (see p271) – this Islington Thai restaurant is a feminised version of the Yau success story, with bookable tables and a less hurried feel.

US-themed diners in London have tended to go more for theme than dining, but not so at **Automat** (see p36) in Mayfair. The dishes are simple, comfort food, but served in a smart setting that the area's pinstripes just lap up.

JULY

Caramba! **Taqueria** (see p46) brought the Cool Chile Co to Notting Hill, with soft tortillas and a choice of toppings at low prices. At last, London has a Mexican restaurant to be proud of. Tom Kime's new take on flavour-combining, based on the Thai principle of hot, salty, sour and sweet, is put into

practice in **Food@The Muse** (see p161), his restaurant inside a part-time art gallery in Notting Hill. Not somewhere for the subtle palate.

Hornsey: not known as a restaurant destination. Until, that is, the **Pumphouse Dining Bar** (see p53) opened in a beautiful conversion of a Brunel-designed (you guessed it) pumphouse. It's run by the same people behind the Mosaica restaurants, who have already done much to improve north London's culinary reputation with their two other restaurants in Wood Green and Tottenham Hale.

A stealthy arrival for one of the West End's biggest openings of the year, **Rhodes W1** (see p55). Gary Rhodes is now running the ground-floor restaurant inside the Cumberland hotel at Marble Arch, feeding footsore tourists lashings of lovely British food.

SE Wonderful

Is there a greater success story in the London food world over the last decade than Borough Market? **Guy Dimond**, who pores over the market's past, present and future, doesn't think so.

ILLUSTRATION | Takako Okuma **PHOTOGRAPY** | Alys Tomlinson

O n Fridays and Saturdays, the top destination for London's food-lovers is unquestionably Borough Market. Each week, around 100 stalls sell a wide variety of foods, from the everyday to the exotic, to heaving crowds; best to arrive early to avoid the crush. Visitors can also munch on sizzling gourmet fast food, and sample cheeses or coffees in the fine food stores that surround the market.

Given such quality and variety, it's little wonder that the accolades keep rolling in. According to *Observer Food Monthly*, Borough Market is the best food market in the UK; it was also recently voted London's most popular tourist attraction in a poll on the VisitLondon website, and won a *Time Out* gong in 2003 as London's top market. It's even spawned *The Borough Market Book* (Civic), an intriguing picture book containing recipes, interviews and essays.

However, while the market itself dates back centuries, its current incarnation is a recent phenomenon. Borough Market in the 20th century was a wholesale fruit and veg operation, selling by quantity not quality; just a decade ago, the weekly retail fine foods market didn't exist. So how did Borough Market become so popular, and a genuine rival to the food markets of Paris?

POTTED HISTORY

A market appeared in or near the current site of Borough Market even before the Romans arrived; the location, on the south bank of an easily navigable section of the Thames and on the main southern route into early London, meant it thrived. By the time Aulus Plautus and his Roman legions invaded London in AD43, a market in the area we now call Borough was well established. No further records of the market exist for two centuries, but it seems probable that the Roman construction of London Bridge, with Borough on the southern shore, only bolstered its position.

A millennium after the Romans left, the market was still a major trading point for fish, grain and cattle. A series of royal charters passed by Edward III formalised the status of Borough Market during the 1400s; in these days, it sold livestock as well as all manner of other foodstuffs. However, the market began to annoy the City of London on the other side of the river, mostly because of the traffic it caused; it was recorded as having being responsible for 'great congestion' on London Bridge as early as 1276. Although the City of London Corporation successfully petitioned to have the place closed in 1755, a replacement market arose the next

year on a nearby four-and-a-half-acre site, just far enough from the main road to ease congestion. It's on this site that Borough Market stands today.

The market survived the creation of the railways (London Bridge station was built in 1843), and even the construction of train lines directly overhead, because of its proximity to the river's wharves, which enabled it to sell exotic fruits and other lucrative foodstuffs during the Victorian era. By the 20th century, it had become a wholesale operation. However, containerisation during the 1970s posed a big threat, and a combination of economic factors and poor management saw the wholesale set-up in decline by the 1980s.

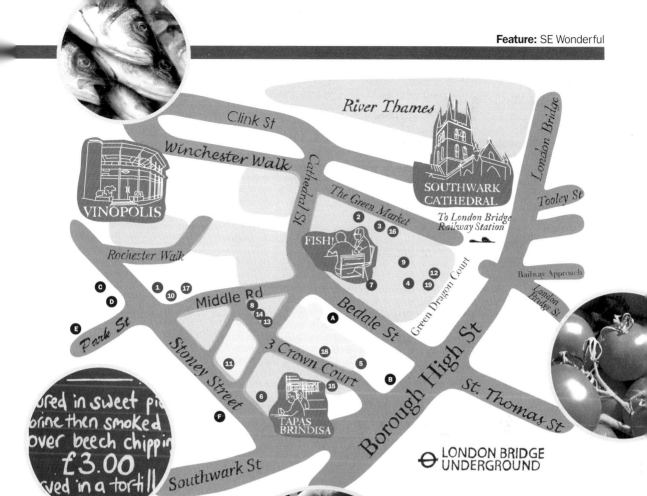

THE MODERN MARKET

The area's renaissance began in the early 1990s, after Brindisa, a Spanish fine foods importer and distributor, moved into a warehouse in nearby Park Street. Owner Monika Linton picks up the story.

'On a Saturday every three months, we'd invite age-old friends of the company to buy. Then, in 1997, Randolph Hodgson [owner of Neal's Yard Dairy] moved into what had been a wine bar on Park Street, and suggested that we do open days at the same time and merge our mailing lists. We felt we needed some fruit and veg there too, so we spoke to Fred Foster of Turnips, a wholesaler at the market, and he agreed to do retail. We got a lot of people coming.'

Such events began to put Borough Market back on the map, but the Food Lovers' Fair, held in November 1998, was perhaps the main catalyst to its resurgence. The organisers invited food producers from across the UK to sell their wares at Borough and attracted large numbers of both visitors and sellers. Linton again:

'We already had a cage in the market that we used just as extra storage, but it was the first time the market trustees had leased a space to a non-traditional wholesaler. After the Food Lovers' Fair, we sold from this stall on Saturdays every three months. One of our team at the time, Leila McAlister, managed the stall and sold from it, and also invented our now-famous hot chorizo roll. She made the stall look very appealing, and people would come to see what was going on. The three of us – Brindisa, Neal's Yard Dairy, and Turnips – set up a selection committee to vet the applications for Saturday stalls at Borough Market, with Neal's Yard doing most of the admin. It took off slowly, but within a year the fine foods market was also opening on Fridays.'

Subsequently, the market was registered as a charity in 1999, and is now administered by 21 trustees, who 'own' the land on which the market is located (along with many of the buildings facing it) and have actively encouraged the market's fine foods retail element. Some stallholders have been there virtually since the start, while others maintain their pitch for a few months before handing it back to the trustees. Finding a specific stall can be a bit tricky, as some stalls change their pitch location from a Friday to a Saturday. But wandering aimlessly and discovering things you'd never dream of looking for is a large part of the fun. It couldn't be more different from the weekly supermarket dash.

Borough Market

8 Southwark Steet (between Borough High Street, Stoney Street, Winchester Walk and Bedale Street), SE1 1TL (7407 1002/www.boroughmarket.org.uk). London Bridge tube/rail. **Open** *noon-6pm Fri; 9am-4pm Sat. Some stalls also open on Thur.*

▶

► SHOPS

Bedales
*5 Bedale Street, SE1 9AL (7403 8853/
www.bedalestreet.com).* **Open** 11am-
8.30pm Mon-Thur; 11am-9pm Fri; 9am-
8pm Sat. **Credit** AmEx, MC, V.
A good wine shop and bar in the heart of
the market. Check online for details of the
regular wine tastings.

De Gustibus
*4 Southwark Street, SE1 1TQ (7407 3625/
www.degustibus.co.uk).* **Open** 7am-5pm
Mon-Fri; 7am-4pm Sat. **Credit** MC, V.
Dan de Gustibus makes excellent breads
following traditional methods, including
varieties from the US, Eastern Europe and
the UK. No flour improvers or emulsifiers
are used. *See also p344.*

Konditor & Cook
*10 Stoney Street, SE1 9AD (7407 5100/
www.konditorandcook.com).* **Open**
7.30am-6pm Mon-Fri; 8.30am-5pm Sat.
Credit AmEx, MC, V.
Fabulous cakes: dark chocolate, lemon
chiffon, coffee walnut, fun 'magic cakes'
(lettered or with messages) and dozens of
others, all top quality. *See also p305.*

Monmouth Coffee Company
*2 Park Street, SE1 (7645 3585/
www.monmouthcoffee.co.uk).* **Open**
7.30am-6pm Mon-Sat. **Credit** MC, V.
An awe-inspiring selection of prime-quality
coffees, plus cakes and other nibbles, and
a great place to sit down and mull over
how good life is. The original outlet is in
Covent Garden (*see p358*).

Neal's Yard Dairy
*6 Park Street, SE1 9AB (7645 3554/
www.nealsyarddairy.co.uk).* **Open**
9am-6.30pm Mon-Fri; 9am-4pm
Sat. **Credit** MC, V.
This second branch of the
Covent Garden original (*see
p347*) is perhaps the best,
and best-loved, cheese shop in
the UK. The cheeses are British
or Irish, all sold in their prime; or
tasting is encouraged. You can also
buy yoghurt, crème fraîche, fromage
frais, butter and excellent oatcakes.

STALLS

**There are over 100 stalls at Borough
Market; here are some of our favourites.**

Brindisa ❶
7407 1036/www.brindisa.com.
A new location under the Floral Hall has
given this excellent Spanish food retailer
better storage. Nothing else has changed:
it still sells its famous bun with char-grilled
chorizo and olive oil-drizzled rocket.
Products to take home include amazing
charcuterie, as well as hams, rice and
paella pans. The outfit also has a new
tapas bar nearby, Tapas Brindisa (*see
p260*) and a shop in Exmouth Market.

Brown & Forrest ❷
01458 250875/www.smokedeel.co.uk.
Smoked meat, game, fish and cheese
from a family-run smokery in Somerset.

Chegworth Valley Juice ❸
01622 859272/www.chegworthvalley.com.
Best-known for its delicious apple juices
(several types, mostly varietal), Chegworth
also makes pear juices and blends such as
apple and rhubarb. There's also an organic
juice, made from sweet russet apples.

Cool Chile Co ❹
0870 902 1145/www.coolchile.co.uk.
Top-quality dried chillies in a mind-boggling
variety of types. You can also buy fresh
corn tortillas and Oaxacan-style chocolate.

Elsey & Bent ❻
7407 1166.
Rare and unusual vegetables, such as
colourful chards and a spectrum of
interesting salad leaves.

Flour Power City ❼
8691 2288/www.flourpowercity.com.
Matt Jones and his team create excellent
handmade organic loaves, from pain au
levain to flavoured breads such as walnut
and apricot. The chocolate brownies and
banana cake are also excellent.

Furness ❽
7378 8899.
Line-caught fish, shellfish such as razor
clams, wild venison, and furred and
feathered game in season.

Gamston Wood Ostriches ❾
*01777 838858/www.gamstonwood
ostriches.co.uk.*
Ostrich meat – lean and more like red
meat than poultry – taken from birds
raised in exotic Nottinghamshire. The
takeaway ostrich burgers are very popular.

Ginger Pig ❿
7403 4721.
Like many of the best stalls at Borough
Market, this butcher has smarter
permament premises (*see p352*). But
the market stall, now under the Floral Hall,
still sells quality pork, free-range ham,
dry-cured bacon, and sausages and beef
from grass-fed cattle.

L Booth Ltd ⓫
7378 8666.
Anthony Booth sells unusual mushrooms in
season, plus other high-quality fruit and veg.

London Honey Company ⓬
7771 9152/www.beesplease.co.uk.
Jill Mead and Steve Benbow have hives
in London, so this is about as local as
your food can get.

Mid-Devon Fallow ⓭
01837 810028.
Venison is good for you: low in fat, and not
nearly as gamey as you might expect. Mid-
Devon Fallow sells venison from fallow deer,
one of the UK's four indigenous species.

Northfield Farm ⓮
01664 474271/www.northfieldfarm.com.
This farm in Rutland, as it says itself,
'produces premium quality beef, lamb and
pork which has been naturally reared, has
lived well and has been humanely killed'.
As recommended by Hugh Fearnley-
Whittingstall, Nigel Slater and others.

Scandelicious ⓰
01728 452880/www.scandelicious.co.uk.
Run by expat Swede Anna Mosesson,
this is the place for Swedish fish, gravlax,
smoked eel, spiced herrings, Swedish
meatballs and other Scandinavian products.
In 2005 Anna opened Glas restaurant
(*see p121*) next to Borough Market.

Sillfield Farm ⓱
015395 67609/www.sillfield.co.uk.
As seen on *Jamie's Kitchen*,
Peter Gott's farm in
Cumbria keeps free-
range wild boar, rare-
breed pigs, Herdwick
sheep and pedigree
poultry. His stall
sells dry-cured
meats, sausages,
fresh wild boar
and cheeses.

Topolski
7729 9789.
Since spring 2005
Leila McAlister and
her team have been
selling five types of
Polish sausage, plus
pickled cucumbers and
horeseradish. Look out too for
plum jam and poppyseed cakes.
Less specialised goods are also available
at Leila's permanent shop (*see p348*).

Turnips ⓲
7357 8356.
Another good place for interesting
vegetables, such as Italian treviso (a type
of radicchio). Not cheap, but the quality
is usually high.

Wyndham House Poultry ⓳
7403 4788.
A poultry specialist rearing and selling
birds that have never seen a battery farm,
such as Label Anglais chickens.

JAMUNA
RESTAURANT & BAR

Upmarket Indian food comes to Paddington
Long regarded as a culinary desert, Paddington has now been given a bright shining star in the guise of a newly launched fine dining Indian restaurant, Jamuna.

At the helm of Jamuna's kitchen is Oberoi trained head chef Jasbinder Singh, who has previously worked at such renowned establishments as the Cinnamon Club and Mint Leaf. Singh's cooking, driven by the freshest, quality ingredients, combines the best of tradition and modernity, culminating in flavours which are both subtle and captivating.

38A Southwick Street, Paddington London W2 1JQ

Tel: 020 7723 5056   Fax: 020 7706 1870

Head Chef: Jasbinder Singh   Seating Capacity: 50

Opening Times: Lunch 12 noon – 2.30pm Dinner 6pm – 11pm Daily

• All major credit cards accepted • Private hire • Fully air-conditioned •
• Nearest stations: Paddington and Edgware Road •

www.jamuna.co.uk

Bottling out

Do you know how much you're paying for a bottle of wine in a restaurant compared to an off-licence? **James Aufenast** investigates the murky world of mark-ups.

PHOTOGRAPHY I Kang Kim

London is one of the most expensive places in the world to drink wine. Paris has a wealth of brasseries that list well-priced, mid-range Bordeaux, Burgundy and Rhône wines; Spain and Italy are even cheaper; and Australia is better priced still. But in the UK's capital, on average, a bottle of wine in a restaurant will cost nearly three times as much as it would in a shop – often more, in fact. Some wines cost over six times as much when you're dining out. Would you spend £36 on a bottle of Jacob's Creek merlot?

'There's some rapacious pricing in London,' says Neil Beckett, editor of *Fine Wine* magazine. 'I don't eat out that much precisely because of what a decent bottle costs. It's a shame, because there are some great places, but you just end up paying through the nose. Mostly, I stay at home and inflict a burnt sausage on people.'

For example, a 2001 Côtes du Rhône from Guigal costs £8.49 from Oddbins. Drink it in a restaurant and you'll pay £30 – over three times the Oddbins' price. That's what this very basic, more or less mass-produced bottle from a large producer in the south-east of France costs at the **Ritz** (*see p129*) on Piccadilly. The Ritz, however, isn't alone in imposing such steep mark-ups.

Other fine dining restaurants, such as Gordon Ramsay's **Angela Hartnett at The Connaught** (*see p127*) and the **Greenhouse** in Mayfair (*see p128*), the **Capital** (*see p126*) in Knightsbridge and **Tom Aikens** (*see p130*) in South Kensington, mark up way beyond what is reasonable. Corinne Michot, head sommelier at Angela Hartnett,

explains her average mark-up of nearly three and a half: 'If I list a wine under £100 our guests think there's something wrong with it. "If it's not expensive enough, it's not going to be any good," is their attitude. As it happens, my prices are no worse than other restaurants in Mayfair.'

Nigel Platts-Martin's group of restaurants – some of the most acclaimed in London, including the **Square** (*see p129*) in Mayfair, **Chez Bruce** (*see p99*) in Wandsworth, **La Trompette** (*see p97*) in Chiswick and the **Glasshouse** (*see p237*) in Kew – used to have a reputation for quite low mark-ups, but that's no longer the case. Dawn Davies, head sommelier at Platts-Martin's latest venture, French restaurant the **Ledbury** (*see p97*) in Notting Hill, says her mark-ups are justified – including one by a factor of four on a South African red wine, Flagstone's 2003 Cellarhand Backchat, priced at £19.50.

'I start by multiplying wine in the middle of the list by three and go up or down from there. That's normal for London, it's what you need to make a profit,' she says. 'Yes, I multiply some [wines] by four, but the 1982 Château Latour isn't even multiplied by one. You can't buy it from a wholesaler for that money.' However, few of us would want to splash out £650 on Latour just to experience its low mark-up. Usually, regional France offers a good refuge for people who can't afford expensive Bordeaux or Burgundy, but Pacherence du Vic-Bilh Sec, by Domaine Berthoumieu, in south-west France, costs three times the wholesale price at the Ledbury.

WHY ARE COSTS SO HIGH?

So are these prices justified? Many restaurateurs would say yes – because of the cost of running a restaurant in central London. 'Someone complained when I was serving a bottle to them at [restaurant] Kensington Place that they could get it much cheaper round the corner,' says Brett Woonton, soon to set up a new wine bar, Vinoteca, in Smithfield. 'So I said, fine, buy it and then pay me for the table when you sit down, the glass you drink it in, and give me some money for the rent and rates that we have to cover as well.'

Few restaurateurs would advocate that their staff be as blunt as this, but many would agree with the sentiment. Add in the cost of breakages, staffing, repairs, phones, stationery, printing, PR and advertising, gas, electricity and water charges, accountants, flowers, insurance and cleaning – and you can see why many try to find ways of increasing turnover. Even refuse collection is a big cost. In Westminster, restaurants pay around £1,000 a month for rubbish removal. Credit card charges, at 2% of turnover, are equally sizeable.

'Some wines cost over six times as much when you're dining out.'

Yet it seems wrong that wine has to bear the brunt of a restaurant's costs. Admittedly, food is marked up significantly too, often by a multiple of three. However, says Martin Lam, owner of Modern European restaurant Ransome's Dock, this is with good reason: 'The labour costs of making even a simple chicken dish soon add up. You buy a bird for £6.50, say, and portion it out, then make money on each part, but it has to pass through two or three people's hands. Paying a sommelier, storing a wine, having a cooling cabinet to keep it at the right temperature and glassware – all cost, but it's nothing like what you spend in a kitchen.'

Shipping and duty on wine is also more expensive in the UK than in France, Italy, Spain and Australia. These countries have large indigenous wine industries and so restaurants don't bring in so many wines from overseas. Furthermore, the whole process of importing wine tends to favour British supermarkets sourcing branded wines, rather than restaurants bringing in smaller, more individual producers. Transporting wine in bulk, whether it comes from France, Australia, South Africa or Chile, costs the least because it travels in huge containers. Wines from unusual parts of Spain and Italy have to be driven by lorry, passing through tolls and consuming petrol. So it's not the distance, but the amount of wine being shipped that counts.

Still, the overall cost of shipping on a case of wine – around £2 for a major brand, £4 for a lesser-known label – doesn't account for the increases currently operational in London. If food received the same treatment as wine, no one would eat out. 'Restaurants can't mark up a steak as much as a bottle of Mouton Rothschild,' says Bill Baker, owner of Bristol-based supplier Reid Wines, 'or they'd be empty within days.' Baker is probably right, but the current situation means there's a huge pricing imbalance in a meal; wine is so expensive that it costs too much to buy the right wine to match the food. Reid thinks there's a need for a change of attitude: 'The customer is as much to blame as the restaurateur. He or she is making an offer; people don't have to accept it.'

THE HOUSE EDGE

So what are diners to do – apart from moaning? First, don't buy that old fall-back, the house wine. This is an area where many restaurateurs pretty much pluck a figure from the air, sit back and rub their hands. Say you pay £16 for a bottle of house wine in a London restaurant. That would cost the restaurateur about £3 from a supplier. The supplier takes a 20 to 30 per cent margin, so he/she would have paid just over £2. After duty and shipping costs of £1.50, 50p is paid to the winemaker. Then there's the labelling and bottling, about 20p per bottle. So the actual wine would have cost 30p to make. It's impossible to make good wine at this price – and bear in mind that some house wines are marked up by a factor of six in London.

'When I was choosing house wine, it was a question of finding something with a bit of oak, and some semblance of fruit,' admits Nick Tarayan, who used to buy wine for a London restaurant and now runs Wine of the Times, which supplies wines to restaurants. 'And it was important to make sure it didn't give people heartburn.'

As well as house wine, many bottles priced at a lower level should be avoided. A bottle of 2004 d'Arenberg the Hermit Crab marsanne/viognier from Australia costs £25 at **Hakkasan** (*see p69*) – but £7.99 at Oddbins. At the **Ivy** (*see p223*), 2000 Marqués de Riscal Rioja Reserva is £31. Compare this with £9.99 at Majestic. Both wines are marked up more than three times the retail price.

Pizza restaurant **Rocket** (*see p310*) in Mayfair commendably adds £10 to the price of every wine, but it's a freak operation. In fact, every pizza restaurant should be able to offer good-value wines in this fashion because of the relatively low production cost of pizza and pasta dishes – but they don't. Usually, cash sums (rather than percentages) are only lumped on at a certain price point, around £60-£100 per bottle – out of reach of most pizzerias.

Matt Skinner, sommelier and wine buyer at **Fifteen** (*see p179*), was shocked by the mark-ups when he first arrived in London from Australia. He thinks adding a cash margin above a ceiling of £50 is the right approach. 'As a restaurant you might take less of a percentage profit,' he says, 'but you'd ultimately make more money, because people would buy your more expensive bottles. The way it is now, people just stick with the safe option. Wine is such an intimidating subject and people are already concerned with how much they're spending, so what they drink is the first to suffer.'

Expensive wines don't necessarily equate to excellent value, however. According to *Fine Wine* magazine's Beckett, 'Some people will have wines just so people can say, "Oh, it's ▶

ALYS TOMLINSON

▶ the most fantastic wine list – it's got 1900 Margaux." The sommelier doesn't really want to sell the wine, so gives it the most ridiculously high price; then, if someone is stupid enough to buy it, they make a vast profit.' A good example of this is a 1870 Château Lafite costing £11,750 at the Greenhouse. More forgivable are those places that mark-up certain wines absurdly, while also providing bottles that are within the reach of most people. Gordon Ramsay (see p130) in Chelsea is one such, offering premium-priced top Bordeaux with plenty of age, but also drinkable wines from the south of France at under £20.

CHOOSE CAREFULLY

Some wines cost a lot for the restaurateur to buy in the first place, so will inevitably be expensive. This applies to the classic French wine regions: Burgundy, Bordeaux, Champagne and parts of the Rhône. It's best to avoid these, as well as cult, fashionable wines from the New World such as Seña from Chile and Penfolds Grange from Australia; big-name wines such as Ornellaia and Sassicaia in Italy; and expensive bottles from the Ribera del Duero and Priorat regions in Spain. They're perfectly good wines, but aimed more at speculators to make a profit on, rather than for people to actually drink with a meal.

Wines from world-famous regions – such as Sancerre, Pouilly-Fumé, Pouilly-Fuissé and Chablis – may cost less, but they can also represent bad value because sommeliers get bored with people ordering the same old wines. Therefore they deliberately price them high, to encourage people to be more adventurous – which could be seen as a laudable approach, in a fashion. Kate Thal – now owner of wine shop-cum-bar **Green & Blue** (see p336) – used to be a buyer for various London restaurants, and still devises lists for the Athenaeum Hotel in Mayfair. 'I put a lower mark-up on something more obscure in order to sell more of it, and make that up with a higher price for a well-known name such as Sancerre,' she says. Thal contrasts this with 'the large hotel groups, who just don't price intelligently. They'll mark up wines that sell and wines that don't sell by over four times, regardless.'

So it's better go for wines and grapes that are not particularly fashionable, but which nonetheless taste delicious. *See below* **Good-value picks** for suggestions.

And ask the advice of the sommelier. Sommeliers tend to have a bad name because people think they only exist to increase diners' spend on wine. Partly that's the case, but a good sommelier should be helpful rather than aggressive. According to Julee Resendez, who buys wine for Aquavit restaurant in New York, 'A lot of people dismiss us when we offer help, but a good sommelier will give a customer three options. One wine at the price they've pointed to, one that's cheaper and one that's more expensive'. Bill Baker of Reid Wines agrees. 'Sommeliers can be very dangerous,' he says, 'but use them well and you won't overspend. People should be more imaginative; tell them that you want a wine to go with your lamb, and that you don't want it to cost more than £25. What can they do then?'

WINE LISTS THAT SHINE

If it's too much bother trying to negotiate the hazards of a wine list – with or without a sommelier – there are some excellent restaurants in London that offer good-value drinking across the board. **Andrew Edmunds** (Modern European, *see p227*) in Soho, **Le Colombier** (French, *see p97*) in Chelsea, **Ransome's Dock** (Modern European, *see p233*) in Battersea, **RSJ** on the South Bank (French, *see p100*) and the **Terrace** (Modern European, *see p229*) in Kensington – all have low mark-ups. A good example is a Morton Estate 2003 sauvignon blanc from New Zealand, which costs £18.50 at Andrew Edmunds – just one and a half times the off-licence price.

Mid-range Italian restaurants also offer well-priced wines, thanks to the close relationship between Italian restaurants and suppliers. **Enoteca Turi** (*see p177*) in Putney, **Metrogusto** (*see p180*) in Islington and **Riva** (*see p176*) in Barnes all have great choice and minimal mark-ups.

As Martin Lam of Ransome's Dock says, 'Costs don't have to affect wine to the extent that they do. All that bleating about central London rents and rates is just a lot of nonsense.'

Good-value picks

Choose an unfashionable grape or a lesser-known region, and you can get away with paying as little as £25 for a good wine. Here are some reliable options.

GRAPES
● **riesling** from Germany
● **grüner veltliner** from Austria
● **sauvignon blanc** from South Africa
● **chardonnay** from Casablanca and Leyda in Chile
● **primitivo** and **negroamaro** from southern Italy
● **grenache** (called **cannonau**) from Sardinia
● **albarino** from Galicia in Spain

REGIONS
● Portugal: non-fortified wines from the **Douro** region
● Italy: **Campania** and the **Val d'Aosta**
● France: **Cairanne**, **Rasteau** and **Costières de Nîmes** in the Rhône and Gaillac, **St Véran** or **Viré-Clessé** in Burgundy, plus the **Côtes du Frontannais** in the south of France
● Spain: **Castilla y León** and **Málaga**

Party on

Arranging a party, large or small, can be a daunting task. Top party planner and caterer to the stars **Lorna Wing** outlines the six essential elements you need to consider.

The more planning you can do for a party the better. And whether your event is in a restaurant, a stately home or the local Scout hut, you'll still need to ask yourself five essential questions: why, when, where, who and what sort of party you want. Each decision will have an impact upon another, and ultimately help you determine your budget.

BUDGET

Different parties require different budgets, so think carefully about the type of event you want to hold as this will inevitably have cost implications. The many variables will have an impact on how you end up spending your money.

The least expensive way to entertain is to have a drinks party, because the food, equipment hire and number of staff required will be considerably less than that of a seated meal. The more choice of food or drink you offer, the more it's going to cost. If you want to keep prices down, remember that less is always best.

Decide what your priorities are, and where you wish to allocate your budget. For some, it's the venue or amazing food or out-of-season blooms. For others, champagne rather than sparkling wine is a must.

VENUE

The entertaining space you choose depends entirely on the kind of party you're giving, as well as the number of guests, the time of year and the budget. Picking a suitable location is probably the biggest initial hurdle to overcome – popular places get booked up months in advance. There's a huge array of venues available, from stylish galleries and village halls, to historic houses and glamorous hotels. Look for them in the 'Yellow Pages', call the National Trust, peruse the newspapers and glossy mags, phone your favourite restaurant, consult dedicated venue guides or go online – www.squaremeal.co.uk is a great site for London venues, and offers helpful virtual tours of many locations.

Your decision about where to go will depend on availability, size and decor. Most venues have rules about what you can and cannot do. Some will accommodate your every need, allowing you to take in your favourite caterer and florist, and letting guests drink, smoke and dance to their hearts' content. But restrictions at others will determine whether you want to hold your party there; for example, many museums and historic houses have very specific rules about their buildings and how they are used by outsiders. In such circumstances, you'll generally have to choose the caterer, lighting people, florist and entertainers from an approved list.

EQUIPMENT HIRE

Numerous companies hire equipment – tables, chairs, china, glassware, tablecloths and mobile kitchens, including ovens, fridges and freezers – from the very mundane to the extremely elaborate. If you're working with a caterer, they will have their tried-and-tested favourites – so it's best to let them get on with organising it all. If you do want to do it yourself, one of the best outfits is **Jones Hire** (24 Creekside, SE8 3DZ, 8320 0600, www.joneshire.co.uk).

▶

► **FOOD**

When it comes to thinking about the food, there are a few fairly logical ground rules about good menu planning:
– Have a varied mix of ingredients, including fish and meat, dairy products, pasta, rice or grains, plus some fruit and vegetables.
– Try not to repeat ingredients in the same menu. Don't serve chicken twice, for example, in a canapé topping and again in a salad.
– Have a contrast of textures: soft and crisp, as well as smooth and rough.
– Include a good spectrum of colours, from pale and interesting, to bold and bright.
– You won't want to have the entire range of the following flavours in one menu, but try to get a balance of sweet versus sour, savoury or bitter, salty or sharp, as well as smoky and flowery.

DRINKS

The drinks, of course, deserve as much attention as the food. The following quantities are a useful guideline.

A bottle of champagne or sparkling wine will yield six glasses, while a bottle of wine will yield only five. For a two-hour drinks party, if the only other drinks you're serving are mineral water and soft drinks, allow three glasses per person. As an aperitif before dinner, allow one and a half glasses of champagne/sparkling wine per person; at a wedding allow a single glass each to toast the happy couple. At drinks parties, white wine is usually more popular than red, so have two-thirds white to one-third red. For lunches and dinners, depending upon the menu, allow each guest two glasses of white and one and a half glasses of red.

A standard bottle of spirits will give about 16 single measures. If spirits or cocktails are the only drinks being served at a party, allow three servings per person. A bottle of liqueur will deliver about 15 glasses for an after-dinner drink, and most people will only want a single glass.

Don't forget to supply non-alcoholic drinks too. Provide a litre bottle of mineral water for every four guests at a two-hour drinks party, and a bottle between three for a seated meal. For soft drinks, a glass per guest will do.

At the end of a party, always ask to do an empty and full bottle count with the caterer to check that quantities marry up with the original amounts, and to make sure that nothing has inadvertently 'walked'.

HIRING EXPERTS

Some large-scale parties need to be treated like a military exercise. This is where caterers, restaurateurs and party planners really come into their own, since they can guide you through entertaining's potential minefields.

Do tell the organiser your true budget – everything hinges on it. Good events organisers will advise you where your money is best spent, and where you can cut costs by doing some of it yourself. They're excellent at lateral thinking, so don't be too rigid about a particular format for your event if you're on a limited budget.

Arrange for three estimates from reputable companies. And confirm, or otherwise, as soon as you can. For large events, once you've agreed everything, ask to taste the food

Checklist

Here's a quick reminder of everything you need to consider when organising a party. Some points only apply to small events, while others are particular to large parties.

● Decide what type of party you want to hold : seated, standing, formal, informal, large or small.
● Determine your budget.
● Compile your guest list.
● Set the date.
● Choose and book the venue.
● Get quotes for caterers/restaurateurs, tents, equipment hire, florists, mobile loos, musicians, dancefloors, lighting, power supplies, mobile air-conditioning and heaters.
● Send out the invitations – but only once you know you can do what you want, where you want and within your budget. Keep a record of acceptances and any special dietary needs.
● Choose the menu (remembering guests with dietary concerns).
● Choose the drinks.
● Have a food and drinks tasting with the caterer/restaurateur.
● Choose all the other services: florists, musicians and so on.
● If having a seated party, get menus and place cards written or printed, and do a table plan.
● Then it's time to hand over to the experts, so you can... party!

and wine that you'll be having, and also to see a table completely laid, with flowers too. Be prepared to be charged if you don't proceed after a tasting.

The following London-based caterers and party planners all have a wealth of experience and can help organise a memorable event.

The Admirable Crichton
5 Camberwell Trading Estate, Denmark Road, SE5 9LB (7326 3800/ www.admirable-crichton.co.uk). **Open** phone enquiries 9am-6pm Mon-Fri.
AC is slick and sophisticated, just like its stunning parties. It organises events in all sorts of exotic locations from Marrakech to Moscow, but is still happy to do bangers and mash in a barn.

De Wintons
Unit 4, Sleaford Street, SW8 5AB (7627 5550/www.dewintons.co.uk). **Open** phone enquiries 8am-7pm Mon-Fri.
De Wintons has a range of delectable canapé, buffet, lunch, dinner party and breakfast menus to tempt and inspire. It can organise set designers, tableware and bar staff to mix the perfect cocktail.

Food Show
22-23 Hackford Walk, Hackford Road, SW9 0QT (7793 1877/ www.foodshow.org.uk). **Open** phone enquiries 8am-6pm Mon-Fri.
An incredibly helpful outfit, Food Show can take care of lighting and luxury loos, and everything else in between: venues, marquees, stylish food and wonderful wines, and the entertainment.

Last Supper
Lazer Building, Lazer Road, King's Cross Goods Yard, off York Way, N1 0UZ (7837 1977/www.lastsupperltd.co.uk). **Open** phone enquiries 9.30am-5.30pm Mon-Fri.
Witty, creative and approachable, Last Supper offers different party styles, from contemporary and minimal, through glamorous and chic, to rustic. Staff are professional and friendly.

Mustard Catering
Unit 5, 1-3 Brixton Road, SW9 6DE (7840 5900/www.mustardcatering.com). **Open** phone enquiries 9am-5.30pm Mon-Fri.
Mustard has arranged every conceivable type of party – from bar mitzvahs to brunches, and society weddings to summer soirées for the great and the good. Renowned for its professionalism, impeccable service and attention to detail.

● **Lorna Wing** is a food writer and food consultant, who for 20 years had a catering company organising thousands of parties: small ones, large ones, glamorous ones and cosy ones, for the rich and famous, and for those who were neither. Her book *Party!* (Conran Octopus, available only from Amazon) is a practical step-by-step guide to planning a party, and a helpful source of ideas, inspiration and menus.

AWARDS 2005
Eating & Drinking

Rounding up the capital's most impressive new restaurants, gastropubs and bars, *Time Out* honoured the very best in ten categories in its 16th annual awards.

Here at *Time Out* we're proud of our reputation for championing the best of London's eating and drinking places. Not just those with the grandest credentials, either, but the little places too, the ones you're not likely to read about anywhere else, that are, in their own field, exceptional. This is the ethos behind our broad coverage of London's gastronomic delights – from weekly reviews in *Time Out* London magazine to our numerous guides. And this is why our annual Eating & Drinking Awards take in not only London's restaurant élite, but also representatives from neighbourhood restaurants, gastropubs and bargain eateries as recommended by *Time Out* readers and selected by *Time Out* judges.

With a fresh crop of new reviews appearing each week in *Time Out* magazine (and on our website), the list of potential candidates can seem dauntingly long, so when the time comes for us to assess and hand out the awards for the year's most impressive new openings, we turn to our readers for help.

The first stage begins in the early summer. In the weekly magazine, we ask you to nominate your favourite bars, pubs and restaurants in several categories. These categories, which vary each year, reflect the diverse needs and tastes of London's diners and drinkers. In 2005 they covered: the best new restaurant; the top spot to take the family; where to eat the city's best vegetarian meal; the pick of local eateries; top-of-the-range gastropubs; the best bar; the slickest design; the best bargain eats; and – new this year – the best burger bar; and the finest alfresco dining spot.

Once the mailbags are nice and full, we embark on stage two. This involves drawing up a series of shortlists based on your recommendations and the views of our independent (and strictly anonymous) reviewers. Since our reviewers visit every establishment as normal paying punters (we never accept PR invitations or freebies of any kind), a consensus of opinion soon emerges.

The results were announced on 29 September 2005 in a glittering ceremony at **Pearl Bar & Restaurant** (*see p126*) – which also is pictured on the cover of this guide.

AND THE
WINNERS ARE...

BEST ALFRESCO DINING
Winner
Petersham Nurseries Café (Cafés) *See p306.*
Runners-up
Le Coq d'Argent (French) *See p91.*
Curve (North American) *See p41.*
Garden Café (Cafés) *See p298.*
Inn The Park (British) *See p56.*

BEST BAR
Winner
Shochu Lounge *See p320.*
Runners-up
Anam *See p327.*
Big Chill Bar *See p325.*
Floridita (also Latin American) *See p44 and p322.*
Graze *See p324.*

BEST BURGER BAR
Winner
Haché *See p296.*
Runners-up
Fine Burger Co *See p296.*
Gourmet Burger Kitchen *See p295.*
Hamburger Union *See p292.*
Ultimate Burger *See p292.*

BEST CHEAP EATS
Winner
Fish Club (Fish & Chips) *See p308.*
Runners-up
Abeno Too (Japanese) *See p181.*
Isarn (Thai) *See p271.*
Ottolenghi (International) *See p165.*
Santa María del Buen Ayre (Latin American) *See p43.*

BEST DESIGN
Winner
Inn The Park (British) *See p56.*
Runners-up
Cocoon (Oriental, Bars) *See p245 and p322.*
Le Cercle (French) *See p91.*
Patara (Thai) *See p265.*
Roka (Japanese) *See p182.*

Maze

Fish Club

Gracelands

kindly supported by

Gordon's

BEST FAMILY RESTAURANT
Winner
Gracelands (Cafés) *See p306.*
Runners-up
Crumpet (Cafés) *See p304.*
Eddie Catz (Cafés) *See p303.*
Tas (Turkish) *See p272.*
Tootsies Grill (North American) *See p39.*

BEST GASTROPUB
Winner
Gun *See p112.*
Runners-up
Bull *See p115.*
Greyhound *See p109.*
Pig's Ear *See p110.*
Princess *See p112.*

BEST LOCAL RESTAURANT
Winner
Chez Kristof (French) *See p97.*
Runners-up
Bistrotheque (French) *See p100.*
The Farm (Modern European) *See p232.*
Morel (Modern European) *See p233.*
Wizzy (Korean) *See p202.*

BEST VEGETARIAN MEAL
Winner
Noura Central (Middle Eastern) *See p215.*
Runners-up
Kathiyawadi (Indian) *See p153.*
Little Earth Café (Vegetarian) *See p285.*
Mangosteen (Oriental) *See p248.*
Salt Yard (Spanish) *See p255.*

BEST NEW RESTAURANT
Winner
Maze (Hotels & Haute Cuisine) *See p128.*
Runners-up
Amaya (Indian) *See p131.*
Bluebird Dining Rooms (British) *See p60.*
The Food Room (French) *See p99.*
The Ledbury (French) *See p97.*

This year's judges: Jessica Cargill-Thompson, Peterjon Cresswell, Claire Fogg, Roopa Gulati, Sarah Guy, Ronnie Haydon, Tom Lamont, Sam Le Quesne, Cath Phillips, Gordon Thomson.

Where to...

For more suggestions, see the **Subject Index**, starting on p394.

SPOT A CELEB

Bar Italia Cafés p300

Le Caprice Modern European p227

Le Gavroche Hotels & Haute Cuisine p128

Gordon Ramsay Hotels & Haute Cuisine p130

Joe Allen The Americas p35

The Ivy Modern European p223

Locanda Locatelli Italian p171

Mr Chow Chinese p70

Nobu Japanese p185

The River Café Italian p173

San Lorenzo Italian p168

J Sheekey Fish p85

Shepherd's British p59

Sketch: The Lecture Room Hotels & Haute Cuisine p129

The Wolseley Modern European p226

Zilli Fish Fish p87

Zuma Japanese p183

ENJOY THE VIEW

Babylon Modern European p229

Blueprint Café Modern European p235

Butlers Wharf Chop House British p61

Le Coq d'Argent French p91

Gun Gastropubs p112

Oxo Tower Restaurant, Bar & Brasserie Modern European p234

Le Pont de la Tour Modern European p236

The Portrait Restaurant Modern European p228

Rhodes Twenty Four British p54

Searcy's Modern European p219

The Tenth Eating & Entertainment p342

Thai Square Thai p268

Top Floor at Peter Jones Brasseries p51

Top Floor at Smiths British p55

Vertigo 42 Eating & Entertainment p342

TAKE A DATE

Almeida French p102

Andrew Edmunds Modern European p227

Aurora Modern European p219

L'Aventure French p102

Café du Marché French p92

Le Caprice Modern European p227

Chez Bruce French p99

Club Gascon French p92

Fino Spanish p255

Julie's Wine Bars p335

Kettners Pizza & Pasta p310

Lightship Ten International p163

Lindsay House British p57

Mango Room African & Caribbean p35

Momo North African p238

Odette's Modern European p237

Orrery Modern European p225

La Poule au Pot French p91

Potemkin East European p83

Quo Vadis Italian p172

The River Café Italian p173

J Sheekey Fish p85

Sugar Hut Thai p268

Les Trois Garçons French p101

La Trompette French p97

La Trouvaille French p96

Villandry Modern European p225

Zetter Italian p166

LOVE THE LOOK

Amaya Indian p131

Asia de Cuba International p159

Baltic East European p83

Benares Indian p132

Le Cercle French p91

Cinnamon Club Indian p136

Cocoon Oriental p245

Crazy Bear Oriental p244

Criterion French p95

Hakkasan Chinese p69

Inc Bar & Restaurant Modern European p234

Inn The Park British p56

Loungelover Bars p327

MVH International p161

Patara Thai p265

Pearl Bar & Restaurant Hotels & Haute Cuisine p126

E Pellicci Budget p294

Pumphouse Dining Bar Brasseries p53

Roka Japanese p182

Shanghai Blues Chinese p70

Sketch: The Gallery Modern European p226

Sketch: The Lecture Room Hotels & Haute Cuisine p129

Smersh Bars p327

Tamarind Indian p133

Trailer Happiness Bars p325

Les Trois Garçons French p101

Wapping Food Modern European p236

Wódka East European p81

Yauatcha Chinese p72

Zuma Japanese p183 ▶

"Good Evening" from *Gordon's*®

Apéritif derives from the Latin word aperititivium meaning 'opener' and whether you're going French and fancy an apéritif or Italian and want an apertivo, this before dinner drink has been enjoyed the world over for centuries.

GORDON'S® believe it's time to reinvigorate apéritif culture into our culinary habits. This is because an apéritif is not only the perfect way to whet the appetite but is also a national custom that endears civility and conviviality by deliberately setting apart time to share a drink and to socialise.

Woven into the fabric of daily home life, of public and private celebrations, and of café and restaurant culture, an apéritif is more than a drink before a meal. The thirty minutes which family, friends, acquaintances and colleagues make a transition from work to world while sipping a **GORDON'S**® Gin and Tonic are welcome moments to be savoured.

What's more the apéritif's purpose is to stimulate the appetite which juniper is particularly effective at doing. And because **GORDON'S**® uses more juniper than any other gin it makes it a great apéritif.

So when you next go for dinner, why not take some time out to order a **GORDON'S**® G&T and enjoy the perfect start to your evening.

THE COLOURFUL GIN

DRINKAWARE.CO.UK

The Cinnamon Club
Re-writing the rulebook

The Old Westminster Library
30-32 Great Smith Street
Westminster
London SW1P 3BU

Tel: 0845 165 8302
Fax: 020 7222 1333
Email: info@cinnamonclub.com
Website: www.cinnamonclub.com

▶ DO BRUNCH

Brunch is offered Sat and Sun, unless stated otherwise. *See also* **Cafés** and **Brasseries**.

The Avenue (Sun) *Modern European p227*

Bank Aldwych *Modern European p222*

Bermondsey Kitchen *Modern European p234*

Bluebird *Modern European p230*

Butlers Wharf Chop House *British p61*

Cantaloupe *Mediterranean p211*

Canyon *The Americas p41*

Christopher's *The Americas p35*

Cru Restaurant, Bar & Deli *Modern European p236*

The Fifth Floor (Sun) *Modern European p223*

Indigo *Modern European p223*

Joe Allen *The Americas p35*

Lundum's (daily) *Global p121*

Notting Grill *British p60*

Penk's (Sat) *International p165*

Ransome's Dock (Sun) *Modern European p233*

Rapscallion *International p163*

Rivington Bar & Grill (Sun) *British p61*

Sam's Brasserie & Bar *Modern European p228*

The Sequel *International p163*

Terminus Bar & Grill *Modern European p221*

Wapping Food *Modern European p236*

Zetter *Italian p166*

TAKE THE KIDS

See also **Cafés**, **Brasseries**, **Fish & Chips**, **Pizza & Pasta**.

Babes 'n' Burgers *Budget p295*

Benihana *Japanese p193*

Blue Elephant *Thai p268*

Blue Kangaroo *Brasseries p50*

Boiled Egg & Soldiers *Cafés p304*

Bush Garden Café *Cafés p303*

Crumpet *Cafés p304*

The Depot *Brasseries p50*

Dexter's Grill *The Americas p40*

Eddie Catz *Cafés p303*

fish! *Fish p89*

Frizzante@ City Farm *Cafés p305*

La Galette *French p95*

Giraffe *Brasseries p53*

Gracelands *Cafés p306*

Inn The Park *British p56*

Marine Ices *Budget p296*

Nando's *Portuguese p252*

Planet Hollywood *The Americas p41*

Rainforest Café *Eating & Entertainment p342*

Smollensky's on the Strand *The Americas p36*

Tas *Turkish p272*

Tootsies Grill *The Americas p39*

Victoria *Gastropubs p110*

Wagamama *Oriental p243*

FIND THE UNFAMILIAR

See also **Global**.

Ali Baba *Middle Eastern p214*

Archipelago *International p158*

Esarn Kheaw *Thai p267*

Fish Hoek *Fish p87*

Hunan *Chinese p62*

Little Earth Café *Vegetarian p285*

MVH *International p161*

Nahm *Thai p263*

Portal *Modern European p222*

Providores & Tapa Room *International p159*

Rong Cheng *Chinese p69*

St John *British p55*

Sichuan Restaurant *Chinese p73*

Stein's *Budget p297*

DINE ALFRESCO

See also p302 **Park cafés**.

Le Coq d'Argent *French p91*

Curve *The Americas p41*

Garden Café *Cafés p298*

The Gaucho Grill *The Americas p43*

Gun *Gastropubs p112*

Inn The Park *British p56*

Petersham Nurseries Café *Cafés p306*

Royal China Docklands *Chinese p74*

EAT LATE

See also **Eating & Entertainment**.

Balans *Brasseries p49*

The Bar & Grill *The Americas p35*

Bar Italia *Cafés p300*

Brick Lane Beigel Bake *Jewish p198*

Café Bohème *Brasseries p49*

Circus *Modern European p227*

Fish in a Tie *Budget p295*

Flaming Nora *Budget p297*

Harlem *The Americas p37*

Istanbul Iskembecisi *Turkish p276*

Mangal II *Turkish p276*

Maoz *Budget p293*

Le Mercury *Budget p297*

Meze Mangal *Turkish p275*

PJ's Grill *The Americas p36*

Sariyer Balik *Turkish p278*

Tinseltown *Eating & Entertainment p342*

Vingt-Quatre *Eating & Entertainment p342*

Published by
Time Out Guides Limited
Universal House
251 Tottenham Court Road
London W1T 7AB
Tel +44 (0)20 7813 3000
Fax +44 (0)20 7813 6001
email guides@timeout.com
www.timeout.com

Editorial
Editor Cath Phillips
Deputy Editor Phil Harriss
Consultant Editor Guy Dimond
Copy Editors Simon Coppock,
Will Fulford-Jones, Ros Sales
Researchers Jill Emeny, Cathy Limb,
Shane Armstrong
Proofer John Pym

Editorial/Managing Director
Peter Fiennes
Series Editor Sarah Guy
Deputy Series Editor Cath Phillips
Business Manager Gareth Garner
Guides Co-ordinator Holly Pick
Accountant Kemi Olufuwa

Design
Art Director Scott Moore
Art Editor Tracey Ridgewell
Designer Josephine Spencer
Junior Designer Pete Ward
Digital Imaging Dan Conway
Advertising Designer Jenni Prichard

Picture Desk
Picture Editor Jael Marschner
Deputy Picture Editor Tracey Kerrigan
Picture Researcher Helen McFarland

Advertising
Sales Director & Sponsorship
Mark Phillips
Sales Manager Alison Wallen
Advertising Sales Ben Holt, Matthew
Salandy, Jason Trotman
Advertising Assistant Lucy Butler
Copy Controller Amy Nelson

Marketing
Marketing Director Mandy Martinez
Marketing & Publicity Manager, US
Rosella Albanese
Marketing Designer Simeon Greenaway

Production
Production Director Mark Lamond
Production Controller Marie Howell

Time Out Group
Chairman Tony Elliott
Managing Director Mike Hardwick
Group Financial Director
Richard Waterlow
Group Commercial Director Lesley Gill
Group General Manager
Nichola Coulthard
Group Art Director John Oakey
Online Managing Director David Pepper
Group Production Director Steve Proctor
Group IT Director Simon Chappell
Group Circulation Director
Jim Heinemann

Sections in this guide were written by
African & Caribbean Fiona McAuslan, Nana Ocran, Sejal Sukhadwala; **The Americas** (North American) Christi Daugherty; (Latin American) Christi Daugherty, Chris Moss, Jenni Muir; **Brasseries** Will Fulford-Jones, Ronnie Haydon, Susan Low, Patrick Marmion, Lesley McCave, Nick Rider, Ethel Rimmer, Pete Watts; **British** Roopa Gulati, Ruth Jarvis, Sam Le Quesne, Patrick Marmion, Lesley McCave, Nick Rider, Ethel Rimmer; **Chinese** Fuchsia Dunlop, Guy Dimond, Ian Fenn, Phil Harriss, Tim Luard; **East European** Janet Zmroczek; **Fish** Terry Durack, Jan Fuscoe, Sarah Guy, Cath Phillips; **French** Tom Coveney, Simon Cropper, Jonathan Cox, Sarah Guy, Ruth Jarvis, Cath Phillips, Simon Tillotson; **Gastropubs** Kevin Ebbutt, Will Fulford-Jones, Jan Fuscoe, Sarah Guy, Ruth Jarvis, Patrick Marmion, Jenni Muir, Cath Phillips, Gordon Thomson; **Global** Susan Low; **Greek** Alexia Loundras; **Hotels & Haute Cuisine** Helen Barnard; **Indian** Guy Dimond, Jim Driver, Roopa Gulati, Phil Harriss, Sejal Sukhadwala; **International** Claire Fogg, Lesley McCave, Nick Rider, Ethel Rimmer; **Italian** Patrick Marmion, Jenni Muir, Nick Rider, Ethel Rimmer; **Japanese** Terry Durack, Kei Kikuchi, Susan Low, Rebecca Taylor; **Jewish** Judy Jackson; **Korean** Susan Low, Sejal Sukhadwala; **Malaysian, Indonesian & Singaporean** Joe Bindloss, Jenny Linford, Wong Hong Suen; **Mediterranean** Claire Fogg; **Middle Eastern** Andrew Humphreys, Vanessa Kendell, Jenny Linford, Ros Sales; **Modern European** James Aufenast, Will Fulford-Jones, Jan Fuscoe, Sarah Guy, Susan Low, Richard Neill, Cath Phillips, Nick Rider, Ethel Rimmer, Ros Sales, Simon Tillotson; **North African** Andrew Humphreys, Janet Zmroczek; **Oriental** Jenny Linford, Sejal Sukhadwala; **Portuguese** Gareth Evans; **Spanish** Ismay Atkins, Elizabeth Carter, Laura Mannering, Lesley McCave, Nick Rider, Ethel Rimmer; **Thai** Joe Bindloss; **Turkish** Ken Olende; **Vegetarian** Sejal Sukhadwala; **Vietnamese** Joe Bindloss, Fuchsia Dunlop, Sarah Guy, Tim Luard, Lam Vo, Yolanda Zappaterra; **Budget** Will Fulford-Jones, Tom Lamont, Holly Pick; **Cafés** Eli Dryden, Roopa Gulati, Ronnie Haydon, Cath Phillips; **Fish & Chips** Jim Driver; **Pizza & Pasta** Jill Emeny, Pendle Harte, Cathy Limb, Pete Watts; **Wine Bars** James Aufenast; **Eating & Entertainment** Jill Emeny; **Food Shops** Simon Coppock, Sejal Sukhadwala; **Courses** Jenni Muir; **Drink Shops** James Aufenast.

Interviews by Jenni Muir except: Matt Skinner and Christine Parkinson (James Aufenast), John Rattagan (Chris Moss), Simon Tang (Fuchsia Dunlop).

Additional reviews written by Ismay Atkins, Henry Archer, James Aufenast, Gabriel Bailey, Simon Coppock, Jonathan Cox, Peterjon Cresswell, Simon Cropper, Guy Dimond, Eli Dryden, Kevin Ebbutt, Jill Emeny, Richard Ehrlich, Stefanie Eschenbacher, Pete Fiennes, Jan Fuscoe, Claire Fogg, Viv Groskop, Roopa Gulati, Elaine Hallgarten, Pendle Harte, Phil Harriss, Ronnie Haydon, Emma Horley, Andrew Humphreys, Ruth Jarvis, Vanessa Kendell, Francisca Kellet, Tom Lamont, Sam Le Quesne, Cathy Limb, Sharon Lougher, Susan Low, Mandy Martinez, Lesley McCave, Jenni Muir, Nana Ocran, Holly Pick, Ros Sales, Veronica Simpson, Sammie Squire, Nick Rider, Ethel Rimmer, Sejal Sukhadwala, Caro Taverne, Pete Watts, Yolanda Zappaterra.

Subject Index Jacqueline Brind.

The Editor would like to thank Katy Attfield, Guy Dimond, Sarah Guy, Mike Harrison, Phil Harriss, Jenni Muir.

Cover photography by Alys Tomlinson, at Pearl (020 7829 7000/www.pearl-restaurant.com).
Openers photography by Beth Evans.
Photography: pages 2, 3, 4, 19, 28, 56, 57, 68, 77, 95, 106, 119, 132, 137, 155, 173, 205, 216, 217, 249, 271, 283, 294, 333 Ming Tang Evans; pages 3, 4, 19, 128 Rob Greig; page 3 Ed Marshall; pages 15, 20, 23, 36, 39, 50, 51, 74, 75, 78, 79, 82, 83, 89, 109, 127, 134, 171, 174, 175, 182, 187, 201, 231, 244, 245, 255, 263, 273, 321, 324, 327, 329, 345 Alys Tomlinson; pages 20, 23, 45, 46, 63, 64, 70, 71, 85, 159, 160, 164, 167, 178, 191, 194, 222, 223, 240, 241, 257, 260, 265, 275, 278, 279, 287, 293, 299, 300, 313, 339 Heloise Bergman; pages 31, 44, 60, 96, 100, 101, 114, 123, 147, 157, 213, 228, 229, 232, 235, 251, 276, 304, 311, 351 Britta Jaschinski; page 46 Brian Daughton; pages 53, 59, 88, 103, 197, 281, 306 Tricia de Courcy Ling; pages 67, 76, 189, 267, 301 Magnus Andersson; page 87 Chris Terry; pages 90, 285, 297 Thomas Skovsende; pages 93, 309, 335 Kevin Nicholson; page 110 Sam Bailey; page 113 Rogan MacDonald; pages 19, 288 Scott Wishart; page 348 Nicole Rowntree.
The following images were provided by the featured establishments: pages 55, 99, 141, 189, 165, 172, 179, 211, 221, 353.

Maps JS Graphics (jsgraphics@wanadoo.fr). Maps 1-18 & 24 are based on material supplied by Alan Collinson and Julie Snook through Copyright Exchange.

Reprographics Icon Reproduction, Crowne House, 56-58 Southwark Street, London SE1 1UN
Printers Copper Clegg Ltd, Shannon Way, Tewkesbury Industrial Centre, Tewkesbury, Gloucestershire GL20 8HB

ISBN 0903 446553

Distribution by Seymour Ltd (020 7396 8000)
Distributed in USA by Publishers Group West

About the Guide
HOW WE REVIEW

The *Time Out Eating & Drinking Guide* is compiled every year by journalists who have a passion for food, and for finding the best places to eat and drink. Many of them also have extraordinary expertise in specialist areas; a few are trained chefs, but most are just enthusiasts. For example, the principal compiler of the Chinese section is an internationally recognised authority on regional Chinese cooking (and a Mandarin speaker to boot). Two of the authors of the Indian chapter are recognised experts in north Indian and Indian vegetarian cookery (they are also, respectively, Hindi and Gujarati speakers).

The restaurants, gastropubs and cafés included in the guide are the best of their type. For the weekly *Time Out* magazine alone, our reviewers visit around 200 new places every year. The better discoveries are then included in this guide. On top of that, reviewers check other new openings, as well as all the restaurants included in the previous edition of the guide. We're also interested in feedback and recommendations from readers and from users of our website. We then eliminate the also-rans to create the list of London's best eateries that this guide represents.

Although our reviewers are often experts in their field, they are in one sense no different from other members of the public: they always visit restaurants anonymously. This is why the reviews in this guidebook are more likely to match your own experience than reviews you might read elsewhere. Recognised critics receive preferential treatment, so it is much harder to trust their judgment. They get better treatment from the staff and more attention from the kitchen, which invariably colours their impressions of a restaurant. However, when *Time Out* reviews restaurants for either this guide or the Food & Drink pages of the magazine, we make every possible effort to do so anonymously. There is no hob-nobbing with PRs, no freebies and no launch parties. We feel our readers have a right to know what eating at that restaurant might be like for them.

Get online!

In addition to our print publications, *Time Out* also has an online service dedicated to providing impartial reviews and information on more than 3,500 of the best restaurants, bars, pubs and budget eateries in London. The website is regularly updated from this guide, plus our bestselling *Cheap Eats in London* and *Bars, Pubs & Clubs* (both annual publications) – as well as with weekly news and reviews about all the latest openings from *Time Out* magazine.

The site offers invaluable information compiled by *Time Out*'s stable of anonymous reviewers. It's as user-friendly as the guides, with an easy search function and an online booking facility. All reviews are listed for those establishments that appear in more than one guide. Registered users can send in their own restaurant recommendations and reviews.

For more information, and to enjoy a 14-day free trial, visit **www.timeout.com/restaurants**.

About the Guide

THE STAR SYSTEM

The star system means you can identify top performers at a glance. A red star ★ next to a restaurant means that it is, of its type, very good indeed. A green star ★ is to help identify London's more budget-conscious eateries. The cut-off point for qualifying for a green star is an average of £15 (for a three-course meal or its equivalent, not including drinks or service).

NEW ENTRIES

The **NEW** symbol makes it obvious which restaurants are new to this edition of the *Eating & Drinking Guide*. In some cases these are brand-new establishments; in other cases we've reviewed a different branch from the last edition, or an existing restaurant for the first time.

AWARD NOMINEES

We've also highlighted the restaurants that were winners or runners-up in *Time Out*'s Eating & Drinking Awards 2005. For more information on the awards, *see p18*.

OPENING HOURS

We've specified if a restaurant serves separate lunch and dinner menus. Times given are for last orders rather than closing times (except in cafés and bars). Restaurants stay open for at least half an hour after last orders, often longer. The times given were correct when we went to press, but hours and days of opening alter frequently. It's always best to book a table by phone and, while doing so, check the opening hours and times of service in advance.

TRANSPORT

Where an underground or rail station is mentioned, it is within a ten-minute walk of the restaurant, unless otherwise implied by the listing (for example: Finsbury Park tube/rail then W7 bus). Where no tube or rail transport is convenient, we've listed the closest and most convenient bus routes. Stations on the Docklands Light Railway have been given a DLR suffix, for example: Cutty Sark DLR.

Central
City EC1

★ ★ Les Invalides **NEW**
2005 RUNNER-UP BEST DESIGN
North Entrance, St Samson's Hospital, Sick Street, EC1 ICU (7654 3210). Old Street tube/rail. **Lunch served** noon-3pm, **dinner served** 6-11pm daily. **Main courses** £8-£13. **Set meal** (noon-3pm, 6-7.30pm Mon-Sat) £12 2 courses, £16 3 courses. **Service** 12.5%. **Cover** £1. **Credit** AmEx, DC, MC, V.
Occupying a site on the ground floor of the now derelict St Samson's Hospital, Les Invalides serves gourmet food in the wittily transformed setting of a former hospital refectory. Starters, or 'Pre Ops' as they appear on the menu, arrive in puréed form (our spicy mousseline of cress, asparagus and white truffle oil was exquisite), while main courses (from the part of the menu simply labelled 'Theatre') are entirely raw. Steak tartare seasoned with an 'infection' of spiced bulgar wheat was a deeply flavourful dish; squid ceviche with a horseradish and yoghurt 'pus' was less impressive. Dessert, however, was quite sensational: the signature dish of chocolate soufflé 'abscess', served with its own biscotti lance, was nothing short of a delight. Regrettably, though, the bed-style seating was not such a success, and the effrontery of the staff who, upon being asked where the toilets were, suggested we might 'draw round the curtain and use the pan', was extraordinary. Oh, and one last thing: the waiting lists are, predictably enough, very, very long.
Babies and children welcome: crayons; high chairs; toys. Disabled: toilet. No smoking. Tables outdoors (10, garden). Vegetarian menu. **Map 11 O6**.

PRICES

We have listed the cheapest and most expensive main courses available in each restaurant. In the case of many oriental restaurants, prices may seem lower, but remember that you often need to order more than one main course to have a full meal. We have also given the price of set meals (if applicable), and specified when they are available and how many courses are offered (for example: **Set lunch** (Mon-Fri) £10 2 courses. **Set dinner** £15 2 courses, £19 3 courses).

MINIMUM CHARGE

Minimum charges are given in the listings, together (where applicable) with the hours when they are in operation. These may be during a busy period or after midnight, for example. Even if we haven't stated a minimum charge, assume that you are expected to have at least a main course. If you want less than that, ask if it's OK. In coffee bars, cafés and brasseries it usually doesn't matter how little you spend.

SERVICE CHARGE

Often the restaurateur adds a percentage to the bill as a service charge. Where this happens we have given that percentage in the listings. Otherwise, tipping is at the customer's discretion. If you are dissatisfied with the level of service provided, you don't have to pay a service charge, even if it is listed on the bill.

COVER CHARGE

This fixed charge may be imposed by the restaurateur to cover the cost of table linen, rolls and butter, crudités and similar extras. Where it is charged, we specify the amount (for example: **Cover £1**).

CREDIT CARDS

The following abbreviations are used: **AmEx** (American Express); **DC** (Diners Club); **JCB** (Japanese credit card); **MC** (MasterCard); and **V** (Visa). If a venue does not accept credit cards, we have said so.

RESTAURANTS BY AREA

After restaurants have been divided by cuisine, they are then listed under the area and district of London in which they are situated.

The main area headings in the order they appear in the guide are:
Central: the area bounded by Marylebone Road in the north, the Thames in the south, Edgware Road in the west and Whitechapel in the east. **West:** Bayswater to Holland Park, Shepherd's Bush, Acton and so on. **South West:** South Kensington, Chelsea, Fulham and over the river to Putney and Wimbledon. **South:** Waterloo, Battersea, Clapham, Brixton, Tooting etc. **South East:** Lewisham, Greenwich, Deptford, Woolwich etc. **East:** from Shoreditch out to Epping. **North East:** Hackney, Stoke Newington and so on. **North:** Camden Town, Archway and northwards. **North West:** Hampstead, Maida Vale, West Hampstead, Kilburn, Willesden etc. **Outer London:** restaurants are listed by borough then by county.

Thus you'll find **The Ivy** (in the Modern European section) listed under Central, then under Covent Garden followed by the postcode, WC2. If you don't know or can't remember what part of town a restaurant is in, just look at the alphabetical index (starting on p417) to find the page number for the review. If you want to check the range of restaurants to be found within a particular area, look at the area index, starting on p401.

In the main body of the guide, as well as in the indexes, restaurants are listed in alphabetical order (ignoring the articles 'the', 'a' in English; 'le', 'la', 'les' in French, and so on). Thus, you'll find **Le Cercle** (in the French section) under C not L.

SERVICES

Babies and children We've tried to reflect the degree of welcome extended to babies and children in restaurants. If you find no mention of either, take it that the restaurant is unsuitable (perhaps because it's a late-night dine and dance place) or that the management is unenthusiastic about kids. 'Babies and children admitted' implies a degree of reluctance on the part of the restaurateur to admit babies and/or children, or a lack of facilities for them, and we've duly recorded any qualifications to admission (children over 6 years admitted early evening, and so on). If kids are welcome, we've said so: 'Babies and children welcome'. We've also pinpointed the facilities provided for kids (children's menu, high chairs, toys, crayons, nappy-changing facilities etc).
Booking advisable/essential are self-explanatory. We also state if a restaurant does not accept bookings.
Disabled: toilet means the restaurant has a specially adapted toilet on the premises, which implies that disabled customers (and wheelchairs) can get into the restaurant. However, we cannot guarantee this, and no matter how good the arrangements appear, we recommend phoning in advance to check feasibility.
Dress rules Many restaurateurs dislike customers turning up shirtless and/or in shorts in summer, but few impose rules. A jacket and tie are demanded only by the more formal establishments, but restaurateurs generally prefer customers to wear 'smart' dress. Where there are rules we state them. 'Dress: smart casual' means that you can wear jeans, but they'd better be clean.
No smoking 'No-smoking tables' means that the restaurant has made some attempt to separate smokers and non-smokers; 'No smoking' means it's banned throughout the venue.
Facilities for parties Almost all restaurateurs will push a couple of tables together for a party. We've listed restaurants with separate rooms, floors, even banqueting suites that are available for parties. Book in advance and check if there is a charge.

Tables outdoors We've tried to be specific about how many tables are available and whether they're out on the pavement or in a back garden. If you want to sit outside, say so when you book, although many restaurants refuse to take bookings for outdoor tables and – irritatingly – allocate them on a first come, first served basis.
Takeaway service We've listed restaurants that run a regular takeaway service. If you can only take food out at certain times, we've said so; otherwise the service is available throughout the restaurant's opening hours. We also mention if there's a **delivery service**, and if there are any limitations on the area served.
Vegetarian menu Most restaurants claim to have a vegetarian dish on the menu. We've highlighted those that have made a concerted effort to attract and cater for vegetarian (and vegan) diners.
Map reference All restaurants that appear on our street maps (starting on p360) are given a reference to the map and grid square on which they can be found.

Anonymous, unbiased reviews

The reviews in the *Eating & Drinking Guide* are based on the experiences of *Time Out* restaurant reviewers. Restaurants, pubs, bars and cafés are always visited anonymously, and *Time Out* pays the bill. No payment or PR invitation of any kind has secured or influenced a review.

Advertisers & sponsors

We would like to stress that advertisers and sponsors have no control over editorial content of the *Eating & Drinking Guide*. No restaurant, bar, café or shop has been included because its owner has advertised in the guide: an advertiser may receive a bad review or no review at all.

Other guides

This is one of a series of eating and drinking guides published by *Time Out*. *Cheap Eats in London* reviews more than 700 eateries where you can dine for under £20 a head; *Bars, Pubs & Clubs* covers the best of the drinking and dancing scene; and *Paris Eating & Drinking* surveys the foodie delights of the French capital.

Get 15% off
your total food and drink bill at these gastropubs

Enjoy a lazy Sunday lunch with friends, or an evening meal à deux. Whatever you choose, it's going to be better value for money when you use this offer.

It's very simple...

To get 15% off your total bill detach the card on the Contents page of this guide and keep it safe. All you have to do when you visit one of the participating gastropubs is buy one main course – then you can eat and drink as much as you like and still save money. Present your card when you ask for the bill.

And remember...

You can use your card as many times as you want at any of the establishments listed below, from the time you buy this guide until 20th September 2006.

Bollo
13-15 Bollo Lane, W4 5LR (8994 6037).
Chiswick Park tube.
Satisfy yourself with some very generously proportioned dishes.
See page 107

Hartley
64 Tower Bridge Road, SE1 4TR (7394 7023/www.thehartley.com).
Borough tube/Elephant & Castle tube/rail then 1,188 bus.
This Bermondsey local buzzes with a crowd who know how to enjoy themselves. **See page 111**

Palmerston
91 Lordship Lane, SE22 8EP (8693 1629).
East Dulwich rail.
A classic gastropub in the heart of East Dulwich.
See page 111

Peasant
240 St John Street, EC1V 4PH (7336 7726/www.thepeasant.co.uk).
Angel tube/Farringdon tube/rail/153 bus.
Low-key and laid-back; ideal for relaxing with friends.
See page 107
Offer applies to downstairs bar only.

Pig's Ear
2005 RUNNER-UP BEST GASTROPUB
35 Old Church Street, SW3 5BS (7352 2908/www.thepigsear.co.uk).
Sloane Square tube.
A satisfying and very homely pub off the Fulham Road.
See page 110

Queen's Head & Artichoke
30-32 Albany Street, NW1 4EA (7916 6206/www.theartichoke.net).
Great Portland Street or Regent's Park tube.
Perfect for a summer snack in the garden or cosying up by the fire in winter. **See page 107**

Salt House
63 Abbey Road, NW8 0AE (7328 6626).
Kilburn Park or St John's Wood tube.
Get a taste of the Med at this St John's Wood favourite.
See page 117

Victoria
10 West Temple Sheen, SW14 7RT (8876 4238/www.thevictoria.net).
Mortlake rail.
There's something for everyone at the Victoria (and that includes the kids).
See page 110

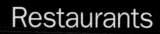

Restaurants

African & Caribbean

In many ways, 2005 was the year of Africa in London. We've had 'Africa 2005', a long-running festival of African arts, crafts, literature and music; an excellent exhibition of modern African art at the Hayward Gallery; and sundry African film festivals – not to mention the G8 Summit and Live8, which have turned international attention on the world's poorest continent.

Time Out has been at the forefront of reviewing African restaurants, but this year, places championed by us such as **Tobia** and **Zigni House** have subsequently garnered rave reviews in the national press. African food is at last getting wider attention. There's now a glorious, burgeoning Ethiopian and Eritrean restaurant scene in parts of north London. Snug Eritrean eaterie **Asmara** also does good business in Brixton, while in west London **Angie's** continues to provide classic Nigerian food as well as a weekly Angolan/Portuguese buffet. In short, more and more Londoners are discovering the delights of spicy wots, crumpet-like enjera bread and the spectacular traditional coffee ceremony. Sadly, though, we have also seen the closure of the unique Sudanese restaurant **Mandola**.

The story is slightly different for Caribbean restaurants. With roughly five per cent of Londoners of Caribbean descent, decent cuisine from the region is somewhat under-represented. While the capital has always had its fair share of takeaway outlets and cafés, there has been a notable paucity of smarter restaurants. Two venues that have always bucked the trend are the long-standing **Mango Room** and **Cottons**, which have prided themselves on their innovative Caribbean food. Recently, their ranks have been swelled by the arrival of **Tyme** in Ealing and **Coco** in Exmouth Market. Alongside traditional dishes, both these restaurants produce a cuisine based on Caribbean ingredients and flavours, but add a modern interpretation and vigour. It's a welcome evolution and is likely to make Caribbean food accessible to a wider audience.

AFRICAN

Central

Covent Garden WC2

★ Calabash
The Africa Centre, 38 King Street, WC2E 8JR (7836 1976). Covent Garden, Embankment or Leicester Square tube/Charing Cross tube/rail. Bar **Open** 5.30-11pm Mon-Sat. *Restaurant* **Lunch served** 12.30-2.30pm Mon-Fri. **Dinner served** 6-10.30pm Mon-Sat. **Main courses** £6.95-£8.10. **Service** 10%. **Credit** MC, V. Pan-African
This once-iconic restaurant inside the Africa Centre (a charity aimed at raising awareness about Africa) is now looking tired and frayed. A generation ago it was pretty much at the cutting edge – a place where many visitors to the centre's bar, gift shop, exhibitions and literary events first discovered African food in London. We were told that refurbishment is on the cards, but there was little evidence of this. Not that there's much wrong with the food. Dishes like groundnut stew and yassa (a Senegalese recipe of chicken marinated in lemon, onions and peppercorns) are fine, but the flavours are toned down, and the pan-African menu seems to be aimed squarely at first-timers. Portions are generous; mains are served with yams, plantains, and rice and peas, and there's a varied selection of African beers and wines. It's been 45 years since Calabash opened, so it's definitely time for a facelift and a smart new menu.
Babies and children admitted. Booking advisable weekends. Separate rooms (in Africa Centre) for parties, seating 80 and 100. Takeaway service. **Map 18 L7**.

Euston NW1

★ African Kitchen Gallery
102 Drummond Street, NW1 2HN (7383 0918). Euston Square tube/Euston tube/rail. **Meals served** 6-11pm Mon; noon-10.30pm Tue-Sun. **Main courses** £5.50-£6.50. **Credit** MC, V. African & Caribbean
A bijou café-restaurant in Euston, the Gallery has dual Nigerian and Iberian ownership. This has resulted in an enjoyable fusion of African and Caribbean food that comes at very reasonable prices and in generous portions. Ackee and saltfish (one of the more expensive items at £7.95), jerk chicken and curry goat stew share the menu with egusi (beef stew), moi-moi, steamed tilapia fish with beans and ground prawns, and groundnut stew. Vegetarian choices include asaro (yam and sweet potato porridge) with mixed herbs, peppers and tomato, as well as jollof rice (or basmati rice and peas). Both these dishes made a perfect combination with an order of wild spinach cooked with melon seed. Freshly made ginger beer was a strong but satisfyingly cleansing accompaniment to the fairly well-spiced dishes; in season there's also olu olu palm tree juice. If space allows, it's worth trying the desserts. These may seem modest in size, but they're packed with flavour – as well as calories. Banana, mango or guava flans are among the temptations.
Babies and children admitted. Booking advisable. No smoking. Table outdoors (4, garden; 1, pavement). Takeaway service. Vegetarian menu. Vegan dishes. **Map 3 J3**.

King's Cross N1

★ Addis
42 Caledonian Road, N1 9DT (7278 0679/ www.addisrestaurant.co.uk). King's Cross tube/ rail/17, 91, 259 bus. **Meals served** noon-midnight Mon-Fri; 1pm-midnight Sat, Sun. **Main courses** £5.95-£8.50. **Credit** AmEx, JCB, MC, V. Ethiopian
Around the corner from the relentless reconstruction of King's Cross, Addis offers a divine slice of eastern Africa, with a choice of some 35 dishes on its Ethiopian menu. The starter list contains a fine assortment of spiced salads, such as the gorgeous selata aswad (deep-fried aubergines with a rich tahini and yoghurt butter sauce). There's a decent balance between meat and non-meat dishes among the main courses. One concession to fish-eaters is the samak muhamar (freshwater snapper cooked in spiced batter with salad or potato), but the mix-and-match choices are wide, with dishes like ayeb be gomen (spinach blended with cottage cheese) and ye beg tibs (lamb cubes fried with onion and pepper spices) combining well on a platter of enjera. Lunchtimes bring £1-off discounts to an already reasonably priced menu, and diners get to sit inside what feels like a peaceful and sunset-hued enclave of N1.
Babies and children welcome: high chairs. Book weekends. No-smoking tables. Takeaway service. **Map 4 L2**.

★ Merkato Restaurant
196 Caledonian Road, N1 0SL (7713 8952). King's Cross tube/rail/17, 91, 259 bus. **Meals served** noon-midnight daily. **Main courses** £5-£10. **Credit** MC, V. Ethiopian
Although Merkato moved from spacious premises to a cosy, caff-like space about a year ago, its popularity hasn't diminished. The buzzy music and lively vibe are a hit with Ethiopian (and non-Ethiopian) bright young things. Inside, there are framed pictures and Ethiopian knick-knacks; outside, a few tables are laid out for alfresco dining. All the dishes we tried – mildly spiced chicken stew, hot marinated grilled lamb, raw beef tartar with seasoned clarified butter and yoghurt cheese, and collard greens cooked with onions and spices – were rich, delicious, and distinctly spiced, and came with gigantic portions of enjera bread. The tej (Ethiopian wine, made with gesho hops and honey) is particularly refreshing here. Service is wonderfully friendly. If you are unfamiliar with Ethiopian food, the knowledgeable staff will be happy to help you navigate the menu. An ideal starting point for those new to Ethiopian cuisine and culture.
Babies and children welcome: high chairs. Booking advisable Fri, Sat. Tables outdoors (4, pavement). Takeaway service. **Map 4 M1**.

RESTAURANTS

West
Shepherd's Bush W12

Piassa
129 Askew Road, W12 9AU (8762 0234). Hammersmith tube then 266 bus. **Meals served** noon-11pm daily. **Main courses** £5.50-£13. **Credit** MC, V. Ethiopian
Formerly known as Demera, this popular Ethiopian restaurant has reverted to its original name Piassa because, we were told, 'regular customers preferred it'. The management (which has remained unchanged throughout all the changes) exhibits similar care when taking into account customer feedback on the food. On our visit, staff were anxious to please and keen to explain the finer points of the cuisine. Of the many dishes we tried, our favourites were a fiery stew of chicken with hard-boiled eggs; mild lamb stew with garlic, ginger and spices; prawns in a hot red chilli sauce; mushrooms stir-fried with onions and green chillies; and a creamy, buttery dish of mashed chickpeas – all brought in little pots to be tipped on to large discs of enjera. There's traditional low-level seating at the front, complete with mosobs (wicker tables), and a conventional dining area at the back. Wherever you sit, the ambience is guaranteed to be relaxed.
Babies and children admitted. Booking advisable. Entertainment: traditional musician & dancer 9pm Fri, Sat. Separate room for parties, seats 30. Takeaway service. Vegetarian menu. **Map 20 A2.**

Westbourne Park W9

Angie's
381 Harrow Road, W9 3NA (8962 8761/ www.angies-restaurant.co.uk). Westbourne Park tube. **Meals served** noon-11pm Mon-Sat; 1-10pm Sun. **Main courses** £10-£15. **Service** 5%. **Credit** AmEx, DC, JCB, MC, V. African & Caribbean
Owner Isaac Namabiri has hit on a good thing with this restaurant. Angie's seems to thrive on its strong west African customer base, which is undeniably family-oriented, hence the popular Sunday buffets where excitable children tuck into the likes of moi-moi, dodo (fried plantain) and jollof rice. The menu is predominantly Nigerian, containing fresh pepper soups, suya (char-grilled beef with dried chilli and onions), vegetarian ewa-aganyi (mashed brown beans), as well as beef or fried fish and egusi. There are also Caribbean choices such as curried goat or chicken, and the global element doesn't end there. Angie's specials include grilled whole fish (£12), whole guinea fowl

(£15), grilled and spiced rabbit (£25) and super lobster (£50), although these dishes require between two and 24 hours' notice. Friday nights are busy, with an open buffet of Portuguese/Angolan food available as well as the regular Nigerian menu.
Babies and children admitted. Booking advisable. Disabled: toilet. No-smoking tables. Takeaway service: delivery service. **Map 1 A4.**

Mosob NEW
339 Harrow Road, W9 3RB (7266 2012). Westbourne Park tube. **Meals served** 6-11pm Mon-Fri; noon-midnight Sat, Sun. **Main courses** £5-£9. **Credit** AmEx, MC, V. Eritrean
This Eritrean restaurant is modern and stylish – not words you would usually associate with African restaurants, which tend to be homely and family-run. Mosob is also family-run – mum's in the kitchen, siblings work front of house – but it's tastefully done up in maroon and cream, with carefully chosen and judiciously placed Eritrean knick-knacks, logos featuring the mosob (traditional low, round, woven dining table), and a charming sheesha room at the back. Food is somewhat mixed. We liked the starters: lamb sambusas (similar to samosas) consisted of well-spiced mince in good pastry, and pinwheels of injera bread stuffed with spinach were fresh and light. Main courses were a let-down, however. Lamb with okra, mixed vegetable alicha (mildly spiced stew), shiro (spicy ground chickpea sauce), and spinach with fresh yoghurt cheese were bland. Dishes lacked individual spicing and distinct identity, and flavours seemed toned down. The traditional coffee ceremony redeemed the evening, though. The aromas of burning frankincense and freshly roasted coffee beans permeated the restaurant, adding to the relaxed, laid-back vibe – and the coffee itself was exquisite. Warm, smiling service was also a plus.
Babies and children welcome: high chairs. Booking advisable. Separate room for parties, seats 24. Takeaway service. **Map 19 C1.**

South
Brixton SW9

★ Asmara
386 Coldharbour Lane, SW9 8LF (7737 4144). Brixton tube/rail. **Dinner served** 5.30pm-midnight daily. **Main courses** £4-£7.50. **Set meal** £25 (vegetarian) 6 courses, £27 (meat) 7 courses. **Credit** MC, V. Eritrean
The spirit of Eritrea in Brixton. This family-run restaurant at the edge of the market is consistently

popular with SW9 diners who want a change from the gastropubs or Caribbean takeaways in the vicinity. Meals are served at neat little tables, with larger communal platters eaten from traditional glass-topped woven baskets. The aroma of hot spices, incense and smoking coffee fills each corner of the fairly compact venue. Meat, vegetarian and vegan food is all included on the menu. Stews are a good choice, with bubbling dishes of well-seasoned lamb, beef or chicken served with portions of sour enjera pancake, seasoned rice or couscous. Spinach with olive oil flavoured with lemon and garlic is excellent with kinche (cracked wheat cooked with butter and yoghurt). As a concession, there's also rigatone and bolognese on the list, perhaps as a reminder that Italians introduced pasta to the Abyssinians a couple of centuries ago.
Babies and children welcome: high chairs. Booking advisable. Separate room for parties, seats 40. Takeaway service. Vegan dishes. **Map 22 E2.**

North
Finsbury Park N4

★ Senke
1B-1C Rock Street, N4 2DN (7359 7687). Finsbury Park tube/rail. **Meals served** noon-midnight daily. **Main courses** £5-£7.50. **No credit cards.** Ethiopian
This welcoming café, bar and restaurant is located in the heart of the Ethiopian community in Finsbury Park, surrounded by food shops that offer everything from ready-to-cook enjera ('just add water') to unusual fresh greens and beans. Like many African restaurants, Senke's dining area is split into conventional tables and traditional low-level seating. Spinach with fresh yoghurt cheese was a good balance of spice, heartiness, creaminess and mineral tang. A spicy lamb stew made with tender meat layered with pieces of enjera was filling yet underwhelming, but a dish that combined enjera, onions and green chillies with a sunflower seed sauce was rich and very tasty. The long and interesting menu also features traditional breakfast dishes rarely seen outside Ethiopia, such as foule (mashed broad beans mixed with seasoned clarified butter, green chillies, shallots, yoghurt cheese and tomatoes, served with french bread), and bula (spicy porridge made with mashed 'false banana' – a variety of Ethiopian root vegetable that's hard to find in the UK). Service, despite some language difficulties, is sweet, and Senke is highly popular with locals.
Babies and children admitted. Booking advisable weekends. Takeaway service.

RESTAURANTS

Lalibela. See p32.

Islington N1

★ **Zigni House** NEW

*330 Essex Road, N1 3PB (7226 7418/
www.zignihouse.com). Angel tube/38, 56, 73,
341 bus.* **Meals served** *7am-1.30am daily.*
Main courses £5-£8.75. **Set buffet** £8.
Credit AmEx, JCB, MC, V. Eritrean & Ethiopian
Once you have adjusted to a few minor obstacles
(the low, hard seating, for one, or the occasional
communication difficulty with the overworked
staff), this charming little restaurant is a rare treat.
The furnishings are unpretentious (there's a small
bar and a colourful buffet at the front, with rows of
squat tables and a smattering of ethnic ornaments
stretching off towards the back), and the same goes
for the clientele, who are clearly dedicated fans of
chef Tsige Haile's cheap and cheerful East African
nosh. And what's not to like? Most people serve
themselves from the buffet of hot stews, pulse-laced
salads and, of course, injera. There's an à la carte
menu too, but these dishes take longer to arrive and
most are included in the buffet anyway. During our
last visit, we preferred the spicier stews (the zignis
from which the restaurant takes its name), which
are laden with sauce and packed with flavour, to
the milder alichas, whose mushier, drier texture is
more of an acquired taste. Speaking of which,
lovers of fine wine take note: stick to beer or water.
*Babies and children welcome: children's menu.
Booking advisable. Entertainment: traditional
musicians Fri, Sat. Separate room for parties,
seats 70-100. Tables outdoors (10, garden).
Takeaway service. Vegetarian menu.*

Kentish Town NW5

★ ★ **Lalibela**

*137 Fortess Road, NW5 2HR (7284 0600).
Tufnell Park tube/134 bus.* **Dinner served**
6pm-midnight daily. **Main courses** £7.50-£8.95.
Service 10% for parties of 6 or more. **Credit**
AmEx, DC, JCB, MC, V. Ethiopian

Eating at Lalibela is always a treat, whether you
sit on the ground floor in the art gallery area, or
upstairs at the low stools by the window that
overlooks Fortess Road. Artefacts adorn the entire
restaurant. Part of the attraction must be the staff,
who switch effortlessly between heart-warming
benevolence and general happy-to-be-there-ness.
Items from the long menu are patiently explained
to any newcomers to Ethiopian cooking. Food is
best ordered in combinations, as in the huge
platters of enjera with separate dishes eaten
directly, by hand, from the sough-dough pancake.
Lamb and pumpkin wot (stew), creamed chicken,
boiled green vegetables, cucumber and yoghurt
sauce, and a side portion of seasoned rice went
down exceptionally well on our most recent visit.
Look out for the pots of traditionally spiced coffee,
the aromas of which waft from table to table by
way of hand-held trays of freshly smoked beans.
*Babies and children welcome: high chairs.
Booking advisable. No-smoking tables.
Takeaway service. Vegetarian menu. Vegan
dishes.* **Map 26 B3.**

★ ★ **Queen of Sheba**

*12 Fortess Road, NW5 2EU (7284 3947).
Kentish Town tube/rail.* **Meals served** 1-11.30pm
Mon-Sat; 1-10.30pm Sun. **Main courses** £5-
£10.50. **Set lunch** £7.50 2 dishes. **Credit** MC, V.
Ethiopian
Named after a much-revered character from
Ethiopian religious mythology, Sheba is certainly
a queen – in terms of its place within north
London's burgeoning Ethiopian dining scene.
There are some interesting dishes on an otherwise
fairly standard menu, such as delicious
mushrooms stir-fried with onions and spices,
crushed roasted chickpeas in hot sauce, and cubes
of lamb cooked in a full-bodied, flavoursome
tomato and chilli sauce. The spicing ranges from
subtle to fiery, and the kitchen doesn't hold back
on flavour. Moreover, everything is prepared fresh
to order, using organic ingredients wherever

possible. Make sure you don't leave without
experiencing the excellent traditional coffee
ceremony, in which deeply aromatic fresh coffee
beans are ground in a mortar, roasted and served
in little cups alongside incense: a theatrical ritual
that's infused with social, symbolic and religious
meaning. Done up in bamboo and wood, the
restaurant has a relaxed, laid-back vibe, and
service is warm and cheerful.
*Babies and children welcome: high chairs. Booking
advisable. Tables outdoors (2, patio). Takeaway
service. Vegetarian menu.* **Map 26 B4.**

North West

West Hampstead NW3

★ ★ **Tobia**

*First Floor, Ethiopian Community Centre,
2A Lithos Road, NW3 6EF (7431 4213/
www.tobiarestaurant.co.uk). Finchley Road tube.*
Meals served noon-midnight Tue-Sun.
Main courses £5-£10.50. **Credit** AmEx, DC,
MC, V. Ethiopian
Since we first reviewed Tobia – a restaurant inside
the dreary-looking Ethiopian Community Centre
off Finchley Road – it has garnered rave reviews
and a consistent media presence. This is thanks,
no doubt, to the marketing nous of its chef-
proprietor Sophie Sirak-Kebede, who has enough
charisma to front her own TV show (isn't Britain
ready for its first Ethiopian celebrity chef?).
Fortunately, the food matches the hype: we've
never had a disappointing meal here. Among the
standard Ethiopian dishes on a reassuringly short
menu, you'll also find ancient family recipes – such
as marinated leg of lamb baked in banana leaves,
cured beef mixed with clarified butter and chilli
sauce, assa kitfo ('Ethiopian sushi' made with raw
tuna), and gouramailia (strips of beef steak and
tongue served with spiced cottage cheese). There's
much choice for vegetarians, and an exclusively
meat-free and dairy-free menu is served on

Wednesdays and Fridays, in accordance with the tenets of the Coptic Christian church. The restaurant has recently been refurbished in a peach and saffron colour scheme. Musicians and regional dancing can be seen on Saturday nights.
Babies and children admitted. Booking advisable weekends. No-smoking tables. Takeaway service. Vegetarian menu. Vegan dishes. **Map 28 A3.**

CARIBBEAN

Central

Clerkenwell & Farringdon EC1

★ Coco NEW
70 Exmouth Market, EC1R 4QP (7833 3332). Angel tube/Farringdon tube/rail/19, 38, 341 bus. Bar **Open** noon-11pm Mon-Thur; noon-midnight Fri, Sat; noon-10.30pm Sun. *Restaurant* **Lunch served** noon-3pm Mon-Fri. **Dinner served** 5-11pm Mon-Fri; 6pm-midnight Sat; 6-10.30pm Sun. **Main courses** £9-£14. **Set lunch** £6.50 1 course. **Service** 12.5%. *Both* **Credit** JCB, MC, V. Caribbean
Attentive service and a friendly, upbeat atmosphere combine with wonderful food to propel this newcomer towards the upper echelons of Caribbean dining. A change in the kitchen has ushered in a new menu, but standards remain high and the new chef is a past holder of the Caribbean Food Emporium 'Caribbean chef of the year' award. For starters, salted cod fritters were lightly fried and succulent; they came with a nicely fiery tomato and scotch bonnet dipping sauce. Equally good, if more hefty, was the red pea soup made with kidney beans and served with heavy dumplings and hardough bread. For a blow-out main, go for the belly kant baal: a choice of three types of either jerk fish or meat, served with succulent plantain and rice and peas. Roast chump of lamb was tender and juicy; mashed plantain made a welcome accompaniment. Also on the menu is curry goat, blue field snapper and oxtail served with sour beans. Desserts have a touch of the nouvelle about them, including creamy mango and lime crème brûlée.
Babies and children welcome: high chairs. Booking essential weekends. Disabled: toilet. Entertainment: jazz 7.30pm Sun. No smoking (restaurant). Separate room for parties, holds 200. Tables outdoors (5, pavement). Takeaway service. **Map 5 N5.**

Soho W1

★ Mr Jerk
189 Wardour Street, W1F 8ZD (7287 2878/ www.mrjerk.co.uk). Tottenham Court Road tube. **Meals served** 9am-11pm Mon-Sat; 10am-8pm Sun. **Main courses** £5-£7.50. **Service** 10%. **Credit** MC, V. Caribbean
A cheap and cheery caff, this Soho branch of Mr Jerk (the older of the two) does a brisk trade throughout the day. This testifies to the filling, tasty meals dished up by friendly staff. Starters and side dishes were a little lacklustre: our saltfish fritter was oily and looked as though it had been sitting around; and the beef patty tasted as if it had been unwrapped from cellophane moments before. Mains were more successful. A plate heaped with brown chicken stew accompanied by rice and peas was appetising and just peppery enough, while a spicy jerk chicken had been flavoured with pimento, black pepper and tomato and came with a crisp salad and coleslaw. Roti is another hearty option; choose from chicken, mutton, prawn or vegetarian. There aren't many desserts, but don't leave without sampling the Guinness punch, which is sweet and creamy with plenty of kick. Mr Jerk is a bona fide option for an impromptu lunch.
Babies and children welcome: high chairs. No-smoking. Takeaway service. **Map 17 J6.**
For branch see index.

West

Ealing W13

BB's
3 Chignell Place, off Uxbridge Road, W13 0TJ (8840 8322/www.bbscrabback.co.uk). Ealing Broadway tube/rail/West Ealing rail. **Lunch served** 11.30am-2.30pm Mon-Fri. **Dinner served** 6.30-11.30pm Mon-Fri; 6.30pm-12.30am Sat. **Main courses** £9.50-£12.95. **Service** 12.5% for parties of 6 or more. **Credit** MC, V. Grenadian
Tucked down an Ealing alley, BB's Caribbean restaurant is an unprepossessing spot easy to miss if you're not paying attention. It's a snug venue with a homely feel; tables line walls that are decorated with graffiti complimenting the chef. Brian Benjamin harnesses the flavours of his homeland Grenada to create novel and delicious dishes. Our starter of crab meat, white wine and cheese was rich and filling; for something lighter, try the callaloo and okra soup, or avocado Perry (a sweet but fresh salad of avocado, pineapple and guava dressing, named after Benjamin's wife). Mains are also inventive. King prawns seretse (cooked in butter with lobster sauce, served with mango and pimentos) was a luxurious meld of flavours. Parrot fish calypso (seasoned with red, green and yellow peppers, served in a citrus sauce) was equally accomplished. Traditionalists are also catered for with goat curry, jerk pork and roti. Irresistible desserts provide the finale. Dig into bananas flamed in rum and lemon, or pineapple la grenade (pineapple in a sticky toffee sauce), or pancakes with tropical stewed fruits.
Babies and children welcome: high chairs. Booking essential Thur-Sat. Disabled: toilet. No-smoking tables. Tables outdoors (4, pavement). Vegan dishes.

★ Tyme
133 Uxbridge Road, W13 9AU (8840 7222/ www.tyme.co.uk). Ealing Broadway tube/rail/ West Ealing rail. **Lunch served** noon-3pm Fri. **Dinner served** 6-11pm Tue-Thur; 6pm-midnight Fri, Sat; 6-10pm Sun. **Main courses** £13.75. **Set lunch** £10 2 courses. **Set dinner** £20 3 courses. **Service** 10%. **Credit** AmEx, DC, MC, V. Caribbean
With a welcoming atmosphere, warm ochre walls, comfortable mauve furniture and effusive and friendly owners, Tyme is a great spot. Start with a light, palate-cleansing appetiser – like sunshine pumpkin soup flavoured with coconut, or an avocado and grapefruit salad – to leave plenty of room for the mains. The inventive menu has Jamaican, Grenadian and European influences, and there's plenty of choice. Kingfish served with a deliciously zesty mango and fresh ginger sauce had just-caught succulence and came with excellent rice and peas – the best we've had in London. An audacious dish of chicken escalope with a glossy bitter-chocolate chilli sauce was a real treat: rich without being cloying and well complemented by a side dish of steamed okra with tomato salsa. Other dishes included chicken with banana and leek sauce, and peppered steak in rum cream sauce, as well as traditional goat curry, jerk chicken and ackee and saltfish. For pudding, try the tropical fruit crumble, a medley of kiwi, prickly pear and mango served with vanilla ice-cream.
Babies and children welcome: high chairs. Booking advisable; essential Fri, Sat. Entertainment: jazz 8pm Fri-Sun. No smoking. Takeaway service.

South

Brixton SW2

★ Bamboula
12 Acre Lane, SW2 5SG (7737 6633). Brixton tube/rail. **Meals served** 11am-11pm Mon-Fri; noon-11pm Sat; 1-8pm Sun. **Main courses** £7-£9.50. **Service** (after 5pm Mon-Sat; 1-8pm Sun) 10%. **Credit** MC, V. Caribbean
Bright yellow walls, a profusion of greenery (both real and artificial) and wicker furniture all create the impression of a surprisingly untacky beach shack. Busy well into the afternoon, Bamboula is a popular choice for lunch – not just with Brixtonians. A quick glance around the restaurant suggests a clientele who travel far and wide to sample the wares. Light meals include jerk chicken sandwich made with hardough bread, and a tasty rich red pea soup. As well as traditional Caribbean dishes such as curried goat, stew chicken and a spicy escoveitched snapper, there's a smattering of vegetarian dishes including 'coconut rundown vegetables' in a rich and creamy sauce, and an aubergine bake. Big eaters should choose the 'hungry man' platter, a huge plate of jerk chicken served with rice and peas and plantain. Bamboula is great value for money, but falls down with woefully inattentive service. We were left waiting nearly half an hour for our food, and a side dish of bammy never turned up, despite us asking three times. A potentially great little eaterie that could, and should, do better.
Babies and children admitted. Booking advisable Fri, Sat (£5 deposit required). No smoking. Tables outdoors (2, garden). Takeaway service. **Map 22 D2.**

South East

Herne Hill SE24

Brockwells
75-79 Norwood Road, SE24 9AA (8671 6868). Herne Hill rail/3, 68, 196 bus. **Open** 5pm-midnight Mon; 5pm-2am Tue, Thur; 5pm-1am Wed; 5pm-3am Fri, Sat; 1pm-2am Sun. **Dinner served** 5-10pm Mon-Sat. **Meals served** 2-10pm Sun. **Main courses** £8.50-£10.95. **Set buffet** (Sun) £9.95. **Service** 10%. **Credit** JCB, MC, V. Caribbean
Restaurant-cum-bar Brockwells is one of the brightest stars in the Herne Hill firmament. The vibe is laid-back and friendly, with food served either at the tables dotted around the expansive dining area or to customers relaxing on the squashy *Miami Vice*-style leather sofas. Much of the menu consists of the standard Caribbean repertoire, but where Brockwells excels is in ensuring that even the familiar and traditional is top-notch: well prepared and well presented. This warrants, we feel, the charging of slightly higher prices than is usual for mid-range Caribbean food. Curry goat was served in a rich glistening sauce spiced with cumin and chilli, while a tender, flavoursome jerk chicken was also enjoyable. Side dishes of rice and peas and juicy plantain were also satisfying. It's unlikely you'll have much room for puddings, given the generous helpings, but the apple pie is notable. The dessert menu is in the process of being updated, though, so keep an eye out for enticing alternatives.
Babies and children welcome (until 8pm): children's buffet. Booking advisable. Disabled: toilet. Dress: smart casual; no caps or trainers. Entertainment: DJs 9pm Tue, Fri-Sun; open mic 7pm Wed, Thur. **Map 23 A5.**

East

Shoreditch E2

★ Anda de Bridge
42-44 Kingsland Road, E2 8DA (7739 3863/ www.andadebridge.com). Old Street tube/rail/26, 48, 55, 67, 149, 242, 243 bus. **Meals served** 11am-midnight Mon-Sat. **Main courses** £5-£10. **Credit** AmEx, DC, MC, V. Caribbean
The hessian banquette seating lining the walls may have worn thin after five years' service, and the bar might be looking a little frayed, but Anda de Bridge is still a great spot to grab a bite and a couple of cool Caribbean beers. The back dining area is now defunct, as is table service, so food is served in the bar at the front, making for a busier, buzzy gastropub feel. The menu stays roughly the same year on year. A starter of plantain was done to a turn: slightly crisp and caramelised. Jerk pork ribs were disappointing, however; the seasoning was tangy, but there was no meat, just chewy gristle. Main courses redeemed matters with a well-seasoned curry goat and a palatable red

RESTAURANTS

snapper served with piquant coconut sauce pepped up with a hint of lemongrass. Both mains came with perfect rice and peas. Other dishes include such favourites as jerk chicken and ackee and saltfish. To drink, the array of prestige rums and Caribbean beers (like hard-to-find Carib) are the top options at this unpretentious venue.
Babies and children admitted. Disabled: toilet. Entertainment: DJs 8pm Fri, Sat. **Map 6 R3.**

North

Camden Town & Chalk Farm NW1

★ Cottons

55 Chalk Farm Road, NW1 8AN (7485 8388/ www.cottons-restaurant.co.uk). Chalk Farm tube. **Lunch served** noon-4pm Sat. **Dinner served** 6pm-midnight Mon-Thur; 6pm-1am Fri, Sat;

Meals served noon-midnight Sun. **Main courses** £10.25-£14.50. **Set meal** £17.95 2 courses, £22.50 3 courses. **Service** 12.5%. **Credit** AmEx, MC, V. Caribbean
Even midweek there's a welcoming and lively scene at Cottons, focused on the front-of-house cocktail bar. Ample seating is dispersed over three dining rooms, and friendly staff are happy to advise on the menu. Our island meze starter consisted of a variety of tasters, including fluffy saltfish fritters, tangy creole prawns and a toasted roti. Caesar salad prepared with a meaty marlin was a successful twist on the original, while ackee and saltfish was delicate and subtly flavoured. Mains were also accomplished. A rack of extremely tender lamb, crisp outside and pink within, was served with curry paste and guava and red onion jam, which, though not especially Caribbean, complemented it perfectly. Red snapper millefeuille with asparagus, served with a rice and smoked fish combination, was excellent:

the fish succulent and the red, green and yellow pepper sauce zesty and fresh. Other mains include curry goat, grilled sea bass and ital vegetable stew with festival. Portion sizes make puddings unlikely, but should you have room there's delicious rum and raisin tart, banana fritters or mango cheesecake.
Babies and children welcome: high chairs. Booking essential weekends. Entertainment: DJ 9pm Fri, Sat; jazz 7pm Sun. No-smoking tables. Separate rooms for parties, seating 20 and 35. Tables outdoors (2, pavement). Vegetarian menu. Vegan dishes. **Map 27 B1.**

Freshh Caribbean Restaurant & Bar

48 Chalk Farm Road, NW1 8AJ (7916 8935). Chalk Farm tube. **Meals served** noon-10.30pm daily. **Main courses** £10.50-£15. **Set lunch** £8 2 courses incl soft drink. **Service** 10%. **Credit** MC, V. Jamaican

Menu

AFRICAN
Accra or **akara:** bean fritters.
Aloco: fried plantain with a hot tomato sauce.
Asaro: yam and sweet potato porridge.
Ayeb or **iab:** fresh yoghurt cheese made from strained yoghurt hung overnight in a piece of muslin.
Berbere: an essential Ethiopian spice mixture made with up to 18 hot and aromatic spices.
Cassava, manioc or **yuca:** a family of coarse roots that are boiled and pounded to make bread and various other farinaceous dishes. There are bitter and sweet varieties (note that the bitter variety is poisonous until cooked).
Egusi: ground melon seeds, added to stews and soups as a thickening agent.
Enjera, enjerra or **injera:** a soft, spongy Ethiopian and Eritrean flatbread made with teff (a grain that was grown only in Ethiopia but, latterly, has been cultivated in the USA), wheat, barley, oats or cornmeal. Fermented with yeast, it should have a distinct sour tang.
Froi: fish and shrimp in an aubergine stew.
Fufu: a stiff pudding of maize or cassava (qv) flour, or pounded yam (qv).
Gari: a solid, heavy pudding made from ground fermented cassava (qv), served with thick soups.
Ground rice: a kind of stiff rice pudding served to accompany soup.
Jollof rice: a kind of hot, spicy risotto, with tomatoes, onions and (usually) chicken.
Kanyah: a sweet snack from Sierre Leone made from rice, peanuts and sugar.
Kelewele or **do-do:** fried plantain.
Kenkey: a starchy pudding that's prepared by pounding dried maize and water into a paste, then steaming inside plantain leaves. Usually eaten with meat, fish or vegetable stews.
Moi-moi or **moin-moin:** steamed beancake, served with meat or fish.
Ogbono: a large seed similar to egusi (qv). Although it doesn't thicken as much, it is used in a similar way.
Pepper soup: a light, peppery soup made with either fish or meat.

Shito: a dark red-hot pepper paste from Ghana, made from dried shrimps blended with onions and tomatoes.
Suya: a spicy Nigerian meat kebab.
Tuo or **tuwo:** a stiff rice pudding, sometimes served as rice balls to accompany soup.
Ugali: a Swahili word for bread made from cornmeal and water.
Ugba: Nigerian soy beans; also called oil beans.
Waakye: a dish of rice and black-eyed beans mixed with meat or chicken in gravy.
Waatse: rice and black-eyed beans cooked together.
Wot: a thick, dark sauce made from slowly cooked onions, garlic, butter and spices – an essential component in the aromatic stews of East Africa.
Doro wot, a stew containing chicken and hard-boiled eggs, is a particularly common dish.

CARIBBEAN
Ackee: a red-skinned fruit with yellow flesh that looks and tastes like scrambled eggs when cooked; traditionally served in a Jamaican dish of salt cod, onion and peppers.
Bammy or **bammie:** pancake-shaped, deep-fried cassava bread, commonly served with fried fish.
Breadfruit: introduced from West Africa in 1792 by Captain Bligh, this football-sized fruit has sweet, creamy flesh that's a cross between sweet potato and chestnut. Eaten as a vegetable.
Bush tea: a herbal tea attributed with anti-toxin or medicinal properties. It can be made from anything from cerese (a Jamaican vine plant) to mint or fennel.
Callaloo: the spinach-like leaves of either taro or malanga, often used as a base for a thick soup flavoured with pork or crab meat.
Channa: chickpeas.
Coo-coo: a polenta-like cake of cornmeal and okra.
Cow foot: a stew made from the foot of the cow, which is boiled with vegetables. The cartilage gives the stew a gummy or gelatinous texture.

Curried (or **curry**) **goat:** more usually lamb in London; the meat is marinated and slow-cooked until tender.
Dasheen: a root vegetable with a texture similar to yam (qv).
Escoveitched (or **escovitch**) **fish:** fish fried or grilled then pickled in a tangy sauce with onions, sweet peppers and vinegar; similar to escabèche.
Festival: deep-fried, slightly sweet dumpling often served with fried fish.
Foo-foo: a Barbadian dish of pounded plantains, seasoned, rolled into balls and served hot.
Jerk: chicken or pork marinated in chilli and hot spices, then slowly roasted or barbecued.
Patty or **pattie:** a savoury pastry snack similar to a pasty, made with turmeric-flavoured short-crust pastry, usually filled with beef, saltfish or vegetables.
Peas or **beans:** black-eyed beans, black beans, green peas and red kidney beans (the names are interchangeable).
Pepperpot: traditionally a stew of meat and cassereep, a juice obtained from cassava; in London it's more likely to be a meat or vegetable stew with cassava.
Phoulorie: a Trinidadian snack of fried doughballs often eaten with a sweet tamarind sauce.
Plantain or **plantin:** a savoury variety of banana that is cooked and used in much the same way as potato.
Rice and peas: rice cooked with kidney or gungo beans, pepper seasoning and coconut milk.
Roti: the Indian flatbread, usually filled with curried fish, meat or vegetables.
Saltfish: salt cod, classically combined with ackee (qv) or callaloo (qv).
Sorrel: not the European herb but a type of hibiscus with a sour-sweet flavour. Used to flavour a traditional Christmas drink.
Soursop: a dark green, slightly spiny fruit; the pulp, blended with milk and sugar, is a refreshing drink.
Sweet potato: most varieties of this tuberous root have a sweetish taste, although some are drier than others.
Yam: a large tuber, with a yellow or white flesh and slightly nutty flavour.

RESTAURANTS

Why the extra 'h' in Freshh? Well, it is Camden, so a bohemian touch is only to be expected. The food is a mixed bag. We liked the melt-in-the-mouth sweet potato korma in mild, rich coconut sauce, and a lamb and chicken curry left our taste buds tingling. However, jerk chicken was a little on the sweet side, grilled pepper steak was flabby and flavourless, and vegetable balls with apple dip were nothing to shout about. Other options include goat curry, braised oxtail, wraps and rotis. We were impressed with the first-floor restaurant for its super-efficient service, and its clean and bright pale-green decor. There's also a bar on the ground floor and a roof terrace where you can bathe in Caribbean-style sunshine (well, English weather permitting), ideally with glasses of freshly produced pineapple juice and Guinness punch. *Babies and children welcome: children's menu; high chairs. Booking advisable. Entertainment: DJ 8pm Fri, Sat. No-smoking tables. Separate rooms for parties, seating 14 and 45. Tables outdoors (12, roof garden). Takeaway service; delivery service (within 2-mile radius).* **Map 27 B1.**

★ Mango Room
10-12 Kentish Town Road, NW1 8NH (7482 5065/www.mangoroom.co.uk). Camden Town tube. **Lunch served** noon-5pm, **dinner served** 5-11pm Mon-Sat. **Meals served** noon-11pm Sun. **Main courses** £9-£13. **Service** 10%; 12.5% for parties of 5 or more. **Credit** MC, V. Caribbean Mango Room has a deserved reputation for great dishes matched by attentive, unobtrusive service. Set apart from the slew of casual drop-in Caribbean restaurants by its ritzier clientele and warm bright decor (all red, blue and yellow hues), it's an intimate and convivial place to enjoy a meal. A starter of ackee with spring onion and sweet pepper was flavoursome and had a good soft texture, even if it was a little heavy on the red pepper. This was outshone by excellent fluffy saltfish fritters with apple chutney. For mains, curry goat was tender and delicately spiced, while seared yellow fin tuna with mango sauce, flavoured with Caribbean spices, was fresh and light. The rice and peas – unusually made with black-eyed beans – was perfectly cooked, boosted by thyme. The menu is strong on fish; sea bass, snapper and salmon fillet all figure. Banana brûlée or banana and coconut cake make a fine finish. The food is complemented by a carefully selected wine list, helping keep Mango Room among London's best restaurants for innovative Caribbean food. *Babies and children welcome: high chairs. Booking advisable weekends. No-smoking tables. Separate room for parties, seats 30.* **Map 27 D2.**

Stroud Green N4

Hummingbird
84 Stroud Green Road, N4 3EN (7263 9690/ www.thehummingbird.co.uk). Finsbury Park tube/ rail. **Meals served** noon-midnight Mon-Sat; 1-11pm Sun. **Main courses** £6.50-£19.95. **Credit** MC, V. Trinidadian
This long-established family-run restaurant, kitted out in pale cream and wood, is the smarter sibling of the slightly dowdier nearby Hannah's (96 Stroud Green Road, 7263 4004). The food is still good. Rich red bean soup with an unusual depth of flavour; densely textured, light dumplings; fragrant, flaky coco bread; and beautifully spiced goat curry – all are hearty, with satisfying rounded flavours. Fish dishes such as lobster, shrimp, coo-coo, and whole red snapper are justly popular. In addition, we can particularly recommend the classic ackee and saltfish, and a meltingly gooey sweet potato bake. Main courses are generously served with plantains, yams, salads and rice and peas. The distinctly flavoured own-made sauces and marinades are a strong point. However, service standards seem to have slipped in recent years. Whereas once Hummingbird attracted repeat visits from its loyal regulars, it has now become a party venue, popular with large groups. Consequently, service can sometimes be a bit slow and staff are occasionally brusque. *Babies and children welcome: high chairs. Booking essential weekends. Tables outdoors (2, pavement). Takeaway service. Vegetarian menu.*

The Americas

NORTH AMERICAN

It's all been happening in the North American sector this year. We say a hearty hello to four new openings: **Curve**, a smart Docklands option that was nominated for Best Alfresco Dining in *Time Out*'s 2005 Eating & Drinking Awards; **The Bar & Grill**, a lovely Smithfields eaterie (with a rather daft generic name); **Missouri Grill**, a reliable steakhouse in the City; and **Automat**, a modish Mayfair take on the US diner.

We also say goodbye to **Ashbell's** and the **Harvard Bar & Grill**, both of which have closed. We applaud the changes to **Christopher's** modern American menu (and hope it lasts), and we absolutely insist that you go have some barbecue at the **Arkansas Café**. Right now. You'll thank us.

Central
City E1, EC1, EC3

★ ★ Arkansas Café
Unit 12, Old Spitalfields Market, E1 6AA (7377 6999). Liverpool Street tube/rail. **Lunch served** noon-2.30pm Mon-Fri; noon-4pm Sun. **Dinner served** by arrangement for parties of 25 or more only. **Main courses** £7-£16. **Service** 10% for parties of 5 or more. **Credit** MC, V.
The most authentic barbecue restaurant in London, the Arkansas Café is where you go if you want the real deal. The atmosphere is redneck chic, with seating made up of whatever Bubba, the gregarious owner, has put out that week (folding chairs, church pews). The art is largely pictures of pigs, although there is a classy painted mirror bearing the unarguable adage, 'Nice girls don't spit'. A sign on the door reads: 'Michael Winner doesn't eat here'. Marvellous though all of that is, the food is the thing. Pork ribs arrived huge, glistening, juicy, perfectly cooked, unbelievably meaty: divinity on a plate. A 10oz steak of Irish beef that was ordered medium arrived startlingly blue. Sent back for a little more time on the grill, it returned well done. Never mind – even overcooked the flesh was so tender it fell apart under the fork. All platters are served with garlicky new potatoes, fresh, light coleslaw, purple cabbage salad, and beans (cooked from scratch in-house). Puddings tend toward the heavy (chocolate cake, pecan pie, cheesecake), but you're not here to diet. *Babies and children admitted. Booking advisable; not accepted Sun. No-smoking tables. Separate room for parties, seats 50. Tables outdoors (30, terrace inside market, Sun only). Takeaway service.* **Map 12 R5.**

★ The Bar & Grill NEW
2-3 West Smithfield, EC1A 9JX (0870 4422541/ www.barandgrill.co.uk). Farringdon tube/rail. **Meals served** noon-midnight Mon-Thur; noon-1am Fri; 5pm-1am Sat. **Main courses** £6.75-£45. **Service** 12.5%. **Credit** AmEx, MC, V.
A new face in Smithfield, this is a gorgeous place, with lots of polished dark wood contrasted with creamy white cushioned chairs, white walls and tasteful modern art. Service is eager and helpful. The menu is heavy on steaks: beef steak, ostrich steak, lamb steak – even Kobe steaks from the famous wagyu breed of cattle, at heart-clutching prices (£45 a serving). Once you've ordered your meat, you choose from a long list of rubs and sauces: lemon and garlic, salt and pepper, rosemary and honey… giving you unusual control over your own meal. There are also pizzas, fish dishes and burgers. A starter of barbecue ribs arrived thick and meaty, lightly doused in a delicate, sweet sauce. Another starter of caesar salad with bacon was crisp and peppery. A T-bone main course arrived smoky and perfectly cooked, while a ribeye was tender and juicy. Sides were less memorable: roast vegetables were mostly peppers and onion on a skewer; french beans were adequate, but unspectacular. Puddings put us back on track. The apple crumble was fresh out of the oven and big enough for two, while the ristretto (vanilla ice-cream doused in espresso) was light and very grown-up. Highly recommended. *Babies and children welcome: children's menu; high chairs. Booking essential. Disabled: toilet. Separate area for parties, seats 10.* **Map 11 O5.**

Missouri Grill NEW
76 Aldgate High Street, EC3N 1BD (7481 4010/ www.missourigrill.com). Aldgate tube. **Meals served** noon-11pm Mon-Fri. **Main courses** £10-£19.50. **Set dinner** £12 2 courses, £16 3 courses. **Service** 12.5%. **Credit** AmEx, MC, V.
Situated on the eastern edge of the City, the Missouri is tailored to the business lunch and, indeed, to the company credit card. Its bare-walled decor even makes the place feel a little like an annex of the boardroom, especially as the general hubbub would be equally at home there. Dishes are also a little businesslike, but they fulfil every expectation: straightforward, served in hearty portions and made with high-quality ingredients. As the restaurant's name implies, grills are the thing. The beefsteaks are American cuts, from the Buccleuch Estates in Scotland, aged for 28 days for flavour and tenderness. Our New York Strip was beautifully cooked, medium rare as requested, served with thin, crisp chips and béarnaise sauce. Starters range from the traditional (clam chowder, Maryland crab cake) to the more contemporary (carpaccio of salmon with key lime dressing), while puds include pecan maple tart and a peach melba with proper grilled peaches. Around us, City suits – almost all male – were making steady progress through the lengthy wine list. The service was consummate. If you could take an office lunch at Missouri every week, you'd be pretty pleased. *Babies and children welcome: children's menu; high chairs. Booking essential lunch. No-smoking tables. Separate room for parties, seats 14.* **Map 12 R6.**

Covent Garden WC2

★ Christopher's

18 Wellington Street, WC2E 7DD (7240 4222/ www.christophersgrill.com). Covent Garden tube. Bar **Open/snacks served** noon-11pm Mon-Sat. **Snacks** £3-£9.
Restaurant **Brunch served** 11.30am-3pm Sat, Sun. **Lunch served** noon-3pm Mon-Fri. **Dinner served** 5-11pm Mon-Sat. **Main courses** £12-£28. **Set meal** (5.30-7pm, 10-11.15pm Mon-Sat) £12.75 2 courses, £16.75 3 courses.
Both **Service** 12.5%. **Credit** AmEx, DC, MC, V.
This first-floor restaurant in the heart of Covent Garden, with a grand Italianate staircase sweeping upwards, is a classic casual-elegant eaterie. Its dining room is spacious, with huge windows and a creamy colour scheme, and staff strike a perfect balance between friendliness and politeness. In recent years the modern American menu has veered from the banal to the elaborate; at the moment it's the best it has been in a long while. We started with a creative take on the waldorf salad, with crisp vegetables neatly encased in thin slices of chilled roasted duck – delicate and delicious. Another starter, ceviche of salmon with lime and tequila, was perfect summer fare, while a 10oz grilled ribeye with buttermilk-fried onions and garlicky mash was cooked to perfection. For dessert, vanilla soufflé with peach ice-cream was so light it fairly flew off the plate. At least, that's what we told ourselves. The wine list is short but inventive, and there's a good bar downstairs, with stylish design and well-meaning (if occasionally hopeless) bar staff. In all, this is a friendly, attractive, useful place.
Babies and children welcome: children's menu; high chairs. Booking advisable Mon-Fri. Separate room for parties, seats 40. **Map 18 L7**.

Joe Allen

13 Exeter Street, WC2E 7DT (7836 0651). Covent Garden tube. **Brunch served** 11.30am-4pm Sat, Sun. **Meals served** noon-12.45am Mon-Fri; 11.30am-12.45am Sat; 11.30am-11.30pm Sun. **Main courses** £8.50-£15. **Set brunch** £18.50 2 courses, £20.50 3 courses incl drink. **Set meal** (noon-3pm Mon-Fri, 5-6.45pm Mon-Sat) £15 2 courses, £17 3 courses incl coffee. **Credit** AmEx, MC, V.
As we waited 45 minutes for our main course, we had ample time for people-watching. At one point, a thin young woman wrapped in a pashmina stormed by us: her large eyes perfectly made up, her departure spectacular – an actress to her

marrow. That's what this place is all about. West End cast and crew, theatre managers and those who love them: all pile in every night. Food is such an afterthought that, frankly, it's no surprise it's not particularly good. You come here hoping to see Lee Evans scoffing the slightly dry pork belly and puzzling over the niggardly portion of bland potato 'hash' – not to eat it yourself. Or you might wish to catch Christian Slater flirting with a make-up artist while trying the slightly dry barbecue ribs, served with what tastes like instant rice and undercooked black-eyed peas. Or Brooke Shields picking at the strawberry shortcake, which treats strawberries like gold dust, giving each serving what seems like less than one large strawberry, sliced. Not that we saw any of them, of course. There was nobody famous around on our visit. Maybe next time. But it remains an institution.
Babies and children admitted. Booking advisable. Entertainment: pianist 9pm-1am Mon-Sat; jazz trio 8-11pm Sun. No-smoking tables. Takeaway service. **Map 18 L7**.

PJ's Grill

30 Wellington Street, WC2E 7BD (7240 7529/ www.pjsgrill.net). Covent Garden tube. **Meals served** noon-1am Mon-Sat; noon-4pm Sun. **Main courses** £8.95-£13.95. **Set meal** (5-7.30pm Mon-Sat) £9.95 2 courses. **Service** 12.5%. **Credit** AmEx, DC, JCB, MC, V.
A favourite with local office workers and the before- and after-theatre crowd, this long, thin restaurant is nicely designed. There's plenty of polished wood, and vintage posters from the theatre and movie worlds. The bar up front can get noisy, so ask for seats at the back if you're hoping for a little peace and quiet. The menu is an appetising blend of old-fashioned dishes and more creative cuisine. A crispy duck starter was delightful and sizeable, but crab cake was greasy and starkly short of crab. Main courses were steadier – a grilled duck salad with rice noodles was light and tasty, the duck well cooked, the dressing delicate. Another main of linguini with spicy tomato sauce was simple, but well executed. Puddings seem somewhat limited, but you can't go wrong with lemon and mango sorbet. Service was friendly, even cheeky, and the wine list had plenty of reasonably priced options. PJ's is a good place to go with a group of laid-back friends.
Babies and children welcome: children's menu; high chairs. Booking advisable. Entertainment: jazz pianist 10.30pm-1am Wed-Sat. No-smoking tables. Tables outdoors (5, pavement). **Map 18 L6**.
For branch see index.

Fitzrovia W1

Eagle Bar Diner ✓

3-5 Rathbone Place, W1T 1HJ (7637 1418/ www.eaglebardiner.com). Tottenham Court Road tube. **Meals served** noon-11pm Mon-Wed; noon-midnight Thur, Fri; 10am-midnight Sat; 11am-6pm Sun. **Main courses** £4-£8.75. **Service** 10% for parties of 6 or more. **Credit** MC, V.
We've loved this arch, modern interpretation of a US diner since it opened a few years back with a milkshake in one metaphorical hand and a cocktail in the other. It still looks beautiful, decked out in sleek leather booths and mood lighting. You'll find a (relatively) healthy approach to fast food here. The menu is heavy on burgers, but with plenty of variations: from grilled beef to tuna and vegetarian. There's a good selection of unusual salads (such as one featuring salt beef and new potatoes), a few huge sandwiches, and hearty breakfasts of the eggs-and-pancakes ilk. On our most recent visit we had barbecue chicken salad, which was light and flavourful with lots of fresh greens. We also enjoyed a perfectly cooked barbecue beef hamburger. The fries are always crisp and not greasy, and it's worth sacrificing your cholesterol count for the shakes – particularly the peanut butter and banana version. In the negatives column: service is a bit offhand, waiters can be hard to track down, and prices for shakes and fruit smoothies are quite high. Otherwise, this is a hip, reliable option.
Babies and children admitted (until 9pm if dining). Booking advisable. Disabled: toilet. Entertainment: DJs 7.30pm Wed-Sat. Takeaway service. **Map 17 K6.**

Mayfair W1

Automat NEW

33 Dover Street, W1S 4NF (7499 3033). Green Park tube. **Meals served** noon-midnight Mon-Fri; 11am-midnight Sat, Sun. **Main courses** £6-£32. **Service** 12.5%. **Credit** AmEx, DC, JCB, MC, V.
Automat isn't an apt name for this new homage to the American diner. Yes, food is freshly prepared, of good quality and served swiftly, but there are no automatons: the service has a distinctly human face. The creation of New York architect and nightclub owner Carlos Almada, it's a brasserie that specialises in simple dishes, many of them nods to US fast food in its heyday – chicken noodle soup, spaghetti with tomato and basil sauce, apple pie. Yet the pricing is for London restaurant food,

Arkansas Café. See p35.

2005. A quarter-wedge of iceberg lettuce, served with ranch dressing: when did you last see that on a menu? Never? Here this 1970s classic is £6, and comes with a creamy buttermilk dressing tasting of dill, with a hint of garlic, pieces of ventrèche (a bit like bacon) and a halved boiled egg. It looked great, and tasted better than you'd think iceberg lettuce ever could. Other standouts were crab cake with guacamole, and a flavoursome hanger steak with crisp chips and decent béarnaise sauce; less successful was a flabby macaroni cheese. The faux railway-carriage interior and perfect tiling are newly built, and everything, from the well-spoken staff to the delicious basket of breads, is terribly, terribly Mayfair.
Babies and children admitted. Booking advisable. Disabled: toilet. No-smoking tables. Takeaway service. **Map 9 H7.**

Soho W1

★ Bodean's
10 Poland Street, W1F 8PZ (7287 7575/ www.bodeansbbq.com). Oxford Circus or Piccadilly Circus tube.
Deli **Open** noon-11pm Mon-Sat; noon-10.30pm Sun.
Restaurant **Lunch served** noon-3pm, **dinner served** 6-11pm Mon-Fri. **Meals served** noon-11pm Sat; noon-10.30pm Sun. **Main courses** £6-£14. **Set meal** (minimum 8) £15.95 2 courses, £18.95 3 courses. **Service** 12.5%.
Both **Credit** AmEx, MC, V.
Bodean's has expanded from its excellent, clubby space in Soho to add a sleek and modern version in Clapham, so clearly its ribs, steaks and brisket platters have found favour. And it's easy to see why. The atmosphere is laid-back class, with leather banquettes, wood-panelled walls and baseball perpetually on the flat-screen TV. Service is professional, and the meat, if you order wisely, is sublimely cooked. Our general advice on Bodean's is to skip the starters – they're not particularly earth-shattering, and they'll fill you up too soon. Among the mains, skip the pulled pork, which is bland, and the chicken, which is dry, and head straight for the ribs. A rack of baby-back ribs was juicy, chewy meat perfection. If that's too undignified for you, try the brisket, which has been marinated and then slowly cooked until it all but dissolves on the tongue. Indulge in a side of tomatoey baked beans and some crispy fries – and that, friends, is what they call down South 'good eatin'. Not a place for vegetarians.
Babies and children welcome: children's area; high chairs. Booking advisable (restaurant). No smoking (restaurant). Restaurant & deli available for hire. Tables outdoors (4, pavement). Takeaway service. **Map 17 J6.**
For branch see index.

★ Ed's Easy Diner
12 Moor Street, W1V 5LH (7434 4439/ www.edseasydiner.co.uk). Leicester Square or Tottenham Court Road tube. **Meals served** 11.30am-midnight daily. **Main courses** £4.40-£5.50. **Minimum** (6pm-midnight Fri-Sun) £4.45. **Service** 12.5%. **Credit** MC, V.
Ed's is everybody's favourite place to indulge in the all-American pastime of eating greasy hamburger and fries. Designed like 1950s diners straight out of *Happy Days*, each branch is more or less the same: counter seating, a few booths, a cheery red and white colour scheme, mini-jukeboxes scattered around, and a menu filled almost exclusively with burgers and 'dogs. The formula rarely changes, but these days we get the feeling a few corners are being cut that were not being cut before. The hamburgers are still made to order, and served hot and fresh, but the meat in ours tasted more processed than it had done in the past. The fries and onion rings are crisp, but the catsup tasted like the cheaper kind – a shame, as such things do matter. Still, the milkshakes and malts were, as always, dangerously delectable, and the waiters were friendlier and more patient than we deserved.
Babies and children welcome: children's menu. No smoking. Tables outdoors (2, pavement). Takeaway service; delivery service (within 1-mile radius on orders over £10). **Map 17 K6.**
For branches see index.

BEST NORTH AMERICAN

For waterfront alfresco dining
Curve. *See p41.*

For impressing a date
The Bar & Grill. *See p35.*

For making Americans homesick
Bodean's. *See below.*

For eating on expenses
Christopher's. *See p36.*

For dinner with loud friends
Big Easy. *See p39.*

For burgers
Eagle Bar Diner. *See p36.* See also
Budget, starting on p292.

Strand WC2

Smollensky's on the Strand ✓
105 Strand, WC2R 0AA (7497 2101/ www.smollenskys.co.uk). Covent Garden, Embankment or Temple tube/Charing Cross tube/rail.
Bar **Open** noon-11pm Mon-Thur; noon-12.30am Fri, Sat; noon-5.30pm, 6.30-10.30pm Sun.
Restaurant **Meals served** noon-11pm Mon-Sat; noon-10pm Sun. **Main courses** £8.50-£19.95. **Set meal** (noon-7pm, after 10.30pm Mon-Fri) £10 2 courses, £12 3 courses. **Service** 12.5%.
Both **Credit** AmEx, DC, MC, V.
This basement eaterie is an old-school steakhouse of the sort you'll find in virtually every US city of any size, doling out Manhattan cocktails, big ribeye steaks and heavy desserts. There's a large bar, but the crowd – a mixture of office workers and professional couples – is rarely rowdy. As they drink and dine, a piano player works his way through the repertoire of Billy and Elton to occasional scattered applause; it's a bit like a cruise ship out of water. We started with grilled wun tuns, which were tasty and light (with a sweet sauce for dipping). Next came ribeye steaks: perfectly grilled to order, and served with fries, creamed spinach and crisp green beans. For pudding, a warm brownie with vanilla ice-cream was exactly the same as in the thousands of other restaurants that serve it. Don't come here looking for anything new, but if you're after reliable old favourites, you won't be disappointed. It's also a good spot for families, with kids' entertainment at weekends and friendly staff.
Babies and children welcome: booster seats; children's menu; entertainment (noon-3pm Sat, Sun); high chairs; toys. Booking advisable. Entertainment: pianist 7.30-10.30pm Mon-Sat; DJ 11pm-12.30am Fri, Sat; jazz 8.15-10.30pm Sun. No-smoking tables. **Map 18 L7.**
For branches see index.

West

Bayswater W2

Harlem
78 Westbourne Grove, W2 5RT (7985 0900/ www.harlemsoulfood.com). Bayswater or Notting Hill Gate tube. **Open** 11am-2am Mon-Thur; 11am-2.30am Fri; 9.30am-2.30am Sat; 9.30am-midnight Sun. **Meals served** 11am-1am Mon-Fri; 9.30am-1am Sat; 9.30am-11.30pm Sat. **Service** 12.5%. **Credit** AmEx, DC, MC, V.
Sitting comfortably amid Notting Hill's glam boutiques, the 'soul food' restaurant Harlem never seems to fit its name. Manhattan maybe, but Harlem? Never. Lately, a new branch has opened in Brixton where, perhaps, it will find its spirit of funk. But will the owners learn that playing soul music does not a soul food restaurant make? The look of both branches is pleasant, with lots of dark wood and big windows, yet the food is another story. A starter of clam chowder was rich and

briny, but another of calamares was small for the price. A main of fried chicken was well cooked, though unaccompanied. If it were true soul food, it would have come with gravy and mashed potatoes, greens or green beans and cornbread. A side dish of macaroni and cheese seemed to have been cooked too long. Another main of hamburger and fries was, by contrast, juicy, big and fresh – but hamburgers are not soul food. Last year we fell in love with the white chocolate and blueberry cheesecake, but this year it was dry and tasteless: symbolic, in a way, of the restaurant itself.
Babies and children welcome: children's portions; high chairs. Booking advisable. Entertainment: DJs 9pm Mon-Sat. Takeaway service. **Map 7 B6.**
For branch see index.

Chiswick W4

The Coyote
2 Fauconberg Road, W4 3JY (8742 8545/ www.thecoyote.co.uk). Gunnersbury tube/rail/ Chiswick rail. **Meals served** 5-10.30pm Mon-Fri; 10am-11pm Sat; 10am-10.30pm Sun. **Main courses** £8-£15. **Service** 12.5% for parties of 6 or more. **Credit** AmEx, JCB, MC, V.
This neighbourhood joint has always had a sharp and creative kitchen with a real knack for complex Southwestern sauces – and that's absolutely still the case. The food is reliably good, but the service is annoyingly amateurish. We'd perused the menu for 15 minutes before the waitress took our order, and only then did she tell us that five dishes on the already small list were not available. We revised our orders to match the limited offerings, and were not disappointed by the result. A starter of marinated chicken brochettes with strawberry sauce was a brilliant mix of flavours. To follow, steak with crispy tobacco onions and smoky chipotle sauce had been perfectly cooked – tender and memorable. Another main course of grilled tuna steak atop squid salad was juicy, with delicate and complex flavours. The only problem all night long was the service. It took half an hour between asking for the bill and paying it, even though the room wasn't as crowded. Nevertheless, the Coyote is a small local venue, and sometimes it's worth suffering for excellent cooking.
Babies and children welcome: children's menu; high chairs. Booking essential dinner. Tables outdoors (7, pavement). Takeaway service.
For branch see index.

Kensington W8

Sticky Fingers
1A Phillimore Gardens, W8 7QG (7938 5338/ www.stickyfingers.co.uk). High Street Kensington tube.
Bar **Open** noon-8pm Mon-Sat.
Restaurant **Meals served** noon-11pm Mon-Sat; noon-10.30pm Sun. **Main courses** £9.25-£17.95. **Service** 12.5%.
Both **Credit** AmEx, JCB, MC, V.
A sort of Hard Rock Café-lite, Sticky Fingers is a loud, determinedly cheerful restaurant. It's co-owned by former Rolling Stone Bill Wyman (as the posters on the tube remind you), so the rock 'n' roll soundtrack and Stonesian decor should come as no surprise. The menu offers your basic nachos, ribs and burgers, and it's all very straightforward. In fact, were it not for the famous name on the bottom line, this place would probably not merit much attention. But famous it is, and so during the day the seats are full of west London yummy mummies with their pricey prams and pampered toddlers, all cheerfully welcomed by the international staff. Those who find other people's kids pesky should come in the evening, when the crowd is more grown up. Prices seem to have been moderated recently, but they're still a bit silly: £13 for a chicken breast with french fries, £12 for a hamburger. We still find the food adequate but unspectacular, and we still marvel at the popularity of this underwhelming venue.
Babies and children welcome: children's menu; entertainment (face-painting & magician 1.30-3.30pm Sat, Sun); high chairs. Booking advisable. No smoking (noon-5pm Sat, Sun). Takeaway service. **Map 7 A9.**

RESTAURANTS

Westbourne Park W2

★ Lucky 7

*127 Westbourne Park Road, W2 5QL (7727
6771). Royal Oak or Westbourne Park tube.*
Meals served 11am-11pm Mon-Thur; 9am-
11pm Fri, Sat; 9am-10.30pm Sun. **Main
courses** £4.25-£7.95. **Service** 12.5%.
Credit MC, V.
Tom Conran's take on the American diner theme
is a classy joint with big booths (which you have
to share with others when it gets crowded), lots
of mirrors, a rolling-dice theme, and a short but
solid menu of burgers, sandwiches, salads and
shakes. The salads are huge and attractive, but
we were lured to the dark side by the smell of
frying meat. The burgers were very dense
creations, with onion-infused beef served with all
the fixings. On the side, skinny fries were
excellent and beer-batter onion rings heavenly.
Milkshakes come in three levels of thickness –
starting at £4 for a regular, with prices climbing
rapidly the thicker they get. The normal is thick
enough for most. Breakfasts are similarly
unhealthy-but-good, with eggs and pancakes
leading the way. Lucky 7 is generally a good
option, but bear in mind the food seems to get
greasier the busier it is. One more niggle: sharing
a booth with strangers feels weirdly intimate, so
try visiting in between rush hours.
*Babies and children welcome: booster seats.
Bookings not accepted. Separate room for
parties, seats 35. Tables outdoors (2, pavement).
Takeaway service.* **Map 7 A5**.

South West

Chelsea SW3

Big Easy

*332-334 King's Road, SW3 5UR (7352 4071/
www.bigeasy.uk.com). Sloane Square tube then
11, 19, 22 bus.*
Bar **Open** noon-11pm Mon-Fri; 11am-11pm Sat;
11am-10.30pm Sun. **Main courses** £7.95-£14.95.
Restaurant **Meals served** noon-11.30pm Mon-
Thur; noon-12.20am Fri; 11am-12.20am Sat;
11am-11.20pm Sun. **Main courses** £8.95-£22.50.
Set lunch (noon-5pm Mon-Fri) £7.95 2 courses.
Service 12.5%.
Both **Credit** AmEx, DC, JCB, MC, V.
This is a raucous restaurant where the borderline-
hilarious Southern US decor (all rustic wood walls
and red and white checked tablecloths) lives up to
its motto – 'put a li'l South in yo' mouth'. Whenever
we've visited Big Easy, it has always been buzzing;
on our most recent trip a two-piece band was
knocking the hell out of a variety of hits from the
1970s and '80s, the crowd had already had a bit to
drink, and the mood was light. Starters include
spicy 'voodoo' chicken wings, and cool snow crab
claws ('imported from Alaska', the website
explains mildly, 'because they're better'). Mains are
served in impossibly huge portions (vast steaks,
hunks of lobster, buckets of shellfish), all perfectly
cooked, and served with cheerful efficiency by the
peppy waiting staff. Wash it all back with a long-
neck beer or a cocktail, and that's good eatin'.
Occasional promotions include the likes of a
lobster festival in July. Not somewhere to go for a
romantic meal, but hard to beat with a group of
friends in good voice.
*Babies and children welcome: children's menu;
crayons; high chairs. Entertainment: musicians
8.30pm daily. No-smoking tables. Tables
outdoors (5, pavement). Takeaway service.*
Map 14 D12.

Gloucester Road SW7

Black & Blue

*105 Gloucester Road, SW7 4SS (7244 7666/
www.blackandblue.biz). Gloucester Road tube.*
Meals served noon-11pm Mon-Thur, Sun;
noon-11.30pm Fri, Sat. **Main courses** £8-£25.
Service 12.5%. **Credit** AmEx, MC, V.
This small but mighty chain of steak restaurants
stepped into a niche a few years ago and filled it
perfectly. Until then we didn't know how badly we

Black & Blue

wanted small, chic steakhouses where dishes are
moderately priced and perfectly prepared. But
clearly we did, as London cannot get enough of
them. Perhaps the key is that there's nothing earth-
shatteringly innovative about the B&Bs. They're
all good-looking places, with rows of green leather
booths to sink into, shared central tables for lone
diners, and an annoying soundtrack of 1980s pop
hits. The food is similarly straightforward; starters
include prawn cocktails and a gooey artichoke and
spinach dip with tortilla chips. But while it may
not win any awards, it's winning the hearts and
minds of London's office classes, who pack the
seats nightly in each of the five branches. They
come for the well-cut steaks (fillet, ribeye, sirloin
and T-bone), which are served with (adequate) fries
and fresh, crisp salads. The service is sharp and
honest (our waitress quietly warned us off one
wine and instead steered us to an excellent South
African merlot), and the food is reliable. A good
place to know about.
*Babies and children admitted. Bookings not
accepted. No-smoking tables. Tables outdoors
(3, pavement).* **Map 13 C10**.
For branches see index.

South Kensington SW7

Tootsies Grill

2005 RUNNER-UP BEST FAMILY RESTAURANT
*107 Old Brompton Road, SW7 3LE (7581 8942/
www.tootsiesrestaurants.co.uk). South Kensington
tube.* **Meals served** noon-11pm Mon-Thur; noon-
11.30pm Fri; 10am-11.30pm Sat; 10am-11pm Sun.
Main courses £6.25-£13.50. **Service** 12.5%.
Credit AmEx, MC, V.
After a high-level meeting with the T-Rex in the
Natural History Museum, hungry families in the
know take a walk to this link in the extensive
Tootsies chain. Other branches, notably Putney
Wharf and Clapham, with their outdoor seating
and children's activities, are heaving at weekends,
but this one, which matches its more frenetic
suburban siblings for friendliness and grub
reliability, has a more relaxed air. Such reliability
is best represented by the classic burger, lean and
thick, served in a sourdough bun with brilliant
fries, salad and relishes. It's the best thing on the
menu, but you can go off-piste with the more exotic
chicken and goat's cheese or chorizo and red

RESTAURANTS

Curve

pepper options, or leave burger country and choose ribs, kebabs or hearty salads. The excellent-value children's menu (£4.95) has the stock quiz-and-colouring-in distractions, but also lists some encouragingly wholesome organic dishes, such as shepherd's pie or 'curly whirly chicken'. Children who can read, however, are more likely to plump for burgers or hot dogs and chips. A riot of ice-creams, sauces and sweetie embellishments is included in the price, as are drinks. Overeating is inevitable, but fun.

Babies and children welcome: children's menu; crayons; high chairs. Booking advisable; not accepted lunch Sat, Sun. No smoking. Tables outdoors (3, pavement). Takeaway service.
Map 14 D11.
For branches see index.

Wimbledon SW19

Jo Shmo's
33 High Street, Wimbledon, SW19 5BY (8879 3845/www.joshmos.com). Wimbledon tube/rail then 93 bus. **Meals served** noon-11pm Mon-Sat; noon-10.30pm Sun. **Main courses** £5.95-£14.50. **Service** 10%. **Credit** AmEx, MC, V.

The chic, modern dining room at Jo Shmo's is all polished dark wood, wide windows and exotic flowers. By day it's popular with mothers with small children; by night, it fills with couples. The menu takes a light approach to American cuisine that manages to be perfect for both sets of folk. Kids are drawn to the hamburgers and fries, adults to the salads, steaks and ribs. We started with a tostada – a flour tortilla topped with slim slices of grilled chicken and cheddar cheese then grilled. It was a bit bland, and quite small for the price. Main courses remedied matters; a sirloin steak was perfectly grilled, and we were given the option of having it with fries or a salad (there you go, Atkins dieters), leaving us no choice but to take the healthy option. Then we cheated, ordering a delicious side helping of crisply fried tobacco onions. A decadent slice of chocolate cake was memorably rich and fresh. A varied choice of house wines also contributes to making Shmo's a classy option down south.

Babies and children welcome: children's menu; high chairs. Disabled: toilet. No-smoking tables. Tables outdoors (2, pavement).
For branch see index.

South
Wandsworth SW17

Dexter's Grill & Bar
20 Bellevue Road, SW17 7EB (8767 1858). Wandsworth Common rail/319 bus. **Meals served** noon-11pm Mon-Fri; 11am-11pm Sat; 11am-10.30pm Sun. **Main courses** £7-£15. **Service** 12.5%. **Credit** AmEx, MC, V.

Owned by the same company that runs the Tootsies chain, Dexter's is similar in style. This outlet near Wandsworth Common is spacious, with exposed brick walls, wood beams and polished wooden floor. During the day, the place is virtually given over to mothers, with pushchairs and toddlers everywhere. So child-friendly is it, there's a kind of kiddie heaven in the back, with sweeties and ice-creams galore. Nobody's going to complain if you set up a crayon colouring station at your table, and nobody will glare at your pram. At night the lights dim, and the venue becomes more romantic. The food is basic Americana that veers from the healthy (big mix-and-match salads, where you can add the meat and dressing of your choice

from a wide selection), to the unhealthy (burgers and divine ice-cream shakes), via somewhere in between (steaks). The atmosphere is casual and relaxing, and the staff are eager to help.
Babies and children welcome: children's menu; crayons; high chairs; toys. Booking advisable weekends. No-smoking tables. Separate rooms for parties, seating 25 and 40. Tables outdoors (9, patio). Takeaway service.
For branches see index.

East
Docklands E14

★ **Curve** NEW

2005 RUNNER-UP BEST ALFRESCO DINING
London Marriott, West India Quay, 22 Hertsmere Road, E14 4ED (7093 1000 ext 2622). Canary Wharf tube/DLR/West India Quay DLR.
Breakfast served 6.30am-11pm Mon-Fri;

7-11am Sat, Sun. **Lunch served** noon-2.30pm, **dinner served** 5-10.30pm daily. **Main courses** £10-£22. **Service** 12.5%. **Credit** AmEx, DC, JCB, MC, V.

Located on the ground floor of the London Marriott hotel, across the dock from Canary Wharf, this slick new modern American restaurant boasts outdoor waterside tables with Manhattan-like views of nearby skyscrapers and streetlife. Already a destination for business types, Curve is overseen by a professional service team and well attuned to dealing with the needs of discerning diners. A reasonably priced menu accents dressed-up classics: clam chowder, caesar salad and seriously meaty steaks. We kicked off with roasted portobello mushrooms, baked with gorgonzola cheese and juicy tomato wedges, topped with concertina-like serrano ham fans – a fitting flourish to a well-executed dish. A satisfying griddled yellowfin tuna, glazed with sticky soy sauce, was served with a sushi

assortment and a winsome accompaniment of crisp-fried vegetable tempura. Don't miss the mini-steel buckets piled high with fabulous fries. Our gold star goes to the puds, including a delectable wedge of pistachio cheesecake, with a silky-smooth texture and subtle, nutty flavour; and a chocolate tower with champagne foam that tasted like a decadent cocktail. Visit at lunch, on a sunny day, to soak in the Docklands vibe from a great vantage point.
Babies and children welcome: children's menu; crayons; high chairs. Booking advisable. Disabled: toilet. No smoking. Tables outdoors (12, terrace).

South Woodford E18

Yellow Book Californian Café
190 George Lane, E18 1AY (8989 3999/ www.theyellowbook.co.uk). South Woodford tube. **Lunch served** noon-2.30pm Mon-Fri. **Dinner served** 6-10pm Mon; 6-11pm Tue-Fri. **Meals served** noon-11pm Sat; noon-10pm Sun. **Main courses** £6.50-£14.50. **Credit** AmEx, MC, V.

This is a relatively sophisticated eaterie in far east London, with wooden floors and a cheery colour scheme. The best seats are in the large breezy courtyard, so a sunny summer's day is the ideal time to visit. Similarly, the extensive menu comes into its own in the hot months, with lots of big crispy salads, and thin-crust pizzas piled with fresh ingredients. The cooking also has a Far East bent, suited to the multicultural nature of California's population. For starters, choose from the likes of ginger tiger prawns – delectable and tender – haddock fish cake, grilled aubergine bruschetta or a generous plate of nachos. For mains, big burritos come stuffed with smoked chicken, peppers and onion, while the pizzas (including some unusual choices such as thai chicken and peking duck) are large, smoky and crisp. There are also assorted burgers, fajitas and quesadillas. Waiters can be a bit brusque, and things tend to slow down when the place gets busy, but this is a strong, steady option.
Babies and children welcome: high chairs. Bookings not accepted Fri, Sat or for parties of fewer than 5. No-smoking tables. Tables outdoors (8, patio). Takeaway service.

Outer London
Richmond, Surrey

Canyon
The Towpath, near Richmond Bridge, Richmond, Surrey TW10 6UJ (8948 2944). Richmond tube/rail. **Brunch served** 11am-3.30pm Sat, Sun. **Lunch served** noon-3.30pm Mon-Fri. **Dinner served** 6-10.30pm daily. **Main courses** £11-£19. **Service** 12.5%. **Credit** AmEx, JCB, MC, V.

Every year Canyon's kitchen seems to lose the plot just a little more. The menu is now desperately pretentious: iced soufflé of English spinach? Tandoori foie gras? What can it all mean? Nothing, that's what. Consider that the 'frozen raspberry soufflé' turned out to be an ordinary sorbet, and you get the picture. With an idyllic riverside location right by the Thames, walls of windows and ample outdoor seating, this restaurant was once one of our favourites, but no more. As the menu has become more ridiculous, the cooking has gone on the skids. Grilled salmon with prawn risotto should have been light, but tasted as if it had been doused in butter. 'Roast corn-fed chicken supreme' was a 'could have done it yourself' sautéed chicken quarter with nothing-to-it saffron rice... for a hefty £16. A side of fine beans was boring, while another of asparagus was soggy and came with partially congealed hollandaise. Puddings were dreadful – the lemon tart tasted as if it hadn't been fresh in some time. Service was as excellent as ever, but the kitchen is crying out for a shake-up.
Babies and children welcome: children's menu; high chairs. Booking advisable. Disabled: toilet. Entertainment: jazz 8.30pm Wed. No-smoking tables. Tables outdoors (12, courtyard; 16, terrace).

Child's play

Sometimes, for reasons we cannot entirely fathom, it is necessary to eat in one of the loud, bright, colourful US-themed chains around town. Generally, the only valid reasons for this are 1) kids or b) drunkenness. If either of these eventualities should occur, these are your options.

Cheers
72 Regent Street, W1R 6EL (7494 3322/ www.cheersbarlondon.com). Piccadilly Circus tube. **Bar Open/snacks served** noon-3am Mon-Sat; noon-12.30am Sun. **Snacks** £6-£8. *Restaurant* **Meals served** noon-10pm daily. **Main courses** £6.95-£12.90. **Minimum** £7. **Set meal** (noon-6pm Mon-Fri) £2.95 1 course. **Service** 12.5% for parties of 6 or more. **Both Credit** AmEx, MC, V.

Arguably the second-best of the chains. The TV theme is relatively muted, and the food can be decent. Stick with the hamburgers, fries and sandwiches; ignore the salads and pizzas. Don't buy a T-shirt.
Babies and children welcome (until 6pm in restaurant): children's menu; crayons; high chairs. Disabled: toilet. Dress: smart casual. No-smoking tables. **Map 17 J7.**

Hard Rock Café
150 Old Park Lane, W1K 1QZ (7629 0382/www.hardrock.com). Green Park or Hyde Park Corner tube. **Meals served** 11.30am-midnight Mon-Thur, Sun; 11.30am-1am Fri, Sat. **Main courses** £8-£13. **Service** 12.5% on bills over £30. **Credit** AmEx, MC, V.

Rock music, rock memorabilia, rockin' waitresses in red-hot miniskirts. Hamburgers (OK), salads (huge and surely not healthy), nachos (not bad). These are what you can expect to find here on Park Lane. Oh, and tourists.
Babies and children welcome: children's menu; high chairs; toys. Booking advisable. Entertainment: musicians 7.30pm Tue. No smoking. Tables outdoors (18, pavement). **Map 9 H8.**

Outback Steakhouse
Dolphin House, Riverside West, Smugglers Way, SW18 1EG (8877 1599/www.outback pom.com). Wandsworth Town rail. **Meals served** 5-10pm Mon-Thur; 5-11pm Fri; 4-11pm Sat; noon-9pm Sun. **Main courses** £8.25-£18.99. **Credit** AmEx, JCB, MC, V.

This is what Americans think of Australia: it's all 'Slap another customer on the barbie'. So pop open a can of Foster's, try a steak, avoid much of the seafood, don't order anything complicated, and, remember, you really don't want a whole fried onion. You just don't.
Babies and children welcome: children's menu; crayons; high chairs; toys. Disabled: toilet. No-smoking tables. Takeaway service.
For branches see index.

Planet Hollywood
Trocadero, 13 Coventry Street, W1D 7DH (7287 1000/www.planethollywood.com). Piccadilly Circus tube. **Meals served** 11.30am-1am Mon-Sat; 11.30am-12.30am Sun. **Main courses** £9.95-£19.95. **Service** 12.5%. **Credit** AmEx, DC, MC, V.

Televisions fill every available corner, all of them blasting out adverts for movies, trailers from movies, snippets of movies – at skull-splitting volume. Order carefully and you won't mind so much. Try the steaks, sandwiches or burgers, but in general avoid the salads, which could be so much better. Kids love this place.
Babies and children welcome: children's menu; high chairs; nappy-changing facilities. Booking advisable. Disabled: toilet. No-smoking tables. Separate room for parties, seats 80. **Map 17 K7.**

TGI Friday's
6 Bedford Street, WC2E 9HZ (7379 0585/ www.tgifridays.co.uk). Covent Garden tube/Charing Cross tube/rail. **Bar Open** noon-11pm Mon-Sat; noon-10.30pm Sun. *Restaurant* **Meals served** noon-11.30pm Mon-Sat; noon-11pm Sun. **Main courses** £7.95-£17.45. **Service** 10% for parties of 8 or more. **Both Credit** AmEx, MC, V.

Probably the best of the lot. The food tastes a bit processed, but comes in huge portions, served by cheerful staff. Try the Jack Daniels ribs or anything off the JD menu, or go with the Tex-Mex dishes. The starters are great and the enormous cocktails taste like puddings.
Babies and children welcome: children's menu; crayons; high chairs. Disabled: toilet. No smoking. Takeaway service.
Map 18 L7.
For branches see index.

Cheers®

LONDON

OPEN TIL 3AM MONDAY TO SATURDAY

RESTAURANT OPEN EVERYDAY FROM MIDDAY

DJ'S EVERYNIGHT FROM 10PM

HAPPY HOUR

MONDAY TO FRIDAY 3PM – 7PM

FOR RESERVATIONS CALL

020 7494 3322

CHEERS, LONDON RESTAURANT & BAR
72 REGENT STREET W1R 6EL

cheersbarlondon.com

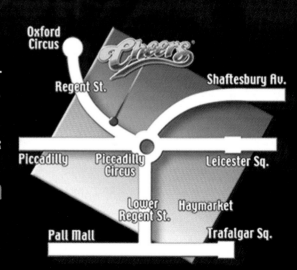

LATIN AMERICAN

London's Latin American scene is small and fairly static, but the past year has seen the opening of two restaurants that target very different markets. In Wardour Street, W1, Conran and its partner Havana Holdings spent millions attempting to replicate the buzz of the Cuban capital's famous **Floridita** bar-restaurant, while on Broadway Market, E8, two Argentinian friends used their savings and a small bank loan to open **Santa María del Buen Ayre**, a down-to-earth local grill that was a contender for *Time Out*'s Best Cheap Eats award in 2005. While Floridita is packed most nights with high-spending, cigar-testing punters downing fabulous cocktails, the Hackney restaurant is altogether more successful as a food experience; its formula of charcoal-grilled Argentine steaks, gently helpful attention and low prices has led to double sittings most nights.

A warm welcome, also, to two new Mexican openings, **Taqueria** and **Mestizo**; the former, in particular, is to be celebrated for bringing an authentic taste of Mexico to the capital. There's a demand for all things South American right now (ask any travel agent), and there's plenty of space for more openings, especially in south London. It would be fantastico if the better venues could set up branches in Brixton, Peckham or Camberwell, where many of London's Colombian and Ecuadorean residents have settled.

Finally, we bid a fond farewell to **Sabor do Brasil**, run by Andrew and Alberina Hunton for the past 13 years. Their success shows the importance of providing a friendly welcome in homely surroundings, and making sure the cooking is faithful to its roots. We wish them a happy retirement.

Argentinian

South West

South Kensington SW7

El Gaucho
30B Old Brompton Road, SW7 3DL (7584 8999). South Kensington tube. **Meals served** 5-11.30pm Mon-Sat; noon-11.30pm Sun. **Main courses** £15-£20. **Credit** AmEx, MC, V.
It's a bit dingy-looking, but El Gaucho's South Kensington basement setting makes for a cosy, bustling little steakhouse. Every one of the diners looks animated as they shout over the pounding cumbia music (ridiculously loud at first, this was turned down on request). There's no swerving from the Argentinian parrilla (grill) menu, but it's all hearty and well prepared. The provolone cheese was nicely melted, and both meat and chicken empanadas were near perfect, though the chorizo sausage lacked bite (and the chimmichurri sauce that accompanied the meat wasn't good enough to enliven it). Sirloin steaks were flavoursome, purple-hued and easy to carve; the other cuts looked lean, large and grilled to perfection. A chicken platter, chosen as a 'lighter option', was immense. Wines are standard New World reds and whites, but that's what this country cooking requires. Ice-cream and pancakes, sugar and stodge dominate the dessert menu. Staff were professional, efficient, but somewhat cooler than the general feel of the place. Customers are left with the impression that, as this is the only decent meat-joint around, the waiters don't have to try too hard. Seven for the steaks, four for effort.
Babies and children admitted. Booking advisable. Entertainment: Latin American musician 7pm Sun. Takeaway service; delivery service (within 1-mile radius). **Map 14 D10.**
For branch see index.

South

Battersea SW11

La Pampa Grill
60 Battersea Rise, SW11 1EG (7924 4774). Clapham Junction rail. **Dinner served** 6-11pm Mon-Fri; 6-11.30pm Sat, Sun. **Main courses** £7.95-£15.50. **Service** 10% for parties of 7 or more. **Credit** MC, V.
Grill restaurants live or die by their meat. Fortunately, La Pampa Grill, where quality has varied greatly over the years, seems to be delivering great steaks again. The fillet was subtle and tender, and covered a large plate; the churrasco (translated as rump) was extremely tasty. Ask for 'a punto' and you get your meat cooked medium-rare: ideal for Argentinian beef, and the topping of fried eggs is a masterstroke. The rest of the meal is so much preamble and postscript. Chorizo sausage was fair (if lacking in peppers) and empanada was dripping with tasty juices. Salads, however, are poor and the chips are too big and stodgy. None of this comes cheap, with steaks £15 and even the empanada a hefty £3.75 – for a glorified pasty. The wine list is strong on full-bodied Mendozan reds. Desserts, should you have space, include pancakes with dulce de leche. Service is friendly and relaxed. The ersatz ranch-style decor gives a warm, welcoming feel to the place, though the fetish for cockerels (which dangle from every angle) is hard to explain.
Booking advisable; essential Sat. Separate area for parties, seats 25. Takeaway service. **Map 21 C4.**
For branch see index.

East

Docklands E14

★ The Gaucho Grill
29 Westferry Circus, Canary Riverside, E14 8RR (7987 9494/www.thegauchogrill.co.uk). Canary Wharf tube/DLR. **Meals served** noon-11pm Mon-Sat; noon-10pm Sun. **Main courses** £14-£38. **Service** 12.5% for parties of 6 or more. **Credit** AmEx, DC, JCB, MC, V.
This branch of Gaucho Grill seems to try harder than the other five in London, as regards both service and steaks. The staff dash around, eager to please, guiding new guests through the longish, fairly exotic menu. They proudly present their main cuts of beef raw on a wooden platter before orders are placed – this helps you select size, hue and fat content. The steaks are magnificent, as are the meat empanadas and hand-cut chips. Frankly, that's what most people come for. However, this Argentinian-themed restaurant chain stands out for its range of alternatives: lobster and oyster starters, ceviches (marinated raw fish), as well as mains of chicken and seafood. Side orders include tasty humitas (corn wraps from north-west Argentina) plus rice and yucca. The wine list has an impressively extensive choice of Argentinian and Chilean labels; for £20 you'll get an excellent young red. With its riverside location (and alfresco eating when weather permits), this is one of the best diners in Docklands and a reliable place to indulge in expertly marbled cow. If you're worried the surroundings might be too corporate, relax: somehow, steakhouses make even bankers unwind, so the atmosphere is never stuffy.
Babies and children welcome: high chairs. Booking advisable. Disabled: toilet. Entertainment: Latin American band 8pm Sun. Tables outdoors (30, terrace).
For branches see index.

Hackney E8

★ ★ Santa María del Buen Ayre ~~NEW~~
2005 RUNNER-UP BEST CHEAP EATS
50 Broadway Market, E8 4QJ (7275 9900/ www.buenayre.co.uk). Liverpool Street tube/rail then 48, 55 bus/26, 106, 277, 394 bus. **Dinner served** 6-10.30pm Tue-Fri. **Meals served** noon-10.30pm Sat; 1-10.30pm Sun. **Main courses** £6.50-£14. **Service** 10% for parties of 5 or more. **Credit** MC, V.
Atkins dieters, longshoremen, Desperate Dan, prick up your ears: this place you must try. The moment you set foot inside Santa Maria, you're treated to the divine cooking smells of the parrilla (a wide grill that can be lowered on to glowing coals), where the steaks, the Argentine sausages, the ribs, the peppers and brochettes are sizzled to slow perfection. This is gaucho food, the kind for which you hang up your spurs, grab a knife and fork in either fist, and tuck the tablecloth into your collar. Steaks are organised by weight and quality of cut (our 8oz prime fillet was a smoky, pink-centred revelation); mixed grills come in various combinations (most of which feature traditional pork and beef sausages); salads are simple (tomato and onion, say); and starters consist of golden empanadas, sliced marinated ox tongue, and cured ham. Non-meat-eaters aren't going to be getting the best of this place, but, hey, even plain vegetables taste good after a spell on the parrilla. Premises-made desserts use a lot of dulce de leche, South America's ubiquitous milk fudge, notably in a very good cheesecake and most indulgently piped around a crème caramel. The wine list makes the most of Argentina's New World credentials.
Babies and children welcome: high chairs. Booking advisable. Disabled: toilet. No-smoking tables. Tables outdoors (5, garden).

Brazilian

Central

Oxford Street W1

★ Brasil by Kilo
17 Oxford Street, W1D 2DJ (7287 7161). Tottenham Court Road tube. **Meals served** noon-9pm daily. **Main courses** 99p per 100g. **Unlicensed. No credit cards.**

RESTAURANTS

On what is perhaps London's most chaotic corner, opposite Oxford Street's Virgin Megastore, this snack bar is a refuge from cold-sandwich culture and big-brand retail. Together, the ground-floor juice and breakfast bar and the pay-as-you-weigh restaurant upstairs offer everything Brazilian – from iced buns and cheese pies for breakfast, to fried bananas, pork-based stews and roast meat for a low-budget lunch. The backdrop is provided by sunny Brazilian national flags and sultry monochrome photographs of the urban tropics. Lunch can be very cheap indeed; the house special of cheesy bread and feijoada (pork stew, black beans and roasted cassava flour) costs just £6, and the Portuguese-speaking staff throw in a cup of filter coffee too. None of this is sophisticated or subtle on the palate, but it's hot, tasty and freshly prepared. The juices, which cover standard apple and orange as well as guava, cashew, papaya and pitanga (Surinam cherry), are sublime, and breakfast time is particularly chilled. How the owners pay the rent on this strip is hard to fathom, but Brazilians love the place – and strapped-for-cash Londoners are following suit.
Babies and children welcome: high chairs. No smoking. Separate room for parties, seats 40. Takeaway service. **Map 17 K6**.

North
Islington N1

Rodizio Rico
77-78 Upper Street, N1 0NU (7354 1076). Angel tube. **Lunch served** noon-3.30pm Mon-Fri; 12.30-3.30pm Sat. **Dinner served** 6-11.30pm Mon-Sat. **Meals served** 12.30-10.30pm Sun. **Buffet** £12.90-£18 meat, £16.90-£23.90 seafood, £9.90-£11.90 vegetarian. **Service** 10%. **Credit** AmEx, DC, JCB, MC, V.
If this new branch of the Brazilian buffet-style restaurant were merely a copy of the Notting Hill original, it would be satisfactory. Yet the bigger, brighter space, the vivacious Latino clientele and the easier access to salads and side dishes combine to make it a superior scion. As is the case with these bustling *espeto corrido* (running skewer) joints, waiters dash about first offering sausage, pork, lamb, chicken wings and chicken hearts and then, finally, tender, succulent cuts of sirloin and flank. But our friendly swordsmen were happy to let us indulge in prime beef and leave the lesser meats for others. Salad items were all crisp, the rice and beans and croquettes were hot and tasty, and there were never queues at the self-service section. There are vegetarian and seafood options, but the meat fest is the thing; it's easy for the ravenous to go on and on eating. Desserts cost extra, but the flans and mousses are well prepared and it's worth saving space for them. Excellent wines from Argentina and Chile add class to this characterful, cheery venue. Small children can sit and pick at their guardians' meal for free.
Babies and children welcome: children's menu; high chairs. Booking advisable. Disabled: toilet. No-smoking tables. Vegetarian menu. **Map 5 O2**. **For branch see index.**

Cuban
Central
Soho W1

Floridita NEW
2005 RUNNER-UP BEST BAR
100 Wardour Street, W1F 0TN (7314 4000). Leicester Square, Piccadilly Circus or Tottenham Court Road tube. **Meals served** 5.30pm-2.30am Mon-Sat. **Main courses** £16-£36. **Service** 12.5%. **Credit** AmEx, DC, JCB, MC, V.
Terence Conran's new venture (styled on its famous namesake in Havana and occupying the cavernous space that was Mezzo) is a cabaret, a cocktail bar, a restaurant, a record label, a travel agent and a cigar promoter. The dark basement restaurant (open evenings only) is a clamorous space. Gangs

of office workers shout for Mojitos, and when the bands play, they shout louder. For all this, the menu is ambitious, offering three types of lobster, and exquisite-sounding concoctions such as meatballs stuffed with quails' eggs. We tested a red snapper ceviche, and then some free-range chicken with peppers, and a ribeye steak. The first two dishes were flawless: the ceviche fresh and tangy, the chicken honeyish and tender, with a side dish of smoky, delicious moros y cristianos (beans and rice; £3.75 extra). The steak was lean and flavoursome, but charred beyond our requested 'well done'. For pudding, baked lime and sultana cheesecake with poached blueberries was a stodgy, bland affair. Excellent New World wines are served by the glass, and the cocktails, as you'd expect, are brilliant. More of a fun night out than a food experience, Floridita is a place to come with lots of mates and lots of money. On the ground floor is Meza (*see p257*), a Spanish tapas bar.
Babies and children admitted. Booking advisable. Disabled: toilet. Entertainment: Cuban band/DJ 7.30pm Mon-Sat. Separate room for parties, seats 56. **Map 17 K6**.

North
Islington N1

Cuba Libre ✓
72 Upper Street, N1 0NY (7354 9998). Angel tube. **Meals served** 11am-11pm daily. **Main courses** £9.95-£11.95. **Service** 12.5%. **Credit** JCB, MC, V.
Post-revolution Cuban cuisine revolves around rice, beans, plantain, yucca and plainly cooked chicken and beef. Cuba Libre serves up all of them, in bite-size tapa form or as mains. Take care if sharing a few dishes or sampler platters, as you're likely to see these ingredients (along with a peppery sausage) appear time and again. Some dishes stood out: the ropa vieja (shredded charqui or jerky-style beef) and smoky beef cuts were tender, the prawns were fresh and well flavoured, and the chicken came in a nice, slightly spicy sauce. Presentation was basic throughout; the 'pijama' dessert of bananas, ice-cream and a red sauce was as garish as a Del Boy cocktail. In all, though, this was a fair rendition of Cuban comfort food, best accompanied by cold beer or perhaps a bottle of cava. Service is friendly, and there's enough staff to handle the hordes who come on warm nights. Eating at Cuba Libre is neither an exotic nor a culinary event, but Islingtonians don't come just for the food. They like the lively vibe, the music, the bar and the pavement terrace.
Babies and children admitted. Booking advisable. Tables outdoors (8, pavement). **Map 5 O2**.

Santa María del Buen Ayre. See p43.

Mexican & Tex-Mex
Central
Covent Garden WC2

Café Pacifico
5 Langley Street, WC2H 9JA (7379 7728/ www.cafepacifico-laperla.com). Covent Garden tube. **Meals served** noon-11.45pm Mon-Sat; noon-10.45pm Sun. **Main courses** £7.95-£16.95. **Set lunch** (Mon-Fri) £10 1 course incl drink. **Service** 12.5%. **Credit** AmEx, MC, V.
This is a cacophonous barn of a restaurant, where the raucous conversation hits ear-splitting volume levels, augmented by a non-stop stream of Latin music blandness. Worse, on our visit, waiters were more interested in socialising than in serving, and that sent the whole system into meltdown. Things went wrong from the beginning, when we were squeezed into a space behind a roaring trio of men lying loudly about their sex lives. Then, getting two Margaritas became an epic struggle – we'd completed our small and uninspiring nachos starter before anybody responded to our pleas, and were promised that the drinks were 'just around the corner'. It was another 15 minutes before two tiny glasses appeared with child-size portions (at £4.50 each). As for the food, the chicken and prawn fajitas appeared to have been sautéed rather than grilled, and the seasoning tasted as if it had come out of a packet. Both our main courses were supposed to come with rice and beans, but one dish arrived with only rice, the other with only beans, and we had to scrape portions on to one another's plates. Suffice it to say, there are better Tex-Mex restaurants in London.
Babies and children welcome: children's menu; high chairs. Bookings not accepted Fri, Sat. No-smoking tables. Takeaway service. **Map 18 L6**.

Fitzrovia NW1, W1

Mestizo NEW
103 Hampstead Road, NW1 3EL (7387 4064/ www.mestizomx.com). Warren Street tube/ Euston tube/rail. **Lunch served** noon-4pm daily. **Dinner served** 6-11.30pm Mon-Sat; 6-10.30pm Sun. **Main courses** £6.50-£12.50. **Credit** MC, V.
A note on the menu at this new restaurant (occupying the space formerly used by Venezuelan café Sol y Luna) says that dishes are prepared with the British palate in mind. At the table behind us, diners were Mexican and American, to the right Spanish. Like us, they probably thought the cooking could do with more kick. The menu is

pleasingly flexible, suited to a formal series of courses or a night of cocktails and grazing. From a long list of tacos and antojitos (appetisers) we chose two tacos with soft maize tortillas, one topped with chorizo, the other with cochinita pibil, a Yucatecan dish of pork marinated with achiote (annatto) seed. Main courses included classic chicken mole, as well as asado negro, a succulent Venezuelan dish of beef cooked in sugar. The only disappointment was the chocolate cake, which was little better than supermarket-standard. Sweetly spiced rice-filled empanadas worked much better. 'Mother Margaritas' are available in lime or strawberry and in the alcoholic ice slushy variety: nothing like we've experienced in Mexico, but tasty and refreshing. Staff are sweet and efficient. Add a modern interior that successfully blends Mayan rustic with ice-cool cream and dark wood, and Mestizo makes a very enjoyable night out among the council estates north of Euston.
Babies and children welcome: high chairs. Booking advisable weekends. Disabled: toilet. No-smoking tables. Separate room for parties, holds 150. Takeaway service. **Map 3 J3**.

La Perla

11 Charlotte Street, W1T 1RQ (7436 1744). Goode Street or Tottenham Court Road tube. Bar **Open** 5-11pm Mon-Sat.
Restaurant **Meals served** noon-10pm Mon-Sat; 5-9pm Sun. **Main courses** £7.95-£13.95. **Service** 12.5% for parties of 8 or more.
Both **Credit** AmEx, MC, V.
A small, tightly run operation, La Perla is fast becoming our top choice for Tex-Mex food. Everything about the place is Lilliputian – the room is barely bigger than a corn tortilla, tables are tiny, and the menu compact – but we always find something to enjoy. On our most recent visit we devoured the free tortilla chips and spicy salsa before deciding to try the 'street tacos': a big platter of half a dozen tacos, each with a different filling ranging from smoky prawns to spicy chicken to rich shredded pork, along with flavourful beans and salsa. Another main of spicy chicken stew was perfectly prepared, with big chunks of chicken breast in a mild but well-spiced tomato-based stew, thickened with shredded tortillas and cheese. It made an ideal lunch on a rainy day, and was served with style by friendly waiters. Other options include fajitas (beef, chicken, prawn or vegetarian) and assorted salads. Of course, the lengthy Margarita menu attracts most of La Perla's customers, but the food is well worth noting.
Babies and children admitted. Booking advisable. **Map 9 J5**.
For branches see index.

Piccadilly W1

Destino

25 Swallow Street, W1B 4QR (7437 9895/ www.destino.co.uk). Piccadilly Circus tube. Bar **Open** noon-3am Mon-Sat.
Restaurant **Meals served** 5pm-midnight Mon-Sat. **Main courses** £10-£21. **Service** 12.5%.
Both **Credit** AmEx, DC, MC, V.
This restaurant, owned by the people behind the Gaucho Grill (*see p43*), has been all over the map of late. Two years ago it was a tacky theme restaurant called Down Mexico Way, then it went upmarket, serving complex Mexican dishes in a gorgeous space with cobalt tiles, heavy hand-carved furniture and a real sense of style. Now it's gone down the tapas route, with a 'grazing menu' that we found disappointingly limited. We started with soup: pollo tortilla (chicken broth topped with avocado and crisp tortillas) was light and creamy; bisque negro featured rich, flavourful lobster stock darkened with squid ink. But from there we lost interest. With only ceviche (tuna with coconut and lime; or salmon, snapper and tuna with soy sauce), skewers (salmon with soy, tuna with sugar cane) and flatbread (pizza-like dishes with toppings such as foie gras and fig) to choose from, we were uninspired. A grazing menu should deliver more freedom, not less, and a small list crammed with rich dishes isn't going to do it. Service is earnest, but can get overwhelmed. The space is still gorgeous, so we hope Destino finds its way soon.
Babies and children welcome (restaurant only): high chair. Booking advisable. Entertainment: DJs 6pm Mon-Sat. Separate room for parties, seats 14. Tables outdoors (3, pavement). Takeaway service. **Map 17 J7**.

Trafalgar Square SW1

Texas Embassy Cantina

1 Cockspur Street, SW1Y 5DL (7925 0077/ www.texasembassy.com). Charing Cross tube/rail. **Meals served** noon-11pm Mon-Wed; noon-midnight Thur-Sat; noon-10.30pm Sun. **Main courses** £7.50-£16.95. **Service** 12.5% for parties of 6 or more. **Credit** AmEx, DC, MC, V.
This big old restaurant at Trafalgar Square can't help but stand out. It always reminds us of walking down the street past a couple of visiting New Yorkers and overhearing one grumble: 'Oh great. Trust Texas to have a bloody embassy. They'll have their own army next.' Indeed. Clearly, given the location, this place isn't immune to trying to attract tourists, but don't let that put you off. What does put us off is its soundtrack: a non-stop cavalcade of country music. And yet we persevere,

Brasil by Kilo. See p43.

Interview
JOHN RATTAGAN

Who are you?
Co-owner (with Alberto Abbate) of **Santa María del Buen Ayre** (*see p43*). My alter ego when working as *parrillero* or head griller is Cacho Gomez.
Eating in London: what's good about it?
Going out for a meal today is as normal as it once was to go to the pub. And the variety on offer makes most other great capitals pale in comparison.
What's bad about it?
Too many restaurants that don't offer value for money. Some places are extortionate; prices don't remotely relate to the quality of the dish. Also: the Stalinist parking schemes adopted by some councils are keeping clients away in areas where the council thinks it can make an easy buck.
Which are your favourite London restaurants?
I like to eat in places that seem authentic. There is a great little Turkish restaurant, **Mangal II** (*see p276*), in Dalston – I've been going there since long before Gilbert & George made it their permanent enclave. For a good drink, and good food, I sometimes visit the **Hartley** (*see p111*), an excellent gastropub.
Any hot tips for the coming year?
The industry will continue to expand and competition will become more fierce, but I think London is still far from reaching its ceiling. Very exciting times, if the economy holds. The trend for smaller premises will also continue.
Anything to declare?
Restaurateurs of London: remember that two out of three complaints are to do with the service. Motivate, train and – last but not least – pay your staff properly. It will show in their faces when looking after your guests. I hear too many stories of managers keeping the tips.

because the tortilla chips are fresh, light and free, the salsa tastes own-made, and the chicken enchiladas are cheesy and well spiced. A platter of tacos was enjoyable: crispy corn shells filled with spicy beef, served with rice and beans. We had greatly looked forward to a starter of nachos (the ones served here are arguably the best in town), but our waitress forgot the order until our mains were ready, and by then it was too late. She meant well, though. Good, touristy fun – and no army.
Babies and children welcome: children's menu; crayons; high chairs. Booking advisable. Disabled: toilet. Separate room for parties, seats 120. Tables outdoors (8, pavement). **Map 17 K7.**

West
Notting Hill W11

★ ★ **Taqueria** NEW
139-143 Westbourne Grove, W11 2RS (7229 4734). Notting Hill Gate tube. **Lunch served** noon-3.30pm, **dinner served** 6-11pm daily. **Main courses** £3-£5.50. **Set lunch** £5.50 1 course. **Credit** MC, V.
With its clean inviting atmosphere, glisteningly fresh ingredients and pocket-petting prices, Taqueria is the sort of place you wish you'd found in Playa del Carmen. The brainchild of Dodie Miller, founder of the Cool Chile Company mail-order service and market stalls (Borough, Portobello), at lunchtime it's a chilled drop-in centre, full of expat North and South Americans, Bill Amberg devotees and home studio workers enjoying a new option for their daily café run. The aguas frescas, including purple-coloured, hibiscus-flavoured flor di Jamaica and a creamy-topped tamarind drink that looks just like Guinness, are a refreshing start. Freshly baked soft corn tortillas might be topped with marinated tuna and black beans, chicken tinga flavoured with tomatoes and chipotle, or roast poblano peppers with potatoes and cheese. We liked all these, and a vibrant side salad of jicama (aka Mexican potato), orange, red onion and coriander. Lunch specials may include huevos rancheros, enfrijoladas or a plate of beans, garlicky greens and rice. There's a brief, affordable wine list, tequilas, Mexican beers and cocktails. Add pleasant, easy-going staff and you'll want to celebrate this opening with a Mexican hat dance.
Babies and children admitted. Bookings not accepted. No smoking. **Map 7 A6.**

South
Clapham SW4

★ **Café Sol**
56 Clapham High Street, SW4 7UL (7498 9319/ www.cafesol.net). Clapham Common or Clapham North tube. **Meals served** noon-midnight Mon-Thur, Sun; noon-2am Fri, Sat. **Main courses** £5.95-£9.95. **Service** 10% for parties of 6 or more. **Credit** AmEx, DC, MC, V.
Things famously move just a bit slower South of the Border, and so it is at Café Sol, where staff are polite but harried when even a few tables are full. We waited more than half an hour for our mains to arrive, while the waiters masterfully resisted our significant glances. Still, the food, when it came, consisted of generous portions of cheesy, Tex-Mex basics. It was almost worth the wait. An order of chicken nachos had been piled so high it was literally sliding off the plate, with cheese, jalapeño peppers, spicy stewed chicken and tortilla chips topped with guacamole. By the time we'd finished it (and we did finish it), we could hardly touch our main courses, which was a shame as the chicken fajitas arrived sizzling on the plate, smoky and delicately marinated, while a trio of enchiladas (chicken, beef and veg) looked alluring, surrounded by beans and rice. The atmosphere here is as sultry as an Acapulco Friday night, and your food will get to you eventually. Just relax.
Babies and children welcome: high chairs. Booking essential dinner Fri, Sat. Disabled: toilet. Entertainment: DJ 11pm Fri, Sat. No-smoking tables. Tables outdoors (6, pavement). Takeaway service. **Map 22 B1.**

Floridita. See p44.

RESTAURANTS

Pan-American

South West

Fulham SW6

★ 1492

404 North End Road, SW6 1LU (7381 3810/ www.1492restaurant.com). Fulham Broadway tube. **Dinner served** 6pm-midnight Mon-Fri. **Meals served** 12.30pm-midnight Sat, Sun. **Main courses** £8.50-£17. **Service** 12.5%. **Credit** AmEx, MC, V.

There's always a buzz at 1492, created by a crowd of Latino regulars and the fact that it has a very laid-back cocktail bar. The setting helps: warm colours, South American motifs (not overdone) and eclectic music from the region. The menu is in the same vein, ranging from simple steaks and mini barbecues, to spicy chicken with mole, pumpkin quesadillas and other Tex-Mex variants. There are also ambitious platters such as the Ecuadorian-Peruvian-Mexican mixed mountain of ceviches – which go down splendidly with Mojitos and Margaritas. The quality is generally excellent, and the sauces are carefully blended, though we've had more tender steaks. Desserts are either refreshingly light (passionfruit mousse) or heavyweight standards based on chocolate and caramel. The underrated Lurton vineyard provides the £15 house wines, and for about £18 you can get an excellent Finca Flichman malbec. Since being a finalist for Best Local Restaurant in the 2004 *Time Out* Eating & Drinking Awards, 1492 has continued to be boldly pan-American. In the absence of any outstanding restaurant specialising in Venezuelan, Colombian or Ecuadorian cuisine, it is particularly *bienvenido*.
Babies and children welcome: children's menu; high chairs. Booking advisable. No smoking. Separate room for parties, seats 30. **Map 13 A13.**

South East

London Bridge & Borough SE1

★ El Vergel

8 Lant Street, SE1 1QR (7357 0057/ www.elvergel.co.uk). Borough tube. **Meals served** 8.30am-3pm Mon-Fri. **Main courses** £3.80-£6. **No credit cards.**

Every year, we half expect this small, out-of-the-way lunchtime hangout to give up on its policy of serving fresh, interesting items from the *vergel* (vegetable patch) and simply provide Borough's office workers with sandwiches and crisps. But, happily, its food and atmosphere just get better and better. Hands-on owners Stella de Garcia and Kiko Sanhueza have turned their snack bar into a catering emporium, and the house standards – tenderloin steak and avocado on flatbread, moist Spanish omelette, meat and vegetarian empanadas, fresh salads – are now devoured by the truckload in boardrooms and council meetings. At the Lant Street HQ, the personnel are warmer than ever. The Colombian waitress-cashier who served us was chatty, curious, cultured and seemed happy to work here as part of an extended pan-Latin American family. For bigger appetites, there's a serious lamb stew, a thick and tasty chicken broth, and pastel de choclo (corn pie, Chile's national vegetarian dish). The only drawback is that El Vergel closes weekdays at around 3pm, and all weekend. Oh, and it gets pretty full soon after opening.
Babies and children admitted. No smoking. Tables outdoors (10, pavement). Takeaway service. Vegan dishes. **Map 11 P9.**

North East

Hackney E8

Armadillo

41 Broadway Market, E8 4PH (7249 3633/ www.armadillorestaurant.co.uk). Bethnal Green tube then 106, 253 bus/26, 48, 55 bus. **Meals**

served 6.30-10.30pm Tue-Sat. **Main courses** £9.50-£16.50. **Service** 12.5% for parties of 5 or more. **Credit** AmEx, DC, JCB, MC, V.

With newly opened Buen Ayre (*see p43*) on the opposite side of Broadway Market, Armadillo has a potential conquistador in its midst. Yet rather than rising to the challenge, it appears to be in a slump. Some dishes – Argentinian fillet steaks, Peruvian ceviche, a slab of suckling pig – were of unquestionably high quality, but there were as many duds as delights when we visited. Sometimes authenticity can be fatal: ensalada rusa (potato salad) was as dreary as the ubiquitous original from Argentina; a polenta starter was tepid and uninspired. Just to emphasise the unevenness of the experience, desserts were exceptional, especially the chocolate truffles and a biggish boat of banana, dulce de leche and 'Mayan' chocolate ice-cream. But there's something lacklustre here. The menu, a single sheet of A4, is perhaps too limited, the music is ineffectually low-key, and the waiters are uncommunicative. It's as if the energy that won the place plaudits at its opening (including Best Local Restaurant in Time Out's 2003 awards) has drained away and left only a residue of Brazilian owner Rogerio David's original idea of a vivacious café-restaurant meeting place. Armadillo certainly isn't beyond rescue, but it needs to apply urgent attention to detail.
Babies and children admitted. Booking advisable; essential Fri, Sat. Separate room for parties, seats 30. Tables outdoors (1, balcony; 4, garden).

North

Islington N1

Sabor

108 Essex Road, N1 8LX (7226 5551/ www.sabor.co.uk). Angel tube/Essex Road rail/ 19, 38, 73 bus. **Lunch served** noon-2.30pm, **dinner served** 6-10.30pm Mon-Sat. **Main courses** £7.50-£14.50. **Set lunch** £10 2 courses, £12.50 3 courses. **Credit** MC, V.

Located on Essex Road rather than restaurant-heavy Upper Street, Sabor is a shiny, happy venue with an alloy ceiling, traffic-light colour scheme, a long bar and a big street window. Reggaeton and cumbia on the sound system add to the cheer. The kitchen is lively too, turning out creative versions of Latin American staples, with special emphasis on Colombia. Instead of the usual spicy minced meat, empanadas come stuffed with cheese and mushroom, beef and potato, or crab and plantain. They're small but moreish. To follow, tender ribeye steak is paired with grilled plantain; and succulent, smoky chicken rests on a bed of corn and blue potato salad. Passionfruit, fish in banana leaf and quinoa grain also figure on the menu. One quibble: the edges of the chicken weren't as hot as the rest – this dish should arrive sizzling. For pudding, tropical fruit ice-cream is all most people can manage, but there's also papaya and cream cheese, and

---

BEST LATIN AMERICAN

For carnivores
The Gaucho Grill (*see p43*),
La Pampa Grill (*see p43*), Rodizio Rico
(*see p44*), Santa María del Buen Ayre
(*see p43*).

For cocktails and cabaret
Floridita. See p44.

For food on the move
Brasil by Kilo (*see p43*),
El Vergel (*see left*).

For authentic Mexican
Mestizo (*see p44*), Taqueria (*see p46*).

For alfresco dining
The Gaucho Grill. See p43.

---

manchego cheese with quince jelly. Wines come from the New World, and are well chosen and fairly priced. One waiter was all over us, the other timid and sleepy. Sabor feels like a work in progress, but tries hard and is far better than other Colombian cantinas in London.
Babies and children welcome: booster seats; high chairs. Booking advisable. Disabled: toilet. **Map 5 P1.**

Peruvian

South East

London Bridge & Borough SE1

Tito's

4-6 London Bridge Street, SE1 9SG (7407 7787). London Bridge tube/rail. **Lunch served** noon-3pm Mon-Fri. **Dinner served** 6-11pm Wed-Fri. **Meals served** noon-11pm Sat, Sun. **Main courses** £7.90-£13.50. **Set lunch** £7.90 3 courses. **Credit** AmEx, MC, V.

Tito's made the national papers following rumours that it served grilled cuy – aka guinea pig, a common dish in Peru – but it doesn't, and never did. Instead, expect staples of seafood, fish soups, fried yucca and rice. Lunchtime customers seem to be gradually veering away from the takeaway sarnies on sale and opting for Peruvian platters. Portions are massive. A starter of ceviche mixto (raw fish and seafood marinated in lemon juice) would have satisfied three, and the king prawn chupe – a milky soup with peas, rice and egg– was simply vast. Food isn't thrillingly tasty (the soup needed salt), but with huge starters at around £5, it's cheap. Desserts look basic, through the alfajor biscuit affair was fresh and tasted like home-baked shortbread. London Bridge's clerical workers are lucky to have this and El Vergel (*see above*) on their doorstep. Perhaps they should try some of Tito's pisco-based cocktails at the next round of office parties.
Babies and children welcome: high chairs. Booking advisable weekends. Separate room for parties, seats 60. Takeaway service. Vegetarian menu. **Map 12 Q8.**

Tower Bridge SE1

Fina Estampa

150 Tooley Street, SE1 2TU (7403 1342). London Bridge tube/rail. **Bar Open** noon-10pm Mon-Fri; 6-10pm Sat. *Restaurant* **Meals served** noon-10.30pm Mon-Fri; 6-10.30pm Sat. **Main courses** £7.95-£14.95. **Service** 10%. *Both* **Credit** AmEx, DC, MC, V.

Two glasses of Pisco Sour – Peru's national cocktail – got things off to a good start. Then came a ceviche, which had the punchy citric tang and fresh fish flavour you'd expect in this classic entrée. But the mains were rather a let-down: lamb seco used good meat but lacked coriander or any other spices and was of poor consistency; and the 'scotch rump steak' employed in the lomo saltado was stringy and oily. Standards have definitely slipped here, as in previous years both these dishes were top-notch. Desserts are uninspiring, and the alfajor (biscuit) and ice-cream with a miserly drop of strawberry sauce was drab. The wine list includes a dozen decent labels but is dominated by Chile: no Argentinian whites and none of the interesting new Peruvian wines. Service was smiling yet desultory; we were shepherded to the back of the bar and our enquiries about upstairs were ignored (in any case, an ugly new office building has obscured the formerly excellent view of Tower Bridge). One waiter struggled with mixing the drinks; a 10% service charge was added.
Babies and children admitted. Booking advisable; essential dinner Sat. Dress: smart casual. Separate room for parties, seats 50. Takeaway service. **Map 12 Q8.**

Brasseries

Londoners have embraced the brasserie – where you can eat a snack or a full-blown meal, throughout the day, in casual, laid-back surroundings – with alacrity. They are often great places for family-eating too. Notable newcomers this year include **Pumphouse Dining Bar**, which, like its Mosaica siblings, has taken advantage of an unexploited industrial site in north London, and **Brasserie l'Auberge**, perhaps the closest thing the capital has to a classic Parisian bistro. Adieu to Camden's **Heartstone**, a much-loved, mellow spot that will be missed.

Central

City EC4

Just The Bridge
1 Paul's Walk, Millennium Bridge North Side, EC4V 3QQ (7236 0000/www.justthebridge.com). St Paul's tube/Blackfriars tube/rail.
Bar **Open** *Easter-Sept* 11am-10pm Mon-Fri; 6-11pm Sat. *Oct-Easter* 11am-10pm Mon-Fri. **Main courses** £4.80-£11.80.
Restaurant **Lunch served** noon-3pm Mon-Fri. **Dinner served** *Easter-Sept* 6-11pm Mon-Sat. *Oct-Easter* 6-10pm Mon-Fri. **Main courses** £9.80-£13.80. **Service** 12.5%.
Both **Credit** AmEx, DC, JCB, MC, V.
As restaurants in the capital were beginning to let go of modernism, Just the Bridge appeared, its stark walls painted in primary colours. Now, with the trend having moved from Middle Eastern to exotica, the brasserie has been kitted out with beige curtains, patterned rugs and Moroccan vases. The menu takes a more global view. Prawns were served atop a tower of frisée lettuce and beansprouts, surrounded by three slices of pink grapefruit and a peanut and soy sauce. The flavours were well thought out and the ingredients separated, Thai-style, for diners to combine while eating. A main course of lamb on a skewer, with couscous, mint and dates – a posh kebab – was let down by overcooked meat and just-warm couscous. The wine list is an acceptable selection of brasserie favourites; the best choices, such as Pascal's Vacqueyras 1998, come in at around £25. Opened to lure in visitors from the neighbouring Millennium walkway, with a pleasant outdoor terrace by the river, Just the Bridge is packed instead with local office workers in shirt sleeves, drinking Chablis. Owner Peter Gladwin is lucky they seem unwilling to walk to the many restaurants across the river.
Babies and children admitted. Booking advisable Wed-Sat. Disabled: toilet. Restaurant and bar available for hire. Tables outdoors (11, terrace). **Map 11 O7.**

Clerkenwell & Farringdon EC1

Brasserie de Malmaison
Malmaison, 18-21 Charterhouse Square, EC1M 6AH (7012 3700/www.malmaison.com). Barbican tube/Farringdon tube/rail. **Brunch served** 11am-3pm Sun. **Lunch served** noon-2.30pm Mon-Sat. **Dinner served** 6-10.30pm daily. **Main courses** £12-£20. **Set lunch** £14.50 3 courses (minimum 2). **Set dinner** £15.95 2 courses, £17.95 3 courses. **Service** 12.5%. **Credit** AmEx, DC, JCB, MC, V.
Its basement location isn't ideal, but the Malmaison hotel's brasserie manages to rise above it: the atmosphere is friendly and standards, on the whole, are high. On our visit, starters included a traditional and successful provençale fish soup with rouille, gruyère and garlic croûtons, its flavours shining through. Conversely, locally smoked salmon blini with herb fromage blanc was inedible, the blini breezeblock-dry and the salmon tasteless. As recompense, we were given (excellent) free fries to go with our escalope of free-range chicken with sautéed spätzle: the meat was beautifully char-grilled and the dumplings light as a feather. Steak tartare, mixed at the table for a touch of theatre, was similarly superlative; the restaurant prides itself on the quality of its matured beef. We then ditched the diet for an assiette aux framboises: gorgeous mini versions of raspberry desserts. Service was charming, though we had a long wait for the bill. Should the imaginative wine list lead you to overdo it, you can always book a room to sleep it off.
Babies and children welcome: high chairs. Booking advisable. Disabled: toilet. No smoking. Separate rooms for parties, seating 12 and 30. **Map 5 O5.**

★ Flâneur Food Hall
41 Farringdon Road, EC1M 3JB (7404 4422). Farringdon tube/rail. **Open** 9am-10pm Mon-Sat; 9am-6pm Sun. **Breakfast served** 8.30-10.30am Mon-Fri. **Brunch served** 9am-4pm Sat, Sun. **Lunch served** noon-3pm Mon-Fri. **Dinner served** 6-10pm Mon-Sat. **Main courses** £8.50-£15.50. **Set menu** £16 2 courses, £21 3 courses. **Service** 12.5%. **Credit** AmEx, DC, JCB, MC, V.
This gorgeous food hall-cum-restaurant on the less-than-gorgeous Farringdon Road is a gem. Tall shelves are lined with well-sourced gourmet products; wines, baked goods, cheeses, charcuterie and deli dishes are further foodie draws. If you'd rather eat in than take away, there are stylish, blond-wood tables set into alcoves, overlooking the street or at the back. The quality of the produce shines through in the menu: terrine of leek with gorgonzola rarebit crostini was delicate yet flavoursome, while san danielle ham with char-grilled peaches, rocket and balsamic was a colourful culinary joy. For mains, slow-roasted Gloucester Old Spot pork belly with apple and goat's cheese tart was variable – the tart burned on the bottom, the meat too fatty – and the accompanying spinach not mentioned on the menu (nor by the waitress), so we ordered an extra side dish of green beans. More successful was pan-fried calf's liver with lentils, bacon and garlic; the meat was well done (we'd requested it pink), though no worse for it, and the lentils cooked to smoky perfection. Service was friendly enough, but so slow we didn't hang around for puds (fig and almond tart, banana walnut cake), tempting though they sounded. The French-heavy wine list features some affordable choices, and there are beers from Sweden, Mexico and even Kenya. A bit of an off-night on our visit, but still a cut above.
Babies and children admitted. Booking advisable. No smoking. Takeaway service. **Map 5 N5.**

Covent Garden WC2

Café des Amis
11-14 Hanover Place, WC2E 9JP (7379 3444/ www.cafedesamis.co.uk). Covent Garden tube.
Bar **Open** 11.30am-1am Mon-Sat.
Restaurant **Meals served** 11.30am-11.30pm Mon-Sat; 11.30am-4pm Sun. **Main courses** £13.50-£20.50. **Set meal** (11.30am-7pm, 10-11.30pm Mon-Sat) £14.50 2 courses, £16.50 3 courses. **Service** 12.5%.
Both **Credit** AmEx, DC, MC, V.
Set on a narrow alleyway behind the Royal Opera House, Café des Amis is a swanky establishment. The decor is expensive and eclectic, with mini chandeliers and boldly coloured walls and upholstery. Fish is a forte, with starters such as fruits de mer, oysters and moules marinières. The latter were over-creamy but plump and fresh; our other starter of foie gras was good quality and nicely caramelised. Mains included a thick chunk of grilled salmon fillet with braised (and somewhat soggy) leeks, and fillet steak with béarnaise sauce – slightly underdone, and not cheap at £20.50, but its quality was outstanding. Among the tempting puds was a smooth and satisfying passionfruit brûlée; the signature dessert, however, is chocolate soup with black pepper ice-cream, the kick of the latter perfectly offsetting the richness of the former. Though prices aren't low, quality is high, and you can cut costs by choosing a set menu and sticking to cheaper wines. Service is friendly, if a little anonymous, and the atmosphere is lively. There's also a wine bar (*see p333*) in the basement.
Babies and children welcome: high chairs. Booking advisable Thur-Sat. Separate room for parties, seats 80. No-smoking tables. Tables outdoors (12, terrace). **Map 18 L6.**

Palm Court Brasserie
39 King Street, WC2E 8JS (7240 2939). Covent Garden tube/Charing Cross tube/rail. **Meals served** noon-11.30pm Mon-Wed; noon-12.45am Thur-Sat; noon-10.30pm Sun. **Main courses** £9.75-£15. **Set meal** (not available 6.30-10pm Fri, Sat) £9.95 2 courses, £12.95 3 courses. **Service** 12.5%. **Credit** AmEx, DC, JCB, MC, V.
With latticed chairs, French posters on the wall and a menu of classics such as snails, french onion soup and coq au vin (plus, er, paella), the Palm Court angles itself as a classic Gallic eaterie. The location might lead one to expect it would be busy, but though the chatty, friendly staff were doing their best to keep things alive, the restaurant was fairly empty and lacking in buzz when we visited. A special of haddock on crushed potatoes was fine, if a little dull, with the thick, good-quality fish slightly overcooked. However, a show-stealing rainbow trout with honey mustard glaze and lentils with spinach, part of the good-value set lunch, was perfect: gorgeous moist fish, accompanied by perfectly al dente lentils with flecks of chilli. Desserts included a blueberry cheesecake which, while not bad, did taste slightly processed; nougat glacé with raspberry coulis seemed more authentic. Not much to write home about, then, but a surprisingly decent bet in this touristy area.
Babies and children welcome: high chairs. Booking advisable Thur-Sat. No-smoking tables. Separate room for parties, seats 50. **Map 18 L7.**

Fitzrovia W1

RIBA Café
66 Portland Place, W1B 1AD (7631 0467/ www.riba.org). Great Portland Street or Oxford Circus tube. **Meals served** 8am-6pm Mon-Fri; 9am-4pm Sat. **Main courses** (noon-3pm Mon-Fri; 9am-4pm Sat) £5.50-£10.50. **Set meal** (Mon-Fri) £12.95 1 course, £16.95 2 courses, £20.95 3 courses. **Credit** AmEx, DC, MC, V.
This casual café/brasserie is on the first floor of the grandiose grade II* listed 1930s headquarters of the Royal Institute of British Architects. There are a few smart banquettes inside, but the best feature is undoubtedly the outside terrace, decked out with sun umbrellas and zinc pots filled with suitably architectural plants. There's even a water feature.

Milburns catering company were in charge on our last visit, resulting in lacklustre food and can't-be-bothered staffing. The set lunch offered a scant two options for each course, none of them particularly enticing: how about tomato and mozzarella salad with pesto sauce and focaccia to start, followed by pan-fried salmon with rocket, tomato dressing and new potatoes, then strawberries with strawberry ice-cream? Dull, dull, dull – and expensive for the quality. Even such straightfoward dishes were poorly executed and lacking in flavour: the salmon was squeaky in texture, the potatoes tepid. Hopefully, it's all change: Charlton House took over in August 2005 and plan gradual improvements to the menu of breakfasts, salads and sandwiches, as well as full lunches. There's also a new stand-up bar/café on the ground floor, suggesting a new solicitousness towards the public.
Babies and children welcome; high chairs. Booking advisable. Disabled: lift, toilet. No smoking. Tables outdoors (20, terrace). Separate rooms for parties, seating 10-400. **Map 3 H4.**

Marylebone W1

Café Bagatelle
The Wallace Collection, Manchester Square, W1U 3BN (7563 9505). Bond Street tube. **Morning coffee served** 10am-noon, **lunch served** noon-2.30pm, **afternoon tea served** 2.30-4.30pm daily. **Main courses** £9-£15.50. **Set menu** (Mon-Fri) £15 2 courses, £20 3 courses. **Credit** AmEx, JCB, MC, V.
Presiding over leafy Manchester Square, this handsomely restored, late 18th-century house contains a fine collection of French masterpieces, furniture, armoury, objets d'art and, not least, one of London's most charming museum restaurants. Located in a spacious, glass-roofed courtyard, dotted with palms, sculptures and well-spaced wicker chairs, Café Bagatelle is a veritable sight for sore eyes: so near to Oxford Street, yet so very far in ambience. The menu is very short, but ambitious, taking in some innovative combinations – a refreshing grilled chicken salad starter, for instance, with juicy chunks of watermelon and papaya – and Asian influences, alongside more standard Modern European fare. A vegetarian main of sticky rice and roasted pumpkin with rich coconut and lime sauce, crowned with just-so pak choi, was simple but effective. The star was grilled swordfish, cooked to perfection and served with spicy chickpeas. Our only gripes about an otherwise very pleasant Saturday lunch concerned the slow, if genuinely friendly, service and the steep prices (the set menu is available only Monday to Friday). Still, there aren't many restaurants in central London offering highly competent cooking in such utterly delightful surroundings.
Babies and children welcome: high chairs. Disabled: toilet. No smoking. Restaurant available for hire (evenings, groups only). **Map 9 G5.**

★ No.6
6 George Street, W1U 3QX (7935 1910). Bond Street tube. **Breakfast served** 8am-noon, **lunch served** noon-3pm, **snacks served** 3-6pm Mon-Fri. **Main courses** £10.50-£15.50. **Minimum** (noon-3pm) £14. **Credit** MC, V.
Perched just off the end of Marylebone High Street, this deli-cum-café attracts its share of genteel locals and smartly dressed workers, but it's elegantly inviting rather than snooty. The small interior is light and furnished with chunky wooden tables, with one wall displaying wine and deli items for sale (own-made tomato and chilli jam, parmesan biscuits, florentines). Young, friendly staff dispense takeaway salads, slabs of quiche, cakes, tarts and huge brownies from the front counter. The daily-changing menu offers around six starters, mains and desserts; all feature fresh ingredients, competently combined and nicely presented. An enjoyable lunch might start with wonderful balsamic figs with prosciutto and parmesan, or gazpacho. For mains, smoked haddock frittata is served simply with flavour-packed peas and new potatoes; similarly, tabbouleh salad and houmous accompanies tender, subtly flavoured lemon-marinated chicken. To round off, there's the

likes of peach and almond tart or creamy ricotta cheesecake with summer fruits. It gets busy at lunchtimes: book ahead if possible.
Babies and children admitted. Booking advisable. No smoking. Restaurant available for hire. Takeaway service. **Map 9 G5.**

Mayfair W1

Truc Vert
42 North Audley Street, W1K 6ZR (7491 9988/ www.trucvert.co.uk). Bond Street tube. **Meals served** 7.30am-9.30pm Mon-Sat; 9.30am-4pm Sun. **Main courses** £12.50-£17. **Service** 10%. **Credit** AmEx, MC, V.
This unpretentious but inescapably classy deli-cum-restaurant lurks on the edge of Mayfair, just opposite the US Embassy. Prices live up to the location, whether for food cooked by the kitchen or for the produce that sits on every shelf, for sale to anyone: you can buy meals to take away and warm up later. We chose to eat on site and kicked off with fish soup, heavy on the aromatics and served with the kind of bread that leaves you in no doubt that you're in good hands (the artisan breads, cheeses and charcuterie are all reliable standbys). Mains were generous: corn-fed chicken breast with steamed new potatoes, french beans and a herb and mustard gravy, and fusilli with smoked chicken, asparagus, mushroom, feta and chilli oil both came in portions that American expats must adore. Desserts – perhaps warm pumpkin pie with clotted cream, or prune and armagnac tart with vanilla ice-cream – are excellent, while the fresh pâtisserie is worth sampling for a special breakfast or brunch. Indeed, it's Truc Vert's very adaptability as a deli and a venue for breakfast, lunch or dinner that makes it so commendable.
Babies and children welcome: high chairs. Booking advisable. No smoking. Tables outdoors (3, pavement). Takeaway service. **Map 9 G6.**

Piccadilly W1

Zinc Bar & Grill
21 Heddon Street, W1B 4BG (7255 8899/ www.conran.com). Piccadilly Circus tube. Bar **Open** noon-midnight Mon-Sat. *Restaurant* **Meals served** noon-11pm Mon-Sat. **Main courses** £9.50-£15.50. *Both* **Service** 12.5%. **Credit** AmEx, DC, JCB, MC, V.
The quietly stylish interior, competent but vaguely sniffy service and poor acoustics immediately mark out Zinc as a Conran restaurant. However, its slightly tucked-away location (on a teensy thoroughfare just off Regent Street, also home to Momo – *see p238*) and capacious dining room means that, unlike some of its sister restaurants, it's rarely ever uncomfortably busy. The menu is a bit of a jumble (steaks, sandwiches, french onion soup, roast chorizo with manchego, grilled halloumi en croute), but staff seem capable of juggling its variety. A pea and ham soup arrived chilled, thick and pleasingly creamy; we followed it with a less characterful but by no means disagreeable roast pork tenderloin with spinach and glazed figs, with a side of fluffy mash. Desserts aren't especially tempting. The occasional special offer – on our last visit, two courses and a sweet if curious Hendrick's cocktail could be had for a very reasonable £15 – can make dining here better value than it might first appear. The lack of cars on Heddon Street mean the pavement tables are an attractive option in warmer weather.
Babies and children welcome: high chairs. Booking advisable. Disabled: toilet. No-smoking tables. Separate room for parties, seats 40. Tables outdoors (9, pavement). **Map 17 J7.**
For branch see index.

Soho W1

Balans
60 Old Compton Street, W1D 4UG (7437 5212/ www.balans.co.uk). Leicester Square tube. **Meals served** 8am-4am Mon-Thur; 8am-6am Fri, Sat; 8am-2am Sun. **Main courses** £8-£14. **Service** 12.5%. **Credit** AmEx, MC, V.

If Balans looks busy from the outside, and it usually does, don't give up. This Old Compton Street fixture, which attracts a largely, though by no means exclusively, gay clientele, is bigger than it first appears, opening out from the pavement into a capacious and casually stylish second room. Smokers will be delighted to learn that the seats set aside for puffing have street views, with non-smokers allocated the tables further back. The menu is long and outrageously varied – everything from spanakópitta to gravadlax, red pepper-crusted mahi mahi to calf's liver and bacon, and that's before you've had chance to clock the list of daily specials – but it's also delivered with a fair amount of success by the efficient staff. After a pleasingly fresh and grease-free quesadilla served with a piquant mango salsa, we tucked into 'Thai chicken', which made up in taste what it lacked in authenticity. Both the dessert and cocktail menus have plenty of appeal. There's a cool feel to the place during the day, but it gets somewhat fizzier after dark.
Babies and children admitted. No-smoking tables. **Map 17 K6.**
For branches see index.

Café Bohème
13 Old Compton Street, W1D 5JQ (7734 0623/ www.cafeboheme.co.uk). Leicester Square tube. **Open** 8am-3am Mon-Sat; 8am-10.30pm Sun. **Meals served** 8am-2.30am Mon-Sat; 8am-10pm Sun. **Main courses** £6-£15. **Set meal** (noon-7pm) £10.50 2 courses, £12.50 3 courses. **Cover** (Fri, Sat) £3 10-11pm, £4 after 11pm. **Service** 12.5%. **Credit** AmEx, DC, MC, V.
We were slightly surprised to learn that Café Bohème opened on this site only 13 years ago, it seems to be so much part of the Soho furniture. Like many places in central London, its popularity seems self-perpetuating (the more people come here, the more people come here). The infectious buzz is helped by low ceilings, dim lighting and small tables that are packed a little too tightly in the long, ground-floor room. But perhaps the main reason for Bohème's success is that the kitchen doesn't get ahead of itself, or its customers. The menu covers all the French brasserie favourites, from generous portions of moules marinière (served as a starter or main) to boeuf bourguignon (unimpressive) and the inevitable steak frites (requested, and served, medium-rare). Prices aren't too bad and given the location, especially if you succeed in nabbing one of the coveted tables with views of Old Compton Street's brilliant parade. Service is laudably efficient. In all, better than you might expect, even if the music is both louder and more modern than the already pulsating atmosphere requires.
Babies and children admitted (before 7pm). Entertainment: jazz 4-6pm Thur, Sun. Tables outdoors (9, pavement). **Map 17 K6.**

Randall & Aubin
14-16 Brewer Street, W1F 0SG (7287 4447). Piccadilly Circus tube. **Meals served** noon-11pm Mon-Sat; 4-10.30pm Sun. **Main courses** £7-£18. **Service** 12.5%. **Credit** AmEx, DC, JCB, MC, V.
The remodelling of this Soho institution was delicate enough to appease even its oldest regulars. A delightful French grocer's for years, it's now a boisterous brasserie, but with the exception of a new mirror ball, the basic, austere look has barely changed. However, one thing that was lost in the transition was the service: once legendarily good, it's now, on the evidence of our meal here, quite shocking. After forgetting our original order, a haughty waiter then retreated into the corner to gossip and munch his lunch, leaving ours on the counter. When the bill arrived, non-optional £1.50 cover charges were levied for bread and olives, neither of which had appeared. It all rather took the gloss off the food, which was pretty impressive. Seafood's the speciality: alaskan blue crab salad (starter) and pan-fried scallops (main) were both daisy-fresh, and if orders of japanese fish cakes and fillet of sea bass weren't quite as strong, they were good enough. Go for a late lunch or very early dinner to avoid the crowds, though you'll still end up shouting over the pulsing music.
Babies and children admitted. Bookings not accepted. Takeaway service. **Map 17 K6.**
For branch see index.

West

Ladbroke Grove W11

Electric Brasserie

191 Portobello Road, W11 2ED (7908 9696/ www.the-electric.co.uk). Ladbroke Grove tube.
Open 8am-midnight Mon-Sat; 8am-11pm Sun.
Meals served 8am-5pm, 6-11pm Mon-Sat;
8am-5pm, 6-10pm Sun. **Main courses** £9.50-£15.
Service 12.5%. **Credit** AmEx, DC, MC, V.
Be persistent, and you'll eventually secure a booking at what is one of the most fashionable restaurants in Notting Hill. In the few years since the opening of this brasserie adjoining the Electric cinema, the wooden floors leading through the cavernous bar to the restaurant have become as worn as the chrome-topped tables. You can hardly hear yourself shout above the background music and well-heeled social clatter. Starters are tempting, with langoustine bisque, or a luxuriant charcuterie of hams, gherkins and sardines (priced at a considerable £9). The latter is served on a rustic wooden board, as is the selection of nibbles such as crab gratin or aubergine bayildi (baked with tomatoes, garlic and onion). Mains are pricey: steak sandwiches cost a tenner, while crispy roast halibut served with clams and spinach was £16.50 and required a £3 side of carbs (mashed, fried and so on). Duck cottage pie is mightily meaty and more than one human being can decently eat. Desserts, which include a good lime soufflé, don't disappoint. Like the wine list, service hails from all over the globe, and is sometimes tart but generally fruity and occasionally sweet.
Babies and children welcome: high chairs. Booking essential. Disabled: toilet. No-smoking tables. Tables outdoors (8, pavement).
Map 19 B3.

Notting Hill W11

★ Notting Hill Brasserie

92 Kensington Park Road, W11 2PN (7229 4481). Notting Hill Gate tube. **Lunch served** noon-3pm daily. **Dinner served** 7-11pm Mon-Sat. **Main courses** £18.50-£23.50. **Set lunch** £14.50 2 courses, £19.50 3 courses. **Service** 12.5%. **Credit** AmEx, MC, V.

Probably one of the best and certainly one of the smartest restaurants in Notting Hill, this brasserie draws in the local bourgeoisie. Starters are mainly of marine life (oysters, scallops and so on), but the crispy duck in a sticky aubergine purée with a hint of harissa and coriander was well worth leaving home for. Mains also concentrate on the sea, one example being roasted monkfish in a creamy broth of lightly cooked mussels, potatoes, onions and tarragon. Of the meat dishes, lamb steak was sublimely seared and served with roasted onions, garlic and potatoes, together with a glorious artichoke purée. For dessert, the too-tempting cheesecake proved lighter than the marinated figs with which it came. One highlight of an excellent evening was the quality of the house wines, especially a red that had the character and depth of a bottle at least twice the price. The stone colour scheme is complemented by small upholstered armchairs at each table, and the classical decor is as assertive and restrained as the warm service.
Babies and children welcome: entertainer (Sun lunch); high chairs. Booking advisable. Entertainment: jazz and blues musicians 7pm daily. Separate rooms for parties, seating 12 and 32. **Map 7 A6.**

South West

Barnes SW14

★ The Depot

Tideway Yard, 125 Mortlake High Street, SW14 8SN (8878 9462/www.depotbrasserie.co.uk). Barnes, Barnes Bridge or Mortlake rail/209 bus. **Open** 11am-11pm Mon-Sat; 10am-10.30pm Sun.
Lunch served noon-3pm Mon-Fri; noon-4pm Sat, Sun. **Dinner served** 6-11pm Mon-Sat; 6-10.30pm Sun. **Main courses** £9.95-£16.50.
Set meal (noon-7.30pm Mon-Fri) £12.50 2 courses. **Service** 12.5%. **Credit** AmEx, DC, JCB, MC, V.
This riverside operation is ever-reliable, thanks to its combination of attractive premises, efficient staff and good-quality cooking. It's had 20 years to get things right, and it does. Pitched perfectly for the neighbourhood, it draws a loyal clientele of affluent locals with blonde bobs (the women) and rugby shirts (the men). Polished wood dominates the interior, with a sunny patio on one side and

lovely sunset views over the Thames on the other. The wide-ranging Mediterranean menu changes with the seasons and offers plenty of simple, well-executed dishes – perhaps a mixed meze plate, serrano ham or steamed asparagus to start, followed by risotto with peas and wild garlic, salade nicoise or corn-fed chicken breast. Good to see pollock (an underused alternative for endangered cod) on the menu; cooked just-so, its mild flavour and smooth texture went well with braised fennel and rich roasted squash. Puds are always a treat; a light panettone bread and butter pudding came topped with rich butterscotch ice-cream. The global wine list is nicely priced, with plenty of bottles for under £20 and plenty of options by the glass. There's also a good-value though limited set menu, and roasts on Sunday.
Babies and children welcome: children's menu; crayons; high chairs. Booking advisable. No-smoking tables. Tables outdoors (10, patio).

Chelsea SW1, SW3, SW6

Blue Kangaroo

555 King's Road, SW6 2EB (7371 7622/ www.thebluekangaroo.co.uk). Fulham Broadway tube/Sloane Square tube then 11, 22 bus. **Meals served** 11.30am-6.30pm daily. **Main courses** £8.50-£16. **Credit** AmEx, MC, V.
The nets, slides, ball ponds and tunnels in the basement of this family diner might dismay traditionalists, but they certainly help hone an appetite. Parents can sit upstairs in the restaurant proper or eat in the midst of the action downstairs; pay a small fee (from £3) for access to the play equipment. The brasserie menu is all modern classics: we enjoyed wild salmon fish cakes served with asparagus, and pumpkin risotto (a saffron-yellow, parmesan-scattered delight), with a leafily diverse but undressed house salad. A starter of sautéed scallops with truffle oil and sun-dried tomato was a treat, as was the firm, white cod in crunchy beer batter with chips. The Sunday roasts, steak sandwiches and chicken ciabattas are all made enjoyable by the high-quality meat used in them. The children's menu has superior versions of kiddy standards: chicken goujons are free-range and organic, salmon fish cakes are miniaturised versions of the adult ones, and burgers are made

Blue Kangaroo

on site with organic beef and served with serious salads. Puddings are, fittingly, nursery favourites: few barrister dads in Sunday-pressed Levi's can resist the bread and butter pudding. Service is affable and unflappable.
Babies and children welcome: children's menu; high chairs; toys. Booking advisable weekends. Disabled: toilet. No smoking. Vegan dishes. **Map 13 C13.**

Cheyne Walk Brasserie
50 Cheyne Walk, SW3 5LR (7376 8787/ www.cheynewalkbrasserie.com). Sloane Square tube.
Bar **Open** 7pm-midnight Mon; noon-midnight Tue-Sat; 11am-6pm Sun.
Restaurant **Brunch served** 11am-4pm Sun. **Lunch served** noon-3pm Tue-Sat. **Dinner served** 7-10pm Mon-Sat. **Main courses** £13-£29.50. **Set lunch** (Tue-Fri) £15 3 courses, (Sat, Sun) £20 2 courses, £25 3 courses. **Service** 12.5%. **Credit** AmEx, MC, V.
After being told to book four to five days ahead for dinner, we settled for Sunday lunch and went with high hopes. In the event, although this prettily decorated former pub offered delightful French service, it ultimately proved a victory of style over content. Tall cream walls and pink lampshades above turquoise leather bench-seats and red leather armchairs give the restaurant a light, elegant feel. But the food lacks this sophistication. Onion tartlet featured a marvellously soft caramelised onion, but tomatoes rolled in aubergine served cold was mundane. The grill is at the physical and thematic centre of the restaurant. Half a grilled chicken was fine, if unadorned; grilled sea bass was fresh, yet not out of the ordinary; and a vegetarian dish billed as 'tartine mozzarella' was a glorified panini. To finish, mousse de fromage blanc with compote de rhubarbe wasn't available, though crème brûlée made a good substitute. The wine list is strong, with a sommelier offering guidance. Mind your wallet, though: even sticking to the set menus resulted in a bill of £100 for three, including a bottle of house wine.
Babies and children welcome: crayons; high chairs. Booking advisable. Separate room for parties, holds 60. **Map 14 E12.**

The Market Place
Chelsea Farmers' Market, 125 Sydney Street, SW3 6NR (7352 5600). South Kensington tube/11, 19, 22, 49 bus. **Meals served** *Apr-Sept* 9.30am-5pm Mon-Fri; 9.30am-7pm Sat, Sun. *Oct-Mar* 9.30am-4.30pm daily. **Main courses** £8-£12. **Service** 12.5%. **Credit** AmEx, MC, V.
The whole of local society passes through this open-air eating and drinking suntrap, which features pub garden tables enclosed within a campsite of Portakabin boutiques. It's as close as a Chelsea restaurant comes to a cattle market. In a gesture of bland multicultural equanimity, the tannoy knocks out the repetitive rhythms of Eddy Grant. But make no mistake, it's useful to know about the Market Place, even if you have to queue for seats on a sunny day. The food is not haute cuisine, but it is agreeably varied as well as reassuringly familiar. Starters range from soup of the day to bresaola; for mains, the juicy burgers are galaxies away from the processed cardboard served at fast-food outlets, while the inch-thick tuna steaks come with thoroughly nourishing green bean, potato and egg salads. The dessert list is comfort food heaven (chocolate pud, cheesecake and the like), and the wine is as good as the wholesome food is affordable.
Babies and children welcome: high chairs. Bookings not accepted. Tables outdoors (35, patio). **Map 14 E12.**

Top Floor at Peter Jones
Sloane Square, SW1W 8EL (7730 3434/ www.johnlewis.com). Sloane Square tube. **Meals served** 9.30am-6.30pm Mon-Sat; 11am-4.30pm Sun. **Main courses** £3.50-£13.50. **Credit** MC, V.
People always look a bit bemused in the top-floor canteen of Peter Jones. The set-up seems simple, yet diners are usually found drifting around the room, wondering how the slightly understaffed, self-service restaurant works. When you've figured it out, you'll find the food good and healthy, even if it doesn't always look as such from the sometimes sweaty 'examples' left out for perusal. At the hot food counter, at least, you're not expected to eat them; indeed, on our visit, the roast beef made a fine Sunday lunch, with potatoes roasted in their skins and al dente veg that showed no signs of wilting. The cold counters offer tasty

light lunches, including tortilla wraps with vegetables and goat's cheese, or summer vegetable pappardelle. But the crown jewels are the desserts, which double up as teacakes and include scones, tiramisu and cheesecakes. Wine is available, as is teabag tea and coffee from a machine. The appeal of the place, with its glorious views towards Kensington Gardens, is clear from the number of people it attracts (along with their infants – high chairs abound). There's a more formal Anglo-European silver-service restaurant downstairs.
Babies and children welcome: children's menu; crayons; high chairs. Bookings not accepted. Disabled: toilet. No smoking. **Map 14 F12.**

Fulham SW10

★ Brasserie de l'Auberge NEW
268 Fulham Road, SW10 9EW (7352 1859/ www.massivepub.com). South Kensington tube then 14 bus. **Meals served** noon-10.30pm Mon-Sat; noon-10pm Sun. **Main courses** £11.95-£15.50. **Set meal** £10.95 2 courses, £14.50 3 courses. **Service** 12.5%. **Credit** AmEx, DC, JCB, MC, V.
Brasserie de l'Auberge is everything that a simple French brasserie-bistro should be, yet so often isn't. You can sit with a coffee reading the papers in the morning, enjoy a beer or a snack during the day, or have a blow-out dinner. It's an unpretentious place, and good value. And the classic French dishes we tried were as good as you find in many Parisian bistros. Coq au vin, cassoulet and French onion soup were textbook-perfect: the meat of the chicken was tender and the sauce rich, the cassoulet was comforting and full-flavoured, and the dark onion soup was so thick it was almost lentil-like. All these dishes are so often traduced elsewhere that it's almost a shock to have the real thing. The desserts were best of all: black specks of real vanilla in the bottom of a crème brûlée, the crust eggshell-thin and crisp; a tarte tatin that the Tatin sisters would have been proud of; and a chocolate fondant that puts most me-too versions to shame. Only the welcoming nature of the French staff and the lack of cigarette smoke detracts from the authenticity of the experience.
Babies and children welcome: high chairs. Booking advisable. Disabled: toilet. No-smoking tables. Tables outdoors (4, pavement). **Map 13 C12.**

South Kensington SW3

Aubaine NEW
260-262 Brompton Road, SW3 2AS (7052 0100/ www.aubaine.co.uk). South Kensington tube. **Meals served** 8am-10.30pm Mon-Sat; 9am-10pm Sun. **Main courses** £12.50-£19.50. **Service** 12.5%. **Credit** AmEx, MC, V.
From the outside, it's difficult to tell whether this is an upmarket kitchen shop or a restaurant. Every bit of spanking-new wood is painted greyish white and 'distressed' in an attempt to give the place an 'authentic' look. Aubaine is more authentic in its execution of French-style, all-day service. The restaurant menu holds rather a lot of pricey Franco-clichés: onion soup, coquilles saint-jacques, duck with Cointreau glaze. Clichés are forgiveable (just) if they're properly and carefully rendered. Our dishes weren't. Salade Aubaine comprised a large bowl of cos lettuce, cut into thin strips, with none of the advertised anchovies or herbs and a grand total of five prawns. Beef tartare came pre-mixed with a choice of Worcestershire sauce or Tabasco on the side. However, beef carpaccio, served with wild rocket and a herby sauce, couldn't be faulted, and a dessert of zesty tarte au citron hit the high notes. Best of all was the bread. Loaves are made on the premises from French flour (as our charming French waitress proudly pointed out) and available to buy from the shop. Despite the mediocre food, Aubaine is likely to be a hit, thanks to its location-location-location smack in the middle of well-heeled shopping nirvana.
Babies and children welcome: children's menu; high chairs. Booking advisable. Disabled: toilet. No smoking. Restaurant available for hire. Tables outdoors (4, pavement). Takeaway service. **Map 14 E10.**

South

Balham SW12

Balham Kitchen & Bar

15-19 Bedford Hill, SW12 9EX (8675 6900/ www.balhamkitchen.com). Balham tube/rail. **Open** 8am-midnight Mon-Thur; 8am-1am Sat; 8am-10.30pm Sun. **Breakfast served** 8am-noon daily. **Meals served** noon-11pm Mon-Sat; noon-10pm Sun. **Main courses** £9-£25. **Service** 12.5%. **Credit** AmEx, MC, V.

Long the butt of opprobrious 'gateway to the South' jokes, Balham is getting revenge and becoming one of south London's hottest eating and drinking spots. Run by the Soho House Group, which also owns Electric Brasserie (*see p50*) and members' club Soho House, the Balham Kitchen & Bar is at the forefront of this change: it's big, brash, busy and noisy. It's also really very good. In addition to the main space, there are various tucked-away seating areas; chefs do their stuff in a central kitchen, in plain view of diners. Breakfast is served until midday, when the French/American-style carte takes over. The menu combines modishness (marinated salmon with cucumber jelly and an oyster beignet, for a well-rendered starter) with brasserie staples such as serious-looking burgers and chips. A spring dish of lamb pot-au-feu with baby vegetables featured tender, rare lamb and a stock tasting of roasted lamb bones. Risotto of shellfish didn't stint on molluscs and the surprise ingredient of tarragon worked a treat. Crisp-crusted lemon tart made a fitting finish. The wine list is commendable in going 'off-piste' with such varietals as Torrontes and Teroldego. Book ahead. *Babies and children welcome (before 6pm, dining only): high chairs. Disabled: toilet. No-smoking tables. Separate rooms for parties, seating 20 and 50. Tables outdoors (6, pavement).*

Clapham SW4

Newtons

33-35 Abbeville Road, SW4 9LA (8673 0977/ www.newtonsathome.co.uk). Clapham South tube. **Lunch served** noon-4pm daily. **Dinner served** 7-10.30pm Mon-Thur, Sun; 7-11pm Fri, Sat. **Main courses** £9.50-£15. **Set lunch** (noon-3pm Mon-Sat) £8 2 courses, £10.50 3 courses; (Sun) £16.50 3 courses. **Set dinner** £15 2 courses; (Sat, Sun) £18.50 3 courses. **Service** 12.5%. **Credit** AmEx, MC, V.

Newtons has been around since before Abbeville Road became trendy, making it something of an elder statesman in these parts. The bare-brick interior hasn't changed in ages, although the menu (about nine starters and nine mains) seems more simple than on previous visits. Vegetarian dishes (such as watermelon and green bean salad, and gnocchi provençal) sound a cut above the average, and we were pleased with the weekend set menu: spring pea soup and a Sunday roast of pork with yorkshire pudding and apple sauce. A starter of warm salad of tender chicken livers and black pudding, lifted by decent balsamic vinegar, overcame the indignity of bagged salad leaves, while a main course of sea bass with citrus and sauce vierge arrived with green beans and a pretty arrangement of pink and yellow grapefruit segments. For dessert, expect the homely likes of hot chocolate brownie or treacle tart. Service is friendly and there's a laid-back feel, making Newtons a local you'll want to frequent. *Babies and children welcome: crayons; high chairs. Booking advisable. No-smoking tables. Tables outdoors (8, terrace).* **Map 22 A3.**

South East

Bankside SE1

Bankside

32 Southwark Bridge Road, SE1 9EU (7633 0011/www.banksiderestaurants.co.uk). Mansion House or Southwark tube/Blackfriars or London Bridge tube/rail. **Brasserie Lunch served** noon-3pm Mon-Fri. **Main courses** £3.50-£7. *Restaurant* **Lunch served** noon-3pm Mon-Fri. **Dinner served** 6-10.15pm Mon-Thur; 6-10.30pm Fri, Sat. **Main courses** £7.50-£11.50. **Service** 12.5%. *Both* **Credit** AmEx, DC, MC, V.

Tucked away in a sidestreet near the Globe, this dark basement dining room resembles a hotel bar, yet caters more to local office workers than passing tourists. Many of them are here to drink and chat as much as eat; the brasserie helps out by buying wine by the barrel and decanting it into its own bottles, which keeps prices down (and didn't seem to mar our decent house red). Food is simple bordering on unadventurous: deep-fried brie came with a spiced apple compote that was really just a plain apple sauce, while tomato and mozzarella salad was just that and nothing more. Main courses of sausage and mash, and haddock in batter emphasised that this is somewhere to come for superior pub grub, but the lack of vegetarian dishes was a major oversight. Eton mess with a fruit coulis ended our meal on a high, yet the increasingly lively atmosphere confirmed our initial impression: Bankside makes a great venue for a group, but isn't ideal for a romantic soirée. *Babies and children welcome: high chairs. Booking advisable Thur-Sat. Brasserie available for parties, seats 40. Disabled: toilet. No-smoking tables.* **Map 11 P8.**

For branch see index.

Tate Modern Café: Level 2

Second floor, Tate Modern, Sumner Street, SE1 9TG (7401 5014/www.tate.org.uk). Southwark tube/London Bridge tube/rail. **Breakfast served** 10-11.30am, **lunch served** 11.30am-3pm daily. **Afternoon tea served** 3-6pm Mon-Thur, Sun; 3-6.30pm Fri, Sat. **Dinner served** 6.30-9.30pm Fri, Sat. **Main courses** £9.50. **Service** 12.5%. **Credit** AmEx, DC, MC, V.

It's actually on the first floor (or even the ground floor, if you're coming from the river), but this superior café/restaurant is easy to find – just follow the queues. There's a distinct lack of art on the walls, but with big windows that offer views of the Thames, and an open kitchen housed behind a sleek long black bar, there's plenty to look at. Three separate daytime menus (breakfast, lunch and tea) are served, as well as tapas when the museum is open late on Fridays and Saturdays. None of it is cheap, but it's a cut above the usual museum fodder. The midday menu has plenty of choice, splitting into 'lunch' and 'light lunch' categories. We tried two dishes from the latter: a lovely, thick pea soup with minted crème fraîche, and a special of twice-baked swede and cheddar soufflé. Food have a modern British slant – braised corn-fed chicken breast with parsley dumplings, say, or Scottish kipper pâté with mustard and dill soda bread – but there's enough choice to suit most palates. And the chips are very decent. A more than impressive pit stop. *Babies and children welcome: crayons; high chairs. Bookings not accepted Sat, Sun. Disabled: toilets. No smoking.* **Map 11 O7.**

Crystal Palace SE19

Joanna's

56 Westow Hill, SE19 1RX (8670 4052/ www.joannas.uk.com). Crystal Palace or Gipsy Hill rail. **Open** 10am-11.15pm Mon-Thur; 10am-11.30pm Fri, Sat; 10am-10.30pm Sun. **Brunch served** 10am-6pm daily. **Meals served** noon-11.15pm Mon-Thur; noon-11.30pm Fri, Sat; noon-10.30pm Sun. **Main courses** £5.95-£18. **Service** 10% for parties of 6 or more. **Credit** AmEx, MC, V.

This bright, welcoming and spacious brasserie has an upbeat soundtrack, attentive staff and a menu with a classic British feel. Reasonably priced lunchtime favourites include Somerset oak-smoked ham, eggs and fries, and traditional roast beef with a giant yorkshire pudding and fresh vegetables, while the pricier carte offers meat lovers a choice of steaks, burgers or lamb cutlets alongside battered fish or moules (served either marinière or with a Thai curry twist). The brunch/lunch menu seems fantastic value and is served alongside an excellent children's version that includes a scoop of creamy Guernsey ice-cream (choose from cinnamon and honey, toffee and hazelnut, and pistachio flavours). For the grown-ups, there's baked honey cheesecake and crème brûlée, as well as a decent selection of cocktails. The wine list offers plenty of options, and there's a pleasing array of continental bottled beers, including Leffe Blonde, Moretti and Bitburger. Book in advance to reserve the old train carriage, perfect for a small party or family. *Babies and children welcome (before 8pm): children's menu; high chairs. No-smoking tables. Separate room for parties, seats 6. Tables outdoors (4, patio).*

East Dulwich SE22

The Green

58-60 East Dulwich Road, SE22 9AX (7732 7575/www.greenbar.co.uk). East Dulwich rail/ 37, 484 bus. **Open** 10am-11pm daily. **Breakfast served** 10am-noon, **lunch served** noon-5pm, **dinner served** 6-11pm daily. **Main courses** £9.95-£11.95. **Set lunch** (Mon-Sat) £8.50 2 courses, £11.50 3 courses, (Sun) £11.95 2 courses, £14.95 3 courses. **Service** 10%. **Credit** AmEx, MC, V.

The fact that East Dulwich is an 'it' location for trendyish parents becomes obvious after a weekend early evening spent in this restaurant/ bar/arts space. The interior has room for high chairs, and a children's menu is available (pasta or cod goujons, a drink and pudding); however, the family groups touting toddlers blend in graciously with loving couples and larger parties. On the main menu, appealing starters of, say, own-made tomato and basil soup, salmon fish cakes or well-dressed gnocchi pave the way for high-quality mains; everything we sampled was attractively presented and carefully seasoned. Calf's liver on crushed, buttery Jersey royals in a fruity gravy was pink and succulent; ostrich steak in tangy onion gravy was the most tender we've had; and salmon steak sported a delicious, crispy, charred skin. Sides shove the prices up (£2.80 for minted peas?), but the inexpensive house red was pleasantly soft. Puddings include a just-tart-enough rhubarb and red plum crumble, and a hot chocolate pudding with an orangey note served with pistachio ice-cream, both delightful. When the live music begins, start pondering the liqueur coffee list. *Babies and children welcome: children's menu; high chairs. Disabled: toilet. Entertainment: jazz 8pm Tue, Thur. Booking advisable. No-smoking area. Separate room for parties, seats 39. Tables outdoors (12, terrace).* **Map 23 C3.**

Greenwich SE10

Bar du Musée

17 Nelson Road, SE10 9JB (8858 4710/ www.bardumusee.com). Cutty Sark DLR. **Bar Open** 11am-midnight Mon-Fri; 11am-1am Sat. *Restaurant* **Brunch served** 11am-4pm Sat, Sun. **Lunch served** noon-5pm Mon-Fri. **Dinner served** 6-10pm daily. **Main courses** £11-£16. **Service** 12.5%. *Both* **Credit** MC, V.

You'll need to venture beyond the low-lighting, rich fabrics and intimate spaces of the bar area, which you encounter on entering, to really get the best from Bar du Musée. The diverse dining and drinking spaces – a cosy, alcoved basement, a welcoming leather sofa in a conservatory, alfresco dining in an extensive patio area – satisfy a range of moods. The glass-roofed main dining area (slate tiles, dark woods, eclectic images on the walls) really comes into its own as darkness falls, with flickering candlelight helping create a charming atmosphere in which to enjoy some good food from a thoughtfully compiled menu. The main successes of our evening were a beautifully cooked loin of lamb with prune and orange couscous and mint yoghurt, and a fluffy brandade of cod with baby potatoes and a citrus dressing. Other favourable points include an extensive wine list and excellent service, all of which go to make up a pleasurable dining experience.

Babies and children welcome: high chairs. Booking advisable weekends. Disabled: toilet. Separate room for parties, seats 20. Tables outdoors (15, garden).

Kennington SW9

The Lavender

24 Clapham Road, SW9 0JG (7793 0770).
Oval tube/59, 155, 159, 333 bus. **Lunch served** noon-3pm Tue-Sun. **Dinner served** 6-11pm daily. **Main courses** £7.50-£11. **Service** 12.5%. **Credit** AmEx, MC, V.

This branch of the Lavender, one of a trio in south London, specialises in pizzas, with a list of about 20. Otherwise, the menu sticks closely to a bready theme, with ranges of bruschettas (toppings served on pizza dough) and calzones ('stuffed' pizzas, with the filling on the inside) alongside a few salads, a selection of oven-cooked dishes and some appealing-sounding specials (grilled squid with polenta, sautéed garlic and green beans) chalked on a board. Unfortunately, our server neglected to point it out to us (one of several slips), so we stuck to the carte, starting with a smoked ham salad and goat's cheese bruschetta. The salad didn't skimp on peppery rocket, but had none of the advertised balsamic vinegar, red onions or olives, while the bruschetta was unremarkable and made a boring prelude to an artichoke and courgette calzone. Oven-baked chorizo with tomato sauce, mushrooms and baby spinach was oversalted. The 20 or so wines cover the basics, with most costing below £20, while the room is comfortable, relaxed and well-scrubbed.
Babies and children welcome: high chairs. Booking advisable. Separate room for parties, seats 20. Tables outdoors (6, garden; 5, patio). Takeaway service.
For branches see index.

North

Crouch End N8

Banners

21 Park Road, N8 8TE (8348 2930). Finsbury Park tube/rail then W7 bus. **Meals served** 9am-11.30pm Mon-Thur; 9am-midnight Fri; 10am-4pm, 5pm-midnight Sat; 10am-4pm, 5pm-11pm Sun. **Main courses** £8.95-£11.50. **Set meal** (10am-6pm Mon-Fri) £6.95 1 course & side dish. **Service** 12.5% for parties of 6 or more. **Credit** MC, V.

The branch off Hornsey Lane has closed, but otherwise, Banners sails on, still drawing a variety of customers. During the day, it's the trusted local for Crouch End's enlightened parents (grumps who

Balham Kitchen & Bar. See p52.

can't take the bar-cum-crêche atmosphere should abstain from visiting in the afternoons), but at night, it's a hipper hangout, with a global beer range and many rums and cocktails to go with the mock tropical-beach decor. The food is an equally broad, multinational mix: bright, colourful, unsubtle and served in big portions. The menu contains everything from snacks and sandwiches via salads up to full main courses, with plenty of choice for kids. We recently enjoyed a jerk chicken burger with hefty salad, and an 'extra' of highly moreish garlic chips. A daily special of vegetarian lasagne with wild mushrooms and goat's cheese was also pleasing, in a hefty home-cooking way, and came with a salad overloaded with rocket (massed leaves is something of a Banners characteristic). Service is always friendly and not as disorganised as it looks.
Babies and children welcome (until 7pm): children's menu; crayons; high chairs. Booking advisable. No-smoking tables (9am-7pm Mon-Fri).

Hornsey N8

★ Pumphouse Dining Bar [NEW]

1 New River Avenue, N8 7QD (8340 0400/ www.mosaicarestaurants.com). Turnpike Lane tube/Hornsey rail.
Bar **Open** 11.30am-11pm Mon-Sat; noon-10.30pm Sun.
Restaurant **Lunch served** noon-3pm Mon-Fri. **Dinner served** 6-9.30pm Mon-Wed; 6-10pm Thur, Fri. **Meals served** noon-10pm Sat; noon-9.30pm Sun. **Main courses** £7.50-£15. *Both* **Service** 10%. **Credit** AmEx, DC, JCB, MC, V.

At this newcomer in Hornsey – part of the Mosaica mini-empire of successful eateries in unlikely industrial surroundings – Italian cuisine is the kitchen's springboard to punchy international flavours. Meaty mains such as lamb shank with parsley mash and gravy, and chicken with mediterranean veg and pesto, are generously proportioned and appetisingly presented. Indeed, our roast was as much potbelly as pork belly: a huge slab spanning the plate, and perfectly cooked with tender meat and evenly crisp crackling. Lighter options include a choice of six pizzas and six pasta/risottos. The tart of the day was chocolate: dark-tasting but not too rich, with satisfyingly crisp pastry and a reasonable vanilla ice-cream. Service was attentive; given that the place had only recently opened when we visited, we decided not to be harsh when staff slipped up with our drinks order, serving us a more expensive glass of wine than the one we'd chosen with no explanation until our second round. One other note: the century-old former waterworks building in which the restaurant is housed has been stylishly converted, but the hard shiny surfaces and open-plan everything do generate a lot of noise, even when the place isn't especially busy.
Babies and children welcome (restaurant and patio only): high chairs. Booking advisable. Disabled: toilet. Entertainment: DJ 7pm Sat. Tables outdoors (10, patio).
For branches (Mosaica) see index.

Muswell Hill N10

Café on the Hill

46 Fortis Green Road, N10 3HN (8444 4957/ www.cafeonthehill.com). Highgate tube then 43, 134 bus. **Meals served** 8am-10.30pm Mon-Sat; 9am-4pm Sun. **Main courses** £7.95-£12.95. **Credit** MC, V.

Looking as much a café as a restaurant, Café on the Hill fulfils several functions perfectly suited to the citizens of Muswell Hill: a call-in spot for a mid-morning or post-school coffee and chat; a good-value lunch venue; and, at night, a full-service restaurant. The food covers an accordingly wide range: get pancakes or a full english breakfast in the morning, pastries and panini nearer the afternoon, or a global mix of main courses, all prepared using mainly organic ingredients, in the evenings. We've previously enjoyed lunching on refreshing mixed salads featuring seafood or char-grilled chicken; this year, we found the evening menu to be satisfying, if not startling. A starter

of pancakes stuffed with garlic mushrooms in asparagus sauce held our interest, as did chicken parfait on a toasted brioche with over-sweet cranberry chutney. Both the mains we ordered – ribeye steak with rösti and portobello mushrooms stuffed with goat's cheese, grilled lamb cutlets with mixed veg – were similarly pleasant without being memorable. The wine list is brief and to the point, and service is capable. The main surprise: on our evening visit, the café was quite smoky.
Babies and children welcome: high chairs; toys. Booking advisable Fri, Sat. No smoking (10am-7pm Mon-Sat). Tables outdoors (4, pavement). Takeaway service.

★ Giraffe

348 Muswell Hill Broadway, N10 1DJ (8883 4463/www.giraffe.net). Highgate tube then 43, 134 bus. **Meals served** 9am-10.45pm Mon-Sat; 9am-10.15pm Sun. **Main courses** £6.95-£12.95. **Set meal** (5-7pm Mon-Fri) £6.95 2 courses, (7-11pm Mon-Fri) £8.95 2 courses. **Service** 12.5%. **Credit** AmEx, MC, V.

The Giraffe chain has hit upon a highly attractive formula: decor that's bright and animal-themed without resembling a nursery, and an approach that manages to be family-friendly without putting off the childless. We've yet to find a branch that doesn't fill up for weekend brunches and lunches (for which you can't book), but the friendly service helps everyone through the queue with little discomfort. The menu runs from brunch favourites (fry-ups, scrambled eggs and smoked salmon), via generous mixed salads, appetisers and burgers, to more sophisticated mains and specials (parmesan chicken and gazpacho salsa, grilled sea bass). All are assembled with the same global mix-and-match style. Our classic Angus burger was excellent, cooked exactly as ordered; 'tangy and spiced turkey enchiladas' were full of interesting flavours; and the creamy, fruity and chocolatey desserts were a real highlight. The drinks list is equally expansive: fruit smoothies, coffees, good-value wines and cocktails. The admirable attention to detail extends to both food (there's plenty of choice for vegetarians) and drink (not one but two fresh mint teas, straight and Moroccan).
Babies and children welcome: children's menu; crayons; high chairs. Bookings not accepted weekend lunch. No smoking. Tables outdoors (3, pavement). Takeaway service.
For branches see index.

RESTAURANTS

British

A pretty good year for British dining saw **Inn The Park** scoop Best Design in *Time Out*'s 2005 Eating & Drinking Awards, as well as runner-up for Best Alfresco Dining, while Conran newcomer **Bluebird Dining Rooms** was a runner-up in the Best New Restaurant category. Other new arrivals are Gary Rhodes' latest venture **Rhodes W1**, Scottish-themed **Albannach**, and the **Paternoster Chop House** (also part of the Conran stable).

The truly outstanding dining experiences tend to be found at a now well-established 'new' generation of restaurants: **Lindsay House**, **St John** and its young mini-me **St John Bread & Wine** have led the way, with **Medcalf** a boisterous recent addition to their ranks. But you can also rely on the old-timers serving traditional Brit cuisine. The **Dorchester Grill Room**, **Simpson's-in-the-Strand**, even doughty old **Rules** keep plugging away, making sure the young whippersnappers know their place and peppery elderly gents can find theirs.

Central

City E1, EC2, EC4

Paternoster Chop House NEW
Warwick Court, Warwick Lane, Paternoster Square, EC4M 7DX (7029 9400/www.conran. com). St Paul's tube. **Food served** 10.30am-10.30pm Mon-Fri; noon-5pm Sun. **Main courses** £9.50-£20.50. **Set lunch** (Sun) £19.50 2 courses; £24.50 3 courses. **Service** 12.5%. **Credit** AmEx, DC, MC, V.
With a great corner location on newly handsome Paternoster Square at the foot of St Paul's, and the concomitant stream of passing tourist and City trade, you'd have thought Terence Conran's new restaurant had everything going for it. A surprise, then, that it felt really quite lacklustre. The interior is light, bright and modern, with huge windows, a curved bar and an open kitchen, but so few diners were there on a Monday night that the atmosphere was very muted; the staff seemed to catch the malaise. The menu changes daily and has some interesting true-Brit offerings alongside signature Conran fish and seafood – lop-eared pig pie, braised piglet, Mendip lamb and faggot, cod cheeks. On our visit it was all pretty standard stuff, though, and what left the kitchen was a catalogue of errors: dressed crab lacked its potato salad; coffee was the colour of beige tights; and the vegetables were variously cold, elderly and overcooked. Mains of (over) buttered plaice and roast beef (at £20 the 'beast of the day') were more acceptable, but not memorable. The charitable view is that there was trouble in't kitchen – since we've previously been attentively served with appetising bar snacks, it's the one we'll adopt for now.
Babies and children welcome: children's menu; games; high chairs. Booking advisable. Disabled: toilet. Tables outdoors (25, courtyard). **Map 11 O6.**

Rhodes Twenty Four
24th floor, Tower 42, Old Broad Street, EC2N 1HQ (7877 7703/www.rhodes24.co.uk). Bank tube/Liverpool Street tube/rail. **Lunch served** noon-2.15pm, **dinner served** 6-8.30pm Mon-Fri. **Main courses** £11.60-£35. **Service** 12.5%. **Credit** AmEx, DC, MC, V.
Unsurprisingly, an overwhelmingly corporate atmosphere pervades this cloud-capped City diner (at lunch, in particular, the requisite captains of industry are very much in evidence). And the pinstripe army gets what must be one of the greatest views of any London restaurant: in the foreground, Foster's 'Gherkin'; beyond it, the grimy, glinting puzzle of east London's streetscape. Gary Rhodes's menu majors on British classics given an innovative twist, but, regrettably, we have not always found the food to be quite as grand as the 24th-floor setting might lead you to expect. On our latest visit, a starter of pea soup with buttered potato and poached egg, for example, tasted as fresh and as comforting as it sounds, but it was hard to see why it should have cost £7.80. Ditto, a little huddle of seared scallops with shallot mustard sauce and mash, also a starter, at £16.50. As for the mains, roast chicken with sage and shallot tart was superb, but gorgeous sea bream was ruined by a slithery salad of marinated cucumber, shallots and oysters. Desserts, however, rarely put a foot wrong – this bread and butter pudding is the definitive version. Staff have a vaguely Stepford-like quality. Champagne-and-oyster bar Vertigo 42 (*see p342*), located higher up the building, offers even more spectacular views.
Babies and children admitted. Booking essential, 2-4 weeks in advance. Disabled: toilet. Dress: smart casual. **Map 12 Q6.**

★ St John Bread & Wine
94-96 Commercial Street, E1 6LZ (7247 8724/ www.stjohnbreadandwine.com). Aldgate East tube/Liverpool Street tube/rail. **Meals served** 9am-10.30pm Mon-Fri; 10am-10.30pm Sat; 10am-5pm Sun. **Main courses** £11-£14. **Service** 12.5% for parties of 6 or more. **Credit** AmEx, MC, V.
The even-more-relaxed branch of St John (*see p55*) is done out in the same airy, pared-down, whitewashed way, right down to the open kitchen, but in a smaller space with the tables slightly closer together. The menu follows the same principles as the original, but allows for more flexibility: breakfast (porridge with prunes, Old Spot bacon sandwich) is served, as is elevenses of seed cake and a glass of Madeira. From midday there are spanking fresh seasonal choices, simply cooked and presented. In summer, this meant plaice with samphire; courgettes; white beans and goat's curd; and beetroot, sorrel and boiled egg. Those lusting after nose-to-tail eating could choose Middlewhite pork and pigeon terrine. No-nonsense puddings might be gingerloaf and butterscotch sauce, or meringue, strawberries and cream, but always include madeleines or eccles cakes. The all-day availability and daily changing menu means that some dishes do run out (tragically, on our last visit, the eccles cakes were all gone). The fabulous bread and cakes are made on site, and sold from a counter next to the kitchen. Wines from the French list are also available as off-sales. In short, it's hard to imagine London's dining scene without the presence and influence of the St John duo – long may they reign.
Babies and children welcome: high chairs. Booking advisable. Takeaway service. **Map 12 S5.**

Clerkenwell & Farringdon EC1

★ Medcalf
40 Exmouth Market, EC1R 4QE (7833 3533/ www.medcalfbar.co.uk). Farringdon tube/rail/ 19, 38, 341 bus. **Open** noon-11pm Mon-Thur, Sat; noon-12.30am Fri; noon-5pm Sun. **Food served** noon-3pm, 6-10pm Mon-Thur; noon-3pm Fri; noon-4pm, 6-10pm Sat; noon-4pm Sun. **Main courses** £9.50-£14. **Credit** MC, V.
Medcalf was an instant hit when it opened in 2004, winning our Best Local Restaurant award. Though success has had its effects, the fundamentals remain in place: top-quality, well-priced British food and a louche, friendly vibe. The former butcher's shop runs back from the street shotgun-style, with a bar on one side flanked by a row of shabby-chic tables. The menu allows you to pick and mix between cheaper, casual dishes/starters and a handful of fully accoutred main courses. The likes of welsh rarebit, ham hock terrine and magnificent beer-battered cod appear frequently, supplemented by seasonal dishes such as, on our visit, dressed crab (a good specimen, coming with an unusually fine green salad) and barnsley chop (thick, succulent and perfectly accompanied by a caper sauce). Medcalf has become something of a destination restaurant; the crowd is less local and a little less casual, and it can now be hard to get a table without booking. But from 10pm, when the kitchen closes, and all night on Fridays, drinkers still prevail; if a planned expansion next door comes off, they'll have a space of their own. Just a shame there are no worthwhile British beers here.
Babies and children admitted (before 7pm). Bar available for hire. Disabled: toilet. Entertainment: DJs 7pm Fri. Tables outdoors (5, garden; 10, pavement). **Map 5 N4.**

Quality Chop House
92-94 Farringdon Road, EC1R 3EA (7837 5093/ www.qualitychophouse.co.uk). Farringdon tube/ rail/19, 38, 341 bus. **Breakfast served** 7.30-10am, **lunch served** noon-3pm Mon-Fri. **Dinner served** 6-11.30pm Mon-Sat. **Meals served** noon-10.30pm Sun. **Main courses** £6.95-£16.25. **Set lunch** (lunch Mon-Fri, 6-7.30pm Mon-Sat) £9.95 2 courses. **Credit** AmEx, JCB, MC, V.
Just around the corner from ever-evolving Exmouth Market, the Quality Chop House may be an older kid on the block, but it shouldn't be overlooked. Occupying two adjoining rooms, with tiled floors, old mirrors and wooden banquette seating, the place lives up to its 'Progressive Working Class Caterer' billing. A starter of yellow-fin tuna loin tartare with black olive and shallot dressing was delightfully fresh, as was a traditional French fish soup, with rouille, gruyère cheese and croutons (and this on a Monday night, typically a bad time for ordering fish). Mains included 'London's noted salmon fishcake' (how could we resist?) and a 28-day-matured Scottish grilled beef chop and chips. A nitpicker might have found the chips a wee bit dry, but otherwise both dishes were faultless. Top-class versions of school dinner puds included an utterly splendid rice pudding with apricot jam. The wine list is mainly French, with a smattering of choice New World offerings. Service was pretty offhand on our visit, but that couldn't detract from what the kitchen was putting out: British food (and some continental variations) at its best. New this year: breakfast during the week, and a bar next door.
Babies and children welcome. Booking advisable. Disabled: toilet. **Map 5 N4.**

★ St John

*26 St John Street, EC1M 4AY (7251 0848/
4998/www.stjohnrestaurant.com). Farringdon
tube/rail.*
Bar **Open/food served** 11am-11pm Mon-Fri;
6-11pm Sat. **Main courses** £4-£15.
Restaurant **Lunch served** noon-3pm
Mon-Fri. **Dinner served** 6-11pm Mon-Sat.
Main courses £13-£21. **Service** 12.5% for
parties of 6 or more. **Credit** AmEx, MC, V.
While we terrify our children with the Grimm
Brothers' fairy tales, our counterparts in the
animal kingdom must sit in their burrows at night
and read aloud from Fergus Henderson's cookbook.
It's gloriously bloodthirsty stuff. Pork is pressed
and paired with gizzards (a great starter, this, by
the way), while main courses might include a plate
of chitterlings or crispy pigs' tails. But it's not all
gore; some of the dishes are downright dainty:
cured sea trout with cucumber and dill, followed
by pigeon with pea purée, perhaps. The point is,
St John takes an exciting, recherché view of British
gastronomy, winkling out delicious (all too often
forgotten) regional dishes from every corner of the
country, while creating whimsical riffs on the
well-worn classics (gooseberry fool, for example,
comes with toasted brioche). Ingredients are
strictly seasonal, presentation of food is simple
(expect scullery china with plain cutlery), and the
uncluttered refectory-style dining room is elegant
without being too formal. So next time some
Frenchman tells you that the British don't know
how to cook, send him along to St John. There
might even be some humble pie on the menu.
*Babies and children welcome: high chair.
Booking advisable. Disabled: toilet. No cigars
or pipes (restaurant). Separate room for parties,
seats 18.* **Map 5 O5**.

★ Top Floor at Smiths

*Smiths of Smithfield, 67-77 Charterhouse Street,
EC1M 6HJ (7251 7950/www.smithsofsmithfield.
co.uk). Farringdon tube/rail.* **Lunch served**
noon-3pm Mon-Fri; noon-3.45pm Sun. **Dinner
served** 6.30-10.45pm Mon-Sat; 6.30-10.30pm
Sun. **Main courses** £19-£28. **Set lunch** (Sun)
£25 3 courses. **Service** 12.5%. **Credit** AmEx,
DC, MC, V.
The rooftop views from this slick third-floor
restaurant opposite Smithfield Market are superb,
the staff are knowledgeable and polite, the decor
is elegant, and the cooking is accomplished. Really,
it's hard to fault the place. Of the Smiths dining
space it's the posh one (the floors below are
comparatively casual bar and brasserie operations
– *see p222* **Smiths of Smithfield**) and the menu
features some suitably high-quality ingredients,
with prices to match. Beef looms large among the
mains, and the provenance of the meat (Islay
Butchers, Chesterton Farm and the like) is listed in
exhaustive detail. Prices are steep: at £28.50 for a
7oz fillet steak, you can feel entitled to expect a
pretty bloody good slice of meat – but, in fairness,
that's what has always arrived on our plate
whenever we have eaten here. Aside from beef,
there are starters like Dorset crab on toast, smoked
eel or meltingly tender salt and pepper squid, while
main courses range from roast halibut with lobster
mash to loin of venison. Desserts include the likes
of rhubarb crumble, and Neal's Yard cheeses with
oatcakes. There's also a fine selection of wines by
the glass on the generally impressive list.
*Babies and children welcome: high chairs.
Booking advisable. Disabled: lift; toilet.
Tables outdoors (8, terrace).* **Map 11 O5**.

Covent Garden WC2

Rules

*35 Maiden Lane, WC2E 7LB (7836 5314/
www.rules.co.uk). Covent Garden tube.* **Meals
served** noon-11.30pm Mon-Sat; noon-10.30pm
Sun. **Main courses** £15.95-£19.95. **Set dinner**
(10-11.30pm Mon-Thur) £18.95 2 courses. **Credit**
AmEx, DC, JCB, MC, V.
When a place has as long a pedigree as 'London's
oldest restaurant' (est. 1798), and such a devoted
clientele of plutocrats and elderly tourists still
figuring out the currency, there's naturally a sense

of dread that it will be just a museum piece,
shamelessly tarting old glories. The lofty ceilings,
original woodwork, stuffed wildlife, Victorian
cartoons and deeply dubious slave-girl statues
certainly give it the look of a monument, but there's
no complacency here: Rules maintains high
standards. The use of first-quality ingredients is a
keynote. Game is the great speciality, sourced from
Rules' own estate in the Pennines, but other menu
stalwarts are classic British dishes, beautifully
done – like the roast beef with really spectacular
yorkshire pud. There's no lack of subtlety, as in the
delicately overlaid flavours of smoked venison with
juniper horseradish and beetroot, or lobster and
asparagus salad. Steaks are cooked exactly right,
and both main players in grilled tuna with scallops
were memorably fresh. Save space for the superbly
light classic English desserts: summer pudding,
lemon possett, hot sponge puddings. One other
special feature of Rules is its private rooms, a
rambling celebrity-warren on the upper floors.
Service is utterly professional and, although prices
are high (especially for wines), Rules also has a
cheaper set menu.
*Babies and children admitted: high chairs.
Booking advisable. Dress: smart casual.
No smoking. Separate rooms for parties
(phone 7379 0258), seating 10, 12, 16 and 20.*
Map 18 L7.

Mayfair W1

★ Dorchester Grill Room

*The Dorchester, 53 Park Lane, W1A 2HJ
(7317 6336/www.dorchesterhotel.com). Hyde
Park Corner tube.* **Breakfast served** 7-11am
Mon-Sat; 7.30-11am Sun. **Lunch served** 12.30-
2.30pm daily. **Dinner served** 6-11pm Mon-Sat;
7-10.30pm Sun. **Main courses** £16-£30.
Set lunch (Mon-Sat) £22 2 courses incl coffee,
£25 3 courses incl coffee; (Sun) £32.50 3 courses.
Set dinner £39.50 3 courses incl coffee.
Credit AmEx, DC, JCB, MC, V.
When a place does old-fashioned full-on luxury as
well as the Dorchester does, there's only one thing
to do: revel in it. Soon after our most recent visit,
the dining room closed for renovation; the new
decor will involve tartan and malt whisky bottles,
but we are confident the service will remain
impeccable without ever being snooty, and have
been reassured the menu will brook no undue
innovation. So expect a bread trolley to arrive
shortly after you are seated, bearing a broad
enough array of fine fresh breads to supply an
entire bakery, and cuisine, a mix of British steaks
and roasts and classic French-style cooking, that's
wonderfully sybaritic. Our coarse country terrine
with foie gras and onion marmalade had a
memorable depth of overlaid flavours, while rump
of veal with summer truffles was supremely
delicate. Very skilfully handled contrasts are a
kitchen hallmark, as in a great guinea fowl with
girolles, or fabulously tender rack of lamb with
shallot purée. Few manage to turn away the
dessert trolley, with two decks of ultra-refined
versions of classic puds. Remarkably, set lunch
menus make it possible to sample Dorchester
indulgence at very decent prices, although you can
be caught out by the wine list, a spectacularly
extravagant collection with little under £30.
*Babies and children welcome: high chairs.
Booking advisable; essential weekends 1 week
in advance. Disabled: toilet. Dress: smart casual.*
Map 9 G7.

Marble Arch W1

Rhodes W1 NEW

*The Cumberland, Great Cumberland Place,
W1A 4RF (7479 3838). Marble Arch tube.*
Bar **Open/snacks served** 11am-11pm Mon-Sat;
11am-10.30pm Sun.
Restaurant **Lunch served** noon-2.30pm,
dinner served 5.30-10pm daily. **Main courses**
£9.75-£38.50. **Service** 12.5%. **Credit** AmEx,
MC, V.
Despite appearing in *Hell's Kitchen*, Gary Rhodes
remains a proper chef: Rhodes W1 now joins
Rhodes Twenty Four (*see p54*) as witness for the
defence. The dining room inside the Cumberland

Interview
TREVOR GULLIVER

Who are you?
Co-owner of the two **St Johns**
(*see p54* and *p55*); also involved
in **Wine Wharf** (*see p336*), **Cantina
Vinopolis** (*see p235*), Bar Blue cocktail
bar, and Brew Wharf microbrewery.
**Eating in London: what's good
about it?**
Diversity. Say what you like about
TV chefs and their programmes but
eating out is part of our life now.
What's bad about it?
Too many poor restaurants. That
includes bad pricing, poor staff, poor
tip policy, poor bread, standardised
wine and beer lists, poor standards
of hygiene. The reliance on overseas
staff that are poorly trained reflects
how catering is seen in this country
in terms of career development.
**Which are your favourite
London restaurants?**
The bar at **J Sheekey** (*see p85*)
is great. I had Saturday lunch at
Le Caprice (*see p227*) recently, and
it was excellent. I also like **Chez
Marcelle** (*see p217*), **Fino** (*see p255*)
and the **Anchor & Hope** (*see p111*).
**What single thing would improve
London's restaurant scene?**
Common sense. To open and maintain
a restaurant is a serious business,
and no one should believe that people
just walk through the door. It's tough
with chains forcing up rents in prime
locations. It takes a restaurant or bar
five years to get really established;
you need to be funded to run for three.
Any hot tips for the coming year?
More of the same from the chains.
I'd like to think there's some legs in
what's happening with pubs. I'd love
to see someone do caffs correctly.
Anything to declare?
Ban prawns. If you want to do
something good for the planet, for
human-kind and farmers, ban prawns.
You can at least put frozen peas on
a bruised leg.

RESTAURANTS

hotel is large enough to feel almost institutional, the service is cheerfully amateurish, and the menu is kept fairly simple, but with Rhodes' signature Modern British approach writ large upon it. Oxtail is a Rhodes favourite, in this case cut into moist and tender chunks that slithered off the bone. Tiny dice of vegetables provided some colour; a side dish of mash was a foil to the rich flavours. Roast skate wing was another simplest-is-best main: roasted and dressed with butter, capers and lemon. Less resolutely British were starters of plump stewed mussels, with appropriately restrained saffron and accompanying gnocchi in the stew; and grilled Bury black pudding garnished with a leafy apple and blue cheese salad. But it's the British classics that are best, as in a sublime steamed sponge pudding, soaked with lemon and blackberry. Served with a lemon-flavoured custard, it was as far away from school dinners as Marble Arch is from Macclesfield. A 'fine dining' Rhodes restaurant is planned next door for autumn 2005, where you can expect more complexity, higher prices and regular sightings of the man himself.
Babies and children welcome: high chairs. Booking advisable. Disabled: toilet. Restaurant available for hire. **Map 9 G6.**

Piccadilly W1

Fortnum & Mason
181 Piccadilly, W1A 1ER (7734 8040/ www.fortnumandmason.co.uk). Green Park or Piccadilly Circus tube.
Fountain (ext 2492) **Breakfast served** 8.30-11.30am, **meals served** 11.30am-7.45pm Mon-Sat. **Main courses** £9-£24.
St James's (ext 2241) **Lunch served** noon-2pm Tue-Sat. **Tea served** 10am-5.30pm Mon; 3-5.30pm Tue-Sat. **Set lunch** £20 2 courses, £23 3 courses.
Patio **Meals served** 10am-5.30pm Mon-Sat; noon-5pm Sun. **Main courses** £10.50-£24.50.
All **Service** 12.5%. **Credit** AmEx, DC, JCB, MC, V.
Less formal than the rather stuffy St James's restaurant, the Fountain is our eaterie of choice at this fabulous Piccadilly store. Its dining room is adorned with whimsical murals depicting the imaginary romps of Messrs F&M as they streaked through the colonies gathering fine teas, feisty pickles and other exotic treats. And there's much

evidence of their hamper-tastic sourcing on the all-day and breakfast menus. From the latter, during a recent early-morning visit, we chose a superb pot of Assam Mohokutie (a sunset-gold liquor of a tea) to accompany 'rare breed' eggs benedict, which turned out to be an artery-furring pile of quality ingredients slathered with a rich, perky hollandaise. If you visit later in the day, you can choose from a self-consciously quaint list of 'savouries' (in other words, the usual brasserie mains and grills, plus the odd welsh rarebit dotted around for granny-sized appetites). There's also an impressive range of ice-creams, sundaes and shakes, intended no doubt as top-drawer bribery material for those parents unlucky enough to have to drag their offspring around Fortnum's food hall.
Babies and children welcome: high chairs. Booking advisable. No-smoking tables (Fountain only). Separate room for parties, seats 32. **Map 17 J7.**

St James's SW1

★ Inn The Park
2005 WINNER BEST DESIGN
2005 RUNNER-UP BEST ALFRESCO DINING
St James's Park, SW1A 2BJ (7451 9999/ www.innthepark.co.uk). St James's Park tube.
Breakfast served 8-11am Mon-Fri; 9-11am Sat, Sun. **Lunch served** noon-3pm Mon-Fri; noon-4pm Sat, Sun. **Tea served** 3-5pm Mon-Fri. **Dinner served** 6-9.30pm daily. **Main courses** £4.50-£18.50. **Credit** AmEx, MC, V.
Nudging the lakefront and surrounded by leafy greens and vibrant blooms, Inn The Park is an oasis for weary tourists and walkers. Architect Michael Hopkins has created a welcoming wood and glass pavilion with a turf-covered sloping roof, generous terrace and glazed walls that slide back in clement weather, so that visitors still feel that they are in the park. The golden larch interior has a classy 1930s feel, and Habitat's creative director Tom Dixon was in charge of the fit-out. Restaurateur Oliver Peyton's simple yet striking menu complements the relaxed atmosphere with full-on lunch and dinner menus, as well as informal teas and breakfasts. In our summery starter, tangy, velvety-smooth goat's curd contrasted with sweet, juicy raisins and was punctuated by the bite of

mildly astringent baby chard leaves – simple food at its best. Other stars included a main course of Cornish hake and creamed roast tomatoes, in which the perfectly textured flesh of the fish was encircled by a moat of equally delicious tomato and red pepper sauce. Puddings fly the flag for the best of British: if you've got room, sink your spoon into the chill of a custardy English Champagne trifle. Staff are relaxed yet professional, and there's a tempting children's menu that will enable you to keep everyone well fed and happy.
Babies and children welcome: children's menu; high chairs. Booking advisable. Disabled: toilet. No smoking (indoors). Tables outdoors (23, terrace). Takeaway service. Vegan dishes. **Map 10 K8.**

Wiltons
55 Jermyn Street, SW1Y 6LX (7629 9955/ www.wiltons.co.uk). Green Park or Piccadilly Circus tube. **Lunch served** noon-2.30pm, **dinner served** 6-10.15pm Mon-Fri. **Main courses** £19-£40. **Credit** AmEx, DC, MC, V.
They don't make 'em like this anymore. Welcome to Wiltons, where a portrait of Edward VII hangs over the bar, gents dining alone are offered a copy of the *Daily Telegraph*, and staff are so ideally attentive you can feel you've acquired your own butler for a couple of hours. In contrast to other grand old British restaurants in town, the speciality is not roasts but fish, especially lobster, sole, plaice, halibut and turbot cooked in several classic styles – although fine steaks are also menu staples, and game features heavily in season. A starter of duck, pork and foie gras terrine was richly enjoyable, even though the strong duck tended to barge the other two ingredients out of the way; to follow, baked cod with a bacon crust was superb, and exquisitely balanced. Desserts are suitably trad. The distinction of the food, though, is less the point here than the seamless, old-world cosseting, much appreciated by regulars – blue-suited gents, ladies who look like they may be duchesses, and a more louche, Mayfair-international set – who know all the senior waiters by name. The cost: astronomical, with a mere bottle of water priced at £5.
Babies and children admitted. Booking advisable. Disabled: toilet. Dress: jacket; no jeans or trainers. Separate room for parties, seats 18. **Map 17 J7.**

Top Floor at Smiths. See p55.

Soho W1

Atlantic Bar & Grill

20 Glasshouse Street, W1B 5DJ (7734 4888/
www.atlanticbarandgrill.com). Piccadilly
Circus tube.
Bar **Open** noon-3am Mon-Fri; 3pm-3am Sat.
Food served noon-3pm Mon-Sat.
Restaurant **Lunch served** noon-3pm Mon-Fri.
Dinner served 5.30-11.30pm Mon-Sat.
Main courses £11.50-£18.50. **Set dinner**
(5.30-7pm, 10-11.30pm Mon-Sat) £14.50 2 courses,
£16.50 3 courses. **Service** 12.5%.
Both **Credit** AmEx, DC, MC, V.
A classic piece of 1990s drop-that-jaw 'event dining'
decor, the Atlantic has walls in decadent burgundy
red, ornate columns, deep-plush banquettes and
glittering chandeliers, spread through three huge,
atmospherically lit spaces (the main bar and grill,
a separate bar and a banqueting room) beneath the
Regent's Palace Hotel. Nowadays, the hip money has
moved on, so there's often a large amount of empty
space beneath the lofty ceilings, and abundant staff
scattered around to point you from one room to the
next can look in need of something to do.
Nevertheless, the food on this visit was excellent.
Menus mix vaguely Modern European dishes with
British classics, all prepared with notable subtlety.
In summer one of the day's specials was first-rate
fresh asparagus, with a beautifully delicate
parmesan sauce; seared scallops came with an
equally suave mix of new potatoes, aïoli and celery.
The main course special was well-flavoured rump
steak with a superbly smooth truffle and wild
mushroom sauce, while the fish and chips from the
main menu offered fine, flaky cod, crisp, light beer
batter and mushy peas tasting, for once, more of
peas than mush. Even the prices – for food and the
excellent wine range – are reasonable, all considered.
Babies and children admitted (daytime only).
Booking advisable. Dress: smart casual; no
trainers. Entertainment: DJ 10pm Fri, Sat.
Separate room for parties, seats 70. **Map 17 J7**.

★ Lindsay House

21 Romilly Street, W1D 5AF (7439 0450/
www.lindsayhouse.co.uk). Leicester Square tube.
Lunch served noon-2.30pm Mon-Fri. **Dinner**
served 6-11pm Mon-Sat. **Main courses** (lunch)

£18-£26. **Set meal** (noon-2.30pm Mon-Fri,
6-6.45pm Mon-Sat) £25 3 courses. **Set dinner**
£48 3 courses. **Tasting menu** £59 6 courses.
Credit AmEx, DC, MC, V.
Ring the buzzer, wait a few seconds and you'll be
ushered into the hallway of Soho's most elegant
townhouse restaurant. The dining area, divided
between ground and first floors, is a pleasant mix
of modern minimalism and discreet period detail,
creating an overall feel of quiet sophistication. Chef
Richard Corrigan's spectacular cooking, on the other
hand, is far more robust and colourful, drawing on
a larder of top-notch European ingredients (with a
particular eye on the produce of his native Ireland).
Among the highlights of a recent dinner visit, a
starter of terrine of foie gras soaked in sherry with
celeriac was crammed with rich textures and
flavours, while ravioli of chorizo and feta with
chinese greens was a vivid, meaty, no-nonsense
dish, upfront and deeply tasty. Main-course steamed
fillets of sole with beurre fondue, salsify and brown
shrimp was a sea-fresh treat; braised pig's cheek
with pork belly, pineapple and pickled endive was
a sophisticated medley yet able, at the same time, to
elicit a resounding 'mmm' from our inner Homer
Simpson. Desserts are the real thing (cinnamon rice
pudding with poached pear and sour apple sabayon,
say) and the farmhouse cheeses 'from our islands'
are to die for. If you're feeling flush, there's also a
six-course tasting menu (including a vegetarian
version). Great wine list, charming staff, good value:
what more could you ask for?
Babies and children admitted. Booking advisable.
Dress: smart casual. Separate rooms for parties,
seating 8, 14 and 20. Vegetarian menu.
Map 17 K6.

Strand WC2

Savoy Grill

The Savoy, Strand, WC2R 0EU (7592 1600/
www.gordonramsay.com). Covent Garden or
Embankment tube/Charing Cross tube/rail.
Lunch served noon-2.45pm Mon-Fri; noon-4pm
Sat, Sun. **Dinner served** 5.45-11pm Mon-Sat;
7-10.30pm Sun. **Set meal** (lunch, 5.45-6.45pm
Mon-Sat) £30 3 courses; (Sun lunch) £18
2 courses, £25 3 courses. **Set dinner** £55
3 courses, £65 tasting menu (7-11pm Mon-Sat).
Service 12.5%. **Credit** AmEx, MC, V.

Popular with those who neither know nor care
what things cost, the Savoy Grill has long been
frequented by gangs of florid gentlemen who seem
determined to discover exactly how much food and
wine it might take to make the buttons ping off
their waistcoats and turn their noses the colour of
Victoria plums. But it's not all Wodehousian
caricature, as Marcus Wareing's modern, delicate
British cooking continues to lure an increasingly
youthful clientele (meaning anyone under 50) into
this sober wood-panelled dining room. Food is
taken very seriously (as well it might be at these
prices), and you can expect dainty amuse-bouches
and all the other trappings of haute cuisine,
including peskily attentive staff. Typical starters
might be baked pithivier of quail's breast and
forest mushroom with crispy quails' legs, walnuts
and Madeira sauce; or fillet of slow-cooked wild
trout with braised fennel hearts. An impressive
choice of main courses yield the likes of pan-fried
fillet of sea bass, braised Wiltshire pork belly, or
pigeon à la bressane with sautéed foie gras.
Desserts come on a trolley, as do the cheeses, which
are impeccably kept and carefully sourced. You'll
struggle to find much below 50 quid on the wine
list, but if that's what you're looking for, this
probably isn't the place for you anyway.
Babies and children welcome: high chairs.
Booking essential. Disabled: toilet. Dress: jacket;
no denim, sportswear or trainers. Vegetarian
menu. Vegan dishes. **Map 18 L7**.

Simpson's-in-the-Strand

100 Strand, WC2R 0EW (7836 9112/
www.simpsons-in-the-strand.com). Embankment
tube/Charing Cross tube/rail. **Breakfast**
served 7.15-10.30am Mon-Fri. **Lunch served**
12.15-2.30pm Mon-Sat; noon-3pm Sun. **Dinner**
served 5.45-10.45pm Mon-Sat; (Grand Divan)
6-9pm Sun. **Main courses** £19.50-£23.50.
Set breakfast £15.50-£17.50. **Set meal** £17.50
2 courses, £20.75 3 courses. **Service** 12.5%.
Credit AmEx, DC, JCB, MC, V.
Eating in Simpson's Grand Divan dining hall is one
of London's classic experiences. The 1890s wood
panelling is magnificently ornate and lightened
by whimsical paintings, done in a Pre-Raphaelite
style, beneath which armies of utterly professional
(but sometimes engagingly cranky) waiters cater

to your every need. It's equally appreciated by tourists, senior lawyers and a scattering of elderly gents, for whom it's probably been a cherished sanctuary for donkey's years. The menu now often includes a few modern items, but to try any of them is to miss the point, which is to sample Simpson's classic roasts and above all the beef, carved with suitable ceremony at your table on giant trolleys. Meat aside, the rest of the cooking can suffer occasional glitches: we were surprised that, while the meat itself was superb, there was not much in the way of accompanying veg. Starters are traditional (including a delightful chicken liver parfait), but desserts are a bit more innovative, with such offerings as cinnamon ice-cream and honey-roast peaches alongside old-school favourites. Simpson's also offers celebrated English breakfasts, and on the floor above there's a seductively comfortable cocktail bar for aperitif-taking before descending to the Divan. *Babies and children admitted. Booking advisable. Disabled: toilet. Dress: smart casual. Separate rooms for parties, seating 15 and 120.* **Map 18 L7**.

Trafalgar Square WC2

Albannach NEW

66 Trafalgar Square, WC2N 5DS (7930 0066/ www.albannach.co.uk). Charing Cross tube/rail.
Bar Open/food served noon-1am Mon-Sat; noon-midnight Sun.
Restaurant **Lunch served** noon-3pm Mon-Sat.
Dinner served 5-10pm Mon-Thur; 5-10.30pm Fri, Sat. **Main courses** (lunch) £9-£17.50.
Set dinner £27.50 2 courses, £32.50 3 courses.
Service 12.50%.
Both **Credit** AmEx, DC, MC, V.
Not much about Albannach is typically Scottish. It's better known as a watering hole for office types and night owl tourists than as a fine dining venue. There are two bars: an informal space on the ground floor, and a dimly lit lounge in the basement. The ground floor, with its wooden floors, expansive windows and pale-blue walls, is cheery enough, but look up and there's an unlikely centrepiece: a mammoth chandelier made from antlers. The mezzanine restaurant is dwarfed by the bar below, giving the impression of being an afterthought. Cooking is a mix of European styles, with a nod to culinary Scotland. Hits include juicy, seared scallops served with heaps of velvety fennel purée. We were also impressed by meltingly soft Buccleuch beef fillet steak, surrounded by a moat

BEST BRITISH

For gaining girth with dignity
Dorchester Grill Room (*see p55*), **Notting Hill Grill** (*see p60*), **Rules** (*see p55*), **Savoy Grill** (*see p57*).

For quality looking
Butlers Wharf Chop House (*see p61*), **Rhodes Twenty Four** (*see p54*), **Top Floor at Smiths** (*see p55*).

For jacket-free guzzling
Medcalf, **St John's Bread & Wine**, **Quality Chop House** (for all, *see p54*).

For the British Isles, not English
Albannach (*see below*), **Boisdale** (*see below*), **Lindsay House** (*see p57*).

of meaty juices. In contrast, asparagus salad was poor – just a straggling heap of leafy greens masking a thrifty helping of artichokes and tired asparagus stems. On a brighter note, the bar boasts well over 100 malt whiskies: an aficionado's paradise, although a shot of 50-year-old Dalmore will set you back £580. For more on the drinking side of things, *see p324*.
Disabled: toilet. Function rooms, seats 20. Tables outdoors (3, pavement). **Map 17 K7**.

Victoria SW1

Boïsdale

13 Eccleston Street, SW1W 9LX (7730 6922/ www.boisdale.co.uk). Victoria tube/rail.
Bar Open/food served noon-1am Mon-Fri; 7pm-1am Sat. **Snacks** £6-£14. **Admission** £10 (£3.95 if already on premises) after 10pm Mon-Sat.
Restaurant **Lunch served** noon-2.30pm Mon-Fri. **Dinner served** 7-11pm Mon-Sat. **Main courses** £13.50-£24. **Set lunch** £14 2 courses.
Set meal £17.45 2 courses. **Service** 12.5%.
Both **Credit** AmEx, DC, MC, V.
Boisdale serves up Romantic Scotland on a plate, for a clientele of office groups, clannish City folk, and curious tourists. Expect dark oak flooring, full-on tartan colours, and a plethora of prints and artefacts across walls. The place has a slightly

sniffy, gentlemen's-club vibe, which is why we prefer the lighter and brighter conservatory with its retractable roof, leafy greenery and crisp white table linen. Cooking is an appealing mix of traditional and modern. If haggis is your thing, look no further; there's also a wide range of steaks, with a choice of three sauces. Marinated Orkney herring won us over with its sweet vinegary flavour, contrasted with mustardy crushed potatoes and pickled beetroot slices. Arbroath fish cake (a main course) was delightfully buttery and exhibited just the right degree of smokiness. Aberdeen Angus rump steak, although well hung, was a little tough and let down by a lacklustre béarnaise sauce. In addition to a well-chosen, if pricey, wine list, you'll find a splendid array of choice whiskies, as well as cocktails, at the two bars. Only the music takes a break from the tartan theme – these guys are big on jazz, so no bagpipes. *Babies and children admitted (restaurant). Separate room for parties, seats 22. Entertainment: jazz 10pm-midnight Mon-Sat.* **Map 15 H10**.
For branch see index.

Westminster SW1

Shepherd's

Marsham Court, Marsham Street, SW1P 4LA (7834 9552/www.langansrestaurants.co.uk). Pimlico or Westminster tube. **Lunch served** 12.30-2.45pm, **dinner served** 6.30-11pm Mon-Fri. **Main courses** £19.50. **Set meals** £26.50 2 courses incl coffee, £29.50 3 courses incl coffee.
Service 12.5%. **Credit** AmEx, DC, JCB, MC, V.
British politicians are notoriously uninterested in food, preferring the safe and unadventurous; Shepherd's, something of a dining room for the 'Westminster Village', gives them what they want. The dining room has a comfortable, rather self-consciously Victorian look, and service is buzzy but obliging. The place has the same owner as Langan's (*see p225*), so the menu has a similar mix of British classics – roasts, fish cakes, grilled halibut – and equally trad brasserie-style dishes. The caesar salad featured quite a lot of juicy marinated anchovies, along with ordinary parmesan and standard-issue lettuce. To follow we looked for something relatively light for a hot day, but found no concessions to the seasons made among the mostly pretty heavy main courses. Venison and wild mushroom sausages with colcannon and white onion sauce sounded robust and certainly was, a powerful plate of nosh with

RESTAURANTS

Bluebird Dining Rooms. See p60.

richly flavoured bangers and an equally rich old-fashioned sauce. Desserts vary between Brit-traditional and slightly fancy. Which was all enjoyable in its old-fashioned way, but hardly justified a cost of £26.50 for just two courses. The wine list is expensive too, and has no half-bottles, which seems a nerve in a restaurant where so many gents dine alone.

Babies and children admitted. Booking advisable. No-smoking tables. Separate room for parties, seats 32. **Map 16 K10**

West

Holland Park W11

Notting Grill

123A Clarendon Road, W11 4JG (7229 1500/ www.awtonline.co.uk). Holland Park tube. ***Bar* Open** 6.30-11pm Mon-Thur; 6.30pm-midnight Fri, Sat; noon-10pm Sun. *Restaurant* **Brunch served** noon-4pm Sat, Sun. **Lunch served** noon-2.30pm Tue-Fri. **Dinner served** 6.30-10.30pm Mon-Thur; 6.30-11.30pm Fri, Sat; 4-10pm Sun. **Main courses** £12.50-£34.95. **Service** 12.5%. *Both* **Credit** AmEx, DC, JCB, MC, V.

With starters that include iberico ham, mains of steak au poivre and desserts of crème brûlée, this is definitely at the Europhile end of British cuisine. It's the sort of robust, satisfying cooking that rendered the proprietor, Antony Worrall Thompson, rich and corpulent. The ambience exuded by the deep red walls is relaxed and bohemian rather than designer fashionable, but black-uniformed staff take their work seriously. Variety is considerable, with a list of around 20 starters (from avocado and prawn cocktail to pork terrine) supplemented by specials that included a scallop, served as a single fat white comma crispily fried in butter. Mains are largely of red meat and the house speciality is suckling pig. Beef is taken extremely seriously too, being exclusively Aberdeen Angus aged for 35 days. Steak au poivre seemed to feature an entire pot of peppercorns yet was a high-quality hunk of flesh, as was the

Berkshire lamb chop that had been singed à point. As expected at an AWT outlet, you're well supplied with veg and potatoes, and there's a decent wine list. So by the time dessert came round we weren't so disappointed by the slightly soggy strawberry and mascarpone tart.

Babies and children welcome: high chairs. Booking advisable. No-smoking tables. Separate room for parties, seats 80. Tables outdoors (6, terrace; closes 10pm). **Map 19 A4**.

For branch (Kew Grill) see index.

Kensington W8

Maggie Jones's

6 Old Court Place, Kensington Church Street, W8 4PL (7937 6462). High Street Kensington tube. **Lunch served** 12.30-2.30pm daily. **Dinner served** 6.30-11pm Mon-Sat; 6.30-10.30pm Sun. **Main courses** £7-£19.50. **Set lunch** (Sun) £15.50 3 courses. **Cover** £1 (dinner). **Service** 12.5%. **Credit** AmEx, DC, JCB, MC, V.

Lore has it that the late Princess Margaret used to dine here, booking under what is now the restaurant's name. You can see the attraction for a hard-living princess: it's a dark little warren where you may expect to remain unaccosted by daylight – although the place is now full of hacks from the nearby *Daily Mail* and *Evening Standard*. The wine list is strong too. The management has created an atmosphere of knick-knack antiquity. Perhaps it's also in honour of Princess Margaret that so much of the food appears to be smoked. The menu is classic old-school British in style. Although there was no evidence of smoke in our cold cucumber soup or our generous prawn cocktail, the chicken in the chicken and avocado salad was lightly fumigated, just as smoked haddock was the dominant flavour in a hearty fish pie. But for the exotic presence of a passionfruit and mango terrine (aka passionfruit jelly with mango), desserts are a typically Anglo Saxon selection, down to the apple crumble. Staff are young, male and well-appointed.

Babies and children welcome: high chairs. Booking advisable. **Map 7 B8**.

Olympia W14

Popeseye Steak House

108 Blythe Road, W14 0HD (7610 4578). Kensington (Olympia) tube/rail. **Dinner served** 7-10.30pm Mon-Sat. **Main courses** £9.95-£45.50. **Service** 12.5%. **No credit cards.**

Vegetarians look away now: there is nothing for you here. In fact, there isn't even anything for non-steak eaters. Popeseye is little more than a converted front room, open for dinner only and operating off an open char-grill, in association with a deep frier for chips. But the meat is very good: better and certainly heartier than the almost spartan conditions of roughly stripped boards and white emulsioned walls. The beef is hung for a minimum of two weeks and is 100% grass-fed Aberdeen Angus delivered daily from Scotland. You can order rump (aka popeseye), sirloin and fillet in 6, 8, 12, 20 and 30 ounce sizes. We reckon the fillet is worth the extra money, being (on the night of our business) an exceptionally fine cut of meat. Don't expect further trimmings. Salad charged at £3.45 was OK and the rhubarb crumble dessert was a nice bijou serving. The only other recommendation is the wine list, which includes some serious appellations costing up to £150. The surroundings make such a charge remarkably cheeky, but the well-hung meat is fair value.

Babies and children admitted. Booking advisable. **For branch see index.**

South West

Chelsea SW3

★ Bluebird Dining Rooms `NEW`

2005 RUNNER-UP BEST NEW RESTAURANT
350 King's Road, entrance in Beaufort Street, SW3 5UU (7559 1129/www.conran.com). Sloane Square tube then 11, 19, 22, 49, 319 bus. **Lunch served** 12.30-3pm Sun. **Dinner served** 7-10.45pm Mon-Sat. **Main courses** £12-£21. **Set lunch** (Sun) £29.50 3 courses. **Service** 12.5%. **Credit** AmEx, DC, JCB, MC, V.

Notting Grill

This wing of the Bluebird complex used to be a private members' club. Now everyone can appreciate the handsome, light-filled first-floor restaurant and bar. Regrettably, on our evening visit, not many were – it was zen-like in its tranquillity, which we quite liked, but can't be doing much for Conran's bank balance. You have to buzz to gain entry, which must deter casual diners. The prices are a disincentive too – even with mains averaging £16.50, side dishes (minted Jersey royals, a flavour-packed Secretts' 'heritage' tomato and herb salad) cost another £3.25. Chef Mark Broadbent's menu is an intriguing read that translates into an equally good read. Potage of Lancashire cauliflower with Colston Basset snippets (cauliflower soup with stilton sort-of-croutons) and potato pancake with smoked Norfolk eel, beetroot, watercress and a slice of crisp bacon were bold starters that hit the mark perfectly. Wild mushroom tart with Jersey cream and summer herbs couldn't quite match this standard, but diver-caught roast plaice with cockles, samphire and parsley sauce did. A good-tasting, if unbalanced, summer berry trifle was heavy on the cream and light on the fruit; British cheeses make a savoury alternative. Staff are charming (but did almost outnumber the diners). For Mod Euro restaurant Bluebird, *see p230*.
Babies and children welcome: high chairs. Disabled: toilet. Separate room for parties, seats 30. **Map 14 D12.**

Foxtrot Oscar

79 Royal Hospital Road, SW3 4HN (7352 7179). Sloane Square tube/11, 239 bus. **Lunch served** 12.30-2.30pm Mon-Fri; 12.30-3.30pm Sat; 12.30-4pm Sun. **Dinner served** 7-11pm Mon-Sat. **Main courses** £8.95-£15. **Service** 12.5%. **Credit** MC, V.
There's something charmingly old-fashioned about Foxtrot Oscar. With its small, warm, bare-brick and worn wood interior, and with dishes on a chalked-up blackboard, the place puts you in mind of a 1970s wine bar. Large mirrors help open it up a little, while a television looms high in the corner as a threat for relaying special events. The menu is more reminiscent of a retro Anglo-American café, containing such delights as avocado with prawns (a steep £6.95). Sesame chicken with sweet chilli mayo is a more up to the minute example. The club menu features classics such as kedgeree, eggs benedict and a brutus salad. But the main courses are dominated by burgers, steaks, sausages and cottage pie. A special of grilled red mullet was on the pink side. Treacle tart from a wholesome pud list was a very standard rendition. More interesting is a wine list that pokes around in unsuspecting corners of the world's wineries and is full of curiosities. Service is excellent: attentive and very laid-back, making you feel more like a guest than a customer.
Babies and children welcome: high chairs. Booking advisable. Separate room for parties, seats 30. **Map 14 F12.**

Fulham SW10

Sophie's Steakhouse & Bar

311-313 Fulham Road, SW10 9QH (7352 0088/ www.sophiessteakhouse.com). South Kensington tube/14, 345, 414 bus. **Meals served** noon-11.45pm Mon-Fri; 11am-11.45pm Sat; 11am-10.45pm Sun. **Main courses** £6.95-£16.50. **Set meal** (noon-6pm Mon-Fri) £9.95 2 courses. **Service** 12.5% for parties of 5 or more. **Credit** AmEx, MC, V.
You can't book a table at Sophie's and even on a Sunday night you have to wait (20-30 minutes), during which time you're encouraged to drink at the bar. Here you can mull over the menu and cast an eye over the minimalist industrial design, as well as the tanked-up Sloanes. Starters such as calamares and chicken liver parfait are nothing special, it's the steaks that are the fleshy jewel in this restaurant's crown. Bottom-of-the-range ribeye at £10.95 wasn't as tasty as it should be, but chateaubriand fillet for two at £29.95 represented reasonable value for this pricey slice of cow and came a rather rare 'medium'. Perhaps we shouldn't

be surprised at the meanness of a green salad priced at £2.25, but main courses are more than satisfying, especially when matched with a good global wine list sensibly priced at £11-£50 a bottle. Desserts are such classic British staples as apple crumble and summer pudding. The most abiding feature of Sophie's, however, is its sheer popularity. As we left at 11pm on a Sunday, most tables remained loaded and the atmosphere scarcely less rocking than when we arrived.
Babies and children welcome: children's menu; high chairs. Disabled: toilet. **Map 14 D12.**

South

Battersea SW11

Jack's Place

12 York Road, SW11 3QA (7228 8519). Clapham Junction rail. **Lunch served** (Sept-Easter) noon-3pm Sun. **Dinner served** 6-11pm Tue-Sat. **Main courses** £10.50-£18.50. **Set lunch** (Sun Sept-Easter) £17.50 3 courses. **Service** 10%. **Credit** MC, V.
Hardly the last word in stylish design, Jack's Place has red tiled floors and lines of plastic chairs and tables that would have been fashionable in a Soho brasserie circa 1960. The Jack in question, a Mr Talkington, has owned the restaurant for 37 years and pictures of his life are everywhere: boxing in the 1950s, mixing with London society in the '60s, supporting Chelsea FC (note the corner shrine). Jack Nicholson and Jimmy Carter's son have all eaten here in years gone by, but now the clientele is mainly friends and locals, which at least makes it a warm, companionable spot. Service is caring, from staff that shift between front-of-house and the kitchen. Unfortunately, the food hasn't moved as well with the times. We passed on a starter of 'egg mayonnaise with Hovis' for an average-tasting bowl of chopped-up melon and a dish of sardines. Main courses were vast: sea bass looked more salmon-sized, and rib of beef was hanging off the plate. But they also appeared suspiciously deep-fried, and the mushrooms that came with both were utterly cremated. Crème caramel with vanilla ice-cream to finish was the best dish by far – try putting that in a fat frier.
Babies and children admitted. Booking essential lunch; advisable dinner. Vegetarian menu. **Map 21 B2.**

South East

East Dulwich SE22

Franklins

157 Lordship Lane, SE22 8HX (8299 9598/ www.franklinsrestaurant.com). East Dulwich rail. **Open** noon-11pm Mon-Wed; noon-midnight Thur-Sat; noon-10.30pm Sun. **Lunch served** noon-4pm Mon-Sat. **Dinner served** 6-10.30pm Mon-Sat. **Meals served** 1-10pm Sun. **Main courses** £11-£15. **Set lunch** (noon-5pm Mon-Fri) £9 2 courses, £12 3 courses. **Credit** AmEx, MC, V.
This capable little restaurant attached to a stylish (albeit diminutive) bar has kept its head while many of the surrounding pubs and bars on Lordship Lane seem to have fallen foul of pseudo-gastro makeovers. More than a gastropub, Franklins' dining room is a pleasingly formal space with smartly set tables. The daily changing menu features some interesting takes on the Modern British theme – which can easily become a bit of a bore these days, but here the kitchen gets it right. Among the starters, Old Spot pork comes with a simple, tangy piccalilli, while cauliflower and roast garlic might be the soup of the day. Hearty mains include dishes like leg of lamb pepped up with anchovies, or hake served with a warming combination of lentils and green sauce. Side dishes add a few quid to the bill but they're generally worth it (the green salad is dressed to perfection). Desserts – brown bread ice-cream, crème caramel, rhubarb crumble and other such staples – are always worth a punt. The wine list might not be big, but it is clever.

Babies and children welcome: high chairs. Disabled: toilet. Separate room for parties, seats 40. Tables outdoors (3, pavement). **Map 23 C4.**

Tower Bridge SE1

Butlers Wharf Chop House

Butlers Wharf Building, 36E Shad Thames, SE1 2YE (7403 3403/www.conran.com). London Bridge tube/rail/Tower Gateway DLR/47, 78, 142, 188 bus. **Bar Open** noon-3pm, 6-11pm Mon-Fri; noon-4pm, 6-11pm Sat; noon-4pm Sun. **Brunch served** noon-4pm Sat, Sun. **Set brunch** (Sat, Sun) £13.95 2 courses, £16.95 3 courses. **Set meal** (noon-3pm, 6-11pm Mon-Fri; 6-11pm Sat) £10 2 courses, £12 3 courses. **Restaurant Lunch served** noon-3pm daily. **Dinner served** 6-11pm Mon-Sat. **Main courses** £13.50-£26. **Set lunch** £22 2 courses, £26 3 courses. **Both Service** 12.5%. **Credit** AmEx, DC, JCB, MC, V.
With its riverside setting and stylish, airy dining room and bar area, this Conran eaterie, a favourite with the City crowd, has a lot going for it. Shame, then, that we can't say the same about the food, which was distinctly average on a recent lunchtime visit. When we arrived staff didn't check whether we wanted the bar or restaurant area, and plonked us in the latter, with its more expensive menu. Also, they'd allowed us to book for 15 minutes before the kitchen closed, so the pressure was on to order quickly. The food was disappointing. A prawn cocktail starter was dull, with less than a dozen weeny crustaceans in an insipid sauce. Of the mains, fish and chips was overcooked and overbattered, and the flabby, simply grilled plaice too small to satisfy even the humblest appetite. Chocolate and vanilla cheesecake was sublime, however, and went some way to make amends, but given the prices, we still felt hard done by. The wine list is ideal for expense accounters, and includes some excellent choices by the glass.
Babies and children welcome: high chairs. Booking advisable. Dress: smart casual. Tables outdoors (12, terrace). **Map 12 R8.**

East

Shoreditch EC2

Rivington Bar & Grill

28-30 Rivington Street, EC2A 3DZ (7729 7053/ www.rivingtongrill.co.uk). Liverpool Street or Old Street tube/rail. **Bar Open/food served** noon-midnight Mon-Sat; noon-11pm Sun. **Restaurant Brunch served** noon-4.30pm Sun. **Lunch served** noon-3pm Mon-Fri. **Dinner served** 6-11pm daily. **Main courses** £10.75-£21.25. **Service** 12.5%. **Credit** AmEx, DC, MC, V.
This airy corner conversion inspires you with confident anticipation. It is plainly but smartly designed, and is co-owned by chef and food writer Mark Hix (though he doesn't work in the kitchen here). The menu looks great on paper (literally: it's your tablemat), offering a dozen simple pleasures in the starter list (gull's eggs in their brief seasonal window, razor clams, steamed artichokes), mains from grill and chef station that tempt in similar vein, and an erudite wine selection. Our experiences here have been decidedly mixed, but this year we were left cold by both food and service. A waitress went off us completely when asked what was on the English meat board. She didn't know and didn't offer to find out, and showed little interest after that. For the record, the board contained tongue, ham and salt beef, but, despite wonderful chutneys, wasn't good or plentiful enough for £6.50. Mains (grilled sea bass with herbs; suckling pig with black pudding) were dried out, and we didn't feel inspired to stay for dessert (though they looked great, particularly the blood orange trifle). It was a Bank Holiday Monday, which may explain this poor showing – but not well enough for paying customers.
Booking advisable. Takeaway service (deli). Vegetarian menu. **Map 6 R4.**

Chinese

The regionalisation of London's Chinese restaurants continues to delight us. Five or ten years ago it was difficult to find anywhere that deviated from the Anglo-Cantonese repertoire. These days, there's a smattering of genuine regional restaurants catering to a growing population of residents from all over China. Some of these don't nail their colours to the mast, but behind their main menus of standard Chinese restaurant fare you'll find separate lists of authentic regional cooking. London now has at least three restaurants serving Sichuanese food – lavish with chilli-and-broad-bean paste and lip-tingling Sichuan pepper – and two Hunanese restaurant. Fujianese cooking, Shanghainese cooking, northern-style boiled dumplings (jiao zi) and food from the north-east (Dong Bei) have all been available to a limited extent for a couple of years. These restaurants are nothing lavish, but offer fascinating opportunities to appreciate something of the diversity of Chinese cuisine. *See p73* **Regional cooking** for more details.

Chinatown remains a cheap, cheery place for a meal; it is frequented largely by tourists, Chinese students and people eating before or after a night on the town. Funky Taiwan- and Hong Kong-style cafés are a hit with the younger generation, and the ever-popular **New Mayflower** serves hearty and delicious Cantonese dishes well into the small hours. An unpopular plan by property developer Rosewheel to reshape the block between Newport Place and Charing Cross Road has struck at the heart of Chinatown, resulting in two grocers, the fishmonger, a kitchenware shop and several other businesses relocating. The main meeting place around the tiny pavilion in Newport Place now has a desolate air, and it's not clear whether the community businesses will be able to return after redevelopment. There are likely to be more changes in the coming months. The rest of Chinatown, however, remains lively, and the shops stock an ever-increasing range of Chinese foodstuffs.

For classier Chinese cooking, you'd be advised to seek out restaurants in other parts of the city, like the consistently excellent **Royal China** chain – with branches in Bayswater, Canary Wharf, St John's Wood and Baker Street – the ever-thrilling **Hakkasan** and the London home of the lobster, **Mandarin Kitchen**.

Dim sum, the dainty snacks that are part of a traditional Cantonese breakfast, have settled into the mainstream as part of a wave of fashionable interest in tapas-style eating (*see p68* **The art of dim sum**). Alan Yau's Hakkasan led the trend, followed by his own **Yauatcha** and other restaurants such as **Shanghai Blues**, **Drunken Monkey** and **Ping Pong**. The Dorchester hotel is even getting in on the act, with a new all-day dim sum restaurant opening in late 2005.

Burgeoning interest in dim sum is also putting Chinese tea on the gourmet map. If you're keen on tea, check out the menu at Yauatcha's ground-floor tea room, which offers many different varieties, of a quality far eclipsing what's generally available (the only problem is that this establishment is too mean to let you brew the leaves more than once – shocking).

A FEW TIPS

Set menus in Chinese restaurants tend to pander to outdated Western stereotypes of Chinese food, featuring only clichéd dishes such as sweet-and-sour pork, chicken in black bean sauce and egg-fried rice. Our advice is avoid them. Order, instead, from the main menu and, if possible, the seasonal specials list. London restaurants with the most enticing chef's specials (translated into English) include **Mr Kong**, **Four Seasons** and **Phoenix Palace**. The main menus at **Yming**, **Mr Chow** and the **Royal Chinas** are inspiring in themselves, and if you really want a walk on the wild side, then put yourself in the hands of Mr Peng at **Hunan**.

The art of ordering a Chinese meal lies in assembling a variety of dishes, differing from one another in terms of their main ingredients, cooking methods and flavours. Because of this, if you are dining with a group it's best to coordinate your ordering. If each guest plumps for a personal favourite you may end up with a lopsided meal. Starters are easy: just order as you please and remember there is life beyond the usual deep-fried snacks (a cold meat platter or steamed seafood can make a delicious beginning to the meal). For main courses, aim to order about one dish for every person in your party, and then one or two extra, and share everything.

Make sure you choose a variety of main ingredients so things don't get repetitive. Then try to balance dry, deep-fried dishes with slow hot-pots and crisp stir-fries; rich roast duck with fresh vegetables; subtle tastes with spicy flavours. And ask your waiter about seasonal greens: you may find the restaurant has pak choi, gai lan (chinese broccoli), pea shoots, water spinach and other marvellous Chinese treats. Most Chinese people fill up on plain steamed rice, which is a good foil to the flavours of the other food and much more comfortable than that old takeaway staple, egg-fried rice.

Desserts are not one of the fortes of Chinese cuisine, and you rarely find much beyond red bean paste pancakes and toffee bananas (Hakkasan and Yauatcha are exceptions, as is Mr Chow, where the French pastries are brought in from a pâtisserie). It's better, in most cases, to order an extra savoury dish and stop at a café afterwards if you want something sweet for dessert.

A useful scheme offers patrons of Chinatown restaurants and supermarkets a 50 per cent discount on parking in the Chinatown Square car park, a boon for those stocking up on heavy Chinese groceries. Look out for the notices in windows of participating businesses, and make sure they stamp your till receipt.

Central
Belgravia SW1

★ **Hunan**
51 Pimlico Road, SW1W 8NE (7730 5712).
Sloane Square tube. **Lunch served** 12.30-2.30pm, **dinner served** 6-11pm Mon-Sat.
Set meal £32-£150 per person (minimum 2).
Service 12.5%. **Credit** AmEx, DC, MC, V.
This eccentric establishment, run by the gregarious Mr Peng and his son, remains one of the most delightful Chinese restaurants in London.

Regulars will know that it's best to ignore the menu and let staff decide what to feed you. Then sit back and wait for a long procession of small and delicious dishes to arrive – 17 on our last visit (and we refused the final beef noodle soup). The meal was superb; it included not only specialities such as a rich, ginger-spiked broth with minced chicken, pork and game (served in bamboo tubes), but also all kinds of concoctions using unusual Chinese ingredients. There were deep-fried 'sandwiches' of sliced lotus root and pork, a fabulous spicy salad of pig's ear and chicken, fried aubergine with gong cai (a juicy stem vegetable), bitter melon stir-fried with salted duck egg, and slivered lamb with garlic stems. The standard of cooking was astonishingly high – every single dish hit the mark – and the feast was much lighter and more delicate than the Chinese norm. We left after this gargantuan repast feeling happy and no more than pleasantly full. The dining room is charming, and service friendly. *Babies and children admitted. Booking essential. No smoking. Separate room for parties, seats 10-15. Vegetarian menu.* **Map 15 G11**.

Ken Lo's Memories of China

65-69 Ebury Street, SW1W 0NZ (7730 7734). Victoria tube/rail. **Lunch served** noon-2.30pm Mon-Sat. **Dinner served** 7-11pm Mon-Sat; 7-10.30pm Sun. **Main courses** £4.50-£27. **Set lunch** £18.50-£21.50 per person (minimum 2). **Set dinner** £30-£48 per person (minimum 2). **Cover** £1.20. **Service** 12.5%. **Credit** AmEx, DC, MC, V.
We remember a time (during the late Ken Lo's life) when the bright and airy dining room of Memories of China offered the best Chinese cuisine in London. Sadly, that's no longer the case judging by our most recent visit. Steamed scallops – large, but with little flavour – made an inauspicious start. We were also disappointed by the hot and sour soup; the flavours were well balanced, but the

ingredients wouldn't have looked out of place in a carton from a cheap takeaway, despite the high price charged. Oil leaked from the three-spiced deep-fried squid, which was both crisp and soggy. This sogginess continued with the kua ta egg-battered chicken. Close to inedible, the sauce tasted strongly of ginger, not garlic. Excess oil also blighted a simple dish of chow mein noodles, which was strangely devoid of the promised sesame seeds. Finally, a 'signature' dish of sichuan double-cooked pork consisted of tough slices of roast barbecued pork stir-fried in a fiery chilli bean sauce. Polite, if occasionally inattentive service was undermined when we overheard staff making derogatory references to diners in Cantonese. *Babies and children admitted. Booking advisable. Separate room for parties, seats 26. Takeaway service.* **Map 15 H10**.
For branch see index.

Bloomsbury WC1

★ Sheng's Tea House

68 Millman Street, WC1N 3EF (7405 3697). Russell Square tube/68 bus. **Lunch served** noon-3pm, **dinner served** 6-10.30pm Mon-Fri. **Main courses** £6.50-£8.50. **Credit** AmEx, MC, V.
Popular with local office workers and members of the nearby legal chambers, Sheng's is an attractive hideaway offering a short but varied range of Chinese and South-east Asian dishes. Hot tossed salt and pepper squid: gently seasoned, tender squid in a soft, flaky batter. Handmade guo tie dumplings also worked well; pan-fried with a similarly sensitive touch, the tiny parcels of pork were delightfully soft and juicy. The restaurant's strict no-MSG or artificial colouring policy was most evident in our main course of char siu barbecued pork on rice. Dark brown, instead of the usual bright red, the thin slices of tender sweet pork had a fine flavour. Like

all our meal, the dish looked attractive too; the pork slices had been carefully staggered on a bed of chinese lettuce, aside an upturned bowl of rice. A good list of wine is augmented by a small range of fresh fruit juices, though guava was the only choice left on our Friday late-afternoon visit. Background jazz piano was accompanied by thoughtful, unobtrusive service. A wonderful spot for lunch. *Babies and children admitted. Booking advisable. No smoking. Tables outdoors (4, pavement).* **Map 4 M4**.

Chinatown W1, WC2

★ Café de HK

47-49 Charing Cross Road, WC2H 0AN (7534 9898). Leicester Square or Piccadilly Circus tube. **Meals served** noon-11pm daily. **Main courses** £4.80-£12. **Credit** AmEx, MC, V.
A favourite with young Chinese, this bright café serves fruit juices, teas and various Eurasian snacks – everything from Cantonese roast meat to spaghetti bolognese and borscht. Loud chatter and pop music fill the main dining room upstairs. A small section down a few steps offers refuge, or would do if it wasn't for hard wooden benches that encourage speedy dining. We've always enjoyed the soup of the day – a rich stock of pork bones and an ever-changing selection of vegetables (on our last visit a gentle combination of chinese mustard cabbage and tofu). Dumplings lack finesse, but not flavour. Spicy chao zhou dumplings of pork, peanut and vegetable had thick wrappers but plenty of filling and crunch. One-dish meals of steamed rice (or spaghetti) with roast meat often sell out. For adventurous diners, 'street hawker' noodle soups of pig's intestine and other offal can be enjoyable, but are displayed only on a Chinese-language menu. Service is friendly if casual; dishes often arrive all at once and with a thump.

Café de HK

RESTAURANTS

Feng Shui Inn

Babies and children welcome. Bookings not accepted. No-smoking tables. Takeaway service. Vegetarian menu. Map 17 K6.

★ Café TPT

21 Wardour Street, W1D 6PN (7734 7980). Leicester Square or Piccadilly Circus tube. **Meals served** noon-midnight Mon-Sat; noon-11.30pm Sun. **Main courses** £6.50-£24. **Set meal** £9.50, £11 2 courses. **Service** 10%. **Credit** MC, V.

Small cafés like this are the life and blood of Chinatown. We single out Café TPT for the sheer friendliness of its well-spoken staff, who carefully weave between the tightly packed tables wearing bright orange sweatshirts. Ask them for the second menu, which contains a wide range of noodle soups and simple rice dishes. Popular with local Chinese, these are quickly prepared by a single chef in a mini-kitchen by the door. Char siu barbecued pork is a great choice at lunchtime, when it's just fresh out of the oven. Deliciously sweet and tender, it almost melts in the mouth. Steamed rice is the traditional accompaniment and is rarely bettered. The wun tun soup is also worth trying; the tiny parcels are folded with a single prawn and little cubes of well-seasoned pork. Ask for explanations of the dishes listed in Chinese on the restaurant's off-white walls; some are featured on the second menu, but there's always the chance of finding something special. Finish with a Malaysian-influenced dessert or some delicious sweet beancurd.

Babies and children welcome: high chair. Takeaway service. Map 17 K6.

★ Canton

11 Newport Place, WC2H 7JR (7437 6220). Leicester Square or Piccadilly Circus tube. **Meals served** noon-11.30pm Mon, Sun; noon-midnight Tue-Thur; noon-12.30am Fri, Sat. **Main courses** £5.20-£9. **Set meal** £10 2 courses. **Credit** AmEx, JCB, MC, V.

One of the best of the old-school Chinatown caffs, Canton is a prime spot for meal-in-one rice or noodle dishes. As if to emphasise the point its modest little interior was full at 6.45pm on a midweek evening yet half empty by 7.30pm. Local Chinese come for a swift after-work bite, then move on. Yet though dishes are served in a trice – by capable staff – this is no fast-food joint. Our favourite dish was stewed beef flank, lengthily simmered to tender, savoury perfection and arriving on a mound of rice for just £4. Usually worth ordering too are the roast meats, chopped in a front kiosk decorated with a fringe of dangling ducks. Roasted pork on fried noodles was a let-down, though: the noodles a mite congealed, the meat char siu (barbecued, rather than roast pork). More complex dishes are listed on the long menu; fried prawns and beancurd managed to successfully balance the textures of the tautly fresh seafood and spongy fried beancurd. This, together with the ultra-fresh gai lan (chinese broccoli) revived our enthusiasm.

Babies and children admitted. Booking advisable. Separate room for parties, seats 22. Takeaway service. Map 17 K6.

ECapital

8 Gerrard Street, W1D 5PJ (7434 3838). Leicester Square or Piccadilly Circus tube. **Meals served** noon-11.30pm Mon-Thur; noon-midnight Fri, Sat; noon-10.30pm Sun. **Main courses** £6.50-£19.80. **Set meal** £8.50-£32 per person (minimum 2). **Service** 12.5%. **Credit** AmEx, DC, MC, V.

When ECapital arrived on the scene in 2002, its speciality eastern Chinese dishes were clearly identified in a separate section of the menu. Nowadays you need to work a little harder, extracting them from a run-of-the-mill list of Chinatown favourites such as crispy shredded beef. If in doubt, consult the knowledgeable staff, many of whom have been here since the opening. The Shanghai cold combination, now much-copied across London, is definitely worth a try. Expect a varied collection of marinated meats, 'smoked' fish, and 'vegetarian tofu' (layers of crisp beancurd). We can also recommend the family

---

banquet soup – a heart-warming milky broth of pork, wood-ear fungus and dried chinese mushroom. We were also excited by the sweet and sour taste of ECapital's hand-shredded roast chicken (a northern speciality); the chicken is gently braised in five-spice before being torn to pieces and doused in vinegar. A dish of snow pea (mangetout) shoots dressed with crab meat and a simple bowl of steamed rice worked well alongside. Pink, bright purple and off-white in colour, the smart dining room is fairly spacious by Chinatown standards.

Babies and children welcome: high chair. Booking advisable weekends. Separate room for parties, seats 50. Takeaway service. Vegetarian menu. Map 17 K6.

Feng Shui Inn

6 Gerrard Street, W1D 5PG (7734 6778/ www.fengshuiinn.co.uk). Leicester Square or Piccadilly Circus tube. **Meals served** noon-11.30pm daily. **Main courses** £6.80-£24.80. **Set lunch** (noon-4.30pm) £3.90 1 course. **Set meal** £12.80-£26.80 per person (minimum 2). **Service** 10%. **Credit** MC, V.

The decor here seems slightly more tongue-in-cheek than at many Chinatown places, with tacky New Year good luck ephemera on every surface. We were especially impressed by a tableau of Snoopy characters wearing Chinese costumes. Although at first glance the menu appears to conform to the Canto-Town norm, closer inspection reveals dishes such as stewed brisket of beef in chu-hua sauce. This might look rather like Irish stew, but the chunks of meat and fat in chrysanthemum sauce are meltingly tender, and taste sweet, with subtle spicing and mouth-watering aroma. We also enjoyed minced pork and aubergine in spicy sauce: a ratatouille-like mixture of cloud-ear fungi, soft aubergine, and shoelace-like strips of pork, with a complex spice flavour in the hot chilli/peppercorn spectrum. Surprising flavours became a pattern in our meal, with duck and preserved plum (served sizzling in a casserole dish) tasting of ginger. Should you fancy a change from Chinese beers or the uninspiring wine list, try one of the excellent fruit juices or other non-alcoholic drinks.

Babies and children admitted. Booking essential weekends. Entertainment: karaoke (call for details). Separate rooms for parties, seating 12, 20 and 40. Takeaway service. Vegetarian menu. Map 17 K7.

★ Fook Sing

25-26 Newport Court, WC2H 7JS (7287 0188). Leicester Square or Piccadilly Circus tube. **Meals served** 11am-10.30pm daily. **Main courses** £3.90-£4.30. **No credit cards.**

Yes, it's a basic caff with Formica tables, two small dining rooms and a rudimentary WC, but look again. Flick to the end of the lengthy menu and you'll find rare treasures from Fujian province (on China's south-eastern coast). How about starting with oyster soup, packed full of the little chaps and veritably singing with seaside flavours? Perhaps you'll then be taken with 'braised hoof' (sliced, tender beef flank in a soy sauce gravy) or even 'roast hairtail' (chunks of bony ribbon-fish with vegetables, also in soy sauce). Portions are huge, prices are low, witness the 'vermicelli in Fujian style', a vast helping of glass noodles dotted with various meats, oysters, prawns and squid – all for only £4. Fish balls are also worth a try; the usual spongy white balls are here stuffed with a tasty pork filling. Come at lunchtime and you can also sample the delectable fried oyster cakes. Friendly service adds to the appeal.

Babies and children admitted. Booking advisable. Takeaway service. Map 17 K6.

Golden Dragon

28-29 Gerrard Street, W1D 6JW (7734 2763). Leicester Square or Piccadilly Circus tube. **Meals served** noon-11.30pm Mon-Thur; noon-midnight Fri, Sat; 11am-11pm Sun. **Dim sum served** noon-5pm Mon-Sat; 11am-5pm Sun. **Dim sum** £1.80-£3.90. **Main courses** £6.50-£25. **Set meal** £12.50-£35 per person (minimum 2). **Credit** AmEx, MC, V.

This huge red and gold restaurant remains popular with tourists and local Chinese, but our concern about falling standards continues this year. Hot and sour soup was reasonably well balanced with heat from both chilli and white pepper, but a clear broth of pork and pickled vegetable was rather lacklustre. In contrast, marinated duck impressed, its moist flesh and chestnut-coloured skin working well alongside the accompanying garlic vinegar dip. Fried yee mein noodles, packed with crab flavour, also hit the spot. We never tasted the house special hot-pot of pork liver and frogs' legs – seconds before our other mains arrived, our waiter told us it was off the menu. A hilarious exchange then ensued à la Monty Python's cheese shop sketch as we requested each of the other specials, only to be told they too had bitten the dust. The waiter's eventual recommendation of paper-wrapped pork proved a bad choice: large pieces of pork in an almost-cooked sauce of red-fermented beancurd. Unlike last year, the bill wasn't slapped on the table the moment we'd finished eating. This time we had to ask for it twice.

Babies and children welcome: high chairs. Booking advisable. Separate rooms for parties, seating 20 and 40. Takeaway service. Map 17 K7.

Harbour City

46 Gerrard Street, W1D 5QH (7287 1526/7439 7859). Leicester Square or Piccadilly Circus tube. **Meals served** noon-11.30pm Mon-Thur; noon-midnight Fri, Sat; 11am-10.30pm Sun. **Dim sum served** noon-5pm Mon-Sat; 11am-5pm Sun. **Dim sum** £1.90-£5.50. **Main courses** £5.50-£20. **Set meal** £13.50-£15.50 per person (minimum 2); £15.50-£16 per person (minimum 4); £16.50-£21.50 per person (minimum 6). **Service** 10%. **Credit** AmEx, JCB, MC, V.

Harbour City is one of our most reliable favourites in Chinatown. Furnishings are nondescript, though tables are large, well spaced and clothed in quality linen. The first floor is lighter and airier than the ground. Dim sum doesn't hit the highest notes, but it's rare to get a bad dish. We like the 'pork pies', which closely resemble British mince pies with their neat pastry cases and lids. We also rate the steamed glutinous rice in lotus leaf, which contained tasty morsels such as succulent, sweet sausage and a few tiny dried prawns. The only low point during a recent meal was some gristly pork that cropped up in a preserved egg and salted pork congee (savoury rice porridge); all other dishes were up to standard. The chef's special dim sum

dishes are still listed only in Chinese, but you can always ask staff for a translation. The full menu has a seafood accent, with (expensive) abalone and fish lips and deep-fried pigeon with mandarin sauce among the more interesting dishes. Service is fine, neither too friendly nor lax. Harbour City is that rare thing in Chinatown – a safe bet.
Babies and children welcome: high chairs. Booking advisable; essential weekends. Separate room for parties, seats 60-70. Takeaway service. Vegetarian menu. **Map 17 K7**.

★ Hong Kong
6-7 Lisle Street, WC2H 7BG (7287 0352/ www.london-hk.co.uk). Leicester Square or Piccadilly Circus tube. **Meals served** noon-11.30pm Mon-Thur; noon-midnight Fri, Sat; 11am-11pm Sun. **Dim sum served** noon-5pm daily. **Dim sum** £2-£3.50. **Main courses** £6-£9. **Set meal** £11.80-£15.80 per person (minimum 2). **Service** 10%. **Credit** AmEx, JCB, MC, V.
Dim sum quality has been steadily increasing here over the past few years. On a recent visit we were stunned by the king prawn cheung fun with its soft, almost translucent, wrapper and firm, not rubbery, prawn. Har gau (prawn dumplings) also impressed us – more firm prawn, and cubes of water chestnut that produced a definite crunch. Pan-fried chive dumplings were perfectly balanced; we loved the eggy batter. Returning to the L-shaped dining room for dinner a few days later, we were similarly impressed. House soup (lai tong) was a comforting broth of pork belly and root veg. A potent dip of red chilli and soy sauce ensured the meat (which had given its all to the broth) wasn't wasted. Sweet and sour chicken was fluorescent-red with food colouring, yet tender, and clad in a crisp batter. The distinctive aroma from our hot-pot of chicken and salted fish filled the room, much to the delight of Chinese customers and the annoyance of others. Perfectly cooked pak choi and steamed rice rounded off an excellent meal. Service was friendly, if at times inattentive.
Babies and children welcome: high chairs. Booking advisable. Separate room for parties, seats 60. Takeaway service. Vegetarian menu. **Map 17 K7**.

Imperial China
White Bear Yard, 25A Lisle Street, WC2H 7BA (7734 3388/www.imperial-china.co.uk). Leicester Square or Piccadilly Circus tube. **Meals served** noon-11.30pm Mon-Sat; 11.30am-10.30pm Sun. **Dim sum served** noon-5pm daily. **Dim sum** £2.20-£3.50. **Main courses** £6-£24. **Set meal** £14.95-£30 per person (minimum 2). **Minimum** £10. **Service** 12.5%. **Credit** AmEx, JCB, MC, V.
Through the tiny alleyway, over the bridge and past the koi carp pond, you're transported away from busy, crowded Lisle Street. Imperial China aims to be a cut above other Chinatown restaurants, and largely succeeds. The wood-panelled interior and attentive service is pitched just right for business meetings, or even smoochy couples who appreciate the generous table spacing. We appreciate the dim sum menu, which, although brief, is prepared with great skill. However, you've got to wonder about a kitchen that puts little faces on the dim sum, and serves 'steamed prawn dumplings in goldfish shape', or even 'steamed custard dumplings in rabbit shape'. Not that the chefs are sentimental, as evidenced by the chicken's feet which were a succulent web of tendon, skin and bone. The full menu includes lots of abalone and lobster dishes, as you might expect of somewhere that appears to be purpose-built for corporate entertainment. We have yet to brave the karaoke rooms, which can be booked for groups.
Babies and children welcome: high chairs. Booking advisable. Disabled: toilet. Entertainment: pianist 7.30-10.30pm Thur-Sat. No-smoking tables. Separate rooms for parties, seating 14 and 70. Tables outdoors (4, courtyard). Vegetarian menu. **Map 17 K7**.

Joy King Lau
3 Leicester Street, WC2H 7BL (7437 1132/ 1133). Leicester Square or Piccadilly Circus tube. **Meals served** noon-11.30pm Mon-Sat; 11am-10.30pm Sun. **Dim sum served** noon-4.45pm Mon-Sat; 11am-4.45pm Sun. **Dim sum** £1.90-£2.90. **Main courses** £6.50-£20. **Set meal** £9.80-£35 per person (minimum 2). **Service** 10%. **Credit** AmEx, DC, MC, V.
A three-storey Chinatown stalwart, Joy King Lau exhibited its old-school credentials the moment we entered, stone-faced staff barking 'Upstairs!' until we reached the top floor. Pale pink tablecloths, dark blue carpet, and pictures of pandas provide the furnishings here; art on the ground-floor walls is moderately more stylish, though space is just as limited. The dim sum has long been well regarded by local Chinese, who account for most custom. The list encompasses bright orange marinated octopus (little ones, and tender too) served with pickled mooli; stuffed mince prawns in beancurd skin (springy prawns, crisp light skin); and red bean cakes (oily grilled pasta with a luscious sweet bean-paste filling). We liked all these, but weren't so taken with the chive cakes (dense discs), the jar leun cheung fun (containing chewy fried bread) or yam croquettes (stodgy). And the house special soup noodles featured dull stock and came in a dauntingly vast portion. The full menu is huge too, including the likes of eel, oysters, abalone (with fish lips) and crab among a myriad stir-fries. A serviceable, if not thrilling, standby.
Babies and children welcome: high chairs. Booking advisable Fri, Sat; essential Sun. Separate area for parties, seats 12-30. Takeaway service. Vegetarian menu. **Map 17 K7**.

Mr Kong
21 Lisle Street, WC2H 7BA (7437 7341/9679). Leicester Square or Piccadilly Circus tube. **Meals served** noon-2.45am Mon-Sat; noon-1.45am Sun. **Main courses** £5.90-£26. **Set meal** £10 per person (minimum 2)-£22 per person (minimum 4). **Minimum** £7 after 5pm. **Credit** AmEx, DC, JCB, MC, V.
The menu at Kong's has several enticing, unusual dishes, and this is surely the draw for the many Chinese who eat here. For once, the list of 'special vegetarian dishes' lives up to the billing; we were wowed by the mock abalone, pasta-like in texture and appearance, but tasting curiously like real mollusc, served with bright-green pea shoots. Braised turbot with shiitake mushrooms and beancurd sticks (aka 'tofu skin') was equally imaginative: the beancurd tasting of ginger, and a black bean sauce not overpowering the rest of the dish. Steamed scallops were served in their shells with glass noodles and garlic, plus a separate bowl of chopped chillies, soy, coriander and shallots – a hot little number. Best of all was the braised pork belly, very rich and laced with a thick sauce, but sandwiched with strata of dark preserved mustard greens. The laminated card of bought-in desserts was the biggest disappointment. Food and service were both up to scratch, though the seating arrangements are still too cramped.
Babies and children welcome: high chairs. Booking advisable. Separate room for parties, seats 30. Takeaway service. Vegetarian menu. **Map 17 K7**.

Laureate [NEW]
64 Shaftesbury Avenue, W1D 6LU (7437 5088). Leicester Square or Piccadilly Circus tube. **Meals served** noon-11.30pm Mon-Sat; 11am-10.30pm Sun. **Main courses** £6.50-£15. **Set meal** £9.50 per person 2 courses (minimum 2). **Credit** AmEx, MC, V.
Laureate sticks to what it does best – serving a Hong Kong-style Cantonese menu in a brightly lit, simple interior, for a fair price. It already has a substantial following among Chinese diners, attracted by the excellent cooking and the range of dishes, which includes specialities such as fish lips with abalone. These large 'fish lips' come from a huge reef fish called wrasse, and are prized for their gelatinous texture. Garnished with abalone and served with Chinese vegetables, this dish was a hit. A whole dover sole was steamed and served with ginger, soy and spring onion, and de-boned at an adjacent table. There was no stinting with ingredients: beancurd with crab had an abundance of crab meat in the slithery sauce. The timing of the cooking, from steamed gai lan (Chinese broccoli) to salt and pepper squid, was spot-on. A plate of slightly rubbery stir-fried beef was the

RESTAURANTS

Interview
CHRISTINE PARKINSON

Who are you?
Wine buyer at **Hakkasan** (*see p69*), **Yauatcha** (*see p72*) and **Busaba Eathai** (*see p265*).

Drinking in London: what's good about it?
The variety; you find just about every wine-producing country in the world. Londoners are spoiled for choice. As sommeliers we're exceptionally lucky with the number of importers and suppliers here.

What's bad about it?
A lot of effort goes into the food and the decor, but restaurateurs don't realise that the wine list can have a personality too. People should taste the food and think about what wines should go with it, even if that means being unconventional.

Which are your favourite London restaurants?
I love what Matt Skinner is doing at **Fifteen** (*see p179*). The wine list is a relaxed, funky interpretation. He has lots of young, ambitious winemakers who are achieving great results, and that matches the ethos of the place.

What single thing would most improve London wine lists?
I'd like to see more restaurants specialising, rather than trying to offer wines from all over the world. It's far better to concentrate on one or two countries, and be known for that.

Any hot tips for the coming year?
There'll be more emphasis on regions from Australia. Customers are becoming more aware of the differences between Adelaide Hills, Margaret River, McLaren Vale and Coonawarra.

Anything to declare?
Restaurant critics should take a bit more notice of what they're drinking. In many restaurants the wine purchase is a quarter of the overall cost. It seems totally unacceptable to be an expert on just 75 per cent of the meal.

only fault. The dim sum are also excellent; there's real finesse in their execution, from the thin, translucent dumpling wrappers of the siu mai to the wonderful detail of tiny threads of vermicelli-like shark's fin used to garnish minced pork and prawn dumplings.

Babies and children admitted: high chairs. Booking advisable. **Map 17 K7**.

New Diamond

23 Lisle Street, WC2H 7BA (7437 2517/7221) Leicester Square or Piccadilly Circus tube. **Meals served** noon-3am daily. **Main courses** £5.80-£22. **Set meal** £10.50-£20 per person (minimum 2). **Minimum** £10 after 5pm. **Credit** AmEx, DC, MC, V.

The smart, quiet and airy interior gave us a moment's welcome respite from the bustle of the narrow pavement outside. But we soon wondered why things were quite so quiet at lunchtime in the heart of Chinatown – with no Chinese among the handful of customers. The service was nothing if not authentic, the waitress giving the impression she'd rather there were no customers at all. Our enquiry as to what types of tea were available was met with a blunt 'Chinese tea'. There turned out to be lots to choose from, both tea-wise and food-wise. Shellfish and particularly clams are a speciality. If spicy salted aubergine and beancurd was on the dry side, chicken with chilli and yellow bean sauce was deliciously moist and sticky, with a hint of sweetness. Then came a pleasant, palate-cleansing soup of clam, pork and beancurd. The grand finale was crab, ginger and spring onion, demanding some serious rolling-up of sleeves. The sauce was a touch gloopy (and the accompanying noodles superfluous), but the crab itself was well worth the effort, with the aid of the various instruments provided (along with a finger bowl).

Babies and children welcome: high chairs. Booking advisable. Takeaway service. Vegetarian menu. **Map 17 K7**.

★ New Mayflower

68-70 Shaftesbury Avenue, W1B 6LY (7734 9207). Leicester Square or Piccadilly Circus tube. **Meals served** 5pm-4am daily. **Main courses** £6.50-£45. **Set dinner** £9.50-£22 per person (minimum 2). **Minimum** £8. **Service** 10%. **Credit** AmEx, MC, V.

This is a genuine Cantonese restaurant of the first order. OK, we had to wait, even though we had booked. And yes, we were finally seated in a cramped and noisy basement next to the kitchen. But the service was then willing, spirited and efficient and the people around us – almost all of them Chinese – were much too busy enjoying the food to worry about their surroundings. We started with a filling snack of spicy deep-fried soft-shelled crab, and moved on to a glorious steamed minced pork and salted egg: the pinkness of the meat and yellow and white of the egg appetisingly speckled with green spring onion. Mixed seafood on an iron plate came sizzling with scallop, squid and prawn, all of a perfect texture and freshness. We also loved the beancurd stuffed with shrimp, the beef noodles, the simple dish of choi sum (chinese cabbage)... oh, and the free juicy oranges served at the end, just as in all the best Hong Kong restaurants. Shaftesbury Avenue, after all, is not just for tourists.

Babies and children welcome: high chairs. Booking essential. Separate room for parties, seats 30. Takeaway service. **Map 17 K7**.

New World

1 Gerrard Place, W1D 5PA (7734 0396). Leicester Square or Piccadilly Circus tube. **Meals served** 11am-11.45pm Mon-Sat; 11am-11pm Sun. **Dim sum served** 11am-6pm daily. **Dim sum** £2-£5. **Main courses** £4.90-£10.50. **Set meal** £9.50-£50 per person (minimum 2). **Minimum** £5 evening. **Credit** AmEx, DC, MC, V.

The dim sum trolley system, as operated at this huge, multi-floored behemoth, has its pros and cons. In its favour, it takes the guesswork out of ordering: what you see is what you get. The drawbacks ('Fried fun gwor? It's very nice') are that you're sometimes barely able to ('Any vegetable cheung fun?') finish a sentence without being

The art of dim sum

The Cantonese term 'dim sum' means something like 'touch the heart', and it is used to refer to the vast array of dumplings and other titbits that southern Chinese people like to eat with their tea for breakfast or at lunchtime. It's an eating ritual simply known as 'yum cha', or 'drinking tea'. Many of London's Chinese restaurants have a lunchtime dim sum menu, and at weekends you'll find them packed with Cantonese families. A dim sum feast is one of London's most extraordinary gastronomic bargains: how else can you lunch lavishly in one of the capital's premier restaurants for as little as £15 a head?

Dim sum are served as a series of tiny dishes, each bearing two or three dumplings, perhaps, or a small helping of steamed spare ribs or seafood. Think of it as a Chinese version of tapas, served with tea. You can order according to appetite or curiosity; a couple of more moderate eaters might be satisfied with half a dozen dishes, while *Time Out*'s greedy reviewers always end up with a table laden with little snacks. Some people like to fill up with a plateful of stir-fried noodles, others to complement the meal with stir-fried greens from the main menu.

interrupted by the trolley dollies. Within 20 minutes of arriving ('Pork and prawn in beancurd sheet?') we were interrupted more than a dozen times. So this is no place for a tête-à-tête. Go on Sunday, however, and the bustle is part of the charm, with queuing the norm and the dim sum – some a little flaccid on our midweek visit – more pert and fresh. Among the highlights of a recent trip were barbecued pork puffs, and glutinous rice with chicken and pork in lotus leaf. The lowest point of the meal was the satay, as the chicken chunks had barely lost their pinkness. The lengthy full menu contains the likes of steamed fish with shredded pork and black mushroom, as well as all the Chinatown standards. For a uniquely Chinese dining experience, you should lunch here at least once.

Babies and children welcome: high chairs. Bookings not accepted lunch Sun. No-smoking tables. Separate rooms for parties, seating 5-200. Takeaway service. **Map 17 K7**.

But however wildly you order, if you stick to the dim sum menu and avoid more expensive specials that waiting staff may wave under your nose, the modesty of the bill is sure to come as a pleasant surprise. The low price of individual dishes (most cost between £1.80 and £3) makes eating dim sum the perfect opportunity to try more unusual delicacies: chicken's feet, anyone?

Two London restaurants serve dim sum Hong Kong-style, from circulating trolleys: the cheerful **New World** (*see below*) and the less-cheerful **Chuen Cheng Ku** (17 Wardour Street, W1D 6PJ, 7437 1398). Some of the snacks are wheeled out from the kitchen after being cooked; others gently steam as they go or are finished on the trolley to order. The trolley system has the great advantage that you see exactly what's offered, but if you go at a quiet lunchtime some of the food may be a little jaded by the time it reaches you. Other places offer snacks à la carte, so everything should be freshly cooked.

Dim sum lunches at the weekend tend to be boisterous occasions, so they are great for children (take care, though, as adventurous toddlers and hot dumpling trolleys are not a happy combination). Strict vegetarians are likely to be very limited in their menu choices, as most snacks contain either meat or seafood – honourable exceptions include **Golden Palace** (*see p78*) which has a generous selection of vegetarian snacks.

HOW TO EAT DIM SUM

Restaurants used to cease serving dim sum at 4pm or 5pm, when the rice-based evening menus took over. However, since the 2004 advent of **Yauatcha** (*see p72*), which serves dim sum in the evening as well, several other new and more established venues have followed suit. Dim sum specialists always list the snacks on separate, smaller menus, which are roughly divided into steamed dumplings, deep-fried dumplings, sweet dishes and so on. Try to order a selection of different types of food, with plenty of light

★ Poons

4 Leicester Street, WC2H 7BL (7437 1528). Leicester Square or Piccadilly Circus tube. **Meals served** noon-11.30pm daily. **Main courses** £4.90-£7.20. **Set meal** £14-£18 per person (minimum 2). **Service** 10%. **Credit** AmEx, MC, V.

There's no easy way to say it. We were immediately concerned when we arrived at Poons to find all the diners were non-Chinese. Based on our many previous visits, it was simply too unusual a sight. Established in Chinatown for more than 35 years, the Poon family has developed renowned specialities featuring wind-dried meat and earthy esoteric dishes involving offal. We started simply, or so we thought, with a portion of steamed scallops. Overcooked, the scallops were tough and had very little flavour. Things picked up momentarily when our friendly waitress delivered a dish of crisp lettuce, stir-fried with sharp-tasting steamed dumplings to counterbalance the heavier deep-fried snacks. If you are lunching with a large group, make sure you order multiples of everything, as most portions consist of about three dumplings.

Tea is the traditional accompaniment to the feast. Some restaurants offer a selection of teas, although they may not tell you this unless you ask. Musty bo lay (pu'er in Mandarin Chinese) or fragrant 'Iron Buddha' (tie guanyin) are delicious alternatives to the jasmine blossom that is normally served by default to non-Chinese guests. Waiters should keep teapots filled throughout the meal; just leave the teapot lid tilted at an angle or upside down to signal that you want a top-up.

London's best dim sum are found at **Hakkasan** (*see below*) and **Yauatcha**, which offer a sublime selection of unusual dumplings in glamorous settings; and the impeccable **Royal China** restaurants in Bayswater (*see p73*), Baker Street (*see p71*), St John's Wood (*see p76*) and Docklands (*see p75*). The dim sum at **Phoenix Palace** (*see p70*) are also impressive, and **Royal Dragon** (*see below*) scores on food if not atmosphere. Outside central London, try friendly **Shanghai** in Dalston (*see p75*), **Yi-ban** in Chelsea (*see p74*), **Local Friends** in Golders Green (*see p76*), **Royal China** in Putney (*see p74*), and **Golden Palace** in Harrow (*see p78*).

The following is a guide to the basic canon of dim sum served in London (spelling may vary depending on the transliteration used).

Char siu bao: fluffy steamed bun stuffed with barbecued pork in a sweet-savoury sauce.
Char siu puff pastry or **roast pork puff**: triangular puff-pastry snack, filled with barbecued pork, scattered with sesame seeds and baked in an oven.
Cheung fun: slithery sheets of steamed rice pasta wrapped around fresh prawns, barbecued pork, deep-fried dough sticks, or various other fillings, splashed with a sweet soy-based sauce. Some non-Chinese dislike the texture.

Chiu chow fun gwor: soft steamed dumpling with a wheat-starch wrapper, filled with pork, vegetables and peanuts. Chiu chow is a regional Chinese cooking style that is popular in Hong Kong.
Chive dumpling: steamed prawn meat and chinese chives in a translucent wrapper.
Har gau: steamed minced prawn dumpling with a translucent wheat-starch wrapper.
Nor mai gai or **steamed glutinous rice in lotus leaf**: lotus-leaf parcel enclosing moist sticky rice with chicken, mushrooms, salty duck-egg yolks and other bits and pieces, infused with the herby fragrance of the leaf.
Paper-wrapped prawns: tissue-thin rice paper enclosing plump prawn meat, sometimes scattered with sesame seeds, deep-fried.
Sago cream with yam: cool, sweet soup of coconut milk with sago pearls and morsels of taro.
Scallop dumpling: delicate steamed dumpling filled with scallop (sometimes with prawn) and vegetables.
Shark's fin dumpling: small steamed dumpling with a wheaten wrapper pinched into a frilly cockscomb shape on top, stuffed with a mixture of pork, prawn and slippery strands of shark's fin.
Siu loon bao: Shanghai-style round dumpling with a whirled pattern on top and a juicy minced pork filling.
Siu mai: little gathered dumpling with an open top, a wheat-flour wrapper and a minced pork filling. Traditionally topped with a little crab coral, although minced carrot and other substitutes are common.
Taro croquette or **yam croquette**: egg-shaped, deep-fried dumpling with a frizzy, melt-in-your mouth outer layer, made of mashed taro with a savoury minced pork filling.
Turnip paste: heavy slab of creamy paste made from glutinous rice flour and white oriental radishes, studded with fragments of wind-dried pork, sausage and dried shrimps and fried to a golden brown on either side.

dishes – and by the bill, which was less than you'd pay at many of the lacklustre Canto-Anglo restaurants in neighbouring streets.
Babies and children welcome: high chairs. Booking advisable. No-smoking tables. Separate room for parties, seats 20. Takeaway service. **Map 17 K7**.

Royal Dragon
30 Gerrard Street, W1D 6JS (7734 0935).
Leicester Square or Piccadilly Circus tube. **Meals served** noon-3am Mon-Sat; 11am-3am Sun. **Dim sum served** noon-5pm Mon-Sat; 11am-5pm Sun. **Dim sum** £1.80-£4.90. **Main courses** £6.30-£9. **Set meal** £11-£18.50 per person (minimum 2). **Service** 10%. **Credit** AmEx, MC, V.
Royal Dragon has just enough room, in various nooks, for diners to feel comfortable rather than hemmed in, but given its prime position on Gerrard Street we were surprised to find the place sparsely populated on a midweek lunchtime. Both the dim sum and full menus are lengthy and interesting, the latter including strong flavours like salted fish and diced chicken fried rice, as well as hot-pots (abalone with duck's web, say). We chose the lunchtime snacks and received some diverting dishes, though execution wasn't always up to par. Baby squid in curry sauce was a tender, tangy success; seaweed rolls were good too, as were the crisp coated taro croquettes. Our waitress – brisk, friendly and attired in a green waistcoat and bow tie – earned extra points for translating the entire Chinese dim sum list. From this, quails' eggs, encased with excellent prawns in overcooked pasta and resting on sheets of beancurd, was a nice idea that required some more thought. Sichuan buns were simply deep-fried doughy bread. A menu with potential, nonetheless. Royal Dragon was under renovation as we went to press, so expect a smarter look in future.
Babies and children welcome; high chairs. Separate rooms available for parties, seating 15 and 30. Takeaway service. Vegetarian menu. **Map 17 K7**.

Fitzrovia W1

★ Hakkasan
8 Hanway Place, W1T 1HD (7907 1888).
Tottenham Court Road tube.
Bar **Open** noon-12.30am Mon, Tue; noon-1.30am Wed-Sat; noon-midnight Sun.
Restaurant **Lunch/dim sum served** noon-2.45pm Mon-Fri; noon-4.30pm Sat, Sun. **Dinner served** 6-11.30pm Mon, Tue, Sun; 6pm-12.30am Wed-Sat. **Dim sum** £3.50-£16. **Main courses** £11.50-£68.
Both **Service** 13%. **Credit** AmEx, MC, V.
There's no questioning the buzz about Alan Yau's flagship. Its dark, roomy, slinky basement interior – all lattice black screens, misty blue or green glass (through which shadowy chefs are discernible), and spotlit tables, with an ultra-stylish bar to the side – resounds with the chatter of enthusiastic diners, both in the evening (when it's hard to book a table) and for lunchtime dim sum (when non-Chinese business diners dominate). The quality of ingredients is also beyond reproach, with luxuries like grilled wagyu beef with enoki mushrooms (a wallet-draining £48) and stir-fried scallops with preserved turnip on the full menu. The dim sum list is cheaper, though still double the price of elsewhere in London (around £5 a snack). Never have dumplings been so packed with innovation, yet to our mind the simple marriage of flavours and textures are the best: witness the delicacy of the Chilean sea bass and yellow chive dumpling; or the cheung fun where fragments of crunchy asparagus are intelligently paired with resilient morsels of shiitake and cloud-ear fungus. Skilful execution is here in abundance, but some snacks are ill-conceived. Blue swimmer crab meat was overwhelmed by its (expertly) deep-fried coating; baby cuttlefish (achingly tender) came with cherry tomatoes and aubergine in a zest-less sauce that floundered between the Mediterranean and South-east Asia. Puddings are European haute cuisine in style: beautifully constructed almond and lavender panna cotta with peach compote, for instance. Staff – watchful, plentiful, multinational – are coolly efficient.

---

fermented beancurd. Then it was back down to earth with a bump. Chicken casserole with salted fish and beancurd lacked substance, and was bereft of the expected earthy aroma. However, the worst was yet to come. The restaurant's signature wind-dried pork was tough and fibrous; it simply hadn't been dried for long enough. We've been extolling the virtues of Poons' wind-dried pork for many years. Let's hope this lacklustre meal was a temporary blip.
Babies and children welcome: high chair. Booking advisable weekends. No-smoking tables. Separate room for parties, seats 20. Takeaway service. Vegetarian menu. **Map 17 K7**.

★ Rong Cheng
72 Shaftesbury Avenue, W1D 6NA (7287 8078).
Leicester Square or Piccadilly Circus tube.
Meals served noon-11pm daily. **Main courses** £4.50-£11.80. **Set meal** £9.50 3 courses per person (minimum 2). **Credit** JCB, MC, V.

Rong Cheng is an anomaly among Chinatown's bustling restaurants. It's tiny, barely more than a few spruce tables. The young women who run the place seem unusually enthusiastic about their jobs. And the menu, as well as containing a sizeable Cantonese list, also has sections for Fujianese dishes and for food from north-eastern China (Dong Bei). Fujian is a coastal region, and the Fujianese dishes here included a remarkably delicate oyster omelette, and a consommé of cucumber and clam that was fresh and evocative of summer at the seaside. The Dong Bei dishes are a of a different order. Dong Bei borders Russia, and the dumplings were a triumph: silky, thin-sheeted pasta encasing delicately flavoured minced pork, prawn and leek. A Korean influence was evident in another Dong Bei dish of 'golden needle' mushroom (enoki) with julienned cucumber and a refreshing dressing of chilli, soy sauce with a hint of vinegar. We were thrilled by all these home-style

Laureate. See p67.

Babies and children admitted. Disabled: toilet. Entertainment: DJs 9pm daily. Restaurant available for hire. Separate room for parties, seats 65. Vegetarian menu. **Map 17 K5**.

Holborn WC1

Shanghai Blues NEW
193-197 High Holborn, WC1V 7BD (7404 1668/www.shanghaiblues.co.uk). Holborn tube. **Meals served** noon-11.30pm, **dim sum served** noon-5pm daily. **Dim sum** £3-£20. **Main courses** £7-£40. **Service** 12%. **Credit** AmEx, JCB, MC, V.

A new addition to the trendy dim sum stable, Shanghai Blues is a bar and restaurant on the ground floor of old Holborn Town Hall. The design is lovely, with dark wooden floors and silk panels painted with foliage. The blue leather chairs are comfortable, the tables well spaced. Staff are kind and attentive, as at other restaurants in the group – Shanghai (*see p75*) and Weng Wah House (*see p76*). The dim sum menu (which we're told might change) includes favourites such as steamed prawn dumplings alongside innovative snacks like potato croquettes with sweetcorn. Vegetable dishes and a fruit platter are also on the list (we loved our wok-fragrant stir-fry of baby pak choi in shrimp sauce). Scallop dumplings, triangular parcels tinted green by spinach juice, were juicily delicious. Shredded duck with yam rolls was a delectable combination of melting crispness and comforting mash (but the sweet sauce inside didn't work so well). The dim sum were generally thoughtful, well cooked and prettily presented. Even the desserts were nice, including a delicate green tea pudding. A selection of teas is served in charming pottery. This was one of the most enjoyable Chinese meals we've had recently. The enticing full menu features more unusual ingredients, such as red dates, Long Jing tea leaves and lily bulbs.

Babies and children admitted. Booking essential dinner. Disabled: toilet. Dress: smart casual. No-smoking tables. Separate room for parties, seats 25. Takeaway service. **Map 18 L5**.

Knightsbridge SW1

★ Mr Chow
151 Knightsbridge, SW1X 7PA (7589 7347/ www.mrchow.com). Knightsbridge tube. **Lunch served** 12.30-3pm, **dinner served** 7pm-midnight daily. **Main courses** £12.50-£25. **Set lunch** £19 2 courses, £22 3 courses. **Service** 12.5%. **Credit** AmEx, DC, MC, V.

Mr Chow is the Ivy of Chinese restaurants: long-established, much-loved, and fabulously glamorous in a lived-in way. The food is surprisingly good and authentic, given that most customers are non-Chinese and the ambience is decidedly Western. But, like the Ivy, this place can make you feel a little excluded if your face doesn't fit. On a Saturday night, we were denied a table in the buzzy ground-floor room (despite the fact that several tables were empty), and were sent to the lovely but nearly deserted upstairs. The menu never seems to change, but its repertoire of dishes is delightful. There are old favourites such as crispy duck with pancakes, alongside fine and authentic renditions of classic Chinese dishes. We especially love the drunken fish (slippy slices of sole and cloud-ear fungus in a sweet, fragrant sauce), and the starter of fresh prawns in a bizarre but delicious mayonnaise glaze, with crisp caramelised walnuts. Order Mr Chow noodles and you'll see a virtuoso display as a chef teases springy dough into spaghetti-thin strands before your eyes. Service tends to be excellent, although it was less than perfect on our last visit.

Babies and children admitted. Booking advisable lunch; essential dinner. Separate rooms for parties, seating 20, 50 and 75. **Map 8 F9**.

Marylebone W1, NW1

Phoenix Palace
3-5 Glentworth Street, NW1 5PG (7486 3515). Baker Street tube. **Meals served** noon-11.30pm Mon-Sat; 11am-10.30pm Sun. **Dim sum served** noon-5pm Mon-Sat; 11am-5pm Sun. **Main courses** £6.50-£25. **Set meal** £14 2 courses per person (minimum 2), £24 3 courses per person (minimum 2). **Service** 12.5%. **Credit** AmEx, JCB, MC, V.

'Palace' is an apt title for this large, splendid-looking restaurant that's kitted out in classic Chinese style, with lacquered panels on the walls and huge round tables for banquets. The menu is impressively long, with over 200 dishes. Many are Cantonese standards, but there are plenty of curiosities, especially on the separate 'chef's special' menu. From this section baked tiger prawns had shells so thin you could eat them – which we did, because the batter coating, piquant dressing and fragments of preserved egg were too good to miss. Another simple but cracking dish was pea shoots with 'loganberries' – actually wolfberries, slightly sweet like sultanas and a surprisingly good match to the spinach-like tang of the pea shoots stems. Thin pieces of venison served with yellow chive and celery added a nice contrast of texture and flavour. The dim sum menu is notable too, including melt-in-the-mouth yam croquettes, octopus patty with vinaigrette, and cheung fun of mixed soya, peanut and sweet yellow bean sauce. Our fellow customers were a surprisingly mixed bunch, from the mullet-haired owner of the Wetherspoon pub chain to a surgically enhanced beauty displaying her assets to a mesmerised date.

Babies and children welcome: high chairs. Booking advisable. Separate rooms for parties, seating 10 and 20. Takeaway service; delivery service (within 1-mile radius on orders over £10). **Map 2 F4**.

Royal China

24-26 Baker Street, W1U 7AB (7487 4688/ www.royalchinagroup.co.uk). Baker Street tube. **Meals served** noon-11pm Mon-Thur; noon-11.30pm Fri, Sat; 11am-10pm Sun. **Dim sum served** noon-5pm daily. **Dim sum** £2.20-£4.50. **Main courses** £7-£30. **Set meal** £28-£38 per person (minimum 2). **Service** 13%. **Credit** AmEx, MC, V.

The Marylebone branch of the much-loved Royal China group moved along the road to this more spacious location in 2004. In last year's guide we called for a revamp and a change in management after experiencing poor service. Today we're repeating the call. This time there were problems with the food too. Opting for the house cold hors d'oeuvres, we were disappointed. Slices of pork hock and marinated beef worked well, but shanghai 'smoked' fish was tired and dry. Chilli prawns also failed to hit the mark, being overcooked and smothered by an unpleasant dressing tasting mainly of tomato ketchup. Deep-fried stuffed squid turned out rubbery with barely any pepper-salt zing. Conversely, an overly salty black bean sauce easily overpowered the lamb chops with dry chilli, honey and black pepper. Worse still, an unacceptably sour taste pervaded our final dish of braised asparagus with egg and garlic sauce. Refusing to believe such poor cooking was the norm at one of London's favourite chains, we returned for dim sum. Mercifully, it was better. *Babies and children welcome: high chairs. Booking essential. Separate room for parties, seats 15. Takeaway service. Vegetarian menu.* **Map 9 G5**.

Mayfair W1

★ Kai Mayfair

65 South Audley Street, W1K 2QU (7493 8988/www.kaimayfair.com). Bond Street or Marble Arch tube. **Lunch served** noon-2.30pm Mon-Fri; 12.30-3pm Sat, Sun. **Dinner served** 6.30-11pm Mon-Sat; 6.30-10.30pm Sun. **Main courses** £13-£39. **Set lunch** £23 2 courses. **Service** 3.5%. **Credit** AmEx, DC, JCB, MC, V.

Why they call it 'Kai Mayfair' we're not sure, because you're left in no doubt as to which part of London this restaurant is located in. Everything about it whispers 'wealth', from the palatial European look of elegant pillars, marble floors, polished mirrors and well-padded chairs, to the ranks of attentive Chinese staff. The monied clientele tend to arrive by limo or taxi. We wonder which of them order the £108 bowl of soup (abalone, shark's fin and other seafood, in case you were wondering). The less extravagant diner might be tempted by a small side dish of 'double-cooked' green beans at £9.50, or the twin portion of mixed rice served in a lotus leaf for £10.50. Of course, the cooking is excellent – we relished the flavours of our iron-pot plum and orange sauce chicken – but you can find food of this standard in the best Chinatown restaurants. You're paying for the surroundings and service (though, to be fair, the service charge is a very low 3.5%); the staff were relaxed and welcoming in a way that is all too rare in Chinese restaurants. *Babies and children welcome: high chairs. Booking advisable. Separate rooms for parties, seating 6 and 12.* **Map 9 G7**.

Soho W1

Chinese Experience NEW

118 Shaftesbury Avenue, W1D 5EP (7437 0377/www.chineseexperience.com). Leicester Square or Piccadilly Circus tube. **Meals served** noon-11pm Mon-Thur; noon-11.30pm Fri, Sat; noon-10.30pm Sun. **Main courses** £6-£22. **Set meal** £19-£23 per person (minimum 2). **Service** 10%. **Credit** AmEx, MC, V.

The picture windows at this new-wave Chinese restaurant are filled most evenings with Londoners and tourists admiring the Japanese-inspired design, decorative calligraphy and bold colours. We've eaten here a few times since it opened, and standards remain high. For dim sum we adore the xiao long bao ('steam pork bun Shanghai-style'), small parcels of pasta which burst open in a flush of savoury stock – but ours had burst before arriving at table. Also excellent was beef shin and white gourd 'in superior soup'. 'Steamed vegetable dumpling' was exquisite: translucent pasta encasing a colourful mix of succulent, pert veg, with the triangular fold at the top garnished with a sweetcorn, a pea, and a dice of carrot. Our spirits sank when we saw our cheung fun had been fried, with beansprouts; but once pepped up with sauces it tasted OK. The most challenging dish was the ducks' tongues: orange-fleshed and resembling stretched mussels, yet with a core of tough cartilage. Service was smiling and attentive, but diners were few on our lunchtime visit. The full menu contains some interest among the usual pairings, but our stir-fried prawns with Chinese tea leaves featured less than top-quality seafood. *Babies and children welcome: high chairs. Booking advisable. Separate room for parties, seats 30. Takeaway service.* **Map 17 K6**.

Ping Pong NEW

44-45 Great Marlborough Street, W1F 7JL (7851 6969/www.pingpongdimsum.com). Oxford Circus tube. **Dim sum served** noon-midnight Mon-Sat; noon-10.30pm Sun. **Dim sum** £2.10-£3.10. **Set lunch** (noon-6pm) £9.90-£11.90. **Service** 10%. **Credit** AmEx, MC, V.

Following the success of Yauatcha (*see p72*), a slew of restaurants now serve all-day dim sum, including newcomer Ping Pong. It certainly looks striking, with curved bars at the entrance, ranks of greeting staff, a central atrium overlooking an

outdoor courtyard (with a huge digital projector showing images of China in the evenings), and multi-level dining. But once we were seated, the smiling service became haphazard and inattentive, with wrong orders brought. The dim sum were mostly adequate, but underwhelming when compared to the best places in nearby Chinatown. The pasta-like cases of har gau (minced prawn) were visibly undercooked, opaque and dry. Worse, the white, floury steamed buns of char siu had fallen apart in the steamer. Shanghai siu loon buns were unusually insipid. Sticky rice loosely wrapped in lotus leaves also fell apart, and the filling was indeterminate. For dim sum, Yauatcha (a five-minute walk away) is in the premier league, Chinatown (ten minutes) first division and Ping Pong barely second. Still, the low prices, evening dim sum menu and proximity to Oxford Street will doubtless keep this place busy.
Babies and children welcome: high chairs. Bookings not accepted. Disabled: toilet. No smoking. **Map 17 J6.**

★ Yauatcha
15 Broadwick Street, W1F 0DE (7494 8888). Leicester Square, Oxford Circus or Piccadilly Circus tube.
Tea house **Tea/snacks served** 10am-11pm Mon-Sat; 10am-10.30pm Sun. **Set tea** £19.
Restaurant **Meals served** noon-11pm Mon-Fri; 11am-11pm Sat; 11am-10pm Sun.
Both **Dim sum served** noon-11pm Mon-Fri; 11am-11pm Sat; 11am-10.30pm Sun. **Dim sum** £3-£14.50. **Main courses** £3.50-£24. **Service** 12.5%. **Credit** AmEx, MC, V.
The most recent venture by star restaurateur Alan Yau, Yauatcha opened to a blaze of publicity in 2004. The Michelin-starred restaurant occupies two floors of Richard Rogers' Ingeni building, and is designed by Christian Liaigre with close attention to detail. In the basement, tropical fish swim the length of the bar in a glowing blue tank; star-like lights twinkle in the ceiling. The ground-floor tea room is cool and light (and you can now

eat-in here, as in the restaurant). Lovely tableware includes serving dishes with ox-blood glazes. Dim sum are the highlight of the menu – served throughout the day and (trailblazingly) in the evening too. Our steamed sea bass dumplings, their cockscomb crests studded with morsels of salty duck egg, were delectable, and we loved also the gently pungent prawn and yellow chive dumplings, and juicy shanghai steamed buns. Yet there were some surprising flaws: undercooked, floury cheung fun, and taro croquettes with rather hard, greasy shells. The tea menu is wonderful (we chose a cooling, delicate green infusion from Taiwan), but staff discard the leaves so they can be brewed only once; this would be a heresy in China. Upstairs, the cakes at the pâtisserie counter are shatteringly beautiful, and delicious too. Getting a mealtime table at Yauatcha can be a hassle, and you're only allowed to keep it 90 minutes (which made the long hiatus between our courses annoying). In the past we've heard bitter complaints about the service, but it seems to have improved immeasurably.
Babies and children admitted. Booking advisable (restaurant). Disabled: toilet. No smoking. Takeaway service (tea house). **Map 17 J6.**

Yming
35-36 Greek Street, W1D 5DL (7734 2721/ www.yming.co.uk). Leicester Square, Piccadilly Circus or Tottenham Court Road tube. **Meals served** noon-11.45pm Mon-Sat. **Main courses** £5-£10. **Set lunch** (noon-6pm) £10 3 courses. **Set meal** £15-£20 per person (minimum 2). **Service** 10%. **Credit** AmEx, DC, JCB, MC, V.
Yming is a Chinese restaurant for people who don't like nearby Chinatown. It looks and feels like a European restaurant, an impression reinforced by urbane service and the emphasis staff place on the above-par wine list. We wondered whether this polish was deceptive, after finding that 'squeamish' ingredients had been expurgated from the menu, and that there were no Chinese customers during our visit. Nevertheless, dishes

are cooked with care and skill, and the regional net is thrown much further than the usual Cantonese classics. From the specials, the double-braised pork in hot-pot featured the fattest rashers of pork belly cooked into melting submission; beneath these slices was a layer of soft vegetables. Also of high quality was a starter of scallops stuffed with prawn, deep-fried then dressed with chilli, garlic and spices. Sizzling prawns in hot sauce was simple but fresh. 'Empress beef' is a poshed-up version of yau nam, a Cantonese dish of beef brisket simmered in a soy stock tasting of star anise and other spices. Although the menu might seem to have had the guts taken out of it somewhat, the flavours and precision of cooking are still impressive.
Babies and children admitted. Booking essential weekends. No-smoking tables. Separate rooms for parties, seating 10 and 18. Takeaway service. **Map 17 K6.**

West
Acton W3

North China
305 Uxbridge Road, W3 9QU (8992 9183/ www.northchina.co.uk). Acton Town tube/207 bus. **Lunch served** noon-2.30pm, **dinner served** 6-11pm daily. **Main courses** £5-£8.80. **Set meal** £14-£18 per person (minimum 2). **Credit** AmEx, DC, MC, V.
Sensibly named, North China specialises in the food of Beijing and northern China. Much of the menu consists of familiar stir-fries, yet interspersed is a peppering of northern food. Last time we relished the classic three-course peking duck (24 hours' notice required), but ordered à la carte on this visit. Smoked chicken with seaweed had strips of smoked breast deep-fried in salty batter, imparting a pork scratching-like flavour. Grilled dumplings featured a nicely chewy covering with a modest (and modestly flavoured) pork and chive filling. To follow, fish in wine sauce

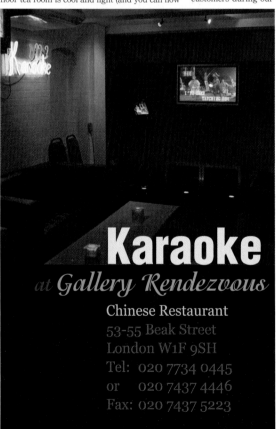

RESTAURANTS

had goujons of first-rate sole covered in a sweet, gloopy (too much cornflour) sauce. Mixed vegetables was an uninspiring Anglo assortment of broccoli, mangetout and baby sweetcorn. The best two dishes were the hand-stretched noodles, perfectly al dente, served with strips of chicken, and the lamb casserole: tender chunks in a rich meaty stock with bamboo shoots. We couldn't resist trying the deep-fried bean paste pancake for pudding. North China is a small place, well liked by Ealing locals. Walls sponged in apricot hues, blue carpets and big wall mirrors create cosiness and an illusion of space. Service was helpful, if a touch on the slow side.
Babies and children welcome: high chairs. Booking advisable; essential dinner Fri, Sat. Separate room for parties, seats 36. Takeaway service; delivery service (within 2-mile radius). Vegetarian menu.

Sichuan Restaurant NEW
116 Churchfield Road, W3 6BY (8992 9473). Acton Central tube. **Meals served** 5.30-10.30pm Tue-Sat. **Main courses** £2-£15. **Set meal** £12.95-£19.95 per person (minimum 2). **Service** 10%. **Credit** (over £10) AmEx, DC, JCB, MC, V.
At last – an authentic and delightful Sichuanese restaurant in London. The chef at this modest eaterie in Acton trained at the famous Sichuanese cooking academy in Chengdu. His cooking is unpretentious, traditional and robustly spicy, with the delicious mixing of flavours for which Sichuan is renowned. True, the menu is limited (with most of the best dishes listed as chef's specials on the last page), the Sichuan pepper lacked zing, and our rice was a bit stodgy, but we thoroughly enjoyed the meal. Gong Bao chicken ('diced chicken with Sichuan sauce') was seductively fragrant and the most authentic we've had in London; stir-fried green beans sizzled; and mapo doufu ('beancurd Sichuan style') luxuriated in spicy red oil, as it should. Corn with salted egg yolk was irresistible, and an off-menu request for fish-fragrant aubergines was nicely done. In short, this is the kind of everyday Sichuanese food that we've been longing to find in London. The restaurant is tiny, with few decorations save some strings of red plastic chillies. Service wasn't entirely professional, but the place has such a friendly family feel that we didn't mind.
Babies and children welcome: high chairs. Booking advisable. No-smoking tables. Takeaway service.

Bayswater W2

Four Seasons
84 Queensway, W2 3RL (7229 4320). Bayswater or Queensway tube. **Meals served** noon-11.15pm daily; noon-10.45pm Sun. **Main courses** £5.50-£25. **Set meal** £13.50-£18.50 per person (minimum 2). **Service** 12.5%. **Credit** AmEx, MC, V.
This chaotic place can be a struggle to get into, even if you've booked. Our advice: make your presence known to staff the moment you arrive, and be prepared to wait in the street for up to 30 minutes before being shown to a large, shared table. If all your party haven't arrived, bad luck – you've missed your turn. The reason for Four Seasons' popularity is its long-established reputation for cantonese roast duck, which also causes a roaring trade in takeaways. However, since a change of ownership last year, we've noticed a worrying move towards smaller ducks dried for less time (the longer the duck dries, the crisper – and better tasting – the skin). Also, char siu barbecued pork was terribly dry on our last visit, though quite tasty. Sweet and sour fish was better, with generous pieces of cod lightly deep-fried and topped by a flavourful bright-red sauce. We also enjoyed the tender belly pork and preserved vegetable hot-pot; a meagre portion left us hankering for more. Service was amiable, but motivated by a need to have people leave (and new diners come in) as quickly as possible.
Babies and children admitted. Booking advisable. Takeaway service. **Map 7 C6.**

Magic Wok
100 Queensway, W2 3RR (7792 9767). Bayswater or Queensway tube. **Meals served** noon-11pm daily. **Main courses** £6-£14. **Set meal** £11.50-£24 per person (minimum 2). **Service** 12.5%. **Credit** AmEx, MC, V.
We've long lauded Magic Wok for its accessibility. Here you'll find a long menu of alluring Cantonese dishes, all translated into English, and served by amenable staff. The food remains of a high standard, yet in recent visits seems to have lost some sparkle. Soup of the day was a comforting pork broth, though the smoked pork loin with special herbs and jellyfish was too cold and the sliced meat lacked flavour. Some sesame seed oil on the jellyfish would have been nice too. For main courses, look to the 'chef's recommendations' and the hot-pot section for best results. From the latter, brisket of beef hot-pot had a gravy of luscious savour and was reasonably tender. Next to this classic dish, portuguese chicken was a curious amalgam: diced breast with potatoes and red peppers in a creamy curry sauce. Better was the stir-fried seasonal vegetables with two kinds of preserved egg (salted, and gelatinous '1,000 year old' egg), though we found the sauce a little sloppy. This comfortable, if hardly showy restaurant has a few round banquet tables at the back and attracts Chinese Londoners and tourists.
Babies and children admitted. Booking advisable dinner. Separate room for parties, seats 30. Takeaway service. **Map 7 C6.**

Mandarin Kitchen
14-16 Queensway, W2 3RX (7727 9012). Bayswater or Queensway tube. **Meals served** noon-11.30pm daily. **Main courses** £5.90-£25. **Set meal** £10.90 per person (minimum 2). **Credit** AmEx, DC, JCB, MC, V.
Even on Monday at 7.30pm, Mandarin Kitchen was turning away customers. The reason? Sensational lobsters – 400 of the giant crustaceans are served every week (beat that, Terence Conran). If you're happy to shell out £28 or so, you can get an impeccable pink-shelled beast served on slithery yellow noodles with a choice of sauce. Other ways of tackling lobster include steamed, deep-fried and even raw, as Japanese-style sashimi. Our lobster was good, but we were underwhelmed by a starter of soft-shell crab, which was watery: odd, considering it was deep-fried. A rice in lotus leaf dish resembled takeaway fried rice, complete with fried egg in it. Presenting the bill as an unitemised total is common practice in many Chinese restaurants, but it makes it impossible to verify the bill's accuracy, or even if a percentage had been added for the brusquely efficient service (it hadn't, we were told). Although our meal was good in parts, on this visit there were sufficient disappointments that we couldn't ignore MK's shortcomings, which include a dreary interior of Artexed walls, wavy ceiling and smoked mirrors that last looked fab in the 1970s.
Babies and children welcome: high chair. Booking essential dinner. Takeaway service. **Map 7 C7.**

★ Royal China
13 Queensway, W2 4QJ (7221 2535/www.royal chinagroup.co.uk). Bayswater or Queensway tube. **Meals served** noon-11pm Mon-Thur; noon-11.30pm Fri, Sat; 11am-10pm Sun. **Dim sum served** noon-5pm Mon-Sat; 11am-5pm Sun. **Dim sum** £2.20-£4.50. **Main courses** £7-£10. **Set meal** £28-£36 per person (minimum 2). **Service** 13%. **Credit** AmEx, DC, MC, V.
Lunching at this restaurant at weekends can be a traumatic experience, what with the lengthy queues, the cramped waiting area, and the brusqueness of many of the staff. But get here early enough to bag a table without fuss, and the food invariably lives up to expectations. On our last visit for dim sum, the sesame prawn rolls were impeccably crisp and fragrant; and the soft turnip cake came enticingly threaded with preserved meats and seared with gold. Steamed chive dumplings glowed greenly through their translucent wrappers, and the scallop dumplings were fresh and juicy. Golden pastry ruptured meltingly to reveal the deliciously sweet saltiness

Regional cooking

Chinese cuisine is conventionally divided into four major schools: the fresh Cantonese cooking of the south; the sweeter, oilier food of Shanghai and the east; the strong spicy cuisine of western China (especially Sichuan and Hunan provinces); and northern cookery, which is typified by a reliance on breads and noodles, and by famous dishes such as mongolian hot-pot and peking duck, rather than by any dominant flavouring style. Beyond these four great culinary regions, many provinces, not to mention cities and towns, have their own special dishes.

London's restaurant scene is still dominated by the Cantonese, many of whom originated in Hong Kong. Cantonese tastes have inevitably influenced the whole development of British Chinese cooking (Cantonese people don't, for example, much like spicy food, and they tend to tone down the flavours of the Sichuanese specialities on their menus).

A growing number of restaurants, however, are offering genuine regional specialities. The chef at **Blue Thames** (Dolphin House, Riverside West, the Boulevard, Smuggler's Way, SW18 1DE, 8874 9878) is Shanghainese, and also spent years in Sichuan, so he can cook a number of dishes from both regions, although you won't find them on the unexciting main menu. But the best Sichuanese food we've tried is at the new **Sichuan Restaurant** (*see left*) in Acton, where the chef turns out some everyday but delicious fare.

There's a modest but real Hunanese venue, the **Shangri-La Hunan Cuisine Restaurant** on the first floor of a shopping complex in Colindale (*see p247* **Oriental City**), and **Hunan** (*see p62*) serves up a sophisticated, Taiwanese version of Hunanese cuisine.

ECapital (*see p65*) offers Shanghainese specialities such as 'vegetarian goose' and 'lion's head' meatballs. **North China** (*see p72*) serves a great cold meat platter and a fine peking duck (prepared in three courses, including not only the familiar duck skin with pancakes, but also a duck-and-vegetable stir-fry and a final duck soup). **Mr Chow** (*see p70*) serves hand-pulled pasta (well-loved by the Muslims of northern China) in spectacular fashion; just watch as a chef comes out of the kitchen to whack a ball of dough into a delicate skein of noodles. Visit **Rong Cheng** (*see p69*) and **Fook Sing** (*see p65*) for Fujianese food (Rong Cheng also has a chef from north-eastern China who cooks Dong Bei specialities).

of barbecued pork inside the roast pork puffs. Staff wander around waving the day's specials under your noses, which might include roast suckling pig or stewed octopus. Drink only tea (several varieties are offered, not just jasmine) and a dim sum lunch remains an extraordinary bargain. Dinner is more expensive, but the standard of cooking is high and the pace more relaxed. Steamed minced pork with salted egg, and 'Royal China fish' (dover sole) are among the enticements.

Babies and children welcome: high chairs. Booking essential Fri, Sat; bookings not accepted lunch Sat, Sun. Separate room for parties, seats 40. Takeaway service. **Map 7 C7**.

South West

Chelsea SW6

Yi-Ban

5 The Boulevard, Imperial Wharf, Imperial Road, SW6 2UB (7731 6606/www.yi-ban.co.uk). Earls Court tube then C3 bus. **Meals served** 6-11pm Mon-Sat. **Main courses** £5-£30. **Service** 13%. **Credit** AmEx, MC, V.

This second branch of Yi-Ban (the other's in Docklands) is housed in the latest riverside development of shops and homes by Chelsea Harbour. It's one of the new wave of Chinese restaurants that appear to be inspired by Hakkasan (*see p69*); dimmed lighting, dark wood and red lanterns make it feel cosy, yet with the use of mirrors and translucent net screens, the dining area appears to stretch to infinity. There's pumping loud music and excellent cocktails in the small bar by the entrance, seats around a hot-plate and grill table, or seats in the main dining area. Skipping past the wagyu beef (£42), we plumped for more traditional Chinese dishes. The peking dumplings and the aromatic duck were standard fare. Much

better were the black bean sizzling seafood clay pot, and the scallops stir-fried in XO sauce. High prices pepper the menu. Sometimes these charges are cheeky (£7 for a small portion of gai lan, aka chinese broccoli), but sometimes it's a fair price, such as £7.50 for an exquisite matcha (green tea) tiramisu, or £8 for a fine banana pudding. The service was outstanding; perhaps it's worth paying a premium for that alone.

Babies and children welcome: high chairs. Booking advisable. Disabled: toilet. Dress: smart casual; no jeans. Entertainment: jazz fortnightly; call for times. No-smoking tables. Tables outdoors (8, pavement). Takeaway service; delivery service (within 5-mile radius). **Map 21 A1**. For branch see index.

Putney SW15

Royal China

3 Chelverton Road, SW15 1RN (8788 0907). East Putney tube/Putney rail/14, 37, 74 bus. **Lunch served** noon-3.30pm Mon-Sat; noon-4pm Sun. **Dinner served** 6.30-11pm Mon-Sat; 6.30-10.30pm Sun. **Dim sum served** noon-3.30pm daily. **Dim sum** £1.80-£5. **Main courses** £5.50-£40. **Set meal** £23-£35 per person (minimum 2). **Service** 12.5%. **Credit** AmEx, DC.

The striking interior of gloss-black walls with gold lacquered artwork are evidence that the Royal China chain invested much effort here. But for a decade this restaurant has had no connection with the other Royal Chinas. Standards, although good, aren't as impeccably high as at the north London namesakes. The dim sum on a recent visit were lacklustre, so we returned in the evening and found the place packed; despite booking, we waited half an hour to be seated (drinks were complimentary). Our order arrived promptly, however. Egg noodles with fresh crab meat were delectably light. Pork belly and preserved vegetables had a gratifying

intensity of flavour, and the slightly sweet sauce wasn't fatty. Tung choi (aka morning glory or water spinach) Malaysian-style had the distinctive aroma of shrimp paste in abundance; when combined with garlic, it made this a dish that only the brave would devour entirely. The most surprising dish was duck covered in a layer of fragrant yam, the lilac-coloured yam paste forming a layer over the lean duck before being fried like a croquette. Most credit cards aren't accepted here; bring cash or a cheque book.

Babies and children admitted. Booking advisable; bookings not accepted lunch Sun. Takeaway service; delivery service (within 3.5-mile radius).

South East

Greenwich SE10

Peninsula

Holiday Inn Express, Bugsby's Way, SE10 0GD (8858 2028/www.mychinesefood.co.uk). North Greenwich tube. **Meals served** noon-11pm Mon-Fri; 11am-11pm Sat, Sun. **Dim sum served** noon-5pm Mon-Fri; 11am-5pm Sat, Sun. **Dim sum** £2.10-£3.50. **Main courses** £6.30-£10.80. **Set meal** £15-£19 per person (minimum 2). **Service** 10%. **Credit** AmEx, MC, V.

Occupying the whole ground floor of a budget commuter hotel, the cream dining room of Peninsula has a blend of the old and the new: vintage photographs of nearby Limehouse (London's original Chinatown), and plasma screens constantly looping adverts and news of monthly specials. These dishes are often the stars of afternoon dim sum. Salted shredded chicken congee was a recent hit. Chefs had roasted a chicken in salt before shredding it into comforting rice porridge. Just one mouthful and we wished it was a regular attraction. An unusual dessert soup

Shanghai Blues. See p70.

of flaked tofu, barley and red dates was similarly soothing. Evening meals are enjoyable too. A request for some roast meat brought an attractive platter of pickled pork knuckle, tender cantonese roast duck, crisp roast pork, soya chicken and shreds of jellyfish. From the Chinese-language menu, lamb and beancurd hot-pot was extremely authentic, featuring fatty slices of lamb and a dip of pungent fermented beancurd. Ong choi (water spinach) stir-fried with shrimp paste also wowed us with its crisp taste and intense flavour. Service is friendly and brisk. Almost all our fellow diners were Chinese.

Babies and children welcome: high chairs. Bookings not accepted before 5pm. Disabled: toilet. Separate rooms for parties, seating 40 and 100. Takeaway service.

East
Docklands E14

★ Royal China

30 Westferry Circus, E14 8RR (7719 0888/ www.royalchinagroup.co.uk). Canary Wharf tube/DLR/Westferry DLR. **Meals served** noon-11pm Mon-Thur; noon-11.30pm Fri, Sat; 11am-10pm Sun. **Dim sum served** noon-5pm daily. **Dim sum** £2.20-£4.50. **Main courses** £7-£40. **Set meal** £28-£36 per person (minimum 2). **Service** 13%. **Credit** AmEx, JCB, MC, V.

When we last popped into this beautiful restaurant for dim sum, most guests, as usual, were ethnic Chinese. This is a venue for serious Chinese dining, and its location means you don't find the long queues and hasty atmosphere of other Royal China branches. Staff tend to be polite and nice to children. The dim sum is reliably excellent. Aside from the main menu – crisp sesame prawn rolls, generously stuffed scallop dumplings seasoned

with coriander, creamy turnip paste, delicate cheung fun – the specials are well worth trying. 'Sliced duck and beancurd in special sauce' turned out to be a splendid version of a dish from the Chaozhou region of Guangdong: duck and fried beancurd stewed in a rich aromatic broth, served with a sharp vinegar dip. A more adventurous sweet soup of 'snowfield frog spawn' was an enchanting melee of longans, wolfberries and the gelatinous fat of a special frog from north-eastern China, sweetened with crystal sugar. The view of the Thames through the picture windows is wonderful, and in warm weather you can dine outside. Highly recommended.

Babies and children welcome: high chairs. Booking advisable; essential lunch Mon-Fri. Disabled: toilet. Separate room for parties, seats 40. Tables outdoors (20, terrace). Takeaway service; delivery service (within 1-mile radius).

Shoreditch E1

Drunken Monkey

222 Shoreditch High Street, E1 6PJ (7392 9606/ www.thedrunkenmonkey.co.uk). Liverpool Street tube/rail/35, 47, 242, 344 bus. **Bar Open** noon-midnight Mon-Fri; 6pm-midnight Sat; noon-11pm Sun. *Restaurant* **Meals served** noon-11.30pm Mon-Fri; 6pm-midnight Sat; noon-11.30pm Sun. **Dim sum served** noon-11.30pm Mon-Fri; 6-11.30pm Sat; noon-10.30pm Sun. **Dim sum** £2.50-£4.50. **Main courses** £4.50-£6.50. **Service** 10%. *Both* **Credit** AmEx, MC, V.

For the Chinese, eating dim sum involves drinking tea. But this popular bar near Liverpool Street station proves that it need not be so. The menu quotes one of the best-loved characters in Chinese literature – Monkey in *Journey to the West* – as saying, 'Enjoy yourself, it's later than you think.' And that's certainly what the young City crowd

were doing on the night we visited, washing down their dumplings with copious amounts of beer and exotic cocktails (with names like Oriental Plymms and Shanghai Sling). Red lanterns hang over the bar and a rear dining area, where the funky music and a riotous hen party combined to produce even more noise than you'd find in a giant family teahouse in Hong Kong on a busy Sunday. But the service was good and the food, believe it or not, was just like the real thing. Besides most of the usual dim sum, there are plates of barbecued meats, and rice or noodles to fill up on. Perhaps the Chinese chef used a little more salt than usual, but this is a bar, right?

Babies and children admitted. Booking essential. Entertainment: DJs 8pm Tue-Sun (bar). Separate room for parties, seats 25. Takeaway service; delivery service (noon-5pm Mon-Fri within 2-mile radius on orders over £10). **Map 6 R4**.

North East
Dalston E8

★ Shanghai

41 Kingsland High Street, E8 2JS (7254 2878). Dalston Kingsland rail/67, 76, 149 bus. **Meals served** noon-11pm, **dim sum served** noon-5pm daily. **Dim sum** £2-£3.90. **Main courses** £5.20-£7.20. **Set meal** £12.90-£14.90 per person (minimum 2). **Credit** AmEx, MC, V.

If you feel like a rest after the rigours of Ridley Road market, try this elegantly refurbished former eel and pie shop just across the street. It's a cool, quiet haven, where friendly staff serve authentic shanghai dumplings and other dim sum delights throughout the day (happy hour 3-5pm). Highly recommended are the chicken and chive pot-sticker dumplings (steamed, then fried until slightly crispy on one side) and the softer scallop

Interview
SIMON TANG

RESTAURANTS

Who are you?
Manager of **Imperial China** (*see p67*) in Chinatown.

Which are your favourite London restaurants?
Because I eat dim sum every day for lunch in my restaurant, I prefer Japanese food on the rare occasions when I go out. **Zuma** (*see p183*) is a personal favourite.

What's your favourite Chinese dish?
Battered prawns stir-fried with salted duck-egg yolk.

And your favourite British dish?
Roast beef with roast potatoes and yorkshire pudding. I love potatoes.

What do you think about Chinese food in London?
Hakkasan (*see p69*) has raised the profile of Chinese food, remodelling traditional dishes in a Western way, using fine ingredients and charging higher prices. Chinese food isn't any longer about 'chop suey', cheap filling food to go with your beer; people realise they can go to a Chinese restaurant for a nice evening meal.

What do you think about your non-Chinese customers?
They are becoming more adventurous in their tastes – especially regular customers. We are able to persuade them to go beyond the tried-and-tested dishes like lemon chicken and sweet-and-sour pork. As they become more confident they are surprised to find Chinese food so varied and healthy.

Any tips for non-Chinese diners who want to make the most of Chinese food in London?
Eat dim sum for lunch – you can try lots of different dishes, and it's never boring. Ask your waiter for recommendations. I don't mean you need to eat chicken's feet: just get beyond the sweet-and-sours. And try some delicious, simple Chinese vegetables like gai lan or choi sum stir-fried with ginger.

dumplings in spinach juice pastry. Also good were the shanghai steamed buns, though the pork was a touch fatty. Stir-fried turnip paste contains egg, pork and beansprouts, all mashed together with XO sauce (made from dried scallops, prawns and chillies). For a bit of green vegetable on the side, you couldn't do better than the tender yet crunchy stir-fried gai lan (chinese broccoli) and ginger. Or, if you want a quick meal-in-one, try a rice-pot, such as chicken and chinese sausage – a bargain at £3.90. In the evening, the rooms at the back can get almost as loud and lively as the market; there's even a 'karaoke set meal'.
Babies and children welcome: high chairs. Booking advisable. Disabled: toilet. Separate rooms for parties, both seating 45. Takeaway service. Vegetarian menu. **Map 25 B5**.

North
Swiss Cottage NW3

★ China Red NEW
O₂ Centre, 255 Finchley Road, NW3 6LU (7435 6888/www.chinaredrestaurant.com). Finchley Road tube. **Meals served** noon-11pm daily. **Main courses** £8.50-£13.50. **Set lunch** (noon-5pm Mon-Fri) £7 2 courses. **Set meal** £16-£28 (minimum 2). **Service** 10%. **Credit** AmEx, JCB, MC, V.
The setting – a capacious room in the O₂ shopping centre at tyre-height to Finchley Road traffic – may lack appeal, but China Red deserves attention. Both its exciting dim sum and its full menus are geared as much to local Chinese as weary shoppers, and execution is of a high order. Take the sensational steamed beef and pineapple dumplings in 'butterfly shape': tender morsels of meat, their flavour skilfully enhanced by almost imperceptible fragments of pineapple and juicy cubes of pepper, wrapped in translucent pastry wittily embellished with tentacle-like stalks of chive. Or the exquisite fresh pasta and flavoursome stock in the 'large prawn and meat dumplings in soup'. We have nothing but praise too for the 'stuffed bamboo web with meat' (delicate bamboo pith fungus wrapped around the meatiest of mushrooms, ham and chicken) and 'deep-fried rice paper with mango flavour rolls' (mango enhancing sweet minced prawns). Only the wizened stuffed beancurd rolls disappointed. The full menu holds such intrigues as foie gras wrapped with prawn paste, to be followed by lobster, sea bass or one of many stir-fries. Staff flit purposefully over the light wooden floor, most with kindly intent. China Red is linked to Imperial China (*see p67*).
Babies and children welcome: high chairs. Disabled: toilet. No-smoking tables. Takeaway service. Vegetarian menu. **Map 28 A/B3**.

North West
Belsize Park NW3

Weng Wah House
240 Haverstock Hill, NW3 2AE (7794 5123/www.wengwahgroup.com). Belsize Park tube/168, 268, C11 bus. **Lunch served** 12.30-2.45pm, **dinner served** 6-11.30pm Mon-Fri. **Meals served** 12.30pm-midnight Sat; 12.30-11.15pm Sun. **Main courses** £5.30-£9.90. **Set lunch** £4.95 2 courses. **Set meal** £12.50-£18.50 per person (minimum 2). **Service** 10%. **Credit** JCB, MC, V.
Local Chinese come here, but most avoid the restaurant in preference to the first-floor karaoke; ground-floor evening diners (monied couples and families) are treated to the muffled fruits of their labours. Service is obliging. There's little natural light, but crisp table linen, art on the walls and two illuminated fish tanks create pleasing environs. On each trip we reach the same conclusion: order classic Chinese dishes and you'll be happy; order 'modern interpretations' and you'll be let down. Most appetisers are thirst-inducing deep-fries. Best was peking ravioli with chilli oil: boiled dumplings encasing a fresh prawn, doused in a fierce garlicky sauce. Next, spinach in preserved beancurd was luscious and pungent, going well with the gloriously fatty duck in the 'special barbecue

combination' (which also featured moist steamed chicken, but tough barbecued pork). Best forgotten, though, was a 'signature dish' of salted egg seafood with enoki mushrooms: bedraggled fungi, barely discernible egg, decent scallop and prawn segments (what a waste) and diced veg (mostly sweetcorn). It looked like something you might tread in outside a pub. Still, free appetisers (nuts, prawn crackers) and desserts (exotic fruit salad) ensure most regulars leave content.
Babies and children welcome: high chairs. Booking advisable dinner. Entertainment: Chinese Elvis and karaoke (call for details). Separate room for parties, seats 70-80. Takeaway service. Vegetarian menu. **Map 28 C4**.
For branch see index.

Golders Green NW11

Local Friends
28 North End Road, NW11 7PT (8455 9258). Golders Green tube. **Meals served** noon-11pm, **dim sum served** noon-10pm daily. **Dim sum** £2.10-£5. **Main courses** £5.50-£8. **Set meal** £11-£19 per person (minimum 2). **Service** 10%. **Credit** AmEx, JCB, MC, V.
The Yauatcha effect has spread to Golders Green, where Local Friends has bucked up its act. So, dim sum are now served until 10pm (virtually unheard of before Alan Yau's trend-setter opened); the list has grown to include several unusual snacks; and the decor has been spruced up with the addition of a blond wood floor (though you'll still find the same crinkly white walls, Chinese pictures, and large windows overlooking the Hippodrome in the modest interior). We concentrated on the dim sum newcomers and can heartily recommend the fried garlic aubergine dumplings (little resilient pieces of eggplant in a pancake-like covering). This came from the alluring vegetarian dim sum list, as did a bland yet interesting stuffed courgette with slightly chewy minced beancurd. Overcooking is a problem, giving har gau a gluey coat and the sesame seed balls a congealed interior. Still, service is sweet (though diners were sparse during a midweek lunch) and new pzazz has been added to lunchtime dim sum. The full menu is workaday in comparison, shredded duck with preserved vegetables being among the more unusual dishes.
Babies and children welcome: high chairs. Booking advisable weekends. Separate room for parties, seats 45. Takeaway service. Vegetarian menu.

St John's Wood NW8

★ Royal China
68 Queen's Grove, NW8 6ER (7586 4280/www.royalchinagroup.co.uk). St John's Wood tube. **Meals served** noon-11pm Mon-Sat; 11am-10pm Sun. **Dim sum served** noon-4.45pm Mon-Sat; 11am-4.45pm Sun. **Dim sum** £2.20-£4.50. **Main courses** £6-£50. **Set lunch** (noon-5pm Mon-Fri) £14 2 courses. **Set dinner** £28-£36 per person (minimum 2). **Service** 13%. **Credit** AmEx, MC, V.
This simple building next to Lord's Cricket Ground gives few outward signs of the delights within. The interior is gilded and lacquered like a Chinese jewel box; treasures are brought from the kitchen by Chinese waitresses wearing smart tunics. The dim sum were as classy as ever. Prawn dumplings, both fried and steamed, were freshly made and models of their kind. Turnip paste was firm on the outside, creamy within, and delicately speckled with wind-dried meats. And the baomiu (beansprout leaves) were stir-fried to perfection with garlic. We also visited for dinner – everything was of a high standard, though perhaps not as notable as the dim sum. Lotus leaf rice was rich with morsels of scallops, duck meat and prawns in its fried rice filling. 'Mixed seafood spicy' also used generous amounts of scallops and other expensive ingredients, plus crunchy shards of bamboo shoot, served in a sizzling dish. Ma po tofu had perfect cubes of beancurd so delicate and slithery they required dexterity with chopsticks to eat, but the moreish sauce, containing minced pork, made it worth the challenge. But don't stray into the set meals, where dishes descend into mediocrity. Service was smooth, and like the glass walls of the private rooms, required no further polishing.

Royal China Docklands. See p75.

Babies and children welcome: high chairs. Booking advisable dinner Mon-Fri; bookings not accepted Sat, lunch Sun. Separate rooms for parties, seating 14 and 21. Takeaway service. **Map 28 A5**.

Outer London
Harrow, Middlesex

★ Golden Palace
146-150 Station Road, Harrow, Middx HA1 2RH (8863 2333). Harrow-on-the-Hill tube/rail. **Meals served** noon-11.30pm Mon-Sat; 11am-10.30pm Sun. **Dim sum served** noon-5pm Mon-Sat; 11am-5pm Sun. **Dim sum** £2.20-£3.20. **Main courses** £5.20-£7.50. **Set meal** £18-£24.50 per person (minimum 2). **Service** 10%. **Credit** AmEx, DC, MC, V.

That Golden Palace was nearly full before midday for Sunday dim sum is testament to its standing among connoisseurs of Cantonese cuisine. A happy mix of diners – many, but not all, Chinese Londoners – populates the two bright modern rooms (spotlights, light wooden flooring, many mirrors) that look on to busy Station Road. Larger parties are treated to big round banqueting tables. The dim sum menu is long and enticing, incorporating various specials (all translated into English), rice and noodle plates, and a vegetarian list. From this, the vegetarian barbecued pork in sweet preserved beancurd was a spongy, dull approximation of the meat version. Yet evidence of great skill was shown in the rest of our order. Highlights included a huge plateful of green leaves and mixed meat ho fun (noodles coated in delectable sesame seed oil, with all manner of meat and seafood titbits), cheung fun with mushroom and chicken (sublime, slithery pasta filled with breast meat and spindly enoki fungi), and exquisitely light baked mini buns with ham, roasted pork and spring onions. Lobster, dover sole and many vegetarian dishes are features of the full menu. Staff are uncommonly approachable, though forgot our custard buns.
Babies and children welcome: high chairs. Booking advisable dinner. Disabled: toilet. Separate rooms for parties, seating 60 and 100. Takeaway service. Vegetarian menu.

Ilford, Essex

★ Mandarin Palace
559-561 Cranbrook Road, Gants Hill, Ilford, Essex IG2 6JZ (8550 7661). Gants Hill tube. **Lunch/dim sum served** noon-4pm, **dinner served** 6.30-11.30pm daily. **Dim sum** £2-£3.80. **Main courses** £2.50-£22. **Set dinner** £19.50-£39 per person (minimum 2). **Service** 10%. **Credit** AmEx, DC, MC, V.

Packed with all manner of vintage chinoiserie, Mandarin Palace continues to grow in popularity as a charming venue with a great line in MSG-free dim sum. Our meal began as usual with complimentary peanuts and pickled cucumber. Our favourite roast pork puff pastries arrived next – small triangles of flaky pastry stuffed with juicy and sweet red pork. King prawn cheung fun was also excellent, with crisp prawns and a light, almost translucent rice wrapper. A new addition to the menu, beef tripe steamed in chilli sauce, delighted us too, as did the crispy seafood croquette of deep-fried tofu stuffed with mouth-watering prawn and crab. Shanghai dumplings failed to excite, though: the filling was moist but bereft of the trademark stock. Sesame oil blighted a plate of otherwise excellent har gau (prawn dumplings). A generous helping of spicy beef brisket noodle soup filled us up, before the complimentary watermelon. At night, a rather dated menu of mainstream choices is now supplemented by a lengthy list of intriguing chef's specials. Fresh fruit juice is available alongside a well-chosen range of wine. Service is friendly and attentive.
Babies and children welcome: high chairs. No-smoking tables. Separate room for parties, seats 30. Takeaway service; delivery service (within 2-mile radius). Vegetarian menu.
For branch see index.

East European

These days, if you go to a London restaurant – be it Italian, Middle Eastern or Turkish – chances are you'll find a Polish waitress or two. However, the increased number of staff from Poland since the European Union was enlarged in 2004 hasn't been accompanied by an explosion in the number of places offering central or eastern European cuisine. For a while now, London has had the gamut of good Polish venues, from simple cafés to glam 'destination' restaurants like **Baltic**. Go for a calorie-fest of pierogi and potato pancakes served by no-nonsense motherly types at **Daquise**, opt for the light touch and modern vibe of **Wódka** or try trad but imaginative **Zamoyski**.

On the Russian front, we think there's still much room for improvement. **Potemkin** scores with some people, but lacked soul for us; many other restaurants are a bit heavy-handed. If you want formal, old-school glamour, there's still no beating the Hungarian **Gay Hussar**. Excellent (and still relatively undiscovered) Georgian outfit **Tbilisi** offers exotic new taste experiences for the uninitiated – though we're sorry to see the departure of equally reliable **Little Georgia** in Hackney. As for vodka bars, you can't do better than unpretentious **Na Zdrowie**, which serves good simple food to soak up all the vodka and beer.

ARMENIAN

South West
Gloucester Road SW7

Jakob's
20 Gloucester Road, SW7 4RB (7581 9292). Gloucester Road tube. **Meals served** 8am-10pm Mon-Sat; 8am-5pm Sun. **Main courses** £6.50-£11. **Credit** AmEx, MC, V.

Jakob's is an eclectic place, a successful deli with a sizeable café attached. Its dual function leads to a degree of chaos. You're supposed to occupy a table, order drinks from a waitress, but order food at the counter: a recipe for mayhem on a busy Saturday lunchtime. There's a choice of hot dishes such as lasagne, spinach and filo pie or Armenian-style dolma with two vegetables, but the highlight is the extensive range of ultra-fresh salads. These include an excellent combo of grilled veg, rice and lentils, tabouleh, and cumin-spiced shredded carrot, among others. The owner is Armenian – evidenced by a

charming hotchpotch of knick-knacks, and pictures of shepherds tending their flocks. The food is reliable and tasty, but not particularly Armenian these days. Other bright spots are the freshly squeezed juices, own-made lemonade and some great cakes (we tried the rich Russian chocolate and organic lemon varieties with a good strong cappuccino). Wine is also served. Jakob's is a decent local haunt with friendly and amenable staff who made the child in our party very welcome, but it's a bit pricey for what it is.
Babies and children welcome: high chairs. Booking advisable. No smoking. Tables outside (2, pavement). Takeaway service; delivery service. **Map 7 C9.**

GEORGIAN

North
Holloway N7

★ ★ Tbilisi
91 Holloway Road, N7 8LT (7607 2536). Highbury & Islington tube/rail. **Dinner served** 6.30-11.30pm daily. **Main courses** £6.95-£8.45. **Credit** AmEx, MC, V.
The fact we were the only diners throughout our thoroughly satisfying evening at Tbilisi was mystifying. With its edge of exoticism, excellent ingredients, charming service and exceptionally fair prices, north Londoners should be flocking here. Dark wooden furniture, a few Georgian paintings and folksy artefacts against dark red walls, subtle lighting – all create a relaxed atmosphere. With so many must-try dishes, it's a relief that starters come in sets, named after regions of Georgia. Our Imereti featured spicy walnut, spinach and aubergine salads. Most include khachapuri (soft yeasty bread filled with light crumbly cheese) or a beany alternative. Walnuts turned up again in chicken satsivi (served at room temperature with ghomi, a sort of polenta). Georgian cookery's generous use of herbs leads to an intensity of flavour demonstrated in dishes such as chakapuli, a robust lamb stew resonating with tarragon and coriander. Our Georgian house white (Tamada Mtsvane) was very easy to drink. A Georgian friend has quibbled about the authenticity of some dishes, but Tbilisi's light touch suited us very well. One of our favourites.
Babies and children admitted. Booking advisable Fri, Sat. Restaurant available for hire. Separate room for parties, seats 40.

HUNGARIAN

Central
Soho W1

Gay Hussar
2 Greek Street, W1D 4NB (7437 0973). Tottenham Court Road tube. **Lunch served** 12.15-2.30pm, **dinner served** 5.30-10.45pm Mon-Sat. **Main courses** £9.50-£16.50. **Set lunch** £16.50 2 courses, £18.50 3 courses. **Service** 12.5%. **Credit** AmEx, DC, JCB, MC, V.
We awaited our night at the Gay Hussar with great anticipation, hoping to spot familiar MPs in hot debate at this favourite political haunt, but it was not to be. Instead, we satisfied ourselves with perusing the walls, full of caricatures of Westminster worthies. The decor and service, both classically old-fashioned and timelessly charming, lend a sense of occasion to a meal here. The menu brims with tongue-twisting Hungarian dishes, while an extensive wine list has Hungarian bottles to suit most pockets (among them an eminently drinkable Disznoko Furmint). Starters include a delicate fish terrine, and marinated herring fillets (served with a pepper salad and soured cream). Our robust mains of stuffed cabbage parcels in a tomatoey sauce, and tender beef fillets on a bed of seriously spicy peppers and fried potatoes, were both relatively simple dishes extremely well executed. To finish, we relished the walnut pancakes: tooth-achingly sweet, but delicious. A new date, an elderly relative or a business companion would all be impressed by the Gay Hussar. Long may it continue.
Babies and children welcome: children's portions; high chairs. Book dinner. Separate rooms for parties, seating 12 and 24. **Map 17 K6.**

POLISH

Central
Holborn WC1

★ Na Zdrowie The Polish Bar
11 Little Turnstile, WC1V 7DX (7831 9679). Holborn tube. **Open** 12.30-11pm Mon-Fri; 6-11pm Sat. **Meals served** 12.30-10pm Mon-Fri; 6-10pm Sat. **Main courses** £5-£7. **Credit** MC, V.

We come back time and again to Na Zdrowie, whether for lunch, after work drinks with a crowd or a good chinwag with a friend. The distressed yellow decor with silver Polish eagles, an eclectic music mix, and helpful staff create a good vibe from the start. This is a small space so can get pretty busy, but earlier in the week you can usually get a table (some low, some high with bar stools) once the after-office crowd have left. You'll also find more than 60 delectable vodkas and a choice of eight Polish beers. The vodka menu is carefully described, and divided into 'dry and interesting', 'nice and sweet', and 'clean and clear'. There are even three kosher varieties. We particularly liked our almond Wyborowa, dry, woody Siwucha and the less common Kminkowa (caraway seed). If you fancy a variation on standard beer, order your Zywiec, Tyskie, Lech and so on with a shot of raspberry syrup: delicious. Excellent simple Polish food is also served: a great peppery barszcz with wild-mushroom uszki; melt-in the mouth herring and beetroot salad; crunchy potato pancakes, and more – all very fresh. To your health, *na zdrowie!*
Bookings not accepted. Tables outdoors (3, pavement). Takeaway service. **Map 18 L5.**

West
Bayswater W2

Antony's
54 Porchester Road, W2 6ET (7243 8743/ www.antonysrestaurant.com). Royal Oak tube. **Dinner served** 6-11pm Mon-Sat. **Main courses** £7.50-£13.80. **Cover** 70p. **Credit** MC, V.
Antony's is blessed with a charming hostess who radiates warmth to both newcomers and regulars. Coupled with high-quality, unpretentious but well-presented food, this makes for a great local. We love the friendly informal/formal mix: starched tablecloths, gleaming cutlery and an authentic Middle European feel, helped along by rich red walls, velvet curtains and jazzy music. Traditional Polish fare shares the menu with steaks and seafood. A well-executed rich, slightly peppery and intensely beetrooty barszcz wowed our Hungarian companion; a smoked-salmon timbale with frizzled leeks also hit the spot. Typical Polish mains include kotlet schabowy and zrazy, but being so spoiled for choice with starters, we opted for two more of these – toothsome potato pancakes with mushroom sauce (crunchy on the outside, moist within) and meltingly tender herrings with onion. Chicken and spinach parcels didn't shine quite so much, unlike the accompanying veg: sautéed potato, tomatoey cabbage and coarsely grated beetroot. With no room for the delectable naleśniki (pancakes) or cheesecake, we settled for cherry and honey vodkas. All this at exceptionally good prices, including a decent house wine.
Babies and children welcome: high chairs. Booking advisable weekends. Restaurant available for hire. **Map 7 C5.**

Ealing W5

★ Café Grove
65 The Grove, W5 5LL (8810 0364). Ealing Broadway tube/rail. **Meals served** 11am-11pm Mon-Sat; 11am-10.30pm Sun. **Main courses** £5-£7.50. **Credit** MC, V.
In a hidden-away parade of half a dozen shops and a pub, Café Grove is the epitome of a decent local, providing a useful array of services to the residents of nearby Victorian terraces, several of whom are Poles. Come here for breakfast (full English, or continental), a drink (there are five Polish bottled beers, eight Polish vodkas, plus a short wine list), a coffee and a perusal of the artworks (displayed on the plain turquoise walls of the simple little interior), a sandwich or salad snack – or a full Polish meal. Soups are superlative, whether you're sampling the complex sweet and savoury flavours of the borscht served with ushka, or perhaps a special of creamy cucumber soup with mushrooms. To follow, we considered the blackboard special of golonka ('it's greasy, it's nice,' beamed our charming Polish waitress), but instead chose bigos: the sauerkraut blessed with

Na Zdrowie

RESTAURANTS

BAVO

authentic mediterranean cuisine

THE BEST TURKISH RESTAURANT IN ISLINGTON

A superb modern restaurant, Bavo is dedicated to offering serious 'well cooked' food in stylish surroundings with quality service.

BAVO
AUTHENTIC MEDITERRANEAN CUISINE
- 105-107 Southgate Road • Islington • N1 3JS •
- Tel: 02072260334 • info@bavo-restaurant.co.uk •
- BR: Essex Road • www.bavo-restaurant.co.uk •

"A superb modern restaurant, Bavo is dedicated to offering serious 'well cooked' food with an emphasis on freshness and a great quality of service".
www.togolondon.co.uk

"It was the main course that really hit the spot. My friend tucked into the Bavo charcoal kebab special (£12.50) a meat-eater's feast, combining lamb, chicken, meatballs and quail, while I went for the stunningly tasty monkfish."
The Islington Gazette, Tom Mackenzie

Experience the magic of authentic mediterranean cusine

The restaurant where customers recommend their friends

Bavo is at your service with its decoration and cuisine. A delicious breeze from the mediterranean. We have combined the rich culture and taste of our traditional Mediterranean cuisine in an authentic atmosphere.

An excellent service awaits you at Bavo Restaurant, where one can choose from a rich menu of traditional Mediterranean cuisine.

Capable of catering for up to 80 people we have a large spacious environment, that suits the most demanding of clientelle. We also specialise in private parties, and all other functions.

The perfect slick and stylish restaurant to bring a date.

the flavours of juniper and smoked sausage, but made a touch prosaic by the addition of three scoops of mash. Cheesecake was partially moist (wonderful), partially dry (tongue-furring). The bill for an enjoyable three-courser for two with wine and service: just £32.

Babies and children admitted. Book Sat, Sun. Separate room for parties, seats 30. Tables outside (2, pavement). Takeaway service.

Hammersmith W6

Lowiczanka Polish Cultural Centre

First floor, 238-246 King Street, W6 0RF (8741 3225). Ravenscourt Park tube.
Café **Open** 9.30am-9pm daily.
Bar/restaurant **Lunch served** 12.30-3pm daily. **Dinner served** 6.30-11pm Mon-Thur, Sun; 7pm-midnight Fri, Sat. **Main courses** £7.30-£14.50. **Set lunch** £8.50 3 courses.
Both **Credit** AmEx, MC, V.

The long-established Polish Centre on King Street is proof of west London's sizeable Polish community; inside the unappealing concrete building is a bookshop, tourist office, art gallery, café and, on the first floor, Lowiczanka restaurant. The decor and vibe is reminiscent of a 1970s hotel eaterie with its anonymous decor, squeaky dance floor and soundtrack of cheesy east European takes on western pop songs. Unfashionable, certainly, but with an unassuming, homely air. Head for the Polish specialities on the menu. We started with bright-tasting barszcz with mushroom dumplings, and succulent herring with chopped onions and an oil and lemon dressing. Flavours are robust, portions hearty: a main of potato pancakes with a rich filling of mushrooms and tender cubed beef, topped with two dollops of sour cream, would have fed two. Other dishes were mixed: plump golabki in tomato sauce were satisfying, but spinach pancakes with dill were rather one-dimensional in flavour. The lone Polish waiter was friendly and efficient, advising on vodka and the best kind of Polish beer to drink. We finished with honey vodka (on the house) and desserts of cheesecake (rather dry) and good makowiec (poppyseed strudel).

Babies and children welcome: high chairs. Book lunch Sat, Sun. Disabled: toilet. Entertainment: gypsy band 8pm-midnight Fri-Sun. No-smoking tables. Separate rooms for parties, seating 60 and 200. Tables outdoors (5, patio). Takeaway service (café). Vegetarian menu. Vegan dishes. **Map 20 A1**.

★ Polanka

258 King Street, W6 0SP (8741 8268).
Ravenscourt Park tube. **Meals served** noon-10pm Mon-Sat; noon-8pm Sun. **Main courses** £4-£7.50. **Unlicensed. Corkage** £1 wine; £5 spirits. **Credit** AmEx, MC, V.

Polanka doubles as a deli and restaurant. The deli counter at the front sells cakes, meats and foodstuffs from the old country, while out back the small, brightly lit restaurant serves homely Polish cooking. The yellow walls are adorned with colourful knick-knacks, service is friendly and the feeling is laid-back and casual. The lengthy menu includes lots of traditional dishes, plus seasonal specials – on our summer visit, fruit-filled pierogi, barszcz and pyzy. We opted for the latter – small, rotund, steamed potato dumplings, topped with cubes of fried bacon. A massive serving of herring in sour cream was rather heavy on the cream, but the salty fish had a firm texture. Mixed pierogi (wild mushroom and sauerkraut, cheese and onion, and meat fillings) featured a generous plate of plump half-moons, the edges neatly pleated like a 1950s skirt, served with a side of sour cream. We managed (just) to find room for a house speciality, zbojnicki pancake: a potato pancake filled with goulash, topped with cheese, then grilled. The flavours of pork, sour cream, dill and potato were inimitably, perfectly Polish. Portion sizes are big, so bring an appetite. The bill, however, is likely to be surprisingly small.

Babies and children welcome: high chairs. Booking advisable. No-smoking tables. Separate room for parties, seats 8. Takeaway service. **Map 20 A1**.

Menu

Dishes followed by (Cz) indicate a Czech dish; (G) Georgian; (H) Hungarian; (P) Polish; (R) Russian; (Uk) Ukrainian. Others have no particular affiliation.

Bigos (P): hunter's stew made with sauerkraut, various meats and sausage, mushrooms and juniper.
Blini: yeast-leavened pancake made from buckwheat flour, traditionally served smothered in butter and sour cream; **blinchiki** are mini blinis.
Borscht: classic beetroot soup. There are many varieties: Ukrainian borscht is thick with vegetables; the Polish version (**barszcz**) is clear. There are also white and green types. Often garnished with sour cream, boiled egg or little dumplings.
Caviar: fish roe. Most highly prized is that of the sturgeon (**beluga, oscietra** and **sevruga**, in descending order of expense), though **keta** or salmon caviar is underrated.
Chlodnik (P): cold beetroot soup, shocking pink in colour, served with sour cream.
Coulebiac (R): see koulebiaka.
Galabki, golabki or **golubtsy**: cabbage parcels, usually stuffed with rice or kasha (qv) and sometimes meat.
Golonka (P): pork knuckle, often cooked in beer.
Goulash or **gulasz (H)**: rich beef soup.
Kasha or **kasza**: buckwheat, delicious roasted: light and fluffy with a nutty flavour.
Kaszanka (P): blood sausage made with buckwheat.
Khachapuri (G): flatbread; sometimes called Georgian pizza.
Knedliky (Cz): bread dumplings.
Kolduny (P): small meat-filled dumplings (scaled-down pierogi, qv) often served in beetroot soup.

Kotlet schabowy (P): breaded pork chops.
Koulebiaka or **kulebiak (R)**: layered salmon or sturgeon pie with eggs, dill, rice and mushrooms.
Krupnik (P): barley soup, and the name of a honey vodka (because of the golden colour of barley).
Latke: grated potato pancakes, fried.
Makowiec or **makietki (P)**: poppy-seed cake.
Mizeria (P): cucumber salad; very thinly sliced and dressed with sour cream.
Nalesniki (P): cream cheese pancakes.
Paczki (P): doughnuts, often filled with plum jam.
Pelmeni (R): Siberian-style ravioli dumplings.
Pierogi (P): ravioli-style dumplings. Typical fillings are sauerkraut and mushroom, curd cheese or fruit (cherries, apples).
Pirogi (large) or **pirozhki (small) (R)**: filled pies made with yeasty dough.
Placki (P): potato pancakes.
Shashlik: Caucasian spit-roasted meat (usually lamb).
Shchi (R): soup made from sauerkraut.
Stroganoff (R): beef slices, served in a rich sour cream and mushroom sauce.
Surowka (P): salad made of raw shredded vegetables.
Ushka or **uszka**: small ear-shaped dumplings served in soup.
Vareniki (Uk): Ukrainian version of pierogi (qv).
Zakuski (R) or **zakaski (P)**: starters, traditionally covering a whole table. The many dishes can include pickles, marinated vegetables and fish, herring, smoked eel, aspic, mushrooms, radishes with butter, salads and caviar.
Zrazy (P): beef rolls stuffed with bacon, pickled cucumber and mustard.
Zurek (P): sour rye soup.

Kensington W8

★ Wódka

12 St Alban's Grove, W8 5PN (7937 6513/ www.wodka.co.uk). High Street Kensington tube.
Lunch served noon-3pm Mon-Fri. **Dinner served** 6.30-11.15pm daily. **Main courses** £10.90-£14.50. **Set lunch** £11.50 2 courses, £14.50 3 courses. **Service** 12.5%. **Credit** AmEx, MC, V.

Wódka – the less showy, calmer, older and smaller sister of Baltic (*see p83*) – was opened by Jan Woroniecki in 1989 and has remained a favourite ever since. Two medium-sized rooms enable intimate service, emphasised by Stan, the portly terrier who greets new arrivals. The place has an upmarket, minimalist look with dark wood and distressed, semi-industrial decor, yet is softened by candles and imaginative lighting. The menu is an adventurous mix of eastern and Modern European dishes: eel in honey and onion sauce with capers juggled a complex set of flavours perfectly; beetroot-marinated gravadlax was simply beautiful, with a subtle taste. Robust mains of char-grilled rump of lamb on a bed of aubergine and carrot salad (said to be Georgian); and braised rabbit with peas, boczek (bacon), sauerkraut and lazanki (a sort of pasta) – were both superlative. Our only quibble was with the chef's promiscuity with the rocket garnish, which has no place in such earthy dishes. Polish puds such as nalesniki (pancakes with sweet cheese), and white chocolate

sernik (cheesecake) vie for attention. There's a good international wine list and a fine choice of vodkas, including own-flavoured versions like caramel and blackcurrant. Staff make a mean vodka cocktail.

Babies and children admitted. Booking advisable. Separate room for parties, seats 30. Tables outdoors (3, pavement). **Map 7 C9**.

Shepherd's Bush W12

★ Patio

5 Goldhawk Road, W12 8QQ (8743 5194). Goldhawk Road tube. **Lunch served** noon-3pm Mon-Fri. **Dinner served** 6-11.30pm daily. **Main courses** £7.50-£9. **Set meal** £14.90 3 courses incl vodka shot. **Credit** AmEx, DC, JCB, MC, V.

Patio is a long-time favourite for home-style cooking. With its slightly faded, fin-de-siècle air, piano and velvet drapes, the place reminds us of an elderly Krakow aunt's apartment, incongruously displaced to the noisy Goldhawk Road. The similarities soon fade, though, once you've been greeted and seated by the warm-hearted Polish owner. The set menu (£14.90 for three courses including complimentary vodka, pre-dessert fruit and coconut cake) is still a great bargain. Starters include potato pancakes, herrings, bigos, a good peppery barszcz, and smoked salmon blini (the latter, an unorthodox deep-fried, torpedo-shaped version, was too dense). Beef gulasz, duck and chicken are among the main courses, but we chose cod in dill sauce, and Polish sausage à la zamoyski (grilled with onions, served with mustard and horseradish). Both were OK, but – like the accompanying red cabbage, roast potatoes, green cabbage with carrots, and surowki (grated raw vegetable salad) – didn't zing with the usual freshness. Puddings include pancakes, fruit and szarlotka (apple cake). Our shared Polish cheesecake was tasty, but not as dense and crumbly as expected. Patio was slightly lacklustre this time, but at these prices we can't be too picky. *Book dinner Fri, Sat. No-smoking tables. Separate room for parties, seats 45. Takeaway service.* **Map 20 C2.**

South West
South Kensington SW7

Daquise
20 Thurloe Street, SW7 2LP (7589 6117). South Kensington tube. **Meals served** noon-11pm daily. **Set lunch** (noon-3pm Mon-Fri) £7.50 2 courses incl glass of wine and coffee. **Credit** MC, V.
A South Ken institution, Daquise has been feeding no-nonsense Polish home cooking to students, tourists, Polish émigrés and lucky locals for over 50 years. The 1970s decor (Formica and leatherette banquettes) is far from depressing, having a cosy, lived-in feel. On a midweek evening the place was heaving with a happy, buzzing crowd. No cool, stylish Polish waiting staff here: instead you'll find more homely types, serving unreconstructed dishes that are all the better for it. Our barszcz with uszka (little dumplings) was vibrantly beetrooty. Blini

with smoked salmon was superb: puffy and light, with a delicious nuttiness from the buckwheat flour. Oblivious to the calories piling up, we worked our way through Russian zrazy (stuffed minced meat roll) with more fluffy roasted buckwheat (kazsa gryczana) and beetroot with horseradish. A mixed Polish platter of potato pancakes, pierogi, golabki and bigos also shone with authenticity. We drank Polish beer and finished up with vodka. For those with gargantuan appetites there's a fine selection of trad pancakes, cheesecakes, apple cake and so on. Low prices, a central location and boundless character – what more can you ask? *Babies and children admitted. Booking advisable. No-smoking tables. Separate room for parties, seats 25.* **Map 14 E10.**

Ognisko Polskie
55 Exhibition Road, Prince's Gate, SW7 2PN (7589 4635/www.ognisko.com). South Kensington tube. *Bar* **Open** noon-11pm daily. *Restaurant* **Lunch served** 12.30-3pm, **dinner served** 6.30-11pm daily. **Main courses** £9-£14. **Set meal** £11 3 courses. *Both* **Credit** AmEx, DC, MC, V.
Ognisko Polskie ('Polish Hearth Club'), located on the ground floor of a grand Kensington residence, started life as a meeting place for Poles in London during World War II. The night we visited, the only Poles in evidence were the waiting staff. Ognisko has a timeless feel, but isn't purely retro. The pink walls, red drapes and pillars have a slightly spare, stylish look despite being adorned with gilt-framed portraits of British royals and the like. The menu is no longer very Polish. Barszcz is offered, along with buckwheat blinis with smoked salmon (large,

rather soggy affairs, but tasty nonetheless), but our favourite starter was a scrumptious warm salad of sautéed prawns and boczek (bacon) with asparagus. Mains didn't excite: fillet of beef 'Czartoryski-style', served on rösti with caramelised onions, was drowned in a very sweet sauce; guinea fowl was dry, but came with excellent red cabbage. The accompanying mixed vegetables were very dull indeed. Things were rescued by an excellent sweet cheese pancake in orange sauce. Although the food wasn't that special, the calm atmosphere and the friendly but proper service won us over. *Babies and children welcome: children's portions; high chair. Booking advisable. Separate room for parties, seats 150. Tables outdoors (10, terrace).* **Map 14 D9.**

South
Clapham SW4

Café Wanda
153 Clapham High Street, SW4 7SS (7738 8760). Clapham Common tube. **Meals served** noon-11pm Mon-Fri; 11am-11pm Sat; 11am-7pm Sun. **Main courses** £4.95-£13.95. **Credit** AmEx, MC, V.
Unpretentious, family-friendly Café Wanda stands out on Clapham High Street for its versatility. It has a reliable, relaxed and refreshingly outmoded air compared to its neighbours. And whether you fancy hearty Polish fare, a sweet treat from the mouth-watering pâtisserie, English breakfast served on wooden platters or pizza, it's difficult to escape unsatiated. There's streetside seating too. During the day, choice but unobtrusive tunes soothe in the background; at night, candles and a

Baltic

piano crooner or similar provide a more intimate vibe. The excellent borscht (as listed on the menu, although more Polish barszcz, really) is clear, light, spicy and comes with a pirogi-style 'croquette'. Meat lovers can tuck into generous portions of stuffed beef rolls, pork knuckle or deep-fried meat dumplings – all genuine and filling, rather than culinary masterpieces. The huge blinis with smoked salmon is a favourite with regulars. Top-notch flavoured vodkas are also worth a tipple. The large cappuccinos and devilish array of cream-tastic creations, Belgian chocolates and Italian ice-creams can leave you struggling to get out of your seat, or tempt you in on a miserable day.
Babies and children admitted. Booking advisable weekends. Entertainment: pianist 8.30-11pm Sat (phone for details). Tables outdoors (3, pavement). Takeaway service. Vegetarian menu. **Map 22 B2.**

Waterloo SE1

★ Baltic
74 Blackfriars Road, SE1 8HA (7928 1111/ www.balticrestaurant.co.uk). Southwark tube.
Bar **Open/snacks served** noon-11pm Mon-Sat; noon-10.30pm Sun.
Restaurant **Lunch served** noon-3pm Mon-Sat. **Dinner served** 6-11.15pm Mon-Sat. **Meals served** noon-10.30pm Sun. **Main courses** £9-£15.50. **Set meal** (noon-3pm, 6-7pm) £11.50 2 courses, £13.50 3 courses. **Service** 12.5%.
Both **Credit** AmEx, DC, MC, V.
Baltic on a hot night had major underfloor heating problems. Huge ceiling fans whirring to combat sweltering temperatures sent menus flying. Apologetic staff could have done more to

compensate; our requests for water and ice were frequently forgotten. The glam vibe and stunning design shone through nonetheless; high ceilings, exposed red brickwork (a potentially noisy combination), and thousands of amber shards aglow in the spectacular chandelier aptly reference Baltic-style à la Gdansk. Food is a modern take on trad central and east European cuisine and ingredients. A starter of vivid saffron-marinated halibut and beetroot- and vodka-cured salmon was a treat for the eyes and taste buds, but blini came with the dullest of herrings. A perfect hunk of roast cod arrived with delicate lemon dumplings and wild mushrooms; roast duck with red cabbage and apples was just right. Afterwards, vodka cherry ice-cream with chocolate sauce was irresistible. A wide range of vodkas includes own-made infusions like ginger and dill, and there's a great cocktail list; Tsar's Toast (with Russkii Standart, fresh ginger, apple juice and champagne) did it for us. The wow factor of the decor is indisputable, kitchen standards generally good, but a little more care in the service would be nice.
Babies and children welcome: high chairs. Disabled: toilet. Entertainment: jazz 7pm Sun. Separate room for parties, seats 30. Tables outdoors (6, terrace). **Map 11 O8.**

North

Hampstead NW3

Zamoyski Restaurant & Vodka Bar
85 Fleet Road, NW3 2QY (7794 4792). Hampstead Heath rail/24 bus. **Lunch served** by appointment. **Dinner served** 6.30-11pm Mon; 5.30-11pm Tue-Sun. **Main courses** £7.95-£11.95. **Set meze** £9.95 9 dishes. **Service** 10% for parties of 6 or more. **Credit** AmEx, MC, V.
Zamoyski was quiet the night we visited – in the past we've found it buzzing – but this made for a relaxing evening. Once a pub, the room has dark wooden furniture and red-brick walls softened by candlelight. The bar has a good selection of Polish and Czech bottled beer, or there's a fairly priced international wine list. We like the idea of 'Polish meze': nine dishes including barszcz, bigos, potato pancakes, herring, cheesecake and so on. It's an ideal way of getting to know traditional Polish cooking, and great value at £9.95 per person. From the carte we loved the lightly pan-fried pierogi selection (filled with wild mushroom, meat, curd cheese and sauerkraut and potato) and the delicious placki (potato pancakes) with smoked salmon, sour cream and chives. Mains were equally satisfying: baked pork ribs with meat falling off the bone, and succulent roast beef with fiery horseradish. They came with perfect Polish-style veg: beetroot, red cabbage, carrot salad and rough mashed potato. Portions are generous, so a shared sour cherry pancake was quite enough, though apple cake and cheesecake also looked spot-on. Rounding off the meal with raspberry vodka and Wisniowka cherry vodka, we left happy.
Babies and children admitted. Booking advisable weekends. Entertainment: Russian music 8.30-11pm Sat. No-smoking tables. Separate room for parties, seats 40. **Map 28 C3.**

RUSSIAN

Central

Clerkenwell & Farringdon EC1

Potemkin
144 Clerkenwell Road, EC1R 5DP (7278 6661/ www.potemkin.co.uk). Farringdon tube/rail.
Bar **Open** noon-11pm Mon-Fri; 6-11pm Sat. **Meals served** noon-10.30pm Mon-Fri; 6-10.30pm Sat.
Restaurant **Lunch served** noon-3pm Mon-Fri. **Dinner served** 6-10.30pm Mon-Sat. **Set lunch** £10 2 courses.

Both **Main courses** £9.50-£16. **Service** 12.5%. **Credit** AmEx, DC, JCB, MC, V.
Potemkin has received such glowing reports we expected great things. The intriguingly curved basement restaurant is very attractive with its padded blue and red banquettes and gilt-framed niches holding Khokhloma vases. But with few other diners present, we found the atmosphere a touch stiff. Potemkin boasts more than 130 vodkas and beers and can rustle up some mean vodka cocktails, including an award-winning Bloody Mary. Suitably cheered after this, we moved on to a good, slightly resinous Georgian white wine, Tamada Mtsvane. Yet the food failed to thrill. We wish the waitress had pointed out that herring as a starter, then pan-fried sturgeon and asparagus as a main were going to be terribly similar. Both were served very plainly with potato and sour cream. Smoked salmon blini, followed by unusually light (almost fluffy) golubtsy in tomato sauce, made for a much better pairing. To finish, a rich chocolate truffle dessert went well with a mocha vodka shot. Next time, we'll opt for staying in the upstairs bar rather than going for the full-on restaurant experience.
Bar available for hire. No smoking (restaurant). **Map 5 N4.**

West

Acton W3

Rasputin
265 High Street, W3 9BY (8993 5802). Acton Town tube/70, 72, 207, 266 bus. **Meals served** noon-midnight daily. **Main courses** £7.50-£12.95. **Service** 10%. **Credit** MC, V.
The sign outside reads 'European', the menu announces 'Russian cuisine' and the ebullient Montenegran hostess and Croatian chef declare the food is 'Eastern European'. Putting such quibbles aside, we kicked straight off with Siberian pelemeni (meat dumplings with sour cream) and borscht of beetroot, cabbage, carrots and herbs. For mains, bigos was a heap of sauerkraut harbouring pieces of unidentified meat, topped with a delicious sausage; and a pepper well stuffed with meat and rice, served with tomato sauce and sour cream. A plentiful array of fresh vegetables came with both dishes. Portions are generous, so we were too full to try the 'Sharlotte Rousse' or cream cheese pancakes. The decor, including a picture of the mad monk himself ('he was like Robin Hood') is as basic and rustic as the food. Some honest Russian black bread would have been more welcome than the brown sliced loaf served with spicy pickled vegetables, but we certainly didn't leave hungry. And we could have left very merry if we'd tried too many of the 18 vodkas.
Babies and children admitted. Booking advisable dinner. Separate room for parties, seats 40.

Bayswater W2

Erebuni
London Guards Hotel, 36-37 Lancaster Gate, W2 3NA (7402 6067/www.erebuni.ltd.uk). Lancaster Gate tube. **Dinner served** 5pm-1am Mon-Sat. **Main courses** £6.50-£18.50. **Set dinner** (Mon-Thur) £15 2 courses. **Service** 10%. **Credit** MC, V.
Our night at Erebuni had a touch of *Fawlty Towers* about it. First, it's a challenge to find the place, cunningly hidden in the breakfast room of an anonymous hotel. The dated red and green decor is redolent of pensioner coach parties, who probably downed many a full English here before the arrival of the new clientele from the East. A pleasant Russian waitress gloomily pronounced most of our choices from the Armenian/Georgian/ Russian menu to be unavailable. That said, cheburekhi (fried lamb dumplings with a clear broth) were crisp and pleasantly spiced; and a salad of garlicky courgettes served with spicy salsa was plain but fresh. Mains of stuffed vine leaves (Echmiadzin-style, so they say) and a garlicky minced lamb kebab were pretty dull. We enjoyed ice-cold Ukrainian Obolon lager and a few vodkas, but beware: buying vodka by the bottle is a pricey business. Though Erebuni's website shows hordes

of merry diners partying, we sat most of the evening alone. Just as we were leaving, a few lively young Russians turned up for a drink to the Russian disco beat. A niche venue, it would seem. *Babies and children admitted. Booking advisable. Entertainment: musicians 7pm Fri, Sat; karaoke Mon-Sat. Restaurant available for hire. Takeaway service.*

South West
Earl's Court SW10

Nikita's
65 Ifield Road, SW10 9AU (7352 6326/ www.nikitasrestaurant.com). Earl's Court tube. **Dinner served** 7-11.30pm Mon-Sat. **Main courses** £9.50-£14.95. **Set meal** £22.50-£36.50 4 courses incl coffee. **Cover** £1.50. **Service** 12.5%. **Credit** AmEx, JCB, MC, V.
So exhaustively decorated it's not impossible to imagine Tsar Nicholas II hiding out in the kitchen, Nikita's is opulent, over the top and utterly charming. A deep red and gold colour scheme gives the basement restaurant a rich, broody character, so intricate that your eye will inevitably wander. Equally impressive are the cavern-like private booths that – with drawn curtains and a bell to get attention – seat parties of up to six. The menu is Russian through and through. Borscht, steak tartar, caviar: all the classics are represented. Gus y zakusky, a chopped salad starter of dill cucumber, egg and smoked goose, was tasty; better still were mains of duck breast in jus and 'shashlyk po-karski' – cubed loin of lamb on an enormous skewer. Caviar is pricey, of course (up to £46 for beluga), though the staff were kind enough to split a portion of the dark and heady ossetrina caviar between two blinis so we could share. The wine list is adequate, but overshadowed by a vast selection of Russian, Polish and Siberian vodkas – to be supped neat with (rather than before) your meal in traditional Russian fashion.
Booking advisable; essential Thur-Sat. Dress: smart casual. Entertainment: gipsy music 8.30-11.30pm Fri, Sat. Separate rooms for parties, seating 6, 15 and 45. Vegetarian menu. Vegan dishes. Map 13 C12.

North
Camden Town & Chalk Farm NW1

★ Trojka
101 Regent's Park Road, NW1 8UR (7483 3765/ www.troykarestaurant.co.uk). Chalk Farm tube. **Meals served** 9am-10.30pm daily. **Main courses** £6-£9.50. **Set lunch** (noon-4pm) £7.95 2 courses. **Corkage** £3 wine; £15-£25 spirits. **Credit** AmEx, MC, V.
This pleasantly laid-back café has very reasonable prices given its Primrose Hill location. Decorated with Chagall-type Russian paintings and the ubiquitous matrioshki dolls, Trojka has a Gypsy violinist playing kitsch folk tunes some nights – fun if you're in the mood after a few vodkas. We've been known to show off our Polish dance steps here. All the usual east European staples are on the menu: herring, blini, russian salad and borscht for starters, and serviceable renditions of salmon koulebiaka, bigos, golubtsy and latkes among the mains. It's all fine and hearty, but somehow lacks a loving hand in the kitchen. This slightly offhand approach extends to the service, which can be patchy and occasionally unfriendly. Pancakes with ice-cream were slightly disappointing; chocolate torte Hungarian-style or Polish apple cake might have been the better choice. Not somewhere to travel far to, Trojka is fine if you happen to be in the neighbourhood. It's also good for parties as you can take your own drink and pay corkage (though this rockets for vodka). In conclusion, it needs to try a bit harder.
Babies and children welcome: high chair. Book dinner Fri, Sat. Entertainment: Russian folk music 8-10.30pm Fri, Sat. No-smoking tables. Tables outdoors (3, pavement). Takeaway service. Map 27 A1.

Fish

Sourcing and simplicity sum up the challenges that top fish restaurants must master. The food-buyer's art reaches its zenith where marine life is concerned. Although we live on an island, top-quality fish aren't easy to come by. The best restaurants might buy some of their stock from a favoured supplier at Billingsgate market (now by West India Docks, E14, though its predecessor off Lower Thames Street, EC3, sold fish to Londoners for 900 years), but increasingly they're having to source their catch directly from fishing ports. Once purchased, these freshest of raw materials need minimal fuss to create the finished dish – though there's much skill involved in presenting precision-cooked specimens à point.

London's best fish restaurants cover a broad spectrum of venues. They include venerable upper-crust establishments such as **Sweetings**, **Wheeler's** and the newer but equally traditional **Green's**. One of the capital's oldest fish outfits, **Scott's**, closed down in the past year – though it should reopen in 2006 under new ownership. Celebrity hangouts like **J Sheekey** also figure in this section, as do celebrity chefs – Aldo Zilli, at **Zilli Fish** – plus high-class City outfits such as **Fishmarket**. A newer phenomenon has been the advent of non-British fish restaurants, and this year the admirable South African specialist **Fish Hoek** has been joined by exciting Scandinavian newcomer **Deep**.

Central
City EC2, EC3, EC4

Chamberlain's
23-25 Leadenhall Market, EC3V 1LR (7648 8690/www.chamberlains.org). Bank tube/ Liverpool Street tube/rail.
Bar **Open** noon-11pm Mon-Fri.
Restaurant **Meals served** noon-9.30pm Mon-Fri. **Main courses** £16-£31. **Set dinner** (5-9pm) £16.95 3 courses.
Both **Credit** AmEx, DC, MC, V.
You'd better be feeling flush or, preferably, on expenses when you visit this smart establishment. It is located in the heart of lovely Leadenhall Market, just around the corner from those twin icons to City commerce, the Lloyds building and the 'Gherkin', and consequently is popular with gents in suits. Lunch is much busier than the evening. Most starters top a tenner and a main course of 'speciality' fish and chips costs £21.50; it had better be pretty special. There's no denying the freshness of the fish – brought in daily from Billingsgate – and portions are generous, with hefty slabs of salmon, tuna, sea bass and halibut making up the mixed grill. But unadorned fish is all you get with that dish: you'll have to pay another few quid for french beans, green salad or chips. A main-course risotto of blue swimmer crab and rocket came with two crab claws and a parmesan crisp circle artfully arranged on top; it was lusciously creamy but on the bland side. Puds are an unthreatening lot: crème brûlée, summer pudding, lemon tart. The ground-floor restaurant with mini mezzanine is flooded with light; otherwise there's a dark brick-lined basement, a first-floor restaurant or (in summer) tables on the cobbled street outside under the market roof.
Booking advisable lunch. Disabled: toilet. No-smoking tables. Separate room for parties, seats 60 (dinner Sat, Sun only). Tables outdoors (18, pavement). Map 12 Q7.

★ Fishmarket
Great Eastern Hotel, Bishopsgate, EC2M 7QN (7618 7200/www.fish-market.co.uk). Liverpool Street tube/rail. **Lunch served** noon-2.30pm, **dinner served** 6-10.30pm Mon-Fri. **Main courses** £11.50-£28. **Service** 12.5%. **Credit** AmEx, DC, MC, V.
Housed in the venerable Great Eastern Hotel, bang next to Liverpool Street station, this is one of the most pleasurable restaurants in the Conran empire. The setting is lovely, for a start. If you're after a quick bite and a glass of champagne, perch at the dramatic, marble-topped oval counter in the airy bar with its elaborate wooden panelling. For a more leisurely meal, take a seat in the dining room, a calming, air-conditioned space of soft grey and white with pretty stained-glass windows framing a display of crustacea. The latter is always a good choice here. We began by sharing a dressed crab (huge and good value at £8) and half a dozen oysters – a mix of Dartmouth rock, Loch Fyne and fine de claire; all plump, top-quality specimens. Expense-accounters can splash out on whole lobster or caviar (three kinds, starting at £25). For mains, a lovely hunk of john dory matched well with sweetish, caramelised onions and smooth, lemony mash; seared salmon (slightly too oily) came on a pile of sautéed leek strips, mixed with flecks of smoked salmon and chunks of prune – a great combination. A simple side dish of green beans was given a summery flavour with slivers of preserved lemon. The amenable staff provide polished service, and are used to business lunchers with limited time.
Babies and children welcome: high chairs. Booking advisable; essential lunch. Disabled: toilet. Map 12 R6.

Sweetings
39 Queen Victoria Street, EC4N 4SA (7248 3062). Mansion House tube. **Lunch served** 11.30am-3pm Mon-Fri. **Main courses** £10.50-£25.50. **Credit** AmEx, JCB, MC, V.

Sweetings really should be snapped up by English Heritage. However, it's more than a working theme park: the three small rooms are busy with City workers (mostly men) downing potted shrimps, smoked cod roe or dressed crab, followed by fish pie, salmon cakes or dover sole, buttressed by brown bread and butter, freshly made condiments and a very decent wine list (white wine and champagne in the main). The food is good: sometimes excellent, as in skate wing poached with black butter, and sometimes more comforting, as with two fillets of Cornish brill, fried and served with old-fashioned buttered spinach and golden chips. Portions are large. The simple but charming interior is just as it should be – there are mosaic floors, white linen-covered tables, old prints (many concerning cricket) and a small bar where the pumps (still very much in use) boast names such as Arkells Best bitter, served in pint and half-pint silver tankards. Pimms is also available and there are savouries such as buck rarebit on offer. Dip your spoon into a bowl of steamed syrup pudding and custard and be transported back in time. A restaurant to be treasured.
Babies and children admitted. Bookings not accepted. Dress: smart casual. Restaurant available for hire, seats 30 (dinner only). Takeaway service. **Map 11 P6.**

Clerkenwell & Farringdon EC1

Rudland & Stubbs
35-37 Greenhill Rents, Cowcross Street, EC1M 6BM (7253 0148). Farringdon tube/rail.
Meals served noon-10.45pm Mon-Fri.
Main courses £10.50-£23. **Service** 12.5%.
Credit AmEx, MC, V.
A former sausage factory, this Clerkenwell fish specialist has a nicely worn-in look with its dark wooden bar, its marble-topped tables and its tiled columns. Standards, however, seem to have slipped a little since our last visit. The fish specials chalked up daily on a blackboard (black bream and dover sole on the evening of our trip) had already sold out, with no replacements forthcoming. This was somewhat strange, considering we were the first customers in for dinner. Adding to our woes, the grilled west coast calamares was alarmingly whiffy. A darne of grilled salmon was dry and overcooked and its accompanying roast vegetables were too oily. Tuna niçoise fared better, although the grey ring around the yolk of the cold hard-boiled egg was not of handsome appearance. On the positive side, our young waiter couldn't have been more charming or helpful, and the welcoming pot of good, marinated mussels with crusty bread was a nice touch.
Booking advisable lunch. Children admitted. Tables outdoors (3, pavement). **Map 5 O5.**

Fitzrovia W1

Back to Basics
21A Foley Street, W1W 6DS (7436 2181/ www.backtobasics.uk.com). Goodge Street or Oxford Circus tube. **Lunch served** noon-3pm, **dinner served** 6-10.30pm Mon-Sat. **Main courses** £12.75-£17.95. **Service** 12.5%.
Credit AmEx, DC, MC, V.
An enormous daily changing menu offered no less than 14 fish specials on our visit (and that's not including all those on the regular list), from lemon sole to codling, via tuna loin and gilt-head bream. Main courses include poached salmon salad at £13.50, and an awesomely portioned, almost unfinishable bowl of delicious king prawns and crustaceans at £17.95. Vegetables cost extra, though our Savoy cabbage vinaigrette gave perfect riposte to all the salty fish. It's all bolstered by a healthy selection of wine (mostly white, as you'd expect), and tailed by dessert: oranges and Grand Marnier pancake with ice-cream, for instance, or Baileys crème brûlée. The street-corner premises are decorated pleasantly enough, but the only feature of note is an enormous blackboard display that highlights the sheer size of the daily menu. Non-fish eaters do get their own 'fish not your dish'

section of the menu, though this consists of only three options, and one of them, a chicken breast in red wine sauce, was very disappointing. Stick to the marine life for the best results.
Babies and children admitted. Booking essential. Tables outdoors (17, pavement). Takeaway service. **Map 3 J5.**

Leicester Square W1, WC2

Café Fish
36-40 Rupert Street, W1D 6DW (7287 8989/ www.santeonline.co.uk/cafefish). Leicester Square or Piccadilly Circus tube.
Bar **Open** noon-11pm Mon-Sat; 2-9pm Sun.
Canteen **Meals served** noon-11pm Mon-Sat; 2-9pm Sun. **Main courses** £9.95-£18.95.
Set meal £10 2 courses.
Both **Service** 12.5%. **Credit** AmEx, DC, MC, V.

Back to Basics

With pristine green and white tiling, banks of dark wooden tables and stainless-steel features, the interior of this branch of Livebait smacks of an upmarket pie and mash franchise. The aromas of garlic and smoked, steamed or fried fish flavour any visit. The main menu (which usually includes separate fish specials) also contains roast chicken and a vegetable pasta dish, as a concession to those wishing to bypass the marine theme (though quite what they're doing here in the first place is anyone's guess). Salmon and cod fish cakes on a bed of wilted spinach with sorrel sauce looked disappointingly small at first, but with a comforting side order of herb mash, it hit the spot perfectly. We needed to send back our char-grilled tuna with guacamole, sour cream and chilli sauce for a little more grilling, but it returned as a perfectly medium-cooked platter. We'd picked a busy Friday evening for our visit, which meant full tables and a steady stream of both after-work and pre-theatre diners. Even so, the service from both table and bar staff was effortlessly friendly and well-choreographed.
Babies and children welcome: children's menu; high chairs. Booking advisable. Disabled: toilet. No-smoking tables. **Map 17 K7.**

★ J Sheekey
28-32 St Martin's Court, WC2N 4AL (7240 2565/ www.caprice-holdings.co.uk). Leicester Square tube.
Lunch served noon-3pm Mon-Sat; noon-3.30pm Sun. **Dinner served** 5.30pm-midnight Mon-Sat; 6pm midnight Sun. **Main courses** £10.75-£29.75.
Set lunch (Sat, Sun) £21.50 3 courses. **Cover** £2.
Credit AmEx, DC, MC, V.
Sister establishment to such perennially talked-about restaurants as the Ivy (*see p223*) and Le Caprice (*see p227*), Sheekey's is – we think – a much more appealing concern. It's less celeb-conscious than the former, less snooty than the latter, and the food is superior. In fact, from the restrained elegance of the decor to the utter professionalism of the staff to the perfectly executed cooking, it's hard to fault the place. The menu majors in top-notch shellfish and crustacea (whole lobster, dressed crab, three kinds of oysters), but there's working-class touches (jellied eels) as well as more rarefied options (beluga caviar at £125 for 50g). For mains, the famous fish pie (there's even a recipe on the website) is always an unctuous delight, and it's hard to top simply cooked classics such as skate wing with brown butter and capers. Desserts are determinedly old-school: spotted dick with golden syrup, or rhubarb pie with clotted cream. The weekend set lunch is not quite the bargain it used to be, but is still exceedingly popular.
Babies and children welcome: colouring books; high chairs. Booking essential. Vegetarian menu. **Map 18 K7.**

Manzi's
1-2 Leicester Street, WC2H 7BL (7734 0224/ www.manzis.co.uk). Leicester Square tube.
Lunch served noon-2.45pm, **dinner served** 5.30-11pm Mon-Sat. **Main courses** £9.95-£32.
Service 12.5%. **Credit** AmEx, DC, MC, V.
This 78-year-old, family-run veteran is no longer the fashionable meeting place it was back in the 1960s and '70s, but it still has a certain charm. The piscine murals, decorative mirrors, long sweeping bar and check-clothed tables are all very Parisian-bistro, but the owners, the waiters and several of the desserts (affogato, tiramisu and cassata) are of Italian descent. The too-huge menu runs from jellied eels and devilled whitebait to full-on fruits de mer platters. A fish soup was an old-fashioned, lightly thickened affair, generously studded with prawns, scallops, mussels, fish and rice; although six rock oysters felt as if they had been rinsed, they were fresh and opened to order. A whole grilled lemon sole ordered from a 'catch of the day' blackboard menu was a little mushy, which balanced out a main course of fair-sized scallops wrapped in bacon that was a retro treat. In spite of the fact that most customers are tourists and theatre-goers, the gregarious waiters show a bit of character and spirit.
Babies and children admitted. Booking advisable. Dress: smart casual. Separate room for parties, seats 45. **Map 18 K7.**

RESTAURANTS

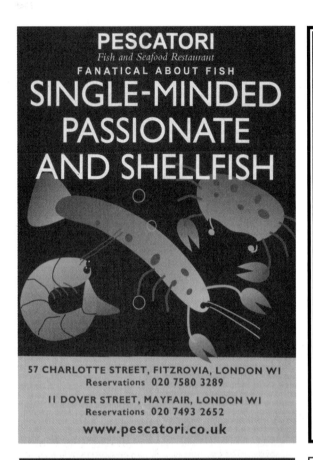

Marylebone W1

★ FishWorks

*89 Marylebone High Street, W1U 4QW
(7935 9796/www.fishworks.co.uk). Baker Street,
Bond Street or Regent's Park tube.* **Lunch
served** noon-2.30pm, **dinner served** 6-10.30pm
Tue-Fri. **Meals served** noon-10.30pm Sat, Sun.
Main courses £10.90-£19. **Credit** AmEx,
MC, V.

Mitchell Tonks' chain of fishmonger-cum-eateries
is expanding apace; as well as this branch, there
are restaurants in Bath (the original), Bristol,
Christchurch, Chiswick, a seafood bar inside
Harvey Nicks, and a new restaurant in Islington
(about to open as we went to press). The formula
is simple: a fishmonger at the front, and a light,
bright, blue and white eating area behind,
decorated with colourful seaside paintings. The
approach – to both setting and food – is casual and
relaxed. Start with good, own-made taramosalata
with chunky bread while you muse over the long
menu. There's a set of always-available 'classic'
dishes (some in both starter and main sizes) plus
seasonal crustacea – native oysters, brown crabs
from Devon and Cornwall, South coast lobsters –
and a blackboard list of daily specials. Or pick
your own fish from the counter at the front. The
emphasis is on super-fresh ingredients, simply
cooked – it's hard to beat succulent roasted skate
with black butter and capers – though the zuppa
del pescatore, a hearty fisherman's stew scented
with thyme and garlic is always a good bet. There
are also salads, both large (greek, or tomato,
mozzarella and basil) and small (green, or fennel
with mint) and creamy mash. The cookery classes
are very popular.
*Babies and children welcome: children's menu;
high chairs. Booking advisable. No smoking.*
Map 3 G5.
For branches see index.

St James's SW1

★ Green's

*36 Duke Street, SW1Y 6DF (7930 4566/
www.greens.org.uk). Green Park or Piccadilly
Circus tube.* **Lunch served** Sept-Apr 11.30am-
3pm Mon-Sat; noon-3pm Sun. *May-Aug* 11.30am-
3pm Mon-Sat. **Dinner served** *Sept-Apr* 6-11pm
Mon-Sat; 6-9pm Sun. *May-Aug* 6-11pm Mon-Sat.
Main courses £11-£40. **Cover** £2. **Credit**
AmEx, DC, MC, V.

With its clubby atmosphere, mahogany panelling,
leather banquettes, family-retainer service and
marble oyster bar, Green's looks as if it has been
around since the 1880s. In fact, it opened in the
1980s, yet still occupies a world in which
gentlemen bear walking sticks, women wear
pearls, and lemons live in muslin negligees. While
there's a surprising amount of meat on the menu
(bangers and mash, loin of venison, fillet of beef),
Green's reason for being is fish, from grilled dover
sole to salmon fish cakes via classic fish and chips.
Seemingly, every second person orders the
meticulously hand-sliced smoked salmon teamed
with very decent scrambled eggs, followed by the
famous smoked haddock Parker Bowles (named
after owner Simon PB), which comes with chive
mash, a perfect poached egg and a creamy white
wine sauce. Wild sea bass with creamed leeks and
peas was an immaculate piece of fish, intelligently
cooked; warmed red mullet fillets with carrot,
onions and saffron was a highly successful take on
escabeche. Staff are helpful and sympathetic.
Sitting up at the busy oyster bar is a joy.
*Babies and children admitted. Booking advisable.
Dress: smart casual; no jeans or trainers.
Separate room for parties, seats 36.* **Map 17 J7.**

Wheeler's

*12A Duke of York Street, SW1Y 6LB
(7930 2460). Piccadilly Circus tube.* **Lunch
served** noon-2.30pm, **dinner served** 5.30-11pm
Mon-Sat. **Main courses** £12.50-£32. **Service**
12.5%. **Credit** AmEx, DC, MC, V.

A few years back, this 77-year-old St James's
institution was taken over by Marco Pierre White,
who handsomely restored the snug (as in tiny)
dining rooms, leaving them gleaming with green
leather banquettes, parquet flooring and walls of
framed prints. In 2004, he handed it over to
Matthew Brown, former chef of the Belvedere in
Holland Park. Wisely, Brown has changed little.
Dover sole comes as véronique, colbert or belle
meunière; the downstairs oyster bar does a roaring
trade in natives; and the fish pie reigns supreme.
Cooking is solid, if uneven. Grilled scallops with
artichokes, parma ham and wild cress was nicely
balanced, and a meaty skate wing grenoblaise
(with capers, lemon and croûtons) was a textural
treat. On the downside, confit rainbow trout was
soft and mushy, and razor clams with merguez
sausage felt bitsy and oily. This is a serious
restaurant, it must be said, with butler-like staff
apparently uninterested in interacting with their
customers. Still, the timeless, steadfastly British
feel of Wheeler's is appealing, and the place
manages a steady trade with the business brigade
by day and American tourists by night.
*Babies and children admitted. Booking advisable
dinner. No-smoking tables.* **Map 17 J7.**

Soho W1

★ Zilli Fish

*36-40 Brewer Street, W1F 9TA (7734 8649/
www.zillialdo.com). Piccadilly Circus tube.*
Meals served noon-11.30pm Mon-Sat. **Main
courses** £8.70-£28. **Service** 12.5%. **Credit**
AmEx, DC, MC, V.

It's refreshing to find that Aldo Zilli, celebrity chef
and friend to the stars, still finds time to rattle the
pots and pans at this Soho stalwart. With its 1970s
turquoise velour chairs, wave-crested banquettes
and giant pepper grinder, Zilli Fish is delightfully
(and deliberately?) retro – when was the last time
you heard *Strangers on the Shore*? It's an endearing
spot, and you can't help but settle into the groove.
Staff are caring and good-humoured, and the fish
is fresh and not overly mucked about with.
Although the menu runs to some Asian-inspired
dishes (squid with chilli sauce, monkfish teriyaki),
every second table orders fish and chips. We found
the Italian food was the best bet: tuna carpaccio
with parmigiano and rocket was fresh, sweet and
clean-tasting; risotto frutti di mare arrived
perfectly al dente; and the signature spaghetti with
lobster was a joyous and decadent triumph. We
weren't the only customers enjoying ourselves,
judging by the girl at the next table: three cheers
for an eight-year-old who can totally demolish an
inky-black squid-ink fettuccine with monkfish,
fagiolini and pesto.
*Babies and children welcome: high chairs. Booking
advisable. Tables outdoors (2, patio).* **Map 17 J7.**
For branch (Zilli Café) see index.

West

Chiswick W4

★ Fish Hoek

*8 Elliott Road, W4 1PE (8742 0766). Turnham
Green tube.* **Lunch served** noon-2.30pm,
dinner served 6-10.30pm Tue-Sat. **Meals
served** noon-9pm Sun. **Main courses** £10-£30.
Set lunch £12 2 courses, £14.50 3 courses.
Service 12.5% for parties of 6 or more.
Credit MC, V.

This South African fish specialist is a real one-off.
Small and bright, its white walls are decorated
with sepia-tinged fishing photos (many belonging
to the owner, Pete Gottgens). The lengthy menu
lists plenty of marine life you won't have come
across elsewhere – stumpnose, kabeljou and
butterfish from South Africa, as well as exotica
from the Caribbean and Indian Ocean –
and more familiar species from closer to home
(Scottish scallops and smoked salmon, English
whitebait and hake). Most dishes are available in
half and full portions: a good idea that more
restaurants should adopt. All our dishes were
excellent; notable were Cape Malay seafood curry
in a gently spiced coconut broth; char-grilled South
Atlantic squid with salad leaves, chunks of orange
and a sweet chilli dressing; and kabeljou (similar
to sea bass) with garlicky butternut squash and a

Interview
MITCHELL TONKS

Who are you?
Founder of **FishWorks** (*see left*), the
Bath-based fish restaurant and retail
chain that now has four branches in
London. Also the award-winning author
of three books on seafood cooking.

**Eating in London: what's good
about it?**
The more my wife and I travel around
the world, the more we come back
and say that London is fantastic. The
whole restaurant scene has exploded,
and the diversity of restaurant
communities, such as Greek and
Indian, is great.

What's bad about it?
Price is an issue, but that's true
all over the UK. I don't think there is
really anything bad – I always seem
to sniff out good spots, and the
more local you become the easier it
is to avoid places that are just in it
for the money.

**Which are your favourite London
restaurants?**
I love **St John** (*see p55*). It's one of
the best places in the world; the food,
service and ambience are perfect.
The **Rivington Bar & Grill** (*see p61*)
is very special. **The Ivy** (*see p223*) and
J Sheekey (*see p85*) are exceptionally
well run – you know you're not going
to be disappointed, and they have a
great sense of occasion. I also like
Cây Tre (*see p288*) in Hoxton.

**What single thing would improve
London's restaurant scene?**
A lot of chefs get very style-led – their
food is all about the way it looks,
rather than how it eats.

Any hot tips for the coming year?
Simplicity is a trend that's been
coming for a long time. We've done
fuss, people don't want it, and
restaurants will respond to that.

Anything to declare?
We only shop for food at farmers'
markets, and go to the supermarket
just for chemicals. It can be done.

RESTAURANTS

Wheeler's. See p87.

sour tamarind sauce. Service is amiable, and the short, all-South African wine list (mostly whites) is nicely priced, with the most expensive white under £30. Don't forget dessert. We recommend the chef's selection: six different puddings, from sorbets to gooey chocolate log, artfully arranged on a large white platter. It's aimed at two, but could easily feed four. The drawback? Fish Hoek's popularity, which means that the closely spaced tables are often uncomfortably rammed, especially for Friday and Saturday dinner when there are two fixed sittings.
Babies and children admitted. Booking advisable. Disabled: ramp. No-smoking tables.

South West
Earl's Court SW5

Lou Pescadou
241 Old Brompton Road, SW5 9HP (7370 1057). Earl's Court tube. **Lunch served** noon-3pm daily. **Dinner served** 7pm-midnight Mon-Fri;

6.30pm-midnight Sat, Sun. **Main courses** £8.90-£18. **Set lunch** (Mon-Fri) £10.90 3 courses. **Set meal** (until 8pm Sat, all day Sun) £14.50 3 courses. **Service** 15%. **Credit** AmEx, DC, MC, V.
The soft lemon and sky-blue colour scheme, French seaside art and fruits de mer platters at this Earl's Court favourite are all very Gallic – as is the host, a tragi-comic performance artist who turns even a request for a lemon into a funny stand-up routine. If anything, the meat dishes are more popular than the fish, so when the table next to us ordered an all-meat meal (lamb and côte de boeuf), the maître d' was moved to comment: 'Are you aware that you have come to a fish restaurant?' (The côte de boeuf looked magnificent, by the way.) Particularly impressive is a list of 'wild fish' of the day, all of which come with vegetables included. A platter of bulots (whelks), bigorneaux (periwinkles) and crevettes gris (shrimp) transported us immediately to Marseilles. John dory, with a red-winey sauce bordelaise, was a little firmly cooked, though skate served with burnt butter was tender and juicy. 'It's even better when it's fresh,' quipped Mr Entertainment. The only downside is the occasional burnt baguette and the steepish 15% service charge added to the bill – but then you do get a floorshow thrown in.
Babies and children welcome: children's menu; high chairs. Booking advisable. Separate room for parties, seats 40. Tables outdoors (8, terrace). Takeaway service. **Map 13 B11**.
For branch (The Stratford) see index.

Fulham SW6

Deep NEW
The Boulevard, Imperial Wharf, SW6 2UB (7736 3337/www.deeplondon.co.uk). Fulham Broadway tube then 391, C3 bus.
Bar **Open/meals served** noon-11pm Tue-Sat; noon-5pm Sun. **Snacks** £4-£11.50. **Set lunch** £6.50 1 course.
Restaurant **Lunch served** noon-3pm Tue-Fri; noon-4pm Sun. **Dinner served** 7-11pm Tue-Sat. **Main courses** £15-£24. **Set lunch** £12.50 1 course, £15.50 2 courses, £19.50 3 courses.
Both **Service** 12.5%. **Credit** AmEx, JCB, MC, V.
Deep is run by Swedish husband and wife team Christian and Kerstin Sandefeldt, and their origins are evident in everything from the modern Scandinavian interior to the choice of 16 akvavits (Swedish schnapps) served in the spacious bar. The long white table linen, white seats and bright lighting focus attention on the dishes, which perform well in the limelight (fish is all sourced from well-managed stocks). Carpaccio of veal and tuna was arranged in a tiled pattern, topped with warm croquettes filled with a béchamel sauce rich in anchovy paste; an excellent dish. Terrine of lobster and veal sweetbreads was slightly less successful, the texture being a little Spam-like. Next, sautéed perch came with morels, onion gnocchi and a bisque with the aroma of vanilla, though the dominant flavour was salt. Wild salmon was also served with a salty broth, but al dente asparagus spears and a topping of sugary caramelised almonds made up for it. Curiously, the best dish was panna cotta with cloudberry jelly, cloudberry sorbet and a tuile (crisp wafer). The excellent own-made breads are Scandinavian-style. With a good wine list and a fascinating menu, Deep is London's most interesting new fish restaurant.
Babies and children welcome: high chairs. Booking advisable. Disabled: toilet. Dress: smart casual. Entertainment: DJ 7pm Thur-Sat. No smoking (restaurant). Tables outdoors (16, terrace).

South Kensington SW3

Bibendum Oyster Bar
Michelin House, 81 Fulham Road, SW3 6RD (7589 1480/www.bibendum.co.uk). South Kensington tube. **Meals served** noon-10.30pm Mon-Sat; noon-10pm Sun. **Main courses** £13-£31. **Service** 12.5%. **Credit** AmEx, DC, MC, V.
Lunches here are buzzier than dinners; during the day, customers at the Conran Shop provide endless people-watching. The evenings have a quiet charm

(as long as you like tiles; don't expect cosiness). The Oyster Bar is split over the foyer and a room directly off it. It's a handsome space with mosaic tiles on the floor, walls tiled with images of the Michelin man, and high ceilings and etched windows. The place has a full licence (and the right atmosphere), so you can just drop in for a drink. Even so, you'll probably be tempted by the short but sweet menu of native or rock oysters, lobster mayonnaise, or gravadlax with pickled cucumber, dill and mustard dressing, or even the plateau de fruits de mer (crab, langoustine, oysters, clams, prawns, crevettes grises, winkles and whelks). There are various non-fish options; thai beef salad was an excellent, clean-tasting special. The cheese plate and puddings (orange and almond cake with confit orange, say) are also a cut above, so it's a shame the bread is unimaginative (plain white stick) and, on one occasion, well below supermarket quality. A stalwart, but a welcome one in an expensive area.
Babies and children welcome: high chairs. Bookings not accepted in bar. Disabled: lift; ramp; toilet. Dress: smart casual. Tables outdoors (5, pavement). **Map 14 E10**.

Poissonnerie de l'Avenue
82 Sloane Avenue, SW3 3DZ (7589 2457/ www.poissonneriedelavenue.co.uk). South Kensington tube. **Lunch served** noon-3pm, **dinner served** 7-11.30pm Mon-Sat. **Main courses** £12.50-£25. **Set lunch** £16 2 courses, £22 3 courses. **Cover** £1.50. **Service** 15%. **Credit** AmEx, DC, JCB, MC, V.
Former Ritz head waiter Peter Rognoli opened this Brompton Cross landmark way back in 1964, when it probably looked much the same as it does today (decor includes timeless gilt-framed nautical oil paintings, a lavish lobster-motif carpet and wood panelling). In its time, the Poissonerie has been a home away from home to the likes of Mary Quant, Maggie Smith and Mick Jagger, who were doubtlessly drawn by the comfort factor of a menu that always seems to include crab salad, garlic prawns, scallops with mornay sauce, and halibut and turbot in various guises. Thanks largely to the adjoining fishmonger's, La Marée, the fish is impeccably fresh: our roasted cod with creamed lentils was plump and succulent, and the grilled tuna, served with a sauce gribiche, boasted a gleaming jewel-like centre, cooked perfectly medium rare as requested. We also liked our almost-provençale fish soup with rouille and grilled baguette, but found a smoked eel starter disconcertingly fridge-cold, and marred by inelegant, undressed batons of celeriac. The waiters here are efficient and proficient, and most diners have the happy air of people who are eating exactly what they feel like.
Booking advisable dinner. Children admitted (babies admitted lunch only). Dress: smart casual. Separate room for parties, seats 20. Tables outdoors (6, pavement).
Map 14 E10.

South
Waterloo SE1

Livebait
43 The Cut, SE1 8LF (7928 7211/www. santeonline.co.uk/livebait). Southwark tube/ Waterloo tube/rail. **Meals served** noon-11pm Mon-Sat; 12.30-9pm Sun. **Main courses** £9.75-£29. **Set meal** (noon-7pm) £14.50 2 courses, £18.50 3 courses. **Service** 12.5%. **Credit** AmEx, DC, JCB, MC, V.
The Livebait chain has expanded and contracted over the years, and moved from independent ownership into the hands of the Chez Gérard Group, but little has changed at the front end: the two remaining London branches still dish up simple shellfish platters and more elaborate fish dishes in a black-and-white tiled café environment. It remains pleasant to be welcomed with bread and spreads, and the decor still works nicely (though warmly in summer – those picture windows are just for effect), but menu mores have moved on since Livebait's was conceived, and it now feels a

little dated. Where simplicity and provenance are the watchwords elsewhere, elaborate dishes of showy global inspiration dominate here. Excellent cooking and outstanding ingredients could have rendered this a quibble, but those weren't to the fore either. After starters of an unremarkable prawn cocktail and ungenerous crab cakes, it was no surprise that puff pastry tart with scallops, monkfish, sun-blush tomatoes and pesto was no better than it sounded – and poor value at £16.75. A simpler barracuda special was better. Come for the good-value set menu (both branches are well placed for pre-theatre meals), but save your seafood blowout for somewhere else.

Babies and children admitted: high chairs. Booking advisable. Disabled: toilet. No-smoking tables. **Map 11 N8.**
For branch see index.

South East
Kennington SE11

The Lobster Pot
3 Kennington Lane, SE11 4RG (7582 5556/ www.lobsterpotrestaurant.co.uk). Kennington tube. **Lunch served** noon-2.30pm, **dinner served** 7-10.45pm Tue-Sat. **Main courses** £14.50-£19.50. **Minimum** (8-10pm) £23. **Set lunch** £11.50 2 courses, £14.50 3 courses. **Set meal** £21.50 3 courses, £39.50 8 courses. **Service** 12.5%. **Credit** AmEx, JCB, MC, V.

This small, intimate and eccentric eaterie is decked out in full nautical attire. The wooden ship interior has portholes through which you can see fish; the upstairs room is painted as the deck; fishing nets and lobster pots are everywhere; and there's a constant soundtrack of ship sound effects (most of which sound like a washing machine in mid-cycle). Waiters, who all wear Breton shirts, offer the loyal local clientele choices from a classically French menu that's big on fish and weak on vegetables. Soupe de poisson was traditional and tasty, a proper fishy infusion served with rouille, gruyère and croûtons, while langoustine cassoulet was creamy and intense. Main courses are simple and pricey: a plate of grilled prawns with garlic butter was good, as it should be for £18.50, though the few accompanying vegetables were tired. Pan-fried grouper with cajun spices and butter sauce was a little bland. Staff are very friendly, and charismatic owner Hervé is a fixture here; as, it seems, is Charles Kennedy, who was fortifying himself post-election on the night we visited.

Babies and children admitted: high chairs. Booking advisable. Dress: smart casual. Separate rooms for parties, seating 20 and 28. **Map 24 O11.**

London Bridge & Borough SE1

fish!
Cathedral Street, Borough Market, SE1 9AL (7407 3803/www.fishdiner.co.uk). London Bridge tube/rail. **Meals served** 11.30am-11pm Mon-Thur; noon-11pm Fri, Sat; noon-10.30pm Sun. **Main courses** £9.95-£19.95. **Service** 12.5%. **Credit** AmEx, DC, MC, V.

The setting, a steel and glass edifice designed by Julyan Wickham, is the most impressive aspect of fish!. On our Sunday evening visit, although the place was nicely busy, the food was average, and service erratic – sometimes attentive, sometimes dopey. The best dish was grilled sea bass, accompanied by spicy salsa (from the mix-and-match list of fish and sauces); everything else we tried was just OK. The prawns in the prawn cocktail wouldn't win any prizes for texture or flavour; calamares with rocket and lemon mayonnaise, though well cooked, was a dull dish;

Deep

RESTAURANTS

RESTAURANTS (sidebar, vertical)

and fish pie was merely comforting. We can see appeal – fish! is a user-friendly place that makes an effort with children – but we were underwhelmed. The restaurant is at its jolliest in the summer, on the days (Friday, Saturday) when Borough Market is in full swing. There are plans to open fish! Kitchen in Kingston in autumn 2005 – check the website for more information.
Babies and children welcome: children's menu; crayons; high chairs. Booking advisable. Disabled: toilet. Tables outdoors (30, pavement). **Map 11 P8.**

Tower Bridge E1

Aquarium
Ivory House, St Katharine-by-the-Tower, E1W 1AT (7480 6116/www.theaquarium.co.uk). Tower Hill tube/Tower Gateway DLR. **Brunch served** *(June-Aug)* noon-4pm Sun. **Lunch served** noon-3pm Mon-Fri. **Dinner served** 6-10pm Tue-Sat. **Main courses** £14-£24. **Set lunch** (Sun) £7-£14 2 courses. **Service** 12.5%. **Credit** AmEx, DC, MC, V.
This boat-shaped restaurant offers one of the best views in the dock area – especially at night, as you look out over the pleasure craft of St Katharine's. Night-time is also when the Aquarium's bar and club come into their own, but don't ignore the food – it's impressive. From a first-rate, predominantly fishy menu, the piled-high seafood platter was spectacular. The flavours of the chef's salt cod and prawn dumplings were married well with marinated daikon (radish) and enoki mushrooms. Succulent char-grilled tiger prawns came with sweet chilli and crème fraîche. Mains included moist slices of delicate grilled tuna combined with crispy shiitake rolls and mixed salad and shaved horseradish, while pea and artichoke risotto with tarragon butter was creamy, well-flavoured and filling. Desserts were no less memorable: raspberry panna cotta with chilli lime syrup and swiss meringue was an explosion of flavours (but looked a little like a messy operation). With so much right, it's a shame there were some hitches: the room is looking pretty tired these days, with chipped paint and flooring, and the service lacked energy and attention to detail.
Babies and children welcome: high chairs. Booking advisable. Dress: smart casual. Entertainment: jazz 1pm Sun (summer). Restaurant available for hire. Separate room for parties, seats 60. Tables outdoors (13, terrace). **Map 12 S8.**

The Fish Shop

East
Bethnal Green E2

Winkles
238 Roman Road, E2 0RY (8880 7450/ www.winklesseafood.com). Mile End tube/ Bethnal Green tube/rail. **Dinner served** 6-10.30pm Mon. **Meals served** noon-10.30pm Tue-Sat; noon-9pm Sun. **Main courses** £7-£22. **Service** 12.5%. **Credit** AmEx, MC, V.
Its location on the grim and gritty Roman Road isn't ideal, but Winkles is usually packed to its gills. Decor is simple: white walls, wicker chairs, wipe-down tables and, most importantly, a wonderful wet fish counter, from which is drawn the menu that balances fishy favourites (oysters, langoustines, fabulous fruits de mer platters) with more adventurous offerings (portuguese espetadas aka fish skewers, Thai prawn omelettes). Starters included a mediocre, mildly spicy prawn laksa soup, and a delicious mound of salt and pepper squid on a chilli dressing. The specials board offered two fine chunks of lemon sole on a bed of rich, tomatoey vegetables, and a reasonable dish of fresh linguine with queen scallops and peppers. Overall, the simpler the dish, the better the result. Desserts are not particularly exciting (pies and cakes, mainly). The wine list offers reasonably priced, light French wines, several by the glass.
Babies and children welcome: children's menu; high chairs. Booking advisable weekends. Disabled: toilet. No-smoking tables. Tables outdoors (3, pavement). Takeaway service.

South Woodford E18

Ark Fish Restaurant
142 Hermon Hill, E18 1QH (8989 5345). South Woodford tube. **Lunch served** noon-2.15pm Tue-Sat. **Dinner served** 5.30-9.45pm Tue-Thur; 5.30-10.15pm Fri, Sat. **Meals served** noon-8.45pm Sun. **Main courses** £8.75-£22.50. **Service** 10% for parties of 6 or more. **Credit** MC, V.
South Woodford's fish-eaters were happy indeed when this airy, open-plan bar-restaurant dropped anchor here last year. The fish is usually faultless. A starter of potted shrimps in basil butter was a good-sized portion, with plenty of brown toast to mop up the delicious buttery juices. Mains are enormous. Light, crispy batter encased huge portions of firm-fleshed cod and plaice, accompanied by nut-brown chips and creamy, mushy peas. More adventurous, but less successful, was a pile of monkfish atop a bigger pile of mash in a sea of pesto – the one-note basil flavour was overwhelming. Puds are firmly old-school: the jam sponge with custard went down very well with the more mature diners in our group. There are kids' menus, and doggy bags are provided on request. No bookings are taken, which can mean waits of up to 40 minutes, but Sunday afternoons are less hectic than Saturday nights.
Babies and children welcome: children's menu; high chairs. Bookings not accepted. No-smoking tables.

North
Finsbury Park N4

Chez Liline
101 Stroud Green Road, N4 3PX (7263 6550). Finsbury Park tube/rail. **Lunch served** 12.30-2pm Tue-Sat. **Dinner served** 6.30-10.30pm daily. **Main courses** £10.95-£17.75. **Set meal** £15 3 courses. **Credit** AmEx, MC, V.
Well-considered lighting, dark wood and orchids give Chez Liline a pleasing ambience. The wide range of fish here almost certainly comes courtesy of the fishmonger (sister) business next door, and a list of specials means there's plenty of choice. A starter of tiger prawns with green curry and lime was wonderfully rich and tangy, while 'fish visnoye' was a take on salade niçoise, here served with red snapper in a chilli and mustard seed dressing. Main courses included mauritian curry with aubergine and rice: robust slabs of monkfish, swordfish and red snapper in a dark, spicy sauce.

'Fricassee des Îles' was also a winner: another firm, piscatorial specimen, this time cooked in its own juices with fresh chilli and herbs. Rice was the only necessary accompaniment to such saucy dishes, and pudding (French classics such as tarte tatin and crème brûlée) was out of the question. The impressive wine list is organised by region, and the house white is a perfectly quaffable sauvignon blanc. Though the menu warns that delays may occur, service was well timed during our meal.
Babies and children welcome: high chairs. Booking advisable. Restaurant available for hire.

Islington EC1

The Fish Shop
360-362 St John Street, EC1V 4NR (7837 1199/ www.thefishshop.net). Angel tube/19, 38, 341 bus. **Lunch served** noon-3pm, **dinner served** 5.30-10.30pm Tue-Sat. **Meals served** noon-8pm Sun. **Main courses** £10.95-£24.50. **Set meal** (noon-3pm, 5.30-7pm Tue-Sat) £13.50 2 courses, £17 3 courses. **Service** 12.5%. **Credit** AmEx, DC, MC, V.
Loudmouth blokes and badly supervised children marred the first 20 minutes of our meal at the Fish Shop. The long-suffering waitresses could hardly hide their impatience to see them go; the lack of soft furnishings means that sound carries here. A light, bright space on three floors, the modern interior looks nothing like the pub it once was. The best tables are in the no-smoking section at the back, with a view of the garden through huge windows. The menu changes daily, though there are some constants, such as grilled plaice with spinach and excellent, nicely browned chips. There's plenty of shellfish, which you can mix and match to suit; non-fish dishes include a soup of the day and steak, served with chips and béarnaise. A generous portion of pale-pink taramasalata served with green olives and grilled bread made a good starter; treacle tart with cream was a sound pudding. In between came lacklustre cod wrapped in undercooked pancetta; we left most of it and, to the staff's credit, it didn't appear on the bill. Overall, an unconvincing performance.
Babies and children welcome: children's portions. Booking advisable dinner Fri, Sat. Disabled: toilet. Tables outdoors (10, terrace). **Map 5 O3.**

Outer London
Barnet, Hertfordshire

Loch Fyne Restaurant
12 Hadley Highstone, Barnet, Herts EN5 4PU (8449 3674/www.loch-fyne.com). High Barnet tube/Hadley Wood rail. **Meals served** 9am-10pm Mon-Fri; 10am-10.30pm Sat; 10am-9pm Sun. **Main courses** £7.95-£15.95. **Set lunch** £9.95 2 courses incl side dish. **Service** 10% for parties of 6 or more. **Credit** AmEx, MC, V.
Stripped floors and a light, spacious feel are the trademarks of this countrywide chain. Supplied by the company's own fisheries and smokehouse, the menu allows the freshest of ingredients, served simply, to speak for themselves. Loch Fyne Ashet was an ultra-fresh platter of bradan rost (kiln-roasted salmon), smoked salmon and marinated raw salmon, with the only accompaniment needed a squeeze of lemon; hot, crunchy whitebait was another hit. A main of poached smoked haddock with mash, spinach, peas and wholegrain mustard sauce made a superb ensemble – chunky fish, creamy mash and plenty of sauce. Salad niçoise with char-grilled tuna (surprisingly fridge-cold, given that we were asked how we'd like it cooked) was also a treat. Trout with shallots, spinach and chilli dressing arrived light and delicately spiced. Delectable sides included great chips, and pink fir-apple potatoes. A selection of ice-cream and sorbets, such as mango and raspberry, rounded off things well. After a meal, stock up on salmon (or a few oysters to shuck at home) from the shop. The wine list, as you'd expect, leads with the whites; the house white is a respectable sauvignon blanc.
Babies and children welcome: children's menu; high chairs. Booking advisable. No-smoking tables. Tables outdoors (7, terrace). Vegetarian menu. **For branches see index.**

French

There are some very fine French restaurants in London, ranging from cosy bistros to stellar performers that are among the capital's most glam destination venues. Every year sees one or two good Gallic openings, with the general standard tending to rise – this time, we welcome the **Ledbury**. It is especially pleasing that some of the top performers are located away from the West End, notably **La Trompette** in Chiswick, the recently rejuvenated **Le Bouchon Bordelais** in Battersea, that consistently excellent Wandsworth operation, **Chez Bruce**, and sister establishments the **French Table** in Surbiton and the **Food Room** in Battersea. The latter, along with the Ledbury, was nominated for Best New Restaurant in the 2005 *Time Out* Awards, while **Bistrotheque** in Bethnal Green and **Chez Kristof** in Hammersmith battled it out for the Best Local Restaurant gong.

As we went to press, **Comptoir Gascon** (63 Charterhouse Street, EC1M 6HA, 7608 0851) – formerly the deli side of the Club Gascon empire – was about to relaunch as a bistro. Regrettably, we've had to say adieu to one of the best local French restaurants, Kentish Town's **Le Petit Prince**, whose owners are heading back over la Manche.

In contrast to such gems, there's still a strand of French restaurants that seems hidebound by the daunting French culinary canon, afraid to experiment (lest they stray into Modern European territory) and trotting out the same over-tested repertoire. These establishments come and go, taking their boeuf bourguignon and escargots with them, but too often it's a case of (dare we say it?) *plus ça change, plus c'est la même chose*. We recommend such chefs restock their creative juices with a visit to the excellent **Le Cercle**. For more French cooking, see **Hotels & Haute Cuisine**, starting on p125.

Central

Belgravia SW1

★ Le Cercle

2005 RUNNER-UP BEST DESIGN
1 Wilbraham Place, SW1X 9AE (7901 9999). Sloane Square tube.
Bar **Open** noon-midnight Tue-Sat.
Restaurant **Lunch served** noon-3pm, **afternoon tea served** 3-5.30pm, **dinner served** 6-11pm Tue-Sat. **Set lunch** (noon-3pm Mon-Sat) £15 3 dishes incl tea or coffee, £19.50 4 dishes. **Set dinner** (6-6.45pm Tue-Sat) £17.50 3 dishes incl tea or coffee, £21.50 4 dishes. **Tapas** £4-£16. **Service** 12.5%. **Credit** AmEx, JCB, MC, V.
This Club Gascon (*see p92*) offshoot follows similar precepts to its much-lauded parent, but interprets them in cleaner, modern mode – very successfully and more cheaply. The restaurant has a satisfying club-like feel, with a discreet entrance leading down to a double-height basement that is sparse on decoration and long on architectural style. An over-abundance of leather, and diaphanous curtains separating galleries, booths and bar from the main central room, certainly lend a frisson to the atmosphere. Staff describe the menu as tapas-style, meaning that to approximate a full meal you need to order three or four dishes, plus dessert. But the description is misleading: there's nothing casual or indeed Spanish about the food, with each dish a perfectly formed modern-French miniature, beautifully served in a just-so receptacle. Of the seven we sampled, tomato variation (zesty sorbet on a fragrant stew); ravioles du royans (cheese) with celery emulsion; foie gras; and steamed plaice with chutney were exquisite – the other three merely good. Wines were similarly immaculate selections served in small measures (for easy matching). Supplying and explaining so many dishes to each table is labour-intensive and just occasionally the otherwise expert service seemed to go AWOL – but then it was sometimes hard to tell the young, black-clad waitstaff and their clientele apart.
Babies and children admitted. Booking advisable. No-smoking tables. **Map 15 G10**.

La Poule au Pot

231 Ebury Street, SW1W 8UT (7730 7763). Sloane Square tube. **Lunch served** 12.30-2.30pm Mon-Sat; 12.30-3.30pm Sun. **Dinner served** 6.45-11pm Mon-Sat; 6.45-10pm Sun. **Main courses** £12-£20. **Set lunch** £15.50 2 courses, £17.50 3 courses. **Service** 12.5%. **Credit** AmEx, DC, MC, V.
A perennial favourite, La Poule au Pot continues to perplex by appearing stylish when by rights (considering the constituent parts of its decor) it should be kitsch. How many other places could carry off a combination of dried flowers, suspended watering cans and harvest memorabilia? More pertinently, how does the room manage to maintain an impression of cosiness when, really, it is cramped? Perhaps by keeping the lighting so low that you can't see the next table. Nevertheless, La Poule manages to create a sense of occasion and has an infectious joie de vivre; it is unfailingly busy with a mainly older, local clientele, plus the occasional dating couple. On our visit the food did nothing to break the spell, but was not quite as striking as the atmosphere. Crab salad (served in a crab shell) was remarkable mainly for its generous size; the asparagus for being plump and crisp. To follow, a supersized cassoulet had all the goose and sausage you could want, while the large entrecôte was good, but upstaged by its frites (which made quite an entrance, wrapped in paper). There are also tables outside, which look on to a pretty square.
Babies and children welcome: high chairs. Booking essential. Separate room for parties, seats 16. Tables outdoors (12, terrace). **Map 15 G11**.

Roussillon

16 St Barnabas Street, SW1W 8PE (7730 5550/ www.roussillon.co.uk). Sloane Square tube. **Lunch served** noon-2.30pm Wed-Fri. **Dinner served** 6.30-10.30pm Mon-Sat. **Set lunch** £23 2 courses, £30 3 courses. **Set dinner** £45 3 courses. **Set meal** £65 7 course tasting menu. **Service** 12.5%. **Credit** AmEx, MC, V.
There's an unexpectedly suburban feel to Roussillon, secreted behind a big bay window on a quiet corner just off Pimlico Road. The somewhat awkward, low-ceilinged space, anonymous decor and hushed tones of the mature clientele don't inspire expectations of culinary greatness – yet this is as accomplished and vital a modern French restaurant as you'll find in London. Executive chef Alexis Gauthier and head chef Gérard Virolle have created a seductive and keenly thought-out seasonal menu (vegetarians have their own dedicated list). On our most recent visit we loved the sweet-tangy subtlety of 'pea and its shoots' with slices of scallops, pickled ginger jelly and crab meat. Another fine jelly, this time of elderflower and chicken, accompanied a silky slab of foie gras parfait. Main dishes were equally well rounded: Anjou squab came perfectly pink, its earthiness complemented by a melting artichoke purée and the crispness of an almond crust; steamed Baltic halibut was served with leeks, black truffle and french dressing. Sommelier Roberto Della Pietro's fine list of 400-plus bins focuses on south and south-west France, and includes several wines by the glass. We did have one criticism: the cheeses with which we finished a memorable meal were served way too cold.
Children over 8 years admitted. Booking advisable. Dress: smart casual. No smoking. Restaurant available for hire. Separate room for parties, seats 26. Vegetarian menu. **Map 15 G11**.

City E1, EC2, EC3

Le Coq d'Argent

2005 RUNNER-UP BEST ALFRESCO DINING
No.1 Poultry, EC2R 8EJ (7395 5000/ www.conran.com). Bank tube/DLR.
Bar & grill **Lunch served** 11.30am-3pm Mon-Fri. **Main courses** £12-£16.
Restaurant **Breakfast served** 7.30-10am Mon-Fri. **Lunch served** 11.30am-3pm Mon-Fri; noon-3pm Sun. **Dinner served** 6-10pm Mon-Fri; 6.30-10pm Sat. **Main courses** £14-£23. **Set lunch** (Mon-Fri, Sun) £23 2 courses, £27 3 courses.
Both **Service** 12.5%. **Credit** AmEx, DC, JCB, MC, V.
Owned by the Conran group, Le Coq d'Argent has a lofty roof-top location that offers unparalleled skyline views from the luxuriant setting of its formal Mediterranean-style garden. A circular walkway around the perimeter is embellished with trailing vines and plants. If privacy is for you, opt for the separate bar and restaurant terraces, which provide a degree of intimacy without isolation. Popular with business-minded types during the day and well-heeled diners after office hours, the regional French cooking is as much a magnet as the restaurant's lush environs. Friendly and on-the-ball staff can't be faulted for their unobtrusive service. White onion tart made an elegant beginning to our meal (in the restaurant); sliced, meltingly soft onions, heaped over crisp

puff pastry and topped with tomatoes, were accompanied by a delicious black olive-studded dressing. A main course of perfectly cooked steamed sea bass fillet, served with a frothy buttery cream of wilted sorrel leaves and lemon, had just the right balance of tangy, tart flavours to offset the mellow sauce. A soothing sight for tired City eyes, Le Coq d'Argent offers respite and calm from the bustling streets below.

Babies and children welcome: high chairs. Booking advisable. Disabled: lift; toilet. Entertainment: jazz 6.30pm Sat, noon-4pm Sun. Restaurant available for hire. Tables outdoors (13, restaurant terrace; 25, bar terrace). **Map 11 P6.**

1 Lombard Street

1 Lombard Street, EC3V 9AA (7929 6611/ www.1lombardstreet.com). Bank tube/DLR. Bar **Open** 11am-11pm Mon-Fri. **Tapas served** 11.30am-10.30pm Mon-Fri. **Tapas** £3.50-£14.50. *Brasserie* **Breakfast served** 7.30-11am, **meals served** 11.30am-10.30pm Mon-Fri. **Main courses** £12.50-£27.50. **Set dinner** (6-10.30pm) £19.50 5 courses. *Restaurant* **Lunch served** noon-3pm, **dinner served** 6-10pm Mon-Fri. **Main courses** £27.50-£29.50. **Set lunch** £34 2 courses, £36 3 courses. **Set dinner** £36 6 courses. *All* **Service** 12.5%. **Credit** AmEx, DC, JCB, MC, V.

As deconsecrated temples of Mammon go, this former bank (grade II listed) is a congenial spot for a nosh-up. For sure, with such history and the Old Lady of Threadneedle Street just across the way, you wouldn't expect it to be cheap; happily, the food and overall experience richly deserve to be written in the 'money well spent' column of a diner's ledger. White walls, big windows and Pietro Agostini's fabulous domed skylight make the expansive brasserie section light and airy, and the vibe is lively but not too raucous. Under the skylight is a (well-stocked) dramatic, circular bar; the restaurant area to one side serves no-nonsense haute cuisine. We enjoyed a high-end lunch in the brasserie. A starter of wild mushroom salad with green beans, celeriac and a rich dressing of pumpkin seed oil and balsamic vinegar was lovely, as was bruschetta of grilled provençal vegetables. To follow, salmon fish cake was expertly done, and lip-smacking goujons of tender sautéed rabbit came with ceps and a sublime garlic and lemon confit. The long-armed international wine list reaches from a 2002 Montepulciano d'Abruzzo at £16.50 to a 1950 Château Pétrus that costs as much as a second-hand car.

Babies and children admitted. Booking advisable lunch. Disabled: lift; toilet. Entertainment: pianist and singer 6.30pm Mon, Fri. No smoking (restaurant). Restaurant available for hire. Separate room for parties, seats 40. **Map 12 Q6.**

★ Rosemary Lane

61 Royal Mint Street, E1 8LG (7481 2602/ www.rosemarylane.btinternet.co.uk). Tower Hill tube/Fenchurch Street rail/Tower Gateway DLR. **Lunch served** noon-2.30pm Mon-Fri. **Dinner served** 5.30-10pm Mon-Sat. **Main courses** £13-£18. **Set meal** £14 2 courses, £17 3 courses. **Set dinner** (Sat) £30 9 courses tasting menu. **Service** 12%. **Credit** AmEx, MC, V.

Word of mouth has helped Rosemary Lane get around its duff location and dull frontage and, judging by the number of suited gents at lunch, it is clearly no longer one of the best-kept secrets in the City. Its reputation has been built on exceptional food, which offers a modern take on French cuisine. Chilled sweetcorn flan was a classic summer starter, the flan's delicacy matched perfectly by a deep green, intensely flavoured basil vinaigrette. Similarly inspired matching came with roast tiger prawns with oven-dried tomatoes and a salad of frisée, mandarin orange and onion marmalade. Trying to find a wine to meet those two head-on was always going to be tricky; the French/Californian list could do with some annotation or, at least, some ordering by style. For mains, slow-roasted Gressingham duck breast was nudged into new territory by an unctuous gratinée of nectarines, sweet potato and brie, while braised monkfish was given a Mediterranean twist with a

colourful ragout of herbs, roast peppers, limes and chickpeas. Strawberry summer pudding finished things on such a high that even the noisy business conversation of our neighbours – the tables in this tastefully converted pub are closely spaced – couldn't dampen our enthusiasm.

Booking advisable lunch. Dress: smart casual. Restaurant available for hire. **Map 12 S7.**

Clerkenwell & Farringdon EC1

Café du Marché

22 Charterhouse Square, Charterhouse Mews, EC1M 6AH (7608 1609). Barbican tube/ Farringdon tube/rail. **Lunch served** noon-2.30pm Mon-Fri. **Dinner served** 6-10pm Mon-Sat. **Set meal** £28.95 3 courses. **Service** 15%. **Credit** MC, V.

Hidden away in a discreet corner of the City, this traditional bistro (complete with candlelight and exposed brickwork) provides a setting that's popular both with canoodling couples and business-account opportunists. The food is generally of a decent quality, but choice is limited and there's the occasional duff dish. We enjoyed starters of refreshing sardine and crab salad, and confit et oeuf de canard (a warming combination of shredded duck, brioche and poached egg). To follow, the plat du jour of rabbit in cep, sage and green peppercorn sauce was exemplary: rich meat cloaked in a kaleidoscope of flavours. In contrast, pork belly cooked with lemon and rosemary was deeply disappointing. The tough meat was drowned in a gelatinous layer of fat, while the bitter citrus flavour did nothing to rescue the dish. Dessert was an equally moist affair: bland pear tart was forgettable, yet white chocolate fondant was the epitome of lip-smacking indulgence. With a long wine list and friendly staff, Café du Marché can offer a great night out, but be prepared to take your chances with the menu.

Babies and children admitted. Booking advisable. Disabled: toilet. Entertainment: jazz duo 8-11pm Mon-Thur; pianist Fri, Sat. Separate rooms for parties, seating 30 and 70. Tables outside (4, pavement). **Map 5 O5.**

★ Club Gascon

57 West Smithfield, EC1A 9DS (7796 0600). Barbican tube/Farringdon tube/rail. **Lunch served** noon-2pm Mon-Fri. **Dinner served** 7-10pm Mon-Thur; 7-10.30pm Fri, Sat. **Main courses** £8.30-£20. **Tapas** £6-£16.50. **Set meal** £38 5 courses. **Service** 12.5%. **Credit** AmEx, MC, V.

BEST FRENCH

For romance
The Belvedere (see p97), **La Trouvaille** (see p96), **Les Trois Garcons** (see p101).

For alfresco dining
The Belvedere (see p97), **Le Bistro** (see p102), **Chez Kristof** (see p97), **Le Colombier** (see p97), **Le Coq d'Argent** (see p91), **Mirabelle** (see p95).

For regional treats
Le Vacherin (see p97), **Chez Lindsay** (see p103), **La Galette** (see p95).

For a touch of tradition
Le Bouchon Bordelais (see p99), **Café du Marché** (see p92), **Elena's L'Étoile** (see p93), **Mon Plaisir** (see p92).

For vegetarians
L'Escargot Marco Pierre White (see p96), **Morgan M** (see p102), **Plateau** (see p101), **Roussillon** (see p91).

For families
Le Bouchon Bordelais (see p99).

Pascal Aussignac's accomplished eaterie is a clubby, dark dining space, with a heavy screen of curved wood at the entrance. The multi-course tasting menu at £38 is a good option – the same menu with matching wines is even better value at £60. If you prefer to go à la carte, staff recommend ordering three savoury dishes each plus a vegetable dish to share – but we found this too much, and wound up foregoing dessert altogether. Foie gras is the house speciality, offered in around eight styles. At the waitress's suggestion, we ordered one cold and one warm plate. The first was a pretty rosette of sliced foie gras accompanied by rose sangria jelly; the second (and best) was seared foie gras scattered with popcorn and garnished at table with powdered popcorn – a startlingly good combination. Ices featured heavily, including a mustard version with 'smooth and crispy' suckling pig, and herb granita with smoked salmon and toasted pine kernels, the simplest dish on the menu. We adored the plate of girolles, sautéed spätzli and cream sauce, and an amuse-bouche of butternut squash soup with pickled sea snails. Bread was first-rate too. The huge wine list is wide-ranging as long as you think France is the centre of the universe; look carefully among the regions and you will find bottles under £25. Sibling Le Cercle (see p91) is much-lauded too.

Babies and children admitted. Booking essential. Restaurant available for hire. **Map 11 O5.**

Covent Garden WC2

Incognico

117 Shaftesbury Avenue, WC2H 8AD (7836 8866/www.incognico.com). Leicester Square or Tottenham Court Road tube. **Lunch served** noon-3pm, **dinner served** 5.30-11pm Mon-Sat. **Main courses** £11.50-£25. **Service** 12.5%. **Credit** AmEx, DC, MC, V.

Since we last visited, Incognico has introduced a cheaper, simpler menu that mixes French brasserie classics and Mediterranean-tinged dishes. The predominantly French wine list has gained new entries from Italy and the New World. Starters of a tian of crab and king prawn salad were delicious: rich crab meat balancing on thick slices of avocado, while plump juicy prawns were slathered in peppery rocket leaves and garlic dressing. Next up, wing of skate combined wonderfully firm fish with tangy caper sauce, while veal milanese was a huge platter of tender meat let down only by the paltry salad that accompanied it. However, by the time we'd finished our mains it became impossible to ignore the fact that we were one of only three tables in a restaurant with a capacity close to 100. At 9pm on a Friday night, most decent West End restaurants ought to be at least half full, and Incognico definitely deserved to be busier (though, to be fair, it attracts a lot of pre- and post-theatre trade). If it had been, we'd have stuck around for a dessert from the range of traditional favourites such as fruit tarts, crumbles and tiramisu.

Babies and children welcome: high chairs. Booking essential. Dress: smart casual. Restaurant available for hire. **Map 17 K6.**

Mon Plaisir

19-21 Monmouth Street, WC2H 9DD (7836 7243/www.monplaisir.co.uk). Covent Garden tube. **Lunch served** noon-2.15pm Mon-Fri. **Dinner served** 5.45-11.15pm Mon-Sat. **Main courses** £13.95-£22. **Set lunch** £12.95 2 courses, £15.95 3 courses. **Set meal** (5.45-7pm Mon-Sat; after 10pm Mon-Thur) £12.50 2 courses, £14.50 3 courses incl glass of wine and coffee. **Service** 12.5%. **Credit** AmEx, MC, V.

There's a certain savoir faire about Mon Plaisir that fits its claim to be the oldest surviving French restaurant in London. On our visit, an efficient army of formally dressed waiters bustled purposefully around the four themed dining rooms while the patron glided from table to table in a tie-dyed T-shirt, chatting affably with the many lunchtime regulars. The rooms reflect the different images non-French diners are assumed to associate with French restaurants, from rive gauche café-bar to the stiff tablecloths of bourgeois dining rooms

La Galette. See p95.

via the avant-garde art of the Mediterranean. There was a shaky nod to modernity in some of our dishes; not content with its celeriac purée, lamb rump was circled with a vivid green slick, a reduction of spinach and broccoli. The onion soup was just what we hoped for – with the onions sweated soft and a thatch of browned emmental so thick you almost needed a knife to cut it. A special of saffron risotto was dense and tangy, and a sharp rhubarb tart was softened with vanilla cream. Mon Plaisir remains a confident operation and the high number of regular diners reflects that consistency.
Booking advisable. Children admitted. Separate room for parties, seats 28. **Map 18 L6.**

Fitzrovia W1

Elena's L'Étoile
30 Charlotte Street, W1T 2NG (7636 7189). Goodge Street or Tottenham Court Road tube. **Lunch served** noon-2.30pm Mon-Fri. **Dinner served** 6-10.45pm Mon-Sat. **Main courses** £14.75-£20.75. **Service** 12.5%. **Credit** AmEx, DC, JCB, MC, V.
From the outside (tiny terrace, brass fittings, blue awnings, glossy blue paintwork) Elena's looks every inch the bijou provincial bistro; inside, the look continues (dark floor, snowy linen, mirrors, butter-yellow globe lamps and nicotine-yellow ceiling), but also makes a swerve in the direction of a theatre foyer. How so? Dozens upon dozens of framed snaps of famous people, many autographed: here's Wogan's signature and signature grin, there's Jamesh Bond beaming at the hostess herself, eightysomething Elena Salvoni. The implied celebrity endorsement can grate, but, then, Elena really does merit the moniker 'institution'. Service can be jerky: there was some funny business with the bread rolls and a disappearing butter dish, and we were brought the wrong bottle of wine. Still, the food arrived on time and was perfectly pleasant: smoked salmon on a warm potato pancake, and 'linguine Elena' with broad beans, herbs and lemon, followed by sea bass on spicy puy lentils, and magret de canard – in France they'd have asked us to specify the *cuisson*, but we had to make it clear – with green beans. The lunchtime crowd was 90% male and 90-decibel guffaws; evenings are, we trust, quieter.
Babies and children admitted. Booking advisable; essential lunch. Separate rooms for parties, seating 10, 16 and 32. **Map 9 J5.**

Knightsbridge SW1, SW3

Brasserie St Quentin
243 Brompton Road, SW3 2EP (7589 8005/ www.brasseriestquentin.co.uk). Knightsbridge or South Kensington tube/14, 74 bus. **Lunch served** noon-3pm daily. **Dinner served** 6-10.30pm Mon-Sat; 6-10pm Sun. **Main courses** £10.75-£23.50. **Set meal** (noon-7.30pm) £15.50 2 courses, £17.50 3 courses. **Service** 12.5%. **Credit** AmEx, DC, JCB, MC, V.
Seductively done out with red vinyl banquettes and sleazy bronzed mirrors, this Knightsbridge stalwart is a disarmingly fun place for a meal. Another surprise is that, behind the Parisian bourgeois decor and friendly French waiting staff,

there's a British theme. Very few ingredients are identified as sourced from France (an exception is 'French chicken', but where in France – Janze? Bresse?). Most come from closer to home (Elwy lamb from Wales, halibut and Buccleuch ribeye from Scotland). On a recent visit, the same careful attention that had been paid to sourcing ingredients was applied to cooking them, which made for a meal that was pure pleasure. The seared duck foie gras was meltingly soft and rich, textured with whole fresh peppercorns and broadened with caramelised apples; the scallops were plump and salty. To follow, Elwy lamb was exquisitely delicate and Buccleuch steak, accompanied by an eggy béarnaise, was tender to the bone. Even the simple steamed potatoes were delicious, served with parsley and a touch of mayonnaise. It was refreshing to be in a French-style restaurant inspired by the traditions of bourgeois cooking without being constrained by them.
Babies and children welcome: high chair. Booking advisable. Separate room for parties, seats 20. **Map 14 E10.**

Drones
1 Pont Street, SW1X 9EJ (7235 9555/ www.whitestarline.org.uk). Knightsbridge or Sloane Square tube. **Lunch served** noon-2.30pm Mon-Fri; noon-3.30pm Sun. **Dinner served** 6-11pm Mon-Sat. **Main courses** £9.50-£22. **Set lunch** (Mon-Fri) £14.95 2 courses, £17.95 3 courses; (Sun) £22.50 3 courses. **Service** 12.5% **Credit** AmEx, DC, MC, V.
We always relish the thought of an evening at Drones, with its retro glamour, classy brown hues and quietly buzzing atmosphere. Patron Marco Pierre White oversees a menu of straight-talking brasserie classics, prepared with precision and panache. Starters brought beautifully dressed fleshy Cornish crab and just-so eggs benedict, with perfect whites and rich, runny yokes. Steak lovers find it impossible to resist a juicy cut of ribeye with plump raisins on top and a delicious jus, accompanied by sensationally creamy pomme purée. Sweet and crispy haricots verts on the side made the perfect counterpart, and our £21 Côtes du Rhône was also spot-on. Drones specialises in rich flavours, and the portions are surprisingly large for such a chic restaurant. After starters and mains we couldn't have managed desserts for love or money – a shame given the impressive proportions served from the cheese trolley, and the tempting mousse au chocolat. As you would expect, prices are high, but they're not outrageous considering the outstanding cuisine, suave service and ritzy location. Reliably excellent.
Babies and children admitted. Booking essential. Restaurant available for hire. Separate room for parties, seats 45. **Map 15 G10.**

★ Racine
239 Brompton Road, SW3 2EP (7584 4477). Knightsbridge or South Kensington tube/ 14, 74 bus. **Lunch served** noon-3pm Mon-Fri; noon-3.30pm Sat, Sun. **Dinner served** 6-10.30pm Mon-Sat; 6-10pm Sun. **Main courses** £12.50-£25.50. **Set meal** (lunch, 6-7.30pm) £15.50 2 courses, £17.50 3 courses. **Service** 14.5%. **Credit** AmEx, JCB, MC, V.
Racine brings a slice of chic, Parisian style to stuffy old Knightsbridge. Push past the heavy curtain into a dark room – all sleek dark leather banquettes, smoked mirrors and immaculate white tablecloths – and settle in for an indulgent treat. Chef Henry Harris is an Englishman, but you'd never know it from his cooking: an array of French bourgeois classics – soupe de poisson, foie gras, steak tartare, cassoulet, calves' brains – alongside somewhat lighter and more rustic dishes. To start, there's the likes of warm garlic and saffron mousse; and Lincolnshire smoked eel, creamy smoked cod's roe, salmon roe mixed with horseradish, and a bright pink cube of beetroot and dill jelly – a wonderful assemblage of fishy flavours (and the most expensive starter, at £12.50). Mains were equally polished: calves' sweetbreads – very rich, very soft – served with broad beans and deep-fried artichokes; and two large pieces of perfect white plaice, with lentils and diced tomato and cucumber

in a champagne sauce. We shared a dessert: velvety lemon pudding topped with a sharp cherry compote. Impossibly elegant, black-clad French waiting staff provide super-professional, unfrosty service (though we still think the 14.5% service charge is a bit steep). You'll need to book.
Babies and children admitted: high chairs. Booking advisable. Dress: smart casual. No-smoking tables. **Map 14 E10**.

Marylebone W1

★ La Galette

56 Paddington Street, W1U 4HY (7935 1554/ www.lagalette.com). Baker Street tube. **Meals served** 9.30am-11pm Mon-Fri; 10am-11pm Sat, Sun. **Main courses** £5.60-£8.95. **Set lunch** (noon-5pm Mon-Fri) £7.95 2 courses. **Service** 10% for parties of 6 or more. **Credit** AmEx, MC, V.
La Galette looks more like a fast-food diner (albeit a stylish one) than a restaurant. And it's certainly possible to have a speedy lunch here. That would mean not lingering over a cider, though. These come from Brittany and Normandy, are served by the bottle or pichet, are drunk from porcelain bowls – and are reason enough to visit. The crêpes (sweet) and galettes (savoury) aren't bad either, but though classy, can't rise above the level of comforting snacks. Starters include tapenade, bayonne ham with celeriac rémoulade, and breton terrine de campagne with cornichons and toast, plus a few salads (goat's cheese and walnut, niçoise), but the galettes are the thing. Choices include forestière (mushrooms, crème fraîche and parsley), complète (ham, cheese and egg) and paysanne (smoked bacon with creamed leeks and parsley). They are filling too: we surrendered long before finishing a rich spinach and emmental galette. It's hard to imagine many diners then sample a crêpe with banana, chocolate sauce and crème chantilly – we assume there's a teatime trade in these. Treat La Galette as you would a pizza place and you won't go far wrong.
Babies and children welcome: high chairs. Bookings accepted for parties of 6 or more. Disabled: ramp. No smoking. Restaurant available for hire. Tables outdoors (2, terrace). Takeaway service. **Map 3 G5**.

Mayfair W1

Mirabelle

56 Curzon Street, W1Y 8DN (7499 4636/ www.whitestarline.org.uk). Green Park tube. **Lunch served** noon-2.30pm Mon-Sat; noon-3pm Sun. **Dinner served** 6-11pm daily. **Main courses** £14.50-£25. **Set lunch** (Mon-Sat) £17.50 2 courses, £21 3 courses; (Sun) £22 3 courses. **Service** 12.5%. **Credit** AmEx, MC, V.
Mirabelle would be fabulously glamorous, were it not for the dominance of male diners in suits. It's a lovely looking place, in a feminine 1940s way – check out the huge mirror ball. So ignore the fact that during the week the restaurant is used as an upmarket works canteen and concentrate on the splendidly retro menu (omelette Arnold Bennett with sauce mornay, for example, followed by ribeye of Aberdeen Angus aux escargots, pomme purée, jus viande). Salmon escabèche in a light, vegetable-packed sauce (a special) and hors d'oeuvres à la muscovite (new potatoes stuffed with fromage blanc and topped with caviar) made contrasting but equally effective starters. Escalope of tuna with aubergine caviar and sauce vierge au basilic came nicely rare and prettily arranged; grilled sea bass au fenouil was a fine choice too. Desserts include pear tarte tatin and crème brûlée, but we're big fans of the gelée of fresh fruits in rosé wine with raspberry syrup. Naturally, the wine list is quite a read (there's also a supplementary fine wine list), but the sommelier is helpful, just like the rest of the well-drilled staff. There are two private dining rooms and an under-publicised patio for summer.
Babies and children welcome: high chair. Booking advisable. Dress: smart casual. Entertainment: pianist dinner Fri, Sat, lunch Sun. Restaurant available for hire. Separate rooms for parties, seating 33 and 48. Tables outdoors (14, patio). **Map 9 H7**.

Chez Kristof. See p97.

★ Patterson's

4 Mill Street, W1S 2AX (7499 1308/ www.pattersonsrestaurant.co.uk). Oxford Circus or Bond Street tube. **Lunch served** noon-3pm Mon-Fri. **Dinner served** 6-11pm Mon-Sat. **Main courses** £13-£17. **Set lunch** £15 2 courses, £20 3 courses. **Service** 12.5%. **Credit** AmEx, MC, V.
A buxom sphere of sphagnum moss sits in a pot in the middle of each table, and the wine menu comes bound in fragrant leather that puts one in mind of a saddler's shop. That's as rustic as this Mayfair restaurant ('with a father for chef and a filial manager') gets, though: Patterson's is low-key, but offers unmistakable class and accomplishment. We visited shortly after noon and opted for the daily-changing lunch menu (the à la carte choice is also available), where starters and desserts cost £5 and mains £10. Even better, on our visit, a special summer promotion meant that the desserts were free. To the crisp accompaniment of a good 2003 pinot grigio, we tucked into starters of potato blini under smoked salmon under a perfect soft-boiled egg (the yolk still gloriously runny); and rich mushroom tart. Next came succulent slices of duck breast on an onion base, and flavourful sea bream. The pudding, served stylishly on a slate rectangle, was a summer fruits millefeuille with ice-cream. With an attractive setting, excellent service and three courses of delicious, expertly cooked food for £15, Patterson's is a corking bargain. We'll most certainly return for the à la carte.
Babies and children welcome: high chair. Booking advisable. Separate room for parties, seats 30. **Map 9 H/J6**.

Piccadilly W1

Criterion

224 Piccadilly, W1J 9HP (7930 0488/ www.whitestarline.org.uk). Piccadilly Circus tube. **Lunch served** noon-2.30pm, **dinner served** 5.30-11.30pm Mon-Sat. **Main courses** £11.50-£29.50. **Set meal** (lunch, 5.30-7pm) £14.95 2 courses, £17.95 3 courses. **Service** 12.5%. **Credit** AmEx, DC, JCB, MC, V.
Criterion hosts an interesting mix of guests, probably due to its location on Piccadilly Circus (the ever-lit neon ad boards shining through the frosted windows lend a sense of perpetual daylight). This melting pot incorporates business suits putting their bill on expenses, older types guffawing through cigar smoke (a heavy presence on our visit), a smattering of awestruck tourists (the Criterion's chandelier-hung, neo-Byzantine hall is spectacular), and casually dressed young things. The menu too marks a fusion: French delights (starters of halved lobster and terrine du foie gras parfait hit the kind of excellence that sets the mains a heavy task) meet Old Boy British classics (we chose roast suckling pig over rabbit, game and cumberland sausages with mash; sticky toffee pudding makes the smaller dessert list). Food is richly flavoured and richly priced, and the wine selection is as vast as the menu itself. The only flaw was the service: the waiters were far too heavy with their attention.
Babies and children welcome: high chairs. Booking advisable. Dress: smart casual. Restaurant available for hire. **Map 17 K7**.

St James's SW1

Brasserie Roux

Sofitel St James, 8 Pall Mall, SW1Y 5NG (7968 2900). Piccadilly Circus tube. **Lunch served** noon-3pm Mon-Fri; 12.30-3pm Sat, Sun. **Dinner served** 5.30-11.30pm Mon-Sat; 6-10.30pm Sun. **Main courses** £6.50-£21.50. **Set dinner** (5.30-7pm Mon-Sat) £15 3 courses; (after 7pm) £24.50 3 courses incl 2 glasses of wine, water & coffee. **Service** 12.5%. **Credit** AmEx, DC, JCB, MC, V.
Far from the brasseries on which it's modelled, this restaurant's location on the ground floor of St James's soulless Sofitel hotel means it's frequented by a mix of monied European and blazered American tourists rather than the late-night bon viveurs of Parisian legend. With the daily menu of hearty French staples such as bouillabaisse and cassoulet having failed to draw in a youthful

crowd, Sunday's Latin-influenced 'jazz brunch' is a misplaced attempt to appeal to a more chi-chi set. To a backing of bossa nova lite, Tex-Mex starters such as goat's cheese quesadillas and red pepper gazpacho were insults to the taste buds. To follow, roast loin of pork with pineapple was fine, although it was a bit too fatty and arrived without the sweet potato offered on the menu. A tuna steak ordered rare came overcooked and tough; it was edible only with large dollops of tomato salsa. For pudding even the simple-sounding dark chocolate mousse with ginger biscuit failed to atone for the preceding failings: the mousse was made with milk chocolate (rather than dark), while the biscuit lacked even a hint of ginger.
Babies and children welcome: children's menu; high chairs. Booking essential. Disabled: toilet (in adjoining Sofitel St James hotel). Dress: smart casual. No-smoking tables. **Map 17 K7**.

Soho W1

L'Escargot Marco Pierre White
48 Greek Street, W1D 4EF (7437 2679/ www.whitestarline.org.uk). Leicester Square or Tottenham Court Road tube.
Ground-floor restaurant **Lunch served** noon-2.15pm Mon-Fri. **Dinner served** 6-11.30pm Mon-Fri; 5.30-11.30pm Sat. **Main courses** £12.95-£14.95. **Set meal** (lunch, 6-7pm Mon-Fri) £15 2 courses, £18 3 courses. **Service** 12.5%.
Picasso Room **Lunch served** 12.15-2pm Tue-Fri. **Dinner served** 7-11pm Tue-Sat. **Set lunch** £20.50 2 courses, £25.50 3 courses. **Set meal** £42 3 courses. **Service** 15%.
Both **Credit** AmEx, DC, JCB, MC, V.
It seems that every second business in Soho is labelled an 'institution'. This Marco Pierre White restaurant has a good claim to the label: there's been a restaurant on this site since the 1920s. As L'Escargot, it's a delight – only the vaguest hint of Old Boy pretension lingers (dead-serious service, guffawing businessmen, cigars 'offered at the discretion of the management') – and the dishes are a pleasure. There are two dining spaces. The ground-floor restaurant is windowless; mirrored walls and high ceilings help, but it suffers for lack of natural light. Upstairs is the more formal Picasso Room, which offers a separate, more expensive menu and plenty of artworks (by guess who?) to gaze at. The highlight of a recent lunch in the ground-floor room was a plate of nine juicy snails (of course) in a dark bordelaise sauce, each mollusc perched on a mini mound of creamed potato. Blenheim Estate lamb followed, sliced to reveal a perfect pink interior, and served over rich risotto and vegetables julienne. Equally satisfying, if more straightforward, was smoked haddock with mustard sauce. Fruit tarts are a dessert speciality. A decent wine selection is let down only by a lack of availability by the glass.
Babies and children admitted (ground-floor restaurant). Booking essential weekends. Dress: smart casual. Separate rooms for parties, seating 24 and 60. Vegetarian menu. **Map 17 K6**.

La Trouvaille
12A Newburgh Street, W1F 7RR (7287 8488/ www.latrouvaille.co.uk). Oxford Circus tube.
Lunch served noon-3pm, **dinner served** 6-11pm Mon-Sat. **Set lunch** £16.95 2 courses, £19.75 3 courses. **Set dinner** £24.50 2 courses, £29.50 3 courses. **Service** 12.5%. **Credit** AmEx, MC, V.
This pint-sized corner restaurant in the heart of Soho is a real charmer, with simple wooden floors, romantic flickering candles and large windows opening on to a cobbled street. La Trouvaille is a wholeheartedly, if by no means doggedly, French restaurant, overseen by an efficient team of charming young French waiters. It seems to revel in its quirkiness, from the eccentric cutlery to the often unusual – but never silly – takes on culinary classics (such as rabbit shepherd's pie). We were bowled over by the explosive flavours of our starter of grilled portobello mushrooms and cured mutton ham, which came gratinéed with blue cheese and served with an exquisite salad dressed with truffle oil. Another starter of celeriac rémoulade with black truffle salsa and marinated

The Ledbury

RESTAURANTS

baby scallops was also highly accomplished. Mains yielded similarly impressive results: so tender and tasty was our cut of grilled beef steak that its accompanying caviar reduction was left surprisingly redundant; and a breast of guinea fowl with roast shallots and cream of port was a sublime combination. With the bill costing under £75 for two courses each (including a cracking bottle of syrah) and providing such a romantic setting, La Trouvaille is a find indeed.
Babies and children admitted. Booking advisable. Separate room for parties, seats 20. Tables outdoors (10, pavement). **Map 17 J6.**
For branch (Brasserie La Trouvaille) see index.

Strand WC2

The Admiralty
Somerset House, Strand, WC2R 1LA (7845 4646/www.somerset-house.org.uk). Embankment or Temple tube/Charing Cross tube/rail. **Lunch served** noon-2.30pm daily. **Dinner served** 6-10.30pm Mon-Sat. **Main courses** £17.50-£23.50. **Service** 12.5%. **Credit** AmEx, DC, JCB, MC, V.
In a great location in a corner of Somerset House by the Thames, the Admiralty was in fine form when we visited for lunch midweek. The decor is playful and fun, from seaside turquoise seating to ship-shaped chandeliers. Light streaming through the high south-facing windows makes for a warm atmosphere. Presentation adds to the food's appeal: scallops were artfully arranged on a plate with an artichoke heart and caramelised onions (the dish tasted as good as it looked), and smoked duck breast slices were served in a shallow bowl of chicken consommé with tomatoes cut small like jewels (even better than the scallops). Next came a delicate dish of halibut with cauliflower purée and firm puy lentils. More successful still was baked sea bass with a delicious saffron sauce, fat mussels and a dramatic razor-shell clam on the side, its flesh chopped into thin slices. Efficient and unobtrusive service added to the sense of occasion. It's all very convivial, even at higher-than-average prices and with no set lunch.
Babies and children welcome: high chairs. Booking advisable. Disabled: toilet. Dress: smart casual. No-smoking tables. Restaurant available for hire. Separate room for parties, seats 30. **Map 10 M7.**

West

Chiswick W4

★ La Trompette
5-7 Devonshire Road, W4 2EU (8747 1836/ www.latrompette.co.uk). Turnham Green tube. **Lunch served** noon-2.30pm Mon-Sat; 12.30-3pm Sun. **Dinner served** 6.30-10.45pm Mon-Sat; 7-10.30pm Sun. **Set lunch** £23.50 3 courses; (Sun) £27.50 3 courses. **Set dinner** £32.50 3 courses, £42.50 4 courses. **Service** 12.5%. **Credit** AmEx, JCB, MC, V.
It may be on the borders of Zones Two and Three, but La Trompette offers a standard of cooking that is striking even by central London standards – and a buzz to match. The owners are Nigel Platts-Martin and chef Bruce Poole, who also run Chez Bruce (see *p99*) in Wandsworth and the Glasshouse (see *p237*) in Kew. Sure, the 1970s retro mushroom walls may not be to everyone's taste, but the menu probably will be. This features old favourite dishes that have been present since the place opened, alongside others added seasonally. We couldn't get enough of starters of warm paysanne salad with shredded duck confit, lentils and poached egg; and chorizo and rolled belly of pata negra pork (despite the blanket of puréed mint on the latter). A sautéed breast of baby chicken was perfectly balanced with french peas, memorable fried foie gras and gnocchi, while a soft veal cheek was matched with crisp fried sweetbreads and a strongly flavoured tarragon sauce. Portions aren't huge, but there's certainly a huge variety of flavours to be sampled. This applies to puddings too. An intense basil granita was attractively presented in a Martini glass with paper-thin slices of candied pineapple, while a

creamy cheesecake was peppered with vanilla seeds – a strong finish. At all times, service was attentive and professional, the sommelier in particular standing out. The wine list is one of London's best.
Babies and children welcome: high chairs. Booking advisable. Disabled: toilet. No smoking. Tables outdoors (7, terrace).

Le Vacherin
76-77 South Parade, W4 5LF (8742 2121/ www.levacherin.co.uk). Chiswick Park tube/rail. **Lunch served** noon-3pm Tue-Sat; noon-5pm Sun. **Dinner served** 6-10.30pm Mon-Thur, Sun; 6-11pm Fri, Sat. **Main courses** (dinner) £11.95-£16. **Set lunch** £13 2 courses, £15.95 3 courses. **Service** 12.5%. **Credit** MC, V.
In the four winter months when vacherin cheese is at its pungent and resiny best, you can enjoy it here in different forms across three courses. For the rest of the year, when it's off the menu, the restaurant loses some of its cachet – but not, apparently, its local popularity. When we visited early in the week, the two mirrored white rooms were packed with middle-aged diners enjoying the relaxed atmosphere. One starter alone was worth our trip: a memorable st marcellin cheese (vacherin's stunt double for late spring) came toasted and molten in a pot with flaked almonds and slices of black truffle, surrounded by such dipping morsels as bayonne ham, pickles and sliced cabbage. Other dishes were pretty good too. Long asparagus came in a loose plait with a thick and salty hollandaise, and an ox cheek had been carefully braised beyond tender to a state where it wobbled when the plate moved. Perhaps too many unseasonal winter dishes were on the menu, but otherwise there was little to fault – especially not the service, which was friendly and effective throughout.
Babies and children welcome: high chairs. Booking advisable. No smoking. Separate room for parties, seats 20.

Hammersmith W6

★ Chez Kristof
2005 WINNER BEST LOCAL RESTAURANT
111 Hammersmith Grove, W6 0NQ (8741 1177). Goldhawk Road or Hammersmith tube. **Deli Open** 8am-8pm Mon-Fri; 8.30am-6pm Sat; 8.30am-7pm Sun. *Restaurant* **Lunch served** 12.30-3pm, **dinner served** 6-11.15pm Mon-Fri. **Meals served** noon-11.15pm Sat; noon-10.30pm Sun. **Main courses** £9-£18. **Service** 12.5%. **Both Credit** AmEx, JCB, MC, V.
Chez Kristof has a fine pedigree, being the latest venture of Jan Woroniecki, proprietor of acclaimed east European restaurants Baltic (see *p83*) and Wódka (see *p81*). The room is elegant and low-key: muted greys and browns are offset by a pretty chandelier and a curtain of golden fairylights in one window. Large french doors at the front open on to pavement tables, shielded from the street by low bamboo planters. The regional French cooking is very good – and varied: everything from oysters to escargots, rabbit to risotto. First-rate starters included satisfyingly earthy haricot beans and clams (large enough for a main course); and a delicate, fresh-tasting crab mayonnaise with celeriac rémoulade. Carnivores are well catered for, *bien sûr*, but there are some immaculate fish dishes (halibut with antiboise sauce was faultless) and vegetarians get a look-in too. A vegetable stew (red peppers, tomatoes, girolles, artichokes, asparagus and butter beans in a light broth) was delicious, each element retaining its shape and flavour. And who'd have thought simple braised puy lentils (a side dish) could be so good? To drink: first-rate cocktails, numerous spirits and a lengthy, mainly French wine list with better-than-average choices by the glass. The only problem? The service, which was indifferent and perfunctory. Next door is a deli, which serves café-style meals during the day.
Babies and children welcome: children's menu; high chairs; films. Booking advisable. Disabled: toilet. Dress: smart casual. No-smoking tables. Separate room for parties, seats 50. Tables outdoors (24, terrace). Takeaway service.
Map 20 B3.

Holland Park W8

The Belvedere
Holland House, Off Abbotsbury Road, in Holland Park, W8 6LU (7602 1238/www.whitestarline. org.uk). Holland Park tube. **Lunch served** noon-2.30pm Mon-Sat; noon-3pm Sun. **Dinner served** 6-10pm Mon-Sat. **Main courses** £10-£18. **Set lunch** (Mon-Fri) £14.95 2 courses, £17.95 3 courses; (Sat, Sun) £21 3 courses. **Service** 12.5%. **Credit** AmEx, MC, V.
The Belvedere is a Marco Pierre White restaurant in a wing of the Jacobean mansion that gives Holland Park its name. Grand isn't the word. Cross the threshold and you're in a high-ceilinged phantasmagoria of opulence and clashing styles: classical arches, chinoiserie, huge scallop lampshades, Moroccan-patterned windows and a vast Warholian mosaic. Despite the setting, diners on our visit were unstuffy and, in several cases, casually attired, and staff were courteous and relaxed. Perhaps too relaxed: our damask tablecloth should have been pristine, but bore a noticeable grubby spot and a wizened flower arrangement. Chef Billy Reid, who has also worked at L'Escargot (see *p96*), joined in late 2004. The daily lunch menu, though reasonably priced, was not a soaring achievement: venison terrine with shallot and thyme marmalade was excellent, and smoked haddock fish cake was comfort food of a high order, but the supreme of organic salmon with fondant potato was merely good. Pork rillettes (from the à la carte) came without the advertised pear chutney. 'Everything OK, chaps?' breezed our waiter at the end – and at just over £50 for four courses and two glasses of white wine, it was, more or less.
Babies and children welcome: high chairs. Booking essential. Restaurant available for hire. Tables outdoors (5, terrace).

Notting Hill W11

★ The Ledbury NEW
2005 RUNNER-UP BEST NEW RESTAURANT
127 Ledbury Road, W11 2AQ (7792 9090/www. theledbury.com). Westbourne Park tube. **Lunch served** noon-2.30pm daily. **Dinner served** 6.30-11pm Mon-Sat; 6.30-10pm Sun. **Set lunch** (Mon-Fri) £19.50 2 courses, £24.50 3 courses; (Sat, Sun) £24.50 2 courses, £29.50 3 courses. **Service** 12.5%. **Credit** AmEx, JCB, MC, V.
Owned by Nigel Platts-Martin and Philip Howard (the team behind the Square; see *p129*), the Ledbury represents a culinary step up for Notting Hill. The chef is Australian Brett Graham, lately of the Square, and he's obviously a young man going places. For example, the sheer loveliness of a dessert of vanilla yoghurt parfait with blueberries and churros was only surpassed by its exquisite taste. A salad of spring vegetables with quail eggs, truffle and pea shoots (a starter), and Glenarm salmon wrapped in pancetta with gnocchi, pea purée and morels (a main) also passed the looks and taste tests with flying colours. Not everything convinced. We weren't persuaded that the flavours involved in a main course of roast sea bass with creamed potato and a vinaigrette of raisins, pine nuts and cockles entirely gelled. There are small niggles too – you pay for three courses even if you only order two – but the place gets most things right (no being left in phone limbo when booking, no sittings policy, a splendid wine list readily explained by an unthreatening sommelier, informed staff who seem happy to be here). This is a handsome restaurant that deserves to be around for a while.
Babies and children admitted. Booking essential. Disabled: toilet. Dress: smart casual. Tables outdoors (37, pavement). **Map 7 A5/6.**

South West

Chelsea SW3

Le Colombier
145 Dovehouse Street, SW3 6LB (7351 1155). South Kensington tube/14 bus. **Lunch served** noon-3pm Mon-Sat; noon-3.30pm Sun. **Dinner served** 6.30-10.30pm Mon-Sat; 6.30-10pm Sun.

Main courses £12-£19. **Set lunch** (Mon-Sat) £14.50 2 courses. **Set dinner** (6.30-7.30pm Sun) £16.50 2 courses. **Service** 12.5%. **Credit** AmEx, JCB, MC, V.

With a corner site and a glazed terrace to one side, Le Colombier looks inviting. And, with so many well-heeled regulars, it's somewhere that doesn't have to try too hard – in fact, during our visit, there were times when it didn't seem to be trying at all. On the positive side, there was a battery of waiters and a personable maître d'. On the negative side, those waiting on our table acted as if their batteries had been taken out. There were some treats among the dishes we tried (a starter of tender tuna was so briefly seared it was like sashimi) and some howlers (a bland 'special' of marinated plaice seemed like something made from leftovers). Fried ris de veau (calves' sweetbreads) with morels trod the line between interesting and curious, while coquilles st-jacques were great, the scallops served separate from their sauce (this separation is a common theme of Le Colombier's take on classic bourgeois dishes). Despite our quibbles, this place clearly has a winning formula that keeps regulars coming back for more.
Babies and children welcome: high chair. Booking advisable; essential Sun. Dress: smart casual. Separate room for parties, seats 30. Tables outdoors (10, terrace). **Map 14 D11**.

Putney SW15

L'Auberge

22 Upper Richmond Road, SW15 2RX (8874 3593/www.ardillys.com). East Putney tube. **Dinner served** 7-10pm Tue-Sat. **Main courses** £11.95-£14.50. **Set dinner** £12.95 2 courses, £16 3 courses. **Service** 12.5%. **Credit** MC, V.

So busy was this family-run restaurant on our Tuesday evening visit that staff were turning away non-bookings. The diverse range of customers (dating couples, groups of medics, thirtysomething friends) seemed to include regulars known by name to patronne Mme Ardilly, so there was a friendly buzz about the place. Food is French with a capital 'F'. We enjoyed an appetising and intense cocotte of fat snails in garlic, cream and white wine with mushrooms, while a delicate plate of savoury veal kidneys was civilised rather than mind-blowing. Cheeses were ripe and well chosen, with a bleu de bresse oozing towards a piquant st marcellin. Puddings are probably chef M Ardilly's forte. A crème brûlée, flavoured with cardamom and almond and named Pondichéry (after the French colony in south India), was warm on arrival, the caramel top still soft from the flames before crusting at the table; it was one of the best crème brûlées we've tasted in years. It's tough to keep to these standards on this slightly bleak stretch of the South Circular (neighbouring restaurants were either empty or closed) and the owners deserve all credit for their success.
Babies and children admitted. Booking advisable for large parties. Restaurant available for hire.

Wandsworth SW17

★ Chez Bruce

2 Bellevue Road, SW17 7EG (8672 0114/ www.chezbruce.co.uk). Wandsworth Common rail. **Lunch served** noon-2pm Mon-Fri; 12.30-2.30pm Sat; noon-3pm Sun. **Dinner served** 6.30-10.30pm Mon-Sat; 7-10pm Sun. **Set lunch** (Mon-Fri) £23.50 3 courses; (Sat) £25 3 courses; (Sun) £29.50 3 courses. **Set dinner** £35 3 courses. **Service** 12.5%. **Credit** AmEx, DC, JCB, MC, V.

Bruce Poole's thoroughbred Wandsworth dining spot celebrated its tenth birthday in 2005 – and you'd be hard pushed to find a single critic or diner with a bad word to say about it over the past decade. The reason? Friendly, knowledgeable service; an unfussy, timeless space hung with low-key art; and, most importantly, classy, classic and 100% reliable cooking. Essentially, this is simple food, free from haute pretensions, but immaculately sourced and cooked with flair and conviction. Classic and regional French cuisine provide the base for the frequently changing menu, with further inspiration drawn from the wider shores of

the Mediterranean. You could go for a Gallic feast of navarin of lamb followed by crème brûlée and the notable cheeseboard, or, like us, head further south for a pair of immaculate Italian starters: vitello tonnato (thin slices of rump of veal with a tuna dressing), and risotto nero with red mullet and meltingly tender baby squid. Mains included silky roast cod with olive oil mash, spinach (unannounced) and an agreeably spiky gremolata; and calf's liver with polenta, buttered asparagus and more unannounced spinach. The wine list is strong on Rhônes, Burgundies and regional French labels, as well as offering rarely encountered gems from Germany and Austria. La Trompette (also French; *see p97*) and the Glasshouse (Modern European; *see p237*) are run by the same team.
Babies and children admitted (lunch). Booking essential. No smoking. Separate room for parties, seats 16 (lunch Mon-Sat; dinner Mon-Thur, Sun).

South
Battersea SW8, SW11

★ Le Bouchon Bordelais

5-9 Battersea Rise, SW11 1HG (7738 0307/ www.lebouchon.co.uk). Clapham Junction rail/ 35, 37 bus. **Bar Open** 10am-11pm Mon-Sat; 10am-10.30pm Sun. **Meals served** 10am-10pm daily. **Main courses** £6.95-£9.95. *Restaurant* **Meals served** noon-11pm Mon-Sat; noon-10.30pm Sun. **Main courses** £14.50-£25. *Both* **Service** 12.5%. **Credit** AmEx, MC, V.

Thanks to Michel Roux's involvement, the once-moribund Le Bouchon Bordelais has transformed into the very essence of a French brasserie. The restaurant and bar sit side by side, with a family room at the back and – a major bonus for parents – a supervised crèche in the basement. The decor consists of classic big mirrors, lashings of dark wood and a chequerboard floor. Eric Landeau's menu is carnivore heaven; beef and lamb are the specialities. It's a delight to see lamb in five versions (gigot, carré, medallions, saddle and shoulder), while the steaks are exemplary: plump, tender and flavour-rich. Romantic red-meat lovers can share an 18oz chateaubriand or rib of beef (both at £37 for two). If you want to go easier on the protein, just about every brasserie standard is here – fish soup, oysters, snails, moules marinière, to be followed by chocolate mousse, tarte tatin, profiteroles, crème brûlée – and all in superior versions. Amiable staff of the 'Antoine de Caunes on speed' variety add a finishing flourish of Gallic bonhomie. Be warned, though: prices are more on the scale of a serious restaurant than a local bistro.
Babies and children welcome: children's menu; crèche (Sat, Sun); high chairs. No-smoking tables. Separate room for parties, seats 80. Tables outdoors (8, terrace). **Map 21 C5.**
For branch (Le Bouchon Lyonnais) see index.

★ The Food Room

2005 RUNNER-UP BEST NEW RESTAURANT
123 Queenstown Road, SW8 3RH (7622 0555/ www.thefoodroom.com). Battersea Park or Queenstown Road rail/137, 156 bus. **Lunch served** noon-2.30pm Tue-Fri. **Dinner served** 7-10.30pm Tue-Sat. **Set lunch** £19.50 2 courses, £24.50 3 courses. **Service** 12.5%. **Credit** MC, V.
The low-key premises on Queenstown Road belie the quality of the food served within. The Food Room is run by Eric Guignard, who also owns the French Table (*see p103*), and while the variations-on-beige interior creates a calm and pleasant backdrop, the food is the star. Guignard is particularly fond of pork belly, and his trilogy of caramelised pork belly (with sweet potatoes and wild mushrooms; broad beans and chorizo; artichoke and foie gras) has pride of place on the modern French menu. On a hot evening, we turned instead to mains of pan-fried sea bass on spinach with croustillant of artichoke and tomato coulis (excellent and inventive), and pastilla of vegetables with mozzarella and pistou (not bad, but it didn't really gel as a dish). Much better were starters of bavarois of petits pois with parmesan and roast

Interview
PASCAL AUSSIGNAC

Who are you?
Chef-patron of **Club Gascon** (*see p92*) and **Le Cercle** (*see p91*).
Eating in London: what's good about it?
It's a great city to eat in. The variety of restaurants is amazing. I've just been to Sicily on holiday, and the restaurant trade all over the island was very boring. In London you can travel all over the world yet stay in the same city.
What's bad about it?
You mean apart from the prices? I don't like the booking system. At Le Cercle we tried not taking bookings after 8pm just to say, look, you don't have to book three weeks in advance, you can come and have a drink and wait for a table – but it didn't work and the critics didn't understand it. People feel frustrated when they have to book three or four months in advance. The other thing I hate is the way some restaurants charge for bread. I don't think it's fair.
Which are your favourite London restaurants?
I love **Busaba Eathai** (*see p265*), **Noura Central** (*see p215*), **Yauatcha** (*see p72*), **Amaya** (*see p131*) and **J Sheekey** (*see p85*).
What single thing would improve London's restaurant scene?
Stop the congestion charge. People don't want to travel and it's hurting the restaurant trade. Public transport takes too long and is too expensive.
Any hot tips for the coming year?
Joël Robuchon is to set up a branch of L'Atelier in Soho. It should be the hit of the year. I welcome Robuchon and hope he'll succeed. He's my super-masterchef.
Anything to declare?
The restaurant trade in London is always evolving. The Paris scene is fantastic, but they're taking no risks. London is not as conservative as Paris – that's why we lost the Olympics!

RESTAURANTS

almonds (an intense blast of flavour), and smoked monkfish salad with tomato confit, curry oil and sesame tuile (full of interest to the last mouthful). And you really can't go wrong with the puds – lemon confit with lemon mousse and raspberry sorbet was a surefire summer hit; cheeses come from La Fromagerie. Staff are smiling and efficient, and the place has the kind of quiet charm that encourages repeat visits.
Babies and children admitted. Booking advisable. No-smoking tables.

Le Petit Max
14 Chatfield Road, SW11 3SE (7223 0999). Clapham Junction rail. **Lunch served** noon-2pm daily. **Dinner served** 7-10pm Mon-Sat. **Main courses** £9.50-£20. **Set lunch** £14.50 2 courses. **Set meal** £18.50 3 courses. **Service** 12.5%. **Credit** MC, V.
This lacklustre eaterie was barely recognisable this year as runner-up for the Best New Restaurant category of the 2004 *Time Out* Eating & Drinking Awards: the exuberance of Max Renzland and his flair for kitchen and service were nowhere to be seen. Perhaps it's because we loved Le Petit Max so much that our recent experience felt so disappointing. From the waiting staff who couldn't explain the menu to the bland and meagre portions, this was an embarrassing display. Asparagus with hollandaise should have been an easy opportunity to please, but there was so little sauce that we looked for signs a cat had got there first. Flavour made a brief appearance with a warmed goat's cheese in an otherwise insipid salad – but that was it. A bavette was so thin, the request for it to be served very rare became irrelevant. Duck confit was ordered with frites and came instead with dull mash. Enticing menus from old restaurants in France adorned the walls by our table; if only we'd been able to order from one of those. In fact, we would rather have been anywhere else than here to witness such a decline.
Babies and children welcome: high chairs. Booking advisable (weekends). Disabled: toilet. Tables outdoors (1, pavement). **Map 21 A3.**

Clapham SW4

Gastro
67 Venn Street, SW4 0BD (7627 0222). Clapham Common tube. **Breakfast served** 8am-3pm, **meals served** noon-midnight daily. **Main courses** £10.45-£16.50. **Service** 12.5%. **No credit cards.**
You have to admire Gastro's *cochon*-headed French swagger: it is the embodiment of the classic Gallic shoulder shrug. Only cash is accepted; the decor is beguilingly dishevelled; wine comes in school canteen-style glasses; the staff's English is thickly accented to the point of incomprehensibility; you never know quite how long it'll take for your order to arrive; and the light levels in the back section beyond the bubbling lobster tank are so low that it's advisable to bring a torch to see the menu. Such eccentricities charm Gastro's many regulars (and irritate less partial diners). But what of the food? A little more French flair would not go amiss on the fairly basic bistro-style menu. A shared assiette bretonne to start offered an unappealing and anaemic selection of cold meats, and was followed by a middling entrecôte and an offputtingly mountainous and bland special of couscous with merguez sausages and veg. The wine list too isn't quite up to scratch – just an unimaginative handful of bottles from the standard regions. Gastro is, alas, a triumph of atmosphere over content.
Babies and children admitted. Booking advisable. Disabled: toilet. No-smoking tables. Separate room for parties, seats 22. Tables outdoors (4, pavement). **Map 22 A2.**

Waterloo SE1

Chez Gérard
9 Belvedere Road, South Bank, SE1 8YS (7202 8470/www.santeonline.co.uk). Waterloo tube/rail. **Meals served** noon-11pm Mon-Sat; noon-9pm Sun. **Main courses** £8.95-£18.95. **Set meal** £13.50 2 courses, £16.75 3 courses. **Cover** £1.50. **Service** 12.5%. **Credit** AmEx, DC, JCB, MC, V.

Positioning itself on the restaurant/brasserie/bar axis, the Chez Gérard chain offers a broad selection of starters, snacks and mains based on popular French classics. Unfortunately, the quality of our recent meal at the South Bank branch was as varied as the choice on the long menu. To start, chicken liver and spinach salad was a warming Gallic joy, whereas queen scallops in shallot vinaigrette were chewy and flavourless. For mains, a marmite (cooking pot) of seafood was a heady creamy stew of monkfish, salmon and shellfish, but the côte de bœuf was sorely disappointing. Nowhere near living up to the menu's boast of 'the best steak-frites this side of Paris', the meat was rare in places but overdone and charred in others, and came accompanied by limp, watery chips. The insipid house red was uninspiring too. We decided to skip dessert and left feeling that while Chez Gérard's atmosphere of mass-production fails to bring out the best in French cuisine, it is probably this that makes the place a popular and lively destination for large groups and office parties.
Babies and children welcome: high chairs. Booking advisable. Disabled: toilet. Separate rooms for parties, seating 20 and 40. Tables outdoors (6, pavement). **Map 10 M8.** For branches see index.

RSJ
33A Coin Street, SE1 9NR (7928 4554/ www.rsj.uk.com). Waterloo tube/rail. **Lunch served** noon-2pm Mon-Fri. **Dinner served** 5.30-11pm Mon-Sat. **Main courses** £12-£17. **Set meal** £15.95 2 courses, £17.95 3 courses. **Service** 12.5%. **Credit** AmEx, DC, MC, V.

Perched in a converted stable just behind the South Bank, RSJ's first-floor dining room has an air of gastronomic calm that is both refreshingly cool on hot summer days and cosily warm on cold winter nights. The seasonally based French menu includes a reasonable prix fixe, but more fun is to be had by paying a little more for the à la carte. To start, foie gras parfait combined indulgent richness with a surprising lightness of texture, while a plateful of seared scallops with hazelnut mash and white truffle sauce was sheer culinary ecstasy. Main courses proved to be just as delicious: hearty chunks of sea bass that flaked easily from the fish's skin were accompanied by forkfuls of tarragon risotto; and juicy strips of belly pork were prised from beneath a shell of crackling and scooped up with mustard mash. We could only glance ruefully at the dessert list wishing we'd left space for warm spiced plum cake. Instead, we consoled ourselves with the last sips of the Vouvray chosen from the restaurant's Loire-specialist cellar.
Babies and children admitted. Booking advisable. Separate room for parties, seats 25. **Map 11 N8.**

East
Bethnal Green E2

Bistrotheque
2005 RUNNER-UP BEST LOCAL RESTAURANT
23-27 Wadeson Street, E2 9DR (8983 7900/ www.bistrotheque.com). Bethnal Green tube/ Cambridge Heath rail/55 bus.

Bistrotheque

Bar **Open** 5.30pm-midnight Mon-Sat; 5.30-10.30pm Sun.
Restaurant **Dinner served** 6.30-10.30pm Mon-Sat. **Meals served** 1-9pm Sun.
Main courses £8-£25. **Service** 12.5%.
Credit AmEx, MC, V.
A dingy Bethnal Green street lined with industrial buildings doesn't look like the setting for a fashionable eaterie, but here it is, through an unmarked door, occupying two floors of a former clothing warehouse. On the ground floor is a small dark bar with excellent cocktails (the passionfruit Caiprinha is recommended); above, a light and spacious dining space that resembles an artist's studio with its with rough white walls and grey-painted concrete floor. The casual vibe extends to the menu, which offers quick snacks (croque monsieur, omelette fine herbes, steak sandwich) as well as straightforward starters and mains. A broad bean, pea and mint salad with soft-boiled egg was a refreshing starter on a hot evening; to follow, poached wild trout was a lovely piece of fish, though its parsley and lemon sauce was too rich for our taste. Side orders – thick-cut chips and roasted cherry vine tomatoes, burst and oozing juices – were exemplary. There's a wry humour at work too, with 1970s classics (prawn cocktail to start, peach melba to finish) putting in an appearance on the menu. Add in genuinely friendly and enthusiastic staff (how rare is that) a fairly priced wine list (including less common grapes such as picpoul), occasional entertainment ('tranny talent show') and you have a real charmer.

Babies and children welcome: high chairs. Booking advisable. Disabled: toilet. Entertainment: cabaret 9pm Wed-Sat. Separate room for parties, seats 50.

Brick Lane E1

★ Les Trois Garçons

1 Club Row, E1 6JX (7613 1924/www.lestrois garcons.com). Liverpool Street tube/rail/8, 388 bus. **Dinner served** 7-10.30pm Mon-Thur; 6.45-11pm Fri, Sat. **Main courses** £18-£32. **Set dinner** (Mon-Wed) £22 2 courses, £26 3 courses. **Service** 12.5%. **Credit** AmEx, DC, JCB, MC, V.
Les Trois Garçons is a splendid venue for a big night out. It's a handsomely converted former pub, easily identified on Bethnal Green Road by its flaming torches. 'Edwardian camp' pretty much describes the interior, accessorised by stuffed animals, chandeliers and idiosyncratic touches such as the display of jewelled evening bags. The place is run with warmth and verve, and – despite appearances – absolute seriousness in the kitchen. Some dishes read a little oddly, but work magnificently (a starter of tartare of bluefin tuna with coconut, grapefruit and soy beans, for example), and some are just tried-and-tested marvellous (witness ratte potato and truffle salad). Mains – cannon of lamb with cipolline onions, cauliflower purée, curry and chocolate sauce; and pan-seared halibut with spring pea purée, shimji mushrooms, grapes and tarragon jus – were just as good and looked exquisite. Very pretty

puddings include the likes of iced coconut parfait with flambéed bananas and chocolate cream. There's caviar and blinis, should you want to push the boat out even further; the wine list reaches out to big spenders too. Very much a one-off, and all the more fun for that.
Booking advisable. Restaurant available for hire. Separate room for parties, seats 10.
Map 6 S4.

Docklands E14

Plateau

Canada Place, Canada Square, E14 5ER (7715 7100/www.conran.com). Canary Wharf tube/DLR.
Bar & Grill **Meals served** noon-11pm Mon-Sat; noon-4pm Sun. **Main courses** £9.50-£33.
Set meal £16.50 2 courses, £20 3 courses.
Restaurant **Lunch served** noon-3pm Mon-Fri, Sun. **Dinner served** 6-10.30pm Mon-Sat.
Main courses £14.50-£27. **Set dinner** £24.75 3 courses, £29.75 4 courses.
Both **Service** 12.5%. **Credit** AmEx, DC, MC, V.
The space-age look of Plateau is exactly right for Canary Wharf. Walls of glass mean light and great views of Docklands, and the groovy designer furniture (it's a Conran joint) is bright white, so by day the place sparkles, but by night clever lighting means it has a soft glow and everyone looks good. Further warmth is injected by the smiley staff. You enter the restaurant through the bar and grill (where cocktails and a less expensive, more international menu of grills and rôtisserie modern standards are served to a muted beat). Prices take a hike in the restaurant: a starter of sweetcorn ravioli with cherry tomatoes and basil oil was £9.50; prawn salad with champagne vinaigrette was £11. Both were good, but too salty. This problem continued with rôtisserie brill with truffle and broad beans; in fact, the only savoury dish to escape this fate was a main course of mixed summer vegetables in a delicate broth. Even a side of – otherwise delicious – herb mash failed the salt test. Chocolate fondant with raspberry chilli sorbet restored our faith in the kitchen. We've had superb meals here in the past, so hope this was a heavy-handed off-night in what is one of east London's most impressive restaurants.
Babies and children welcome: high chairs. Booking advisable. Disabled: toilet. Dress: smart casual. Separate room for parties, seats 24. Tables outdoors (12, terrace). Vegetarian menu.

Shoreditch EC2

South

128 Curtain Road, EC2A 3AQ (7729 4452). Old Street tube/rail. **Lunch served** noon-3pm, **dinner served** 6-10.30pm Mon-Sat. **Main courses** £9.50-£14. **Set lunch** £12.95 3 courses. **Service** 12.5%. **Credit** JCB, MC, V.
South is unusual in Shoreditch in that it's a straightforward French restaurant, rather than a style bar or designer statement. The exterior is painted an unwise almost-peppermint green; inside is much nicer (calming cream and white), although the effect was spoiled on our visit by disco beats coming from the sound system. The place has been around for a couple of years, but can still feel slightly makeshift. On a hot evening more than one person ordered rosé, so the restaurant ran out. The cooking was also patchy. A starter of grilled squid with chilli, parsley and garlic was a large portion expertly cooked and flavoured, and the hors d'oeuvres plate was a diverting and summery mix of tastes. Mains were less satisfactory: stuffed aubergine with peppers was a bit nothingy, while pan-fried salmon was also underwhelming. Maybe we should have plumped for steak (ribeye with chips and peppercorn butter). Puddings were the likes of gateau au chocolat or fresh grilled apricots, but by this stage we weren't convinced they'd be a good investment. We've had better meals here, so we hope this was a blip. In South's favour, prices are very reasonable.
Babies and children welcome: high chair. Booking advisable. Disabled: toilet. No-smoking tables. Restaurant available for hire.

RESTAURANTS

North

Crouch End N8

Les Associés

172 Park Road, N8 8JT (8348 8944). Finsbury Park tube/rail then W7 bus. **Lunch served** noon-3pm Sun. **Dinner served** 7.30-10pm Tue-Sat. **Main courses** £11-£16. **Set dinner** (Tue-Fri) £10.50 2 courses, £14.50 3 courses. **Credit** AmEx, MC, V.

You can't help but feel a tingle of excitement as you discover Les Associés amid the terraced houses on Park Road. An unlikely spot it may be for French dining, but nevertheless the restaurant draws you in with its arched leafy entrance and delightful terrace, complete with outdoor seating and bushy lavender edging. Inside is homely, and the cream and burgundy theme lends a touch of elegance. Our meal got off to a good start with a warm welcome and delectable bread and butter. Starters were excellent: cream of jerusalem artichoke soup was sublime, and roasted langoustines (from the impressive list of daily specials) came bursting with flavour. Main courses seemed to have been cooked in a different kitchen, though. Chicken with a morel cream sauce lacked appeal, while a parcel of brill with duck's liver was pallid and overcooked. Luckily a good bottle of house wine kept us amused, and a pleasant chocolate mousse meant that our meal ended on a higher note.
Babies and children admitted. Booking advisable. No-smoking tables. Restaurant available for hire. Tables outdoors (5, garden).

Bistro Aix

54 Topsfield Parade, Tottenham Lane, N8 8PT (8340 6346/www.bistroaix.co.uk). Finsbury Park tube/rail then W7 bus/91 bus. **Lunch served** noon-3pm, **dinner served** 6.30-11pm Tue-Sun. **Main courses** £9.99-£17.99. **Set lunch** £10 1 course incl glass of wine or soft drink, salad and coffee; £11.50 2 courses. **Set meal** (Sun) £13.50 2 courses, £16.50 3 courses. **Service** 12.5%. **Credit** AmEx, MC, V.

There's plenty of classic bistro dishes to choose from at this narrow, rather cramped restaurant. You'll find everything from straightforward salads to foie gras, with grilled meats and fish predominating for main courses, plus various vegetarian dishes. The set menu seemed like good value, but wasn't entirely successful; the first-course terrine lacked flavour, though this was compensated for by a main course of succulent stuffed breast of guinea fowl with pumpkin purée. From the carte, fish soup was bland, while grilled sea bass 'filet' on a bed of spinach with a side order of dauphine potatoes was well cooked. For dessert, we decided against ordering one of the old-fashioned sundaes, but the mango sorbet we did select had negligible mango flavour. The mainly Gallic wine list, reminded us that Bistro Aix is indeed a French restaurant. But the variable quality of food and service – and a problem with the bill – left us disappointed.
Babies and children admitted. Booking essential weekends. Restaurant available for hire. Tables outside (11, conservatory).

Holloway N7

★ Morgan M

489 Liverpool Road, N7 8NS (7609 3560/www.morganm.com). Highbury & Islington tube/rail. **Lunch served** noon-2.30pm Wed-Fri, Sun. **Dinner served** 7-10.30pm Tue-Sat. **Set lunch** £19.50 2 courses, £23.50 3 courses. **Set dinner** £32 3 courses. **Set meal** £36 (vegetarian), £39 (non-vegetarian), tasting menu. **Service** 12.5%. **Credit** DC, MC, V.

It was a bold move on the part of chef/proprietor Morgan Meunier to open his first solo venture in this Holloway hinterland. But it seems to be paying off, as his small temple gastronomique is well worth a journey. The airy dining room is a hushed haven in which to sample some of London's best French cooking. The dinner menu uncompromisingly offers a minimum of three courses, plus a six-course tasting menu – including, unusually, a vegetarian version. Dishes are classic French with more than a dash of the modern and the Mediterranean. Amuses-bouche set the pace, with perhaps a minute saucerful of chilled beetroot purée topped with delicate horseradish crème fraîche. To follow, there might be just-seared scallops with a white chicory tarte tatin and onion-infused sauce soubise, or foie gras in various seasonal guises (always served with toasted brioche). Mains are moderately sized and beautifully presented, whether pink and juicy rack of lamb with caramelised apple and garlic, or tender veal loin with tiny sweetbreads, onions and morels. Puddings are a further highlight, theatrically presented, and the wine list ranges from vins de pays to grands cru, mainly from France. None of this comes cheap, but it's worth it.
Babies and children admitted. Booking essential. Dress: smart casual. No smoking. Separate room for parties, seats 12. Vegetarian menu.

Hornsey N8

Le Bistro

36 High Street, N8 7NX (8340 2116). Turnpike Lane tube/Hornsey rail/41, W3 bus. **Brunch served** 12.30-5pm Sun. **Dinner served** 6-11pm Mon-Sat; 5-10pm Sun. **Main courses** £10.95-£15.50. **Set meal** £10.95 2 courses, £12.95 3 courses. **Service** 10%. **Credit** MC, V.

This enduring north London bistro has been plying locals with its inimitable Gallic charm for over 20 years. You'll find a friendly, but not overbearing welcome from the patron, who will settle you into one of the restaurant's colourful corners while a soothing French soundtrack drifts from the stereo. On a recent visit we started with delicious cold mussel salad – a tightly packed disc of shelled seafood on a bed of crunchy leaves – and a chunky gazpacho made with vine tomatoes, prawns and basil: a bowlful of freshness. For main courses, navarin (stew) of lamb combined wonderfully dark hunks of flaky meat with crisp spring vegetables, while meaty sea bass with a flavoursome ratatouille of pine nuts, peppers and onions would have been even better without its accompanying (slightly overpowering) chilli sauce. With the kitchen out of its signature lavender crème brûlée, fig and almond tart with vanilla ice-cream was an excellent way to round off a memorable meal. Visit in the summer to enjoy the garden at the rear of the restaurant.
Babies and children welcome: high chairs. Booking advisable. Tables outdoors (15, garden).

Islington N1

Almeida

30 Almeida Street, N1 1AD (7354 4777/www.conran.com). Angel tube/Highbury & Islington tube/rail. **Lunch served** noon-2.30pm Mon-Fri; noon-3pm Sat, Sun. **Dinner served** 5.30-10.45pm Mon-Sat; 5.30-9.30pm Sun. **Main courses** £12-£19. **Set meal** (lunch, 5.30-7pm daily; 10-10.45pm Mon-Sat) £14.50 2 courses; £17.50 3 courses. **Service** 12.5%. **Credit** AmEx, DC, MC, V.

It's hard to believe that the Almeida (part of the Conran empire) has only been open since November 2001, so assured does it seem. The furnishings are modern without being flashy, the seats are sleek but comfortable, and the staff are unpushy and adept. The menu is traditional (right down to the plat du jour) with delicious results. Six snails (à la bourguignonne) were just so – and a good, light starter to have before one of the weightier mains, such as coq au vin; herring salad was much meatier, but too moreish to leave. For those unable to contemplate the magnificence of 'chateaubriand à la moëlle, sauce béarnaise' (for two, priced at £19 a head), the likes of grilled halibut with hollandaise sauce means you can make it through to the 'trolley of tarts', a Billy Bunter-esque experience of French baking. The cheese is worth ordering too. A tapas menu (on offer at the sunken bar and the pavement terrace) features the likes of oysters, serrano ham, tapenade, anchoïade en croûte, with nothing costing more than steak tartare at £4.50. Needless to say, the wine list doesn't stray far from French soil. Still Islington's best restaurant at this level.
Babies and children welcome: high chairs. Booking advisable. Disabled: toilet. No-smoking tables. Restaurant available for hire. Separate room for parties, seats 20. Tables outdoors (8, pavement). **Map 5 O1.**

Palmers Green N13

Café Anjou

394 Green Lanes, N13 5PD (8886 7267/www.cafeanjou.co.uk). Wood Green tube then 329 bus/Palmers Green rail. **Lunch served** noon-2.30pm, **dinner served** 6.30-10.30pm Tue-Sun. **Main courses** £8.55-£11.25. **Set lunch** (noon-2pm Tue-Sat) £7.45 1 course incl coffee & beverage. **Set meal** (Tue-Fri, lunch Sat) £12.95 2 courses, £14.45 3 courses. **Service** 10% for parties of 7 or more. **Credit** AmEx, MC, V.

Family-run Café Anjou gallantly flies the Gallic flag in Palmers Green, continuing to produce consistently good French cooking. On our most recent visit, the summer menu had just come in; we got into the seasonal swing of things with a mouth-watering timbale of Cornish crab meat stacked with crème fraîche and caviar. Equally delicious streaky parma ham was wrapped around peppery rocket and sprinkled with shavings of parmesan. For mains, the juicy spiciness of lamb meatballs was offset by cooling yoghurt mixed with apple and green peppercorns, while the Périgord favourite of magret de canard with honey and ginger delivered the correct balance of sweetness and acidic tartness. To finish, we shared a generous crêpe stuffed with irrepressibly fresh summer berries and vanilla ice-cream, and drizzled with raspberry coulis. Replete with these delights, we polished off our fruity bottle of Brouilly and left highly satisfied.
Babies and children welcome: children's portions (Sun); high chairs. Booking essential dinner Fri, Sat. Restaurant available for hire.

North West

St John's Wood NW8

L'Aventure

3 Blenheim Terrace, NW8 0EH (7624 6232). St John's Wood tube/139, 189 bus. **Lunch served** 12.30-2.30pm Mon-Fri. **Dinner served** 7.30-10.30pm Mon-Fri; 7-10.30pm Sat. **Set lunch** £18.50 3 courses incl coffee. **Set dinner** £32.50 3 courses. **Service** 12.5%. **Credit** AmEx, MC, V.

This neighbourhood restaurant might have been transported straight from France, complete with fixtures, fittings and service. From the menu of Gallic classics, written in copper-plate, to the charming and earnest staff who arrive to translate it, the place exudes a French provincial air. This is reinforced by the surroundings, with a pretty, shaded front terrace and a cosy interior filled with heavy drapes, tapestries, cornucopias of dried flowers, and iron candlesticks cast in the shape of frogs. Make no mistake, though: this is a serious restaurant where top-notch ingredients are expertly combined. To start, we went for a special of saucisse de suprême de volaille (delicate discs of chicken breast flecked with pistachios, served with a bitter-sweet chicory salad); and a huge plateful of fresh artichoke salad, beautifully dressed and presented. Among the main courses were classics such as ris de veau, magret de canard offset by a fruity sauce, a succulent pink carré d'agneau, and some excellent lotte (monkfish) with a textbook sauce vierge. Prices seem reasonable for the quality of cooking, although wine pushes up the cost rapidly. Altogether a grown-up sort of place, well suited to its slightly elderly St John's Wood clientele. But don't let that put you off.
Babies and children admitted. Booking advisable dinner. Tables outdoors (6, terrace). **Map 1 C2.**

Outer London

Surbiton, Surrey

★ The French Table

85 Maple Road, Surbiton, Surrey KT6 4AW (8399 2365/www.thefrenchtable.co.uk). Surbiton rail. **Lunch served** noon-2.30pm Wed-Fri, Sun. **Dinner served** 7-10.30pm Tue-Sat. **Main courses** £10.80-£15.80. **Set lunch** (Wed-Fri) £13.50 2 courses, £16.50 3 courses; (Sun) £17.50 3 courses. **Credit** MC, V.

The people of Surbiton are lucky. We left the French Table, after paying under £50 for a fabulous lunch for two with wine, wishing we had a local as good as this. A bright, unfussy dining room; friendly, unobtrusive service; a varied, well-annotated wine list with plenty to offer under £20 and a good handful of wines by the glass; homemade bread – the right mood was set even before the starters arrived. Croustillant of confit duck and wild mushrooms delivered tender shreds of meat in paper-thin pastry with a richly flavoured smoked duck dressing, while deep-fried plaice and courgette with sauce gribiche received ticks all round: the freshest of fish, featherweight batter, and a delicious, caper-speckled accompaniment. Mains were equally on song. Baked cod with saffron pasta and smoked haddock was a classic brunch dish in the making, each element cooked to perfection. And if pork fillet with roast sweet potato, spinach, garlic confit and port sauce sounded one ingredient too many, a clean plate suggested otherwise. To finish, we shared tangy apricot compote with crème de

tonka (cream infused with almond-flavoured liqueur) and apricot sorbet. If you're heading south down the A3, this is well worth a detour.
Babies and children welcome: children's portions; high chairs. Booking advisable; essential weekends. No smoking.

Kew, Surrey

Ma Cuisine

9 Station Approach, Kew, Surrey TW9 3QB (8332 1923). Kew Gardens tube/rail. **Meals served** 10am-10.30pm daily. **Main courses** £8.95-£14. **Set lunch** (noon-3pm Mon-Sat) £12.95 2 courses, £15.50 3 courses; (noon-4pm Sun) £15 2 courses, £18 3 courses. **Service** 10%. **Credit** MC, V.

This former Post Office near Kew Gardens station houses the second branch of Ma Cuisine, itself an offshoot of Mod Euro restaurant McClements (*see p237*). The decor shouts 'French bistro' in ringing tones: black and white checked floor, plasticised gingham tablecloths and Toulouse-Lautrec posters on yellow walls. The mix of diners – commuters on their way home, locals out for an impromptu supper, and a lone gent with a newspaper – attests to the casual, drop-in vibe. During the day there are baguettes, salads and croissants, with a full-blown menu of unfussy bistro classics at lunch and dinner. Expect the likes of boudin noir or french onion soup for starters, and cassoulet, calf's liver or steak to follow. Finish with decent crêpes suzette or crème brûlée. The food is enjoyable, but not spectacular (the Twickenham original, by all reports, is still the best). A starter

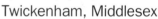

Ma Cuisine

of skate pâté was possibly too subtle in flavour (and unappealingly pale yellow, though that's no fault of the chef). Blanquette de lapin with vegetables and mash was generous in size, but the rabbit was on the tough side. Best was a strong-tasting fish soup, with all the trimmings, crammed with thick chunks of fish. The shortish, all-French wine list offers good-value carates.
Babies and children welcome: children's menu (Sun lunch); high chairs. Booking advisable. No smoking. Tables outdoors (6, pavement).

Richmond, Surrey

Chez Lindsay

11 Hill Rise, Richmond, Surrey TW10 6UQ (8948 7473). Richmond tube/rail. **Crêperie Meals served** noon-11pm Mon-Sat; noon-10pm Sun. **Main courses** £3.30-£8.95. **Restaurant Meals served** noon-11pm daily. **Main courses** £11.75-£15.75. **Set lunch** (noon-3pm Mon-Sat) £6.75 2 courses, £14.50 2 courses, £17.50 3 courses. **Set dinner** (after 6.30pm) £16.50 2 courses, £19.50 3 courses. Both **Service** 12%. **Credit** MC, V.

Chez Lindsay's yellow brick walls and simple furnishings conjure up an English church hall, though the food is regional French (specifically from Brittany and Normandy, areas with which the eponymous Lindsay has strong connections). The menu is extensive: tantalising fruits de mer with oysters, whelks, bigorneaux (periwinkles) and more, followed by starters and then grands plats (including scallops, duck, steak). And of course the signature dish of northern France, galettes, which come savoury (buckwheat) or sweet (wheatflour). There are also two very reasonable set menus and most delicious cidres de France. Soupe de poissons was good; a galette, enclosing a layer of cheese and topped with a pale ratatouille, was excellent. The tepid, but tasty, magret de canard with honeyed brandy sauce had the duck beautifully presented with a mound of sweet potato purée studded with spears of vegetables. We finished with a perfect apple and caramel crêpe. Apparently the place is heaving at weekends, but for our midweek visit it was peaceful; the river view is a bonus.
Babies and children welcome: high chairs. Booking advisable. No cigars or pipes. Separate room for parties, seats 36.

Twickenham, Middlesex

Brula

43 Crown Road, Twickenham, Middx TW1 3EJ (8892 0602/www.brulabistrot.co.uk). St Margaret's rail. **Lunch served** 12.30-3pm, **dinner served** 7-10.30pm daily. **Main courses** £11.75-£19.50. **Set lunch** £11 2 courses, £13.50 3 courses. **Credit** MC, V.

Stained-glass windows, worn parquet flooring, cream walls adorned with watercolours and mirrors, soft lighting from chandeliers and tea lights – all lend this small neighbourhood bistro a lovely lived-in air. It's popular too: it was packed on a Tuesday evening in high summer (which led to rather slow service). Brula finds favour thanks to its longevity and welcoming staff, and also because of the cooking, a reliable mix of French classics (foie gras, escargots, onglet steak) and dishes with a more Modern European touch. A half-dozen juicy, plump scallops worked well as a starter, though the accompaning prunes and leeks were too muddled together; aubergine and red pepper roulade with basil dressing was clean and summery. Fish dominated the main courses: trout went brilliantly with dill-scented cucumber and olive tapenade, but the Asian promise of lime, coriander and chilli failed completely with (perfectly cooked) john dory, and was swamped in oil. To finish, choose from the likes of cheeses, crème brûlée, Eton mess – familiar dishes, but well executed – or refreshing mint tea. Wines, most French, include wallet-friendly carafes. A smattering of pavement tables is a bonus in clement weather. La Buvette, Brula's sister establishment in Richmond, is also worth a visit.
Babies and children admitted. Booking advisable. Separate room for parties, seats 24. Tables outdoors (6, pavement).
For branch (La Buvette) see index.

DINING OUT IN PARIS AND LONDON?

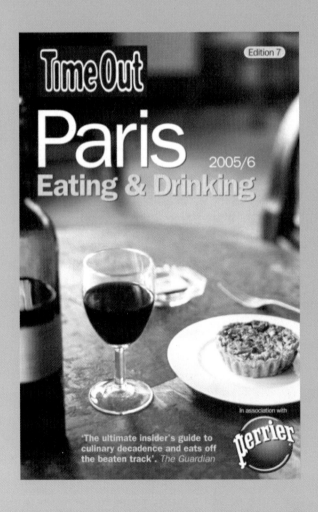

Gastropubs

London's gastropub scene is now well established. After all, it's been nearly 15 years since the arrival of the **Eagle** in Farringdon, usually cited as the first example of the genre, and there are few corners of the capital that remain ungastrofied. The original formula of an all-in-one boozing/eating space, with stripped floorboards, mismatched tables and chairs, the odd battered sofa, bar service and hearty portions of relatively simple food, remains popular, but splinter groups have emerged too. The trend upmarket that we identified in the last edition continues, with many venues having a separate, restaurant-like dining room that offers a different, more sophisticated (and more expensive) menu accompanied by a superior wine list and table service. You could almost forget you were in a pub. In fact, some places have dropped the pub element completely, dealing in rarefied cocktails rather than real ale. Change isn't always for the good, of course, but the competitive kick provided by fresh faces and new ideas can prevent a slide into stagnation.

Notable newcomers this year include the **Gun** in Docklands, **Greyhound** in Battersea, **Pig's Ear** in Chelsea, **Princess** in Shoreditch and **Bull** in Highgate – all nominated for Best Gastropub in the 2005 *Time Out* Awards.

Central
Belgravia SW1

★ Ebury
11 Pimlico Road, SW1W 8NA (7730 6784/ www.theebury.co.uk). Sloane Square tube/ Victoria tube/rail/11, 211 bus.
Bar **Open** noon-11pm Mon-Sat; noon-10.30pm Sun.
Brasserie **Lunch served** noon-3.30pm Mon-Fri; noon-4pm Sat, Sun. **Dinner served** 6-10.30pm Mon-Sat; 6-10pm Sun. **Main courses** £9.95-£18.
Restaurant **Dinner served** 6-10.30pm Tue-Sat.
Set dinner £25 2 courses, £29.50 3 courses.
All **Credit** AmEx, MC, V.
The Ebury is surely the Rolls-Royce of gastropubs. From the moment you pass the velvet ropes outside, you know this is not your typical junkshop-chic conversion. The light and airy bar, with its refulgent floral displays and sleek, low-

BEST GASTROPUBS

For alfresco eating
Bull (*see p115*), **Drapers Arms** (*see p115*), **Dartmouth Arms** (*see p111*), **Ealing Park Tavern** (*see p108*), **Gun** (*see p112*), **Hill** (*see p117*), **Junction Arms** (*see p116*), **Ship** (*see p111*), **Westbourne** (*see p109*), **William IV** (*see p117*).

For oenophiles
Greyhound (*see p109*).

For families
Victoria (*see p110*).

For waterside views
Gun (*see p112*), **Ship** (*see p111*).

For a bar vibe
Ebury (*see above*), **Hartley** (*see p111*).

slung furniture is more *Wallpaper** than wayside tavern. And the upstairs dining room painted deep brown with glossy wood floors and glittering pink chandeliers is so 'now' it's tomorrow. Amazingly for such a flash gaff, staff are absolutely charming, and although prices are in line with posh restaurants, the cooking is up to it. Starters include ceviche of Glenarm salmon, mackerel and diver-caught scallops, or a perfect bresaola with parmesan and rocket. Mains cover perfectly grilled sea bream with provençal veg, marjoram gnocchi and aubergine caviar, as well as a fine roast duck with foie gras, butternut squash purée, chicory salad and duck heart brochette. It would have been indecent not to broach desserts and marmalade ice-cream, ginger cake and orange sauce was as gorgeous as it was original. And each dessert is matched with a dessert wine from a list complete with helpful tasting notes.
Babies and children admitted. Disabled: toilet. Separate room for parties, seats 60.
Map 15 G11.

City EC4
White Swan Pub & Dining Room
108 Fetter Lane, EC4A 1ES (7242 9696/ www.thewhiteswan.com). Chancery Lane or Holborn tube.
Bar **Open** 11am-11pm Mon-Fri. **Lunch served** noon-3pm Mon-Fri. **Dinner served** 6-10pm Tue-Fri. **Main courses** £8.95-£15.
Dining Room **Lunch served** noon-4pm, **dinner served** 6-10pm Mon-Fri. **Main courses** £14-£17. **Set lunch** £20 2 courses, £25 3 courses. **Service** 12.5%.
Both **Credit** AmEx, MC, V.
The White Swan is a Jekyll and Hyde establishment in every way, except for the food. Upstairs is a jewel of a restaurant, with attentive service, sparking glassware and a sense of calm. On the ground floor is a traditional-looking pub room (wooden furniture, brick walls, huge mirror) enlivened by a boar's head and a flatscreen TV. There's a decent choice of beers, plenty of wines by the glass, a cocktail list and

even a Herefordshire perry. That's where the good news ends. On a Monday lunchtime, house music was blaring out, despite the fact that the clientele largely consisted of men in suits. Staff were slow and inefficient, but that was nothing to the incompetence of the kitchen. After an hour's wait, first and second courses came at once – we were too hungry to argue, so quickly ate chilled avocado soup and grilled asparagus with balsamic and parmesan before moving on to Thai salmon salad and a (now rather cold) five-spice roast cod with mint, coriander and mizuna. There's no denying the quality of the cooking, but eat in the restaurant (many dishes are served in both rooms) if you value your digestion or your blood pressure. Sister establishments are the Well (*see p107*) and Docklands newcomer the Gun (*see p112*).
Booking essential (restaurant). Restaurant available for hire (Sat, Sun). **Map 11 N5.**

Clerkenwell & Farringdon EC1, WC1

★ Coach & Horses
26-28 Ray Street, EC1R 3DJ (7278 8990/ www.thecoachandhorses.com). Farringdon tube/rail/19, 38, 55, 63, 243 bus. **Open** 11am-11pm Mon-Fri; 6-11pm Sat; noon-3pm Sun. **Lunch served** noon-3pm Mon-Fri, Sun. **Dinner served** 6-10pm Mon-Fri. **Main courses** £10.50-£14. **Credit** AmEx, MC, V.
Charmingly updated (as opposed to refurbished), the Coach & Horses is a refreshingly unposey spot to have anything from a pint to a full meal. The menu changes daily: on our most recent lunch it featured asparagus with boiled duck egg, potted prawns with chilli and garlic, Long Ghyll (the farm where all the rare-breed meat comes from) black pudding and apple, and twice-baked Milleens soufflé with chicory and grapes. The black pudding and the soufflé were particularly good, but the cooking is so reliable that it's hard to go wrong. The menu makes no concessions to the squeamish: crispy pig's ear and dandelion salad, and grilled ox tongue sandwich were other options. Praise is also due to a traditional English salad – simple but delicious. We finished with medlar and pear tart (wondrous) and – the only low point – a bland cheese plate. And make sure you try the addictive bread, made on the premises. Real effort is also made with the drinks. The interesting wine list has loads by the glass (including two rosés), while ales include Timothy Taylor Landlord. Winner of Best Gastropub in the 2004 *Time Out* Awards, this pub has its heart in the right place.
Babies and children welcome: high chairs. Tables outdoors (16, garden). **Map 5 N4.**

★ Eagle ✓
159 Farringdon Road, EC1R 3AL (7837 1353). Farringdon tube/rail/19, 38, 63, 341 bus. **Open** noon-11pm Mon-Sat; noon-5pm Sun. **Lunch served** 12.30-3pm Mon-Fri; 12.30-3.30pm Sat, Sun. **Dinner served** 6.30-10.30pm Mon-Sat. **Main courses** £5-£15. **Credit** MC, V.
Generally recognised as London's first gastropub, the Eagle continues to show everyone else how it's done. You'll find fancier cuisine and more formal settings elsewhere, but nobody has improved on the basic formula of decently priced, simple, seasonal food that's pretty much cooked in front of you in a pubby environment. So straightforward is the menu that it's not divided into courses, and there are no side dishes or even desserts: you takes your choice from a handful of tapas for £3, a soup, half a dozen mains for under a tenner, and cheese or a Portuguese tart to finish. Oh, and you get free bread and oil. The flavours are big and brash, and the styles a mix of simple Mediterranean and hearty British, with lots of roasting and piquant accompaniments. An Old Spot chop was huge and hearty, with salsa verde to cut nicely through the fat; linguine alio olio was just right. Ales are by Charles Wells; there's also a choice of continental white beers and a good selection of

Peasant

wines. All this is enjoyed in a slightly raffish, music-infused environment: this is one gastropub that hasn't had the pub gastroed out of it.
Babies and children admitted. Tables outdoors (4, pavement). **Map 5 N4.**

★ Easton ✓
22 Easton Street, WC1X 0DS (7278 7608/ www.theeaston.co.uk). Farringdon tube/rail/19, 38 bus. **Open** noon-11pm Mon-Thur; 12.30pm-1am Fri; 5.30pm-1am Sat; noon-10.30pm Sun. **Lunch served** 12.30-3pm Mon-Sat; 1-4pm Sun. **Dinner served** 6.30-9.30pm daily. **Credit** MC, V.
The Easton has the gastropub thing down to a T: it's a one-room place, not over-renovated, with lovely retro wallpaper, big windows, pub-style tables, the menu on a blackboard behind the bar, and food that majors in big flavours in generous portions, without fuss or frippery. We loved a robust lamb, chorizo and sausage cassoulet with Spanish white beans – a vivid, hearty dish, great with a glass of Rioja; and organic Saltmarsh lamb – beautifully cooked and crammed with juices – with champ, zingy braised red cabbage and spicy mustard seed gravy. It's not all meaty stuff, either. Vegetarian dishes can be imaginative (vegetable and halloumi kebab with chermoula and sweet potatoes, say), there's often a soup, and fish comes in some lively combos, such as char-grilled bream with tarragon, potato salad and broad bean salsa verde. Staff are young, and seem infinitely good-natured. Perhaps a crucial attraction is the friendly, local kind of vibe that builds up as the evening progresses. The Easton was a runner-up for Best Gastropub in the 2004 *Time Out* Awards, and it's keeping up the good work; newer sibling the Princess (*see p112*) is also worth checking out. If only they'd get in some real ales.
Babies and children admitted (daytime). Entertainment: DJs 9pm Fri. Tables outdoors (5, pavement). **Map 5 N5.**

★ Peasant 15% off
240 St John Street, EC1V 4PH (7336 7726/ www.thepeasant.co.uk). Angel tube/Farringdon tube/rail/153 bus. **Open** noon-11pm daily. **Meals served** noon-10.45pm Mon-Sat; noon-10pm Sun. **Main courses** £9-£15. **Service** 12.5%. **Credit** AmEx, DC, JCB, MC, V.
It's hard to choose between the low-key, laid-back downstairs area, with battered leather sofas, red walls, huge fireplace and menu of bar snacks and sharing plates, and the upmarket dining space upstairs, a lovely room with cream walls, candelabras and circus-themed posters. We opted for the latter, and while staff were friendly, we were left for a while before our order was taken. Seared king scallops with black rice risotto, wakame and cucumber salad and harissa oil was a good kick-off: the scallops weren't the fattest in the world, but had a lovely char-grilled taste, and went brilliantly with the risotto. For mains, smoked paprika-roast pork fillet with sage came with an apple and confit shallot tart – gorgeously gooey, but so rich we couldn't finish it. We also chose an inventive-sounding pan-fried barbary duck breast with broad beans, peas and black truffle dressing, and weren't disappointed in the fine match of flavours. There's a good selection of desserts, including a mini versions of own-made marshmallow, chocolate ganache, fudge and lemon-curd doughnuts. Wines start at just £11.75 a bottle, with a great selection by the glass. We'll be back.
Babies and children welcome: high chairs. Booking advisable. Tables outdoors (4, garden terrace; 5, pavement). **Map 5 O4.**

Well
180 St John Street, EC1V 4JY (7251 9363/ www.downthewell.com). Farringdon tube/rail. **Open** 11am-11pm Mon-Sat; 10.30am-10.30pm Sun. **Lunch served** noon-3pm Mon-Fri; noon-4pm Sat. **Dinner served** 6-10.30pm Mon-Sat. **Meals served** 10.30am-10pm Sun. **Main courses** £9.95-£15.95. **Credit** AmEx, DC, MC, V.
Refurbishments carried out during summer 2005 have smartened up the Well, but the place remains recognisable as the easy-going gastropub it always was. Big windows and high ceilings mean it's bright and airy inside (the basement looks

altogether more clubby), and there are also tables out on the pavement. A new chef has added a level of sophistication to the menu, but you could just order a pint of prawns with mayonnaise if that's all you fancy. Some dishes don't live up to expectations (which are high, given that the vegetarian dish of that day cost £11.50): chicken burger with thin-cut chips lacked flavour, and gorgonzola gnocchi tasted much more like mozzarella gnocchi (and so pretty bland). Much better was buffalo mozzarella with vine tomatoes and peperonata – simply but beautifully done – and seared tuna caesar salad, which had quality ingredients and a great dressing. Sides cost extra (£3 in the case of buttered spinach); puddings – crème brûlée, chocolate tart with clotted cream – are around a fiver; and a plate of Neal's Yard cheeses with quince jelly and oatcakes costs a stonking £9. A good neighbourhood joint, but with restaurant prices that the food struggles to justify.
Babies and children welcome: high chairs. Tables outdoors (6, pavement). **Map 5 O4.**

Holborn WC1

Perseverance
63 Lamb's Conduit Street, WC1N 3NB (7405 8278). Holborn or Russell Square tube. **Open** 12.30-11pm Mon-Sat; 12.30-10.30pm Sun. **Lunch served** 12.30-3pm Mon-Fri; 12.30-4pm Sun. **Dinner served** 5.30-10pm Mon-Sat. **Main courses** (lunch) £10-£13.50. **Tapas** £4-£6. **Set tapas** £12 3 dishes. **Credit** AmEx, DC, MC, V.
It might have been the longest day of the year, but when we visited the handsome, intimate dining room above this buzzing Bloomsbury boozer (the same owners operate the Endurance in Soho; *see below*), the menu seemed more suited to the middle of winter. The six summery portions of skate fillet were taken by the first group of seven diners, leaving us to choose from an array of hearty starters and red-meat mains. We wouldn't have minded so much if the kitchen had made a better job of cooking them. By far the most impressive dish was a delectable terrine of foie gras and ham knuckle served with apple chutney; steamed asparagus, our other starter, was fine. But fillet of beef en croute, served as a main, was decidedly overcooked (the accompanying potato gratin was rather better), while the pasta main du jour was forgettable, a token vegetarian option from the old school. Service too was amateurish. Disappointing, all told; we might have been better off staying downstairs and munching on the good-value tapas. The Perseverance has a comprehensive wine list; Old Speckled Hen is among the ales on tap.
Babies and children admitted (lunch). Booking advisable. Tables outdoors (6, pavement). **Map 4 M4.**

Marylebone NW1 *Okay, good*

Queen's Head & Artichoke 15% off
30-32 Albany Street, NW1 4EA (7916 6206/ www.theartichoke.net). Great Portland Street or Regent's Park tube. **Open** 11am-11pm Mon-Sat; noon-10.30pm Sun. **Lunch served** 12.30-3pm, **dinner served** 6.30-10.15pm Mon-Sat. **Meals served** 12.30-10.15pm Sun. **Tapas served** 12.30-10.15pm daily. **Main courses** £9-£13.50. **Tapas** £2-£5. **Service** 12.5%. **Credit** AmEx, MC, V.
This lovingly refurbished (if strangely named) Victorian boozer is a joy to behold: big leather sofas, wood-panelled walls, large windows that let the sun stream in, and a beautiful tiled fireplace that looks like it would work wonders on cold winter nights. A huge, dark wood central bar delivers a host of real ales and reasonably priced wines (several by the glass), but it's the food that's the real reason to head here. On the first-floor is a swankier dining room, where proceedings are overlooked by an ornate ormulu clock, chandeliers and, gazing down from the walls, a host of sultry maidens. There's a full-blown menu, which changes daily, offering nicely executed gastro classics: oysters or chicken liver pâté to start, say, followed by lamb juniper berry and mint ragout or pan-fried sea bass. Rhubarb clafoutis with

passionfruit sorbet is typical of the inventive puds. There's also a Spanish-led tapas menu – the likes of chicken kebabs marinated in lemon and rosemary, grilled halloumi, roasted peppers, patatas bravas and marinated anchovies – perfect for a summer snack in the tiny, walled garden. Service was a little eccentric on our visit, but we'll be heading back regardless. *Definitely*
Babies and children admitted. Booking advisable. Separate room for parties, seats 45. Tables outdoors (6, garden; 6, pavement). **Map 3 H4.**

Soho W1

Endurance
90 Berwick Street, W1F 0QB (7437 2944). Leicester Square, Oxford Circus or Tottenham Court Road tube. **Open** noon-11pm Mon-Sat; 12.30-10.30pm Sun. **Lunch served** 12.30-4pm Mon-Sat; 1-4.30pm Sun. **Main courses** £6-£12. **Service** 12.5%. **Credit** MC, V.
Mercifully, the Endurance is not another out-of-the-box gastropub, but something a little more ramshackle. Its position by Berwick Street market helps, but so does the designer's enthusiasm for brown: brown horseshoe bar, tables and benches; brown wooden floors; nicotine-hued flock wallpaper; and even the stuffed head of a (brown) bear on the wall. Still, the impression remains of an old-style boozer, helped by a clientele that mixes market traders with yapping media types and solitary Soho codgers. There's a fair selection of ale and wine to go with the erratic cooking. Fish and chips is a good choice: invariably light and flakey, with a deluge of soft peas; beef and mushroom pie packs a good, meaty punch, but taste was compromised by a stodgy, outsized lozenge of mash. We've had a very good mushroom risotto here, and puddings (try the tangy lemon tart) are successful, but we have been less lucky with the starters. Slushy potted prawns in gritty, curried butter were not pleasant; and what should have been a simple mozzarella and tomato salad was overwhelmed by a boatload of salt. Still, this is a fine place to while away the hours on a lazy afternoon.
Babies and children admitted (before 5pm). Tables outdoors (8, garden). **Map 17 J6.**

West

Chiswick W4

Bollo 15% off
13-15 Bollo Lane, W4 5LR (8994 6037). Chiswick Park tube. **Open** noon-11pm Mon-Sat; noon-10.30pm Sun. **Lunch served** noon-3pm Mon-Fri, Sun; 12.30-4pm Sat. **Dinner served** 6-10.15pm daily. **Main courses** £6.50-£12.95. **Set lunch** £10 2 courses. **Credit** MC, V.
This corner pub, with a green-tiled exterior and picture windows, is a capacious spot. The usual mismatched wooden tables and chairs sit on one side, with a separate carpeted dining area towards the back under a circular skylight. On a warm summer's evening, the interior was largely deserted, with customers preferring to sit at the pavement tables outside. A shame it was so empty: there's a good choice of drinks (real ales plus well-priced wines), and the food is a notch above average. Especially size-wise: Desperate Dan would have had problems finishing our whopping slab of tuna (not cooked rare, as requested, but still tender) with garlicky mash and sweet, chewy caramelised onions. An ample salmon fish cake, with green salad and fluffy, chunky chips, was also robustly flavoursome. The Bollo changed hands as we went to press, but the new menu seems to continue in a similarly straightforward vein. Expect the likes of battered calamari, or caesar salad with bacon and chicken to start; followed, perhaps, by cumberland sausages and mash, or, more inventively, by roast suckling pig and pork sausages with figs and rosemary mash. The admirable practice of offering smaller dishes (wild mushroom risotto, smoked haddock) continues.
Babies and children welcome (until 7pm); high chairs. Booking advisable weekends. Tables outdoors (12, pavement).

Ealing W5

Ealing Park Tavern
222 South Ealing Road, W5 4RL (8758 1879).
South Ealing tube.
Bar **Open** 5-11pm Mon; 11am-11pm Tue-Sat;
noon-10.30pm Sun. **Tapas served** 5-10pm
Mon-Sat; 5-9pm Sun.
Restaurant **Lunch served** noon-3pm Tue-Sat;
noon-4pm Sun. **Dinner served** 6-10.30pm
Mon-Sat; 6-9pm Sun. **Main courses** £8.50-£15.
Service 12.5% for parties of 5 or more.
Both **Credit** AmEx, MC, V.
This massive, popular corner pub has plenty of
dining space indoors, and a spacious garden area
(without much greenery) with large interlocking
stone benches (and rugs), huge umbrellas, heaters
and barbecue facilities. Evening diners can choose
from a tapas selection – ranging from mixed olives
to large charcuterie plates – and a daily-changing
menu. There's little out of the ordinary on it, but
the standards are rendered very well indeed.
Following a shared tapas starter (a very generous
helping of quality gravadlax and pickled
cucumbers), our large piece of tuna was seared
perfectly, and a juicy steak came with a mound of
great chips. For dessert, the chocolate nemesis and
berry compote wouldn't have been out of place in
higher-class establishments. Having heard mixed
reviews about the service, we were wary, but it was
a joy: all of the staff were bubbly, friendly and
completely on the case. Drinks include a decent
selection of real ales. Definitely worth hunting
down if you're in the area.
Babies and children welcome: high chairs; toys.
No smoking (restaurant). Tables outdoors
(25, garden).

Hammersmith W6

Anglesea Arms
35 Wingate Road, W6 0UR (8749 1291).
Goldhawk Road or Ravenscourt Park tube.
Bar **Open** 11am-11pm Mon-Sat; noon-10.30pm
Sun.
Restaurant **Lunch served** 12.30-2.45pm
Mon-Sat; 12.30-3.30pm Sun. **Dinner served**
7-10.30pm Mon-Sat; 7-10pm Sun. **Main courses**
£8.95-£15.95. **Set lunch** (Mon-Fri) £9.95
2 courses, £12.95 3 courses. **Credit** MC, V.
This small corner pub has got the lot. Dark and
cosy area for drinkers and smokers at the front?
Check. Cheerful (no-smoking) dining area at the
back? Check. Real fire for wintry nights? Check.
Outdoor tables for summery lunches? Check. Add
a clutch of real ales (Old Speckled Hen, London
Pride), a lengthy wine list and excellent food, and
you have a blueprint for successful gastropubbery.
The short menu (chalked on a large blackboard
next to the open kitchen) is a seasonal delight. For
starters, a dish of salad leaves, watermelon, mint,
feta and tomatoes was zingily refreshing, while
rich and creamy pea risotto came sprinkled with
chives and parmesan (though the peas weren't as
fresh-tasting as we would have liked). Mains
feature the likes of calf's liver with baby turnips,
spinach, capers and shallots; or pearly white cod
with new potatoes and green beans, which came
with an inventive gremolata using cucumber,
tomato and samphire (a variant on the traditional
Italian version). Finish with the likes of vanilla
panna cotta or raspberry cream tartlet with crisp
sweet pastry and a gooey filling. Staff run
proceedings smoothly even when the place is full,
which it often is (there's no booking).
Babies and children welcome: high chairs.
Bookings not accepted. No-smoking area.
Tables outdoors (5, pavement). **Map 20 A3.**

Ladbroke Grove W10

Golborne Grove
36 Golborne Road, W10 5PR (8960 6260/
www.groverestaurants.co.uk). Westbourne
Park tube.
Bar **Open** 11am-11pm Mon-Thur; 11am-11.30pm
Fri, Sat; noon-10.30pm Sun. **Snacks served**
4-7pm daily.
Restaurant **Lunch served** noon-3.45pm
Mon-Sat; noon-3.30pm Sun. **Dinner served**

6.30-10.15pm Mon-Thur; 6.30-10.45pm Fri, Sat;
6.30-9.45pm Sun. **Main courses** £8.50-£15.
Set lunch £13 2 courses. **Service** 12.5%.
Both **Credit** DC, MC, V.
Heartier than it is sophisticated, Golborne Grove
is a likeable place, with an open-plan layout and a
warm, woody decor with terracotta colouring. The
£13 set lunch for two courses seemed a fair price,
especially when it featured such varied starters as
merguez sausages or Thai-style fish cakes. But
seafood salad with tuna, salmon, cod, swordfish
and mussels tasted more like a creamy tomato and
wine soup, with the lettuce long since drowned
somewhere beneath fish and sauce. Roasted pork
loin, a gigantic doorstop reminiscent of a Barnsley
chop, was a surprisingly wintry dish in
midsummer when served with garlic mash, braised
red cabbage, mangetout, broccoli and a red wine
sauce. You certainly can't fault the generosity of
the management, though; and with big heavy
puddings to finish, an afternoon siesta seemed a
copper-bottomed certainty. Service is sweet and the
wine list is admirably democratic, but don't expect
culinary revelation.
Babies and children admitted. Booking advisable.
Separate room for parties, seats 40. Tables
outdoors (6, pavement). **Map 19 B1.**

Olympia W14

Cumberland Arms
29 North End Road, W14 8SZ (7371 6806/
www.thecumberlandarmspub.co.uk). West
Kensington tube/Kensington (Olympia) tube/rail.
Open noon-11pm Mon-Sat; noon-10.30pm
Sun. **Lunch served** 12.30-3pm Mon-Sat;
12.30-3.30pm Sun. **Dinner served** 7-10.30pm
Mon-Sat; 7-10pm Sun. **Main courses** £7-£13.
Credit MC, V.
Flower power reigns at this welcoming corner
pub, such is the riot of colourful foliage spilling
out of the hanging baskets and window boxes
covering its exterior. Inside, it's all warm wood
and battered furniture, globe lighting (dimmed to
a cosy glow in the evening) and big windows. It's
a proper boozer as much as a gastro enterprise,
with as many drinkers as diners and three draught
ales on top of a globetrotting wine list. The place
is buzzy but never too crowded, so you'll find a
table even on a Friday night. The shortish
Mediterranean/North African menu isn't divided
into starters and mains, so cost is the best
indication of the size of a dish – and prices are
keen, with nothing over £12.50 (for whole sea
bass). All our choices were good, with strong,
earthy flavours and fresh ingredients to the fore.
Highlights included a chunky soup of puy lentils,
tomatoes and pepper; a light, summery salad of
feta, roast fennel and polenta croutons; and grilled
Italian sausages – three plump, peppery specimens
– served with simple sautéed broccoli and
cauliflower. And whoever 'Donald' is, we like his
chocolate and almond cake. Genial staff keep
things trucking along nicely.
Babies and children admitted. Tables outdoors
(10, pavement).

Shepherd's Bush W14

Defectors Weld **NEW**
170 Uxbridge Road, W12 8AA (8749 0008/
www.defectors-weld.com). Shepherd's Bush tube.
Open noon-11pm Mon-Thur; noon-midnight
Fri, Sat; noon-10.30pm Sun. **Lunch served**
noon-3pm, **dinner served** 5-9.30pm Mon-Fri.
Meals served noon-9.30pm Sat, Sun.
Main courses £7-£10. **Credit** MC, V.
Retreat from the traffic fumes of ever-unpleasant
Shepherd's Bush Green into this corner venue,
formerly a joyless chain pub, but now a buzzing
gastro-style enterprise. It's a huge space – all green-
on-green paint and dark wood – ranged around a
central bar, made comfortable with groupings of
sofas and, at the rear, more private booths. Upstairs
there is also a high-ceilinged dining room. Drinkers
fuel up on cocktails, lagers, ales (among them
London Pride) and wine; many also partake of the
short, Mediterranean-slanted food menu. Dishes
come piled high, but tend to look better than they
taste. Pan-fried halloumi with piquillo peppers and

tsatsiki was surpisingly dull, while penne with
pesto and roasted vegetables was no better than
you'd make at home, and the addition of frozen
peas did nothing for the flavour. Better were
chunky, fluffy salmon fish cakes with a tangy
caper mayo. Other options include burgers and –
a clever idea, this – pies from the acclaimed Square
Pie Company. Weekends bring roasts and class DJ
sets. Oh, and the name? Supposedly a reference to
the Cambridge spy circle; Kim Philby's portrait
hangs on the stairs.
Disabled: toilet. Entertainment: DJs 9pm Fri-Sun.
No-smoking area. **Map 20 C2.**

Westbourne Park W2

★ Cow Dining Room
89 Westbourne Park Road, W2 5QH (7221
0021). Royal Oak or Westbourne Park tube.
Bar **Open** noon-11pm Mon-Sat; noon-10.30pm
Sun. **Lunch served** noon-3.30pm daily.
Dinner served 6-10.30pm Mon-Sat; 6-10pm Sun.
Main courses £10-£14.
Restaurant **Lunch served** noon-3pm Sun.
Dinner served 7-11pm Mon-Sat; 7-10.30 Sun.
Main courses £14-£18.
Both **Service** 12.5%. **Credit** MC, V.
It may be just a small 1950s-styled room over a
pub, but the Cow is surely one of the best
restaurants in Notting Hill. It's the mix of the
classical and the inventive on the short menu
which is most to be admired. Starters featured a
summery chilled avocado and smoked paprika
soup, and perfectly juicy braised baby octopus and
samphire salad. There are pasta dishes – goat's
cheese and broad bean ravioli – and lobster risotto,
but these are serious dishes rather than cheap
padding to the menu (especially at prices of about
£9 as a starter and over £17 as a main). Other main
courses included a no less pricey but immaculate
fillet of sea trout with braised fennel, while Welsh

black beef ribeye with artichoke and potato gratin was as fine a steak as you'll find anywhere. Gooseberry fool, alas, had been struck off the menu by the time we reached dessert stage, but the chocolate truffle cake would make anyone happy. You can splash out if you want on the strong wine list, but the house bottles are good; or you can enjoy one of the best-kept pints of ale in London ferried up from the pub downstairs. Service is relaxed and attentive, setting a laid-back tone loved by the boozy, voluble media types who flock here to get pickled and talk shop.
Babies and children admitted (lunch, restaurant). Booking essential (restaurant). Restaurant for hire. Tables outdoors (4, pavement). **Map 1 A5.**

Westbourne
101 Westbourne Park Villas, W2 5ED (7221 1332). Royal Oak or Westbourne Park tube. Bar **Open** 5-11pm Mon; 11am-11pm Tue-Fri; noon-11pm Sat; noon-10.30pm Sun. **Snacks served** 3.30-6.30pm Mon-Fri.
Restaurant **Lunch served** 12.30-3pm Tue-Thur; 12.30-3.30pm Sat, Sun. **Dinner served** 7-10pm Mon-Sat; 7-9.30pm Sun. **Main courses** £9-£15. **Credit** MC, V.
It's so ridiculously popular here that even if you do get a table, you'll be fighting for elbow space as a nonstop stream of drinkers push past. The merest glimmer of sunshine is enough to attract huge crowds; the frighteningly beautiful are now outnumbered by wannabes and loud City boys. Such is the price of fame, and the standard of the Westbourne's food has declined distinctly as a result. Still, you could try your luck at a midweek lunch. A pint of prawns was a nice fresh starter, and a main course of sea bass with bean salad was tasty, the salad in particular. However, lamb tagine came unexpectedly and disappointingly as a huge lamb shank with a bit of dryish couscous. We would have fancied pudding (chocolate brownie),

but you have to queue at the bar, and with an estimated waiting time of half an hour and the likelihood of losing your seat, it just wasn't worth it. There's a good beer selection, including Leffe, Dortmunder Union and Old Speckled Hen, along with bottled Belgian beers and some good wines.
Babies and children admitted. Tables outdoors (14, terrace). **Map 7 B5.**

South West
Battersea SW11

★ Greyhound NEW
2005 RUNNER-UP BEST GASTROPUB
136 Battersea High Street, SW11 3JR (7978 7021/www.thegreyhoundatbattersea.co.uk). Clapham Junction rail/49, 319, 344, 345 bus. **Open** noon-11pm Tue-Sat; noon-5pm Sun. **Lunch served** noon-2.30pm, **dinner served** 7-9.30pm Tue-Sat. **Meals served** noon-5pm Sun. **Main courses** £6.60-£8.50. **Set dinner** £27 2 courses, £31 3 courses. **Service** 10%. **Credit** AmEx, MC, V.
Offering more of a fine dining experience than merely a quick stop-off point for a pint and some potted shrimps, the Greyhound is a tastefully renovated pub in the heart of Battersea. It's owned by Australian-born sommelier Mark van der Goot, so the wine list is splendid; clearly laid out according to grape variety, it offers more than 300 Old and New World bottles, including many from interesting Austrian and new-style Italian producers, and 20 wines by the glass. Chef is Tom Martinovic (also an Aussie), whose CV boasts apprenticeships with Eric Chavot and Heston Blumenthal – and there is a definite whiff of the master food boffin about the menu. Witness Argentinian beef tartare with cucumber, popcorn and oyster beignet; or Golden Valley goat's curd salad with red pepper mousse – both starters on the dinner menu. Mains featured

intense, gamey four-year-old organic Herdwick mutton, served with houmous, baby aubergine and broccoli. It's bold and brilliantly executed cooking, impeccably sourced, and astutely proportioned to allow indulgence in a full three courses. The only real downside to the whole experience is the insistence on square plates (a needless stroke of fussiness) and the slightly tepid atmosphere. Otherwise, a real find.
Booking advisable. Disabled: toilet. No smoking. Separate room for parties, seats 25. Tables outdoors (12, patio). **Map 21 B2.**

Chelsea SW3, SW10

Lots Road Pub & Dining Room
114 Lots Road, SW10 0RJ (7352 6645). Fulham Broadway tube then 11 bus/Sloane Square tube then 11, 19, 22 bus. **Open** 11am-11pm Mon-Sat; noon-10.30pm Sun. **Lunch served** noon-3pm Mon-Fri. **Dinner served** 5.30-10pm Mon-Thur; 5.30-10.30pm Fri. **Meals served** noon-10.30pm Sat; noon-10pm Sun. **Main courses** £8-£13. **Set meal** (6-10pm Sun) £12.50 main course & dessert. **Credit** MC, V.
How an Irish Mint Milkshake (crème de menthe, fresh mint, Baileys, cream) qualifies as a 'summer special' is anyone's guess. Still, we had time to ponder as much while we waited for a table on a busy midweek night at this Chelsea staple (which, non-locals should note, is a bit off the beaten track unless you're en route to check on your boat at Chelsea Harbour). The menu is stocked with standards – spring rolls, burgers, sausage and mash – but we plumped for more adventurous options. A starter of mixed seafood with avocado salad had just the right acidity of dressing. Roasted lamb rump on salad niçoise was a strange (and expensive) combination, but the decent chunk of meat was cooked with skill. Stuffed chicken breast on garlic spinach with gnocchi and saffron

Greyhound

Pig's Ear

sauce was excellent. Our enthusiastic waitress encouraged us to finish with a sticky toffee pudding she'd 'sell her grandmother for'. The acoustics weren't great at our table by the bar, but there's a more pleasant and intimate alcove area if you book or arrive early. The Sunday deal, any main course and dessert for £12.50 from 6pm, is popular and good value.
Babies and children admitted. Disabled: toilet. No smoking (restaurant). Restaurant available for hire. Takeaway service. **Map 13 13C.**

★ Pig's Ear NEW 15% off

2005 RUNNER-UP BEST GASTROPUB
35 Old Church Street, SW3 5BS (7352 2908/ www.thepigsear.co.uk). Sloane Square tube. Bar **Open** noon-11pm Mon-Sat; noon-10.30pm Sun. **Lunch served** 12.30-3pm Mon-Fri; 12.30-4pm Sat, Sun. **Main courses** £8-£14.50. *Restaurant* **Lunch served** 12.30-4pm Sun. *Both* **Dinner served** 7-10pm Mon-Sat. **Main courses** £8-£14.50. **Credit** AmEx, DC, MC, V.
A tidy corner boozer off the Fulham Road that has retained its homely feel despite the arrival of bone marrow and other fashionable delights on its menu, the Pig's Ear is a low-key and satisfying venue. The menu is astonishingly varied: we had baby octopus salad, the eponymous fried pig's ears and bone marrow to start (mainly because we couldn't settle on just two choices), followed by a deliciously fatty pork chop with cubes of chorizo, and duck with pak choi (the duck was slightly tough). Firm and tasty new potatoes worked well on the side, and the own-made walnut bread is almost worth the trip alone. Each generously proportioned dish arrived carefully prepared and lovingly crafted. The decor – battered Formica burgundy table-tops, faded brass-framed mirrors and colourful signs and portraits – is finely judged, and staff are friendly and fun. The place was quiet on a midweek lunchtime, but locals still enjoy

having a pint or two in there as well, which makes it feel still very much like a genuine pub that happens to serve great grub.
Babies and children welcome: high chairs. Booking advisable (restaurant). **Map 14 E12.**

East Sheen SW14

★ Victoria 15% off

10 West Temple Sheen, SW14 7RT (8876 4238/www.thevictoria.net). Mortlake rail. **Open** 8am-11pm Mon-Sat; 8am-10.30pm Sun. **Breakfast served** 7-9.30am Mon-Fri; 8-10am Sat, Sun. **Lunch served** noon-2.30pm Mon-Fri; noon-3pm Sat; noon-4pm Sun. **Dinner served** 7-10pm Mon-Sat; 7-9pm Sun. **Main courses** £9.95-£16.95. **Service** 12.5%. **Credit** AmEx, MC, V.
A huge sunlit space that's been decorated with great attention to detail, the Victoria looks more like a country hotel than a gastropub (and does, in fact, have bedrooms). There's a cosy bar area for everything from evening cocktails to afternoon coffee and cakes, a spacious restaurant and a garden for the children. A plate of own-made bread, olives and dip set the tone with generous, exotic flavours. A starter of English asparagus with St George's mushrooms and a fried duck egg was done simply, but with great care. A main of Charolais rump steak with spring garlic leaf butter, chips and salad was stunning: top-notch meat and zinging spring flavours. Grilled salmon with broad beans, chorizo, Jersey royals and salsa verde was almost as good. None of the dishes are messed around with or overdone. Profiteroles with crème chantilly and hot seville orange chocolate sauce were infused with real vanilla, and the sauce had a sumptuous fruitiness. The wine list is also good: a recommended glass of house rosé was very acceptable. At first glance, the Victoria's menu looked expensive, but after such a feast it seemed a complete bargain.

Babies and children welcome: high chairs; children's menu; books; children's play area (garden). Booking essential weekends. Restaurant available for hire. Separate area for parties, seats 34. Tables outdoors (10, garden).

Southfields SW18

Earl Spencer

260-262 Merton Road, SW18 5JL (8870 9244/ www.theearlspencer.co.uk). Southfields tube. **Open** 11am-11pm Mon-Sat; noon-10.30pm Sun. **Lunch served** 12.30-2.30pm Mon-Sat; 12.30-3pm Sun. **Dinner served** 7-10pm Mon-Sat; 7-9.30pm Sun. **Main courses** £7.50-£12.50. **Credit** AmEx, MC, V.
With its U-shaped bar, impressive high ceiling and gilt features, the Earl Spencer has a touch of grandeur. Large blackboards chalked with appetising dishes dominate the walls and immediately indicate that the emphasis is on quality food. The daily-changing menu has an international flavour. On our visit, starters included crispy lamb pancakes with cucumber, spring onions and hoisin sauce, and chicken liver parfait with 'Indian military piccalilli' and toast; a spiced red lentil soup was surprisingly light and flavoured beautifully with coriander. For mains, Italian-style veal meatballs with troffie pasta, and tomato, parmesan and rocket tempted, but we opted for the seared tuna, cooked perfectly and accompanied by a delicious spicy black bean salad and guacamole. If you can manage a dessert, you might have a choice of pavlova with griottine cherries, sticky ginger pudding, or the cheese plate with British and Irish varieties. There's a good wine list, cask-conditioned ales, and seasonal own-made drinks (elderflower pressé, lemon barley, ginger soda). The comfortable atmosphere seems to be enjoyed mostly by couples and groups of thirtysomethings.

Babies and children welcome: high chairs.
Bookings not accepted. Separate room for parties,
seats 70. Tables outdoors (10, patio).

Wandsworth SW18

Alma ✓ *good sunday roast 3/06*

499 Old York Road, SW18 1TF (8870 2537/
www.thealma.co.uk). Wandsworth Town rail.
Open 11am-11pm Mon-Sat; noon-10.30pm
Sun. **Lunch served** noon-4pm daily. **Dinner
served** 6-10.30pm Mon-Sat; 6-10pm Sun.
Main courses £8-£13. **Service** 12.5% for
parties of 6 or more. **Credit** AmEx, MC, V.
Walk out of Wandsworth Town station and you
might as well step straight in through the front
door of this ever-lively gem. Don't be put off by
the boozy after-work crowd in the bar – push on
through to the back where you will find a
charming, green-accented oasis of candlelight,
wooden tables and homely food. With a note on the
table about the owners' Surrey farm (where some
of the meat is sourced) and a charming welcome
from the staff, we couldn't wait to get stuck in. The
menu has a robust, rural ring to it: we enjoyed a
fine haddock and mussel chowder with saffron,
and an enormous portion of herb-stuffed pork loin
on a bed of lentils, potato and cabbage, with a
gooseberry and cider sauce. Our only criticism of
the latter was a slight overload of strong flavours,
where greater simplicity would have better served
the fine ingredients. After such a high-volume
feast, we didn't have a hope of finding room for
desserts, lovely though the apple and berry
crumble sounded. Sister pub is the Ship (*see below*).
Babies and children welcome: high chairs.
Booking advisable. Disabled: toilet. Separate
room for parties, seats 50. **Map 21 A4.**

Freemasons

2 Wandsworth Common Northside, SW18 2SS
(7326 8580). Clapham Junction rail. **Open**
noon-11pm Mon-Sat; noon-10.30pm Sun. **Lunch
served** noon-3pm Mon-Fri; 12.30-3.30pm Sat;
12.30-4pm Sun. **Dinner served** 6.30-10pm
Mon-Sat; 6.30-9.30pm Sun. **Main courses**
£8-£11.50. **Credit** AmEx, MC, V.
This building has been a Café Med and a Livebait
in previous lives, but it now seems to have found
its feet as an upmarket gastropub in the no-man's
land between Wandsworth Common and Clapham
Junction. The set-up is standard gastropub (open
kitchen, wooden floors), supplemented by some
outdoor seating, but the Freemasons' excellent
wine list (including fine dessert wines and aged
Armagnacs) and calm, professional service help
give it an edge. Our salt and chilli squid starter was
good, while own-made tortellini stuffed with
chorizo in a delicious tomato sauce vierge set our
juices flowing. Oven-roasted chicken breast,
sautéed new potatoes, ruby chard and coarse grain
mustard with a very seasonal broad bean jus was
the ideal gastropub main, while char-grilled ribeye
with oven-roasted tomatoes, shallot and béarnaise
sauce came with impeccable chunky chips. Figs
with honey ice-cream were a sensuous delight.
The only letdown was an Eton mess minus
meringues, which we sent back. The chef emerged
to apologise that he was training staff that night,
though the second effort wasn't a huge
improvement. There's only so much double cream
you can handle.
Babies and children welcome: high chairs.
Disabled: toilet. No-smoking area
(restaurant). Tables outdoors (11, patio).
Map 21 B4.

Ship

41 Jew's Row, SW18 1TB (8870 9667/
www.theship.co.uk). Wandsworth Town rail.
Open 11am-11pm Mon-Sat; noon-10.30pm Sun.
Meals served noon-10.30pm Mon-Sat; noon-
10pm Sun. **Main courses** £7.50-£14.75.
Credit AmEx, DC, MC, V.
Residents of Wandsworth are lucky to have the Ship
(sister to the Alma, *see above*). Its fabulous Thames-
side garden is the perfect spot to enjoy a pint in the
sunshine, and its kitchen serves decent seasonal
food made with ingredients from the proprietors'
own farm. We followed summery starters of

English asparagus with hollandaise, and a fine
gazpacho with fillet steak served with crushed new
potatoes and béarnaise sauce – a tender piece of
meat, cooked with precision. Alternative mains
might include artichoke tortellini, or scallops with
spinach mousse. Desserts tend towards the
traditional: chocolate cake, summer pudding and an
excellent crème brulée, say. On our visit the interior
was almost empty, as most customers were having
a lively time in the garden taking advantage of the
gourmet barbecue that takes place every summer
weekend. Restaurant customers can also eat
alfresco; if the weather's not up to scratch, head for
the main dining room, which is candlelit and more
comfortable than the rather low-key conservatory.
Staff are friendly and swift, and there's a good, fairly
priced wine list.
Babies and children admitted (before 7pm).
Separate room for parties, seats 20. Tables
outdoors (30, riverside garden). **Map 21 A4.**

South
Waterloo SE1

★ Anchor & Hope ✓

36 The Cut, SE1 8LP (7928 9898). Southwark
tube or Waterloo tube/rail. **Open** 5-11pm Mon;
11am-11pm Tue-Sat. **Lunch served** noon-
2.30pm Tue-Sat. **Dinner served** 6-10.30pm Tue-
Sat. **Main courses** £10.80-£14. **Credit** MC, V.
The much-praised Anchor & Hope takes an almost
fundamentalist approach to gastropubbery.
There's the no-booking policy, for instance, which
means both prince and pauper have to take pot
luck on tables when they turn up (the place is
deservedly popular, so the only way to avoid a
lengthy wait in the adjacent bar is to arrive early).
Then there's the food: the roast beef rump, we were
told pointedly, comes pink, because that's how chef
cooks it. No concessions. It's an attitude that shows
how seriously the British-slanted food is taken.
And the cooking is marvellous. Bold but simple is
the key, as with starters such as duck heart on
toast, or whole artichoke (leaves and heart) with
accompanying vinaigrette. For mains, we passed
on tripe and chips, and instead tried the beef rump
(served too pink, we maintain) and an earthy stew
of slow-cooked Tamworth pork, bacon and
turnips. A huge dessert of chocolate and hazelnut
cake closed off a hearty meal. Staff are friendly
and totally in control of proceedings. One of
London's finest gastropubs.
Babies and children admitted. Bookings not
accepted. No smoking. Tables outdoors
(4, pavement). **Map 11 N8.**

South East
Bermondsey SE1

Garrison

99-101 Bermondsey Street, SE1 3XB (7089
9355/www.thegarrison.co.uk). London Bridge
tube/rail. **Open** noon-11pm Mon-Sat; noon-
10.30pm Sun. **Lunch served** noon-3pm Mon-Fri;
12.30-4pm Sat, Sun. **Dinner served** 6-10pm
Mon-Sat; 6-9.30pm Sun. **Main courses** £6.90-
£16. **Service** 12.5%. **Credit** AmEx, MC, V.
The interior of this bright, light gastropub is an
appealingly eclectic mix of retro and antique, with
classic novels and wall sconces mixed up with
leather diner-style seating and stripped wooden
flooring. Friendly, efficient staff and a decent
kitchen recommend it further to a young local
crowd. Menu-wise, the simpler dishes work best.
Fresh asparagus with a moreish béarnaise was
delicious. But tempura vegetables was not: soggy
veg in a heavy batter that was more suited to a
fillet of cod. Things improved with a splendid slab
of roast trout on sage polenta, while a similarly
large chunk of pork loin was a fine lean/fat
balance and sat happily in a root vegetable broth.
Desserts of Neal's Yard cheeses and own-made
sorbets and ice-creams round things off nicely. A
decent wine list offers a few by the glass (including
a full-bodied Argentinian Malbec Alamos and a
delicate South African chenin blanc). It's advisable
to book at weekends, when brunch is added to the

menu. The intimate downstairs cinema can be
booked for private viewings.
Babies and children admitted (lunch Sat, Sun
only). Booking advisable. Disabled: toilet.
No-smoking area. Separate room for parties,
seats 40. **Map 12 Q9.**

Hartley 15% off

64 Tower Bridge Road, SE1 4TR (7394 7023/
www.thehartley.com). Borough tube/Elephant
& Castle tube/rail then 1, 188 bus. **Open**
noon-midnight Mon-Thur; noon-1am Fri, Sat;
noon-11pm Sun. **Lunch served** noon-3pm
Mon-Fri; 11am-5pm Sat. **Dinner served** 6-10pm
Mon-Sat. **Meals served** noon-8pm Sun.
Main courses £7.50-£13.50. **Credit** AmEx,
MC, V.
More gastrobar than gastropub, the Hartley is a
very appealing spot, with a convivial vibe,
inoffensive decor (zinc bar, jolly colour scheme),
reasonable prices and cheery staff. The food has
been highly praised, but on our most recent visit
results were mixed. The best dish was a generously
sized plate of salmon fish cakes; fat chips with
sweet chilli sauce were good too, and beef stew,
while not sensational, did the job on a cold night.
Butternut squash covered in a tomato sauce with
almonds on top wasn't up to the usual standard,
however. The wine list is limited, but ungreedily
priced and offers plenty of options by the glass;
there are more beers in bottles than on tap, and
even a few cocktails. It's not the sort of place for
a quiet conversation, though. There's not much
choice in these parts, despite luxury apartments
going up all over the borough, so the place was
full, but a bit of competition might be just what
the Hartley needs.
Babies and children admitted (before 6pm).
Entertainment: DJ 7.30pm Sun; jazz 8pm Tue.
No-smoking tables.

Dulwich SE22

Palmerston 15% off

91 Lordship Lane, SE22 8EP (8693 1629).
East Dulwich rail. **Open** noon-11pm Mon-Sat;
noon-10.30pm Sun. **Lunch served** noon-
2.30pm Sat; noon-4pm Sun. **Dinner served**
7-10pm Mon-Sat. **Main courses** £9-£14.
Credit MC, V.
When it was originally converted to a gastropub,
the Palmerston perhaps pitched itself a touch high
for its constituency. It's now a little less pricey and
a little more casual, but it retains high standards
of presentation and, particularly, service. It's a
corner property, a showcase of pub design: wood
panelling, fireplaces, an 1865 mosaic floor and
brewers' names trumpeted in red glass. The menu
is classic gastropub: starters that also do nicely as
snacks (soups, spreads, salads), hearty and
interesting main courses, and desserts that can
stand alone. We ordered the duff starter,
wondering how white crab would fare with a thai
dressing; the answer was obscured by a painful
amount of chilli. But tomato broth with pistou was
nicely defined; a risotto milanese with pungent
fonduta (cheese fondue sauce) was unashamedly
rich and intense; and spring lamb was plentiful if
uninteresting. If the cooking was a little mixed,
everything else hummed with commitment, from
the staff's anticipatory abilities to the lively
discussion over the next day's menu we overheard
taking place over coffee. Enough people come here
to drink for the pub decor to be more than just a
theme: the wines are interesting, and there are
three real ales on tap.
Babies and children welcome: high chairs.
Booking advisable weekends. No smoking rooms.
Tables outdoors (5, pavement). **Map 23 C4.**

Lewisham SE23

Dartmouth Arms NEW

7 Dartmouth Road, SE23 2NH (8488 3117/
www.thedartmoutharms.com). Forest Hill rail/
122, 176, 312 bus. **Open** 11am-11pm Mon-Sat;
noon-10.30pm Sun. **Lunch served** noon-4pm,
dinner served 6.30-10pm Mon-Sat. **Meals
served** noon-9pm Sun. **Main courses** £9-£14.
Credit AmEx, MC, V.

The owners of the Dartmouth Arms, former Fire Station and Livebait partner Michael Richards and wife Violeta, have recruited chef Paul Newbury, who's conjured up a creative, British-inspired menu. To start, black pudding and squid risotto was subtly flavoured and fragrant with truffle oil, while smoked haddock and leek tart with roasted peppers was a tangy delight. For main courses, a Somerset smoked eel, served with pancetta, spring onion mash and beetroot chutney, was an inspirational combination of flavour and form. However, pan-fried calf's liver, white bean and jerusalem artichoke purée proved too starchy, weighed down by the liver's breadcrumb coating. Lamb chump chop (with dauphinois potatoes and flageolet beans) was undercooked, but was quickly rectified by the charming staff. We finished on a high note: both lemon posset with raspberry coulis and vanilla shortbread, and a British cheese plate with own-made plum chutney and oatcakes were spot on. Thankfully, the Dartmouth Arms hasn't sold its pub soul for the gastro element. The front half of the cavernous building is for drinkers, who sup from a well-picked, accessible wine list, and several good ales (London Pride, Speckled Hen, Bombardier).
Babies and children welcome: high chairs. Disabled: toilet. No-smoking tables. Restaurant available for hire. Tables outdoors (10, garden).

East

Bow E3

Morgan Arms
43 Morgan Street, E3 5AA (8980 6389/ www.geronimo-inns.co.uk). Mile End tube. **Open** noon-11pm Mon-Sat; noon-10.30pm Sun. **Lunch served** noon-3pm Mon-Sat; noon-4pm Sun. **Dinner served** 7-10pm Mon-Sat. **Main courses** £12.95-£18. **Credit** MC. V.
A pub this fancy in Bow? It makes sense when you realise the Morgan is mere yards from long-gentrified Tredegar Square. Its residents must have quite a thirst: the place is permanently busy, even the drinking area with its mix-and-match wooden tables. As for the restaurant, we had to wait over two hours for a table (there are no bookings). Staff were coping with the crush with varying degrees of grace, though their explanation as to why we couldn't eat outside or in the bar made sense: the tiny kitchen, open for all to see, has a limited capacity. The food, when it arrived, was exuberant, unexpectedly complex and graphically presented. At first taste, of a wonderful crumbly/smooth tart, we knew the kitchen could perform; at second, of a less impressive brioche-baked brie, we knew it was patchy. Generally, though, flavours were fresh and cooking assured. Puddings, all sets of mini variations on a theme (ours was 'sooo toffee'), made a perky finish. The well-organised wine list is broad. A small extension into the patio should be in place by autumn 2005, in time to rescue the Morgan from its own success.
Babies and children admitted (dining). Disabled: toilet. Tables outdoors (11, garden; 4, pavement).

Docklands E14

★ Gun NEW
2005 WINNER BEST GASTROPUB
27 Coldharbour, Isle of Dogs, E14 9NS (7515 5222/www.thegundocklands.com). Canary Wharf tube/DLR/South Quay DLR. **Open** 11am-11pm Mon-Sat; 11am-10.30pm Sun. **Lunch served** noon-3pm Mon-Fri; noon-4.30pm Sat, Sun. **Dinner served** 6-10.30pm Mon-Sat. **Meals served** noon-10pm Sun. **Main courses** £10-£17. **Service** 12.5%. **Credit** AmEx, MC, V.
Perched on the south-east corner of Canary Wharf, with spectacular views across the Thames to the Millennium Dome, the Gun is an oasis in a desert of iron, steel and glass. Owned by Tom and Ed Martin (who also run the White Swan, *see p105*, and the Well, *see p107*), it's a wonderfully inviting place, full of cosy nooks and crannies, battered leather sofas, distressed wood and a stunning river terrace that buzzes with noise and is illuminated

at night with flickering candles. There's also a separate sun-deck, with its own bar and barbecue food. The pub – there is a separate dining room too, with a more formal menu – offers wonderful interpretations of British classics, as well as touches of French bistro cuisine. A generous bowl of fresh whitebait with tartare sauce arrived crunchy and salty (all the Gun's fish is bought daily from nearby Billingsgate Market); Old Spot bacon with eggs and brown sauce was the best sandwich we've ever had. Other dishes included gamey potted duck with apricot, and Gun fish pie, both of which we witnessed being enjoyed by a happy throng of City types and chirpy locals. Service was not exactly slick, but the busy staff were attentive. The wine list is impressive without being daunting. One disappointment: the roast suckling pig with apple sauce had run out on our visit (clearly, it's a favourite), but there were still more than enough treats to recommend many repeat visits. A true gem.
Babies and children welcome: high chairs. Disabled: toilet. Separate room for parties, seats 12. Tables outdoors (12, terrace; 15, sun deck).

Shoreditch EC2

Fox Dining Room
28 Paul Street, EC2A 4LB (7729 5708). Old Street tube/rail. **Open** noon-11pm Mon-Fri. **Lunch served** 12.30-3pm, **dinner served** 6.30-10pm Mon-Fri. **Main courses** £10.25. **Set meals** £15 2 courses, £19.75 3 courses. **Credit** MC, V.
The Fox is a proper drinkers' pub downstairs with a (very different) large dining room above, dotted with random rugs and tables bearing wax-encrusted candelabra that compete atmospherically with the deep, dark colour scheme. It's all pleasingly ramshackle, but the indiscipline doesn't extend to the kitchen, which issues a short, sharp daily menu of four options per course, all so appetising that the choice is unlikely to feel limited. Dishes are simple but full-on and packed with interest: grey mullet might come with samphire, serrano ham with well-garlicked lamb tomaquet, and duck with sautéed potatoes or ratatouille. Everything savoury that we tasted was spot on – good ingredients well handled – but, mysteriously, our desserts were duds. Lemon syrup cake was dull and dry, and pinenut and thyme semi freddo apparently devoid of the billed flavourings. But neither that deficiency, nor the occasional lapse from the T-shirted servers, detracted from a charming dining experience overall. There's a short, well-chosen wine list, with several by the glass. The tiny canopied terrace is one of the few good options for outdoor eating in the area.
Babies and children admitted (dining). Booking advisable. Restaurant available for hire. Tables outdoors (6, terrace). **Map 6 Q4.**

★ Princess NEW
2005 RUNNER-UP BEST GASTROPUB
76 Paul Street, EC2A 4NE (7729 9270). Old Street tube/rail. *Bar* **Open** noon-11.30pm Mon-Fri; 5.30-11pm Sat; noon-5.30pm Sun. **Lunch served** 12.30-3pm Mon-Fri; 1-4pm Sun. **Main courses** £5-£9.50. *Restaurant* **Lunch served** 12.30-3pm Mon-Fri. **Main courses** £10-£15. *Both* **Dinner served** 6.30-10.30pm Mon-Sat. **Credit** AmEx, MC, V.
Australian expats Zim Sutton and Andrew Veevers made an impressive debut with their first gastropub, the Easton (*see p107*) in Clerkenwell. Now they have taken over the former Princess Royal on the fringes of Shoreditch, creating a two-tiered eating venue that provides fabulous food, simply cooked, with a solid drinks selection (including Timothy Taylor Landlord and Fuller's London Pride on tap, and an international wine list helpfully organised by flavour characteristics). From the short pub menu we chose crispy beer-battered cod and home-cut chips with basil mayonnaise – all excellent – and butternut squash risotto, which had nutty flavours, a solid texture and a smooth unctuous finish. Other tasty options

included barbecue lamb flatbread sandwich with harissa and yoghurt, and springbok sausages with pancetta gravy and mash. Staff were accomodating when we requested the Spanish cheese with figs from the menu in the more formal first-floor dining room. Accessed by a wrought-iron spiral staircase, this has an art deco flavour, with cream-upholstered chairs, floral wallpaper and a huge convex mirror above the fireplace. Here you can feast on such dishes as pata negra pork cheeks braised in morcilla and Rioja; flash-fried cuttlefish salad; and meringues with cardamom mascarpone and rosewater raspberries.
Babies and children admitted. Booking advisable. **Map 67 Q4.**

Royal Oak NEW
73 Columbia Road, E2 7RG (7729 2220). Old Street tube/rail/Bethnal Green tube/26, 48, 55 bus. **Open** 6-11pm Mon-Thur; noon-11pm Fri; 11am-11pm Sat; 9.30am-10.30pm Sun. **Meals served** 6-10.30pm Mon-Thur; noon-4pm, 6-10.30pm Fri, Sat; 9.30am-4pm, 6-9.30pm Sun. **Main courses** £7-£14. **Credit** AmEx, MC, V.
Columbia Road's smoky old gay boozer has been spruced up into a smoky new gastropub. Happily, the beautiful interior remains intact. Light streams through the windows on to a big island bar and dark wood panelling crowned with references to the pub's previous brews (Truman's Eagle Ale, Imperial Stout, Trubrown Ale). These days, there's a short, well-chosen wine list, and even a choice of cocktails. The menu is short, simple and – on our visit – well executed. Firm asparagus came with a creamy, own-made hollandaise and a beautifully poached egg, while a huge steak sandwich was stuffed with a perfectly cooked piece of meat, plus cheese, tomatoes, rocket, red onion and chutney, and accompanied by a pile of chunky chips. A cheeseboard with a good hunk of stilton, crumbling mature cheddar and creamy brie arrived with a pile of biscuits, pickled onions and

own-made chutney. Our neighbour was making quick work of a fine-looking roast dinner, complete with yorkshire. Already popular, particularly when the Sunday morning flower market is in full swing, the Royal Oak is now busier than ever, which may have attributed to our only gripes: an out-of-action loo and slightly distracted service. There's also a cafe at the rear, and the upstairs room will become a dining area later in autumn 2005.

Babies and children admitted. Bookings accepted (upstairs). No-smoking tables (upstairs). Separate room for parties, seats 40. Tables outdoors (4, courtyard). **Map 6 S3**.

Victoria Park E3

Crown

223 Grove Road, E3 5SN (8981 9998/ www.singhboulton.co.uk). Mile End tube/277 bus. **Open** 5-11pm Mon; noon-11pm Tue-Sat; noon-10.30pm Sun. **Lunch served** noon-4pm Tue-Fri; 12.30-4pm Sat, Sun. **Dinner served** 6.30-10.30pm Mon-Sat; 6.30-10pm Sun. **Main courses** £8-£14.50. **Credit** MC, V.
Sister of the Duke of Cambridge (*see p116*) in Islington, the Crown sits on a prime spot next to green Victoria Park and alongside the Regents Canal. It's very proud of its organic and ethical credentials: ingredients are sourced from small, independent suppliers; fish are line-caught; tea and coffee is fair trade; even the tampons in the loos are organic. Drinks (all organic, of course) include beers from Pitfield, Freedom and St Peter's breweries, proper ginger ale and a 40-strong wine list. All very worthy, but don't worry: the results are far from dull. The menu mixes British and Mediterranean influences in an inventive manner, and changes seasonally; thus autumn might bring wild mushroom risotto or braised oxtail with swede purée, while summer sees roast cod in salsa verde, new potato and mussel stew, or bacon-wrapped scallops. Ingredients are good, flavours

earthy. You can eat downstairs in the spacious, noisy pub area or upstairs, which is quieter, has table service and a cute roof terrace overlooking the park entrance. Staff coped well under pressure on a packed Saturday lunchtime; we hadn't booked, but they found us a table upstairs within minutes, and weren't fazed by asking for changes to a dish for dietary reasons.

Babies and children welcome: high chairs. Disabled: toilet. No smoking (restaurant). Restaurant available for hire. Separate rooms for parties, seating 20 and 30. Tables outdoors (8, terrace; 5, balcony).

North East

Hackney E8

Cat & Mutton

76 Broadway Market, E8 4QJ (7254 5599). Bethnal Green tube/rail then 106, 253 bus/ London Fields rail/26, 48, 55 bus. **Open** 6-11pm Mon; noon-11pm Tue-Sat; noon-10.30pm Sun **Lunch served** noon-3pm Tue-Sat; noon-5.30pm Sun. **Dinner served** 6-10pm Mon-Sat. **Main courses** £8.50-£14.50. **Set dinner** (Mon) £12.50 2 courses, £15 3 courses. **Credit** AmEx, MC, V.
The first gastropub in these parts is maturing into a fine local hangout. Some Fridays and Saturdays it's a little too rumbustious to make eating a pleasure, and sometimes during the day at weekends there are too many small children wandering around. However, on the whole the Cat & Mutton gets it right. The furnishings are simple – wooden chairs and tables, bare brick walls, the odd bit of art – with huge windows on two sides really making the room. Food, prepared in a tiny on-view kitchen, changes daily, but usually includes steak and chips; otherwise there might be chilled tomato soup or feta, pea and mint salad, grey mullet with radishes, sorrel and new potatoes, or rocket and basil risotto with confit garlic and

ricotta. We've rarely been disappointed with the cooking, although the best dish of a recent meal (Cantabrian anchovies with sourdough toast, capers and lemon) didn't require much preparation, just great ingredients. To finish, there are cheeses from Neal's Yard, or indulgent puddings such as chocolate mousse cake with cream and hazelnut caramel. Adnams Bitter or Greene King IPA are the beers; the wine list is tempting . Service is willing, and more efficient than the casual demeanour suggests.

Babies and children welcome: high chairs. Disabled: toilet. Entertainment: DJs 5.30-10.30pm Sun. Tables outdoors (6, pavement).

North

Archway N19

★ St John's

91 Junction Road, N19 5QU (7272 1587). Archway tube. **Open** 5-11pm Mon; noon-11pm Tue-Sat; noon-10.30pm Sun. **Lunch served** noon-3.30pm Tue-Fri; noon-4pm Sat, Sun. **Dinner served** 6.30-11pm Mon-Sat; 6.30-9.30pm Sun. **Main courses** £9-£14.50. **Service** 12.5% for parties of 5 or more. **Credit** AmEx, MC, V.
Junction Road is a dismal setting for this large and lovely old pub with a buzzing front bar and an equally lively dining room at the back. The space is painted murky green and maroon, with a high gold ceiling and a wall hung with the oddest assemblage of slightly freakish portraits. The mood stays light thanks to ever-full tables (bookings are a must) and chatty, personable staff – we were impressed when a guy on the next table asked a question about the Bordeaux and the waitress fetched a hefty book on wines to search for the answer. (The imaginative wine list, incidentally, even includes an English bottle.) We've eaten here a couple of times in the last 12

Gun

RESTAURANTS

Princess. See p112.

months and have yet to be disappointed – the food is terrific, marrying solid cooking skills with flashes of invention. Last time round we enjoyed a lamb shank with couscous prepared with chopped veg, and a baked sea bass, served with head and tail intact and no silly sauces. The real highlights are the puddings; expect the likes of panettone bread pudding with vanilla custard; chocolate and caramel tart; or mixed berry pavlova.
Babies and children welcome: booster seats. Booking advisable. Tables outdoors (7, patio). **Map 26 B1.**

Camden Town & Chalk Farm NW1

Engineer
65 Gloucester Avenue, NW1 8JH (7722 0950/ www.the-engineer.com). Chalk Farm tube/31, 168 bus. **Open** 9am-11pm Mon-Sat; 9am-10.30pm Sun. **Breakfast served** 9-11.30am Mon-Fri; 9am-noon Sat, Sun. **Lunch served** noon-3pm Mon-Fri; 12.30-4.30pm Sat, Sun. **Dinner served** 7-11pm Mon-Sat; 7-10pm Sun. **Main courses** £10.50-£16.50. **Service** 12.5%. **Credit** MC, V.
Dilapidated, *deshabillé*, its glory days a bittersweet memory… there's an air of Blanche DuBois about the Engineer. Once the hottest place in town, it's now simply a decent local in a cool neighbourhood. The menu is truly international and experimental, and uses free range or organic meat. Some dishes, such as watermelon, grape, feta and mint salad, or salt and pepper squid with green papaya salad, could be ordered as starters or mains. A main course of red pimento stuffed with orange sweet potato and served with plantain, asparagus and black olive dressing looked spectacular. Indeed, all our food was well executed, with the exception of a chocolate ganache with coffee granita, vanilla ice-cream and chocolate brownie, which was served sundae style, but arrived more like a milkshake with a dry slab of cake on the side. One of the cheapest bottles on the excellent wine list, Viu Manent Malbec 2004 from Chile (£13.50), lived up to a flowery description promising five or six flavours. The atmosphere among customers was convivial, and the service prompt and friendly. We'd happily return. One gripe: on booking, we were granted a two-hour time slot for our Sunday lunchtime visit, yet there were many tables free.
Babies and children welcome: high chairs. Booking advisable. Disabled: toilet. Separate rooms for parties, seating 20 and 32. **Map 27 B2.**

★ Lansdowne
90 Gloucester Avenue, NW1 8HX (7483 0409). Chalk Farm tube/31, 168 bus. **Bar Open** 6-11pm Mon; noon-11pm Tue-Sat; noon-10.30pm Sun. **Lunch served** 12.30-3pm Tue-Sat; 12.30-4pm Sun. **Dinner served** 7-10pm Mon-Sat; 7-9.30pm Sun. *Restaurant* **Lunch served** 1-4pm Sat, Sun. **Dinner served** 7-10pm Tue-Sat. **Service** 12.5%. *Both* **Main courses** £8.50-£15.50. **Credit** MC, V.
The bustling ground-floor bar of the Lansdowne serves full meals, but has not, like many of its rivals, gone for full table service – that's restricted to the upstairs restaurant. Ordering more than one course, and all your drinks, at the bar can be a bit of a faff, though staff do their best. There are some fine beers on tap, plus an impressive list of wines, aperitifs and digestifs. We took ages deciding what to eat – mainly because evening light shining on the hand-scrawled blackboard menu made it difficult to read. There's also a separate bar food list on a blackboard behind the bar, and, on a third board above the kitchen entrance, a list of gourmet pizzas (very popular, these looked terrific). Choices ranged from the sublime (white gazpacho with green grapes) to the ridiculous (wheatgrass sorbet). Ribeye with chips and béarnaise sauce was great. Roast halibut on a bed of minty yellow and green courgettes, with vine tomatoes, was very nicely cooked too – but a tad heavy-handed with the olive oil. Desserts were less impressive: chocolate biscuit cake was too firm, and they had run out of the lovely ice-creams advertised (rose, jasmine). Regrettably, the substitutes were mediocre.

Babies and children welcome (restaurant; until 7pm in bar). Disabled: toilet. Restaurant available for hire. Tables outdoors (8, pavement). **Map 27 B2.**

Queens
49 Regent's Park Road, NW1 8XD (7586 0408/ www.geronimo-inns.co.uk). Chalk Farm tube/ 31, 168, 274 bus. **Open** 11am-11pm Mon-Sat; noon-10.30pm Sun. **Lunch served** noon-3pm Mon-Sat; 12.30-4pm Sun. **Dinner served** 7-10pm Mon-Sat; 7-9pm Sun. **Main courses** £9-£17. **Credit** MC, V.
With its own first-floor dining room, complete with a balcony overlooking leafy Primrose Hill, this popular local boozer competes with the restaurants of Regent's Park Road. The Modern British menu struck an aspirational note on a recent visit, with oysters alongside white asparagus risotto. Our simple choices failed to impress, though. Stodgy battered 'codling' came with frozen peas instead of the advertised mushy peas, while the 'thick-cut chips' (more like wedges) were soggy, and tasted reheated rather than freshly cooked. A griddled chicken sandwich with salad was pleasant enough, though over-generous with the raw onion. Desserts also disappointed: an uninspired panna cotta arrived with strawberries instead of the promised 'fennel caramel', while strawberries and semi-freddo was bizarrely topped with 'Iranian saffron floss', a strange concoction that looked like hair from a grey wig and had little flavour to compensate for its unappealing appearance. Overall, the whole meal felt perfunctory and half-hearted, surprising given the competition in the area. The wine selection is good, with 15 available by the glass.
Babies and children admitted (restaurant). Booking advisable; essential Sun. Tables outdoors (3, balcony; 3, pavement). **Map 27 A2.**

Highgate N6

Bull NEW
2005 RUNNER-UP BEST GASTROPUB
13 North Hill, N6 4AB (0845 4565 033/ www.inthebull.biz). Highgate tube. *Bar* **Open** 11am-11pm Mon-Sat; 11am-10.30pm Sun. *Restaurant* **Lunch served** noon 2.30pm Tue-Fri; noon-3.30pm Sat, Sun. **Dinner served** 6-10.30pm Mon-Sat; 6.30-9.30pm Sun. **Main courses** £10.50-£20. **Set lunch** (Tue-Fri) £14.95 2 courses, £17.95 3 courses. **Service** 12.5%. *Both* **Credit** MC, V.
In the 16th century, Highgate's position at the top of the hill on the main northern route out of London made it the ideal place for toll collecting, and for innkeepers to trade. Hence the plethora of pubs on North Hill – including this grade II listed building, now home to the Bull. The ground floor holds the dining room – banquette seating, wooden tables, mahogany bar and an open fire – and, in summer, an outside terrace. Upstairs is the pub area. Cask ales include Timothy Taylor and Highgate Bitter, and the wine list offers chilled reds for hot days. Unusually for a gastropub (though not for Highgate), you can also get traditional afternoon tea with scones. The food is generally of good quality; from past visits, we have fond memories of ribeye topped with wholegrain mustard and crispy shallots; and smooth foie gras and chicken liver parfait with Armagnac. However, the fillet of beef we asked for medium rare arrived medium and lukewarm, and john dory with summer vegetables and asparagus sauce was just bland. Service is quick – a little too quick! – but also slightly muddled, suggesting the staff haven't quite gelled yet. Still, given time to bed in, the Bull has the potential to excel.
Babies and children welcome: high chairs. Disabled: toilet. No smoking (restaurant). Separate room for parties, seats 70. Tables outdoors (12, terrace).

Islington N1

Barnsbury
209-211 Liverpool Road, N1 1LX (7607 5519/ www.thebarnsbury.co.uk). Angel tube/Highbury & Islington tube/rail. **Open** noon-11pm

Mon-Sat; noon-10.30pm Sun. **Lunch served** noon 3pm Mon Fri; noon-4pm Sat, Sun. **Dinner served** 6.30-10pm Mon-Sat; 6.30-9.30pm Sun. **Main courses** £8.50-£14. **Service** 12.5%. **Credit** AmEx, MC, V.
Don't judge the Barnsbury by its strange, thrust-out frontage. Inside, it's a handsome rectangular space retreating back via two dining rooms and a square central bar to a small but sweet sunken garden. All is dark wood, duck-egg paint and dining room tables, plus the odd contemporary flourish. It's a generalist operation: people come here variously to snack, dine, drink or have coffee, alone or in (birthday) parties. The menu is international, with some interesting flavour combinations: starters include tuna carpaccio with guacamole, for example, or a salad of chilli-pickled oranges, spinach, feta and olive oil. Mains are a little more predictable, with de rigeur roast chicken breast and mash and merely predictable ribeye, pork loin and roast cod. The cooking was competent but not knock-out, the food looking (and tasting) like something a talented friend might serve; it matched the comfortable, relaxed atmosphere, but slightly disappointed the palate, and the pocket. We intended to have a full meal, but gave up on dessert when forgotten by our previously attentive waiter. It's a free house, with three good ales and plenty of wines by the glass.
Babies and children welcome: high chairs. Disabled: toilet. No-smoking area. Restaurant available for hire. Tables outdoors (4, pavement; 6, garden). **Map 5 N1.**

Drapers Arms
44 Barnsbury Street, N1 1ER (7619 0348/ www.thedrapersarms.co.uk). Highbury & Islington tube/rail. **Open** noon-11pm Mon-Sat; noon-10.30pm Sun. **Lunch served** noon-3pm; noon-3pm Sun. **Dinner served** 7-10pm Mon-Sat. **Main courses** £9-£15. **Service** 12.5%. **Credit** AmEx, MC, V.
It looks like a pub and sounds like a pub, but the crisp, airy Drapers Arms doesn't really feel like one. Thriving despite a tucked-away Islington location, the Drapers is very much at the 'gastro' end of the gastropub scale; the prices, a couple of quid above expectations for most mains, confirm suspicions that this is a kitchen within a pub rather than the other way round. In years gone by, we've generally found that the cooking lived up to these expectations; this time, however, results were a little more mixed. A starter of caramelised five-spice pork belly was immaculate, and the chips into which we regularly dipped were divine. But lamb kleftico, served with garlicky new potatoes, was lacking in lustre, and though the crab mash that accompanied organic brown trout was splendid, the trout itself was perhaps not as fresh as it might have been. But we know that higher standards are the norm and have little hesitation recommending the Draper's, whether you choose to eat in the main pub space, the upstairs dining room or the lovely garden out back.
Babies and children welcome: high chairs. No smoking. Tables outdoors (18, garden). **Map 5 N1.**

Duchess of Kent
441 Liverpool Road, N7 8PR (7609 7104/ www.geronimo-inns.co.uk). Highbury & Islington tube/rail. **Open** noon-11pm Mon-Sat; noon-10.30pm Sun. **Lunch served** noon-3pm Mon-Fri; noon-4pm Sat, Sun. **Dinner served** 7-10pm daily. **Main courses** £7.95-£14.95. **Credit** MC, V.
Formerly a do-nothing corner pub, the Duchess of Kent was reincarnated a couple of years ago by the flourishing Geronimo mini-chain as a gastro-local. It retains a clubbable feel, with red velvet sofas, carpet and generous tables. Staff are helpful and charming, the flowers are fresh, there are board games on offer… it's all very pleasant. And yet the carefully interesting but non-distracting soundtrack, the ringing-all-bells menu, and the fact that a Heathrow Airport branch will have opened by the time you read this evoked a whiff of focus group. Such niggles might have been assuaged by a good feed, but the unfancy gastro standards were a disappointment: they looked good, but didn't

actually taste that nice, with miscued flavourings and textures. Thumbs up for a delicate salmon ballontine (sic), with lovely pickled cucumber and rich, fragrant mussels, but down for a distinctly odd tomato and (tasteless) mozzarella tart, a burger of unpleasant consistency, and a pork belly braised clean away from its flavour. Drinks were better, with a couple of real ales on tap, a decent Bloody Mary (free with Sunday lunch) and an estimable number of wines by the glass.
Babies and children welcome (until 6pm). Disabled: toilet. No-smoking area. Tables outdoors (10, pavement).

★ Duke of Cambridge

30 St Peter's Street, N1 8JT (7359 3066/ www.singhboulton.co.uk). Angel tube. **Open** noon-11pm Mon-Sat; noon-10.30pm Sun. **Lunch served** 12.30-3pm Mon-Fri; 12.30-3.30pm Sat, Sun. **Dinner served** 6.30-10.30pm Mon-Sat; 6.30-10pm Sun. **Main courses** £9.50-£15. **Service** 12.5% for parties of 5 or more. **Credit** MC, V.
Now that quality ingredients are the norm, the Duke of Cambridge's organic/ethical-only schtick isn't really enough to set it apart. Fortunately, the previously patchy cooking is rising to the challenge. Only one dish was typical of the old-style Duke, a dry and taste-free scallop, butter bean and chorizo salad, steeply priced at £9. But both our main courses were in a different class – cod and aïoli, airily subtle and gorgeously textured on top of an intense, rough-hewn caponata; and a moist rump steak with lovely horseradish crème fraîche. Puddings were good too, particularly the soft orange cake with intense kiwi sorbet. The surroundings – it's a dark and woody corner pub enlived by huge windows and, soon, a conservatory – along with the busy local vibe and the charming and efficient service (the latter greatly improved over our last few visits), made dinner an all-round pleasure. People come to sip as much as eat, and the buying policy is particularly interesting when it comes to the drinks, with some unusual non-alcholic options, organic wines (the Horsemondon dry white, from Sussex, tastes like May in a glass) and moderately well-kept cask ales.
Babies and children welcome; high chairs. Booking advisable. No smoking. Restaurant available for hire. Tables outdoors (5, courtyard; 5, pavement). **Map 5 O2.**

House

63-69 Canonbury Road, N1 2DG (7704 7410/ www.inthehouse.biz). Highbury & Islington tube/rail. **Open** 5-11pm Mon; noon-11pm Tue-Sat; noon-10.30pm Sun **Lunch served** noon-2.30pm Tue-Sun. **Dinner served** 6-10.30pm Mon-Fri; 6.30-10.30pm Sat, Sun. **Main courses** £12.95-£45. **Service** 12.5%. **Credit** MC, V.
The House makes good use of its awkward triangular site, with a beer garden at the entrance and bay windows on the long sides looking on to a pleasant narrow terrace. The bar takes up one side and the fairly formal restaurant the other, effectively separating the two functions – appropriate, as the food demands attention. The menu is at the fine-dining end of the gastropub spectrum: expect modest portions, carefully presented, of (mainly) modern European and British standards, and expect it to be good – as it should be for the money. On our most recent visit, though, the crab rolls' lovely filling was let down by unlovely deep-frying oil, and the fennel salad with red snapper was a non-event. Still, bubble and squeak with haddock, and pea risotto were both very fine. The House is usually full with a well-heeled crowd, and its popularity occasionally results in poor service. This time round, we could find no real fault, except for being ignored when it was time for the bill. The drinks selection is highlighted by an extensive wine list.
Babies and children admitted. Disabled: toilet. Entertainment: musicians 8pm Sun; free. No smoking. Tables outdoors (6, garden).

Northgate

113 Southgate Road, N1 3JS (7359 7392). Essex Road rail/38, 73 bus. **Open** 5-11pm Mon-Thur; 5pm-midnight Fri; noon-midnight Sat; noon-10.30pm Sun. **Lunch served** noon-4pm Sat, Sun. **Dinner served** 6.30-10.30pm Mon-Sat; 6.30-9.30pm Sun. **Main courses** £9-£13.50. **Set lunch** (Sun) £12.50 2 courses. **Credit** MC, V.
The Northgate's new owners had only been in place for a couple of months when we visited, so it was perhaps too early to judge its direction: it was still very much the pub we know, a likeable local serving unpretentious comfort food. It's a big corner palace, with typical gastro decor – sofas, wood, globe lighting, large windows, plus a slightly more formal, duck-egg blue dining room – and a laid-back feel that can border on the raffish (late opening will do that to you). We went for lunch, when the menu is truncated to flourish-free favourites: a decent piece of steak in a sandwich; good Spanish meats; a mozzarella, beetroot and walnut salad, the ingredients of which didn't quite meld. Everything was fine rather than exciting. In the evening, the menu goes up a notch: dishes might include pan-roast duck with polenta, goat's cheese risotto or chicken breast stuffed with olive tapenade. Look out for the lovely macadamia parfait, generously nutted. The new management is improving the drinks: along with a good range of wines available by the glass (including prosecco and rosé cava), there are three real ale regulars plus a guest, and a cocktail list promised for the future.
Babies and children admitted (patio, restaurant). Booking advisable. Disabled: toilet. Tables outdoors (10, patio). **Map 6 Q1.**

Social

33 Linton Street, Arlington Square, N1 7DU (7354 5809/www.thesocial.com). Angel tube/ 38, 56, 73 bus. **Open** 5-11pm Mon-Fri; noon-11pm Sat; noon-10.30pm Sun. **Dinner served** 5-10.30pm Mon-Fri. **Meals served** 12.30-10.30pm Sat; 12.30-9.30pm Sun. **Main courses** £7-£13.50. **Credit** AmEx, MC, V.
We'd booked for 8.30pm, having been assured that the kitchen stays open on Sundays until 9.30pm. By the time the last member of our party had arrived, a little over ten minutes late, the waiter had vanished; when he re-emerged, the kitchen staff had packed up, and we were told all we could order was a pie or a lamb burger. So much for reservations. Turning up at 7pm a few weeks later, we at least succeeded in getting served, but service was still scatty: on a quiet night, the kitchen delivered our mains barely two minutes after our starters had been cleared, presumably in another rush to knock off early. It's a pity, as the food itself is pretty decent. Starter salads (beetroot, orange, green bean and goat's cheese; chicory, walnut, stilton and pear) were both very fresh, and though the list of mains doesn't offer much adventure (steaks, burgers, bangers), baked leek and spinach tart was tasty and the chips were as good as you'd hope. Twenty wines are offered; beers include Kirin and Bombardier. DJs play at weekends; at other times, the impeccably stocked jukebox is cranked to pub rather than gastropub levels.
Babies and children admitted (until 6pm weekends). Entertainment DJs occasional eves; 4.30pm Sun. Separate room for parties, seats 30. Tables outdoors (2, pavement). **Map 5 P2.**

Kentish Town NW5

Highgate

53-79 Highgate Road, NW5 1TL (7485 8442). Tufnell Park tube/Kentish Town tube/rail. Bar **Open** noon-11pm Mon-Fri; noon-midnight Sat; noon-10.30pm Sun. **Main courses** £6.50-£9.50.
Restaurant **Main courses** £8.50-£14. **Service** 12.5%.
Both **Lunch served** 12.30-3pm Mon-Sat; 12.30-4pm Sun. Dinner served 6.30-10.30pm Mon-Sat; 6.30-10pm Sun. **Credit** AmEx, MC, V.
We've had mixed experiences of late at this former *Time Out* award-winner. On Sundays, when staff are stretched, the menu is focused on roasts and burgers, and the room is full of young tanked-up mums hoping someone else is watching their children, the Highgate does surprisingly well. Weekday dinner à deux, however, was a disappointment. It started well enough, with a

gracious welcome, a quiet table and a chilled bottle of French rosé. The bread was a little dry, but we surveyed the modern eclectic menu with optimism. However, a starter of shaved artichokes with rocket and parmesan was disappointing: the artichokes large, spotty and cut too thickly, the parmesan too scarce. Gnocchi of garlic confit and parsley served with ceps sounded delicious, but arrived as ugly brown dumplings. Still, roast beef (although cooked longer than asked) proved highly enjoyable and generously portioned; it came with girolles, spinach and a tasty sauce. Chicken ballottine was nicely juicy too. A decor of rich colours, ornate wallpaper, old sofas and vintage posters warms up the warehouse space, although the look is growing into a bit of a cliché these days.
Babies and children admitted (until 8pm). Bar available for hire. Booking advisable. Disabled: toilet. Separate room for parties, holds 150. Tables outdoors (3, pavement). **Map 26 A4.**

Junction Tavern

101 Fortress Road, NW5 1AG (7485 9400/ www.junctiontavern.co.uk). Tufnell Park tube/Kentish Town tube/rail. **Open** noon-11pm Mon-Sat; noon-10.30pm Sun **Lunch served** noon-3pm Mon-Fri; noon-4pm Sat, Sun. **Dinner served** 6.30-10.30pm Mon-Sat; 6.30-9.30pm Sun. **Main courses** £7.50-£14. **Set lunch** (Sun) £14 2 courses. **Credit** MC, V.
You can eat in any of the Junction Tavern's various spaces: the outdoor tables in the balmy garden, the wood-panelled, pub-like back room or the relaxed dining room with its large glass frontage overlooking the street. Just make sure you avoid the grim conservatory tacked on the back by the toilets. The menu changes daily. A nice choice of starters included a fine, hearty gazpacho and delicious seared scallops undermined by a lump of guacamole. Sometimes the food tries too hard: the flavours of lamb chops with sweet potatoes and salad were camouflaged by the addition of a generous portion of feta cheese and coriander leaves, while chorizo was an unnecessary element in monkfish with spinach and puy lentils. There's no doubting the quality and freshness of the ingredients, though. For afters, a cheesecake was very ordinary, but others have raved about the chocolate desserts that weren't on the menu when we visited. There's an excellent choice of beers, and a changing wine list.
Babies and children admitted. Booking advisable. Tables outdoors (15, garden). **Map 26 B4.**

Oxford NEW

256 Kentish Town Road, NW5 2AA (7485 3521/www.realpubs.co.uk/theoxford). Kentish Town tube/rail. **Open** noon-11pm Mon-Sat; noon-10.30pm Sun. **Lunch served** noon-3.30pm Mon-Fri; noon-5pm Sun. **Dinner served** 6-10pm Mon-Sat. **Meals served** 12.30-9.30pm Sun. **Main courses** £8.50-£12.50. **Credit** MC, V.
There's a lot to love about the Oxford, the most recent gastropub to liven up Kentish Town. Most loveable of all: charming and efficient service. Our waitress kept her cool (and her smile) despite being in sole charge of the large, busy dining room. Also very likeable: the high-ceilinged, minimally decorated room, with a bar at the front and dining at the back. Third pleasing item: some very good cooking from a menu that's almost defiantly brief. Grill and frying pan do most of the work, and no main course costs more than £12.50. On Sunday lunch, roasts join the list; weekday lunches add a few extra cheaper, lighter items. The no-nonsense approach is mirrored in the short, interesting wine list. There is one unloveable problem, though: patches of frankly embarrassing cooking. A salad of watercress, squid and chorizo had around eight minuscule scraps of squid, some half-raw. 'French onion soup' was nothing of the kind: gloopy, industrial-tasting broth, accompanied by a half-hearted slab of half-melted cheese on toast. We were told that a new chef had recently arrived, so we hope these failures were teething problems.
Entertainment: jazz Mon 8.30pm. Tables outdoors (6, pavement). **Map 26 B5.**

Tufnell Park NW5

Lord Palmerston
33 Dartmouth Park Hill, NW5 1HU (7485 1578/www.geronimo-inns.co.uk). Tufnell Park tube. **Open** noon-11pm Mon-Sat; noon-10.30pm Sun. **Lunch served** 12.30-3pm Mon-Sat; 1-4pm Sun. **Dinner served** 7-10pm Mon-Sat; 7-9pm Sun. **Main courses** £8.75-£13. **Credit** MC, V.
A model of the old-pub-stripped-down-to-become-foodie-venue, the Lord Palmerston also has a very nice balance of easy-going, comfortable vibe and imaginative, consistently enjoyable food. Seating is at austere wooden tables – in the airy main bar, in the rear conservatory or on the pavement outside (where some tables are on a pronounced slope, for playing 'slide the glass'). The blackboard menu doesn't really offer any starters; instead, there are a few smaller dishes (BLTs, grilled chicken sandwiches) as alternatives to the more sophisticated modern Brit-meets-Mediterranean mains (toulouse sausage and mash, grilled swordfish, pastas). Prices are a bit higher than the local gastropub norm, but dishes are put together with distinct panache, using quality ingredients. A parma ham salad featured finely grilled asparagus, just-right avocado and lively, nicely sharp rocket; grilled confit of duck with bean cassoulet and red wine juice contained overcooked meat, but the whole concoction still had plenty of full-on flavour. Fruity, creamy yet light desserts complete the offerings. To keep up its pub credentials, the Lord P offers excellent beers, from Adnams of Southwold.
Babies and children admitted. Separate room for parties, seats 35. Tables outdoors (5, garden; 13, pavement). **Map 26 B3.**

North West

Belsize Park NW3

Hill
94 Haverstock Hill, NW3 2BD (7267 0033/www.geronimo-inns.co.uk). Belsize Park or Chalk Farm tube. **Open** 11am-11pm Mon-Sat; 11am-10.30pm Sun. **Lunch served** noon-3pm Mon-Sat. **Dinner served** 7-10.30pm Mon-Sat. **Meals served** 12.30-9pm Sun. **Main courses** £8.95-£13.95. **Credit** MC, V.
An outpost of gastropub mini-empire Geronimo Inns, this big old boozer has been given one of the more original and decadent foodie-pub makeovers. Think Victorian pub meets ancien régime: pastel green woodwork and baroque details picked out in gilt look down on ultra-comfy plush banquettes, studded leather chairs and tables, and smart table settings. Amid all this quirky ornateness, though, the atmosphere is amiably laid-back. Food sticks to a familiar gastropub style – grills, salads, pasta, imaginative risotto variations – with nice original touches: sausages and mash featured leeks and cheddar cheese in the mash, and meaty pork and leek sausages, and was served in a merlot jus; the 'Hill burger' came in focaccia instead of a bun; and a summer salad included artichoke hearts and good dry manchego. Menus are varied and change frequently, with a new set of specials each day; tempting seasonal desserts might include fresh strawberries and raspberry coulis. One suspects there may have been a company decision to appear 'less pub-like' by having no real bitters among the lager-heavy beer range, but at least there's a respectable choice of wines.
Babies and children admitted. Tables outdoors (20, garden). **Map 28 C4.**

Hampstead NW3

Wells
30 Well Walk, NW3 1BX (7794 3785/www.thewellshampstead.co.uk). Hampstead tube. **Bar Open** noon-11pm Mon-Sat; noon-10.30pm Sun. **Lunch served** noon-3pm Mon-Fri; noon-4pm Sat; noon-3pm Sun. **Dinner served** 5-10pm Mon-Fri; 7-10pm Sat; 7-9.30pm Sun. **Main courses** £9.95-£13.95. **Set lunch** (Mon-Fri) £12.95 2 courses, £13.95 3 courses.
Restaurant **Lunch served** noon-4pm Sun.
Dinner served 7-10pm Mon-Sat; 7-9.30pm Sun. **Set lunch** £12.95 2 courses, £13.95 3 courses. **Set dinner** £24.50 2 courses, £29.50 3 courses. *Both* **Service** 12.5%. **Credit** MC, V.
The Wells has planted its foot firmly in the table-service camp and even customers choosing to eat in the downstairs bar might find there is no bar service available. We've previously enjoyed meals here (the romantic first-floor restaurant is good for special occasions), but were underwhelmed on our most recent visit. A query as to whether they had any fruit beers was met with the response, 'Is fruit-flavoured beer made?' and an offer to put some lime cordial in a lager. Disconcerting clattering noises came from the open-plan kitchen, and service, although well intentioned, was remarkably slow given the few customers. We'd be prepared to forgive and forget if the food had been terrific, but it wasn't. A dreary rump steak with béarnaise came with poor chips; better was a slab of roast salmon on crushed potatoes speckled with peas. Decent crème caramel was prettily decorated with prunes and berries, but chunky carrot and walnut cake with strawberry sorbet was a dud. The Wells charges restaurant-level prices for what, on this experience, was disorganised pub service and fairly ordinary gastropub fare. There is a balance to be struck, but it isn't hitting it.
Babies and children admitted. Booking advisable. Disabled: toilet. Entertainment: musicians 8.30pm Mon. No smoking. Separate room for parties, seats 12. Tables outdoors (15, patio). **Map 28 C2.**

Kensal Green NW10

William IV
786 Harrow Road, NW10 5LX (8969 5944). Kensal Green tube. **Open** noon-11pm Mon-Wed; noon-midnight Thur-Sat; noon-10.30pm Sun. **Tapas served** noon-3pm, 6-10.30pm Mon-Wed; noon-3pm, 6-11pm Thur, Fri; 12.30-4pm Sat; noon-9.30pm Sun. **Tapas** £3.75-£7.25. **Set lunch** (Sun) £15 2 course, £18 3 courses. **Service** 10% for parties of 5 or more. **Credit** AmEx, DC, MC, V.
Always maintaining high standards, the William IV continues to thrive as a handsome, panelled 1930s pub with a Spanish kitchen attached. Anyone concerned that this might mean high-priced, stingily proportioned tapas should be assured that the comprehensive menu is as you would find it in Spain. A huge array of vegetarian tapas includes ample plates of beetroot and potato salad or spicy aubergine (more onion than eggplant) alongside patatas bravas. An immaculately grilled swordfish steak (served, oddly, with a sweet chutney), and six juicy giant tiger prawns bathed in a piquant tomato sauce hailed from a long list of fish dishes. Meatballs languished in a rather similar sauce to the prawns and could have been tastier, but confit belly of pork with caramelised onions was satisfying, and also of generous size. Quibbles aside, it all amounts to good value. There's also a full wine list, a well-stocked bar and service is spirited, efficient and charming. If you can, head to the rear garden, which has become a walled haven with newly established potted plants.
Babies and children welcome: high chairs. Entertainment: DJ 9pm Fri, Sat. Tables outdoors (30, garden).

Kilburn NW6

Osteria del Ponte NEW
77 Kilburn High Road, NW6 6HY (7624 5793). Kilburn Park tube. **Open** 4-11pm Mon-Thur; noon-11pm Fri, Sat; noon-10.30pm Sun. **Lunch served** noon-3.30pm Mon-Thur; noon-4.30pm Fri-Sun. **Dinner served** 6.30-11pm Mon-Sat; 6.30-10.30pm Sun. **Main courses** £9-£12. **Credit** MC, V.
Although there are a few osteria-style dishes on the specials menu at Osteria del Ponte (lamb stew with root vegetables, say), this is really a gastropub with a pizzeria attached. After sitting down in the prettily lit dining area, we started with a mushroom and pecorino crostini (more bruschetta than crostini, but who's arguing). It came laden with too much topping, but it tasted good so we

didn't mind. Char-grilled vegetables were less successful: courgettes, aubergines and peppers were cooked in what tasted like chicken stock, rolled around sliced mozzarella, drizzled with an excess of balsamic vinegar, and served chilled. Next, pizza topped with gorgonzola, pear and spinach just didn't work: fruit, blue cheese and greens is a classic French combination, but doesn't quite come together as a pizza topping. A margherita with extra anchovies was tastier. Good points: the pizza base was properly crisp and bubbled, and round, crusty loaves of rosemary focaccia were moreish. Indeed, Osteria del Ponte works best when it lets its wood-fired oven – rather than its chef – do the talking.
Babies and children welcome: high chairs. Tables outdoors (5, pavement).

Queens Park NW6

Salusbury
50-52 Salusbury Road, NW6 6NN (7328 3286). Queens Park tube/rail. **Open** 5-11pm Mon; noon-11pm Tue-Sat; noon-10.30pm Sun. **Lunch served** 12.30-3.30pm Tue-Sun. **Dinner served** 7-10.15pm Mon-Sat; 7-10pm Sun. **Main courses** £9.50-£16.50. **Set lunch** (Mon-Fri) £5 1 course incl 1 drink. **Credit** MC, V.
Furnished with battered wooden chairs and tables, the bar at the Salusbury still has a pretty boozer-ish feel. The dining area is similarly scuffed, with rustic-style tables and aged mirrors. Both spaces can get pretty smoky (while the law still allows), and the convivial atmosphere can be as important as the food, which has its ups and downs. We've had some great meals here, choosing from a classic, crowd-pleasing, good-value foodie pub menu, but our last visit was a tad disappointing. Asparagus risotto was the low point – deeply dull, sloppily cooked and, at £7, pretty poor value. Octopus salad with red onion and chickpeas (actually houmous) was better; the octopus was on the chewy side, but came with a refreshing mix of herbs. Lamb chop was lacking in flavour, but the accompaniments of roast sweet potatoes and mint were nicely fresh and tangy; a very trad ribeye steak was a lot better, with a suitably rich béarnaise sauce. Desserts are a strong suit, with the likes of sgrappino (lemon sorbet and grappa) or chocolate mousse with blackcurrant sauce. There's also an excellent, multinational wine list, at reasonable prices.
Babies and children welcome (before 7pm); high chairs. Booking advisable weekends. Tables outdoors (4, pavement).

St John's Wood NW8

Salt House 15% off
63 Abbey Road, NW8 OAE (7328 6626). Kilburn Park or St John's Wood tube. **Open** 5-11pm Mon; noon-11pm Tue-Fri; noon-11pm Sat; noon-10.30pm Sun. **Lunch served** noon-4pm, **dinner served** 7-10.30pm daily. **Main courses** £9.50-£17. **Credit** MC, V.
This venerable old pub has run through several guises in the past few years. Formerly called the Salt House, it then became the Abbey Road Pub & Dining Room, and has now (as we went to press) reverted back to its old name. The new owners – who have also taken over the Bollo (*see p107*) in Chiswick – have spruced the place up, introducing a light, bright, cream and red colour scheme, as well as tablecloths to the main dining area and (newly opened) upstairs room. Sofas give the bar area a more loungey feel. Draught Greene King beers remain, and there's a choice of 60 or so wines and a short cocktail list. The stylish terrace outside gains a cover, so that it can be used in all weathers. The new menu has a Mediterranean slant, with the likes of Sardinian vegetable and tomato soup with poached egg, or pan-fried squid to start, followed by whole sea bass baked in a salt and herb crust, or asparagus risotto. There are also specials, such as roast guinea fowl with ratatouille.
Babies and children welcome (before 7pm); high chairs. Booking advisable dinner. Separate room for parties, seats 24. Tables outdoors (12, terrace). **Map 2 D2.**

RESTAURANTS

Global

This is where London excels. Within the boundaries of our metropolis, you'll find a wealth of the world's cultures – a multinational mix unequalled in history. And many, many of these diverse groups have their national cuisines celebrated in the form of a London restaurant. In this section you'll find a few of the more esoteric representatives (fancy a quick Burmese, anyone?), some of them catering largely to nostalgic expats, others to culinary adventurers. Where else in the world could you relish a Danish brunch (**Lundum's**), swiftly followed by an Afghan lunch (**Afghan Kitchen** or **Kabul**) and then enjoy a South African feast for dinner (**Chakalaka**)?

Afghan

North
Islington N1

★ Afghan Kitchen
35 Islington Green, N1 8DU (7359 8019).
Angel tube. **Lunch served** noon-3.30pm,
dinner served 5.30-11pm Tue-Sat.
Main courses £4.50-£6. **Service** 10%.
No credit cards.
History and geography have played crucial roles in forming the complexities of Afghan food. The country was traversed by the ancient Silk Road and over the centuries has been invaded by Alexander the Great, Genghis Khan, the Moghuls, the British and the Soviet Union. Central Asian and Middle Eastern (particularly Persian) flavours dominate the indigenous, but there are also tangible influences from China and the Indian subcontinent. The result is a cuisine that values subtlety; spices are used to give fragrance and flavour, but never to overpower. This bijou little restaurant (be prepared to squeeze in and share the communal tables) in Islington claims to offer 'traditional Afghan home cooking'. The menu is very brief and the food (prepared in advance) is straightforward. The best dishes, such as tender lamb cooked with spinach, show good use of spicing. We were impressed with bright-orange wedges of pumpkin, spiked with chilli and dressed with cooling yoghurt. Central Asian-style flatbread was dusted with sesame and nigella seeds. Dessert, however – dry baghlava – was a definite let-down. Given the dimensions of the room, this isn't the place for a romantic meal à deux, but it's a decent, affordable pit-stop. Cash or cheques only.
Babies and children admitted: high chairs.
Booking advisable. Takeaway service.
Map 5 O2.

Outer London
Southall, Middlesex

★ Kabul
First floor, Himalaya Shopping Centre, 65-67
The Broadway, Southall, Middx UB1 1LB
(8571 6878/www.thekabulrestaurant.com).
Southall rail. **Meals served** noon-midnight
daily. **Main courses** £1.75-£7.99. **Credit** AmEx, MC, V.
The cooking at Kabul is more authentic than at London's other Afghani restaurant, Afghan Kitchen (*see above*) – as it should be, since it's located in Southall, home to a sizeable Afghan community. If you have magpie tendencies, the

Himalaya Shopping Centre is well worth a look, as it's packed with glimmery, shimmery fabrics and trinkets. Upstairs is this rather staid, brightly lit restaurant, done out in aqua blue. On the night we dined, a Bollywood film featuring an exotic landscape – Scotland – blared in the background. If Afghan food can be defined by one dish, it's pilau; the selection of rice dishes here, based on vegetables, chicken or lamb, is substantial. We chose Quabuli pilau. The rice was coloured with browned onions and flavoured with pistachio, raisins, shredded carrot and tender lamb. Starters included a very good version of ashak, an Afghani pasta dish similar to ravioli, filled with leeks and green onions, steamed then topped with melted butter, dried herbs, yoghurt, fried minced lamb and a few pinches of sweet chilli flakes. Delectable. Mantu gosht, dumplings similar to Turkish manti, served with yogurt and toor dahl, were meaty and moreish. There's also an Indian menu for the less adventurous.
Babies and children welcome: high chairs.
No-smoking tables. Takeaway service; delivery
service (within 8-mile radius).

Austrian

West
Bayswater W2

Tiroler Hut
27 Westbourne Grove, W2 4UA (7727 3981/
www.tirolerhut.co.uk). Bayswater or Queensway
tube. **Open** 6.30pm-1am Tue-Sat; 6.30pm-
midnight Sun. **Dinner served** 6.30pm-midnight
Mon-Sat; 6.30-11.30pm Sun. **Main courses**
£9.70-£16.90. **Set dinner** £15.50 2 courses,
£18.50 3 courses. **Cover** £1. **Service** 10%.
Credit AmEx, DC, MC, V.
Camp, corny, and cacophonous: that just about sums up an evening at Tiroler Hut. But don't get us wrong – we're not dissing the Hut. This long-standing party venue (established way back in 1967) is located in a dark basement on Westbourne Grove, but it does its level best to look like an Alpine ski lodge, with *gemütlich* wooden tables and faux-wooden beams. The whole set-up is presided over by lederhosen-clad host and musician extraordinaire Josef, who plays the accordion, keyboards and cowbells. Against this kitsch background, the food can sometimes seem an afterthought, but it's worth more consideration than most diners probably give it. The menu preserves such 1970s stalwarts as prawn-stuffed avocado and breaded fried mushrooms, but the main story is meat: there are wursts, schnitzels and fillets galore, most served with a rib-sticking side

of potatoes, noodles or sauerkraut. Main courses of roast pork (served with a semmelknodel, a tennis ball-sized bread dumpling, and nicely flavoured sauerkraut) and jagerschnitzel (pan-fried pork with mushroom sauce and spätzle) conjure up the taste of skiing holidays. Desserts are the likes of chocolate fondue for two or apple strudel. And be prepared to sing along to a *Sound of Music* tune or two.
Babies and children admitted. Booking advisable;
essential weekends (2 weeks in advance).
Entertainment: cowbell show 9pm Wed-Sat.
Map 7 B6.

Belgian

North
Camden Town &
Chalk Farm NW1

Belgo Noord
72 Chalk Farm Road, NW1 8AN (7267 0718/
www.belgo-restaurants.com). Chalk Farm tube.
Lunch served noon-3pm Mon-Fri. **Dinner
served** 6-11pm Mon-Thur; 6-11.30pm Fri.
Meals served noon-11.30pm Sat; noon-10.30pm
Sun. **Main courses** £8.95-£17.95. **Set lunch**
£5.95 1 course incl drink. **Service** 12.5%.
Credit AmEx, DC, JCB, MC, V.
Belgo Noord is the big sister to Belgo Centraal in Covent Garden. However, while there's definitely a strong family resemblance – both specialise in Belgian-style cuisine (most notably moules frites) served in industrial-chic surroundings – the ambience is very different. Eating at Centraal can feel like you've crashed a frat party. Noord, on the other hand, is for grown-ups – and their offspring; two children can eat free from the kids' menu per paying adult, which can make Noord seem like a crèche at times. On our visit, the rye bread was stale and the moules were unremarkable, as were the frites. The 'bisque' sauce was watery and distinctly un-bisquelike, even if the mussels were plump and fresh. We had better luck with other dishes, though, such as a monster-sized starter of salad Brabaconne with smoked bacon, shredded duck, sautéed potatoes, lentils, black pudding, garlic croutons (and, yes, some lettuce), with a good dijon mustard dressing. A veggie main of globe artichoke stuffed with chanterelles, asparagus and pine nuts, with a carrot butter sauce, was a treat. The beer list, from sharp but food-friendly gueuze to refreshing fruit beers, is irresistible – one of the best selection of Belgian beers in London, served at fair prices.
Babies and children welcome: children's menu;
colouring books; high chairs. Booking advisable.
Map 27 B1.
For branches see index.

Burmese

Central
Edgware Road W2

★ ★ Mandalay
444 Edgware Road, W2 1EG (7258 3696).
Edgware Road tube. **Lunch served** noon-
2.30pm, **dinner served** 6-10.30pm Mon-Sat.
Main courses £3.90-£6.90. **Set lunch** £3.90
1 course, £5.90 3 courses. **Credit** AmEx, DC,
JCB, MC, V.
The road to Mandalay – otherwise known as the Edgware Road – is gritty and unpretty. It's a good job, then, that Mandalay itself is such a welcoming, friendly destination. The restaurant is run by two Burmese brothers who both clearly love food. Show an interest in the ingredients in, say, prawn balachong (a spicy condiment made from pounded dried prawn, garlic and red chillies, topped with crisp-fried shallots), and you'll get an

explanation of how this version differs from the Indian version. You'll also be guided around the menu to ensure that your meal takes in all the sharp, hot, salty and sweet flavours that make up Burmese food. And what food it is. A light, clear bottle gourd soup will prove extremely refreshing on a warm summer evening. Tea-leaf salad, a Burmese favourite that's not always on the menu, features tea leaves imported from Burma, with crunchy lentils and a red-chilli kick. Twice-cooked fish has a lively red sauce flavoured with tomato and tamarind, while a vegetable kaukswe (a one-pot noodle dish) is served with a flavoursome coconut sauce. All the dishes cost under £7.50, many of them substantially so, making a meal here incredibly good value. It's little wonder that Mandalay has a loyal following, so be sure to book.

Babies and children welcome: high chairs. Booking essential. No smoking. Takeaway service. **Map 2 D4.**

Irish

Central

Marylebone W1

O'Conor Don

88 Marylebone Lane, W1U 2PY (7935 9311/ www.oconordon.com). Bond Street tube. Bar **Open** noon-11pm Mon-Wed, Fri; noon-1am Thur. **Meals served** noon-3pm, 6-10pm Mon-Fri. *Restaurant* **Lunch served** noon-2.30pm, **dinner served** 6-10pm Mon-Fri. **Main courses** £9.95-£16. **Service** 12.5%.
Both **Credit** AmEx, MC, V.

'The food is wholesome rather than sophisticated,' explained a guest at a nearby table loudly to his rather deaf companion. That hits the nail on the head: the O'Conor Don does a fine line in unpretentious comfort cooking. Upstairs from a 'proper' pub, the restaurant is equally old-fangled, with heavy drapery, dark wood floors and framed pictures on dark red walls. The food is not completely Irish. There are a few Asian-influenced dishes, but we passed in favour of a heftily portioned starter of chicken liver pâté, studded with rum-soaked raisins and served with soda bread. For mains, the batter on our cod and chips was far too heavy to pass for 'tempura' style, as the menu claimed, but it served the purpose of steaming the beautiful piece of cod it enrobed to pearly perfection. A beef and Guinness stew was made with an inexpensive cut of beef (just as it should be), which had been slow-cooked to melting tenderness and served with a huge mound of champ. Portions like these tend to leave little room for cosy desserts such as treacle tart and chocolate, and Bailey's mousse.
Babies and children admitted. Booking advisable. Entertainment: DJ 10pm Thur. Restaurant available for hire; all areas available for hire Sat, Sun. Separate bar for parties. **Map 9 G5.**

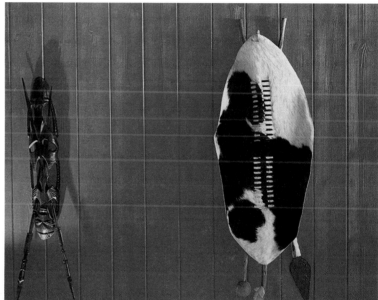

Chakalaka. See p121.

Laotian

Central

Pimlico SW1

Page NEW
*11 Warwick Way, SW1V 4LT (7834 3313/
www.frontpagepubs.com). Pimlico tube/Victoria
tube/rail.*
Bar **Open** noon-11pm Mon-Sat; noon-10.30pm
Sun.
Restaurant **Lunch served** noon-3pm, **dinner
served** 6-10pm daily. **Main courses** £6-£10.
Laotian set meal (dinner Sat, Sun) £24.95
per person.
Both **Credit** AmEx, MC, V.
The British pub/Thai restaurant combo has been a
successful formula in many a London pub,
including this spot in Pimlico – but here there's a
twist. Thai food is served all week, but on Saturday
and Sunday evenings, if you book in advance, you
can enjoy a multi-course Laotian feast. Laotian food
has similarities to Thai food, but uses less coconut
and favours sticky (glutinous) rice. To make the
most of the feast, go with a group of friends so that
you can try a range of dishes. Our meal began with
prawn and tomato skewers, served with a blazing,
garlicky chilli sauce. Next came a coconut-based
fish soup flavoured with galangal, lime leaves and
lemongrass, with cooked vermicelli, beansprouts
and julienned carrot to be added, DIY-fashion, to
the broth. To follow, sticky rice in bamboo steamers,
along with the main dishes: duck breast, sliced and
topped with red chilli, mint, green onion and sliced
lemongrass; fried sea bass served on a banana leaf
with chilli sauce; sliced chicken breast cooked on a
bed of lemongrass with red chillies and fried onion;
and a prawn and beef curry-style dish with long
beans, flavoured with holy basil. The chef came out
at the end of the meal to see if we'd enjoyed our
food, although the empty plates and happy faces
probably said it all.
*Babies and children admitted (before 6pm).
Booking advisable. Tables outdoors (4, pavement).*
Map 15 J11.

Scandinavian

Central

Marylebone W1

Garbo's
*42 Crawford Street, W1H 1JW (7262 6582).
Baker Street or Edgware Road tube/Marylebone
tube/rail.* **Lunch served** noon-3pm Mon-Fri,
Sun. **Dinner served** 6-11pm Mon-Sat.
Main courses £6.50-£13.50. **Set lunch** £10.95
2 courses, £11.95 3 courses; £12.95 smörgåsbord.
Set buffet lunch (Sun) £13.95. **Cover** £1
(à la carte only). **Credit** AmEx, MC, V.
If the mention of Swedish cuisine has you thinking
of flat-packs and lengthy queues for Swedish
meatballs, think again. The aesthetic at Garbo's is
almost studiedly un-designery, with pale yellow
tablecloths, sensible cutlery and a propensity for
1970s touches such as curly parsley garnishes and
paper doilies. Nor will you catch the menu straying
off into an unknown, experimental hinterland.
They like to stick to the classics, although there's
a worrying tendency toward ultra-kitsch names
('Viking Sword', aka fish brochette, anyone?).
The cooking is of the solid, Volvo-driving school
rather than being inspirational. A two-toned carrot
and pea soup was pronounced 'not bland', but
fish dishes, such as the herring selection and
gravadlax, are exemplary. The classic Swedish
smörgåsbord stalwart, Jansson's temptation – a
potato and anchovy casserole – lacked the
creaminess we'd hoped for and a main course of
pytt i panna (potato and beef 'hash' served with a
fried egg on top and cooked beetroot on the side)
was merely workmanlike. Our faith was restored
by stuffed cabbage, the white leaves filled with a
toothsome meat mixture complemented by a very

Swedish-tasting slightly sweet sauce. Abba-era
desserts tend to towards vanilla ice-cream, apple
crumble and other well-rehearsed tunes.
*Babies and children welcome: high chair. Booking
advisable. Separate room for parties, seats 35.*
Map 8 F5.

South West

South Kensington SW7

★ Lundum's
*117-119 Old Brompton Road, SW7 3RN (7373
7774/www.lundums.com). Gloucester Road
or South Kensington tube.* **Brunch served**
9am-noon Mon-Sat. **Lunch served** noon-4pm
Mon-Sat; noon-1.30pm Sun. **Dinner served**
6-11pm Mon-Sat. **Main courses** £11.75-£24.25.
Set lunch (Mon-Sat) £13.50 2 courses, £16.50
3 courses; (Sun) £21.50 buffet. **Set dinner** £17.25
2 courses, £22.50 3 courses. **Service** 13.5%.
Credit AmEx, DC, MC, V.
North European cuisine may be experiencing
something of a renaissance. If so, long-established
Lundum's demonstrates what we've been missing.
The cooking and flavour combinations are as
tasteful and well turned-out as the carefully coiffed
clientele. Our ravioli of langoustine and papaya
(actually a single, large raviolo) was stuffed with
chunky pieces of langoustine and set off by an
orange beurre blanc sauce. Fish is a speciality, with
shoals of herring (served three ways at lunchtime)
and salmon dishes, including a starter of petal-like
slices of firm-textured salted salmon, served with
horseradish cream, cucumber brunoise and
salmon caviar. Mains such as European catfish
wrapped in Skagen ham and served with puy
lentils, spinach and lime yoghurt are likely to
feature superb quality fish, cooked to perfection.
The house special dessert, a massive portion of
crème brûlée, was nearly good enough to justify its
£8.25 price tag, but the accompanying vanilla ice-
cream was merely average. The expanded wine list
has some well-chosen bottles, and service is
professional and friendly. Prices can be steep, but
the quality of the produce is excellent. At Sunday
brunch, a feast of fishy and meaty Danish
specialities is served at the 'det kolde bord' buffet.
*Babies and children welcome: high chairs.
Booking advisable brunch, dinner. Tables outdoors
(8, patio). Separate room for parties, seats 18.*
Map 14 D11.

South East

London Bridge & Borough SE1

★ Glas NEW
*3 Park Street, SE1 9AB (7357 6060/www.glas
restaurant.com). Borough tube or London Bridge
tube/rail.* **Lunch served** noon-2.30pm, **dinner
served** 6.30-10pm Tue-Fri. **Meals served**
1-10pm Sat. **Dishes** £3.95-£8.95. **Credit** MC, V.
After a short stint at the Lindsay House, then at a
restaurant back home in Sweden, Patric Blomquist
(a former Swedish Chef of the Year) is running this
new restaurant in partnership with Swedish-born
Anna Mosesson, best known as the face of the
Scandelicious stall at Borough Market. It's a small
but smart place, with linen tablecloths, polished
glasses and too many tables crammed into a
narrow room. The smörgåsbord-style menu gives
you a choice of several tapas-like plates. Herring
never goes out of fashion in Sweden, and here you
can have it pickled with cloves, allspice, bay leaves
and carrots; marinated in lime and vodka; or as
'matjes' (pickled with sandalwood, among other
things), all served with nutty Västerbotten cheese.
All these preparations are, unusually, made on the
premises. Gravadlax – salmon marinated in sugar,
salt and dill for a couple of days – was served with
hot brioche and a twist of lemon. A duck liver and
pig's cheek terrine had a gorgeously melting
texture, but was a little bland; a relish of sweet-
sour apple and lingonberry pepped it up. Boiled,
unsalted brisket of beef is another 'home-style'
dish, served with horseradish to give it some kick.

Drinks extend from Swedish beers through a
diverse but reasonably priced wine list to akvavits
and dessert wines.
*Babies and children welcome: high chairs. Booking
essential. No smoking.* **Map 11 P8**.

South African

South West

Putney SW15

Chakalaka NEW
*136 Upper Richmond Road, SW15 2SP
(8789 5696/www.chakalakarestaurant.co.uk).*
Dinner served 6-10.45pm Mon-Fri. **Meals
served** noon-10.45pm Sat, Sun. **Main courses**
£9.95-£16.95. **Service** 12.5%. **Credit** MC, V.
You can't miss Chakalaka. Just look out for the
massive zebra stripes that mark the exterior – and
interior – of this South African eaterie. On the night
we visited, all the staff and most of the customers
were South African, tucking into the flavours of
home with the likes of boerwors with chakalaka
and mealie pap. Chakalaka, incidentally, is a hot
sauce based on chillies, tomato and onions that here
lent a (rather too mild) capsicum kick to the mound
of mealie pap (maize meal) on which the flavourful,
meaty sausages rested. At first we thought our lamb
bobotie (a Cape Malay dish of minced lamb baked
with raisins and almonds in a savoury custard)
looked a bit effete, served in three smallish rounds
with some yellow rice. However, the sweet/savoury
flavour, enhanced by Mrs Ball's chutney and some
desiccated coconut, convinced us otherwise. We
were too full for the classic South African dessert of
Dom Pedro, a kind of boozy milkshake for grown-
ups, here made with Amarula. The wine list is all
South African, apart from a rogue Italian pinot
grigio; there's a reserve list for aficionados, with
some top Cape producers, sold at lower than usual
mark-ups. Service comes with a smile.
*Babies and children welcome: high chairs.
Booking advisable. No-smoking tables.
Separate room for parties, seats 25.*
For branch (The Boom Bar) see index.

Swiss

Central

Soho W1

St Moritz
*161 Wardour Street, W1F 8WJ (7734 3324/
www.stmoritz-restaurant.co.uk). Tottenham
Court Road tube.* **Lunch served** noon-3pm
Mon-Fri. **Dinner served** 6-11.30pm Mon-Sat.
Main courses £8.95-£18. **Service** 12.5%.
Credit AmEx, DC, MC, V.
St Moritz was established in 1974 and not much –
from the menu to the decor to the music – has
changed since. There are the same dark timber
beams, red and white checked curtains and
outrageously large cowbells hanging up as
ornaments. Similarly, the menu makes no
concessions to contemporary obsessions. There's
none of that low-fat, GI-diet nonsense here – just
good, honest, artery-clogging Swiss grub that
manages to be even cheesier than the music. A
starter of melted raclette cheese was perhaps not
the wisest prelude to a fondue, but a plate of nicely
textured air-dried beef provided alternative
protein. To miss out on the fondues would be
criminal. Not a scrap of our fondue Valaisanne,
with gruyère and vacherin cheeses, flavoured with
tomatoes and white wine, went to waste. Likewise,
bratwurst with rösti and onion gravy was the
genuine article. Our one gripe was with the
patronising receptionist who grudgingly took our
reservation but warned of dire consequences
should we be 15 minutes late – all the more galling
when diners turn up to a near-empty restaurant.
*Babies and children admitted. Book dinner.
Separate room for parties, seats 30.* **Map 17 K6**.

RESTAURANTS

RESTAURANTS

Greek

The past few years have been rather good for Greeks. Aside from triumphs like unexpectedly winning the Euro 2004 football championships and stupendously hosting the 2004 Olympics (not to mention that fabulous 2005 Eurovision victory), top Greek cuisine has also been on the rise. Good Greek food is not about decadent sauces, intricate cooking methods or exotic ingredients. It's about keeping things simple: bringing out the best natural flavours from the harvest of the Mediterranean land and sea. The tricky part, of course, is to do it well.

A truly great Greek dining experience is about more than just the food. Meal times are a social occasion and the capital's Greek restaurants for the most part reflect this, with buzzing but laid-back atmospheres. All this is helped by improved Greek wine lists and the increased availability of Greek spirits, from ouzo and Metaxa brandy to rarer home-grown tipples such as tsipouro (a spirit distilled from the must residue of the wine press).

London certainly has its share of decent tavernas. While some restaurants – **Mario's**, **Vrisaki** – let Mama's, or as the Greeks would say, Mana's, traditional cooking speak for itself, others – **Café Corfu**, the **Real Greek** restaurants – have played with their food and given fun, modern twists to old-fashioned dishes.

Central

Clerkenwell & Farringdon EC1

★ The Real Greek Souvlaki & Bar
140-142 St John Street, EC1V 4UA (7253 7234/ www.therealgreek.co.uk). Farringdon tube/rail. **Meals served** noon-11pm Mon-Sat. **Main courses** £3.85-£8.30. **Service** 12.5%. **Credit** MC, V.
The hip sister of Hoxton's Real Greek looks more like a trendy Athenian bar than a humble souvláki joint. But although it boasts a fine ouzo Mojito – near sacrilege in the old country – it's also responsible for the best souvláki west of Corfu. Traditional dishes are given a modern edge; grilled meat is wrapped in flatbread and served in grease-proof paper, as it should be, but there are twists. Herby sauces replace the expected tzatzíki, while smoked haddock souvláki and vegetarian dishes (offered alongside the traditional chicken, lamb and pork variations) cater to non-meat eaters. The haddock had too subtle a flavour to work, but the chicken souvláki was perfect. Aside from seemingly deep-fried spanakópittas, mezédes were also good: gigantes, served cold, had a nice dill flavour; grilled octopus in lemon and olive oil was gloriously plump. Desserts (baklavá, yoghurt and honey) are fairly basic, but the choice of Greek wines and beers is vast and includes the criminally underrated Mythos lager. The verdict? Swish but authentic: even the bill arrived in a shot glass. The Real Greek is no longer owned by its creator, Theodore Kyriakou; the new owners have ambitious expansion plans, so expect more outlets to appear in central London soon.
Babies and children welcome: high chairs. Booking advisable. Disabled: toilet. Separate room for parties, seats 40. Tables outdoors (2, pavement). Takeaway service. **Map 5 O4.**
For branches see index.

West

Bayswater W2

Aphrodite Taverna
15 Hereford Road, W2 4AB (7229 2206). Bayswater, Notting Hill Gate or Queensway tube. **Meals served** noon-midnight Mon-Sat. **Main courses** £8.50-£27.50. **Mezédes** £17 vegetarian, £19.50 meat, £27.50 fish. **Cover** £1. **Service** 10%. **Credit** AmEx, DC, JCB, MC, V.
Step into the busy Aphrodite and be enveloped in the ever-welcoming bosom of its bubbly owner, Rosana. Decked out with gourds, brass lamps and hanging copper pots, this Cypriot taverna is at once tacky and inviting, and therein lies its charm. The extensive menu pretty much covers the Greek-Cypriot culinary repertoire, along with a few international favourites. The avocado vinaigrette was exemplary: ripe and served with a sharp semi-viscous dressing. Dolmádes were hot, moist and comforting. Main courses range from stifádo, kléftiko and traditional grills, to quail and fillet steaks. A large portion of grilled kalámari cones was pleasingly unadorned and full of natural flavour, while sea bass – a chef speciality – arrived nicely grilled and with its head considerably lopped off. Both mains came with a crunchy, steamed vegetable garnish and disappointingly chewy rice. We were appeased for this by an excellent bottle of light Boutari Santorini from the moderately priced wine list. The loukoúmi and mint humbugs that arrived with the bill reiterated Aphrodite's something-for-everyone hospitality.
Babies and children welcome: high chairs. Booking advisable dinner. Tables outdoors (12, terrace). Takeaway service. Vegetarian menu. **Map 7 B6.**

Notting Hill W8

★ Greek Affair
1 Hillgate Street, W8 7SP (7792 5226). Notting Hill Gate tube. **Lunch served** noon-3pm, **dinner served** 5.30-11pm Mon-Fri. **Meals**

served noon-11pm Sat, Sun. **Main courses** £5.50-£12. **Unlicensed. Corkage** £1.50. **Service** 10%. **Credit** AmEx, MC, V.
Walking into this cosy spot is like stepping into a Greek country kitchen – a sensation emphasised by the welcoming service and the BYO bottle policy. The subtle homely decor is complemented by a dare-to-be (just a bit) different menu that offers alternatives to standard dishes: fish moussaká, for instance. The emphasis is on meze and the selection (both hot and cold) is extensive. The houmous, taramósalata and tzatzíki were excellent. Gigandes, though advertised as cold, arrived hot, but the beans were plump and sat in an authentically thick and tasty tomato sauce. Apart from a flavoursome kléftiko, main courses were slightly disappointing. The vegetarian moussaká was overwhelmed by its rich béchamel topping, and the psári plaki (fish baked with tomatoes) was dry and chewy. For pudding, in addition to Greek treats like baklavá, galaktoboúreko (custard pie), and kataïfi, there's a range of cheesecakes and tiramisu. While the food might be hit or miss, Greek Affair is a charming place worth a visit for its atmosphere and starters.
Babies and children welcome: high chairs. Booking advisable. No-smoking tables. Separate room for parties, seats 30. Tables outdoors (5, roof garden). Vegetarian menu. **Map 19 C5.**

Shepherd's Bush W12

Vine Leaves
71 Uxbridge Road, W12 8NR (8749 0325). Shepherd's Bush tube. **Lunch served** noon-3pm, **dinner served** 5pm-midnight Mon-Thur. **Meals served** noon-1am Fri, Sat; noon-11.30pm Sun. **Main courses** £5.95-£14.95. **Set meal** £9.95 3 courses incl coffee (Mon-Thur, Sun), £13.95 3 courses incl coffee (no fish or steak), £17.95 3 courses incl coffee. **Mezédes** £9.95 mini, £13.95 mixed, £16.95 fish. **Service** 10% for parties of 5 or more. **Credit** AmEx, JCB, MC, V.
This laid-back taverna may lack intimacy, but it has a cheery, buzzing atmosphere. Contemporary Greek pop pulses from the speakers and staff are friendly and attentive. Portions are large. We started with a fresh, light, mini-mountain of kalámari. In contrast, the dolmádes, though plump, lacked sharpness, and the complimentary chicken in filo pastry was dry. Meat, predominately lamb, features heavily among the main courses, but the selection of fish (mainly grilled) is good. Grilled sea bass, stuffed with peppers, onions, celery and chilli, was nicely cooked if light on the chilli. Nevertheless, the kotópoulo (chicken) lemonáta with mushrooms tasted comfortingly home cooked: the moist pieces of grilled chicken nicely complemented by the delicately tangy sauce. The crisp side-salad that arrived with the mains, in addition to the usual rice or potatoes, was a nice touch. Neither the dessert nor the wine menu is particularly adventurous. Puddings include baklavá and Greek honey with yoghurt, and there's a reasonable selection of well-priced, standard Greek labels among the wines.
Babies and children welcome: children's menu. Booking advisable weekends. No-smoking tables. Takeaway service. Vegetarian menu. **Map 20 B2.**

South West

Earl's Court SW5

★ As Greek As It Gets NEW
233 Earl's Court Road, SW5 9AH (7244 7777/ www.asgreekasitgets.com). Earl's Court tube. **Meals served** noon-midnight daily. **Main courses** £6.50-£9. **Mezédes** £1.50-£2.20. **Service** 10%. **Credit** AmEx, MC, V.
Despite its name, this laid-back newcomer is not the orthodox joint it markets itself as. Decked out in brown and gold with wall-mounted TV screens spinning Greek pop videos, and reassuringly full of young Greek diners, it's more trendy Athenian hangout than traditional taverna, and sports a short but sufficient menu to match. The specialities – souvláki and plates of tender gyros – were

excellent. As was the large, fresh horiátiki salad. But a bland spinach pie disappointed, as did the dips: tzatziki, though pleasingly thick, was overpowered by garlic, while the taramósalata was near-fluorescent pink in colour and tasted artificially fishy. Dessert was either Greek yoghurt (with honey and walnuts or sour cherry sauce) or a passable galaktoboúreko (custard pie). The rudimentary drinks menu includes Greek beers, ouzo and tsipouro plus a limited choice of Greek wines (served in small bottles). As Greek As It Gets is more fast-food diner than restaurant and as such far exceeds the competition (try to ignore the menu's cringe-worthy puns). Recommended for kids or grown-ups looking for a relaxed, quick bite.
Babies and children welcome: children's menu. No-smoking tables. Tables outdoors (2, pavement). Takeaway service. Vegetarian menu.

East

Shoreditch N1

★ Mezedopolio
14 Hoxton Market, N1 6HG (7739 8212/ www.therealgreek.co.uk). Old Street tube/rail/ 26, 48, 55, 149, 243 bus. **Meals served** noon-10.30pm Mon-Sat. **Mezédes** £2.10-£6.95. **Service** 12.5%. **Credit** MC, V.
Located next door to sister establishment, the Real Greek, Mezedopolio buzzes with sociability. It is set in an old Victorian mission hall. An impressive mosaic-like mural at the far end, modern chandeliers seemingly styled on Greek Orthodox church lighting, and high, stained-glass windows give the place a unique character. A mezedopolio is the Greek equivalent of a tapas bar and features a menu of small seasonal dishes – six are about the right number for two diners. Our selection didn't disappoint: gigandes were plump and buttery; spinachy hórta was offset by sweet beetroot; and fat dolmádes were filled with herby rice. Yet these tasty treats were bettered by perfectly textured grilled octopus, delicately doused in olive oil, and fleshy prawns served in a rich tomato sauce and melted feta cheese. Puddings also tempted, particularly the warm kataïfi filled with fresh cream cheese and honey. It has by far the best Greek wine list in London, with many (unusual) Greek grape varieties and boutique producers. Service can be a bit impatient, but even so, Mezedopolio adds a fun and modern twist to this traditional Greek meal.
Babies and children welcome: high chairs. Booking advisable; essential weekends. Tables outdoors (6, pavement). Takeaway service. **Map 6 Q/R3.**

The Real Greek
15 Hoxton Market, N1 6HG (7739 8212/ www.therealgreek.com). Old Street tube/rail/ 26, 48, 55, 149, 243 bus. **Lunch served** noon-3pm, **dinner served** 5.30-10.30pm Mon-Sat. **Main courses** £13.50-£17.90. **Mezédes** £7.70-£8.95. **Service** 12.5%. **Credit** MC, V.
This funky Hoxton mainstay is a cut above the city's more humble Hellenic establishments. All warm wood and glass, the Real Greek (which shares its door with Mezedopolio, *see above*) is understatedly swish. Service on our visit was top-notch as was presentation; both the mezédes were expertly layered concoctions. Soutzoúki plaki served on a base of gigandes and a fried egg was bitingly flavoursome thanks to the accompanying tyrokafteri (spicy cheese dip). However, a gorgeously textured grilled octopus was let down by sticky, bland fáva (mashed lentils) and unexciting xerotigana (horta pancakes). Instead of the fagakia (light second courses) we opted for the heftier mains. There were no vegetarian choices, but the grilled fish (hake) was thick and fleshy. Biggest disappointment was a chewy lamb fricassee. From the excellent all-Greek wine list, a light Kellaria red did not disappoint. From a list of inspired-sounding desserts, baklavá with cardamom ice-cream was a real palate-pleaser. The Real Greek succeeds in giving an haute twist to traditional recipes – but it's a shame that with such haute prices it sometimes fails to deliver.

As Greek As It Gets

Babies and children welcome: high chairs. Booking advisable. Disabled: toilet. Separate rooms for parties, seating 8 and 20. Tables outdoors (6, pavement). Takeaway service. Vegan dishes. **Map 6 Q/R3.**

North

Camden Town & Chalk Farm NW1

Andy's Taverna
81-81A Bayham Street, NW1 0AG (7485 9718). Camden Town or Mornington Crescent tube. **Lunch served** noon-2.30pm Mon-Fri. **Dinner served** 6pm-midnight Mon-Fri; 5.30-11.30pm Sat. **Meals served** 1-11pm Sun. **Main courses** £8.95-£14. **Mezédes** £13.95 per person (minimum 2). **Service** 10% for parties of 6 or more. **Credit** AmEx, DC, JCB, MC, V.
With its pleasant white-walled courtyard out back and its warm, beamed interior, there's more than a hint of island charm to this understated taverna. The menu is similarly homely, offering simple traditional food served by the Greek proprietors. On a midweek evening, the place was fairly quiet, but studded with regulars who chatted with their amiable host. The food is indeed worthy of return visits. In addition to the usual cover nibbles of olives and chillies there was a basket of delicious Turkish-style pide bread. Starters of light and delicate spanakópitta and cold gigandes in a rich tomato sauce were good – though the latter was pricey at £4.95 and not vastly superior to the tinned version. A hearty chunk of lamb kléftiko served with potatoes made a very satisfying main course, as did an almost fluffy, grilled Aegean sea bass (fish is imported from the Greek islands three times a week). The wine list is rather modest, but the house white from Kambas was cool and crisp. In all, a relaxed dining experience.
Babies and children welcome: crayons; high chairs. Booking advisable Fri, Sat. Separate rooms for parties, seating 30 and 40. Tables outdoors (7, garden). Takeaway service. **Map 27 D2.**

★ Café Corfu
7 Pratt Street, NW1 0AE (7267 8088/ www.cafecorfu.com). Camden Town or Mornington Crescent tube. **Meals served** noon-10.30pm Tue-Thur, Sun; noon-11.30pm Fri; 5-11.30pm Sat. **Main courses** £7.95-£12.95. **Set meal** £16.75 3 courses, £20 4 courses. **Service** 12.5%. **Credit** MC, V.
Down-to-earth but effortlessly stylish, Café Corfu is London's finest purveyor of modern Greek cuisine. Staff put a bright, creative slant on everything – from the Hellenic-tinged cocktails to the inspired pistachio-encrusted take on psári plaki (fish baked with tomatoes). Starters were faultless.

The four-dip pikilia was excellent, as was a dreamy slice of creamy spanakópitta with greek yoghurt. The mouth-watering mains focus on grilled and oven-roasted meat and fish, but also include a few inventive vegetarian dishes. Grilled tuna steak was expertly cooked and sat on a plump pillow of butter beans, while a thick wild salmon fillet was complemented by a sharp lime and caper sauce and lay on a bed of chunky mash. Desserts too were traditional with a twist, but a bougátsa pastry, served separately from its custard filling, was dryish. Still, presentation throughout was impeccable, as was the efficient but warm service. The Greek wine list is superb; so too is the choice of native beers. The rarely seen tsipouro (a strong spirit) earns this family-run establishment still more well-deserved points.
Babies and children welcome: high chairs. Booking advisable; essential weekends. Entertainment: belly dancer, DJ, dancing 9pm Fri, Sat; musicians 8pm Sun. No-smoking tables. Separate rooms for parties, seating 50-150. Tables outdoors (6, forecourt). Takeaway service. **Map 27 D2.**

Daphne
83 Bayham Street, NW1 0AG (7267 7322). Camden Town or Mornington Crescent tube. **Lunch served** noon-2.30pm, **dinner served** 6-11.30pm Mon-Sat. **Main courses** £7.50-£13.50. **Set lunch** £6.75 2 courses, £8.25 3 courses. **Mezédes** £13.50 meat or vegetarian, £17.50 fish. **Credit** MC, V.
There's a warm, welcoming glow to this quietly bustling taverna. On a midweek evening the place was full, the small tables and booths filled with Greek and Cypriot regulars. But despite the numbers, the staff were friendly and attentive. Emphasis here is on simplicity done well. A meze starter was impeccable: eight little dishes that included a gloopy but moreish tzatziki, creamy taramósalata, palate-cleansingly fresh beetroot and a good, grainy houmous. Having devoured the accompanying warm pitta, we were immediately offered a fresh round. Among the menu of familiar grills and oven-cooked main courses, the kléftiko, served with fluffy rice, was succulent and herby. Grilled xifias (swordfish), which came with steamed spinach and potatoes, was nice and fleshy. The Greek wine list is short and sweet, but there's a homely choice of desserts: from figs with cream and seasonal fruit, to old-school treats such as rice pudding. A nice bolt-hole for a dose of well-cooked comfort food.
Babies and children welcome: high chairs. Booking essential Fri, Sat. Disabled: toilet. Separate room for parties, seats 50. Tables outdoors (8, roof terrace). **Map 27 D2.**

Lemonia
89 Regent's Park Road, NW1 8UY (7586 7454). Chalk Farm tube. **Lunch served** noon-3pm Mon-Fri; noon-3.30pm Sun. **Dinner served**

Dishes followed by (G) indicate a specifically Greek dish; those marked (GC) indicate a Greek-Cypriot speciality; those without an initial have no particular regional affiliation. Menu spellings often vary.

Afélia (GC): pork cubes, ideally from filleted leg or shoulder, stewed in wine, coriander and other herbs.

Avgolémono (G): a sauce made of lemon, egg yolks and chicken stock. Also a soup made with rice, chicken stock, lemon and whole eggs.

Baklavá: a pan-Middle Eastern sweet made from sheets of filo dough layered with nuts.

Dolmádes (G) or **koupépia (GC)**: young vine leaves stuffed with rice, spices and (usually) minced meat.

Fasólia plakí or **pilakí**: white beans in a tomato, oregano, bay, parsley and garlic sauce.

Garídes: prawns (usually king prawns in the UK), fried or grilled.

Gígantes or **gígandes**: white haricot beans baked in tomato sauce; pronounced 'yígandes'.

Halloumi (GC) or **hallúmi**: a cheese traditionally made from sheep or goat's milk, but increasingly from cow's milk. Best served fried or grilled.

Horiátiki: Greek 'peasant' salad of tomato, cucumber, onion, feta and sometimes green pepper, dressed with ladolémono (oil and lemon).

Hórta: salad of wild greens.

Houmous, hoúmmous or **húmmus (GC)**: a dip of puréed chickpeas, sesame seed paste, lemon juice and garlic, garnished with paprika. Originally an Arabic dish, not Hellenic.

Htipití: tangy purée of matured cheeses, flavoured with red peppers.

Kalámari, kalamarákia or **calamares**: small squid, usually sliced into rings, battered and fried.

Kataïfi or **katayfi**: syrup-soaked 'shredded-wheat' rolls.

Keftédes or **keftedákia (G)**: herby meatballs made with minced pork or lamb (rarely beef), egg, breadcrumbs and possibly grated potato.

Khtipití another name for **htipití** (see above).

Kléftiko (GC): slow-roasted lamb on the bone (often shoulder), flavoured with oregano and other herbs.

Kopanistí (G): a cheese dip with a tanginess that traditionally comes from natural fermentation, but is often boosted with chilli.

Koukiá: broad beans.

Loukánika or **lukánika**: spicy coarse-ground sausages, usually pork and heavily herbed.

Loukoúmades: tiny, spongy dough fritters, dipped in honey.

Loukoúmi or **lukúmi**: 'turkish delight' made with syrup, rosewater and pectin, often studded with nuts.

Loúntza (GC): smoked pork loin.

Marídes: picarel, often mistranslated as (or substituted by) 'whitebait' – small fish best coated in flour and flash-fried.

Melitzanosaláta: purée of grilled aubergines.

Meze (plural mezédes, pronounced 'mezédhes'): a selection of either hot or cold appetisers and main dishes.

Moussaká(s) (G): a baked dish of mince (usually lamb), aubergine and potato slices and herbs, topped with béchamel sauce.

Papoutsáki: aubergine 'shoes', slices stuffed with mince, topped with sauce, usually béchamel-like.

Pastourmá(s): dense, dark-tinted garlic sausage, traditionally made from camel meat, but nowadays from beef.

Pourgoúri or **bourgoúri (GC)**: a pilaf of cracked wheat, often prepared with stock, onions, crumbled vermicelli and spices.

Saganáki (G): fried cheese, usually kefalotyri; also means anything (mussels, spinach) made in a cheese-based red sauce.

Sheftaliá (GC): little pig-gut skins stuffed with pork and lamb mince, onion, parsley, breadcrumbs and spices, then grilled.

Skordaliá (G): a garlic and breadcrumb or potato-based dip, used as a side dish.

Soutzoúkákia or **soutzoúki (G)**: baked meat rissoles, often topped with a tomato-based sauce.

Soúvla: large cuts of lamb or pork slow-roasted on a rotary spit.

Souvláki: chunks of meat quick-grilled on a skewer (known in London takeaways as kebab or shish kebab).

Spanakópitta: small turnovers, traditionally triangular, stuffed with spinach, dill and often feta or some other crumbly tart cheese.

Stifádo: a rich meat stew (often rabbit) with onions, red wine, tomatoes, cinnamon and bay.

Taboúlleh: generic Middle Eastern starter of pourgoúri (qv), chopped parsley, cucumber chunks, tomatoes and spring onions.

Taramá, properly **taramósalata**: fish roe pâté, originally made of dried, salted grey mullet roe (avgotáraho or botárgo), but now more often smoked cod roe, plus olive oil, lemon juice and breadcrumbs.

Tavás (GC): lamb, onion, tomato and cumin, cooked in earthenware casseroles.

Tsakistés (GC): split green olives marinated in lemon, garlic, coriander seeds and other optional flavourings.

Tyrópitta (G): similar to spanakópitta (qv) but usually without spinach and with more feta.

Tzatzíki, dzadzíki (G) or **talatoúra (GC)**: a dip of shredded cucumber, yoghurt, garlic, lemon juice and mint.

6-11.30pm Mon-Sat. **Main courses** £7.75-£12.95. **Set lunch** (Mon-Fri) £7.50 2 courses incl coffee, £8.50 3 courses. **Mezédes** £16.25 per person (minimum 2). **Service** 10% for parties of 10 or more. **Credit** MC, V.

On a sunny Thursday evening every table – both in the vine-roofed conservatory-like interior and the window-lined front room – was taken. Yet despite the considerable traffic (and impressive table turnover) this bustling modern taverna deserves its popularity. Lemonia's classic Greek menu is expertly delivered. For starters, our houmous was authentically grainy, and rich in flavour: the perfect companion to a side of warm, fluffy pitta. The plump and light kalámari were also excellent. Next, we considered moussaká and stifádo but opted for chicken shashlik and a traditional vegetarian dish, gemistá (vegetables stuffed with rice). The grilled chicken pieces (interspersed with peppers, tomatoes and onions) were moist and aromatic and came with chilli-hinted rice. The gemistá (a tomato and courgette) were too sweet, however: the delicate flavours of rice and pine nuts overpowered by raisins. A dessert of warm kataïfi better satisfied the sweet tooth. Lemonia's choice of Greek wines continues to impress. The service, although friendly, was a little erratic; we had to ask for our bill five times. Still, this was a pleasant meal out.

Babies and children admitted. Booking essential. Separate room for parties, seats 40. Tables outdoors (6, pavement). Vegetarian menu. **Map 27 A1.**

Limani
154 Regent's Park Road, NW1 8XN (7483 4492). Chalk Farm tube. **Lunch served** noon-3pm Sat. **Dinner served** 6-11.30pm Tue-Sat; 3.30-10.30pm Sun. **Main courses** £7.75-£14.50. **Mezédes** £14.50 meat or vegetarian, £17.50 fish, per person (minimum 2). **Credit** MC, V.

Early on a drizzly Sunday evening, the older sister of neighbouring Lemonia (*see above*) was already packed to its wooden rafters. Such trade might explain the under-par service – abrupt at best – but it doesn't excuse it. The food exceeded the hospitality, but only just. Aside from a soft, zingy oktapodi (octopus) in lemon juice and olive oil, starters were a let-down: taramósalata was heavy on the mayo and lacking in roe; fish salad was little more than sandwich-filler; whitebait was soggy. Fresh-tasting fried tiger prawns and crisp kalámari raised the standard somewhat. Limani offers a good choice of vegetarian mains (though meat and fish dominate). The horiátiki was mainly lettuce – not right at all – and was hardly the summer salad it ought to have been. Servings of kléftiko were fairly small, but the excellently grilled sea bass

was more than adequate. There's a decent wine list, yet with more French and New World producers than Greek. Considering there's not much to recommend it, Limani remains bafflingly popular; as we left, people were queuing in the rain for a table. *Babies and children admitted. Booking essential weekends. Separate room for parties, seats 30. Takeaway service.* **Map 27 A1.**

Wood Green N22

★ Vrisaki
73 Myddleton Road, N22 8LZ (8889 8760). Bounds Green or Wood Green tube. **Lunch served** noon-4pm, **dinner served** 6-11.30pm Mon-Sat. **Main courses** £9.50-£18. **Mezédes** £18 per person (minimum 2). **Service** 10%. **Credit** AmEx, MC, V.

Secreted behind a busy kebab shop, this north London gem is imbued with old-school charm. The bustling, family-friendly taverna has no natural light, but no matter. The walls are decorated with trompe-l'oeil island scenes, and the vibe is so cosy you hardly notice the lack of real windows. Both food and drink menus are short but more than adequate. House wines (Andreas, white; Tsantali, red) easily pass muster, and the simple but good food tastes as if it's from recipes that have been handed down generations. Starters were superb.

RESTAURANTS

Served with an array of complimentary meze, the grilled halloumi was moist and tasty, and tzatziki was pleasantly zingy, enlivened by crunchy cucumber chunks and enjoyed with warm pitta. A hearty main course of moussaká served with saffron rice was abundant with herbs and vegetables. Grilled halibut – not on the menu but recommended by our amiable Greek waiter – was thick, fleshy and delicious. We had no room for any of the tempting cream cakes and baklavá from the dessert trolley. No frills, and wholeheartedly traditional, Vrisaki is well worth a trip across town. *Babies and children admitted. Booking advisable; essential weekends. Takeaway service (8881 2920).*

North West
Belsize Park NW3

Halepi
48-50 Belsize Lane, NW3 5AN (7431 5855). Belsize Park or Swiss Cottage tube. **Meals served** 4-11pm Mon; noon-11pm Tue-Sun. **Main courses** £9.50-£24. **Set lunch** £10 2 courses. **Mezédes** £16.90 meat, £25 fish. **Cover** £1. **Credit** AmEx, DC, MC, V.
From its airy, minimalist decor, this Belsize Village eaterie seems to pride itself on being a cut above the average taverna. Such ambitions are also reflected in its old-meets-new menu – and its prices. Yet considering all this, the food was less than impressive. The crisply fried spanakópitta triangles were overpowered by dill. And while the halloumi ravioli was a nice idea, it needed more halloumi. To follow, we opted for grilled giant prawns (without the garlic sauce) and a portion of kalámari stuffed with crab, lobster and other seafood. The prawns (five in all) were nicely cooked with a hint of chilli, but quite small: more king than giant. The kalámari, however, were chewy and swimming in a greasy tomato sauce that obliterated the flavour of the stuffing. The international wine list contains a good selection of Greek and Cypriot bottles – the Tsantili house red was ripe and fruity – and service is courteous. But a dessert of stale-tasting rose-flavoured baklavá confirmed our un-rosy verdict on Halepi.
Babies and children welcome: high chairs. Booking advisable; essential weekends. Separate room for parties, seats 66. Takeaway service. **Map 28 B3.**
For branch see index.

West Hampstead NW6

★ Mario's
153-155 Broadhurst Gardens, NW6 3AU (7625 5827). West Hampstead tube/rail/28, 139, C11 bus. **Lunch served** noon-3pm Thur. **Dinner served** 6-11pm Mon-Thur. **Meals served** noon-midnight Fri, Sat; noon-11pm Sun. **Main courses** £6.95-£13.95. **Service** 10% for parties of 8 or more. **Credit** AmEx, DC, MC, V.
Despite a name that recalls a Sicilian trattoria, this West Hampstead local makes a fine, welcoming Cypriot taverna. Traditional Greek Laiki songs breeze through its speakers, vines hang from its slanted beamed roof. The atmosphere is relaxed, and matched by courteous, unfussy service. We opted for meze, which started promisingly. Of the six cold platters the tzatziki was nice and chunky, the mavromátika (greens with black-eyed beans) was fresh, and a moussey-looking taramósalata tasted better than it appeared. Light, herby meatballs were the highlight of the warm hors d'oeuvres, but over filo-ed spanakópittas let the side down. The fish dishes – kalámari, tiny marides and king prawns – were all excellent. To follow, we chose a plate of succulent grilled meats (lamb, pork and chicken souvláki) which came with a large greek salad. The wine list is short yet decent, though only one of the two advertised Greek beers was available. Desserts sounded decadent, including baklavá and warm kataifi with ice-cream or brandy; if only we had space for them.
Babies and children admitted. Booking essential. Separate area for parties, seats 35. Tables outdoors (6, garden). Takeaway service. **Map 28 A3.**

Hotels & Haute Cuisine

Why pay a small fortune to eat at a haute cuisine restaurant? Well, there are plenty of reasons. Fine dining establishments are often housed in unique and beautiful buildings, adding a sense of pomp and circumstance that isn't easily reproduced in more casual establishments. At best, they also represent the pinnacle of culinary innovation and glamour, wooing with flavour combinations that you won't have eaten elsewhere, dazzling with presentation, while waiters smooth the whole performance along with impeccable, unobtrusive, non-threatening guidance. Still, competition is increasing, and the heat is on for such venues to stay well ahead of the game.

Farewell this year to **Putney Bridge** (the premises now taken over by the Thai Square chain), and welcome back to **Pied à Terre** (7636 1178), which reopens in autumn 2005 (regrettably, too late for us to visit) following a major fire at the end of 2004. **Le Soufflé** (7318 8577) is undergoing a revamp (not before time) and will re-emerge, into the 21st century we hope, in early summer 2006.

A round of applause for **Maze**, part of the Gordon Ramsay empire, but under the command of Jason Atherton, which arrived in 2005 and promptly picked up *Time Out*'s Best New Restaurant award. Other notable performers include **Mju** for great-value, clean-tasting and innovative dishes with an oriental twist; **Pétrus** for outstanding glamour and luxury; **Pearl** for hitting some real culinary high notes; and **Sketch** for pure theatre. What a great place London is.

Central
City EC2

Bonds
Threadneedles, 5 Threadneedle Street, EC2R 8AY (7657 8088/www.theetoncollection.com). Bank tube/DLR. **Lunch served** noon-2.30pm, **dinner served** 6-10pm Mon-Fri. **Main courses** £17.50-£25. **Set lunch** £20 2 courses, £25 3 courses. **Service** 12.5%. **Credit** AmEx, MC, V.
Bonds at lunchtime is packed with the grey and chalk-stripe suits of City stockbrokers and fund managers – talking in hushed yet collectively noisy tones about the latest hirings, firings and relocations rippling through London's banking institutions. Still, man cannot live on rumour alone, and this marbled, no-nonsense and echoey restaurant is superbly placed to provide sustenance. Bread, wine and a lot of puddings (pistachio soufflé with ice-cream, or mango bavarois with chocolate sorbet, coconut foam and rose water tapioca, for instance) are served with due discretion by soft-shoed diplomatic waiters, to be demolished with gusto. We began with a simple yet refreshing gazpacho, pooled around a fluffy island of goat's cheese, and an à la carte starter of new-season asparagus, lightly charred and sprinkled with parmesan. To follow, fantastically tasty and butter-tender 'Lakes and Dales' lamb was a generous portion served with niçoise garnish and excellent aromatic couscous, but a

more diminutive mackerel dish consisted of just a few small fillets sluiced with a fiery coating of lime pickle and a single spoonful of spiced aubergine. The menu speak is uncluttered and simple, but disguises some appealingly well-thought-out combinations of fine ingredients arranged with contemporary flair.
Disabled: lift; toilet. Dress: smart casual. No smoking. Separate rooms for parties, seating 9, 12 and 20. **Map 12 Q6.**

Embankment WC2

Jaan
Swissôtel London, The Howard, 12 Temple Place, WC2R 2PR (7300 1700/http://london.swissotel.com). Temple tube. **Lunch served** noon-2.30pm Mon-Fri. **Dinner served** 5.45-10.30pm daily. **Set lunch** £19 2 courses, £23 3 courses. **Set dinner** £33 2 courses, £38 3 courses, £41 5 courses, £48 7 courses. **Service** 12.5%. **Credit** AmEx, DC, JCB, MC, V.
Early in 2005 this distinctly Swiss hotel with an enviable London skyline view closed its restaurant for a refit. Jaan then reopened without discernible change to those of us on the outside, apart from the few quid that's been added to each set meal. The restaurant could do with a more fundamental refurbishment, since the cool calm beige of yesteryear is looking bland and battered. There are some intriguing features to executive chef Paul Peters' menu, though. The menu may have started out as a shaky, wacky French-Cambodian hybrid,

but has settled more comfortably, and perhaps inevitably, into a fashioning of European ingredients into Asian vogue. Lobster consommé with two types of seaweed was a delicious example of this, intensely flavoured with sweet sea tones and luxurious aroma. It was followed on the seven-course tasting menu by a trio of raw scallop sashimi in lime dressing, roasted scallop on rich duck confit, and a shot of duck consommé. Quail with crispy pig's ear and artichoke foam failed to win us over to the cause of pig's peripherals, since cooked cartilage is an acquired taste and the foamed artichokes tasted of nothing at all. But a more simple plate of roasted cod on cod brandade and spinach was excellent. Full up by this time, we found the main course of roast beef, horseradish and pak choi garnished with raw beef ravioli and foie gras just too heavy, but desserts such as carpaccio of Asian pineapple, or white and dark chocolate casket, finish on a high note for those with room.

Book dinner. Children welcome: high chairs. Disabled: ramp; toilet. Dress: smart casual. Entertainment: pianist in bar dinner daily. Restaurant available for hire. Tables outdoors (28, garden). Map 10 M7.

Holborn WC1

★ Pearl Bar & Restaurant
Chancery Court Hotel, 252 High Holborn, WC1V 7EN (7829 7000/www.pearl-restaurant.com). Holborn tube.
Bar **Open** 11am-11pm Mon-Fri; 6-11pm Sat *Restaurant* **Lunch served** noon-2.30pm Mon-Fri. **Dinner served** 7-10pm Mon-Sat. **Set lunch** £23.50 2 courses, £26.50 3 courses. **Set dinner** £45 3 courses, £55 5 courses (£100 incl wine). *Both* **Service** 12.5%. **Credit** AmEx, DC, JCB, MC, V.
Jun Tanaka, a Japanese-American chef from whom we've seen occasional flashes of brilliance, has stuck with the Chancery Court Hotel's lofty ceilinged restaurant through its various guises. He has finally, we hope, rested upon a style of cooking that suits both his natural talent and the taste of London diners. Waiting staff have taken on a friendlier air while remaining professional; the vast former banking hall has a warmer, more peopled atmosphere; and in this instance the food was, without exception, exceptionally good. From an inspiring carte, beef oxtail raviolo with char-grilled fillet and truffle consommé captured every nuance of beefiness, from delicately light to intensely rich, along with consummate texture and presentation. Thin slices of monkfish and clams gratinated in their shells topped a sensational herb risotto, brought neatly into focus by lemon and caper dressing. Main courses followed to equal delight: fabulous succulent Limosin veal three ways (roast loin, braised cheek and confit breast) served with orange-spiked dressing, own-made macaroni, wild asparagus and smoked bacon; and a superb vegetarian pithivier (elaborate pie) of butternut squash and oozing taleggio cheese, which featured fine, golden-glazed puff pastry and baby honey-roast vegetables on the side, bathed in frothy and fragrant garlic velouté. Original desserts such as banana tarte tatin with aged balsamic vinegar and peanut caramel ice-cream compete with simpler assemblies like rice pudding and cherry parfait; don't even think of leaving without trying one. Now's certainly the time to savour Pearl.
Babies and children welcome (before 7pm): high chairs. Disabled: toilet. Entertainment: pianist 6pm daily. No smoking (restaurant). Map 10 M5.

Knightsbridge SW1, SW3

★ Boxwood Café
The Berkeley, Wilton Place, SW1X 7RL (7235 1010/www.gordonramsay.com). Hyde Park Corner or Knightsbridge tube. **Lunch served** noon-3pm Mon-Fri; noon-4pm Sat, Sun. **Dinner served** 6-11pm daily. **Main courses** £13.50-£25. **Service** 12.5%. **Credit** AmEx, MC, V.

More haute couture than haute cuisine, Boxwood Café comes complete with a darkly furnished and sleekly illuminated bar. From here, you descend into a sea of faces in the restaurant below – all gawping to check whether the latest arrival is some hot celeb. If you're not an attention-magnet this can be slightly intimidating, but the relaxed atmosphere soon soothes. Although Boxwood shares the same address as the Berkeley hotel, it feels young, individualistic and a long way removed from any hallowed and gilded establishment. Staff on the door, at the bar and in the restaurant are easy-going yet knowledgeable and quick to get on with the job, making the whole experience a real pleasure. The dining room is as well lit and comfortable as you could wish. Furthermore, there's the pleasure of contemplating a menu stuffed with slightly naughty foods that feel out of place in such a classy joint, such as burger and chips or a bowl of sugar-dusted doughnuts – except that the burger is made with English veal and foie gras and costs £22.50, and the doughnuts are served on linen folded into a water lily and accompanied by a mini silver tankard of espresso sorbet. Everything we tried was perfect, aside from a portion of tough squid. Some dishes, such as char-grilled tuna on red onion salad doused in a light peppery sauce, are offered in both starter and main course sizes, and plenty of vegetable extras and great rolls bolster what's already a generous menu.
Babies and children welcome: children's menu; high chairs. Booking essential. Disabled: toilet. No smoking. Separate room for parties, seats 12-16. Map 9 G9.

The Capital
22-24 Basil Street, SW3 1AT (7589 5171/7591 1202/www.capitalhotel.co.uk). Knightsbridge tube.
Bar **Open** noon-11pm daily.
Restaurant **Breakfast served** 7-10.30am Mon-Sat; 7.30-10.30am Sun. **Lunch served** noon-2.30pm daily. **Dinner served** 7-11pm Mon-Sat; 7-10.30pm Sun. **Set breakfast** £12.50 continental, £16.50 full English. **Set lunch** £29.50 3 courses. **Set dinner** £48 2 courses, £55 3 courses, £68 7 courses. **Service** 12.5% (lunch, dinner). **Credit** AmEx, DC, MC, V.
Finally the Capital basks in the glory of a long overdue makeover. The obscure wooden sculptures have gone (exposing acres of beautiful blond wood panelling), the patriarchal chairs have been upstaged by shimmery new ones, and the windows are now adorned with miles of glamorous duck-egg blue silk. Eric Chavot's fabulous cuisine hasn't changed, thank goodness, but last year's impeccable service was marred this time by an individual who was annoyed at waiting for our order, and voiced disapproval when we selected only two of the three set-lunch courses (we were charged for three anyway). Unsurprisingly, given its class and position on the main drag of retail heaven, the place is awash with groomed shoppers, Knightsbridge old-timers and those just dropping by for a chilled Martini in the pocket handkerchief of a bar, so you'd do well to book ahead. Appetisers and pre-desserts are included within the set lunch, all the better to sample Chavot's ethereal touch on some terrific ingredients, such as exemplary lemon sole on pod-poppingly fresh vegetables with a whiff of mint about them, or fine char-grilled fillet of halibut with exquisite 'gnocchettini' (baby dough balls) mingled with creamy morel foam and minuscule mushrooms packed with flavour and aroma. This unfettered lightness, together with pure essence-like flavour, continues in desserts such as rhubarb and custard, which here means poached fruit encapsulated in glistening rhubarb jelly, contrasting with cool mouthfuls of milky ice-cream, crisp traceries of caramel and smooth vanilla froth. The disagreeable one finally displayed a tray of petits fours, which we dared not disturb, but despite this we left replete and entertained.
Booking advisable; essential weekends. Children over 10 admitted. Dress: smart casual; no jeans or trainers. Restaurant available for hire. Separate rooms for parties, seating 12 and 24. Map 8 F9.

★ Foliage
Mandarin Oriental Hyde Park Hotel, 66 Knightsbridge, SW1X 7LA (7201 3723/www.mandarinoriental.com). Knightsbridge tube. **Lunch served** noon-2.30pm, **dinner served** 7-10.30pm daily. **Set lunch** £25 3 courses (£32 incl wine). **Set meal** £47.50-£50 3 courses. **Service** 12.5%. **Credit** AmEx, DC, JCB, MC, V.
Foliage has been hotshot-designed in tones of butterscotch and rosewood with a leafy theme reflecting the restaurant's matchless location overlooking Hyde Park, but the decor isn't what you come for. In true red-carpet style, this Knightsbridge hotel is crammed with staff from pavement through to reception, staggeringly trendy bar and both restaurants. All of them wear an immaculate uniform and genuine smile. What's more, they can usually find you a table with just a few days' notice – seemingly in contrast to everywhere else in London of this magnitude. How we love Foliage! Appetisers are sensationally presented and do exactly what they are supposed to: excite your senses in readiness for your starter. What follows might be captivating little frogs' drumsticks, crisply battered and served with Alsace bacon, spinach purée and a hint of garlic; or possibly a spellbindingly white and al dente risotto charged with freshly unearthed Piedmont truffles and scantily dressed with truffled honey for a lick of sweetness so good it induces goose-bumps. Mains followed the same course of seduction, with rare roast fillet of Scottish beef and head-over-heels lovely cannelloni of the deepest, richest, juiciest braised oxtail, plus a dash of white onion soubise and red wine jus. Pot-roasted rabbit with a dinky mushroom pie was also a resounding success, while desserts flirt with tonka beans, pearl barley, grue (the husk of the cocoa bean) and the like, weaving them eloquently into soufflés, mousses, ice-creams and parfaits, along with some more general sweetnesses. Altogether, unmissable.
Babies and children welcome: high chairs. Booking advisable. Disabled: toilet. Dress: smart casual. Vegetarian menu. Map 8 F9.

★ Mju
The Millennium Knightsbridge, 16-17 Sloane Street, SW1X 9NU (7201 6330/www.millennium hotels.com). Knightsbridge tube. **Lunch served** noon-2.30pm, **dinner served** 6-10.30pm Mon-Sat. **Main courses** £15-£19.50. **Set lunch** £17.50 2 courses. **Set dinner** £38 3 courses, £46 6 courses (£71 incl wine); £60 tasting menu (£95, £130, £210 incl wine). **Service** 12.5%. **Credit** AmEx, DC, JCB, MC, V.
There's an abundance of menu options available at this comfortable, gently oriental restaurant, carefully selected and deftly prepared by chef Tom Thomsen. Each course of the chef's tasting menu comes with modest, special or celebratory wines by the glass for an additional £35, £70 or £150: a great way to sample spot-on pairings of adventurous food and wine, which is a dicey game that most of us shy away from. Our visit coincided with a special offer of a two-course lunch for a tenner, a monumental bargain. The food was so good we'd have been happy to pay twice the price. Sashimi of tuna and wild sea bass, thinly sliced and served in opaquely raw pink and white alternating squares, was delicate and delicious: dusted with citrus peel and seaweed and accompanied by a barely-there dressing for a virtuous starter. More fulsome was a twirl of lobster linguine, the pasta handmade and of proper Italianate consistency, the dressing (of kombu seaweed and spices) utterly gorgeous and sheening every strand of pasta for complete flavour satisfaction. Such wonderful pasta doesn't come along often, even in the best restaurants, and that was without the tender, sweet lobster generously strewn throughout. Other perks of the meal included – unbelievably for a mere £10 – an amuse-bouche and notably good cleansing froth of semi-frozen watermelon, simply but sensationally seasoned with a hint of salt and lime. A return to great form; don't leave Mju off your must-visit list.
Babies and children welcome: high chairs. Booking advisable. Disabled: lift; toilets. No smoking. Restaurant available for hire. Map 8 F9.

RESTAURANTS

Pearl Bar & Restaurant

One-O-One

101 William Street, SW1X 7RN (7290 7101). Knightsbridge tube. **Lunch served** noon-2.30pm, **dinner served** 7-10.30pm daily. **Main courses** £22-£26. **Set lunch** £25 3 courses. **Set dinner** £70 7 courses. **Credit** AmEx, DC, JCB, MC, V.

Daylight is not especially kind to the hard turquoise and maple colour scheme in this superbly well sited Knightsbridge restaurant, making the place look more like a hotel add-on. In the kinder light of evening, tables glow warmly with candles, the street outside looks less like a race track, and more diners create more atmosphere. Still, you'll pay twice as much for the privilege in the evening, unless sticking parsimoniously to one or two options from the carte. Pascal Proyart is a talented chef who landed in Britain years ago, bringing with him a passion for his beloved Brittany and the feasts for which that region is renowned. Native oysters and dramatically prehistoric-looking royal king crab legs from the Barents Sea are two exceptionally fine specialities, served a dozen different ways with classic and not so classic garnishes, such as almond and garlic butter, spring onions and sweet chilli, or wasabi mayonnaise. They made an impressive start to an impressive piscine adventure, and at £19 per head were on a par with most of the à la carte starters. To follow, a hearty portion of creamy textured, beautifully white brill was roasted on the bone for added succulence and flavour, and paired with a luxurious tarragon-rich variant of sauce béarnaise: pink and piquant with tomato to form sauce choron. Baby monkfish was also a fabulous example of tender, juicy, sea-scented loveliness, albeit slightly overpowered by its raw-tasting saffron and cumin crust. Desserts are good too – warm chocolate fondant with raspberry sorbet and raspberry coulis is a favourite – but really aren't the point in comparison to the exceptional fish.
Babies and children welcome; high chairs. Booking advisable Thur-Sun. Disabled: toilet. Dress: smart casual. No-smoking tables. **Map 8 F9.**

★ Pétrus

The Berkeley, Wilton Place, SW1X 7RL (7235 1200/www.petrus-restaurant.com). Hyde Park Corner or Knightsbridge tube. **Lunch served** noon-2.30pm Mon-Fri. **Dinner served** 6-11pm Mon-Sat. **Set lunch** £30 3 courses. **Set dinner** £60 3 courses, £80 tasting menu. **Credit** AmEx, MC, V.

This velvety purple restaurant is deliciously glamorous in both broad daylight or darkness. Its soft-edged, tranquillising interior is punctuated by the polished trappings of haute cuisine: gleaming silverware and white linen, ice clinking in champagne buckets, cut-crystal baskets swaying heavy with jewel-coloured bonbons. Head chef Marcus Wareing, known to all by now, is one of Gordon Ramsay's protégés and so Pétrus is naturally one of the brighter luminaries in our culinary solar system. It lives up to its starry status, though, as skilfully demonstrated in an à la carte lunch comprising two 'speciality' dishes of 24-hour-cooked belly pork and slow-cooked sea bass. The former appeared as three neat squares of pale, silkily fatted and milky-fleshed meat dusted with five spice and daubed with streaks of complex mustard-spiked apple purée, fresh coriander seed shoots adding shots across the bows of sweetness. Sea bass was brilliantly succulent, yielding and subtly flavoured, contrasting with a pungent, garlic-infused arsenal of frogs' legs splashed with vivid green basil oil and nestling in roasted garlic purée. This seductive £60 à la carte menu is the backbone of the kitchen's talent. At half the price, the set lunch is understandably simpler and slightly humdrum, relying on ingredients like chicken and salmon (impeccably sourced, no doubt). The tasting menu has six real courses, plus the amuse-bouche, pre-dessert and bonbons offered on each menu, and cheese for an additional £8. Opera, a delicately layered coffee and chocolate gateau served with espresso ice-cream, was visually artful but lacked any great flavour – but don't let that put you off trying this or anything else at Pétrus. You won't be disappointed.
Babies and children welcome: high chairs. Booking essential. Dress: smart jacket preferred. No smoking. Separate room for parties, seats 16. Vegetarian menu. **Map 9 G9.**

Marble Arch W1

The Crescent

Montcalm Hotel, Great Cumberland Place, W1H 7TW (7402 4288/7723 4440/ www.montcalm.co.uk). Marble Arch tube. **Lunch served** 12.30-2.30pm Mon-Fri. **Dinner served** 6.30-10.30pm daily. **Set lunch** (incl half bottle of wine) £21 2 courses, £26 3 courses. **Set dinner** (incl half bottle of wine) £24.50 2 courses, £29.50 3 courses. **Credit** AmEx, DC, JCB, MC, V.

Tucked improbably away from the bustle of Oxford Street, the serene Montcalm Hotel is always awash with overseas visitors busy lapping up London life and meeting friends and business colleagues. Hence the in-house restaurant is a sociable kind of place, lacking pretension and marked by consistently approachable, helpful staff. The menu is approachable too, not just because of its no-nonsense set lunch and dinner options (which both include a half bottle of wine per person, red or white, and no questions asked), but also in that food is refreshingly straightforward and fits its description. Grilled black bream with warm endive and asparagus salad was ideally fresh and pan-fried, and a more imaginative starter than we've sampled on recent visits, while roasted scallop atop black pudding and mushy peas was a complementary array of earthy, vibrant and sweet taste-sensations. To follow, tiger prawn and chive risotto with chilli jam was reluctantly sidelined; instead we chose roasted cod with crab cake and sweetcorn emulsion. This latter arrangement saw a great piece of fish matched to a surprisingly fragrant and mellow sauce, but the crab cake that should have subtly clinched the partnership was a disaster of stodgy rice containing barely a whiff of crab within its breadcrumbed and deep-fried fortification. Desserts appeal to senses of humour and comfort, featuring combinations such as warm chocolate brownie with pecan brittle ice-cream and Valhrona milkshake, or roasted banana and caramel parcel served with a shot glass of vanilla smoothie. Good value, friendly – and central.

Mayfair W1

Angela Hartnett at the Connaught

The Connaught, 16 Carlos Place, W1K 2AL (7592 1222/www.gordonramsay.com). Bond Street or Green Park tube. **Breakfast served** 7-10.30am Mon-Fri; 7-11am Sat, Sun. **Lunch served** noon-2.45pm Mon-Fri; noon-3.15pm Sat, Sun. **Dinner served** 5.45-11pm Mon-Sat; 7-10.30pm Sun. **Set lunch** £30 3 courses. **Set dinner** £55 3 courses, (tasting menu) £70 6 courses. **Service** 12.5%. **Credit** AmEx, DC, MC, V.

The Connaught is a gorgeous place in which to eat and luxuriate. Glossy oak panelling and mossy green blinds work brilliantly in a dining room of this size. The overall effect is stunning, warm and elegant. Angela Hartnett arrived in 2003, waving away the fine porcelain, silverware and High Church cooking of previous legendary French chef Michel Bourdin, and bringing in Italian peasant fare and rustic earthenware. Then the food took a more refined Italian turn, and now we're back into porcelain and light classical French dishes with cross-European leanings. We don't mind, as long as the victuals live up to the surroundings, which on this occasion they didn't. An amuse-bouche clouded the taste buds with an overload of creamy celeriac and sweet blur of syrupy truffle reduction. 'Minestrone di Parma' was deeply flavoured and deeply delicious: a clear ham broth poured over a few lettuce leaves and sliced asparagus stalk, garnished with fine ham and parmesan ravioli. Main courses weren't successful: a marmalade goo dotted with raisins turned a good piece of john dory into a peculiarly fishy pudding; and pigeon, described by the waiter as fully boned, was barely so, leaving us to tackle the carcass with a steak knife and to finish with a plate of bloodied bones and onion skins (left on the garnish). A novel Spanish-themed dessert, catalan cream with Pedro Ximénez jelly and roasted quince, suffered again from the dullness of cream – despite a knockout sherry jelly that hypnotised the palate after three or four mouthfuls. Three slices of quince plonked on the plate like an afterthought failed to add interest. So near, yet so far from perfection.
Babies and children welcome: high chairs. Booking essential. Disabled: lift; toilet. No smoking. Separate rooms for parties, seating 14 and 22. **Map 9 H7.**

Brian Turner Mayfair

Millennium Hotel Mayfair, 44 Grosvenor Square, W1K 2HP (7596 3444/www.millenniumhotels. com). Bond Street tube.
Bar **Open** noon-midnight Mon-Fri; 6.30-11.30pm Sat.
Restaurant **Lunch served** 12.30-2.30pm Mon-Fri. **Dinner served** 6.30-10.30pm Mon-Sat. **Main courses** £12.50-£28.50. **Set lunch** £22.50 2 courses, £25.50 3 courses. **Service** 12.5%.
Both **Credit** AmEx, DC, MC, V.

The glitzy Millennium Hotel is well placed in lovely Grosvenor Square. In its cavernous reception hall adults in suits and their kids in jeans drift around, parking themselves on vast sofas. In one dark corner, marked by a discreet podium and greeter, is the entrance to Brian Turner's restaurant, striking a relaxing tone with its sea-coloured decor, comfy leather chairs and crisp, capacious tables. Waiters were merely coasting on a half-full Saturday evening, not paying attention to empty glasses and finished plates, and sending wine to a table when they had confirmed among themselves that it was unsuitable. The pace increased whenever a suited and booted Brian Turner strode through. Food plays safe, with well-thumbed British ideas (so why no accompanying British beer?). Decent pieces of meat are cooked with a degree of skill. What does blow you away is the menu's salt content. An otherwise nice starter of squid on tomato concassé with chive butter sauce came with a religiously dry wafer so solidly encrusted with salt that one tiny fragment wiped out any other sensation for 15 minutes. Main courses were traditional and pleasant, other than the seasoning (we overheard another squid-eater asking for his next dish to be made without salt). Duck breast was tender, juicy and served with a spoonful of mashed peas, fig chutney and truffle-oiled potato mash, while an equally nicely cooked loin of lamb lay alongside a humble potato cake, three sliced beans and a salty jus. Fudge and blueberry bread and butter pudding might be among the desserts. Brian Turner's is good for a laid-back, reasonably priced Sunday lunch, but probably won't rock your world.

Babies and children admitted. Booking advisable. Disabled: toilet. Dress: smart casual. No-smoking tables. Separate room for parties, seats 45. Tables outdoors (5, terrace). **Map 9 G7.**

★ Le Gavroche

43 Upper Brook Street, W1K 7QR (7408 0881/ www.le-gavroche.co.uk). Marble Arch tube.
Lunch served noon-2pm Mon-Fri. **Dinner served** 6.30-11pm Mon-Sat. **Main courses** £27-£40. **Minimum** £60 (dinner). **Set lunch** £44 3 courses incl half bottle of wine, mineral water, coffee. **Service** 12.5%. **Credit** AmEx, DC, JCB, MC, V.

Since 1970 Le Gavroche has been widely regarded by those in the know as London's premier purveyor of epicurean luxury. Service is virtually unimpeachable, the aura is one of a vintage Bentley, and the food Mayfair-streets ahead of anyone else's. The fatly, darkly upholstered room divides opinion as decisively as does a jar of Marmite, though: into people who can only eat in cutting-edge spaces, and those who genuflect over good food wherever it be found. Needless to say, the former go elsewhere while the latter keep this place constantly buzzing – and a regular feature at food award ceremonies. Despite the set lunch being great value at £44 for three courses (with wine, water, coffee and petits fours included, and no corners cut in any of these departments), plenty of midday diners gorge themselves on the à la carte and tasting menus. Here, a starter of artichoke stuffed with foie gras and chicken mousse will set you back £34; a main course of whole roasted john dory with smooth olive oil mash costs £64; and poached Bresse chicken with truffles and Madeira sauce is £96 for two. It has to be good. Michel Roux Junior has 21st-century lightness built into his classical French genes, and his kitchen excels at cooking delicious vegetables deliciously and concentrating big flavours into small packages. For example, fabulous Aberdeen Angus is char-grilled to tender perfection and served with a small yet wonderfully intense onion tart glazed with roquefort: the onions sweet, the cheese piquant yet not over the top, and the dissolvingly good pastry blended with a hint of cheddar cheese in a subtle re-emphasis that might escape the notice of an untrained palate. But frankly, not many such palates visit Le Gavroche.

Children admitted. Booking essential. Dress: jacket; no jeans, shorts or trainers. No pipes or cigars. Restaurant available for hire. **Map 9 G7.**

Gordon Ramsay at Claridge's

Claridge's, 55 Brook Street, W1A 2JQ (7499 0099/www.gordonramsay.com). Bond Street tube. **Lunch served** noon-2.45pm Mon-Fri; noon-3pm Sat, Sun. **Dinner served** 5.45-11pm Mon-Sat; 6-11pm Sun. **Set lunch** £30 3 courses. **Set dinner** £60 3 courses, £70 6 courses. **Credit** AmEx, JCB, MC, V.

Trying to secure a table here on a Friday or Saturday evening proved impossible – we were told that nothing was available for the next 16 weeks and that the restaurant would then be closed for a month. Marvellous! We persevered and secured a 5.45pm Wednesday slot instead, and found ourselves virtually alone for an hour, apart from 17 waiters (yes, 17). Let's face it, not many people want to eat an evening meal before their kids have had tea. Eventually we were fed and watered à la Gordon, in spite of the annoying

quantity of staff faffing around. Super-clean crockery and slick presentation are Ramsay trademarks that add yet another layer of glamour to the vintage sparkle of this beautiful and beautifully restored art deco hotel. Of the three courses, dessert continues to linger seductively in the mind: apple sorbet, parfait, jelly and tatin – each component artistically arranged, of fragile flavour and searching mouth-feel, the perfect ending. Main course Cornish lamb fillet and confit with a niçoise garnish of three cherry tomatoes, one sliced bean, a few olives and a £6 supplement was curiously average in flavour for all its good looks, while a starter of duck egg was most disappointing: the outer 2mm of the egg white peculiarly tough, the rest of the white and the yolk cold and completely raw, served on a textureless pap of warm broccoli purée, melted goat's cheese and a smattering of shaved truffle. A mixed bag for £186.

Babies and children welcome: high chairs. Booking essential. Disabled: toilet. Dress: smart /jacket preferred/no jeans or trainers. Separate rooms for parties, seating 6, 10 and 30. **Map 9 H6.**

★ Greenhouse

27A Hay's Mews, W1J 5NY (7499 3331/www. greenhouserestaurant.co.uk). Green Park tube.
Lunch served noon-2.30pm Mon-Fri. **Dinner served** 6.45-11pm Mon-Sat. **Set lunch** £28 2 courses, £32 3 courses. **Set meal** £60 3 courses. **Service** 12.5%. **Credit** AmEx, DC, MC, V.

If you're in search of an innovative, elegant and challenging yet not intimidating dining experience, the Greenhouse makes a sophisticated choice. Chef Bjorn van der Horst is a fusion-food meister. He spent years practising his art on New Yorkers before arriving here in 2004, throwing down the gauntlet to our native British talent. We're very impressed: think Heston Blumenthal grown up and calmed down. To illustrate, take one of the signature dishes, foie gras with coffee and amaretto foam. Mentally this doesn't sound promising, but once in the mouth the butter-soft liver is hot, tender, titillated by a savoury coffee bitterness and licked over with a delicate almond alcoholic pouffe of nothingness, in much the same – but different – way as we accept and celebrate the marriage of port, Sauternes or Madeira with foie gras. Sounds wild, but it's sure-footed nonetheless. Clever play is made on contrasting temperatures throughout the meal. Little extras crop up delightfully. We recommend the tasting menu to make the most of the occasion and to experiment as much as possible. Outstanding too, among our seven (modest) portions, was a vividly refreshing cool pea soup, poured around a hot creamy bacon essence and a superior, meaty mini crab cake. In a nod to seasonality, the carte also offered Cornish lobster at a supplement of £40 for two. Not your common-or-garden greenhouse, this.

Babies and children admitted. Booking essential. Dress: smart casual. No-smoking tables. Separate room for parties, seats 10. **Map 9 H7.**

★ Maze NEW

2005 WINNER BEST NEW RESTAURANT
Marriott Grosvenor Square, 10-13 Grosvenor Square, W1K 6JP (7107 0000/www.gordon ramsay.com). Bond Street tube.
Bar **Open** noon-1am daily.
Restaurant **Tapas** £5-£8.50. **Main courses** £13.50-£16.50.
Both **Lunch served** noon-3pm, **dinner served** 6-11pm daily. **Service** 12.5%. **Credit** AmEx, MC, V.

Ignore the fact it's in a Marriott hotel, be patient with the seemingly endless wait for the phone to be answered by a real person, and endure being told you can dine at 6.45pm or 9.30pm only. It's all worth it. Jason Atherton, installed here by Gordon Ramsay, has cooked at El Bulli in Spain and is now showing London what he can do. Attentive but friendly staff put everyone at ease. People come here to enjoy themselves; there's more laughter and chatter in this sleek, beige and cream L-shaped dining room (designer David Rockwell) than at many high-falutin' establishments. The menu lists 20 or so tapas-sized dishes (though the hopelessly

Maze

challenged can revert to a starter and main course combo). The wine list has taster portions too; all is explained by the charming, unpushy sommelier. Menu high points were too many to mention – even the lesser dishes were praiseworthy – but plaudits have to go to risotto of carnaroli with peas, broad beans, wood sorrel and grated truffle (every mouthful a glorious melding of flavours); aged English beef with foie gras, parsley, snail and garlic aligot de marinette (amazingly rich and filling for such a compact dish); and peanut butter and cherry jam sandwich with salted nuts and cherry sorbet (the most unexpectedly lovely dessert we've ever had). In short, whether you order the more unusually flavoured dishes, say Valrhona chocolate fondant with green cardamom caramel, sea salt and almond ice-cream, or play safe with the likes of salad of violet artichoke with fresh truffle and truffle mayonnaise, we can guarantee your dining pleasure.
Babies and children welcome: high chairs. Booking advisable. Disabled: toilet. No smoking. Separate room for parties, seats 10. **Map 9 G6.**

★ Sketch: The Lecture Room
9 Conduit Street, W1S 2XZ (0870 777 4488/ www.sketch.uk.com). Oxford Circus tube. **Lunch served** noon-2.30pm Tue-Fri, **dinner served** 7-10.30pm Tue-Fri. **Main courses** £45-£59. **Set lunch** £35 3 courses. **Set dinner** £80-£140 3 courses. **Service** 12.5%. **Credit** AmEx, DC, MC, V.
As with many restaurants, lunch at Sketch is a completely different experience to dinner, although in this case both are equally stunning. Designed by Gabhan O'Keefe, the first-floor dining room features juicy fruit colours that positively glow as sunlight filters down through a central atrium. Fewer front-of-house bodies at lunchtime result in a more relaxed, albeit still very correct, progression through the courses. And, if anything, dishes served at midday benefit from a touch of simplicity that throws the juxtaposition of curious ingredients into starker relief. Consider, for example, an à la carte vegetarian carrot custard with red radish glazed in spicy beetroot juice, cream of quinoa, stilton and paprika. You'll not have eaten it anywhere else. Aside from dramatic food, the Lecture Room sets out to deliver all the theatre, expectation, choreography and ostentatious menu-speak it can shoehorn into a single meal – starting with the electric-blue entrance, taking in 'langoustines addressed four ways', and ending with all the day's desserts displayed in a cigar box (from which you ditheringly make a choice and wait with bated breath as a fresh one is spirited from the remarkably good pastry kitchen). It's not all show and no substance, though. Common sense and hospitality win you over from the start with a firm, welcome handshake, capacious tables, and three rolls delivered to each guest in a feel-good gesture. Portions are fair at lunchtime, the set meal a snip at £35 for three good and unusual courses, and the starter and dessert are likely to be a combination of several dishes for your additional delectation.
Babies and children admitted. Booking essential (no entrance without a table reservation after 5pm for non-members). Dress: casual. Entertainment: DJs 10.30pm-2am Mon-Sat (bar). Restaurant available for hire. **Map 9 J6.**

★ The Square
6-10 Bruton Street, W1J 6PU (7495 7100/ www.squarerestaurant.com). Bond Street or Green Park tube. **Lunch served** noon-2.45pm Mon-Fri. **Dinner served** 6.30-10.45pm Mon-Sat; 6.30-9.45pm Sun. **Set lunch** £25 2 courses, £30 3 courses. **Set dinner** £60 3 courses; £75 8 courses. **Service** 12.5%. **Credit** AmEx, DC, JCB, MC, V.
Fine dining restaurants are likely to fall short of perfection on a Bank Holiday, even at this hallowed venue richly decorated in tones of burnished copper, spicy orange and chocolate. In all likelihood, the head chef will be having a rare night off, leaving the kitchen to the second or third in command. There will be fewer punters around; staffing levels in general will be skeletal; and fresh food deliveries, well, there won't have been any, so

some dishes may be off the menu. To be fair, only the lobster with its stately £20 supplement was missing from the Square's full and fabulous menu on the night we visited. That aside, the front of house team was running on half empty and was half-enthused; a few mistakes cropped up in what is normally a faultless gourmet indulgence. What you will usually encounter here is poised, sometimes surprising yet earth-motherly dishes with a seasonal bent, such as roast Orkney scallops with rustic curried cauliflower and a dressing of pomegranate and lime. Main courses might be light and airy (turbot with langoustines, samphire and champagne, for instance), or gently visceral as in aged fillet of beef with oxtail ravioli and bone marrow. Finish with sumptuous yet fragile desserts like summer berry soup with blackcurrant cornetto (but not as you know it), or an intriguing selection of chocolate goodies described only as 'bitter, milk and white, warm hot and cold'. It's difficult to make a bad choice here, but steer clear of Bank Holidays.
Babies and children admitted. Booking essential. Disabled: toilet. Dress: smart. No cigars. Restaurant available for hire. Separate room for parties, seats 18. **Map 9 H7.**

Windows
The London Hilton on Park Lane, Park Lane, W1K 1BE (7493 8000/www.hilton.co.uk). Green Park or Hyde Park Corner tube. **Bar Open** noon-2.30pm Fri; 5.30pm-2.30am Sat; noon-10.30pm Sun. **Restaurant Lunch served** 12.30-2.30pm Mon-Fri, Sun. **Dinner served** 7-10.30pm Mon-Thur; 7-11.30pm Fri, Sat. **Main courses** £26.50-£33.50. **Set lunch** £39.50 3 courses, £45.50 4 courses. **Set dinner** £59.50 5 courses, £77.50 7 courses incl wine. **Service** 12.5%. **Both Credit** AmEx, DC, MC, V.
We keep trying to be kind to Windows. The view from the 28th floor is mesmerising, and the separate bar pretty groovy, but the restaurant is dull and dominated by a pianist on Friday and Saturday evenings, turning up on your bill in the form of a £7.50 'entertainment charge'. Credit where credit is due, though, and Windows has improved its front-of-house team over the past couple of years, with staff on this occasion courteous and the timing perfectly acceptable. A grand buffet attracts plenty of diners at midday – when daylight is also more fully shed on London's scope, parks and architecture. A genuine à la carte menu is offered for lunch and dinner, so you can order just a main course if you wish. From the carte, beef fillet (£32.50), and pan-fried sea bass (£29.50) were well cooked and adequately if not memorably accompanied, the former with beef confit and the latter with apple and celery salad. Starters, though, were a cream-based puréed 'minestrone' that no Italian would dare label minestrone, and wild mushroom terrine of basic egg crêpe wrapped around scrambled egg and mushrooms (£15). Further disappointments came with the bill. The minestrone was charged at £10; on the menu it was £9 (this was rectified on enquiry). And two glasses of very ordinary wine came to £25 plus service, well above comparable hotel prices. Someone is gazing through Windows on the poor mugs inside and having a laugh.
Babies and children welcome: 50% discount for under-10s; high chairs (restaurant only). Disabled: toilet. Entertainment: musicians 7pm-1.30am Mon-Sat. No-smoking tables (restaurant). **Map 9 G8.**

Piccadilly W1

The Ritz
150 Piccadilly, W1J 9BR (7493 8181/ www.theritzhotel.co.uk). Green Park tube. **Bar Open** 11.30am-11pm Mon-Sat; noon-10.30pm Sun. **Restaurant Breakfast served** 7-10.30am Mon-Sat; 8-10.30am Sun. **Lunch served** 12.30-2.30pm daily. **Tea served** (reserved sittings) 11.30am. 1.30pm, 3.30pm, 5.30pm, 7.30pm daily. **Dinner served** 6-10.30pm Mon-Sat. **Main courses** £25-£56. **Set lunch** £45 3 courses. **Set tea** £34 . **Set dinner** (6-7pm,

10-10.30pm) £45 3 courses; (Mon-Thur) £65 4 courses; (Fri, Sat) £75 4 courses. **Both Credit** AmEx, MC, V.
London's fading debutantes (or that's what they look like) are eking out their last years at the Ritz, enjoying the morning-suited waiters, weighty swish of silver trolleys weaving to and fro, beholding the ever-wondrous pink and gilded ballroom with an air of smug familiarity and, in the case of their menfolk, taking constant puffs of a fat cigar. Few places now dare serve food so unyieldingly British, so belt and braces traditional (despite claims of 'contemporary accents' to its classical cuisine), so reassuringly plain yet exorbitantly priced to a clientele so intent on hanging on to the past. The back page of the menu lists dishes always available – lest a rebellion occur – such as grilled whole dover sole for £39, beef wellington at £78 for two sharing, and beluga caviar at £185 a pop. A dinner dance with four-piece band is held on Friday and Saturday evenings, and yes, plenty do cha-cha between courses. The Summer Menu (everything has to have a capital letter) offered a retro jellied tomato consommé nicely flavoured and studded with a generous helping of langoustine tails, while apple and celery soup from the à la carte was smooth, fragrant and daringly garnished with sunflower seeds. From the always available list, an organic grilled steak was accompanied by six unremarkable chips and béarnaise sauce for £35, and navarin of lamb wallowed in a rich but sticky meat gravy. Pineapple flambéed at table was the star of the show, and a show is really what your money is buying you at this iconic hotel.
Babies and children welcome: children's menu; high chairs. Disabled: toilet. Booking advisable restaurant; essential afternoon tea. Dress: jacket and tie; no jeans or trainers. Entertainment: dinner dance Fri, Sat (restaurant); pianist daily. Separate rooms for parties, seating 22 and 55. Tables outdoors (8, terrace). Vegan dishes. Vegetarian menu. **Map 9 J7.**

Pimlico SW1

Allium
Dolphin Square, Chichester Street, SW1V 3LX (7798 6888/www.allium.co.uk). Pimlico tube. **Lunch served** noon-3pm Tue-Fri; noon-2.30pm Sun. **Dinner served** 6-10.30pm Tue-Sat. **Main courses** £12.50-£24.10. **Set lunch** £17.50 2 courses, £22.50 3 courses. **Set meal** (6-7pm) £28.50 3 courses. **Set dinner** £32.50 3 courses. **Service** 12.5%. **Credit** AmEx, DC, MC, V.
The plush royal-blue dining room, with its art deco details, dramatic flowers and spiky allium sculpture, seems at odds with the distant shrieks of children splashing about in the adjacent, though hidden, swimming pool. However, the fact that Allium's executive chef is Anton Edelmann, a man of long and impressive culinary repute, is enough to allay any worries. Contemporary European is how the food is described, which translates as seasonal ingredients, continental recipes and newfangled lightness. Our Bank Holiday meal was slightly marred by the few staff barely coping with more diners than they had anticipated, but at a special price of £29.50 for a four-course dinner with wine we were not about to complain. In quick succession came a scrambled egg and onion velouté freebie, followed by tuna tartare with a thick lid of crème fraîche, lobster mousse stuffed into a courgette flower, grilled halibut on braised lettuce with red wine reduction, and finally a rich chocolate mousse on coffee granita. Yes, the meal lacked a little of the sophistication of à la carte dishes we've enjoyed in the past, but Allium is nonetheless a great place to entertain families and groups. Top marks also go to the marketing department for offering tempting little extras such as free river cruise tickets with a Sunday lunch menu, monthly specials and the ability to order two pre-theatre courses and return after the show for dessert. Check the website for details.
Babies and children admitted. Booking advisable. Disabled: toilet. No-smoking tables. Separate rooms for parties, seating 24 and 70. **Map 15 J12.**

RESTAURANTS

St James's SW1

L'Oranger

*5 St James's Street, SW1A 1EF (7839 3774).
Green Park tube.* **Lunch served** noon-2.30pm
Mon-Fri. **Dinner served** 6-10.30pm Mon-Sat.
Main courses £24-£29 (lunch); £22-£29
(dinner). **Set lunch** £25 2 courses, £29 3 courses.
Set dinner £40 3 courses, £70 6 courses.
Service 12.5%. **Credit** AmEx, DC, MC, V.
Charming isn't a word that's used too often these
days, but it aptly describes L'Oranger, which is
traditional without being old-fashioned and elegant
without being stuffy, successfully combining both
the comfort and formality due a dining room of
this calibre. Last year chef Laurent Michel took to
the kitchen, promising great things and delivering,
we found, assured and sound if not staggeringly
original dishes on the remodelled menu. Prices are
unchanged, not that you'd know this if you are
female, since in an archaic move ladies are now
given menus sans prix. Portions and garnishing
match the substantial cost of the à la carte menu
(starters £13-£25, mains £22-£29), which relies on
plenty of well-rehearsed and classic combinations.
A more modest set menu on our visit proved light,
fruity and mostly delicious, if less challenging to
the kitchen. Wafer-thin pasta wrapped around
nuggets of buttery, caramelised foie gras made a
great starter, served with a jus here, a froth there
and copious slicings of fresh truffle. Mains went
from roast chicken and mash to excellent poached
salmon with warm potato and egg salad sprinkled
with salty bursts of salmon caviar. Cheese was
generously offered as one of three dessert options
(often it is only featured with a supplement), but
watermelon soup was basic in the extreme: blitzed
melon, diced melon and iced melon with an
imperceptible dash of vodka. Still, L'Oranger is a
reliable, secluded and dignified venue.
*Children over 7 admitted. Booking essential.
Dress: smart casual; no trainers. Separate
room for parties, seats 32. Tables outdoors
(6, courtyard).* **Map 9 J8.**

South West

Chelsea SW3, SW10

Aubergine

*11 Park Walk, SW10 0AJ (7352 3449). Bus 14,
345, 414.* **Lunch served** noon-2.15pm Mon-
Fri. **Dinner served** 7-11pm Mon-Sat. **Set lunch**
£34 3 courses incl half bottle of wine, mineral
water, coffee. **Set dinner** £60 3 courses, £74
7 courses. **Service** 12.5%. **Credit** AmEx, DC,
JCB, MC, V.
Changes and improvements have sneaked in since
our last review. Complicated-sounding dishes are
now simply described by listing a few key elements:
duck with prunes and Madeira jus, for example,
ham hock in jelly with mustard mayonnaise, or
chocolate tart with bottled cherries. But don't think
fewer words on the page equates to less interest on
the plate – far from it. Asking questions will reveal
how carefully ingredients are sourced. Lunch is
exceptional value given the high-quality service,
lovely wine choices, coffee and petits fours thrown
in, and the overall generosity. Germini of lobster
was a fragrant, flavoursome and creamy shellfish
soup with neatly diced lobster claw, potato, peas
and mint. It paired well with the white burgundy
of the day. There followed a great example of what
Aubergine does best: classic French dishes that
should never have gone out of fashion. Blanquette
de veau, or white veal stew (no need to be
squeamish about this byproduct of British dairy
farming) was gently casseroled in a pale silky
sauce flavoured with silverskin onions and served
with baby spring vegetables and creamed potato.
It was hot, savoury, succulent, sexy and completely
fulfilling. Choice is plentiful, even on the set lunch,
and will include some of William Drabble's
favourite offal and game. Come here to remind
yourself how satisfying classic, well-cooked food
and excellent service is.
*Babies and children admitted. Booking advisable;
essential weekends. Dress: smart casual. No pipes
or cigars. No-smoking tables.* **Map 14 D12.**

BEST LUNCH DEALS

View the bill at the restaurants here
as you would at your local pizza place;
the menu might say a margherita
costs £6.95, but you don't expect
the final bill to be just shy of seven
quid. You know that once you've
added a couple of glasses of wine,
coffee and service, it will be closer to
£15. Ditto these lunch menus, where
the actual cost can easily double per
head. However, they're our favourites
this year, and to any food lover they
represent money very well spent.

Allium
£17.50 2 courses,
£22.50 3 courses. *See p129.*

Aubergine
£34 3 courses including half bottle of
wine, mineral water, coffee. *See below.*

Bonds
£20 2 courses,
£25 3 courses. *See p125.*

The Crescent
£21 2 courses, £26 3 courses, both
including half bottle of wine. *See p127.*

Foliage
£25 3 courses
(£32 including wine).*See p126.*

Mju
£17.50 2 courses. *See p126.*

Pearl Bar & Restaurant
£23.50 2 courses,
£26.50 3 courses. *See p126.*

Gordon Ramsay

*68-69 Royal Hospital Road, SW3 4HP (7352
4441/3334/www.gordonramsay.com). Sloane
Square tube.* **Lunch served** noon-2pm, **dinner**
served 6.30-11pm Mon-Fri. **Set lunch** £35
3 courses. **Set meal** £65 3 courses, £80
7 courses. **Credit** AmEx, DC, JCB, MC, V.
After Claridge's (*see p128*) couldn't find us a
remotely convenient table for weeks, we knew that
making a booking at Ramsay's premier restaurant
would be equally troublesome. A dull, preachy voice
on the reservations line droned that there was no
table available when we wanted one and that we
would have to book one month in advance, to the
day. When we asked for any table in the foreseeable
future, she maddeningly answered they weren't
taking bookings because in one month's time it
would be a Sunday and therefore the restaurant
would be closed. We finally secured a Monday
lunchtime spot. Winning the lottery is easier. As
usual, though, we were bowled over by the
experience on the day, and found that the three-
course set lunch menu had perked up considerably,
making GR's now a viable option for those of us not
yet millionaires. Of note too were a few 'Fat Duck-
alike' touches: a mini Martini glass appetiser of
potato and chive salad, baked potato jelly (served
cold), horseradish mousse and langoustine tails.
Such cooking also crept into one of the set lunch
desserts in the shape of pear tarte tatin with brave
gorgonzola ice-cream and walnut foam. Main
courses were generous, faultless and had the wide
appeal of roasted Welsh lamb or novelty value of
braised Gloucester Old Spot pig's cheeks. We're not
saying that the booking system isn't a complete pain
– or the waiters aren't still patronising with their
interminable descriptions of dishes, and checking
that we knew what beef carpaccio was – but you
can expect just reward for your perseverance.
*Booking essential. Children admitted. Dress:
smart. No smoking.* **Map 14 F12.**

Gloucester Road SW7

1880

*The Bentley Hotel, Harrington Gardens, SW7 4JX
(7244 5555/www.thebentley-hotel.com). Gloucester
Road tube.* **Dinner served** 6-10pm Mon-Sat.
Set dinner £45 3 courses; £48-£60 5-10 courses.
Credit AmEx, DC, MC, V.
From the look of them, the Bentley's residents all go
shopping at Chanel during the day. In the evening,
when they arrive dressed up to the nines, there's a
whole lot of bling going on: in both the outfits and
the restaurant's own decor. The room seems to have
sunk into the basement under the sheer weight of
its sculpted carpets, gilt-edged mirrors, two-tone
marble and opulent light fittings. With the
razzmatazz to match, chef Andrew Turner offers us
(via some nattily turned out and word-perfect front
men) a flight of menus and accompanying wines
designed to impress the socks off you with their
plethora of ingredients, preparations and saucings.
Fairly enough, portions are small on the tasting
menus, but the process of describing each course
takes too long, leaving food cool or melted by the
time you grab your eating irons. So we chose from
the standard carte (which mostly contains larger
versions of the tasting menu dishes). A few
gustatory niceties were overshadowed by poor
timing, resulting in one meal arriving at table
several minutes before the second (the garnish of
which arrived separately after another five
minutes). Desserts were disastrous. A quadruplet of
crème brûlées failed to hit any of the right spots,
with barely glazed tops and ill-matched flavours.
Lemon tart fared even worse: the pastry too soft, the
filling shrunken and mouth-furringly acidic; no
relief was given by a sharp berry ripple sorbet. We
mentioned to staff the bad timing of the main
courses, but our complaint was ignored, no apology
was offered and nothing taken off the bill.
*Booking advisable. Disabled: toilet. Dress: smart
casual; no trainers. No smoking. Vegetarian menu.*
Map 13 C10.

South Kensington SW3

Tom Aikens

*43 Elystan Street, SW3 3NT (7584 2003/
www.tomaikens.co.uk). South Kensington tube.*
Lunch served noon-2.30pm, **dinner served**
7-11pm Mon-Fri. **Set lunch** £29 3 courses.
Set meal £60 3 courses, £75 7 courses.
Service 12.5%. **Credit** AmEx, JCB, MC, V.
If the contemporary restaurant's aim is to soothe
the eye and shock the palate, then Tom Aikens is
up there with the best of them. Sleek and severely
pared down, the L-shaped room packs in tables,
eschews daylight behind secretive screens, and
allows vapid green charger plates barely a
moment's limelight against their backdrop of stark
white linen and sombre walnut veneer. What colour
there is comes in edible form, boldly going where
no foam, juice and jelly has ever gone before and
showcasing exotic fruits and seasonal vegetables.
One particularly novel starter was a vast plateful
of shimmering viscidity, which looked like
something from *Dr Who*, but in reality was just
three poached oysters under a wobbly pillow of
cucumber and lemon mousse and gewürztraminer
jelly, flanked by splashes of green and white
vegetable purée. Almost equally nonconformist
was cured red mullet surrounded by a carnival of
red and orange root vegetables, squiggles of orange
sauce and fabulously meaty mushrooms. A main
course simply titled 'piglet' on the menu could have
been called 'squidlet', given that more squid than
pig was involved. Light squid tempura
complemented two dinky pig cutlets, which in turn
rested on a sweet and hearty shredded pork raviolo.
Veal sweetbreads were given similar treatment: hot
and crisply battered and sitting astride veal belly,
braised and encased in fine pasta and served with
rosemary polenta 'chips'. Airy-fairy puddings such
as coconut foam with poached lychee and
pomegranate jelly round off a dramatic eating
experience that's not for the fainthearted.
*Babies and children admitted. Booking essential
dinner. Disabled: toilet. Dress: smart casual.
No smoking. Vegetarian menu.* **Map 14 E11.**

Indian

North Indian curries still form the mainstay of most local 'Indian' restaurants in the capital (the majority of which are Bangladeshi-run), yet now it's easier to get an authentic roghan gosht or biriani, where spices have been mixed and ground in-house and meat has been simmered to tenderness. And London has now discovered the glorious variety to be found in regional specialities from across the subcontinent (including Pakistan, Bangladesh, Nepal and Sri Lanka, as well as the modern state of India). Today we can dip into such gems as creamy coconut broths from Kerala, tamarind-infused Gujarati lentils and Mumbai beach snacks, not to mention first-rate Pakistani tandoori food, Bangladeshi fish dishes and fiery curries and relishes from Sri Lanka.

The heightening of standards at London's Indian restaurants owes much to the British government's relaxation of visa restrictions for trained chefs. As Iqbal Wahhab, former owner of the **Cinnamon Club**, points out: 'The improvement seen in restaurants has come primarily from more talent arriving from India, and restaurants employing more chefs trained by catering colleges and five-star hotels. Restaurateurs have also invested more in their businesses and this too has reaped significant rewards.'

The past year has seen an expansion of smart café and restaurant chains serving affordable cooking without compromising on quality. A tasty meal at any one of **Masala Zone**'s three-strong chain won't set you back much more then a well-spent tenner. Not all the chains are home-grown either. Delhi's long-standing restaurant group **Moti Mahal** was about to open a branch in Covent Garden as we went to press (45 Great Queen Street, WC2B 5AA, 7240 9329), and plans are also afoot for a London outlet of Indian Bollywood singer Asha Bhosle's successful Dubai-based chain, called Asha's.

London is the world leader in spotlighting the culinary diversity of the subcontinent. No other city has such a wealth of Indian fine-dining destinations – among them Knightsbridge newcomer **Amaya**, nominated for Best New Restaurant in the 2005 *Time Out* Awards – while at the same time celebrating the earthy appeal of homely community caffs like the **New Asian Tandoori Centre (Roxy)**, **Five Hot Chillies** and **Apollo Banana Leaf**. Wembley arrival **Dadima**, the revamped Chiswick branch of **Woodlands** and Gujarati specialist **Kathiyawadi** (also up for an award, for Best Vegetarian Meal) are worth highlighting too.

Central
Belgravia SW1

Salloos
62-64 Kinnerton Street, SW1X 8ER (7235 4444). Hyde Park Corner or Knightsbridge tube. **Lunch served** noon-2.15pm, **dinner served** 7-11.15pm Mon-Sat. **Main courses** £10.90-£14.90. **Set lunch** £12 2 courses, £16 3 courses. **Service** 12.5%. **Credit** AmEx, DC, MC, V. Pakistani
This Pakistani stalwart has a club-like charm, boosted by the restrained bonhomie that flourishes between the regular clientele and Salloos' long-standing service team. The restaurant occupies a first floor, above a sleepy Belgravia backstreet. It's a popular destination for civil servants, Pakistani bureaucrats and wealthy local residents. Islamic grilles on windows, heavy white tablecloths and the hum of genteel conversation add to the Raj-style atmosphere. Top billing goes to the mouth-watering tandoori lamb chops. Succulent and delectably charred on the surface, ours had the perfect degree of pinkness inside, but what really scored was the superlative marinade of ginger and thick yoghurt. Lamb gosht, with its tender meat chunks, was also a winner; we particularly liked the smooth-as-silk ground onion masala, topped with ginger shreds. Nans are among the best in town: light and fluffy, even at the edges. In contrast, vegetable dishes don't usually deliver the goods, tending to be overcooked and lacklustre. Meat-eaters, however, are in for a treat.
Booking advisable. Children over 8 years admitted. Dress: smart casual. Takeaway service. **Map 9 G9.**

Fitzrovia W1
★ **Indian YMCA**
41 Fitzroy Square, W1T 6AQ (7387 0411/ www.indianymca.org). Great Portland Street or Warren Street tube. **Lunch served** noon-2pm Mon-Fri; 12.30-1.30pm Sat, Sun. **Dinner served** 7-8.30pm daily. **Main courses** £2-£5. **Credit** AmEx, JCB, MC, V. Pan-Indian
There's a corner of Fitzroy Square that remains forever India. Housed in a nondescript concrete block, the YMCA offers great-value meals to a multicultural mix of office workers, students and medical staff. The staff, kitted out in dapper spotless white tunics, add a touch of class and quirkiness to this loveable institution. Expect school-style tables, a self-service counter and all the charm of a conference hall. Get here soon after noon for the best pickings. You'll find a small selection of staples, meat and vegetarian curries, plus fried munchies. Our favourite has to be the fish curry – weighty hunks of white fish, simmered in smooth tomato, tamarind and curry leaf masala. It takes some beating. Another highlight is the ginger and cumin spicing in the Punjabi vegetarian classics; the green beans cooked with turmeric-coated potatoes are particularly delicious. Fried snacks can be iffy: bullet-like vadas (fried white lentil dumplings) and bouncy bhajis aren't for the faint-hearted. In the evenings, there's a prepaid set dinner menu worth dropping in for.
Babies and children welcome: high chairs. No smoking. Separate rooms for parties, seating 30 and 200. Takeaway service. Vegetarian menu. **Map 3 J4.**

★ **Rasa Samudra**
5 Charlotte Street, W1T 1RE (7637 0222/ www.rasarestaurants.com). Goodge Street tube. **Lunch served** noon-3pm Mon-Sat. **Dinner served** 6-10.45pm daily. **Main courses** £6.25-£12.95. **Set meal** £22.50 (vegetarian), £30 (seafood). **Service** 12.5%. **Credit** AmEx, JCB, MC, V. South Indian
Rasa's cochineal-pink frontage might seem more attuned to a sweet shop than a Keralite seafood restaurant, but everything else about the place is true to tradition. The flagship restaurant of a five-strong chain, this is a choice destination for adventurous, deep-pocketed diners. It is spread over two levels, dotted with South Indian statues and artefacts; we prefer the first floor for its lighter, more spacious feel. Our samudra rasam (seafood and black pepper broth) was the catch of the day, studded with crab flakes and perfectly cooked prawns; we loved the gentle turmeric spicing of soupy simmered lentils and creamy coconut milk. Crab varuthathu was another corker: peppery stir-fried crab pieces, in their shell, combined with explosive mustard seeds, crisp-fried chillies and a glorious tangle of squidgy onions. Roll up your sleeves and use the crab cleavers provided by the ever-helpful staff. Vegetarian specials included a delicious leafy green thoran: stir-fried cabbage, seasoned with curry leaves and topped with a shower of coconut shreds. A marvellous meal of memorable Keralite flavours.
Babies and children welcome: high chairs. Booking advisable. No-smoking tables. Separate rooms for parties, seating 15, 20 and 40. Takeaway service. Vegetarian menu. **Map 9 J5.**
For branches see index.

Knightsbridge SW1

★ **Amaya** NEW
2005 RUNNER-UP BEST NEW RESTAURANT
Halkin Arcade, SW1X 8JT (7823 1166/ www.realindianfood.com). Knightsbridge tube. **Lunch served** 12.30-2.15pm Mon-Fri; 12.30-2.30pm Sat; 12.45-2.45pm Sun. **Dinner served** 6.30-11.15pm Mon-Sat; 6.30-10.15pm Sun. **Main courses** £8.50-£25. **Credit** AmEx, DC, JCB, MC, V. Modern Indian
Amaya is one of the best of London's top-end Indian restaurants. Swish with its gorgeous interior of terracotta statues, dark wood fittings, flickering

candles and glimmering chandeliers, it's the acclaimed new venture from the Panjabi sisters (of Chutney Mary fame – *see p139* – among other restaurants). It specialises in kebabs; they're cooked either in a tandoor (clay oven), sigri (charcoal grill) or tawa (cast-iron griddle). We adored dori kebab (a Lucknowi classic made with spiced lamb), which resembles a smooth, skinless sausage, de-threaded at table. Also surprisingly good are the stuffed tinda: tomato-sized squashes stuffed with halloumi then griddle-fried. Hamour (a grouper from the Arabian Sea) was our favourite, served on a skewer with an amazing marinade of mustard, chilli and peanut. Make sure you try the sublime desserts, such as plum compote with chilli custard and rose sorbet. Recent awards have set up Amaya for a fall: not everyone likes the way 'celebrity' guests get the best tables, for example, and noisy acoustics and large round tables mean this isn't the most romantic venue. But there's no doubt that Amaya is doing for Indian food what Nobu did for Japanese – namely making it cool, even fashionable.
Babies and children admitted. Booking advisable. Disabled: toilet. Dress: smart casual. No-smoking tables. Separate room for parties, seats 14. **Map 9 9G.**

Marble Arch W1

Chai Pani

64 Seymour Street, W1H 5BW (7258 2000/ www.chaipani.co.uk). Marble Arch tube. **Lunch served** noon-2.30pm Mon-Fri; noon-4.30pm Sat, Sun. **Dinner served** 6-10.30pm daily. **Main courses** £5-£7. **Set buffet** (lunch Mon-Fri) £6. **Thalis** £8-£20. **Credit** AmEx, JCB, MC, V. Rajasthani vegetarian

Rajasthani cooking now frequently features in food festivals held in London's Indian restaurants – but this is the only venue specialising in the cuisine of the Marwaris, a merchant community of the Shekhawati region in Rajasthan (a desert area in north-west India). It's a curious place, full of contradictions: the dining room is smart and elegant, yet rustic and homely (filled with Rajasthani knick-knacks like peacock feathers, soft drapes, puppets and ornaments); the service is both businesslike and amateurish; and the menu contains dishes ranging from exciting to mundane. Dishes we enjoyed: kanji vada (deep-fried savoury lentil doughnuts soaked in a thin spicy gravy), kuttoo (potato slices fried in buckwheat flour) and ker sangri (stir-fried cluster beans with wild baby melon). Less successful were aam ki launji (green mangoes in sweet and sour sauce – too sweet and too sour) and an insipid rabri (millet and yoghurt soup). Rajasthani food is renowned for its spiciness, but the flavours here are mild and timid overall. Nevertheless, Chai Pani is worth a visit if you're curious about this little-known cuisine.
Babies and children welcome: high chairs. Booking advisable weekends. Disabled: toilet. Takeaway service. Vegan dishes. Vegetarian menu. **Map 8 F6.**

Deya

34 Portman Square, W1H 7BH (7224 0028/ www.deya-restaurant.co.uk). Bond Street or Marble Arch tube. **Lunch served** noon-2.45pm Mon-Fri. **Dinner served** 6.30-10.45pm Mon-Sat. **Main courses** £9.50-£14.50. **Set lunch** £14.95 2 courses. **Set meal** £22-£40 5 courses. **Service** 12.5%. **Credit** AmEx, JCB, MC, V. Modern Indian

A strikingly colourful mural – like an enlarged version of an Indian miniature painting – lends vibrancy to what is otherwise a rather staid but spacious venue with huge picture windows, funky chandeliers, and elegant bucket chairs arranged around tables covered in crisp white linen. Deya's menu is a more conventional, more health-conscious version than that at Zaika (*see p139*), which is under the same ownership. Goat's cheese samosa was similar to (but not a patch on) those at Zaika. Grilled sea bass marinated in garlic and chilli featured fleshy, flavoursome fish, but the flavours didn't marry well with the accompanying uppama (savoury semolina), and coconut and curry leaf sauce. Wild mushroom biriani with a flaky pastry lid lacked the magic of Zaika's take on this dish, but the accompanying pomegranate raita added a touch of welcome luxury. Chicken pieces cooked in fennel, cardamom and chilli sauce would have been tasty, had it not been for the tough, gristly chicken. Deya (which means 'lamp') fails to light up the Indian fine-dining scene. In fact, this restaurant, which is co-owned by Michael Caine, left us wondering 'what's it all about?'
Babies and children welcome: high chairs. Booking advisable. Dress: smart casual. Vegetarian menu. **Map 9 G6.**

Mayfair W1

Benares

12A Berkeley Square House, Berkeley Square, W1J 6BS (7629 8886/www.benaresrestaurant. com). Green Park tube. **Lunch served** noon-2.30pm Mon-Fri. **Dinner served** 5.30-10.30pm Mon-Sat; 6-10pm Sun. **Main courses** £15-£22.

Pan-Indian menu

Spellings of Indian dishes vary widely; dishes such as gosht may appear in several versions on different menus as the word is transliterated from (in this case) Hindi. There are umpteen languages and several scripts in the Indian subcontinent, the most commonly seen on London menus being Punjabi, Hindi, Bengali and Gujarati. For the sake of consistency, however, we have tried to adhere to uniform spellings. The following are common throughout the subcontinent.

Aloo: potato.
Ayre: a white fish much used in Bengali cuisine.
Baingan: aubergine.
Balti: West Midlands cooking term for karahi cooking (qv, North Indian menu), which became all the rage a decade ago. Unfortunately, many inferior curry houses now apply the name to dishes that bear little resemblance to real karahi-cooked dishes.
Bateira, batera or **bater**: quail.
Bengali: Bengal, before Partition in 1947, was a large province covering Calcutta (now in India's West Bengal) and modern-day Bangladesh. 'Bengali' and 'Bangladeshi' cooking is quite different, and the term 'Bengali' is often misused in London's Indian restaurants.
Bhajia or **bhaji**: vegetables dipped in chickpea flour batter and deep-fried; also called pakoras.
Bhajee: vegetables cooked with spices, usually 'dry' rather than sauced.
Bhindi: okra.
Brinjal: aubergine.

Bulchao or **balchao**: a Goan vinegary pickle made with small dried prawns (with shells) and lots of garlic.
Chana or **channa**: chickpeas.
Chapati: a flat wholewheat griddle bread.
Chat or **chaat**: various savoury snacks featuring combinations of pooris (qv), diced onion and potato, chickpeas, crumbled samosas and pakoras, chutneys and spices.
Dahi: yoghurt.
Dahl or **dal**: a lentil curry similar to thick lentil soup. Countless regional variations exist.
Dhansak: a Parsi (qv) casserole of meat, lentils and vegetables, with a mix of hot and tangy flavours.
Dhaniya: coriander.
Ghee: clarified butter used for frying.
Gobi: cauliflower.
Gosht, josh or **ghosh**: meat, usually lamb.
Gram flour: chickpea flour.
Kachori: crisp pastry rounds with spiced mung dahl or pea filling.
Kadhi or **khadi**: yoghurt and chickpea flour curry.
Lassi: a yoghurt drink, ordered with salt or sugar, sometimes with fruit. Ideal to quench a fiery palate.
Machi or **machli**: fish.
Masala or **masaladar**: mixed spices.
Methi: fenugreek, either dried (seeds) or fresh (green leaves).
Murgh or **murg**: chicken.
Mutter, muter or **mattar**: peas.
Nan or **naan**: teardrop-shaped flatbread cooked in a tandoor (qv, North Indian menu).
Palak or **paalak**: spinach; also called saag.

Paan or **pan**: betel leaf stuffed with chopped 'betel nuts', coconut and spices such as fennel seeds, and folded into a triangle. Available sweet or salty, and eaten at the end of a meal as a digestive.
Paneer or **panir**: Indian cheese, a bit like tofu in texture and taste.
Paratha: a large griddle-fried bread that is sometimes stuffed (with spicy mashed potato or minced lamb, for instance).
Parsi or **Parsee**: a religious minority based in Mumbai, but originally from Persia, renowned for its cooking.
Pilau, pillau or **pullao**: flavoured rice cooked with meat or vegetables. In most British Indian restaurants, pilau rice is simply rice flavoured and coloured with turmeric or (rarely) saffron.
Poori or **puri**: a disc of deep-fried wholewheat bread; the frying makes it puff up like an air-filled cushion.

Set lunch £14.95 2 courses. **Set dinner** £52 tasting menu. **Service** 12.5%. **Credlt** AmEx, DC, MC, V. Modern Indian

The luxurious Benares exudes rarefied style, epitomised by the seductively lit, shiny black granite bar area. Decorations include impressive flower-filled water tanks and a rich assortment of colonial-style wooden furniture. Unsurprisingly, this is popular with the silk and chiffon set, also attracting plenty of sharp suits on expense accounts. Chef-patron Atul Kochhar makes a mean pot of lentils, and our gold star goes to the delectable makhani dahl – simmered black lentils, enriched with cream, tomatoes and dollops of butter. A main course of perfectly cooked, griddle-fried dover sole fillet spoke volumes for tasteful simplicity. We also appreciated the accompaniment of buttery, cumin-scented mashed potatoes, sharpened with the tang of tamarind – a subtle match for the plainly cooked fish. In contrast, a starter of jal tarang (seafood fritters with grapes, dressed in ginger and lemon juice) was poor: dense batter masked the delicate mussels, and a heavy scattering of toasted nigella and sesame seeds lent bitterness. Equally disappointing, lamb biriani had an overpowering floral aroma and lacklustre spicing. Chaotic service was yet another letdown. So, on this occasion, Benares failed to live up to expectations.
Booking advisable dinner weekends. Dress: smart casual. No smoking. Restaurant available for hire. Separate rooms for parties, seating 8, 16 and 20. Vegetarian menu. **Map 9 H7.**

★ Tamarind
20 Queen Street, W1J 5PR (7629 3561/ www.tamarindrestaurant.com). Green Park tube. **Lunch served** noon-3pm Mon-Fri; noon-2.30pm

Popadom, poppadom, papadum or **papad:** large thin wafers made with lentil paste, and flavoured with pepper, garlic or chilli. Eaten in the UK with pickles and relishes as a starter while waiting for the meal to arrive.
Raita: a yoghurt mix, usually with cucumber.
Roti: a round, sometimes unleavened, bread; thicker than a chapati and cooked in a tandoor or griddle. Roomali roti (literally 'handkerchief bread') is a very thin, soft disc of roti.
Saag or **sag:** spinach; also called palak.
Tamarind: the pods of this East African tree, grown in India, are made into a paste that imparts a sour, fruity taste – popular in some regional cuisines, including Gujarati and South Indian.
Thali: literally 'metal plate'. A large plate with rice, bread, containers of dahl and vegetable curries, pickles and yoghurt relishes.
Vadai or **wada:** a spicy vegetable or lentil fritter; dahi wada are lentil fritters soaked in yoghurt, topped with tamarind and date chutneys.
Vindaloo: originally, a hot and spicy pork curry from Goa that should authentically be soured with vinegar and cooked with garlic. In London restaurants, the term is usually misused to signify simply very hot dishes.
Xacuti: a Goan dish made with lamb or chicken pieces, coconut and a complex mix of roasted then ground spices.

Sun. **Dinner served** 6-11.30pm Mon-Sat; 6-10.30pm Sun. **Main courses** £14.50-£26. Set lunch £16.95 2 courses, £18.95 3 courses. **Set meal** (6-7pm) £22.50 2 courses. **Service** 12.5%. **Credit** AmEx, DC, MC, V. North Indian

This classy, sumptuous, subterranean restaurant specialises in Mogul tandoori cuisine from north-west India, and is currently the only Michelin-starred Indian restaurant in the UK. Head chef Alfred Prasad's cooking is cautious rather than flamboyant, leaving the theatrics to the kebab chefs in the open-view kitchen. Peshawari champen were exquisite: lamb chops tenderised with green papaya, and marinated in garlic, ginger, paprika, peppercorns, nutmeg, coriander and star anise. The flavour was like an explosion of fireworks in the mouth, and the meat was falling off the fork. A scrumptious mixed vegetable chat comprising light lentil dumplings, chickpeas and batter-fried baby spinach came drizzled with lovely mint and blackcurrant-yoghurt chutneys. Pan-fried sea bass was juxtaposed with spicy coconut and red chilli sauce and crispy spinach; the flavours worked very well together. Roomali roti was silky-smooth and feather-light, just as it should be. The only disappointments were paneer makhani – the addition of black cherries made this classic dish too sweet, and the fresh fenugreek and tomato sauce lacked personality – and a nan stuffed with date and almonds, which would probably work better as a dessert. Slick, superb service helps make this a highly enjoyable dining experience. A branch called Imli is planned for Soho in autumn 2005.
Babies and children welcome (over 2 years): high chair. Booking advisable; essential dinner. Dress: smart casual. No-smoking tables. Restaurant available for hire. Takeaway service; delivery service (within 1-mile radius). **Map 9 H7.**

Yatra
34 Dover Street, W1S 4NF (7493 0200/ www.barbollywood.net). Green Park tube. **Lunch served** noon-3pm Mon-Fri. **Dinner served** 6.30-11pm Mon-Wed; 6-11.30pm Thur-Sat. **Set meal** £21.50-£24.50 2 courses. **Set buffet** (lunch Mon-Fri) £9.95. **Service** 12.5%. **Credit** AmEx, JCB, MC, V. Modern Indian

Unquestionably cool, Yatra features sleek staff, modish decor and aesthetic dish presentation. There's even a club, Bar Bollywood, in the basement. Yet we found shortcomings. The menu is now set-price; it reads well, mixing innovation (basil and mustard infused paneer and peppers, hot smoked) and tradition (roghan gosht on the bone), but we found it of uncommon rigidity. The bored waiter didn't allow us a side dish of dahl (such nonsense has now been rectified and side dishes are served). Worse, the new chef seems to have dumbed down his cooking to pander to the non-Asian expense-account clientele. Burmese lamb kebab had nothing to distinguish it from any patty you'd find at a good Punjabi pit stop. To follow, pot-roasted leg of lamb boasted tender slices of meat, but these were covered in a thick tomato-based sauce resembling the dreaded tikka masala. There's still talent here – bread and rice were impeccable, barwan aloo tikki were delicate potato cakes stuffed with cashews, over chickpeas in tamarind relish – but it's hard to justify the prices and the 12.5% service charge.
Babies and children admitted. Booking advisable. Disabled: toilet. Entertainment: DJs Fri, Sat (Bar Bollywood). Restaurant available for hire. Separate room for parties, seats 50. **Map 9 H7.**

Paddington W2

Jamuna NEW
38A Southwick Street, W2 1JQ (7723 5056/ www.jamuna.co.uk). Edgware Road tube/ Paddington tube/rail. **Lunch served** noon-2.30pm, **dinner served** 6-11pm daily. **Main courses** £11-£27. **Service** 12.5%. **Credit** AmEx, DC, MC, V. North Indian

Tucked down a sidestreet off Edgware Road, this smart new restaurant is worth tracking down for its food. Ragada patties (a popular Mumbai street snack, this version containing potato and paneer,

topped with white marrow-fat pea stew and tamarind sauce) were sensational – the presentation cried out 'Modern Indian', but the authentic flavours carried real street cred. There's a lot of fish on the menu, including black cod, halibut and sea bass; our monkfish tikka marinated in fresh mint and coriander was pleasingly light. Lamb shank sikandari was a huge chunk of meltingly tender lamb in a mustard-spiked gravy. Side dishes are variable: saag paneer and mixed vegetable curry were good, but goda batata lacked authentic Maharashtrian spicing (goda masala) and was more like the curry house staple, 'bombay aloo'. The dining room and the basement bar, decorated with cream paintwork and blond wood furniture, are easy on the eye. The major drawback was the service. The owner kept interrogating us about how we had heard of the restaurant, wanted feedback on each dish, and seemed too keen to join in our conversation.
Babies and children admitted. Booking advisable Mon-Thur. No-smoking tables. Separate room for parties, seats 25. **Map 8 E5.**

St James's SW1

Quilon
41 Buckingham Gate, SW1E 6AF (7821 1899/ www.thequilonrestaurant.com). St James's Park tube. **Lunch served** noon-2.30pm Mon-Fri. **Dinner served** 6-11pm Mon-Sat. **Main courses** £8.50-£23. **Set lunch** £12.95 2 courses, £15.95 3 courses. **Service** 12.5%. **Credit** AmEx, DC, MC, V. South Indian

Swish Quilon (named after the Keralite backwaters trading town) is part of Taj Hotel Group's St James's Court Hotel. As such it has highly talented chefs at its disposal, yet also attracts business diners and perma-tanned tourists with bouffants (no Indians on a midweek evening). We've found the food to pull its punches; if you want South Indian heat, you must ask the smart, plentiful staff – one Nepali, one Punjabi, one English on our visit. Even the complimentary rasam lacked pepperiness. The menu is mostly South Indian. We'd recommend avoiding North Indian dishes if our lamb shank (a pricey £18) was typical: overcooked to stringiness, it came in a sauce of

Amaya. See p131.

undistinguished tomato paste. Best was the fish. Both the starter of cochin mixed seafood broth (cockles, mussels, squid and prawn, all taut and tender) and the keralan fish curry (exquisitely cooked white halibut and snapper) were beyond reproach. Good too was the intense Grover Vineyards wine from Bangalore. And though the large L-shaped dining room is unmistakably hotel-lounge plush, murals of South Indian life humanise it. Still, 'Keralite lite' sums up Quilon these days.
Babies and children welcome: high chairs. Booking advisable. No smoking. Takeaway service. Vegetarian menu. **Map 15 J9.**

Soho W1

Chowki

2-3 Denman Street, W1D 7HA (7439 1330/ www.chowki.com). Piccadilly Circus tube. **Meals served** noon-11.30pm Mon-Sat; noon-10.30pm Sun. **Main courses** £5.95-£9.95. **Set meal** £11.95 3 courses. **Credit** AmEx, DC, MC, V. Pan-Indian
One of four London-based restaurants owned by Kuldeep Singh – the others are 3 Monkeys (*see p145*), Soho Spice and Mela – Chowki stands out from the others because of its changing monthly menu: three different styles of regional cooking every month. Don't be put off by its gloomy appearance; an abundance of dark wood, regimented rows of red leatherette stools, and industrial piping across the ceiling do it few favours. No matter: customers, mainly small office groups, tourists and nostalgic Asians, come here for affordable, authentically prepared meals, overseen by attentive staff. On our visit, flavours of the month were from Rajasthan, Mangalore and Kashmir. We adored the mackerel fillets, simmered in a broth-like curry, seasoned with toasted coriander seeds, zesty cardamom and warming black peppercorns, though starters of dense-textured banana dumplings dunked in yoghurt were as unyielding as golf balls. But we soon forgot this hiccup after dipping into a deliciously pungent rajasthani lamb curry, laced with ginger and fennel seeds. Chowki is one of the few spots where you can happily taste your way around India without leaving the comfort zone of W1.
Babies and children welcome: high chairs. Booking advisable. Disabled: toilet. Vegetarian menu. **Map 17 K7.**

★ Masala Zone

9 Marshall Street, W1F 7ER (7287 9966/ www.realindianfood.com). Oxford Circus tube. **Lunch served** noon-3pm Mon-Fri; 12.30-3.30pm Sun. **Dinner served** 5.30-11pm Mon-Fri; 6-10.30pm Sun. **Meals served** 12.30-11pm Sat. **Main courses** £5.50-£7.45. **Thalis** £7-£11.55. **Service** 10%. **Credit** MC, V. Pan-Indian
In addition to running the Masala Zone mini chain, the Panjabi sisters also own upmarket restaurants Amaya (*see p131*) and Chutney Mary (*see p139*). A stomping ground for young office types on a limited budget, this café does chic on the cheap. Affable staff deliver meals in a jiffy. We loved our pau bhaji starters: a hearty Mumbai snack of soft, buttered rolls, served with mashed gingery potatoes, flecked with tomatoes and softened root vegetables. Mains weren't quite as memorable. Roghan josh (a Kashmiri lamb curry) didn't get accolades for authenticity, but it did score points for its smooth onion masala and meltingly tender lamb chunks. Butter chicken was poor, though, swimming in a moat of sweet tomato sauce that had much in common with tinned tomato soup. Yet despite occasional gripes, we reckon the Zone is good value for money.
Babies and children welcome: high chairs. Bookings not accepted. No smoking. Separate area for parties, seats 40. Takeaway service. **Map 17 J6. For branch see index.**

★ Red Fort

77 Dean Street, W1D 3SH (7437 2115/ www.redfort.co.uk). Tottenham Court Road or Leicester Square tube. **Lunch served** noon-2.15pm Mon-Fri. **Dinner served** 5.45-11pm

Chutney Mary

London's most beautiful and romantic Indian restaurant with refined gourmet cooking. Open daily for dinner and on Saturday and Sunday for lunch. Private salon seating 24 for lunch and dinner everyday.

535 Kings Road, Chelsea, London SW10. Tel: 020 7351 3113

Amaya

The ultimate Indian grill with lighter food. Luxurious interiors and chic cocktails. In fashionable Knightsbridge. Private salon seats 14.

Halkin Arcade, Motcomb Street, Knightsbridge, London SW1. Tel: 020 7823 1166

London's finest Indian restaurants.

From gourmet to everyday.

Veeraswamy

Established in 1926, celebrating its 80th anniversary as the oldest Indian restaurant in the UK. We are undergoing a transformation and reopening at the end of October 2005.

Mezzanine Floor, Victory House, 99 Regent Street, London W1 (entrance on Swallow Street). Tel: 020 7734 1401

Masala Zone

Delicious street foods and traditional home style cooking in a lively atmosphere. No reservations required.

Marshall Street, Soho, London W1. Tel: 020 7287 9966
80 Upper Street, Islington, London N1. Tel: 020 7359 3399
147 Earls Court Road, London SW5. Tel: 020 7373 0220

Mon-Sat; 5.30-10pm Sun. **Main courses** £12.50-£20. **Set lunch** £12 2 courses. **Set meal** (5.45-7pm) £16 3 courses incl tea or coffee. **Service** 12.5%. **Credit** AmEx, MC, V. North Indian
Popular with local media babes, Red Fort is beautiful to behold. Its Jaipuri red sandstone walls with Mogul alcoves are supposedly modelled on Lal Quila, the Red Fort in Delhi. Walls are festooned with Indian art, the floors are mosaic, the lighting is subtle, and there's an attractive water feature based on Mogul design, filled with floating marigolds. The basement Bar Akbar – a pretty spot with stone floors, colourful rugs, leather armchairs and charming bar staff – serves Indian-style cocktails. In the ground-floor restaurant, we kicked off with tandoori fruit chat: green bananas, avocados, guavas and sweet potatoes have never tasted more appetising. Very fresh, gently spiced prawns, clothed in crisp, tempura-like batter, were light and delectable. A main-course vegetable biriani, though, was devoid of the complexity and flamboyance of the real thing, like pilau rice in Sunday clothes. Dum ki bater (quail in a creamy yoghurt, almond and cashew nut sauce) was more convincing, and a stir-fry of okra and green mango was superb. Red Fort showcases the Avadhi cuisine of Lucknow, so the spicing is subtle, and flavours rich and regal.
Babies and children admitted. Booking advisable. Disabled: toilet. Dress: smart casual. Entertainment: DJ 8pm Thur-Sat (bar). Vegan dishes. Vegetarian menu. **Map 17 K6**.

Strand WC2

★ India Club
Second floor, Strand Continental Hotel, 143 Strand, WC2R 1JA (7836 0650). Temple, Covent Garden or Embankment tube/Charing Cross tube/rail. **Lunch served** noon-2.30pm, **dinner served** 6-10.50pm daily. **Main courses** £3.50-£7.80. **Set meal** £12-£15 4 courses (minimum 2). **Unlicensed. Corkage** no charge. **No credit cards.** Pan-Indian
High-quality photos of Punjabi life (for sale) now adorn this cherished second-floor dining room. Only one dusty portrait of an Indian worthy remains: saved, we hope, by the admirable length of his beard. Walls are now a cheerful yellow, but the worn red lino, stackable metal-framed chairs and wood-veneer tables have seen decades of service; the Club has notched up over half a century. Staff are civil gents in white tunics, patient beyond reason with a table of guffawing nitwits on our visit. Sadly, no Indians were dining on a midweek evening; perhaps more lunch here, as the High Commission is opposite. The menu is a remarkable period piece, split into veg and non-veg sections, and including such retro classics as egg curry. We found portions quite small, and haven't enjoyed the masala dosais in the past, but the keema peas and soup-like dahl were savoury treats, the breads more than passable, and the prices astonishingly low. Best, though, is the nostalgic aura (think Ealing Studios, by way of Calcutta) created by this shabby-genteel classic. Bring your own alcohol.
Babies and children admitted. Booking advisable. No-smoking tables. Takeaway service. Vegetarian menu. **Map 10 M7**.

Victoria SW1

Sekara
3 Lower Grosvenor Place, SW1W 0EJ (7834 0722/www.sekara.co.uk). Victoria tube/rail. **Lunch served** noon-3pm Mon-Sat; noon-3.30pm Sun. **Dinner served** 6-10pm daily. **Main courses** £5.95-£10.95. **Set lunch** (Mon-Sat) £4.95 1 course. **Set buffet** (Sun) £9. **Service** 10%. **Credit** AmEx, MC, V. Sri Lankan
It's likely Sekara has introduced some new set meals on to its menu. It's hard to be sure, as the list has always been lengthy and confusing: curry house chaff (in the minority), interspersed with Sri Lankan wheat. We can vouch for the quality of mutton lamprais: a good-value biriani-like meal including fried meat morsels in an attractive mound of rice, plus tender mutton curry, and a tangy-sweet aubergine number. Enjoyable too were

North Indian menu

Under the blanket term 'North Indian', we have included dishes originating in the Punjab (both in Pakistan and the modern state of India), Kashmir and all points down to Hyderabad. **Southall** (*see p154*) has some of London's best Punjabi restaurants, where breads cooked in the tandoor oven are often preferred to rice, marinated meaty kebabs are popular, and dahls are thick and buttery.

Bhuna gosht: a dry, spicy dish of lamb.
Biriani or **biryani**: a royal Moglai version of pilau rice, in which meat or vegetables cooked together with basmati rice, spices and saffron. It's difficult to find an authentic biriani in London restaurants.
Dopiaza or **do pyaza**: cooked with onions.
Dum: a Kashmiri cooking technique where food is simmered slowly in a casserole (typically a clay pot sealed with dough), allowing spices to permeate.
Gurda: kidneys.
Haandi: an earthenware or metal cooking pot, with handles on either side and a lid.
Jalfrezi: chicken or vegetable dishes cooked with fresh green chillies – a popular cooking style in Mumbai.
Jhingri, jhinga or **chingri**: prawns.
Kaleji or **kalezi**: liver.
Karahi or **karai**: a small iron or metal wok-like cooking dish. Similar to the 'balti' dish made famous in Birmingham.
Kheema or **keema**: minced lamb, as in kheema nan (stuffed nan).
Kofta: meatballs or vegetable dumplings.
Korma: braised in yoghurt and/or cream and nuts. Often mild, but rich.
Magaz: brain.
Makhani: cooked with butter (makhan) and sometimes tomatoes, as in murgh makhani.
Massalam: marinated, then casseroled chicken dish, originating in Muslim areas.

Moghul or **Mogul**: from the Moghul period of Indian history, used in the culinary sense to describe typical North Indian Muslim dishes.
Nihari or **nehari**: there are many recipes on the subcontinent for this long-simmered meat stew, using goat, beef, mutton or sometimes chicken. Hyderabadi nihari is flavoured with sandalwood powder and rose petals. North Indian nihari uses nutmeg, clove, dried ginger and tomato. In London, however, the dish is made with lamb shank (served on the bone).
Pasanda: thin fillets of lamb cut from the leg and flattened with a mallet. In British curry houses, the term usually applies to a creamy sauce virtually identical to a korma (qv).
Paya: lamb's feet, usually served on the bone as paya curry (long-cooked and with copious gravy); seldom found outside Southall.
Punjabi: Since Partition, the Punjab has been two adjoining states, one in India, one in Pakistan. Lahore is the main town on the Pakistani side, which is predominantly Muslim; Amritsar on the Indian side is the Sikh capital. Punjabi dishes tend to be thick stews or cooked in a tandoor (qv).
Roghan gosht or **rogan josh**: lamb cooked in spicy sauce, a Kashmiri speciality.
Seekh kebab: ground meat, skewered and grilled.
Tak-a-tak: a cooking method – ingredients (usually meat or vegetables) are chopped and flipped as they cook on a griddle.
Tandoor: clay oven originating in north-west India in which food is cooked without oil.
Tarka: spices and flavourings are cooked separately, then added to dahl at a final stage.
Tikka: meat, fish or paneer cut into cubes, then marinated in spicy yoghurt and baked in a tandoor (qv).

the meaty seer fish, the exceptionally light prawn kothu roti (a large portion of tagliatelle-like strips of bread mixed with prawns, spices, leek and egg), the zingy sambols (coconut and lime especially) and the creamy, calming kiri hodi. Approach the devilled dried fish with care: we were warned of its chilli-heat, but not its fierce saltiness. Sekara has a well-loved bistro feel to it, helped by kindly staff, tea-lights on tables, yellow walls sporting elaborately framed pictures, and an agreeable blend of multinational regulars. We hardly noticed the main road outside. Pity about the open credit card slip, though.
Babies and children welcome: high chairs. Booking advisable. No-smoking tables. Restaurant available for hire. Takeaway service. Vegan dishes. Vegetarian menu. **Map 15 H9**.

Westminster SW1

★ The Cinnamon Club
The Old Westminster Library, Great Smith Street, SW1P 3BU (7222 2555/www.cinnamonclub.com). St James's Park or Westminster tube. **Breakfast served** 7.30-9.30am, **lunch served** noon-2.30pm Mon-Fri. **Dinner served** 6-10.45pm Mon-Sat. **Main courses** £11-£26. **Set lunch** £19 2 courses, £22 3 courses. **Set dinner** £60 5 courses (£95 with wine). **Service** 12.5%. **Credit** AmEx, DC, JCB, MC, V. Modern Indian
Housed inside a converted 19th-century library, this elegant and spacious restaurant has a gentlemen's club feel, with a cosy lounge bar, a gallery lined with books, parquet flooring, spice-coloured banquettes and contemporary Indian art. Little wonder, then, that the Cinnamon Club is more popular with MPs and business suits than for romantic dates. Chef Vivek Singh's regularly changing menu is a show-stopper. We enjoyed the curious flavours of roast 'Oisin red deer' with a potato and fenugreek stir-fry and a piquant sauce flavoured with pickling spice. Tandoor grilled cauliflower was permeated with a delicious smokiness, and was accompanied by spicy stuffed potatoes and morel mushrooms. However, red kidney beans in tomato and onion sauce lacked the robustness of this classic Punjabi dish. Save room for desserts: spicy pineapple and tapioca payasam

Sarkhel's. See p141.

Babies and children welcome: high chairs. Booking advisable weekends. Restaurant available for hire. Separate room for parties, seats 40. Tables outdoors (2, pavement). Takeaway service. **Map 20 A4.**
For branches see index.

Hammersmith W6

★ Agni NEW

160 King Street, W6 0QU (8846 9191/ www.agnirestaurant.com). Hammersmith or Ravenscourt Park tube. **Lunch served** noon-2.30pm Mon-Fri. **Dinner served** 6-11pm Mon-Fri; 4-11pm Sat. **Meals served** noon-10.30pm Sun. **Main courses** £5.50-£8.50. **Thalis** £6.50-£9.95. **Service** 10%. **Credit** MC, V. Pan-Indian

Agni is housed in a diminutive, narrow building, enhanced by mirrors, orange-themed decor and wispy wall hangings. When busy, the ground floor gets a tad noisy – best to head upstairs for a more laid-back experience, and to watch chefs wielding skewers and tossing rotis through the glassed-in open kitchen. Chef Gowtham Karingi used to be the head honcho at Utsav (*see below*) in Kensington. Cooking styles embrace India's regional dishes – though there's more emphasis on stylised presentations than a homely vibe. No fanciful flourishes with traditional lamb biryani, though. Rich with fragrant basmati rice, gentle cardamom spicing and succulent lamb, ours was a great rendition of a classic dish from Hyderabad's royal palaces. Goan balchao – fried tilapia fillet, cloaked in chilli-ginger masala, sharpened with palm vinegar, was satisfyingly hearty. Street snacks also scored: samosas filled with a tasteful mash of cumin-spiced potatoes, encased in shortcrust-like, crisp pastry, were as good as you'd get in a New Delhi market. Despite occasional stumbles (bhel poori was way too salty and stodgy), cooking remains resoundingly good value, and service is commendable.
Babies and children welcome: high chairs. Booking advisable. No smoking. Separate room for parties, seats 30. Takeaway service. **Map 20 B4.**

★ ★ Sagar

157 King Street, W6 9JT (8741 8563). Hammersmith tube/266 bus. **Lunch served** noon-2.45pm Mon-Fri. **Dinner served** 5.30-10.45pm Mon-Thur; 5.30-11.30pm Fri. **Meals served** noon-11.30pm Sat; noon-10.45pm Sun. **Main courses** £5-£10. **Thalis** £8.95-£11.45. **Credit** AmEx, DC, JCB, MC, V. South Indian vegetarian

Attracting a loyal following, Sagar is one of the best places to sample vegetarian food from India's southern states. Modern blond-wood furnishings, a glass-paned entrance and elegant Indian artefacts lend a light, airy and upmarket feel, while the 'mum's own' traditional cooking style provides an earthy contrast. Masala dosais are the biggest hits. These legendary pancakes (made from ground lentils and rice) are crisp and golden on one side, and spongy on the other – perfect for scooping up the crushed potato and peppy mustard seed accompaniment. Many of the substantial snacks and main courses are served with tongue-tingling sambar: soupy yellow lentils, sharpened with tamarind water and simmered with tomatoes, chopped aubergines and various vegetables. For a South Indian-style all-day breakfast, order a bowl of steamy rasam (a peppery broth), along with uppama (savoury fried semolina). It's a winning combo: we loved the bland creamy texture of the semolina, flecked with crunchy lentils, cashew nuts and crackling curry leaves. The affable staff get a trifle harried on occasion, but that's a glitch in the context of such outstanding cooking.
Babies and children welcome: high chairs. Booking advisable. No-smoking tables. Takeaway service. Vegetarian menu. **Map 20 B4.**

Kensington W8

Utsav

17 Kensington High Street, W8 5NP (7368 0022/www.utsav-restaurant.co.uk). High Street Kensington tube. **Lunch served** 11.30am-3pm

was a wonderful take on the classic festive South Indian pudding, and the somewhat stodgy plantain and coconut fritters were redeemed by the delightful accompanying almond sorbet. Yes, Cinnamon Club gets our all-party vote.
Babies and children welcome: high chairs. Booking advisable. Disabled: toilet. Separate rooms for parties, seating 30 and 50. **Map 16 K9.**

West

Chiswick W4

★ ★ Woodlands

12-14 Chiswick High Road, W4 1TH (8994 9333/www.woodlandsrestaurant.co.uk). Stamford Brook tube. **Lunch served** noon-2.45pm, **dinner served** 6-10.45pm daily. **Main courses** £4-£7. **Thali** £13.95-£15.25. **Service** 12.5%. **Credit** AmEx, DC, MC, V. South Indian vegetarian

Hugely popular in India, the Woodlands chain is somewhat underrated in the UK, but serves some of the best and most authentic food from Chennai (Madras). However, it does depend on which venue

you visit. The quality of food in the two central London branches is variable, and the excellent Wembley outpost closed this year. However, the chef from Wembley now works in the Chiswick branch. This has resulted in the happy marriage of pleasant surroundings (brightly painted walls, chunky furniture, wood carvings and fresh flowers) and excellent food. Although the thalis and vegetable curries are admirable, we recommend South Indian breakfast snacks like idlis and dosais. Kancheepuram idli was wonderful: light, soft as cushions, and pepped up with green chillies, peppercorns and cashew nuts. Uppama (savoury semolina cooked with ginger, mustard seeds and curry leaves) was perfect. Onion rava masala dosai (onion and chilli-flecked semolina pancakes stuffed with potato and pea curry) had been beautifully spiced, and the contrasting textures were delectable. We also enjoyed a memorable rendition of the classic festival dish, bisi bele huliana (available only at weekends) – rice, lentils and vegetables, tempered with whole spices.

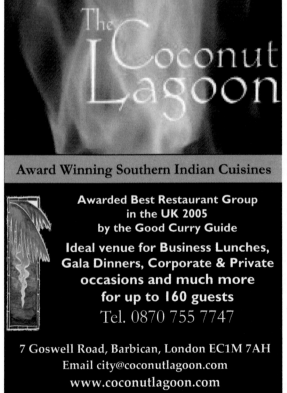

daily. **Dinner served** 6-11pm Mon-Thur; 6-11.30pm Fri, Sat; 6-10.30pm Sun. **Main courses** (lunch) £4.95-£5.95, (dinner) £9.75-£12.75. **Service** 12.5%. **Credit** AmEx, MC, V. Pan-Indian

Utsav can't compete for the same clientele as Zaika (*see below*), its fine-dining neighbour, but it does appeal to business travellers. Decor is based on a blue-tinted colour scheme, even the lighting has a surreal sci-fi glow. Cane furniture and cushions soften the sharp lighting, adding a welcome homely touch to this glass-fronted restaurant. On our visit, most folk gave the pan-Indian menu a miss and played safe by ordering North Indian skewered kebabs, birianis and nans. Our starters of nariyali jhinga (king prawns, steeped in garlicky coconut cream), although succulent, didn't have any trace of coconut flavour. Saag gosht (lamb and spinach curry) was an improvement, winning approval for its tender lamb chunks, its lush green spinach and its cardamom masala. However, chicken varuthatha (supposedly a South Indian curry with tamarind and curry leaves) was a cop-out, having a sweet, tomato ketchup-like masala. Service was slow, and the staff needed a dash more enthusiasm. We've had much better meals here in the past.
Babies and children welcome: high chair. Booking advisable. No-smoking tables. Restaurant available for hire. Separate rooms for parties, each seating 50. Takeaway service. Vegetarian menu. **Map 7 B8**.

★ Zaika

1 Kensington High Street, W8 5NP (7795 6533/www.zaika-restaurant.co.uk). High Street Kensington tube. **Lunch served** noon-2.45pm Mon-Fri, Sun. **Dinner served** 6.30-10.45pm Mon-Sat; 6.30-9.45pm Sun. **Main courses** £12.50-£19.50. **Set lunch** £15 2 courses, £18 3 courses, £20 4 courses. **Set meal** £38-£58 tasting menus. **Service** 12.5%. **Credit** AmEx, DC, JCB, MC, V. Modern Indian

After launching Deya (*see p132*), head chef Sanjay Dwivedi returned to Zaika to try to reinstate the Michelin star it lost early in 2005. Owned by Claudio Pulze and Raj Sharma, Zaika couldn't be more different from its sister restaurant. The high-ceilinged, split-level dining room of this converted bank – decorated in warm jewel colours of ruby, amethyst, emerald and gold – is alive with the buzz of contented diners. Dwivedi has introduced an ambitious new menu, which mirrors some of the ideas from Deya and Rasoi Vineet Bhatia (*see p141*). Rich, creamy coconut soup, with shiitake mushroom pakora and wild mushroom and truffle-oil nan, was unusual, but the flavours worked seamlessly together. A prawn platter comprised crispy tiger prawns, grilled king prawns marinated in chilli and rosemary, and a red onion and shrimp risotto, served with coconut chutney: absolutely delicious. A vegetable thali was more conventional, with some items (black urid dahl, pan-fried okra) very tasty, and others (paneer makhani, saffron pilau) a bit dull. More exciting was the imaginative pairing of mustard-marinated grilled guinea fowl with asparagus tikki and aubergine mash. Our main criticism? Too much truffle oil.
Babies and children welcome: high chair. Booking advisable. Dress: smart casual. Restaurant available for hire. Vegetarian menu. **Map 7 C8**.

South West
Chelsea SW3, SW10

Chutney Mary

535 King's Road, SW10 0SZ (7351 3113/ www.realindianfood.com). Fulham Broadway tube/11, 22 bus. **Lunch served** 12.30-2.30pm Sat; 12.30-3pm Sun. **Dinner served** 6.30-11pm Mon-Sat; 6.30-10.30pm Sun. **Main courses** £13.50-£25.50. **Set lunch** £16.50 3 courses. **Service** 12.5%. **Credit** AmEx, DC, JCB, MC, V. Pan-Indian

Run by the Panjabi sisters – of Amaya (*see p131*) and Masala Zone (*see p134*) fame – this fine-dining basement restaurant is a favourite haunt of businessmen on expense accounts and well-heeled Chelsea residents. An airy, colonial-style conservatory, embellished with greenery and cane

South Indian menu

In recent years South Indian cuisine in London has come of age. Cooking standards are higher and more sophisticated places are now serving varied regional specialities little known outside South India. The well-publicised expansion of both the **Woodlands** (*see p137*) and the **Rasa** (*see p131 and p149*) chains has played no small role in this. Chefs tend to be from either Chennai (formerly Madras) or Kerala, though **Sagar** (*see p137*) specialises in the famed vegetarian cuisine of Karnataka.

Much of London's South Indian food consists of rice-, lentil- and semolina-based dishes. Fish features strongly in non-vegetarian establishments, and coconut, mustard seeds, curry leaves and red chillies are widely used as flavourings.

Adai: fermented rice and lentil pancakes, with a nuttier flavour than dosais (qv).
Avial: a mixed vegetable curry from Kerala with a coconut and yoghurt sauce. Literally, 'mixture' in Malayalam (the language of Kerala).
Bonda: spiced mashed potatoes, dipped in chickpea flour batter and deep-fried.
Dosai or **dosa**: thin, shallow-fried pancake, often sculpted into interesting shapes – the very thin ones are called **paper dosai**. Most dosais are made with fermented rice and lentil batter, but variants include **rava dosai**, made with 'cream of wheat' semolina. **Masala dosais** come with a spicy potato filling. All variations are traditionally served with sambar (qv) and coconut chutney.
Gobi 65: cauliflower marinated in spices, then dipped in chickpea flour batter and deep-fried. It is usually lurid pink due to the addition of food colouring.
Idli: steamed sponges of ground rice and lentil batter. Eaten with sambar (qv) and coconut chutney.
Kadala: black chickpea curry.
Kalan: a thin curry from the southern states made from yoghurt, coconut and mangoes.
Kancheepuram idli: idli (qv) flavoured with whole black peppercorns and other spices.
Kappa: cassava root traditionally served with kadala (qv).
Kootu: mild vegetable curry in a creamy coconut and yoghurt sauce.
Kozhi varutha: usually consists of pieces of chicken served in a medium-hot curry sauce based on garlic and coconut – it is very rich.
Moilee: Keralite fish curry.
Rasam: consommé made with lentils; it tastes both peppery-hot and tamarind-sour, but there are many regional variations.
Sambar or **sambhar**: a variation on dahl made with a specific hot blend of spices, plus coconut, tamarind and vegetables – particularly drumsticks (a pod-like vegetable, like a longer, woodier version of okra).
Thoran: vegetables stir-fried with mustard seeds, curry leaves, chillies and fresh grated coconut.
Uppama: a popular breakfast dish in which onions, spices and, occasionally, vegetables are cooked with semolina using a risotto-like technique.
Uthappam: spicy, crisp pancake/pizza made with lentil- and rice-flour batter, usually topped with tomato, onions and chillies.
Vellappam: a bowl-shaped, crumpet-like rice pancake (same as appam or hoppers, qv, Sri Lankan menu).

furniture, contrasts with the more formal dining area, furnished with silks and elegant flickering candles. We began with shorba, a broth of good strong lamb stock (known as a yakhini) with a blend of delicate, well-balanced spices. We especially appreciated the citrusy, cardamom infusion, cut-through with astringent ginger, warming cumin and rich bone marrow. lush green goan chicken curry was flavoured with creamy coconut milk, perky green chillies and just-picked coriander leaves. The tandoori platter was good, but only in parts: succulent chicken tikka pieces, filled with figs, worked well, but lamb koftas were undercooked. Dense, ginger-laden prawn seekh kebabs (skewered and grilled minced prawns) were equally lacklustre. Service is unobtrusive, yet sound, and there's a superb and carefully chosen wine list. Despite our gripes, we still rate Chutney Mary highly.
Babies and children welcome: high chairs. Booking advisable. Dress: smart casual. Entertainment: jazz 12.30pm Sun. No-smoking tables. Separate room for parties, seats 24. **Map 13 C13**.

Painted Heron

112 Cheyne Walk, SW10 0TJ (7351 5232/ www.thepaintedheron.com). Sloane Square tube/ 11, 19, 22, 319 bus. **Lunch served** noon-2.30pm Mon-Fri. **Dinner served** 6-11pm daily. **Main courses** £10-£15. **Thalis** £12-£14. **Credit** AmEx, JCB, MC, V. Modern Indian

Cheyne Walk's affluent residents have done well out of this upmarket, modern restaurant. Artistic monochrome prints across cream walls are set off by crisp white table linen, flickering candles and light-wood flooring. In contrast, the daily changing menu is wildly flamboyant – expect curiosities such as sweetly spiced strawberry curry, kebabs topped with silver leaf, and herby rosemary nans. We especially relished the first course of potato cake filled with goat's cheese: the delicious buttery mashed potato, flecked with crisp-fried yellow lentils and curry leaves, worked well with the tang of soft warm cheese. As wacky as the strawberry curry sounded, it tasted wonderful – the puréed strawberries studded with fruity chunks, enhanced by toasted cumin, and sharpened with a dash of lime juice. Not everything was as memorable: the diced lamb curry (cooked with black lentils and broad beans) was stodgy, and let down by tough meat. Service was friendly but inefficient, and could do with tightening up. Chef Yogesh Datta has his hands full, running the Kennington branch as well as this flagship. Perhaps that's why the standard of cooking has slipped a few notches.
Babies and children admitted. Booking advisable weekends. No-smoking tables. Separate room available for hire, seats 25. Tables outdoors (5, garden). Vegetarian menu. **Map 13 D13**.
For branch see index.

152-156 Shaftesbury
Avenue, London
WC2H 8HL

Tel : 020 7836 8635
Fax : 020 7379 0527
www.melarestaurant.co.uk

"The best food I have ever had"
- *Sir Andrew Lloyd Webber*

"Upmarket Indian Food at bargain prices"
- *Zagat*

HOMESTYLE
INDIAN FOOD

2-3 Denman Street,
London, W1 7HA

Tel : 020 7439 1330
Fax: 020 7287 5919
www.chowki.com

Excellent Indian home cooking on a shoe string"
- *Guardian Guide*

"Indian dream, a very honest and good value place"
- *Charles Campion, Es Magazine*

SOHO SPICE

124-126 Wardour Street,
Soho, London, W1F OTY

Tel : 020 7434 0808
Fax : 020 7434 0799
www.sohospice.co.uk

Come and enjoy a fusion between the vibrant soho scene and exquisite Indian spice

After dinner relax at The Spice Bar & Lounge, open till 3am (live performers & DJ's)

3 MONKEYS
VINTAGE INDIAN
CUISINE

3 Monkeys Restaurant
136/140 Herne Hill
London, SE24 9QH

Tel : 020 7738 5550
Fax : 020 7738 5505
www.3monkeysrestaurant.com

"Top 50 Curries in London"
- *Time Out*

"3 Monkeys is a serious contender as one of South London's best Indian restaurants"
- *Time Out*

MELA EVENTS

From dinner parties, business lunches, or social gatherings to lavish wedding receptions, Mela Events dedicated team will tailor each package to the requirements of the individual customer. For more information contact: 020 7495 4800.

★ Rasoi Vineet Bhatia

10 Lincoln Street, SW3 2TS (7225 1881/ www.vineetbhatia.com). Sloane Square tube. **Lunch served** noon-2.30pm Mon-Fri. **Dinner served** 6.30-10.30pm Mon-Sat. **Main courses** £14-£36. **Set meal** £58-£69 tasting menus. **Service** 12.5%. **Credit** AmEx, JCB, MC, V. Modern Indian

Ex-Zaika chef Vineet Bhatia's Michelin-chasing baby lies within an elegant townhouse, its somewhat staid black and cream interior enlivened by framed antiques. We started with a medley of samosas. Some fillings (asparagus with coconut and curry leaves, and shiitake mushroom with roasted peanut) worked better than others (Mediterranean-influenced spinach and raisin). Trio of chicken was an unmitigated triumph, though; two types of succulent chicken tikka (one marinated in saffron and spices, another in fresh coriander and mint paste) were accompanied by a crispy chicken nugget stuffed with a delectable mixture of paneer, spices and roasted sesame seeds. We also loved the juicy lobster flavoured with chilli and ginger, which came with creamy broccoli khichadi dusted with pickling spice and cocoa powder. Roast potatoes stuffed with spicy paneer, sweetcorn and pine kernels were less razzle-dazzle, but still delicious – the accompanying coconut and kokum gravy and South Indian-inspired beetroot rice accentuated the flavours. Not everything works: spicy blue-cheese nan, some of the savoury ice-creams, and mundane vegetable accompaniments got the thumbs-down. Moreover, the cooking is over-elaborate and the prices cheeky. But for dazzling inventiveness, audacity and vision, this postmodern Indian – with a slight nod to Blumenthal-style gastro-jiggery pokery – gets our red star.
Babies and children admitted. Booking advisable. Dress: smart casual. No smoking. Separate rooms for parties, seating 8 and 15. Vegetarian menu. **Map 14 F11.**

Vama

438 King's Road, SW10 0LJ (7351 4118/ www.vama.co.uk). Sloane Square tube then 11, 22 bus. **Lunch served** noon-3pm daily. **Dinner served** 6.30-11.30pm Mon-Sat; 6.30-10.30pm Sun. **Main courses** £6.25-£18.50. **Set buffet** (lunch Sun) £12.95. **Service** 12.5% for parties of 6 or more. **Credit** AmEx, DC, MC, V. North Indian

Andy Varma's Vama – which, they claim, means 'the essence of womanhood' in Sanskrit – was once one of the most talked about Indian restaurants in town. Yet over the years, the quality of Indian fine dining has improved, while standards have slipped at this former Chelsea favourite. The restaurant still looks stylish with its deep-ochre walls, old paintings, stone floor, potted plants, handcrafted teak furniture, and handmade crockery. The menu is mainly Punjabi, with influences from Afghanistan, Pakistan and Rajasthan. Til wale paneer tikka featured cotton-soft own-made paneer, but the creamy sesame and chilli marinade was bland. Salmon tikka was better: flavoursome wild salmon, glossy with clarified butter and infused with lemon juice and ajwain seeds, was a successful marriage of flavours. Crab kofta curry contained insipid balls of crab and vegetables, redeemed by a well-flavoured tomato sauce. Ma ki dahl (black urid lentils and red kidney beans in a creamy, gingery tomato sauce) was an instant hit, but a spinach, pea and fenugreek curry was nothing to shout about. Pilau rice and roomali roti ('handkerchief bread') made with roasted cumin were both excellent, though, and service was lovely.
Babies and children welcome: high chairs. Booking essential weekends. Separate room for parties, seats 35. Tables outdoors (4, patio). Takeaway service. **Map 14 D12.**

East Sheen SW14

Sarkhel's

199 Upper Richmond Road West, East Sheen, SW14 8QT (8876 6220/www.sarkhels.com). Mortlake rail. **Lunch served** noon-2.30pm daily. **Dinner served** 6-10.30pm Tue-Thur; 6-11pm Fri, Sat. **Main courses** £6.95-£9.95. **Set lunch** £5 2 courses. **Credit** MC, V. Pan-Indian

Just as we were starting to get reports of the original Sarkhel's in Southfields occasionally losing its grip, we visited the new branch in East Sheen. Unlike chef Udit Sarkhel's other restaurants, this one has a menu that is cloned from the original – which is a good thing, because it is filled with perfectly rendered and finely tuned dishes picked from all regions of India. Jardaloo ma ghosht is a mouth-watering Parsi dish of lamb chunks cooked with apricots then topped with crunchy fried potato straws. It goes particularly well with dark-coloured dhansak rice. Even the simplest dishes, such as a cashew, tomato and aubergine number, sing with flavour when spiced here: in this case with ginger and a chilli masala. A further bonus is that there are no lakes of ghee. Dishes were noticeably low in fat; even the deep-fried gade pakore were greaseless little fish fingers. Easily one of the best Indian restaurants to have opened in 2005.
Babies and children welcome: children's menu; high chairs. Booking advisable weekends. Disabled: toilet. No smoking. Takeaway service; delivery service (within 3-mile radius). Vegetarian menu. **For branch see index.**

Gloucester Road SW7

Bombay Brasserie

Courtfield Road, SW7 4QH (7370 4040/ www.bombaybrasserielondon.com). Gloucester Road tube. **Lunch served** 12.30-3pm, **dinner served** 7.30-11.45pm daily. **Main courses** £16-£21. **Minimum** (dinner) £25. **Set buffet** (lunch) £18.95 incl tea or coffee. **Service** 12.5%. **Credit** AmEx, DC, JCB, MC, V. Pan-Indian

In existence well before the term 'Modern Indian' was invented, the Bombay Brasserie sports plush colonial decor that's either charmingly retro or old-fashioned, depending on your point of view. The spacious dining room boasts ornate gilded ceilings, patterned carpets, kitsch ornaments, framed monochrome pictures of the Raj, and a wall half-covered with a monkey mural. There's also a large conservatory filled with wicker furniture, hanging baskets and potted palms, as well as a verandah. The pan-Indian menu is apparently a hit with Hollywood celebrities. Sev batata puri (a classic Mumbai street snack made with crisp pooris topped with potatoes, sprouted mung, sev and three chutneys) was tongue-tingling and refreshing, but grilled scallops marinated in honey and ginger, served with red pimento sauce and 'burnt garlic' were less successful. The Lucknowi speciality, lamb nihari, was very tasty: tender lamb shank in a rich, robust sauce. We also liked paneer akbari (paneer stuffed with mint and coriander chutney), but the accompanying tomato sauce was superfluous. Recalling a Merchant Ivory film set, they just don't make them like this anymore.
Babies and children admitted: high chairs. Booking advisable; essential weekends. Dress: smart casual. Entertainment: pianist 9pm Mon-Sat; 12.30-3pm, 9pm Sun. No-smoking tables. Restaurant available for hire. Separate conservatory for parties, seats 150. Vegetarian menu. **Map 13 C10.**

Putney SW15

Ma Goa NEW

242-244 Upper Richmond Road, SW15 6TG (8780 1767/www.ma-goa.com). East Putney tube/Putney rail/74, 337 bus. **Lunch served** 1-4pm Sun. **Dinner served** 6.30-11pm Mon-Sat; 6-10pm Sun. **Main courses** £7-£11. **Set meal** (6.30-8pm daily) £10 2 courses. **Set buffet** (Sun lunch) £10. **Service** 12.5%. **Credit** AmEx, DC, JCB, MC, V. Goan

This amazingly friendly, family-run restaurant has had a makeover, and now boasts lively contemporary art on cream walls, black leather chairs, crisp white linen and fresh flower arrangements. There's a buzz to the place, which is hugely popular with locals. Little wonder, as the food on our visit was delicious. Goan cuisine marries Central and South Indian flavours with Portuguese-introduced ingredients such as vinegar and pork; dishes tend to be hot and sour (here, though, chillies are used judiciously). We loved

Interview
NAMITA PANJABI

Who are you?
Director of Masala World, co-owner of three **Masala Zone** restaurants (*see p134*) as well as **Chutney Mary** (*see p139*) and **Amaya** (*see p131*).
Eating in London: what's good about it?
I've been involved in the eating scene in London for 15 years it has changed dramatically. Different kinds of people are becoming restaurateurs – educated people who want to express themselves and say something about food.
What's bad about it?
We've had a huge battle since we entered the scene, in which everyone, including the guides, would say 'it's expensive for Indian food'. At Chutney Mary we were the first to plate Indian food glamorously, and even senior media people would tell us it should be served in bowls so that people could mix it all together on the plate. The chef has spent two hours on each dish, so why would you mix them?
Which are your favourite London restaurants?
I visit a lot of restaurants for work and don't have the luxury of going back again, but I do have some old favourites. I love **Langan's Brasserie** (*see p225*) and the **River Café** (*see p173*).
What single thing would improve London's restaurant scene?
Service. We look to America in an effort to continually improve standards.
Any hot tips for the coming year?
I think spice has come to stay. We'll see more European chefs veer towards adding spice – not fusion, but using spice to bring an additional excitement or dimension to European food. **Maze** (*see p128*) is already beginning to do that. The entire Asian food scene is very exciting, and there are some wonderful Chinese places now.
Anything to declare?
I have things to talk and chat about, but nothing to declare.

RESTAURANTS

baked aubergines topped with a smooth garlicky yoghurt sauce, and Goan pork chorizo cooked with garlic, mild kashmiri chillies, palm vinegar and potato and onion salsa. Mixed vegetable caldine contained a few unconventional vegetables such as broccoli, sugar-snap peas and baby corn in a spicy, creamy coconut gravy infused with curry leaves and palm vinegar. More curry leaves and palm vinegar featured in Konkan-style galinha, a lovely dish of tender chicken breast jazzed up with tangy and fiery roasted red chilli sauce. Coconut rice made with fresh coconut and nigella seeds provided a perfect foil to the punchy flavours. *Babies and children welcome: high chairs. Booking advisable; essential weekends. Dress: smart casual. No smoking. Restaurant available for hire. Separate room for parties, seats 35. Takeaway service; delivery service (within 3-mile radius).*

Raynes Park SW20

★ Cocum
9 Approach Road, Raynes Park, SW20 8BA (8540 3250/8542 3843). Morden tube then 163 bus/Raynes Park rail. **Lunch served** noon-2.30pm Mon-Thur, Sat, Sun. **Dinner served** 5.30-11pm Mon-Thur; 5.30-11.30pm Fri, Sat; 5.30-10.30pm Sun. **Main courses** £4-£8. **Service** 10%. **Credit** AmEx, DC, JCB, MC, V. South Indian
Cocum's location, on a barren shopping parade facing a railway junction, does it few favours. Keralite knick-knacks try to create atmosphere, but this isn't easy in a boxy shop unit. However, spirits lift when you read the Keralite menu, which

is the culinary full monty. Kick off with the pickles and snacks. The prawn and fish pickles are mouth-watering, but snacks such as achappams (flower-shaped papads) would be better if freshly fried instead of cold. Meen manga puli was our best dish: white chunks of fish flesh with the smoky flavour and whisky-like, phenolic aroma of fish tamarind (aka cocum). Other dishes, such as lemon rice and a vegetable dish of slowly simmered spring onion and okra, were more workaday. We skipped the card of bought-in desserts and instead ordered pal payasam: like a rice pudding, but tasting of coconut milk laced with cashews. Our big disappointment was the way 10% service was illegibly added to the bill – then we were presented with the credit card slip left open for a further gratuity.
Babies and children welcome: high chairs. Booking advisable weekends. Restaurant available for hire. Takeaway service; delivery service (within 3-mile radius on orders over £15).

South Kensington SW3

Shikara NEW
87 Sloane Avenue, SW3 3DX (7581 6555/ www.shikara.co.uk). South Kensington tube. **Lunch served** noon-3pm, **dinner served** 6-11.30pm daily. **Main courses** £6.50-£12.95. **Set meal** £8.95-£35.95 2-5 courses. **Credit** AmEx, JCB, MC, V. North Indian
Newish Shikara is fitted out with plush dark-leather seating and a well-stocked bar, no doubt with the aim of establishing it as a fine-dining destination. However, on our visit most people seemed to be ordering takeaways. In an endeavour

to attract healthy eaters, the menu enthuses about the beneficial effects of spices and herbs; the chefs even offer to cook dishes in olive oil. We're not convinced that the gimmick pays off. Our tandoori mixed grill consisted of an assortment of nibbles, including chicken and lamb tikka, tandoori chicken and lamb seekh kebabs. Although carefully spiced and cooked to the right degree of smokiness, each item was made with below-par, supermarket-standard meat. Having been charged £12.95 a platter, we expected better. Tok dahl also disappointed, the tart dried mango flavouring lending it a bitter taste. If Shikara wants to earn its spurs as a cutting-edge establishment, it needs to move away from stodgy, British-inspired balti dishes, and think more about sourcing top-quality ingredients.
Babies and children welcome: high chairs. Booking advisable. No-smoking tables. Takeaway service; delivery service (within 3-mile radius). Vegetarian menu. **Map 14 E10.**

South

Balham SW12

★ Sadya NEW
90 Bedford Hill, SW12 9HR (8673 5393/ www.sadya.co.uk). Balham tube/rail. **Lunch served** noon-3pm daily. **Dinner served** 6-11pm Mon-Thur, Sun; 6pm-midnight Fri, Sat. **Main courses** £4-£8. **Service** 10%. **Credit** MC, V. South Indian
Sadya's menu is Keralite, with all the dosais, idlis and vadais you might expect. Besides snacks, it also has a varied choice of vegetable dishes, such

Gujarati menu

Londoners aren't exactly queuing up to visit Gujarati restaurants: possibly, we suspect, because none are in the West End. Most are in north-west London, mainly Hendon, Wembley, Kingsbury, Kenton, Harrow and Rayners Lane – not exactly glamorous hotspots – and they tend to be garish, low-profile family-run eateries.

Unlike North Indian food, Gujarati dishes are not usually cooked in a base sauce of onions, garlic, tomatoes and spices. Instead they're tempered – whole spices such as cumin, red chillies, mustard seeds, ajwain (carom) seeds and curry leaves are sizzled in hot oil for a few seconds. The tempering is added at the start or the end of cooking, depending on the dish. Commonplace items like grains, beans and flours – transformed into various shapes by boiling, steaming and frying – form the basis of many dishes. Coriander, coconut, yoghurt, jaggery (cane sugar), tamarind, sesame seeds, chickpea flour and cocum (a sun-dried, sour, plum-like fruit) are also widely used.

Each region has its own cooking style. Kathiyawad, a humid area in western Gujarat, and Kutch, a desert in the north-west, have spawned styles that are less reliant on fresh produce. Kathiyawadi food is rich with dairy products and grains such as dark millet, and is pepped up with chilli powder. Kutchis make liberal use of chickpea flour (as do Kathiyawadis) and their staple diet is based on khichadi. In central Gujarat towns such as Ahmedabad and Baroda, grains are

widely used; they form the basis of snacks (chats) that are the backbone of menus in London's Gujarati restaurants.

The gourmet heartland, however, is Surat – one of the few regions with heavy rainfall and lush vegetation. Surat boasts an abundance of green vegetables like papadi (a type of broad bean) and ponk (fresh green millet). A must-try Surti speciality is undhiyu. Surti food uses 'green masala' (fresh coriander, coconut, green chillies and ginger), as opposed to the 'red masala' (red chilli powder, crushed coriander, cumin and turmeric) more commonly used in western and central regions.

In our opinion, there are no Gujarati restaurants in London that serve truly top-notch dishes (and none specialising in genuine Surti cuisine). However, **Dadima** (*see p157*) serves a decent rendition of central Gujarati food; **Kathiyawadi** food is showcased by the restaurant of that name (*see p153*); and **Chowpatty** (*see p156*) and **Sakonis** (*see p153*) offer good Kenyan versions of Mumbai street snacks.

Bhakarvadi: pastry spirals stuffed with whole spices and, occasionally, potatoes.
Bhel poori: a snack originating from street stalls in Mumbai, which contains crisp, deep-fried pooris, puffed rice, sev (qv), chopped onion, tomato, potato and more, plus chutneys (chilli, mint and tamarind).
Farsan: Gujarati snacks.
Ganthia: Gujarati name for crisply fried savoury confections made from chickpea flour; they come in all shapes.

Ghughara: sweet or savoury pasties.
Khadi: yoghurt soup.
Khichadi or **khichdi:** rice and lentils mixed with ghee and spices.
Mithi roti: round griddle-cooked bread stuffed with a cardamom- and saffron-flavoured lentil paste. Also called puran poli.
Mogo: deep-fried cassava, often served as chips together with a sweet and sour tamarind chutney. An East African Asian dish.
Pani poori: bite-sized pooris that are filled with sprouted beans, chickpeas, potato, onion, chutneys, sev (qv) and a thin, spiced watery sauce.
Patra: a savoury snack made of the arvi leaf (colocasia) stuffed with spiced chickpea flour batter, steamed, then cut into slices in the style of a swiss roll. The slices are then shallow-fried with sesame and mustard seeds.
Pau bhajee: a robustly spiced dish of mashed potatoes and vegetables, served with a shallow-fried white bread roll.
Puran poli: see mithi roti.
Ragda pattice or **ragada patties:** mashed potato patties covered with a chickpea or dried pea sauce, topped with onions, sev (qv) and spicy chutney.
Sev: deep-fried gram-flour vermicelli.
Thepla: savoury flatbread.
Tindora: ivy gourd, a vegetable resembling baby gherkins.
Undhiyu: a casserole of purple yam, sweet and ordinary potatoes, green beans, Indian broad beans, other vegetables and fenugreek-leaf dumplings cooked with fresh coconut, coriander and green chilli. A speciality of Surat.

as thorans (vegetable stir-fries), and a few other classic dishes from Kerala's Nair clan. Erissery was a mush of dun-coloured pumpkin, green banana and yam, flavoured with cumin and mustard seeds. Olan (shards of onion-like gourd with aduki beans) is another dish we've seen better versions of elsewhere; grey-coloured coconut milk lessened its eye-appeal. Meen polichathu was meant to be kingfish, but pomfret appeared (unannounced) instead, scored chevron-style and slathered in a spicy marinade that kept it moist and filled it with flavour during grilling. The best dish by far, though, was the appams: perfect saucers of fermented batter, light, fresh and browned just so. Pickles and chutneys are a matter of pride in Keralite kitchens, and the selection here sums up the effort overall: some were own-made, others bought-in. Although Sadya's food is of a good standard and the prices are low, leading Keralite restaurants such as the Rasa chain have nothing to fear from Balham.
Babies and children welcome: high chairs. Booking advisable. No-smoking tables. Takeaway service; delivery service (within 2-mile radius on orders over £15). Vegetarian menu.

Norbury SW16

★ Mirch Masala

1416-1418 London Road, SW16 4BZ (8679 1828/8765 1070). Norbury rail. **Meals served** noon-midnight daily. **Main courses** £3-£10. **Set buffet** (noon-4pm Mon-Sat) £6.99. **Unlicensed. Corkage** no charge. **Credit** AmEx, JCB, MC, V. East African Punjabi
This plain white café, popular with Asian families and large groups, offers fuss-free cooking at low prices. It certainly lives up to its name – which translates as 'chilli and spice', and is a slang term loosely meaning 'excitement, embellishment and buzz'. However, the dishes we tried were a mixed bag. We liked the fresh patra (colocasia leaves, stuffed with spicy chickpea flour paste, steamed, sliced into spirals and fried). It's a rare treat to find a fresh (rather than tinned), home-style version of this dish in a restaurant. Chicken bhajia (fritters), on the other hand, were bland and greasy. More successful were the imaginatively rendered masala karela dahl bhajee (spicy bitter gourd scrambled with split peas) and karahi valpapdi baingan (aubergines stir-fried with Indian broad beans cooked in their pods). Two karahi dishes with fresh fenugreek – butter beans methi, and lamb keema methi with peas and potatoes – were very oily and short on fenugreek. And pilau rice was a throwback to the days of flock wallpaper, speckled as it was with red food colouring.
Babies and children welcome: high chairs. Booking advisable. Takeaway service; delivery service (within 2-mile radius). Vegetarian menu.
For branches see index.

Tooting SW17

Tooting has an unusually diverse range of restaurants from the Indian subcontinent. In the 15-minute walk from Tooting Bec tube to Tooting Broadway (and beyond), you'll find excellent cafés and restaurants serving dishes that are East African Asian, Gujarati, Pakistani, Sri Lankan and Keralite. Best of all, they're cheap. But why Tooting?

The first well-educated immigrants from the Indian subcontinent came to study at the South West London College (which still specialises in accountancy, business and management studies) in the 1960s. Some of these white-collar workers stayed in the area, settled and raised families. The first South Indian restaurant, Sree Krishna, opened here in 1973.

A wave of nationalism swept through East Africa in the 1970s, forcing many successful Asians to flee their adopted countries (Tanzania, Kenya, Uganda). A lucky break for Tooting was the arrival of the Thanki family, who run **Kastoori**, moving from Uganda and bringing their Gujarati vegetarian cooking with them; their East African heritage is evident in the cassava and sweetcorn dishes on the menu.

In the late 1980s, a civil war between the Sinhalese majority and a minority of Tamil separatists in Sri Lanka created a new wave of Tamil refugees – and many moved to the stretch between Tooting Broadway and Colliers Wood. Tooting is now home to around 30,000 Tamil people (of an estimated 100,000 living in London), which makes them the largest Asian community in the area. While most of the Tamil caffs that stretch towards Colliers Wood are cheap and very basic, **Apollo Banana Leaf**, opened in 2004, upped the stakes by attempting to be more like a restaurant. It is currently our favourite place for proper Sri Lankan cooking, but still charges astoundingly low prices.

★ ★ Apollo Banana Leaf

190 Tooting High Street, SW17 0SF (8696 1423). Tooting Broadway tube. **Meals served** noon-11pm daily. **Main courses** £3.50-£6.25. **Credit** AmEx, MC, V. Sri Lankan
This simple, unassuming caff offers hot and fiery Sri Lankan and South Indian dishes at low, low prices. From an extensive menu, we enjoyed pittu (Sri Lankan red rice and fresh coconut steamed in a hollowed-out bamboo log) with a rich vegetable curry laced with cinnamon, black cardamom and star anise – mouth-watering. Mutton kothu was a beautifully flavoured melange of tender lamb pieces mixed with chopped veechu roti, onions and chillies in a heavily spiced gravy. Devilled chicken lacked the chilli heat and tanginess for which this dish is known, but featured tender breast meat coated in roasted spices. Prawn curry was crammed with juicy king prawns in a mild, creamy coconut gravy with onion and turmeric. We mopped this up with egg hoppers and string hoppers, both delicate and lacy, and made with red rice. Relishes such as seeni sambol and lunnu miris are beautifully flavoured. Service, though, was slow and rather hampered by language difficulties.
Babies and children welcome: high chairs. Booking advisable weekends. No smoking. Takeaway service.

★ Jaffna House

90 Tooting High Street, SW17 0RN (8672 7786/ www.jaffnahouse.co.uk). Tooting Broadway tube. **Meals served** noon-midnight daily. **Main courses** £2.25-£9. **Set lunch** (noon-3pm Mon-Fri) £4-£5 2 courses incl drink. **Credit** AmEx, MC, V. Sri Lankan
This small no-frills eaterie, with café at the front and restaurant at the back, won't win style awards with its garish red and cream decor and patterned carpet. However, the food from Jaffna, a port in northern Sri Lanka, is certainly worth a second look. To start, we had perfectly cooked devilled liver, which was enveloped in a delicious coating of spices, chilli and tomatoes. Fish cutlets were a bit potato-heavy, but otherwise fine. Much more successful was pittu (steamed red rice and fresh coconut 'log') fried in butter with eggs and vegetables. We also enjoyed a fiery seafood kothu (squid and prawns mixed with chopped veechu roti, eggs, onions and lots of green chillies). For pudding, wattalappan was intensely sweet, dense and gooey. There are many North Indian and South Indian dishes on the huge menu, as well as curry house standards like chicken tikka masala – but we suggest sticking to Sri Lankan dishes. Service from overstretched staff can be rushed.
Babies and children admitted. Booking advisable. Separate room for parties, seats 25. Takeaway service. Vegetarian menu.

★ Kastoori

188 Upper Tooting Road, SW17 7EJ (8767 7027). Tooting Bec or Tooting Broadway tube. **Lunch served** 12.30-2.30pm Wed-Sun. **Dinner** served 6-10.30pm daily. **Main courses** £4.75-£6.25. **Thalis** £8.50-£16.25. **Minimum** £7. **Credit** MC, V. East African Gujarati vegetarian
This unassuming restaurant – with blue chairs, yellow tablecloths and Hindu wall sculptures – is hugely popular with vegetarians and vegans. Owned by the friendly and efficient Thanki family (who hail from Kathiyawad in Gujarat, via East Africa), Kastoori offers an ambitious menu strewn with East African vegetables like cassava and green banana cooked with sweetcorn, peanuts, sesame seeds, coconut and lots of tomatoes – a quintessentially East African Gujarati cooking style. Mogo bhajia was a generous portion of rather heavy cassava fritters. Corn bhel (a modern classic from Mumbai, usually made with coriander, coconut, whole spices, a variety of sauces and sev) was a fairly mundane mix of sweetcorn, potatoes and tomatoes in a too-sweet tamarind sauce. Kastoori kofta were tired-looking vegetable balls (hard and dry) in indifferent gravy. Chilli banana contained beautifully spiced stuffed bananas and green chillies – but hot, sweet tomato sauce ruined the dish. However, a potato and cabbage curry, soft pooris and chapatis were good. Overall, we found the restaurant overpriced, and the balance of sweet, hot and tangy flavours askew.
Babies and children admitted. Booking essential. Takeaway service. Vegan dishes.

★ ★ Radha Krishna Bhavan

86 Tooting High Street, SW17 0RN (8682 0969). Tooting Broadway tube. **Lunch served** noon-3pm daily. **Dinner served** 6-11pm Mon-Thur, Sun; 6pm-midnight Fri, Sat. **Main courses** £1.95-£6.95. **Thalis** (Sun) £5.95-£7.95. **Minimum** £5. **Service** 10%. **Credit** AmEx, DC, MC, V. South Indian
The interior of this popular neighbourhood restaurant is totally bonkers: eye-popping photographic wallpaper of sunsets, beaches, forests and foliage; wacky furniture; and some rather unsettling kathakali masks. Thank goodness for the food. To start, idli vadai sambar contained feather-light idli soaked in snazzily spiced sambar, along with savoury lentil doughnuts, which were a little hard. Egg dosai was a rich, buttery pancake topped with beaten eggs and fresh coriander, and the accompanying coconut chutney was OK. Next, Malabari-style biriani with king prawns featured fragrant rice and rich stock, but lacked the complex flavour of individually roasted spices for which this Keralite Muslim classic is renowned. Avial was spot-on though; crunchy green beans, carrots, green bananas, potatoes and drumsticks were cooked in a coconut and yoghurt sauce, pepped up with mustard seeds and curry leaves. Beetroot thoran, made with an abundance of fresh coconut, had a gorgeous colour. We scooped it up with crisp, flaky, layered Malabar paratha.
Babies and children admitted. Booking advisable. Takeaway service; delivery service (within 3-mile radius). Vegetarian menu.
For branch (Sree Krishna Inn) see index.

South East
Herne Hill SE24

★ 3 Monkeys NEW

136-140 Herne Hill, SE24 9QH (7738 5500/ www.3monkeysrestaurant.com). Herne Hill rail/ 3, 37, 68 bus. **Lunch served** noon-2.30pm, **dinner served** 5.30-10.30pm Mon-Sat. **Meals served** noon-10.30pm Sun. **Main courses** £8.95-£10.95. **Set lunch** (Mon-Thur, Sun) £7.95 2 courses. **Set dinner** (Mon-Thur, Sun) £12.95 2 courses. **Service** 12.5%. **Credit** AmEx, DC, JCB, MC, TC, V. Pan-Indian
After opening in 1998, with Udit Sarkhel as consultant chef, 3 Monkeys was the culinary talk of Herne Hill. But as time went on Sarkhel left, standards slumped, and on our visits in 2003 and 2004 we found the food mediocre and overpriced, and felt the place was faltering. This all changed late in 2004 when the restaurant changed ownership. It is now in the capable hands of chef-proprietor Kuldeep Singh, of Chowki fame

(*see p134*). The menu and staff have changed and the cooking has improved by several notches. Mastery of Mogul courtly cooking is demonstrated in the shikampuri kebab, a finely textured patty that's delicately spiced with cinnamon and cardamom. An understanding of regional Indian cooking is evident in a thaaravu roast, a Syrian Christian dish from Kerala where duck breast is pot-roasted with spices, and served with a moreish orange sauce. Even the stir-fries are memorable, such as the peppery tiger prawns. The combination of excellent cooking, good service and a very striking minimalist interior now makes 3 Monkeys a serious contender for the title of south London's best Indian restaurant.
Babies and children welcome: high chairs. Booking advisable. Disabled: toilet. No-smoking tables. Separate rooms for parties, seating 16 and 40. Takeaway service; delivery service. **Map 23 A5.**

Lewisham SE13

★ **Arru Suvai** NEW
19 Lee High Road, SE13 5LD (8297 6452). Lewisham rail/DLR. **Meals served** 10am-11pm daily. **No credit cards.** Sri Lankan
This spacious cream-painted caff comes with light-enhanced waterfall pictures, shrines and even a fruit machine. In the short time since opening, it has become a busy centre of expat life in central Lewisham. The menu encompasses the usual Sri Lankan array – kothu, pittu, dosais, bonda, devilled mutton, fried fish – offered at prices that would shock most restaurant accountants. Spend more than six quid a head and you're in danger of exploding. We were impressed by rich and chilli-hot devilled potato, beautifully spiced tomato kulambu and well-flavoured dahl: each at just £1.50 for quite generous portions. The huge, fluffy and well-stuffed masala dosa (£2.25) almost filled our table; onion and egg dosais are even cheaper. In fact, the most expensive dish on the menu is just

£4.50. High-street curries appear under the guise of 'South Indian style curry dishes', but the predominantly Sri Lankan family and male groups that haunt the place ignore such distractions. Service is friendly and café-style (no bow-ties and hot towels here). Lovers of Sri Lankan soaps are well catered for by the satellite TV.

Peckham SE15

Ganapati NEW
38 Holly Grove, SE15 5DF (7277 2928). Peckham Rye rail/B13 bus. **Meals served** noon-10.45pm Tue-Sun. **Main courses** £7.95-£10.95. **Set lunch** £4.50-£5.50 1 course. **Service** 10%. **Credit** MC, V. South Indian
The corner site that used to be Holly has become Peckham's latest sign of regeneration. Ganapati – named after the elephant-headed god – is a simply furnished café, with incense smouldering and staff, both European and Indian, wearing kadhi ('homespun') shirts. The menu is brief and mainly Keralite. The larger size of thali has all the requisite components: a tangy sambar, a thoran (colourful grated vegetable stir-fry), a peppery rasam (consommé-like soup), olan (black-eyed bean and pumpkin stew) and a pungent kingfish curry. But staff might have warned us that some of these dishes would recur in our meal, as separate side orders. The cooking was adequate rather than anything worth crossing town for, but at least the bill was agreeably low. Service on our visit was painfully slow, but well-meaning.
Babies and children welcome: high chairs. Booking advisable Fri, Sat. No smoking. Tables outdoors (4, garden; 4, pavement). Takeaway service.

East

Those who stick to the notion that Brick Lane is synonymous with good curries are merely holding on to blurry-eyed nostalgia

(*see p151* **Brick Lane**). Brick Lane does still offer excellent Indian food: not in its restaurants, but in its bustling food shops, which sell an amazing array of authentic Bangladeshi ingredients seldom seen elsewhere, and in the tiny snack shops piled high with Bengali sweets like rasgulla.

If you want good old Brick Lane-style curries, however, try **Kasturi** in Aldgate High Street. While the more upmarket Indian restaurants have turned up their noses at City boy favourites' lamb vindaloo and chicken tikka masala, this smart restaurant isn't too proud to put them on the menu – and what's more, here they're cooked with care.

However, if you're looking for authentic curry in East London, you can't beat the long stretch of Little India that is Green Street in Upton Park. This street positively bristles with virtually every community from the subcontinent, and the colour and vibe (particularly at weekends) are like nowhere else in London. It's lined with dozens of amazing grocers, butchers, fishmongers, greengrocers and sweet shops that provide a wealth of exotic ingredients – from squat Bangladeshi lemons to malai kulfi, and from parrot fish to red spinach.

There's also a vibrant restaurant scene, popular with both Indian families and (increasingly) non-Indian groups. Perennial favourites include the excellent **Vijay's Chawalla** and the somewhat hit-or-miss **Mobeen**. From tangy Mumbai-style chats to smoky charcoal-grilled kebabs, here's a high-street restaurant that caters to everybody's taste.

3 Monkeys. See p145.

Upton Park E6, E7

★ Lazzat Kahari

18 Plashet Grove, E6 1AE (8552 3413).
Upton Park tube. **Lunch served** 11am-midnight
daily. **Main courses** £3.95-£4.95. **Unlicensed**.
No alcohol allowed. **No credit cards.**
Punjabi

This friendly Punjabi café has recently doubled in
size and been given a clean, bright, white-painted
look, accented with light wood and chrome fittings.
The short menu remains a constant, offering a
basic variety of kebabs, breads and pungently
spiced curries, prepared in batches in the semi-
open kitchen/serving area. Steady turnover
ensures that most dishes aren't left long in their
large metal troughs, and we've always found the
place a hive of activity. A large complimentary
salad of onion, tomato, lettuce and whole pickled
chilli sets the tone, and is best followed by rich and
meaty shami kebabs and crisp and plump (if ever
so slightly oily) samosas. Main courses, such as the
thickly reduced and aggressively spiced karahi
gosht, come with fluffy nan bread and/or a
mountain of rice, and the type of dahl your mother
might warn you against: thick and well infested
with fried red chillies. Vegetable dishes are pretty
decently cooked, but – as they tend to be treated
as supports to the main acts – less aggressively
spiced than their meaty cousins.
Babies and children welcome: high chairs.
Takeaway service.

★ Mobeen

224 Green Street, E7 8LE (8470 2419).
Upton Park tube/58 bus. **Meals served** 11am-
10pm daily. **Main courses** £2-£5.50. **Credit**
MC, V. Pakistani

On our Saturday lunchtime visit, this bright, clean,
self-service caff with glass counter, Formica tables
and kitsch decor was heaving with Indian families
– some dressed in elaborate wedding outfits. Up to
half a dozen cooks get busy flipping nan breads,
grilling kebabs over charcoal and flash-frying
curries in flaming karahis. Yet sometimes food is
heated up in microwaves, and ours wasn't hot
enough in terms of either chillies or temperature.
Vegetable samosas were plump triangles of dry,
thick pastry, stuffed to bursting with potatoes and
peas, laced with amchur (sun-dried mango
powder) and dried pomegranate seeds. Lamb tikka
was more timidly spiced, but the meat was
meltingly soft and beautifully charred. Chicken
biriani was more like a curry house version: dry
rice with insipid chunks of chicken, cloying
masala paste and flavourless stock. Vegetable
mince curry (made with soya mince) was better,
with a good grainy texture. Chickpea curry had
been flavoured with cinnamon, black cardamom,
fennel seeds and fresh ginger: delicious. Service,
from no-nonsense but efficient women, was
friendly yet rushed. Mobeen is fine for mid-
shopping sustenance, but not somewhere to linger.
Babies and children welcome: high chairs.
No smoking. Separate room for parties, seats 200.
Takeaway service.
For branch see index.

★ Vijay's Chawalla

268-270 Green Street, E7 8LF (8470 3535).
Upton Park tube. **Meals served** 11am-9pm
daily. **Main courses** £4-£7. **Thalis** £6-£7.
Unlicensed. **Corkage** no charge. **Credit** JCB,
MC, V. Gujarati vegetarian

If you're shopping in Green Street, a visit to this
bustling fast-food caff and snack shop is a must.
With its worn pink decor and non-stop showing of
Bollywood films, Vijay's is not so much a
destination restaurant as somewhere to chill your
heels. Chhole bhature (chickpea curry with large
pooris) was spot on: the curry had thick, robustly
flavoured gravy, and the pooris were light as air.
A potato curry was also delicious, the humble
tuber transformed by the addition of cinnamon,
cloves, ginger and fennel. The various chats,
samosas and bhel poori are also a good bet, and
the chilli paneer is a must-try. Some people find the
food here too hot and spicy, and South Indian
staples like sambar can be a little too sweet – but
on our most recent visit, we had no complaints.
True to its name (chawalla means 'tea seller'), the
masala tea is fabulous. And don't forget to pick up
sweets and savouries from the snack counter on
your way out.
Babies and children welcome: high chairs.
Disabled: toilet. No smoking. Takeaway service.
Vegetarian menu.

Whitechapel E1, EC3

Café Spice Namaste

16 Prescot Street, E1 8AZ (7488 9242/
www.cafespice.co.uk). Aldgate East or Tower
Hill tube/Tower Gateway DLR. **Lunch served**
noon-3pm Mon-Fri. **Dinner served** 6.15-
10.30pm Mon-Fri; 6.30-10.30pm Sat. **Main
courses** £9.95-£15.95. **Set meal** £25-£40
(minimum 2). **Service** 12.5%. **Credit** AmEx,
DC, JCB, MC, V. Parsi

Set in a former magistrate's office, Cyrus
Todiwala's upmarket restaurant makes a vibrant
spectacle, with an abundance of bright Bollywood
colours across walls. The clientele, mainly City
types, come here for such adventurous dishes as
beetroot samosas, ostrich tikka and spiced wild
boar sausages. Best bets are Todiwala's Parsi
dishes, notable for their distinctive, sweet-tart
flavours, inspired by a Middle Eastern heritage.
Our seal of approval went to jardaloo ma murghi:
chicken morsels, simmered in a toasted cumin and
onion masala along with intense hits of dried
apricots. The result – a sweet, mild curry, topped
with crunchy fried straw potatoes – was
particularly winsome. Equally satisfying, an
authentic goan pork vindaloo scored for its
vinegar, garlic and red chilli base. Our meal wasn't
all sunshine cooking, however: a South Indian vada
(fried lentil dumpling) was disappointingly dry
and dense, and the baingan bhartha (aubergine
purée, simmered with onions and tomato) didn't
carry any trademark smokiness. Service is helpful
and friendly, even when the place gets busy.
Babies and children welcome: high chairs.
Booking advisable. Disabled: toilet. Tables
outdoors (8, garden). Takeaway service; delivery
service (within 2-mile radius). Map 12 S7.

Kasturi

57 Aldgate High Street, EC3N 1AL (7480 7402/ www.kasturi-restaurant.co.uk). Aldgate tube. **Meals served** 11am-11pm Mon-Fri. **Dinner served** 5.30-11.30pm Sat. **Main courses** £6.95-£10. **Set buffet** (11am-3pm Mon-Fri) £9.99. **Credit** AmEx, MC, V. Pan-Indian

Those bemoaning Brick Lane's declining star should head to this City restaurant, popular with local suits. The look is standard 'smart Indian restaurant' – cream walls, bright artwork, potted palms, crisp white napery, wooden floors. The menu includes many familiar, none-too-ambitious curry house staples, but Kasturi specialises in Pakhtoon cuisine from India's north-west frontier, so kebabs and grills are a must-try. Shammi kebab (minced lamb patties laced with fresh mint and coriander) had a meltingly soft texture that did this classic dish justice. Paneer tikka was less successful: the cheese was too hard, and the stuffing (chillies, garlic, fresh herbs) and marinade (olive oil, cumin seeds) were indistinct. For mains, we had chicken afghani lababdar – strips of chicken, onions, green peppers, chillies and tomatoes stir-fried into hot, melting deliciousness. Baghare baingan (baby aubergines in a peanut and poppyseed sauce) lacked the usual richness and spiciness of this Hyderabadi dish, but was fine. We'd no complaints about the wonderfully flavoured black urid dahl, though, which had smoky undertones and the perfect texture that comes from long simmering. Service was amateurish, yet eager.
Babies and children welcome: high chairs. Booking advisable. Disabled: toilet. Separate rooms for parties, seating 20 and 40. Takeaway service; delivery service (within 3-mile radius on orders over £15). Vegetarian menu. **Map 12 S6.**

North East
Stoke Newington N16

★ Rasa

55 Stoke Newington Church Street, N16 0AR (7249 0344/www.rasarestaurants.com). Stoke Newington rail/73, 243, 393, 426, 476 bus. **Lunch served** noon-3pm Sat, Sun. **Dinner served** 6-10.45pm Mon-Thur, Sun; 6-11.30pm Fri, Sat. **Main courses** £3.65-£6.85. **Set meal** £16 4 courses. **Service** 12.5%. **Credit** AmEx, DC, JCB, MC, V. South Indian vegetarian

After adding an extension at the back, this bright pink restaurant, fragrant with incense and fresh flowers, is still packing 'em in. No wonder, as the vitality of ingredients and the vibrancy of cooking are outstanding. No concessions are made on the menu to the vindaloo-and-lager brigade – making this chain unique in terms of integrity. We started with mixed lentil and tomato soup, delicately laced with garlic, coriander and black pepper. Nair dosai (festive rice and black urid lentil pancake stuffed with beetroot and other vegetables) was light but earthy, and came with great sambar and coconut chutney. Two thorans – savoy cabbage and tindori (like baby gherkins) – were first-rate, the cashew nuts in the latter providing a contrasting crunch. Tamarind rice with peanuts and dried red chillies was deeply savoury, and we loved uzhunappam (rice flour flatbread flavoured with coconut, shallots and cumin). Save room for scrumptious desserts such as kesari (semolina and mango pudding with nuts and raisins). Special mention must go to the crunchy pre-meal snacks and own-made pickles and chutneys, without which no visit to Rasa would be complete.
Babies and children welcome: high chairs. Booking essential weekends. No smoking. Takeaway service. Vegan dishes. Vegetarian menu. **Map 25 B1.**
For branches see index.

North
Archway N19

The Parsee

34 Highgate Hill, N19 5NL (7272 9091/ www.theparsee.com). Archway tube. **Dinner served** 6-10.45pm Mon-Sat. **Main courses**

Sri Lankan menu

Sri Lanka has three main groups: Sinhalese, Tamil and Muslim. Although there are variations in the cooking styles of each community and every region, rice and curry form the basis of most meals, and curries tend to be hot and spicy.

The cuisine has evolved by absorbing South Indian, Portuguese, Dutch, Arabic, Malaysian and Chinese flavours over the years – so aromatic herbs and spices like cinnamon, cloves, nutmeg, curry leaves and fresh coriander are combined with South-east Asian ingredients like lemongrass, pandan leaves, sesame oil, dried fish and rice noodles. Fresh coconut, onions, green chillies and lime juice (or vinegar) are also used liberally, and there are around two dozen types of rice – from short-grained white to several long-grained burgundy-hued kinds.

Curries come in three main varieties: white (with coconut milk), yellow (with turmeric and mild curry powder) and black (with roasted curry powder, usually used with meat). Hoppers are generally eaten for breakfast with kithul palm syrup and buffalo-milk yoghurt, or (more often in London's restaurants) with fiery curries and relishes.

Despite the increasing number of Sri Lankan restaurants in Tooting, Southall, Wembley and Harrow, Londoners aren't as familiar with the food as they are with other Asian cuisines. This is a pity because the gorgeous tropical flavours of this beautiful island will be a revelation to adventurous palates.

Ambul thiyal: sour fish curry cooked dry with spices.
Appam or appa: see hoppers.
Badun: black. 'Black' curries are fried; they're dry and usually very hot.
Devilled: meat, seafood or vegetable dishes fried with onions in a sweetish sauce; usually served as starters.

Godamba roti: flaky, thin Sri Lankan bread, sometimes wrapped around egg or potato.
Hoppers: confusingly, hoppers come in two forms, either as saucer-shaped, rice-flour pancakes (try the sweet and delectable milk hopper) or as string hoppers (qv). Also called appam.
Idiappa: see string hoppers.
Katta sambol: onion, lemon and chilli relish; fearsomely hot.
Kiri: white. 'White' curries are based on coconut milk and are usually mild.
Kiri hodi: coconut milk curry with onions and turmeric; a soothing gravy.
Kuttu roti, kottu or kothu roti: strips of thin bread (loosely resembling pasta), mixed with mutton, chicken, prawns or vegetables to form a 'bread biriani'; very filling.
Lamprais or lumprice: a biriani-style dish where meat and rice are cooked together, often by baking in banana leaves.
Lunnu miris: a relish of ground onion, chilli and maldives fish (qv).
Maldives fish: small, dried fish with a very intense flavour; an ingredient used in sambols (qv).
Pittu: rice flour and coconut steamed in bamboo to make a 'log'; an alternative to rice.
Pol: coconut.
Pol kiri: see kiri hodi.
Pol sambol: a mix of coconut, chilli, onions, maldives fish (qv) and lemon juice.
Sambols: strongly flavoured relishes, often served hot; they are usually chilli-hot too.
Seeni sambol: sweet and spicy, caramelised onion relish.
Sothy or sothi: another name for kiri hodi.
String hoppers: fine rice-flour noodles formed into flat discs. Usually served steamed (in which case they're dry, making them ideal partners for the gravy-like kiri hodi, qv).
Vellappam: appams (qv) served with vegetable curry.
Wattalappan or vattilapan: a version of crème caramel made with kithul palm syrup.

£9.95-£12.95. **Set dinner** £25 3 courses, £30 4 courses. **Service** 10%. **Credit** AmEx, MC, V. Parsi

Parsi cuisine is a fusion of flavours from Iran, Gujarat and Mumbai. Fresh coriander, mint, cumin, meat, fruit and eggs are used liberally to create a subtle balance of savoury, sweet and tangy flavours. Dishes aren't usually chilli-hot. Chef-proprietor Cyrus Todiwala's stark yet cosy restaurant – all creams, browns, bright artwork and wooden floors – is a one-off, showcasing classic Parsi home-style and wedding dishes. Regrettably, we found the cooking variable, the service rushed when busy, and cooking standards seem to have slipped. Eeda na kavaab were savoury cutlets of hard-boiled eggs, spiked with green chillies and coriander leaves. Although tasty, they were too filling for a starter. In contrast, mumbai no frankie (spicy lamb nuggets encased in pancakes) was among the best versions we've had of this retro-trendy snack from Mumbai. Papeta purr eeda (potatoes, sliced and spiced, topped with eggs) was deliciously hearty, but lamb dhansak had been too timidly flavoured and

indistinctly spiced. The accompanying rice, aromatic with browned onion and star anise, was excellent, though, and the own-made wedding pickles would be worth getting married for.
Babies and children admitted. Booking advisable weekends. No-smoking tables. Separate rooms for parties, seating 18-35. Takeaway service; delivery service (within 3-mile radius on orders over £25). **Map 26 B1.**

Swiss Cottage NW3

Cumin NEW

O2 Centre, 255 Finchley Road, NW3 6LU (7794 5616). Finchley Road tube. **Meals served** noon-11pm Mon-Wed, Sun; noon-midnight Thur-Sat. **Main courses** £5.95-£8.95. **Service** 10%. **Credit** MC, V. Pan-Indian

This bright new canteen inside the O2 shopping centre has Wagamama-style bench seating, interesting wrought-iron artefacts, huge pictures of Indian men and women in traditional costumes, and multicoloured lighting. Somewhat bizarre decor aside, it provides decent, mid-priced Indian classics in contemporary surroundings. Lately,

though, the cooking has been hit and miss. We liked hara bhara kebab (coriander-laden spinach and vegetable kebab served with mint chutney) and succulent prawns in red chilli sauce flecked with caraway and sesame seeds. A velvety paneer curry in fresh fenugreek and tomato sauce, and a distinctly spiced chana masala were also a success. However, hara masala ka gosht (roast lamb with fresh mint, green chillies and spices) wasn't as tender as it should have been. On previous visits, we've enjoyed a silky-smooth nan, yet this time it had a dried-out texture. Cumin has a great atmosphere at weekends when it's busy, but otherwise looks a little dreary. To attract a regular flow of customers, the cooking needs to be much more consistent.

Babies and children welcome: children's menu; crayons; high chairs. Booking advisable weekends. Disabled: toilet. No smoking. Tables outdoors (2, balcony). Takeaway service; delivery service (within 3-mile radius). Vegan dishes. Vegetarian menu. **Map 28 A/B3.**

★ Eriki

4-6 Northways Parade, Finchley Road, NW3 5EN (7722 0606/www.eriki.co.uk). Swiss Cottage tube. **Lunch served** noon-3pm Mon-Fri, Sun. **Dinner served** 6-11pm daily. **Main courses** £7.95-£11.95. **Set lunch** £6.95 1 course. **Service** 12.5%. **Credit** AmEx, JCB, MC, V. Pan-Indian

Good Indian restaurants tend to fall into two categories: cheap and cheerful, or upmarket and expensive. Eriki is different in being a smart neighbourhood restaurant offering reasonably priced aimed at the local market. We like the funky orange and fuchsia paintwork, ornate wooden screens and fabulously groovy cutlery (imported from Rajasthan). Goan head chef Jude Pinto's ambitious menu covers all bases: chats, curries, kebabs, birianis and regional specialities. A salad of squid stir-fried with onions, curry leaves and mustard seeds made an excellent start to the meal, the squid perfectly cooked and the spices judiciously deployed. Pastry cups filled with spiced vegetables and tamarind sauce were fine, if nothing special. Paneer stir-fried with peppers, dried fenugreek leaves and whole spices was absolutely scrumptious, but lamb biriani lacked the meatiness of the real thing (the stock was thin in flavour). Breads such as spinach and fenugreek roti, and layered fresh mint parathas, were exquisite. We've occasionally found the spicing here timid, but food is generally beautifully presented and carefully prepared with top-notch ingredients. Warm, professional service is another plus.

Babies and children admitted. Booking advisable. Restaurant available for hire. Takeaway service. Vegetarian menu. **Map 28 B4.**

North West
Hendon NW4

★ Lahore Original Kebab House NEW

148-150 Brent Street, NW4 2DR (8203 6904). Hendon Central tube. **Meals served** 11am-11.30pm daily. **Main courses** £5-£6.50. **Credit** MC, V. Pakistani

The Lahore chain of basic caffs used to serve authentic Pakistani food until around a decade ago, then standards seemed to slip as competition from other similarly named restaurants intensified. This is the better branch. It has a plain cream and black interior, garnished with a few kitsch ornaments. Chilli mogo was an excellent starter; here the cassava is stir-fried with whole spices, fresh coriander and lots of red and green chillies, then drizzled with a wonderfully tangy tamarind sauce. Paneer pakora were light, fluffy pillows of very soft own-made cheese fried in chickpea flour batter: delicious. Garlic king prawns, juicy little specimens, had been pepped up with lots of garlic and chilli. Karahi chicken keema contained delicately minced chicken in a dark, robust gravy. Spicing is punchy and assertive, as further evidenced by vegetable dishes like karahi bhindi

(okra) and mung makhani (a velvety mung dahl). The only disappointment was egg curry: hard-boiled eggs with a grey rim around the yolks aren't very appetising.

Babies and children welcome: high chairs. Booking advisable. No-smoking tables. Separate room for parties, seats 35. Restaurant available for hire. Takeaway service. Vegetarian menu. **For branch see index.**

Kilburn NW6

Kovalam

12 Willesden Lane, NW6 7SR (7625 4761/ www.kovalamrestaurant.co.uk). Kilburn tube/ 98 bus. **Lunch served** noon-2.30pm daily. **Dinner served** 6-11pm Mon-Thur, Sun; 6-midnight Fri, Sat. **Main courses** £4.35-£7.95. **Set meal** (vegetarian) £18-£35 serves 2-4, (non-vegetarian) £26-£48 serves 2-4. **Credit** AmEx, JCB, MC, V. South Indian

On a stretch of Willesden Lane that's lined with better-known, longer-established South Indian restaurants, Kovalam is king; its popularity never seems to wane. This year the premises have undergone refurbishment (but retain a kitsch look) and the menu has been revamped. Some people still come here for curry house staples like lamb vindaloo – but Keralite classics are really the point. We started with a delicious, fiery seafood soup, crammed with succulent king prawns, tomatoes, ginger, tamarind, garlic and fresh coriander. Pazham pori (ripe plantain fritters) were soft, crunchy and delightful. Lamb fry (marinated nuggets of lamb fried with black peppercorns, onions and curry leaves) had rather tough meat, but the dish was packed with flavour. Chickpea thoran (with shallots, curry leaves and a gentle snowstorm of freshly grated coconut) featured a fabulous marriage of flavours and textures. The main disappointment was a dry lemon rice that lacked the distinctive citrus fragrance and tang. Staff are eager to please and alert.

Babies and children admitted. Booking advisable. No-smoking tables. Takeaway service; delivery service (within 3-mile radius on orders over £15). Vegetarian menu. **Map 1 A1.**

Neasden NW9

★ Tandoor NEW

232-234 Kingsbury Road, NW9 0BH (8205 1450/www.tandoorrestaurant.co.uk). Kingsbury tube/83, 183, 302, 204 bus. **Lunch served** noon-3.30pm, dinner served 6-11.30pm daily. **Main courses** £5-£7.50. **Set lunch** £6.99 1 course. **Credit** AmEx, MC, V. North Indian

One of Kingsbury's culinary heroes, Tandoor is a popular destination with South Asian families. This modern, split-level restaurant, housed in a pub, is furnished with swish silk drapes, crisp table linen and ornate lamps. Affordable North Indian specialities, earthy curries and some of the more unusual griddle kebabs are what to look for on the menu. A first course of kathi kebabs made an auspicious beginning to our meal – they came as soft chapatis, coated with a spicy omelette on one side, enveloping delicious, lime-drenched slivers of tandoori chicken and crisp raw onion slices. Bara kebab – succulent seared lamb chops, steeped in a tart yoghurt and ginger masala – was another winner. Vegetables were the only let-down: our paneer saagawala (fried spinach with paneer) was heavy on oil and overspiced. Service, though, was spot-on. We'll be back for piles of the flaky parathas and platters of meat kebabs.

Babies and children welcome: high chairs. Booking advisable weekends. Disabled: toilet. No smoking. Separate room for parties, seats 60. Takeaway service. Vegetarian menu.

Willesden NW10

★ Saravanas

77-81 Dudden Hill Lane, NW10 1BD (8459 4900/2400/www.saravanas.co.uk). Dollis Hill tube. **Meals served** noon-10.30pm Tue-Sun. **Main courses** £4.45-£7. **Thalis** £5.95-£7.95. **Set buffet** (noon-3.30pm Fri, Sun) £4.75. **Credit** JCB, MC, V. South Indian

Brick Lane

Brick Lane's fame as a centre for 'Indian' restaurants – they are almost all Bangladeshi-run – grew during the 1970s as small neighbourhood caffs began catering for edge-of-City diners. By the 1980s they were thriving, earning a growing reputation for good-value meals. The Bangladeshi owners were quick to capitalise on this. By 2005 the total number of restaurants in 'Banglatown' (if you include venues in neighbouring streets) exceeded 50, probably the largest 'curry-house cluster' in Europe. Brick Lane's fame has even reached New York, where an upmarket restaurant has named itself after the most famous street in Spitalfields.

Yet if you study the menus displayed in Brick Lane windows, one thing quickly becomes clear: originality is not a strong point of most kitchens. The same dishes tend to recur. Chicken tikka masala, chicken or lamb madras/bhuna/ korma, tandoor-cooked meats, various vegetable and seafood dishes – they all start to taste very similar after you've eaten in Brick Lane a few times. Try finding a real Bangladeshi dish, let alone authentic Indian cooking, and you'll need to look hard.

Not that you get much chance to scrutinise window menus. Hesitate, and touts are likely to pounce. In 100 metres we must have been approached more than a dozen times, before stopping at one restaurant with a neon sign proudly proclaiming 'Best In Brick Lane, *Time Out* 2001'. News to us, as *Time Out* has never had a 'Best In Brick Lane' award.

In fact, for years *Time Out* has been warning readers of the pitfalls of eating in Brick Lane. Namely, while the food can be cheap, most restaurants aren't going to win any awards for their cooking. Year after year our reviewers have found culinary standards on Brick Lane inconsistent, and service also highly variable. Even when *Time Out*'s reviewers have had a good meal, return visits have seen standards slump.

By all means, go to Brick Lane looking for a relatively inexpensive and fun night out. Savour the aromas, the vibrancy of the neighbourhood, the loud music and party atmosphere, and the often memorable decor (our favourite is the large Bollywood-style portrait of Lady Di in one restaurant). Just don't expect to find London's most 'authentic' or 'best' South Asian food – because back in Bangladesh, which has a strong and distinctive culinary tradition, most people wouldn't recognise the dishes served on Brick Lane.

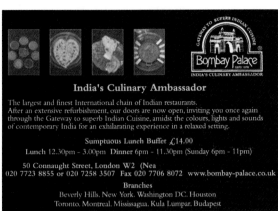

Overcoming a less-than-glamorous location, Saravanas has made its mark by serving affordable South Indian spreads to local Asian residents. It is partitioned into two linked areas: the main dining room is geared for families, and furnished with basic seating and easy-wipe tables; the other area, aimed at Asian businessmen, is more of a bar, with its dark-hued mix of rattan and cane seating. Cooking is variable: we've had memorable dishes in the past, but also mediocre ones. The sambar has been consistently excellent; this soupy lentil dish, tart with tamarind, is studded with South Indian vegetables such as drumsticks and squishy aubergines. This time we plumped for the Saravanas thali – a complete meal of four vegetable dishes, plus munchies, rice, a poori and a milky pud. We especially liked the crushed potatoes combined with crunchy yellow lentils and curry leaves, for its gentle spicing. Not all dishes were as worthy: an excessively salty rasam (peppery soup) and densely textured idlis (spongy, steamed rice dumplings) did the restaurant no favours. Service, although well-meaning, needs a nudge now and again.
Babies and children welcome: high chairs. Booking advisable. Disabled: toilet. No smoking Restaurant available for hire. Takeaway service.

Outer London
Edgware, Middlesex

★ **Haandi**
301-303 Hale Lane, Edgware, Middx HA8 7AX (8905 4433/www.haandi-restaurants.com). Edgware tube. **Lunch served** 12.30-3pm Wed-Sun. **Dinner served** 6-11pm Mon-Thur, Sun; 6-11.30pm Fri, Sat. **Main courses** £3.50-£7.90. **Service** 12.5%. **Credit** AmEx, MC, V. North Indian
The latest link in a four-strong chain of restaurants in Nairobi, Kampala, Knightsbridge and now Edgware, this Haandi doesn't do fine dining in the same way as its dressier sibling in SW3. It's not a plain establishment – adorned with foliage, a water feature, cane seating and skylights – but most Asian families and curious local residents come here for the cooking and not the fetching glass-plated exterior. The Punjabi spicing scores every time. Kake di lamb was a delight, well worth the lengthy wait for its arrival at table: cooked on the bone, the meltingly tender meaty chunks were surrounded by a moat of bone marrow-rich masala, delicately flavoured with cardamom, ginger and garlic. If you order one dish, make it this one. Tandoori chicken, well marinated in tartly spiced yoghurt, was another winner. Only the chickpea dish disappointed, with its mundane masala of undercooked tomatoes and onion. And we were baffled by the tomato ketchup squiggles of modern art on our platters. The service team, although friendly, could do with supervision and a better understanding of the menu.
Babies and children welcome: high chairs. Booking advisable weekends. No-smoking tables. Takeaway service; delivery service (within 3-mile radius on orders over £20). Vegetarian menu.
For branch see index.

Harrow, Middlesex

★ **Blue Ginger** NEW
383 Kenton Road, Harrow, Middx HA3 0XS (8909 0100/www.vijayrestaurant.com). Kenton tube/rail. **Lunch served** noon-3pm Tue-Sun. **Dinner served** 6-11pm daily. **Main courses** £5.25-£9.95. **Credit** AmEx, MC, V. North Indian
An affluent British Asian crowd has struck gold with this neighbourhood watering hole. It's a spacious, light and airy spot, furnished with low-slung, comfy sofas in the lounge area, a sleek black granite bar in the main restaurant, and a plethora of flat-screen TVs. Two separate menus celebrate Indo-Chinese and mainly North Indian cooking styles. On our visit, the Chinese bites were as bold and brassy as the Bollywood dancers on the TV. We kicked off with honey chicken – deep-fried meaty morsels, dunked in a lovely honey glaze. Though hardly subtle, it made an appetising bar

snack, enjoyable for its pungent root ginger and a wake-up call of red chilli. Staying closer to North Indian roots, we loved the rich, russet-brown masala, spiked with toasted garlic paste, in a simple main course of keema curry (fried lamb mince, simmered with onions, garlic and ginger). The service team set the tone: professional, personable and enthusiastic. At last there's somewhere decent that bridges the chasm between pricey Indian fine-dining restaurants and budget high-street joints.
Babies and children welcome: children's menu; high chairs. Booking essential. Disabled: toilet. Dress: smart casual. No-smoking tables. Restaurant available for hire (Mon-Thur). Tables outdoors (7, terrace). Takeaway service.

★ **Ram's**
203 Kenton Road, Harrow, Middx HA3 0HD (8907 2022). Kenton Road tube. **Lunch served** noon-3pm, **dinner served** 6-11pm daily. **Main courses** £3.30-£4.50. **Thalis** £4.99 (lunch), £8.99 (dinner). **Set meal** £15 unlimited food and soft drinks. **Service** 10%. **Credit** AmEx, DC, JCB, MC, V. Gujarati vegetarian
This unassuming café with plain white walls and statues of Hindu gods specialises in Surti food from southern Gujarat. It's popular with vegetarians and vegans, but the cooking doesn't live up to the hype. What's more, it's not the real deal. Surti dishes are usually cooked with green masala (coriander leaves, fresh coconut, green chillies, ginger and – most importantly – Indian green garlic, which is rarely found in the UK). However, loaded with crushed tomatoes and red chilli powder, Ram's dishes are hardly distinguishable from London's other East African Gujarati restaurants, and the flavours are too fiery and too sweet. Kand (purple yam fritters) are often a good bet, but this time the yam was undercooked. Stuffed banana fritters were better – though the spicing was not specifically Surti. Karela-ravaiya (bitter gourd with aubergines) was interesting for its texture more than its flavour. Bhindi kadhi (okra in spicy yoghurt sauce) was delicious, yet too thin in consistency, but khichadi (a rice and lentil mix) was authentically mushy and rich with ghee. Stick to snacks and savouries rather than cooked meals, and don't expect absolute authenticity.
Babies and children welcome: high chairs. Booking advisable weekends. Disabled: toilet. No smoking. Restaurant available for hire (Mon-Thur). Takeaway service. Vegetarian menu.

Safari NEW
14A Broadwalk, Pinner Road, North Harrow, Middx HA2 6ED (8861 6766). Harrow rail/ 183, 350 bus. **Dinner served** 6pm-midnight Mon-Thur. **Meals served** 1pm-midnight Fri-Sun. **Main courses** £4.50-£9.50. **Credit** MC, V. North Indian
Darkened windows and a nondescript façade aren't the best advertisement for pulling in punters – but looks aren't everything. This joint is chiefly a meeting place and watering hole for local Asian men and (at weekends) their families. The interior is dimly lit and decor distinctly low-key, except for a nod towards a safari-style big game theme. Cooking, however, is a couple of notches above average. Keema mutter (fried lamb mince, studded with green peas) was simmered with browned onions and ginger, and seasoned with pounded cardamom seeds – great comfort cooking. On the other hand, chicken tikka pieces, although juicy and well marinated in garlicky yoghurt, had a disconcerting radioactive-red hue. Our advice is to stick with the no-nonsense curries and mop up the lot with nans. Service is a little slow, but there's plenty of Bollywood action on the flat-screen TVs to help you build up an appetite.
Babies and children welcome: high chairs. Booking advisable. Disabled: toilet. Dress: smart casual. No-smoking tables. Takeaway service; delivery service (within 5-mile radius on orders over £15). Vegetarian menu.

★ **Sakonis**
5-8 Dominion Parade, Station Road, Harrow, Middx HA1 2TR (8863 3399). Harrow rail/140, 182, 186, 342 bus. **Meals served** noon-9.30pm

Tue-Thur, Sun; noon-10pm Fri, Sat. **Main courses** £3.95-£6.75. **Set buffet** £6.50 (lunch), £8.99 (dinner). **Service** 10%. **Credit** MC, V. Gujarati vegetarian
Most Gujaratis have their favourite Sakoni dish. Many swear by crispy bhajia (garlicky potato slices in a batter so crisp the recipe is a trade secret) and chilli paneer (an Indo-Chinese modern classic, made with paneer stir-fried with green pepper, onions, tomatoes, garlic, soy sauce and chilli sauce). However, we gave the hugely popular Indo-Chinese dishes and the busy self-service buffet a miss in favour of traditional Gujarati savouries. Dahl bhajia (lentil fritters) were hot, soft and crunchy; we couldn't stop eating them. Pau bhaji (spicy, buttery, mashed vegetables, accompanied by a white bread roll) was beautifully flavoured, if a little rich. Avoid the South Indian dishes, which can be too sweet, and stick to Mumbai-style chats. Fresh juices, milkshakes and sundaes make perfect accompaniments to the fried food. All the caffs in the ever-expanding Sakonis chain have simple and functional decor, a counter serving sweets and savouries, a self-service buffet, and a lively atmosphere. It can be hard to get a table at the flagship Wembley branch; this outlet is quieter.
Babies and children welcome: crayons; high chairs. Booking advisable. Disabled: toilet. No smoking. Separate room for parties, seats 100. Takeaway service. Vegan dishes. Vegetarian menu.
For branches see index.

Rayners Lane, Middlesex

★ ★ **Kathiyawadi**
2005 RUNNER-UP BEST VEGETARIAN MEAL
434 Rayners Lane, Middx HA5 5DX (8868 2723/ www.kathiyawadi.co.uk). Rayners Lane tube. **Meals served** 5-11pm Tue-Fri; noon-11pm Sat, Sun. **Main courses** £4.75-£6.25. **Credit** AmEx, JCB, MC, V. Gujarati vegetarian
The design of this no-frills restaurant – complete with patterned carpet and plasma screens showing Bollywood movies – won't set your pulse racing. No matter: here you'll find the authentic fiery cuisine of Kathiyawad, a hot, arid region in west Gujarat. Dishes tend to be mushy, and contain lots of chickpea flour, red chilli powder and own-made dairy products (thick buttermilk, creamy yoghurt, white butter). To start, we shared a light, ungreasy platter of mixed bhajia: potato slices, hot green chillies, stuffed mild chillies, and urid lentil balls flavoured with fresh fenugreek and chilli, dipped in batter and fried until crisp. Curries like sev and fresh tomato, and chana dudhi (bottle gourd with split Bengal chickpeas) were equally delicious. Breads such as rotlo (millet bread) and chilli paratha are authentically rustic, and there's a wide range of lovely own-made pickles. The restaurant bustles with Indian families at weekends when there's a special menu – but on our Friday evening visit, it was quiet except for a few couples, though the kindly proprietor still allowed us to order from the weekend menu.
Babies and children welcome: high chairs. Booking advisable. Takeaway service. Vegetarian menu.

Papaya
15 Village Way East, Rayners Lane, Middx HA2 7LX (8866 5582/www.papayauk.com). Rayners Lane tube/H10, H12 bus. **Meals served** noon-midnight Mon-Sat; noon-11pm Sun. **Main courses** £6-£10. **Service** 10%. **Credit** MC, V. Sri Lankan
Glass-fronted Papaya has lost its cosy community-caff feel and bright sassy colours. The decor has been revamped in favour of leatherette banquettes, a neutral colour scheme and rows of varnished tables, sacrificing quirky charm for a regimented canteen vibe. Thankfully, the cooking still has plenty of soul, making up for any shortcomings in the interior design. Fried kingfish steak, steeped in turmeric and lime juice, was surrounded by a delectable, dark-hued moat of satiny-smooth tamarind and ginger curry. We also approved of the mutton biriani, its cardamom-rich base cloaking the perfectly cooked rice and enveloping tender pieces of meat. This is no run-of-the-mill curry house – cooking styles are typically Sri

Lankan and dishes are embellished with own-ground toasted spices. Expect chilli-heat, coconut milk sauces and an array of rice-based staples. Service is smooth and our East European waitress was impressively clued-up on menu choices. *Babies and children welcome: high chairs. Booking essential weekends. No-smoking tables. Restaurant available for hire. Takeaway service; delivery service (within 3-mile radius on orders over £15). Vegetarian menu.*

Southall, Middlesex

Noisy, brash and beautiful, Southall doesn't just imitate a Punjabi town centre – it does it better than back home. The place is more like a perennial village fair than a shopping centre, but there's little you can't get here.

It's the food that makes Southall special; baltis, more Birmingham than Pakistan, aren't given stove space here. Instead, you'll discover stacks of nans, black creamy dahls, and skewer-wielding chefs spearing marinated meats. For the best kebabs and superb yoghurt-based snacks, take a brisk walk away from the Broadway, down South Road, and head for **New Asian Tandoori Centre (Roxy)**. Its wholesome cooking is not only astonishingly cheap, but also as authentic as they come.

Yes, Southall is cursed with maddening traffic at weekends. If driving, use the main car park behind the Broadway's Himalaya Centre. Better still, take the train or bus – shops are close by and there's plenty to see on the way. Check out **Kwality Foods** (47-61 South Road, UB1 1SQ, 8917 9188) for groceries and extremely cheap vegetables such as gourds and greens.

For local residents going about their business, old Southall still has its well-worn charm. **Glassy Junction** (97 South Road, UB1 1SQ, 8574 1626), a Punjabi pub, has the vibe of a working men's club with its patterned carpet and pints of keg beer – except here you'll also get hot parathas. **Madhu's** restaurant, located down the road, boasts black granite floors and a super-stylish Indo-Kenyan menu; this is where the well-heeled hang out. For more down-to-earth munchies, grab a bag of samosas from **Ambala** (107 The Broadway, UB1 1LNT, 8843 9049); they're a bargain at under 50p each. Finally, there's always **Moti Mahal** (94 The Broadway, UB1 1QF, 8571 9443) for hot, syrupy jalebis made from whirls of deep-fried batter – one is never enough.

Brilliant

72-76 Western Road, Southall, Middx UB2 5DZ (8574 1928/www.brilliantrestaurant.com). Southall rail. **Lunch served** noon-2.30pm Tue-Fri. **Dinner served** 6-11.30pm Tue-Sun. **Main courses** £4.50-£13. **Credit** AmEx, DC, JCB, MC, V. Punjabi
To name your restaurant Brilliant, you have to be either arrogant or confident – and it seems that this much-loved, well-established restaurant falls in the latter camp. It's immensely popular with large groups and families out celebrating birthdays, and consequently sparkles with a constant buzz. The food is fairly basic, and the flavours are strong and assertive: don't expect subtle spicing. Meat kofte were flavoursome, melt-in-the-mouth meatballs in a sassy gravy, and vegetable keema was a delicious vegetarian version of the archetypal minced lamb curry with peas. Nor do popular classics like butter chicken, jeera chicken and the various karahi dishes disappoint. And don't miss the aloo paratha or the own-made lemon pickle, which are simply scrumptious. To drink, we recommend the Penfolds shiraz, which is a perfect match to the food. Service

is very friendly and eager to please, but the decor – worn patterned carpet, somewhat uncomfortable seating, plasma screens blaring Indian pop music – could do with a 21st-century makeover. *Babies and children welcome: high chairs. Booking advisable weekends. No-smoking tables. Restaurant available for hire. Separate room for parties, seats 120. Takeaway service. Vegetarian menu.*

Madhu's

39 South Road, Southall, Middx UB1 1SW (8574 1897/www.madhusonline.com). Southall rail. **Lunch served** 12.30-3pm Mon, Wed-Fri. **Dinner served** 6-11.30pm Mon, Wed, Thur, Sun; 6pm-midnight Fri, Sat. **Main courses** £6-£12. **Set meal** £17.50-£20 16 dishes incl tea or coffee. **Credit** AmEx, DC, MC, V. East African Punjabi
A popular destination with Punjabi families and adventurous non-Asians, Madhu's looks very much the part as an upmarket Indian restaurant. It is fronted by an expansive glass-paned entrance, and sprawls over two floors. Furnishings include shiny black granite flooring, water features and crisp, white table linen. Sari-clad waitresses add to the elegance. Cooking is Punjabi, but there's a noticeable East African twist to signature dishes. We plumped for machuzi kuku, a satisfying chicken curry, flavoured with a subtle cinnamon and clove infusion. The more classic Punjabi dishes, although passable, aren't quite as memorable. Papri chat – crisp pastry discs, coated in yoghurt, and streaked through with sweet tamarind chutney and a tart mint and coriander relish – made a refreshing start to our meal. But main courses such as makhani chicken and keema mutter bordered on the banal, having more in common with a curry house rendition than a restaurant of this repute. Almond kulfi saved the day: this Indian ice-cream, rich with cooked-down cream and fudgy almond flavour, was quite divine. We'll be back for the East African dishes and, of course, for pud. *Babies and children welcome: high chairs. Booking advisable. Disabled: toilet. Dress: smart casual. Separate room for parties, seats 35. Takeaway service.*

★ ★ New Asian Tandoori Centre (Roxy)

114-118 The Green, Southall, Middx UB2 4BQ (8574 2597). Southall rail. **Meals served** 8am-11pm Mon-Thur; 8am-midnight Fri-Sun. **Main courses** £3-£7. **Credit** MC, V. Punjabi
In common with many Southall diners, this Punjabi favourite has moved upmarket over the years. There's still a canteen-style takeaway section, its stainless-steel counter displaying bhajis, sweets and curries (the latter microwaved before serving), its back wall bedecked with backlit photos of the dishes. Adjacent, though, is a large waiter-served dining room with frosted-glass windows, long communal tables (popular with Sikh families and groups of young Southallians), uplit, honey-hued walls and modern wooden furniture. Next to this is a still-swisher bistro-like room, similarly decorated but with a bar, smaller tables, lower lighting and fresh flower arrangements. Happily, the service (polite, friendly) and the food (low priced, large portions) remains of a high order. Best are the curries: thick, savoury dahl; sag meat featuring tender lamb in luxuriant, mousse-like spinach. Not far behind are the breads (hard-to-refuse methi paratha, feather-light rotis and nans) and the snacks/starters (especially the papdi chat: chickpeas and popadom fragments in a sweet-sour sauce). Best avoid the greasy birianis, but otherwise the Roxy is a treat. *Babies and children admitted: high chairs. Booking advisable. Disabled: toilet. No smoking. Separate room for parties, seats 60. Takeaway service. Vegetarian menu.*

★ Palm Palace

80 South Road, Southall, Middx UB1 1RD (8574 9209). Southall rail. **Lunch served** noon-3pm daily. **Dinner served** 6-11pm Mon-Thur; 6-11.30pm Fri-Sun. **Main courses** £3-£5.50. **Credit** AmEx, JCB, MC, V. Sri Lankan

Perhaps nudged into action by the sleek refurb undergone by nearby Madhu's (*see above*), Palm Palace unveiled its spanking new interior in June 2005. You'll now find parquet flooring, stylish narrow-backed wooden chairs, granite-effect table tops, a wooden bar, and violet and green refracted light playing down beige walls. Little could be done about the modest size of the place or the plate-glass windows looking on to busy South Road, though. No matter: the waiters are now smartly attired in black shirts and ties, yet they're still models of quiet congeniality. The high food quality and low prices have remained too. From the long list of Sri Lankan and South Indian dishes, we can enthusiastically recommend the brinjal jaffna-style (lovely smoky flavours of aubergine in a spicy tomato sauce), the squid ceylon (tender as mercy), the idiappa special mix biriani (a string hopper biriani with mutton, chicken, prawns, cashew nuts and boiled egg), the flavour-packed sambar and the large portions. The devilled mutton was chewy, but otherwise we had no complaints. Sri Lankans and increasing numbers of Westerners provide the happy mix of customers. *Babies and children welcome: high chairs. Booking advisable weekends. Takeaway service. Vegetarian menu.*
For branch see index.

Sudbury, Middlesex

★ ★ Five Hot Chillies

875 Harrow Road, Sudbury, Middx HA0 2RH (8908 5900). Sudbury Town or Sudbury Hill tube. **Meals served** noon-midnight daily. **Main courses** £3.50-£9. **Unlicensed. Corkage** no charge. **Credit** MC, V. Punjabi
Everything about this jolly caff hits home – from the earthy Punjabi dialects to the no-frills, brilliantly executed cooking and the boisterous, backslapping bonhomie between regular diners. Five Hot Chillies is frequented mainly by Punjabi and Pakistani families. The atmosphere can be summed up as vibrantly chaotic, but there's method in the madness; the clued-up waiters rarely miss a thing. There has been some attempt to convey a contemporary feel to the decor, with a glass-plated frontage and plenty of green-hued fittings and fixtures, but mercifully the cooking remains wholesome, traditional and remarkably cheap. Delicious chicken tikka, served straight from the skewer, came unadorned: a simple dish, where the focus was on the full flavour of thick yoghurt spiked with garlic and ginger, rather than fussy garnishing. Deighi gosht (an earthy, North Indian lamb curry, cooked on the bone) benefited from a slow-fried onion masala, and was finished with a shower of crisp raw ginger strips. No question: this place is the jewel in Sudbury's culinary crown. *Babies and children welcome: high chairs. Booking advisable. Takeaway service. Vegetarian menu.*

Twickenham, Middlesex

★ Pallavi

Unit 3, Cross Deep Court, Heath Road, Twickenham, Middx TW1 4QJ (8892 2345/4466/www.mcdosa.com). Twickenham rail. **Lunch served** noon-3pm daily. **Dinner served** 6-11pm Mon-Thur, Sun; 6pm-midnight Fri, Sat. **Main courses** £4.50-£7.95. **Service** 10%. **Credit** AmEx, MC, V. South Indian
Owned by the company that also runs Radha Krishna Bhavan (*see p145*), Pallavi is located on the first floor of a shopping arcade. With its worn carpet, kitsch knick-knacks and artificial plants, the interior is in urgent need of a makeover. Despite this, the food is good. We started with delectable adai (spicy pan-fried griddle cakes made with a fermented rice and mixed lentil batter), which had the appropriate spongy texture and sour tang. Meat masala dosai featured crisp, lacy pancakes stuffed with a tasty mix of minced lamb and mashed potatoes. The accompanying sambar and coconut chutney were OK, but lacked oomph. Cochin prawn curry was made with prawns that tasted less than fresh, though the coconut sauce,

Cumin. See p149.

pepped up with cumin, mustard seeds, chillies and curry leaves, was flavoursome. Dahl with spinach was delightfully creamy, and green bean and fresh coconut thoran arrived at table vibrant and pleasingly al dente. Lemon rice and pilau rice were both made with fragrant basmati. Service is sweet-natured, if a little dreamy and languorous.
Babies and children welcome: high chairs. Booking advisable. No-smoking tables. Takeaway service; delivery service (within 3-mile radius on orders over £20).

Tangawizi NEW

406 Richmond Road, Richmond Bridge, East Twickenham, Middx TW1 2EB (8891 3737). Richmond tube/rail. **Dinner served** 6.30-11pm Mon-Sat. **Main courses** £6.95-£12.95. **Credit** AmEx, MC, V. Modern Indian
It's rare for a neighbourhood Indian restaurant to boast a chef 'trained by, and strongly recommended by, Vineet Bhatia'. But Tangawizi ('ginger' in Swahili) does just that. The chef is Krishnapal Negi, formerly of Mayfair's Yatra (*see p133*). This smart venue – done up in saffron and blackberry, with backlit panels and judicious use of sari fabric – buzzes with well-heeled locals. We've visited twice, and were largely impressed with the food: authentic North Indian dishes reinterpreted for a 21st-century Western clientele. Crisp, light, chilli-flecked button mushroom pakoras were delicious; spicy yoghurt-marinated lamb chops were butter-soft; and a sauté of cauliflower in tamarind and tomato sauce sparkled with layers of flavour. For mains, the best dishes were spicy marinated red snapper dipped in light tempura-like batter, served with cheddar and parmesan risotto; and saag paneer enlivened with fresh ginger. The dahls (black urid with kidney beans, and yellow split peas) were excellent: rich and beautifully spiced, with exemplary texture. Less admirable were the dry pilau rice, lacking in fragrance; Andhra-style potatoes masked with too much tomato purée; and an odd-tasting mango ice-cream 'with a hint of chilli'. Nonetheless, flavours here are generally fresh, light and perky.
Babies and children welcome: high chairs. Booking advisable Fri, Sat. Entertainment: musicians 8-10pm Fri. No smoking (before 10pm). Takeaway service; delivery service (within 3-mile radius on orders over £15). Vegetarian menu.

Wembley, Middlesex

Until fairly recently, Ealing Road in Wembley could be described as the capital's 'Little Gujarat'. It's where Gujarati businessmen and their families – most of them second- or third-generation Asians from Kenya or elsewhere in East Africa, plus a few from India – had settled in the 1950s and set up shops, cafés and restaurants. The road shimmers with shops selling peacock-coloured saris, wedding jewellery, kitchen utensils, Bollywood films and Indian celebrity magazines. The pavements heave with displays of exotic fruit and vegetables; elsewhere there are paanwallahs selling paan (mouth-fresheners), ice-cream vans dishing out kulfi (Indian 'ice-cream') or falooda (thick, sundae-like milky drinks), and little makeshift stalls offering boxes of mangos. Gujarati food shops include **Prashad Sweets** (222 Ealing Road, HAO 4QL, 8902 1704), and grocery stores **VB & Sons** (147 Ealing Road, HAO 4BU, 8795 0387) and **Wembley Exotics** (133-135 Ealing Road, HAO 4BP, 8900 2607).

Yet change is afoot, with Sri Lankan and Somali businesses making inroads into the area. **Bismillah Butchers** (6 Plaza Parade, Ealing Road, HAO 4YA, 8903 4922), a Sri Lankan meat and fish emporium, is one such enterprise. Gujarati families are gradually moving out to more affluent areas like Kingsbury, Kenton, Harrow and Rayners Lane; consequently, there has been a spate of new Gujarati shops, cafés and restaurants opening in those districts.

★ Chowpatty NEW

234 Ealing Road, Wembley, Middx HAO 4QL (8795 0077). Alberton tube/83, 297 bus. **Lunch served** 11am-3pm, **dinner served** 5.30-10pm Mon-Wed, Fri. **Meals served** 11am-11.30pm Sat; 11am-10pm Sun. **Main courses** £2.49-£4.25. **Thalis** £3.99-£8.95. **Set buffet** (11am-4pm Sun) £4.50. **Service** 10%. **Credit** MC, V. Gujarati vegetarian
Named after the popular Mumbai beach, Chowpatty is one of the best Gujarati restaurants to have opened in Wembley in recent months. It looks garish: there are gigantic colourful murals of Chowpatty beach, complete with its famous food stalls. Mumbai street food and Kutchi specialities (from the north-west desert region of Gujarat) are the draw here. Bhel puri is the real thing, a rare treat in London – hot, tangy, crispy and correctly spiced. Chats, pakoras and kebabs are also tasty; try, for instance, the vegetable kathi kebabs (spiced

Sweets menu

Sweetmeats and puddings aren't usually served during everyday meals on the Indian subcontinent. You're more likely to be treated to fragrant mangoes, heaps of chilled lychees or perhaps a wedge of lush red watermelon. A selection of sweet, syrupy confectionery is more likely to be offered at religious and festive occasions; these are enjoyed throughout the day, even sometimes at breakfast.

Once in a while, though, home cooks will set aside an afternoon to make huge amounts of fudge-like carrot halwa, flavoured with cardamom and sweetened cooked-down milk. Other sweets contain semolina, wholewheat flour, lentils or pumpkin. Most take time to make, which is why many people prefer to visit sweetmeat stores, the best known of which is **Ambala**'s flagship emporium (112 Drummond Street, NW1 2HN, 7387 3521). Here, an impressive array of traditional eye candy for the seriously sweet-toothed includes soft cheese-based dumplings immersed in rose-scented syrup, cashew-nut fudgy blocks, toasted gram-flour balls and marzipan-like rolls. Expect floral flavours, shed-loads of sugar and a good whack of calorie-laden ghee (clarified butter). It's hard to believe that, with all the varieties offered, specialist sweet-makers (known as 'halwais') cook with so few ingredients – milk products, dried fruit, sugar and ghee being the key components.

For more adventurous tastes, upmarket restaurants have upped the stakes and fine-tuned their dessert repertoire. Newcomer **Amaya** (*see p131*) surpasses itself with such winning numbers as dreamy rose sorbet, served with chilli-spiked custard, and a peppery Bollywood-red plum compote. There has also been a growing trend among more innovative chefs in top-end restaurants to combine classic Indian flavours and Western-style desserts. Shining examples include the dried apricot ice-cream served at **Café Spice Namaste** (*see p147*) and **Chutney Mary**'s garam masala crème brûlée (*see p139*). For a really wacky combination, visit **Rasoi Vineet Bhatia** (*see p141*) and sample the unusual chocolates, crammed with Indian aromatics.

On the flip side, many smaller establishments are buying in ready-made kulfis and pre-packed sweets from caterers on the cheap – results, in the main, are underwhelming.

Barfi: sweetmeat usually made with reduced milk, and flavoured with nuts, fruit, sweet spices or coconut.
Bibenca or **bibinca**: soft, layered cake from Goa made with eggs, coconut milk and jaggery.
Falooda or **faluda**: thick milky drink (originally from the Middle East), resembling a cross between a milkshake and a sundae. It's flavoured with either rose syrup or saffron, and also contains agar-agar, vermicelli, nuts and ice-cream. Very popular with Gujarati families, faloodas make perfect partners to deep-fried snacks.
Gajar halwa: grated carrots, cooked in sweetened cardamom milk until soft, then fried in ghee until almost caramelised; usually served warm.
Gulab jamun: brown dumplings, deep-fried and served in rose-flavoured sugar syrup, best served warm. A traditional Bengali sweet, now ubiquitous in Indian restaurants.
Halwa: a fudge-like sweet, made with semolina, wholewheat flour or ground pulses cooked with syrup or reduced milk, and flavoured with nuts, saffron or sweet spices.
Jalebis: spirals of batter, deep-fried and dipped in syrup, best eaten warm.
Kheer: milky rice pudding, flavoured with cardamom and nuts. Popular throughout India, where there are countless regional variations.
Kulfi: ice-cream made from reduced milk, flavoured with nuts, saffron or fruit.
Payasam: a South Indian pudding made of reduced coconut or cow's milk with sago, nuts and cardamom. Semiya payasam is made with added vermicelli.
Rasgullas: soft paneer cheese balls, simmered and dipped in rose-scented syrup; served cold.
Ras malai: soft paneer cheese patties in sweet and thickened milk, served cold.
Shrikhand: hung (concentrated) sweet yoghurt with saffron, nuts and cardamom, sometimes with fruit added. A traditional Gujarati favourite, eaten with pooris.

Five Hot Chillies. See p154.

potatoes and vegetables dolloped inside soft flatbreads) and khichi (steamed lentil flour dumplings doused in oil). The menu lists (Gujarati versions of) South Indian, Punjabi and Chinese dishes, but we suggest you skip these in favour of Kutchi specialities like baingan oro (grilled, mashed aubergines), kadhi (yoghurt 'soup'), khichadi (lentil and rice mixture) and bajra roti (millet bread). In fact, breads are the kitchen's strong point: we can particularly recommend methi thepla (savoury flatbread flavoured with fresh fenugreek) and missi roti (spicy maize flour flatbread flecked with chillies).
Babies and children welcome: high chairs.
Booking advisable Fri-Sun. No smoking.
Takeaway service; delivery service (within 5-mile radius on orders over £12). Vegan dishes.
Vegetarian menu.

★ ★ Dadima NEW

228 Ealing Road, Wembley, Middx HA0 4QL (8902 1072). Alperton tube/83, 79 297 bus.
Lunch served noon-3pm, **dinner served** 5-10pm Mon, Wed-Fri. **Meals served** noon-10pm Sat, Sun. **Main courses** £3-£4.50. **Thalis** £2.99-£5.99. **Credit** MC, V. Gujarati vegetarian
One of the best restaurants to have opened on Ealing Road recently, Dadima ('grandmother' in Gujarati) is a small, unpretentious, family-owned venue with warm, welcoming service. It specialises in Gujarati food from Ahmedabad (home of Mahatma Gandhi) in central Gujarat. As with many Gujarati restaurants, the menu encompasses slightly sweet versions of Punjabi and South Indian dishes. Avoid these and head straight for the speciality Gujarati food. We particularly like dadi ni thali ('grandma's thali') in which a large metal plate comes with little metal containers crammed with freshly cooked seasonal vegetables and dahls. On our most recent visit, we enjoyed toor (pigeon pea) dahl, yoghurt kadhi, potato

curry, spinach curry, sprouted mung beans, soft fluffy pillows of pooris, and pilau rice. The flavours are distinctively Ahmedabadi – that is, dishes are cooked with a 'red masala' mixture of chilli powder, turmeric, ground cumin and crushed coriander seeds. Gujarati food has incorporated 'fusion' flavours over the years, but the dishes here are the real deal. They're the kind of food that Gujarati grannies of yesteryear used to make. Recommended.
Babies and children welcome: high chairs.
Booking essential weekends. Disabled: toilet.
No smoking. Takeaway service. Vegan dishes.
Vegetarian menu.

★ Jashan

1-2 Coronet Parade, Ealing Road, Wembley, Middx HA0 4AY (8900 9800/www.jashan restaurants.com). Wembley Central tube/rail.
Lunch served noon-3.30pm, **dinner served** 6-11pm Mon-Fri. **Meals served** noon-11pm Sat, Sun. **Main courses** £3.50-£4.95. **Set buffet** (lunch Mon-Fri) £4.99. **Credit** JCB, MC, V. Pan-Indian vegetarian
A contemporary-styled café, catering mainly to Gujarati customers and local shoppers, Jashan offers substantial snacks at fair prices. A large, plate-glass frontage looks on to a bright interior, seasoned with colourful motifs and East African artefacts. The extensive menu features pan-Indian classics, but also includes the latest vegetarian fads, such as spicy sichuan mogo chips, sweet and sour vegetables, and a fusion of Indo-Italian spaghetti dishes. We chose a selection of more traditional food. South Indian dosa (paper-thin lentil and ground-rice pancake) was crisp and golden, accompanied by potato mash seasoned with softened onions and popped mustard seeds. We especially liked the fresh-tasting coconut chutney, pounded with mild green chillies and white lentils. Regrettably, our somewhat stingy helping of sambar didn't match the dosa in quality,

being too bland. Breads are excellent, served straight from the tandoor by helpful staff. We highly recommend the fresh lime sodas (sweet or salty) – they're icy cold and a great pick-me-up.
Babies and children welcome: high chairs.
Bookings not accepted weekends. No smoking.
Takeaway service.
For branch see index.

Karahi King

213 East Lane, North Wembley, Middx HA0 3NG (8904 2760/4994). North Wembley tube/245 bus. **Meals served** noon-midnight daily.
Main courses £3.50-£12. **Unlicensed**.
Corkage no charge. **Credit** AmEx, DC, JCB, MC, V. Punjabi
Local residents hold this homely caff in great esteem – and for good reason. Notable for hearty Punjabi grub, Karahi King is valued for its array of kebabs, especially those seared in a smoky tandoor. The premises are divided into two main dining areas. An attempt has been made to dress up the decor with rattan-work chairs, wooden tables and a lick of paint, but flamboyance is reserved for the roti-rolling, skewer-wielding chefs working behind the steel-fronted open-kitchen counter. Tandoori chicken, deliciously charred on the surface, yielded a full-bodied garlicky flavour within; a light dusting of chat masala (dried mango powder mixed with various spices including ginger and toasted cumin) added an appealing tartness. Aloo paratha (flaky griddle-cooked flatbread, filled with spiced, gingery mashed potato and lashings of ghee) was a meal in itself, needing only a simple pot of yoghurt and a dab of pickle to round things off. Vegetarian main dishes are hit and miss, and meaty curries tend to be oil-rich. Service, even when things get busy at the weekends, is attentive.
Babies and children welcome: high chairs.
Separate room for parties, seats 60-80.
Takeaway service. Vegetarian menu.

International

Welcome to the culinary laboratory. In this section we include restaurants that combine ingredients and cooking styles from around the world on to a single menu. This doesn't mean you'll find only outrageous flavour combinations and the messy by-products of globalisation. Several restaurants offer classic dishes within the European repertoire, but will stray across national boundaries. Others provide tried-and-tested Asian dishes alongside European or North African standards. However, the most exciting places boast chefs who have forged a new fusion cuisine, where ingredients and cooking techniques are synthesised into innovative combinations. It's a risky approach and doesn't always work, but the best venues – **The Providores & Tapa Room**, **Ottolenghi**, **Cinnamon Cay** and new arrival **Food@The Muse** are our current favourites – produce menus that fizz with originality.

Central
City EC4

Bar Bourse

67 Queen Street, EC4R 1EE (7248 2200/ 2211). Mansion House tube.
Bar **Open** 11.30am-11pm Mon-Fri. **Lunch served** 11.30am-3pm, **dinner served** 5.30-8.30pm Mon-Fri. **Main courses** £6.50-£7.50. *Restaurant* **Lunch served** 11.30am-3pm Mon-Fri. **Main courses** £14-£20. **Service** 12.5%. *Both* **Credit** AmEx, JCB, MC, V.
A textbook City wine bar, the basement Bar Bourse sticks to bar snacks in the evening and provides a play-safe menu at slightly inflated prices for weekday lunchtimes. The wood-panelled venue bustles with business folk between 1pm and 2pm. It's a speedy, streamlined operation – unless you roll up towards the end of service, when staff noticeably step down a gear. Some dishes are akin to high-quality English pub fare (fish and chips, salmon en croûte, ribeye steak with chips and béarnaise sauce), while others look further afield for their inspiration. The elegant 'Asian plate' was a substantial starter of rare tuna, crisp tempura prawns and dainty spring rolls. To follow, the heartier thai green curry had a rich, fragrant broth that wasn't overly strong, while grilled cod with a buttery prawn crust came with asparagus spears and a fruity mango dressing. A short dessert menu featured eton mess and chocolate mousse. As a dining stop-off, Bar Bourse is better than fine; as you might expect, the wine list is suitably pleasing. *Babies and children admitted. Bar and restaurant available for hire. Booking advisable. Dress: smart casual.* **Map 11 P7**.

Clerkenwell & Farringdon EC1

Vic Naylor Restaurant & Bar

38-42 St John Street, EC1M 4AY (7608 2181/ www.vicnaylor.com). Barbican tube/Farringdon tube/rail.
Bar **Open** 5pm-1am Tue-Sat.
Restaurant **Meals served** noon-10pm Mon-Fri. **Dinner served** 5-11pm Sat. **Main courses** £8-£15.50. **Service** 10% for parties of 5 or more. **Credit** AmEx, MC, V.
Sam Taylor-Wood once worked here and Tracey Emin used to hang out here – but now? Given its heritage, weekdays at this restaurant and bar have a disappointingly suited-and-booted vibe. Come the weekend, though, Vic's undoes its top button and loosens its tie, as groups of clubby diners rev up for a riotous night out. Decor is a little Dante-esque, the high walls daubed in burnished rusts and reds, complete with towering mock torches. By comparison, head chef Rebecca St John Cooper's menu is positively puritanical. No-fuss dishes change daily and mix the quintessentially British with Italian. Sharing a plate of charcuterie (air-cured ham, sausage, lomo) whetted our appetite, though the fig relish had a pungent aniseed note that might not suit everyone's taste. Mains were robust: the lamb chops (all three) were thick and bloody, with plump broad beans and a zingy cucumber, mint and feta salad; roast chicken was heaped with saffron potatoes. To finish, bramley apple and blackberry crumble was deliciously fruity, though lacked crunchiness on top. Tasty stuff, and a decent international wine list. *Babies and children admitted. Booking advisable. Separate room for parties, holds 100.* **Map 5 O5**.

Covent Garden WC2

Le Deuxième

65A Long Acre, WC2E 9JH (7379 0033/ www.ledeuxieme.com). Covent Garden tube.
Lunch served noon-3pm, **dinner served** 5pm-midnight Mon-Fri. **Meals served** noon-midnight Sat; noon-11pm Sun. **Main courses** £11.50-£16. **Set meal** (noon-3pm, 5-7pm, 10pm-midnight Mon-Fri; noon-11pm Sun) £10.95 2 courses, £14.50 3 courses. **Service** 15%. **Credit** AmEx, MC, V.
Le Deuxième impresses from the off with its suave looks: a part-frosted glass front provides passers-by with glimpses of the stylish beige interior, punctuated by purple heather on the tables and a vast amethyst rock feature. It sports a predominantly Modern European menu with occasional Asian flourishes. On our latest visit the results were consistently competent and well presented, starting with a refreshing tian of crab with spinach and fondant tomatoes, and a richly flavoured lasagne. A steak frites main was fully functional, but the highlight was undoubtedly a super-juicy roast duck breast with potato beignet and blackberry sauce. With its combination of smart decor and ambitious cuisine, Le Deuxième makes the grade in a part of London where competition is fierce and often touristy. That said, the à la carte prices are high for what is very good, but not always exceptional, cooking. On these grounds we recommend trying the superb-value set menus for a cheap, chic eat. Nearby is French sister restaurant Café du Jardin (28 Wellington Street, 7836 8769). *Babies and children admitted. Booking advisable.* **Map 18 L6**.

Fitzrovia W1

Archipelago

110 Whitfield Street, W1T 5ED (7383 3346). Goodge Street or Warren Street tube. **Lunch served** noon-2.30pm Mon-Fri. **Dinner served** 6-10.30pm Mon-Sat. **Main courses** £14-£19.50. **Set lunch** £15.50 2 courses. **Service** 12.5%. **Credit** AmEx, DC, JCB, MC, V.
Not for the squeamish, Archipelago's weird and wonderful menu tempts you to eat the kind of exotic beasties more usually encountered on the Discovery Channel. So prepare to be both challenged (crispy bugs) and delighted (crocodile fillet seared in vine leaves – astonishingly juicy). We tried gnu, which tasted like a cross between rabbit and beef, and a spicy frogs' legs and cashew stir-fry. Judging from the appreciative sighs at a neighbouring table, we would also have enjoyed cambodian marinated kangaroo, or peacock-on-a-date with tomato and vanilla coulis. To finish, the 'baby bee alaska' was a hive-shaped confection complete with a 'honeycomb' of white chocolate and (you guessed it) a small bee: dead, minus its sting and edible. The dishes and the drinks list (which includes hemp beer and Château Pétrus) scream 'novelty' and 'rare delicacy' in equal measure. Archipelago's ethnic decor, however, is firmly in the former category; the deluge of African and Indian artefacts (crude wooden figures, ornate mirrors, jangly candle-stands, even a decorative birdcage) is a little too reminiscent of a student backpacker's idea of palatial furnishings. Prices are palatial too. *Babies and children admitted. Booking advisable. No smoking. Tables outdoors (2, patio).* **Map 3 L4**.

Mash

19-21 Great Portland Street, W1W 8QB (7637 5555/www.mashbarandrestaurant.co.uk). Oxford Circus tube.
Bar **Open** 11am-2am Mon-Sat.
Restaurant **Breakfast served** 7.30-11.30am, **lunch served** noon-3pm Mon-Fri. **Dinner served** 6-11pm Mon-Sat. **Main courses** £9-£15. **Set meal** £22.50-£28.50 3 courses. *Both* **Credit** AmEx, DC, MC, V.
With its own microbrewery, Mash's plasticky street-level bar is handy for grabbing a decent beer, and is usually heaving with the hyper-trendy Soho Square brigade. Upstairs, the open, functional restaurant is noticeably more sedate. Huge metal vats of brew glint temptingly at you from the far corner. The menu here had a revamp in late summer 2005, but it doesn't seem to have changed hugely in style: it's still pretty gastropubby in tone, albeit slightly dressier, offering a mix of appetising salads (avocado, herb shoots, peas, feves and spring onions), meaty plates (lamb chops and sautéed potatoes, rib-eye steak), fishy dishes (roasted sea bass with mussels and mixed beans) and the long-renowned pizzas. We've found the burgers make real monster mains: sometimes a little too well done for our taste, but otherwise lovely. However, the grilled chicken and rosemary skewers, available in the bar (along with pizzas, sandwiches and other smaller dishes), are a little less impressive. Service could be improved, especially those Pinter-esque pauses between courses, but as a convenient central stop-off, Mash does the trick. *Babies and children welcome: high chairs. Bar available for hire. Disabled: toilet. Dress: smart casual. Entertainment: DJs 10pm Thur-Sat. Separate room for hire, seats 28. Tables outdoors (4-8, pavement).* **Map 9 J6**.

Spoon+ at Sanderson

The Sanderson, 50 Berners Street, W1T 3NG (7300 1444/www.spoon-restaurant.com). Oxford Circus or Tottenham Court Road tube.
Breakfast served 6.30am-noon, **lunch served** noon-2.30pm, **tea served** 3-5pm daily.

Dinner served 6-11pm Mon-Sat; 6-10.30pm
Sun. **Main courses** £21-£49. **Service** 15%.
Credit AmEx, DC, MC, V.
From the onyx-topped Long Bar to the tiny
spoon motif denoting the signature dishes, this
glamorously styled restaurant is concept first, food
second. Designed by Philippe Starck and located
inside Ian 'Studio 54' Schrager's exclusive
Sanderson hotel, the tailor-made chic can feel
achingly pretentious – unless, of course, you're
someone who likes 'to arrive' for dinner, rather
than just turn up. Annoyingly for those not in the
know, Alain Ducasse's costly menu confusingly
divides up components of the main courses and
displays them across three columns. In theory, you
can mix and match as you see fit, but in practice
you'd be unlikely to risk the stranger combinations.
Suggested dishes are adequate but misfire on the
details, so a sensible-sounding crab cake starter (at
a less than sensible £25) had a cloying honey
vinaigrette; rotisserie chicken came with a runny
devilled marmalade; and sea bass and paella
ruined the inviting texture by moulding the rice
into two uniform rods. The wine list is terrifyingly
expensive and the service is unctuous. In summer,
though, you can make like the A-list and enjoy the
louche luxury of a central terrace, where you'll find
pillows strewn over benches.
Babies and children welcome: high chairs.
Booking advisable. Disabled: toilet. Separate
room for parties, seats 50. Tables outdoors
(15, terrace). **Map 17 J5.**

Leicester Square WC2

Asia de Cuba

St Martins Lane, 45 St Martin's Lane, WC2N
4HX (7300 5588/www.asiadecubarestaurant.
com). Leicester Square tube. **Breakfast served**
6.30-11am Mon-Fri; 7am-noon Sat, Sun. **Lunch**
served noon-2.30pm daily. **Dinner served**
5.30pm-midnight Mon-Wed; 5.30pm-12.30am
Thur-Sat; 5.30-10.30pm Sun. **Tea served**
3-4.30pm daily. **Main courses** £16.50-£48.
Set meal (lunch, 6-7pm daily) £24 bento box.
Service 15%. **Credit** AmEx, DC, MC, V.
Style comes at a price. Or, at least, it does in
Asia de Cuba, the futuristic-looking, startlingly
expensive restaurant at St Martins hotel. Designed
by Philippe Starck, it's a prepossessing, dazzlingly
white two-tier space. The unusual decorative
flourishes really stand out: tatty books, pot plants
and black and white photos encircling the room's
colossal pillars. Staff are attentive veering on
obsequious, though they do usefully explain the
playful Latino-Asian menu's biggest quirk: most
dishes are for sharing, and a couple of starters, one
entrée, sides and a single dessert are appropriate
for two diners. At £18, the lobster pot-stickers
appetiser should have been superlative, but in the
event, the neat parcels were simply good, their
spiced rum sauce appealingly speckled with
vanilla pod. It was a similar story for the wok-fried
tofu dumplings. Cuban spiced chicken with a
swoosh of tamarind sauce was fine, but we craved
more variety. Why not a main course each? You
are, it seems, paying for the experience, the
gimmick, the thrill of navigating a fun fusion
menu. You'll want to say you've been there, done
that: but the real test is, would you do it again?
Babies and children welcome: high chairs. Booking
advisable. Disabled: toilet. No-smoking tables.
Separate rooms for parties, seating 48 and 120.
Vegetarian menu. **Map 18 L7.**

Marylebone W1

★ The Providores & Tapa Room

109 Marylebone High Street, W1U 4RX
(7935 6175/www.theprovidores.co.uk).
Baker Street or Bond Street tube.
The Providores **Lunch served** noon-2.45pm
daily. **Dinner served** 6-10.45pm Mon-Sat;
6-10pm Sun. **Main courses** £15-£22.
Cover (lunch Sat, Sun) £1.50.
Tapa Room **Breakfast served** 9-11.30am
Mon-Fri; 10am-3pm Sat, Sun. **Meals served**
noon-10.30pm Mon-Fri; 4-10.30pm Sat; 4-10pm
Sun. **Tapas** £1.50-£13.
Both **Credit** AmEx, MC, V.

Refuel. See p160.

Ottolenghi. See p165.

The buzzy street-level Tapa Room on Marylebone High Street is frequently packed to capacity, the crowds attracted by the exquisite global tapas and breakfasts. Upstairs, the restaurant itself is small and refined, the crisp white walls and elegant simplicity dictating that you focus solely on the food. That said, New Zealander Peter Gordon's dishes are so good that little could detract from their rarefied fusion of mainly Asian and Middle Eastern ingredients. A starter of berbere spiced kangaroo fillet on shiitake, basil and halloumi fritter with chickpea tahini purée, argan oil and greek yoghurt sounded complicated, but the succulent centrepiece of fillet was not remotely overshadowed. A main of gilt-head bream was a beautiful piece of fish, the samphire, fennel and chinese cabbage salad a substantial accompaniment alongside a gentle nectarine and chipotle chilli salsa. 'Welsh Black' beef fillet was, unusually, served with good, thick cassava chips and, quite deliciously, puy lentils sweetened with pomegranate molasses. The Kiwi wine list is also well thought out. When it comes to fusion cooking, this is exceptional, a fact that's reflected in the prices: with mains costing around £23, even a modest meal for two tops £100.
Babies and children welcome: high chairs. Booking advisable (Providores); bookings not accepted (Tapa Room). Disabled: toilet. No smoking (Providores). Tables outdoors (2, pavement). **Map 9 G5.**

Soho W1

Refuel NEW
The Soho Hotel, 4 Richmond Mews, W1D 3DH (7559 3007/www.refuelsoho.com). Tottenham Court Road tube.
Bar **Open** 11am-midnight Mon-Sat; 11am-10.30pm Sun.
Restaurant **Meals served** 7am-11pm Mon-Fri; 7am-11am, 5.30-11pm Sat; 8am-10.30pm Sun.
Main courses £16.50-£29. **Set lunch** (noon-6.30pm Mon-Fri) £19.95 3 courses; (noon-3pm Sun) £24.95 3 courses. **Service** 12%.
Credit AmEx, JCB, MC, V.
Housed within the stylish new Soho Hotel, Refuel strikes the perfect pitch for a hip clientele of media and business types. Partially divided from a handsome zinc bar by shelves of rustic amphoras, the restaurant mixes gently distressed kitchen tables with more formal furniture. From the à la carte, a starter of grilled morcilla with roasted aubergine, watercress, slices of roasted garlic and parmesan dressing impressed; a main of salmon and smoked haddock fish cake, big and round as an anarchist's bomb, was nearly as good. Although the £19.99 set lunch offered dismal paucity of choice (three courses: quiche or salad, polenta-crusted haddock or pesto pasta, bakewell tart or ice-cream), the cooking again delighted. Blue cheese quiche was perfect, with broccoli blackened on top for a pleasing crunch without any loss of

moist firmness. Fragrant fresh mint tea provided solace when we had no room for an intriguing cheeseboard – although we couldn't pass on the complimentary petits fours. Staff were a pleasant bunch, but over-eager to clear and pour, and lacking in focus (we were offered a potato side for the potato-based – and already ample – fish cake). Prices are high too, with most à la carte mains costing around £20.
Babies and children welcome: high chairs. Booking advisable Thur, Fri. Disabled: toilet. No-smoking tables. Separate room for parties, seats 45. Takeaway service (breakfast until 11am daily). **Map 17 K6.**

Victoria SW1

Ebury Wine Bar & Restaurant
139 Ebury Street, SW1W 9QU (7730 5447/ www.eburywinebars.co.uk). Sloane Square tube/ Victoria tube/rail.
Bar **Open** 11am-11pm Mon-Sat; noon-3pm, 6-10.30pm Sun.
Restaurant **Lunch served** noon-2.45pm daily. **Dinner served** 6-10.15pm Mon-Sat; 6-9.45pm Sun. **Main courses** £10-£19.50. **Set meal** (noon-2.45pm, 6-7.30pm) £13.50 2 courses, £17.50 3 courses. **Service** 12.5%. **Credit** AmEx, MC, V.
The Ebury first opened its doors back in 1959, and while we wouldn't accuse it of being a 1950s throwback, it does feel perilously out of step with today's expectations. The decor is a big sticking

point: a trompe l'oeil surrounds you, complete with books bearing such gruesome jokes as 'The Art of Etiquette' by Alex Higgins. The menu has also escaped the onslaught of change, improvement and modernity. Rabbit and prune terrine with plum chutney tasted as if it had been served with Branston pickle, while the crumb on the veal cutlets merely concealed the lacklustre meat within. Best was ostrich steak, char-grilled into submission amid a plate awash with violently coloured beetroot lyonnaise. A wedge of coconut tart was a little dry, but, less forgiveably, the accompanying raspberry sauce possessed a fizzy tang that suggested it was past its best. Surprisingly, the Ebury is often full. Could this be a case of location, location, location? Either that or the lure of a drink or two: the wine list is both long and fairly priced. *Babies and children admitted. Booking advisable. No-smoking tables.* **Map 15 H10.**

Westminster SW1

The Atrium

4 Millbank, SW1P 3JA (7233 0032/ www.atriumrestaurant.com). Westminster tube. **Lunch served** noon-3pm, **dinner served** 6-9.45pm Mon-Fri. **Main courses** £7.50-£14.95. **Service** 12.5%. **Credit** AmEx, DC, MC, V.
Although the Atrium serves dinner only until 9.45pm, the waitresses seem less than enthused by the late shift. No wonder: lunchtimes are fairly busy, but the evenings are virtually dead. The Westminster politico's unofficial canteen, this café/restaurant benefits from a lofty glass roof, but little can disguise its underwhelming likeness to the impersonal lobby of a chain hotel. Dishes cover a variety of bases, from spaghetti bolognese to aubergine charlotte via paprika smoked monkfish. They are, however, too pedestrian to justify the prices (mains cost around £14). The cigar-shaped ham and asparagus starter, snugly wrapped in filo pastry and accompanied by salsa, tasted like a superior bar snack, a sort of posh sausage roll. A thick seared tuna steak with salsa verde, and a surprisingly trim-looking lamb shank, were too well done for our liking (and no one took the trouble to ask how we wanted them cooked). Saving graces were a reasonable wine list and a chocolate terrine with cherry compote and subtly orange-infused cream. Had the service been a little more friendly, we might have warmed to the place. *Booking essential lunch. Disabled: lift; toilet. No-smoking tables. Separate rooms for parties, seating 12 and 24.* **Map 16 L10.**

West

Kensington W8

Abingdon

54 Abingdon Road, W8 6AP (7937 3339). Earl's Court or High Street Kensington tube. **Bar Open** 12.30-11pm Mon-Sat; 12.30-10.30pm Sun. *Restaurant* **Lunch served** 12.30-2.30pm Mon-Fri; 12.30-3pm Sat, Sun. **Dinner served** 6.30-10.30pm Mon, Sun; 6.30-11pm Tue-Sat. **Main courses** £11.75-£17.50. **Set lunch** (daily) £14.75 2 courses; (Sun) £17.50 3 courses. **Service** 12.5%. *Both* **Credit** AmEx, MC, V.
A terrific buzz hits you as you push through the thronged bar to the restaurant of this deservedly popular spot. Here, a pleasing international menu allows you to travel from Thailand to Italy, Spain and home again. A perfect risotto of braised leeks and stilton, and a smoked halibut with shallot and mint dressing, started us off with tingling taste buds. Our gravelly voiced South African waitress persuaded us to try the pan-fried butterfish – firm and juicy – in a soupy sauce of lemongrass, ginger and coconut on pak choi; excellent, as it turned out. Chicken breast swimming in a flame-red chorizo and butter bean casserole tasted as exciting as it looked. Research decreed we ought to share a splendid sticky toffee pudding, obligingly served with ice-cream and clotted cream. With a delightful, well-trained team of young staff, and a varied wine list (starting at £10.75 up to some high-price oldies and including six by the glass from £3)

the Abingdon has all the ingredients for a delicious and relaxing evening. Good value, considering the all-round quality.
Babies and children welcome: high chairs. Booking essential. No-smoking tables. Tables outdoors (4, pavement). **Map 13 A9.**

Ladbroke Grove W11

★ Food@The Muse NEW

269 Portobello Road, W11 1LR (7792 1111). Ladbroke Grove tube. **Dinner served** 6-11pm Mon. **Meals served** 11am-11pm Tue-Thur; 10am-11pm Fri, Sat; 10am-6pm Sun. **Main courses** £9.50-£14. **Set lunch** £5.95 2 courses. **Service** 12.5%. **Credit** MC, V.
In deepest Ladbroke Grove, gastropubs are already so last century; the latest 'in' place occupies the corridor of an art gallery. White tables are jammed together, refectory-style, to fit the narrow white space – which made our dinner a lot more convivial than we'd expected. Chef Tom Kime has worked at David Thompson's Darley Street Thai, in its day one of Sydney's most influential restaurants – and it shows. Witness a starter salad of roasted prawn and watermelon, spiked with ginger, red chilli and lime, then garnished with roasted peanuts. It was a stunner, with multiple flavours exploding on the palate. Also good: figs marinated in sherry vinegar and thyme, with plump olives, salted almonds, blue picos cheese and some tip-top Spanish lomo (cured pork loin). This combination was inspired by a classic dish at the River Café, where Kime worked for five years. Main courses were not as successful. Roasted pork belly was oddly dry and dull, despite an elaborate three-stage cooking process. And tuna was cut far too thick to merit its 'carpaccio' tag, though its salted lemon and caper dressing was a fine match. The short wine list is well chosen.
Babies and children admitted. Disabled: toilet. No smoking. **Map 19 B2.**

South West

Barnes SW13

★ MVH

5 White Hart Lane, SW13 0PX (8392 1111). Barnes Bridge or Mortlake rail/209 bus. **Bar Open** 6-11pm daily. *Restaurant* **Lunch served** noon-2.30pm Thur-Sun. **Dinner served** 6-10.30pm daily. **Main courses** £15. **Set meals** £26 2 courses, £29 3 courses. **Service** 12.5%. *Both* **Credit** AmEx, JCB, MC, V.
MVH is a real one-off. The ground-floor dining area was undergoing renovations when we visited, so we ate upstairs, in what is normally the bar. It's a tiny space, with room for barely a dozen diners in a dimly lit, dark red interior crammed with enough kitsch to hold a jumble sale. It was utterly charming, like being at a private dinner party hosted by a particularly eccentric friend, an ambience enhanced by ultra-enthusiastic staff. Chef-patron Michael von Hruschka's cooking lives up to the surroundings; it's a riot of international influences. The set dinner is not cheap (and it's cheeky to charge extra for side dishes), but value comes in the array of amuse-bouches that punctuate the meal. Some of these were marvellous, notably a drink of cucumber, cactus, lime and ginger (served in test tubes). An intense seaweed soup. Starters were stellar: a rich, spicy 'soup' of flaked halibut and tuna yielded myriad complex flavours; and soft-shell crab came atop a zingy salad of bean sprouts, grapefruit and papaya. Mains faltered by comparison – honey-glazed cod with garlic mash, lemongrass sauce and beetroot purée was a flavour too far – but the whole experience is huge fun, and an antidote to the po-faced attitude of so many resturants. Women beware: the ladies' loo (the exterior encrusted with fake roses) contains a truly alarming distorting mirror. A café-cum-deli was about to open across the road as we went to press.
Babies and children welcome (lunch): high chairs. Booking advisable. No-smoking tables. Separate room for parties, seats 25-30. Tables outdoors (4, terrace).

South Kensington SW3

The Collection

264 Brompton Road, SW3 2AS (7225 1212/ www.the-collection.co.uk). South Kensington tube. **Bar Open** 5-11pm daily. *Restaurant* **Dinner served** 6-11.15pm Tue-Sat. **Main courses** £13-£22. **Set dinner** (6-7.15pm Mon-Fri) £15 2 courses, £20 3 courses. **Service** 15%. **Credit** AmEx, MC, V.
Torch flames mark the entrance, and an illuminated catwalk-style bridge leads into a vast brick warehouse space. A long downstairs bar is overlooked by a large mezzanine dining room. The Collection is a strange transformation of a former factory into a bamboo tiki bar. It's an odd mix, and so's the crowd: after-work suits dominate the bar, while rather bling young diners sit upstairs (along with the odd hen-night party). On our visit, an enormous screen was showing a no-volume film, presumably for folk tired of people-watching. Despite describing itself as 'modern British', the menu is mostly Asian, but there are European touches. To start, we tried sesame tiger prawns with peanut sauce, and parma ham-wrapped scallops; both were competent and prettily served. Oriental duck with soba noodles was on the small side, but featured tender duck. Thai red chicken curry was nicely spicy, arriving with a thick coconut sauce. Desserts sounded exotic: salted caramel mousse, or an impressive-looking chocolate plate for two. We couldn't find serious fault with the food, but given the prices (starters are around a tenner), you might expect something more special.
Babies and children admitted: high chairs. Booking advisable. Entertainment: DJ 8pm daily. Vegetarian menu. **Map 14 E10.**

Wimbledon SW19

Light House

75-77 Ridgeway, SW19 4ST (8944 6338). Wimbledon tube/rail then 200 bus. **Lunch served** noon-2.30pm Mon-Sat; 12.30-3pm Sun. **Dinner served** 6.30-10.30pm Mon-Sat. **Main courses** £12-£16.50. **Set lunch** (Mon-Sat) £14 2 courses, £16.50 3 courses; (Sun) £18 2 courses, £23 3 courses. **Service** 12.5%. **Credit** AmEx, MC, V.
Bright and airy, all blond wood and unobtrusive styling, the Light House attracts a mature local crowd. Waiters seemed to want diners to question them about the Italian-inspired menu (they kept asking, but we had no queries), which is divided into antipasti, primi and secondi. On our visit, salad starters were very impressive, made with flawless ingredients. Avocado, green bean, baby gem, marcona almond and piquillo pepper was a near-perfect combination, generous on the avocado and tasty almonds. Bocconcini (balls of mozzarella), beetroot and asparagus with pumpkin seeds was almost as good, but were let down by an over-vinegary dressing. Mains were more mixed. The waiter argued in favour of fettuccine with asparagus, cream and parmesan in a starter size, but it turned out to be far too small. A dish of char-grilled tuna with oven-dried tomato, spinach and green peppercorn sauce was disappointing: char-grilled proved to be an understatement (a burnt taste infused the entire dish), while the sauce was more suited to steak than fish. Still, this is a professional outfit and a popular place.
Babies and children welcome: children's menu (Sun); high chairs. Booking advisable weekends. Disabled: toilet. No-smoking tables.

South

Battersea SW11

★ Cinnamon Cay

87 Lavender Hill, SW11 5QL (7801 0932/ www.cinnamoncay.co.uk). Clapham Junction rail then 77A, 156, 345 bus. **Dinner served** 6-10.30pm Mon-Sat. **Main courses** £9.50-£14.50. **Set meal** (Mon, Tue) £12 2 courses. **Service** 12.5%. **Credit** AmEx, DC, MC, V.
This haven of fusion food tucked away on Lavender Hill goes way beyond the call of duty for a neighbourhood restaurant, with ambitious

THE BRITISH MUSEUM

Court Restaurant

ENGLISH

MEDITERRANEAN

AFRICAN

THAI

CLASSIC VENUE

WORLD-CLASS MENU

OPEN FROM 11.00

RIGHT: A SET OF SILVER 'APOSTLE' SPOONS
FROM LONDON, ENGLAND, AD 1536–37

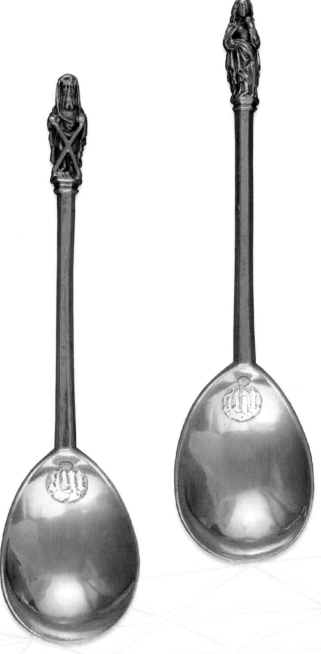

Information & reservations +44 (0)20 7323 8990
Thursday and Friday late opening until 23.00
courtrestaurant@digbytrout.co.uk

⊖ Tottenham Court Road, Holborn, Russell Square
Great Russell Street, London WC1B 3DG

food, professional staff and sleek decor – all the while keeping prices affordable. The menu is eye-catchingly international, introducing SW11 to such exotic delicacies as crocodile croquettes, black rice sushi, and barramundi. The list can be bewildering, but helpful waitresses are on hand (we're sure we weren't the first to ask what crocodile tasted like). The highlights of our latest visit were the roasted halibut with a tangy pine-nut and caper sauce and lemon risotto cake (an inspired combination), and a starter of chicken skewers with chickpea and ginger dip. Though the innovative culinary pairings are very well-judged, traditionalists may struggle to come to terms with delicate rose-roasted quail served with a sweet chilli sauce. As you might expect, the wine list whisks you around the world: our Argentinian red (£12.95) was outstanding value. Deservedly, Cinnamon Cay is a hit with the smart young locals of Lavender Hill, so book ahead at weekends.
Babies and children welcome: high chairs. Booking advisable. Tables outdoors (5, patio).

Clapham SW4

Polygon Bar & Grill
4 The Polygon, SW4 0JG (7622 1199/ www.thepolygon.co.uk). Clapham Common tube/ 35, 37, 345 bus. **Lunch served** noon-3pm Fri; 11am-3.30pm Sat; 11am-4pm Sun. **Dinner served** 6-11.30pm Mon-Sat; 6-11pm Sun. **Main courses** £8-£15. **Service** 12.5%. **Credit** AmEx, MC, V.
The Polygon, which is tucked away behind a pub in the centre of Clapham Old Town, has become particularly popular for weekend breakfasts and brunches: eggs benedict with bacon, for instance, or blueberry pancakes with maple syrup. However, we visited for dinner. Penne pasta with prawn and lobster in a white wine and cream sauce was excellent; however, char-grilled salmon steak with spinach, lime and tamarind aïoli could have had more flavour, despite the innovative use of ingredients. Side orders are generously sized, with skinny french fries, garlic mash and roasted sweet potatoes being particular favourites. The children's menu includes pork sausage, chicken and fish fingers with chips or mash; luscious desserts include pear and champagne sorbet, strawberry panna cotta and banoffi pie. The bright interior of features smooth bleached-wood tables, plenty of painted glass, a gleaming bar and a bevy of black-clad waiting staff.
Babies and children welcome: children's menu; high chairs. Booking advisable weekends. Disabled: toilet. No smoking tables. **Map 22 A1.**

The Rapscallion
75 Venn Street, SW4 0BD (7787 6555/ www.therapscalliononline.com). Clapham Common tube. **Breakfast served** 10.30am-noon, **lunch served** noon-4pm Mon-Fri. **Brunch served** 10.30am-4pm Sat, Sun. **Dinner served** 6-11pm Mon-Sat; 6-10.30pm Sun. **Main courses** £6-£11. **Service** 12.5%. **Credit** AmEx, DC, JCB, MC, V.
Small and stylish, the Rapscallion is a popular place with a high-quality kitchen, though it does feel more like a bar. The premises are bright (with big windows), feeling summery on long July evenings and cosy in winter. The food is creative and unusual, impressively made and appealingly presented. Crab frittata surprised us by being served chilled, with an interesting sweet-sour pineapple salsa. Risotto with broad beans, asparagus and mint was very fresh, seasonal and tasty. To follow, an unusual dish of roasted pork belly with chilli feta, chickpeas and tomato relish worked well: the meat was sweet and infused with flavour, and the feta was creamy and luxurious. Sirloin steak with caramelised tomato, sweet potato, oyster mushrooms, watercress and port juice sounded like a bumper combo and was a large, satisfying dish; the sweet potatoes were especially good, but the port sauce was a bit too sweet. The kitchen is tiny yet produces surprisingly good food; the long bar is said to mix a mean cocktail too. *See also below* the Sequel.
Babies and children admitted. Booking advisable. Tables outdoors (8, pavement). **Map 22 A2.**

The Sequel
75 Venn Street, SW4 0BD (7622 4222/ www.thesequelonline.com). Clapham Common tube/35, 37, 355 bus. **Bar Open** 5pm-midnight Tue-Thur; 5pm-1am Fri; 11am-1am Sat; 11am-midnight Sun. **Restaurant Brunch served** 11am-4pm Sat; 11am-6pm Sun. **Dinner served** 6-11pm Tue-Thur; 6pm-midnight Fri, Sat; 6-10.30pm Sun. **Main courses** £9-£12. **Set meal** £16.50 2 courses. **Service** 12.5%. **Both Credit** AmEx, DC, JCB, MC, V.
Opposite the Rapscallion (*see above*), which is under the same ownership, the Sequel is decorated in shades of brown and caramel that create a stylish post-cinema environment. The place is atmospheric in a mildly retro way, with suedette banquettes and dim lighting; old movies play discreetly on a screen. Staff go slightly too far out of their way to make sure you're comfortable. We lost count of how many times they checked that everything was OK with our meal, and grew tired of interrupting our conversation to reassure them. Still, everything was OK and the food is always beautifully presented. We tried three starters, all of them fine. Sichuan salt and pepper squid with roast garlic mayonnaise was crisp and tasty; tuna carpaccio with rocket and parmesan was fresh and beautifully thin; and caramelised onion and goat's cheese tatin was creamy and sweet, with the pastry spot on. A main course of marinated lamb cutlets with potato gratin and rosemary was less exciting: on the hefty side, but competently made. Our only complaint concerns the unpleasant state of the toilets, which put a real downer on proceedings. Still, that's not hard to correct.
Babies and children admitted. Booking advisable. Tables outdoors (2, pavement). **Map 22 A2.**

Waterloo SE1

Laughing Gravy
154 Blackfriars Road, SE1 8EN (7721 7055). Southwark tube/Waterloo tube/rail. **Bar Open** noon-11pm Mon-Fri; 7-11pm Sat. **Restaurant Meals served** noon-11pm Mon-Fri; 7-10pm Sat. **Main courses** £12.25-£15.95. **Both Credit** MC, V.
It's hard to pin down exactly what it is that makes Laughing Gravy so special. The food is good but not mind-blowing and certainly not cheap; service is informal and pleasant, but not outstanding; and the location leaves a lot to be desired. But there's something in the combination of subtly eccentric decor, laid-back atmosphere, beautifully lit dining space and pleasantly satisfying cooking that sees us return time and again. Taking its name from 1920s slang for alcohol, and hiding behind an unobtrusive door in an unexceptional part of town, Laughing Gravy has a sophisticated European feel. Food is international: fresh pea soup with bacon slivers, or cajun freshwater crayfish cocktail, to start; quail on sweet potato hash with wilted greens, mushrooms, pomegranates and balsamic, or pan-fried bison tournedos on potato rösti with vodka cranberry sauce, for mains; and caramelised banana rice pudding to close. All very fine – but we wish the restaurant would change its policy of listing prices without VAT on the menu. It's misleading, and always makes the bill more of a shock than it should be.
Babies and children welcome: high chairs. Booking advisable. Disabled: toilet. Restaurant available for hire. Tables outdoors (2, pavement). **Map 11 O9.**

South East

Tower Bridge E1

Lightship Ten
5A St Katharine's Way, St Katharine's Dock, E1W 1LP (7481 3123/www.lightshipx.com). Tower Hill tube. **Lunch served** noon-3pm Tue-Fri. **Dinner served** 6-10pm Mon-Sat. **Main courses** £11-£18.90. **Service** 12.5%. **Credit** AmEx, MC, V.
The setting is superb: moored on St Katharine's Dock, a beautifully restored 'sea-going lighthouse' has been transformed into a stylish restaurant.

Discreet lighting combines with old wooden timbers and original portholes to create a warm, romantic atmosphere. Those lucky enough to sit on deck (we were unceremoniously ushered below, despite free tables) can enjoy the views of moored yachts. The Modern European/Scandinavian menu included a fresh, spicy chilled salmon tartare topped with moreish basil mousse, but the tender seared scallops in sesame seeds benefited little from a pea mash and an unremarkable red wine and anchovy reduction. Next, three medallions of monkfish wrapped in pancetta rested on a huge portion of lentils in an unusually good coffee and ginger cream. Well-cooked red mullet with a herb filling lay on a bed of sweet pepper compote. Sides of garlicky green beans arrived on time; frites took longer. Offered an extra portion as recompense, we were disappointed to see it added to the bill. Desserts include a classic crème brûlée with mango coulis, and warm brownie with custard cream. A short wine list includes reasonable bin ends and a perfectly good peachy Bordeaux sauvignon blanc.
Booking essential. Entertainment: jazz 7-10pm Mon, Wed. Separate room for parties, seats 35. Tables outdoors (23, top deck). **Map 12 S8.**

Westcombe Park SE3

Thyme Restaurant & Bar
1A & 3 Station Crescent, SE3 7EQ (8293 9183/ www.thymerestaurant.co.uk). Westcombe Park rail. **Bar Open** 5-11pm Tue-Sat. **Restaurant Dinner served** 7-9.30pm Tue-Sat. **Main courses** £10.95-£12.95. **Service** 10% for parties of 6 or more. **Credit** V.
It may be a bit off the beaten track, but Thyme is a classy, unpretentious gem. Neat, simple decor and super-friendly service accompany high-quality cooking and very reasonable prices to make this a local favourite in a quiet spot. A starter of parma ham and watermelon salad was refreshing and tasty, while salmon and cod fish cakes were generous with the fish, if slightly dry. Main courses were huge. Pan-fried chicken breast with minted pea risotto was highly satisfying: the risotto fresh and minty, and the chicken corn-fed and juicy. Roast pepper, tomato and basil tatin was full of flavour, with rich sweet peppers, and a nice crispy base for the tart; the accompanying salad had a lovely dressing. A cherry and blackcurrant crumble was slightly too sweet yet, on the whole, hard to fault. Be warned, though: the kitchen has been known to shut ahead of schedule on quiet nights, so get here relatively early or book ahead.
Babies and children admitted. Bar and restaurant available for hire. Booking advisable. No-smoking tables.

East

Bethnal Green E2

Perennial
110-112 Columbia Road, E2 7RG (7739 4556/ www.perennial-restaurant.co.uk). Old Street tube/ rail then 55 bus. **Dinner served** 7-11pm Tue-Sat. **Meals served** 8.30am-4pm Sun. **Main courses** £10.50-£14.50. **Credit** AmEx, MC, V.
On Sundays, when Columbia Road flower market transforms this narrow East End thoroughfare into a vibrant riot of blooms, stems and foliage, Perennial makes a handy brunch-time retreat. It's particularly good in the summer months, when just sitting alfresco on the leafy patio can feel like a refined version of the pollen-raising pandemonium outside. Less pleasing, though, is the evening experience. Friday night, a time that should smell as sweet as honeysuckle to any budding restaurateur, can be ultra quiet, as in fact can any weekday evening. The problem: the dishes are often below par. Given that this is straightforward bistro cooking, we felt that only minimum effort had been expended. Seared tuna loin was coated in a dusty layer of seasoning that did little to disguise its lifeless texture, while grilled medallions of venison were tough, their accompanying 'aubergine caviar' disturbingly acidic. Nothing tasted freshly cooked, and the

toffee-smothered profiteroles arrived still semi-frozen. It's a shame, as the atmosphere is pleasant enough, but the food just doesn't impress.
Babies and children admitted. Booking advisable weekends. No-smoking tables. Separate room for parties, seats 30. Tables outdoors (6, garden). **Map 6 S3.**

Victoria Park E9

Frocks

95 Lauriston Road, E9 7HJ (8986 3161/ www.frocks-restaurant.co.uk). Mile End tube then 277 bus. **Lunch served** noon-4pm Sat. **Dinner served** 6.30pm-midnight Mon-Sat. **Meals served** noon-9pm Sun. **Main courses** £11-£17. **Service** 12.5%. **Credit** MC, V.
A fire in 2004 resulted in an emergency rethink and a refit, which, in the long run, has turned out for the best. No longer a country pine affair, Frocks has introduced sleek wood panelling and, along with it, a small but smart dose of urban modernity. The gentility is still here, of course – not least in the dandy Hackney types who float in, all boho rags and Sienna chic. Dishes, too, display a casual charm, taking their inspiration ad hoc from around the globe. Own-made gnocchi was a decent starter, arranged as an artistic circle with each dumpling supporting a crispy fragment of deep-fried baby squid. Three chewy tofu and wakame fritters, on the other hand, seemed a little stranded in a sea of black-eyed beans. Best was the crispy sea bass, which arrived with a pleasing blend of baby artichokes, girolles and broad beans. Portions are smaller than of old, but service is friendly, drinks are reasonable and those decadent desserts remain: Baileys and walnut cheesecake with chocolate sauce, anyone? It's good, overall, but we do wish Frocks wouldn't include service and then leave our credit card slip blank for the tip.
Babies and children welcome: high chair. Booking advisable weekends. Separate room for parties, seats 40. Tables outdoors (6, pavement; 6, walled garden).

Wanstead E11

Hadley House

27 High Street, E11 2AA (8989 8855). Snaresbrook or Wanstead tube. **Breakfast served** 10am-noon daily. **Lunch served** noon-6.30pm, **dinner served** 7-10.30pm Mon-Sat. **Meals served** 12.30-9pm Sun. **Main courses** £9-£16.95. **Set dinner** (Mon) £17.95 3 courses. **Credit** MC, V.
Fuchsia-pink drapes and sunshine-yellow walls evoke a fresh, summery vibe at the popular, pine-furnished Hadley House. You can't judge a restaurant by its decor, though. All year round the menu is characterised by the kind of huge, hearty dishes you'd most hunger for in winter: roasted beef ribeye with scallops and breaded potato cake; honey-glazed Gressingham duck breast with thai noodles; rack of lamb with roquefort dauphinoise potatoes and roasted peppers and pumpkin. Scallops with courgette purée and crispy lardons was decent, but what if you hated parmesan? From parmesan crisp to parmesan crumbs, the cheese featured in four of the five starters. For mains, calf's liver came with sweetbreads fried together as one, while the gamy hare didn't deliver on its 'cooked pink' promise. What we ate, right down to the overly sweet vanilla and mascarpone cheesecake with glazed banana and caramel sauce, was agreeable, but not brilliant. The problem is, for these prices (most mains are £16.95) and no West End location, you'd expect more.
Babies and children welcome (lunch and Sun): high chairs. Booking essential. Tables outdoors (7, patio). Takeaway service (lunch).

North
Islington N1

The Commissary

49-50 Eagle Wharf Road, N1 7ED (7251 1155/ www.holbornstudios.com). Angel tube/Old Street tube/rail.
May-Sept **Breakfast served** 8-11am, **lunch served** noon-3pm, **bar snacks served** 4-10pm Mon-Fri. *Oct-Apr* **Meals served** 8am-8pm Mon-Fri. **Main courses** £5.50-£12.95. **Credit** MC, V.
On our visit to the Commissary, set on an anonymous Islington backstreet, there was a choice of just two main courses, the third having run out. Good job, then, that there were also a couple of starters on offer, plus a selection of sandwiches. One of our mains was excellent: pan-fried pollock with savoy cabbage and fennel mashed potatoes with caper, lemon, parsley and butter sauce. The fish had been cooked for just the right length of time, retaining its texture and moisture. On the other hand, merguez sausages with 'mustard and baby spinach mashed potatoes' and rosemary gravy was undistinguished. Both servings of mash tasted virtually identical. Desserts included apple pie and promising-sounding lime, orange, lemon and strawberry crème brûlée, but they didn't manage to lure us. The restaurant's real draw is its canalside location, perfect for a glass of wine or two on a summer's evening.
Babies and children welcome: high chairs. Disabled: toilet. No-smoking tables. Separate room for parties, seats 20. Tables outdoors (11, pontoon). **Map 5 P2.**

Frederick's

Camden Passage, N1 8EG (7359 2888/ www.fredericks.co.uk). Angel tube.
Bar **Open** 11am-11pm Mon-Sat. *Restaurant* **Lunch served** noon-2.30pm, **dinner served** 5.45-11.30pm Mon-Sat. **Main courses** £11.50-£17.50. **Set meals** (lunch, 5.45-7pm) £14 2 courses, £17 3 courses. *Both* **Service** 12.5%. **Credit** DC, JCB, MC, V.
Frederick's continues to pull in the local smart set. There's a stylish bar at the front, opening on to Camden Passage, and the restaurant proper is spacious and airy, with huge artworks and a conservatory at the back. The food seems to have improved since last year, though weaknesses in

Penk's

other areas remain: we were seen by no less than six serving staff by the time our orders were taken, after we'd been ignored for 15 minutes from being given the menu. Thankfully, the starters arrived quickly. Sweet chilli roast crispy duck with spring onion and cucumber was no more than the sum of its parts, but the meat was moist and tender. Other dishes were very good. Pan-fried lambs' kidneys on toast with grain mustard sauce was excellent, the quality of the kidneys shining through. For mains, dover sole meunière was simple yet superlative, while scotch fillet of beef with confit of garlic and courgettes with enoki mushrooms and foie gras sauce worked well, despite the plethora of ingredients. Dessert of black cherry and almond tart, however, was a dry, cloying let-down. The French-heavy wine list features some stunners, but with little under £20. *Babies and children welcome: children's menu (lunch Sat); high chairs. Booking advisable weekends. No-smoking tables. Separate rooms for parties, seating 18 and 32. Tables outdoors (12, garden).* **Map 5 O2.**

★ Ottolenghi

2005 RUNNER-UP BEST CHEAP EATS
287 Upper Street, N1 2TZ (7288 1454). Angel tube/Highbury & Islington tube/rail. **Meals served** 8am-11pm Mon-Sat; 9am-10pm Sun. **Meze** (dinner) £4.50-£8. **Set meze** (lunch) £10.50 3 meze, £11.50 4 meze. **Credit** MC, V.
To look at, Ottolenghi is a 24-carat Upper Street product: the chairs appear to have been rescued from the set of *Barbarella*, and long, communal tables add the necessary touch of farmhouse chic. But top-quality food and pastries, displayed in a sunburst of Mediterranean colours, prove that this operation is as much about substance as style. If you're going to have a proper meal (as opposed to a snack, soup or salad), you'll need several dishes to keep you going; in other words, portions are on the small side. The quality of cooking, though, is beyond reproach. Last time we ate dinner at this branch – there's another, the original, in Notting Hill (of course) – a portion of perfectly seared tuna with nori and panko crust left us weak at the knees. Char-grilled lamb cutlets with spicy bulgar salad and cucumber yoghurt had a similar effect. Delicious artisanal breads, for dipping into peppery green olive oil, make for a memorably warm welcome. The staff are never less than charming and efficient.
Babies and children welcome; high chairs. Booking advisable evening, not accepted lunch. No smoking. Takeaway service. **Map 5 O1.** **For branch see index.**

Swiss Cottage NW3

Globe

100 Avenue Road, NW3 3HF (7722 7200/ www.globerestaurant.co.uk). Swiss Cottage tube/ 13, 31 bus. **Lunch served** noon-3pm Mon-Fri, Sun. **Dinner served** 6-11pm Mon-Sat. **Main courses** £9.50-£13.50. **Set lunch** (Sun) £15 2 courses. **Set dinner** (6-7pm, 10-11pm Mon-Sat) £12 2 courses, £15 3 courses. **Service** 12.5%. **Credit** MC, V.
Globe has a curious double identity. It's owned by a bunch of drag artistes (the Globe Girls) who host shimmering cabaret nights each Thursday. But at other times, it's a calm, discreet restaurant, the only signs of high camp being some pictures on the walls and the occasional flounce by staff. Housed in a spacious conservatory next to the Hampstead Theatre, it's a light, airy, comfortable and modern space, and the seasonally changing contemporary menus are well-executed. From the spring menu, a warm goat's cheese salad was made original by the addition of wonderful beetroot, and precisely cooked lentils with lovely mint dressing. Globe salad was full of good, fresh things (grilled asparagus, shaved parmesan, mozzarella) with, again, a delicate dressing. Of our main courses, pan-fried tuna came in a crunchy coriander-seed crust, nicely complemented by a salad of butter beans, mint and spring onion; roast duck breast with sweet potato mash and

raspberry balsamic sauce was beautifully balanced. Desserts include Malteser and Crunchie bar ice-cream, both of which are more refined than you'd think. There's also an imaginative, well-priced wine list. The pre- and post-theatre and Sunday lunch menus are exceptional value.
Babies and children welcome: children's menu (Sun); high chairs. Booking advisable. Entertainment: cabaret 8.30pm Thur (not Aug). No smoking. **Map 28 B4.**

North West
Queen's Park NW6

Hugo's

21-25 Lonsdale Road, NW6 6RA (7372 1232). Queen's Park tube/rail. **Meals served** 9.30am-11pm daily. **Main courses** £10.80-£14.80. **Service** 12.5%. **Credit** MC, V.
It's easy to see why Queen's Park locals are fond of Hugo's. On a cobbled street of old workshops now housing small businesses, it has a long frontage with seating outside, leading into an ample, shady space with wooden tables, quirky decorative details and a mellow atmosphere that invites you to relax and glance through the papers. Weekend brunch is highly popular, and Hugo's also hosts jazz sessions every Sunday night. The often-ditzy service would be annoying in some places, but here it doesn't seem to matter so much. With these assets, the food (a modern-bistro mix, highlighting organic ingredients) doesn't have to work too hard to please, and is accordingly enjoyable without being exceptional. The all-day weekend brunch menu offers plentiful choices – fry-ups, salads, snacks, steaks, pancakes and more – and every day there's a tasty vegetarian pasta special. A Hugo's organic burger with chips and salad was nicely savoury and juicy. In ribeye steak with hollandaise, the peppery meat was well-flavoured, if a bit tough, but the sauce was bland. Fresh fish, such as grilled tuna with niçoise salad, is often better. Drinks include decently priced wines and organic beers.
Babies and children welcome: high chairs. Booking advisable dinner. Entertainment: dinner dance 8pm Thur; jazz musicians 8.15-10.30pm Sun. No-smoking tables. Tables outdoors (14, pavement). Takeaway service. **Map 1 A1.** **For branch see index.**

Penk's

79 Salusbury Road, NW6 6NH (7604 4484/ www.penks.com). Queen's Park tube/rail. **Brunch served** 10.30am-3pm Sun. **Lunch served** noon-3pm Mon-Fri. **Dinner served** 7-11pm Mon-Thur; 7-11.30pm Fri, Sat. **Meals served** 10.30am-11pm Sun. **Main courses** £9.95-£15.95. **Service** 10% for parties of 8 or more. **Credit** MC, V.
Occupying what at first looks like one of London's smallest restaurant spaces, this much-loved local is easy to miss. The tiny frontage is deceptive, for the narrow former shop opens up into a slightly bigger space at the back and then a more spacious conservatory, but the small scale adds to the friendly intimacy. The appetising food is French bistro-based, but with ample British and more global touches. Tempura tiger prawns, a near-fixture on the menu, are served with a skilfully balanced, sweet but never excessive honey, ginger and saké sauce. We love them. A richly meaty country-style veal terrine with wild mushrooms and herb salad was different but just as good. The kitchen's fine way with sauces was evident in our mains: a spot-on roast turbot with a piquant hollandaise; and grilled pork chop with cider and crème fraîche sauce, and potato and celeriac croquettes. Desserts and the wine list don't disappoint, service is pleasantly unflustered (staff get used to squeezing past tables) and there are well thought-out lunch and weekend brunch menus as further signs that Penk's knows how to stay on top of its game.
Babies and children welcome: high chairs. Booking advisable. No-smoking tables. Separate room for parties, seats 22. Tables outdoors (1, pavement). **Map 1 A2.**

Interview
PETER GORDON

Who are you?
Executive chef and co-owner of **The Providores & Tapa Room** (*see p159*), originally from New Zealand.
Eating in London: what's good about it?
London's not the greatest food city in the world, but it's hugely improved in the 15 years I've been here, and I'd rather be here than in Paris or Madrid. If you want to blow a lot of money on an upmarket meal, you can, but I love Pret a Manger and I like pubs with a bit of character and really nice food.
What's bad about it?
There's not a lot of mid-priced stuff. It's also a shame that so many British chefs want to do French food – Fergus Henderson [of **St John**; *see p55*] is one of their heroes, yet comparatively few are following in his footsteps.
Which are your favourite London restaurants?
At the moment, **Roka** (*see p182*) and the **Ledbury** (*see p97*). I love the service at both. I love the decor at Roka – it's probably my favourite place to sit – and their crab hotpot with wasabi tobiko is the best single dish I've eaten in the past year. I also love **Tapas Brindisa** (*see p260*), and **Parlour at Sketch** (*see p299*).
What single thing would improve London's restaurant scene?
Lower rents for restaurants. If rents were less, restaurants wouldn't have to turn tables so much and they would have more space. I'd also like to see more restaurant reviewers whose only agenda is the food and the way the restaurant operates.
Any hot tips for the coming year?
I think more people will be looking to China for inspiration.
Anything to declare?
Thank heaven for Borough Market. People's awareness of foods has improved tremendously in the past couple of years.

RESTAURANTS

Italian

Italians are often thought to be staunchly traditional about their national and regional cuisine, but in London the molecular gastronomy movement is certainly making an impact on Italian chefs. For some years, the capital has welcomed Italian eateries that are more reminiscent of Milan than Montefalco, but suddenly it's normal to find half of your starter dish being presented in a shot glass, meaty main courses accompanied by ice-cream, and vegetables in the dessert. Rectangular white plates with sauces smeared like thick paint down the centre are almost compulsory. Yet the venues in this section that attract a red star – and, we suspect, the most business – tend to be those firmly rooted in authenticity, even if they do at times like to present food elegantly.

Central

Belgravia SW1

Il Convivio

143 Ebury Street, SW1W 9QN (7730 4099/ www.etruscagroup.co.uk). Sloane Square tube/ Victoria tube/rail. **Lunch served** noon-2.45pm, **dinner served** 7-10.45pm Mon-Sat. **Set lunch** £15.50 2 courses, £19.50 3 courses. **Set dinner** £26.50 2 courses, £32.50 3 courses, £38.50 4 courses. **Service** 12.5%. **Credit** AmEx, DC, JCB, MC, V.

Cash has been lavished on fitting out Il Convivio, but the owners seem to have got value for money as its colourful elegance has stood the test of time. A table in a shady corner of the glass-roofed dining room is one of the best places to spend a peaceful Saturday lunch. The menu features prime ingredients such as Buccleuch beef and salt marsh lamb used in ways that are artful but not tricksy. Of the eight antipasti, we could have ordered several. Scallops came with pea purée and semi-dried figs, plus a little fresh fig sauce – a sublime combination. Less good was the pasta stracci: a generous serving, yes, but with very little fresh crab among the spinach, tomatoes and bisque sauce. Remarkably tender ribeye was served very simply with runner beans and jus. More typical of the kitchen's output were the inventive desserts, such as caramelised apple tart with green tea ice-cream. Wines start at an approachable £13.50 per bottle, though there are plenty of premium options for those who want to flex the credit card.
Babies and children admitted. Booking advisable dinner. Restaurant available for hire. Separate room for parties, seats 14. **Map 15 G10.**

Olivo

21 Eccleston Street, SW1W 9LX (7730 2505). Sloane Square tube/Victoria tube/rail. **Lunch served** noon-2.30pm Mon-Fri. **Dinner served** 7-11pm Mon-Sat; 7-10.30pm Sun. **Main courses** £14.50-£16. **Set lunch** £17 2 courses, £19 3 courses. **Cover** £1.50. **Credit** AmEx, DC, JCB, MC, V.

Sardinian food is quietly promoted amid the boldly painted walls of this stylishly rustic restaurant. The concise wine list has a special section devoted to Sardinian bottles, including the pleasing house red Arenada Monica di Sardegna DOC 2002. Much use is made of the char-grill, as in generous main courses of veal escalopes with wilted spinach and sautéed potatoes. Steak is made interesting with crunchy juniper berry flavouring. First-timers should order spaghetti with bottarga, Sardinia's cured grey mullet roe, here dusted prettily over a buttery pile of tasty pasta. Linguine with crab, chilli, garlic and parsley is another winning classic, though we also enjoyed unusual gnocchi stuffed with tangy pecorino cream and served with a textbook tomato sauce. Service from white-shirted staff with colourful neckties was attentive and professional, though the degree of pleasure to be extracted from an evening at Olivo does depend on the position of your table. Given a choice, opt for one near the front window. The back is a little cramped and the well-fed business and government types who (understandably) eat here do tend to amplify the effect.
Children admitted. Booking advisable.
Map 15 H10.
For branch (Olivetto) see index.

City E1, EC3, EC4

Caravaggio

107 Leadenhall Street, EC3A 4AA (7626 6206/ www.etruscagroup.co.uk). Aldgate tube/Bank tube/DLR/25 bus. **Lunch served** 11.45am-3pm, **dinner served** 6.30-10pm Mon-Fri. **Main courses** £11.75-£21. **Set meal** £19.50 2 courses, £23.50 3 courses. **Cover** £1.50. **Service** 12.5%. **Credit** AmEx, DC, JCB, MC, V.

On a hot summer evening all the after-office diners at Caravaggio had removed their jackets, creating a parade of striped shirts. One of a London-based group of swish Italian restaurants (also including Il Convivio, *see above*), it occupies a former bank branch, done up with the extra dose of flash often seen in City venues – a curious mix of 1990s chic and art nouveau, with abundant mirrors. Service was smooth and sharp; it seemed at first as if the Neapolitan sommelier was being somewhat over-keen in pushing only wines over £35 – from a huge, all-Italian list – but he turned out to be very helpful. The modern Italian cuisine is delicately done: trofiette semolina pasta with beans and pesto had a lovely, rich, mellow flavour. Parma ham and mozzarella – from the day's set menu – was enjoyable, even though the ham didn't seem as exciting as its 'prosciutto 16 mesi' status had implied. Star of our main courses was roast fillet and belly of pork with an unusual, delicately sweet melon-infused sauce. Hake baked in foil (al cartoccio) with baby tomatoes was more simple, but also finely flavoured. A pleasant meal, if nothing exceptional for the lofty prices – although this probably doesn't bother the locals.
Babies and children admitted. Booking advisable. Disabled: toilet. Dress: smart casual; no shorts. Restaurant available for hire. **Map 12 R6.**

1 Blossom Street

1 Blossom Street, E1 6BX (7247 6530/ www.1blossomstreet.com). Liverpool Street tube/rail.

Bar **Open/snacks served** noon-11pm Mon-Fri. *Restaurant* **Lunch served** noon-3pm, **dinner served** 6-9pm Mon-Fri. **Main courses** £12.50-£17. **Set meal** £17.95 2 courses, £20 3 courses. *Both* **Service** (on food) 12.5%. **Credit** AmEx, DC, JCB, MC, V.

If you've previously written off this spacious basement bar and restaurant in the increasingly gentrified residential area near Spitalfields, now is the time to reconsider. A new chef has improved the food, so that the modern Italian menu tastes as good as it reads, and important details such as the standard of bread and oil have been brought into line with the rest of the proposition. Generous starters put an intriguing twist on deli ingredients. Bresaola was rolled into cones and stuffed with goat's cheese mousse before being scattered with strips of orange zest. Tuscan smoked wild boar fillet came with baby onions, semi-mature pecorino and delicious, rosemary-flavoured Sardinian bread. Radicchio and dill purée had an unusual jammy taste that threatened to overpower a main course of char-grilled sea bass, but we were astounded by the sublime richness of pistachio ice-cream that came with warm almond and chocolate cake. Reading the premium-priced wine list is a challenge – it's large and offers little inspiration to the untrained eye – but there are some great bottles, such as the good-value unoaked cabernet franc from Giovanni Puiatti's Le Zuccole label.
Babies and children admitted. Booking advisable. Disabled: lift; toilet. Dress: smart. Restaurant and bar available for hire. Separate rooms for parties, seating 6, 12 and 26. Tables outdoors (16, garden). **Map 6 R5.**

Refettorio

Crowne Plaza Hotel, 19 New Bridge Street, EC4V 6DB (7438 8052/www.tableinthecity.com). Blackfriars tube/rail. **Lunch served** noon-2.30pm Mon-Fri. **Dinner served** 6-10.30pm Mon-Sat. **Main courses** £5.50-£17.50. **Service** 12.5%. **Credit** AmEx, MC, V.

An identikit modern interior of chunky dark wood and leather suggests someone got overexcited flicking through the Ocean catalogue, but given Refettorio's hotel setting, this sleek refectory is refreshingly relaxed and unpompous. As we went to press, Giorgio Locatelli announced he would no longer be acting as consultant chef, but the suggestion was that there would be no dramatic changes as the new chef was coming from Locanda Locatelli. Staff endeavoured to take our order promptly, but, once they intuited our intention to eat leisurely, were happy to let us linger. There was much to like, especially the sharing plates of artisan cheeses, cured meats and own-made antipasto pickles of baby beetroot, artichoke and courgette. The bread basket (charged at £3.50) offered a nice selection. We opted for a starter of tagliatelle with broad beans, broccoli and clams, which arrived with too many pasta strands stuck together. A main of stuffed char-grilled squid was a little bland, while juicy roast breast of guinea fowl with pine nuts and sultanas had an over-reduced sauce. The highlight was a coppa with spicy chocolate, coffee, liquorice and cherry flavours expertly melded in a sophisticated ice-cream sundae. It made the fancy sbrisolona (almond and polenta crumble cake) that arrived with creamy, almond-dusted pyramid and pointless passionfruit foam look foolish. Classy simplicity is the way forward here.
Babies and children admitted. Booking advisable. Separate room for parties, seats 30. **Map 11 O6.**

Clerkenwell & Farringdon EC1

Zetter

The Zetter, 86-88 Clerkenwell Road, EC1M 5RJ (7324 4455/www.thezetter.com). Farringdon tube/rail. **Breakfast served** 7am-10.30pm Mon-Fri; 7.30am-11pm Sat, Sun. **Brunch served** 11am-3pm Sat, Sun. **Lunch served** noon-2.30pm Mon-Fri. **Dinner served** 6-11pm Mon-Sat; 6-10.30pm Sun. **Main courses** £12.50-£17. **Service** 12.5%. **Credit** AmEx, DC, JCB, MC, V.

Hotel restaurants may typically be stilted, formal environments, but the Zetter is a friendly, easy going brasserie with open kitchen. Huge windows with zinc alloy frames provide a panoramic view of the surrounding streets, and walls are decorated with black and red artistic flourishes. Service was efficient and unobtrusive, though it was a slow Sunday – which also accounted for the brunch menu on offer, with plenty of tempting breakfast dishes. But it was still possible to order a hearty Italian meal. Big flavours and simple cooking are the key tenets. Exceptionally tender ribeye came with peppery jus and a well-balanced combination of roasted radicchio with melted gorgonzola. Simpler still was tuna steak with roasted red peppers, new potatoes and a big, sunny wedge of lemon. Desserts need work, though a soft chocolate and almond tart included excellent pastry. It's worth planning for pre-meal drinks in the cosy bar with its funky floral fabrics, vintage panelling and soft leather lounges.
Babies and children welcome: children's portions; crayons; high chairs. Booking advisable. Disabled: toilet. Separate rooms for parties, seating 10 and 40. Tables outdoors (4, pavement). **Map 5 O4.**

Covent Garden WC2

Neal Street

26 Neal Street, WC2H 9QW (7836 8368/ www.carluccios.com). Covent Garden tube. **Lunch served** noon-2.30pm, **dinner served** 6-10.30pm Mon-Sat. **Main courses** £12.50-£25. **Set meal** (lunch, 6-7pm Mon-Sat) £21 2 courses, £25 3 courses. **Service** 12.5%. **Credit** AmEx, DC, JCB, MC, V.

A refreshing contrast to the detached presence that so many celebrity chefs become, Antonio Carluccio is clearly still involved in the day-to-day running of this seminal London restaurant (he was lunching and amiably chatting to customers at a nearby table during our most recent visit). Attention to detail is apparent throughout the operation, from the attentive (but laid-back) staff to the giant pre-prandial olives and fragrant artisanal breads through to the menu itself and the sun-kissed (mostly) Italian wine list. From a good-value set menu, we enjoyed deliciously simple starters of green salad with marinated mushroom and crispy pancetta; and hand-cut tagliolini with butter, lemon and parmesan. Main-course rabbit legs baked with black olives, thyme, lemon and cherry tomatoes, served with potato cake, was poetry on a plate, totally eclipsing a passable but not memorable second main of Sicilian stuffed swordfish. For dessert, house tiramisu and orange brûlée showed that the chef has a handle on the sweet stuff too. All in all, then, Neal Street remains a worthwhile, inventive and, perhaps most impressive, unpretentious destination restaurant.
Babies and children welcome: high chairs. Booking advisable. Dress: no shorts. No-smoking tables. Separate room for parties, seats 24. **Map 18 L6.**

Fitzrovia W1

Camerino

16 Percy Street, W1T 1DT (7637 9900/ www.camerinorestaurant.com). Goodge Street or Tottenham Court Road tube. **Lunch served** noon-3pm Mon-Fri. **Dinner served** 6-11pm Mon-Sat. **Set lunch** £17.50 2 courses, £21.50 3 courses. **Set dinner** £22.50 2 courses, £26.50 3 courses, £30.50 4 courses. **Service** 12.5%. **Credit** AmEx, DC, MC, V.

Beautiful faux-embroidery murals, long drops of red fabric, and crisp white linen bring a fresh feel to this modern yet restrained restaurant. Cordial, soberly dressed staff strive to be all present and correct, making this a fine choice for business lunches and after-work liaisons. We could have had a billowy pile of scrambled eggs on toast with prawns – which looked lovely – or an asparagus salad, which also featured eggs. We opted, however, for a special of scallops with raw radicchio and light saffron vinaigrette. With five plump specimens, it was too generous for a first course; fewer shellfish of better quality would be

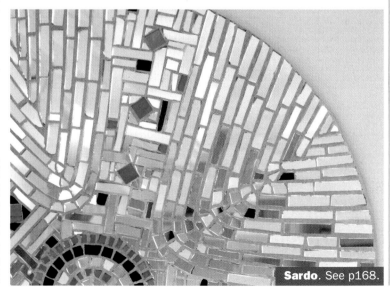

Sardo. See p168.

RESTAURANTS

preferable. Another special of pan-fried cod with broccoli and anchovy sauce was nicely done. Own-made gelato in Kentish cherry, chocolate and hazelnut, and Malaga raisin flavours made a nice light finish, along with good strong espresso served in stylish little cups. Comino Bianco from Sicily and Comino Rosso from Puglia are decent wines to enjoy by the glass. The highlight was the bread basket, featuring homemade grissini and flavoured breads, including lovely focaccia with a warm, moist cherry tomato embedded in it.
Babies and children welcome: high chairs. Booking advisable. Restaurant available for hire. Tables outdoors (3, pavement). **Map 10 K5.**

Carluccio's Caffè
8 Market Place, W1W 8AG (7636 2228/ www.carluccios.com). Oxford Circus tube. **Meals served** 7.30am-11pm Mon-Fri; 10am-11pm Sat; 10am-10pm Sun. **Main courses** £5.95-£10.95. **Service** 10% for parties of 8 or more. **Credit** AmEx, MC, V.
With nearly 15 branches around London, Carluccio's may feel like a bit more chain-like than a few years ago, but it's still pushing the right buttons if our recent visit was typical. This branch – set on a semi-pedestrianised area behind Oxford Circus, with plenty of outside tables – is a great spot in warm weather. Eating inside, where pasta, wines, oils and other deli produce is for sale, feels rather like chowing down in a supermarket (albeit a posh one). Staff were inviting, and the diners a mix of tourists taking a breather, businessmen grabbing a power-lunch and young families. The menu blends classic and innovative regional Italian food, plus a few daily specials. Swordfish, pan-fried with parmesan and breadcrumbs, was perfect summer fare: light, crisp and fresh, with garlicky green beans on the side. A mushroom risotto was huge, but so delicious we motored through it with little difficulty; the chef had gone overboard with the garlic, but otherwise it was a beautifully unctuous dish. Desserts include own-made gelati and sorbets, but we couldn't resist tiramisu. It was dinky in size, if not price (£4.25), and wonderfully heavy on the cream. The Italian wine list is short, but has some interesting choices.
Babies and children welcome: children's menu; high chairs. Disabled: toilet. No-smoking tables. Tables outdoors (16, pavement). Takeaway service. **Map 17 J6.**
For branches see index.

Latium
21 Berners Street, W1T 3LP (7323 9123/ www.latiumrestaurant.com). Oxford Circus tube. **Lunch served** noon-3pm Mon-Fri. **Dinner served** 6.30-10.30pm Mon-Fri; 6.30-11pm Sat. **Main courses** £11-£15. **Set meal** £21.50 2 courses, £25.50 3 courses. **Service** 12.5%. **Credit** AmEx, JCB, MC, V.
Black leather seating, white tablecloths and dark-suited waiters lend a smartness to this restaurant located just a stone's throw from Oxford Street's takeaways. The generosity of kitchen and staff was exemplified in the canapé selection, which included arancini (rice balls), pizzetta and baby calzone, as well as a plate of briny olives. Service was astonishingly swift too; we ate comfortably in record time, yet staff left us alone when it came to the bill, not wanting to push us out. House wines come from Sardinia and are versatile choices to accompany Latium's high-quality, refined cooking. Borlotti bean ravioli with guinea fowl ragù, from a long list of pastas and risottos, was much lighter than it sounded – the ragù a few simply cooked pieces of poultry and fine strands of vegetables in a rich stock sauce. The waiter talked us out of having the intriguing stracci with aubergine, mussels and salted ricotta, instead insisting we try a more classic special of tagliatelle with fresh tuna, olives, capers and tomato sauce. Main of slow-roast pork with mash and cod 'crust' tasted much better than it looked, and featured a good sticky gravy in addition to savoy cabbage and bacon. For afters, there's the likes of chocolate and almond tart or a fine list of cheeses.
Babies and children welcome: high chairs. Booking advisable weekends. **Map 17 J5.**

★ Passione
10 Charlotte Street, W1T 2LT (7636 2833/ www.passione.co.uk). Goodge Street tube. **Lunch served** 12.30-2.15pm Mon-Fri. **Dinner served** 7-10.15pm Mon-Sat. **Main courses** £14-£22. **Service** 12.5%. **Credit** AmEx, DC, JCB, MC, V.
Passione is aptly named. Amalfi-born chef Gennaro Contaldo's deep commitment and enthusiasm for the food of his native southern Italy shines through in every dish at this tiny Charlotte Street haven. Such dedication to the best, freshest – and most authentic – ingredients, and the wizardry involved in their combination, doesn't come cheap. You can rapidly find a simple, seasonal lunch with a single glass of wine topping the £40 mark. This doesn't deter the determined foodies and business diners who pack the cramped, contemporary space on a regular basis. Start with a huge, fresh plateful of vegetali alla griglia with melt-in-the mouth fresh mozzarella di bufala, or perhaps sea-fresh carpaccio of octopus served with a chicory salad. Move on to one of the mainstays of Amalfi coastal cooking: tagliatelle con vongole, packed with garlicky clams and fresh tomatoes. Or perhaps try a dish of branzino (sea bass) served with spring onions, cherry tomatoes and basil oil, with some mash to mop up all the juices. And save room for the legendary tiramisu.
Babies and children admitted. Booking advisable. Restaurant available for hire. Separate room for parties, seats 18. Tables outdoors (2, patio; 1, pavement). **Map 10 K5.**

★ Sardo
45 Grafton Way, W1T 5DQ (7387 2521/ www.sardo-restaurant.com). Warren Street tube. **Lunch served** noon-3pm Mon-Fri. **Dinner served** 6-11pm Mon-Sat. **Main courses** £8.90-£18. **Credit** AmEx, DC, MC, V.
Even if you haven't been to Sardinia, it's easy to imagine this is how a top-ranking Sardinian restaurant should be. The walls are bright white; there's a welcome area/bar in the narrow front room, behind which sun-kissed staff bob and beam; and customers are kicking back in holiday mode. In short, the place seems to be suffused with enough Mediterranean light to drive out the severest London gloom. We've said before that Sardo is where restaurant critics are happy to spend their own money – but it's partly because the place is such good value. The menu changes monthly, but is also built around a few staple dishes that you'll want to revisit. Calamari stuffed with herbs and their own meat was a wonderful starter, as was carpaccio di pesce: thin slices of flavourful fish, accompanied by soft, own-baked breads. Seafood is the strength. Linguine with crab meat and chilli oil sauce worked well as a light main course; fresh tuna or swordfish steaks are served simply, with rocket. If you do crave meat, calf's liver with balsamic vinegar was very succulent. There's nothing heavy about the food, so you'll find room for panna cotta, lemon tart or maybe even the sebadas (puff pastry with cheese and honey) . The wines are Sardinian, and staff will be happy to steer you to the right bottle.
Babies and children admitted. Booking advisable. No-smoking tables. Separate area for parties, seats 30. Tables outdoors (3, patio). **Map 3 J4.**
For branch (Sardo Canale) see index.

Knightsbridge SW1, SW3

Emporio Armani Caffè
191 Brompton Road, SW3 1NE (7823 8818). Knightsbridge tube. **Open** 10am-6pm Mon-Sat. **Breakfast served** 10am-noon Mon-Sat. **Lunch served** noon-3.30pm Mon-Fri; noon-4pm Sat. **Main courses** £12.50-£17.50. **Credit** AmEx, DC, JCB, MC, V.
Don't be fooled by the term caffè, or the in-store location. This is Armani, after all, and much as you might like to think people in fashion don't eat, someone here certainly understands food. You can visit for simple coffee (the puffy cappuccino is spectacularly decorated with chocolate powder and flakes, the macchiato may arrive with a smiley face drawn in the foam), but the lunch menu is restaurant-calibre. A starter of grilled squid with chorizo typifies the modern approach to Italian cuisine. So too peppered goat's cheese crostata, served with rocket and a finger-licking glaze of fig balsamic. Excess vegetables in the mix, especially celery, overpowered a crab and chard risotto, but sea bream cooked in a salt crust and served with caponata was pleasing. Staff didn't hesitate to push their favourite dishes and the daily specials. There was some confusion over the range of ice-creams available on our visit, and service was very slow, but staff were unerringly friendly and polite.
Babies and children admitted. Booking advisable. Disabled: toilet (in shop). **Map 14 E9.**

San Lorenzo
22 Beauchamp Place, SW3 1NH (7584 1074). Knightsbridge tube. **Lunch served** 12.30-3pm, **dinner served** 7.30-11.30pm Mon-Sat. **Main courses** £14.50-£28.50. **Cover** £2.50. **No credit cards.**
Celebrity culture has nothing to do with quality. Take San Lorenzo. For over 40 years this has been a haunt of London's glitterati (though, today, celeb-watchers may outnumber actual celebs). It still has the same 'Museum of Swinging London' decor to prove it. There's nothing wrong with the food, which is pleasant, but considering the place's fame and the prices (£40-plus per head), a bit more effort could be made. Best of our starters was warm asparagus with a simple, well-blended oil and lemon dressing. Insalata di gamberoni featured just one fat, very juicy prawn; we looked in vain for another (isn't 'gamberoni' plural?). To follow, taglierini with prawns and lobster sauce was a juicy pasta dish, and fritto misti di mare a very generous platter of fried prawns, squid, rather chewy hake and more. Throughout, there was none of the culinary finesse expected in a top-flight restaurant. Similarly, the wine list sticks to time-honoured Italian labels at premium rates. Still, the customers don't seem to mind. Service is efficient, but inclined to get brusque (unless, of course, you're famous) as the place fills.
Babies and children welcome: children's portions; high chairs. Booking advisable Fri, Sat. Dress: smart casual; no shorts. Restaurant available for hire. Separate room for parties, seats 30. **Map 14 F9.**
For branch see index.

Zafferano
15 Lowndes Street, SW1X 9EY (7235 5800/ www.zafferanorestaurant.com). Knightsbridge tube. **Lunch served** noon-2.30pm Mon-Fri; 12.30-3pm Sat, Sun. **Dinner served** 7-11pm Mon-Sat; 7-10.30pm Sun. **Set lunch** £25.50 2 courses, £29.50 3 courses, £33.50 4 courses. **Set dinner** £29.50 2 courses, £37.50 3 courses, £41.50 4 courses. **Service** 12.5%. **Credit** AmEx, DC, MC, V.
Service at Zafferano is impeccable: a perfect combination of friendliness, courtesy, buzziness and a readiness to answer every need. This creates a nicely pampered feeling in customers, which must be one reason why the place is always full. The restaurant is no longer quite the foodie target of old, since star chef Giorgio Locatelli moved on. Nor does the menu change as frequently, but it continues to provide highly enjoyable modern Italian food. The key is in doing simple things very well, with prime-quality ingredients. Salads, such as a summer mix including fennel, asparagus, crisp carrot and beetroot, are wonderfully refreshing; malfatti (large ravioli) contained a delicately flavoured mix of ricotta and aubergine (though the pasta wasn't quite al dente, a surprise in such a high-end venue). To follow, veal cutlet with fungi and rösti was a richly flavoured mix, and tuna plainly cooked 'alla griglia' was superb. Zafferano sticks to a set-price formula, although several dishes carry supplements; if you have the full three courses, go for any dessert involving great fresh fruit. An enticing list of classic and modern Italian wines, very correctly served, adds to the comfortable feel.
Babies and children welcome: high chairs. Booking essential, at least 1wk in advance for lunch, 4-6wks in advance for dinner. Dress: smart casual; no shorts (dinner). Separate room for parties, seats 20. **Map 15 G9.**

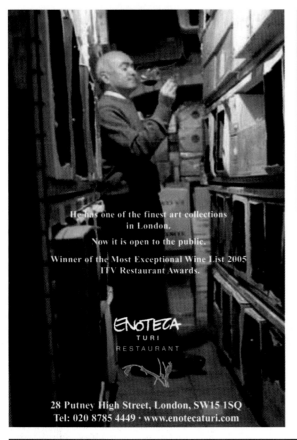

Marble Arch W2

Arturo NEW

*23 Connaught Street, W2 2AY (7706 3388/
www.arturorestaurant.co.uk). Marble Arch tube.*
Lunch served noon-2.30pm Mon-Sat;
12.30-3.30pm Sun. **Dinner served** 6-10.30pm
Mon-Sat; 6-9.30pm Sun. **Main courses** £12-£16.
Set meal £12.95 2 courses, £15.95 3 courses.
Service 12.5%. **Credit** MC, V.
Snake-hipped waiters work conscientiously at this
sleekly designed yet relaxed restaurant with
downstairs bar. The decor, with its simple lines and
elegant pots of flowers, hints at the Orient, but the
menu has its feet firmly planted in Italy. Chef
Ginetto Morganti hails from a Tuscan fishing
village, although owner Anthony Brown also runs
Buchan's, a modern Scottish restaurant in
Battersea. The à la carte menu typically offers a
choice of six dishes across each category, and
there's also a limited-choice set menu. Balsamic
vinegar and olive oil were brought for dunking the
authentically bland bread, though there was a
sense of nanny-knows-best in the manner of
serving one slice at a time. Generosity, however,
was the hallmark of Arturo's main courses. The
plump, juicy, 10oz char-grilled fillet of beef that
featured in tagliata di manzo was impressive, if
not sliced. Starters were strikingly presented,
though we felt the vitello tonnato suffered from too
delicate a hand with the tuna mayonnaise. Risotto
with black truffles was fine, as was the house red.
We were too full to enjoy desserts such as panna
cotta or tiramisu, but left content.
*Babies and children admitted. No-smoking tables.
Tables outdoors (3, pavement).* **Map 8 F6.**

Marylebone W1

Eddalino

*10 Wigmore Street, W1U 2RD (7637 0789/
www.eddalino.co.uk). Bond Street or Oxford
Circus tube.* **Lunch served** noon-3pm, **dinner
served** 6-10.30pm Mon-Sat. **Main courses**
£10.50-£28.50. **Service** 12.5%. **Credit** AmEx,
MC, V.
Eddalino's conservative appearance – clean lines,
dark blue accents and suited waiters – belies an
eye-catchingly creative menu, crafted by its young,
talented chef Francesco Pesce, who hails from Le
Marche. We were wholeheartedly impressed by the
results. Own-made ravioli was deliciously al dente,
filled with aubergine caviar and served with a
wonderfully fresh tomato sauce; char-grilled
scallops (skewered with pumpkin and sweet white
asparagus) were cooked to perfection with delicate
smoky flavours; and spaghetti with lobster was
sensational, with first-rate pasta, upfront
seasoning and tender morsels of flesh. Eddalino
also boasts a serious wine list with a small but
robust selection in the lower price range. Wine is
served in super-thin, oversized glasses – and
swilled around in a theatrical manner by the waiter
before being delivered. If you're tired of robotic
staff, you'll love the characterful, suavely attentive
service, from individuals who clearly understand
– and are passionate about – the menu. So smooth
an operation as this will cost you dear, but the
rewards are rich.
*Babies and children welcome: high chairs.
Booking advisable. No-smoking tables. Restaurant
available for hire. Tables outdoors (2, pavement).*
Map 9 H5.

★ Locanda Locatelli

*8 Seymour Street, W1H 7JZ (7935 9088/
www.locandalocatelli.com). Marble Arch tube.*
Lunch served noon-3pm Mon-Fri; noon-
3.30pm Sat, Sun. **Dinner served** 7-11pm
Mon-Thur; 7-11.30pm Fri, Sat; 6.45-10pm
Sun. **Main courses** £16-£30. **Credit** AmEx,
JCB, MC, V.
Lunch at Locanda Locatelli feels naughty. Not only
is the meal guaranteed to seem like wanton
indulgence when you survey the prices (no
bargain-priced set menus here), the sensuous
surfaces of the dimly lit interior evoke a very
exclusive nightclub. Many Locatelli dishes are
contemporary spins on Italian classics, but the

Osteria dell'Arancio.
See p176.

menu's breadth of choice lends an old-school vibe.
Don't hesitate to order ravioli – these are probably
the best in the country. Our lovely courgette and
oregano version featured a sauce of prawns and
courgette blossoms. The 'pickled aubergine with
anchovies' that accompanied pan-fried sea bream
fillets was a tasty mixed veg caponata with toasted
pistachios. Veal cutlet came with half-moons of
crunchy saffron risotto. Most Italian restaurants
devote little effort to desserts, but Locanda
Locatelli lists 12, including cheese. There is a
wealth of ices inspired by garden and tropics, plus
well-considered treats such as hot chocolate and
banana doughnuts. The encyclopaedic wine list
starts at an impressively low £12, then takes
sizeable leaps upwards. Our only complaint is with
the service, which can be achingly slow, even when
the restaurant is not especially busy.
*Booking essential. Disabled: toilet (hotel).
Dress: smart casual.* **Map 9 G6.**

Mayfair W1

★ Alloro

*19-20 Dover Street, W1X 4LU (7495 4768).
Green Park tube.*
Bar **Open** noon-midnight Mon-Fri; 6pm-
midnight Sat. **Main courses** £8-£16.
Restaurant **Lunch served** noon-2.30pm
Mon-Fri. **Dinner served** 7-10.30pm Mon-Sat.
Set lunch £26 2 courses, £29 3 courses.
Set dinner £28.50 2 courses, £33 3 courses,
£36 4 courses. **Service** 12.5%.
Both **Credit** AmEx, DC, JCB, MC, V.
Serene, quietly classy and hugely enjoyable –
Alloro may not be the flashiest Italian in town, but
there are times when Valentino is more appropriate
than Versace. Our Friday evening visit saw one
large table of businessmen, and an incongruous
birthday party, but most of the customers were
couples with romance in mind. The charming staff
are perfectly attentive and enthusiastic about both
menu and wine list. The maître d' diplomatically
recommended a delicious Dolcetto d'Alba to match
our divergent choice of dishes. A special of mixed
seafood grill came with an unusual base of pearl
barley, lentils and pickled onions that nourished
while complementing the exquisitely fresh pieces
of sea bream, red mullet, mackerel and prawn.
Black truffles featured strongly in the tempting list
of pastas, including a satisfying special of own-
made penette with duck ragout and truffle
shavings, and rich, truffle-flavoured gnocchi with
veal ragout. Fine tiramisu came in a tuile basket
with dark chocolate sauce. It was also impossible
to resist the warm cherry and cinnamon tart with
vanilla ice-cream. When you need to impress,
Alloro's number is the one to ring.
*Babies and children welcome: high chairs.
Booking advisable. Restaurant and bar
available for hire. Separate room for parties,
seats 16. Tables outdoors (3, pavement).*
Map 9 J7.

Giardinetto

*39-40 Albemarle Street, W1S 4TE (7493 7091).
Green Park tube.* **Lunch served** 12.30-3pm
Mon-Sat. **Dinner served** 6-10.30pm daily.
Set lunch £22 3 courses. **Service** 12.5%.
Credit AmEx, DC, JCB, MC, V.
Giardinetto's basement location on Charlotte
Street was certainly looking shabby, so the move
in 2005 to Mayfair seems sensible. However, the
restaurant has lost the rustic charm of the menu
along with the vintage fittings. It was always a
premium-priced place, but the new Giardinetto
has molecular-gastronomy affectations to the
dishes and few bottles of wine under £25. A
starter of cold passionfruit and vegetable soup
with olive oil ice-cream exemplifies the new mood.
So too 'chlorophyll' tagliolini with a fresh tomato
sauce and carefully arranged side servings of
finely diced onion and carrot. Fanciful
presentation does seem high on the new venue's
agenda. Juicy guinea fowl breast with cherry
sauce was accompanied by an edible lidded pot of
chopped vegetables, and crisp, light toffee-coated
fresh apricot and redcurrants were the decorative
highlight of apricot jam crostata. The tall dark

RESTAURANTS

Interview
GIORGIO LOCATELLI

Who are you?
Chef-patron of **Locanda Locatelli** (*see p171*), and star of the TV series *Tony & Giorgio*, with Tony Allan. My next book, *Made in Italy*, will be published by Fourth Estate in September 2006.
Eating in London: what's good about it?
The variety is unbelievable. If only the quality was half as good as the variety, it would be absolutely outstanding. No other European city has Chinese, Indian and Japanese restaurants rated in the Michelin guide.
What's bad about it?
I'm a peasant, not a businessman. I hate the chain restaurants' system, where the financial men take over the day-to-day running of a restaurant. It's restrictive – not for the corporation, but for the customer. It's very much an American model, when we should look more to Europe for inspiration.
Which are your favourite London restaurants?
I haven't eaten in any big shiny restaurants recently – I'm over it – but my wife and I sometimes go to **Nobu** (*see p185*). I've never had a bad meal there. Occasionally we walk across Hampstead Heath to the **Wells** gastropub (*see p117*).
What single thing would improve London's restaurant scene?
The delivery and transport system should be reconsidered. Now, we all suffer and pay enormous amounts of money. Yet supermarkets send big vans full of crap food across the country, and you can eat a sandwich that was made 300 miles away.
Any hot tips for the coming year?
Ingredients. Let's all concentrate on what we eat – and feel responsible for it and for the people who've produced it. With supermarkets we're not responsible, and we don't care about what has happened to the animal or vegetable on the plate.

brown leather chairs are deep and comfortable. Waiters were keen, but with more staff than customers the formality of the service felt laboured. Hopefully, when nearby Brown's Hotel eventually reopens, the place will be so busy that it won't seem awkward.
Babies and children admitted. Booking advisable. No-smoking tables. Separate rooms for parties, seating 10 and 14. **Map 9 J7**.

Sartoria
20 Savile Row, W1S 3PR (7534 7000/ www.conran.com). Oxford Circus or Piccadilly Circus tube.
Bar **Open/snacks served** noon-11pm Mon-Sat.
Restaurant **Lunch served** noon-3pm Mon-Fri. **Dinner served** 6-11.30pm Mon-Sat. **Main courses** £15-£18.50. **Set meal** (6.30-8pm) £17.95 2 courses, £21.95 3 courses.
Both **Service** 12.5%. **Credit** AmEx, DC, JCB, MC, V.
Many Conran restaurants fail to deliver on all that their style-defining design seems to promise, but we've never found this the case here. Sartoria is exceptionally spacious, cool and relaxing, with ultra-comfy long sofas as well as more conventional chairs. Service is keen and charming, and there's a helpful, expert sommelier to guide you through a wine list that's a giant catalogue of modern Italian labels. Food is a nice blend of traditional Italian simplicity with modern subtleties and fashionable notes, based on first-rate ingredients. Tagliatelle with mixed fungi, available as starter or main, was an eminently satisfying mix with delicate grades of flavour. In marinated tuna with avocado and tomato, the fish was deliciously smooth-grained, although its dressing was a bit overcharged with lemon. Next, seafood spaghettini was an excellent, light version of an Italian classic, packed with fine mussels, prawns and other good things; Gressingham duck with castelluccio lentils and roast peach was gratifyingly full-bodied, even though a slight oiliness again suggested a tendency to overdo the dressings. Desserts are refined, fresh and indulgent. For once, style and quality go together.
Babies and children welcome: high chairs; nappy-changing facilities. Booking advisable; essential lunch. Disabled: toilet. Entertainment: pianist 7-10pm Thur-Sat. Restaurant available for hire. Separate rooms for parties, seating 20 and 45. **Map 9 J7**.

St James's SW1

Al Duca
4-5 Duke of York Street, SW1Y 6LA (7839 3090). Piccadilly Circus tube. **Lunch served** noon-2.30pm Mon-Fri; 12.30-3pm Sat. **Dinner served** 6-11pm Mon-Sat. **Set lunch** £17.50 2 courses, £20.50 3 courses, £23.50 4 courses. **Set dinner** £20 2 courses, £24 3 courses, £28 4 courses. **Service** 12.5%. **Credit** AmEx, DC, MC, V.
This St James's Italian was packed to bursting with business diners on our summer lunchtime visit. Indeed, we had to wait for our table outside. But after a shaky start (the waiters are much nicer than the meeters-and-greeters), we reckoned Al Duca pretty much delivered what it promised: dependable, classic Italian food at Mayfair prices. From a page-long menu divided into antipasti, pasta, fish and meat mains, and dolce, we tried a rotunda of grilled vegetables (a stack of peppers, aubergines and courgettes interspersed with discs of grilled goat's cheese) and a pale and slightly production-line plate of traditional vitello tonnato (cold veal with tuna and caper sauce, which came with a sweet/sour carrot and fennel garnish). Fish of the day was rolls of grilled squid served with pesto and a slashed julienne of carrots and courgettes. Pasta was pappardelle with beef ragù and parmesan. Puddings are a notch up from the main courses, including a textbook panna cotta with summer berries, and a fresh, tangy plateful of slivered pineapple with mint and passionfruit.
Babies and children welcome: high chair. Dress: no shorts. Restaurant available for hire (Sun). **Map 17 J7**.

Fiore NEW
33 St James's Street, SW1A 1HD (7930 7100/ www.fiore-restaurant.co.uk). Green Park tube. **Lunch served** noon-2.30pm Mon-Fri; 12.30-3pm Sat, Sun. **Dinner served** 6-10.30pm daily. **Main courses** £14-£16. **Set lunch** £18 2 courses, £22 3 courses, £26 4 courses. **Set dinner** £45 5 course tasting menu. **Service** 12.5%. **Credit** MC, V.
Fiore is in the premises previously occupied by Marcus Wareing's Pétrus, then by Ramsay's short-lived Fleur. It's now part-owned by respected restaurateur Claudio Pulze, who has had more than one Michelin-starred restaurant to his name. We started with risotto 'Milano-Tokyo' – an intriguing title. Golden, saffron-scented risotto was the perfect mix of chewy and creamy, with a rich, succulent flavour. The 'Tokyo' element was a parmesan basket filled with finely minced raw tuna, which sat in the centre of the risotto. It worked – just – thanks to careful juxtaposition of flavours and textures. The daily special of oven-baked leg of lamb with sautéed potatoes and onions was not so impressive; and millefoglie of veal with chilli-flavoured braised lettuce, sautéed mushrooms and black truffle was smothered in a flavourless brown sauce. The kitchen didn't stint on mushrooms and truffle, but the dish was confused. Yet beneath such gussied-up, misjudged offerings, there is real technique and ability. Dessert held a surprise: treviso parfait with red fruit sauce. What alchemy did the chef use to turn a bitter salad leaf into a sumptuous dessert? This semi-frozen blend of sweet and bitter tasted utterly Italian and quite delicious. Quite what the buttoned-up denizens of St James will make of it all we're not sure.
Babies and children welcome: high chairs. Restaurant available for hire. **Map 17 J7**.

Soho W1

Quo Vadis
26-29 Dean Street, W1T 6LL (7437 9585/ www.whitestarline.org.uk). Leicester Square, Piccadilly Circus or Tottenham Court Road tube. **Lunch served** noon-2.30pm Mon-Fri. **Dinner served** 5.30-11pm Mon-Sat. **Main courses** £10.50-£19. **Set meal** (lunch, 5.30-6.30pm) £14.95 2 courses, £19.95 3 courses. **Service** 12.5%. **Credit** AmEx, DC, JCB, MC, V.
Quo Vadis's curious yet relaxing decor blends art nouveau features with clubby bench seating and an eccentric art collection featuring skeletal sculptures and butterflies. Since our last visit the menu has become similarly wacky – yet in this environment it works. Fruit featured in an astonishing number of dishes, from raisin oil used to dress prawn ravioli with porcini and pistachios, to a rhubarb soup that provided a sauce for fillet of turbot. Lobster ravioli came with mandarin and vanilla sauce, duck capelletti with lentils and pomegranate. Even grilled beef fillet with chestnut crêpes featured a filling of soft cheese and apricot, and we were easily persuaded to try the special salad of crab and green apple. Orange and carrot sorbet with a zingy garnish of shiso leaves was delicious, but the accompanying sweet confit of carrot was a triumph of chemistry over taste. Generous linguine with scallops, rocket and chilli, an excellent dark chocolate fondant and a lavish choice of Italian wines were the few examples of Quo Vadis playing safe. Still, staff and customers seem to enjoy the creativity – everyone on our visit was having a good time.
Booking advisable. Children admitted. Dress: smart casual. Separate rooms for parties, seating 12, 14, 30 and 80. **Map 17 K6**.

Vasco & Piero's Pavilion
15 Poland Street, W1F 8QE (7437 8774/ www.vascosfood.com). Oxford Circus, Piccadilly Circus or Tottenham Court Road tube. **Lunch served** noon-3pm Mon-Fri. **Dinner served** 6-11pm Mon-Sat. **Main courses** £9.50-£17. **Set dinner** £22 2 courses, £26 3 courses. **Service** 12.5%. **Credit** AmEx, DC, JCB, MC, V.
The tapestry-covered chairs and yellow walls may look rather jaded these days, and the tables and

Pomino. See p179.

chairs are still squashed a little too close together, but V&P is busy most nights with a crowd looking for quality Italian food, a buzzy atmosphere and friendly, efficient service. Fresh pasta features often, as do the ingredients (cheeses, meats, even herbs) of Vasco's beloved native Umbria. The set dinner is excellent value and offers the likes of own-made sea bass tortelloni served in a buttery asparagus sauce; or a fresh summer salad of beetroot, tomato, mixed leaves, anchovy and egg. A main course of salmon fish cakes was full of chunky salmon pieces, served with fried potatoes and a spicy tomato and avocado 'guacamole'. Aubergine tortelloni in tomato sauce were a little overwhelmed by the accompanying goat's cheese and rosemary, but satisfied us nonetheless. The tempting array of desserts included simple, delicious marinated peaches in lemon and sugar. The wine list contains a number of reasonable offerings under £20.
Booking advisable. Children over 6 years admitted. Separate room for parties, seats 36. **Map 17 J6.**

Westminster SW1

★ Quirinale
North Court, 1 Great Peter Street, SW1P 3LL (7222 7080). St James's Park or Westminster tube. **Lunch served** noon-2.30pm, **dinner served** 6-10.30pm Mon-Fri. **Main courses** £12.50-£16. **Service** 12.5%. **Credit** AmEx, DC, MC, V.
This creamy-coloured basement restaurant makes clever use of pale stone and wood, and a sneaky little skylight. Even a full room with birthday party table did not detract from Quirinale's sense of calm, though we did find service slowing slightly as the large group received its dishes. Our food was tremendous. Baked sea bream in salt crust was filleted tableside by the expert staff. Intriguing combinations made the pasta dishes seem compulsory. A special of chitarra (square spaghetti) came with duck and pistachio nuts, while triofe was sublimely partnered with braised veal sweetbreads, porcini and spinach. The stupendous cheese list includes rarely seen moro di bufala, though it's hard to pass on desserts such as champagne and strawberry semifreddo. Quirinale offers a choice of four house wines, starting at £16.50, but the list on the whole does not hit alarming heights. We went with a Sicilian bottle made with the primitivo grape, but could have had Trebbiano d'Abbruzzo, Soave, or Montepulciano. Set in deepest Westminster, this lovely restaurant gets a vote of confidence from ministers and bureaucrats too.
Babies and children admitted. Booking advisable. **Map 16 L10.**

West

Bayswater W2

L'Accento NEW
16 Garway Road, W2 4NH (7243 2201). Bayswater or Queensway tube. **Lunch served** noon-2.30pm, **dinner served** 6.30-11.15pm Mon-Sat. **Main courses** £14-£16.50. **Set meal** £13.50 2 courses. **Service** 12.5%. **Credit** AmEx, JCB, MC, V.
In a rather down-at-heel part of Notting Hill near Bayswater, this slightly scruffy Italian continues to survive. Beaten-up wooden chairs and tables are set amid classic sponge-and-wipe swirly paint. True, there are minimalist white walls, but these look like an attempt to justify main courses that are in the £14-£17 bracket. The owner seems to feel he has to attract business too, standing outside the entrance like a Greek taverna or curry house operator. But he needn't worry. Lovestruck couples and large family groups fill the compact room, sensibly concentrating on each other rather than the food. A starter of aubergine with a rich tomato sauce, basil and parmesan was the high point. Risotto with zucchini came swimming in a cheesy sauce, without any hint of the billed saffron. For mains, veal was perched attractively on well-cooked spinach and decent sliced potatoes, but was overwhelmed by its lemon sauce. The wine list, by contrast, is excellent. Falanghina's Sannio Beneventano, Feudi di San Gregorio (2004), at £21.50, is a great choice: one of the best-value white wines in southern Italy.
Babies and children admitted. Booking advisable dinner Fri, Sat. No-smoking tables. Separate room for parties, seats 30. Tables outdoors (5, pavement). **Map 7 B6.**

★ Assaggi
First floor, 39 Chepstow Place, W2 4TS (7792 5501). Bayswater, Notting Hill Gate or Queensway tube. **Lunch served** 12.30-2.30pm Mon-Fri; 1-2.30pm Sat. **Dinner served** 7.30-11pm Mon-Sat. **Main courses** £16.95-£19.50. **Credit** MC, V.
A simple colourful room set above a pub, Assaggi is refreshingly free of wood laminate, leather banquettes and trendy decoration, and still manages to be more fashionable than most restaurants. A couple of oversized flower arrangements, a trompe l'oeil mantelpiece and fabric-covered picture frames are the extent of the embellishments – the rest of the small space is devoted to tables and practical matters. The menu relies on a succession of classics that Assaggi has made its own, and several Sardinian accents including the excellent carta di musica (crispbread). Generously proportioned starters

include grilled prawns – meaty specimens – with pea purée, and courgette flowers stuffed with a whole egg yolk. We revelled in guinea fowl breast with rich potato purée and shavings of black truffle. Among the desserts are a light spongy ricotta cheesecake with berries, and a white chocolate mousse turned out and topped with confit orange rind. The wine list is mercifully brief, and not too expensive, though it starts with Monica di Sardegna at £17.95. Our Saturday lunchtime visit saw the restaurant busy, with three tables of families and groups of friends. We left when Michael Winner arrived, though he's clearly a man of excellent taste.
Babies and children welcome: high chairs. Booking advisable. **Map 7 B6.**

Hammersmith W6

★ The River Café
Thames Wharf, Rainville Road, W6 9HA (7386 4200/www.rivercafe.co.uk). Hammersmith tube. **Lunch served** 12.30-3pm daily. **Dinner served** 7-9.30pm Mon-Sat. **Main courses** £23-£32. **Service** 12.5%. **Credit** AmEx, DC, MC, V.
While it's all too easy to be disenchanted by the restaurants of celebrity chefs, the River Café rarely disappoints. Indeed, this practised operation, which opened in 1987, seems only to improve with age (though large posters advertising Rose Gray and Ruth Roger's latest cookbook do seem an unnecessary addition to the minimalist decor). Signature starters such as curls of char-grilled squid with red chilli and rocket are hard to pass up, you may well have the recipe at home. We opted instead for luscious black truffle risotto from the brief list of primi. A main course of monkfish showed the River Café ethos – first-rate ingredients cooked simply – at its best: a hunky piece of wood-roasted fish accompanied by fresh green peas, broad beans and other summery veg. Pan-roasted limousin veal chop was superbly juicy and tender. The wine list is low on detail, but in egalitarian style offers a wide range of price points to suit all pockets. To finish, the famous chocolate nemesis does not disappoint; neither does the lovely big bowl of anything-but-plain caramel ice-cream. Friendly, easy-going staff are the syrup on the sponge. The River Café is pricey, but a sweet deal.
Babies and children welcome: high chairs. Booking essential. Disabled: toilet. Dress: smart casual. Tables outdoors (15, terrace). **Map 20 C5.**

Holland Park W11

Edera
148 Holland Park Avenue, W11 4UE (7221 6090). Holland Park tube. **Coffee served** 10am-noon, **lunch served** noon-2.30pm, **dinner**

served 6.30-11pm Mon-Sat. **Meals served** 12.30-10pm Sun. **Main courses** £11-£18. **Service** 12.5%. **Credit** AmEx, MC, V.

A Sardinian restaurant decorated to spartan standards, Edera is fitted with oak floors and white walls relieved only by a scattering of walnut-effect cubic lampshades. All colour is provided by the cooking. At first glance some of the menu appears to resemble that of a standard trattoria, but on the plate the food proves a cut above the ordinary. A starter of wild sea bass carpaccio was eye-catching at £9, but aubergine and parmesan bake was gloriously lush. The pastas (not priced higher if ordered as a main) featured own-made malloreddusu came with an intense saffron sauce of sausage and tomato, while perfectly al dente pappardelle was served with a light rabbit ragù. Fish and meat main courses are all healthy, but tempting combinations, such as cod with asparagus, olives and tomato, or pan-fried calf's liver with crispy polenta. Desserts too were the usual Italian examples, produced by a refined and classical kitchen. Customers are a discriminating bunch, with plenty of Italian being spoken and not only by the staff. House wines are fine, but there's also plenty to distract the flashier drinker.
Babies and children admitted. Booking advisable dinner. Restaurant available for hire. Separate room for parties, seats 15. Tables outdoors (4, pavement). Map 19 B5.

Kensington SW7, W8

Brunello

Baglioni Hotel, 60 Hyde Park Gate, Kensington Road, SW7 5BB (7368 5700/www.baglioni hotellondon.com). High Street Kensington tube. **Breakfast served** 7-10.30am, **lunch served** noon-2.30pm, **dinner served** 7-10.30pm daily. **Set lunch** £15 1 courses, £20 2 courses, £24 3 courses. **Main courses** £11-£26. **Service** 12.5%. **Credit** AmEx, MC, V.

Compared to Chianti, Brunello di Montalcino is the lesser known of Tuscany's speciality wines, but some argue it is the king. This richly decorated restaurant named after it certainly suggests regal glamour, with its long black and gold silk curtains, ornate Murano glass chandeliers and huge gilded napkin rings that look like ancient Roman artefacts. And like the wine, the restaurant is expensive – even for this upmarket location: starters and pastas reach well over £15. However, the cooking can be exquisite. Take our deep-fried courgette flower, stuffed so deliciously with creamy scamorza that it made us wonder why anyone bothers using other cheeses. Fresh scallops were absolutely huge, divinely fresh, fastidiously seared. There was an authentic fluidity to the risottos, one featuring clams, another deliciously flavoured with watercress and gorgonzola and garnished with poached pear. Service was well meaning, though staff did sit customers very close together in what is a spacious dining area. Even the bread basket was stunning – we couldn't resist accepting a second, but were ashamed when offered a third. Still, at these prices, copious amounts of flour and yeast is the very least they could provide to suggest value for money.
Babies and children admitted. Booking essential Fri, Sat. Disabled: toilet (hotel). Tables outdoors (5, terrace). Map 7 C9.

★ Timo

343 Kensington High Street, W8 6NW (7603 3888). High Street Kensington tube. **Lunch served** noon-2.30pm Mon-Sat; noon-3pm Sun. **Dinner served** 7-11pm Mon-Sat; 7-10.30pm Sun. **Main courses** £11.50-£18.50. **Service** 12.5%. **Credit** AmEx, JCB, MC, V.

The extra treats included with a meal at Timo make it feel like a destination restaurant, even if the destination's more Olympia than Kensington. It's a lovely serene space, with a fresh mood thanks to pale walls, fun lighting and artwork depicting an enchanting walled garden. Service is pleasant if a little stiff, thanks to the dance of cutlery and frequent wine top-ups – and staff have much to bring to the table, what with the plentiful bread and oil, appetisers such as potato pancakes with egg and bacon, and petits fours. The well-chosen wine list starts with a Le Marche red for £15. Dishes are a similarly judicious mix of the innovative and the approachably familiar. Light starters included grilled vegetables with cooked orange must, and sardine fillets with breadcrumb crust. Tagliata di manzo used Angus steak, and came with celeriac purée and a red wine sauce. Black cod, sliced and pan-fried, was accompanied by petals of tomato flesh, a little oregano and just-picked rocket – very simple, but carefully prepared. A pudding of chocolate soufflé with wild berry sauce and vanilla ice-cream was overcooked and pretentiously served, but that's a rare slip-up from this reliably smart outfit.
Babies and children admitted. Booking advisable. No-smoking tables. Restaurant available for hire. Separate room for parties, seats 18. Map 13 A9.

Ladbroke Grove W11

Essenza

210 Kensington Park Road, W11 1NR (7792 1066/www.essenza.co.uk). Ladbroke Grove tube. **Meals served** 12.30-11.30pm Mon-Sat; 4-10.30pm Sun. **Main courses** £13-£14.50. **Set lunch** £10 2 courses. **Service** 12.5%. **Credit** MC, V.

There are four Italian restaurants within 100 yards of one other on this stretch of road – including Essenza's sister establishments Mediterraneo (*see below*) and Osteria Basilico. This is the smallest and most chic: a simple white cube of a room furnished with brown upholstered benches and stiff linen tablecloths. The menu is as small and neat as the restaurant, but it's also a little short on inspiration. You certainly can't fault the generosity of a starter that includes four char-grilled Scottish scallops served on petals of finely sliced courgette for £8. Otherwise, the choices were beef or tuna carpaccio, calamares or the inevitable buffalo mozzarella, artichoke, tomato and basil salad. There's a fair selection of pastas (which attract a £2 supplement

if taken as a main). These include seafood linguine, penne bolognese and a reasonable aubergine and parmesan bake. The four meat main courses are all staples. Baked monkfish served with prawns and langoustines in a shallot sauce was heavily cooked and rather too rich. Desserts don't present any surprises either, and the wine list, though fair, doesn't offer especially good house choices. The £10 express lunch seemed better all-round value.
Babies and children welcome: high chairs. Booking essential Wed-Sun. Tables outdoors (2, pavement). **Map 19 B3**.
For branch (Osteria Basilico) see index.

Mediterraneo

37 Kensington Park Road, W11 2EU (7792 3131/www.osteriabasilico.co.uk). Ladbroke Grove or Notting Hill Gate tube. **Lunch served** 12.30-3pm Mon-Fri; 12.30-4pm Sat; 12.30-3.45pm Sun. **Dinner served** 6.30-11.30pm Mon-Sat; 6.30-10.30pm Sun. **Main courses** £8-£16.50. **Set lunch** £12.50 2 courses incl coffee. **Service** 12.5%. **Credit** AmEx, JCB, MC, V.

Success has brought some annoyances to Mediterraneo. Despite being a small local restaurant offering reasonably good food, the management has discovered airs and graces. Phoning (admittedly, only a day) in advance, we were offered a 7pm slot with the requirement to be out by 9pm. And staff seemed focused on the second sitting from the moment we arrived. It's not like this down the road at sister restaurant Osteria Basilico, where the food is notably better and service less impatient. Starting with lobster and prawn salad, we were given an ordinary thatch of rocket scattered with prawns and a single small lobster claw. To follow, char-grilled lamb chops with mash came with a lush porcini sauce from an enticing selection of meat and fish dishes. Pasta is surcharged if ordered as a main; while offering tasteful combinations, the bolognese special was too salty. From a mundane dessert list, cheesecake was topped by tired raspberries that seemed to share the staff's lack of interest. This isn't the

priciest Italian in town, but after spending £75 on two courses (including wine) for two people for a meal served inside an hour, we felt like fodder for profit margins.
Babies and children welcome: high chairs. Booking advisable; essential dinner. Tables outdoors (3, pavement). **Map 19 B3**.
For branch (Osteria Basilico) see index.

Maida Vale W9

Green Olive

5 Warwick Place, W9 2PX (7289 2469). Warwick Avenue tube/6 bus. **Lunch served** noon-2.30pm Mon-Sat; noon-3.30pm Sun. **Dinner served** 6.30-10.30pm Mon-Sat. **Main courses** £9-£21. **Service** 12.5%. **Credit** AmEx, JCB, MC, V.

God, they say, is in the details. Peek through the window and you'll think Green Olive hasn't changed since last year; walk through the door and you'll know everything is different. Management is suddenly all 'prego prego', the waiting staff are shy teenage girls, Italian pop music shimmies in the background, and there's a new pricing system on the menu. It's naff – soup of the day was 'cream of carrot', for goodness sake – and yet busier than we've ever seen it. The keen staff tried hard to promote the side veg, water, aperitifs and coffee, but their inexperience meant we did not hear about a special of buffalo mozzarella ravioli with wild mushroom sauce until after we'd ordered the meat ravioli with stock-based sauce. Fat ribbons of own-made tagliatelle were dressed with veal ragù, broad beans and baked ricotta: a nice combination. The choice of mains was notable for the lack of poultry, and two of the three fish dishes contained bacon. Desserts were not great: the 'spiced' rice pudding served with peppered pineapple seemed to be flavoured with nothing but vanilla, while the chocolate fondant was simply chilled chocolate cake. It doesn't matter how many rectangular white plates they use, this is homely fare aspiring to be stylish.

Babies and children welcome: high chairs. Booking advisable. Restaurant available for hire. Separate room for parties, seats 20. **Map 1 C4**.

Notting Hill W8

★ The Ark

122 Palace Gardens Terrace, W8 4RT (7229 4024/www.thearkrestaurant.co.uk). Notting Hill Gate tube. **Lunch served** noon-3pm Tue-Sat. **Dinner served** 6.30-11pm Mon-Sat. **Main courses** £10-£18. **Set truffle tasting menu** (winter only) £55 5 courses. **Service** 12.5%. **Credit** AmEx, MC, V.

Slinky tones and textures and Hempel-esque design make the Ark feel like a place to go two by two. The restaurant wasn't busy on our lunchtime visit – but why? We were mightily impressed with the food, right down to the superlative breads. Exquisitely fresh seafood included langoustine from the Isle of Skye, and dishes such as saffron-cured salmon with pomegranate and lemon confit indicated that the kitchen was prepared to cut loose from classic Italian moorings. We loved our tangle of soft-shell crab with linguine, chilli and garlic, and also pan-fried sea bream served with a cooling 'cucumber gazpacho' and yellow cherry toms. Clams were classily combined with castelluccio lentils to provide a bed for a nugget of monkfish wrapped in parma ham. Desserts, including jellied citrus fruit terrine with greek yoghurt ice, were also very pleasing. The manager knew that his easy-going staff were too laid-back and apologised: arriving with the main courses before removing the starter plates was too obvious an error to conceal. Other restaurants would do well to emulate the Ark's excellent wine list, which not only provides an educational map of the country, but inspiring, informative descriptions of each bottle.

Babies and children welcome: high chairs. Booking advisable. Restaurant available for hire. Tables outdoors (4, terrace). **Map 7 B7**.

Matilda. See p178.

Olympia W14

Cibo

*3 Russell Gardens, W14 8EZ (7371 6271/
2085/www.ciborestaurant.co.uk). Shepherd's
Bush tube/Kensington (Olympia) tube/rail.*
Lunch served noon-2.30pm Mon-Fri, Sun.
Dinner served 7-11pm Mon-Sat. **Main
courses** £10.50-£23.50. **Set lunches** (Mon-Fri)
£16.50 2 courses; (Sun) £18.95 2 courses,
£24.95 3 courses. **Service** 12.5%. **Credit**
AmEx, DC, JCB, MC, V.
Someone has an, ahem, unusual sense of design at
this popular restaurant tucked around the back of
Olympia Exhibition Centre – witness the bizarre
paintings inset with 3D cherubs, and the huge
colourful plates on which the food arrives. Still,
don't let aesthetics put you off. Seafood is the
speciality, with or without pasta, though the likes
of veal, lamb and calf's liver are available for
diners who prefer meatier fare. Baby octopus
stewed in wine and tomatoes, with rocket, was
crammed with little gastropods, but the broth was
far too salty; not a problem affecting the wine and
herb sauce with a frutti di mare platter. Portions
are large – and complimentary appetisers (quality
bread, chunky olives) are plentiful – so you may
not have room for tiramisu, zabaglione or Italian
cheeses. The boisterous, all-Italian staff were
focused on chatting among themselves, but that
didn't marr the service, which was attentive. Cibo
is a popular spot for celebrations – a birthday
party was in full swing the night we visited; call
for details of the various party menus.
*Babies and children welcome: high chair.
Booking advisable dinner. Dress: smart casual.
Restaurant available for hire. Separate rooms
for parties, seating 12 and 16. Tables outdoors
(4, pavement).*

Westbourne Grove W11

Zucca

*188 Westbourne Grove, W11 2RH (7727 0060).
Notting Hill Gate tube/23 bus.* **Brunch served**
noon-3.30pm Sun. **Lunch served** 12.30-3pm
Mon-Fri; 12.30-3.30pm Sat. **Dinner served**
7-11pm Mon-Sat; 7-10.30pm Sun. **Main courses**
£7.75-£14. **Set lunch** (Mon-Fri) £12.50 2 courses,
£14.50 3 courses. **Service** 12.5%. **Credit** MC, V.
Low lighting and a lack of customers at street level
always has us wondering if this place is still open.
Fortunately, it is, for Zucca offers a great mix of
delicious food, keen prices and a relaxed, stylish
atmosphere. It may be just a single shopfront, but
it extends over three levels, the best tables being
near the quietly efficient kitchen. Pleasant staff
quickly offered us bread, which we accepted
without thinking that the generously filled basket
would be charged at £1.75. But, as gripes go, that's
all we have. From the nicely descriptive wine list,
Rosso Salento 2003 from San Marzano proved to
be a good, inexpensive choice. Risotto with sun-
dried tomatoes, lemon and rocket was scattered
with toasted sesame seeds, and typical of the
clever twists on fashion the kitchen can produce.
We also enjoyed a hearty starter of four-cheese
calzoncini, and linguine with prawns, chilli and
garlic. Desserts are good too, particularly the ice-
cream. As we dined, a steady stream of Sunday
evening customers turned up for takeaway pizzas.
This is something of an insider secret: Zucca
doesn't publish a takeaway menu, but if you ring
they'll tell you what varieties of pizza are available
that day and prepare it for you to collect.
*Babies and children welcome: high chairs.
Booking essential dinner; bookings not accepted
lunch Sat. Separate room for parties, seats 40.
Tables outdoors (2, pavement). Takeaway service.*
Map 7 A6.

South West

Barnes SW13

Riva

*169 Church Road, SW13 9HR (8748 0434).
Barnes or Barnes Bridge rail/33, 209, 283 bus.*
Lunch served noon-2.30pm Mon-Fri, Sun.

Dinner served 7-11pm Mon-Sat; 7-9.30pm Sun.
Main courses £11.50-£19.50. **Service** 12.5%.
Credit AmEx, MC, V.
Riva is perennially popular. On a sultry midweek
night, the discreetly decorated room was packed
with well-off Barnes locals, no doubt discussing
their complicated child-care arrangements and/or
Italian holiday homes. Or what to eat: the seasonal
menu offers much to mull over. Ingredients are top-
quality; take the smoky olive oil brushed over
grilled vegetables, or the silky creaminess of
super-fresh burrata (a kind of mozzarella) – both
among the starters. A main of spaghetti alle
vongole came heaving with fat, fresh, juicy clams;
creamy creole risotto with plump freshwater
shrimps and velvety red peppers delivered a
paprika kick. Pasta dishes are available as starters
or mains; non-pasta options include calf's liver,
roast lamb, tuna and sea bass. The tempting
dessert list majors on inventive ice-cream and
sorbet concoctions; we couldn't get enough of the
cinnamon ice-cream sitting in a pool of balsamic
vinegar, honey and crushed amaretti biscuits. The
young waiting staff were exemplary, coping
admirably with a sudden lack of ice and even
welcoming a couple of late-comers seconds before
closing time. Best to drink by the bottle; only house
wines on the all-Italian list are available by the glass.
*Babies and children admitted (lunch): high chairs.
Booking essential dinner. Tables outdoors
(3, pavement).*

Chelsea SW3, SW10

★ Daphne's

*112 Draycott Avenue, SW3 3AE (7589 4257/
www.daphnes-restaurant.co.uk). South Kensington
tube.* **Lunch served** noon-3pm Mon-Fri; noon-
3.30pm Sat; 12.30-4pm Sun. **Dinner served**
5.30-11.30pm Mon-Sat; 5.30-10.30pm Sun.
Main courses £12.25-£24.75. **Set meal** (until
7.15pm daily) £16.75 2 courses, £19.75 3 courses.
Service 12.5%. **Credit** AmEx, JCB, MC, V.
A surprising member of Caprice Holdings (also
owner of the Ivy and Le Caprice), Daphne's interior
is evocative of a Tuscan villa with its smudgy
terracotta coloured walls and olive bushes. On a
sunny day in the glass-roofed area at the rear you

BEST WATERSIDE

Riverside

There are tables by the Thames
at **Canyon** (North American) in
Richmond, the **Depot** (Brasseries)
in Barnes, **Kwan Thai** (Thai) near
London Bridge, **Ransome's Dock**
(Modern European) in Battersea, the
River Café (*see p173*) in Hammersmith,
Riverside Vegetaria (Vegetarian)
in Kingston, the **Ship** (Gastropubs)
in Wandsworth and **Thai Square**
(Thai) in Putney. Or you can just
have a pint next to the water the
Dove (Pubs) in Hammersmith.

Dockside

Plenty of options in Docklands,
including **Elephant Royale** (Thai),
Gaucho Grill (Latin American), **Royal
China Docklands** (Chinese), and
newcomers **Curve** (North American)
and the **Gun** (Gastropubs). There's
also **Aquarium** (Fish) in St Katherine's
Dock and **Deep** (Fish) at Imperial
Wharf. **Yi-Ban** (Chinese) has two
waterside branches: in Docklands
and at Imperial Wharf.

Canalside

It can be tricky to find, but the
Commissary (International) rewards
with lovely views of Regent's Canal.

Afloat

For the ultimate in river dining, climb
aboard **Lightship Ten** (International).

---

can almost imagine you're in Italy, although the
menu's dedication to seasonal produce can hint
more at Lowestoft than Lucca. Samphire is a
favourite ingredient, and you'll often find some sort
of unusual fungi. Comforting Italian classics are
not forgotten, however, such as deliciously buttery
spaghetti with bottarga, and delectable meatballs
in tomato sauce. Our plate of gnocchi was a
blissful combination of featherlight dumplings,
spinach and creamy gorgonzola sauce. The carte
typically includes a choice of five salads in
addition to six or so contorni (vegetable side
dishes), such as roasted squash with pesto, and
potatoes cooked in prosciutto fat with rosemary
and parmesan. It's worth browsing the set menu
for well-executed treats like chicken skewers with
soft polenta and black olives, and bitter chocolate
ice-cream. The wine list offers seven bottles for
under £20, though these are mostly whites; there's
also a good choice by the glass and half bottles. A
friendly welcome and discreet service confirm
Daphne's as a winner.
*Babies and children welcome: high chairs. Booking
advisable. Separate room for parties, seats 40.*
Map 14 E10.

Manicomio

*85 Duke of York Square, SW3 4LY (7730 3366/
www.manicomio.co.uk). Sloane Square tube.*
Deli **Open** 8am-7pm Mon-Fri; 10am-7pm Sat;
10am-6pm Sun.
Restaurant **Lunch served** noon-3pm Mon-Fri;
noon-5pm Sat, Sun. **Dinner served** 6.30-10.30pm
Mon-Sat; 6.30-10pm Sun. **Main courses**
£10.50-£19.75. **Service** 12.5%. **Credit** AmEx,
JCB, MC, V.
There's no such thing as a free lunch, nor really
free bread and oil, but it is unusual these days to
see a contemporary restaurant charging for it.
Manicomio does: £1.50 per person. Given the
restaurant's premium pricing in general (starter-
sized pasta dishes reach £15, and main courses of
meat and fish cost £16.50-£22.75), this does seem
rather mean. However, there was little else to fault
on a recent visit. Sitting at a courtyard table,
protected from gusts of wind by a well-positioned
glass screen, we enjoyed exquisitely light herb
gnocchetti with brown shrimp, lemon and parsley.
Grilled tuna was slightly overcooked, but worked
nicely with horseradish, fennel and beetroot. Start
with a tasting plate comprising your choice of
three antipasti: grilled sardines and cured meats
were superb, though veal carpaccio was
disappointing. Around 25 wines are available by
in two glass sizes on a list that takes in California,
France, Spain and New Zealand, as well as Italy.
We were too full for dessert, but tempted by
options such as chocolate fondant with apricot
compote, and grilled nectarines with vanilla,
amaretto and yoghurt sorbet.
*Babies and children welcome: booster seats.
Booking advisable. No-smoking tables. Separate
room for parties, seats 30. Tables outdoors
(30, terrace).* **Map 14 F11**.

Osteria dell'Arancio NEW

*383 King's Road, SW10 0LP (7349 8111/
www.osteriadellarancio.co.uk). Gloucester Road
or Sloane Square tube.* **Lunch served** noon-
2.30pm Mon-Sat; noon-4pm Sun. **Dinner
served** 7-11pm Mon-Sat. **Main courses**
(lunch) £12-£14. **Set dinner** £24 2 courses,
£30 3 courses, £35 4 courses. **Credit** MC, V.
In Italy, osterias are generally low-key, informal
places serving home-style, local food. On first
appearances, Osteria dell'Arancio fits the casual,
family-friendly bill. There are a profusion of bright
colours in the front bar, while the rear restaurant
has a few children's crayon drawings tacked up on
the wall. There's a temperature-controlled wine
cellar that holds the fun stuff for grown-ups, with
bottles on full view. The wine list is all-Italian,
meticulously selected and the first clue that this
isn't an osteria as we know it. The tiny menu (seven
choices plus cheese, on our visit) offers a
succession of small dishes. Each has quite a lot
going on. A 'lasagna' made of thin pieces of
polenta was served with octopus, swiss chard and
tomato sauce, while pasta noodles with broccoli,
bacon and chickpeas had a chicken broth

Party pieces

An Italian restaurant is the ideal choice when you're trying to find a venue suitable for a group meal, such as an office party or a family gathering. There'll be something reassuringly familiar for fusspots (grilled chicken and spinach), something for the diet-obsessed (seared tuna and rocket salad), truffles for the foodies, and pasta for the kids. These user-friendly restaurants are all in the West End, so no one has to panic about travelling across town to get home either.

Aperitivo
41 Beak Street, W1F 9SB (7287 2057/ www.aperitivo-restaurants.com). Piccadilly Circus tube. **Tapas served** noon-11pm Mon-Sat. **Tapas** £2.95-£9.95. **Service** 12.5%. **Credit** AmEx, MC, V.
Sofa seating near the front, a sizeable choice of cocktails and finger-food designed for sharing make this 'Italian tapas' joint a great choice for lounge-lovers. Food is unusually high calibre for such a casual eaterie.
Babies and children welcome: high chairs. Booking advisable Wed-Sat. Separate room for parties, seats 35. **Map 17 J6.**

Bertorelli
19-23 Charlotte Street, W1T 1RL (7636 4174/www.santeonline.co.uk). Goodge Street tube.
Bar **Open** 3-11pm Mon-Sat.
Café **Meals served** noon-11pm Mon-Sat. **Main courses** £7.50-£14.95.
Restaurant **Lunch served** noon-3pm Mon-Fri. **Dinner served** 6-11pm Mon-Sat. **Main courses** £13.75-£16.50. **Set meals** £15.50 2 courses, £18.50 3 courses. *All* **Service** 12.5%. **Credit** AmEx, DC, MC, V.
The upstairs restaurant at the multi-faceted Charlotte Street branch is a popular location for office parties of a formal but not too expensive bent. A grown-up crowd dines here – so no snogging under the table.
Babies and children welcome: high chairs. Booking advisable. No-smoking tables.

Restaurant available for hire. Separate rooms for parties, seating 22 and 44. Tables outdoors (5, terrace). **Map 9 J5.**
For branches see index.

Caffè Caldesi
118 Marylebone Lane, W1U 2QF (7935 1144/www.caffecaldesi.com). Bond Street tube.
Deli/bar **Breakfast served** 8.30-11am Mon-Sat. **Meals served** 11am-11pm Mon-Sat; 10.30am-5pm Sun. **Main courses** £7-£9.50. **Set brunch** (Sat) £20 3 courses.
Bistro **Lunch served** noon-3pm, **dinner served** 6-11pm Mon-Sat. **Main courses** £9.50-£17.50. **Set brunch** (Sat, Sun) £20 3 courses.
Both **Service** 12.5%. **Credit** AmEx, JCB, MC, V.
Friendly, accommodating staff and plenty of space between the tables make the upstairs restaurant at Caffè Caldesi a fine (if rather noisy) destination for groups. The street-level bar is the place to meet for wines by the glass and homemade stuzzichini (bar snacks).
Babies and children welcome: high chairs; nappy-changing facilities. Booking advisable (bistro). Disabled: toilet. Restaurant and bar available for hire. Tables outside (7, pavement). Takeaway service (deli). **Map 9 G5.**
For branch (Caldesi Tuscan) see index.

Orso
27 Wellington Street, WC2E 7DB (7240 5269/www.orsorestaurant.co.uk). Covent Garden tube. **Meals served** noon-midnight daily. **Main courses** £8.50-£16. **Set lunch** (noon-5pm Sat, Sun) £18.50 2 courses, £20.50 3 courses, incl a glass of champagne or cocktail. **Set meal** (5-6.45pm Mon-Sat) £16 2 courses, £18 3 courses incl coffee. **Credit** AmEx, MC, V.
A colourful restaurant that owes as much to Californian cuisine as it does to regional Italian gastronomy. Expect fresh fare in hearty portions and plenty of pizzas, making Orso a favourite haunt of families.

Babies and children admitted: booster seats. Booking advisable. No-smoking tables. **Map 18 L7.**

Quod
57 Haymarket, SW1Y 4QX (7925 1234/ www.quod.co.uk). Piccadilly Circus tube. **Coffee served** 10.30am-noon, **afternoon tea served** 3-4.30pm, **meals served** noon-midnight Mon-Sat. **Main courses** £8.35-£16.75. **Set meal** (4-7pm, 10pm-midnight) £10.95 2 courses. **Service** 12.5%. **Credit** AmEx, DC, JCB, MC, V.
A rambling contemporary restaurant and bar with a choice of private rooms, plus plenty of subtly segregated areas in the main dining room. Food, including afternoon tea, is available all day. Quod offers a sensible children's menu as well as an approachable set meal for groups of 16 or more.
Babies and children welcome: children's menu; high chairs. Disabled: toilet. No-smoking tables. Restaurant available for hire. Separate rooms for parties, seating 10-120. **Map 17 K7.**

Signor Zilli
40-41 Dean Street, W1V 5AB (restaurant 7734 3924/bar 7734 1853/www.zilli aldo.com). Leicester Square, Piccadilly Circus or Tottenham Court Road tube.
Bar **Open** noon-midnight, **meals served** noon-11pm Mon-Sat. **Main courses** £9.50-£16.50.
Restaurant **Lunch served** noon-3pm Mon-Fri. **Dinner served** 6-11.30pm Mon-Sat. **Main courses** £8.50-£22.50.
Both **Credit** AmEx, DC, JCB, MC, V.
Enquire about the small, vividly frescoed basement dining room with aquarium, as it allows you to have a good (if noisy) time without disturbing ground-floor diners. Premium prices reflect the location rather than the cooking, but the cod-Italian service is fun.
Babies and children welcome: high chairs. Bar available for hire. Booking advisable (restaurant). Tables outdoors (4, pavement). **Map 17 K6.**

ceremoniously poured over it at the table. Monkfish tail came stuffed with artichoke and parsnip, with a black truffle sauce. 'Tutto alle clementine' was three clementine-based desserts – a moist cake, a rich crème catalan and a soufflé, served together on a rectangular white plate. Some dishes worked superbly, but others lacked focus – surely not the intention with such a tightly honed menu. A risky undertaking, perhaps, but not just another Italian.
Babies and children admitted: high chairs. No-smoking tables. Separate room for parties, seats 30. Tables outdoors (9, terrace). **Map 14 D12.**

Fulham SW10

La Famiglia
7 Langton Street, SW10 0JL (7351 0761/ 7352 6095/www.lafamiglia.co.uk). Sloane Square tube then 11, 22 bus/31 bus. **Lunch served** noon-2.45pm, **dinner served** 7-11.30pm daily. **Main courses** £10.50-£20.50. **Cover** £1.75. **Minimum** £18.50 dinner. **Credit** AmEx, DC, JCB, MC, V.
We've had many good meals at this enjoyably traditional, blue and white tiled restaurant, but this year's performance was very disappointing. Service is old-world Italy, as are the packets of grissini on each table. It's certainly popular: the joint was buzzing, and the marquee area out back

was full of couples and groups enjoying themselves. Deep-fried artichokes were a popular special, and simply grilled sea bass with new potatoes a frequently ordered main. We opted for pasta starters. Black spaghetti with cuttlefish was fine, but there was too much chilli in asparagus spaghettini, overwhelming it almost to the point of inedibility. Veal chop came with so much sage in its buttery sauce that it looked like a salad, giving the dish an unwelcome medicinal kick. Better was fresh tuna with a vivid, creamy emulsion of mint, lemon and oil. Even the bodacious dessert trolley provided little consolation. Apple tart was unpleasantly dry; chocolate torte had a decent dark flavour, but an unusual crumbly base made extra-crunchy with sugar crystals. Everyone seems to fall under La Famiglia's spell eventually, so we hope our negative experience won't be repeated.
Babies and children welcome: children's menu; high chairs. Booking advisable dinner and Sun. Separate room for parties, seats 30. Tables outdoors (30, garden). **Map 13 C13.**

Putney SW15

Enoteca Turi
28 Putney High Street, SW15 1SQ (8785 4449/ www.enotecaturi.com). East Putney tube/ Putney rail/14, 74, 270 bus. **Lunch served** noon-2.30pm; **dinner served** 7-11pm Mon-Sat. **Main courses** £14-£17. **Set lunch** £13.50 2 courses, £16.50 3 courses. **Service** 12.5%. **Credit** AmEx, DC, MC, V.
Light and spacious, Enoteca Turi is the ideal local Italian – it does smart and romantic, but also has the personal touch. The interior is beautifully designed, predominantly white and minimalist, yet welcoming and cosy at the same time. The menu and wine list smack of professionalism; virtually everything is sourced from Italy, and all the staff (who provide excellent, unobtrusive service) are Italian. We started with vegetarian mixed antipasti (marinaded peppers, artichokes, olives, houmous, aubergines), which was fabulously fresh and came in a generous portion arranged with attention to detail. A simple dish of artichokes drizzled with oil was unbelievably good. From a huge and well-balanced choice of mains, the calf's liver was first-rate, but lacked the spectacular presentation of the starters. Ravioli of creamy potato and leek was surprisingly exciting: melting pasta and subtle flavours. Side vegetables (£3 each) tend to push up costs, but were super-fresh, including impeccable spinach and green beans. Own-made bread sticks and bread flowed freely (and gratis) throughout. A restaurant in a class of its own in Putney.
Babies and children admitted. Booking advisable. Disabled: toilet. No-smoking tables.

Rosmarino. See p180.

South

Battersea SW11

Matilda NEW

*74-76 Battersea Bridge Road, SW11 3AG
(7228 6482). Clapham Junction rail then 319
bus/South Kensington tube then 45 or 345 bus.*
Lunch served noon-3pm Mon-Fri; 11am-4pm
Sat, Sun. **Dinner served** 6-10.30pm daily.
Main courses £9-£15.50. **Service** 12.5%.
Credit MC, V.
A large corner venue with a bar, restaurant, outside
space and rooms upstairs for parties, Matilda is
adorned with chandeliers and palm-fronded
wallpaper, and has the distressed look of a Tuscan
inn. It's co-owned by Charlie McVeigh, the man
behind such ventures as Bush Bar & Grill (*see
p230*). The simple menu includes such Tuscan
classics as acquacotta (vegetable soup) and bistecca

fiorentina (a huge steak), various grills, and rare
regional specialities like delicious lardo di
colonnata (aged pork fat rubbed in herbs). The
'Matilda boards' of cured meats and cheeses with
pickles and own-made savoury jelly are the best
bet for sharing starters with friends, or to
accompany the decently priced Italian wines (the
house Sicilian is tremendous value at £10.50). On
our last visit, a shared starter of octopus and
artichoke salad was OK, while meatballs with own-
made tagliatelle was standard at best. A well-
cooked sea bass with lovely peppers left nothing
to complain about, but tiramisu was hugely
disappointing: it lacked liquor and was barely
touched. Things were disturbingly quiet for a
Friday night; service was fine, but not stretched.
*Babies and children admitted. Disabled: toilet.
No-smoking tables. Separate room for parties,
seats 40. Tables outdoors (5, garden;
5, pavement).* **Map 21 B1**.

Osteria Antica Bologna

*23 Northcote Road, SW11 1NG (7978 4771/
www.osteria.co.uk). Clapham Junction rail/35, 37,
319 bus.* **Lunch served** noon-3pm Mon-Fri.
Dinner served 6-11pm Mon-Thur; 6-11.30pm
Fri. **Meals served** 11am-11.30pm Sat; 11am-
10.30pm Sun. **Main courses** £13.80-£18.50. **Set
lunch** (Mon-Sat) £10.50 2 courses, £13 3 courses.
Cover 90p. **Service** 12.5%. **Credit** AmEx, MC, V.
Battersea's Northcote Road on a Friday night
positively rocks with young, upwardly mobile
twentysomethings. Bars bulge and music pumps,
with every venue seemingly bursting at the seams.
This long-standing, cheap and cheerful Italian,
with a dark woody interior, is no exception. The
menu is fairly middlebrow, but this is fully
accounted for in the prices, turnover and the brisk
but pleasant service. Starters cover basic Italian
options presented in their most rudimentary form.
Pastas sound good, but are more straightforward

than the menu suggests: spaghetti bolognese was a thinnish ragù; giant ravioli filled with langoustine and scallops was rather too leathery to live up to its enticing billing. Fish and meat mains come in ample servings, where, as with the mountainous side dish of spinach, quantity outweighs quality. The wine list is at least an eminently negotiable and drinkable line-up, and very appealing to the enthusiasm and wallets of the lively, not to say intoxicated, customers who heartily endorse OAB. *Babies and children admitted. Booking essential dinner Fri, Sat. Restaurant available for hire. Tables outdoors (6, pavement).* **Map 21 C4.**

Tooting SW17

Pomino NEW

35 Bellevue Road, SW17 7EF (8672 5888/ www.pomino.co.uk). Tooting Bec tube. **Lunch served** noon-3pm, **dinner served** 6-10.30pm daily. **Main courses** £8.75-£14.75. **Set lunch** £7.50 1 course incl glass of wine. **Set dinner** (6-7pm) £12.95 2 courses, £16.95 3 courses. **Service** 12.5%. **Credit** AmEx, MC, V.
Residents of Nappy Valley are still inclined to think that a couple of weeks at a Tuscan villa is the ultimate in holiday chic, so opening a restaurant here that focuses on the food and wine of central Italy is potentially a clever idea. Pomino's lovely outdoor tables make the most of its position opposite Wandsworth Common, but the cavernous interior is an unsuccessful mix of rustic patterned tiles with funky designer fittings more suited to Shoreditch than this capital-C conservative hamlet. We've enjoyed good meals here in the past, but found little to compliment on our most recent visit. The list of starters draws heavily on deli items, partnering cured meats with fresh items in mouth-watering combinations, such as finocchiona (fennel-flavoured salami) with celery hearts, and Tuscan prosciutto with peaches. How we wished we'd ordered these instead of the bland, overcooked pasta dishes. Mains were an improvement, with tender roast meats and succulent gravies – though the roast plum accompanying suckling pig with roast potato cake and cavolo nero did nothing to enhance the dish. Tuscan Sangiovese was one of two house reds available by the glass, bottle or 50cl pot. As we were the only customers on a Sunday evening, staff struggled to strike a balance between being too attentive and too relaxed.
Babies and children welcome: children's menu; high chairs. Booking advisable weekends. Disabled: toilet. Tables outdoors (8, terrace).

South East

Bermondsey SE16

Arancia

52 Southwark Park Road, SE16 3RS (7394 1751/www.arancia-uk.co.uk). Bermondsey tube/ Elephant & Castle tube/rail then 1, 53 bus/ South Bermondsey rail. **Lunch served** 12.30-2.30pm, **dinner served** 7-11pm Tue-Sat. **Main courses** £9-£10.50. **Set lunch** £7.50 2 courses, £10.50 3 courses. **Credit** AmEx, MC, V.
The view from this corner restaurant stretches down a dual carriageway, which isn't very enticing. But in this part of town, where housing estates rub along with Georgian terraces, Arancia has come up with just the right take on the trattoria look. Candles, paper tablecloths and exposed brickwork make for a cosy atmosphere, helped along by chatty groups of diners. The restaurant, billed as Italian, has an Irish chef and owner and a Colombian waiter. Food isn't always entirely Italian either; a 'parma' tart was certainly of northern European extraction, and seemed rather thrown together. Lamb steak was better, nicely char-grilled and served with a fair romesco sauce. To finish, peach sorbet had an enjoyable flavour, but the texture of snow; it came with a tooth-crunchingly hard lemon biscuit. The wine list is excellent for the price. It includes a lovely 2003 blend from the Accademia del Sol in Puglia, which uses native negroamaro and sangiovese grapes and tastes of spicy blackcurrants.

Babies and children welcome: high chair. Booking advisable dinner. Separate room for parties, seats 8.

Tower Bridge SE1

Cantina del Ponte

Butlers Wharf Building, 36C Shad Thames, SE1 2YE (7403 5403/www.conran.com). Tower Hill tube/London Bridge tube/rail. **Lunch served** noon-3pm daily. **Dinner served** 6-11pm Mon-Sat; 6-10pm Sun. **Main courses** £9.50-£14.50. **Service** 12.5%. **Credit** AmEx, DC, JCB, MC, V.
Despite being part of the Conran stable, Cantina del Ponte feels surprisingly low-key, with terracotta tiles and a colourful mural replacing the usual chrome and glass. The after-work clientele spills on to the riverside terrace in summer. Service is relaxed and friendly, if a little intrusive – our wine glasses were topped up every few minutes. The suitably rustic menu is reasonably priced, although most of the Italian-only wine list hovers around £20. Starters included a rather crumbly carpaccio, but the chitarrina pasta served with new season lamb and peas was delicious, the tender chunks of meat balanced by the bite of the peas. Pizza primavera, topped with young asparagus spears and a wonderfully dry parma ham, was oily and lacked the crispy base you'd expect from a wood-fired oven. Highlight was the slow-roasted pork with baby carrots; the meat fell from the skin. The desserts on our outing seemed unseasonably heavy, with the exception of a velvety panna cotta, served with sweet-sour berries that provided a refreshingly sharp end to a robust meal.
Babies and children welcome: children's portions; high chairs. Booking advisable. Dress: smart casual. Restaurant available for hire. Tables outdoors (20, terrace). Takeaway service (pizza only, noon-3pm, 6-10pm daily). **Map 12 S8.**

Tentazioni

2 Mill Street, SE1 2BD (7237 1100/ www.tentazioni.co.uk). Bermondsey tube/ London Bridge tube/rail. **Lunch served** noon-2.30pm Tue-Fri. **Dinner served** 7-10.45pm Mon-Sat. **Main courses** £12-£22. **Set dinner** £28 3 courses, £36 5 courses, £38 5 courses. **Service** 12.5%. **Credit** AmEx, MC, V.
Waiting staff at Tentazioni give a warm welcome to regulars, who appreciate the high-quality food and fair prices. The decor is a combination of steel girders and exposed brickwork: industrial rather than rustic, Milan rather than Tuscany. The ambience is suitably Everyman, catering equally well to casually dressed Japanese tourists and a couple in celebratory mode. The all-Italian wine list ranges from the moderate (a £15 Masciarelli Montepulciano 2001) up to £55 premium bottles. At £28, the three-course set dinner was excellent value for such a hearty feast, but offered no choice: tagliatelle amatriciana, a generous serving of grilled lamb chops, and a savoury dessert of pecorino cheese with young broad beans. An à la carte starter of gnocchi with black truffles was perfect; cooked to perfection, the little dumplings were rich yet light, the truffles making the dish special without being overly fussy (a balance typical of Tentazioni's cooking). Mains from the carte feature the likes of roasted rack of lamb with hazelnut sauce and red pepper tartlet; or breaded skate wing with sun-dried tomatoes and courgettes. Desserts include upmarket ice-creams, cheeses and tiramisu. The only disappointment was a 45-minute wait for the bill.
Babies and children admitted. Booking advisable dinner Fri, Sat. Restaurant available for hire. Separate room for parties, seats 24. **Map 12 S9.**

East

Shoreditch N1

Fifteen

15 Westland Place, N1 7LP (0871 330 1515/ www.fifteenrestaurant.com). Old Street tube/rail. **Trattoria Breakfast served** 8.30am-11pm Mon-Sat. **Lunch served** noon-5pm Sun. **Dinner served** 6-10pm Mon-Sat. **Main courses** £12-£15.

Interview
MATT SKINNER

Who are you?
Sommelier and wine buyer at **Fifteen** (*see left*), originally from Australia.
Drinking in London: what's good about it?
Gastropubs like the **Anchor & Hope** (*see p111*) and the **Garrison** (*see p111*) have been a revelation, with inspired wine lists. You also see wines from Spain, Greece and Austria that you'd never find in Australia.
What's bad about it?
It's still a bit of an old boys' club, with French and Italian sommeliers banding together to list the same old wines, regardless of whether or not they're good. It's far too conservative.
Which are your favourite London restaurants?
Chez Bruce (*see p99*) is phenomenal. It's a bible of all the great names, but not necessarily all their greatest wines. This means you can get really good, aged bottles for a not-ridiculous amount of money – such as a 1998 Jamet Côte Rôtie.
What single thing would most improve London wine lists?
When I came here, I found the mark-ups jaw-dropping. If all restaurants had a mark-up to £50, then went with a cash margin above that price, it would be so much better.
Any hot tips for the coming year?
There are some great dry whites coming out of Greece. Sauvignon blanc and semillon are performing well, and there are some bizarre things like the assyrtiko grape, which is really clean, fresh and dry. People will continue to drink more rosé, from southern Italy, Spain, Chile, and Bruce Jack's Semaphore from South Africa.
Anything to declare?
Sommeliers need to understand what the customer wants. It's either 'don't speak to me, I'm the sommelier and I know best', or they want to tell you absolutely everything they know.

Restaurant **Lunch served** noon-2.30pm daily. **Dinner served** 6.30-10pm Mon-Sat. **Main courses** £25-£29. **Set meal** £60 tasting menu. *Both* **Service** 12.5%. **Credit** AmEx, JCB, MC, V.
It's not everywhere that a waiter's response to an order for medium-rare steak would be 'coolio', but if you were expecting buttoned-up formality at the trattoria part of Jamie Oliver's training scheme for unemployed youth, you must have been asleep for the six years since he first burst on to our screens as the Naked Chef. The Fifteen Foundation's aim is to change the lives of 30 youngsters each year by training them to become 'the next generation of star chefs'; if our meal was representative of the emerging talent, Jamie may be able to retire sooner rather than later. That medium-rare ribeye was eye-openingly tender, cloaked in a delicious rosemary-anchovy butter and accompanied by watercress subtly enhanced with horseradish. Pan-fried calf's liver was also superb, and made the most of summer's freshest and plumpest black figs, mingled with balsamic, pancetta and rocket. Classic pastas of linguine carbonara made with guanicale (cured pig's cheek) and Tuscan eggs, and orecchiette with beef ragù, were decent – and of huge proportions. No wonder we couldn't face desserts like Baileys panna cotta or raspberry tart. Our only complaint lies with the wine list, which starts at £20 a bottle. We know it's for 'charidee', but the entry point seems a little high.
Babies and children welcome: high chairs. Booking essential. Disabled: toilet (Trattoria). Dress: smart casual. No smoking. **Map 6 Q3.**

North

Crouch End N8

Florians
4 Topsfield Parade, Middle Lane, N8 8PR (8348 8348/www.floriansrestaurant.com). Finsbury Park tube/rail then W7 bus/91 bus.
Wine bar **Open/meals served** noon-11pm Mon-Fri; 11am-11pm Sat; 11am-10.30pm Sun. **Main courses** £6.50. **Set meal** £8.95 2 courses.
Restaurant **Lunch served** noon-3pm daily. **Dinner served** 7-11pm Mon-Sat; 7-10.30pm Sun. **Main courses** £9.50-£16.
Both **Credit** MC, V.
The secluded courtyard tables were proving popular on our visit to this discreet eaterie tucked behind the noisy streetside wine bar of the same name. To reach the baby-blue restaurant you need to head straight through the bar and up the stairs. A list of specials – including sea bream with avocado pesto, and saffron risotto with goat's cheese and artichokes – was chalked up on a blackboard. Portions from the semi-open kitchen tend to be generous. We enjoyed black seafood ravioli with lemon butter and dill sauce. 'Fresh and cured' cod cakes, a popular choice that evening, arrived coated in bright orange breadcrumbs, accompanied by a tangy eggy orange aioli and lemon wedges. Main courses included duck with honey and grape sauce and sweet potato mash, and chicken breast stuffed with aubergine and scamorza. Desserts were commonplace offerings such as panna cotta and chocolate pud, but looked good. Cheery, proficient staff brought our wine bucket close to the table so that we could grab the bottle whenever we wanted – the kind of easy informality that, combined with good food, makes an ideal local restaurant.
Babies and children welcome: high chairs. Booking advisable dinner. Separate rooms for parties, seats 15 and 40. Tables outdoors (8, patio).

Islington N1

Casale Franco
Rear of 134-137 Upper Street, N1 1QP (7226 8994). Angel tube/Highbury & Islington tube/rail.
Lunch served noon-2.30pm Sun. **Dinner served** 6-11.30pm Tue-Sat. **Meals served** noon-10pm Sun. **Main courses** £8.50-£17.50. **Cover** £1. **Credit** AmEx, JCB, MC, V.
Casale Franco opened in the late 1980s – the era of goodbye trattoria, hello groovy modern Italian – and this place epitomised the brave new trend. Fifteen or so years on and no one would describe

it as trendy, but this restaurant has discovered the secret of longevity: giving people what they want. The twisted copper-pipe ceiling decoration amid bare brickwork stands as a monument to those heady days, but now CF is a warm and buzzing neighbourhood restaurant. Fish and meat get fairly classic treatment (pan-fried calf's liver with butter and sage, parmesan polenta and balsamic onions; or chicken breast in mushroom and cream sauce with prosciutto and Marsala), and there are also pasta and risotto dishes and Casale Franco's signature pizzas. A special of squid in its own ink was a generous portion of soft, well-cooked squid, though the ink was slightly overpowering; polenta was a nicely bland accompaniment. Seafood ravioli – filled with sea bass, served in a light fish sauce with scallops – was suitably delicate and light. A 'chocolate pyramid' pud was a hard mousse, which tasted as if it had come straight from the freezer. But we don't want to end on a negative note: the vibe's the thing at Casale Franco, and it won us over.
No-smoking tables. Restaurant available for hire (Mon-Thur, Sun). Separate room for parties, seats 50. Tables outdoors (32, courtyard). **Map 5 O1.**

Metrogusto
13 Theberton Street, N1 0QY (7226 9400/ www.metrogusto.co.uk). Angel tube. **Lunch served** noon-2.30pm Fri, Sat. **Dinner served** 6.30-10.30pm Mon-Thur; 6.30-11pm Fri, Sat; 7-10pm Sun. **Main courses** £10-£15.50. **Set lunch** £19.50 2 courses, £24.50 3 courses. **Service** 12.5%. **Credit** AmEx, JCB, MC, V.
This upmarket Italian restaurant draws equally upmarket locals for its well-executed, interesting menu and eclectic dining room (furnished with striking artworks and chunky tables). But after a hearty Italian-style welcome, we were shoved in a corner and forgotten about, waiting ages between courses. The menu is in a league of its own, with no sign of the dull Italian classics seen elsewhere. Starters included a gnocchi with smoked ricotta, almonds and tomato sauce – rich and intense. Fish of the day was a lightly crumbed sea bass (high quality, if not especially exciting), and caramelised duck breast with sour sauce and tempura: a successfully inventive idea. The laudably lengthy choice of desserts included a thin apple tart with parmesan ice-cream (a brilliant pairing), and a glass of soft cheesecake with sweet chestnut: great to taste, too rich to finish. The wine list is an Italian oenophile's dream; our waiter suggested a not-too-pricey Orvieto Classico. Service is undeniably friendly, but staff should be quicker.
Babies and children welcome: high chairs. Booking advisable; essential weekends. No-smoking tables. Separate room for parties, seats 24. Tables outdoors (4, pavement). **Map 5 O1.**

North West

Golders Green NW2

Philpotts Mezzaluna
424 Finchley Road, NW2 2HY (7794 0455/ www.philpotts-mezzaluna.com). Golders Green tube. **Lunch served** noon-2.30pm Tue-Fri; noon-3pm Sun. **Dinner served** 7-11pm Tue-Sun. **Set lunch** £10 1 course, £15 2 courses, £19 3 courses, £23 4 courses. **Set dinner** £15 1 course, £22 2 courses, £25 3 courses, £30 4 courses, £35 5 courses. **Service** 12.5%. MC, V.
Set deep in residential Golders Green, this reliable stayer attracts an older, monied crowd that prizes value for money above flash, but appreciates formal add-ons such as amuse-bouches that are not typical of neighbourhood restaurants. Week nights can see it packed to the picture rails, so don't turn up on spec. David Philpott's cooking seems to be increasingly experimental, without indulging in molecular-gastronomy clichés. Take the swede and haggis ravioli with roast meat sauce of lamb and rosemary – absolutely brilliant. So too was penne with char-grilled chicken livers, spring onions and tarragon. Less innovative, but equally delicious was veal with porcini and roast potatoes; but roast halibut with salsa verde, green lentils and spinach

featured overcooked fish. House wine is the reliable Borgo Selenes. The room, though lined with tiles, is prone to stuffiness, and the position of our dinky round table made us feel as though we were sitting in a corridor. Still, the kindly staff and ebullient maitre d' made it an enjoyable evening.
Babies and children welcome: high chairs. Booking advisable dinner Sat. Restaurant available for hire. Tables outdoors (3, terrace).

St John's Wood NW8

★ Rosmarino
1 Blenheim Terrace, NW8 0EH (7328 5014). St John's Wood tube. **Lunch served** noon-2.30pm Mon-Fri; noon-3pm Sat, Sun. **Dinner served** 7-10.30pm Mon-Thur; 7-11pm Fri, Sat; 7-10pm Sun. **Set lunch** (Mon-Thur) £19.50 2 courses, £24.50 3 courses. **Set meal** (lunch Fri-Sun; dinner daily) £22.50 2 courses, £27.50 3 courses, £32.50 4 courses. **Service** 12.5%. **Credit** AmEx, JCB, MC, V.
Aim for a seat in the glass-walled conservatory area of this romantic neighbourhood restaurant lit by thick white candles. The rear dining room near the kitchen door and loos is functional, but not as calming or attractive. Rosmarino's kitchen is more experimental than the NW postcode might suggest, serving prune sorbet in a cocktail glass alongside roast rack of lamb, and a shot measure of tomato froth with seasonal vegetable salad and onion toast. Whether these affectations are amusing culinary diversions or simply pretentious is arguable; the flavours worked, even if serving and eating the dishes proved awkward. Starter of baby squid stuffed with creamy broccoli purée and accompanied by tempura broccoli floret and toasted bread sauce was delicious. Similarly impressive were desserts of chocolate fondant with banana ice-cream, and caramelised apricots with 'clotted milk chocolate' ice-cream and bright yellow vanilla sauce. We chose Puglian Salice Salentino from the well-considered wine list. Attentive service fell off as the restaurant got busier, but this is a small complaint about an otherwise very pleasant evening.
Babies and children welcome: high chairs. Booking advisable dinner Fri-Sun. Restaurant available for hire. Separate room for parties, seats 20. Tables outdoors (7, terrace). **Map 1 C2.**

Outer London

Twickenham, Middlesex

★ A Cena
418 Richmond Road, Twickenham, Middx TW1 2EB (8288 0108). Richmond tube/rail. **Lunch served** noon-3pm Tue-Sun. **Dinner served** 7-11pm Tue-Sat. **Main courses** £13.75-£18.50. **Set lunch** (Tue-Sat) £10 2 courses, £12 3 courses. **Credit** AmEx, MC, V.
A gloriously sophisticated restaurant, A Cena has made clever use of its space. For pre-dinner drinks, the small bar near the entrance is ideal: a 1950s Sinatra kind of spot, with a great cocktail list. The place buzzes at evenings and weekends, but few tables were taken on our lunchtime visit and the menu comprised a handful of dishes (three or four choices compared to eight or nine at night). Yet somehow everything was right. A huge plate of complimentary own-made focaccia with great olive oil for dipping arrived without a word. A glass of 2004 pinot grigio was a good choice from the splendid wine list. Typical lunchtime starters include a delicious cherry tomato and borlotti bruschetta. The à la carte starter of asparagus with prosciutto, parmesan and balsamic vinegar was flawless: fat asparagus spears, plenty of ham. Whole roast lemon sole with capers, mixed leaves and new potatoes (the daily special) was excellent too; fine fish, simply cooked. For dessert, own-made bacio (chocolate and hazelnut) and strawberry ice-creams were sublime. The friendly, helpful staff had a touching pride in their menu. This place knows its stuff.
Babies and children welcome: high chairs. Booking advisable dinner Thur-Sat. Restaurant available for hire.

Japanese

The beauty of Japanese food – aside from all those low-fat and high-omega goodies – is that you can indulge in it to extremes in London. From a humble bento to a kaiseki banquet, it's all here. In fact, there are so many budget choices in the West End that we have corralled ten of the best bets into an at-a-glance box (*see p185* **Bargain central**).

At the high end of the market, **Nobu, Zuma, Matsuri, Tsunami** and **Sumosan** are still going strong, with **Nobu Berkeley** (the third London restaurant for the global Nobu empire) opening in summer 2005. They also have a new contender in their midst since **Umu** opened its discreet doors. However, you might hesitate to cross Umu's threshold at the prospect of kaiseki sets that take off at £60 and soar to a stratospheric £250 (yes, that's for one person).

Over the past couple of years, several Korean-run Japanese restaurants have sprung up in London (rather than in the Seoulful Surrey enclave of New Malden; for which, *see* **Korean**, starting on p200). These include **Hana** in Holloway, **Matsuba** in Richmond, **Samurai** off Leicester Square, **Centrepoint Sushi** by Tottenham Court Road tube station and **Kyoto** in Chinatown. So look out for more regular opportunities to splice your sushi and sashimi with bibimbap and bulgogi.

Central

City EC2

★ K-10
20 Copthall Avenue, EC2R 7DN (7562 8510/ www.k10.net). Moorgate tube/rail.
Restaurant **Lunch served** 11.30am-3pm Mon-Fri. **Main courses** £1.25-£5.
Shop **Open** 11am-6pm Mon-Fri.
Both **Credit** AmEx, DC, JCB, MC, V.
The tiny, ground-floor takeaway on Copthall Avenue gives no clue to the hi-tech kaiten-zushi bar that occupies the large basement below. Blue light bathes the clinically white room, fast beats play over the sound system, and the smiling service keeps pace with the brisk tempo. We were flabbergasted by the sheer variety of dishes rolling past us on a peak-time, lunch-hour visit, many of which we only glimpsed before they were snapped up by someone else. Hot dishes are usually a bad bet in conveyor-belt sushi bars, but a delicately battered vegetable tempura was still piping. The classic sashimi and sushi dishes were present and correct, but it was the 'gourmet sashimi' that triumphed: slivers of seared tuna edged with a roast-sesame crust and accompanied by a miso and mustard vinaigrette proved an excellent combo. The Chinese- and European-influenced dishes were also outstanding, especially the fruit parfait-esque desserts, served in glass espresso-style cups allowing you to see the contrast of jewel-bright colours. K-10 manages to be modern without being muddled, and is a cut above most other kaiten contenders.
Babies and children admitted. Bookings not accepted. No smoking. Takeaway service (11am-6pm); delivery service (11am-3pm).
Map 12 Q6.
For branch see index.

Miyabi
Great Eastern Hotel, Liverpool Street, EC2M 7QN (7618 7100/www.great-eastern-hotel.co.uk). Liverpool Street tube/rail. **Lunch served** noon-2.30pm Mon-Fri. **Dinner served** 6-10.30pm Mon-Fri; 6-10pm Sat. **Main courses** £6.50-£14. **Set lunch** £17-£25. **Service** 12.5%. **Credit** AmEx, DC, MC, V.
Sir Terence Conran meets Japan in this compact, moody little restaurant. As you would expect when two great design freaks get together, the result is aesthetically pleasing, coolly confident and utterly functional. At night the crowd is a mix of tourists and corporate types, who pick and peck their way through freebie starters of chicken tatsuta-age (saké-marinated and deep-fried), artfully presented platters of sushi, and dainty, modern salads with a Japanese twist. Sea bass and tuna nigiri were expertly made and sweetly fresh-tasting, while an unagi temaki was generously proportioned, the nori wrapper providing a crisp, satisfying crunch. Sir Terence himself could have designed the crab and avocado salad: a pretty wheel of juicy crab meat with an avocado lid. An overcooked beef teriyaki was not so appetising, and neither was the Miyabi maki, which came filled with deep-fried prawn and cod mousse but tasted more of Japan's Worcester-style sauce. Staff here are unfailingly pleasant, food is well paced, and Miyabi is a nice place to be.
Babies and children admitted. Booking advisable. Takeaway service (noon-2.30pm, 6-9pm Mon-Sat). **Map 12 R6.**

Noto
2-3 Bassishaw Highwalk, off London Wall, EC2V 5DS (7256 9433/www.noto.co.uk). Moorgate tube/rail. **Lunch served** 11.30am-2.30pm, **dinner served** 6-9.45pm Mon-Fri. **Main courses** £7.80-£9. **Set lunch** £7-£9.90. **Set dinner** £8.90-£22. **Credit** JCB, MC, V.
Impressed by Noto's sushi outlets in Harrods and Oriental City, we raced in to visit the group's flagship restaurant, tucked away in the charmless, upper-level walkways of corporate planet Moorgate. At lunchtime, the place is sardine-packed with Japanese suits early and Anglo suits late, most of whom stick to platefuls of authentically gloopy Japanese curry and rice, crumbed pork and prawns, and tempura. This branch is a bit like the Japanese equivalent of a chippy, with its busy deep-fryers, fridges full of cola, plastic chairs and easy-wipe tables. At dinner, you can go for broke with an extensive à la carte menu and an impressive selection of sushi, but lunch is limited to the above-mentioned tempura sets and curry dishes plus sushi platters and noodles. It's all super-fast, cheap and cheerful, so don't expect the sushi to have the sparkle of made-to-order stuff, or the tempura to be light-as-air crisp, and you won't be disappointed.
Children admitted. Booking advisable. Disabled: toilet. No smoking (lunch). Takeaway service.
Map 11 P5.
For branches (Harrods Sushi Bar, Noto Sushi) see index.

Covent Garden WC2

★ Abeno Too NEW
2005 RUNNER-UP BEST CHEAP EATS
17-18 Great Newport Street, WC2H 7JE (7379 1160/www.abeno.co.uk). Leicester Square tube. **Meals served** noon-11pm Mon-Sat; noon-10.30pm Sun. **Main courses** £6.50-£7.80. **Set lunch** £5.95-£9.95. **Credit** AmEx, DC, JCB, MC, V.
Its discreet exterior makes it easy to miss, but this modest offspring of the successful Abeno in Bloomsbury is always packed with hungry local workers, Japanese regulars and those lucky enough to have stumbled across it. The furnishings are simple (most diners sit at stools surrounding the horseshoe-shaped serving station), the staff are polite and efficient, and the food is heartily delicious. Pride of place on the menu goes to okonomiyaki, the Japanese equivalent of a Spanish omelette. To a base of cabbage, egg and batter (with spring onions, ginger and tempura crumbs stirred in) is added any number of more substantial ingredients, ranging from pork, prawns or squid to lotus root, salmon... even cheese and bacon. The results are deeply satisfying. Our favourite is the feisty Osaka Mix, packed with pork, prawns and zingy kimch'i, while the London Mix (pork, bacon, cheese and salmon – trust us, it's delicious) comes a close second. There are rice and noodle dishes too, as well as teppanyaki and salads. And to drink? Saké, shochu or ice-cold Kirin.
Babies and children admitted. Bookings not accepted. Disabled: toilet. No smoking. Takeaway service. **Map 18 K6.**
For branch see index.

Hazuki
43 Chandos Place, WC2N 4HS (7240 2530). Charing Cross tube/rail. **Lunch served** noon-2.30pm Mon-Fri; 12.30-3pm Sat. **Dinner served** 5.30-10.30pm Mon-Sat; 5.30-9.30pm Sun. **Main courses** £5.50-£18. **Set meal** £16-£40. **Service** 10%. **Credit** AmEx, MC, V.
If they gave awards for niceness, this compact, no-frills Japanese all-rounder would romp it. Service comes not only with a smile, but with a gentle, caring attitude that makes the rest of Covent Garden look positively surly. The you-name-it menu runs from yosenabe (one-pot stew) to yakitori, but the raw is superior to the cooked. Sushi is the star here, especially translucent amaebi (sweet shrimps) nigiri sushi that actually were sweet. Also good were taut but tiny inside-out salmon and avocado maki and super-fresh, satiny tuna nigiri. Of the cooked dishes, the best was the barely cooked: a glistening salad of tuna tataki (seared) with a crisp cabbage and lettuce salad. Agedashidofu felt overly firm and came without its customary toupee of bonito flakes, while tara (cod) teriyaki lacked depth of flavour. Nevertheless, Hazuki makes a fine stop for a quick lunch or a bite before a show, and we loved how the manager kept topping up our green tea from a communal pot.
Babies and children admitted. Booking advisable; essential dinner. Separate room for parties, seats 25. Takeaway service; delivery service (within 2-mile radius). **Map 18 L7.**

RESTAURANTS

Fitzrovia W1

★ Ikkyu

67A Tottenham Court Road, W1T 2EY (7636 9280). Goodge Street or Tottenham Court Road tube. **Lunch served** noon-2.30pm Mon-Fri. **Dinner served** 6-10.30pm Mon-Fri, Sun. **Main courses** £6-£13. **Set lunch** £6.20-£9.60. **Set dinner** £6.10-£13.50. **Service** (dinner) 10%. **Credit** AmEx, MC, V.

Head down into this long-established, well-worn basement gaff and the carpet might look offputting, but the cooking smells will entice. The atmosphere has improved since the introduction of 'no smoking' signs that now confine the once-prevalent tobacco fumes to one corner of the room. Lunch is a limited but inexpensive affair of shioyaki (salt-grilled) fish sets, sushi, sashimi and a couple of noodle choices. Pickles fans should note: £2.50 gets you an almost too generous helping of green and pink cucumber, and white and yellow radish. There's a wider choice on the dinner menu, with interesting dishes involving ingredients such as yamaimo (mountain yam) and natto (fermented soy beans – an acquired taste). At night, Ikkyu is particularly good for grazing on grilled chicken and fish dishes. Judging by our most recent visit, the waitresses seem better able to speak English. Nevertheless both the food and surroundings remain true to their Japanese origins. When it comes to closing time, staff don't mess about – though they did mess up our bill. In all, though, this remains a battered old favourite.
Babies and children admitted. Booking essential dinner. No-smoking tables. Separate room for parties, seats 12. Vegetarian menu. **Map 4 K5.**

Roka

2005 RUNNER-UP BEST DESIGN
2005 RUNNER-UP BEST BAR

37 Charlotte Street, W1T 1RR (7580 6464/ www.rokarestaurant.com). Goodge Street or Tottenham Court Road tube.
Bar **Open** 5pm-midnight daily. **Meals served** 5.30pm-midnight daily.
Restaurant **Lunch served** noon-2.30pm Mon-Sat. **Tea served** 2.30-5.30pm Mon-Sat. **Dinner served** 5.30-11.30pm Mon-Sat; 5.30-10.30pm Sun. **Main courses** £3.60-£21. *Both* **Service** 12.5%. **Credit** AmEx, DC, MC, V.
Rainer Becker's Zuma (*see p183*) took London by storm in 2002, and Roka, its beautiful little sister, created respectable ripples when it opened in 2004. Both were designed by hip Japanese firm Super Potato. Occupying a corner site and enclosed on its street sides by floor-to-ceiling glazing, Roka has been conceived as 'a restaurant without walls'. Some people may feel like they're eating in a goldfish bowl, but on warmer days the windows can be folded back and the place takes on the atmosphere of an upmarket street café. The real star, however, is the robata (charcoal grill) at the heart of the dining room. Head chef Nicholas Watt insists on the finest ingredients, not only in the dishes but beneath them. The charcoal is shipped from Osaka, while the ice is made from purified water. So, not cheap – but not disappointing. A glistening seaweed salad boasted five varieties in a zesty vinaigrette. Also outstanding was the quail: sticky, meaty and exquisitely juicy. Grilled aubergine, smoky and sweet, arrived in squares on a platter, like a draughts board. Even the rice was a pleasure. The only bum note was sea urchin tempura: its flavour too bitter. Desserts are worth trying, as are the interestingly

flavoured shochu shots (honey and lavender, for instance), which can also be enjoyed in Shochu Lounge, the lovely basement bar.
Babies and children welcome: high chairs. Booking advisable. Disabled: toilet. No smoking (restaurant). Tables outdoors (10, pavement). **Map 9 J5.**

Holborn WC1

★ Aki ⟨NEW⟩

182 Gray's Inn Road, WC1X 8EW (7837 9281/ www.akidemae.com). Chancery Lane tube. **Lunch served** noon-3pm Mon-Fri. **Dinner served** 6-11pm Mon-Fri; 6-10.30pm Sat. **Main courses** £4.50-£11.50. **Set lunch** £7.80-£14.70. **Set dinner** £18-£40.50. **Service** 10%. **Credit** AmEx, JCB, MC, V.

Cracked floor tiles, dog-eared slips of paper on the walls, faux-cottage beams across the ceiling… yes, Aki is tatty, but the worn furnishings and happi coat-clad waitresses make you feel right at home. As this is an izakaya (think tapas bar), the idea is to pick your poison (beer, saké, shochu, umeshu) then smack your lips over the full gamut of Japanese cuisine, from raw fish, simmered noodles and grilled chicken to lesser-spotted dishes like tomoe-don (sea urchin, salmon and salmon roe on rice). Or you could have a hamburger and a tomato salad. Then there are the daily specials. While the richness of monkfish foie gras was suitably counterbalanced by a sharp dressing, 'special deep-fried beancurd' was novel yet a bit too special with its heavy coatings of sesame and shaved fish under a blanket of grated daikon. But grilled yellowtail jaw was beautifully cooked and yielded an amazing amount of succulent flesh. From the red lantern hanging outside to the bottle-keep system inside, Aki is definitely old-school and certainly tasty.

Abeno Too. See p181.

Babies and children admitted. Booking advisable. No-smoking tables. Separate room for parties, seats 30. Takeaway service. Vegetarian menu. **Map 4 M4.**

★ Matsuri

71 High Holborn, WC1V 6EA (7430 1970/ www.matsuri-restaurant.com). Chancery Lane or Holborn tube. **Lunch served** noon-2.30pm Mon-Sat. **Dinner served** 6-10pm Mon-Sat. **Main courses** £8.50-£15 lunch, £13-£28 dinner. **Set lunch** £8.50-£33. **Set dinner** £70-£80. **Service** 12.5%. **Credit** AmEx, DC, JCB, MC, V.
Unlike its older St James's sibling (where the decor and service are conservative and the focus is on teppanyaki), Holborn's Matsuri is style-conscious, with polished surfaces, white walls, slatted wooden screens and lots of glass. Although both venues have a sushi counter, teppan and restaurant seating, this branch seems more of an all-rounder. The cooking and ingredients are superb whichever place you choose. Brilliantly fresh and tender fish feature in the sushi and sashimi. The star dish was tuna yukke (raw tuna served in the style of Korean yuk hwe: a kind of steak tartare), with sesame oil and seeds, green onion, a touch of sugar and tiny strips of nori. Stunning. The presentation is beautiful. Eel and cucumber and spicy tuna maki looked as good as they tasted; wasabi was presented in the shape of a tiny leaf. Less successful was takoyaki: balls of chopped octopus in batter, cooked in an iron mould and served with a Worcestershire-like sauce. Service is slick and the drinks list will appeal to burgundy lovers and saké fans. Expensive, but worth it.
Babies and children admitted. Booking advisable. Disabled: toilet. Separate rooms for parties, seating 10 and 30. **Map 10 M5.**
For branch see index.

Knightsbridge SW3, SW7

Nozomi NEW

14-15 Beauchamp Place, SW3 1NQ (7838 1500/ www.nozomi.co.uk). Knightsbridge tube. **Lunch served** 12.30-3pm, **dinner served** 6.30-11pm Tue-Sat. **Main courses** £12-£18. **Service** 12.5%. **Credit** AmEx, JCB, MC, V.
In spite of bemusing menu descriptions, unavailable choices and worryingly Western-looking dishes appearing on neighbouring tables, our meal was surprisingly good at this Knightsbridge newcomer. Eschewing lamb with avocado soy sauce, roast parsnip and Gengis Khan chicken in favour of scallop sashimi, marinated yellowtail and wagyu tataki probably helped. The shellfish needed only to be fresh, which it was. The fish was deliciously dressed in ponzu and finely chopped spring onion. The marbled fillet steak was tender and came with an equally moreish dip. Layout and design are less welcoming. Set over split levels, the three separate areas have some weak points. The bar is spacious, but has the air of a hotel foyer, an impression compounded by the top-hatted and liveried doorman. The main dining room boasts a large skylight (which must be lovely to lunch under) yet lacks interesting decor to comepensate for having no windows. The sushi room offers gleaming cream coolness by way of contrast to the lower main room's greys and browns – but not the full menu. The clientele are monied, of course, but whether Nozomi attracts the 'discerning A-list crowd' vaunted in its publicity is another matter. And the food: not so much fusing as confusing – but worth some careful exploring.
Babies and children welcome: high chairs. Booking essential. Dress: smart casual. Entertainment: DJ 8pm-1am Tue-Sat. No-smoking room. Separate room for parties, seats 20-25. Vegetarian menu. **Map 14 F9.**

★ Zuma

5 Raphael Street, SW7 1DL (7584 1010/ www.zumarestaurant.com). Knightsbridge tube. **Bar Open** noon-10.45pm Mon-Sat; noon-10.15pm Sun. *Restaurant* **Lunch served** noon-2pm Mon-Fri; 12.30-3pm Sat, Sun. **Dinner served** 6-10.45pm Mon-Sat; 6-10pm Sun. **Main courses** £3.80-£54.80. **Set lunch** £8.30-£21.80. **Service** 12.5%. **Credit** AmEx, DC, MC, V.

The pleasures of this Knightsbridge high-flyer don't come cheap, but that hasn't stopped Zuma being packed to its designer rafters every lunch and dinnertime. Most of the flibbertigibbets seem to be here for the scene, which just shows how silly they are, because the food is seriously good. The big attraction is super-talented sushi chef Shinji Tani. Grab a seat at the sushi bar to watch him shape slender nigiri, an exemplary Dynamite Spider Roll (soft-shell crab), and the less flashy but even more delicious prawn tempura roll. For a taste of how the other half eat, try the silky scallop sashimi with soy, saké and sevruga caviar. The menu cleverly caters for high- and low-rollers, so you can tuck into grilled wagyu beef if you can afford it, and a tender, highly marbled, well-grilled ribeye with wafu sauce if you can't. The wine list is sophisticated and food-friendly, and the saké selection is dangerously extensive. If you come for the food, do lunch, as the overly loud and lively bar scene at night can get tiresome.
Babies and children welcome: high chairs. Disabled: toilet. Function rooms. No smoking (restaurant). Separate room for parties, seats 14. Tables outdoors (5, pavement). Vegetarian menu. **Map 8 F9.**

Leicester Square SW1

Samurai NEW

6 Panton Street, SW1Y 4DL (7930 8881). Leicester Square or Piccadilly Circus tube. **Meals served** noon-11pm daily. **Main courses** £5.50-£12.50. **Set lunch** £8-£12. **Credit** MC, V.
The swordsman paraphernalia against white walls here is pretty, rather than medievally macho; the black, faux-leather upholstered chairs are smart and comfortable; and although chef-owner Sung Lew is Korean, there's a satisfying ring of truth to the Japanese food. Sushi set B was a crowd-pleasing combination of salmon, tuna and prawn rolled every which way (nigiri, maki and temaki). Moist prawn and chive gyoza (Chinese-style dumplings) were delicious and evidently whisked straight from pan to plate to table. There is some Seoul food too, including a decent bibimbap (assorted veg, beef and egg on rice). A detour from the traditional path proved ill-advised; sliced roast duck breast on green beans looked appetising, but the meat was tough and the yuzu sauce too sweet. In contrast, the edamame, enlivened by ginger and chilli and served still warm, went down a treat with cold draught Kirin. With welcoming staff and reasonable prices, Samurai lays on good food in a comfortable setting. And proximity to Leicester Square serves it well.
Babies and children admitted. Tables outdoors (1, pavement). Takeaway service. **Map 17 K7.**

Yo! Sushi

St Albans House, 57 Haymarket, SW1Y 4QX (7930 7557/www.yosushi.com). Leicester Square or Piccadilly Circus tube. **Meals served** noon-10.30pm Mon-Thur; noon-11pm Fri, Sat; noon-10pm Sun. **Main courses** £1.50-£5. **Credit** AmEx, DC, MC, V.
This is the newest outlet in the Yo! kaiten empire, and they don't come funkier – iPods attached to the table that download music while you eat; 1960s-style white leather booths; and staff (mostly non-Japanese) kitted out in tomato-red outfits, looking like Scotty ready to beam you up, never mind take your order. So far, so hip. And the food? Yo! Sushi gave its menus a makeover in May 2005 and there is now much greater choice, including a host of new cooked dishes. A serving of 'hairy prawn', coated in feathery strands of batter and looking like a hat fit for Ascot, was crisp and succulent. However, prawn gyoza were too crisp and rather bland. The sushi fared little better: a hand roll of yellowtail ceviche was mushy, its flavours indistinguishable; an inside-out roll of soft-shell crab and yuzu tobiko (flying fish roe) was rich in colour but lacked flavour; only the avocado and crab hand roll impressed. Come for the fun, upbeat atmosphere and friendly staff, but leave your tastebuds at home.
Babies and children welcome: high chairs. Disabled: toilet. No smoking. Takeaway service. **Map 17 K7.**
For branches see index.

BEST JAPANESE

For kaiten-zushi
Catch some maki on the move at **K-10** (*see p181*), **Kulu Kulu** (*see p186*), **Moshi Moshi Sushi** (*see p192*), **Yo! Sushi** (*see below*) – and **Itsu** (*see p245*, in the **Oriental** section).

For that old-school izakaya vibe
Eat, drink and be merry, and then drink a bit more at **Aki** (*see p182*), **Asakusa** (*see p192*), **Donzoko** (*see p186*) and **Ikkyu** (*see p182*).

For grill thrills
Seek out searing delights at **Ikkyu** (*see p182*), **Jin Kichi** (*see p193*), **Roka** (*see p182*) and **Zuma** (*see below*).

For Korean on the side
Mix and match neighbouring cuisines at **Hana** (*see p192*), **Kyoto** (*see p185*), **Makiyaki** (*see p189*), **Matsuba** (*see p194*) and **Samurai** (*see below*).

For the high life
For special occasions and expense-account spectaculars, splash out at **Nobu** (*see p185*), **Nobu Berkeley** (*see p186*), **Roka** (*see p182*), **Sumosan** (*see p186*), **Tsunami** (*see p189*), **Umu** (*see p186*) and **Zuma** (*see below*).

For low costs
See p185 **Bargain central** for West End options that are easy on your wallet.

Mayfair W1

★ Chisou

4 Princes Street, W1B 2LE (7629 3931). Oxford Circus tube. **Lunch served** noon-2.30pm, **dinner served** 6-10.15pm Mon-Sat. **Main courses** £3.50-£22. **Set lunch** £9-£17. **Service** (dinner) 12.5%. **Credit** AmEx, DC, JCB, MC, V.
London now has a large number of inexpensive but good-value Japanese restaurants. Chisou isn't one of them. But, while the food at this stylish slate-and-glass Mayfair establishment doesn't come cheap, the high quality of the dishes ensures you won't be disappointed. We would recommend dining in the evening (and booking, since a loyal and mostly Japanese following tends to fill the place), when an intriguing variety of chef's specials are available. We chose several of these, including: monkfish liver with dashi and ponzu; grilled cod's roe with okra tempura and spicy mayonnaise; and diced octopus with wasabi. Each dish was tiny and exquisitely presented, but packed a powerful punch of flavour. A less recherché dish of mixed tempura was delightfully light and crisp. Service, which tends towards formality, is well oiled and eager to please. This is a place where the quality of ingredients – from sushi and sashimi to select sakés and fundamentals like dashi – matters. They say you get what you pay for; Chisou proves the point.
Babies and children admitted. Booking advisable. Separate room for parties, seats 12. **Map 9 J6.**

★ Miyama

38 Clarges Street, W1Y 7EN (7499 2443). Green Park tube. **Lunch served** noon-2.30pm, **dinner served** 6-10.30pm Mon-Sat. **Main courses** £9-£25. **Set lunch** £13-£22. **Set dinner** £30-£35. **Service** 12.5%. **Credit** AmEx, DC, JCB, MC, V.
The dining room is a bright, not especially Japanese oasis of calm, with cream walls, potted palms and wooden partitions. However, both food and service are rooted firmly in Japanese tradition. The menu is free of Nobu-esque novelties and the waitresses wear pretty blossom-print kimonos. A complimentary appetiser of cauliflower in a refreshing mayo-based sauce was followed by some A-grade à la carte sushi (from £1.80 a piece). Yellowtail, fatty tuna and salmon nigiri were

velvety soft. Chirashi sushi was generously laden with succulent olivers of tuna, salmon, prawn and mackerel. Grilled black cod in miso sauce arrived slick with juice and sprinkled with pine nuts, the sweet oily flesh contrasting beautifully with the charcoal-bitter skin. There are some nice touches: the oshibori (hot flannels) that greet you; the bamboo tray of individually decorated saké cups to choose from; and the restrained, silver-brushed lacquerware. So we feel churlish complaining, but service was intrusive and could have proceeded at a more leisurely pace. It seems criminal to hurry food this good (and this expensive).

Babies and children admitted. Booking advisable. Takeaway service. **Map 9 H8.**
For branch (City Miyama) see index.

★ **Nobu**
Metropolitan Hotel, 19 Old Park Lane, W1K 1LB (7447 4747/www.noburestaurants.com). Hyde Park Corner tube. **Lunch served** noon-2.15pm Mon-Fri; 12.30-2.30pm Sat, Sun. **Dinner served** 6-10.15pm Mon-Thur; 6-11pm Fri, Sat; 6-9.30pm Sun. **Main courses** £5-£27.50. **Set lunch** £25. **Set dinner** £70-£90. **Service** 15%. **Credit** AmEx, DC, JCB, MC, V.

It's still the most famous Japanese restaurant in town, yet Nobu is no longer the most fashionable (*see p183* **Zuma**) or the most expensive (*see p186* **Umu**). With siblings in New York, Paris and other cities as well as London, it's practically a chain. You still need to book well ahead, though. Opulent bums were on nearly every seat for our early midweek dinner. It's not essential to 'do' Nobu (for instance spend £70/£90 each on the Omakase – chef's choice). Judicious selection of dishes, backed by a bowl of rice, yielded a varied and filling meal costing under £90 for two,

Bargain central

Since the first wave of budget Japanese eateries washed over London in the early 1990s, affordable Japanese food has been easy to find in many parts of the city (especially the north and west), but the highest concentration of such cut-price cooking is to be found in central London. They might not win awards for culinary excellence, and their seating may discourage lingering, but these reliable spots offer good deals on all the mainstream options (sushi, sashimi, noodles, yakitori, teriyaki, tempura, katsu and bento combinations) at bargain prices all day – not just for lunch. Some throw in free green tea too.

For specialist cheap treats in and around Soho, try **Ryo** (*see p186*) for noodles, **Kulu Kulu** (*see p186*) for traditional kaiten-zushi, **Itsu** (*see p245* **Oriental**) for modern kaiten and **Abeno Too** (*see p181*) for okonomiyaki.

Centrepoint Sushi
20-21 St Giles High Street, WC2H 7LN (7240 6147/www.cpfs.co.uk). Tottenham Court Road tube. **Meals served** noon-10pm Mon-Sat. **Main courses** £7.50-£15. **Set lunch** £8-£13.50. **Service** 10%. **Credit** MC, V.
Surprisingly plush and prim for a humble eaterie, tucked away above a Korean-Japanese grocery store. Good food too.
Best for Comfy booths.
Babies and children welcome: high chairs. Booking advisable. Takeaway service. Vegetarian menu. **Map 17 K6.**

Japan Centre NEW
212 Piccadilly, W1J 9HG (7255 8255/ www.japancentre.com). Piccadilly Circus tube.
Shops **Open** 10am-7pm Mon-Fri; 10.30am-8pm Sat; 11am-7pm Sun.
Restaurant **Meals served** noon-9pm Mon-Sat; noon-8.30pm Sun. **Main courses** £2.50-£14. **Set lunch** £6.90-£14.30. **Set dinner** £7.90-£14.80. **Service** 12.5%. **Credit** JCB, MC, V.
The Toku restaurant sits next to a travel shop on the ground floor. There are unusual brown-rice options on the menu.
Best for Well-dressed side salads.
Babies and children welcome: high chairs. Bookings not accepted. Disabled: toilet. No smoking. Takeaway service. Vegetarian menu. **Map 17 J7.**

Kintaro Sushi NEW
26-27 Lisle Street, WC2H 7BA (7437 4549). Leicester Square tube. **Meals served** noon-11.30pm daily. **Main courses** £6-10. **Set lunch** £5-£9. **Set dinner** £6-£15. **No credit cards.**

Space and the menu are minimal, but this open-all-day newcomer is second only to **Misato** (*see below*) for vast set-meal portions.
Best for A pre-cinema quicky (though service can be slow).
Babies and children welcome: high chairs. No-smoking tables. Takeaway service. **Map 17 K7.**

Kyoto NEW
27 Romilly Street, W1D 5AL (7437 2262). Leicester Square or Piccadilly Circus tube. **Lunch served** noon-3pm Mon-Fri. **Dinner served** 5-11pm Mon-Fri, Sun. **Meals served** noon-11pm Sat. **Main courses** £6-£12. **Set lunch** £7.99. **Credit** AmEx, DC, JCB, MC, V.
Another good-value newcomer, this Korean-run restaurant has made itself attractive with floor pebbles and table calligraphy. Try the delicately steamed pork gyoza.
Best for Interesting decor and polite service.
Babies and children admitted. Booking advisable. Separate room for parties, seats 20. Tables outdoors (2, pavement). Takeaway service. **Map 17 K6.**

Misato
11 Wardour Street, W1D 6PG (7734 0808). Leicester Square or Piccadilly Circus tube. **Lunch served** noon-2.45pm Mon-Fri; noon-3pm Sat, Sun. **Dinner served** 5-10.30pm daily. **Main courses** £4.90-£8.60. **Set lunch** £5.60-£7.20. **No credit cards.**
No frills and no credit cards, small menu, breathtakingly big portions (mostly katsu and teriyaki) served on plastic plates. The sushi is fine too, but steer clear of the tori kara-age (deep-fried chicken).
Best for Pigging out.
Babies and children admitted. Bookings not accepted. No smoking. Takeaway service. **Map 17 K7.**

Ramen Seto
19 Kingly Street, W1B 5PY (7434 0309). Oxford Circus tube. **Meals served** noon-10pm Mon-Sat; 5.30-8pm Sun. **Main courses** £5.50-£8.80. **Set meals** £5.50-£8.80. **Credit** JCB, MC, V.
Decor and crockery couldn't be plainer nor the menu simpler, but ten slices of salmon and tuna for £7 is top value.
Best for Generous sashimi portions.
Babies and children welcome: high chairs. Booking advisable weekends. Takeaway service. **Map 17 J6.**

Satsuma
56 Wardour Street, W1D 3HN (7437 8338/www.osatsuma.com). Piccadilly Circus tube. **Meals served** noon-11pm Mon, Tue; noon-11.30pm Wed, Thur;

noon-midnight Fri, Sat; noon-10.30pm Sun. **Main courses** £8-£16. **Service** 12.5%. **Credit** AmEx, DC, JCB, MC, V.
Not the cheapest of the cheap eats, but Royal China Group's take on Wagamama is a slick and tasty affair.
Best for Modernity and style.
Babies and children welcome: high chairs. Bookings not accepted. Disabled: toilet. No smoking. Takeaway service. **Map 17 K6.**

Taro NEW
10 Old Compton Street, W1D 4TF (7439 2275). Leicester Square or Tottenham Court Road tube. **Lunch served** noon-2.45pm daily. **Dinner served** 5.30-10.30pm Mon-Sat; 5.30-9.30pm Sun. **Main courses** £5.50-£8.50. **Set meal** £8-£13. **Credit** JCB, MC, V.
A double-height basement of cream walls and blond furniture purveying the expected batch of treats. You'll find its older sister in Brewer Street.
Best for Room to manoeuvre, and delectable tori kara-age.
Booking advisable. No smoking. Separate room for parties, seats 30. Takeaway service. **Map 17 K6.**
For branch see index.

Tokyo Diner
2 Newport Place, WC2H 7JP (7287 8777/ www.tokyodiner.com). Leicester Square tube. **Meals served** noon-midnight daily. **Main courses** £3.90-£12.90. **Set lunch** (noon-6.30pm Mon-Fri) £4.40-£8.80. **Credit** JCB, MC, V.
Open 365 days of the year, this veteran has three floors (smoking on the first only). The menu is helpfully annotated, but quality is erratic, service can be off-hand and the stools are titchy. Tipping discouraged.
Best for Novice diners.
Babies and children admitted. Bookings not accepted Fri, Sat. No smoking (ground floor and basement). Takeaway service. **Map 17 K7.**

Zipangu
8 Little Newport Street, WC2H 7JJ (7437 5042). Leicester Square tube. **Meals served** noon-11pm Mon-Thur; noon-11.30pm Fri, Sat; noon-10.30pm Sun. **Main courses** £4.50-£14. **Set lunch** (noon-5.30pm) £6-£12. **Set dinner** £9.50-£14 5 courses. **Credit** AmEx, MC, V.
Three floors (all no-smoking) of limited space and zero atmosphere – but good, authentic Japanese food.
Best for Bargain set meals.
Bookings not accepted Fri, Sat. No smoking. Separate room for parties, seats 15. Takeaway service. **Map 17 K7.**

including two Kirin Ichibans. The Osusume list offers exciting possibilities: 'soft-shell crab harumaki with creamy wasabi and balsamic' vying with 'wagyu beef and foie gras gyoza with goma ponzu sauce'. Some innovations work, some don't. Tuna tataki with ponzu did, simply by tweaking the toppings on a traditional dish (replacing chopped spring onions and grated ginger with shiso, sliced garlic and orange-infused grated daikon). But the gyoza were a foie gras too far. The trim, young, efficient staff seem less bossy these days, but are quick to clear plates. So don't get distracted by the views over Hyde Park. Sister restaurant Ubon in Docklands serves the same menu in less striking surroundings; and there's also new Nobu Berkeley (*see below*).
Babies and children welcome: high chairs. Booking essential. Disabled: toilet. No-smoking tables. Separate room for parties, seats 14-40. **Map 9 H8**.
For branch (Ubon) see index.

★ Nobu Berkeley NEW
15 Berkeley Street, W1J 8DY (7290 9222/ www.noburestaurants.com). Green Park tube. **Bar Open** 6pm-2am Mon-Sat. *Restaurant* **Dinner served** 6pm-1am Mon-Sat. **Main courses** £2.25-£26.60. **Service** 15%. *Both* **Credit** AmEx, MC, V.
Nobu Berkeley is the latest London opening of US-based restaurateur Nobu Matsuhisa. We visited in its first week and it was already heaving with big-spending Mayfair gents in dark suits. You can't book by phone unless you're in a party of six or more; instead, you have to show up and put your name down, then wait, expensive drink in hand, in the vast bar. It's a convenient system for the restaurant, but very inconvenient for diners. From the bar, a sweeping staircase leads to the stylish dining room, with its hibachi grill and sushi bar. The Japan-meets-Peru menu is as good as at Nobu, with some extra 'wood oven' dishes, such as 'aubergine steak'. Or there's 'shishito anti cucho Peruvian-style skewer', which translates as a few sweet little green peppers grilled on a skewer and served with a dip. Dishes are undoubtedly inventive, from sea bass sashimi served on wafer-thin slices of white turnip, garnished with shavings of dried bonito, to a dessert of 'chocolate bento box' with green tea ice-cream. Nobu Berkeley is a place to impress clients, with its New York-style buzz, glamorous David Collins interior, good-looking waiting staff (all female) and startlingly different dishes. The phone is already permanently engaged.
Babies and children welcome: high chairs. Bookings accepted for parties of 6 or more. Disabled: toilet. Dress: smart casual. Entertainment: DJ 9pm Thur-Sat. No smoking. Vegan dishes. **Map 9 H7**.
For branch (Ubon) see index.

Sumosan
26 Albemarle Street, W1S 4HY (7495 5999/ www.sumosan.com). Green Park tube. **Lunch served** noon-3pm Mon-Fri. **Dinner served** 6-11.30pm Mon-Sat. **Main courses** £7.50-£22.50. **Set lunch** £19.50; £45 per person 6 courses (maximum 4). **Set dinner** £65 per person 8 courses (maximum 4). **Service** 12.5%. **Credit** AmEx, DC, MC, V.
Sumosan belongs to the Zuma/Nobu school (*see p183 and p185* respectively) of modern Japanese restaurants and charges similarly high prices. In fact, there's something a bit bling about the place. Maybe it's the highly polished wooden tables or the conspicuous-consumption feel of the drinks list (lots of champagne and, incidentally, one of the most impressive saké selections in town). Although the now-classic black cod with miso is inevitable (£22.50), you can, unusually, sample it as a maki (£7.50). Alternatively, splash out on wagyu beef teppanyaki for £55. The menu strays far from its Japanese roots into dishes such as roast wild duck leg with girolles; or lamb with courgettes, carrots and potatoes. Rock shrimp and tofu tempura come with a difficult-to-dislike spicy mayonnaise dipping sauce. Our sashimi was sea bass and sea bream was nicely presented, yet merely adequate. Goose liver nigiri sushi sounded like a gamble, but this was one case in which the French-Japanese fusion paid off. In general, though, Sumosan is

perhaps best described as 'Japanese lite'. The cooking is of a decent standard, but flavours and textures are mostly unchallenging.
Babies and children welcome: high chairs. Booking advisable. No-smoking tables. Separate area for parties, seats 30. Takeaway service. **Map 9 H7**.

Umu NEW
14-16 Bruton Place, W1J 6LX (7499 8881). Bond Street or Green Park tube. **Lunch served** noon-2.30pm, **dinner served** 6-11pm Mon-Sat. **Main courses** £12-£45. **Set lunch** £22-£44. **Set dinner** £60-£250. **Service** 12.5%. **Credit** AmEx, DC, JCB, MC, V.
When we emerged from Umu, through its touch-activated sliding door, a curious passer-by asked what we'd just done behind that enigmatic façade. Eaten our most expensive meal ever was the answer. Kaiseki sets (several courses that arrive separately and in strict order) go from £60 to a heart-stopping £250 per head. Head chef Ichiro Kubota hails from Kyoto and brings 'a modern twist' to that city's traditional cuisine. Our Special Kaiseki (£90) peaked at the start with saké-flavoured orange jelly, topped by salty grey caviar and a flowering sprig of red shiso, laid upon sweet pink raw prawns resting on a minty green shiso leaf and cool white daikon threads – fabulous flavours and colours. The subsequent fish courses were wonderful too. But the miso soup and pickles were disappointing, partly because they come under closer scrutiny when counted as a separate course. Umu cocoons customers in dark, classy surroundings and crisp, courteous service, concocting food of the highest order in the poshest of locations. Then it raises the stakes even higher with handmade pottery, generous staffing levels and flown-in ingredients (even water from Kagoshima to avoid cooking with harsh London H_2O). Too rich for us.
Babies and children welcome: high chairs. Booking advisable dinner. Disabled: toilet. Dress: no trainers. No smoking. **Map 9 H7**.

Soho W1

Donzoko
15 Kingly Street, W1B 5PS (7734 1974). Oxford Circus or Piccadilly Circus tube. **Lunch served** noon-2.30pm Mon-Fri. **Dinner served** 6-10.15pm Mon-Sat. **Main courses** £6.50-£28. **Set lunch** £12-£30. **Credit** AmEx, MC, V.
Lined with hanging wooden menu slats and traditional noren curtains, this appealing izakaya-style restaurant has a charming, homey interior. The menu features an extensive saké list, including regional varieties, as well as different types of shochu and chu-hai (shochu and fruit juice cocktails). There's a fair choice of sashimi, sushi and temaki, with sets starting at around £15. From the à la carte sushi menu, toro (fatty tuna), maguro (tuna) and salmon nigiri were uninspiring, and the toppings quite small, while the california roll was bland, mushy and seemed bereft of mayonnaise. Only the ikura gunkan maki was more than mediocre. The mackerel and salmon grilled sets were similarly bland. On the upside, miso soup was nicely brothy and not too salty, and a cold dish of sansai (mountain vegetables) udon was a treat, with its delicate, fresh flavours. Such an erratic performance from the kitchen, combined with incredibly slow service, made for a mixed experience during our lunchtime visit, the food failing to match up to the delightful surroundings.
Booking advisable. Disabled: toilet. Takeaway service. **Map 17 J6**.

★ Kulu Kulu
76 Brewer Street, W1F 9TX (7734 7316). Piccadilly Circus tube. **Lunch served** noon-2.30pm Mon-Fri; noon-3.45pm Sat. **Dinner served** 5-10pm Mon-Sat. **Main courses** £1.20-£10. **Credit** MC, V.
Now numbering three branches – Soho (the oldest), South Ken (the smallest), Covent Garden (the newest and brightest) – Kulu Kulu qualifies for mini-chain status. All have a conveyor belt, fixed padded stools, help-yourself free green tea and some of the lowest kaiten prices around (plates start at £1.20, which includes two salmon nigiri). This original is still going strong, evidenced on the

day we visited when there were no places free at the kaiten and we were seated in the shabbier downstairs room. There's plenty of sushi, but KK is pretty good at hot dishes too, such as agedashidofu and tori-kara-age. Our raw fish was mostly good, but the squid was a surprise. Oh-so-chewy in the wrong hands, it came sliced to wafer-thin perfection with a delectably creamy texture. Functional and flexible (except for the 45-minute time-limit at lunch), Kulu Kulu is a handy pit stop and one of the easier places to go off-kaiten with personal orders. Its all-rounder mother restaurant, Ten Ten Tei (*see below*), is up the street.
Babies and children welcome: high chairs. Bookings not accepted. No-smoking tables. Takeaway service. **Map 17 J7**.
For branches see index.

★ Ryo
84 Brewer Street, W1F 9TZ (7287 1318). Piccadilly Circus tube. **Meals served** 11.30am-midnight Mon-Wed, Sun; 11.30am-12.30am Thur-Sat. **Main courses** £5-£20. **Set meal** £5.50-£10. **No credit cards.**
Bar the widescreen TV, Ryo has remained resistant to change over the years – and that's mostly a good thing. The functional, monochrome interior is slightly shabby, but the down-to-earth ambience and low prices are popular with both Japanese students in the evening and harried Japanese businessmen who pop in to grab a bowl of noodles for lunch. The noodle menu is extensive, ranging from basic miso and shoyu ramen to kimch'i and curry varieties. Vegetable ramen (tanmen) boasted springy noodles with a mountain of beansprouts, bamboo shoots, leek, cabbage and mushrooms. The gyoza set was similarly satisfying. We also tried unadon (eel and egg on rice), a favourite in Japan for its supposed energy-giving properties. Because this dish is so rich, it can be difficult to get right, but Ryo's version is spot-on. Other favourites include hiyashi chuka and a host of rice dishes, among them nira reba (chinese chives and liver). Friendly and unpretentious, Ryo is still one of the best places for cheap, fast food in true Japanese style.
Babies and children admitted. Bookings not accepted. Disabled: toilet. Takeaway service. **Map 17 J7**.

★ Ten Ten Tei
56 Brewer Street, W1R 3PJ (7287 1738). Piccadilly Circus tube. **Lunch served** noon-2.30pm Mon-Fri; noon-4pm Sat. **Dinner served** 5-10pm Mon-Sat. **Set lunch** £6.50-£12. **Set dinner** £13.80-£17.80. **Service** (dinner) 10%. **Credit** JCB, MC, V.
What this cheery, slightly scruffy place lacks in aesthetics (if you like lots of brown varnish, you'll be in your element here), it generally makes up for on the plate. Take time to examine the extensive menu, which lists a staggering range of dishes. Play safe with noodles and katsu curry, or take a walk on the wild side with grilled salmon head and ox tongue. The best approach is to decide on a teishoku (which comes with the full works – agedashidofu, rice, miso soup, pickles and ice-cream), then order a few complementary dishes to fill any gaps. We wouldn't say our set-dinner tempura was the lightest or best we've eaten, but we had better luck with other dishes. A starter of mentaiko (spicy cod's roe) packed a chilli hit that was nicely offset by lemon and shiso leaf; a surf clam nigiri was spot-on, as were natto maki rich in umami. Service is quick and on the ball. Not really a place to linger, but like its kaiten sister Kulu Kulu (*see above*), Ten Ten Tei delivers the goods.
Babies and children admitted. Bookings not accepted Fri, Sat. Takeaway service. **Map 17 J7**.

West
Ealing W5

★ ★ Sushi-Hiro
1 Station Parade, Uxbridge Road, W5 3LD (8896 3175). Ealing Common tube. **Lunch served** 11am-1.30pm, **dinner served** 4.30-9pm Tue-Sun. **Set lunch** £5-£14. **Set dinner** £5-£14. **No credit cards.**

Samurai. See p183.

Despite its unassuming, almost secretive frontage of frosted glass, Sushi-Hiro's star shines brightly. The restaurant has earned a reputation for low-priced, top-quality sushi – and on the evening we visited, it didn't disappoint. Amid blond wood and white walls, the chefs work away behind the sushi bar, immaculately kitted out in starched blue uniforms, contributing to the minimalist effect. Of the sashimi (sets from £10) we tried, highlights included silky-soft slices of tuna and rich, robustly flavoured mackerel: all beautifully decorated with seaweed and a shiso leaf on a wooden slab. A bowl of chirashi sushi was warm, moist and slid down in seconds. A la carte nigiri also hit the spot: toro (tuna belly) was delectably soft and delicately favoured; tamago (egg) suitably fluffy and slightly sweet; even the tako (octopus) was on the right side of chewy. Miso soup arrived with a pungent aroma, while the rice was firm but sticky. Japanese diners were out in force on our visit. They obviously caught on to Ealing's delicious, well-kept secret long ago.
Babies and children welcome: high chair. Booking advisable. Takeaway service.

South West
Battersea SW11

Tokiya
74 Battersea Rise, SW11 1EH (7223 5989/ www.tokiya.co.uk). Clapham Junction rail. **Lunch served** 12.30-3pm Sat, Sun. **Dinner served** 6.30-10.30pm Tue-Sun. **Main courses** £7-£16. **Set lunch** £7-£15 3 courses. **Set dinner** £15-£20 5 courses. **Credit** AmEx, JCB, MC, V.
The look of this little neighbourhood sushi bar is best described as shabby-chic. There are black-painted tables, cast-off chairs, a pale blue sushi bar and battered wooden floors. The sunny yellow walls are sparsely adorned with pictures and blackboards, upon which daily specials are hand-written. The menu rounds up the regulars: a rather limited list of sushi and sashimi, tempura, starters such as seaweed salad, gyoza, yakitori and so on. On our winners' list were the inside-out rolls, with sesame seed-encrusted rice on the outside. The grilled eel and cucumber maki and the grilled salmon skin version were well rendered too, while seaweed salad, served with a sesame dressing, was substantial and flavourful. Yet not all the dishes impressed. Although fresh and of good quality, yellowtail and toro sashimi arrived tooth-numbingly cold. Deep-fried aubergine served in tsuyu had an unpleasant taste resembling used cooking oil. Tuna tataki was watery and, like the sashimi, too cold. In contrast, service was warm and friendly.
Babies and children admitted. Booking essential weekends. No smoking. Takeaway service; delivery service (on orders over £20). **Map 21 C4.**

Fulham SW10

Feng Sushi
218 Fulham Road, SW10 9NB (7795 1900). South Kensington tube then 14, 414 bus. **Meals served** 11.30am-10pm Mon-Wed; 11.30am-11pm Thur-Sat; noon-10pm Sun. **Main courses** £2.50-£15.25. **Set meal** £9.50-£14.25. **Service** 12.5%. **Credit** AmEx, DC, JCB, MC, V.
There are now five Feng Sushis in London. This tiny branch on the busy Fulham Road follows the Feng formula: one long, tall table meant for sharing, plus a few smaller tables and a trendy colour scheme. There's non-stop business news on a plasma screen for those who can't tear themselves away from their portfolios, and a fish tank, behind which the sushi chefs work. The menu contains udon, salad and tempura, but the focus is on sushi including a selection made with brown rice (together with dishes suitable for vegans). For the best choice, order à la carte. For the best prices, order one of the 'value boxes'. Our 'bento box deluxe' featured predictable sashimi (salmon, tuna and hamachi of adequate quality) and sushi. Tempura held surprises; baby sweetcorn and okra lurked beneath the batter. 'Nippon duck' (actually tofu skin) with pancakes,

hoi sin sauce, cucumber and green onion, was fun and flavourful. Service lacks polish and on our visit was distracted, with waiters spending much time handing out takeaways to delivery men.
Babies and children admitted. Bookings not accepted. No smoking. Takeaway service; delivery service (on orders over £10). Vegetarian menu. **Map 13 C12.**
For branches see index.

Putney SW15

★ Chosan
292 Upper Richmond Road, SW15 6TH (8788 9626). East Putney tube. **Lunch served** noon-2.30pm Sat, Sun. **Dinner served** 6.30-10.30pm Tue-Sat; 6.30-10pm Sun. **Main courses** £3.30-£19.90. **Set lunch** £7.90-£13.90 incl miso soup, rice. **Set dinner** £18.90-£20.90 7 courses, £19.90-£24.90 bento box. **Service** 12.5%. **Credit** MC, V.
Forget Zen-style minimalism and reverential silence – Chosan is filled with knick-knacks, and the Japanese soundtrack can be less than calming. Yet it's one those places that every lover of Japanese cuisine cherishes simply because the food is so good. Squeezed into the premises are a sushi bar and a dozen or so wooden tables. The names of the day's raw fish are written on wooden placards hung on the wall, and there's a lengthy list of chef's specials. Of these, horse mackerel and seaweed, served in salty-sharp ponzu, was light and flavourful. A small dish of simmered dried radish and beancurd provided contrasting textures. From the range of kushiage (breadcrumbed and skewered) dishes, the aubergine, served like a savoury ice-cream, with hot mustard and lemon, was a fun-to-eat treat. Neat little tuna maki were enlivened with chilli sauce. With grilled dishes also available, the choice here is varied enough to keep diners returning for many visits, and there are seasonal specials too.
Babies and children admitted. Separate area for parties, seats 25. Takeaway service.

Wimbledon SW19

Makiyaki
149 Merton Road, SW19 1ED (8540 3113). South Wimbledon tube. **Lunch served** noon-3pm Mon-Sat. **Dinner served** 6-10.30pm Mon-Thur; 6-11pm Fri, Sat. **Main courses** £5.50-£12. **Set lunch** £7.50-£11.50. **Credit** JCB, MC, V.
When it opened a few years ago, Makiyaki seemed a quiet, unassuming place in a less-than-fashionable part of Wimbledon. It has since grown into a busy, buzzy spot. The simple, bright dining room is popular with locals, especially families and members of the substantial Korean community. Innovation seems to be favoured over tradition. Take the maki menu. There are 45 kinds, and many have jokey names, such as the Kentucky (topped with breadcrumbs), Lambada (served with spicy sauce) and Titanic (deep-fried prawns, tuna, salmon, crab and tobiko – flying fish roe), although we didn't try the last one, so can't say how well it went down. Makiyaki is Korean-owned, hence the likes of bulgogi (barbecued marinated beef) and bibimbap (rice, veg and meat with an egg on top) make an appearance too. With so much going on, flavours get a bit confused, attention to detail is not a strong point, and some jokes go too far – whose idea was it to put banana in the tempura? Overall, though, the quality of the fish and craftsmanship are pretty high, the prices fairly low.
Babies and children welcome: high chairs. Booking advisable dinner Fri, Sat. No smoking. Takeaway service.

South
Clapham SW4

★ Tsunami
5-7 Voltaire Road, SW4 6DQ (7978 1610/ www.tsunamijapaneserestaurant.co.uk). Clapham North tube. **Dinner served** 6-11pm Mon-Fri. **Meals served** 12.30-11.30pm Sat. **Main courses** £6.95-£16.50. **Service** 12.5%. **Credit** AmEx, MC, V.

Interview
RAINER BECKER

Who are you?
Chef-proprietor of **Roka** (*see p182*) and **Zuma** (*see p183*).
Eating in London: what's good about it?
The variety, quality and the fact that the restaurant scene is so competitive, which constantly pushes up standards.
What's bad about it?
The restrictions of the planning and licensing laws, which make it difficult for restaurateurs to contribute to London as a world-class city. Modern planning regulations tend to favour outmoded notions of protecting residential character. Government departments need to understand that restaurants, if managed professionally, add character and diversity.
Which are your favourite London restaurants?
The Wolseley (*see p226*), **Racine** (*see p93*), **Club Gascon** (*see p92*), **Maroush** (*see p213*) in Beauchamp Place, and the **Knightsbridge Express** sandwich bar (17 Knightsbridge Green, SW1, 7589 3039). When I eat out, I'm essentially looking for quality of product: the straightforward, clean taste of the ingredients. Unpretentious, good service is also important.
What single thing would improve London's restaurant scene?
A major revision of the congestion charge. It restricts the individual's freedom to drive to a central London location, for lunch, say – something that many people would like to do, but now might think twice about.
Any hot tips for the coming year?
If I knew what was going to be hot, I certainly wouldn't tell you – I'd bottle it and sell it...
Should smoking be banned in restaurants?
I leave it to the individual restaurateur to make this decision, though I prefer dining in a non-smoking environment.
Anything to declare?
Zuma Events, our new catering division, will give people the chance to experience Zuma in their own venue, whether it's a private dinner party for 20 or a wedding reception for 200.

Tsunami sits in its less than salubrious surroundings like a flower on a rubbish heap. Inside, bright yellow chrysanthemums adorn sleek brown tables. A lampshade like an overgrown dandelion hangs from the ceiling. Tsunami won the Best Japanese category of the *Time Out* Eating & Drinking Awards when it opened in 2002 and, bar the odd minor blip, has continued to impress. Despite haphazard but well-intentioned service on our most recent visit, the modern Japanese cooking seemed back on form. Fresh, tender yellowtail jalapeño sashimi, served on a large white plate with a tangle of grated mooli at its centre, tasted as good as it looked. Not quite as successful were grilled scallops with smelt eggs in a spicy, creamy sauce, which arrived dramatically aflame; the sauce served only to mask the delicate flavour of the scallops. Better were the snow crab shumai dumplings, served simply in a bamboo steamer. A main course of beef fillet with foie gras and sea urchin butter (£14.50) was good value: three large pieces of rare, meltingly tender meat with an intriguing depth of flavour. Don't expect austere quiet; Tsunami attracts a lively following, amplified by its smooth flooring and airy design.
Babies and children welcome: high chairs. Booking advisable weekends. No-smoking tables. Takeaway service (6-7.30pm Mon-Fri; noon-7.30pm Sat). **Map 22 B1.**

Waterloo SE1

Ozu

County Hall, Westminster Bridge Road, SE1 7PB (7928 7766/www.ozulondon.com). Embankment tube/Charing Cross or Waterloo tube/rail. **Lunch served** noon-3pm, **dinner served** 5.30-10.30pm Mon-Sat. **Main courses** £12-£15. **Set lunch** £9.50-£18.50. **Set dinner** £23.50-£44.50. **Service** 12.5%. **Credit** AmEx, DC, JCB, MC, V.
Having lost its chef soon after opening in 2004, Ozu has settled down as a rock-solid purveyor of old-school cuisine at mid-market prices in a rock-solid behemoth (it sits on the Belvedere and Westminster Bridge Road corner of the vast County Hall). Apart from 'restaurant japonais' inscribed on its frontage and a Franco-leaning wine list, there's scant evidence of its French owner. The eel and cheese spring roll may be the strangest of chef's recommendations, but traditional food prevails. Less common dishes include kamameshi: rice with veg and/or meat and fish simmered in a subtle stock and served in a wooden-lidded metal pot. Decor is equally orthodox; the sturdy bamboo poles and flimsy privacy screens are soothing to sit amid while glancing up at a movie projected on to the high ceiling – *Belleville Rendez-Vous* on our visit, rather than a Yasujiro Ozu gem. Service was provided by blonde waitresses with Euro accents who couldn't have been more charming, even if their pronunciation did confound at times.
Babies and children admitted. Booking advisable. Disabled: toilet. No-smoking tables. **Map 10 M9.**

South East

Catford SE6

★ Sapporo Ichiban

13 Catford Broadway, SE6 4SP (8690 8487). Catford rail. **Lunch served** noon-3pm Mon-Fri; noon-4pm Sat, Sun. **Dinner served** 6-10.30pm daily. **Main courses** £5-£8. **Set meal** £8.30 per person 2 courses (minimum 2), £12 per person sushi (minimum 2). **Credit** MC, V.
This friendly, casual restaurant is deservedly busy. During the week it's popular with office workers (Lewisham Town Hall is a stone's throw away); at weekends it attracts families. Seating is at the sushi counter, at pale wooden tables or in the tatami room, which is decorated with kimonos and red lanterns. The menu covers bentos, tempura, sushi, sashimi, and rice and noodle dishes. Our sashimi set of tuna, salmon and sea bass was of decent quality. A la carte sushi of surf clam, mackerel, eel and a hand roll of fried salmon skin all used high-quality ingredients and were well presented. A salmon teriyaki bento was let

Umu. See p186.

For further reference, Richard Hosking's *A Dictionary of Japanese Food: Ingredients & Culture* (Tuttle) is highly recommended.

Agedashidofu: tofu (qv) coated with katakuriko (potato starch), deep-fried, sprinkled with dried fish and served in a shoyu-based broth with grated ginger and daikon (qv).

Amaebi: sweet shrimps.

Anago: saltwater conger eel.

Bento: a meal served in a compartmentalised box.

Calpis or **Calpico** (brand name): a sweet soft drink derived from milk, similar in taste to barley water. Dilute to taste and serve ice cold.

Chawan mushi: savoury egg custard served in a tea tumbler (chawan).

Daikon: a long, white radish (aka mooli), often grated or cut into fine strips.

Dashi: the basic stock for Japanese soups and simmered dishes. It's often made from flakes of dried bonito (a type of tuna) and konbu (kelp).

Dobin mushi: a variety of morsels (prawn, fish, chicken, shiitake, ginkgo nuts) in a gently flavoured dashi-based soup, steamed (mushi) and served in a clay teapot (dobin).

Donburi: a bowl of boiled rice with various toppings, such as beef, chicken or egg.

Edamame: fresh soy beans boiled in their pods and sprinkled with salt.

Gari: pickled ginger, usually pink and thinly sliced; served with sushi to cleanse the palate between courses.

Gohan: rice.

Gyoza: soft rice pastry cases stuffed with minced pork and herbs; northern Chinese in origin, cooked by a combination of frying and steaming.

Hamachi: young yellowtail or Japanese amberjack fish, commonly used for sashimi (qv) and also very good grilled.

Hashi: chopsticks.

Hiyashi chuka: Chinese-style (chuka means Chinese) ramen (qv noodles) served cold (hiyashi) in tsuyu (qv) with a mixed topping that usually includes shredded ham, chicken, cucumber, egg and sweetcorn.

Ikura: salmon roe.

Izakaya: 'a place where there is saké': An after-work drinking den frequented by Japanese businessmen, usually serving a wide range of reasonably priced food.

Kaiseki ryori: a multi-course meal of Japanese haute cuisine, first developed to accompany the tea ceremony.

Kaiten-zushi: 'revolving sushi' (on a conveyor belt).

Katsu: breaded and deep-fried meat, hence tonkatsu (pork katsu) and katsu curry (tonkatsu or chicken katsu with mild vegetable curry).

Maki: the word means 'roll' and this is a style of sushi (qv) where the rice and filling are rolled inside a sheet of nori (qv).

Mirin: a sweetened rice wine used in many Japanese sauces and dressings.

Miso: a thick paste of fermented soy beans, used in miso soup and some dressings. Miso comes in a wide variety of styles, ranging from 'white' to 'red', slightly sweet to very salty and earthy, crunchy or smooth.

Miso shiru: classic miso soup, most often containing tofu and wakame (qv).

Nabemono: a class of dishes cooked at the table and served directly from the earthenware pot or metal pan.

Natto: fermented soy beans of stringy, mucous consistency.

Nimono: food simmered in a stock, often presented 'dry'.

Noodles: second only to rice as Japan's favourite staple. Served hot or cold, dry or in soup, and sometimes fried. There are many types, but the most common are **ramen** (Chinese-style egg noodles), **udon** (thick white wheat-flour noodles), **soba** (buckwheat noodles), and **somen** (thin white wheat-flour noodles, usually served cold as a summer dish – hiyashi somen – with a chilled dipping broth).

Nori: sheets of dried seaweed.

Okonomiyaki: the Japanese equivalent of filled pancakes or a Spanish omelette, whereby various ingredients are added to a batter mix and cooked on a hotplate, usually in front of diners.

Ponzu: usually short for ponzu joyu, a mixture of the juice of a Japanese citrus fruit (ponzu) and soy sauce; used as a dip, especially with seafood and chicken or fish nabemono (qv).

Robatayaki: a kind of grilled food, generally cooked in front of customers, who make their selection from a large counter display.

---

down by a dull salad; and though vegetable tempura was a generous serving, it came without grated daikon for its tsuyu. Yet these are mere cavils in what was an enjoyable meal. Catford may not be the first place you'd look for authentic, good-value Japanese food, but you will find it here – with the added benefits of bright, clean surroundings and super-friendly service. Beats a night 'down the dogs' any day.
Babies and children admitted. Booking advisable. Disabled: toilet. Takeaway service.

East

Docklands E14

Moshi Moshi Sushi

Waitrose, Canary Wharf, Canada Place E14 5EW (7512 9201/www.moshimoshi.co.uk). Canary Wharf tube/DLR. **Meals served** 11.30am-9pm Mon-Fri; 11.30am-8.30pm Sat; noon-6pm Sun. **Main courses** £1.20-£3.50. **Credit** JCB, MC, V.
Wedged between the deli counter and the bakery of Waitrose's vast basement food hall, the Canary Wharf branch of Moshi Moshi might not be the most glamorous place in which to dine. Yet it's still better than being caught amid the frenetically smoking and drinking suits that pack out the terraces along Mackenzie Walk. Kaiten-zushi is the deal here, as blue-capped chefs maintain the flow of colour-coded plates. Regulars know to request a made-to-order temaki – perhaps salmon and avocado or unagi – if they can't find what they want on the conveyor belt. On the downside: some of the salads looked tired; the sushi rice felt solid and joyless; and we'd like a word with whoever thought a maki of sun-dried tomato, feta and cucumber was a good idea. Best bets are sashimi – especially the velvety, fatty sake (salmon) and the ruby-hued, jewel-like maguro (tuna) – and mochi (chewy, sweet glutinous rice cakes). While the wine list is limited, it's pleasing to see a choice of no less than five different sakés.
Bookings not accepted lunch. Disabled: toilet. No smoking. Takeaway service.
For branches see index.

North

Holloway N7

Hana NEW

150A Seven Sisters Road, N7 7PL (7281 2226). Finsbury Park tube/rail/4, 29, 253, 254 bus. **Lunch served** noon-3pm Mon-Sat. **Dinner served** 6-11pm daily. **Main courses** £2.50-£10.50. **Set lunch** £2.90-£14.50. **Set dinner** £16.50-£23 4 courses. **Credit** MC, V.
A surprise find, this: a Japanese restaurant in Holloway, and a Korean-run one at that. So it's less surprising that the menu includes some Korean staples (bibimbap, bulgogi). The modest premises run to a small sushi counter and half a dozen tables. The plush, suedette seats seemed spanking new, though the baby's high chair had seen better days. Gyoza were more crispy-fried than stretchy-steamed and the filling was mushy, but the rest of our meal was easily up to scratch. The bountiful sushi and salmon bento included a heap of good mixed sushi. We had fun perusing the zany list of maki – from local 'speciality' Seven Sisters (deep-fried salmon, tuna and snapper) to Peter Pan (eel, avocado and flying-fish roe), Philadelphia (salmon, cream cheese, avocado and cucumber) and Shrek (tuna, snapper, salmon, avocado and cucumber). Quite a roll-call. And if that line-up doesn't raise a chuckle, try the Red Rose Comedy Club across the road.
Babies and children welcome: high chairs. Booking advisable. Takeaway service; delivery service (within 2-mile radius). Vegetarian menu.

Camden Town & Chalk Farm NW1

★ Asakusa

265 Eversholt Street, NW1 1BA (7388 8533/ 8399). Camden Town or Mornington Crescent tube. **Dinner served** 6-11.30pm Mon-Fri; 6-11pm Sat. **Main courses** £5.50-£12. **Set dinner** £5.20-£19. **Service** 12%. **Credit** AmEx, MC, V.
With its busy carpet, 1970s-style studded banquettes and faded ambience, the ground-floor dining room of Asakusa is like a 'Before' shot to the 'After' of the current delirium of Japanese designer diners. Still, far better to be upstairs than down in the basement, even if you are, as we were, seated at the sushi counter next to (unbelievably) a smoker. More frustration came in trying to get someone to translate the Japanese specials, which are plastered over the walls like gastro patches; though, in fact, many of them are items on the English menu written in Japanese. So you can do well enough ordering from the all-encompassing carte. Sashimi moriawase was a treat – a mixed plate of magnificently fresh tuna, salmon, sea bream and mackerel – as was nasu dengaku (grilled aubergine with miso). Agedashidofu was perfectly crisp outside and creamy within. Next came wafu steak, surprisingly tender, cooked perfectly rare, and accompanied by a likeable Japanese coleslaw. Fortunately, the refreshingly fair prices more than make up for the grumbles.
Babies and children admitted. Booking essential Fri, Sat. Separate room for parties, seats 20. Takeaway service. **Map 27 D3.**

Saké: rice wine, around 15% alcohol. Usually served hot, but may be chilled.

Sashimi: raw sliced fish.

Shabu shabu: a pan of stock is heated at the table and plates of thinly sliced raw beef and vegetables are cooked in it piece by piece ('shabu-shabu' is onomatopoeic for the sound of washing a cloth in water). The broth is then portioned out and drunk.

Shiso: perilla or beefsteak plant. A nettle-like leaf of the mint family that is often served with sashimi (qv).

Shochu: Japan's colourless answer to vodka is distilled from raw materials such as wheat, rice and potatoes.

Shoyu: Japanese soy sauce.

Sukiyaki: pieces of thinly sliced beef and vegetables are simmered in a sweet shoyu-based sauce at the table on a portable stove. Then they are taken out and dipped in raw egg (which semi-cooks on the hot food) to cool them for eating.

Sunomono: seafood or vegetables marinated (but not pickled) in rice vinegar.

Sushi: combination of raw fish, shellfish or vegetables with rice – usually with a touch of wasabi (qv). Vinegar mixed with sugar and salt is added to the rice, which is then cooled before use. There are different sushi formats: **nigiri** (lozenge-shaped), **hosomaki** (thin-rolled), **futomaki** (thick-rolled), **temaki** (hand-rolled), **gunkan maki** (nigiri with a nori wrap), **chirashi** (scattered on top of a bowl of rice), and **uramaki** or **ISO maki** (more recently coined terms for inside-out rolls).

Tare: general term for shoyu-based cooking marinades, typically on yakitori (qv) and unagi (qv).

Tatami: a heavy straw mat – traditional Japanese flooring. A tatami room in a restaurant is usually a private room where you remove your shoes and sit on the floor to eat.

Tea: black tea is fermented, while green tea (ocha) is heat-treated by steam to prevent the leaves fermenting. **Matcha** is powdered green tea, and hasa high caffeine content. **Bancha** is the coarsest grade of green tea which has been roasted; it contains the stems or twigs of the plant as well as the leaves, and is usually served free of charge with a meal. **Hojicha** is lightly roasted bancha. **Mugicha** is roast barley tea, served iced in summer.

Teishoku: set meal.

Tempura: fish, shellfish or vegetables dipped in a light batter and deep-fried. Served with tsuyu (qv) to which you add finely grated daikon (qv) and fresh ginger.

Teppanyaki: 'grilled on an iron plate' or, originally, 'grilled on a ploughshare'. In modern Japanese restaurants, a chef standing at a hotplate (teppan) is surrounded by several diners. Slivers of beef, fish and vegetables are cooked with a dazzling display of knifework and deposited on your plate.

Teriyaki: cooking method by which meat or fish – often marinated in shoyu (qv) and rice wine – is grilled and served in

a tare (qv) made of a thick reduction of shoyu (qv), saké (qv), sugar and spice.

Tofu or **dofu:** soy beancurd used fresh in simmered or grilled dishes, or deep-fried (agedashidofu), or eaten cold (hiyayakko).

Tokkuri: saké flask – usually ceramic, but sometimes made of bamboo.

Tonkatsu: see above katsu.

Tsuyu: a general term for shoyu/mirin-based dips, served both warm and cold with various dishes ranging from tempura (qv) to cold noodles.

Umami: the nearest word in English is tastiness. After sweet, sour, salty and bitter, umami is considered the fifth primary taste in Japan, but not all food scientists in the West accept its existence as a basic flavour.

Unagi: freshwater eel.

Uni: sea urchin roe.

Wafu: Japanese style.

Wakame: a type of young seaweed most commonly used in miso (qv) soup and kaiso (seaweed) salad.

Wasabi: a fiery green paste made from the root of an aquatic plant that belongs to the same family as horseradish. It is eaten in minute quantities (tucked inside sushi, qv), or diluted into shoyu (qv) for dipping sashimi (qv).

Yakimono: literally 'grilled things'.

Yakitori: grilled chicken (breast, wings, liver, gizzard, heart) served on skewers.

Zarusoba: soba noodles served cold, usually on a bamboo draining mat, with a dipping broth.

Zensai: appetisers.

North West

Golders Green NW11

★ Café Japan

626 Finchley Road, NW11 7RR (8455 6854). Golders Green tube/13, 82 bus. **Lunch served** noon-2pm Sat, Sun. **Dinner served** 6-10pm Wed-Sat; 6-9.30pm Sun. **Main courses** £12-£17. **Set lunch** £8.50. **Set dinner** £12-£17. **Credit** MC, V.
This long, narrow café gets packed out quickly, so book early. Our seat, at the corner of the counter and by the door, wasn't in the most relaxing position. A man next to us, talking loudly into his mobile, didn't help. But any shortcomings in ambience were more than made up for by the food. Inside-out maki, filled with prawn tempura or soft-shell crab and served on tasteful wooden platters, were deliciously moreish. The mayonnaise used in the maki is Japanese (less eggy than the western stuff), which adds a smooth, creamy texture to the food. The superb sushi (à la carte, £2.30-£2.80) made us feel quite Lilliputian – Café Japan must do the biggest nigiri toppings in London. Most stunning of all was the miso-marinated black cod (£12): sweet, succulent and suffused with rich, warm flavours. Service, care of a waitress with oriental features and striking long, peroxide-blonde hair, was brisk and friendly. A stone's throw from Golders Green station, Café Japan is worth the price of a Travelcard any day of the week.
Babies and children admitted. Booking advisable. No smoking. Takeaway service.

Hampstead NW3

Jin Kichi

73 Heath Street, NW3 6UG (7794 6158/ www.jinkichi.com). Hampstead tube. **Lunch served** 12.30-2pm Sat, Sun. **Dinner served**

6-11pm Tue-Sat; 6-10pm Sun. **Main courses** £5.40-£12.70. **Set lunch** £7.30-£13.80. **Credit** AmEx, DC, JCB, MC, V.
This intimate (some might say cramped) izakaya-style restaurant is a long-time favourite with north Londoners. Kitted out with worn wooden tables and traditional Japanese knick-knacks, it has a welcoming, unpretentious atmosphere. The food is similarly down to earth, with house specialities arriving hot from the char-grill. As you tuck into dainty portions on pretty earthenware, it can feel like being in a doll's house at times. But that didn't stop us wolfing down yakitori featuring aromatic chicken, crunchy asparagus, creamy chicken liver, and pieces of glistening duck – all suffused with a warm, charcoal flavour. Only ox tongue was a little tough and salty for our taste. From the rest of the long and varied menu, chicken and shiso leaf with plum paste arrived tender and delicately flavoured; tuna and salmon-and-avocado sushi was moist and fresh, with rice just the right side of sticky. Although friendly and unobtrusive, service was slow, but in such a convivial atmosphere, with a cup of hot saké (from £3.30 a tokkuri) in hand, we found it easy to forgive.
Babies and children admitted. Booking essential Fri-Sun. Takeaway service. Map 28 B2.

Swiss Cottage NW3

Benihana

100 Avenue Road, NW3 3HF (7586 9508/ www.benihana.co.uk). Swiss Cottage tube. **Lunch served** noon-3pm daily. **Dinner served** 5.30-10.30pm Mon-Sat; 5-10pm Sun. **Set lunch** £11-£15. **Set dinner** £17-£55. **Service** 12.5%. **Credit** AmEx, DC, JCB, MC, V.
You don't go to Benihana for a meal – you go for a performance. At this branch of the international teppanyaki chain founded by ex-Olympic wrestler

Rocky Aoki, photos of Aoki with Hollywood celebs adorn the entrance. The restaurant has the feel of a 1980s business hotel, an impression reinforced by our fellow diners who were either in suits or variations of 'Dress Down Friday' attire. Seating is arranged in a horseshoe around a hotplate table. There are various set menus, which start at £17 for teriyaki chicken and rise to £55 for lobster and sea bass. Sushi and sashimi can be ordered as side dishes. Our allocated chef theatrically introduced himself, asked 'Are you ready?', and whipped up a selection of seared juicy prawns and tuna steak, accompanied by asparagus, mushrooms and spinach – all fresh and healthy-tasting. Mustard and ginger dips spiced up the fare. The chef rounded off with a culinary juggling act that sent spoons, spatulas and knives flying, and had us all applauding loudly. Not the most authentic Japanese experience, but great fun.
Babies and children welcome: children's menu (Sun); high chairs. Booking advisable; essential weekends. No smoking. Tables outdoors (6, garden). Takeaway service. Vegetarian menu. Vegan dishes. **Map 28 B4.**
For branches see index.

Wakaba

122A Finchley Road, NW3 5HT (7586 7960). Finchley Road tube. **dinner served** 6.30-11pm Mon-Sat. **Main courses** £4.50-£19.80. **Set buffet** £6 (lunch). **Set dinner** £22.50-£34. **Service** (buffet) 10%. **Credit** AmEx, DC, JCB, MC, V.
When Wakaba opened in 1987, the whiteout design, by minimalist architect John Pawson, caused a sensation. Nearly 20 years on, that celebrated interior is looking worse for wear. There are Sellotaped signs on the elegant curved glass front and scuff marks on the once-pristine paintwork. Such a lack of attention does little to

inspire confidence, particularly in Japanese restaurants where the delight is in the detail. Our initial doubts were thankfully dispelled by the quality of the food. Pawson would probably cringe at the garish, green, padded menus, but the dishes listed therein show that food is taken seriously. There are the usual sushi, sashimi and noodle choices and much more besides – such as a nicely textured turbot 'fringe' with natto. Monkfish liver nigiri, one of the weekly specials, was a hit, as were hosomaki of sour-plum paste and shiso leaf. The batter on our prawn tempura, served with cold soba, could have been crisper, but that was a minor gripe. With a good scrub behind the ears and some investment in repair and maintenance, Wakaba could just make a return to form.

Babies and children admitted. Booking advisable Fri, Sat. Restaurant available for hire. Takeaway service. **Map 28 B3**.

Willesden NW2

★ Sushi-Say

33B Walm Lane, NW2 5SH (8459 2971).
Willesden Green tube. **Lunch served** 1-3.30pm Sat, Sun. **Dinner served** 6.30-10.30pm Tue-Fri; 6-11pm Sat; 6-10pm Sun. **Main courses** £6-£19. **Set dinner** £19-£29.50. **Credit** AmEx, JCB, MC, V.
With its wooden beams, plain white interior and staff kitted out in blue happi suits, Sushi-Say exudes homeliness. So it's a surprise to find such a wide-ranging and imaginative menu. We started with the basics: a selection of nigiri (£11 for nine pieces). This featured moist, delectable toro (fatty tuna), clams bursting with sweet juices, and smoky, rich eel. Specialities include various ponzu-dressed dishes; we tried rare grilled salmon, the rich, fishy flavours of which contrasted wonderfully with the ponzu's zesty citrus kick. Buri daikon (yellowtail and mooli in a shoyu, saké and sugar-based sauce) was a delicious combination of rough-cut fish pieces and smooth-textured radish. A portion of kabocha netsuke (steamed pumpkin) was comfortingly mushy. The insipid miso soup was our only gripe. Otherwise, Sushi-Say offers a delightfully authentic menu (including natto, renowned for its fearsome smell and mucous texture) and friendly, efficient service. It definitely merits a trip to Willesden.

Babies and children welcome: high chairs. Booking advisable. No smoking. Takeaway service.

Outer London

Richmond, Surrey

Matsuba NEW

10 Red Lion Street, Richmond, Surrey TW9 1RW (8605 3513/www.matsuba.co.uk).
Richmond tube/rail. **Lunch served** noon-3pm, **dinner served** 6-11pm daily. **Main courses** £15-£20. **Set lunch** £9-£15. **Set dinner** £30-£40. **Service** 10%. **Credit** AmEx, JCB, MC, V.
One of several Korean-run Japanese restaurants to have sprung up in London over the last year or so, Matsuba is a neat, compact oasis of modern design, traditional cooking and polite service. Outside, the view is of M&S's rear. Inside, grey slate tiles, dark brown tables and narrow-backed, black, faux-leather chairs and soft lighting conspire to soothe. Consequently this feels more of a couples' place in the evening, when muted violin concertos replace blaring Far Eastern pop. A seat at the counter affords a fine view of the ultra-fresh fish to be had, if not much space for your plate. Maybe that was why our meltingly splendid scallops came teetering precariously on two coiled piles of daikon string that dwarfed the modest dish beneath. Agedashidofu sported two flamboyantly large bonito flakes writhing in the heat coming off three perfectly coated cubes of curd. But despite Matsuba's Korean credentials, na mool (a side dish of beansprouts, spinach and kimch'i radish) was only so-so. Small yet well-rounded, Matsuba has just seven tables, so yes, you should book.

Babies and children admitted. Booking advisable. No smoking. Takeaway service.

Jin Kichi. See p193.

RESTAURANTS

Jewish

The laws of kashrut – what defines food as kosher – can be briefly summarised: no pork or shellfish; cows, sheep and poultry killed in accordance with strict rules; no dairy products served with, or shortly after, meat. The restaurants that follow these laws are supervised. A few others listed here that serve Jewish-style food are designated 'not kosher'.

In central London, the two most ambitious establishments, **Six-13** and **Bevis Marks**, serve elaborate, well-presented dishes with respectable wine lists and inventive desserts. **Eighty-Six Bistro Bar**, a newcomer in north-west London, has some innovative cooking but is let down on the management side. Also in the area is **Mr Baker**, a bright establishment adding to the number of excellent kosher bakeries. Further out in Edgware, **Aviv** and **Penashe** provide attractive cooking and superb value.

CAFÉS

North West
East Finchley NW11

★ Parkview
56 The Market Place, NW11 6JP (8458 1878).
East Finchley tube. **Meals served** 8am-6pm
Mon-Fri, Sun. **Main courses** £4.50-£6.50.
Credit (over £10) MC, V.
Recently refitted in dark wood and chrome, this corner café in East Finchley is now separate from the food shop. It looks good, but the noise at a busy lunchtime is intense. Try to sit near the picture window for a good view of the park. The menu still features houmous and Israeli salads, but there's also a wider choice: toasted bagels and french toast for breakfast, pastas and pizzas and even tortillas. Fish is also on the list, but when we visited, few people seemed to be ordering the salmon or sea bass. The food was filling and appetising, if unexceptional. Onion soup and a dish of stir-fried vegetables with rice came promptly with a smile. Dessert cakes are flown in from Israel. A cinnamon danish pastry was unremarkable, but a caramel gateau layered with mousse was silky and sweet.
Babies and children welcome: high chairs.
Kosher supervised (Beth Din). No smoking.
Tables outdoors (7, pavement). Takeaway service.

Golders Green NW11

Café Also
1255 Finchley Road, NW11 0AD (8455 6890).
Golders Green tube. **Lunch served** noon-5pm
daily. **Dinner served** 6-10pm Mon-Thur, Sat,
Sun. **Main courses** £8.25-£12.95. **Set lunch**
£9.95 2 courses. **Set dinner** £17.50 3 courses.
Credit MC, V. Not kosher
The café is under the same ownership as the bookshop next door, so bibliophiles can pop in for a coffee and cake. The food isn't kosher, but Also doesn't serve meat and caters well for vegetarians. The cold meze (tabouleh, beans, taramosalata, houmous) went well with a dish of olives. A pleasant main course of roasted vegetables in a tomato sauce came with couscous and yoghurt, but was marred by tough aubergine slices. In contrast, trout with almonds was pink and moist – a deliciously fresh dish. Salmon and a fresh tuna salad are also on the menu. There's a large choice of pasta options, as well as an unusual okra and chickpea casserole. After a quick browse around the bookshop, you may have room for a piece of cheesecake too.
Babies and children welcome: high chairs.
Booking advisable. No smoking. Tables outdoors (2, pavement).

Milk N Honey [NEW]
124 Golders Green Road, NW11 8HB
(8455 0664). Golders Green tube. **Meals**
served 10.30am-10.30pm Mon-Fri, Sun.
Main courses £5.95-£10.95. **Service** 10%.
Credit AmEx, MC, V.
Sandwiched in between several meat restaurants, Milk N Honey is the only supervised dairy café on the busy Golders Green Road. The name conjures up visions of sweetness and plenty, but too many of the dishes here aren't quite right: soup a bit salty, lukewarm falafel, noodles in a stir-fry overcooked. A starter of spring rolls had a spicy red pepper filling; fried, crumbed mushrooms were crisp. Main courses are listed under pizza, pasta, oriental dishes and fish. Cannelloni, made, alas, with frozen spinach, came with a redeeming cheesy tomato sauce. Perhaps grilled tuna or fried haddock would have been a better choice. Service was rushed and not particularly charming, but a good coffee ice-cream and a chocolate truffle cake saved the day.
Babies and children welcome: high chairs.
No smoking. Takeaway service.

RESTAURANTS

Central
City EC3

Bevis Marks Restaurant
Bevis Marks, EC3A 5DQ (7283 2220/www.
bevismarkstherestaurant.com). Aldgate tube/
Liverpool Street tube/rail. **Lunch served**
noon-3pm Mon-Fri. **Dinner served** 5.30-7.15pm
Mon-Thur. **Main courses** £9.50-£15.90.
Service 12.5%. **Credit** AmEx, MC, V.
High-quality tableware and the general aura of the place make Bevis Marks London's most stylish kosher venue. Through its windows you can view the chandeliers of the adjoining 18th-century synagogue. The wine list (mostly French, Israeli and Californian bottles) has helpful annotations. 'Kosher fusion' might describe the cooking, with dishes such as crispy thai salt beef and caribbean chicken with mango. Starters don't seem to stretch the chef's skills, but the accompaniments – gooseberry compote with pâté de foie gras; fennel and samphire salad with cured salmon – are certainly interesting. On our visit the service was desultory and the food, though competent, never rose to starry heights. A grilled veal chop was delicious but small, while char-grilled ribeye steak had a good flavour yet was spoilt by oversized, slightly soggy chips. Perhaps sea bass with artichoke, or bream with fennel, would have been better choices. Desserts are innovative: black pepper ice-cream, lavender shortbread and rosewater macaroons. Lockshen pudding featured a warm circle of noodles with excellent crème anglaise and an ice-cream tasting just like a frozen Passover cinnamon ball.
Babies and children admitted. Booking advisable
lunch. Disabled: toilet. Kosher supervised
(Sephardi). Restaurant available for hire.
Tables outdoors (4, courtyard). Takeaway service.
Vegetarian menu. **Map 12 R6.**

Marylebone W1

Reuben's
79 Baker Street, W1U 6RG (7486 0035).
Baker Street tube.
Deli/café **Open** 11.30am-4pm, 5-10pm Mon-Thur,
Sun; 11.30am-1hr before Sabbath Fri.
Restaurant **Lunch served** 11.45am-1hr before
Sabbath Fri. **Meals served** 11.45am-4pm,
5-10pm Mon-Thur, Sun. **Main courses** £10-£20.
Minimum £10 per person (restaurant).
Credit MC, V.
The ground-floor cafeteria at Reuben's is bustling at lunchtime: it's the only kosher deli in the West End. (There's also a basement restaurant, which has a similar menu but is pricier.) It's a shame there isn't more competition, as the food is unexceptional and the atmosphere rather stark. A safe bet is to stick with the traditional. You won't go far wrong with chopped liver, a salt beef or chicken sandwich and coleslaw. The salads looked brighter than the cold meats. The soups, served from covered containers, were barely hot, and though portions were generous, the taste was far from homemade. A better choice was grilled lamb – two large skewers served with good chunky chips. We weren't tempted by the desserts: a very meringuey lemon pie and rather solid-looking chocolate cake or apple strudel. But a lockshen pudding addict couldn't resist trying a large cube of the saffron-coloured noodles. It tasted of apple and raisins, but, as with the rest of the food here, lacked the touch of a real Jewish mother.
Babies and children welcome: high chairs. Booking
advisable (restaurant). Kosher supervised
(Sephardi). No-smoking tables. Tables outdoors
(3, pavement). Takeaway service. **Map 3 G5.**

Six-13
19 Wigmore Street, W1U 1PH (7629 6133/
www.six13.com). Bond Street or Oxford Circus
tube. **Lunch served** noon-2.30pm Mon-Thur.
Dinner served *Summer* 5.30-10.30pm Mon-
Thur; 7.30-10.30pm Fri. *Winter* 5.30-10.30pm
Mon-Thur. **Main courses** £14.50-£24.
Set meal (lunch) £20 2 courses, £24.50
3 courses. **Credit** AmEx, MC, V.
The name refers to Judaism's 613 biblical commandments. The owners are clearly meticulous and the cooking is well above standard, yet the decor (both inside and out) is unimpressive, and the service not welcoming enough. A basket of bread arrived at the same time as the starters (chicken pâté with toast; borscht with ravioli), by which time we were ravenous. Chicken, lamb and beef all came with thoughtful additions: buckwheat mushroom risotto, saffron couscous and excellent vegetables – though (regrettably) potatoes aren't included with main courses. Duck breast and steak arrived deliciously rare, with well-executed, rich sauces. Lamb (a smoked loin or lamb burger) was less successful. There are several fish options: salmon and sea bass brightened with tapenade, pesto or salsa verde. But desserts are where 613 excels; highlights included warm

RESTAURANTS

orange cake, deep chocolate fondant and berry parfaits with a real fruity taste. The 'grand cru' platter included all these plus a coffee crème brûlée and a strangely flavoured poached pear. Our meal was way over the London kosher average, but high prices and occasional lapses rob 613 of star quality. *Babies and children welcome: high chairs. Kosher supervised (Beth Din). Separate room for parties, seats 22. Takeaway service; delivery service.* **Map 9 H6.**

North West

Golders Green NW11

Bloom's

130 Golders Green Road, NW11 8HB (8455 1338). Golders Green tube. **Meals served** noon-10.30pm Mon-Thur, Sun; noon-3pm Fri. **Main courses** £7.50-£17.50. **Credit** AmEx, DC, MC, V.
The mural depicting an old shtetl (village) tells you what to expect: Ashkenazi home cooking. The long-established Blooms employs waiters who have been here for 30 years; ours was a 'junior' with a mere 15 years' service. Immediately we sat down he brought iced water, matzo crackers and fresh rye bread. The menu is traditional. The hors d'oeuvres include a reassuringly constant chopped liver, egg and onion, and a huge ball of sweet and moist poached gefilte fish. Chicken soup lacked the touch that makes knaidlach and kreplach tender. Salt beef, with the requested ripple of fat, came with passable chips. Beef blintz, one of the specials, featured a hefty meat pancake sitting on a sauce reminiscent of tinned soup. A whole breast of lamb on the bone arrived succulently roasted with crisp-on-the-outside potatoes. Meat portions – this is no place for vegetarians – are generous, and main courses include salad and rice or potatoes (avoid the heavy latkes). Lemon tea made a good end to a rib-sticking meal, but if you're determined to complete the haimishe experience, take away some strudel or lockshen pudding. *Babies and children welcome: children's menu; high chairs. Kosher supervised (Beth Din). Tables outdoors (2, pavement). Takeaway service.*

★ Dizengoff's

118 Golders Green Road, NW11 8HB (8458 7003/www.dizengoffkosherrestaurant.co.uk). Golders Green tube. **Meals served** *Summer* noon-midnight Mon-Thur, Sun; noon-3.30pm Fri. *Winter* noon-midnight Mon-Thur, Sun; noon-3.30pm Fri; 7pm-midnight Sat. **Main courses** £12-£18. **Credit** MC, V.
Maroon-on-white tablecloths are among the many improvements made at this Tel Aviv-style restaurant. Dizengoff's was one of the few kosher places to open in Passover week and was rewarded by increased business. Service is slick and cheerful. Customers are welcomed with complimentary olives and pickles, and crisp little latkes. Orange slices are provided at the end of the meal. The menu is large yet not over-ambitious. Most orders are for grilled meat rather than the more elaborate tongue or lamb in wine sauces. Starters are as good as they sound: six dishes with houmous, spicy or traditional soups, and crisp kibbe without a trace of oil. A stuffed artichoke in mushroom sauce made a pleasant change. Pâté de foie gras, dolmas and broad beans in oil are alternatives. Even on a night when the owners weren't there, the grills were perfect: tender lamb chops with garlicky potatoes, and chicken Dizengoff (a flattened thigh cooked to the right succulence). Salads and vegetables were less inspired, but then this is a place for meat eaters seeking an authentic Israeli experience. *Babies and children welcome: high chairs. Book weekends. Kosher supervised (Sephardi). Tables outdoors (3, pavement). Takeaway service.*

La Fiesta

239 Golders Green Road, NW11 9PN (8458 0444). Brent Cross tube. **Lunch served** noon-3pm Mon-Thur. **Dinner served** 6-10.30pm Mon-Thur, Sun. **Main courses** £7.50-£22. **Set lunch** £15.50 3 courses. **Credit** MC, V.
La Fiesta overlooks the orthodox section of the Golders Green Road. Choose a table with a view of the street. The food is Argentinian, with the emphasis on beef. We started with empanadas: fried pastries filled with meat or mushroom and enriched with olives and peppers. Beef chorizo is an alternative. A brochette of chunky grilled vegetables was appealing, but soups – apart from the pepper and tomato – were indifferent. On to the serious part: the meat. Asado ribs, lamb cutlets and boned chicken were all well grilled, but unless you want tough steak avoid the mixed brochette, as the beef has to be overdone if the chicken and chorizo are to be cooked through. The famed saltenia (sautéed potatoes with garlic) never seems to be available when we visit, so we opted for chips and a soggy sweet potato. Desserts are often covered with mock cream, so after all that meat it's better to end with a glass of fresh mint tea. *Babies and children welcome: high chairs. Booking advisable dinner. Kosher supervised (Beth Din). No-smoking tables. Separate area for parties, seats 90. Takeaway service.*

Met Su Yan

134 Golders Green Road, NW11 8HP (8458 8088/www.metsuyan.co.uk). Golders Green tube. **Lunch served** noon-2.15pm Mon-Thur;

Menu

There are two main strands of cooking: Ashkenazi from Russia and eastern Europe; and Sephardi, originating in Spain and Portugal. After the Inquisition, Sephardi Jews settled throughout the Mediterranean, in Iraq and further east. London used to contain mainly Ashkenazi restaurants, but now Hendon and Golders Green are full of Sephardi bakeries and cafés, specialising in the Middle Eastern food you might find in Jerusalem. You can still get traditional chicken soup and knaidlach or fried latkes, but these are never as good as you'll find in the home. Nor will you find the succulent, slow-cooked Sabbath dishes that are made in many homes every Friday. The Israeli-type restaurants are strong on grilled meats and offer a range of fried or vegetable starters.

Since most kosher restaurants serve meat, desserts are not a strong point. Rather than non-dairy ice-cream, it's better to choose baklava or chocolate pudding. Though, by the time you've got through the generous portions served in all these places, you may not have room for anything more than a glass of mint or lemon tea.

Bagels or **beigels**: heavy, ring-shaped rolls. The dough is first boiled then glazed and baked. The classic filling is smoked salmon and cream cheese.
Baklava: filo pastry layered with almonds or pistachios and soaked in scented syrup.
Blintzes: pancakes, most commonly filled with cream cheese, but also with sweet or savoury fillings.
Borekas: triangles of filo pastry with savoury fillings like cheese or spinach.
Borscht: a classic beetroot soup served hot or cold, often with sour cream.
Calf's foot jelly (also called **petchah** or **footsnoga**): cubes of jellied stock, served cold.
Challah or **cholla**: egg-rich, slightly sweet plaited bread for Sabbath.
Chicken soup: a clear, golden broth made from chicken and vegetables.
Chopped liver: chicken or calf's liver fried with onions, finely chopped and mixed with hard-boiled egg and chicken fat. Served cold, often with extra egg and onions.
Chrane or **chrain**: a pungent sauce made from grated horseradish and beetroot, served with cold fish.

Cigars: rolls of filo pastry with a sweet or savoury filling.
Falafel: spicy, deep-fried balls of ground chickpeas, served with houmous and tahina (sesame paste).
Gefilte fish: white fish minced with onions and seasoning, made into balls and poached or fried; served cold. The sweetened version is Polish.
Houmous: chickpeas puréed with sesame paste, lemon juice, garlic and oil.
Kataifi or **konafa**: shredded filo pastry wrapped around a nut or cheese filling, soaked in syrup.
Kibbe, kuba, kubbeh or **kobeiba**: oval patties, handmade from a shell of crushed wheat (bulgar) filled with minced meat, pine nuts and spices. Shaping and filling the shells before frying is the skill.
Knaidlach or **kneidlach**: dumplings made from matzo meal and eggs, poached until they float 'like clouds' in chicken soup. Also called matzo balls.
Kreplach: pockets of noodle dough filled with meat and served in soup, or with sweet fillings, eaten with sour cream.
Latkes: grated potato mixed with egg and fried into crisp pancakes.
Lockshen: egg noodles boiled and served in soup. When cold, they can be mixed with egg, sugar and cinnamon and baked into a pudding.
Matzo or **matzah**: flat squares of unleavened bread. When ground into meal, it's used as a coating for fish or schnitzel to make it crisp.
Parev or **parve**: a term describing food that is neither meat nor dairy.
Rugelach: crescent-shaped biscuits made from a rich, cream cheese pastry, filled with nuts, jam or chocolate. Popular in Israel and America.
Salt beef: pickled brisket, with a layer of fat, poached and served in slices.
Schnitzel: thin slices of chicken, turkey or veal, dipped in egg and matzo meal and fried.
Schwarma or **shwarma**: layers of lamb or turkey, cooked on a spit, served with pitta.
Strudel: wafer-thin pastry wrapped around an apple or soft cheese filling.
Tabouleh: cracked wheat (bulgar) mixed with ample amounts of fresh herbs, tomato and lemon juice, served as a starter or salad.
Viennas: boiled frankfurter sausages, served with chips and salt beef.

RESTAURANTS

Bevis Marks Restaurant. See p195.

noon-2.30pm Sun. **Dinner served** 6-10.30pm Mon-Thur, Sun. **Main courses** £12.95-£15.95. **Set meal** £19.50 2 courses, £25-£29.50 3 courses, £39.50 4 courses. **Credit** AmEx, MC, V. The name means 'excellent' in Hebrew and this is no doubt the aim. The range of food is ambitious including sushi, Thai vegetables, curries and satays. Yet standards seems to have slipped a bit. A spicy peanut sauce came with an overcooked chicken skewer; vegetable tempura was so heavy on the batter you could hardly tell a courgette from a carrot. Main courses (delivered by a smiling waitress five minutes apart) were equally variable. Aromatic peking duck arrived with excellent pancakes and green trimmings, but the meat was dry. A generous serving of duck with plum sauce was tasty, though the dish was dominated by fresh pineapple with barely a hint of plum. Side dishes were enough for two, but the crispy noodles were so garlicky that most were left. It's hard to judge such a wide range

of dishes from the few chosen. Could the sushi be good with no visible Japanese chef? Perhaps the tuna or sea bass lift the standard. It might be worth going back to find out – but we're not sure. *Babies and children welcome: high chairs. Booking advisable. Kosher supervised (Federation). No smoking. Takeaway service.*

★ **Solly's Exclusive**
148A Golders Green Road, NW11 8HE (ground floor & takeaway 8455 2121/ first floor 8455 0004). Golders Green tube. Ground floor **Lunch served** noon-3pm Fri. **Meals served** noon-11pm Mon-Thur, Sun; 1hr after Sabbath-1am Sat. **Main courses** £10-£15. **Set meal** £22 3 courses. *First floor* **Dinner served** 6.30 11.30pm Mon-Thur, Sun. *Winter* 1hr after Sabbath-midnight Sat. **Main courses** £10-£15. **Set dinner** £24 3 courses. *Both* **Credit** MC, V.

Both the menu and the prices are the same in the ground-floor and upstairs restaurants. 'Exclusive' may refer to the eclectic decor, which has a hint of Middle Eastern kitsch, but the Israeli food is down to earth: generous, well-spiced starters and appetising grilled meats. The pitta bread is of a superior quality; it comes bubbling and crisp from the brick oven, yet is soft inside. A piled-high portion of houmous with fuul was deliciously creamy and smooth. Tabouleh had the required abundance of herbs and delivered a fresh tanginess. A good test of the main courses was the mixed grill: a shish kofta (minced lamb skewer), schwarma, turkey kebab and crisp-skinned chicken wings. The grilled meat was full of flavour, though the schwarma was oily and too salty. Chips, rice and a cabbage salad were adequate. To finish we had refreshing lemon and mango sorbet (no accompanying berries, alas) and mint tea with honeyed filo

Bakeries

Delicious fresh breads, crisp and tasty danish pastries, and some excellent pâtisserie are all to be had at London's Jewish bakeries. Staff at the shops listed here bake on the premises and it shows: it's hard to leave without being tempted by something sweet or savoury.

Bonjour
84 Brent Street, NW4 2ES (8203 8848). Hendon Central tube. **Open** 7am-11pm Mon-Thur, Sun; 7am-6pm Fri. **No credit cards**.
An enticing smell wafts out of this small shop. French flour and imported Israeli dough are used in the pastries and biscuits; taste the difference in the cappuccino rugelach and jam danish. The pitta is puffy and superb too.
Kosher supervised (Beth Din). Takeaway service.

Brick Lane Beigel Bake
159 Brick Lane, E1 6SB (7729 0616). Liverpool Street tube/rail/8 bus. **Open** 24hrs daily. **No credit cards**. Not kosher
This time-honoured survivor of the once-substantial East End Jewish community is still a magnet for those who know their bagels. The smoked salmon filling is generous and the cakes – try the cheesecake and chocolate fudge – are terrific value at 60p each.
Takeaway service. **Map 6 S4**.

Carmelli
128 Golders Green Road, NW11 8HB (8455 2074/www.carmelli.co.uk). Golders Green tube. **Open** 6.30am-1am Mon-Wed; 6am Thur-1hr before Sabbath Fri; 1hr after Sabbath Sat-1am Mon. **No credit cards**.

Temptation is laid out before you at Carmelli: appealing breads on one side; creamy gateaux in the middle; and savouries and pizzas (nice crust, adequate filling) by the door. We recommend the pain au chocolat, custard millefeuille and the fruity danish pastries.
Kosher supervised (Beth Din and Kedassia).

Daniel's Bagel Bakery
12-13 Hallswelle Parade, Finchley Road, NW11 0DL (8455 5826). Golders Green tube. **Open** 7am-9pm Mon-Wed; 7am-10pm Thur; 7am-1hr before Sabbath Fri. **No credit cards**.
The rye bread at Daniel's is airy and scrumptious, and the smoked salmon bagels are well filled and lemony. Also on offer here are large gateaux, pies and fluffy custard doughnuts. The bakery also supplies the small café next door.
Kosher supervised (Beth Din).

Hendon Bagel Bakery
55-57 Church Road, NW4 4DU (8203 6919). Hendon Central tube. **Open** 7am-11pm Mon-Wed; 7am-midnight Thur; 7am-6pm Fri; 11pm Sat-11pm Sun. **No credit cards**.
The wide range of excellent breads here includes generous smoked salmon bagels and soft challah rolls. Best sweet items: walnut pastry and chocolate rugelach. The newly refurbished shop also sells appetising takeaway platters.
Kosher supervised (Federation).
For branches (Orli) see index.

Mr Baker [NEW]
119-121 Brent Street, NW4 2DX (8202 6845). Hendon Central tube. **Open** 7am-midnight Mon-Thur, Sun; 1hr after Sabbath-3am Sat. **No credit cards**.
There's a great display of borekas, pastries and breads in this huge airy space (with coffee bar). The danish are a little light on fillings, but the pastry is flaky. An olive and cheese- or pizza-flavoured puff is a good savoury choice.
Babies and children admitted. Tables outside (4, pavement). Takeaway service.

Rinkoff's
79 Vallance Road, E1 5BS (7247 6228). Whitechapel tube. **Open** 7am-4.45pm Mon-Fri; 7am-3pm Sun. **No credit cards**. Not kosher
An old established bakery, now also catering for business lunches and parties. Smoked salmon bagels are well filled; cheesecake and lemon cake are both light and delicious.
Babies and children admitted. No smoking. Tables outdoors (2, pavement). Takeaway service.
For branch see index.

Roni's Bagel Bakery [NEW]
250 West End Lane, NW6 1LG (7794 6663). West Hampstead tube. **Open** 7am-midnight daily. **No credit cards**. Not kosher
Roni's bagels are deliciously chewy, and the black rye roll is superlative. Sweet highlights include creamy gateaux, honey-soaked konafa, good apple tart and carrot cake.
Babies and children admitted. Takeaway service. **Map 28 A2**.

---

pastries. The waiters were prompt in bringing relishes and orders to the table, but rather less attentive later on, and positively languorous when bringing the bill. Solly's Takeway (see p199 **Takeaways**) adjoins the ground-floor restaurant.
Babies and children welcome; high chairs. Booking advisable (upstairs). Kosher supervised (Beth Din). No smoking. Separate room for parties, seats 100. Takeaway service.

Hendon NW4

Eighty-Six Bistro Bar [NEW]
86 Brent Street, NW4 2ES (8202 5575). Hendon Central tube. **Lunch served** noon-3pm, **dinner served** 6-11pm Mon-Thur, Sun. **Main courses** £9.95-£22.95. **Credit** MC, V.
The painted mural outside shows that some care has gone into this new venture, but casual waitresses, a misspelt menu and unlit candles on the tables display a lack of professionalism. Yet the food is inventive and successful, including dishes unlike any others in kosher London. Seared foie gras with apple slices and caramelised Calvados sauce was dreamily soft. A salad of smoked turkey, salami and goose breast looked good too. Steaks were grilled to the requested pinkness and a baby chicken with arrabbiata sauce came pleasingly charred and tender. Only veal chops were disappointing, as the delicate meat was slightly overwhelmed by dried herbs. To compensate, chips were crisp, and bread and olives arrived with speed. The bistro menu is strange. Gourmet burgers, chorizo (made from beef) with chimichurri sauce and spaghetti bolognese share space with more ambitious items like sea bass in a salt crust and lamb chops in red wine and fennel sauce. The proprietors have got the food right, to judge by the full tables, but they need to be more

welcoming on the phone and should address the management side of the business.
Babies and children welcome: high chairs. Booking advisable. Kosher supervised (Federation). No smoking. Takeaway service.

Isola Bella Café
63 Brent Street, NW4 2EA (8203 2000/www.isolabellacafe.com). Hendon Central tube. **Meals served** 8am-11pm Mon-Thur, Sun; 8am-4pm Fri. **Main courses** £10-£18. **Set lunch** £15-£18 3 courses. **Credit** AmEx, DC, MC, V.
New York is the place for kosher dairy restaurants, where food is rich and comes in huge helpings. In similar vein, Isola Bella has a massive menu of 287 dishes, and gigantic portions. Yet we found both the variety on offer, and the size of the plates, offputting. To test the ambitious range of food – Thai, Italian, fish – you'd need to stay here from breakfast through lunch and tea to dinner. A starter of smoked salmon and cream cheese crêpe, generously filled and garnished with salad, was enough for two. A rickshaw (a huge basket of fried potato straws) overflowed with at least seven crunchy vegetables. Another dish big enough for a sumo wrestler was the egg noodles with stir-fried vegetables, Thai barbecue sauce and roasted cashews. Bread arrives as a whole fresh loaf with butter. Desserts are better tackled on their own, mid-afternoon, with one of a dozen types of coffee; the choice of cakes is vast. A smiling waitress brought a hazelnut gaya, with swirls of creamy caramel. This was too good to share.
Babies and children welcome: high chairs. Booking advisable. Kosher supervised (Beth Din). No smoking. Separate room for parties, seats 70. Takeaway service. Vegetarian menu.

Mama's Kosher Restaurant & Takeaway
53 Brent Street, NW4 2EA (8202 5444). Hendon Central tube. **Meals served** 11am-11.30pm Mon-Thur, Sun; 11am-5pm Fri (1pm in winter). **Main courses** £8-£16. **Set lunch** (Mon-Fri) £9.99 1 course. **Credit** AmEx, MC, V.
A year after Mama's opening, the café-style tables are not as full as they were, but this reflects less on the cooking than the proliferation of eateries in the area. There really is a mama in the kitchen, working with a chef to produce Sephardi food. Vegetarians are well catered for, with couscous, spicy cigars, aubergines and dark-brown slow-cooked eggs. A whole sea bream on the bone also looked good. The pitta that came with the houmous and falafel was deliciously puffy, but fried kibbe was pale and greasy. Our suggestion is to pass on the schwarma and schnitzel, and go for the 'homemade' dishes. Yemenite soup was spicy and thick with potatoes and vegetables, while Iraqi beetroot kibbe – semolina dumplings filled with meat – had chunks of beetroot in a rich red stock. Side dishes of rice and chips were better than the unseasoned salad. If you don't have room for chocolate cake or baklava, the Special Lemon cocktail (£1) will leave you with a pleasant taste of fresh juice and mint.
Babies and children welcome: booster seats; children's menu. Booking advisable. Kosher supervised (Federation). No smoking. Tables outdoors (1, pavement). Takeaway service.

Sami's Kosher Restaurant
157 Brent Street, NW4 4DJ (8203 8088). Hendon Central tube. **Meals served** noon-11pm Mon-Thur, Sun. **Set lunch** (Mon-Thur) £9.95 2 courses, £12.95 3 courses. **Main courses** £11.95-£14.50. **Credit** MC, V.

The yellow plastic benches at Sami's Kosher Restaurant have been replaced with a new look: mirrors and glass, dark wood tables and stylish crockery. Regrettably, the service doesn't match the surroundings; our waiter even forgot to bring any cutlery. Like many Israeli-type restaurants, Sami's is uncertain of its role. Is it Middle Eastern, south Asian, Ashkenazi or Iraqi? The menu boasts houmous and falafel, lamb tikka masala, chicken soup and knaidlach, and stuffed kibbe. But the chef can't be expert in all four cuisines, so our advice is to make a meal of the substantial starters and avoid the chicken nuggets or New Delhi mixed grill. Greek aubergine salad was deliciously oily and rich; matbucha (tomato and red pepper salad) was smooth and sweet. The fried kibbe, though crisp, were bland and didn't taste of bulgar. Schwarma in a puffy pitta wrap looked good, as did the creamy houmous and the array of fresh salads by the entrance. Main courses were less inviting: the lamb cutlets overcooked, the tikka masala strangely dry. For dessert, try baklava rather than the ubiquitous chocolate pudding.

Babies and children welcome: children's menu; high chairs. Kosher supervised (Beth Din). No smoking. Takeaway service.

St John's Wood NW8

Harry Morgan's

31 St John's Wood High Street, NW8 7NH (7722 1869/www.harryms.co.uk). St John's Wood tube. **Meals served** 11.30am-10pm Mon-Fri; noon-10pm Sat, Sun. **Main courses** £8.95-£11.50. **Service** 12.5%. **Credit** AmEx, MC, V. Not kosher

In a street full of fashionable boutiques and Mediterranean cafés, Harry's still attracts customers who prefer to eat chopped liver and calf's foot jelly. The menu is eastern European: egg and onion for a starter; chicken soup, or bean and barley soup, followed by salt beef with chips or latkes. But the soup, though tasty, had what one customer called 'balls like stone'. The beef was disappointingly dry; many people prefer it without fat, but this affects the succulence. A generous portion of fried gefilte fish came garnished with salad and was flavoursome if a bit firm. Haddock and chips was faultless: the fish with a crisp coating of matzo meal, melting flakes inside, served with a pile of perfect chips. Newer items on the menu looked appealing, especially a hot chicken salad piled high with onions and peppers on a bed of well-dressed greens. Leave room for dessert. Maybe the chef has a Jewish grandma, because the sweet blintzes were just what these soft cheese pancakes should be.

Babies and children welcome: high chairs. Booking advisable (taken on weekdays only). Tables outdoors (5, pavement). Takeaway service. **For branch see index**.

Outer London
Edgware, Middlesex

★ Aviv

87-89 High Street, Edgware, Middx HA8 7DB (8952 2484/www.avivrestaurant.com). Edgware tube. **Lunch served** noon-2.30pm Mon-Thur, Sun. **Dinner served** *Winter* 5.30-11pm Mon-Thur, Sat, Sun. *Summer* 5.30-11pm Mon-Thur, Sun. **Main courses** £9.95-£13.95. **Set lunch** noon-2.30pm Mon-Thur) £8.95 2 courses. **Set meals** £14.95, £18.95, 3 courses. **Service** 10%. **Credit** AmEx, MC, V.

What sets Aviv apart from other kosher restaurants is its professionalism; staff scrutinise a computer to check the progress of each table. At 7pm on a Sunday night the room was almost full. The food is excellent value with set menus at £16 and £20. Starters include houmous with lamb and pine nuts, chicken satay and meat cigars. Kibbe, though well filled, didn't quite taste homemade. Duck pancakes were crisp and aromatic, but the meat could have been more succulent. Grills were the best bet; tender rib or T-bone steaks came with

good chips. A lamb shank (kevas batanur) was slightly overwhelmed by a spicy sauce, but the meat fell off the bones. Barbecued chicken seemed a bit dry; a grilled sole looked more promising. The set menu includes puffy pitta bread, crudités, tea or coffee and a dessert. We should have avoided the nut-topped apple crumble (piping hot yet too sweet) and the tiramisu, which simply can't be made well if it's parev. Fruit salad was the best way of ending this charmingly served, high-quality meal.

Babies and children welcome: children's meal; high chairs. Booking essential. Kosher supervised (Beth Din). No smoking. Tables outdoors (14, patio). Takeaway service.

★ B&K Salt Beef Bar

11 Lanson House, Whitchurch Lane, Edgware, Middx HA8 6NL (8952 8204). Edgware tube. **Lunch served** noon-3pm, **dinner served** 5.30-9.15pm Tue-Sun. **Main courses** £4-£9.50. **Unlicensed**. **Corkage** no charge. **Credit** MC, V. Not kosher

Although the B&K Salt Beef Bar is somewhat off the beaten track, it's usually packed (with about 20 regulars). The furnishings are unfussy; there's no fine china or linen here. The customers come for the food and the smiles of the owner as he cuts the huge joint of salt beef. He presides over the deli counter, serving herring, egg and onion and chopped liver. Pickled cucumbers nestle among the traditional salads, but there's not much else for vegetarians. After a starter of chicken soup you're expected to continue a meal with a hefty plate of meat. Cold options include tongue and turkey, but it's the warm salt beef that is the star of the show. A sandwich is generously filled with thick slices oozing out of the rye bread. Don't bother with the latkes or the lockshen

pudding (both look better than they taste), but leave with the richly consoling taste of the beef in your mouth.

Babies and children welcome: high chairs. Bookings not accepted. No smoking. Takeaway service (11.30am-9.15pm).

Stanmore, Middlesex

★ ★ Madison's Deli

11 Buckingham Parade, Stanmore, Middx HA7 4ED (8954 9998). Stanmore tube. **Lunch served** noon-3pm, **dinner served** 5.30-10pm daily. **Main courses** £4.95-£9.95. **Set lunch** £5.95 2 courses. **Credit** MC, V.

The decor at Madison's Deli still shines brightly, and lunchtime specials cost the same as last year. On offer is a large choice of terrific-value Jewish food. In winter, warming chicken soup and hot salt beef would fortify the most determined local shopper. On a hot day, meanwhile, a refreshing glass of beetroot borscht and a plate of salads would make an ideal lunch for the weight-conscious. But forget the diet and go for the specialities: chopped liver, egg and onion, a pastrami or tongue sandwich in rye bread, fish fried in matzo meal, or a pile of tomato-sauced meatballs with rice. The chips are more appealing than the not-quite-right latkes. Each of the four desserts looks scrumptious. The lockshen pudding has a creamy vanilla flavour and the apple strudel is well-filled and tasty. Both the chocolate cake and the cheesecake look extremely sweet, but this is the eastern European style – sugar in the fish balls, the borscht and the desserts. There's a takeaway counter too.

Babies and children welcome: children's menu; high chairs. Booking advisable. Disabled: toilet. No-smoking tables. Takeaway service.

Takeaways

Buying hot Jewish food to take out is tricky in London: standards vary. Don't just go for a kosher certificate (some supervised establishments aren't so appetising); instead, try one of the following places, which produce quality falafel, pizza, schwarma or grilled meat.

Chap A' Nash [NEW]

41 Greville Street, EC1N 8PJ (7831 2224). Chancery Lane tube/Farringdon tube/rail. **Open** 7am-3pm Mon-Fri. **No credit cards.**

The name means 'Grab a Bite' in Yiddish. Hatton Garden's only kosher venue for sandwiches and salads also does a pretty good hot latke.

Babies and children admitted. Takeaway service. **Map 11 N5.**

Dizengoff's Fried Chicken

122 Golders Green Road, NW11 8HB (8209 0232/www.kosherfriedchicken. co.uk). Golders Green tube. **Meals served** noon-midnight Mon-Thur, Sun; noon-1hr before Sabbath Fri; 1hr after Sabbath-3am Sat. **Main courses** £3.99-£6.49. **No credit cards.**

Forget the overspiced chicken wings and don't expect a cheap meal, but the fried chicken (freshly cooked, if you're lucky) will be sizzling hot and crispy.

Babies and children welcome: high chairs. Kosher supervised (Sephardi). No smoking. Tables outdoors (4, pavement). Takeaway service.

★ Penashe

60 Edgware Way, Mowbray Parade, Edgware, Middx HA8 8JS (8958 6008/ www.penashe.co.uk). Edgware tube.

Lunch served noon-3pm, **dinner served** 5-10pm Mon-Thur. **Meals served** 1hr after Sabbath-midnight Sat; noon-10pm Sun. **Main courses** £2.85-£7.50. **Credit** MC, V.

Worth a visit for the freshly grilled meat. Lockshen soup with real matzo balls will keep you going while you wait for a rib steak sandwich or marinated chicken wings. Waffles and maple syrup complete the New York experience.

Babies and children welcome: children's menu; high chairs. Kosher supervised (Beth Din). No smoking. Takeaway service.

Slice [NEW]

8 Princes Parade, NW11 9PS (8458 9483). Brent Cross tube. **Open** 11am-11pm Mon-Thur, Sun; 11am-5pm Fri; 1hr after Sabbath-midnight Sat. **No credit cards.**

Not a place to relax over a whole pizza, but Slice is fine for a quick, tasty takeaway. Pizzas are precooked and finished to order. The basic cheese and tomato topping is pleasant, but a large cheese pretzel was bland.

Babies and children admitted. Kosher supervised (Federation). No smoking. Takeaway service.

★ Solly's Takeaway [NEW]

For listings, see p197.

You could order a beefburger or tandoori chicken, but the Israeli specialities are the best. Falafel, schwarma, houmous and tabouleh are all fresh and tasty. Chicken or lamb skewers are also grilled to order. Also in the same building is Solly's Exclusive restaurant (*see p197*).

RESTAURANTS

Korean

Can it be that Londoners are finally beginning to catch on to the joys of Korean food? If so, at least part of the reason for this change of heart may be down to the opening in spring 2005 of **Wizzy**, the first 'modern' Korean restaurant in the capital. Chef Hwi Sim (aka Wizzy) counts two of London's trendiest and best Asian eateries – Nobu and Hakkasan – among the kitchens in which she has worked. In her eponymous venture in Parsons Green she has taken London's Korean food to a new level of upmarket refinement, helping to broaden the appeal of Korean cooking. Contemporary interpretations of traditional dishes, such as the classic ginseng chicken and kaysan (marinated crab), are exquisitely prepared and presented.

Elsewhere, one of our favourite Korean restaurants, **Cah Chi** in Raynes Park, seems to be attracting a substantial non-Asian following too. Its new menu makes a point of explaining the basics of Korean food to a receptive audience, and the place is always busy. Despite these advances, the casual, inexpensive, café-style Korean eateries in central London still attract a mainly Korean or Japanese clientele.

So, if you haven't tried Korean food yet, what are you waiting for? Eating a Korean meal is an interactive experience. Many of the dishes, from casseroles to bulgogi, are cooked for you at your table. Ingredient-wise, comparisons with Chinese and Japanese are inevitable, but Korean food has its own very definite character. Chillies and chilli pastes are used liberally, but a meal should always strike a balance between spicy, bland, sour, salty and sweet. Garlic, chilli and sesame are the holy trinity of Korean cooking, and these will appear at every meal, as will the famous spicy pickle, kimchi.

There are two main centres of Korean cooking in London: Soho and New Malden. **Nara** and **Woo Jung** are among the best in Soho, but if you really want a taste of Korean food at its best, head to the deep south-west. London's Korean community is centred in New Malden, so this is where you'll find the best food, from homely, no-frills places such as **You-Me** and **Yeon-Ji** to higher-end restaurants like **Asadal** and **Han Kook**.

Central
Covent Garden WC2

★ Woo Jung
59 St Giles High Street, WC2H 8LH (7836 3103). Tottenham Court Road tube. **Meals served** noon-midnight Mon-Sat; 5pm-midnight Sun. **Main courses** £6-£8. **Set meal** £10-£30. **Credit** MC, V.
The best of the three Korean restaurants located near Centrepoint in St Giles High Street, this small and unassuming eaterie is something of an undiscovered gem – unless you're Korean, in which case you probably already know how popular it is. The extensive menu incorporates special dishes such as cod, vegetable, chilli and tofu casserole cooked in seafood stock, as well as a wide range of astonishingly good value set meals. Main courses, priced at around £6 to £8, are particularly good value. We started with tangy pickled radish and crispy toasted seaweed, swiftly followed by raw seafood (salmon, turbot, squid, sea bream and mackerel) in a lively chilli sauce. The slithery texture of ox tongue seasoned with sesame oil and lemon could be an acquired taste, but vegetable bindaedok (made with crushed mung beans and an array of colourful vegetables) was fabulous. The restaurant can be noisy and the service – although friendly – is slow during peak periods. However, the generous portions, consistently good food and low prices more than make up for it. *Babies and children admitted. Takeaway service.* **Map 18 K6.**

Fitzrovia W1

Han Kang
16 Hanway Street, W1T 1UE (7637 1985). Tottenham Court Road tube. **Lunch served** noon-3pm, **dinner served** 6-10.30pm Mon-Sat. **Main courses** £6.50-£28. **Set lunch** £6.50 3 courses. **Credit** AmEx, MC, V.
One of the best-known Korean restaurants in the capital, this lively venue is enormously popular with Korean Society students from UCL and nearby office workers, and enjoys something of a cult following. It's almost like a fast-food joint, busy during lunchtimes and quieter in the evenings, with quick-quick service to match. There's a small dining room on the ground floor, a private room upstairs and a karaoke bar in the basement (complete with loud Korean pop music). Does it live up to the hype? Sadly, no. The all-important kimchi – the benchmark dish on which a Korean chef's skills are invariably judged – is a disappointment, being too bland and chilled (it should be fiery and served at room temperature). Seafood is the kitchen's strong point, and neither the raw squid nor the marinated seafood in spicy sauce disappointed. The luscious flavour of wafer-thin slices of pork bulgogi also appealed, but a vegetable bibimbap was short on vegetables and heavy on rice. We have enjoyed eating here for many years, but on our most recent visit it seemed the kitchen was resting on its laurels. *Babies and children welcome: high chair. Separate room for parties, seats 20. Takeaway service.* **Map 17 K5.**

Mayfair W1

Kaya
42 Albemarle Street, W1X 4JH (7499 0622/ 0633). Green Park tube. **Lunch served** noon-3pm, **dinner served** 6-11pm Mon-Sat. **Main courses** £9-£18. **Set lunch** £12-£15. **Service** 15%. **Credit** JCB, MC, V.
One of very few smart Korean restaurants in London, this lovely Mayfair venue boasts pretty, minimalist, contemporary decor – all white walls, paper lanterns and moody lighting. A lively, animated vibe belies the tranquillity of the surroundings. We liked vegetable p'ajeon (here made with unhusked green mung beans), and jellyfish with seafood in mustard sauce was like discovering a long-standing secret affair between succulent texture and sharp piquancy. The kimchi and namul were particularly exquisite; a parade of spinach, beansprouts, cucumber and whole sesame-studded Chinese leaves were in turns hot, tender, crunchy and refreshing. Pork with kimchi was tasty, but the spicy broth it was cooked in could have done with more body and kick. Unusually, there's also a small selection of desserts on offer – mainly of the fresh fruit and ice-cream variety, rather than the nutty, fruity, occasionally bean-, vegetable- and egg-based concoctions you would find in a Korean home. Service from traditionally attired female staff is excellent, and even the set menus are regal. A refurbishment and a new chef may herald changes later in 2005. *Booking advisable. Separate rooms for parties, seating 8 and 12. Takeaway service. Vegetarian menu.* **Map 9 J7.**

Soho W1

Jin
16 Bateman Street, W1D 3AH (7734 0908). Leicester Square or Tottenham Court Road tube. **Lunch served** noon-3pm, **dinner served** 6-11pm Mon-Sat. **Main courses** £8-£38. **Set lunch** £7.50-£10 5 dishes. **Set dinner** £30-£35 6 courses. **Service** 10%. **Credit** AmEx, MC, V.
This buzzy restaurant located in the heart of Soho is a marriage of western and traditional oriental design concepts: behind a stylish cream exterior, you will find a soothing dining room with magnolia walls, framed pictures, fresh flower arrangements, black marble tables and leather upholstery. We enjoyed jajang myun (black bean noodles) with sesame-flavoured spinach and assertively spiced kimchi. Rice with vegetables and seafood was studded with sea squirts (which are like miniature squid) and sliced whelk, and permeated with a punchy, garlicky flavour. Barbecue dishes are good as long as you stick to meat – seafood bulgogi, in our experience, is a mishmash of undercooked, overcooked and almost raw seafood, and is best avoided. Soups, kimchis, noodles and claypot dishes are, on the whole, very spicy and well-flavoured. Service from waiters in white shirts is friendly, although sometimes hampered by language difficulties. The menu is also notable for a good selection of Korean-style Chinese food – which is different from traditional Chinese food, and very popular in Korea. *Babies and children admitted. Booking advisable weekends. Separate room for parties, seats 10. Takeaway service.* **Map 17 K6.**

Asadal. See p203.

RESTAURANTS

Myung Ga

1 Kingly Street, W1B 5PA (7734 8220).
Oxford Circus or Piccadilly Circus tube.
Lunch served noon-3pm Mon-Sat. **Dinner served** 5.30-11pm Mon-Sat; 5-10.30pm Sun.
Set lunch £9.50-£12.50 2 courses. **Set dinner** £25-£35 3 courses. **Credit** AmEx, DC, MC, V.
Located off Regent Street, this homely restaurant is something of a hit or miss experience. The decor is unexceptional – an area with low wooden tables, divided from the main dining area (cream walls, black tables, black vinyl chairs) by glass screens – and the menu comprehensive, listing standard dishes from all over Korea, including rice, noodles, kimchi, stir-fries and hot-pots. Some dishes we liked: deep-fried oysters in a light egg batter, bright red (just as it should be) kimchi stir-fried with pork belly, and bibimbap made with raw ground beef, vegetables, rice and egg. Prawn barbecue was less successful – the small crustaceans were overcooked and came with an undercooked pile of spring onions, mushrooms and peppers. Noodles with chinese leaves, carrots and cloud ear mushrooms were no better than an ordinary Chinese stir-fry. There's a good selection of vegetarian dishes, and tabletop barbecues are a speciality of the house – but we find the flavours here a bit rough around the edges. Service from beautifully dressed, somewhat motherly, waitresses is variable. Other minus points include smokiness (the restaurant is poorly ventilated), loud Korean pop and meagre portions. *Babies and children admitted. Booking advisable. No-smoking tables. Separate room for parties, seats 14.* **Map 17 J6.**

Menu

Chilli appears at every opportunity on Korean menus. Other common ingredients include soy sauce (different to both the Chinese and Japanese varieties), sesame oil, sugar, sesame seeds, garlic, ginger and various fermented soy bean pastes. Until the late 1970s eating meat was a luxury in Korea, so the quality of vegetarian dishes is high.

Given the spicy nature and overall flavour of Korean food, drinks such as chilled lager or vodka-like soju/shoju are the best matches. A wonderful non-alcoholic alternative that is always available, although not always listed, is barley tea (porich'a). Often served free of charge, it has a light dry taste that perfectly matches Korean food.

Korean restaurants don't generally offer desserts (some serve half an orange or some watermelon at about the same time as the bill) – though **Wizzy** is a notable exception.

Spellings on menus vary hugely; we have given the most common.

Bibimbap or **pibimbap**: rice, vegetables and meat with a raw/fried egg dropped on top, often served on a hot stone.
Bindaedok, **bindaedoek** or **pindaetteok**: a mung bean pancake.
Bokum: a stir-fried dish, usually including chilli.
Bulgogi or **pulgogi**: slices of marinated beef barbecued at the table, then sometimes rolled in a lettuce leaf; eaten with vegetable relishes.
Chang, **jang** or **denjang**: various fermented soy bean pastes
Chapch'ae, **chap chee** or **jap chee**: mixed vegetables and beef cooked with transparent vermicelli or noodles.
Cheon or **jon**: the literal meaning is 'something flat'; this can range from a pancake containing vegetables, meat or seafood, to thinly sliced vegetables, beancurd and so on, in a light batter.
Chigae or **jigae**: a hot stew containing fermented bean paste and chillies.
Gim or **kim**: dried seaweed, toasted and seasoned with salt and sesame oil.
Gu shul pan: a traditional lacquered tray with nine compartments containing individual appetisers.
Hobak chun or **hobak jun**: sliced marrow in a light egg batter.

Jjim: fish or meat stewed for a long time in soy sauce, sugar and garlic.
Kalbi, **galbi** or **kalbee**: beef spare ribs, marinated and barbecued.
Kimchi, **kim chee** or **kimch'i**: pickled vegetables, usually chinese cabbage, white radishes, cucumber or greens, served in a small bowl with a spicy chilli sauce.
Kkaktugi or **kkakttugi**: pickled radish.
Koch'ujang: a hot, red bean paste.
Kook, **gook**, **kuk** or **guk**: soup. Koreans have an enormous variety of soups, from consommé-like liquid to meaty broths of noodles, dumplings, meat or fish.
Ko sari na mool or **gosari namul**: cooked bracken stalks dressed with sesame seeds.
Mandu kuk or **man doo kook**: clear soup with steamed meat dumplings.
Namul or **na mool**: vegetable side dishes.
P'ajeon or **pa jun**: flour pancake with spring onions and (usually) seafood.
Panch'an: side dishes; they usually include pickled vegetables, but possibly also tofu, fish, seaweed or beans.
Pap, **bap**, **bab** or **pahb**: cooked rice.
Pokkeum or **pokkm**: stir-fry. For example, **cheyuk pokkeum** (pork), **ojingeo pokkeum** (squid) **yach'ae pokkeum** (vegetable).
Shinseollo, **shinsonro**, **shinsulro** or **sin sollo**: 'royal casserole'; a meat soup with seaweed, seafood, eggs and vegetables, all cooked at the table.
Soju or **shoju**: a strong Korean rice spirit, often drunk as an aperitif.
Teoppap or **toppap**: 'on top of rice'. For example, **ojingeo teoppap** is squid served on rice.
Toenjang: seasoned (usually with chilli) soy bean paste.
Tolsot bibimbap: tolsot is a sizzling hot stone bowl that makes the bibimbap (qv) a little crunchy on the sides.
Tteokpokki: bars of compressed rice (tteok is a rice cake) fried on a hot-plate with veg and sausages, in a chilli sauce.
Twaeji gogi: pork.
T'wigim, **twigim** or **tuigim**: fish, prawns or vegetables dipped in batter and deep-fried until golden brown.
Yuk hwe, **yukhoe** or **yukhwoe**: shredded raw beef, strips of pear and egg yolk, served chilled.
Yukkaejang: spicy beef soup.

★ Nara

9 D'Arblay Street, W1F 8DR (7287 2224).
Oxford Circus or Tottenham Court Road tube. **Lunch served** noon-3pm Mon-Sat.
Dinner served 5-11pm daily. **Main courses** £6.50-£40.50. **Set lunch** £6.50. **Set dinner** £7.50. **Credit** MC, V.
This relative newcomer remains one of the best spots in central London for high-quality Korean food. Nara bills itself as Japanese/Korean, but stick to the Korean dishes and you'll be in for some pleasant surprises. The cooking is exemplary, with dishes radiating freshness and packed with flavour. Namul, including zingy kimchi and cubes of chestnut jelly, set a cracking pace. To follow, a starter of bindaedok was hot, crisp and grease-free. The house specials list is the place to look for the most interesting dishes: if tofu stir-fried with kimchi or tteokpokki doesn't appeal, how about skate wing in chilli sauce or soon-dae (Korean-style black pudding) with vegetables? We couldn't resist the somen noodles with whelks, despite the appropriate warning ('very spicy!') from the waiter. A barbecue dish of marinated kalbi, cooked at the table, packed a strong garlic kick. Yuk hwe, flavoured with pine nuts and sesame, was a tad cold, but otherwise impressive. There's a selection of set lunches (including tofu with chilli sauce, bulgogi and pan-fried pork), all at £6.50. In the evening, though, be prepared for some bustle. The ventilation isn't the greatest – on our visit, there was a fug of smoke from countless tabletop barbecues and the sound system blared cloying, tinny Asian pop.
Babies and children welcome: high chairs. **Map 17 J6.**

South West
Parsons Green SW6

★ Wizzy NEW

2005 RUNNER-UP BEST LOCAL RESTAURANT
616 Fulham Road, SW6 5PR (7736 9171).
Parsons Green tube. **Lunch served** noon-3pm, **dinner served** 6-11.30pm daily. **Main courses** £8.50-£15. **Credit** AmEx, MC, V.
Welcome to the first 'modern Korean' restaurant in London, the brainchild of chef Hwi Shim, aka Wizzy. Most of the diners were Western on our visit, so the cross-cultural message must be getting through. Although the small room is plain, great attention is paid to presentation, with food artfully arranged on striking tableware (huge celadon plates, wooden boxes, stone bowls). A starter based on kaysan (marinated crab) produced a tower of rice and crab meat, topped with bright orange flying-fish roe, and two sauces – pomegranate-yoghurt and soy – arranged in concentric circles around its base. Bibimbap – super-fresh vegetables (and, usually, strips of beef; we had the vegetarian version), rice and egg served sizzling in a stone bowl to be mixed together at the table – was a superior example. And a bargain at £6. Ginseng chicken was a delicate, reviving broth laced with red dates, chestnuts and discs of ginseng. Desserts are not a big feature of Korean cuisine, but they're great here: don't miss the red-bean tiramisu and gooey chocolate pot. Not everything works: portion sizes are variable, the menu is badly translated into English, and service can be amateurish, but these are endearing rather than irritating traits thanks to the enthusiasm behind the venture.
Babies and children welcome: high chairs. Booking advisable.

Raynes Park SW20

★ Cah Chi

34 Durham Road, SW20 0TW (8947 1081).
Raynes Park rail/57, 131 bus. **Lunch served** noon-3pm, **dinner served** 5-11pm Tue-Fri.
Meals served noon-11pm Sat; noon-10.30pm Sun. **Main courses** £4.50-£14. **Set dinner** £18 3 courses. **Corkage** (wine) 10%. **No credit cards**.
Cah Chi has had a facelift since our last visit. Nothing major, mind you, just some new pale wood chairs and new tables with inset gas cookers. The friendly vibe has been maintained, though: kids' drawings are still tacked up on the walls and the

welcome is as smiling as ever. Also new are the menus, which seem to cater for an increasingly Western clientele, with explanations about Korean food and how to put together a meal. The food is still fabulous, starting with top-notch namul: kimchi, pickled radish and sticky-sweet soya beans. Our starters of fried mung bean pancakes with perilla leaves and spring onions, and steamed tofu (with a delectable topping of sliced green onions, thin strips of nori, perilla seeds and the ubiquitous soy, sesame and red chilli) sang with freshness. Classic kalbi, cooked at the table and served with a pile of fresh lettuce leaves, some thinly sliced spring onion, bean paste and soy sauce for dipping, was lip-smackingly good. A side dish of cold buckwheat noodles with sliced courgette and hard-boiled egg came with a bright-red chilli sauce and packed a kick. The food's unbeatable – and you can bring your own wine.
Babies and children welcome: high chairs. Booking essential. Separate room for parties, seats 18. Takeaway service.

North West
Golders Green NW11

★ Kimchee
887 Finchley Road, NW11 8RR (8455 1035). Golders Green tube. **Lunch served** noon-3pm Tue-Fri; noon-4pm Sat, Sun. **Dinner served** 6-11pm Tue-Sun. **Main courses** £6.50-£8.50. **Set lunch** £6.50 6 dishes. **Credit** JCB, MC, V.
Named after Korea's national dish, this popular neighbourhood restaurant conjures up a contemporary feel with walls the colour of vanilla ice-cream, dark wood furniture and a floor of glazed tiles. Shigumchi (spinach and tofu) soup didn't contain enough denjang (fermented soy bean paste), and therefore lacked the body and roundedness a thick Korean soup should have. However, mandu (meat dumpling) soup was cooked in a rich beef stock and utterly delicious. Kimchi and namul are a strong point: sliced radish with chilli and vinegar, beansprouts doused in sesame oil, and lettuce with denjang were all beautifully flavoured. A casserole of cod, seafood, tofu and vegetables was made with good stock and spiked with Korean chilli pepper threads – fabulous. The barbecued vegetables were somewhat prosaic, and barbecued beef ribeye with garlic and sesame oil slightly rubbery. Over many visits, we have found the quality of cooking here to be inconsistent, but, on the whole, it delivers more often than not. The main downside is the price: for instance, lettuce leaves that accompany barbecued meat should be given free (as in most Korean restaurants), but here they are charged extra; thus the cost of a meal can spiral upwards.
Babies and children admitted: high chairs. Booking essential Fri-Sun. No-smoking tables. Takeaway service. Vegetarian menu.

Outer London
New Malden, Surrey

★ Asadal
180 New Malden High Street, New Malden, Surrey KT3 4EF (8942 2334/8949 7385). New Malden rail. **Lunch served** noon-3pm Mon-Fri. **Meals served** noon-11pm Sat. **Dinner served** 5-11pm Sun. **Main courses** £7-£25. **Set dinner** £15 2 courses; £50 per person 5 courses (minimum 2). **Service** 10%. **Credit** MC, V.
This much-loved, long-established restaurant was one of the first to open in New Malden, and almost single-handedly kick-started the metamorphosis of a sleepy suburban district into the capital's 'Korea Town'. Asadal looks more contemporary than other Korean eateries in the area, with prices to match. However, the portions are large, the lively atmosphere makes it ideal for group or family dining, and the smartly dressed staff radiate sunshine smiles. And did we mention the food? We adored seafood p'ajeon studded with scallops, squid and spring onions, as well as raw beef with sesame oil and Korean pear (similar to Japanese nashi pear). Vegetable chapch'ae was a delicious tangle of chewy sweet potato noodles and crisp vegetables.

Tabletop barbecue, although a fun way to eat, can be difficult to get right: in many Korean restaurants you will find your meat or seafood overcooked or undercooked, but not here. We dolloped morsels of spicy barbecued chicken into lettuce leaves along with some rice and vegetables, and were in instant culinary heaven. Infused with vibrant chilli and garlic flavours, the food here is some of the best and most authentic Korean you'll find in London.
Babies and children welcome: high chairs. Takeaway service.
For branch see index.

Hamgipak
169 High Street, New Malden, Surrey KT3 4BH (8942 9588). New Malden rail. **Meals served** 11am-10pm Mon, Tue, Thur-Sun. **Main courses** £5-£20. **Credit** MC, V.
Small but perfectly formed – with less than half a dozen tables plus bar stools – this lovely glass-fronted café, with slate floors and blond wood furniture, is ideal for family dining. Don't be fooled by its size: a separate trailer at the back can accommodate large group bookings, although it lacks the lively ambience of the main restaurant. Interesting fish such as saury, croaker and pollock feature on the large menu, but we decided to stick to meat and vegetables. Pork bulgogi was rich, fatty meat in a good marinade, perfectly barbecued. Similarly, vegetable bulgogi comprised a plethora of multicoloured vegetables – peppers, mushrooms, carrots, spring onions and baby corn – that had just kissed the sizzling hotplate and thus retained their crunchiness. The best thing about this eaterie, however, is that pickles and side dishes, such as enticingly flavoured baby cucumber kimchi stuffed with grated radish, arrive automatically with the main courses. Unlike most Korean restaurants in central London, they don't have to be ordered separately and are included in the price. This is quintessential Korean hospitality – why don't more restaurants do the same?
Babies and children admitted. No smoking. Takeaway service.

Han Kook
Ground floor, Falcon House, 257 Burlington Road, New Malden, Surrey KT3 4NE (8942 1188). Raynes Park rail. **Lunch served** noon-3pm Mon, Tue, Thur, Fri. **Dinner served** 6-11pm Mon-Fri. **Meals served** noon-11pm Sat, Sun. **Main courses** £5.90-£27.90. **Set meal** £20 3 courses. **Credit** MC, V.
Behind its dull exterior, Han Kook is surprisingly chic, all paper screens and bamboo touches. Sit cross-legged at one of the low tables, or go for one of the large chunky ones, and come with a group: the menu seems designed for sharing, with many dishes serving two to four. 'Soju sets' – meals (such as steamed whelks and chilli) made for drinking with soju, the Korean-style rice spirit – are another hint that this is a place to gather friends. Still, Han Kook is pretty upmarket, with traditionally clad waitresses (sporting incongruous smiley name badges) and friendly, attentive service. The menu is extensive, with fried, grilled and hot-pot dishes, as well as 'lid-pan' barbecues. Our barbecued spicy belly pork came to the table in a shallow wok-like pan with red chillies, onion, courgette, mushroom and sweet-hot chilli sauce. We made delicious, flavour-packed little parcels by wrapping the pork and veggies in lettuce leaves with fermented bean paste. A p'ajeon starter was bursting with seafood and green onion, while stir-fried octopus in chilli sauce with noodles had an enticing, smoky flavour and plenty of tender octopus. Excellent namul, including seaweed with chilli sauce and potato in cold sesame sauce, kept pace with the other dishes.
Babies and children welcome: high chairs. Booking essential dinner Fri, Sat.

Korea Garden NEW
73 Kingston Road, New Malden, Surrey KT3 3PB (8336 1208). New Malden rail. **Lunch served** noon-3pm, **dinner served** 6-10.30pm Mon-Sun. **Main courses** £6.40-£35. **Service** 10%. **Credit** AmEx, MC, V.
Tabletop barbecues are standard at many Korean restaurants, but none do the barbecue thing better than Korea Garden. The secret? Real, proper

charcoal. Most restaurants use gas-fuelled cookers, but not here, where the fragrant smoky charcoal gives food an unbeatable aroma. Choose from the lengthy selection of barbecue choices: there's beef, chicken, pork, lamb and seafood, including an enticing seafood selection that features the likes of whelks and razor clams. Make your order and the hot coals will be delivered straight to your table. Our 'lamb chop' (actually a leg steak) was served with lettuce leaves, soy bean paste and sesame oil/salt dip. Squid marinated in chilli paste was flavoursome, but we made the mistake of cooking it too long. For starters, fried dumplings, stuffed with pork, green onion and rice vermicelli, were firm, well textured and full of flavour, as was a kimchi pancake made with mung bean flour. Plentiful namul were little dishes of cucumber kimchi, beansprouts, courgette, mushroom and onion – and, of course, cabbage kimchi. Tolsot bibimbap, served in a hot stone bowl, was cooked to a crunchy crust. Service is friendly and the waiting staff happy to advise on what to order.
Babies and children admitted. Takeaway service.

★ Yeon-Ji
106 Burlington Road, New Malden, Surrey KT3 4NS (8942 7184). New Malden rail. **Meals served** noon-10pm Mon-Sat. **Dinner served** 5.30-10pm Sun. **Main courses** £5.50-£7. **Unlicensed. Corkage** no charge. **No credit cards.**
Yeon-Ji is as no-frills as Korean caffs in New Malden come. There are 'wood-look' Formica tables, lino floors and wipe-clean Perspex-mounted menus that sit on the tables; decor consists of a few jumble-sale pictures hung on the walls. It's an ultra-friendly place, with scatty but endearing service and, generally, good food. The cooking tends to be gutsy – literally, in the case of lamb entrails in hot sauce or 'beef and gut soup' – and there's a fair amount of choice. Our sirloin barbecue, cooked at our table on a portable gas cooker, arrived with a few mushrooms and a moreish dipping sauce of salt and sesame oil, but was on the tough side. Potato-starch noodles, translucent and irresistibly stretchy, were served with shiitake and plenty of veggies: carrot, cabbage, courgette and green onion. Namul, which comprised crunchy yellow mooli and some so-what beansprouts, were saved by lively, ultra-spicy kimchi that packed a wonderful ginger/chilli kick. Yeon-Ji is unlicensed, so bring your own booze.
Babies and children admitted. Takeaway service.

★ You-Me
96 Burlington Road, New Malden, Surrey KT3 4NT (8715 1079). New Malden rail. **Meals served** 11.30am-10.30pm Mon, Wed-Sun. **Main courses** £5.90-£13. **Set lunch** £11.90 6 dishes. **Credit** MC, V.
Home-style Korean cooking is the name of the game at You-Me, and the homely atmosphere extends well beyond the plate. In the smaller room at the front (there's a larger space to the rear) you'll find wooden furniture, a selection of Korean-language books and mags, and a TV wittering on in the background. It's all brightly lit and convivial, popular with families, but on our most recent visit service seemed a bit rushed and less friendly than usual. The namul were as varied and as good as ever, including sour-spicy cucumber and cabbage kimchi and crunchy, sweetish cubes of pickled daikon. The menu is pretty extensive, with a solid range of barbecue dishes, plus rice and noodle options, soups and one-dish meals. Look around and you're likely to see people tucking into the house special noodles with black bean sauce, impossibly long and succulent noodles that would doubtless cause bewilderment in Italy. The variation we chose featured those noodles in a rich, savoury brown sauce with lots of slow-cooked onions. Pork and bean-paste stew, packed with vegetables, was hearty and filling, but a rather boring starter of stir-fried mushrooms was less impressive . Still, You-Me (named after the owner's daughter) generally gets things right.
Babies and children welcome: high chairs. Separate room for parties, seats 6. Takeaway service.

Malaysian, Indonesian & Singaporean

During the past decade, restaurants specialising in the cooking of Malaysia, Indonesia and Singapore have rarely figured at the cutting edge of London dining. Yet that's not to say the cuisine is unpopular. These days, cross-border cooking is the trend, so Singaporean laksa could find itself sharing a menu with pad Thai, Vietnamese pho, or even sushi. You'll find venues with such menus listed in the **Oriental** section of the guide, starting on p243.

Nevertheless, there are still several restaurants that concentrate on the food of this particular region of South-east Asia, and there's a pleasing diversity of establishments. For a quick, cheap meal, try Soho's **Melati**, which has been serving Indonensian-Malaysian dishes for a quarter of a century. Our choice for a mid-range meal would be **Satay House** with its varied, entirely authentic cooking. But for a celebratory feast, the two best upmarket restaurants are **Singapore Garden**, an old-stager that carries on producing first-rate renditions of Malaysian and Singaporean food, and the newer **Champor-Champor**, which offers an especially creative take on Malaysian cuisine.

Central

City EC4

Singapura
1-2 Limeburner Lane, EC4M 7HY (7329 1133/ www.singapuras.co.uk). St Paul's tube/Blackfriars tube/rail. **Meals served** 11.30am-10.30pm Mon-Fri. **Main courses** £8.25-£13.75. **Set lunch** £10-£15 2 courses. **Set meal** £20-£25 per person (minimum 2). **Service** 12.5%. **Credit** AmEx, DC, MC, V.
Once you get beyond the slightly corporate decor, Singapura impresses with its fine Malacca Straits cuisine. The menu features dishes from Singapore, Malaysia, Thailand and Indonesia, skilfully prepared and served by polite waitresses in red silk uniforms. The black and white colour scheme and starched white tablecloths add class, but this is a venue designed to appeal to City high-fliers. We visited on a weekday night and found the cavernous dining room empty apart from a handful of after-office couples and American businessmen; it's busier at lunchtime. The Laotian larb (minced chicken salad) seemed a little insipid, and the Indonesian-style chicken satay was competent but unremarkable. We were more impressed with the mains, including a rich, spicy ayam lemak (Malaysian chicken curry) and an inspired char kway teow (fried ho fun noodles, tiger prawns, fish cakes, sweet soy sauce and diced chillies). Regrettably, we were too full to try the earl grey tea ice-cream for dessert. This is a good choice for a business lunch, less so for a romantic dinner. *Babies and children admitted. Booking advisable lunch. Disabled: toilet. Tables outdoors (15, terrace). Takeaway service; delivery service. Vegetarian menu. Vegan dishes.* **Map 11 O6.**
For branches see index.

Edgware Road W2

★ Mawar
175A Edgware Road, W2 2HR (7262 1663). Edgware Road tube.
Buffet **Meals served** noon-10.30pm Mon-Sat; noon-10pm Sun. **Set meal** £4-£5 1 course.
Restaurant **Dinner served** 6-10.30pm Mon-Sat; 6-10pm Sun. **Main courses** £5-£9. **Unlicensed**. **Corkage** no charge. **Service** 10%.
Both **Credit** (over £10) AmEx, MC, V.
Hidden at the bottom of some steps leading down from Edgware Road, Mawar has been serving inexpensive, authentic Malay food to an appreciative local crowd – including many Malaysians, always a good sign – for a number of years. Painted in Islamic green, the dining hall is divided into two parts, with a canteen-like staggeringly cheap counter meals – you can get rice with veg and three curries or stir-fries for just £5 – and a cosier à la carte section with tablecloths and waitress service, open from 6pm. We went for the full sit-down dining experience, starting with roti canai and soto ayam: both tasty if uninspired. More interesting was the kambing berlada: crispy fried lamb in a sweet, Cantonese-influenced chilli sauce. In contrast, the beef rendang was oily and dry. We ended the meal on a high, with iced kacang: a huge mound of ice shavings, sago, lychees and sweetcorn drenched in sweet rose syrup. Staff were friendly, but service was slow and not quite deserving of the 10% service charge. Nevertheless, Mawar makes a good choice for a low-priced canteen meal. *Babies and children welcome: high chair. Booking essential weekends. No-smoking tables. Takeaway service; delivery service (on orders over £30).* **Map 8 E5.**

Marylebone NW1

Rasa Singapura
Regent's Park Hotel, 154-156 Gloucester Place, NW1 6DT (7723 6740/www.regentspkhotel.com). Baker Street tube/Marylebone tube/rail. **Lunch served** noon-3pm, **dinner served** 6-11.30pm daily. **Main courses** £5.50-£25. **Set meal** £14.50-£30 3 courses. **Service** 12.5%. **Credit** AmEx, DC, JCB, MC, V.
Its basement location and kitsch entrance may not be immediately appealing, but venture into Rasa's dining room and you'll find a conservatory-style glass roof, and walls adorned with monochrome photos of 1950s Singapore. Authentic Singaporean food and amiable service confirm you've made the right choice. Tuck into fragrant hainanese chicken rice with gusto; smother every chicken slice with the dish's essence – chilli – spot on in its combination with chicken stock, garlic and ginger. Allow the silky, tender chicken to slither down your throat. Leave space for desserts or you'll miss the Malay kueh tayap; it would be hard to find a better version in London. This pièce de résistance of a pandan-flavoured coconut crêpe is wrapped thinly over a generous filling of fragrant, slightly crisp and wonderfully sweet grated coconut; drizzle the masterpiece with thick, warm coconut cream provided in an accompanying jar. The Nigerian couple celebrating their engagement with friends on the night of our visit must also have overlooked Rasa's slightly contrived surroundings, having been won over by the superior cooking. *Babies and children welcome: high chairs. Booking advisable. No-smoking tables. Takeaway service; delivery service (within 2-mile radius). Vegetarian menu.* **Map 2 F4.**

Soho W1

★ C&R Café
3-4 Rupert Court, W1D 6DY (7434 1128). Piccadilly Circus tube. **Meals served** noon-11pm daily. **Main courses** £5-£7.50. **Set meal** £12 vegetarian, £16 per person (minimum 2). **Credit** MC, V.
Much like its location in a back lane, and its stark and fuss-free interior, C&R produces food that is nondescript and falls short of the bold claims made of it. The restaurant purports to sell 'authentic cuisine': not only Singapore-Malaysian, but also Thai (though the menu contains few recognisably Thai dishes). The essential ingredients of coconut milk and shrimp paste were under-represented in our watered-down, salty version of Singapore laksa. However, we were relieved to find the char kway teow (seafood noodles stir-fried in black bean sauce) familiar and pleasantly peppery, even if drenched in oil. The drinks list includes a variety of fresh fruit juices and own-made concoctions. For pudding, we managed only a few spoons of what was supposed to be boo boo cha cha (yam and sweet potato in coconut milk), which was again severely lacking in coconut milk. Prompt service and generous portions aside, there are better places to have South-east Asian food in Soho. We left disgruntled. *Babies and children admitted. Bookings not accepted dinner Fri, Sat. Takeaway service. Vegetarian menu.* **Map 17 K7.**

Melati
21 Great Windmill Street, W1D 7LQ (7437 2745). Piccadilly Circus tube. **Meals served** noon-11.30pm Mon-Thur, Sun; noon-midnight Fri, Sat. **Main courses** £6.35-£11.35. **Set meals** £20-£23.50 per person (minimum 2). **Service** 10%. **Credit** AmEx, MC, V.
Melati has been around for 25 years, and it's not difficult to see why. The à la carte menu (over 100 dishes including a varied choice for vegetarians) offers a combination of Indonesian-Malaysian street food, as well as more generic hotel-restaurant dishes, and there's an extensive wine list. Perhaps the spotlit furnishings and Norah Jones soundtrack sit uneasily with the old portraits of Malay royalty that line the stairs. However, the food (prepared by an Indonesian-Malaysian duo) is unashamedly aimed at South-east Asian taste

RESTAURANTS

Nyonya. See p207.

buds, and is dished out in generous portions. Lamb satay was a little burnt in places, but the accompanying gravy, which we smothered over the meat, was perfect: freshly crushed peanuts providing crunch to a concoction of spices blended into a paste. The grilled squid (cumi cumi bakar), though wonderfully fresh, needed less sweet soy sauce and more lime leaf and ginger for fragrance. Service comes from an affable hostess. This gem of a restaurant shines brightest on weekday lunchtimes; tables are a little too close for privacy during the crowded evenings.

Babies and children admitted. Book dinner Fri, Sat. Separate rooms for parties, both seating 40. Takeaway service. Vegetarian menu. **Map 17 K7**.

West
Ladbroke Grove W10

★ **Makan**
270 Portobello Road, W10 5TY (8960 5169). Ladbroke Grove tube. **Meals served** 11.30am-9pm daily. **Main courses** £4-£6. **No credit cards**.

A basic caff sheltering under the Westway flyover, Makan looked promising when we counted a number of Malay families among its patrons. There was also a few backpackers present, attracted by its laid-back style. However, perhaps we should have ordered from the choice of ten ready-made dishes displayed at the counter (a good mix of meat and vegetarian, spicy and non-spicy), because the made-to-order food proved disappointing. We could hardly discern the coconut in the rice of the nasi lemak, and were aghast when chicken noodle soup turned out to

be a bowl of scraggly noodles with a few pieces of chicken and roughly cut carrots and celery immersed in bland stock. We quizzed the friendly staff about whether this dish was specifically Malay, but they responded with blank looks. Roti canai was a reliable bet, however, the bread light and crisp. Makan is also great for a quick bite of tasty Malay cakes, spring rolls and curry puffs. For mains, however, other Malay cafés serving similar fare (albeit at slightly higher prices) offer far better value for money.
Babies and children admitted. No-smoking. Takeaway service. Vegetarian menu.
Map 19 B2.

Notting Hill W11

★ Nyonya
2A Kensington Park Road, W11 3BU (7243 1800/www.nyonya.co.uk). Notting Hill Gate tube. **Lunch served** 11.30am-2.45pm, **dinner served** 6-10.30pm Mon-Fri. **Meals served** 11.30am-10.30pm Sat, Sun. **Main courses** £5.50-£8.50. **Credit** AmEx, DC, MC, V.
The pestle and mortar icon of Nyonya promises that the restaurant's Peranakan food will emulate that prepared in the days when Nyonyas (Peranakan women) painstakingly pounded spices fresh in a mortar. And, on the whole, so it does. Sambal brinjal was soft, silky and impregnated with the flavour of the sambal belachan (though this could have been spicier). The various spices in the curry tumis prawns were allowed to blend carefully so that each of the 15 (gasp!) prawns was wonderfully flavoured, with the fruity, sour taste of tamarind predominating. Replete as we were, we finished off a dessert of savoury and sweet kueh in no time – a delightful treat of contrasting flavours, colours and textures. Single diners might enjoy the communal eating on the ground floor, in a chic monochromatic setting enlivened by splashes of fuchsia. But take a cue from Nyonya's trendy old-timers and dine in a group on the more intimate first floor where you can linger over food and enjoy a window view overlooking three buzzing Notting Hill thoroughfares. Staff tend to be over-zealous in clearing dishes.
Babies and children welcome: high chair. Booking advisable. No smoking. Takeaway service. **Map 7 A7.**

Paddington W2

★ Satay House
13 Sale Place, W2 1PX (7723 6763/ www.satay-house.co.uk). Edgware Road tube/ Paddington tube/rail. **Lunch served** noon-3pm, **dinner served** 6-11pm daily. **Main courses** £5-£18.50. **Set meal** £13.50, £18, £25 per person (minimum 2). **Service** 10%. **Credit** AmEx, MC, V.
Initially, we were a trifle disconcerted that we had been seated too close to Satay House's semi-open kitchen for comfort. However, we soon bucked up as familiar aromas began to waft from the hob in our direction. Ikan bilis – fried until brown and crispy with pungent petai beans, then caramelised with sugar and sambal – was piquant and wonderful. Rojak achieved the essential balance between salty, sweet and sour, even if the dressing was too thin and the dried tofu lacked crunch. It was a pity that the chicken cooked in coconut milk and spices (ayam percik) wasn't allowed to simmer long enough for the spices to penetrate beneath the skin. Satay House is no place to linger and chat. Its regulars gave the menu only cursory glances before ordering their favourite dishes, then tucked into the food with relish, leaving soon after they had finished. The decor is forgettable too. But all of this matters little: the food will have you coming back to the Satay House time and again, especially given the reasonable prices. Promise yourself that next time you'll leave more room for one of the rich desserts.
Babies and children welcome: high chairs. Book weekends. Separate room for parties, seats 35. Takeaway service. **Map 8 E5.**

South East
London Bridge & Borough SE1

★ Champor-Champor
62-64 Weston Street, SE1 3QJ (7403 4600/ www.champor-champor.com). London Bridge tube/rail. **Lunch served** by appointment Mon-Sat. **Dinner served** 6.15-10.15pm Mon-Sat. **Set meal** £19.90 2 courses, £26 3 courses. **Service** 15%. **Credit** AmEx, JCB, MC, V.
With lush decor and inventive fusion-Malaysian cooking, Champor-Champor offers a unique and unexpected treat down a Southwark sidestreet. Props ranging from a serene Buddha to old wooden carved windows and doorways add a touch of Asian exoticism to the two intimate dining rooms, which were filled with diners on a weekday evening. Our starters – deliciously textured soft-shelled crab nigiri and an intriguing chekodok bilis rojak (dried fish fritter salad) with an authentic South-east Asian salty fishy kick – got the meal off to a flying start. Main courses proved just as impressive. A banana and turmeric curry audaciously served with petai bean rice (pungent petai beans are notoriously an acquired taste) was a rich, flavourful combination, while the tender holy basil-marinated veal fillet with hibiscus rice combined chilli-heat with sweetness. Given cooking of this standard we were unable to resist dessert. Pumpkin and cinnamon cheesecake managed to be both light in texture and gloriously indulgent, while steamed ginger cake with smoked banana ice-cream was simply heavenly. The drinks menu takes in saké, wines from around the world (including China, Georgia and Lebanon), cocktails and Asia-Pacific beers. Pleasantly attentive service completed what had been a great meal out.
Babies and children welcome: high chair. Booking essential. Disabled: toilet. Separate room for parties, seats 8. **Map 12 Q9.**

Georgetown
10 London Bridge Street, SE1 9SG (7357 7359/ www.georgetownrestaurants.co.uk). London Bridge tube/rail. **Lunch served** noon-2.30pm, **dinner served** 5.30-11pm daily. **Main courses** £7.75-£12.95. **Service** 10%. **Credit** AmEx, DC, MC, V.
If *Time Out* gave points purely for appearance, Georgetown would score highly, but we found it a little institutional: something not entirely out of keeping with the colonial theme. It's styled like a colonial Malay mansion, with wicker chairs, chandeliers, piped classical music and waiters in white tuxedos. The menu is divided into Malaysian, South Indian, Straits Chinese and vegetarian sections, with starters, mains and desserts for each genre. There were few lunchtime diners. The two-course set menu (£10) started well with soto ayam: a full-flavoured chicken soup with a hint of coriander. Another starter, trengganu rojak (spiced fruit salad with prawn paste), was a gamble, but it was tasty and fresh and served, unexpectedly, over flakes of white fish. To follow, the Butterworth nasi ayam was certainly authentic, with soy, garlic and chilli dipping sauces, a mound of soy-seasoned rice, and a bowl of unseasoned chicken broth, yet we found it a bit pedestrian. Service was impeccable, though, and we certainly got our money's worth for a tenner.
Babies and children welcome: high chairs. Booking advisable. Disabled: toilet. No-smoking tables. **Map 12 Q8.**

North
Crouch End N8

Satay Malaysia
10 Crouch End Hill, N8 8AA (8340 3286). Finsbury Park tube/rail then W7 bus. **Dinner served** 6-10.45pm Mon-Thur, Sun; 6-11.45pm Fri, Sat. **Main courses** £5.50-£12.50. **Set dinner** £11.50-£13.50 per person (minimum 2). **No credit cards.**
Like many of its competitors, Satay Malaysia is decked out in batik tablecloths and wall/ceiling hangings, but here the furnishings are somewhat

past their best. Nevertheless, the restaurant is several notches above the norm in terms of service – and food. The menu offers the usual Malaysian classics, but is more heavily tilted towards Chinese dishes. Sambal squid was impressive; the spankingly fresh squid stir-fried in a potent sambal chilli had us eating much more of the accompanying rice than intended. Sliced ginger, soy sauce and parsley garnishing were all that was needed for the fresh steamed trout. Less accomplished was the satay; the prawn was much too salty, and the gravy (an unsatisfying thin blend) suffered from too much tamarind and too few peanuts. Service, though, was attentive and winning; when quizzed about the ingredients, the waitress showed she knew the dish intimately. Good food, charming staff, low prices: not bad.
Babies and children welcome. Book weekends. Takeaway service. Vegetarian menu.

Swiss Cottage NW6

★ Singapore Garden
83A Fairfax Road, NW6 4DY (7624 8233). Swiss Cottage tube. **Lunch served** noon-2.45pm daily. **Dinner served** 6-10.45pm Mon-Thur, Sun; 6-11.15pm Fri, Sat. **Main courses** £5.50-£32.50. **Set lunch** (Mon-Fri) £7.50 2 courses, £9 3 courses. **Set meal** £22-£32.50 per person (minimum 2). **Minimum charge** £10 per person. **Service** 12.5%. **Credit** AmEx, DC, MC, V.
Although discreetly positioned on a Swiss Cottage backstreet, this established restaurant has no problem pulling in punters. A Sunday lunchtime visit found the two light, neat rooms filled with diners, tucking in with gusto. One reason for the continuing success undoubtedly lies in the parallel menus, which offer around 70 Chinese dishes plus a large range of Singaporean and Malaysian 'specialities'. Service, as on past visits, was polite and efficient, with dishes brought to our table with admirable timing. To start, daging otak otak proved to be deliciously spiced fish paste neatly wrapped in banana leaf parcels then grilled; and the exemplary chicken satay reminded us of just how good this dish can be. Main courses didn't disappoint either, from a rich rojak (fruit and vegetable salad tossed in a shrimp paste dressing), authentically featuring fresh pineapple and yambean, to tasty mee goreng (stir-fried noodles in a chilli sauce). Our favourite was the daging curry – tender beef and new potatoes in a fragrant, spicy coconut gravy – which had us fighting over the last spoonful. To drink, we chose chendol, a Malaysian coconut milk concoction, and the inevitable Tiger beer.
Babies and children welcome: high chairs. Booking advisable. Separate rooms for parties, seating 6 and 100. Tables outdoors (4, pavement). Takeaway service; delivery service (within 1-mile radius). **Map 28 A4.**

Turnpike Lane N8

Penang Satay House
9 Turnpike Lane, N8 0EP (8340 8707). Turnpike Lane tube/29 bus. **Dinner served** 6-11pm Mon-Thur; 6pm-midnight Fri, Sat. **Main courses** £4-£8.50. **Set meal** £11.90, £13.50 per person (minimum 2) 3 courses. **Credit** MC, V.
You're likely to emerge from here gratified, even if the food was nothing to rave about. The reason? Impeccable service, which comes with warm smiles. The manager bantered with his customers as he led them to their tables; an Indian family celebrated a birthday; and an African-American couple cosied up in a corner. The batik fabrics adorning the walls and tables prepare you for Indonesian cuisine, but instead the restaurant offers Malaysian-Singaporean and Chinese dishes. Roast duck was tasty, though its accompanying pancakes were starchy and parched; by the waiter's admission, they were bought from a supermarket. Prawn satay was a refreshing addition to the usual meat ensemble, yet the meats and seafood were grilled too evenly, lacking any flavoursome searing. Still, the peanut sauce was given a nice lift by pineapple purée. The waiter

RESTAURANTS

rightly steered us towards the spinach fried in sambal belachan; it must have been lifted from the wok at just the right instant, as its vibrant-green crunchiness and fresh flavours testified. *Babies and children welcome: high chairs. Booking essential. Takeaway service; delivery (within 2-mile radius on orders over £10). Vegetarian menu.* **For branches see index.**

Outer London
Croydon, Surrey

★ **Malay House**
60 Lower Addiscombe Road, Croydon, Surrey CR0 6AA (8666 0266). East Croydon rail then 197, 312, 410 bus. **Lunch served** noon-3pm Fri.

Dinner served 6-11pm Tue-Sat. **Meals served** 1-9pm Sun. **Main courses** £3.80-£9. **Set lunch** (Fri) £5.25 2 courses. **Buffet** (Sun) £7. **Unlicensed. Corkage** £1 per person. **Credit** MC, V.

Pretty watercolours of Malay village life adorning the walls; table mats made up of squares bearing photographs of South-east Asian spices; a relaxed vibe; and a menu with accurate and detailed descriptions of dishes – all immediately attracted us to this restaurant. But it was the traditional Malay food that won us over. Malay House, like Satay House (*see p207*) in Paddington, doesn't offer Chinese or pan-Asian dishes, and this specialisation in Malay classics pays off. Mee goreng, though not as spicy as promised, was a beguilingly tasty plate of springy noodles fried in chilli, curry powder and onions, sweetened with tomato slices and made tangy with a squeeze of lime. The taste of freshly grated coconut came through strongly in the coconut rice, and rendang chicken had been simmered just long enough for the chicken to absorb the spices (making it redolent with the fragrant scent of lemongrass and lime leaves) while retaining its moisture and tenderness. Customers were thin on the ground during a Friday lunchtime: surprising for a restaurant that serves really good food at reasonable prices.
Babies and children welcome: high chairs. Booking advisable Fri, Sat. Takeaway service; delivery service. Vegetarian menu.

Menu

Here are some common terms and dishes. Spellings can vary.

Acar: assorted pickled vegetables such as carrots, beans and onions, which are often spiced with turmeric and pepper.
Assam: tamarind.
Ayam: chicken.
Bergedel or **pergedel:** a spiced potato cake.
Blachan, belacan or **blacan:** dried fermented shrimp paste; it adds a piquant fishy taste to dishes.
Bumbu bali: a rich, chilli-hot sauce from Bali.
Char kway teow or **char kwai teow:** a stir-fry of rice noodles with meat and/or seafood with dark soy sauce and beansprouts. A Hakka Chinese-derived speciality of Singapore.
Chilli crab: fresh crab, stir-fried in a sweet, mild chilli sauce.
Daging: beef.
Ebi: shrimps.
Gado gado: a salad of blanched vegetables with a peanut-based sauce on top.
Galangal: also called lesser ginger, Laos root or blue ginger, this spice gives a distinctive flavour to many South-east Asian dishes.
Goreng: wok-fried.
Hainanese chicken rice: poached chicken served with rice cooked in chicken stock, a bowl of light chicken broth and a chilli-ginger dipping sauce.
Ho jien: oyster omelette, flavoured with garlic and chilli.
Ikan: fish.
Ikan bilis or **ikan teri:** tiny whitebait-like fish, often fried and made into a dry sambal (qv) with peanuts.
Kambing: actually goat, but in practice lamb is the usual substitute.
Kangkong or **kangkung:** water convolvulus, often called water spinach or swamp cabbage – an aquatic plant often steamed and used in salads with a spicy sauce.
Kari: curry.
Kecap manis: sweet dark Indonesian soy sauce.
Kelapa: coconut.
Kemiri: waxy-textured candlenuts, used to enrich Indonesian and Malaysian curry pastes.
Kerupuk: prawn crackers.

Laksa: a noodle dish with either coconut milk or (as with penang laksa) tamarind as the stock base; it's now popular in many South-east Asian cities.
Lemang: sticky Indonesian rice that is cooked in bamboo segments.
Lengkuas or **lenkuas:** Malaysian name for galangal (qv).
Lumpia: deep-fried spring rolls filled with meat or vegetables.
Masak lemak: anything cooked in a rich, red spice paste with coconut milk.
Mee: noodles.
Mee goreng: fried egg noodles with meat, prawns and vegetables.
Mee hoon: rice vermicelli noodles.
Murtabak: an Indian-Malaysian pancake fried on a griddle and served with a savoury filling.
Nasi goreng: fried rice with shrimp paste, garlic, onions, chillies and soy sauce.
Nasi lemak: coconut rice on a plate with a selection of curries and fish dishes topped with ikan bilis (qv).
Nonya or **Nyonya:** the name referring to both the women and the dishes of the Straits Chinese community. *See below* peranakan.
Otak otak: a Nonya (qv) speciality made from eggs, fish and coconut milk.
Pandan leaves: variety of the screwpine plant; used to add colour and fragrance to both savoury and sweet dishes.
Panggang: grilled or barbecued.
Peranakan: refers to the descendants of Chinese settlers who first came to Malacca (now Melaka), a seaport on the Malaysian west coast, in the 17th century. It is generally applied to those born of Sino-Malay extraction who adopted Malay customs, costume and cuisine, the community being known as 'Straits Chinese'. The cuisine is also known as Nonya (qv).
Petai: a pungent, flat green bean used in Malaysian cooking.
Poh pia or **popiah:** spring rolls. Nonya or Penang popiah are not deep-fried and consist of egg or rice paper wrappers filled with a vegetable and prawn medley.
Rempah: generic term for the fresh curry pastes used in Malaysian cookery.
Rendang: meat cooked in coconut milk, a 'dry' curry.
Rijsttafel: an Indonesian set meal of several courses; it means 'rice table' in Dutch.
Rojak: raw fruit and vegetables in a spicy sauce.

Roti canai: a South Indian/Malaysian breakfast dish of fried round, unleavened bread served with a dip of either chicken curry or dahl.
Sambal: there are several types of sambal, often made of fiery chilli sauce, onions and coconut oil; it can be served as a side dish or used as a relish. The suffix 'sambal' means 'cooked with chilli'.
Satay: there are two types – terkan (minced and moulded to the skewer) and chochok ('shish', more common in London). Beef or chicken are the traditional choices, though prawn is now often available too. Satay is served with a rich spicy sauce made from onions, lemongrass, galangal, and chillies in tamarind sauce; it is sweetened and thickened with ground peanuts.
Sayur: vegetables.
Soto: soup.
Soto ayam: a classic spicy Indonesian chicken soup, often with noodles.
Sotong: squid.
Tauhu: tofu, beancurd.
Tauhu goreng: deep-fried beancurd topped with beansprouts tossed in a spicy peanut sauce, served cold.
Telor: egg.
Tempeh or **tempe:** an Indonesian fermented soy bean product; similar to tofu, it has a more varied texture and can look like peanut butter.
Terong: aubergine.
Tersai or **trassie:** alternative names for blachan (qv).
Udang: prawns.

DESSERTS
Bubor pulut hitam: black glutinous rice served in coconut milk and palm sugar.
Cendol or **chendol:** mung bean flour pasta, which is coloured and perfumed with essence of pandan leaf (qv) and served in a chilled coconut milk and palm sugar syrup.
Es: ice; a prefix for the multitude of desserts made with combinations of fruit salad, agar jelly cubes, palm syrup, condensed milk and crushed ice.
Es kacang: shaved ice and syrup mixed with jellies, red beans and sweetcorn.
Gula melaka: palm sugar, an important ingredient with a distinctive, caramel flavour added to a sago and coconut-milk pudding of the same name.
Kueh or **kuih:** literally, 'cakes', but used as a general term for many desserts.
Pisang goreng: banana fritters.

RESTAURANTS

Mediterranean

The health claims made for the Mediterranean diet, coupled with a general move towards the fusing of cuisines, has led to a strong showing for London's Med restaurants over the past few years. Though olive oil is de rigueur, flavours can come from the southern European, the North African and the Middle Eastern sides of the sea. So expect anything from harissa to provençal sauce to accompany your fresh tuna steak.

Central

City EC3

Royal Exchange Grand Café & Bar
The Royal Exchange, EC3V 3LR (7618 2480/ www.conran.com). Bank tube/DLR. **Breakfast served** 8-11am Mon-Fri. **Meals served** 11.30am-10pm Mon-Fri. **Main courses** £6.50-£14.50. **Service** 12.5%. **Credit** AmEx, DC, MC, V.
The astoundingly grand Royal Exchange building (the current edifice dates from 1844) makes an impressive dining spot. It comes complete with delicately carved stonework and high arches that are now home to boutiques such as Tiffany's. And you can indeed breakfast here, on crumpets, muffins, brownies and fruit compote. The café occupies the centre of a spacious courtyard, its circular bar flanked by steel tables. Upstairs, the mezzanine's twin bars are a little removed from the majestic setting, but prove admirably relaxed despite the sometimes noisy chinwagging City workers. Running contrary to the splendidly chic Conran decor, dining is a casual experience. Cold snacks, such as antipasti and charcuterie boards, predominate: stylishly assembled but unexciting. A slightly dry rose-harissa chicken came with roast vegetable couscous. Good chips are a mainstay, as is seafood (lobster sandwich, crab tartine, langoustine mayonnaise). All are treated with courtesy here, but the sevruga caviar (£55) will probably remind you that this is the Square Mile. *Babies and children admitted (restaurant). Bookings not accepted. Disabled: toilet. Dress: smart casual.* **Map 12 Q6.**

Soho W1

Aurora
49 Lexington Street, W1F 9AT (7494 0514). Oxford Circus tube. **Lunch served** 12.30-3pm Mon-Sat. **Dinner served** 6.30-10pm Mon, Tue; 6.30-10.30pm Wed-Sat. **Main courses** £11.95-£13.50. **Service** 12.5%. **Credit** MC, V.
In terms of atmosphere, this quaint little restaurant is glorious, the kind of unaffected place where you instantly feel at home. Housed in one of Soho's more venerable 18th-century houses, it sports unfussy decor and deep-red walls that convey an air of shabby chic. Where Aurora falls down is in the quality of its food – much of the eclectic menu resembles something you could knock up at home. The highlight was pan-fried kesslar ham on warm puy lentils: a hearty starter that went some way towards sating our appetite. Smoked mackerel salad with fennel and raisin coleslaw was less appealing, too much vinaigrette sitting alongside the mayo. On to the mains, where a tough duck breast was eclipsed by good carrot, swede and turnip mash with salsa verde; grilled tuna steak on pak choi with oyster mushrooms and jasmine rice was unremarkable. An unadventurous wine list further deters lingering. *Babies and children admitted. Booking advisable. Separate room for parties, seats 18. Tables outdoors (10, courtyard).* **Map 17 J6.**

West

Brook Green W6

Snow's on the Green
166 Shepherd's Bush Road, W6 7PB (7603 2142/ www.snowsonthegreen.co.uk). Hammersmith tube. **Lunch served** noon-3pm Mon-Fri. **Dinner served** 6-11pm Mon-Sat. **Main courses** £10.50-£16. **Set meal** £12.50 2 courses, £16.50 3 courses. **Service** 12.5% for parties of 6 or more. **Credit** AmEx, DC, MC, V.
A popular spot for more than a decade, Snow's has always seemed a smart, well-managed local, fresh and airy, decorated with a few Bill Brandt nudes. On this occasion, though, our evening was tainted by carelessness. Service came with a smile. Unfortunately, that smile extended to everyone

Sarastro Restaurant
"The Show After The Show"

A sumptuous treasure trove hidden within a Grade II listed Victorian townhouse, Sarastro is perfectly locate in the heart of London's Theatreland. A wide selection of delicious Mediterranean dishes are served with theatrical flair and passion against the elaborate backdrop of golden drapes and decorative frescoed walls. Sarastro is ideal for pre- and post-theatre dining with a menu available at **£12.50**.

Lunch is served every day.

A private function room is available for corporate and red carpet occasions (for up to 300 guests).

126 Drury Lane, London WC2
Tel: 020 7836 0101 Fax: 020 7379 4666
www.sarastro-restaurant.com E: reservations@sarastro-restaurant.com

Papageno Restaurant & Bar
"Seeing is believing"

Nestling in the heart of London's bustling Covent Garden, Papageno is dedicated to pre- and post-theatre dining. Open all day, seven days a week, guests are invited to eat from an exclusive a la carte menu or choose from special set theatre meals available from £12.50.

Available for private functions, weddings, parties and other events for up to 700 guests, Papageno has one of London's most exquisite rooms with its own private entrance and bar.

29-31 Wellington Street, London WC2
Tel: 020 7836 4444 Fax: 020 7836 0011
www.papagenorestaurant.com E: reservations@papagenorestaurant.com

simultaneously, meaning our waiter would wander off – even midway through pouring the wine. Behind the scenes (but in earshot), voices were raised; dishes, we heard, had been getting mixed up all week. If you repeat ingredients when ordering (starters of courgette and lemon soup, and deep-fried courgette flower with ricotta, mint and peperonata, for instance), staff need to be alert. The Italian-influenced menu swung from brilliant (a parmesan starter topped with al dente seasonal veg and a perfectly poached egg) to horrid (crab lasagnette, which had shards of brittle shell), and averaged around fair (rabbit leg had too much sun-dried tomato stuffing; raspberry brioche bread and butter pudding lacked much fruit). Music was loud and clubby. We hope this was simply an off night. *Babies and children welcome: high chair. Separate rooms for parties, seating 15 and 26. Vegetarian menu.* **Map 20 C3**.

South West
South Kensington SW7

★ Bistrot 190
190 Queensgate, SW7 5EU (7584 6601/ www.gorehotel.co.uk). Gloucester Road or South Kensington tube. **Meals served** 7am-11.30pm Mon-Fri; 7.30am-midnight Sat; 7.30am-11.30pm Sun. **Main courses** £10.50-£19.95. **Service** 12.5%. **Credit** AmEx, DC, MC, V.
The 'Bistrot' name-tag belies this restaurant's upmarket setting: within the Gore, a luxurious hotel that prides itself on Victorian grandeur. The surroundings are duly resplendent, including the walnut and mahogany-panelled Bar 190 (opposite the bistro) and some rather ornate bedrooms. The restaurant is charming, its walls congested with dozens of old pictures, the service informal and unhurried. The Franco-Italian dishes are simply presented but quite inventive. A starter of spiced yellow split-pea soup was thick and dahl-like; goat's curd chilli added extra pep. Smoked mackerel was robust enough to be paired with a strongly flavoured herby salad. Mains were also impressive: grilled bream had a lively combo of capers, raisins and almonds blended with parsley and a little lemon; duck leg, beautifully slow roasted, offset the expected orange with caramelised endive. Don't skip dessert. Chocolate brownie, already good, came with salted caramel ice-cream that took it to another level. Prices are perhaps over the odds (the substantial wine list is costly too), but the dishes have indisputable flair. *Babies and children welcome: high chairs. Booking advisable. No-smoking tables. Separate room for parties, seats 24.* **Map 8 D9**.

South East
Crystal Palace SE19

Numidie
48 Westow Hill, SE19 1RX (8766 6166/ www.numidie.co.uk). Gypsy Hill rail. **Meals served** 10am-10.30pm Tue-Sun. **Main courses** £7.25-£12.50. **Credit** MC, V.
With its dark-hued walls, aged mirrors, strings of plastic veg and token chandelier, Numidie has the appealing air of a French bistro muddled with a slightly shabby English dining room. Dishes are many and varied, predominantly French and North African, and, for the most part, enjoyable. To start, courgette fritter was tasty, the vivid green slices glued together with molten roquefort offset by a slim swirl of sweet black cherry sauce. A simple main course of lamb shank proved yielding and tender; steamed couscous and buttery seasonal veg increased its comfort-food status. Red mullet stuffed with an aubergine and anchovy tapenade was marred by an onslaught of garlic. A crêpe enrobing a tantalising scoop of own-made honey and cinnamon ice-cream came from a handful of simple desserts. Overall, Numidie's food is above average, but it's the one-offness of the place that locals love. Downstairs is a popular and equally characterful bar. *Babies and children welcome: high chairs. Booking advisable. No-smoking tables. Separate room for parties, seats 20.*

East
Shoreditch EC2

Cantaloupe
35 Charlotte Road, EC2A 3PB (7613 4411/ www.cantaloupe.co.uk). Old Street tube/rail/55 bus. Bar **Open** 11am-midnight Mon-Fri; noon-midnight Sat; noon-11.30pm Sun. *Restaurant* **Lunch served** noon-3pm Mon-Fri. **Brunch served** noon-5pm Sun. **Dinner served** 6-11pm Mon-Fri; 7-11pm Sat. **Main courses** £9.50-£16.50. **Service** 12.5%. *Both* **Credit** AmEx, DC, JCB, MC, V.
Space, buzz, modernity – all three qualities are nicely realised within the sprawling crimson interior of Cantaloupe. This open-plan bar-cum-restaurant is the landmark Shoreditch venue from the group behind Cargo and W1's equally stylish Market Place. Food is a fashionable Spanish-North African mix, served mainly as tapas-size portions, alongside lamb or beef burgers and a few steaks. Kibbeh, a handful of heavily spiced lamb and bulgar wheat patties, were dense and fragrantly spiced; succulent chicken chermoula brochettes proved a lighter option, the tasty skewered cubes fired up by a sweet piquant dipping sauce. But vegetable empaniditas were unexciting, the thick puff pastry drowning the filling. Such finger food is ideal for dipping into with a gang of pals, but most tables are for twos, which seems curious given the group mentality of the place. Packs of trendsters swamp the bar, and dining is a noisy experience. You chomp along to a backdrop of bar chat and either DJs or their specially selected iPod playlists. *Babies and children admitted. Disabled: toilet. Entertainment: DJ 8pm Fri-Sun.* **Map 6 R4**.

★ Eyre Brothers
70 Leonard Street, EC2A 4QX (7613 5346/ www.eyrebrothers.co.uk). Old Street tube/rail. **Lunch served** noon-3pm Mon-Fri. **Dinner served** 6.30-11pm Mon-Sat. **Main courses** £13-£22. **Service** 12.5%. **Credit** AmEx, DC, MC, V.
Mahogany panels extend across the floor, walls and ceiling, lending the Eyre Brothers' understated dining area a retro edge. With one side devoted to a long bar, the other a window, it feels spacious. Robert and David Eyre serve high-quality Iberian food. Service was professional and informative. Our softly spoken waiter described the amuse bouche (cubes of pork on clams in a piquant tomato sauce), but hovered no longer than necessary. The appetising menu changes often, but always displays the Eyres' fondness for Spanish flavours and Portuguese regional cooking, the latter developed during their childhood in colonial Mozambique. Dishes are delicious and unapologetically hearty: stewed rabbit, tangy in wine vinegar with strong herbs, was complemented by the plainness of boiled potatoes simply garnished with parsley; caldeirada, a thick Portuguese fish soup, combined a good mix of clams, mussels, prawns, monkfish, dorada (sea bream), tuna and halibut in a nourishing broth. Difficult to fault, and a grown-up find in this DJ bar-strewn side of town. *Babies and children admitted. Booking advisable. No-smoking tables. Restaurant available for hire.* **Map 6 Q4**.

North East
Stoke Newington N16

Mesclun
24 Stoke Newington Church Street, N16 0LU (7249 5029/www.mesclunrestaurant.com). Bus 73. **Open** 7-11pm Tue-Thur; noon-11pm Fri-Sun. **Main courses** £8.80-£13.50. **Set lunch** £8.50 2 courses, £11.50 3 courses. **Service** (dinner) 10%. **Credit** AmEx, MC, V.
Abstract canvases and giant coloured glass panels lit by strings of spotlights would give this high-ceilinged neighbourhood favourite a chilled, urbane vibe, were it not for the inordinately jolly welcome. Having sat precisely where we wanted (at the back by the french windows), we then shifted to another, less draughty spot, yet the waitress's smile remained undiminished. The menu offers simple

Interview
ROBERT EYRE

Who are you?
Manager of **Eyre Brothers** (*see p211*), run with chef and brother David Eyre.
Eating in London: what's good about it?
Eating locally is very good. We all have our own little routes and go to the same restaurants all the time.
What's bad about it?
Service – which is what I'm in charge of at Eyre Brothers. It can be unpredictable. Waiting lists seem to be unavoidable. As a restaurateur, everyone wanting to eat at the same time is a problem. And everyone following the trend for the latest place.
Which are your favourite London restaurants?
My local restaurants. That means the bar at the **Rivington Bar & Grill** (*see p61*). I like proper char-grilling, such as at **Mangal** (*see p276*), especially at 2am. My two favourite 'proper' restaurants are the **Capital** (*see p126*) for lunch, and **J Sheekey's** (*see p85*) for eating at the bar, because it's easy and I know them.
What single thing would improve London's restaurant scene?
I think we'd all like to be able to eat a lot later, or at different times, without being told that there is no wine available or only bar food. I'd like 18-hour restaurants, a bit like the **Wolseley** (*see p226*). I'd also like the green belt of London to be used by people who grow produce – lovely lambs and suckling pigs for us – instead of having brownfield sites and housing developments.
Any hot tips for the coming year?
People need to be more adventurous when buying wine. It would be nice if people knew their vintages for Rioja as well as they know their vintage clarets and Burgundies.
Anything to declare?
I'm quite partial to a pork pie, homemade, and late-night salt beef.

appetisers like smoked haddock fish cakes, deep-fried mozzarella and grilled sardine fillets. It buttresses these humble beginnings with about ten eclectic mains (the mesclun being a not very authentic version of a kind of provençal salad). Potato walnut gnocchi had a heavy, pungent gorgonzola and basil sauce, while grilled sirloin steak came with Marsala jus and a carrot purée nicely seasoned with nutmeg. All meat is organic and free-range. Desserts are a boon if you've a 'more is more' mentality about chocolate; fresh strawberry trifle, for instance, favours the unusual addition of white chocolate crème anglaise. Note: a 10% cover charge is added to your bill at dinner, but the credit card chit reads 'service not included'. *Babies and children welcome: high chairs. Booking advisable.* **Map 25 C1**.

North
Islington EC1

Café Med
370 St John Street, EC1V 4NN (7278 1199/ www.cafemed.co.uk). Angel tube. **Meals served** noon-11pm Mon-Sat; noon-10.30pm Sun. **Main courses** £8.50-£16.50. **Set lunch** (noon-5pm Mon-Fri) £9.95 2 courses. **Set dinner** (5-7pm Mon-Fri) £11.95 2 courses. **Service** 12.5%. **Credit** AmEx, MC, V.
Converted from an old boozer, but with precious little in the way of added sparkle, this is a dark, cavernous restaurant. Dishes are modern bistro standards (risotto, salmon fish cake, caesar salad, breaded veal escalope, duck confit), but what they lack in flair, they compensate for with quantity. Take the fries – wafer-thin, yes, but piled to the rafters. Warm halloumi and tabouleh salad? An epic chomp through slabs of grilled cheese, chunky roasted peppers, courgette and red onion. And the steak? You can choose up to 22oz of beef on the bone (serves two). Spicy moroccan lamb sausages qualify as a starter, but would probably do better as a light main. To finish there is a fine array of puds such as apple pie, baked cheesecake and a lovely creamy affogato, proving that when it comes to iced concoctions, the Italian approach is hard to beat. Service is friendly.
Babies and children welcome: children's menu; high chairs. Booking advisable. Disabled: toilet. Separate room for parties, seats 40. **Map 5 O3**. **For branches see index.**

North West
Hampstead NW3

Base
71 Hampstead High Street, NW3 1QP (7431 2224/www.basefoods.com). Hampstead tube. **Lunch served** noon-4pm Mon-Fri; noon-5pm Sat. **Dinner served** 6-10.45pm Tue-Sat. **Meals served** noon-10.30pm Sun. **Main courses** £6.95-£16.95. **Credit** AmEx, MC, V.
When a restaurant website boasts that 'famous international sports stars and celebrities' are among the regulars, you'd be forgiven for thinking it has pretensions, or worse, pretentious customers. Thankfully, Base has neither. A down-to-earth affair with plain white walls and red banquettes, it is a café by day, but come the evening it keeps the Hampstead hordes swinging in through its narrow doors with a well-executed selection of standards. You won't be surprised by the food – pan-fried cod with crushed new potatoes, and ribeye steak with pepper sauce and potato wedges – but you will be satisfied. Pappardelle with asparagus and beans was pasta perfection: gloriously rich and creamy with wide, evenly coated ribbons. Pudding-wise, profiteroles with freshly made vanilla ice-cream are a stand-out. A couple of minor quibbles – the wine list is quite short and, on our last visit, service was a little harassed and slow.
Babies and children welcome: high chairs. Booking advisable. No-smoking tables. Tables outdoors (8, pavement). Takeaway service (noon-4pm Mon-Fri). Vegetarian menu. Vegan dishes. **Map 28 B2**. **For branches see index.**

Middle Eastern

The Middle East may be composed of a dozen or more countries, but when it comes to cuisine you're really talking Lebanese. The Egyptians, Syrians, Jordanians and Gulf Arabs may have their own regional specialities, but much of the food is similar, and in any case the Lebanese often do it better. More to the point, it is the entrepreneurial Lebanese who took the restaurant business out of their own country to cater for Arabs worldwide, where it was discovered by other discerning diners.

Lebanese food is all about meze. The typical meal involves a table of these small hors d'oeuvres shared between all. It's an extremely social way of dining. Grilled meats arrive at the end of the meal and, again, are meant for sharing. Dessert options rarely extend beyond the honey-soaked nutty pastries that are generically known as baklava.

The only Middle Eastern cuisine that differs significantly is Iranian. Many Iranian restaurants in London devote themselves to kebabs: lamb or chicken, fillet or minced. The marinated and tenderised meat comes with mounds of fluffy, saffron-stained long-grain rice, a grilled tomato and vast discs of taftun, a chapati-like bread. It's a working-class meal, and a delicious one, and London's best Iranian restaurants are all modest affairs. Kebabs are sometimes supplemented with a daily special, typically a stew of some description, but that's about as far as the options extend. Which is a shame as it is in the stews that you find the full flowering of Persian cuisine: courtly and exquisite combinations where powdered walnuts and meat juices combine to make a luxuriant sauce, and pomegranate adds another level of flavour. Spices like cinnamon, cloves, cardamom and fenugreek also feature.

Most of London's Middle Eastern restaurants are clustered along the Edgware Road, but you'll find smaller enclaves in Bayswater and Olympia. The healthy nature of much Middle Eastern food – lots of salads, pulses and puréed veg – seems to be proving a hit with Londoners, and in recent times Lebanese 'fast food' outlets such as **Ranoush** and **Al-Dar** have expanded across the city.

Central
Edgware Road NW1, W1, W2

★ Al-Dar
61-63 Edgware Road, W2 2HZ (7402 2541/ www.aldar.co.uk). Marble Arch tube. **Meals served** 8am-1am daily. **Main courses** £8.95-£10.50. **Set meze** £9.50-£10.50. **Service** 10%. **Credit** (over £10) AmEx, MC, V. Lebanese
Though spacious, Al-Dar now looks a little worn around the edges. Nevertheless, its orangey marble table tops are still home to generous platefuls of honest Lebanese food. All the standards are here: a full range of meze dishes, as well as kebabs. The speciality is fruit juices, fruit cocktails and milkshakes – whopping portions of vitamin C in appetising combinations, served in sundae glasses. Juices, and food, are prepared behind a long counter on one side of the space (there's a shisha lounge, also belonging to Al-Dar, next door). Dishes tend to be a notch below best restaurant standards, and the reasonable prices (for Edgware Road) reflect this. Our favourite meze on a recent visit was a zesty bitinjan rahib: mashed aubergine dip flavoured with garlic, with a good lemony tang. We accompanied it with tabouleh (a large portion, a bit rough and ready, but tasty) and chicken livers in a light lemony sauce. Al-Dar is perfect for a grabbed snack or a satisfying lunch, but doesn't have the kind of ambience to make you want to spend an evening here.
Babies and children welcome: high chairs. Takeaway service; delivery service. **Map 8 F6**. **For branches see index.**

★ ★ Kandoo
458 Edgware Road, W2 1EJ (7724 2428). Edgware Road tube. **Meals served** noon-midnight daily. **Main courses** £5.60-£10.30. **Unlicensed. Corkage** no charge. **Service** 10%. **Credit** MC, V. Iranian
Prettily decorated with apricot-coloured walls, potted plants and colourful tiles, this friendly Iranian restaurant provides a welcome haven from a gritty stretch of the Edgware Road. As Kandoo doesn't serve alcohol (though diners can bring their own booze), we opted instead for doogh (a

Al Waha. See p216.

creamy, minted yoghurt drink) and freshly squeezed carrot juice. Sitting near the window close to the tiled oven gave us a prime view of the bread-making ritual. Watching the attention the chef devoted to rolling out the dough into a flatbread, then seeing it brought freshly baked to our table added a nice touch of theatre. With it we enjoyed simple, fresh, flavoursome starters, including spinach with yoghurt, a garlicky aubergine dip and fragrant tarragon, mint and white cheese. Main courses were also lovingly cooked, with the minced lamb kebab dangerously moreish. Dish of the day proved to be a generous portion of tender chicken covered with saffron-yellow rice and a generous sprinkling of red barberries. We left too full to eat another mouthful, but keen to return soon.

Babies and children welcome: high chairs.
Tables outdoors (10, garden). Takeaway service.
Map 2 D4.

★ Maroush Gardens
1-3 Connaught Street, W2 2DH (7262 0222/ www.maroush.com). Marble Arch tube. **Meals served** noon-midnight daily. **Main courses**

£12-£22. **Set dinner** £21-£35 per person (minimum 2) 3 courses. **Credit** AmEx, DC, MC, V. Lebanese
There are now eight Maroush outlets in London, plus four Ranoushes and one Beirut Express, all part of the same chain, and with more promised. We prefer this one for its big main dining room, which, when busy – and it usually is – buzzes like a mainline train station. Troops of black-jacketed waiters service the dozens of big round tables. The space is light, airy and full of greenery. Paunchy Middle Eastern businessmen dine here. As one of the oldest Lebanese restaurants in town, Maroush has had time to get the food right, and it does. The menu runs to around 60 hot and cold meze, plus mains. It's strong on offal (kidneys, liver, tongue, testicles) and preparations involving raw minced meat. Lots of lemon and pomegranate juice is used in the flavouring, as well as mint and cumin. The results are superb; this is some of the most refined Lebanese cooking you'll find in London. The wine list is also good, or there's the Levantine aniseed spirit arak. While the original Maroush, at 21 Edgware Road, remains popular for its belly dancing, this branch is where to treat your taste buds.

Babies and children admitted. Booking advisable.
Map 8 F6.
For branches (Maroush, Ranoush, Beirut Express) see index.

★ Meya Meya NEW
13 Bell Street, NW1 5BY (7723 8983). Edgware Road tube. **Meals served** 9am-11pm daily. **Main courses** £3.50-£7.25. **Unlicensed**. **Corkage** £5. **Service** 15%. **No credit cards**. Egyptian
There's nothing quite like Egyptian peasant food to give outstanding value for money. Here at Meya Meya, whose name implies you're getting 100%, you feel as though you're in the heart of Cairo. The shop, which also operates a free local delivery service, prides itself on serving the only fiteer (Egyptian pizza) in Britain. The fiteer are prepared and baked in full view at the front of the shop where the dough gets tossed in the air and then filled with all manner of ingredients. Our khan el khalili variety was deliciously doughy and came stuffed with savoury mince and onions, along with tomato and olives. A bowl of kushari, another salubrious Egyptian speciality, is a dream for vegetarians with its layers of macaroni, rice, lentils,

tomato sauce and crispy fried onions. A complimentary glass of tamarhindi (a dark, syrupy tamarind drink) added an authentic touch, as did the karkadeh (a ruby-red infusion of hibiscus flowers). The loud Egyptian TV may put off those wanting a quiet meal, but the downstairs dining area is nevertheless clean and cosy, featuring plush cushions and traditional inlaid furniture.
Babies and children admitted. No-smoking tables. Takeaway service; delivery service. **Map 2 E5.**

★ Patogh
8 Crawford Place, W1H 5NE (7262 4015). Edgware Road tube. **Meals served** 1pm-midnight daily. **Main courses** £6-£12. **Unlicensed. Corkage** no charge. **No credit cards**. Iranian
Patogh's interior is, well, unusual. Nicotine coloured paint covers the rough-hewn walls of the small space (there's a second room upstairs). This is a classic kebab restaurant: food is reliable; portions are huge. Dishes are prepared behind a corner counter that encloses a traditional mosaic bread oven. Massive flatbread discs, big enough to hang over the largest plate, emerge from here and are served warm at the table. We began a recent meal in typical style with sabzi, a plate of leaves (mainly twigs of mint) served with radishes and a square of feta – used as a palate cleanser. We also sampled masto moosir (a yoghurt dip with shallots), great with some of that bread. Next came a superb chicken kebab: soft cubes of meat marinated in saffron and served with rice Iranian-style. Perfect rice is integral to Iranian cuisine. Cooked to a fluffy but non-sticky consistency and served with a knob of butter and a grilled tomato, it was superb sprinkled with warm red sumac spice. A great venue for classic Persian food.
Book weekends. Takeaway service. **Map 8 E5.**

★ Ranoush Juice Bar
43 Edgware Road, W2 2JR (7723 5929/ www.maroush.com). Marble Arch tube. **Meals served** 8am-3am daily. **Main courses** £3-£10. **No credit cards**. Lebanese

An Edgware Road classic, Ranoush serves shawarma sandwiches, fruit juices (a long list including the likes of melon and mango), and meze dishes to folk who dash in and out of the often busy café and takeaway. Things can get frenetic and the staff aren't noted for friendliness; mind you, they're often absorbed filling huge shawarma takeaway orders. You make your choice, pay at the till, then take your receipt to the juice man or the food man. The few marble-topped tables and the counter, where customers can eat-in, can be full. In Ranoush's favour, portions are huge. A heaped bowl of tabouleh, for example, is meant to be shared and is always served carefully with a lettuce garnish; houmous usually comes with a dip in the middle, filled with olive oil. Ranoush is part of the Maroush chain, and although its approach is very different to the bow-tied formality of the restaurants, the food is consistently good. Choices also include falafel, sujuk, batata hara and warak einab.
Babies and children welcome. Takeaway service; delivery service. **Map 8 F6.**
For branches see index.

Marylebone W1, NW1

Al Fawar
50 Baker Street, W1U 7BT (7224 4777/ www.alfawar.com). Baker Street tube. **Meals served** noon-midnight daily. **Main courses** £12.50-£13.90. **Set meal** £25 3 courses incl coffee and dessert. **Cover** £2 (à la carte). **Credit** AmEx, DC, JCB, MC, V. Lebanese
Despite being housed in a modern block on Baker Street, this large restaurant has a traditionally decorous interior. Murals of Lebanese scenery add a distinctly colourful note. Prompt professional service from smartly clad waiters, overseen by a besuited maître d', made for a smooth-running meal. A complimentary bowl of notably fresh salad vegetables and olives (presumably paid for by the £2 a head cover charge) arrived with our

drinks as a welcome nibble. Opting to graze, we chose a selection of meze dishes, accompanied by warm flatbread solicitously served and replenished throughout the meal. Cold meze included parsley-rich tabouleh, smooth creamy labneh and houmous shawarma topped with tender, full-flavoured lamb; the hot dishes comprised robust, tasty fuul medames, baby okra in tomato sauce, and savoury lamb pastry parcels. In all, it proved to be a highly satisfying meal. Lebanese coffee and rosewater-flavoured hot water – served with a plateful of traditional sweet pastries – rounded off our repast nicely.
Babies and children welcome: high chairs. Book dinner. Dress: smart casual. Restaurant available for hire. Takeaway service; delivery service (within 3-mile radius). **Map 9 G5.**

★ Ali Baba
32 Ivor Place, NW1 6DA (7723 7474/5805). Baker Street tube/Marylebone tube/rail. **Meals served** noon-midnight daily. **Main courses** £8-£10. **Unlicensed. Corkage** no charge. **Service** 10%. **No credit cards**. Egyptian
Egyptian food, on its own, may never become the height of fashion, but that's not to say it can't be deeply satisfying. Don't be put off by Ali Baba's kebab-shop front. Walk through to the simple dining room at the back. With Egyptians chatting around you, papyrus paintings on every wall, and the sound of upbeat Arabic music, it's hard to believe you're just around the corner from Baker Street. The food is true to its roots, delicious and just what you'd find in a typical home in Cairo. The national dish of fuul (brown beans) and ta'amia (falafel) were brought out in the traditional way, accompanied by a plate of torshi (pickles). Stuffed vine leaves arrived warm, which was a nice surprise, but in keeping with the meze style of this cuisine our other dishes came very shortly afterwards. Egypt's ancient peasant soup, molokhia, was garlicky. Bamia, a tomato-based stew with okra, had chunks of meat so tender it

alone would give us reason to come back. A great place for a quick and thoroughly tasty bite to eat. *Babies and children welcome: high chairs. Booking advisable. Takeaway service; delivery service.* Map 2 F4.

Fairuz
3 Blandford Street, W1H 3AA (7486 8108/ 8182/www.fairuz.uk.com). Baker Street or Bond Street tube. **Meals served** noon-11.30pm Mon-Sat; noon-10.30pm Sun. **Main courses** £9.95-£18.95. **Set meze** £18.95. **Set meal** £26.95 3 courses. **Cover** £1.50. **Credit** AmEx, DC, MC, V. Lebanese
For several years Fairuz was a favourite of ours, serving great Lebanese food in homely rustic-bistro surroundings. On this visit, the place still looked the same – yellow walls, a few artefacts, wooden tables – but something was awry. The maître d' was the first problem. At around 7pm in an almost empty restaurant he insisted we'd have to be out by 8.30pm: just in case other diners happened by. Having grudgingly agreed to seat us, he handed us over to other staff who were as pleasant and professional as ever. We remained hopeful about the food, but this time it didn't have that sharp edge of colour and zest. Foul moukala (broad beans fried in olive oil, with lemon juice) was rather sludgy, bland and overcooked; bitinjan bil laban (aubergine in yoghurt) was something of a nonentity. Arayes bil jibneh (pitta bread stuffed with grilled cheese) was better, and a main of farouj moussahab was a well-grilled boneless chicken with satisfyingly thick garlic mayonnaise. So not all bad, but the unfriendly greeting put us off; we hope this was just an off-night.
Babies and children welcome: high chairs. Book dinner. Takeaway service; delivery service. Map 9 G5.

Levant
Jason Court, 76 Wigmore Street, W1U 2SJ (7224 1111/www.levant.co.uk). Bond Street tube. Bar **Open** noon-1am daily. *Restaurant* **Meals served** noon-11.30pm Mon-Fri. **Dinner served** 5.30-11.30pm Sat, Sun. **Main courses** £11.25-£25. **Set lunch** (noon-6pm Mon-Fri) £12.50 2 courses. **Set dinner** £24.50-£35 3 courses. **Service** 15%. *Both* **Credit** AmEx, DC, JCB, MC, V. Lebanese
The waft of incense as we made our way down the dimly lit steps to this basement bar and restaurant hinted at exotic things to come. Levant opts for opulence à la *Arabian Nights*, decked out as it is with dark wooden carvings, crimson rose petals scattered on the table, and hypnotic music. The exotic setting pulls in a lively, cosmopolitan crowd, with diners ranging from large youthful parties to couples. The menu is predominantly Lebanese, though with a few original touches. We opted for meze, and a series of prettily presented dishes were brought to our table: tabouleh, silky houmous with lamb, and fried aubergine with pomegranate sauce. A highlight was the octopus salad: tender chunks of octopus in a savoury dressing flavoured with fresh coriander. The only dish that didn't work was the crab kibbeh: the crab's delicate flavour was lost because of the thick bulgar wheat coating. Staff were polite, and one waitress was particularly attentive, yet as the restaurant filled, service became more sporadic. Overall, though, we were favourably impressed. We're rather less keen on sister restaurant Levantine in Paddington, which pushes the oriental fantasia shtick even further and serves disappointing food.
Booking advisable. Entertainment: belly dancer 8.30pm. Separate area for parties, seats 12. Takeaway service. Map 9 G6.
For branch (Levantine) see index.

Mayfair W1

Al Hamra
31-33 Shepherd Market, W1Y 7HR (7493 1954/ www.alhamrarestaurant.com). Green Park or Hyde Park Corner tube. **Meals served** noon-11.30pm daily. **Main courses** £14-£22.50. **Minimum** £20. **Cover** £2.50. **Credit** AmEx, DC, JCB, MC, V. Lebanese

On a corner site in Shepherd Market, Al Hamra is a hardy perennial on the elite Lebanese dining circuit, packed most nights with an international Mayfair clientele. Its popularity – combined with closely packed tables in the middle of the room (better to choose the banquettes around the edges) and a low ceiling – can make it seem claustrophobic. Decor remains unchanged; it's still all crisp white linen, patterned curtains, carpeted floor. Food consistently hits the high notes. Star of a recent meal was a simple 'Lebanese salad'. Very ordinary ingredients (lettuce, tomato, cucumber) of the utmost freshness arrived doused in a lemony, slightly spicy dressing: fantastic. Other hits included a mellow fuul medames, delicious mushed up with the olive oil that had been generously poured on top; sabanak bil zeit (spinach cooked with oil), garnished with caramelised onions; a thick, nutty houmous; crispy falafel with tahina sauce; and smoky grilled chicken wings. We enjoyed it all. Our only gripe was that waiting staff seemed overstretched. A waiter drifted away while telling us about the pastries – but these moist little parcels went nicely with a cup of turkish coffee.
Babies and children welcome: high chairs. Book dinner. Tables outdoors (24, terrace). Takeaway service; delivery service (orders over £20). Map 9 H8.

Al Sultan
51-52 Hertford Street, W1J 7ST (7408 1155/ 1166/www.alsultan.co.uk). Green Park or Hyde Park Corner tube. **Meals served** noon-midnight daily. **Main courses** £12-£13.50. **Cover** £2. **Minimum** £20. **Credit** AmEx, DC, MC, V. Lebanese
Al Sultan is resolutely old school: carpeted floors, tables dressed with white starched tablecloths and set with heavy cutlery and a pink rose in a vase. Nothing wrong with that, except that the old-school attitude extends to the black-jacketed staff who, on our recent visit, were surly going on outright rude. The menu – all but tossed on to our table – impresses, with close to 50 kinds of meze, but quality varies. No complaints about the rich houmous, parsley-infused tabouleh or tart shinklish (a salad of diced tomatoes, parsley and feta cheese doused in olive oil and lemon juice), but the fuul medames was watery and both bitter and bitty because the dish had been prepared with the beans still in their skins. The grilled meat dishes that constitute the mains are unexceptional. At these prices – not to mention a £2 cover charge and a minimum £20 spend per head – you'd expect better. Which perhaps explains why Al Sultan was only half full on a Saturday night while that Shepherd Market landmark Lebanese, Al Hamra (*see above*), was full.
Babies and children welcome: high chairs. Book dinner. Tables outdoors (4, pavement). Takeaway service; delivery service (within 2-mile radius on orders over £35). Vegetarian menu. Map 9 H8.

Piccadilly W1

Fakhreldine
85 Piccadilly, W1J 7NB (7493 3424/ www.fakhreldine.co.uk). Green Park tube. **Meals served** noon-midnight Mon-Sat; noon-11pm Sun. **Main courses** £13-£23. **Set lunch** £17 2 courses, £22 3 courses. **Service** 12.5%. **Credit** AmEx, DC, JCB, MC, V. Lebanese
Two years ago Fakhreldine jettisoned the velour and went modish; the menu headed the same way. Since then we've heard mixed reports, but a recent visit left us in good cheer. Picture windows and a first-floor location make the most of impressive views over Green Park. The subdued colour scheme of the eating area is mitigated by a brighter adjacent bar with comfy sofas. We opted for modern mezes. Basturma samak was a pungent, enjoyable swordfish version of the classic smoked beef dish. Pumpkin kibbe (another variant on a Lebanese standard) successfully substituted minced meat for pumpkin inside a hard bulgar wheat case. Manaeesh zaatar came cutely presented as tiny rounds of warm pitta

BEST MIDDLE EASTERN

For fruity heaven
Al-Dar (*see p212*), **Ranoush Juice Bar** (*see p214*) and **Fresco** (*see p216*) have juices, fruit cocktails and milkshakes galore.

For a taste of the real Iran
Marinated kebabs and saffron rice are cooked to perfection at **Alounak** (*see p216*), **Hafez** (*see p216*), **Kandoo** (*see p212*), **Mohsen** (*see p217*), **Patogh** (*see p214*) and **Yas** (*see p217*).

For idiosyncratic charm
We love unpretentious **Abu Zaad** (*see p217*), where appreciative locals enjoy good-sized helpings of 'Damascene cuisine'.

For Lebanese food with a twist
Fakhreldine (*see below*) serves modish takes on traditional Lebanese dishes in stylish surroundings.

For eating Egyptian-style
Ali Baba (*see p214*) and **Meya Meya** (*see p213*) are nothing if not authentic.

dusted with olive oil and dried zaatar spice mix. To follow, we chose a mixed grill: a fine, if unexceptional and modestly sized selection of meat and offal. Inflated prices (in this case £19.50) suddenly didn't seem so justified. More esoteric choices include beef marinated in pomegranate sauce, sautéed with onions, potatoes and mushrooms; and – more authentic – roast chicken stuffed with smoked green wheat. Price gripes aside, the sleek vibe and thoughtful staff made our meal memorable.
Babies and children welcome: high chairs. Booking advisable. Takeaway service; delivery service. Map 9 H8.

St James's SW1

★ Noura Central
2005 WINNER BEST VEGETARIAN MEAL
22 Lower Regent Street, SW1Y 4UJ (7839 2020/ www.noura.co.uk). Piccadilly Circus tube. **Meals served** noon-midnight Mon-Thur, Sun; noon-1am Fri, Sat. **Main courses** £9.75-£18.50. **Set meal** (noon-6.30pm) £14.50 2 courses incl coffee; £25, £30, £34 per person (minimum 2) 3 courses incl coffee. **Credit** AmEx, DC, MC, V. Lebanese
To find fine Levantine cooking at reasonable prices just off the fast-food fleapit of Piccadilly Circus is a godsend. Add the fact that this new branch of the Parisian chain is a glam, air-conditioned sanctuary, offering numerous tasty hot and cold mezes and around 20 mains, and it's hard to go wrong. Vegetarians will appreciate the range of mezes open to them, thanks to the tradition of Lebanese meat-free festivals. Omnivores have the likes of pungent batrakh (salted and dried grey mullet roe) and kebbeh nayeh (lamb tartare, the raw mince as smooth as pâté). To make the most of it, pick several dishes, dive in and share – group dining is the norm, though there's a cushion-strewn bank of seats under plush drapes for the romantically inclined. Chilled okra came with a thick tomato sauce fragrant with fresh coriander; fava beans had a mellow garlicky flavour; and the mana'eesh, flatbread topped with thyme and sesame seed, was excellent. Mains consist of simple grilled meat and fish dishes (veggie choices are typically big versions of the mezes). It's the ice-creams that really impress: milk and orange blossom was so dense and creamy you'll want to resist that Cornetto and pop in after the movies.
Babies and children welcome: high chairs. Booking advisable; essential dinner. Disabled: toilet. Takeaway service. Map 17 K7.
For branches see index.

RESTAURANTS

West

Bayswater W2

★ Al Waha

*75 Westbourne Grove, W2 4UL (7229 0806/
www.waha-uk.com). Bayswater or Queensway
tube.* **Meals served** noon-midnight daily.
Main courses £9-£18. **Set lunch** £12.50
5 dishes. **Set dinner** £21 (minimum 2) 3 courses,
£25 (minimum 2) 4 courses. **Cover** £1.50.
Credit MC, V. Lebanese
With consistently excellent food, Al Waha is
probably the most reliable Lebanese restaurant in
town. We've eaten here perhaps a dozen times in
the last few years and have yet to leave
disappointed. This is a smart little place all done
out in a warm mellow yellow, with tables separated
by potted greenery (plastic: the one false note),
arrayed on two levels, both patrolled by elegant,
fragrant waiters in charcoal suits. Meze choices
run to 50 or more. It's all good and it's all good-
looking: creamy houmous is spiced up with
carefully cut diamonds of crisp red pepper; minty
labneh is studded with half slices of cucumber;
sambousek shaped like mini cornish pasties have
their tops lopped off to expose the fillings of
cheese and pastry. Even the mains – a let-down in
most Lebanese restaurants – are superb. We love
the kafta yogurtliyeh, slices of minced lamb on a
base of toasted pitta drowned in a warm yoghurt
sauce, with a side dish of shareya ('hairy') rice –
which is rice cooked in butter with vermicelli.
Baklava comes on the house.
*Babies and children welcome (until 7pm): high
chairs. Booking advisable; essential dinner. Tables
outdoors (4, patio). Takeaway service; delivery
service (within 5-mile radius).* **Map 7 B6.**

★ Fresco

*25 Westbourne Grove, W2 4UA (7221 2355/
www.frescojuices.co.uk). Bayswater tube.* **Meals
served** 8am-11pm daily. **Main courses** £5.95-
£7.95. **Set meze** £9.95. **Credit** MC, V. Lebanese
At first glance Fresco, with its bright yellow walls
and huge photos of fruit, looks merely like a juice-
cum-snack bar. Make your way towards the back,
though, and it opens out into a café dining area with
friendly service. Juices are made to order: delicious
medleys of mango, melon and watermelon arrived
promptly. The menu moves from scrambled eggs
at breakfast, through sandwiches and wraps for
lunch, and a range of meze dishes and main
courses. Starters of moutabal (aubergine purée
topped with pomegranate seeds) and tabouleh
served with hot pitta bread were excellent. Main
courses came in huge portions, accompanied by
rice cooked with vermicelli, and green salad.
Chicken kebab, pre-grilled, then reheated, let the
side down, but the loubieh (green beans in a tomato
sauce) was a tasty homely dish. We couldn't resist
sampling mohalabia (a blancmange-like creation
made from ground rice, served surrounded by a
rosewater syrup speckled with chopped pistachio),
and fragrant cardamom and mint teas. Great value.
*Babies and children welcome: high chairs.
Bookings not accepted. Takeaway service
(within 3-mile radius). Vegetarian menu.*
Map 7 B6.
For branches see index.

Hafez

*5 Hereford Road, W2 4AB (7221 3167/7229
9398/www.hafez.com). Bayswater tube/328 bus.*
Meals served noon-midnight daily. **Main
courses** £6-£14.50. **Service** 10%. **No credit
cards.** Iranian
Hafez faces the silent, stuccoed elegance of Leinster
Square. It's a lovely, peaceful location and on a
warm summer's evening the restaurant's forecourt
tables are prime seating. The interior is pleasant
too, enlivened by a trompe l'oeil pink sunset sky
painted across the ceiling. Shame then that the food
is variable. Despite the presence beside the front
window of a large beehive-shaped oven for baking
bread, ours was anything but fresh – cold,
cardboard-like and chewy. A starter of kashk-e
badejan (baked aubergines) was worse: an oily
brown slurry with a musty taste. The houmous and
salad olivieh, however, are fine. Where Hafez does
score is with its kebabs. The meat is superb and the
accompanying rice is fantastically light and fluffy,
served with a pat of butter on top. Hafez is unusual
among Iranian restaurants for offering a regular
selection of stews, a couple of fish options, plus a
few vegetarian dishes. We've also seen staff rustle
up a plate of chips and a bottle of tomato ketchup
on request, although we wouldn't have held it
against them had they said no.
*Babies and children welcome: high chairs.
Tables outdoors (4, pavement). Takeaway service;
delivery service.* **Map 7 B6.**
For branch see index.

Olympia W14

★ ★ Alounak

*10 Russell Gardens, W14 8EZ (7603 7645).
Kensington (Olympia) tube/rail.* **Meals served**
noon-midnight daily. **Main courses** £5.60-
£11.10. **Unlicensed. Corkage** no charge.
Service 10%. **Credit** MC, V. Iranian
Of London's many Iranian restaurants, Alounak
remains our favourite. It scores highly for its bright,
cheerful, family-friendly air and for the consistency
of the kitchen. As with all Iranian restaurants, its
menu is a paean to marinated fillets of lamb and
chicken, served plainly alongside mounds of rice.
Take it or leave it. (Although you can substitute
bread or salad for the rice.) The rice is always light
and fluffy, the meat always tender and flavourful.
On such things are Iranian restaurants judged.
Vegetarians are not catered for, though there's a fish
option – marinated grilled sea bass, served with
head and tail intact. Starters include the usuals,
such as mirza ghazemi (char-grilled aubergine with
fried onion and garlic), halim bademjan (mashed
char-grilled aubergine with onions, herbs and
walnuts) and salad olivieh (potato salad with
shredded chicken). All these, plus houmous, olives
and chillies, come as part of a mixed starter (good
value at £8.90). Booking is recommended; couples
should ask for a table in the cosy front area
(rusticated brickwork, hanging bauble lights)
rather than the rear (large tables, loud parties).
*Babies and children welcome: high chairs. Booking
advisable. Takeaway service; delivery service.*
For branch see index.

★ ★ Chez Marcelle

34 Blythe Road, W14 0HA (7603 3241).
Kensington (Olympia) tube/rail. **Meals served**
5-10pm Tue-Thur; noon-10pm Fri-Sun. **Main
courses** £7-£9.50. **No credit cards**. Lebanese
Far from the Anglo-Lebanese heartlands of
Bayswater and Edgware Road, this humble little
restaurant behind Olympia's exhibition halls turns
out some of the best Levantine food this side of the
Mediterranean. The cooking is done by Marcelle
herself, who bustles between kitchen and front-of-
house, rushing to greet diners with kisses. She gets
a lot of repeat custom. The menu is a laminated
card of 36 meze, plus grilled meat mains. At
Marcelle's the falafel are the size of tennis balls
(they are also the finest in town); the batata hara
(highly spicy diced potato) is a mountainous heap;
and houmous and labneh arrive in deep, deep
dishes. Four meze will make more than a meal for
two. Shame to miss out on the mains, though,
especially the 'stuffed lamb', which isn't stuffed but
baked and cut thinly to be layered on cinnamon rice
and topped with sliced pistachios and almonds.
The house wines are Lebanese and nowhere near
as good as the food. Note that Chez Marcelle is cash
or cheque only, with the nearest ATM a 20-minute
walk away on Kensington High Street.
*Babies and children admitted. Booking advisable.
Separate room for parties, seats 40. Takeaway
service.* **Map 20 C3.**

Mohsen

152 Warwick Road, W14 8PS (7602 9888).
*Earl's Court tube/Kensington (Olympia) tube/
rail.* **Meals served** noon-midnight daily. **Main
courses** £12-£15. **No credit cards**. Iranian
Once, Mohsen drew an almost exclusively Iranian
crowd, but thanks to numerous glowing reviews it
has been discovered by the rest of London. Punters
trek in numbers to this no-man's-land location,
opposite a Homebase car park. The restaurant
provides far more convivial surroundings of white
walls, terracotta tiles and round blue tables. Out
back there's an alfresco dining area, complete with
plants, colourful kilims and chirping caged
songbirds. An oven beside the front door fills the
air with the smell of fresh-baked bread, which is
served hot and crisp as an accompaniment to any
of the 14 starters. Beyond these, the menu is the
standard Iranian kebabs: barg, chenjeh, joojeh or
koubideh (that's lamb fillet, lamb pieces, chicken
or minced lamb). The meat is marinated in lime
juice (saffron in the case of chicken), seasoned and
served with a huge mound of gorgeous rice and a
grilled tomato. Specials (mainly stews) explore
Iranian cuisine further, but we've found them
variable. Desserts include faloodā (sweet noodles
in rosewater sorbet) and syrupy pastries, but a
main course here is sufficient for most.
*Babies and children admitted. Tables outdoors
(2, yard).* **Map 13 A10.**

Yas

7 Hammersmith Road, W14 8XJ (7603 9148).
Kensington (Olympia) tube/rail. **Meals served**
noon-4.30am daily. **Main courses** £6-£12.
Service 10%. **No credit cards**. Iranian
Amid a small row of Iranian eateries on a busy
road, this veteran restaurant provides a mellow
dining experience. Bright yellow walls and a blue-
tiled dome-shaped oven in the corner create a
cheerful atmosphere. Service, though leisurely, was
friendly. Having ordered persian bread, we
watched the chef roll out the dough and slap it on
to the roof of the oven. A few minutes later we
were tucking into it with mirza ghasemi (a
deliciously smoky aubergine dip), masto mousir
(creamy yoghurt flavoured with shallot) and sabzi
e paneer (aromatic herbs with feta-like cheese).
Main courses consist of kebabs or Iranian stews
known as 'khoresht', with lamb the favoured meat.
A mixed kebab, consisting of minced lamb and a
fillet, was freshly cooked and tasty, served on a bed
of fluffy rice. The classic lamb, aubergine and split-
pea stew was good too, with limoo (dried limes)
adding sourness. Generous portions meant that
dessert was out of the question, so we enjoyed
refreshing tea, served in dainty glasses, and left
feeling all was well with the world.
*Babies and children admitted. Booking advisable.
Takeaway service.*
For branch see index.

Shepherd's Bush W12

★ Abu Zaad

29 Uxbridge Road, W12 8LH (8749 5107).
Shepherd's Bush tube. **Meals served** 11am-11pm
daily. **Main courses** £4.50-£7.90. **Credit** MC, V.
Syrian
A local restaurant for local people, and in
Shepherd's Bush that means Sudanese, Levantines,
more Sudanese, westerners… and they all seem to
be on first-name terms with the staff. Abu Zaad
claims to offer 'Damascene cuisine', but since
Levantine food is pretty uniform, you'll find the
meze dishes here similar to those of Edgware
Road's glitziest establishments. Surroundings are
modest, with photos of old Damascus on the walls,
and pottery scattered here and there. Mezes are
carefully presented and very good. A huge portion
of tabouleh was packed with zest; bitinjan rahib
(roughly mashed aubergine with peppers and
onions, lemon juice and olive oil) was a super-fresh
melding of taste and texture. Mashi (here called
'Sheikh Almashi') is a household staple, a comfort
food not usually found in restaurants, made with
courgettes or cabbage leaves stuffed with mince.
Granted, it appeared in a bizarre 'sauce' (more like
milk than white sauce) but our equilibrium was
restored once we fished out the mashi: firm little
masterpieces, with lean, spicy mince. And fabulous
with the rice, traditionally cooked with oil and
fragments of vermicelli. Not a glamorous venue,
but great for real roots food.
*Babies and children welcome: high chairs.
Book weekends. No-smoking tables. Separate
room for parties, seats 30. Takeaway service.*
Map 20 B2.

South West

Fulham SW6

Aziz

24-32 Vanston Place, SW6 1AX (7386 0086).
Fulham Broadway tube. **Lunch served** noon-
3pm, **dinner served** 6pm-midnight Mon-
Fri. **Meals served** noon-midnight Sat; noon-

Mohsen

RESTAURANTS

11pm Sun. **Main courses** £7.50-£14.50.
Set lunch (Mon-Fri) £12.50 2 courses.
Set dinner (Mon-Fri) £16.50 2 courses.
Service 12.5%. **Credit** AmEx, MC, V.
Modern Middle Eastern

Aziz is an attractive restaurant; the exterior is discreet, but inside it's fashionably furnished with sage-green leather seats and brocade banquettes, striking deep orange and pink walls, and a spacious bar area. A doorway offers a glimpse through to its colourful sister-shop, which exudes a bazaar-like atmosphere. On our weekday lunchtime visit, a handful of well-dressed diners formed the clientele. The menu, offering an array of meze dishes and tagines, seems promising. Yet starters, served with olive bread, failed to scintillate, with sardines chermoula lacking zest, and a fridge-cold portion of baba ganoush simply so-so. Main courses were a let-down too: grilled merguez were dry and tough; chicken tagine with preserved lemons lacked fragrance. It also seems rather mean-spirited not to include couscous with the tagine; instead this had to be ordered as a £3 side dish. Much thought has gone into creating the interior decor, so it's a shame the same attention hasn't been paid to the quality of the food.

Babies and children welcome: high chairs. Booking essential weekends. Disabled: toilet. Tables outdoors (6, pavement). Takeaway service (deli). **Map 13 A13.**

South Kensington SW7

Al Bustan

68 Old Brompton Road, SW7 3LQ (7584 5805). South Kensington tube. **Meals served** noon-10.30pm daily. **Main courses** £11.50-£16.
Set meal (lunch Mon-Sat; noon-10.30pm Sun) £10 3 courses. **Credit** AmEx, DC, JCB, MC, V.
Lebanese

Small and intimate, Al Bustan brings a welcome touch of Middle Eastern class to the Old Brompton Road. The decor is light and clean, with cream-painted walls brightened by large mirrors and colourful prints, and tables tastefully clothed in taupe linen. Downstairs things become even cosier, with two alcoves tucked in beside a small bar. An excellent-value £10 lunch, offering two courses from a generous range of dishes, ensured that, on a Sunday lunchtime, the restaurant filled quickly (with smartly dressed, cosmopolitan couples). The menu lists a pared-down selection of classic

Lebanese dishes, including lamb both charcoal-grilled and raw. We opted for a selection of meze. These arrived promptly and prettily presented, accompanied by warm, napkin-wrapped pitta bread. Standards were high, from the refreshing tabouleh and a smooth lamb-topped houmous to the garlicky finger-lickin' chicken wings and delicious muhamara (spiced nuts). Star of the show, however, was the fatayer: freshly baked, dainty pastry parcels filled with tasty spinach. Cardamom coffee and rich, buttery baklava rounded off a very pleasant meal.
Babies and children admitted. Takeaway service; delivery service. **Map 14 D10.**

South

Balham SW12

Dish-Dash

11-13 Bedford Hill, SW12 9ET (8673 5555/ www.dish-dash.com). Balham tube/rail. **Meals served** 11am-11pm Mon-Sat; 11am-10.30pm Sun. **Main courses** £7.50- £9.50. **Service** 12.5%.
Credit MC, V. Iranian

With its modish furnishings, cocktail menu, wooden flooring and bar, Dish-Dash is very much a contemporary Persian restaurant. The decor seems more suited to night-time drinking and dining, since by day, even with sunshine outside, the place seemed dark and gloomy. Lunchtime diners are offered an express menu featuring a small choice of wraps and sandwiches. This ploy is obviously designed to pull in local office workers, but had only managed to attract one other couple. Our charming waiter informed us apologetically that both soup dishes were off that day. Then we tried a bottle of sparkling water; it was warm, and came without ice or lemon. Not a promising start. A large, tasty feta cheese sandwich (with crisp flavourful bread) and a minced lamb 'pizza' topped with onion and tomato cheered us up, yet our spirits sank again after sampling a fattoush salad coated in a thick mayonnaise-style dressing and without a trace of sumac. Perhaps in the evening, Dish-Dash pulls out the stops, but our lunch was a desultory affair.
Babies and children welcome: children's menu; high chairs. Book weekends. Disabled: toilet. Separate room for parties, seats 30. Tables outdoors (2, pavement). Takeaway service. Vegetarian menu.

North

Camden Town & Chalk Farm NW1

Le Mignon

98 Arlington Road, NW1 7HD (7387 0600). Camden Town tube. **Meals served** noon-midnight daily. **Main courses** £9.50-£18.50.
Service 12.5%. **Credit** MC, V. Lebanese

Le Mignon made a bizarre move a couple of years ago, deserting its atmospheric little premises for a small corner space a couple of doors down. It's now furnished with all the accoutrements of a 1970s sit-com: pink tablecloths, rustic granite cladding. To our relief, the friendly proprietor is still in charge and the food hasn't changed a bit; Le Mignon remains an outpost of classic Lebanese cooking in Camden. Freshness flashed through all our starters: a spicy fattoush salad with crunchy toasted pitta; bitinjan rahib (mashed aubergines with peppers, onions, oil and lemon juice), which had an abundance of texture and bite; a dense, smoky houmous with plenty of olive oil; foul moukala, with perky green broad beans and plenty of fresh coriander and lemon juice. As is so often the way, mains were more ordinary: spatchcocked firri (quail) was a bit dry; a mixed grill was competent yet not special. Concentrate on mezes to enjoy the full flowering of the chef's talent. We accompanied our meal with a modestly priced but perfectly drinkable Nakad Lebanese rosé.
Babies and children admitted (daytime). Booking advisable. Tables outdoors (4, pavement). Takeaway service. **Map 27 D3.**

Menu

See also the menu boxes in **North African** and **Turkish**. For more information, get hold of a copy of *The Legendary Cuisine of Persia*, by Margaret Shaida (Grub Street).

MEZE

Baba ganoush: Egyptian name for moutabal (qv).
Basturma: smoked beef.
Batata hara: potatoes fried with peppers and chilli.
Falafel: a mixture of spicy chickpeas or broad beans ground, rolled into balls and deep fried.
Fatayer: a soft pastry with fillings of cheese, onions, spinach and pine kernels.
Fattoush: fresh vegetable salad containing shards of toasted pitta bread and sumac (qv).
Fuul or **fuul medames:** brown broad beans that are mashed and seasoned with olive oil, lemon juice and garlic.
Kalaj: halloumi cheese on pastry.
Kibbeh: highly seasoned mixture of minced lamb, cracked wheat and onion, deep-fried in balls. For meze it is often served raw (**kibbeh nayeh**) like steak tartare.
Labneh: Middle Eastern cream cheese made from yoghurt.
Moujadara: lentils, rice and caramelised onions mixed together.
Moutabal: a purée of char-grilled aubergines mixed with sesame sauce, garlic and lemon juice.
Muhamara: spiced and crushed mixed nuts.
Sambousek: small pastries filled with mince, onion and pine kernels.
Sujuk: spicy Lebanese sausages.
Sumac: an astringent and fruity-tasting spice made from dried sumac seeds.
Tabouleh: a salad of chopped parsley, tomatoes, crushed wheat, onions, olive oil and lemon juice.
Torshi: pickled vegetables.
Warak einab: rice-stuffed vine leaves.

MAINS

Shawarma: meat (usually lamb) marinated then grilled on a spit and sliced kebab-style.
Shish kebab: cubes of marinated lamb grilled on a skewer, often with tomatoes, onions and sweet peppers.
Shish taouk: like shish kebab, but with chicken rather than lamb.

DESSERTS

Baklava: filo pastry interleaved with pistachio nuts, almonds or walnuts, and covered in syrup.
Konafa or **kadayif:** cake made from shredded pastry dough, filled with syrup and nuts, or cream.
Ma'amoul: pastries filled with nuts or dates.
Muhallabia or **mohalabia:** a milky ground-rice pudding with almonds and pistachios, flavoured with rosewater or orange blossom.
Om ali: bread and butter pudding.

IRANIAN DISHES

Ash-e reshteh: a soup containing noodles, spinach, pulses and dried herbs.
Halim bademjan: mashed char-grilled aubergine with onions, herbs and walnuts.
Kashk-e badejan: baked aubergines mixed with herbs.
Kuku-ye sabzi: finely chopped fresh herbs mixed with eggs and baked in the oven.
Masto khiar: yoghurt mixed with finely chopped cucumber and mint.
Masto musir: shallot-flavoured yoghurt.
Mirza ghasemi: crushed baked aubergines, tomatoes, garlic and herbs mixed with egg.
Sabzi: a plate of fresh herb leaves (usually mint and dill) often served with a cube of feta.
Salad olivieh: a bit like a russian salad, with chopped potatoes, chicken, eggs, peas and gherkins, plus olive oil and mayonnaise.

Modern European

Modern European remains one of London's favourite and most fought-over cuisines. The potential dining experiences are many and varied, covering the perennially celebrated (**The Ivy**, **Le Caprice**), the currently celebrated (**The Wolseley**), Soho stalwarts (**Andrew Edmunds**, **Alastair Little**), Conran's finest (**Blueprint Café**, **The Orrery**), foodie favourites (**Clarke's**, **Villandry**) and local maestros (**The Glasshouse**, **McClements**). As for changes to the scene in the past 12 months, the move upmarket and uptown, from Clapham to the West End, proved a mistake for **Thyme**, which closed in 2005. Its Clapham site has been taken over by **Morel** – a contender for Best Local Restaurant in the *Time Out* Awards 2005, along with **The Farm** in Fulham. Other arrivals include stylish **Island Restaurant & Bar** in Bayswater, Portuguse-inflected **Portal** in Clerkenwell, and two fine examples of neighbourhood restaurants: **Sam's Brasserie & Bar** in Chiswick and **Dylan's Restaurant** on the capital's outskirts, in Barnet.

Central

Barbican EC2

Searcy's

Level 2, Barbican, Silk Street, EC2Y 8DS (7588 3008/www.searcys.co.uk). Barbican tube. **Lunch served** noon-2.30pm Mon-Fri. **Dinner served** 5-10.30pm Mon-Sat. **Set meal** £22.50 2 courses, £26.50 3 courses. **Service** 12.5%. **Credit** AmEx, DC, JCB, MC, V.

The Barbican's classiest restaurant is all clean lines and modern furniture, which can make the place look a little corporate. Striking flowers, sympathetic lighting and a great view over the lake offset this, and welcoming, efficient staff add to a feeling of well-being. Searcy's is not as busy as it could be; perhaps diners are deterred by the obligation to have at least two courses, which, good though they are, might be a course too many pre- or post-concert. Starters such as goat's cheese ravioli with tomato confit and pomegranate dressing, or chilled Heirloom tomato and basil terrine with fromage blanc, slip down easily enough. Of the mains, wild mushroom risotto cake with poached egg and lemon dressing was a better choice than a lacklustre pan-fried bream with olive tapenade and fricassée of jerusalem artichoke. Iced nougat parfait with fresh raspberries was a much perkier offering, and the cheese plate a generous one, with plenty of crackers. Worth investigating – just don't expect culinary fireworks.
Booking advisable. Dress: smart casual. No-smoking tables. **Map 11 P5.**

Bayswater W2

Island Restaurant & Bar [NEW]

Lancaster Terrace, W2 2TY (7551 6070/ www.islandrestaurant.co.uk). Lancaster Gate tube. **Lunch served** noon-3pm, **dinner served** 6-10.30pm daily. **Main courses** £11.50-£40. **Set meal** (noon-7pm) £12 2 courses, £15 3 courses. **Credit** AmEx, DC, MC, V.

A traffic island in the middle of the swirling one-way system around Lancaster Gate tube is hardly the obvious location for a stylish new restaurant, so the backers of Island, which opened in late 2004, deserve credit for their belief in the project. The large space has been given an emphatically sleek makeover by Wagamama designers Stiff + Trevillion. Giant windows keep out traffic noise, and on a hot evening the air-con was so powerful we were chilly. The food is adventurous. The standard Mod Euro approach of taking a French classic and chucking in unusual ingredients is becoming a cliché, but Island's cooking ascends to a higher level of refinement. An ultra-smooth gazpacho was offset by a delicate scoop of basil sorbet; in crab salad with artichoke and shellfish mayonnaise, everything was ideally matched. Mains were as impressive: roast tuna with cherry tomatoes was perfectly cooked; and while a scallop tartlet with baby carrots, peas and cumin oil was maybe less exciting, the quality of ingredients was excellent. The dessert of goat's cheese ice-cream was intriguing, but possibly too cheesy. The wine list offers a sophisticated range, at very fair prices. Service was keen to the point of being overeager.
Babies and children welcome: children's menu; high chairs. Booking advisable. Disabled: toilet. No-smoking tables. **Map 8 D6.**

City E1, EC2, EC3, EC4

Aurora

Great Eastern Hotel, 40 Liverpool Street, EC2M 7QN (7618 7000/www.aurora.restaurant.co.uk). Liverpool Street tube/rail. **Lunch served** noon-2.30pm, **dinner served** 6.45-10pm Mon-Fri. **Main courses** £15.50-£29.50. **Set lunch** £28 3 courses. **Set meal** (2-9pm) £50 7 courses tasting menu (£75 with wine). **Service** 12.5%. **Credit** AmEx, MC, V.

The impressive hall of the Great Eastern Hotel, with its Victorian domed ceiling, provides a very grand setting for Aurora, the flagship of Conran's restaurants here. Attentive service is another aspect of the dining experience (popular with a City clientele), though on this visit there were some glitches. The (expensive) menu reads well, but execution was at times disappointing: white gazpacho with coriander cress and almonds should have been a refreshing summer soup, but came laden with cream; confit of sea trout, English asparagus and truffle dressing was little more than an overly chilled fillet that tasted little better than supermarket fare. Mains were better, although the accompaniments were a little too reminiscent of the starter ingredients (both snails and asparagus got a second look in). Typical was fillet of aged Highland beef with braised snails; it looked a treat, but was both overcooked and over-caramelised, drowning the flavour. The extensive wine list will keep everyone happy. Aurora has the potential to be a great dining experience – we've had some wonderful meals here – but this time it wasn't firing on all cylinders.
Babies and children admitted. Booking advisable. Disabled: toilet (in hotel). **Map 12 R6.**

The Chancery

9 Cursitor Street, EC4A 1LL (7831 4000/ www.thechancery.co.uk). Chancery Lane tube. **Meals served** noon-2.30pm, **dinner served** 6-10.30pm Mon-Fri. **Main courses** £12-£16. **Set menu** £14.50 2 courses, £19.50 3 courses, £32 3 courses incl coffee & petits fours. **Service** 12.5%. **Credit** AmEx, DC, JCB, MC, V.

That the Chancery's stylishly tall, leather-clad chairs also provide excellent lower-back support exemplifies the combination of discreet sobriety – suitable for a lawyer-heavy area – and modern chic at this compact restaurant. The cooking of head chef Andrew Thompson similarly offers a nice mix of refined innovation and established virtues. The £32 three-course set menu is excellent value, with coffee, petits fours and appetisers (escabeche of red mullet and anchovy on toast, on our visit) all included. In a smoked duck salad, the almost-sweet meat was nicely offset by apple crisps and walnuts. Conventional-seeming baked goat's cheese was enlivened by the use of fine cheese and an original beetroot and asparagus salad. Highlight of our mains was perfectly cooked chicken complemented by rich merguez sausage and mint yoghurt dressing. Roast lamb shank was very tender, but the accompanying wild mushroom risotto needed more defined flavours. Only in the desserts did inventiveness seem to get ahead of execution, with a trio of crèmes brûlées (rhubarb, blueberry and vanilla) that didn't quite work, and an oddly tart elderflower ice-cream. The wine list offers a good balance of sophistication and value. Service is efficient, if a bit anonymous.
Babies and children welcome: high chairs. Booking essential. No-smoking tables. Separate room for parties, holds 20. **Map 11 N6.**

The Don

The Courtyard, 20 St Swithin's Lane, EC4N 8AD (7626 2606/www.thedonrestaurant.com). Bank tube/DLR.
Restaurant **Lunch served** noon-2.30pm, **dinner served** 6.30-10pm Mon-Fri. **Main courses** £12.95-£23.95.
Bistro **Lunch served** noon-3pm, **dinner served** 6-10pm Mon-Fri. **Main courses** £8.95-£14.95.
Both **Service** 12.5%. **Credit** AmEx, DC, MC, V.

George Sandeman took over the cellars at 20 St Swithin's Lane in 1798 for his port, sherry and wine company. Now it's the home of restaurant and bistro the Don. The cobbled entrance is charming, and there's a warm welcome inside – for City and non-City diners alike. This year we ate in the restaurant – an intimate dining space with tall ceilings that resembled a banqueting hall – but the cellar bistro is worth a visit too. To start, a mediterranean fish soup was rich and flavoursome, served with freshly grated gruyère and a delectable rouille. Terrine of foie gras and duck confit with orange and beetroot dressing, served with a warm brioche, was less stunning, but a good and hearty portion nonetheless. Next: perfectly cooked grilled calf's liver, topped with sage polenta squares and curly kale; braised fennel in saffron oil and a sweet pepper coulis added a sweet and sour twist to ballotine of sea bass. Lastly, if you can resist the likes of chocolate fondant with white chocolate schnapps sorbet, the cheese board may seduce you into a Sandeman nightcap. The attentive sommelier is typical of the friendly service.
Children over 10 years welcome. Booking essential. Dress: smart casual. Separate room for parties, seats 24. **Map 12 Q7.**

Lanes

East India House, 109-117 Middlesex Street, E1 7JF (7247 5050/www.lanesrestaurant.co.uk). Liverpool Street tube/rail.
Bar **Open** 10am-11pm Mon-Fri.

J O A N N A ' S

A stylish, traditional restaurant with an exceptional and varied, modern, international menu.

A unique venue with a friendly atmosphere, we are open from 10am (cocktail bar from 11am) until late, seven days a week.

Joanna's 56 Westow Hill Crystal Palace SE19 1RX
T 020 8670 4052 **F** 020 8670 8306 **www.joannas.uk.com**

The County Hall Restaurant

Situated on the South Bank, with stunning views overlooking the Thames, The County Hall Restaurant offers you the opportunity to savour modern cooking at its best, in an environment of understated warmth and friendliness.

The restaurant is housed in the former Greater London Council where the original rooms are kept with grandeur serving pre-theatre and a la Carte meals. Afternoon tea and light meals are also available in The Rotunda Lounge and The Library.

Marriott
LONDON COUNTY HALL

The County Hall Restaurant
Westminster Bridge Road, London, SE1 7PB
Tel: 0207 902 8000
Fax: 0870 400 7300 www.marriott.com/lonch

allium

Contemporary European cooking with depth of flavours and simplicity, from the kitchen of Chef Patron Anton Edelmann, served in the relaxed but sophisticated atmoshphere of the restaurant's elegant Art Deco dining room.

Lunch
Tuesday to Friday, 12.00pm - 3.00pm
Set menu from £17.50

Sunday Lunch
12.00pm - 2.30pm
2 & 3 course set menu from £17.50

Dinner
Tuesday to Saturday, 6.00pm - 10.30pm
a la carte also available

Allium is also available for private dining and exclusive use.

Allium
Dolphin Square Chichester Street London SW1V 3LX
T. 020 7798 6888 F. 020 7798 5685
E. info@allium.co.uk www.allium.co.uk

The
CLERKENWELL

69-73 St.John Street London EC1M 4AN
Tel: 0207 253 9000   Fax: 0207 253 3322
www.theclerkenwell.com

The Clerkenwell Dining Room, under the direction of Chef Andrew Thompson and Co-owner Zak Jones, is a calm, inviting room of intimate proportions offering friendly, spiffy service. The style is cool modern, with grays and blues predominating, and it's a bit of an oasis for the business folk who frequent this spot. The pan-European menu offers terrifically high standards of preparation and presentation with surprising affordability.

Take advantage of the wonderful 2 course/ 3 course du jour menu reasonably priced at £14.50 or £19.50 or perhaps you may be tempted by the sumptuous a la carte menu. With a large modern ground floor restaurant, stylish and comfortable bar/lounge area and a wonderful first floor mezzanine level private dining room you are spoilt for choice at The Clerkenwell

Due to popular demand The Clerkenwell are now open through the winter months only for Sunday brunch.

Fans of The Clerkenwell will be thrilled to now that the duo have recently opened an intimate fine dining restaurant off Chancery Lane, called
The Chancery – www.thechancery.co.uk t. 0207 831 4000

Restaurant **Lunch served** noon-3pm, **dinner served** 5.30-10pm Mon-Fri; 6-10pm Sat. **Main courses** £12.50-£18.50. **Set dinner** £15 2 courses, £21.50 3 courses. **Service** 12.5%. **Credit** AmEx, DC, JCB, MC, V.

Lanes pitches itself as a relaxed place to eat serious food at less-than-City prices. It's certainly a good-looking restaurant – high ceilings and plentiful natural light help you forget you're dining below street level – and the staff are friendly, if perhaps a little amateurish (our water glasses were filled up far too regularly and three different people served us). But prices seem to have nudged upwards, the menu could do with a change, and small details are letting things down. Two glasses of French sauvignon blanc were not served cold enough. A starter of smoked swordfish with lemon risotto and pickled lemon looked beautiful and the thin slices of fish were divine, but it was marred by risotto served so cold it was clumped solid. Both our mains tasted far better than they looked (colourless). Brill stuffed with mussels and clams, with a potato crust, leeks and asparagus, was a creative match, the hollowed-out brill bulging with a lovely dill-flavoured filling. And fillet of halibut with fennel, asparagus and pancetta-wrapped potatoes was excellent. To finish, peaches and cream came as a delicious layered sandwich of crunchy thin pastry, thick peach-speckled cream and fresh peach slices.

Bar and restaurant available for hire (weekends). Booking essential lunch. Disabled: toilet. Separate room for parties, seats 28. **Map 12 R6**.

Novelli in the City

London Capital Club, 15 Abchurch Lane, EC4N 7BW (7717 0088/www.londoncapitalclub.com). Cannon Street tube/rail/Bank tube/DLR. **Lunch served** noon-2.30pm, **dinner served** 5.30-9pm Mon-Fri. **Main courses** £7.50-£21. **Set meal** £17.50 2 courses, £20 3 courses. **Credit** AmEx, MC, V.

The latest move by an old-fashioned London establishment to bring in a celebrity chef is working at this gentlemen's club. Jean-Christophe Novelli might spend more time in the Hertfordshire countryside at haute cuisine restaurant Auberge du Lac, but his London dining room is packed out most lunchtimes. The dark wood panelling, mirrors and banquettes are an improvement on the swirling carpets and framed hunting pictures of the upstairs members' area, although the clientele remains pretty much the same – mainly chaps in a striped shirt and tie. The kitchen helps punters feel right at home by serving posh club food given a southern European twist: sirloin steak came with stacked fat chips and vine tomatoes; langoustine bisque was served with a gorgeous spray of Pernod foam. The best thing about the goodish wine list is the inclusion of decent second wines from well-known properties: 2000 Château Charmes de Kirwan, from Margaux, for example. Note that there are two lists, though. Pieropan's 2002 Soave is a much better drop than his 2003, but the 2002 is only offered on the more extensive of the two lists – if you want a look, you must request it specially.

Children over 8 years admitted. Booking essential. Dress: smart casual. Separate rooms for parties, seating 6-70. **Map 12 Q7**.

Prism

147 Leadenhall Street, EC3V 4QT (7256 3888/www.prismrestaurant.co.uk). Monument tube/Bank tube/DLR. *Bar* **Open** 11am-11pm Mon-Fri. **Meals served** 11.30am-3pm, 6-10pm Mon-Fri. **Main courses** £9-£11. *Restaurant* **Lunch served** noon-3pm, **dinner served** 6-10pm Mon-Fri. **Main courses** £17.50-£22. *Both* **Service** 12.5%. **Credit** AmEx, DC, JCB, MC, V.

Harvey Nicks-owned Prism makes optimum use of the former Bank of New York's hall. Imposing columns and stark white walls are offset by plenty of red leather and bustling waiting staff dressed in black and white. It's popular with City gents in grey attire, but a raft of bright, modern art keeps things interesting. The menu offers fresh

ingredients, simply prepared and beautifully presented. Asparagus with poached egg, hollandaise and truffle shavings was perfectly executed. Quality gravadlax with sweet mustard dressing came with crayfish salad (though describing three crayfish on a shred of lettuce as 'salad' is slightly cheeky). Roasted pavé of salmon was served with sorrel sauce, salmon confit and spring veg salsa; though individually faultless, each component failed to complement the other. Better was roast monkfish with rich, seafood paella and parsley jus. Portions were small enough to allow us a dessert of manchego cheesecake with an orange and port sorbet: warm savoury cheese paired perfectly with the cool, sweet yet slightly acidic sorbet. Service is polished. The extensive wine list is thin at the lower end (a fine if unexceptional Seresin sauvignon blanc was £24).

Disabled: toilet. Separate room for parties seating 20 and 40. **Map 12 Q6**.

Terminus Bar & Grill

Great Eastern Hotel, 40 Liverpool Street, EC2M 7QN (7618 7400/www.terminus-restaurant.co.uk). Liverpool Street tube/rail. **Breakfast served** 7-11am Mon-Fri; 7.30-11am Sat, Sun. **Brunch served** 11am-4pm Sat, Sun. **Lunch served** noon-4pm daily. **Dinner served** 5-11pm Mon-Fri; 5-10pm Sat, Sun. **Main courses** £9.50-£20. **Service** 12.5%. **Credit** AmEx, DC, MC, V.

Of all five Conran venues within the Great Eastern Hotel – including Aurora (*see p219*), Fishmarket (*see p84*) and Miyabi (*see p181*) – Terminus is most closely associated with the railway below: down to the occasional floor-rumbling as the 17.50 to Norwich heads out from platform six. The interior resembles a stylish railway station buffet: from the lines of tables to the lines on the staff shirts, crockery and even ashtrays. Service is on time too. And the food, thankfully, is way better than standard train fare. A starter of green pea and mint soup was delightfully fresh, while tagliolini with crab and chilli was tasty and filling. A huge portion of perfectly moist and tender roast Haughley Farm chicken arrived in a flavoursome savoy cabbage, leek and thyme broth. Only a minuscule trout salad lacking diverting ingredients disappointed. Desserts include warm chocolate pudding, and popcorn vanilla parfait with roast plums. A short wine list keeps it simple, with prices from £14.50 for a perfectly reasonable sauvignon blanc. This is simple fare, well cooked, with plenty of choice for vegetarians. Tapas, salads and sandwiches make Terminus the perfect stop for lunchtime dining, as well as for parties and after-work dinners.

Babies and children welcome: high chairs. Booking essential lunch Mon-Fri. Disabled: toilet. No-smoking tables. **Map 12 R6**.

Vivat Bacchus

47 Farringdon Street, EC4A 4LL (7353 2648/www.vivatbacchus.co.uk). Chancery Lane tube/Farringdon tube/rail. *Bar* **Open/snacks served** noon-11.30pm Mon-Fri. *Restaurant* **Lunch served** noon-2.30pm, **dinner served** 6.30-9.30pm Mon-Fri. **Main courses** £13-£20. **Set lunch** (noon-2.30, 6.30-7pm) £13.50 2 courses, £15.50 3 courses. **Service** 12.5%. *Both* **Credit** AmEx, DC, MC, V.

Classy food and even classier wines are served at Vivat Bacchus, yet in a delightfully relaxed manner. Staff are friendly and down to earth, but know their stuff. The modern basement space is sparingly decorated with wine memorabilia, and there are views into the glassed-off cellars and cheese room. Diners are invited to go into both to make their selection. The restaurant sprang from one in Johannesburg, and there's a great selection of wines from South Africa (other wine-growing areas are amply covered too). The menu has less of a South African influence – although judging by the grilled springbok steak with corn fritters and pinotage jus, we wish there was more. Other successes included a very refined gazpacho, and a zingy, generous grilled mancheg and prawn brochette with watermelon salsa. Less pleasing was seared foie gras with braised endive tart tatin

Interview
MARTHA GREENE

Who are you?
Owner of **Villandry** shop, restaurant and bar (*see p225*).

Eating in London: what's good about it?
The variety. And there is great Middle Eastern food in this country – I love Persian food because I spent part of my childhood in Iran.

What's bad about it?
The hours are very provincial. You can't eat all day. London is sophisticated, but it's not a 24-hour city at all.

Which are your favourite London restaurants?
Generally, I go for neighbourhood restaurants rather than the trendy ones. I love **Yas** (*see p217*), which does very authentic Persian food. For Italian I like **Locanda Locatelli** (*see p171*) and **La Famiglia** (*see p177*), and **Yauatcha** (*see p72*) for Chinese.

What single thing would improve London's restaurant scene?
Making the prices easier. London is really expensive, and it's really a problem. Landlords want a great covenant, so they would rather have a chain than an independent business like ours, so you wind up with chains – and I don't like chains.

Any hot tips for the coming year?
I'd like to see us move more towards seasonal food, for people to stop wishing that a peach would taste great in December. We should stop wanting what nature doesn't give us. I'd also like to see a really great Cuban restaurant here.

Anything to declare?
The congestion charge is a disaster. Ultimately it's forcing up prices in shops. We used to get mothers from Camden picking up their kids after school and just popping over the Marylebone Road to shop, but it's no longer convenient for them. And you still can't get a good bagel here, that I'm sure of – I'm told it might be because of the water.

RESTAURANTS

(unrelentingly rich). Finally, the lure of the cheese room overcame the temptation of Eton mess or chocolate and ginger cheesecake, and for just £6.50 we got a magnificent array of perfectly pungent pieces, plus crackers, fruit and chutney. A very welcome, nicely different, addition to City dining.
Babies and children admitted. Booking advisable. Disabled: toilet. Dress: smart casual. No-smoking tables. Separate room for parties, seats 45. **Map 11 N5**.

Clerkenwell & Farringdon EC1

Clerkenwell Dining Room

69-73 St John Street, EC1M 4AN (7253 9000/ www.theclerkenwell.com). Farringdon tube/rail.
Lunch served noon-2.30pm Mon-Fri. **Dinner served** 6-11.30pm Mon-Fri; 7-11.30pm Sat.
Main courses £12-£16. **Set meal** £14.50 2 courses, £19.50 3 courses. **Service** 12.5%.
Credit AmEx, DC, JCB, MC, V.
From the crisp, white table linen and designer flowers to the informed, efficient service, the Clerkenwell shows itself to be a smart dining establishment. Chef Andrew Thompson of the Chancery (*see p219*) is co-owner, but head chef here is Nelson Reposo. He got us off to a good start with his amuse-bouche: a confection of cucumber, crème fraîche and lobster dumpling. A starter of tuna, avocado and ginger tartare with a shot glass of chilled tomato gazpacho was fresh, light and perfectly balanced, though the fennel purée was superfluous. Own-made potato gnocchi with pancetta, shaved pecorino cheese and broad beans made good use of seasonal beans in an attractive but simple combination. For mains, a well-cooked fillet of sea bass was stuffed with crab meat and herbs and served with ratatouille and steamed new potatoes, while grilled monkfish tail, layered with crispy chorizo, was beautifully put together with razor clams, tomatoes and fresh herbs, plus saffron potato purée. Superb desserts included hot chocolate fondant, Pina Colada and rum ice-cream or praline and white chocolate bavarois. Coffee comes with a half-dozen petits fours. Prices are high, but the reasonably priced (and extensive) wine list helps keep the bill down.
Babies and children admitted. Booking advisable. Separate room for parties, seats 40. Vegetarian menu. **Map 5 O4**.

Portal NEW

88 St John Street, EC1M 4EH (7253 6950/ www.portalrestaurant.com). Farringdon tube/rail.
Lunch served noon-3.30pm Mon-Fri. **Dinner served** 6.30-10.30pm Mon-Sat. **Main courses** £11.50-£29.50. **Service** 12.5%. **Credit** MC, V.
The trademark of Quinta do Portal, an acclaimed Douro wine company, appears on this restaurant's plates, so Portal must be its flagship London restaurant, right? Wrong. But there's an imaginatively chosen, unusual and Iberian-accented wine list that includes such food-friendly grapes as Spanish albariño and even assyrtiko from Greece. The spacious premises are broken into bar, private rooms, a huge glass conservatory and airy dining room. Service is professional yet friendly, the feel of the place very smart. And the Modern European menu, both in the restaurant and the small dishes (petiscos) served in the bar, takes some inspiration from Portugal. You won't find bacalhau (salt cod) much better than this – thoroughly soaked and rinsed to get rid of excessive saltiness, but with a firm, chewy texture. Tender, full-flavoured pork cheeks had been marinated in red wine for 12 hours then slow-cooked for nearly a day. Some aspects of our dishes seemed curiously old-fashioned, such as the 1970s-style medley of vegetables served with the main courses, but the details were all correctly prepared, from a flavoursome complimentary appetiser of duck sausage to a drizzle of Madeira sauce reduction. London's Portuguese restaurant scene was moribund until Tugga (*see p251*) opened in 2005; Portal is a worthy accomplice.
Babies and children welcome: high chairs. Disabled: toilet. No-smoking tables. Separate room for parties, seats 10. **Map 5 O4**.

Smiths of Smithfield

67-77 Charterhouse Street, EC1M 6HJ (7251 7950/www.smithsofsmithfield.co.uk). Farringdon tube/rail.
Ground-floor bar/café **Meals served** 7am-5pm Mon-Fri; 10am-5pm Sat; 9.30am-5pm Sun.
Main courses £3.50-£6.
Cocktail bar **Open** 5.30-10.30pm Mon-Wed; 5.30pm-1am Thur-Sat.
Dining Room **Lunch served** noon-3pm Mon-Fri. **Dinner served** 6-11pm Mon-Fri; 6-10.45pm Sat.
Main courses £10.50-£11.75.
All **Credit** AmEx, DC, MC, V.
Smiths is an entire building (four floors) given over to eating and drinking. There's a ground-floor bar serving brunch and snacks during the day, a cocktail bar on the first floor, and dining on the two levels above (for the Top Floor, *see p55*). We tried the informal, second-floor Dining Room. It's loud – an industrial-scale space with bare-brick walls set around a large central well that's open down to the lower-floor revellers. The menu features well-tried standards, with plenty of meat. A starter of seared tuna with aubergine and miso paste featured two miniature just-seared squares of tuna on aubergine cooked like Turkish imam bayıldı, with dabs of miso paste fringing the plate; the flavours were sound (we loved the smoky aubergine), but the dish was no more than the sum of its parts. 'Lucky' squid was squidgy and fresh, but its flavour was compromised by too much chilli jam. A main of grilled sea bream with fennel was cooked just-so, but there was a lot of fat on a ribeye steak (though the meat was tender) and the chips were dryish. The food is variable, then, but youthful zest and a lively atmosphere go a long way to compensate.
Bar available for hire. Booking advisable. Disabled: lift; toilet. Entertainment: DJ 8pm Wed-Sat. Separate room for parties, seats 26. Tables outdoors (8, terrace; 6, pavement). Takeaway service (café). **Map 5 O5**.

Covent Garden WC2

Axis

One Aldwych, 1 Aldwych, WC2B 4RH (7300 0300/www.onealdwych.com). Covent Garden or Embankment tube/Charing Cross tube/rail.
Lunch served noon-2.45pm Mon-Fri. **Dinner served** 5.45-10.45pm Mon-Fri; 5.45-11.30pm Sat.
Main courses £13.95-£28. **Set meal** £16.75 2 courses, £19.75 3 courses. **Service** 12.5%.
Credit AmEx, DC, JCB, MC, V.
We rather relished the mini-trek to our table at Axis. Once through the velvet-curtained entrance, several grand spiral staircases take you into the depths of the swanky One Aldwych hotel. This is no poky basement, though. In line with the rest of the super-chic hotel (also home to Indigo; *see p223*), Axis is an impressive space, with soaring ceilings and a cutting-edge, art deco-accented look. Fashionable it certainly is, but its countenance remains largely restrained, with sober black leather, white linen and marble floors – a style that attracts plenty of suited and booted diners. Australian chef Mark Gregory oversees an unintimidating Modern European menu, with some interesting global accents and, true to his homeland, a sizeable grill section. On our latest visit, each dish was well executed, including a moist pan-fried Canadian halibut with asparagus and new potatoes, a tangy gruyère soufflé, and – our favourite – a fantastically crispy duck noodle salad starter. The superb service helped further to justify the high-end prices. The sleek toilets, for those who care about such things, are in a league of their own.
Babies and children welcome: high chairs. Booking advisable. Disabled: toilet. Entertainment: jazz 8pm Tue, Wed. Restaurant available for hire. Vegetarian menu. **Map 18 M7**.

Bank Aldwych

1 Kingsway, WC2B 6XF (7379 9797/ www.bankrestaurants.com). Holborn or Temple tube.
Bar **Open** 11.30am-11pm Mon-Sat; 11.30am-10.30pm Sun.
Restaurant **Breakfast served** 7.30-10.30am Mon-Fri. **Brunch served** 11.30am-4.30pm Sat, Sun. **Lunch served** noon-3pm Mon-Fri. **Dinner served** 5.30-11pm Mon-Sat; 5.30-9.30pm Sun.
Main courses £10.80-£21. **Set meal** (lunch, 5.30-7pm, from 10pm) £13.50 2 courses, £16 3 courses.
Both **Service** 12.5%. **Credit** AmEx, DC, MC, V.

Occupying a giant former bank at the foot of Kingsway, Bank Aldwych has been one of the most successful of London's 1990s high-style makeovers. Huge glass doors open into a sleek bar, beyond which you walk past long, metal chefs' stations and mirrored walls, to reach the ample dining area. There you'll find groovy soft red seats and murals recalling the New Jersey seaboard. Airy, with loads of light, the restaurant is big enough to be buzzy without becoming overpowering. The wine list and separate menus for lunch, dinner and weekend brunch (similar dishes recur in each) offer a something-for-everyone mix, presented with style. The brunch list is divided into 'light' and 'large', although a good-value set menu is still available. Classic eggs benedict and scrambled eggs with smoked salmon (both 'light') hit all the right notes. From 'large', roast chicken with char-grilled peach, herb salad and pear dressing was very well handled; and grilled chicken crostini included generous additions of bacon and imaginative salad. Desserts provide intriguing variations on classics; we enjoyed a fine apple sorbet and a smart sticky toffee pudding. Staff were unflustered on a quiet lunchtime, but we wondered how they'd manage at full stretch.
Babies and children welcome: children's brunch menu; high chairs; nappy-changing facilities (restaurant). Booking advisable. Disabled: toilet. Entertainment: jazz 11.30am-3pm Sun. Separate room for parties, seats 28. **Map 10 M6.**

Indigo

One Aldwych, 1 Aldwych, WC2B 4RH (7300 0400/www.onealdwych.com). Covent Garden or Embankment tube/Charing Cross tube/rail. **Breakfast served** 6.30-11am daily, **dinner served** 6-11.15pm daily. **Brunch served** 12.30-3pm Sat, Sun. **Lunch served** noon-3pm Mon-Fri. **Main courses** £13.95-£21. **Set dinner** (6-7pm, 10-11.15pm) £16.75 2 courses, £19.75 3 courses. **Service** 12.5%. **Credit** AmEx, DC, JCB, MC, V.
The more discreet of the two restaurants in One Aldwych hotel, Indigo sits on a mezzanine above the lobby and so, unlike its neighbour Axis (*see p222*), doesn't have its own entrance. Like the rest of the enterprise, it strives after a stylish 'boutique hotel' feel of modern luxury (all clean lines and

subdued colours), without straying into anything too radical. Staff – polite young men in crisp shirts and ties – dash about a lot, though often with little apparent purpose. The menu is as modishly European-eclectic as the surroundings, with some distinctive features such as a list of salad ingredients from which to create your own. There's an emphasis on organic sourcing. The organic chorizo and truffled mozzarella tart was a nicely smooth quiche, but the chorizo seemed mundane. The day's special starter, chicken, beetroot and asparagus salad, was more memorable, with a smooth balance of flavours. Summer pea risotto with fresh mint and basil was also a bright, refreshing mix. In the house speciality, beef fillet on a potato blini with asparagus and red pepper hollandaise, the accompaniments made more of a mark than the meat. A pleasant meal, but hardly one to make a date for.
Babies and children welcome: high chairs. Booking advisable. Disabled: toilet (hotel). Separate rooms for parties, seating 45 and 48. **Map 18 M7.**

The Ivy

1 West Street, WC2H 9NQ (7836 4751/ www.caprice-holdings.co.uk). Leicester Square tube. **Lunch served** noon-3pm Mon-Sat; noon-3.30pm Sun. **Dinner served** 5.30pm-midnight daily. **Main courses** £9.75-£38.50. **Set lunch** (Sat, Sun) £22.50 3 courses. **Cover** £2. **Credit** AmEx, DC, JCB, MC, V.
It's still possible to go to the Ivy and feel pretty damn good about the world, its works and your place in it. Which is why it remains such a hard table to book and so popular with a heady mix of local ad execs, management consultants stiffing their clients and, oh yes, a celeb list that runs the gamut from Z to A. Station yourself at a table by the bar near the stained-glass entrance if you want to observe the tidal flow of this menagerie; or head into the soberly decorated main room and nestle next to Ricky Gervais. The determinedly unfazed waiting staff are equal to their rather peculiar job, but, more importantly, the food's just what it should be. Beef and lamb shepherd's pie is spot-on – moist, meaty, unfussy – while the mixed grill, which comes with a slab of bubble and squeak, contains top-notch sausages, kidneys and chops.

The emphasis is on simple, often British classics (kedgeree, dressed crab with celeriac, corned beef hash), but you can also build your meal around three kinds of caviar and a curry. Of the dozen or so starters, we've recently tried some splendid seared scallops with a salty garlic/parsley sauce, and a light, nicely nuanced risotto with peas and gorgonzola. Puddings are defiantly trad (sticky toffee or rice pudding), but we'd suggest the Brit cheese plate and maybe a welsh rarebit to round off an enduringly memorable occasion.
Babies and children welcome: high chairs. Booking essential, several wks in advance. Separate room for parties, seats 60 (minimum 25). Vegetarian menu. Vegan dishes. **Map 18 K6.**

Knightsbridge SW1

★ The Fifth Floor

Harvey Nichols, Knightsbridge, SW1X 7RJ (7235 5250/www.harveynichols.com). Knightsbridge tube.
Café **Breakfast served** 10am-noon, **lunch served** noon-3.30pm, **dinner served** 6-10.30pm Mon-Sat. **Brunch served** 11am-5pm Sun. **Tea served** 3.30-6pm Mon-Sat; 3.30-5pm Sun. **Main courses** £9.50-£15.
Restaurant **Brunch served** 11.30am-3.30pm Sat, Sun. **Lunch served** noon-3pm Mon-Fri. **Dinner served** 6-11pm Mon-Sat. **Main courses** £15-£24. **Set dinner** £34.50 2 courses, £39.50 3 courses incl unlimited house wine. **Service** 12.5%. **Credit** AmEx, DC, JCB, MC, V.
The Fifth Floor has had a revamp and a new chef since we last visited – both successful changes. From the pale blue, rounded, feminine space to the staff's professionalism tempered with friendliness, everything seemed right. Then there was the choice of champagnes for an aperitif; the extras (warm cheese straws, petits fours); and, of course, the food, under the auspices of Finnish-born chef Helena Puolakka. To start, carpaccio of halibut brought exquisite, citrusy, paper-thin slices sprinkled with dill. Squid salad came with astonishingly soft squid; a scattering of chickpeas and pomegranate made a good three-way contrast, and delicate little stalks of samphire lurked under the salad leaves. Main-course portions are small, and serving plates big, but the density of flavours meant that each dish was truly ample. Ballotine of chicken, stuffed with girolles and spinach, rested on a creamy, pearl barley risotto, with little flurries of extra frothed-up creaminess around the edges – texture heaven. Lamb loin with girolles, lambs' tongues, merguez and borlotti beans was just as good: plump little rectangles of lamb on spinach, with other touches of robust meatiness, mellow beans and a tangy onion marmalade. Perhaps surprisingly, there are some well-priced wines on the list. Our £16.50 rioja rosé was a great accompaniment to an all-round good time.
Babies and children welcome: high chairs. Booking advisable. Disabled: lift; toilet. Tables outdoors (15, café terrace). Vegetarian menu. **Map 8 F9.**

Marylebone W1

Blandford Street

5-7 Blandford Street, W1U 3DB (7486 9696/ www.blandford-street.co.uk). Baker Street or Bond Street tube. **Lunch served** noon-2.30pm Mon-Fri. **Dinner served** 6.30-10.30pm Mon-Sat. **Main courses** £11-£17.50. **Service** 12.5%. **Credit** AmEx, MC, V.
White linen tablecloths, a maître d' in a pin-striped suit and, on our visit, an almost empty dining room occupied by an eager American couple and two locals laughing self-consciously – Blandford Street is soldiering on. A recent redesign has improved the compact main room, with the dark walls and abstract paintings replaced by red banquettes and hand-painted Cath Kidston-style floral patterns. The food is still good, consisting of prime ingredients from named sources. Thin slices of meltingly soft, cured Glenarm salmon were well matched with celeriac coleslaw and chives, and a wholegrain mustard dressing. A main course assembly of pork belly, morteaux sausage and choucroûte was lifted by wine-accentuated pan juices. Desserts are simple, with Valrhona

Bank Aldwych

chocolate used expertly in a pastry-based tart, light and mousse-like to go with vanilla sauce and pistachio ice-cream. The wine list could improve its choice of Chilean labels, vins de pays, and bottles under £30, but Campbell's 2001 Rutherglen chardonnay/semillon from Australia (£22) showed good orange blossom scents and rounded texture. Blandford Street deserves to be more popular.
Babies and children admitted. Booking advisable lunch. Dress: smart casual (dinner). No-smoking tables. Separate area for parties, seats 18. Tables outdoors (3, pavement). **Map 9 G5.**

Orrery

55 Marylebone High Street, W1U 5RB (7616 8000/www.orrery.co.uk). Baker Street or Regent's Park tube. **Lunch served** noon-3pm daily. **Dinner served** 7-11pm Mon-Sat; 7-10.30pm Sun. **Main courses** £16.50-£30. **Set lunch** £25 3 courses. **Set dinner** (Sun) £30 3 courses incl glass of champagne. **Service** 12.5%. **Credit** AmEx, DC, JCB, MC, V.
Of all Conran's restaurants, Orrery has the grandest ambitions, with the result that it can, on occasion, get rather giddy with a sense of its own importance. From the self-consciously vast digestif trolley to the army of flunkies committed to the opening of doors, the folding of napkins and so on, very few haute cuisine clichés are left undisturbed. It's a shame, as the dining room has Sir Tel's stamp of refined modernism and the Marylebone High Street setting is wonderfully exclusive. Still, the deft Modern European cooking almost always passes muster (provided that paying high prices won't ruin your appetite). A typical seasonal starter would be scallops, apple, avocado and potato salad with summer truffles. Among the mains, wild salmon with pea purée and Jersey royals was outstanding. Desserts such as chocolate and cherry cake with crunchy milk chocolate mousse and cherry sorbet are guaranteed to put a smile on your face. The sommelier takes the selling part of his job seriously, so don't be surprised to find yourself nursing a dessert wine you never really wanted.
Babies and children welcome: high chairs. Booking essential. Disabled: toilet. No-smoking tables. Tables outside (12, bar roof terrace). **Map 3 G4.**

★ Villandry

170 Great Portland Street, W1W 5QB (7631 3131/ www.villandry.com). Great Portland Street tube. **Bar Open** 8am-11pm Mon-Fri; 9am-9pm Sat. **Breakfast served** 8am-noon Mon-Sat. **Lunch served** noon-3.30pm Mon-Fri; noon-3pm Sat. **Snacks served** 5-11pm Mon-Fri; 5-9pm Sat. **Snacks** £5.50-£10.
Restaurant **Lunch served** noon-3pm Mon-Fri. **Dinner served** 6-10.30pm Mon-Sat. **Main courses** £10.50-£22.
Both **Service** 12.5%. **Credit** AmEx, MC, V.
Villandry's troika of mouth-watering deli, slick modern restaurant and bar continues to keep it at the head of the pack of central London's more affordable, quality foodie destinations. Walk through the food hall, past the piled cheeses and orchard fruits, the exotic tins and jars, to reach the pared minimalism of the restaurant. The daily menu capitalises on the importing arm of the business, with assembly-job starters like buffalo mozzarella, grilled aubergines, tomatoes and basil, or red chicory, pear, celeriac and blue cheese salad, letting the quality of the ingredients speak for themselves. Mains are heartier: slow-roasted pork belly, wilted baby gem, roseval potatoes, pancetta and red wine sauce was an intensely flavoured highlight of a recent meal. The likes of lemon and rhubarb tart with crème fraîche, or fresh berries with greek yoghurt and shortbread, are on hand for dessert, but the only way to wrap up a meal at Villandry is to opt for the cheese plate (£11.50 for five, £5.50 for one). Where else would you get the chance to tuck in to perfectly kept organic Godminster cheddar and tome des quatre reines at the same time? A class act.
Babies and children welcome: children's menu (restaurant); high chairs. No smoking (restaurant). Tables outdoors (13, pavement). **Map 3 H5.**

Mayfair W1

Berkeley Square Café

7 Davies Street, W1K 3DD (7629 6993/ www.theberkeleysquare.com). Bond Street tube. **Lunch served** noon-2.30pm, **dinner served** 6-10pm Mon-Fri. **Set meal** £17.95 2 courses, £20.95 3 courses. **Set dinner** £49.50 3 courses, £55 7 courses. **Service** 12.5%. **Credit** AmEx, DC, MC, V.
Owned by music mogul Vince Power, Berkeley Square Café is a rather hit or miss affair. Upstairs, the linen tablecloths, chocolate velvet curtains and soft lighting contrast with a lacklustre basement bar (retro meets garage). Food divides into a reasonably priced set menu and a pricier à la carte, both offering star-quality cooking; the extensive wine list holds little under £20. Chef Steven Black provided a couple of amuse-bouches; a tasty ham-wrapped goat's cheese outdid a rather uninspiring melon 'soup'. First courses were more consistent: chilled pea and mint soup was fresh, creamy and delicious; smoked trout paired well with a smooth avocado purée and aromatic shisu leaves. Mains included a perfectly cooked sea bream lifted by a red pepper sauce, and moist and flavourful organic chicken that was overwhelmed by a busy mound of aubergine, celery and pine nuts. With no desserts left on the set menu we were offered the à la carte, and opted for five well-kept cheeses served with oatcakes. Coffee arrived with petits fours. This is a popular destination for families and pre-casino diners, but was deserted by 10.30pm.
Babies and children admitted. Booking advisable lunch. No-smoking tables. Separate room for parties, seats 30. Tables outdoors (8, terrace). **Map 9 H7.**

Embassy

29 Old Burlington Street, W1S 3AN (7851 0956/ www.theembassygroup.co.uk). Green Park or Piccadilly Circus tube. **Lunch served** noon-3pm Tue-Fri. **Dinner served** 6-11.30pm Tue-Sat. **Main courses** £14.50-£25. **Set meal** (lunch, 6-8pm) £19.50 2 courses, £22.50 3 courses. **Service** 12.5%; 15% for parties of 10 or more. **Credit** AmEx, MC, V.
On hot summer evenings Embassy opens its run of floor-to-ceiling windows, letting in the sounds of an occasional parking Ferrari; these meld, in the golden light of the long ground-floor dining room, with crass (if quiet) disco music and, on our visit, a loud and uncouth conversation about 'clients' in the members bar behind it. All told, it feels rather like a footballer's idea of luxury: low gilded ceiling, high-backed cream leather chairs and gold cloth drapes. Still, we were warmly welcomed on arrival for dinner, and there's little to quibble about with the food, prepared by chef and co-owner Garry Hollihead. We weren't given the option of the à la carte menu, just a choice of three starters, three mains and three desserts. Salmon sashimi with ginger was a delight, beef carpaccio with confit tomatoes and flakes of parmesan likewise; roast ribeye with fried egg, spinach and wild mushrooms, and seared tuna steak with lemon-scented couscous and a garnish of soft broad beans and olives, were well presented, tasty and fresh. Service was attentive and polished, if a little lugubrious, and our 2002 sangiovese (£28.50), from a medium-sized and slightly pricey wine list, made good drinking.
Babies and children admitted (lunch). Booking advisable. Dress: smart casual. Restaurant available for hire. Tables outdoors (6, terrace). **Map 9 J7.**

Langan's Brasserie

Stratton Street, W1J 8LB (7491 8822/ www.langansrestaurants.co.uk). Green Park tube. **Meals served** 12.15-11.45pm Mon-Fri. **Dinner served** 7pm-midnight Sat. **Main courses** £12.50-£18.50. **Cover** £1.50. **Service** 12.5%. **Credit** AmEx, DC, JCB, MC, V.
Peter Cook wasn't the only one who used to abuse Dudley Moore; the late Peter Langan did it in spades when the actor came in to his restaurant in the 1980s. Nowadays staff may be dressed as the French brasserie norm of white tie and jackets (as

they buzz competently between tightly packed tables), but the flipside to Langan's approach – an emphasis on informality – lives on. Businessmen smoke cigars and drink Armagnac long after lunch, while women in Margaret Thatcher-style dress suits and large beaded necklaces chat away merrily. It's like the last 20 years never happened, and the food is stuck in the 1980s too. A caesar salad with iceberg lettuce was combined with burned croûtons. Lashings of cream smothered a monkfish, scallop and prawn fricassée. The wine list is short but not sweet; someone has made the mistake of following up the excellent 2002 vintage in Burgundy with the same wines from the extremely poor 2003 harvest. Choose the 2003 pinot gris, otherwise known as pinot grigio, from Matakana and taste how much better Kiwis aare with this grape than Italians.
Babies and children welcome: booster chairs. Booking advisable; essential dinner. Entertainment: band 10.30pm Wed-Sat. **Map 9 H7.**
For branches see index.

Nicole's

158 New Bond Street, W1F 2UB (7499 8408). Bond Street or Green Park tube. **Bar Open** 10am-10.45pm Mon-Fri; 10am-6pm Sat. **Meals served** 11.30am-5.30pm Mon-Sat. **Main courses** £9-£12.50.
Restaurant **Breakfast served** 10-11am Mon-Fri; 10-11.30am Sat. **Lunch served** noon-3.30pm Mon-Fri; noon-4pm Sat. **Afternoon tea served** 3-6pm Mon-Sat. **Dinner served** 6.30-10.30pm Mon-Fri. **Main courses** £12.50-£22.50. **Cover** (noon-4pm, 6.30-10.45pm Mon-Sat) £1. **Minimum** £15.
Both **Service** 15%. **Credit** AmEx, DC, JCB, MC, V.
The clientele at Nicole's at lunchtime, when the place is at its busiest, will come as no shock. Housed in the basement of the Nicole Farhi store on swish New Bond Street, the restaurant is every bit as chic and elegant as you'd expect. As are the diners – ladies who lunch and, very occasionally, the men who love them. The surprise, perhaps, is that the food lives up to its surroundings; certainly, this is several placs cuts above the popular stereotype of in-store dining. You can choose something as prosaic as a steak, but there are usually a number of more exciting options. A starter of tiger prawns, artichoke and rocket salad came served on a gentle bed of skordalia, but was let down a little by the fridge-cold (and, thus, not totally tender) prawns. However, a main course of pan-fried duck breast was spectacular; it was served with a tangy peach compote and a red rice and almond salad that was as crunchily tasty as the duck was deliciously tender. Prices are high, but portions are generous: the duck breast had plainly been culled from a bird of Dolly Parton-esque proportions. Wear Farhi to blend in.
Babies and children admitted. Booking advisable lunch. No-smoking tables. Restaurant available for hire. **Map 9 H7.**

noble rot

3-5 Mill Street, W1S 2AU (7629 8877/ www.noblerot.com). Oxford Circus tube. **Lunch served** noon-3pm Mon-Fri. **Dinner served** 6-11pm Mon-Sat. **Main courses** £17-£25. **Set lunch** £18 2 courses, £22.50 3 courses. **Service** 12.5%. **Credit** AmEx, DC, JCB, MC, V.
Having a name that demands explanation ('noble rot' is a grape fungus that's used in making the finest sweet wines – which feature among the house specialities) and insisting it's written in lower case indicates a certain pretentiousness, but this aspirational Mayfair venue has its attractions too. Service can wander off-track on weekend evenings, but at lunchtime things are much calmer. The fashionably international menu changes frequently. For our lunch, several dishes shared an emphasis on creaminess: a plus for some, but not others. Nicely smoky haddock was served with french beans, quails' eggs and a creamy mustard sauce; fine-flavoured sautéed scallops were a little overpowered by their back-up of macaroni in basil and cream. Porcini risotto was a similarly rich, highly enjoyable mix, but our best choice was the

RESTAURANTS

meaty merguez sausages with tomato couscous and cinnamon and fruit sauce, in which creaminess was mercifully absent. The wine list is huge, yet not just out to impress, with good labels at accessible prices. The dining room has a stylishly mellow look; the members' bar in the basement is far more baroque. *Babies and children admitted. Booking advisable. Separate room for parties, seats 40. Tables outdoors (6, terrace).* **Map 9 H6.**

Sketch: Gallery

9 Conduit Street, W1S 2XG (0870 777 4488/ www.sketch.uk.com). Oxford Circus tube. **Dinner served** 7-10.30pm Mon-Sat. **Main courses** £18-£33. **Service** 12.5%. **Credit** AmEx, DC, MC, V.
Fashionistas are still flocking to Gallery more than two years after it opened. The big attraction is the cool vibe and audacious design. Should you arrive early and get past the self-important door staff, you can sit in the pod-like bar and enjoy a *Barbarella* moment before admiring the egg-shaped toilet cubicles. Moving images projected on to the dining room's white walls give a nightclub feel, an effect aided by throbbing ambient music. The cooking is mostly OK, though it's frequently a triumph of style over substance, and at high prices (starters typically £8-£24, mains £18-£30). A starter of aubergine was served three ways, one of them cut wafer-thin then oven-dried, the result chewy and flavourless; the stuffed and stewed versions were fine, but the white chocolate garnish was pointless. Pretentious descriptions litter the menu: in gnocchi with 'scents of Costa Rica and dried ceps', the 'scents' referred to an odourless shake of ground coffee that made an otherwise good dish gritty. The best dish was the simplest – organic salmon, slow-cooked and served with noodles. Desserts at £7.50 seemed like a bargain, and green sponge cake with rocket, pistachio cream and green apple sorbet was much nicer than it sounds. The wines by the glass are dreary and expensive. Gallery is a good place to go for a dramatic meal when someone else is paying, though.

Booking essential. Dress: smart casual. Entertainment: DJs 11.30pm-2am Mon-Sat. Restaurant available for hire. **Map 9 J6.**

Sotheby's Café

Sotheby's, 34-35 New Bond Street, W1A 2AA (7293 5077). Bond Street tube. **Breakfast served** 9.30-11.30am, **lunch served** noon-3pm, **afternoon tea served** 3-4.45pm Mon-Fri. **Main courses** £12.50-£17. **Set lunch** £15.50 2 courses. **Set tea** £5.25. **Credit** AmEx, DC, MC, V.
How distinctly, delightfully 1930s is this swish refectory on the ground floor of the famous auction house: big, Beatonesque black and white portraits, tiled mirrors, geometrically judicious dark wood panelling, a long leather banquette and waiters who say Monsieur and Madame a lot (although there's no particular French bias in evidence). Fellow lunchers speak in quiet, cultured tones, but the mood is unstuffy – in keeping with the short, user-friendly menu and wine list: three starters, three mains and a few more desserts. Celery soup with blue cheese cream was suitably autumnal, and moroccan chicken with roast sweet potato and tomato and onion salad was tasty and nicely presented. Another table's pesto risotto cakes with grilled vegetables looked just as appetising. Still, prices are quite high and service wasn't faultless: a glass of red Côtes du Rhône was served too warm, and the waiters bantered too audibly and inappropriately for the setting (even, at one point, commenting ironically on the size of a previous customer's tip). Dinner isn't served, but you can also come for breakfast or afternoon tea.
Babies and children admitted. Booking essential lunch. Disabled: toilet. No smoking. **Map 9 H6.**

Piccadilly W1

The Wolseley

160 Piccadilly, W1J 9EB (7499 6996/ www.thewolseley.com). Green Park tube. **Breakfast served** 7-11.30am Mon-Fri; 9-11.30am Sat, Sun. **Lunch served** noon-2.30pm

Mon-Fri; noon-3pm Sat, Sun. **Tea served** 3-5.30pm Mon-Fri; 3.30-6pm Sat, Sun. **Dinner served** 5.30pm-midnight Mon-Sat; 5.30-11pm Sun. **Main courses** £9.50-£23. **Cover** £2. **Credit** AmEx, DC, JCB, MC, V.
This handsome building was built in 1921 as a car showroom, and its huge windows, luxury decorations and high vaulted ceilings doubtless befitted the role. But its current incarnation as a European-style grand café is surely the one it was born for, so perfectly does it frame the buzz of a score of waiters and a hundred-plus customers rehearsing the interconnected dramas of dining. That the Wolseley's owners are alumni of the Ivy (*see p223*) and Le Caprice (*see p227*) explains why it provides an experience as much as sustenance – indeed, sheer pleasure in our surroundings tided us over a couple of lapses during our dinner visit. From a largely French menu (with guest appearances from other European cuisines), starters of lobster bisque and celeriac remoulade were excellent, but the main courses sagged – particularly an expensive (£16.75) steak frites that Le Caprice would have been ashamed to serve. There are multiple menus: you can come here just for the cake of the day (*see p299*), or breakfast, or caviar, or a brasserie snack. The black-clad staff will treat you with just the same ringmaster efficiency, tinged with hauteur. We recommended booking in the evening: the Wolseley may be big, but, boy, is it popular.
Babies and children welcome: crayons; high chairs. Disabled: toilet. Takeaway service. **Map 9 J7.**

Pimlico SW1

Tate Britain Restaurant

Tate Britain, Millbank, SW1P 4RG (7887 8825/ www.tate.org.uk). Pimlico tube/77A bus. **Breakfast served** 10-11.30am, **lunch served** 11.30am-3pm, **afternoon tea served** 3-5pm daily. **Main courses** £14.50-£17.50. **Service** 12.5%. **Credit** AmEx, DC, MC, V.

The elder Tate's restaurant talks up its Rex Whistler mural, but the painting seemed to us in need of a little TLC – it wasn't helped by being too severely lit to be easily seen at close quarters. The rather short Sunday lunch menu (further limited because several of the main-course specials were available by 1.30pm) struck a neat compromise between traditional and modern. Succulent Tom Wilson lamb cutlets came with fresh mint instead of mint sauce; salmon was served as seared maple-cured cubes, glossily gelatinous on top and conventionally flaky beneath, along with a delicious baby leaf salad (although the advertised apple was indiscernible). You could even have ox tongue – served in a truffled salad with bresaola. Puddings range from apple and gooseberry crumble to chocolate and chilli tart with orange and passionfruit. Not everything came off (the deconstructed scotch egg on potted ham terrine with a strip of rarebit toast was ponderous), but service was great from the off. Our waitress greeted our choice from a good wine list with informed enthusiasm, and was on hand whenever required, yet never intruded. Amid the dignified chatter of other diners (decidedly grown-up, if predominantly dressed-down), our meal proved a cheerful one.

Babies and children welcome: high chairs. Booking advisable. Disabled: toilets. No smoking. Tables outdoors (8, terrace). **Map 16 L11.**

St James's SW1

The Avenue
7-9 St James's Street, SW1A 1EE (7321 2111/ www.egami.co.uk). Green Park tube.
Bar **Open** noon-11pm Mon-Fri; 6-11pm Sat; noon-10pm Sun.
Restaurant **Brunch served** noon-3.30pm Sun. **Lunch served** noon-3pm Mon-Sat. **Dinner served** 5.45pm-11.30pm Mon-Thur; 5.45pm-12.30am Fri, Sat; 5.45-10pm Sun. **Main courses** £13.50-£18. **Set meal** £17.95 2 courses, £19.95 3 courses. **Service** 12.5%. **Credit** AmEx, DC, MC, V.
Compared to the usual oak panels of St James, the Avenue is a contemporary space: a cavernous white box with occasional decoration (modern paintings, long illuminated bar-top, grand piano). It's a successful operation and was fairly full when we visited early in the week – a good sign, even if the hard acoustics work against easy conversation, and the rotation of waiting staff makes for a less personal service. At first we thought the portions just looked small, in the context of such a large room, but we soon realised they sometimes were. Tiny pieces of bread looked lost in their basket and, when we had eaten them, they were replaced by even smaller morsels. A starter of wild mushroom risotto was intensely concentrated in size as well as flavour – as if arborio rice was a rare ingredient. Calf's liver was pretty good, keeping pink despite the thin slices. Roast pollack was a highlight, featuring deliciously textured fish, though, again, garnished with strictly rationed peas and beans. To finish, a fun sundae in a tall glass topped with Carnation milk ice-cream certainly meant we left with a good impression.
Babies and children welcome. Disabled: toilet. **Map 9 J8.**

Le Caprice
Arlington House, Arlington Street, SW1A 1RT (7629 2239/www.caprice-holdings.co.uk). Green Park tube. **Lunch served** noon-3pm Mon-Sat; noon-4pm Sun. **Dinner served** 5.30pm-midnight Mon-Sat; 6pm-midnight Sun. **Main courses** £14.25-£26.50. **Cover** £2. **Credit** AmEx, DC, MC, V.
Nothing we can write will ever deter Le Caprice's natural constituency (ladies who lunch, local fat cats and older celebrities) from dining here, but for anyone looking to the place for a special meal out – think twice. The supercilious manner in which bookings are dispensed sets the tone (staff are pretty pleased with themselves in general), one that the £2 cover charge for indifferent bread does nothing to dispel. Our most recent lunch was a fairly average affair at a not inconsiderable price. A special of fillet of brill with wild orach (a leaf

---

vegetable) and beetroot for £22.75 was fine, but oversalted; much better was the Caprice menu stalwart salmon fish cake with buttered spinach and sorrel sauce – too rich to finish, but good. Accompanying chips were poor things – anaemic and tasteless; better was a green herb salad. Tried-and-tested starters include caesar salad, eggs benedict and steak tartare; dessert-wise, it's hard to go wrong with Scandinavian berries with white chocolate sauce, though summer fruits with raspberry sorbet meant our meal finished on a pleasant note. The room is glam in a 1930s black-and-white way that works as well at lunch as it does later in the day. The bottom of the menu advertises the book *Le Caprice*, written by AA Gill; if you like the idea of that, you'll have a great time here.
Babies and children welcome: high chairs. Booking essential, several wks in advance. Entertainment: pianist 7pm-midnight daily. Vegetarian menu. Vegan dishes. **Map 9 J8.**

Quaglino's
16 Bury Street, SW1Y 6AJ (7930 6767/ www.conran.com). Green Park tube.
Bar **Open** 11.30am-1am Mon-Thur; 11.30am-2am Fri, Sat; noon-11pm Sun.
Restaurant **Lunch served** noon-3pm daily. **Dinner served** 5.30-11.30pm Mon-Thur; 5.30pm-12.30am Fri, Sat; 5.30-10.30pm Sun. **Tea served** 3pm-5.30pm daily. **Main courses** £12.50-£22.50. **Set meal** (noon-3pm, 5.30-6.30pm daily) £17 2 courses, £19 3 courses. **Service** 12.5%.
Both **Credit** AmEx, DC, JCB, MC, V.
The stylish staircase is the focal point here, with shiny Qs wrought into the elaborate banisters. It was designed for making a big entrance in Quaglino's mid-1990s heyday, when this huge lower-ground restaurant was as much a place for entertainment as dining. When we visited, we felt like part of a production line. The factory image was intensified by the wall of sound (despite the place being half empty), the corporate diners and the roof (resembling that of a bus garage). The team of stressed waiters rotated as if each had only one task to perform at each table, emphasising the impersonal, dining-by-numbers touch. The food was more miss than hit. Seared tuna was cold and dry and had been plated some time in advance – the decorative sesame squiggle had skinned over. Warm scallops were attractively presented on their shell with grapefruit vinaigrette, but the sole meunière, while tasty, should have been dredged in flour before being cooked in butter. A tomato and shallot salad was ornate, but lacking in flavour. Some ground was regained by a decent lamb rump, only to be lost

---

by a lacklustre chocolate mousse. Service was pressingly prompt and we were back up those stairs in little more than an hour.
Babies and children welcome: children's menu; high chairs. Booking advisable. Disabled: toilet. Entertainment: musicians daily (call for details). Separate room for parties, seats 44 (7389 9619). **Map 17 J7.**

Soho W1

★ Alastair Little
49 Frith Street, W1D 4SG (7734 5183). Leicester Square or Tottenham Court Road tube. **Lunch served** noon-3pm Mon-Fri. **Dinner served** 6-11.30pm Mon-Sat. **Main courses** £24.50. **Set lunch** £31 2 courses. **Set dinner** £38 3 courses. **Service** 12.5% for parties of 8 or more. **Credit** AmEx, JCB, MC, V.
This diminutive Soho stalwart is still going strong after 20-odd years, since the 1980s when Little (no longer at the helm) was a key figure in the redefinition of Modern British cooking. The short menu now – as then – draws on notable ingredients and influences, but the food is never pretentious. Indeed, simplicity is one of the restaurant's selling points. The culinary peaks of our latest visit (which isn't to imply there were troughs) were a superb starter of smoked eel with potato cakes, beetroot and horseradish, and a super-fresh main of wild sea trout, samphire, Jersey royals, shrimp and cucumber butter sauce. But the real show-stopper was something much more simple: a ball of own-made vanilla ice-cream swimming in a rich pool of Pedro Ximenez sherry, served in a wine glass. Suffice to say we can't remember the last time we found ourselves daydreaming about a dessert several days later. Some find the decor a little plain, but we rather like the homely, unshowy look, with a bookcase in the corner and bright paintings. Prices are fairly steep at £38 for three courses, but we rate Alastair Little very highly for its beautiful food, unpretentious attitude and the charming, refreshingly un-intrusive service.
Babies and children admitted. Booking advisable. Separate room for parties, seats 25. **Map 17 K6.**

★ Andrew Edmunds
46 Lexington Street, W1F 0LW (7437 5708). Oxford Circus or Piccadilly Circus tube. **Lunch served** 12.30-3pm Mon-Fri; 1-3pm Sat; 1-3.30pm Sun. **Dinner served** 6-10.45pm Mon-Sat; 6-10.30pm Sun. **Main courses** £7.95-£15. **Service** (over £50) 12.5%. **Credit** MC, V.
This long-running Soho establishment could show many a young pretender how it should be done. The whole operation – from the unaffected decor to the straightforward menu to the casual bonhomie of the staff – runs with an effortless ease that can only result from years of practice polished to perfection. The premises are small, with wooden pew seating upstairs and closely packed tables in the dark basement; cramped, yes, but with a vibe of intimate exclusivity. The short menu offers high-quality seasonal ingredients, cooked simply and with aplomb. And prices are exceedingly fair for both wine and food; when did you last see a starter for £2.95 (french onion soup with goat's cheese crostini)? An early summer visit brought starters of impeccable English asparagus with hollandaise; and rough-textured salt cod and green bean fritters with a spicy tomato and black olive salsa. To follow: a comfortingly earthy game pie crammed with succulent meat, accompanied by creamy mash; and seared tuna cooked just right (the inside almost raw) with aioli. It's worth saving space for pud: a long list offers enticing favourites such as lemon tart, sticky toffee pudding and Neal's Yard cheeses. Come in a suit or in torn jeans; you'll feel equally special.
Babies and children admitted. Booking advisable; essential weekends. Tables outdoors (2, pavement). **Map 17 J6.**

Circus
1 Upper James Street, W1F 9DF (7534 4000/ www.egami.co.uk). Piccadilly Circus tube.
Bar **Open** noon-1am Mon-Wed; noon-3am Thur, Fri; 6pm-3am Sat. **Admission** (after 11pm) £5 Mon-Sat.

Restaurant **Lunch served** noon-3pm, **dinner served** 5.45pm-midnight Mon-Sat. **Main courses** £6-£18.80. **Set meal** (lunch, 5.45pm-midnight Mon; 5.45-7.15pm, 10.30pm-midnight Tue-Sat) £14.50 2 courses, £16.50 3 courses. **Service** 12.5%. **Credit** AmEx, DC, MC, V.
Occupying a prominent corner site just south of Carnaby Street, Circus is surrounded by advertising agencies. Execs pack in here for a midday bite, amid the minimalist white walls, large windows and spotlights. There's an attempt at frivolity with pinned-up quotations, such as Miss Piggy's 'Don't eat more than you can lift' – hard to do at Circus where portions are on the small side of acceptable. Not much has changed in ten years. Smoked haddock with risotto cake, spinach and soft-poached egg has been on the menu from the start – and the fish still needs poaching rather than pan-frying, to give a contrast in textures. A slab of feta completely overwhelmed a few pieces of roasted pepper, and the dish was without the billed olives. Missing in action too was parmesan, promised with provençal vegetables and small pieces of lamb saddle, though the meat was well cooked. The superb wine list is the legacy of former sommelier Matthew Bradford, the pick being an interesting blend of two grapes normally kept apart – pinot noir and gamay – in Domaine du Salvard's 2002 Cheverny, from the Loire.
Babies and children admitted. Booking advisable. Entertainment (bar): DJ 9pm-3am Thur-Sat. Separate room for parties, seats 16. **Map 17 J6.**

Strand WC2

Adam Street

9 Adam Street, WC2N 6AA (7379 8000/ www.adamstreet.co.uk). Charing Cross tube/rail.
Lunch served noon-2.30pm Mon-Fri. **Dinner served** (members only) 6-11pm Mon-Sat.
Main courses £9-£17.90. **Set lunch** £16.50 2 courses, £19.50 3 courses. **Cover** (lunch) £5. **Service** 12.5%. **Credit** AmEx, MC, V.
This private club opens its restaurant to non-members at lunchtime. For the £5 a head cover charge, you do get a more laid-back and distinctive experience than is generally available locally at these prices. Ring on the black door to be let in, head downstairs past modern art on white walls, then onward to the spacious, attractive dining room (vaulted to support the road above). The menu features some items that nod towards the fustier end of clubland: macaroni cheese and shepherd's pie are among the comfort foods; and the novelty breads (sun-dried tomato, walnut) reminded us of teacakes. Otherwise, the range is more enterprising. The highly fragrant truffle oil on a fresh green pea soup could be smelled several feet away and the parmesan crisps that went with it were savoury perfection. Equally successful was a succulent duck confit scattered with soft sultanas and a touch of lime; less so a slab of grilled salmon, brought down by an oily taint. Adam Street is a good place if you're after a sense of

occasion without prohibitive prices. You should book a few days in advance to secure your place among the members and others in the know.
Babies and children admitted (lunch). Booking advisable. Separate room for parties, seats 45. **Map 18 L7.**

Trafalgar Square WC2

The Portrait Restaurant

National Portrait Gallery, St Martin's Place, WC2H 0HE (7312 2490/www.searcys.co.uk).
Leicester Square tube. **Open** 10am-5pm Mon-Wed, Sat, Sun; 10am-9pm Thur, Fri. **Lunch served** 11.45am-2.45pm Mon-Fri; 11.30am-3pm Sat, Sun. **Tea served** 3-5pm daily. **Dinner served** 5.30-8.30pm Thur, Fri. **Main courses** £11.95-£17.95. **Service** 12.5%. **Credit** AmEx, JCB, MC, V.
When it comes to location, the Portrait has it made: perched on top of the National Portrait Gallery, it offers a pigeon's-eye view of the rooftops around Trafalgar Square. A window runs the length of the long thin space – modishly decorated in grey, white and black – so everyone gets a view. Catering company Searcy's (which also operates a restaurant at the Barbican; *see p219*) is in charge, hence you get competent, but unspectacular cooking. Endive, roquefort, walnut and pear salad was an adequate starter; a more interesting option was black pudding with a poached egg and wild mushrooms on toast. Mains include a decent range of fish (halibut, salmon, tuna, sea bass) and meat (chicken, beef, lamb), plus a couple of vegetarian choices, but prices are high for the quality, with most dishes topping £16. And errors are made: gnocchi with peas, beans, mint and rocket was almost inedible, with the gnocchi badly charred on one side. Staff have a corporate air. The serviceable wine list offers a generous 18 options by the glass. Our main criticism? The space gets unpleasantly noisy when full, thanks to the low, angled ceiling and hard surfaces. Handy for the nearby cultural institutions, then, but not destination dining.
Babies and children welcome: children's menu; high chairs. Booking advisable. Disabled: lift; toilet. No-smoking tables. **Map 18 K7.**

Westminster SW1

Bank Westminster

45 Buckingham Gate, SW1E 6BS (7379 9797/ www.bankrestaurants.com). St James's Park tube.
Bar **Open** 11am-11pm Mon, Tue; 11am-1am Wed-Fri; 5pm-1am Sat.
Restaurant **Lunch served** noon-3pm Mon-Fri. **Dinner served** 5.30-11pm Mon-Sat. **Main courses** £15.95-£21.50. **Set lunch** £13.50 2 courses, £15 3 courses. **Set dinner** £15.95 2 courses, £17.95 3 courses. **Service** 12.5%. *Both* **Credit** AmEx, DC, MC, V.
Busy at lunchtime, this outpost of the Aldwych original (*see p222*) is a little quieter in the evenings, although the dearth of decent eating options in the area means that the expansive space – less atmospheric than its sister, but brighter, thanks to

huge picture windows – rarely feels empty. The menu changes regularly, although some dishes, such as a surprisingly sensual starter of soft, delicious black pudding, seared foie gras and a fried duck egg, appear to be mainstays. Cornish crab cannelloni, served with avocado and cumin dressing and mango salsa, wasn't as interesting as its description, but enjoyable nonetheless. For mains, pan-fried lamb's liver with sautéed sweetbreads was strong and edifying, though – perhaps unsurprisingly – a 'poppiette' of lemon sole and shrimps with a delicate potato fondant was subtler. Two knocks on the place. One, the slightly higher-than-they-should-be prices – though it's unlikely the expense-accounters who make up most of the clientele really notice. And two, while the fish and meat selections are always strong, the vegetarian options – perhaps a salad, perhaps a gnocchi – feel like an afterthought. Service was careful and competent, if slightly fussy.
Babies and children welcome: high chairs. Booking advisable. Disabled: toilet. Separate room for parties, seats 50. Tables outdoors (4, terrace). **Map 15 J9.**

West

Chiswick W4

Sam's Brasserie & Bar **NEW**

11 Barley Mow Passage, W4 4PH (8987 0555/ www.samsbrasserie.co.uk). Chiswick Park or Turnham Green tube.
Bar **Open** 9am-11pm Mon-Sat; 9am-10.30pm Sun.
Restaurant **Brunch served** 9am-3pm Sat, Sun. **Lunch served** noon-3pm daily. **Dinner served** 6.30-10.30pm Mon-Sat; 6.30-10pm Sun. **Main courses** £9.50-£16.50. **Service** 12.5%. *Both* **Credit** AmEx, MC, V.
The beautifully sparse conversion of this former paper factory in Chiswick has been done with élan. The muted colour scheme, huge pendant lighting and clever retro-industrial design were overseen by Sam Harrison, the charming young owner. Harrison used to work as a restaurant manager for Rick Stein in Padstow; now Stein is one of his financial backers. It seems a good move: Sam's is the kind of place that turns a meal out locally into a special treat. Young leeks were char-grilled until tender, then dressed with sherry vinegar and shavings of parmesan, topped with a soft-boiled egg: simple, but perfect. Fish soup was a rich, dense purée served with rouille and croutons; we're sure Rick would approve. A main course of Italian ossobuco comprised shin of veal steaks cut across the bone, served with risotto alla milanese. It was a proper risotto, but too strongly scented with saffron. Heavy spicing (this time garam masala) also marred another main, of diver-caught plaice. Puddings range from crème brûlée to raspberry millefeuille. There's a good selection of interesting wines by the glass, the atmosphere is very convivial, and the well-appointed staff were smiling and efficient.

Babylon

Babies and children welcome: children's menu, high chairs. Booking advisable (restaurant). Disabled: toilet. Entertainment: magician 9am Sat, Sun. No smoking (restaurant). Separate room for parties, seats 25.

Gloucester Road SW7

L'Etranger

36 Gloucester Road, SW7 4QT (7584 1118/ www.etranger.co.uk). Gloucester Road tube. **Lunch served** noon-3pm Mon-Fri. **Dinner served** 6-11pm Mon-Sat. **Main courses** £12-£20. **Set meal** (noon-3pm, 6-7pm Mon-Fri) £14.50 2 courses, £16.50 3 courses. **Service** 12.5%. **Credit** AmEx, MC, V.

This upmarket French-Japanese fusion restaurant continues to thrive, with a diverse mix of well-heeled locals savouring such stimulating curiosities as foie gras tempura with tamarind sauce, and pollen madeleines on pandanus leaves. The regulars clearly enjoy themselves, but any public school antics are restrained by the soothing and pervasive lavender and grey decor (even the loo paper is lavender). Though occasionally eccentric, the food is of a high standard: a peach soufflé was so exquisite and fresh you could smell the blush; a confit of milk-fed pork was delicately addictive; and the purple and brown concentric rings of each venison medallion looked sumptuous. Perhaps, the Japanese twists are distracting rather than improving (the tempura foie gras wasn't as successful as the more mainstream pan-fried portion that came with it) and sometimes the fusion extends only so far as serving a French dish on a Japanese plate (witness the crème brûlée). Overall, this is a confident and indulgent dining venue, though food prepared with so much care and labour doesn't come cheap.
Babies and children welcome: high chairs. Booking essential dinner. Dress: smart casual. Restaurant available for hire. Vegetarian menu. **Map 13 C9.** **For branch see index.**

Kensington W8

Babylon

The Roof Gardens, seventh floor, 99 Kensington High Street, W8 5SA (7368 3993/www.virgin. com/roofgardens). High Street Kensington tube. **Lunch served** noon-3pm daily. **Dinner served** 7-11pm Mon-Sat. **Main courses** £11-£20. **Set lunch** (Mon-Fri) £14 2 courses, £16 3 courses; (Sun) £18.50 2 courses, £21 3 courses. **Service** 12.5%. **Credit** AmEx, DC, JCB, MC, V.

Planes, trains and hot-air balloons – Richard Branson has a go at most things, but until recently he had never owned a restaurant above a department store. Yet, thanks to this dining room perched over the swaying trees and pink flamingos of a roof garden, Virgin has another successful business. Babylon is like a buzzy downtown New York diner. It has sleek white walls and banquettes filled with groups of well-dressed women with jewellery and time on their hands. Chef Oliver Smith has improved on his work at Bank Aldwych (*see p222*), now serving super-charged brasserie food with a twist. Steak tartare was surrounded by piles of tomato, parsley, capers and lemon juice. A juicy, thyme-stuffed coquelet was topped with a small block of butter stuffed with pine nuts and sun-dried tomatoes, plus fresh chervil. For dessert, a half-set plum wine jelly was surrounded by blackberries and pieces of kiwi fruit, crowned by a pear and amaretto sorbet. In comparison to all this invention, the wine list was a let down – the best choice being a newly listed Santa Isabel 2003 gewürztraminer, from Chile's Casablanca Valley.
Babies and children welcome: children's menu; entertainer; high chairs (Sun). Booking advisable. Disabled: lift; toilet. Separate room for parties, seats 14. Tables outdoors (15, balcony). **Map 7 B9.**

★ Clarke's

124 Kensington Church Street, W8 4BH (7221 9225/www.sallyclarke.com). Notting Hill Gate tube. **Brunch served** 11am-2pm Sat. **Lunch served** 12.30-2pm Mon-Fri. **Dinner served** 7-10pm Tue-Sat. **Main courses** (lunch) £14-£16. **Set dinner** £32-£36 2 courses; £49.50 4 courses incl coffee, truffles & service. **Credit** AmEx, DC, JCB, MC, V.

A long-standing favourite, Sally Clarke's restaurant has retained consistently high standards, a commitment to fresh, simple cooking and a long line of appreciative regulars over more than 20 years. The restaurant occupies a modest shop-front space, unpretentiously decorated in pastel shades, with starched white tablecloths, wicker chairs and plenty of fresh flowers. Next door, a bakery/grocery sells Sally Clarke goodies. Menus change daily, with the option of two or three courses at lunchtime and the now-legendary no-choice set dinner menu. Fresh, seasonal and meticulously sourced ingredients are the order of the day. Influences dip in and out of France, the Mediterranean and California. A spring menu might offer simply poached fillet of halibut with zingy aïoli, served with grilled fennel, marinated beetroot and wild rocket. This could be followed by juicy new-season Welsh lamb, roasted and served with a creamy tarragon sauce, peas, fava beans, cabbage, asparagus and puréed potatoes. Simple salads show off the freshest ingredients. To finish, there are Neal's Yard cheeses and a dark, bitter chocolate brownie served with maple syrup ice-cream. The wine list is one of London's best, and the expert, charming maître d', Paul Baldwin, is usually on hand to explain it.
Babies and children welcome: high chair. Booking advisable; essential weekends. No smoking. **Map 7 B7.**

Kensington Place

201-209 Kensington Church Street, W8 7LX (7727 3184/www.egami.co.uk). Notting Hill Gate tube. **Lunch served** noon-3.30pm daily. **Dinner served** 6.30-11.45pm Mon-Sat; 6.30-10.15pm Sun. **Main courses** £14-£22.50. **Set lunch** (Mon-Fri) £18.50 3 courses; (Sun) £21.50 3 courses. **Set dinner** £24.50 3 courses, £39.50 3 courses incl wine. **Service** 12.5%. **Credit** AmEx, DC, JCB, MC, V.

A Notting Hill landmark, which now finds itself described as a veteran, Kensington Place (est. 1987) reliably delivers on both food and atmosphere. Sometimes the latter can be a little deafening (with locals wining and dining during the week, and returning with their many small offspring for Sunday lunch). And service can be distracted. But the seasonal menu and eclectic, wide-ranging wine list, rarely disappoint. The menu might offer some new-season asparagus with a poached duck's egg and herb butter to start, followed by venison cutlets served with parmesan and pesto, or roast bream with a citrus tang and fruity olive oil. Puddings are classics with a twist: pears poached in Beaujolais matched with black pepper ice-cream, or perhaps bitter chocolate mousse served hot, with coffee ice-cream. The set menus, both at lunch and dinner, offer excellent value.
Babies and children welcome: high chairs. Booking advisable; essential weekends. Disabled: toilet. Separate room for parties, seats 45. **Map 7 B7.**

Launceston Place

1A Launceston Place, W8 5RL (7937 6912/ www.egami.co.uk). Gloucester Road or High Street Kensington tube. **Lunch served** 12.30-2.30pm Mon-Fri, Sun. **Dinner served** 6-11pm Mon-Sat; 6-10.30pm Sun. **Main courses** £17.50-£19.50. **Set lunch** £15.50 2 courses, £18.50 3 courses; (Sun) £22.50 3 courses. **Service** 12.5%. **Credit** AmEx, DC, JCB, MC, V.

It's a fair bet that the classic decor here – pale colours, traditional landscape paintings; seating as from a country-house hotel – mirrors that of many of the smart homes nearby. Accordingly, affluent local residents seem to regard the restaurant as a cosy neighbourhood dining room and trusted standby. Service is correct, unstuffy and charming; we appreciated receiving full guidance on what each main course came with, instead of (as so often happens) being lured into taking on unnecessary side orders. The food offers an enjoyable balance between familiarity and innovation. As a refreshing summer starter, peach and tomato salad with capers and basil was lovely; seared scallops and fennel salad had a welcome tang of quality ingredients. Mains were just as pleasant, featuring unusual flavours and combinations: first-rate veal escalopes was richly matched with parma ham and sage; and (slightly dry) sea bass was set off by a perky basil mayonnaise. Desserts are fairly trad, with plenty of bright fresh fruit. Wines are very properly served. This will never be a place of radical innovation, but it's easy to see why Launceston Place is popular.
Babies and children welcome: children's portions. Booking advisable. Dress: smart casual. Separate rooms for parties, seating 14 and 30. **Map 7 C9.**

The Terrace

33C Holland Street, W8 4LX (7937 3224/ www.theterracerestaurant.co.uk). High Street Kensington tube. **Lunch served** noon-2.30pm Mon-Sat; noon-3pm Sun. **Dinner served** 6.30-11pm Mon-Sat. **Main courses** £11.50-£20. **Set lunch** (Mon-Fri) £14.50 2 courses, £17.50 3 courses. **Set brunch** (noon-3pm Sat; noon-3.30pm Sun) £17.50 2 courses, £21.50 3 courses. **Service** 12.5%. **Credit** AmEx, JCB, MC, V.

This neat little restaurant is ideally suited to its location, deep in Kensington's cosy web of smart mews and historic cottages. The dining room is snug, light and understated, while in front is the pretty shrub-lined terrace that gives the place its name. This is also the restaurant's greatest asset, a charming spot for outdoor dining. Food follows the now-common Euro-eclectic style, with a few Middle Eastern and Pacific Rim touches; it's decent without being anything special. Our starters were best: smoked duck breast with pancetta, parma ham and sesame-dressed leaves had good, rounded flavours, though the ham seemed to have got lost; the house salad was a great fresh mix including celeriac and grilled courgettes, with a lively pesto dressing. Mains – most of which sounded pretty

RESTAURANTS

busy – were less successful. Pan-fried fillet of sea bass with parsnip purée, garlic spinach and lime beurre blanc was less exciting than it sounded; and in citrus-marinated char-grilled guinea fowl with parsley tabouleh, poached egg and rocket, the meat was overshadowed by all the rest, and the egg was considerably overcooked. Wines are a plus, with plenty of good labels at fair prices, and service is charming, if inexperienced.
Babies and children welcome: children's portions; high chairs. Booking advisable. No smoking (terrace). Tables outdoors (7, terrace).
Map 7 B8.

Maida Vale W9

The Vale

99 Chippenham Road, W9 2AB (7266 0990). Maida Vale or Westbourne Park tube. **Brunch served** 11am-3pm Sun. **Lunch served** 12.30-2.30pm Tue-Fri. **Dinner served** 7-11pm Tue-Sat. **Main courses** £8.50-£14. **Set dinner** £15.50 2 courses, £18.50 3 courses. **Service** 12.5%. **Credit** AmEx, DC, JCB, MC, V.
The Vale specialises in family groups celebrating birthdays, with coloured balloons, dads in shorts and moody grandparents – all in a rambling, glass-roofed corner site. The peeling wood frames and frosted glass cover the view of Billy's Dry Cleaning and the local paper shop. But the food is way above home-cooked fare. A minted pea soup with lettuce was a great, fresh-tasting and well-made dish. Perfectly cooked scallops came with a taste of the sea, as well as pieces of monkfish, and a cumin-spiced avocado and tomato pile. The Vale's version of using an ingredient 'three ways' took the form of vodka in a ginger Moscow Mule granita, an outstanding and alcoholic crème brûlée White Russian, and vodka and raspberry jelly. The only bum note in our meal was puy lentils stewed with smoked bacon (far too salty and not fresh enough) as the bed for juicy roasted quail. The wine list is excellent, including the great 2003 Laughing Magpie from Aussie winemakers d'Arenberg. And don't miss the 20-year-old Vin Santo from Italy, Villa di Vetrice Chianti Rufina, at £6 a glass.
Babies and children welcome: children's portions; high chairs. Booking advisable. No-smoking tables. Separate rooms for parties, seating 12 and 23.
Map 1 A3.

Olympia W14

Cotto

44 Blythe Road, W14 0HA (7602 9333). Hammersmith or Shepherd's Bush tube/ Kensington (Olympia) tube/rail. **Lunch served** noon-2.30pm Mon-Fri. **Dinner served** 7-10.30pm Mon-Sat. **Set lunch** £14.50 2 courses, £17.50 3 courses. **Set dinner** £18 2 courses, £20.50 3 courses. **Service** 12.5%. **Credit** AmEx, JCB, MC, V.
Beneath the looming hulk of the Olympia Exhibition Centre, Cotto has occasional business from convention-goers, but isn't quite close enough to residential Shepherd's Bush to attract locals. A refit has given it a warm chocolate-brown colour scheme, producing a homely gastropub look. The night we visited, diners were sparse. Service came from two well-meaning waiters dressed in black. One bowed like a page boy every time he offered the bread, blocking the path of the other arriving with the starters and mains. Chef James Kirby scatters seasonal ingredients across a good-value three-course menu, but there's the occasional glitch. Too much white pepper in an opening mini-dish of celeriac soup could have been shifted to the under-seasoned main course of Hereford lamb, served with garlic and broad beans. Risotto was rich and delicious in a starter with scallops, wild garlic and leeks, but sea trout, in a main dish with morels, fennel and dill velouté, was overcooked. The wine list, put together by consultant Tim McLaughlin-Green, is full of superb choices over £20, including Tamaya's cabernet sauvignon, merlot and syrah 2001 blend from Chile's up-and-coming Limari region.
Babies and children welcome: high chairs. Separate room for parties, seats 35. Tables outdoors (4, pavement). **Map 20 C3**.

Shepherd's Bush W6, W12

Brackenbury

129-131 Brackenbury Road, W6 0BQ (8748 0107). Goldhawk Road or Hammersmith tube. **Lunch served** 12.30-2.45pm Mon-Fri; 12.30-3.30pm Sun. **Dinner served** 7-10.45pm Mon-Sat. **Main courses** £9-£16. **Set lunch** (Mon-Fri) £12.50 2 courses, £14.50 3 courses. **Service** 12.5%. **Credit** AmEx, MC, V.
How pleasant to book a table at a time of one's choosing. Equally cheering: a French waiter singing the praises of Sheffield chef Noel Capp (who was dining alfresco). There's an ample choice of starters on the Brackenbury's daily menu: perhaps foie gras and quail, leek confit and salmon terrine, or artichoke with roasted tomato purée risotto. We settled for thai-spiced crab and salt cod, guacamole, flavoured with curry and vanilla oil: a lip-smacking dish. So too was the pan-fried mackerel with brandade-stuffed piquillo pepper and (a rather dry) couscous and raita. We ate more fish for mains – pan-fried sea bass with a lively niçoise bourride; and roasted hake atop pea croquette, with a hint of tomato and chive beurre blanc – both dishes bursting with flavour, well presented and generous. If there's a tendency towards too many ingredients, it's a small cavil. Add a very attractive wine list starting at £12, and a chef who's confident to leave his kitchen in good hands, and it's not surprising there's a happy bunch of (mainly young) diners at this justifiably favourite local.
Babies and children welcome: high chair. Booking advisable. Tables outdoors (7, patio).
Map 20 B3.

Bush Bar & Grill

45A Goldhawk Road, W12 8QP (8746 2111/ www.bushbar.co.uk). Goldhawk Road tube. **Bar Open** noon-11.30pm Mon-Sat **Restaurant Lunch served** noon-3pm Mon-Sat. **Dinner served** 5.30-11.30pm Mon-Sat. **Main courses** £8.50-£17. **Set lunch** £12.50 2 courses, £14 3 courses. *Both* **Service** 12.5%. **Credit** AmEx, MC, V.
Bush Bar & Grill is a veritable Tardis of a restaurant, with its metal entrance on grimy Goldhawk Road giving no hint of the stylish and cavernous space within. Smart furnishings (green banquettes, blue chairs, dark wood tables) combine with a lofty ceiling strewn with white pipework to give an air of semi-industrial chic that appeals to a buzzy, youngish crowd. The bar side of the business is lively too, with drinks running from champagne and wine (plenty of choices by the glass) to well-made cocktails, and food in the form of sharing platters. The monthly changing restaurant menu is long (possibly too long) covering starters, salads, steaks and plenty of fish and meat dishes. Cooking was mixed on our visit, with simpler dishes faring better than fancier ones – but nothing really show. Grilled sardines were acceptable; organic salmon fish cakes were hearty; swordfish was toughish (and too big to finish). A side of beetroot dauphinoise sounded an unlikely combination – as it should; it didn't work at all, being far too cloying. Staff were a bit clueless, though friendly. Owner Charlie McVeigh is also behind Italian newcomer Matilda (*see p178*).
Babies and children welcome: children's menu; high chairs. Booking advisable Fri, Sat. Disabled: toilet. Separate room for parties, seats 50. Tables outdoors (9, courtyard).
Map 20 B2.

South West

Barnes SW13

★ Sonny's

94 Church Road, SW13 0DQ (8748 0393/ www.sonnys.co.uk). Barnes or Barnes Bridge rail/33, 209, 283 bus. **Café Open** 10.30am-6pm Mon-Sat. **Lunch served** noon-4pm Mon-Sat. **Main courses** £3.95-£9. **Restaurant Lunch served** 12.30-2.30pm Mon-Sat; 12.30-3pm Sun. **Dinner served** 7.30-11pm

Mon-Sat. **Main courses** £10.75-£16. **Set lunch** (Mon-Sat) £13 2 courses, £16.50 3 courses; (Sun) £21 3 courses incl coffee. **Set dinner** (Mon-Thur) £16.50 2 courses, £19.50 3 courses. **Service** 12.5%. **Credit** AmEx, MC, V.
Lucky Barnes to have two excellent restaurants within spitting distance of one another: Italian restaurant Riva (*see p176*) and this quietly elegant affair. Modern artworks and pale turquoise woodwork enliven the white space; especially soothing is the half-sunken back room, with its subtle lighting and widely spaced tables. Families, couples, birthday parties and local celebs (Tim Henman, on our visit) mingle happily. The seasonal menu wears its French, Italian and British influences lightly. Dishes often have elaborate twists, but simple works well too, as with featherlight gnocchi in a tomato, garlic and caper sauce. A starter of Cornish crab rémoulade was a super-fresh concoction with big chunks of tasty crab meat, topped with zingy lemon sorbet; to follow, flaky wild halibut was a good match for its sweet potato purée and samphire accompaniments. Occasional lapses occur: linguine with brown shrimps, mussels and shellfish butter (more of a soup, actually) was too salty and the mussels overcooked, and the usually excellent skinny fries were dried out. Straightforward desserts – sorbets, meringue with strawberries, vanilla rice pudding – round off matters nicely. Other good points: a well-judged wine list; and cordial, observant staff, happy to adjust the air-conditioning, and bringing fresh jugs of tap water without being asked.
Babies and children welcome: high chairs. Booking advisable (restaurant). Restaurant available for hire. Separate room for parties, seats 22.

Chelsea SW3

Bluebird

350 King's Road, SW3 5UU (7559 1000/ www.conran.com). Sloane Square tube then 11, 19, 22, 49, 319 bus. **Bar Open** 11am-11pm Mon-Thur; 11am-12.45am Fri, Sat; 11am-10.45pm Sun. **Restaurant Brunch served** noon-3.30pm Sat, Sun. **Lunch served** 12.30-3.30pm Mon-Sat. **Dinner served** 6-11pm Mon-Sat; 6-10pm Sun. **Main courses** £13.50-£25. **Service** 12.5%. **Credit** AmEx, DC, JCB, MC, V.
Just booking a table here is a marathon. It took at least five minutes to get through the Conran telephone holding pattern, and for that sort of patience you expect a packed dining room and terrific food. Neither of which we got. The lovely sky-lit restaurant was worryingly empty and despite the best efforts of our friendly South African waiter, we wished we were downstairs eating alfresco on the packed forecourt. A starter of clams, chorizo and chickpeas was a watery disappointment, and hardly justified the name 'Catalan' stew. Iced gazpacho andaluz was exactly what we wanted, but again, the textureless soup tasted as if it had been sitting in a fridge too long. Mains were good, but no better than you'd get at a decent gastropub for half the price. Roast rump of lamb with couscous salad and apricot relish was tender and well matched by the waiter's suggestion of a pinot noir. And roast fillet of sea bass with parsley salad and tapenade disproved our fears about ordering seafood on Mondays – the fish was beautifully fresh. An excellent dessert of orange honey mousse with red berries couldn't sweeten the arrival of a triple-figure bill. For the Bluebird Dining Room, *see p60*.
Babies and children welcome: children's menu (weekends); high chairs. Disabled: toilet. Entertainment: DJs Fri, Sat. Separate rooms for parties, seating 15 and 42. **Map 14 D12**.

East Sheen SW14

Redmond's

170 Upper Richmond Road West, SW14 8AW (8878 1922/www.redmonds.org.uk). Mortlake rail then 337 bus/33 bus. **Lunch served** noon-2.30pm Sun. **Dinner served** 6.30-10pm Mon-Thur; 7-10pm Fri, Sat. **Set lunch** (Sun) £18.50 2 courses, £23 3 courses. **Set dinner**

RESTAURANTS

The Farm. See p232.

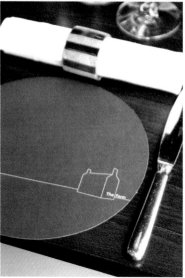

Delfina. See p235.

(6.30-7.45pm Mon-Thur) £12.50 2 courses, £15.50 3 courses; (Mon-Fri) £27.50 2 courses, £32 3 courses. **Service** 10% for parties of 6 or more. **Credit** JCB, MC, V.

This polished neighbourhood operation continues to please affluent locals with its inventive seasonal cooking. Biscuit-coloured table linen and soft lighting add to the air of discreet gentility. Highlights of a recent dinner included starters of tuna carpaccio with wasabi, cucumber and sushi ginger, and asparagus salad with oven-baked tomatoes, boiled egg and parmesan: both light, summery dishes, made with first-rate ingredients. Almost as good was an earthy main of tender pork belly with superb crackling, black pudding, aromatic cumin mash and green beans. But goujons of lemon sole were a waste of space – just five thin pieces that tasted more of their breadcrumb coating than of fish, atop a pedestrian salad of cos lettuce, potatoes and peas – neither tasty nor filling. Roast wild salmon, although a classy piece of fish, was also meagre, with just sugar snaps and watercress sauce as accompaniment. That's the problem with fixed-price menus (there's no à la carte): the absence of side dishes to bulk out inadequate portions. Hunger was partly sated by cheese (all excellent British varieties) for dessert. Redmonds still has a great wine list (and regular wine-related events), but management should rethink the balance of its menu: £27.50 for what amounted to two salads was distinctly poor value. *Babies and children welcome: children's portions; high chair. Booking advisable; essential weekends. No smoking. Restaurant available for hire.* **For branch (Burlington) see index.**

Fulham SW6

★ The Farm
2005 RUNNER-UP BEST LOCAL RESTAURANT
18 Farm Lane, SW6 1PP (7381 3331/ www.thefarmfulham.co.uk). Fulham Broadway tube/11, 14, 211 bus.
Bar **Open** noon-11pm Mon-Sat; noon-10.30pm Sun. **Meals served** noon-10pm Mon-Sat; noon-9.30pm Sun.
Restaurant **Lunch served** noon-3pm Mon-Sat; noon-3.30pm Sun. **Dinner served** 6-10.15pm Mon-Sat; 6-10pm Sun. **Service** 12.5%.
Both **Main courses** £10-£15. **Credit** AmEx, JCB, MC, V.
Gastropub-like but with a smarter edge, the Farm shares similarities with its sibling, the slick Ebury (see p105) in Pimlico. Both are owned by Tom Etridge, who has a practised knack with sophisticated but casual eateries. It's a venue of two parts: a square wooden bar forms the divide between the drinking area at the front (luxurious brown leather sofas, dark oak panelling and modern chrome fireplaces) and the dining area at the back (polished wooden tables, silver-tinted floral wallpaper and a glass back wall). Logoed table mats and exquisite shell-and-silver salt containers reveal an eye for detail. Chef Paul Merrett has form too, having attained a Michelin star while at the Greenhouse, and it shows. The seasonal dinner menu is short – only five dishes for each course – and fairly priced. Haddock fish cakes, grilled ribeye, risotto – these aren't complicated dishes, but execution and presentation raised them well above the norm. Top marks to a juicy chunk of salmon baked in light puff pastry, with potato salad and mustard and honey dressing; a classy salad nicoise; and excellent chips. For puds, there's the likes of tropical pineapple with mango and passionfruit sorbet, or comforting almond and apricot tart. Other bonuses: gracious service and drinks for all-comers, from cocktails to real ales.
Babies and children admitted. Disabled: toilet. Tables outdoors (4, pavement). **Map 13 A13.**

Putney SW15

★ Phoenix Bar & Grill
162-164 Lower Richmond Road, SW15 1LY (8780 3131/www.sonnys.co.uk). Putney Bridge tube/22, 265 bus. **Lunch served** 12.30-2.30pm Mon-Sat; 12.30-3pm Sun. **Dinner served** 7-11pm Mon-Thur; 7-11.30pm Fri, Sat; 7-10pm Sun.

Main courses £9.50-£16.50. **Set lunch** (Mon-Sat) £13.50 2 courses, £15.50 3 courses. **Set meal** (7-7.45pm Mon-Thur, Sun) £15.50 2 courses, £17.50 3 courses. **Service** 12.5%. **Credit** AmEx, MC, V.

Tucked away on the Lower Richmond Road, this is a glamorous restaurant that makes good use of its outside space – a surprisingly atmospheric terrace with fairylights, warmed up by plenty of outdoor heaters. The staff are a major asset. Hugely knowledgeable and passionate, they know the excellent menu and vast wine list inside out. The Phoenix also has one of the biggest wine-by-the-glass menus in London: a treat. Starters and desserts were outstanding. Crab salad with basil mayonnaise managed to be creamy and light at the same time, while the house speciality starter, vincisgrassi maceratesi (a Franco Taruschio 18th-century lasagne recipe with mushrooms, prosciutto and truffle oil), seemed brave but was extremely successful: it melted in the mouth. Mains were a little ordinary by comparison, but well executed. Roast duck breast with bacon, peas, and bubble and squeak was tasty, though not amazing; roasted monkfish with cherry tomatoes, olives and garlic had excellent fish and was full of fresh flavours. Desserts pushed the standard back up: own-made chocolate and crème fraîche ice-creams were absolutely gorgeous, while apricot pavlova with roasted almond cream was soft and sumptuous. Sister establishment Sonny's (*see p230*) is located in nearby Barnes.

Babies and children welcome: children's menu (Sun); crayons; high chairs. Booking essential summer; advisable winter. Disabled: toilet. No-smoking tables. Tables outdoors (19, terrace).

South Kensington SW3

★ Bibendum

Michelin House, 81 Fulham Road, SW3 6RD (7581 5817/www.bibendum.co.uk). South Kensington tube. **Lunch served** noon-2.30pm Mon-Fri; 12.30-3pm Sat, Sun. **Dinner served** 7-11.30pm Mon-Sat; 7-10.30pm Sun. **Main courses** £19-£42. **Set lunch** £28.50 3 courses. **Service** 12.5%. **Credit** AmEx, DC, MC, V.

It was only on leaving Bibendum that we realised what a tremendously good-value meal we had just enjoyed. At lunch, there is a three-course price-fixe menu at £28.50. When they later posted the à la carte at the door, with starters of foie gras terrines and escargot hitting £19.50, and roast chicken for two at £48, we felt decidedly smug. Our meal was faultless. Roast beef and high-rise yorkshire pud, or haddock and chips for traditionalists; rump of lamb with choux farci, or roast chicken with artichoke barigoule and trompettes de mort for those with Continental leanings. Oxtail ravioli was rich and moist; pickled anchovies came with salad and a fluffy Spanish-style tortilla of egg and potato. Desserts were also excellent: chocolate marquise topped with tangy orange sorbet and a crown of chocolate sheets, and richly eggy cherry clafoutis with vanilla-packed ice-cream. Service was pitch-perfect, though the sommelier blanched when we tried to discuss the merits of their cheapest bottles. The wine list has a whole page of house wines at various price points, and although France dominates there are interesting diversions to Austria, Germany and the New World. It's a glorious room too – one of Conran's first, and in terms of decor, probably still the best.

Babies and children welcome: high chair. Booking essential, 2wks in advance for dinner. Dress: smart casual. **Map 14 E10.**

South

Balham SW12

★ Lamberts

2 Station Parade, Balham High Road, SW12 9AZ (8675 2233/www.lambertsrestaurant.com). Balham tube/rail. **Lunch served** 11am-3pm Sat. **Dinner served** 7-10.30pm Tue-Sat. **Meals served** 11am-9pm Sun. **Main courses** £12-£17. **Set meal** (Tue-Thur) £15 2 courses, £18 3 courses. **Service** 12.5%. **Credit** JCB, MC, V.

The menu at this well-turned-out Balham local takes provenance seriously, name-checking producers with the likes of Secrett's Farm asparagus (served with a poached duck's egg and silky hollandaise sauce) and dedicating a dish to Farmer Sharp's Herdwick mutton, wether and lamb. There's plenty more to entice, from the good own-made breads, served with tiny purple olives, to tender, perfectly cooked char-grilled chump of lamb with aubergine, tomato and roast potatoes, which comes from the set menu. Combinations of flavours on the seasonally inspired carte are well considered, as in a spring dish of steamed halibut with baby leeks, Jersey royals and lobster cream. Desserts, such as lavender and honey crème brûlée served with crumbly shortbread biscuits, follow in the same well-judged vein, and cheeses come from Neal's Yard. The sensibly priced wine list suggests that the buyers here know their stuff, with some respected producers from Europe and the New World, as well as a section of sherries, whiskies and Armagnacs. The young, professional staff provide spot-on service.

Babies and children welcome: children's menu (weekends); high chair. Booking advisable. No smoking. Restaurant available for hire.

Battersea SW11

Louvaine NEW

110 St John's Hill, SW11 1SJ (7223 8708/www.louvaine.com). Clapham Junction rail. **Dinner served** 6-10.30pm Tue-Sat. **Meals served** noon-5.30pm Sun. **Main courses** £8-£13.50. **Service** 12.5%. **Credit** AmEx, MC, V.

This small neighbourhood corner bar-bistro, housed in what looks like a former tapas bar, keeps things simple. The menu is short – four starters, six mains and five desserts, plus a few daily specials, all at relatively affordable prices – and there's nothing too challenging on it. Despite this, not all our dishes were successful: the flavours in red pepper and lemongrass soup were confusing and conflicting; and the tomato tart, which comprised a very thin crisp crust topped with four under-ripe tomato halves, was poorly judged. Happily, mains were better prepared. You can't really go wrong with a decent ribeye steak, and this was a pretty good version: tender, juicy and lean, served with a green peppercorn sauce (50p extra) and fine chips. Confit duck leg, with spicy red cabbage and mashed potatoes, was also a reassuring dish. All told, we liked Louvaine's lack of pretension, not to mention its good value.

Babies and children admitted. Booking advisable. Tables outdoors (5, pavement). **Map 21 B4.**

Niksons

172-174 Northcote Road, SW11 6RE (7228 2285). Clapham Junction rail. *Bar* **Open** 5-11pm Mon; noon-11pm Tue-Sat; noon-10.30pm Sun. *Restaurant* **Lunch served** noon-3pm Tue-Fri. **Dinner served** 6-10pm Mon-Sat. **Meals served** 11am-10.30pm Sun. **Main courses** £10-£15.50. **Cover** £1. **Service** 12.5%. *Both* **Credit** AmEx, DC, MC, V.

Niksons is a slick operation, from the front bar area, with its leather sofas and notable cocktail list, to the smoke-free conservatory dining room at the rear (all beautiful flower displays and jewel-toned paintings). Our foie gras and brioche starter was actually a terrine, served in a thick slice with toasted brioche. A main course of steamed sea bass with scallop mousse was wrapped in fresh tarragon and sat on a bed of asparagus velouté. Less impressive was a starter of 'sautéed' red mullet and scallops with ratatouille and lentils; the scallops were lovely, the lentils fine, but the mullet had been fried, which did nothing for the flavour or texture of this delicate fish. The only vegetarian main course, wild mushroom risotto, didn't skimp on mushroom, but perhaps overdid the cheese. We weren't at all keen on the cover charge, which, with prices for main courses topping £15, seems a bit rich, particularly when one of the two breads served, like the brioche, was stale. The drinks list is nothing special, offering just a few predictable wines by the glass.

Babies and children welcome: high chairs; nappy-changing facilities. Booking advisable. Disabled: toilet. Separate room for parties, seats 30. Tables outdoors (4, pavement). **Map 21 C5.**

Ransome's Dock

35-37 Parkgate Road, SW11 4NP (7223 1611). Battersea Park rail/19, 49, 319, 345 bus. **Brunch served** noon-3.30pm Sun. **Meals served** noon-11pm Mon-Sat. **Main courses** £10.50-£21.50. **Set meal** (noon-5pm Mon-Fri) £14.75 2 courses. **Service** 12.5%. **Credit** AmEx, DC, JCB, MC, V.

In an era of 'concept' restaurants, a veteran such as Ransome's Dock – where the concept is merely serving good food and great wine in simple surroundings – is a relief. The wine list is easily one of London's best for quality, range and pricing. Wine-loving owner/chef Martin Lam believes in encouraging experimentation with lower-than-usual mark-ups. The short menu changes frequently. Ingredients (many of them organic) are carefully sourced. Flavour combinations are well considered, as in a starter of char-grilled spiced quail with carrot and preserved lemon, but on our visit, on a busy Saturday evening, timings were less accurate than in the past. Pan-fried English veal (cut into thin slices and served with penne, broad beans, cream and fresh tarragon) was on the tough side; and the quail had also spent too long on the grill. Fortunately, the Shorthorn sirloin with roquefort butter and chips (not cheap at £21.50) was cooked perfectly rare as requested, and was tender and flavourful. Finger-burning chips were crisp, crunchy and incredibly moreish. To finish, prune and Armagnac soufflé was fluffy and light, with rich Armagnac-spiced custard on the side. At weekends, a brunch-style menu is served throughout the day.

Babies and children welcome: high chairs. Booking advisable. No-smoking tables. Tables outdoors (12, terrace). **Map 21 C1.**

Clapham SW4

Morel NEW

2005 RUNNER-UP BEST LOCAL RESTAURANT

14 Clapham Park Road, SW4 7NN (7627 2468/www.morelrestaurant.co.uk). Clapham Common tube. **Dinner served** 6-10.30pm Tue-Sat. **Meals served** noon-4pm Sun. **Set meal** £16 1 course, £20 2 courses, £25 3 courses. **Service** 12.5%. **Credit** MC, V.

Morel's site is both good (the former occupant was ever-popular Thyme) and bad (off Clapham's main drag, so not much passing traffic). At the front a wavy red banquette dominates the small bar area; beyond lies the dining room, with slatted wooden blinds, soft lighting, walls of cream and rich ruby, and a striking abstract painting on the back wall. It's muted but modish – much like the food. Highlights included celeriac velouté to start (full-bodied and velvety smooth) and a main of nicely cooked haddock with poached egg, spinach and a raviolo with a creamy jerusalem artichoke stuffing. In general, the kitchen could do with a bit more oomph, however. A terrine of pressed foie grass, duck and chicken with fig compote was too bland; desserts of fruit (roasted figs, poached pear) accompanied by ice-cream (honey, cinammon) were similarly mild in flavour. Still, amuse-bouches and (awkwardly) geometric tableware indicate aspirations above a conventional neighbourhood eaterie, and the courteous staff were helpful in answering questions. There's a good-value set menu, and roasts on Sunday.

Babies and children welcome: high chairs. Booking advisable. No smoking. **Map 22 B2.**

Tooting SW17

Rick's Café

122 Mitcham Road, SW17 9NH (8767 5219). Tooting Broadway tube. **Lunch served** 12.30-3pm daily. **Dinner served** 6.30-11pm Mon-Sat; 6.30-10.30pm Sun. **Main courses** £6-£12. **Set lunch** (Sun) £10.95 2 courses. **Service** 12.5%. **Credit** MC, V.

It's a simple concept. Start with a modest dining room at the front and an open kitchen at the back. Add a small, frequently changing menu, a decent

RESTAURANTS

wine list, some wooden tables and chairs. Then hang a few paintings by local artists on the walls. The result? That London rarity: a good, casual neighbourhood restaurant. The owner of Rick's, according to our waitress, is Spanish-British. There's an Iberian influence in several of the dishes: Spanish charcuterie platter with olives, for example; or piquillo peppers with Spanish anchovies. There were hits and misses in our food. To start, a smoked salmon tart with Jersey royals and dill was well conceived, but the crust was overcooked and the whole thing a bit dry. We leapt at the chance to try garfish, an Australian coastal specimen not frequently seen here; the long thin fish was served with gutsy aïoli, but the chips were rather greasy and limp. More impressive was a dish of undyed smoked haddock over creamy rice, topped with a perfect poached egg and smooth butter sauce. Desserts lean towards British nursery food: sticky toffee pudding or steamed sponge with sauce anglaise.
Babies and children welcome: children's portions; high chairs. Booking advisable dinner and weekends. Disabled: toilet.

Waterloo SE1

County Hall Restaurant
London Marriott Hotel County Hall, Westminster Bridge Road, SE1 7PB (7902 8000/ www.marriott.com). Embankment or Westminster tube/Charing Cross or Waterloo tube/rail. **Breakfast served** 6.30-11am Mon-Fri; 7-11am Sat, Sun. **Lunch served** 12.30-3pm, **afternoon tea served** 2.30-5.30pm, **dinner served** 5.30-10.30pm daily. **Main courses** £14-£32. **Set meal** £23.50 2 courses, £26.50 3 courses. **Credit** AmEx, DC, MC, V.
With an enviable riverside location, this should be a hotel restaurant with potential. Unfortunately it remains unfulfilled. Middle-of-the-road decor, dreadful lift music, sloppy service (broken corks laboriously extracted in front of us), even that river view was spoiled by dirty windows. All of which might have been forgiven had the food been first-rate (it wasn't) or the prices reasonable (they weren't). A starter of smoked haddock and spinach tart with herb oil looked and tasted no better than an M&S bung-it-in-the-oven offering and left us playing hunt the haddock. Gravadlax of salmon with a red onion and caper relish was unimaginatively presented and, again, there was what looked like supermarket uniformity to the slices of salmon. Mains were better. Roast chicken breast with truffle mash, celeriac remoulade and pancetta was let down only by the sad-looking strip of pancetta balanced circus-like on top of the chicken. And an excellent piece of roast turbot with delicate spring greens and puy lentils showed how good it could have been. The puds sounded uninspiring, so we paid our bill and left, with the young Italian waiter asking whether he had seen us before at his other job at Wetherspoons. Very disappointing.
Babies and children welcome: children's menu; high chairs. Booking advisable. Disabled: lift; toilet. Entertainment: pianist/guitarist 6.30-10.30pm Thur, Fri. No-smoking tables. Takeaway service (breakfast). **Map 10 M9**.

Oxo Tower Restaurant, Bar & Brasserie
Eighth floor, Oxo Tower Wharf, Barge House Street, SE1 9PH (7803 3888/www.harvey nichols.com). Blackfriars or Waterloo tube/rail. **Bar Open** 11am-11pm Mon-Sat; noon-10.30pm Sun.
Brasserie **Lunch served** noon-3.15pm Mon-Sat; noon-3.45pm Sun. **Dinner served** 5.30-11pm Mon-Sat; 6-10.15pm Sun. **Main courses** £10.25-£17. **Set meal** (lunch, 5.30-6.45pm Mon-Fri) £16.50 2 courses, £21.50 3 courses.
Restaurant **Lunch served** noon-2.30pm Mon-Sat; noon-3pm Sun. **Dinner served** 6-11pm Mon-Sat; 6.30-10pm Sun. **Main courses** £17.50-£26. **Set lunch** £29.50 3 courses.
All **Service** 12.5%. **Credit** AmEx, DC, JCB, MC, V.
The two restaurants on the eighth floor of the Oxo Tower, run by Harvey Nichols, are no longer the

destination eateries they once were, but the public don't seem to have been put off: at a midweek lunchtime, the restaurant was doing a decent trade and the brasserie appeared virtually full. Negatives are the appalling acoustics, particularly in the brasserie – where we ate – and a slight but tangible laziness in the kitchen. Our most enjoyable dish was a straightforward starter of lime-pickled chicken with mango salsa, a lively combination that put a more forgettable fried squid, rocket and parmesan salad in the shade. Main courses were unexceptional: roasted rack of lamb with couscous was framed around a fairly nondescript cut of meat, while braised pork belly served with steamed jasmine rice and green papaya chutney wasn't as flavoursome as it perhaps ought to have been. Still, service was fine, and the views remain fantastic.
Babies and children welcome: children's menu; high chair. Booking advisable. Disabled: lift; toilet. Entertainment: pianist/singer 7.30pm daily (brasserie). Restaurant available for hire. Tables outdoors (27, restaurant terrace; 34, brasserie terrace). Vegetarian menu (brasserie). **Map 11 N7**.

Blackheath SE3

Chapter Two
43-45 Montpelier Vale, SE3 0TJ (8333 2666/ www.chaptersrestaurants.co.uk). Blackheath rail. **Lunch served** noon-2.30pm Mon-Sat; noon-3pm Sun. **Dinner served** 6.30-10.30pm Mon-Thur; 6.30-11pm Fri, Sat; 6.30-9pm Sun. **Set lunch** (Mon-Sat) £14.50 2 courses, £18.50 3 courses. **Set dinner** (Mon-Thur, Sun) £16.95 2 courses, £19.95 3 courses; (Fri, Sat) £23.50 3 courses. **Service** 12.5%. **Credit** AmEx, DC, JCB, MC, V.
Chapter Two is a touch too much Modern European by numbers. Its looks are smart, though undistinguished (an aubergine and mid-blue colour scheme incorporating anonymous abstracts); service is efficient, but equally anonymous; and the menu reads well, yet doesn't quite deliver on its promises. The Monday to Saturday lunch menu offers plenty of choice, but, on our last visit, lacked conviction in the execution. Crab raviolo with roast fennel, prawn velouté and saffron oil was light and refreshing, but the crab was short on flavour and definition. To follow, monkfish with broad beans, brown shrimps, white asparagus and horseradish velouté needed a sharp counterpoint to the creamy blandness of the dish – there was no discernible horseradish tang to the velouté, and the unannounced extra beans (cannellini? haricot?) were undercooked. Nor did the desserts live up to their billing: honeycomb ice-cream appeared to have been made with Crunchies rather than honeycomb, and the accompanying banana was certainly not caramelised as advertised. There was, though, one indisputable mark of class: Charlie Mingus on the sound system. Blackheath's affluent burghers have remained loyal to Chapter Two, but this won't last if the kitchen fails to keep its eye on the ball.
Babies and children welcome: high chairs. Booking advisable. Disabled: toilet. No-smoking.

Greenwich SE10

Inc Bar & Restaurant
7 College Approach, SE10 9HY (8858 6721). Cutty Sark DLR/177, 180, 286 bus. **Bar Open** 6pm-midnight Mon-Thur, Sun; 6pm-1am Fri, Sat. **Tapas served** 6-10pm daily. *Restaurant* **Dinner served** 6-10pm daily. **Main courses** £10-£17.
Both **Service** 12.5%. **Credit** MC, V.
Inspired by the 'slum and splendour' of Georgian Greenwich, the decor at Inc – courtesy of Laurence Llewelyn-Bowen – is worth a visit in its own right. The 'divan', complete with flickering fire, low lighting, sofas and saucy wallpaper that comes with a warning, contrasts brilliantly with the cavernous main bar, where carriage clocks and colourful glass chandeliers work alongside plasma screens playing (bizarrely) *Finding Nemo* and *The*

Matrix on our visit, together with black and white stills of Greenwich life gone by. It sounds disjointed, but it works. The dining area is on a mezzanine. The menu is short and a little unadventurous, but every dish is beautifully presented. Service was excellent. To start, seared tuna with salad leaves, honey and lime was light and delicious. Marmalade-glazed duck breast was plump and succulent; stuffed chicken breast with puy lentils and mushroom sauce was tasty, though the lentils were undercooked. The wine list is short; cocktails are the thing here (there are at least 60). Inc is popular with a young and funky crowd, and although the food is on the pricey side and secondary to the drinks, for a local night out it can't be faulted.
Babies and children admitted. Booking advisable. Dress: smart casual. Entertainment: DJs 9pm-1am Sat. Vegetarian menu.

Inside
19 Greenwich South Street, SE10 8NW (8265 5060/www.insiderestaurant.co.uk). Greenwich rail/DLR. **Brunch served** 11am-2.30pm Sat. **Lunch served** noon-2.30pm Tue-Fri; noon-3pm Sun. **Dinner served** 6.30-11pm Tue-Sat. **Main courses** £10.95-£16. **Set meal** (lunch, 6.30-8pm) £14.95 2 courses, £17.95 3 courses. **Credit** AmEx, MC, V.
What makes Inside special is the thought that evidently goes into the whole dining experience: crisp white linen, gentle music, colourful, atmospheric art on the walls, the way the decor captures the light and somehow transforms a relatively small room into an open, light, airy space. The menu has a Franco-Italian bent and offers some rich specialities: a starter of seared scallops with black pudding, and pea and mint velouté, for instance. While steak and chunky chips may seem an ordinary option, the delicacy with which the steak (requested rare) had been cooked turned it into an fine dish. Corn-fed chicken was plump, golden and succulent, and well matched with garlic spinach, thyme jus and fondant potato. On previous visits, we've seen some outstanding desserts; pecan tart with vanilla and bourbon ice-cream is a current example. The wine list offers a carefully selected array – for example, a good Rioja from a family-run bodega. Inside is a great neighbourhood restaurant, quietly treasured by locals, yet it seems a shame not to shout about the place just a little.
Babies and children admitted. Booking advisable. Disabled: toilet. No-smoking tables.

London Bridge & Borough SE1

Bermondsey Kitchen
194 Bermondsey Street, SE1 3TQ (7407 5719). Borough tube/London Bridge tube/rail. **Brunch served** 9.30am-3.30pm Sat, Sun. **Lunch served** noon-3pm Mon-Fri. **Dinner served** 6.30-10.30pm Mon-Sat. **Main courses** £9-£13. **Service** 12.5% for parties of 6 or more. **Credit** AmEx, DC, MC, V.
'The morning after the night before' described the look and feel of Bermondsey Kitchen on the Saturday of our brunch. Staff seemed dreamy, and the loos needed tidying. An open kitchen with a bar around it looks out on to a non-designer mix of wooden chairs and tables. Luckily, the kitchen crew were fully awake, so good Bloody Marys and lovely, chewy bread were followed by a whole sea bass on a tangle of rocket and grilled, chillied sardines – both very adept versions – accompanied by harissa new potatoes. These were slightly undercooked: the only flaw in a meal that culminated in glorious hot chocolate pudding with crème fraîche. Such food is typical of the evening menu; more brunchy options include eggs florentine, or a big breakfast of poached eggs, Tamworth sausage and bacon, mushrooms, roast tomatoes, new potatoes and spinach. There's a Spanish slant too: tapas (boquerones, chorizo and so on, much of it from Brindisa) are chalked on a blackboard, and many of the regular dishes have Spanish ingredients. The cocktail list is notable, and the range of wines global (including sherry,

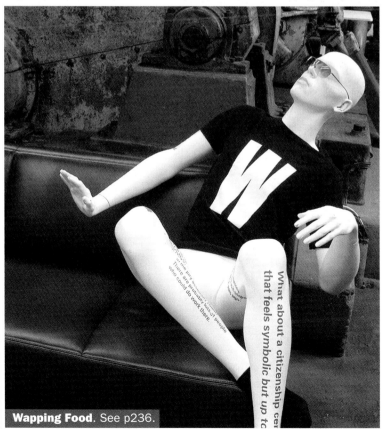

Wapping Food. See p236.

and a decent choice by the glass). The easy-going vibe encourages kicking back and staying for just one more. A great local.
Babies and children welcome: high chairs. Booking advisable. Disabled: toilet. No-smoking tables. Restaurant available for hire. **Map 12 Q9**.

Cantina Vinopolis
1 Bank End, SE1 9BU (7940 8333/www.cantina vinopolis.com). London Bridge tube/rail.
Bar **Open** 11am-11pm Mon-Sat; 11am-4pm Sun. *Restaurant* **Lunch served** noon-3pm Mon-Sat; noon-4pm Sun. **Dinner served** 6-10.30pm Mon-Sat. **Main courses** £8.50-£19. **Service** 12.5%. **Credit** AmEx, DC, JCB, MC, V.
You can't fault the location of this restaurant, tucked among the railway arches by Borough Market and next door to Vinopolis wine museum and wine bar Wine Wharf (*see p336*). It's co-owned by Trevor Gulliver of St John (*see p55*), who's transformed the glass and steel ticket area into a new, swirling-patterned, blue-coloured bar and improved what was once a wine list heavy with bottles from the Majestic off-licence chain. Gulliver's influence is also evident in the decor (a simple, brick arch interior) and the emphasis on provincial French reds. A few deals can be found on a page of bin ends – wines approaching their sell-by-date. Surprises abound, with a very good 2003 dry riesling from Dr Bürklin Wolf, from Pfalz in Germany, with superb mineral and white peach flavours. Customers include wine nerds, grumpy older couples or smiling tourists who have just visited Vinopolis. The food is the sort of decent fare you'd find in many galleries or museums. Red pepper soup was smoky, rich and peppery. To follow, a fillet of halibut was covered in too much cream, but came with potatoes, squash, green beans and mushrooms. Monkfish was much better, cooked on the bone in spicy batter, with potatoes, asparagus and spring onions.
Babies and children admitted. Booking advisable. Disabled: toilet. No-smoking tables. Restaurant available for hire. Separate room for parties, seats 80-100. **Map 11 P8**.

Delfina
50 Bermondsey Street, SE1 3UD (7357 0244/ www.delfina.org.uk). London Bridge tube/rail.
Lunch served noon-3pm Mon-Fri. **Dinner served** 7-10pm Fri. **Main courses** £9.95-£12.95. **Service** 12.5%. **Credit** AmEx, MC, V.
Delfina is a spacious restaurant-cum-art-gallery, quintessentially minimalist from the varnished wood floor to the bright, white walls bearing nicely chosen abstracts. Surrounded by a smattering of elegantly slumming aesthetes and crisp-suited businessmen, we started with succulent miso-marinated scallops with edamame, oyster mushrooms, coriander sprouts and chinese pickled cabbage; and an equally delicious Asian braised pork belly with char-grilled pineapple, coriander and black bean salad. Main courses ranged from the directness of a surprisingly light and herby meatloaf, served with puréed mash and a (perhaps oversweet) cherry vine tomato sauce, to the complications of smoked paprika- and garlic-marinated halloumi with flatbread, a salad of chickpeas, cherry tomatoes, cucumber, parsley and mint, and halves of soft-boiled egg. We were also tempted into over-indulgence by sweet potato chips cooked in ginger and curry oil – a brilliant mix of flavours. The short but beguiling dessert list reinforced the menu's Asian slant with a fine lemongrass and ginger brûlée with lemongrass ice-cream. Service was impeccably friendly, although the staff were so preoccupied setting up for the evening that they neglected to bring us the dessert menu. No matter: Delfina is firmly recommended.
Babies and children welcome. Booking advisable. Disabled: toilet. No-smoking tables (on request). Separate rooms for parties, seating 12 and 30 (7564 2400). **Map 12 Q9**.

Tower Bridge SE1

Blueprint Café
Design Museum, 28 Shad Thames, SE1 2YD (7378 7031/www.conran.com). Tower Hill tube/ Tower Gateway DLR/London Bridge tube/rail/

47, 78 bus. **Lunch served** noon-3pm daily. **Dinner served** 6-11pm Mon-Sat. **Main courses** £12.50-£22. **Service** 12.5%. **Credit** AmEx, DC, MC, V.

Calming, clean and spacious interior design cleverly focuses attention on Blueprint's two best assets: a panoramic Thameside view taking in Tower Bridge and the 'Gherkin', and the cooking of popular Dundonian chef Jeremy Lee. Although the menu incorporates influences from the Mediterranean and northern Europe, ingredients such as lovage, elderflower and mint smack deliciously of the English summer garden. To start, there was a choice of chilled soups, as well as an appealing squid with coriander chutney, and a salad of smoked eel, potato and bacon. For mains, tart of potato, rosemary and ardrahan cheese from Ireland was tempting, but we opted for a fillet of brill with fresh peas and bacon, and roast shoulder of lamb. The latter arrived as an uncompromising plate of meat, topped with a mustardy herb and breadcrumb crust. For balance, we should have had a side plate of greens instead of the excellent roast new potatoes with garlic. We finished with strawberry shortcake and rich, fresh apricot trifle. A special promotion on Australian wines expanded the drinks options greatly, although we picked a forward, fruity Argentinian white. Attentive service slacked off come bill time. Still, we appreciated being allowed to linger – the view is worth the money, even on cloudy days.
Babies and children welcome: high chair. Booking advisable dinner. Disabled: toilet (Design Museum). Restaurant available for hire. Tables outdoors (4, terrace). **Map 12 S9**.

Le Pont de la Tour

Butlers Wharf Building, 36D Shad Thames, SE1 2YE (7403 8403/www.conran.com). Tower Hill tube/Tower Gateway DLR/London Bridge tube/rail/47, 78 bus.
Bar & grill **Lunch served** noon-3pm, **dinner served** 6-11pm daily. **Main courses** £11.50-£22. **Set lunch** £13.95 2 courses, £16.95 3 courses.
Restaurant **Lunch served** noon-3pm, **dinner served** 6-11pm daily. **Main courses** £11.50-£35.50. **Set lunch** £29.50 3 courses.
Both **Service** 12.5%. **Credit** AmEx, DC, JCB, MC, V.

There's a sense of occasion here, but it isn't a result of Conran-style brashness. We walked in through the lively bar (where a pianist plays) to a graceful white-tableclothed dining room with opened windows overlooking the Thames. Service aims high: when it was good, it was very good – from the helpful young French sommelier to our friendly waitress – but at times we felt like we were in the outpatients' department and they'd lost our notes. Cooking is assured, characterful and even cheeky. We knew crayfish with marie rose sauce was a homage to prawn cocktail, but didn't realise quite what an accurate replication it would be: right down to the strips of iceberg lettuce. Another starter of langoustine with pork cheek, leaves and fresh anchovies was awesome; the meat juices melded well with firm langoustine flesh, while the anchovies added another dimension. Pigeon with beetroot and turnips seemed unseasonal, yet was brilliant; the squidgy red meat made an excellent contrast with a crunchy salty crust, the sharp beetroot and bland turnip mixing well with the juices. Halibut with caper leaves, tomatoes and fennel was equally successful, and our bottle of Pouilly-Fumé (at £25 one of the cheapest on an extensive list) very fine.
Babies and children welcome: high chairs. Booking advisable. Entertainment: pianist 7pm daily (bar & grill); duos/trios 7pm Thur-Sat. Separate room for parties, seats 20. Tables outdoors (22, terrace). **Map 12 S8**.

East

Shoreditch N1

Cru Restaurant, Bar & Deli

2-4 Rufus Street, N1 6PE (7729 5252/ www.cru.uk.com). Old Street tube/rail. **Brunch served** noon-3.30pm Sat, Sun. **Lunch served** noon-3pm Tue-Fri. **Dinner served** 6-11pm Mon-Sat; 6-10.30pm Sun. **Main courses** £9.50-£15.50. **Set lunch** £10 2 courses, £14 3 courses. **Service** 12.5%. **Credit** AmEx, MC, V.

Since November 2004, Cru has had a new head chef: American Matthew Boudreau. His short, reasonably priced menu is served to an often-raucous Hoxton clientele in a well-designed contemporary and convivial space – part-bar, part-restaurant (the 'deli' is merely a corner of the bar selling bread and a few vegetables). Tables are close together, which can be irritating if your neighbour is a whinnying wench with an unnatural attachment to her mobile phone. Service is laid-back, yet courses are delivered promptly. Seared scallops were beautifully tender, but their delicate flavour wasn't enhanced by a highly seasoned pepper and mushroom salad; poached egg with asparagus and béarnaise sauce was a more familiar, happier combo. Organic Buccleuch sirloin steak was chewy, but a main of roast pork loin was a huge lump of perfectly cooked, tender meat, which benefited from a tart sage rice with haricots verts. A short but varied wine list contains several well-priced bottles. Desserts include chocolate fudge brownie à la mode and warm rhubarb tart with balsamic strawberries. Cru is a fairly reliable Hoxton option, but hardly ground-breaking and a little patchy.
Babies and children welcome: high chairs. Booking advisable. Disabled: toilet. No-smoking tables. Takeaway service (deli). **Map 6 R4**.

Hoxton Apprentice

16 Hoxton Square, N1 6NT (7739 6022/ www.hoxtonapprentice.com). Old Street tube/rail.
Bar **Open** noon-11pm Tue-Sun.
Restaurant **Lunch served** noon-4pm, **dinner served** 7-10.30pm Tue-Sun. **Main courses** £4.50-£7.50. **Credit** MC, V.

Appropriately housed in a former school, Hoxton Apprentice trains student chefs in-house, then provides them with an opportunity to exhibit their skills. The interior is warm and red-curtained, with a glass-fronted mezzanine, soft lighting, linen tableclothes and friendly service. Midweek, every table was filled. The menu (advised upon by Prue Leith) is split into small and large portions of 'bowls & breads' (including houmous, raita and baba ganoush), 'colds' and 'hots' (oak-smoked salmon with sourdough, chive and dill crème fraîche; or seared tuna niçoise salad), and side dishes (roasted garlic mash, wilted seasonal greens and peas). A 'small' of crab, fennel, pomegranate and mixed herb salad was a well-composed pile of fresh, complementary ingredients. This was followed by two more 'smalls': perfectly cooked tuna strips intensely flavoured with soy and sesame; and salmon fish cakes simply bursting with salmon flakes, matched with creamy spiced tartare. Sticking with the small dishes leaves room for delicious-sounding desserts; the outrageously chocolatey date and hazelnut truffle torte was superb. Wines are well-priced (nothing over £26) with plenty of mid-range options, such as a peachy viognier 2002 for £14.50. We'll definitely be coming back for these school dinners.
Babies and children admitted. Disabled: toilet. No-smoking tables. Separate room for parties, seats 40. Tables outdoors (6, pavement). **Map 6 R3**.

Wapping E1

★ Wapping Food

Wapping Hydraulic Power Station, Wapping Wall, E1W 3ST (7680 2080). Wapping tube/ Shadwell DLR. **Brunch served** 10am-12.30pm Sat, Sun. **Lunch served** noon-3.30pm Mon-Fri; 1-4pm Sat, Sun. **Dinner served** 6.30-11pm Mon-Fri; 7-11pm Sat. **Main courses** £11-£19. **Service** 12.5%. **Credit** AmEx, MC, V.

First things first: this really is a stunning spot. The building housing the Wapping Project was formerly a hydraulic power station, and its dramatic conversion makes little effort to hide its origins. The

---

BEST RESTAURANT COOKBOOKS

Just visited a restaurant, tasted something great, and want to recreate it at home? That's what the restaurant cookbook is for. Here are some of our favourites.

The Blue Elephant Cookbook
By John Hellon (Pavilion).
Recipes from the international Thai chain are simplified and explained. *See p268.*

The Cinnamon Club Cookbook
By Iqbal Wahhab & Vivek Singh (Absolute Press).
From the creators of one of Britain's leading Modern Indian restaurants. *See p136.*

Big Flavours & Rough Edges
By David Eyre & the Eagle cooks (Headline).
Recipes from the pioneering Farringdon gastropub. *See p105.*

FishWorks Seafood Café Cookbook
By Mitchell Tonks (Absolute Press).
Stunning and easy fish dishes from the owner of the FishWorks group. *See p87.*

The Gate Vegetarian Cookbook
By Adrian & Michael Daniel (Mitchell Beazley).
Be inspired by one of London's finest veggie restaurants. *See p284.*

Le Gavroche Cookbook
Le Gavroche (Ten Recipes)
Both by Michel Roux Jr (Weidenfeld & Nicolson).
Michel Roux reveals his personal approach to classic French food in these two books. *See p128.*

Moro: The Cookbook
Casa Moro
Both by Sam & Sam Clark (Ebury Press).
The original *Cookbook* from the much-praised Spanish restaurant, spawned a follow-up. *See p253.*

New Kosher Cooking
By Jason Prangnell (Absolute Press).
New ways with kosher food, from the chef at Bevis Marks, to be published in 2006. *See p195.*

Nobu: The Cookbook
Nobu Now
Both by Nobu Matsuhisa (Quadrille).
Two books by the master behind acclaimed Japanese restaurant Nobu. *See p185.*

The Real Greek at Home
By Theodore Kyriakou & Charles Campion (Mitchell Beazley).
Modern Greek cooking from the pioneering Real Greek. *See p123.*

River Café Cookbook
By Rose Gray & Ruth Rogers (Ebury Press).
Four to choose from: yellow, blue, green and easy. Version 2 of 'easy' is the latest. *See p173.*

Sally Clarke's Book
By Sally Clarke (Grub Street).
The subtitle says it all: 'Recipes from a Restaurant, Shop & Bakery'. *See p229.*

The Wagamama Cookbook
By Hugo Arnold (Kyle Cathie).
Learn the secrets of the mega-successful noodle bar chain. *See p243.*

huge industrial space, actually made up of several interconnecting rooms, offers art exhibitions, a bar area and even, in summer, screenings of classic movies (outdoors if it's warm and dry, inside on mountains of cushions if it's not). However, on the evidence of our Saturday-night visit, it's the restaurant operation that really steals the show. The appetising, quietly inventive menu changes constantly, and the kitchen staff cook as though they're genuinely engaged by the challenge. To start, a tender portion of char-grilled pigeon with delectable caramelised swedes; and immaculate tiger prawns with crispy noodles and salmon roe. Mains were just as good: a sizeable scallop and prawn ravioli, and perfectly grilled swordfish with pea and mint risotto; ingredients in both could not have been fresher. The lively, well-regarded wine list is wholly Australian, and there are also cocktails. Staff strike just the right note in genuinely extraordinary surroundings. Exemplary destination dining.
Babies and children welcome: high chairs. Disabled: toilet. Entertainment: performances and exhibitions (phone for details). Tables outdoors (20, garden).

North
Camden Town & Chalk Farm NW1

★ Odette's
130 Regent's Park Road, NW1 8XL (7586 5486). Chalk Farm tube/31, 168, 274 bus. **Lunch served** 12.30-2.30pm Tue-Sun. **Dinner served** 7-11pm Mon-Sat. **Main courses** £15-£23. **Set lunch** £16.50 2 courses, £20 3 courses. **Service** 12.5%. **Credit** AmEx, JCB, MC, V.
Although lined with a huge collection of gilt-framed mirrors, Odette's interior exudes understated simplicity. It's quietly romantic (when the women of a certain age in the downstairs wine bar stick a cork in it) and there are plenty of French accents – not just from a couple of the waiters, but in the wine list, and a menu incorporating snails, frogs' legs and chicken ballotine. Carved roast rack of lamb with crushed potatoes and artichokes was exceedingly good – the meat juicy, fat and pink, with little bones scraped perfectly clean to invite nibbling. Honeyed breast of barbary duck was slightly tough and, given the thin pieces of ripe black fig, tiny onion tart and pak choi that were also on the plate, didn't need its accompanying slice of foie gras. Still, we enjoyed it. At £14, a very good Chilean merlot seemed more wallet-conscious than the food pricing. Odette's finished on a high note with a first-class chocolate fondant – a low, wide disc all the better to ooze with deeply tangy chocolate filling. Mild pistachio ice-cream and black cherry compote made pretty garnishes on the long oval plate. Like the appreciative couples surrounding us, we look forward to returning.
Babies and children admitted. Booking advisable. Restaurant available for hire. Separate rooms for parties, seating 8 and 30. Tables outdoors (7, conservatory). **Map 27 A1**.

Islington N1

Lola's
The Mall Building, 359 Upper Street, N1 0PD (7359 1932/www.lolas.co.uk). Angel tube. **Lunch served** noon-2.30pm Mon-Fri; noon-3pm Sat, Sun. **Dinner served** 6-11pm Mon-Sat. **Main courses** £13.50-£18.50. **Set lunch** £15.75 3 courses. **Set dinner** (6-11pm Mon-Wed; 6-7pm Thur-Sat) £18.75 3 courses. **Service** 12.5% for parties of 5 or more. **Credit** AmEx, DC, JCB, MC, V.
Only a handful of tables were occupied on our Thursday night visit to Lola's, which is a shame, as the restaurant occupies a lovely upstairs atrium space in the old London Electricity building, with a large picture window overlooking Upper Street. The comfortably elegant ambience was enhanced by a pianist. Service was cheerful and efficient, and the food excellent, if pricey. A large basket of

varied breads was followed by starters of pea and mint soup with a seared scallop, crème fraîche and caviar (all the ingredients tasted market-fresh); and asparagus with poached egg (simple yet sublime). Both mains also hit the spot: chicken breast with houmous, fattoush and flatbread (though the bread was dry and heavy-going); and fillet steak with chips (costing a hefty £24). Two courses is easily enough, but we couldn't resist roasted pineapple with coconut sorbet (perfect for summer) and café liégeois (a wonderful concoction of frozen coffee, ice-cream and chocolate). The à la carte prices will dent the wallet, but set meals are available at convenient times.
Babies and children welcome: high chairs. Booking advisable. Dress: smart casual. Separate room for parties, seats 16. **Map 5 O2**.

North West
West Hampstead NW6

Walnut
280 West End Lane, NW6 1LJ (7794 7772/ www.walnutwalnut.com). West Hampstead tube/ rail. **Dinner served** 6.30-11pm Tue-Sun. **Main courses** £9.50-£12.95. **Credit** DC, JCB, MC, V.
Here's just what a local restaurant should be – friendly and good value, in a stylishly furnished (if curiously shaped) space. There's plenty to praise at Walnut, with starters including scallops, fish soup and crispy chorizo salad. To start, a tart of wild mushrooms was a generous heap of fungi on a dryish pastry slab, while three-salmon mousse (poached, smoked and gravadlax) was simple but good. Vegetarians have the option of own-made aubergine and sorrel sausages, or mushroom risotto with coriander pesto. Otherwise, there's a choice of lamb shanks, ribeye and various fish dishes. Fish cakes tasted of salmon and cod rather than (far too frequently encountered) mashed potato, and chicken breast came deliciously stuffed with stilton and lovage. With a side order of garlic mashed potato, we too were well stuffed. A light dessert of fresh cherry mousse was a flavourful, if rather chunky, purée. A Côtes de Gascogne house wine from a decently priced list, and a cheerful, hard-working waitress sent us away satisfied. Note that Walnut is not open at lunch.
Babies and children welcome: children's portions, high chairs. Booking advisable weekends. No-smoking tables. Restaurant available for hire. Tables outdoors (4, pavement). **Map 28 A2**.

Outer London
Barnet, Hertfordshire

Dylan's Restaurant NEW
21 Station Parade, Cockfosters Road, Barnet, Herts EN4 0DW (8275 1551/www.dylans restaurant.com). Cockfosters tube. **Lunch served** noon-3pm Mon-Sat; noon-4pm Sun. **Dinner served** 6-10pm Mon-Sat; 6-9pm Sun. **Main courses** £10.95-£15.90. **Set lunch** (Mon-Sat) £12.50 2 courses, £15.50 3 courses. (Sun) £15.50 2 courses, £19.50 3 courses. **Set dinner** (6-7pm Mon-Sat) £12.50 2 courses, £15.50 3 courses. **Service** 12.5% for parties of 6 or more. **Credit** AmEx, JCB, MC, V.
Cockfosters was a village until the 1933 opening of the Piccadilly line made it one of the original suburbs. Now it's received a sizeable injection of city slickness with the opening of this sophisticated restaurant decked in hot pink and shades of grey. Manager Dylan Murray and chef Richard O'Connell are both formerly of One Aldwych, and their well-trained staff dressed in smart black uniforms would not look out of place in the West End. There is a hint of fusion cuisine on the modish menu (lemongrass with the pasta, guacamole with the stir-fry) but the only suggestion of O'Connell's Irish upbringing is the addictive soda bread in the bread basket. Roast fillet of beef is offered in a choice of three appetising ways. On our visit, iced Maltesers parfait with raspberry sorbet was proving a

popular pud, though we opted for satisfyingly full-flavoured chocolate marquise. The wine list starts at £12.90 for French red and white, then journeys round the Old and New Worlds without topping £52, except for champagnes. The diners packing the place on a Tuesday night certainly seemed to appreciate the good deal they were getting.
Babies and children admitted. Booking advisable weekends. No smoking.

Kew, Surrey

★ The Glasshouse
14 Station Parade, Kew, Surrey TW9 3PZ (8940 6777/www.glasshouserestaurant.co.uk). Kew Gardens tube/rail. **Lunch served** noon-2.30pm Mon-Sat; 12.30-2.45pm Sun. **Dinner served** 7-10.30pm Mon-Thur; 6.30-10.30pm Fri, Sat; 7.30-10pm Sun. **Set lunch** (Mon-Sat) £23.50 3 courses; (Sun) £27.50 3 courses. **Set dinner** £35 3 courses, £45 7 courses. **Service** 12.5%. **Credit** AmEx, MC, V.
Forget the hot, hissing sprays in the leaf-filled Palm House at nearby Kew Gardens: this glasshouse is more like a conservatory extension from one of the local mansions. Pale gold blinds pull down from a padded ceiling, with air-conditioning pouring out of tiny grates, and spotlights casting an attractive light on the middle-aged clientele. The Glasshouse offers neighbourhood dining par excellence. Chef Anthony Boyd combines classical French training with Mediterranean ingredients and Heston Blumenthal-style playfulness. A large glass came filled with layers of gorgeously smoky salmon mousse, shrimps, salmon and gazpacho jelly. Main course fibrous pork belly sat on a thin layer of apple tarte fine: a novel way to serve this combination of meat and fruit. For dessert, own-made yoghurt was scattered with space dust that crackled on the palate amid the mango and melon. The Glasshouse has a place among the 4WDs and health-food shops on Kew's Station Parade, but the owners need to take care that it doesn't slip into cruise control. Staff were uncertain about an exceptional wine list; luckily we chose well with a half bottle of Bernard Gripa's 2002 St Joseph (Rhône).
Babies and children welcome (lunch): children's menu; high chairs. Booking essential. No smoking.

Twickenham, Middlesex

★ McClements
2 Whitton Road, Twickenham, Middx TW1 1BJ (8744 9610). Twickenham or Whitton rail/ 33, 110, 267, 281, 290, 490, 904, 942 bus. **Lunch served** noon-2pm daily. **Dinner served** 7-9.30pm Tue-Sat. **Set lunch** £25 3 courses. **Set dinner** (Mon-Thur) £34 2 courses, £38 3 courses. **Set meal** £60 6 courses. **Service** 10%. **Credit** AmEx, MC, V.
Midweek lunchtime visitors are clearly a summer rarity at McClements; the headwaiter was still getting dressed when we arrived. We dined alone to the sound of a dreadful 'Hits on Classics' medley and despite the best efforts of one extremely friendly (now suited) Frenchman, and two very good glasses of Petit Chablis, we wished we'd come in the evening. Appetites whetted by delicious breads and an amuse-bouche of foie gras with fig chutney, we then had two faultless starters. Mullet escabeche with tapenade potatoes and baby leaves was mopped to the last dribble of dressing, while chicken and foie gras boudin with caramelised apple and potato tuile deftly managed the trick of being both rich and light. For mains, tender pink strips of roasted veal loin with crushed potatoes were so good we hardly noticed the absence of the listed beetroot fondant. And fillet of sea bream and deep-fried lobster claw was great, except for a slightly overpowering garlic purée. Desserts didn't quite hit the same mark. An apricot soufflé was too big and rather bland, and delicious roasted peaches weren't improved by two dry slices of caramelised brioche. The wine list is a francophile's delight – but make sure your boss is paying.
Babies and children admitted. Booking advisable. Disabled: toilet. No smoking.

North African

There are two types of North African restaurant in London: the ones with striped rugs on the walls and sequinned throw cushions everywhere, and the ones that do good food. Rarely are the two combined.

North African cooking is practical and unfussy. The overriding principle is to throw all the ingredients into a pot then leave to cook slowly. Prime exhibit is the signature dish of tagine (also spelled tajine), which is essentially a stew of meat (usually lamb or chicken) and vegetables slow-cooked over a charcoal fire. Olives, tangy preserved lemon, almonds or prunes are typical flavourings. The name tagine describes both the food and the pot it's cooked in – a shallow earthenware dish with a conical lid that traps the rising steam and stops the stew from drying out. The other defining local staple is couscous, which is again the name of the basic ingredient (coarse-ground semolina) and of the dish; the couscous is slow-cooked and accompanied with a rich meat or vegetable stew.

The menu rarely strays much beyond these two items, except for perhaps some grilled brochettes and a pastilla. Starters take the form of hot and cold small dishes – called salads, but which are more usually spiced purées of carrots, peppers, aubergine, tomatoes and the like. Reliable exponents include **Moroccan Tagine**, **Original Tagines**, **Pasha** and **Safir**, though there's not a lot of experimentation, and even somewhere as hip and fashionable as **Momo** is very conservative when it comes to the kitchen. The one notable exception is the newly opened **Occo** in Marylebone, which is pioneering what it calls 'modern Moroccan'.

Central
Covent Garden WC2

Souk
27 Litchfield Street, WC2H 9NJ (7240 1796/ www.soukrestaurant.net). Leicester Square tube. **Meals served** noon-11.30pm Mon-Thur, Sun; noon-2am Fri, Sat. **Main courses** £7.95-£8.95. **Set meal** (noon-5pm) £12.50 3 courses incl mint tea; (after 5pm) £15 3 courses incl mint tea. **Service** 12.5%. **Credit** AmEx, MC, V.
We know lots of people who love Souk, and we can see why, but it's got nothing to do with the food. The food is dreadful. We're not talking just the odd off-night; we've eaten here on several occasions and the standard has been woeful every time. Most recently we endured a plate of houmous that had the consistency of gruel, and a yoghurt and cucumber dip that was like cold soup. The couscous royale was soggy. The only palatable thing was a lamb and prune tagine. Even the beer was off. So what's the appeal? Well, Souk's interior is pure oriental fantasy: a ground-floor dining room filled with silky throw cushions and filigree lanterns, and a brick-lined basement with a ceiling draped in black sheets, kilim-covered benches and a bazaar's worth of oriental trinketry. African staff sport flowing jellabas, there's belly dancing and the air is heavy with the sweet scent from glass-bowled waterpipes. It's probably the most fun-looking basement in the West End and perfect for parties. We just recommend having a few drinks before ordering food.
Babies and children admitted. Booking essential. Entertainment: belly dancing 11pm Wed-Sat. Separate room for parties, seats 40. Vegetarian menu. **Map 18 K6**.

Leicester Square SW1

Saharaween
3 Panton Street, SW1Y 4DL (7930 2777). Leicester Square or Piccadilly Circus tube. **Meals served** 4pm-1am daily. **Main courses** £7.50-£11. **Unlicensed. Corkage** no charge. **Credit** MC, V.
Saharaween is a definite find in this tourist-rammed part of town, located just off Leicester Square. A great mix of traditional and modern Maghrebi music plays unobtrusively. From the ground-floor tea-room with shishas, you descend a perilous spiral staircase to a cosy basement restaurant with low seating and the usual decor of rugs, gilded leather cushions and drapes. The place feels slightly shabby, but is all the more homey for it. There's no alcohol licence, though you will find imaginative fresh fruit cocktails – the Touareg has mounds of fresh pineapple, ginger and orange flower water – or you can bring your own wine. To eat, mixed meze include zaalouk and shredded chicken with honey and ground nuts. Our Tunisian companion praised his fresh, coriander-infused chorba (soup). Tagine bahri featured two giant prawns and red snapper in an excellent tomatoey fish sauce. Tagine of lamb, prunes and apples, intense in flavour, sweet but not cloying, was too watery; the pitta bread (why no North African bread?) was inadequate to mop it up. Crêpes berbere were reminiscent of shop-bought pancakes, though the rich honey, butter and almond sauce that accompanied them was good. Finish your meal with mint tea – refreshing but pricey at £7 a pot.
Babies and children admitted. Separate room for parties, seats 40. Tables outdoors (2, pavement). Takeaway service. **Map 17 K7**.

Marylebone W1

Occo [NEW]
58 Crawford Street, W1H 4NA (7724 4991/ www.occo.co.uk). Edgware Road tube/Marylebone tube/rail. **Lunch served** noon-3pm Mon-Sat. **Dinner served** 6.30-10pm daily. **Main courses** £9.75-£13.95. **Service** 12.5%. **Credit** AmEx, MC, V.
That's Occo as in 'Morocco'. But not quite. 'The food here is modern Moroccan,' said the waiter. Modern Moroccan perhaps more accurately describes Occo's interior. Chandeliers resembling squashed daddy longlegs echo the caps of caidal tents; cushions are clay-brown in hue; basins in the toilets are of beaten copper. The bar has a tapas menu of modern Moroccan meze, along with a cocktail list that includes fig Bellini. But diners should head for the small sunken well of a restaurant at the back. What constitutes a modern Moroccan menu? Apparently, it's things like goat's cheese and rocket salad, deep-fried calamares, duck breast with wild mushrooms, and cod and king prawn brochettes. North Africa is there, but only in the details. For instance, the salad comes with a dressing of oil extracted from the nuts of the argan tree from southern Morocco. The cod served on the brochette is marinated in a jus saturated with cumin and ginger and presented with a gorgeous purée of fig and orange blossom; it's very Moroccan in flavour and never has cod tasted so good. Just like the name, Occo is a place that leaves us wanting Mor.
Disabled: toilet. No-smoking tables. Separate room for parties, seats 20. Tables outdoors (6, pavement). **Map 2 F5**.

★ Original Tagines
7A Dorset Street, W1H 3SE (7935 1545/ www.originaltagines.com). Baker Street tube. **Lunch served** noon-3pm, **dinner served** 6-11pm daily. **Main courses** £9.50-£11.95. **Set lunch** £10 2 courses. **Credit** MC, V.
Original Tagines is a great little neighbourhood restaurant that happens to be Moroccan. It's slotted just off the top end of Baker Street among red-brick mansion blocks and mews, next to the Barley Mow pub. The restaurant is blessedly free of ethnic knick-knacks, favouring instead a minimal aesthetic of yellow calligraphy on yellow walls (they read 'Peace', 'Thanks', 'Blessings' and other expressions of goodwill). Mosaic-topped tables add a splash of colour. The standard double act of couscous (five varieties) and tagines (11 types) is lent support by an atypically good selection of starters including briouettes, broad bean and red pepper salads, merguez, sautéed kidneys and an excellent pastilla (shredded chicken in filo pastry dusted with icing sugar and cinnamon). Main-course portions tend to be modest, with the emphasis on flavour and quality, as in a beautiful sweet and savoury lamb and pear tagine – we suggest ordering a side dish of couscous with the tagines to avoid leaving hungry. Moroccan wine by the glass comes in red, white and rosé varieties, although the beer is Turkish (Efes).
Babies and children welcome: high chairs. Booking advisable. Tables outdoors (5, pavement). Takeaway service. **Map 3 G5**.

Mayfair W1

★ Momo
25 Heddon Street, W1B 4BH (7434 4040/ www.momoresto.com). Piccadilly Circus tube. **Lunch served** noon-2.15pm Mon-Sat. **Dinner served** 7-11.15pm Mon-Thur; 7-11.45pm Fri, Sat; 7-10.45pm Sun. **Main courses** £14.50-£19.50. **Set lunch** £11 2 courses, £14 3 courses. **Service** 12.5%. **Credit** AmEx, DC, MC, V.
We love Momo, but anyone who comes for the food is missing the point. You come here for the scenery – the place is both chic and exotic, decked out like Rick's Café Américain of *Casablanca* fame, with lattice-screen windows and hanging brass lanterns. You come for the crowd: almost without exception tall and leggy (men and women both) with a smattering of imposing Nubians and North

RESTAURANTS

Africans. Staff, in their custom-designed kasbah pop art T-shirts, seem to have been chosen for their looks rather than their table-waiting skills. Come for the energy too. The vibe is club-like, with diners hyper-animated, knocking back minty house cocktails; staff knifing between densely packed tables; and music to the fore (rattling, clattering and pounding). And OK, while you're here, you can eat. The menu consists of the standard tagines and couscous, supplemented by Med-style dishes such as baked cod, duck breast and sea bass. Yet good as the food is – and it is very good – it's unlikely to be the most memorable aspect of your evening. Next door is the Mô Tea Room, another glitzy, seductive spot filled with lanterns, kaftans, jewellery, antiques, books – many of which are for sale. Do head there for the atmosphere, but don't bother with the food.

Babies and children admitted. Booking essential. Separate room for parties, seats 80. Tables outdoors (8, terrace). **Map 9 J7.**

For branch (Mô Tea Room), see index.

Oxford Street W1

Momo at Selfridges

2nd floor, Selfridges, 400 Oxford Street, W1C 1JT (7318 3620/www.momoresto.com). Bond Street tube. **Breakfast served** 10am-noon, **lunch served** noon-3pm, **meze served** 3-7pm daily. **Main courses** £8-£17.50. **Set meal** £17 2 courses, £20 3 courses. **Service** 12.5%. **Credit** AmEx, DC, JCB, MC, V.

A restaurant in a department store. Not a cafeteria or a canteen, but a restaurant. Fitting then that it should be a branch of Momo (*see p238*), a restaurant that goes about selling you a whole branded lifestyle. Page one of the menu lists not soups and salads but accessories: the cookbook, the CDs, the clothing. The food at Selfridges is designed to match the surroundings, so it's big on style and presentation, and pricey. Pick of the minimal line-up of starters is the Momo kemia, an artful pairing of two filled savoury pastries, mashed aubergine and a mixed pepper salad; it looks pretty but there's little on the plate for £8.50. Otherwise, you'll find full-blown fare including a couscous dish, one tagine and, recently, a couple of fish options. It all looks splendid but isn't it a bit overblown for snacking between the boutiques? If you're paying £30 a head do you really want to eat surrounded by window-shoppers? However, we love the idea of the cocktail bar, a big glamorous affair with plenty of bar counter seating. And the tent for smoking waterpipes is certainly novel.

Babies and children welcome: children's menu. Disabled: toilet. No-smoking tables. **Map 9 G6.**

For branch (Mô Tea Room), see index.

West

Bayswater W2

Couscous Café

7 Porchester Gardens, W2 4DB (7727 6597). Bayswater tube. **Meals served** noon-11pm Mon-Thur, Sun; noon-midnight Fri, Sat. **Main courses** £9.95-£15.95. **Service** 10%. **Credit** AmEx, MC, V.

We'd heard some positive reports of the Couscous Café, so entered full of hope. It's an intimate little spot, decorated in the usual *Road to Morocco* style – henna lamps with folksy artefacts and rugs scattered about. At first our Morroccan host's effusive welcome seemed sweet, but by the end of the evening his purple prose about every item on the menu grated. Plus points include an extensive Moroccan wine list that ranges widely in price and contains bottles rarely found in London. The food, though, didn't live up to its exalted description. A borek with minced lamb and coriander was cold in the middle; and chicken bastilla, despite being tasty and warmly spiced with cinnamon, was a real heavyweight. Mixed brochette of lamb, chicken and merguez was OK, but the couscous royale tasted odd – perhaps it suffered from over-generous use of smen (preserved butter), though even our butter-loving companion wrinkled his

nose at it. To finish, fresh pastries and good mint tea partially saved the evening. Nevertheless, this place needs to lighten up (in all regards) if it wants diners to return.

Babies and children admitted. Booking essential. Tables outdoors (2, pavement). Vegetarian menu. **Map 7 C6.**

Hammersmith W6

Azou

375 King Street, W6 9NJ (8563 7266). Stamford Brook tube. **Lunch served** noon-2.30pm Mon-Fri. **Dinner served** 6-11pm daily. **Main courses** £7-£13. **Set meal** £12-£15 3 courses. **Service** 12.5%. **Credit** MC, V.

Geographically, the menu at Azou is all over the place. The restaurant bills itself as 'Moroccan, Algerian and Tunisian' but there's also some Egyptian (fuul medames) and generic Middle Eastern (houmous, baba ganoush, falafel) too. 'Meze menus' have recently been introduced. There's nothing wrong with this cross-border cuisine, it's just that traditional Moroccan dishes (couscous and tagines account for the bulk of the menu) tend to be pretty substantial and don't need padding. The kitchen is more than a little shaky. In the past we've enjoyed the Tunisian starters of chakchouka (baked peppers, tomato and onion) and brik, but this time the former was swamped in thick tomato sauce, while the latter was oily and heavy. The mains weren't much better: the lamb in a lamb couscous was too hard, and the chickpeas were cold. Tagine romanne – chicken simmered in a pomegranate sauce – was crude and overcooked. A shame, as Azou is a nice, little casual place with a café-like ambience and a bright pleasant interior. The management have always been charming. Maybe it's time they got more ruthless in the kitchen.

Babies and children admitted. Booking advisable. Entertainment: belly dancers (phone for details). Takeaway service. Vegetarian menu. **Map 20 A4.**

Fez

58 Fulham Palace Road, W6 9BH (8563 8687). Hammersmith tube. **Meals served** noon-midnight daily. **Main courses** £7.50-£9.95. **Set lunch** £5.95-£8.95 2 courses. **Set meal** £12.95 2 courses. **Meze** £22.95-£24.95. **Credit** MC, V.

Fez is a Moroccan restaurant for those who aren't sure they like Moroccan food. The menu offers familiar Lebanese meze as starters, including the supermarket staples of houmous and falafel. The couscous dishes (from a choice of seven) are Anglicised versions of the true North African recipe, limiting themselves to safe ingredients such as lamb, chicken, carrots and potatoes, served dry and with minimal spicing. There are just two tagines, with none of that beef-and-fruit nonsense. And if this fails to reassure timid palates, the menu also includes pepper steak and entrecôte, with apple pie and black forest gateaux for dessert. But it seems to work. Always when we've visited, the restaurant has been host to large parties (hence the crowd-pleasing menu), drawn here by the ethnicky frills (low cushioned seating, lots of rugs and things with tassles) and good-time vibe, helped by a great sound system. It's designed to appeal to anyone who's ever bought a Buddha Bar CD – which is obviously many people given that the place was completely full on a midweek evening.

Babies and children admitted. Booking advisable weekends. Entertainment: belly dancers Fri, Sat (phone for details). Takeaway service; delivery service (orders over £25 only). **Map 20 C4.**

Ladbroke Grove W10

★ Moroccan Tagine

95 Golborne Road, W10 5NL (8968 8055). Ladbroke Grove or Westbourne Park tube/23 bus. **Meals served** noon-11pm daily. **Main courses** £5.50-£7.90. **Unlicensed**. No alcohol allowed. **Credit** MC, V.

For a no-frills street café, Moroccan Tagine boasts an ambitious and excellent menu. Tagines and couscous form the backbone, of course, but there

Menu

North African food has similarities with other cuisines; see the menu boxes in **Middle Eastern** and **Turkish**.

Bastilla or **pastilla**: an ouarka (qv) envelope with a traditional filling of sliced or minced pigeon, almonds, spices and egg, baked then dusted with cinnamon and powdered sugar. In the UK chicken is often substituted for pigeon.

Brik: minced lamb or tuna and a raw egg bound together in paper-thin pastry, then fried.

Briouats or **briouettes**: little envelopes of deep-fried, paper-thin ouarka (qv) pastry; these can have a savoury filling of ground meat, rice or cheese, or be served as a sweet flavoured with almond paste, nuts or honey.

Chermoula: a dry marinade of fragrant herbs and spices.

Chicken kedra: chicken stewed in a stock of onions, lemon juice and spices (ginger, cinnamon), sometimes with raisins and chickpeas.

Couscous: granules of processed durum wheat. The name is also given to a dish where the slow-cooked grains are topped with a meat or vegetable stew like a tagine (qv); couscous royale usually involves a stew of lamb, chicken and merguez (qv).

Djeja: chicken.

Harira: thick lamb and lentil soup.

Harissa: very hot chilli pepper paste flavoured with garlic and spices.

Maakouda: spicy potato fried in breadcrumbs.

Merguez: spicy, paprika-rich lamb sausages.

Ouarka: filo-like pastry.

Tagine or **tajine**: a shallow earthenware dish with a conical lid; it gives its name to a slow-simmered stew of meat (usually lamb or chicken) and vegetables, often cooked with olives, preserved lemon, almonds or prunes.

Zaalouk or **zaalouk**: a cold spicy aubergine, tomato and garlic dip.

are no less than six kinds of lamb tagine, for instance – including with okra, with prunes, with roasted almonds, and with green peas and artichoke. Chicken is cooked with olives, or onions and sultanas, or in a 'secret sauce'. Soon to come is beef with orange. Mmm. Unsurprisingly with one of London's best fishmongers up the street, there's also a good showing of seafood: sardines stuffed or grilled, calamares, fish tagine and a fish platter with salad. Again, the quality of the food belies the humble setting. Everything's prepared by the genial, bearded Hassan, a Berber from the mountains of Morocco, using family recipes. We relish the olives, which come as a complimentary starter; they're imported by Hassan from his homeland and then marinated to his own recipe. No alcohol is served, but the mint tea is powerfully refreshing, especially on a hot day.

Babies and children welcome: high chairs. Book weekends. No-smoking tables. Tables outdoors (4, pavement). Takeaway service; delivery service (within W10). **Map 19 B1.**

RESTAURANTS

Safir

Shepherd's Bush W12

Adam's Café

77 Askew Road, W12 9AH (8743 0572).
Hammersmith tube then 266 bus. **Dinner**
served 7-11pm Mon-Sat. **Set dinner** £10.50
1 course incl mint tea/coffee, £13.50 2 courses,
£15.50 3 courses. **Service** 12.5%. **Credit** AmEx,
MC, V.

London's only Tunisian restaurant (the owner is
from Djerba in Tunisia) is an unimposing little
place, justly popular with west London locals, not
least for its child-friendliness. The menu is
extensive. Our meal started brilliantly: tiny cumin-
infused kefta (meatballs); pickled vegetables in
spicy, oily dressing; and bread to dip in the
obligatory fiery harissa with oil. We know of no
other venue in town that serves authentic Tunisian
brik a l'oeuf (a fan-like ouarka shell filled with
tuna, potato, egg and parsley); other places
substitute filo, which lacks the proper, delicately
brittle crispness. Equally praiseworthy was the
odja: rich scrambled egg mixed with peppers,
tomato and harissa, here served with good spicy
merguez. We were sorry not to find many Tunisian
main courses, all-purpose North African being the
norm. Fish tagine (Moroccan, rather than
Tunisian-style) with swordfish, peppers and

potatoes was richly tomatoey and well spiced. We
weren't so pleased with our stuffed baby calamares
with couscous, the calamares lacking in fresh
tender juiciness. But with friendly, attentive service
from the owners, very reasonable prices and a
good, well-priced wine list (including a citrusy,
refreshing Macon for £12), we'd certainly visit
Adam's again.
Babies and children admitted. Book weekends.
Separate room for parties, seats 24. Vegetarian
menu. **Map 20 A1.**

South West

Gloucester Road SW7

★ Pasha

1 Gloucester Road, SW7 4PP (7589 7969/
www.pasha-restaurant.co.uk). Gloucester Road
tube/49 bus. **Lunch served** noon-3pm Mon-Sat.
Dinner served 6-11pm Mon-Sat; 6.30-10pm Sun.
Main courses £9.75-£16.75. **Set lunch** £13.50
2 courses, £15.75 3 courses. **Service** 15%.
Credit AmEx, DC, MC, V.

As soon as you step through Pasha's imposing
marble entrance you know you're in for a sensory
treat. A flower-strewn marble fountain with blue
and white mosaic surround; bevvies of huge brass

lanterns suspended on high; and sumptuously
cushioned intimate alcoves, gently candlelit – all
help create a most romantic venue, with rhythmic,
relaxing music as a backdrop. Even the loos are
gorgeous. Service has sometimes been found
snooty and unhelpful, but our waitresses were
amiable and attentive. Pasha plays with traditional
elements of Maghrebi cuisine, often creating
something new. Tunisian borek was pronounced
rather heavy and cheesy by our Tunisian
companion. Yet we enjoyed the light crispy prawn
and egg briouat, enlivened by fresh coriander.
Tagine d'Essaouira (snake fish with mussels and
prawns) came with an intense bouillabaisse-style
sauce of perfect consistency. Couscous royale was
also exemplary, with succulent grilled chicken and
lamb, spicy lean merguez, a hunk of meltingly
tender stewed lamb and a light, flavoursome broth
with vegetables. The drinks list encompasses some
imaginative cocktails, and a few Moroccan options
– we enjoyed Casablanca beer and Gris de
Guerrouane rosé by the glass. Other bonus points:
there's an enterprising vegetarian menu, and the
set lunch gives a wider-than-average choice of
dishes. An all-round winner.
Babies and children admitted. Book weekends.
Separate room for parties, seats 18. Vegetarian
menu. **Map 7 C9.**

South
Balham SW12

Tagine NEW
*1-3 Fernlea Road, SW12 9RT (8675 7604).
Balham tube/rail.* **Meals served** noon-11pm
daily. **Main courses** £6.90-£11.99. **Set lunch**
(noon-5pm) £5.99 1 course. **Set dinner** (after
5pm) £11.99 2 courses. **Unlicensed**. No alcohol
allowed. **Credit** MC, V.
A simple room just off Balham's burgeoning
restaurant strip (Bedford Hill) has been given the
Moroccan makeover with leather pouffes, low
tables, stained-glass lanterns, sheesha pipes and
some excellent North African music on the CD
player. There's no alcohol, just a straightforward
menu of classic dishes. Chicken pastilla, heavily
dusted in icing sugar, was so rich with fruit, meat
and sugar it was almost like a Christmas pudding.
After this, the much subtler flavours of vegetable
couscous and lamb tagine were very welcome. The
meat of the orika tagine was excellent, served on
the bone and very tasty, with green peas and
artichokes. Couscous was also exemplary, with
distinct, perfectly steamed grains and a turmeric-
yellow vegetable stew. For dessert, a dried fig cake
layered with mascarpone and drizzled with a

fudge-like caramel sauce was inventive, though the
icing sugar had again been used very liberally. A
real taste of Morocco, with genuine hospitality.
*Babies and children welcome: high chairs. Booking
advisable. No-smoking tables. Tables outdoors
(6, pavement).*

North
Islington N1

Fez
*70 Upper Street, N1 0NU (7359 1710/
www.fez-islington.co.uk). Angel tube.* **Meals
served** noon-11pm Mon-Wed; noon-2am Thur-
Sat;noon-midnight Sun. **Main courses** £6.95-
£23.95. **Credit** MC, V.
Fez's heavy wooden door leads into a soothing
terracotta room – all henna lamps and red woven
fabrics. The low lighting is relaxing, but beware of
dark spots; reading our menu and seeing the food
was tricky. Service was more attentive than on
previous visits. Choose from tempting cocktails,
several beers including Moroccan Casablanca, and
a fairly priced wine list with Moroccan bottles.
Meze kemia gives the chance to sample a few
starters: zaalouk, mini pastilla and salade mechoui
(grilled peppers, tomatoes, garlic and parsley). Or

try lightly spiced lamb kefta (meatballs). We
usually swear by the tagine de rouget fruit de mer,
with mussels, clams, prawns and an intense
reduced fish sauce, but this time it was incredibly
salty, as was couscous brochette d'agneau. The
latter was just right in terms of tender moist lamb
skewers, with vegetable broth and harissa served
separately, but both dishes left us gasping for
water. Serviceable desserts include pancake with
honey and almonds, and Moroccan rice pudding.
The mint tea is the real thing; enjoy it with a shisha
upstairs or in the downstairs disco bar.
*Babies and children admitted. Booking advisable.
Tables outdoors (3, pavement). Vegetarian menu.*
Map 5 O2.

Maghreb
*189 Upper Street, N1 1RQ (7226 2305/
www.maghrebrestaurant.co.uk). Highbury &
Islington tube/rail.* **Meals served** 6-11.30pm
daily. **Main courses** £6.95-£11.95. **Service**
12.5% for parties of 6 or more. **Credit** AmEx,
JCB, MC, V.
A chilly evening seemed a good time to allow
Maghreb to transport us to warmer climes with its
vibrant drapes against yellow walls and glowing
red silk lanterns. In the past we've praised the
zingy spicing and fresh ingredients, but this time
some dishes, like the decor, seemed tired. Zaalouk
was served too cold, stifling the usually intense
aromatic coriander-cumin fusion. Merguez on a
bed of cumin-infused chickpea salad were better,
but slightly burned on one side as if reheated. The
same could be said of the mixed grill couscous; the
grilled meat (chicken, lamb, merguez, kefta) was
dry, verging on burnt in parts. The couscous was
fine, but accompanied by too stingy a portion of
an albeit flavoursome vegetable stew. Baked sea
bass marinated in chermoula worked better. The
fairly priced wine list features several Moroccan
choices; our basic Trois Domaines Guerrouane red
was smooth and drinkable. Unlike many Moroccan
venues, there's a good choice of puddings,
including baghrir (spongy pancakes with a honey
and butter sauce) and Moroccan rice and almond
pudding. We hope Maghreb returns to form soon.
*Babies and children welcome: high chairs. Booking
advisable. No-smoking tables. Restaurant available
for hire. Separate areas available for parties,
seating 38 and 44. Takeaway service.* **Map 5 O1.**

North West
Hampstead NW3

★ Safir
*116 Heath Street, NW3 1DR (7431 9888/
www.safir-restaurant.co.uk). Hampstead tube.*
Dinner served 6pm-midnight Mon-Wed.
Meals served noon-midnight Thur-Sun.
Main courses £8.85-£17.50. **Set meal** £11.95
2 courses. **Credit** MC, V.
Saturday night at Safir is usually busy; earlier in
the week it's supremely calm. A mixed crowd is
drawn by sweet, attentive staff through the heavy,
studded door into a traditional green and yellow
tented room with chairs and divans upholstered in
bright striped satin. Safir distinguishes itself with
well-executed traditional cuisine. Success lies in
the food's simplicity – no overloading of flavours
or ingredients. Garlicky zaalouk, carrot chermoula
(nicely piquant) and light, crispy prawn briouat
were all just right. Couscous with chicken,
caramelised onions and sultanas was simply but
perfectly done, the sweetness foiled by the
delicately spiced broth with veg. Tagine of lamb
with prunes is always a hit here too; the chef
achieves that perfectly reduced, sweet but not
sickly, gloopy sauce that others often serve too
watery. Weekend diners are entertained by a belly
dancer; unlikely-looking types are sometimes lured
on to the floor, but fear not, the mood is always well
judged with no sense of embarrassing compulsion.
One of our favourite Moroccan venues.
*Babies and children welcome: high chairs. Booking
essential Fri, Sat, dinner Sun. Entertainment:
belly dancer 8pm Thur-Sat; band 7.30pm Fri.
Separate room for parties, seats 25. Takeaway
service.* **Map 28 C1.**

Oriental

The origins of pan-oriental cuisine in London can be traced back to the late 1980s, when Chinese restaurateurs saw the popularity of various other Asian cuisines – Malaysian at first, then Thai – and began offering versions of these dishes on their menus. Some even dreamed up a new name, carried out a quick refurb, and changed their restaurant's national identity.

The blossoming of the Vietnamese restaurant scene in the 1990s, coupled with the dramatic increase in inexpensive Japanese cafés, added to the chance of cross-fertilisation. A further boost came with the opening of the first **Wagamama** in 1992. By 1996 there was a sufficient number of oriental restaurants for us to give this generic new cuisine its own chapter in our guide.

The phenomenal success of Wagamama led to an array of imitators buying in bench seating, and brushing up their meal-in-one pan-Asian rice and noodle dishes. More recently, the cutting edge of oriental cuisine has moved upmarket. Will Ricker set the ball rolling with the opening of **Cicada** in 1997. He continues to be a major player today, with a batch of stylish, good-looking restaurants that includes **Great Eastern Dining Room**, **E&O** and **Eight Over Eight**.

Such venues have moved away from providing classic dishes of specific oriental countries, and instead fashioned a new 'Modern Asian' cuisine where Korean pickles might share a plate with a Thai salad, or Vietnamese spicing might pep up a bowl of Japanese noodles. This year, developments have captured the imagination of top chefs and restaurateurs, such as Gordon Ramsay and Ian Pengelley at **Pengelley's**, and ex-Sugar Club maestros Vivienne Hayman and Ashley Sumner at the **Grocer on Warwick Café**. And the advent of **Cocoon** proves, at least, that oriental cuisine is now a hot tip in the fashion stakes.

Central
City EC2, EC4

Silks & Spice
Temple Court, 11 Queen Victoria Street, EC4N 4UJ (7248 7878/www.silksandspice.com). Mansion House tube/Bank tube/DLR. **Meals served** 11.30am-10.30pm Mon-Fri. **Main courses** £5.50-£20. **Set meals** £15.95 (vegetarian) 3 courses, £16.95 3 courses, £19.95-£25.85 4 courses (minimum 2). **Service** 12.5%. **Credit** AmEx, MC, V.
Down the road from the Bank of England, Silks & Spice caters for its City clientele with a large bar and an express meal dining area, complete with blaring satellite TVs. We opted to eat in the sedate (TV-free) back-room restaurant instead– a large but oddly gloomy space that felt distinctly like a hotel lounge, with only a handful of besuited male diners at lunch. To kick off, pandan-leaf wrapped chicken was dull, while Thai fish cakes were tasty but oily. Butterflied charcoal-grilled prawns (ordered as the sea bass we'd originally wanted 'hadn't been delivered yet') looked spectacular, but were overcooked and therefore chewy. Thankfully, the rest of the meal came up trumps: coconutty Thai green chicken curry and stir-fried morning glory with garlic and chilli both went down well. No doubt it gets busier in the evening, adding some much-needed atmosphere, but the patchy cooking was a disappointment from a chain that has performed so well in the past.
Babies and children admitted. Booking advisable; essential for parties of 10 or more. Disabled: toilet. Entertainment: DJs 10.30pm Thur, Fri. Separate room for parties, seats 20. Takeaway service. Vegetarian menu. **Map 11 P6.**
For branches see index.

Wagamama
1A Ropemaker Street, EC2V 0HR (7588 2688/ www.wagamama.com). Moorgate tube/rail. **Meals served** 11.30am-10pm Mon-Fri. **Main courses** £6.10-£9.95. **Set meal** £11.50-£12.75 incl drink. **Credit** AmEx, DC, JCB, MC, V.
This no-frills eating formula has been oft repeated, but seldom bettered. Long communal refectory tables and shared benches may not be everyone's cup of green tea, but for those looking for quick, cheap, wholesome oriental food, Wagamama is the place to come. And with 21 branches in London, there's probably one near you. The menu is simply divided into various noodle and rice dishes: ramen (big bowls of noodles in soup), kare noodle (in a coconut-based soup), chilli men (in a spicy sauce) and teppan (cooked on a griddle). Vegetarians should look for anything prefaced with yasai; the rest can choose from chicken, seafood, beef and chicken combos. Extras include gyoza (grilled dumplings with cabbage, carrot and water chestnut); miso soup and raw salads. Not everything works. Our 'summer special' salad with chicken and mandarin looked delicious, but tasted bland. Yasai cha han (fried rice, veg and tofu, with vegetarian miso soup and pickles) was comforting,

if a bit dull, but ebi chilli men (stir-fried prawns in chilli sauce) was excellent. Kids have their own mini menu, which includes a chicken and sweetcorn ramen. Drinks include Japanese beer, saké, freshly made juices and as many cups of free green tea as you like. Service is brisk and efficient.
Babies and children welcome: high chair; children's menu. Disabled: toilet. No smoking. Takeaway service. Vegetarian menu. Vegan dishes. **Map 12 Q5.**
For branches see index.

Clerkenwell & Farringdon EC1

Cicada
132-136 St John Street, EC1V 4JT (7608 1550/www.cicada.nu). Farringdon tube/rail. **Bar Open** noon-11pm Mon-Sat. **Restaurant Lunch served** noon-3pm Mon-Fri. **Dinner served** 6-10.45pm Mon-Sat. **Dim sum served** noon-3pm, 6-10pm Mon-Sat. **Dim sum** £3-£6. **Main courses** £8-£14. **Service** 12.5%.
Both **Credit** AmEx, DC, JCB, MC, V.
Although no longer a one-off – see also Great Eastern Dining Room (*see p248*), E&O (*see p245*) and Eight Over Eight (*see p247*) – this bar-restaurant is still the cheapest in the chain and still buzzing. Restaurateur Will Ricker's baby is spacious and glass-fronted, with a chic bar leading to a dining area that is set on a raised platform, and outside seating on a terrace. A stunning catwalk of Japanese, Chinese, Thai and Korean fashion plates includes soups, salads, futo maki rolls, sashimi, curries, barbecue dishes and oriental-inspired desserts. Edamame and 'pomegranate & pomelo betel leaf' (a fruitier, less complex version of Thai miang) are both listed under 'dim sum' – but, hey, this is no place for authenticity. The latter was more Nigella than Bangkok street market, but tasted exquisite. Rock shrimp tempura with ponzu (citrus-soy dipping sauce) were light and as pretty as snowflakes. However, the steamed sea bream, although featuring perfectly cooked fish, was let down by the clashing flavours of yellow bean sauce and cinnamon. Service ranged from slow to chatty (or perhaps it was slow because it was chatty?). Vietnamese lemonade and guava cooler make for an exciting drinks list, which also includes seductive oriental cocktails.
Babies and children admitted. Booking advisable lunch. No-smoking tables. Separate room for parties, holds 75. Tables outdoors (6, pavement). **Map 5 O4.**

Fitzrovia W1

Bam-Bou
1 Percy Street, W1T 1DB (7323 9130/ www.bam-bou.co.uk). Goodge Street or Tottenham Court Road tube. **Bar Open** 6pm-1am Mon-Sat. **Restaurant Lunch served** noon-3pm Mon-Fri. **Dinner served** 6-11.30pm Mon-Sat. **Main courses** £9.80-£14. **Service** 12.5%.
Both **Credit** AmEx, JCB, MC, V.
There's a playful exoticism to Bam-Bou, whose French colonial decor (plenty of teak and bamboo, eastern iconography and French-Vietnamese furnishings) work well in the tall narrow confines of its Georgian townhouse setting. The menu too manages to sidestep any kind of theme-park tackiness by matching its vivid, tropical flavours to a range of comfortingly moreish pan-Asian dishes. For openers, steamed soya beans with spiced salt, or superb giant prawn crackers make delicious menu-browsing finger food, while more substantial starters include fragrant chicken salad with lime and chilli or asparagus and crab soup. The main course that we keep coming back for is seared scallops with lacquered pork (a plump, sweet, fleshy treat), although seafood options such as 'drunken' lemon sole or the delicious house roast duck often distract us. Desserts are inventive, with the flavours of kaffir lime brûlée or chilli chocolate and ginger nougat bombe lingering on the palate long after the

meal is finished. The staff could perhaps learn to recognise when diners just want to be left alone, but other than this, we have no complaints.
Babies and children admitted. Booking advisable; essential lunch and weekends. Separate rooms for parties, seating 12, 14 and 20. Tables outdoors (4, terrace). **Map 10 K5**.

Crazy Bear
26-28 Whitfield Street, W1T 2RG (7631 0088/ www.crazybeargroup.co.uk). Goodge Street or Tottenham Court Road tube.
Bar **Open** noon-11pm Mon-Fri; 6-11pm Sat.
Restaurant **Meals served** noon-10.45pm Mon-Fri. **Dinner served** 6-10.45pm Sat. **Dim sum** £2.50-£3.50. **Main courses** £7-£18.50. **Set lunch** £7.50 1 course. **Set meal** (tasting menus) £25 8 dishes, £30 10 dishes. **Service** 12.5%.
Both **Credit** AmEx, MC, V.
A branch of an Oxfordshire gastropub with rooms, this elegant restaurant offers modern Thai cuisine with Chinese, Japanese and Vietnamese influences. The somewhat awkward ground-floor layout combines a sleek ecclesiastical style with art deco. Padded monochrome seating surrounds tables that are too small, and design quirks include oversized menus and long cutlery designed to double up as chopsticks. The ambitious menu takes risks with the likes of rich, tender slow pot roast of ox cheek with Thai lettuce, coriander and spring onions. A beautifully smoky, seared charolais beef salad was enlivened with the colours and flavours of cherry tomatoes, cucumber, mint, chilli and lime. Vegetable massaman curry had a depth of flavour that you would be hard pushed to find in a more traditional Thai restaurant. Our only complaint is variable service: on the whole, staff were friendly, but they were also over-attentive, sometimes slow and occasionally brusque. The glamorous lounge bar in the basement is one of the most beautiful in London, and don't neglect the smoke-and-mirror loos, almost a destination in their own right.
Babies and children admitted (lunch only). Booking advisable. **Map 4 K5**.

★ dim T café
32 Charlotte Street , W1T 2NQ (7637 1122/ www.dimt.co.uk). Goodge Street tube. **Meals served** noon-midnight daily. **Dim sum** £2.50-£2.75. **Main courses** £6.85-£8.95. **Credit** MC, V.

Dim T's formula is obviously working: its West End branch was heaving on a midweek lunchtime. The look is clean-lined and rather feminine – white walls, pink-tinged mirrors, lilac banquettes strewn with floral cushions, and dark wood tables. Dim sum is the thing, with 20 varieties to choose from: prawn, peanut and coriander, say or spicy cod or chicken, wasabi and mushroom. The quality might not be up to Chinatown standards, but they're fresh, tasty and delivered promptly in bamboo baskets by smiling staff. The one-price DIY noodle options are popular too: choose your ingredient (meat, prawns or tofu), then either noodles (rice, egg, wheat versions) or rice, then your topping, and finally the cooking method (stir-fried or in a soup). An egg noodle stir-fry came with beansprouts, baby corn and plenty of plump prawns, but the Thai topping was gloopy and over-dependent on coconut. Alternatively, you can take a whistlestop tour through Asia with the à la carte dishes – Indonesian chicken satay, Chiang Mai red duck curry, Japanese teriyaki salmon. Portions are generous, prices fair. To drink, there are ten kinds of oriental tea (served in Japanese cast-iron teapots) and a few wines and beers.
Babies and children welcome: children's portions; high chairs. Booking advisable lunch. No-smoking tables. Tables outdoors (2, pavement). Takeaway service. **Map 9 J5**.
For branches see index.

Knightsbridge SW1

Pengelley's NEW
164 Sloane Street, SW1X 9QB (7750 5000/ www.pengelleys.com). Knightsbridge tube.
Bar **Open** noon-1am daily. **Dim sum served** noon-midnight daily. **Dim sum** £3.50-£12.
Restaurant **Lunch served** noon-3pm, **dinner served** 6-11pm daily. **Main courses** £12-£18. **Set lunch** £15 3 courses.
Both **Service** 12.5%. **Credit** AmEx, MC, V.
There are fashionable restaurants, and then there are fashionable chefs. Ian Pengelley – who was the chef behind E&O (*see p245*) when it started, and before that worked at Cicada (*see p243*), Birdcage and the Hempel – has been elevated to the status of the latter, not least because Gordon Ramsay is behind this new restaurant. The menu is more hit

than miss, but that's usually the case with pan-Asian restaurants, where individual dishes rarely match the standard of the best dedicated Thai, Japanese or Chinese restaurants. Sushi and tempura were fresh and pert, but a side dish of morning glory was overcooked and flaccid. Chilli salt squid was not as tender as the versions found in most Chinatown restaurants, yet a Hakkasan-style steamed vegetable dim sum, served as an appetiser with steamed soy beans, was perfect. The most inventive dishes were, surprisingly, the most enjoyable. A salad of smoked duck was served with blanched slivers of scallops, fresh herbs and even pieces of lychee: the pea shoots, holy basil and mint sang when combined with a topping of fried shallots, garlic and a dressing of Chinese black vinegar and sesame oil. Service was slow on our visit, but staff were well meaning, and the place had a very convivial buzz. Pengelley's is attractively designed, with a beautiful upstairs bar and a private members club downstairs.
Babies and children admitted. Bar and restaurant available for hire. Booking essential dinner. Disabled: toilet. Entertainment: DJ 9pm Thur-Sat (bar). No smoking (restaurant). **Map 14 F9.**

Mayfair W1

Taman Gang
141 Park Lane, W1K 7AA (7518 3160/www. tamangang.com). Marble Arch tube. **Dinner served** 6-10.30pm Mon, Sun; 6-11.30pm Tue-Thur; 6.45-11.45pm Fri, Sat. **Dim sum served** noon-3.30pm Sun. **Dim sum** £8.50 (vegetarian), £11.50 (fish). **Main courses** £12.50-£45. **Service** 15%. **Credit** AmEx, JCB, MC, V.
Taman Gang – which means 'Park Lane' in one of the Indonesian languages – has a team installed by Gary Yau (brother of restaurateur Alan Yau). It combines a drinking, eating and clubbing experience under one roof, an approach that is already big in New York and just taking off in the UK. The star-studded subterranean restaurant is notable for its design: hand-crafted limestone carvings, richly coloured silk banquettes, water features and bronze Kama Sutra statues create a look that combines sumptuous palaces and the temple ruins of ancient Indonesia. The modern Asian menu incorporates Japanese, Chinese, Thai

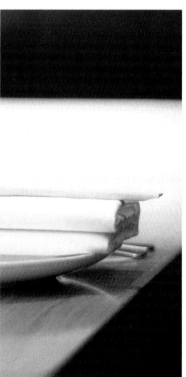

and Modern European influences. Delicious lamb chops, glazed with champagne, plum wine and wild honey, were soft as marshmallows, but a vegetable clay pot of tofu, cloud ear mushrooms, daikon, wild bamboo, wolf berries and star anise tasted more mundane than its ingredients would suggest. Attractive, designer-clad staff are a delight, and there's a lively atmosphere when the DJ comes on. Taman Gang isn't for those looking for authentically prepared, reasonably priced food; it's aimed squarely at the party crowd and, as such, fulfils its brief.
Babies and children admitted (before 8pm). Booking essential. Disabled: toilet. Entertainment: DJ 9pm Wed-Sat. **Map 9 G6.**

Piccadilly W1

Cocoon NEW

2005 RUNNER-UP BEST DESIGN

65 Regent Street, W1B 4EA (7494 7609/ www.cocoon-restaurants.com). Piccadilly Circus tube. **Lunch served** noon-3pm Mon-Fri. **Dinner served** 5.30pm-1am Mon-Sat; 5.30-10.30pm Sun. **Main courses** £7.50-£18.50. **Set meal** (lunch, 5.30-7pm daily) £12.50-£24 2 courses (minimum 2). **Service** 12.5%. **Credit** AmEx, MC, V.
Showcasing the current trend for 'small eats', this new bar-restaurant offers Japanese, Chinese and Thai dishes designed for sharing. There are six intimate dining areas, separated by diaphanous curtains, and a dimly lit, set-aside lounge area. The look, created by American designer Stephane Dupoux, is low-key kitsch: glass-topped dining tables decorated with artificial rose petals, quilted walls, cosy ball-shaped chairs, and cocoon motifs on walls and curtains. We kicked off with cocktails in the bar, which has a beguiling list of perfumed rosewater and saké concoctions. And the food is pretty good. The sushi was a mixed bag: yellowtail nigiri was fresh and elegant, but california roll was standard, with too much mayonnaise, and pickled vegetable roll too tart. Vegetarian dim sum were silky and moreish, though, and lotus leaf-wrapped seafood and chicken rice delicately flavoured. Next, batter-fried prawns in wasabi sauce, despite their glow-in-the-dark appearance, were featherlight and mouth-

Pengelley's

puckeringly sharp, and a dish of spinach-topped fried and silken tofu in pumpkin sauce marvellously austere. Saké and shochu made an ideal accompaniment. We can particularly recommend the chestnutty yam ice-cream.
Babies and children admitted. Booking advisable; essential weekends. Disabled: toilet. No smoking. Separate room for parties, seats 14. **Map 17 J7.**

Soho W1

★ Grocer on Warwick Café NEW

21 Warwick Street, W1B 5NE (7437 7776). Piccadilly Circus tube. **Meals served** 8am-11pm Mon-Sat. **Main courses** £5.50-£9.80. **Service** 12.5%. **Credit** AmEx, DC, JCB, MC, V.
A restaurant that describes itself as 'a new concept in casual dining and food retail' might produce a sinking feeling in some. But when you know that the concept belongs to Vivienne Hayman and Ashley Sumner, on the site of their former success, the Sugar Club, you can feel more confident. And the Grocer – east-meets-west eaterie, bakery and ready meals – doesn't disappoint. There's some great food on sale at the front, but it's the artfully constructed restaurant menu that really scores. Served in dark, oriental teahouse-style surroundings by enthusiastic Antipodean staff, the page-long list merges lunch, dinner, snacks, first and second courses, all produced in tapas-size portions, into a continuous all-day serving. Don't miss the crisp, succulent pork belly with a hint of chilli, or the delicate sea bass fillet with harissa and lemon miso vinaigrette. There are also oriental classics such as green papaya salad with shrimp and peanut dressing, or spring rolls with tamarind dressing, with only the occasional bum note – as in a fairly pedestrian pad Thai and so-so vegetable tempura. Take your waiter's advice on the best way to mix and match, then sit back and enjoy the results as they are delivered to your table in batches.
Babies and children admitted. Booking advisable lunch. No smoking. Separate room for parties, seats 70. Takeaway service. **Map 17 J7.**

Itsu

103 Wardour Street, W1F 0UQ (7479 4790/ www.itsu.com). Piccadilly Circus tube. **Meals served** noon-11pm Mon-Thur; noon-midnight Fri, Sat; 1-10pm Sun. **Main courses** £1.95-£6.95. **Credit** AmEx, MC, V.
This must have been how the future of eating looked, back in the wide-eyed 1950s. Little labelled containers of attractive, fresh food, moving as if by magic in front of your eyes via a smooth, silent conveyor belt. Gleaming surroundings, all silver and red, with brown leather seating. Polite, smiling staff who appear at the touch of a red button, anxious to explain how everything works. Aldous Huxley would have hated it, but we think Itsu is great fun. There are five colour-coded price ranges on the belt, as well as a list of hot and made-on-demand dishes that you order from the staff, including succulent eel sushi in a sweetish sauce. There's plenty of standard Japanese fare – sashimi, sushi, crystal rolls, miso soup – all of good if not top quality, plus a smattering of non-oriental puds (fresh fruit with yoghurt, crème brûlée). Prices are reasonable, but those little plates do mount up – especially the top-priced gold ones. To drink, choose from green tea, fruit juices, a few wines, Asahi beer and even cocktails. The takeaway sushi boxes are extremely popular at lunch. The side-by-side seating works for pairs, but larger groups should grab one of the four-seater booths.
Babies and children admitted. Bookings not accepted. No smoking. Takeaway service. **Map 17 K6.**
For branches see index.

West

Bayswater W2

I-Thai

The Hempel, 31-35 Craven Hill Gardens, W2 3EA (7298 9001/www.the-hempel.co.uk). Lancaster Gate tube/Paddington tube/rail.

Lunch served noon-3pm Mon-Sat. **Dinner served** 7-11.30pm Mon-Wed; 7pm-1am Thur-Sat. **Main courses** £19.25-£24.50. **Set lunch** £30 3 courses. **Service** 12.5%. **Credit** AmEx, DC, JCB, MC, V.
Housed in a spacious basement room at the minimalist Hempel hotel, I-Thai, with its striking black and white decor, certainly looks the part. White orchids and muted lighting soften what could otherwise be an austere space; once our only fellow lunchtime diners, an office party, had left, the restaurant did take on a rather cavernous feel. From an Asian-inspired menu, we tried starters of prawn and asparagus tempura, attractively presented on the (inevitable) large white platter, and fish cakes, let down by an over-sickly dipping sauce and uninspired green papaya salad. Mains were similarly patchy: miso-glazed salmon was pleasant, but the boiled 'saffron potatoes' were overcooked and bland. Sesame tuna, on stir-fried 'Asian greens' was similarly lacking in flavour and overly greasy, while its 'roast fig' garnish was undercooked. Verdict: what should have been a stylish dining experience was marred by careless cooking, which allowed the vivid flavours and vitality of authentic oriental food to seep away.
Babies and children welcome: high chairs. Booking advisable. Disabled: toilet. No-smoking tables. Separate room for parties, seats 35. Tables outdoors (50, terrace). **Map 7 C6.**

Ladbroke Grove W10, W11

★ E&O

14 Blenheim Crescent, W11 1NN (7229 5454/ www.eando.nu). Ladbroke Grove or Notting Hill Gate tube.
Bar **Open/dim sum served** noon-11pm Mon-Sat; noon-10.30pm Sun. **Dim sum** £3-£6.50.
Restaurant **Lunch served** noon-3pm Mon-Sat; 1-3pm Sun. **Dinner served** 6-10.30pm Mon-Sat; 6-10pm Sun. **Main courses** £6-£21.50. **Service** 12.5%.
Both **Credit** AmEx, DC, MC, V.
Perhaps the best loved of Will Ricker's chain of Asian-lite restaurants – Cicada (*see p243*), Eight Over Eight (*see p247*) and Great Eastern Dining Room (*see p248*) – this hip New York-style venue is still pulling in Prada-clad A-listers by the taxi-load. The design is suffused with understated cool: striking dark wood (on walls, furniture and tiny bar) contrasts with cream walls; large lampshades scatter light and shadows on to caramel-coloured banquettes. Date and water chestnut gyoza concealed a crunchy, tasty filling within squidgy, sticky-soft rice flour dumplings. Chilli-salt squid is a must-try – a dish that E&O's original head chef Ian Pengelley (now at his own restaurant, Pengelley's; *see p244*) made his own. These days the concoction is ubiquitous, appearing on restaurant menus from Scotland to Sussex, but this hot crisp version, served in cute oriental newspaper cones, was simply divine. A coriander-laden aubergine salad was light and refreshing, and the black cod with miso was sweet and rich – perhaps not as lovely as Nobu's, but still satisfying. Staff were welcoming and efficient, and there's an inspired list of wines, spirits and Asian-themed cocktails.
Babies and children admitted. Booking essential weekends. Separate room for parties, seats 10-18. Tables outdoors (5, pavement). Vegan dishes. **Map 19 B3.**

Number 10 NEW

10 Golborne Road, W10 5PE (8969 8922/ www.number10london.com). Ladbroke Grove or Westbourne Park tube.
Bar **Open** 5pm-midnight Mon-Fri; noon-midnight Sat; noon-10.30pm Sun.
Restaurant **Dinner served** 6-11pm Mon-Fri. **Meals served** noon-10.30pm Sat, Sun. **Main courses** £4.50-£6.
Both **Credit** AmEx, DC, JCB, MC, V.
After mixed reviews during its previous incarnation serving Modern European/gastropub fare, the kitchen made an abrupt change in spring 2005 and re-emerged, surprisingly, as a specialist

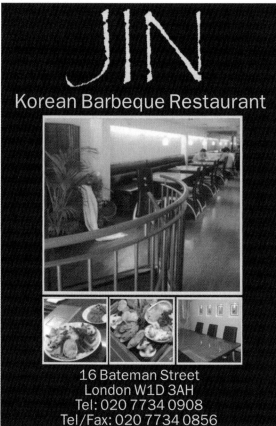

in modern Japanese cuisine, much to the delight of tempura-starved locals. The lively atmosphere (there's a popular ground-floor cocktail bar and a top-floor members club), regular live music policy and retro-funky decor haven't changed, though. The restaurant is on the first floor, in a large, boldly decorated room rendered slightly oppressive by frosted-glass windows that deny views of the iconic Trellick Tower opposite. While a jazz guitarist and double bassist noodled away in the background, helpful staff explained that the menu is designed for sharing. We tucked into fine gyoza (pork dumplings with shiitake and cabbage) and mixed vegetable tempura; decent sake nanban (deep-fried salmon marinated in sweet vinegar with chilli); and excellent beef nambudare (marinated in sesame and miso paste) and buta kakuni (pork belly slow-braised in sweet soy sauce). To finish: explosive deep-fried green tea ice-cream. This is a bold venture for an unusual location, and now it might have a kitchen to match its manifold ambitions.
Babies and children welcome: high chairs. Booking advisable. Entertainment: bands/DJs 9pm Thur-Sat (bar); jazz 7.30pm Fri, Sat (restaurant). Restaurant and bar available for hire. Tables outdoors (6, pavement). **Map 19 B1.**

★ Uli
16 All Saints Road, W11 1HH (7727 7511). Ladbroke Grove or Westbourne Park tube. **Dinner served** 6.45-11.15pm Mon-Sat. **Main courses** £6.75-£9. **Service** 12.5%. **Credit** MC, V.
Located on fashionable All Saints Road, Uli was brimming with customers on a weekday evening; a stream of regulars was greeted by the affable owner and ushered through to the popular courtyard dining area. From a menu of Thai and Chinese dishes, we opted to kick off with tom yum kung (hot and sour soup with prawns), which, though aromatically flavoured with galangal, was noticeably oversweet. Salt-peppered soft-shell crab was also disappointing; the deep-fried crab was distinctly on the soggy side. The quality of the cooking was cranked up a notch for the main courses: a tasty Thai green chicken curry, stir-fried Chinese broccoli with garlic and ma po beancurd (stir-fried with pork), which had a deliciously smoky saltiness. The Tiger beers were refreshingly chilled, but it was a bit of a surprise that all the soft drinks were warm, not ideal on a torrid summer evening. Despite these caveats, the restaurant obviously functions well as a pleasant neighbourhood local – it's a place to drop in to, rather than a special occasion venue.
Babies and children admitted. Booking essential. Restaurant available for hire. Tables outdoors (6, patio). Takeaway service. Vegan dishes. **Map 19 B2.**

South West
Battersea SW11

★ Banana Leaf Canteen NEW
75-79 Battersea Rise, SW11 1HN (7228 2828). Clapham Junction rail. **Lunch served** noon-3pm, **dinner served** 6-11pm Mon-Fri. **Meals served** noon-11pm Sat, Sun. **Main courses** £5.45-£8.75. **Service** 10%. **Credit** AmEx, MC, V.
Banana Leaf is a keenly priced and popular South-east Asian eaterie situated on the corner of Northcote Road and Battersea Rise. At peak times you should expect to queue before being ushered to one of the shared benches and tables (they do take bookings for six or more people). The concrete floor and bare walls are a touch stark, but the service is perky and friendly, and there's always a bustling atmosphere. It's easy to fill up on the fine range of starters such as tiger prawns in crispy beancurd pastry or pork and prawn dumplings, but the mains menu also provides intriguing possibilities. Alongside familiar favourites (pad Thai, nasi goreng, laksa) are more interesting selections, such as Vietnamese pork stew (with lemongrass and cinnamon bark) and chicken bakar jawa (grilled thighs in Javanese spices). The Banana Leaf specials are good value, and come with glass noodle salad, jasmine rice and other extras, at just a couple of quid more than a normal main course. Chilli blackened pork and stuffed pancakes for dessert were the highlights of our most recent visit, the food proving to be filling rather than exceptional.
Babies and children welcome: children's menu; high chairs. Booking advisable (accepted for 6 or more). Disabled toilet. No-smoking tables. **Map 21 C4.**

Chelsea SW3

Eight Over Eight
392 King's Road, SW3 5UZ (7349 9934/ www.eightovereight.nu). Sloane Square tube then 11, 22 bus. **Lunch served** noon-2.45pm Mon-Fri; noon-4pm Sat. **Dinner served** 6.15-10.45pm Mon-Fri; 6.15-11pm Sat; 6.15-10.30pm Sun. **Main courses** £10-£26. **Service** 12.5%. **Credit** AmEx, DC, JCB, MC, V.
This popular restaurant offers Japanese, Thai, Chinese and Korean fare very similar to that produced at its sister restaurants Cicada (*see p243*), E&O (*see p245*) and Great Eastern Dining Room (*see p248*). Indeed its name is based on a Chinese proverb that means 'lucky forever'. The design is strikingly minimalist: the bar and the restaurant are divided by a beautiful wrought-iron screen with floral pattern, and there are two-tone oak walls, parasol-like silk ceiling lamps, dark brown leather banquettes, and red neon signage. Start with the fragrant oriental cocktails in the bar, then move on to 'small plates' designed for sharing. Duck, watermelon and cashew was a perfect salad: a contrast of soft and crunchy, jazzed up by the liveliness of super-fresh ingredients. Aubergine and lychee curry was beguilingly aromatic, but Sichuan-style sea bass with Shaoxing wine lacked zip. The tables are cramped and the restaurant can be smoky, but the friendliness of beautiful young staff and the excitement generated by a monied, manicured and made-up clientele make it worth a visit.
Babies and children admitted. Booking advisable. Dress: smart casual. Separate room for parties, seats 14. **Map 14 D12.**

Fulham SW6

★ Zimzun
Fulham Broadway Retail Centre, Fulham Road, SW6 1BW (7385 4555/www.zimzun.co.uk). Fulham Broadway tube. **Meals served** noon-10.30pm Mon-Thur, Sun; noon-11pm Fri, Sat. **Main courses** £5.50-£7.95. **Set lunch** £5.95 1 course & side dish. **Service** 12.5%. **Credit** AmEx, MC, V.
Despite its rather soulless location on the first floor of the shopping centre above Fulham Broadway tube station, Zimzun is distinctly smart. On a sultry summer day, the spacious dining room, stylishly decked out with lattice woodwork, eye-catching beaded chandeliers and wooden furniture – and, thankfully, air-conditioned – was a welcome oasis. Efficient, friendly service meant that a freshly made smoothie appeared swiftly. From a predominantly Thai-inspired menu, succulent king prawns with aromatic holy basil were excellent, while green papaya salad, though lacking the chilli kick one might expect from a street stall portion in Thailand, had a pleasant salty-sweetness, authentically flavoured with dried shrimp. Jasmine tea made a pleasant end to our meal. On our lunchtime visit the place was largely deserted except for a handful of smartly dressed young Fulhamites; a shame considering the quality of the food and service.
Babies and children admitted. Booking advisable weekends. Disabled: toilet. No-smoking tables. Takeaway service. **Map 13 B13.**

South
Balham SW12

★ The Paddyfield
4 Bedford Hill, SW12 9RG (8772 1145). Balham tube/rail. **Dinner served** 6-11pm daily. **Main courses** £4.50-£6.95. **Unlicensed**. **Corkage** £1. **No credit cards**.

Oriental City

Oriental City is a huge complex of shops, restaurants and snack stalls in the north-western suburb of Colindale. Here you can stock up on groceries from all over Asia, buy Japanese tableware, check out traditional Chinese qi pao dresses in patterned brocade, browse among giant porcelain vases, treat your cold with Chinese medicine, have your hair cut or even sing karaoke in Chinese. The centre is a magnet for East Asians and anyone else with an interest in oriental food and cultures, most of all for its wonderful food.

On the ground floor is a Hong Kong-style **food court**; it's a huge central dining space filled with canteen-style chairs and surrounded by a dizzying variety of snack stalls. There's Vietnamese pho, Singaporean puddings,

Malaysian halal curries, 'Yummy yummy Thai' cooking, sushi and bento boxes, Beijing boiled dumplings, Cantonese roast meats, dim sum, 'Chairman Mao's family cuisine' – and just about everything else you could think of. The food is freshly prepared, often tasty and stunningly cheap, especially the set meals. Ordering is easy because most items are either on display or pictured in glorious technicolour on the stall fronts. The only snag is that there's so much choice that you may find yourself walking in endless circles, unable to decide what to eat.

If this happens, you could simplify things and go upstairs, where there's a large dim sum outfit called **China City** (8201 3838) and the **Shangri-La Hunan Cuisine Restaurant** (8200 9838),

possibly the only restaurant in London run and staffed by immigrants from Hunan. Or you could eat hot-pot at the **Steamed Boat Buffet** (8358 3568) downstairs. Or snack on a Japanese pancake or an English teacake at the Hong Kong-style café near the supermarket. Hmm. Visit with a hearty appetite.

★ Oriental City
399 Edgware Road, NW9 0JJ (8200 0009). Colindale tube/32, 142, 204, 303 bus. **Meals served** 10.30am-9pm Mon-Sat; 10am-8.30pm Sun. **Main courses** £3.50-£7.50. **No credit cards**.
Babies and children welcome: high chairs. No-smoking tables. Tables outdoors (6, garden). Takeaway service. Vegetarian menu.

RESTAURANTS

Small and rather sparsely decorated, the Paddyfield thrives as a reliable local restaurant. Food is served on contemporary white porcelain that mirrors the clean lines of the mint-coloured decor. The menu offers Vietnamese and Thai noodle dishes, stir-fries and curries. Crispy, vegetable-filled pastry triangles with plum dipping sauce, or zingy salads with fresh herbs and chilli make great snacks or starters. From the concise list of mains, green curry served with plump, perfectly cooked king prawns had a good chilli kick and was full of flavour. A creamy chicken, coconut and Thai basil stir-fry was equally impressive. Other classics include pad Thai and Vietnamese pho (noodle soup). Desserts offer the likes of lychees and ice-cream or indulgent banana and pineapple fritters. Eminently reasonable prices add to the general feeling of bonhomie.
Babies and children admitted. Booking advisable weekends. No smoking. Takeaway service.

Brixton SW9

★ New Fujiyama

7 Vining Street, SW9 8QA (7737 2369). Brixton tube/rail. **Meals served** noon-11pm Mon-Thur, Sun; noon-midnight Fri, Sat. **Main courses** £5.10-£6.70. **Service** 10%. **Credit** MC, V.

Combining canteen-style seating with a funky house and jazz soundtrack, this relaxed Japanese eaterie is a popular and rather trendy local spot. Anyone familiar with Wagamama (*see p243*) will spot the similarities in the menu, although New Fujiyama offers plenty more to choose from, be it ramen, don buri or sushi, and mostly at under £6 per dish. There is also a selection of pan-fried noodle and curry noodle dishes, and rice dishes (cha han, for example, is fried rice wth shredded carrot and chicken, onion, prawns, eggs, mushrooms and spring onions). Side dishes offer bite-sized tasters with platters of prawn gyoza, dumplings and vegetable croquettes. A skewer of tasty chicken came with a mountain of rice and sweet yakitori sauce, as well as miso soup and a small selection of pickles. Big appetites should be satisfied with the healthy portions of rice and noodles. There are a few Japanese drinks such as plum wine, saké and green tea alongside the usual beverages.
Babies and children welcome: high chairs. Booking advisable. No-smoking tables. Separate rooms for parties, seating 14-35. Takeaway service; delivery service (7737 6583; within 3-mile radius on orders over £10). **Map 22 E2.**

Waterloo SE1

Inshoku

23-24 Lower Marsh, SE1 7RJ (7928 2311). Waterloo tube/rail. **Lunch served** noon-3pm Mon-Fri. **Dinner served** 6-10.30pm Mon-Sat. **Main courses** £6-£15. **Set lunch** £4-£8 2 courses. **Set dinner** £10-£30 3 courses. **Credit** AmEx, MC, V.

A stone's throw from Waterloo station, Inshoku's deceptively small façade opens up into a long room decorated with Japanese paper parasols and colourful prints. It filled up rapidly with hungry office workers on our weekday lunchtime visit. The bewilderingly long menu is predominantly Japanese, though 'Thai-style' curries and noodles also feature. A piping hot serving of gyoza (dumplings), with a tasty cabbage filling, arrived promptly and was a promising start. Prawn and vegetable tempura was a generous portion, but proved to be on the greasy side. There was then a very long wait before our sushi set was served. Accompanied by a so-so miso soup, this was the most disappointing dish of the meal. Over-generous lashings of mayo made the avocado and crabstick roll unpleasantly greasy – not at all the clean flavours one looks for in sushi. So, a distinctly patchy meal, though friendly service and reasonable prices are obviously a draw.
Babies and children welcome; high chairs. Booking advisable Thur, Fri. Takeaway service; delivery service (within 3-mile radius on orders over £15). Vegetarian menu. **Map 10 M9.**

South East
Gipsy Hill SE27

Mangosteen NEW
2005 RUNNER-UP BEST VEGETARIAN MEAL

246 Gipsy Road, SE27 9RB (8670 0333). Gipsy Hill rail/3 bus. **Lunch served** 11am-3pm, **dinner served** 6-8pm Mon-Sat. **Main courses** £7.50-£10. **Set lunch** £6 2 courses. **Service** 10% (dinner only). **Credit** JCB, MC, V.

Mangosteen (no relation to the W1 restaurant of the same name) is a bright, diminutive place, co-owned by two Vietnamese sisters and almost café-like in its simplicity. Don't be deceived by appearances, though; the pan-oriental menu is short but well executed, with more attention paid to presentation (carefully stacked salads, neatly crimped vegetable dumplings) and exacting cooking (a slice of the grilled Sichuan pork bore a perfect pink tidemark) than we've come to expect from a neighbourhood restaurant. Slightly frustrating, then, was the lack of balance across the menu. Start with the tomato tofu steak salad with marinated lemongrass, say, and move on to the vegetable peanut curry, and the same green beans and pungent sweet Thai basil will appear in both. Both dishes were decent, but a vegetarian might feel short-changed by the lack of variety. Service was unfailingly polite if occasionally misguided, sometimes barely allowing a pause for breath between courses, at other times leaving tables stranded. Try a few crisp Tsing Tao beers and the knockout lemon and ginger tart, however, and you'll leave happy.
Babies and children welcome: children's menu; high chairs. Booking advisable weekends. No smoking. Tables outdoors (5, terrace). Takeaway service.

Herne Hill SE24

★ Lombok

17 Half Moon Lane, SE24 9JU (7733 7131). Herne Hill rail/37 bus. **Dinner served** 6-10.30pm Tue-Thur, Sun; 6-11pm Fri, Sat. **Main courses** £6-£8.50. **Service** 10%. **Credit** MC, V.

Nothing much changes at Lombok. It's still purple without, white clapboard within. The tables are still too close together and the staff's level of friendliness remains variable. And its pan-Asian greatest hits menu is still as popular as ever with Herne Hill's increasingly affluent diners. Thailand weighs in with fiery tom yam soup, pad Thai and impressively authentic red and green curries, with genuine pea aubergines. Vietnam is represented by delicate crab and prawn lettuce wraps and toothsome sugar cane prawns. Nasi goreng, prawns Malay and chicken satay front the Indonesian and Malaysian contributions. There's also Singapore chilli crab with crisp noodles (a whole crab wok-fried with ginger, spices and chilli), and even a tasty offering from Burma – 'Rangoon curry', a subtle, soothing yellow curry with fish, cumin, star anise, lime leaves and coconut milk. In truth, there's nothing particularly remarkable about Lombok; its secret lies in its consistency.
Babies and children admitted. Booking essential weekends. Takeaway service.

East
Shoreditch EC2

★ Great Eastern Dining Room

54-56 Great Eastern Street, EC2A 3QR (7613 4545/www.greateasterndining.co.uk). Old Street tube/rail/55 bus.
Below 54 bar **Open/meals served** 7.30pm-1am Fri, Sat. **Main courses** £4.50-£10.50.
Ground-floor bar **Open/meals served** noon-midnight Mon-Fri; 6pm-midnight Sat. **Main courses** £4.50-£10.50.
Restaurant **Lunch served** 12.30-3pm Mon-Fri. **Dinner served** 6.30-10.45pm Mon-Sat. **Main courses** £9-£14.50. **Service** 12.5%.
All **Credit** AmEx, DC, MC, V.

Admirably living up to its hip Hoxton credentials, the Great Eastern Dining Room (part of the Will

Ricker empire) is a stylish, spacious venue with dark wood floors and striking contemporary chandeliers. On the menu are a modish range of pan-Asian dishes, so sushi sits alongside curries, spicy soups, salads and noodle dishes. Soft-shelled crab salad was a winner, combining crisp deep-fried crab with juicy star fruit, water spinach and fresh coriander to make an attractive, multi-textured dish. Pad Thai, attractively presented with a pile of beansprouts and sliced red chilli, and generously studded with chicken, was very moreish, while mirin-dressed edamame (soy beans) made a pleasant side dish. For pudding, coconut panna cotta was a delightfully smooth and creamy coconut milk creation resting on a layer of ruby-red rhubarb jelly with three peanut-coated pieces of rhubarb on the side. It was almost too pretty to eat, but somehow we forced ourselves.
Babies and children admitted (restaurant only). Bars available for hire. Booking advisable; essential Fri, Sat. Entertainment: DJs 8pm Fri, Sat (bar). **Map 6 R4.**

North East
Stoke Newington N16

★ Itto

226 Stoke Newington High Street, N16 7HU (7275 8827). Stoke Newington rail/67, 73, 76, 149, 243 bus. **Meals served** noon-11pm daily. **Main courses** £3.90-£6.20. **Credit** MC, V.

Nestled opposite the entrance to Abney Park Cemetery, Itto is a little off the Stoke Newington main drag, but serves as a useful pit stop for lunch or a quick supper. The emphasis is on homey; benches dotted around two tiny rooms (a café-style front room and a more intimate restaurant-like rear) are tended by helpful and solicitous staff. The cooking could be described as oriental fusion, café-style. It brings together assorted tempura, various soups and fried noodles, and popular one-plate rice dishes (sweet and sour pork, roast duck, satay chicken, Thai green curry with prawns). Chicken katsu curry rice was a substantial, though rather greasy portion, but came with a warming miso soup – and all for a reasonable £5.90. There's a choice of udon, ramen or ho fun noodles with the soup dishes. A bowl of roast duck and barbecue pork with ramen noodle soup was perfectly adequate without reaching the heights you'd find in Chinatown. With oriental beers at £2.50, Itto is a decent enough local eaterie that won't dent your wallet.
Babies and children welcome: high chairs. No smoking. Tables outdoors (4, pavement). Takeaway service; delivery service (within 2-mile radius on orders over £10). **Map 25 C1.**

North
Camden Town & Chalk Farm NW1

★ ★ Lemongrass

243 Royal College Street, NW1 9LT (7284 1116). Camden Town tube. **Dinner served** 5.30-11pm daily. **Main courses** £5.50-£8.60. **Set dinner** £16.50-£18.50 per person (minimum 2). **Credit** JCB, MC, V.

For a fine taste of Cambodian cuisine, head to this small, homely restaurant, simply but daintily decorated with pale yellow walls and clusters of fairylights. The white-hatted chef is the star of the show, working busily at his woks in a tiny back kitchen, sending out one freshly cooked dish after another. Our meal got off to a fine start with a tasty leek-filled pancake and superb aromatic Cambodian prawn soup. We decided to share the main courses, South-east Asian style, as the menu advised. A charming waitress brought out each stir-fried dish to our table as it was cooked: succulent whisky prawns; al dente asparagus with black pepper; Phnom Penh chicken, with a chilli paste bite; and tender chunks of garlicky lok luk beef, plus a fresh mango and coriander side salad. For the finale we fell upon the 'banana cake', a

scrumptious banana leaf-wrapped sticky rice and banana concoction, topped with coconut cream. Highly recommended.
Babies and children admitted. Booking advisable weekends. No smoking. Vegetarian menu. **Map 27 D1.**

Primrose Hill NW3

★ Café de Maya

38 Primrose Hill Road, NW3 3AD (7209 0672). Chalk Farm tube/31 bus. **Brunch served** 8am-3pm, **dinner served** 6-11pm Tue-Sun. **Main courses** £4-£6.50. **Service** 10%. **Credit** MC, V.

Very much a mellow neighbourhood local rather than a destination diner, Café de Maya, now a decade old, adds a pleasant touch of conviviality to a Primrose Hill backstreet. Bright yellow walls, cheerfully gaudy pictures and an eccentric collection of ornaments make for a cheerful setting, while a huge stack of prominently displayed CDs ensured a varied range of background music, from Clapton to reggae. Customers on a midweek evening visit ranged from solo diners to groups of friends. An assortment of Thai and Chinese-Malaysian dishes are served. Our meal was pleasant rather than stunning. Tamarind prawns were on the sweet side, and the curry spicing in the

penang beef was a tad harsh, but the Thai green chicken curry was fragrant, and stir-fried bok choy and broccoli in oyster sauce made a tasty side dish. Jasmine tea came with complimentary melon, a hospitable touch totally in keeping with Café de Maya's welcoming vibe.
Babies and children welcome: high chairs. Booking advisable weekends. No-smoking tables. Restaurant available for hire. Tables outdoors (2, pavement). Takeaway service; delivery service (within 3-mile radius on orders over £15). **Map 28 C5.**

Outer London
Barnet, Hertfordshire

★ Emchai

78 High Street, Barnet, Herts EN5 5SN (8364 9993/www.emchai.co.uk). High Barnet tube. **Lunch served** noon-2.30pm Mon-Thur; noon-3pm Fri-Sun. **Dinner served** 6-11pm Mon-Thur; 6pm-midnight Fri, Sat; 5-10pm Sun. **Main courses** £4.90-£6.50. **Credit** AmEx, JCB, MC, V.
Now in its sixth year, Emchai continues to serve enjoyable cuisine to a loyal local following on High Barnet's high street. Striking flower displays, an open-plan kitchen and a large dining room with a bright turquoise wall make for an attractive space. The pan-oriental menu is wide-ranging. We opted for two soup noodle dishes, both served in generous portions. Chicken noodles in a light stock was enjoyable comfort food, while laksa – a generous portion of noodles in coconut broth, garnished with prawns, fiery raw red chilli and crisp fried shallots – was authentically tasty. Freshly stir-fried salt and spicy soft-shell crab was a winning dish: deliciously crispy crab with a moreish flavouring. Spare ribs were also finger-lickin' good. Full marks to the attentive staff, who brought complimentary prawn crackers promptly to our table and topped up our iced tap water with charming courtesy. A neighbourhood local to be cherished.
Babies and children welcome: high chairs. Disabled: toilet. No-smoking tables. Restaurant available for hire. Takeaway service.

Kingston, Surrey

Cammasan

8 Charter Quay, High Street, Kingston upon Thames, Surrey KT1 1NB (8549 3510/ www.cammasan.co.uk). Kingston rail.
Meinton noodle bar **Lunch served** noon-3pm, **dinner served** 5.30-11pm Mon-Fri. **Meals served** noon-11pm Sat, Sun. **Main courses** £5.50-£8.90. **No credit cards.**
Chaitan restaurant **Lunch served** noon-3pm, **dinner served** 5.30-11pm Mon-Fri. **Meals served** noon-11pm Sat, Sun. **Minimum** £15. **Main courses** £5.50-£30. **Set meal** £13.90-£21 3 courses (minimum 2). **Service** 10%. **Credit** AmEx, MC, V.
Back in 2001 Kingston became only the second place outside central London to get a branch of Wagamama. The fact that Cammasan, which arrived not long after, has been mostly full every time we've visited shows that there's demand for more than one noodle bar in the area. The ground-floor space is small, bright and friendly (as befits any independent alternative) and serves generous portions of recognisable and simple noodle soups, curries and stir-fries. Chicken mixed with cashew nuts in a yellow bean sauce came with a well-presented heap of boiled rice. Pad Thai jay – flat rice noodles with a sprinkling of scrambled egg yolk, tofu, tamarind, chai po (a type of radish), peanuts and beansprouts in a thick vegetarian stock – was tasty and almost too large to finish. The upstairs dining room is a little more formal – and more expensive – with a wider choice of main dishes (in particular, fish, duck, vegetarian and rice options) that show a predominantly Chinese influence. A handy spot; come with an out-of-town relative for a leisurely meal (upstairs) or with your mates for a pre-film filler (downstairs).
Babies and children welcome: high chairs. Booking advisable. Disabled: toilet. Restaurant available for hire. Tables outdoors (12, terrace). Takeaway service.
For branch (China Royal) see index.

Cocoon. See p245.

RESTAURANTS

Portuguese

The heartland of Portuguese dining in London is in the south, notably around Vauxhall and Stockwell, where there seems to be a never-ending supply of friendly neighbourhood drop-in bars with a casual café, an ever-present TV screen and a more formal restaurant attached. In west London, particularly around Golborne Road, the Portuguese flag still flutters as locals divide themselves into those who take their coffee and cake at **Oporto** and those who prefer **Lisboa**.

Top-end Portuguese restaurants have always been rare beasts, but this looks to change with the arrival, within a couple of months of each other in 2005, of upmarket **Tugga** and Portuguese-slanted **Portal** (in the Modern European section). At last, new doors are opening to better Portuguese food and drink in London.

PASTELARIA

West

Ladbroke Grove W10, W11

Lisboa Patisserie
57 Golborne Road, W10 5NR (8968 5242).
Ladbroke Grove or Westbourne Park tube/23,
52 bus. **Open** 8am-7.30pm daily. **Credit** MC, V.

Golborne Road is a world in a few hundred metres, with a whole stack of eateries and cafés from across the globe. But Portugal can boast two pitches, of which this bustling sit-down and takeaway venture is ahead by a fair way. As befits its capital city name, Lisboa (spelled Lisbona on the wall-tiled historical cityscape) delivers a wide range of taste experiences, centred around superb pasteis de nata and equally impressive pasteis de bacalhau. There are plenty of other savoury and sweet choices, all displayed but strangely unsigned in the glass display counter. Almond tarts, ham and cheese slices, chicken fritters and prawn pasties all deliver well, and prices are very reasonable. Sit outdoors if you can, although the pressure's on the seating both inside and out, but if you're market-trawling, then just drop in and carry away a fresh taste of the old country.
Babies and children admitted. Tables outdoors
(3, pavement). Takeaway service. **Map 19 B1**.
For branches see index.

Oporto Patisserie
62A Golborne Road, W10 5PS (8968 8839).
Ladbroke Grove or Westbourne Park tube/23,
52 bus. **Open** 8am-7pm daily. **No credit cards**.
Just as the settlement in question suffers second-city status to Portugal's luminous capital, so this west London café dips below the undoubted charms of its rival, Lisboa, across the road. Cheaper on all fronts, this is a brisk and busy snack stop whose national culinary credentials are certainly present but not the whole story. Lavazza is the coffee of choice, and there are generic rolls and croissants on offer, as well as a solid range of Portuguese regulars (pasteis, fritters, pastries). These are somewhat uneven: chicken fritters were bland, prawn pastry limp and short on filling, and a milky galão coffee was uninvigorating. But it's unfair to impose high bars on what is a straightforward, unassuming and seemingly well-supported venture.
Babies and children admitted. Tables outdoors
(3, pavement). Takeaway service. **Map 19 B1**.

Tea's Me NEW
129A Ladbroke Grove, W11 1PN (7792 5577).
Ladbroke Grove tube. **Open** 8am-7pm Mon-Sat.
No credit cards.
With its colourful awning and kitsch interior, Café Algarve was a long-term fixture on this cul-de-sac just off Ladbroke Grove, but now the awning has vanished and in its place is Tea's Me, fresh from a minimalist makeover. One look at the menu shows the Portuguese spirit lives on, though, in mains

such as feijoada and bacalhau, but after traipsing around nearby Portobello Market, another famous Algarve staple was required – the all-day breakfast. The tiny ground-floor room has a cosy feel, but it wouldn't take too many wayward tourists to turn cosy into cramped. Although the fry-up was pretty good and the latte even better, the real stars here are the pastries – tocinho de ceu (almond cake), pasteis de nata (custard cake) and the seriously sweet and seriously tasty pasteis de feijao (bean cake). Naughty, but very, very nice. **Map 19 B3.**

South
Vauxhall SE1

Café Madeira
46A-46B Albert Embankment, SE1 7TN (7820 1117). Vauxhall tube/rail. **Open** 7am-9pm daily. **Main courses** £6.50-£15. **Credit** MC, V.
The smell of freshly baked bread hits you some distance from this massively popular café/ sandwich shop, which has a bakery and deli attached. Happily, the promise contained in that enticing scent is more than delivered on. Take your pick from a huge, and hugely imaginative, array of fresh sandwich breads and fillings laid out at the counter; alternatively, partake of one of the hot special dishes of the day. These can include the likes of paella, lasagna and chilli, but we settled for a mild, fruity curry that contained enormous pieces of succulent chicken – utterly delicious, as well as being superb value. It was impossible to resist finishing off with a pasteis de nata, which tasted as if it had been freshly made five minutes before, and a strong coffee. There's plenty of room inside the internet café, but on a blisteringly hot weekend afternoon a large, relaxed crowd had spilled out to the pavement tables positioned under a canopy of trees; a perfect shady spot to enjoy the excellent food and service.
Babies and children admitted. Disabled: toilet. No-smoking tables. Separate room for parties, seats 15. Tables outdoors (10, pavement). Takeaway service. **Map 16 L11.**

RESTAURANTS

Central
Knightsbridge SW3

★ O Fado
49-50 Beauchamp Place, SW3 1NY (7589 3002/ www.restauranteofado.co.uk). Knightsbridge or South Kensington tube. **Lunch served** noon-3pm daily. **Dinner served** 6.30pm-1am Mon-Sat; 6.30pm-midnight Sun. **Main courses** £10.95-£16.95. **Cover** £1.50. **Service** 12.5%. **Credit** AmEx, JCB, MC, V.
The perfect place for a long lunch or a dignified evening of live fado, conducted in the old-fashioned Portuguese manner, this intimate basement dining room just off the Knightsbridge drag is a welcome discovery. From the quality tablecloths and settings to the quietly alert waitering, it keeps to tradition. Extensive choices across all courses make initial deliberation difficult. The tried and trusted sardines and prawns in tomato and white wine were comfortable openers, while the mains – bacalhau with mussels, prawns and potato, and monkfish and prawn tamboril – were both vast and flavoursome. Indeed the guilt attendant on dishes that were genuinely impossible to finish was the only downside to our visit: management could easily cut back on the portions without complaint. After these, desserts were out of the question, but a very good Irish coffee found its way to the table. The result? A high scorer on all fronts, O Fado left us feeling anything but melancholy.
Babies and children admitted. Booking advisable; essential dinner weekends. Entertainment: guitarists 8pm Tue-Sun. Separate room for parties, seats 75. Takeaway service. **Map 14 F9.**

Tugga

South West
Chelsea SW3

★ Tugga NEW
312 King's Road, SW3 5UH (7351 0101/ www.tugga.com). Sloane Square tube then 11, 19, 22 bus. **Meals served** noon-11pm Mon-Sat; noon-10.30pm Sun. **Main courses** £13.50-£22. **Service** 12.5%. **Credit** AmEx, MC, V.
The chef at Tugga (the name is from 'Portugga', meaning a person from Portugal) is Miguel Castro e Silva, the highly respected chef of the Bull & Bear in Oporto, which is known for refined, updated Portuguese cooking. We began with three tapas. Pickled pig's ears, flavoured with celery and carrot, slightly jellied and served cold, were firm without being too cartilaginous. The Portuguese sausage selection comprised meaty, paprika-spiked chouriço, some smooth-textured morçela (a kind of blood sausage) flavoured with cumin, and gently smoked farinheira, a super-smooth Alentejan speciality made with pork belly. Our final choice, tuna and black-eyed bean salad, was perked up with a bit of apple. Tugga's main courses tend to be less overtly Portuguese, such as a distinctly French-influenced confit of duck parmentier. The potatoes were infused with black truffles and the duck richly flavoured. We couldn't pass up the excellent bacalhau, served with spicy cabbage and a 'mash' made of moistened bread and ripe tomato, formed into two quenelles. The wines are all from Portugal, which means, inevitably, that reds are better than whites. Tugga is simply light years away from the Portuguese caffs in Vauxhall/ Stockwell, and prices aren't out of order for the posh neighbourhood or the quality of cooking. Somewhere to overcome your possibly negative preconceptions about Portuguese food.
Babies and children admitted. Booking advisable. Disabled: toilet. Entertainment: 6pm Wed-Sat. Separate room for parties, seats 12. Tables outdoors (3, pavement). **Map 14 D12.**

South
Brixton SW2

The Gallery
256A Brixton Hill, SW2 1HF (8671 8311). Brixton tube/rail/45, 109, 118, 250 bus. **Dinner served** 7-10.30pm Tue-Sun. **Main courses** £8.50-£14. **Credit** AmEx, MC, V.
First impressions are misleading at the Gallery. Push through the door marked 'Restaurant' in the corner of an unimpressive takeaway joint, serving piri-piri chicken and other sizzling meat dishes, and you enter a delightful new realm – a cantinho decorated with kitsch murals, with a wooden gallery that overlooks the main dining area. A warm, relaxed atmosphere prevailed among our fellow diners (a mixed bunch comprised mainly of families and couples), and service was prompt and friendly. We plumped for prawn cocktail and quails for starters, both fresh and tasty, if a little smothered in their respective sauces. You'll be spoiled for choice on the main course: several versions of bacalhau, plus various cataplana dishes, a speciality we've sampled here before and

can heartily recommend. We eventually opted for simpler pleasures: dover sole and grilled rare steak with accompanying vegetables (which were fine, although the fish was a touch overcooked), washed down with a glass or two of passable house white. Not a place you'd travel to, but a decent local.
Babies and children welcome: high chairs. Book weekends. Takeaway service (5-10.30pm daily). **Map 22 D3.**

Stockwell SW8, SW9

Bar Estrela
111-115 South Lambeth Road, SW8 1UZ (7793 1051). Stockwell tube/Vauxhall tube/rail. **Meals served** noon-11pm daily. **Main courses** £8-£15. **Credit** AmEx, MC, V.
On a hot summer's evening the confines of the indoor restaurant and café seemed very much inferior to the large pavement terrace, where a noisy scrum from the bar merged with a mixed crowd of diners; our waiter was more than happy to oblige us with a move outside. Would the food match the fine service and friendly atmosphere? The menu certainly offered a good helping of the usual London-Portuguese standards, plus a decent accompanying wine list – the young 'green' wine we opted for was light, sharp and almost fizzy, perfect for the sweltering weather. Starters were mixed: the fish cakes were bland and dry, and what little taste they had was killed off by the tartare sauce. The broad bean, chorizo and pork stew, on the other hand, was a tasty treat. Main courses diverged too: tender, perfectly cooked fried squid in white wine sauce won hands down, with the calf's liver and bacon again a bit dry and failing really to excite the taste buds. In a word, patchy.
Babies and children welcome: high chairs. Booking advisable. Tables outdoors (10, pavement). Takeaway service. **Map 16 L13.**

Grelha D'Ouro
151 South Lambeth Road, SW8 1XN (7735 9764). Stockwell tube/Vauxhall tube/rail. **Meals served** 7am-11pm daily. **Main courses** £4.50-£12.35. **Credit** MC, V.
We all know it's the little details that count, but it's a lesson the proprietors of this fine restaurant have obviously absorbed. At the front is the typical bar and café serving drinks and tapas, but push through the swing doors into the restaurant at the back and you could be in old Oporto: it's a simple, classic space with dark wood decor and walls lined with wine bottles. The bread and olives, which appeared instantly, were excellent, as was the house white. A shared starter of king prawns impressed with its freshness and meant we gave those proper cloth napkins a run for their money. To follow: generous portions of chicken in white wine and mushroom sauce, and squid with chilli – both dishes fresh, succulent and tasty. The 'Molotov' dessert, less threatening than it sounds, is a local favourite concocted out of egg whites and smothered in toffee sauce, and made the perfect finale. For authentic Portuguese dining, you need look no further.
Babies and children welcome: high chairs. Booking advisable weekends. No-smoking tables. Separate room for parties, seats 100. Takeaway service. **Map 16 L13.**

O Cantinho de Portugal

135-137 Stockwell Road, SW9 9TN (7924 0218).
Stockwell tube/Brixton tube/rail/2, 322, 325,
355 bus.
Bar **Open** 11am-11pm daily.
Restaurant **Meals served** noon-midnight daily.
Main courses £4-£10. **Credit** AmEx, MC, V.
Both Closed 1st 3wks Aug.

Be warned that Sunday lunch is generally a busy time in this popular local eaterie. A communion and birthday party meant the place was buzzing, but the friendly atmosphere meant we felt more than happy to hang fire in the bar/café area and chat to the locals until a place was ready. The menu offered some interesting surprises, the wine list turned out to be much better than average, and the food was all well worth the wait. A plateful of whelks for starters were as fresh as if you'd bought them at the pier. The rabbit in wine sauce was succulent and flavoursome, while lemon sole came with a spicy kick and was cooked to perfection. The nicest surprise was the bill: such generous portions, such value for money. Despite the sheer volume of people, service was quick and efficient. Everyone we talked to in the restaurant raved about it – one couple had even come down from near Wembley. We'll be joining them on a regular basis from now on.
Babies and children welcome: high chairs.
Booking advisable weekends. Disabled: toilet.
Takeaway service. **Map 22 D1.**

★ O Moinho

355A Wandsworth Road, SW8 2JH (7498 6333).
Stockwell tube/Vauxhall tube/rail/77, 77A bus.
Meals served 10am-11pm daily. **Main courses**
£6.50-£9.50. **Credit** MC, V.

O Moinho's light, airy space felt just right on a hot summer's evening. To one side there's a café adorned with football shirts and other knick-knacks; on the other there's the restaurant, impeccably turned out with plants, crisp tablecloths, and azulejo tiles on the walls. Our dinner came with a number of thoughtful touches: tuna and sardine pâté arrived with bread and olives, and a fingerbowl was provided for cleaning up after the delicious opener, king prawns with chilli and garlic. The full menu contained an eye-opening selection of meat and fish dishes (plus, of course, hearty seafood stews), as well as some choice wines. We decided to veer off the standard path and opted for the duck in orange sauce, which was cooked to juicy perfection. The tuna was just as tasty, although the accompanying carrots and spinach were disappointingly tasteless. Service had been fastidious until we asked for the bill, which took an age to arrive. All things considered, O Moinho is definitely worth a visit.
Babies and children admitted. Booking advisable.
Separate area for parties, seats 50. Tables
outdoors (5, pavement). Takeaway service.

North East
Dalston E8

★ Nando's

148 Kingsland High Street, E8 2NS (7923 3555/
www.nandos.co.uk). Dalston Kingsland rail/
38, 76, 149, 236, 243 bus. **Meals served**
noon-11.30pm Mon-Thur, Sun; noon-midnight
Fri, Sat. **Main courses** £4.95-£7.75. **Credit** JCB,
MC, V.

King of the roost when it comes to peri-peri chicken chains, this international outfit offers a spicy fast-food feast with an easygoing charm that manages not to feel manufactured. There's a relaxed atmosphere as soon as you enter – large and airy rooms, vibrant designs and a soundtrack that is lively without becoming intrusive, all good for families eating out. This Dalston branch dominates the corner with Shacklewell Lane just north of the Rio cinema, and does a brisk trade with all parts of the community. It's easy to see why: you assemble your preferred size and part of the bird, throw in fries, corn, spicy rice and your own scale of spicy heat, before opting to down bottomless soft drinks or one of a dozen wines, and then sign it all off with very reasonable desserts. There are minor negative points (the dressing on the green salad was a little tart, 'medium spicy' lacked a bit of zip), but if you don't expect too much you should be pretty happy. It all feels fresh and is far from pricey, and the chocolate mousse was great. An efficient meal solution when you're pushed for time.
Babies and children welcome: children's
menu; crayons; high chairs. Booking advisable
for parties of 8 or more. Disabled: toilet.
No-smoking tables. Takeaway service.
Map 25 C4.
For branches see index.

North
Camden Town & Chalk Farm NW1

Pescador

23 Pratt Street, NW1 0BG (7482 7008).
Camden Town or Mornington Crescent tube/
24, 29 bus. **Dinner served** 6-11pm Tue-Fri.
Meals served 1-11pm Sat; 1-10pm Sun.
Main courses £9.50-£16. **Set lunch** (1-5pm
Sat, Sun) £10.50 2 courses. **Credit** JCB, MC, V.

Welcome for being one of just a couple of Portuguese restaurants away from the familiar stamping grounds of Ladbroke Grove and Lambeth, Pescador is a resolutely local affair, its neutral decor of yellow walls and generic framings a little at odds with the undeniable origins of the menu. Specialising in fish and seafood, it certainly plays to its strengths in those areas, but the evidence was not weighted towards the starters. Last year's visit had found hugely impressive pasteis de bacalhau (fried potato and salt cod balls); this time around they had slipped significantly down the league. Similarly, the mixed salad was only average. We ignored the 'free' (not) bread and factory butter openers. Things certainly improved with the mains: packed arroz de marisco (soupy seafood rice) and a tender, complete squid (the only time we've seen one so served). However, the standard accompanying vegetables were boiled free of any flavour. The Portuguese might keep their supporting dishes simple, but potatoes, carrots and beans can steal the plate if freshly done. Not here. Solid fare, but would you travel for it? Regrettably, one thinks not.
Babies and children welcome: high chairs.
Booking advisable; essential weekends.
Takeaway service. **Map 27 D2.**
For branch see index.

Menu

If you think the cooking of Portugal is just poor man's Spanish cuisine, you haven't eaten enough Portuguese food. Despite sharing the Spanish love for chorizo-style sausages (chouriço), dry cured ham (presunto) and salt cod (bacalhau), the Portuguese have developed a cooking style that has a character, a culture and a cachet all its own. Take the famous arroz (rice) dishes that appear on practically every Portuguese menu. While they are often compared to paella, they are, in fact, far soupier, with the rice used almost as a thickening agent.

Portuguese cooking is in essence a peasant cuisine: the food of farmers and fishermen. Pork, sausages and charcuterie figure prominently, as does an abundance of fresh fish and seafood and olive oil (azeite). There's a strong tradition of charcoal-grilled fish and meats. The hearty bean stews from the north and the thick bready soups (açordas) are also worth trying, as is the coastal speciality of caldeirada, Portugal's answer to bouillabaisse. Garlic, lemon juice, wine and wine vinegar are much used in marinades, with favoured spices being piri-piri (hot peppers, often used to flavour oil in which chicken is basted) and, for the cakes, cinnamon – both the latter showing the culinary influence of Portugal's colonial past. To finish, there is always a lush arroz doce (rice pudding), a wobbly pudim flan (crème caramel) or the world's most loved custard tart, the deliciously scorched pastel de nata.

Açorda: a bread stew, using bread that's soaked in stock, then cooked with olive oil, garlic, coriander and an egg. Often combined with shellfish or bacalhau (qv).
Amêijoas à bulhão pato: clams with olive oil, garlic, coriander and lemon.
Arroz de marisco: soupy seafood rice.
Arroz de tamboril: soupy rice with monkfish.
Arroz doce: rice pudding.
Bacalhau: salt cod; soaked before cooking, then boiled, grilled, stewed or baked, and served in myriad variations; Portugal's national dish.
Bifana: pork steak, marinated in garlic, fried and served in a bread roll.
Caldeirada: fish stew, made with potatoes, tomatoes and onions.

Caldo verde: the classic soup of finely sliced spring cabbage in a potato stock, always served with a slice of chouriço (qv).
Caracois: boiled snails, eaten as a snack with beer.
Carne de porco alentejana: an Alentejo dish of fried pork, clams and potato.
Cataplana: a special copper cooking pan with a curved, rounded bottom and lid.
Chouriço assado: a paprika-flavoured smoked pork sausage cooked on a terracotta dish over burning alcohol.
Cozido à portuguesa: the traditional Sunday lunch of Portugal – various meats plus three types of sausage, cabbage, carrots, potatoes and sometimes white beans, all boiled together.
Dobrada: tripe stew.
Feijoada: bean stew, cooked with pork and sausages.
Pastel de bacalhau (plural **pasteis**): salt cod fish cake.
Pastel de nata: a rich egg custard tart made with crisp, thin, filo pastry.
Piri piri or **peri peri:** Angolan hot red pepper.
Pudim flan: crème caramel.
Sardinhas assadas: fresh sardines, roasted or char-grilled.

Spanish

Spanish dining in London has received a fillip with the arrival of two excellent, authentic tapas bars: **Café García** and **Tapas Brindisa**. Significantly, both are linked to Spanish food importers: long-standing R García & Sons in Portobello, and Brindisa, which has a shop in Exmouth Market and a stall at Borough Market. Also squeezing new zest into a scene once dominated by sangria and flamenco joints are **Salt Yard**, which adds an Italian accent to the Spanish tapas repertoire (and was a runner-up for Best Vegetarian Meal in the 2005 *Time Out* Awards), and stylish **Meza**, part of the Conran stable. Maintaining their popularity, and superlative standards of cooking, are three more established restaurants: **Moro**, whose North African-tinged menu is as enticing as ever; stylish, tapas-only **Fino** and fashionable yet traditional **Cambio de Tercio**.

Central

Bloomsbury WC1

Cígala

54 Lamb's Conduit Street, WC1N 3LW (7405 1717/www.cigala.co.uk). Holborn or Russell Square tube.
Bar **Open/tapas served** 5.30-10.45pm Mon-Sat; 5.30-9.45pm Sun. **Tapas** £2-£8.
Restaurant **Meals served** noon-10.45pm Mon-Fri; 12.30-10.45pm Sat; noon-9.45pm Sun. **Main courses** £10-£17. **Set lunch** (noon-3pm Mon-Fri) £15 2 courses, £18 3 courses. **Set meal** (Sun) £10.50 1 course.
Both **Credit** AmEx, DC, MC, V.
Chef-proprietor Jake Hodges has blessed Cígala with some extremely plain decor: bare boards, plain wood tables and white walls. Such surroundings inevitably help focus diners' attention on the food, which is surely the point: Hodges' brilliant interpretation of classic Spanish cooking takes the food out of the theme bar ghetto. Crab salad with spring onions, parsley, tomato and cucumber was sparkling and fresh, well matched to a glass of chilled Galician albariño from an above-average list of modern Spanish wines (there are also impressive selections of sherries, cavas and Spanish brandies). Of the main courses, grilled sea trout with baby vegetables and alioli was a highlight, while roasted chicken breast with new potato, pepper and mushroom salad was simple but immaculate. Orange sorbet sprinkled with chopped black olives proved a very refreshing way to finish. Despite the busy lunchtime crowd, staff were clued up and unflaggingly attentive, and prices are reasonable for the quality of the food. Tapas-sized dishes are also available at pavement tables, in the basement bar in the evening, and, if it's not busy, in the restaurant itself.
Babies and children welcome: high chairs. Bar available for hire. Booking advisable. Tables outdoors (10, pavement).
Map 4 M4.

City E1, EC3

Barcelona Tapas Bar y Restaurante

15 St Botolph Street, entrance at 1 Middlesex Street, EC3A 7DT (7377 5222/www.barcelona-tapas.com). Aldgate tube/Liverpool Street tube/rail. **Tapas served** 11am-11pm Mon-Fri. **Tapas** £2.95-£13.95. **Service** 12.5%.
Credit AmEx, DC, MC, V.
Step off the dingy street and straight on to the Costa Brava: the bright blues and yellows of the decor in this popular City haunt are authentic, as is the music. With a long menu of traditional (and pricey) tapas, paellas and Spanish cheeses, and an even longer list of Spanish wines, our expectations were high, but the food didn't match up. The grilled butterflied sardines verged on the unpleasant, and tasted as though they'd been cooked hours before they arrived at our table. The pork in the pincho moruno was dry and tasteless, the patatas bravas were insipid, and the pulpo a la gallega was almost rubbery. Only freshly cooked tacos de berenjenas (deep-fried aubergines) stood out, though we had to ask for the salt; the albóndigas, billed as a house speciality, boasted meaty, rich flavours. This may be a pleasant place to hang out with a bottle of excellent Freixenet merlot, and the cheery staff do a good job, but in the main the food is merely an add-on after one bottle too many during *hora loca*.
Babies and children admitted. Booking advisable lunch. Restaurant available for hire. Separate floor for parties, seats 80. **Map 12 S6.**
For branches see index.

Mesón Los Barriles

8A Lamb Street, E1 6EA (7375 3136). Aldgate East tube/Liverpool Street tube/rail. **Tapas served** 11am-11pm Mon-Fri; noon-4pm Sun. **Closed** 3 wks Aug. **Tapas** £2.75-£21.90.
Credit AmEx, JCB, MC, V.
It's easy to miss this old-fashioned bar-restaurant, set down a quiet street on the edge of Spitalfields Market. Yet both the dark wood bar, with hams hanging overhead and barrels for tables, and the cheerful dining room, with less eye-catching decor, were crowded with office workers on the Wednesday lunchtime we visited. The order of the day are generously sized tapas, which arrived on our table within minutes of ordering. The highlights: decent butterflied sardines; a dish of garlic chicken that looked dull but proved to be pretty good; rich, robust albóndigas; and wedges of fresh bread with olive oil. Less impressive: the flavour of ham or cheese in fiercely deep-fried croquetas proved elusive; battered halibut was a reasonable if bland rendition (the tartare sauce had a synthetic taste); and the missable range of desserts. Still, add in the bustlingly efficient Spanish staff and the reasonably priced, straightforward Spanish wine list, and Mesón Los Barriles comes out with more positives than negatives.
Babies and children welcome: high chairs. Booking advisable. Separate room for parties, seats 60. Tables outdoors (5, market). **Map 12 R5.**
For branch see index.

Clerkenwell & Farringdon EC1

Anexo

61 Turnmill Street, EC1M 5PT (7250 3401/www.anexo.co.uk). Farringdon tube/rail/55, 243 bus.
Bar **Open** 11am-1am Mon-Thur; 11am-2am Fri; 4pm-2am Sat.
Restaurant **Lunch served** 11.30am-2.30pm Mon-Fri. **Dinner served** 6-11pm Mon-Sat. **Tapas served** 11am-11pm Mon-Sat. **Main courses** £6.50-£12.50. **Tapas** £2.95-£5.25. **Set lunch** £6 2 courses, £8 3 courses.
Both **Credit** AmEx, MC, V.
Apparently, Anexo can rival legendary gay club Trade, which ran for years just next door at Turnmills, for buzz factor on a busy night. On a wet Tuesday in summer, however, things are a lot quieter. The local, after-work crowd are unfazed by the dated Spanish-style decor (Gaudi-esque geckos, wrought iron twisted organically around windows, doors and the bar), but they're more likely to be here for Bacardi Breezers than sangria and tapas. Their loss, we reckon. With the exception of an ordinary pollo al ajillo (garlic chicken), the dishes recommended by our friendly, attentive waiter ranged from decent (patatas bravas, calamari fritos, spinach fritters topped with parmesan) to excellent (pimiento piquillos, albóndigas, gambas al ajillo). Other options include various wraps, paninis and fajitas. Upstairs is a Spanish restaurant, Topfloor at Turnmills, with a full à la carte menu; it was deserted on our visit. There's a salsa club downstairs, if you want to work off your dinner.
Babies and children admitted (lunch only). Booking advisable dinner. Entertainment: DJs (Topfloor) from 8pm Thur-Sat. Restaurant available for hire. Separate floor available for parties. Tables outdoors (10, pavement). **Map 5 N4.**

★ Moro

34-36 Exmouth Market, EC1R 4QE (7833 8336/www.moro.co.uk). Farringdon tube/rail/19, 38 bus.
Bar **Open/tapas served** 12.30-11.45pm Mon-Sat (last entry 10.30pm). **Tapas** £2.50-£9.
Restaurant **Lunch served** 12.30-2.30pm, **dinner served** 7-10.30pm Mon-Sat. **Main courses** £13.50-£17.50. **Set lunch** (1-3.30pm Sat) £40 4 course tasting menu incl sherries. **Service** 12.5% for parties of 6 or more.
Both **Credit** AmEx, DC, MC, V.
After nearly a decade, Sam and Sam Clark's Spanish restaurant is still one of London's best, so it was no surprise to find it (very) bustling on a Friday night. The look is bare but sleek, with a long zinc bar stretching down one side, and the kitchen open to view at the far end. You can pop in for a snack (tapas are available all day) or settle down for a full meal from the Moorish-slanted menu, which changes weekly. Tables are on the small side and can get quickly crowded with plates and glasses, but that didn't stop us from enjoying a feast; similarly, staff

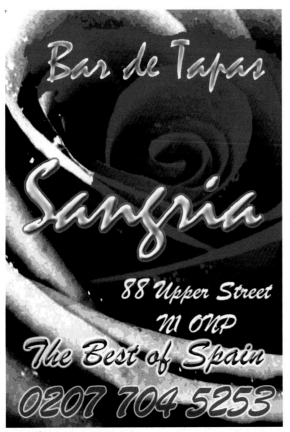
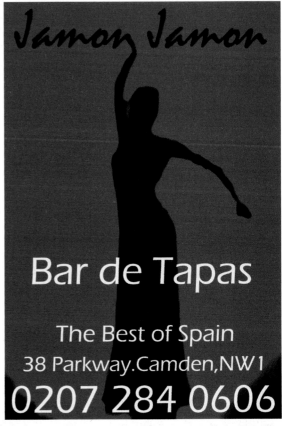

can get overstretched on busy nights, but are always friendly. To start, calves' kidneys with farika and cinnamon yoghurt was good, if unremarkable, and sopa de ajo with quail's eggs was fine (though the garlic flavour was overpowered by chopped bacon). The kitchen's charcoal grill and wood-fired oven are put to good use – a main course of charcoal-grilled lamb with bulgar, tomato and aubergine pilav and walnut tarator was outstanding, the pilav so moreish we could have eaten another plateful. Fruit-and yoghurt-based dishes often feature for pudding; our rosewater and cardamom ice-cream was subtle yet divine. The drinks list is a forte, including sherries, hard-to-find Spanish wines and the best frozen Margaritas in town. Note too that Moro is now open on Saturday lunchtimes, offering tasting menus with matching sherries.
Babies and children welcome: high chairs. Booking essential. Disabled: toilet. Tables outdoors (6, pavement). **Map 5 N4.**

Fitzrovia W1

★ Fino
33 Charlotte Street, entrance on Rathbone Street, W1T 1RR (7813 8010/www.finorestaurant.com). Goodge Street or Tottenham Court Road tube. **Lunch served** noon-2.30pm Mon-Fri; 12.30-2.30pm Sat. **Dinner served** 6-10.30pm Mon-Sat. **Tapas** £4-£15.50. **Set tapas meal** £17.95 6 tapas. **Service** 12.5%. **Credit** AmEx, MC, V.
Those tired of the slow service and limp tortillas afflicting many a London tapas bar will be dazzled by Fino, a runner-up for *Time Out*'s Best New Restaurant award in 2004. Despite the basement setting, the place is far from gloomy, with sleek blond wood fittings and colourful flourishes. Tantalising presentation – 'we'll have that', we pointed excitedly at our neighbour's baby plum tomato and chorizo salad – is clearly a priority, but Fino keeps its feet firmly on the ground, majoring in simple, uncontrived dishes with direct flavours. From our formidable tapas spread, highlights included the pimientos de padrón (just salty and piquant enough), patatas bravas and a surprisingly delicious green side salad, beautifully cold and crisp with a just-so dressing. We wrapped up with a trio of banana, mango and coconut sorbet, all bursting with natural flavour. The wine list is strong and, true to the restaurant's name, has a fine sherry selection. Service, from an army of beige-clad, mainly Hispanic staff, is slick. We'll be back – often.
Babies and children welcome: high chair. Booking advisable. Disabled: lift; toilet. **Map 9 J5.**

Navarro's
67 Charlotte Street, W1T 4PH (7637 7713/ www.navarros.co.uk). Goodge Street or Tottenham Court Road tube. **Lunch served** noon-3pm Mon-Fri. **Dinner served** 6-10pm Mon-Sat. **Tapas** £1.50-£15.50. **Service** 10%. **Credit** AmEx, MC, V.
A neighbourhood haunt of many years vintage, Navarro's is much-loved by the local workforce. It provides a reliable lunch and after-work spot in which to knock back a decent Rioja mopped up with a selection of tapas. To be fair, it also has a fine wine list, where the Riojas get way beyond decent. The food, however, never rises above pretty good. Into this category fall dishes such as sardines (four lovely fresh ones, grilled), spinach sautéed with cumin and chickpeas, and tuna empanadillas. Too many dishes were simply there to make up the numbers (patatas bravas, squid in Rioja) and a few were actively horrid – deep-fried potato balls topped with what tasted like salad cream, for example. The bread is good, the faux-rustic decor jolly and the service is willing (though there can be language difficulties) – but with local competition that now includes Salt Yard (*see below*), Navarro's might just have to try a little harder.
Babies and children welcome: high chairs. Booking essential dinner. **Map 3 J5.**

★ Salt Yard NEW
2005 RUNNER-UP BEST VEGETARIAN MEAL
54 Goodge Street, W1T 4NA (7637 0657/ www.saltyard.co.uk). Goodge Street tube. **Open** noon-11pm Mon-Fri; 5-11pm Sat. **Tapas served** noon-3pm, 6-11pm Mon-Fri; 5-11pm Sat. **Tapas** £2.75-£7. **Set lunch** £6.50 4 dishes. **Credit** MC, V.

Stylishly pared down, with a few elegant design flourishes (a mirrored stairwell, a striking wooden bar top), the compact Salt Yard is unusually restrained for a tapas bar/restaurant (the ground floor is for drinkers only). Then again, this is no ordinary tapas joint. Where Spanish tapas typically plunge headlong into seafood, jamón and chorizo, the menu here brazenly adds Italian cuisine to the mix, emerging with an enhanced (if hardly vast) vegetarian snack selection. Courgette flowers drizzled with honey and stuffed with nutty monte enebro cheese had a delicate, crisp batter; the richness of spinach and ricotta gnocchi was offset by a piquant tomato sauce; inventive bruschettas included a marriage of roast beetroot and caraway. Meat-eaters can savour perfectly cooked confit of Gloucester Old Spot pork belly with cannellini beans or morcilla croquetas, a velvety Spanish black pudding in breadcrumbs. Among the innovative desserts, a delicious rice pudding was given a twist with a brûlée topping and a scoop of wonderful rhubarb ice-cream. Aside from the inclusion of only two sherries, the wine list is well chosen, and service is cheerful and unaffected, even at the busiest times.
Babies and children admitted. No-smoking tables. Tables outdoors (3, pavement). **Map 9 J5.**

Mayfair W1

El Pirata
5-6 Down Street, W1J 7AQ (7491 3810/ www.elpirata.co.uk). Green Park or Hyde Park Corner tube. **Meals served** noon-11.30pm Mon-Fri; 6-11.30pm Sat. **Main courses** £10-£13.50. **Tapas** £2.50-£8. **Set lunch** (noon-3pm) £8 2 dishes incl glass of wine. **Set meal** £13.95-£17.75 per person (minimum 2) 8 dishes. **Service** 10%. **Credit** (over £10) AmEx, DC, JCB, MC, V.
This tapas bar is a Mayfair fixture. There's an '80s-style bar on the top floor; the ground floor is lighter and airier and the basement can feel like an afterthought, but on a busy Saturday night we

Don Fernando's. See p261.

were happy just to get a table. The food is generally good, a roster of dishes that taste home-cooked and authentic. Boquerones were thick, fresh and not too garlicky; albóndigas were excellent; pollo al ajillo had a thick, tasty gravy and moist cuts of meat; and langostinos al chef were good-quality, sizeable prawns. Indeed, the only duff dish was patatas a la pobre, which turned out to resemble a dry, tasteless version of potato dauphinois. Service is a little on the brusque side (we were kept waiting for one dish with no explanation), despite there being approximately one waiter for every two diners. The lengthy menu also lists specialities and a few more substantial dishes such as suckling pig and sea bass. A reliable option, all in all.
Babies and children admitted. Booking advisable dinner. Separate room for parties, seats 65. Tables outdoors (4, pavement). Takeaway service. **Map 9 H8.**

Piccadilly W1

Mar i Terra
17 Air Street, W1B 5AF (7734 1992/www.mari terra.co.uk). Piccadilly Circus tube. **Tapas served** noon-3pm, 5-11pm Mon-Fri; **Tapas** £2.50-£7.75. **Service** 12.5%. **Credit** AmEx, DC, JCB, MC, V.
After a bit of a blip, Mar i Terra seems to be back on form. With cheap-looking wooden tables and a dingy back area, the room isn't the smartest, but that doesn't seem to put off the mix of couples, pals, workmates and the occasional family who eat here. Virtually everything we tried during a lunchtime visit was successful: ham croquetas were wonderfully squidgy, albóndigas came in an excellent tomato sauce, boquerones were fresh and garlicky, sautéed chicken livers were lively, and crisp pork belly was rich and accompanied nicely by a slab of potato dauphinois. The weakest links were patatas bravas (a bit limp and bland), tortilla española (steaming and runny in the middle) and the poor beer selection (there's only Estrella). But

LONDON'S PREMIER TAPAS BAR AND RESTAURANT

Fuego

Launched in 1993, just a short distance from where the Great Fire of London started is 'Fuego

Fuego brought a touch of spain to London's Square Mile and now become internationally famous for its authentic food, va for money and the operatic style red and gold interior.

Opening Times:
Lunch: 11.30am to 4.00pm Mon-Fri
Dinner: 6.00pm to 2.00am Mon to Wed
6.00pm to 3.00am Thurs & Fri
Happy Hours: 5.00pm to 7.00pm
Food served till close (selected dishes)

Resident DJ every week night

Available for hire on Saturdays for special events and partie

Choose from our wide range of freshly prepared hot or cold Tapas, Paella, Patatas Bravas, Tortilla Espanola, Chorizo, Calamares Fritos and many more.

Fuego is :

- about flavour
- about tastes, delightfully simple and daringly different
- about the seduction of chillies and fragrant and aromatic spic
- about food that is sensuous, imaginative and stylish
- about the mediterranean
- about late night entertainment
- and very definitely about you

Fuego
1a Pudding Lane
London EC3R 8LB

Tel: 020 7929 3366
Fax: 020 7283 4142
www.fuego.co.uk

at least Mar i Terra shows imagination, with both harder-to-find dishes (fabada asturiana, tarta de Santiago) and drinks (agua de valencia, like an ultra-boozy Buck's Fizz) on the menu. Service is young and friendly.

Babies and children admitted. Booking advisable. Restaurant available for hire, seats 40. Separate room for parties, seats 8. Map 17 J7. For branch see index.

Pimlico SW1

Goya

34 Lupus Street, SW1V 3EB (7976 5309/ www.goyarestaurant.co.uk). Pimlico tube. **Lunch served** noon-3pm, **dinner served** 6-11.30pm daily. **Main courses** £10.90-£16.95. **Tapas** £1.80-£6.85. **Credit** AmEx, DC, JCB, MC, V.
Spanish-owned and Spanish-run, Goya is the Pimlico version of a neighbourhood tapas bar. We declined a table in the spacious but empty basement restaurant, preferring the sociable atmosphere created by besuited after-work drinkers and Spanish-speaking locals in the mustard-yellow ground-floor bar. Here, tapas classics – patatas bravas, chorizo in red wine, kidneys in sherry – are served alongside mainstream dishes such as steak in pepper sauce, and duck with orange. Bland meatballs and rubbery chipirones (baby squid) failed to transport us to Spain, but bacalao con patatas, chosen from a list of specials scrawled in Day-Glo colours on the mirror behind the bar, proved to be first-class fish and chips served with a pungent bowl of alioli. Flan de la casa was still in the oven, but the proffered alternative, tarta de Santiago, was a more than acceptable almond tart. In general, the food's a little rough around the edges, and staff may take a little prompting unless you've got your Spanish off pat. However, prices are reasonable and the house Rioja is superb, and there's nothing in the area to compare.

Babies and children welcome: high chairs. Booking advisable Mon-Fri. No-smoking tables. Tables outdoors (7, pavement). Takeaway service. Map 15 J11. For branch see index.

Soho W1

★ Meza [NEW]

100 Wardour Street, W1F 0TN (7314 4002/www. conran.com). Tottenham Court Road or Leicester Square tube. **Open** noon-2.30pm, 5pm-2am Mon-Thur; noon-2.30pm, 5pm-3am Fri, Sat. **Tapas served** noon-2.30pm, 5pm-1.30am Mon-Thur; noon-2.30pm, 5pm-2.30am Fri, Sat. **Tapas** £1.50-£12.50. **Service** 12.5%. **Credit** AmEx, MC, V.
In overhauling his old Mezzo restaurant site, Terence Conran has created something of a Latin Quarter in the heart of Soho (for Cuban-themed Floridita downstairs, *see p44*). As you might expect, the design tycoon has gone for a modish look at this Spanish lounge bar-restaurant, with its sea blues, creamy marble floors, stained oak and striking Miró-inspired mural. The atmosphere is spirited and loud, with upbeat music and up-for-it patrons. But this doesn't mean the food – all tapas – is incidental. Quite the opposite, in fact: our crop of classic tapas was superb, and presented with splendid simplicity. Highlights included white slabs of smooth monte enebro goat's cheese on a wooden board, plump skewered king prawns with super-fresh alioli, steamed asparagus with melted manchego cheese and – our waiter's favourite, with good reason – fried balls of goat's cheese with honey. The same attention to detail is applied to the drinks, with an impressively long sherry list and an extensive selection of Spanish wine. Tired of putting up with lousy bar snacks for the sake of drinking in a sassy bar? Or of eating fine food in a stuffy atmosphere? Then book yourself into Meza, which does a fine job at bridging the gap.

Babies and children welcome: high chairs. Booking advisable. Disabled: lift; toilet. Separate room for parties, seats 38. Map 17 K6.

West
Brook Green W6

Los Molinos

127 Shepherd's Bush Road, W6 7LP (7603 2229). Hammersmith tube. **Lunch served** noon-3pm Mon-Fri. **Dinner served** 6-10.45pm Mon-Sat. **Tapas** £3.50-£7.90. **Service** 10%. **Credit** AmEx, DC, MC, V.
The owner of this amiable local out on the Shepherd's Bush Road hails from Andalucía, and you might guess as much from the rather sweet rustic decor of the place. It follows, then, that the restaurant's forte is traditional tapas, cooked with care, verve and due attention paid to ingredients. Working to these relatively simple aims, Los Molinos has managed to build a strong neighbourhood following: when we visited one lunchtime, a business crowd was tucking enthusiastically into higado de pollo salteado, albóndigas a la bilbaina, fabada asturiana, and patatas al andalucia. The food was great: mouth-watering huevos revueltos (scrambled eggs with red peppers, artichokes and gulas, a form of pasta) and truly sublime dorada a la plancha, all matched by the sound house Rioja (£3 a glass) and tarta de Santiago, which went perfectly with a heart-stopping espresso. Service is easy-going, friendly and fast. With the Gypsy Kings playing in the background, what more could you want?

Babies and children welcome: high chairs. Booking advisable dinner Fri, Sat. Restaurant available for hire. Separate room for parties, seats 50. Map 20 C3.

Fino. See p255.

RESTAURANTS

Ladbroke Grove W10, W11

★ Café García [NEW]

246 Portobello Road, W11 1LL (7221 6119).
Ladbroke Grove tube. **Tapas served** 8am-7pm
Mon-Thur; 8am-11pm Fri, Sat; 10am-7pm Sun.
Tapas £1.50-£5. **Credit** AmEx, MC, V.
R Garcia & Sons, one of London's most respected
Spanish food importers, has just opened a café and
tapas bar next door. Set over two floors, it's a piece
of Spain in Notting Hill, with Eurotrash music and
real Spanish food and drink. The simple, functional
design is brightened with prints of posters for the
Feria de Seville and the air buzzes with chatter
from the predominantly Spanish clientele. There is
an outstanding selection of raciones and tapas,
pastries, fruit tarts and cream cakes. You have to
queue at the counter to order, but even on a busy
Saturday lunchtime, the sassy all-Spanish staff
had it under control. Everything we ate was
superb. The daily special was paella negra,
seafood paella made deliciously dark with squid
ink. Habas con jamón salad combined sweet, fresh
broad beans and shavings of quality serrano ham.
Tortilla was perfectly balanced – firm on the
outside, slightly gooey in the middle – and
albóndigas were dense and spicy. A moist slice of
tarta de Santiago, washed down with creamy café
con leche, topped off what has to be one of the best
Spanish eating experiences you'll have in London.
Babies and children admitted. Takeaway service.
Map 19 B2.

Galicia

323 Portobello Road, W10 5SY (8969 3539).
Ladbroke Grove tube. **Lunch served** noon-3pm
Tue-Sun. **Dinner served** 7-11.30pm Tue-Sat;
7-10.30pm Sun. **Main courses** £7-£12.
Tapas £2.95-£6. **Set lunch** £7.50 3 courses;
(Sun) £8.50 3 courses. **Credit** AmEx, DC, MC, V.
Of all the Spanish restaurants in London, Galicia
can lay a strong claim to having the most authentic
atmosphere. Castilian greeted us as we pushed our
way through the lunchtime drinkers bellying up to
the long wooden bar; as waiters straight out of
Central Casting showed us to the one remaining
table in the airless back room, we could have been
in any Spanish town. We started with tapas,
thinking to order main courses later, but any idea
of a long, Spanish-style Sunday late lunch was
dispelled by a biro-tapping waiter, who informed
us that the kitchen was about to close. As the tapas
hadn't amounted to much – stale tortilla, dry and
not very garlicky chicken, a plate of dull-tasting
grilled sardines, poor quality baguette – we gave
up on the mains, then found ourselves wondering
what to do with the rubbery, overcooked flan we
had ordered for dessert. There was little consolation
in the wine list, either, an average collection of
mainstream Spanish labels. A shame; for ten
minutes, we really thought we were going to like it.
*Babies and children admitted. Booking essential
weekends.* **Map 19 B1.**

Maida Vale NW6

Mesón Bilbao

33 Malvern Road, NW6 5PS (7328 1744).
Maida Vale tube. **Lunch served** noon-3pm
Mon-Fri. **Dinner served** 6-11pm Mon-Thur;
7-11.30pm Fri; 6-11.30pm Sat. **Main courses**
£9.95-£11.75. **Tapas** £2.50-£6.95. **Credit** MC, V.
Its rustic taverna look is rather old-fashioned, but
it's not the decor that's kept Mesón Bilbao alive for
15 years: it's the gracious service and the authentic
Basque cooking. The food here may lack the
sophistication on offer at the likes of Fino (*see
p255*), but no matter. Our tapas – spicy grilled
chorizo sandwiched between thin slices of grilled
aubergine, and tender pieces of octopus tossed in
olive oil and paprika – arrived in generous portions;
while simple dishes, they could nonetheless only
have been made by someone who knew not
just what they were doing, but where to find the best
ingredients with which to do it. Fish, though, is the
backbone of Basque cooking. The day's offerings
were chalked up on the blackboard: dover sole,
whole sea bass, or – our choice – a spot-on merluza
(hake) a la plancha served with olive oil, parsley and
garlic. Only bacalao vizcaina, the Basque national
dish, wasn't up to scratch, the salt cod smothered in
a thick and rich-looking but ultimately bland sauce.
We passed on the not very Spanish-sounding
desserts. Prices are kind, and the easy-drinking
wines, especially the house Rioja, are good company.
*Babies and children welcome: high chairs.
Booking advisable dinner Fri, Sat. Tables
outdoors (2, pavement).* **Map 1 A3.**

South West

Fulham SW6, SW10

Lomo

*222-224 Fulham Road, SW10 9NB (7349 8848/
www.lomo.co.uk). South Kensington tube then
14 bus.* **Tapas served** 5pm-midnight daily.
Tapas £2.95-£7.95. **Set meal** £6.95 paella incl
glass of wine. **Service** 12.5% for parties of
6 or more. **Credit** AmEx, DC, MC, V.
The list of around 40 tapas on the menu at this
pleasant, airy and sharply designed tapas bar,
popular with casually clad locals, is modern rather
than old-fashioned: the likes of crispy battered
chicken with honey, mustard and pine nuts, and red
peppers stuffed with feta cheese are included
among the calamares a la romana and fabada
asturiana. Unfortunately, the food doesn't taste as
good as it reads. Slices of aubergines in batter
topped with cheese were a little on the dull side;
what should have been a delicate, garlicky dish of
baby eels in sizzling oil was overpowered by an
excess of dried chilli peppers; and a plate of pata
negra offered some good quality ham but proved
pricey given the size of the portion. On the upside,
the welcome is very warm; there's a good supply of
bread and olives; the crema catalana, though more
crème brûlée in style, was delicious; and for £11.50
you can get a decent bottle of house tempranillo.

Babies and children admitted. Bookings not accepted after 8.30pm. Entertainment: guitarist 8-10pm Wed-Fri. **Map 13 C12**.

Olé

Broadway Chambers, Fulham Broadway, SW6 1EP (7610 2010/www.olerestaurants.com). Fulham Broadway tube.
Bar **Open** 5-11pm Mon-Sat. **Tapas** £1.65-£6.45.
Restaurant **Dinner served** 5-11pm Mon-Sat.
Main courses £12-£14. **Service** 10% for parties of 6 or more.
Both **Credit** AmEx, DC, JCB, MC, V.
From Olé's hard-edged modern look and location (a dour junction close to Fulham Broadway tube), we weren't expecting much. It looks more like a bar than a restaurant; the bar area was dead when we arrived in the early evening, with most of the restaurant tables cramped at the back. However, the tapas menu reads well, an interesting mix of Spanish specialities with some international influences. And what's more, the dishes – tasty croquettes of jamón ibérico, egg and spinach, freshly made tortilla with chorizo, a plate of hard goats' cheese, tomatoes, salty anchovies and sweet membrillo (quince jam) – tasted pretty good. Carne de buey a la plancha (steak), served with a stir-fry of vegetables and a sun-dried tomato and date sauce, was the only disappointment among those we sampled. Even the desserts are great, at least if a chocolate and almond crêpe is anything to go by, and at £11 a bottle, the house Rioja is a steal.
Babies and children welcome: high chairs.
Book weekends. Disabled: toilet. Restaurant/ bar available for hire. **Map 13 B13**.

Putney SW15

La Mancha

32 Putney High Street, SW15 1SQ (8780 1022/ www.lamancha.co.uk). Putney Bridge tube. **Meals served** noon-11pm Mon-Thur; noon-11.30pm Fri, Sat; noon-10.30pm Sun. **Main courses** £8.85-£12.95. **Tapas** £3.95-£6.95. **Set lunch** (noon-2.45pm) £7.95 2 courses. **Credit** AmEx, DC, MC, V.
Putney High Street isn't exactly short of casual bar-restaurants, but the long-established La Mancha still manages to draw the crowds: despite being told by phone that there was no need to book, we only just got a table on a Friday night. It's a large, garishly modern place on two floors, with the enormous ground floor dominated by a long bar. Although the high noise levels indicated that everyone was having a good time (it was hard to hear the resident guitarist), we put it down to the very reasonable drinks prices and the good selection of Spanish wines, as the food seems to have fallen by the wayside. There's a long list of tapas and some main courses, but everything we tried was dull. Beef and chorizo meatballs were tasteless, served with the same cloying tomato sauce that turned up on a main of envuelto de espinacas y queso gratinada (rubbery pancakes stuffed with a tasteless mix of spinach and cheese). Apart from the synthetic alioli, chuletas de cordero (three tender lamb chops) was the only dish we actually finished; staff removed the barely touched pancakes without comment.
Babies and children welcome: high chairs.
Separate room for parties, seats 60.

South Kensington SW5

★ Cambio de Tercio

163 Old Brompton Road, SW5 0LJ (7244 8970/ www.cambiodetercio.co.uk). Gloucester Road or South Kensington tube. **Lunch served** 12.30-2.30pm Mon-Fri; 12.30-3pm Sat, Sun. **Dinner served** 7-11.30pm Mon-Sat; 7-11pm Sun. **Main courses** £13.50-£16.75. **Service** 12.5% for parties of 6 or more. **Credit** AmEx, DC, MC, V.
Cambio celebrated its tenth anniversary in 2005, and though the 1990s decor (designer variations on bullfight themes) might be looking a bit tired, the Spanish cooking – modern, but with traditional roots – is as good as ever. Foodie trends make occasional appearances – doses of fashionable foam, for example, as decreed by Catalan master chef Ferran Adrià – but the essential, enjoyable virtues of each dish are never lost. In the fried 'caramelos' (mini croquettes) of cheese with prawns, redcurrant sauce and raspberry vinegar, the mix of sweet and savoury was absolutely right; grilled fresh spring vegetables with a smooth romesco sauce made a very different, beautifully simple starter. Mains offered similarly skilful and imaginative combinations of strongly contrasting, expertly sourced ingredients. Solomillo of Iberian pork came with full-on morcilla blood sausage, mangetout and rice noodles; grilled tuna arrived with leeks, broad beans and white cheese in a subtle tomato jus. Desserts are exquisite and highly inventive, and the wine list is an encyclopaedia of modern Spanish labels (albeit at hefty prices). Service can be over-speedy at busy times, but every meal we've had here has been interesting and enjoyable, and many have been exceptional.
Babies and children admitted. Booking advisable dinner. Restaurant available for hire. Separate room for parties, seats 22. Tables outdoors (3, pavement). **Map 13 C11**.

Tendido Cero

174 Old Brompton Road, SW5 0BA (7370 3685/ www.cambiodetercio.co.uk). Gloucester Road or South Kensington tube. **Tapas served** noon-11pm daily. **Tapas** £4.50-£14. **Set tapas meal** £25 per person (minimum 8). **Unlicensed. Corkage** £3. **Service** 12.5%. **No credit cards**.
This casual tapas-bar offshoot of Cambio de Tercio (*see above*), located right across the street, is even more successful than its parent. The tapas follow the same cooking style as Cambio – some choices, such as the unbeatable ham croquettes, are the same on both sides of the street – but there are fewer culinary adventures here. Tapas portions are on the tastefully small side, but choosing five or six will provide an enjoyable mix of vibrant flavours: a salpicón de mariscos (seafood salad) with delicately satisfying scallops, octopus, mussels and more; a nicely done classic tortilla; refined but crunchy patatas bravas; and a lovely fresh pisto of courgettes, peppers and manchego cheese. Only chorizo cooked in cider disappointed: the chorizo was of a high quality, but most of the cider's flavour had gone missing. Perhaps predictably, Tendido is more stylish than most tapas bars: like the good-looking staff, who rush about in an often chaotic but friendly way, it's sleek and clad mostly in black. One peculiar feature is that it still doesn't have a licence to serve alcohol; you're welcome to bring your own, though you'll be charged £3 for the privilege of using their corkscrew and glasses.
Babies and children admitted. Booking advisable dinner Tue-Sat. Restaurant available for hire. Tables outdoors (5, pavement). **Map 13 C11**.

South
Clapham SW4

El Rincón Latino

148 Clapham Manor Street, SW4 6BX (7622 0599). Clapham Common tube. **Dinner served** 6.30-11.30pm Tue-Fri. **Meals served** 11am-11.30pm Sat; 11am-10.30pm Sun. **Main courses** £9.95-£14.95. **Service** 10% for parties of 6 or more. **Credit** AmEx, MC, V.
This cheap and cheerful pan-Hispanic joint is absurdly popular with Clapham's youthful hordes, who, encouraged by the super-friendly service and salsa soundtrack, lend the place a lively atmosphere. It was a shame, then, that patchy food marred our most recent visit. The menu covers an array of Spanish tapas standards, with a few Latin American flourishes (plantain, yucca, guacamole). We were pleased with our plump king prawns a la plancha, delicately flavoured yellow potatoes with melted cheese on top and meatballs with tasty 'granny-style' tomato sauce. But an overly dry pollo al ajillo wasn't up to scratch, the artichoke hearts were a tad bitter for our tastes, and the reasonably priced Chilean red wine was overwhelmingly sweet. That said, we got the impression from the other diners that to analyse the dining experience too closely would perhaps be to miss the point. Come here for a boozy, affordable evening with a large group, and a merry time will be had by all.

Babies and children welcome: high chairs; nappy-changing facilities. Booking essential dinner. Disabled: toilet. Vegetarian menu (tapas). **Map 22 B1**.

Vauxhall SW8

Rebato's

169 South Lambeth Road, SW8 1XW (7735 6388/www.rebatos.com). Stockwell tube.
Tapas bar **Open** 5.30-10.45pm Mon-Fri; 7-11pm Sat. **Tapas** £2.95-£5.50.
Restaurant **Lunch served** noon-2.30pm Mon-Fri. **Dinner served** 7-10.45pm Mon-Sat. **Main courses** £11.95. **Service** 10% for parties of six or more.
Both **Credit** AmEx, DC, MC, V.
Rebato's hasn't really changed its style since it opened 22 years ago, and why would it? Few restaurants are held in as much affection by their regulars. The main menu attractions are traditional tapas served at bargain prices (mostly £2.95-£3.95), ranging from plump grilled sardines and spicy chorizo, which went well with a couple of thick slices of Spanish omelette, to specials such as salmon, artichoke and red pepper salad. The portions are generous, but if you want more, head beyond the dimly lit bar, with its tiled floor and ornate ceiling, to the light, cream and leafy-green dining room. There you can enjoy no-frills cooking of dishes such as parrillada de pescado and garlic chicken. The highlight of our meal was paella valenciana, strong in saffron and well stocked with meat and seafood, but we were also impressed by the excellent house wines and a very reasonable bill. The Spanish-speaking staff are all charming and obliging models of efficiency, adding to the buzzy, open-to-all-comers atmosphere. No wonder Rebato's is nearly always full.
Babies and children admitted. Booking essential (restaurant). **Map 16 L13**.

South East
Herne Hill SE24

Number 22 NEW

22 Half Moon Lane, SE24 9HU (7095 9922/ www.number-22.com). Herne Hill rail/3, 37, 68 bus. **Meals served** noon-11pm Mon-Fri; 10am-11pm Sat; noon-10.30pm Sun. **Main courses** £8-£17. **Tapas** £3.50-£7. **Set lunch** (noon-4pm Sun) £10 1 course, £13 2 courses, £16 3 courses. **Credit** MC, V.
The opening of Number 22 is further proof of the continuing rise of Herne Hill. Clad in a fetching sky-blue and brown colour scheme, this Spanish-slanted bar and restaurant literally packs in the locals: it's a tiny space, with barely room for 20 or so diners. (There's also a small patio out back for fine weather dining.) If you're not a claustrophobe, you'll almost certainly appreciate the sensibly short menu that offers appealing and essentially simple, rustic dishes such as baked sardines with chickpeas, coriander, garlic and cumin, and the classic Spanish seafood stew zarzuela. A little more precision is needed in the kitchen – the couscous accompanying rump of lamb with harissa was undercooked, and the bacon wrapped around calamari with rocket and a squid ink dressing was too salty – but staff get full marks for their good intentions. The dessert menu is short: why not just order vanilla ice-cream and a glass of chocolatey, raisiny Pedro Ximenez sherry and pour the latter over the former? Perfect. Tapas are available in the evening if you don't want a full meal, and the cocktails are first-rate.
Babies and children admitted. No smoking. Tables outdoors (4, patio; 2, pavement). **Map 23 A5**.

Kennington SE11

The Finca

185 Kennington Lane, SE11 4EZ (7735 1061/ www.thefinca.co.uk). Kennington tube/rail.
Bar **Open** noon-midnight Mon-Wed, Sun; noon-1am Thur-Sat.
Restaurant **Tapas served** noon-3pm, 6-11.30pm Mon-Fri; noon-11.30pm Sat, Sun.
Both **Tapas** £3.50-£7.95. **Service** 10%.
Credit MC, V.

The Finca is part laid-back lounge bar, part Spanish taverna, with chill-out tunes or Spanish guitar music filling the cavernous space. On one side, punters (mostly young, good-looking locals) sink into banquettes strewn with cushions, while psychedelic slides are projected above their heads. Opposite there is a raised eating area, simply furnished with tables made from barrels and softly lit with candles. The restaurant does some dishes well. Discs of pulpo (octopus) topped with an explosion of paprika were cooked to perfection, and a hearty chicken in cider casserole was tender with a zing of apples. Less impressive was a raft of skewered langoustines, wrapped in tough serrano ham and smothered in batter of chip-shop proportions – a bizarre, greasy combination. Also disappointing was the Spanish classic, huevos estrellaos. Instead of thin, golden potato slices topped with a fried egg, crisp at the edges and gooey in the middle, it was an oil-fest of soggy boiled potatoes crowned with a flabby egg. The good things about the Finca is the relaxed, chatty vibe and lovely Spanish staff. The food is hit and miss, although the occasional star dish might tempt you back for more.
Babies and children welcome: high chairs. Booking essential. Entertainment: DJ 8pm-1am Thur-Sat. Separate room for parties, seats 25. Vegetarian menu.

London Bridge & Borough SE1

★ Tapas Brindisa NEW
18-20 Southwark Street, SE1 1TJ (7357 8880/ www.brindisa.com). London Bridge tube/rail. **Tapas served** 11am-11pm Mon-Thur; 9am-11pm Fri, Sat. **Tapas** £3-£6.75. **Service** 12.5%. **Credit** MC, V.
This stylish tapas bar on the edge of Borough Market has been packed to the gills since it opened in October 2004. With good reason too. The tapas bar set-up marks a logical progression by the owners from importing and selling high-quality

Spanish produce to showcasing that same produce in a restaurant-like setting. Many of the items on sale (at Brindisa's stall in Borough Market and shop in Exmouth Market) take centre-stage on the menu: beech-smoked mackerel in olive oil, cured Cantabrian anchovies, cured gran reserve Joselito ham. Yet there are plenty of dishes that require more than slicing meat or opening a tin. Gazpacho, served with cucumber slices and fried bread, and anointed with flavourful olive oil, tasted like Spanish summer in a bowl. Another seasonal offering was tomato salad with cabernet sauvignon vinaigrette; in the past, we've enjoyed battered salt cod with garlicky alioli, and Iberian ham croquettes. To drink, there's sherry and a well-chosen, all-Spanish wine list. As in tapas bars in Spain, there's an area for standing only and another for sitting. No reservations are taken though, so be prepared to wait at busy times.
Babies and children admitted. No-smoking tables. Tables outdoors (6, pavement). **Map 11 P8.**

East

Bethnal Green E2

Laxeiro
93 Columbia Road, E2 7RG (7729 1147). Bethnal Green tube/Liverpool Street tube/rail/ 8, 26, 48, 55 bus. **Tapas served** noon-3pm, 7-11pm Tue-Sat; 9am-3pm Sun. **Tapas** £2.95-£9.50. **Credit** AmEx, DC, MC, V.
This unpretentious Columbia Road favourite has a bright, almost caff-like interior with cheerful, neat wood decor, and a scattering of pavement tables. It's pretty small and does get hectic, especially when the flower market is in full swing on Sundays, but the alert, friendly staff ensure you're never forgotten for long. With a glass of excellent Rioja in hand, we resisted the paella (the only main course available) and chose a variety of tapas from a list (chalked on a blackboard) that mixes good-value standards such as pinchos and garlic prawns with some contemporary updates – coriander and chilli clams, beef in black pepper – and a number of vegetarian

options. A light, freshly made tortilla, rich, meaty albóndigas and a surprisingly delicate butterbean and mozzarella salad were great, and the chicken and chickpea stew was supreme. The only tapas left half-eaten was a bland, disappointing patatas bravas, a heap of fried potatoes with a bit of red sauce on top, but we suspect this is just a minor glitch. A great choice for pit stop dining.
Babies and children admitted. Booking advisable; not accepted Sun. Tables outdoors (3, pavement). Takeaway service. **Map 6 S3.**

Leytonstone E11

Elche
567-569 Leytonstone High Road, E11 4PB (8558 0008/www.elcherestaurant.co.uk). Leytonstone tube. **Lunch served** 12.30-2.30pm Mon-Sat. **Dinner served** 6.30-11pm Mon-Thur; 6.30pm-midnight Fri, Sat. **Meals served** 12.30-10pm Sun. **Main courses** £8.50-£15. **Tapas** £2.50-£5. **Set tapas meal** £12. **Set buffet** (12.30-4pm Sun) £12 incl half-bottle of wine or sangria. **Credit** AmEx, MC, V.
The suit of armour at the door; the white stucco walls hung with guitars, brass saucepans and Dali prints; and the soft twanging of Spanish muzak create a cosily kitsch environment – the perfect setting for some tapas-like-mother-makes. But instead of moreish comfort food, our dishes were consistently lacklustre. A slice of tortilla was dry and crumbly, the chorizo was bland and the paella valenciana was scattered with a sad, shrivelled collection of prawns and calamares. Succulent boquerones were better, though it's hard to go wrong with these. The pollo Elche, a creamy chicken casserole with sweet red pepper, was the only truly enjoyable dish, giving a tantalising taster of the homemade Spanish flavour we were craving. Desserts hardly improved on the tapas: both apple tart and berry cheesecake were soggy, with only a cinnamon arroz con leche really going down well. Elche once had a reputation for good-quality, good-value tapas, and it still maintains its popularity with families and groups of friends.

Salt Yard. See p255.

But with this food, and surprisingly grumpy staff, it seems only to be affection for what it used to be that keeps the place going.

Babies and children welcome: half-price Sun buffet; high chairs. Booking advisable; essential dinner Fri, Sat. Entertainment: flamenco 8.30pm Fri. Restaurant available for hire. Separate room for parties, seats 30. Takeaway service.

North

Camden Town & Chalk Farm NW1

Bar Gansa

2 Inverness Street, NW1 7HJ (7267 8909/ www.gansa.co.uk). Camden Town tube. **Open** 10am-midnight Mon-Wed; 10am-1am Thur-Sat; 10am-11pm Sun. **Main courses** £5-£21. **Tapas** £3.25-£4.50. **Service** 10% before 5pm; 12.5% after 5pm. **Credit** MC, V.

Young, loud and unfeasibly busy, even very early on a Saturday evening, Bar Gansa is not the place to come if you're looking to linger over a bottle of Rioja and a roster of exciting Iberian delicacies. However, it is a decent spot from which to appreciate the diversity of Camden's lively market crowd, along with some decent if unspectacular Spanish cooking. Pinchitos morunos (lamb skewers) came up slightly over-charred but very thoughtfully spiced, and salt and pepper squid was incredibly tender; chickpeas and spinach, though, didn't have enough of a spicy edge. Chorizo with beans and the tortilla were up to scratch. Beer bottles vastly outnumber wine glasses most nights, but even so more thought could be put into a decidedly unadventurous and highly priced wine list on which a standard Rioja costs a good £20. Despite the crowds, there's nothing intimidating about the room: the dark, red and orange decor gives it a warmth that echoes the vibrancy of the clientele and the friendliness of the staff.

Babies and children admitted. Booking advisable weekends. Entertainment: flamenco 8pm Mon. Tables outdoors (2, terrace). **Map 27 C2**.

Jamón Jamón

38 Parkway, NW1 7AH (7284 0606/ www.jamónjamón-tapas.co.uk). Camden Town tube. **Meals served** noon-11.30pm Mon-Thur, Sun; noon-12.30am Fri, Sat. **Tapas** £2-£6.95. **Set meal** (noon-5pm Mon-Fri) 2 dishes for the price of 1. **Service** (over £40) 10%. **Credit** AmEx, DC, MC, V.

This Camden bar began with a nice idea that differentiated itself from the familiar tapas bar routine: Spanish cheeses, serrano ham and cold meats served on tablas (wooden slabs), a traditional style that's very popular in Spain. Nice idea, but if you're going to do things this simply, you really do need to get top-quality ingredients: the anticipated punchy Spanish country flavours were lacking in the tablas of manchego and the promised jamón. The conventional tapas were no better. Interest was aroused by croquettes of cabrales, normally one of the world's most pungent and instantly recognisable cheeses, but they seemed to be made with bog-standard blue. Patatas alioli were lardy and short on garlic; only lomo adobado (marinated pork loin) had a decent tang. Still, the long narrow space is quite cool and pretty, with a roof that opens in summer to form a kind of internal patio. The young Spanish staff, while a bit ditzy, are very friendly, and the place was buzzing when we visited. Obviously you don't need to work too hard in this location to draw a crowd.

Babies and children welcome: high chairs. Booking advisable dinner and weekends. Vegetarian menu. **Map 27 C2**. **For branches (La Siesta, Tapeo) see index.**

El Parador

245 Eversholt Street, NW1 1BA (7387 2789). Mornington Crescent tube. **Lunch served** noon-3pm Mon-Fri. **Dinner served** 6-11pm Mon-Thur; 6-11.30pm Fri, Sat; 6.30-9.30pm Sun. **Tapas** £3-£6. **Service** 10% for parties of 5 or more. **Credit** MC, V.

El Parador keeps its ample fan base with frequently changing menus of imaginative tapas that are very different from the routine lists of so many London bars. Of our larger tapas, gambas del parador (tiger prawns with garlic, ginger, coriander and butter) was a perfectly balanced mix of spices and juicy seafood, and purée de batata (sweet potato purée with goats' cheese, leeks and butter) was an interesting veggie option. We also enjoyed the roasted almond, garlic and chilli-based 'romanesco' (romesco) dipping sauce served with fresh bread. From the classic tapas list, traditional albóndigas were enjoyably succulent. Not everything is so successful – our col con pimentón (savoy cabbage cooked with roast tomatoes and paprika) was burnt and greasy, and service is often abrupt. However, there's an above average and decently priced wine list, and the little garden at the back is enormously popular in summer. Note that staff don't take bookings for parties of fewer than three people, so if two of you turn up at a busy time, you'll probably be confined to the basement, the least attractive of the Parador's three dining spaces.

Babies and children admitted. Bookings accepted for 3 or more only. Separate room for parties, seats 30. Tables outdoors (10, garden). Vegetarian menu. **Map 27 D3**.

Crouch End N8

La Bota

31 Broadway Parade, Tottenham Lane, N8 9DB (8340 3082). Finsbury Park tube/rail then 91, W7 bus. **Lunch served** noon-2.30pm, **dinner served** 6-11.30pm Mon-Fri. **Meals served** noon-11.30pm Sat, Sun. **Tapas** £2-£4.50. **Credit** MC, V.

The notion of 'authenticity' in London restaurants is a pretty vague one these days. However, visitors to La Bota really will find something close to authentic Spanish street-corner bar food, with classic flavour combinations such as tuna-heavy ensaladilla rusa and cold beer that can evoke Spain more effectively than any memory of sunset over the Alhambra. The authenticity extends to the occasional duffness of some of the dishes, but there were no such disappointments on our last visit. Serrano ham croquettes were creamy and richly flavoured, raxo (marinated pork) was properly strong and punchy, and espinacas a la catalana (spinach with raisins and pine kernels) was pleasantly sweet and savoury. A few main courses complement the extensive tapas list, and there's a decent Spanish wine and drinks list. The good-value menu and comfortable atmosphere help make La Boca a very adaptable spot, drawing everyone from shoppers in need of a breather to rambunctious weekend parties. Service is quickfire and deadpan (also quite authentic), but few places are more co-operative when it comes to accommodating pushchairs in small spaces.

Babies and children welcome: high chairs. Booking advisable dinner Fri, Sat. Takeaway service.

Harringay N4

La Viña

3 Wightman Road, N4 1RQ (8340 5400). Harringay rail/29, 341 bus. **Meals served** 5pm-midnight Mon-Sat; 5-10.30pm Sun. **Main courses** £8.45-£10.50. **Tapas** £3-£5. **Credit** MC, V.

This charming little tapas restaurant in the Harringay Ladder maintains its popularity by taking good care of its customers. Staff are friendly and unflustered, and deal well with bookings of all sizes (even kids' parties) without ever letting diners in ones or twos feel neglected. The setting is comfortable, with a few Spanishy knick-knacks spread around the mellow, dark-shaded space. And the tapas list has something for everyone, with innovations alongside the classics and plenty of vegetarian options to boot. With over 45 tapas to choose from, there are bound to be highs and lows, but our albóndigas were nicely moist and meaty; chicken croquettes, while a bit over-toasted on the outside, were otherwise full of flavour; and 'cuernas de toro' – nothing to do with bulls: these were prawns and manchego wrapped in piquillo peppers – were an intriguing combination. The only thing

that disappointed was hot squid stuffed with chewy prawns. As alternatives to tapas there are a few main courses and paellas, especially on Monday and Tuesday. Wines (Spanish standards) are served at the right temperature, prices are amenable, and the complimentary liqueurs after each meal make one last nice touch.

Babies and children welcome: high chairs. Booking advisable; essential dinner. No-smoking tables. Restaurant available for hire (Sun).

Muswell Hill N10

Café Loco

266 Muswell Hill Broadway, entrance on Muswell Hill, N10 2QR (8444 3370). Highgate tube then 43, 134 bus. **Dinner served** 6-10.30pm Mon-Sat (open until 2am); 4.30pm-midnight Sun. **Main courses** £7-£10.50. **Tapas** £2.50-£5.50. **Service** 12%. **Credit** AmEx, DC, MC, V.

With a name like this, it's unlikely to be aiming for dinner-for-two romancers, and so it goes: Café Loco is a key stop on Muswell Hill's party circuit, with heaving DJ sessions (Thur-Sat), hot-tropical decor and a fly-me-to-the-binge drinks list that includes 'loco jugs' of cocktails ('more alcohol, less ice!'). However, in its quieter moments, it's an almost unrecognisably cosy and relaxing spot. None of the food is hugely elaborate, but it's all put together with a likeably generous style. Mains, specials and large salads are as global-eclectic as the spelling on the menu (cajun steak with 'marscoponi' mustard, niçoise salad, char-grilled salmon in teriyaki spices), but the tapas stick a bit closer to Spanish originals. The stars of our selection were pimientos rellenos, filled with a brandade-like mix of cod, salmon, potato and herbs; emparedados (battered cheese parcels, nicely crunchy); chicken pinchitos; and a fresh-tasting ensaladilla, made rather oddly with cocktail sauce instead of mayonnaise. Portions are bigger than the tapas norm; when we visited, there was an offer of any three tapas for £8.50 during happy hour (6-8pm Mon-Thur, Sun).

Babies and children welcome (until 9.30pm): high chairs. Booking essential dinner Fri, Sat. Dress: no tracksuits or caps. Entertainment: DJ 10pm-2am Thur-Sat. Restaurant available for hire. Takeaway service.

Outer London

Richmond, Surrey

Don Fernando's

27F The Quadrant, Richmond, Surrey TW9 1DN (8948 6447/www.donfernando.co.uk). Richmond tube/rail. **Lunch served** noon-3pm, **dinner served** 6-11pm Mon, Tue. **Meals served** noon-11pm Wed-Sat; noon-10pm Sun. **Main courses** £8-£13. **Tapas** £3-£5. **Set meal** £15.75-£19.95 2 courses. **Service** 10% for parties of 6 or more. **Credit** AmEx, MC, V.

This veteran Spanish restaurant is bang next to Richmond train/tube station. The light and airy ground-floor room declares its owners' Andalucian roots through a riot of exuberant wall tiles, wood and terracotta. Coupled with an easy-going atmosphere and a lengthy something-for-everyone menu, the place was doing brisk business when we arrived for a late Sunday lunch. We opted for tapas – from a highly traditional collection – rather than variations on the paella theme (including a vegetarian version) or main courses such as lamb steak with rosemary, and swordfish Andalucian-style. While we couldn't complain about the size of the portions, the food, regrettably, didn't quite square up with the enterprising Spanish wine list, which opens at £12.75. Lentejas caseras (lentil stew with vegetables) was dull, pincho pollo tasteless, and grilled squid with garlic rubbery. Better were chorizo cooked with white wine, habas (broad beans) con jamón, and jamón serrano with manchego. Triangulitos de queso frito seemed a livelier choice than any of the pedestrian desserts, but turned out to be deep-fried brie with cranberry sauce and sweetened cream.

Babies and children welcome: high chairs. No-smoking tables. Tables outdoors (4, pavement).

Thai

Thai food is one of the most popular budget cuisines in the capital, with every neighbourhood, it seems, having its own cheap and cheerful purveyor of green and red curries, fish cakes, pad Thai and other firm favourites. Cooking standards tend to be reliable rather than spectacular, which is why we've hived off the best of these into a box, **Local Thais**.

But there is plenty of excellent Thai cooking to be experienced, from the communal seating, fresh flavours and budget prices of Alan Yau's mini chain, **Busaba Eathai** (its third central London outlet opened in 2005) to the extravagances of swankier establishments, such as **Nipa**, **Nahm** and **Patara** (also with a new branch). Newcomer **Isarn** in Islington – runner-up for Best Cheap Eats in the 2005 *Time Out* Awards – shows that the demand for stylish venues, classy cooking and reasonable prices remains strong. The **Thai Square** chain has moved upmarket with its takeover of a riverside architectural showpiece in Putney.

Don't expect chopsticks at a Thai restaurant; food is usually eaten with a fork and spoon, although fingers are acceptable if that is convenient.

Central
Belgravia SW1

★ Nahm
The Halkin, Halkin Street, SW1X 7DJ (7333 1234/www.nahm.como.bz). Hyde Park Corner tube. **Lunch served** noon-2.30pm Mon-Fri. **Dinner served** 7-11pm Mon-Sat; 7-10pm Sun. **Main courses** £11-£16.50. **Set lunch** £26 3 courses. **Set dinner** £49.50 4 courses. **Service** 12.5%. **Credit** AmEx, DC, JCB, MC, V.

Poor acoustics slightly mar the dining experience at this ultra-stylish Thai restaurant in Belgravia's exclusive Halkin hotel; other people's conversations create a confusing muddle of sound. Still, this is a small failing for a restaurant serving inspired modern Thai cooking. Kitchen maestro David Thompson – formerly of Sydney's Darley Street Thai, and author of the award-winning book *Thai Food* – has put together a thought-provoking menu of royal Thai classics made with first-rate ingredients. The minimalist dining room bustles with theatrical waiting staff. The wine list is ostentatious: a bottle of the £900 Hermitage La Chappelle, perhaps? Despite Thompson's credentials, the modernist Thai cooking can be variable (pork fried with shrimp paste and lime leaves was too fishy, and flavours didn't gel), but when it works, it's spectacular. Take the yam pak salad: a flavour-safari of basil, mint, coriander, fried aubergine, tart greens, star fruit and physalis. We also relished Nahm's monkfish green curry: not too sweet and satisfyingly spicy. Jet-setters, hotel guests and ladies with Gucci bags dine here. *Book dinner. Disabled: toilet. Dress: smart casual. No smoking. Separate room for parties, seats 36. Vegetarian menu.* **Map 9 G9**.

City EC2

Nakhon Thai
10 Copthall Avenue, EC2R 7DJ (7628 1555/ www.nakhonthai.co.uk). Moorgate tube/rail. **Meals served** 11.30am-10pm Mon-Fri. **Main courses** £5-£19. **Set meal** £19.95-£24.95 3 courses. **Service** 12.5%. **Credit** AmEx, MC, V.
With the City location and stylish corporate interior, Nakhon Thai looks expensive. Fear not – prices are very fair for food of this quality. Tucked away on a City backstreet, the dining room is primarily set up for one-to-one business lunches, with rows of tables for two facing the inevitable pagoda-roofed bar. Walls are decorated with Thai montages and curious flat-framed Buddhas; the glass-topped tables contain offerings from the spirit houses found outside Thai homes. The menu holds few surprises, but all the Thai standards we tried were well done. Crispy parcels were a good marker for the rest of the meal: crispy wun tun pastry wrapped around minced prawns and water-chestnut, and tied up with a strand of edible grass. Poh pia (fried spring rolls) were fairly unexciting, but the chicken kraprao restored our confidence: complex, spicy and packed with hot peppercorns. Beef penang curry was also a pleasant surprise; for once, flavours weren't swamped by sugar and coconut milk. Fancy a break from satay and green curry? Order the soft-shell crabs or some stir-fried scallops.
Babies and children admitted. Booking advisable. No-smoking tables. Separate room for parties, seats 15. Takeaway service. **Map 12 Q6**.
For branch see index.

Thai Square. See p268.

Marylebone W1

★ ★ Busaba Eathai

8-13 Bird Street, W1U 1BU (7518 8080). Bond Street tube. **Meals served** noon-11pm Mon-Thur; noon-11.30pm Fri, Sat; noon-10pm Sun. **Main courses** £5.10-£9. **Set meal** £13.70-£14.90. **Service** 10% for parties of 5 or more. **Credit** AmEx, MC, V.

Comparisons with Wagamama (*see p243*), also created by Alan Yau, are inevitable, but Busaba Eathai does something altogether more impressive with the template of no-smoking communal tables and no reservations. This is the third branch; as at the others, the mod-colonial design is beautiful: the dark wood and judiciously deployed candles and low-hung cylindrical lights make it surprisingly intimate, given it aims to serve one-course meals within the confines of a lunch hour. Streetside window seating, with heavy-wood stools, offered fresh air – and a view of a barren street. We especially enjoyed properly smoky char-grilled duck with stir-fried chinese broccoli and tamarind sauce, but the lychee-like rose-apple stir-fry was equally moreish. Temptations resisted included blue swimmer crab and prawn pomelo in betel leaves. Individual pots of excellent lemongrass and pandan leaf tea were a worthy substitute for pudding. Pretty much empty for our early lunch, the restaurant nonetheless conjured a chatty buzz; the shirt-sleeved workers and casual-chic shoppers clearly felt lucky to have discovered the place. Despite minor niggles (a little too much atmospheric incense, and service that disappeared when it came to paying up, although it was otherwise impeccable), we concur. Another branch opens at the end of 2005.
Babies and children admitted. Disabled: toilet. No smoking. **Map 9 G6.**
For branches see index.

Eat-Thai.net

22 St Christopher's Place, W1U 1NP (7486 0777/www.eatthai.net). Bond Street tube. **Lunch served** noon-3pm, **dinner served** 6-10.30pm daily. **Main courses** £7.95-£16.95. **Set lunch** £8.95 2 courses. **Service** 12.5%. **Credit** AmEx, MC, V.

This charming restaurant goes by several names, including Eat-Thai.net, Eat-Thai and Chaopraya (the name of the river that winds through Bangkok). Dining is an intimate experience; couples come here for romantic dinners. Groups of wealthy west Londoners also frequent the place. Most choose the elegant upstairs dining room over the plainer bistro-like area downstairs. Chef Nipa Senkaewsai has put together an impressive menu of royal Thai classics, Esarn dishes from north-east Thailand and fusion food that blends Thai and western cuisine. Our starters set a high standard, particularly the steamed crystal spring rolls stuffed with prawn and roast duck, served with a dreamy sweet soy dipping sauce. In comparison, green papaya salad disappointed (a noticeable lack of chilli), but the penang curry with sticky rice was flawless and the green curry was delightfully rich and fragrant. Flavours were well complemented by a bottle of Monsoon Valley: a crisp, fruity Thai white wine. Presentation was spectacular throughout, with attractive garnishes and unusually shaped Thai porcelain dishes. Service could have been speedier, but the heated celadon plates for the main course were a nice touch.
Babies and children welcome: high chairs. Booking advisable. No-smoking tables. Takeaway service. **Map 9 H6.**

Soho W1

★ Patara

2005 RUNNER-UP BEST DESIGN
15 Greek Street, W1D 4DP (7437 1071). Leicester Square or Tottenham Court Road tube. **Lunch served** noon-2.30pm Mon-Sat. **Dinner served** 6.30-10.30pm daily. **Main courses** £12.95-£15.50. **Set lunch** £11.95 2 courses, £14.95 3 courses. **Set dinner** (6.30-7.30pm) £13.95 2 courses. **Service** 12.5%. **Credit** AmEx, DC, JCB, MC, V.

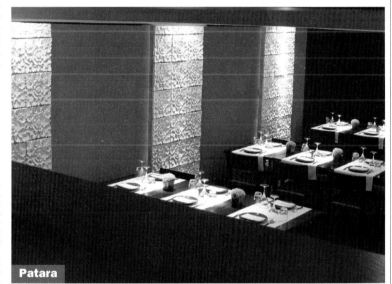

Patara

THAI THO
RESTAURANT

Tennis player Maria Sharapova described Thai Tho as her favourite restaurant during th
Wimbledon Championships. Those who have eaten here and return time and time agai
would certainly agree. Thai Tho is a stylist restaurant, serving some of the best Thai food
outside of Thailand

The Staff are delightful, the decor calm, the food delicious. The ingredients are fresh,
many are flown from Thailand each week. It is rare to find a restaurant of such quality at
such reasonable prices.

Thai Tho
20 High Street, Wimbledon Village, London SW19 5DX

Tel: 020 8946 1542 / 020 8296 9034

Open: Lunch 11.30 am – 3.30 pm
            Dinner 6.30 pm – 11.30 pm
            Sunday: Open all day

" We look forward to serving you.

This is the fourth London branch of upmarket Patara, a Thai-based international chain. This Soho flagship takes its design from traditional Thai royal pavilions, with elaborately carved palmwood columns, chiselled sandstone lining the walls, sumptuous red seating, and spotlights on white linen; it looks stunning. The centrepiece is the huge model of a teak palace, finished with gold leaf and lit from above. The menu is refreshingly like 'real' Thai food, but with plenty of innovation, such as black cod with yellow bean sauce; crab meat and grilled aubergine salad; or curried sea bass grilled in coconut leaves. Flavours are strong but well balanced, just as they should be. The chilli-heat of a salad of shredded chicken and julienned mango was a an assault on the palate, but sour lime juice, salty fish sauce and notes of sweet and bitter also vied for attention. Fresh mint and fried garlic added to the taste explosion. Even basics such as fish cakes and rice were perfectly rendered, and a vividly orange curry of duck with diced pineapple wasn't a as sickly sweet as it might sound. The set menus are particularly good value, considering the quality of the cooking.
Booking advisable. No-smoking tables. Vegetarian menu. **Map 17 K6.**
For branches see index.

West

Bayswater W2

★ Nipa

Royal Lancaster Hotel, Lancaster Terrace, W2 2TY (7262 6737/www.royallancaster.com). Lancaster Gate tube.
Bar **Open** 11am-11pm Mon-Sat; 11am-10.30pm Sun.
Restaurant **Lunch served** noon-2pm Mon-Fri. **Dinner served** 6.30-10.30pm Mon-Sat.
Main courses £8.50-£13.50. **Set meals** £25-£28 4 courses; khantoke (lunch, 6.30-7.30pm) £14.90.
Both **Credit** AmEx, DC, MC, V.
The atmospheric dining room at Nipa wouldn't look out of place in a royal palace in Bangkok – a surprising thing to find behind the façade of a 1960s towerblock hotel. Carved wooden details and cabinets of gilded Benjarong china grace the walls, and the window tables look out over Hyde Park (soundproofed glass cuts traffic noise to a whisper). Prices are high, but the classic Thai food is exquisite. Chefs pay great attention to detail; even the carved vegetable garnishes are works of art. We started with moist Thai fish cakes, laced with shredded lime leaves and served with deep-fried basil leaves and an incendiary sweet chilli dip. Also a big hit was the pla phad ped: tender flakes of battered white fish stir-fried with curry paste, lime leaves and searing bird-eye chillies. Compared to these delights, the chicken pad kraprao (chicken fried with chilli and basil) failed to excite, but the pad Thai was perfectly judged, with melt-in-the-mouth butterfly prawns and al dente rice noodles. Service was punctual and unobtrusive. The meal ended with hot towels and an impressive mound of after-dinner chocolates. Highly recommended.
Babies and children welcome: high chairs. Booking essential Fri, Sat. Disabled: toilet. Dress: smart casual. Takeaway service. Vegetarian menu. **Map 8 D6.**

Tawana

3 Westbourne Grove, W2 4UA (7229 3785/ www.tawana.co.uk). Bayswater tube. **Lunch served** noon-3pm, **dinner served** 6-11pm Mon-Sat. **Meals served** noon-10pm Sun.
Main courses £5.75-£17.95. **Set meal** £15.95 2 courses. **Minimum** £10. **Service** 10%. **Credit** AmEx, DC, MC, V.
Tawana has an airport-lounge-meets-the-east style: Waitresses glide around in Thai clothes, between comfortable chairs edged with faux-bamboo, pagodas, wood carvings, ceiling fans and the odd orchid. It's all rather dated, but a welcome haven from the frenetic pace of Queensway. To begin, tom yum goong was thin, sharp and hot, with plenty of lemongrass and a wicked chilli kick. But other starters – morning glory in batter and a

mixed plate for two (with fried prawn wun tun, vegetable spring rolls, corn patties and kratong thong, with plum sauce) – were batter-heavy, dry and rather boring. A main of whole baby squid steamed in garlic, lime juice and chilli (pla uek phad prig sod) brought fresh, squidgy little squid with tart, chilli-hot juices. Stir-fried mixed veg was a let-down, though, and expensive too: £4.95 for Sunday dinner-style vegetables, plus chinese leaves, sitting in what tasted like watered-down soy sauce. There are plenty of trad dishes (pad Thai, curries), as well as a vegetarian menu. Good in parts, but really quite pricey.
Babies and children admitted. Booking advisable. Separate room for parties, seats 50. Takeaway service. Vegetarian menu. **Map 7 B6.**
For branches (Thai Hut, Thai Kitchen) see index.

Kensington W8

Papaya Tree

209 Kensington High Street, W8 6BD (7937 2260). High Street Kensington tube. **Lunch served** noon-3.30pm, **dinner served** 6-11pm daily. **Main courses** £7.95-£9.95. **Set lunch** £5-£6 1 course. **Set dinner** £18-£24 3 courses. **Service** 10%. **Credit** AmEx, DC, JCB, MC, V.
When we visited early on a Saturday night, this restaurant was empty: a shame, as the food was perfectly respectable, if a little pedestrian. Papaya Tree may lose points for its basement location – after all, this is a neighbourhood where people go out to be seen. However, the room is done out very nicely: white tablecloths and chair covers, ball topiary, onion flowers in steel vases and whisper-thin spotlights on the ceiling. The menu includes loads of set meals and a decent vegetarian section. Familiar Thai standards are spruced up with novel ingredients and given exotic-sounding names (dizzy prawns, anyone?). To start, the chicken satay was tasty enough, with an unusual hint of lime, but the khanom jeep (minced meat parcels) were a little too close to packet dim sum for our taste. The presentation of the mains wasn't great, but the penang beef curry had plenty of zip. Easily the best dish was the drunken noodles: fat pad Thai noodles scented with chilli and stir-fried with chicken and bamboo shoots. Service was fine – but so it should have been as we were the only diners.
Babies and children admitted: high chairs. Booking advisable. No-smoking tables. Takeaway service; delivery service (7644 6666). Vegetarian menu. **Map 7 A9.**

Shepherd's Bush W12

★ ★ Esarn Kheaw

314 Uxbridge Road, W12 7LJ (8743 8930). Shepherd's Bush tube/207, 260, 283 bus. **Lunch served** noon-3pm Mon-Fri. **Dinner served** 6-11pm daily. **Main courses** £5.95-£8.95. **Credit** AmEx, DC, MC, V.
An unassuming, rather grungy place that feels like an Indian restaurant, Esarn Kheaw boasts some of the best Thai food in London. After last year's aberration, this time we found the service friendly but modest; staff hate recommending anything in case you won't like it (or in case it's too hot for you), so it helps to know your stuff. There are some fabulous versions of Thai staples; tod mun pla fish cakes were prepared immediately and came with a superb, fresh sauce, as piquant as it was sweet. Kai bang tauy (chicken in pandanus leaves) was marginally less successful (the chicken could have been more tender), but still delicious. Despite the fact the owners are from Bangkok, there's an array of hard-to-find northern specialities including son-in-law's eggs (omelette with shallots, tamarind and coriander) and chiang mai sausage. All are recommended, but best are the typical dishes; red chicken curry was the best we've ever tasted. Even the coconut rice is something special. Taro yam (hot coconut custard) rounded off a simple meal that felt like a feast. Limited drink options (albeit including Thai wine) don't spoil the effect.
Babies and children admitted. Booking advisable. Takeaway service. **Map 20 B1.**

Interview
DAVID THOMPSON

Who are you?
Buggered if I know. I'm a consultant at **Nahm** (*see p263*), and I'm in a partnership in Sailor's Thai in Sydney.
Eating in London: what's good about it?
You can do it now. A revolution has occurred in the past 20 years. You used to have to eat *before* you came to London – now you come here to eat. It really has become one of the food centres of the world. I spend four to six months in London each year; if I could, I'd make it eight months.
What's bad about it?
It's one of the ironies of life that if you go to eat in an English restaurant, English is usually not the mother tongue. It's hard to order off-menu, and explaining to the waitperson what you want is going to take longer than cooking the meal. There is a desperate shortage of staff.
Which are your favourite London restaurants?
I go back to **Locanda Locatelli** (*see p171*) all the time. I like **Hakkasan** (*see p69*), **Yauatcha** (*see p72*) and also **Le Cercle** (*see p91*). For me, they are local and easy. People tend to eat where they live or work in this city – **Club Gascon** (*see p92*) or **St John** (*see p55*) are too much effort to get to.
What single thing would improve London's restaurant scene?
I'm tempted to say get rid of food critics, but I've been very lucky, and I get on well with a few food critics.
Any hot tips for the coming year?
I'm in a culinary cul-de-sac. We get all our ingredients from Thailand; what's interesting for me are the magical things I find there – great fish noodles, great white sesame oil that's organic but not roasted. Things that taste good, that I'd like to bring over to London. I'm currently researching a new book and for me, that means eating and being able to relax.

RESTAURANTS

South West
Fulham SW6

★ Blue Elephant
4-6 Fulham Broadway, SW6 1AA (7385 6595/ www.blueelephant.com). Fulham Broadway tube. **Lunch served** noon-2.30pm Mon-Fri; noon-3pm Sun. **Dinner served** 7pm-midnight Mon-Thur; 6.30pm-midnight Fri, Sat; 7-10.30pm Sun. **Main courses** £10.60-£28. **Set meals** £33-£39 3/4 courses. **Set buffet** (lunch Sun) £22 adults, £11 children. **Service** 12.5%. **Credit** AmEx, DC, MC, V.

Imagine a Vegas floorshow in the middle of Fulham and you'll have some idea of what to expect from Blue Elephant. This hugely successful Thai restaurant chain has branches as far afield as Bangkok and Copenhagen. The London incarnation is a veritable jungle, with hundreds of potted ferns and palms, trickling fountains, wooden bridges and cascades of fresh-cut flowers – the daily orchid bill doesn't bear thinking about. Waiters in bellboy uniforms and waitresses dressed like maids hover attentively, and tables are set with Blue Elephant's trademark Thai steel cutlery and ink-splash dishes. For once, this isn't a case of presentation compensating for mediocre food. The som tam (green papaya salad) was on fire, with powerful flavours of shrimp, chilli and lime, while the menam chicken soup (basically tom kha gai) was rich, creamy and indulgent. For main course, we were impressed by the pork chiang rai, a spicy blend of pork, red chilli, basil leaves and strands of fresh green peppercorns. We accompanied this with the house white (adequate, and one of just a few wine choices). Our only criticism: with all the pot plants and water features, there isn't much elbow room for diners.
Babies and children welcome: colouring books; face painting (Sun); high chairs. Booking advisable. Disabled: toilet. Dress: smart casual;
no shorts. Entertainment: colouring books, face-painting Sun. Takeaway service; delivery service. Vegetarian menu. **Map 13 B13**.

Sugar Hut
374 North End Road, SW6 1LY (7386 8950/ www.sugarhutfulham.com). Fulham Broadway tube. **Dinner served** 7-11.30pm Tue-Thur, Sun; 7pm-midnight Fri, Sat. **Main courses** £9.50-£19.50. **Set meal** £28.50-£35 4 courses (minimum 2). **Service** 12.5%. **Credit** AmEx, MC, V.

If reviews were based entirely on style, Sugar Hut probably would be the best Thai restaurant in London. Sadly, style rather wins out over content, though this is still an impressive place to take a first date. Full of moody lanterns and flickering candles, the interior looks like a Thai summer palace that has collided with a Moroccan kasbah. Islamic tiles are juxtaposed with Thai Buddhas on the walls, and the pre-dinner bar has upholstered divans where you can sip on a Mai Tai or puff on a scented hookah. As for the food – a secondary consideration for many – the house chicken satay was up to the mark, and the larb (spicy chicken salad) had rich flavours of fresh coriander. However, mains were less memorable. The tom yam soup was flat and insipid, and the pad Thai was only so-so. Beef penang curry was an improvement, though closer to a Malaysian rendang than the authentic Thai article. So, bring someone you want to impress, and concentrate on the ambience and drinks menu instead of the food.
Babies and children admitted. Booking advisable weekends. Dress: smart casual. Entertainment: musicians 9pm Sun. Vegetarian menu. **Map 13 A13**.

Putney SW15

Thai Square
Embankment, 2 Lower Richmond Road, SW15 1LB (8780 1811/www.thaisq.com). Putney Bridge tube/14, 22 bus.

Bar **Open/snacks served** noon-midnight Mon-Thur; noon-2am Fri, Sat; noon-10.30pm Sun.
Restaurant **Lunch served** noon-2pm daily. **Dinner served** 5.30-11pm Mon-Sat; 5.30-10.30pm Sun. **Main courses** £7-£20. **Set dinner** £25 per person (minimum 2) 3 courses; £30 per person (minimum 2) 4 courses. **Service** 12.5%.
Both **Credit** MC, V.

Former fine-dining establishment Putney Bridge has gone all oriental: the space is now the flagship of restaurant chain Thai Square. Architecturally, it's impressive: a wave-like white wall leads up from the ground-floor bar to the split-level dining area, where floor-to-ceiling windows offer views over the Thames (still the ideal place from which to watch the start of the Boat Race). A touch of the East comes in the form of a striking gold Buddha, huge floral arrangements, ancient bells by the entrance, and waitresses in traditional silk garments. Multicoloured lighting adds drama in the evening. A shame, then, that the food doesn't live up to the setting. The long menu offers all the Thai standards – fish cakes, assorted curries, pad Thai, green papaya salad and so on – plus a few more unusual creations; all competently cooked but no better than in any decent neighbourhood Thai. Although tasty enough, green curry with prawns was too thin and lacking in crustaceans; best was crispy black cod with a sweetish, fiery topping of chilli and garlic. Dishes also arrived alarmingly quickly, suggesting a production-line approach in the kitchen; a feeling reinforced by the solicitous but uncoordinated army of staff (we were asked by three separate waitresses if we wanted drinks). What a waste: it could be so much more special.
Babies and children welcome: high chairs. Disabled: lift; toilet. No-smoking tables. Separate room for parties, seats 70. Takeaway service. Vegetarian menu.
For branches (Thai Square, Thai Pot) see index.

South East
Blackheath SE3

★ Laicram
*1 Blackheath Grove, SE3 0DD (8852 4710).
Blackheath rail.* **Lunch served** noon-2.30pm,
dinner served 6-11pm Tue-Sun. **Main
courses** £4.50-£13.90. **Service** 10%.
Credit AmEx, MC, V.
One of those neighbourhood Thais that look as if
they might once have been Italian bistros, Laicram
keeps Blackheath supplied with red curry and pad
Thai. Inside, it's all very homely, with pebble-dash
walls, framed prints of Thai royalty and a wooden
trellis on the ceiling. The place can get pretty busy,
but staff stay on top of things and everything we
ordered arrived on cue. To test the mainstream
Thai menu, we ordered tod mun pla – elegantly
spiced fish cakes, let down by a vinegary dipping
sauce. However, the red-hot yam nua (beef and
chilli salad) was marvellous: holy basil, hot slivers
of chilli and sliced lemongrass providing
wonderful depth of flavour. Mains were also right
on the button: a fiery, coconut-free jungle curry
served on a miniature charcoal brazier; and an
excellent weeping tiger (don't be put off by the
name, it's a char-grilled steak, marinated in spices,
sliced thinly and served with a sweet dipping
sauce). Paying by credit card was held up by
technical difficulties (it seemed this wasn't
unusual), but we left feeling full and satisfied.
*Babies and children admitted (until 8pm).
Booking essential Fri, Sat. Takeaway service.
Vegetarian menu.*

London Bridge & Borough SE1

Kwan Thai
*The Riverfront, Hay's Galleria, Tooley Street, SE1
2HD (7403 7373/www.kwanthairestaurant.co.uk).
London Bridge tube/rail.* **Lunch served**
11.30am-3pm Mon-Fri. **Dinner served** 6-10pm
Mon-Sat. **Main courses** £8-£14. **Set lunch**
£7.95-£8.95 2 courses. **Set dinner** £20-£28 per
person (minimum 2) 3 courses. **Credit** AmEx,
DC, MC, V.
Elegant and sophisticated, Kwan Thai is where
South Bank executives take clients they want to
impress. Overlooking the Thames from the back of
Hay's Galleria arcade, the restaurant is styled like
a colonial mansion, with framed Thai paintings on
the walls. Fitting the colonial mood, starched
napkins are placed on your lap as soon as you sit
down. The menu covers familiar ground for an
upmarket Thai restaurant, but portions are
generous and the food is artfully prepared. We hit
the jackpot with the moist, tender pork satay – one
of the best in London. Tasty, but less outstanding,
were the toon tong or 'golden balls', deep-fried
parcels of wun tun pastry filled with minced
chicken, prawns and garlic. Of the mains, the yam
nua (a spicy salad of char-grilled beef tossed with
chillies, mint, tomatoes and sweet lime dressing)
was delicious, but let down slightly by the use of
iceberg lettuce instead of Thai greens. Despite the
high quality of the food, the lunchtime service was
indifferent. A smile would have added a lot to our
dining experience.
*Babies and children welcome: high chairs. Booking
advisable. No-smoking tables. Tables outdoors (20,
riverside terrace). Takeaway service. Vegetarian
menu.* **Map 12 Q8**.

New Cross SE14

★ Thailand
*15 Lewisham Way, SE14 6PP (8691 4040).
New Cross or New Cross Gate tube/rail.* **Lunch
served** noon-2.30pm Mon-Fri. **Dinner served**
5-11.30pm daily. **Main courses** £4.95-£10.
Set meal (noon-2.30pm, 5-7pm) £3.95 2 courses;
£10 2 courses and glass of wine. **Credit** MC, V.
Busy, cheap and authentic, Thailand is a dream
come true for students across the road at
Goldsmiths College. From noon to 2.30pm and 5pm
to 7pm, you can dine on authentic Thai classics

Menu

We've tried to give the most useful
Thai food terms here, including variant
spellings. However, these are no more
than English transliterations of the
original Thai script, and so are subject
to considerable variation. Word
divisions vary as well: thus, kwaitiew,
kwai teo and guey teow are all
acceptable spellings for noodles.

USEFUL TERMS
Khantoke: originally a north-eastern
banquet conducted around a low table
while seated on traditional triangular
cushions – some restaurants have
khantoke seating.
Khing: with ginger.
Op or **ob:** baked.
Pad, pat or **phad:** stir-fried.
Pet or **ped:** hot (spicy).
Prik: chilli.
Tod, tort, tord or **taud:** deep-fried.
Tom: boiled.

STARTERS
Khanom jeep or **ka nom geeb:** dim
sum. Little dumplings of minced pork,
bamboo shoots and water chestnuts,
wrapped in an egg and rice (wun tun)
pastry, then steamed.
Khanom pang na koong: prawn
sesame toast.
Kratong thong: tiny crispy batter cups
('top hats') filled with mixed vegetables
and/or minced meat.
Miang: savoury appetisers with a
variety of constituents (mince, ginger,
peanuts, roasted coconut, for instance),
wrapped in betel leaves.
Popia or **porpia:** spring rolls.
Tod mun pla or **tauk manpla:** small
fried fish cakes (should be lightly
rubbery in consistency) with virtually
no 'fishy' smell or taste.

SOUPS
Poh tak or **tom yam potag:** hot and
sour mixed seafood soup, sometimes
kept simmering in a Chinese
'steamboat' dish.
Tom kha gai or **gai tom kar:** hot and
sour chicken soup with coconut milk.
Tom yam or **tom yum:** a hot and sour
consommé-like soup, smelling of
lemongrass. **Tom yam koong** is with
prawns; **tom yam gai** with chicken;
tom yam hed with mushrooms.

RICE
Khao, kow or **khow:** rice.
Khao nao: sticky rice, from the
north-east.
Khao pat: fried rice.
Khao suay: steamed rice.
Pat khai: egg-fried rice.

SALADS
Laab or **larb:** minced and cooked meat
incorporating lime juice and other
ingredients like ground rice and herbs.
Som tam: a popular cold salad of
grated green papaya.
Yam or **yum:** refers to any tossed salad,
hot or cold, but it is often hot and sour,
flavoured with lemon and chilli. This

type of yam is originally from the north-
east of Thailand, where the Laotian
influence is greatest.
Yam nua: hot and sour beef salad.
Yam talay: hot and sour seafood salad
(served cold).

NOODLES
Generally speaking, noodles are eaten
in greater quantities in the north of
Thailand. There are many types of
kwaitiew or **guey teow** noodles.
Common ones include **sen mee:** rice
vermicelli; **sen yai** (river rice noodles):
a broad, flat, rice noodle; **sen lek:** a
medium flat noodle, used to make pad
Thai; **ba mee:** egg noodles; and **woon
sen** (cellophane noodle): transparent
vermicelli made from soy beans or
other pulses. These are often prepared
as stir-fries.
The names of the numerous noodle
dishes depend on the combination of
other ingredients. Common dishes are:
Khao soi: chicken curry soup with egg
noodles; a Burmese/Thai dish,
sometimes referred to as the national
dish of Burma.
Mee krob or **mee grob:** sweet crispy
fried vermicelli.
Pad si-ewe or **cee eaw:** noodles fried
with mixed meat in soy sauce.
Pad Thai: stir-fried noodles with
shrimps (or chicken and pork),
beansprouts and salted turnips,
garnished with ground peanuts.

CURRIES
Thai curries differ quite markedly from
the Indian varieties. Thais cook them
for a shorter time, and use thinner
sauces. Flavours and ingredients
are different too. There are several
common types of curry paste; these
are used to name the curry, with the
principal ingredients listed thereafter.
Gaeng, kaeng or **gang:** the generic
name for curry. Yellow curry is the
mildest; green curry (**gaeng keaw wan**
or **kiew warn**) is medium hot and uses
green chillies; red curry (**gaeng pet**)
is similar, but uses red chillies.
Jungle curry: often the hottest of the
various curries, made with red curry
paste, bamboo shoots and just about
anything else to hand.
Massaman or **mussaman:** also known
as Muslim curry, because it originates
from the area along the border with
Malaysia where many Thais are
Muslims. For this reason, pork is never
used. It's a rich, but mild concoction,
with coconut, potato and some peanuts.
Penang, panaeng or **panang:** a dry,
aromatic curry made with 'Penang' curry
paste, coconut cream and holy basil.

FISH & SEAFOOD
Hoi: shellfish.
Hor mok talay or **haw mog talay:**
steamed egg mousse with seafood.
Koong, goong or **kung:** prawns.
Maw: dried fish belly.
Pla meuk: squid.

Local Thais

It was at the beginning of the 1990s that Thai food first gained widespread popularity in London. Yet unlike many other cuisines whose moment in the fashion limelight was brief and involved just a few West End restaurants, Thai cooking went out into the suburbs and beyond. The phenomenon of the 'neighbourhood Thai' took root.

Many of these restaurants formed a partnership with London boozers – a trend started in 1988 when the manager of the Churchill Arms on Kensington Church Street, who enjoyed holidaying in Thailand, recruited a Thai chef to cook in the pub. It was a big success, and other pubs in the same chain began offering Thai food too. Others followed suit. Perhaps the reason lay behind the link between spicy food and a healthy thirst; perhaps pub landlords wanted to provide their drinkers with an alternative to the 'local Indian'.

You won't find all the intricacies of first-rate Thai cuisine at these places, and ingredient-substitution is common, but the establishments listed below are reliable sources of an inexpensive meal where you can sample at least some of the zesty flavours of South-east Asia.

Ayudhya
14 Kingston Hill, Kingston upon Thames, Surrey KT2 7NH (8546 5878). Norbiton rail. **Lunch served** noon-2.30pm Tue-Sun. **Dinner served** 6.30-11pm Mon-Sat; 6.30-10.30pm Sun. **Main courses** £5.95-£9.95. **Set meal** £19.95 per person (minimum 2) 2 courses incl tea or coffee. **Credit** MC, V.
Babies and children admitted. Booking advisable. Separate rooms for parties, both seating 30. Takeaway service. Vegetarian menu.

Bangkok Room
756 Finchley Road, Temple Fortune, NW11 7TH (8731 7473/www.bangkokroom.co.uk). Golders Green tube. **Lunch served** noon-3pm, **dinner served** 6-11pm daily. **Main courses** £6.95-£7.95. **Set lunch** £3.50 vegetarian, £3.95 meat, £4.95 seafood, 1 course. **Set dinner** £15.95 3 courses incl tea or coffee; £18.95 4 courses incl tea or coffee. **Credit** AmEx, MC, V.
Babies and children welcome: high chairs. Booking advisable. Tables outdoors (4, courtyard). Takeaway service; delivery service (within 2-mile radius). Vegetarian menu.

Ben's Thai
Above the Warrington, 93 Warrington Crescent, W9 1EH (7266 3134). Maida Vale or Warwick Avenue tube. **Lunch served** noon-2.30pm, **dinner served** 6-10.30pm daily. **Main courses** £5-£7.50. **Set dinner** £13.95-£15.95 per person (minimum 2) 3 courses. **Service** 10%. **Credit** MC, V.
Babies and children welcome: high chairs. Booking advisable; essential dinner. No-smoking tables. Takeaway service. Vegetarian menu. **Map 1 C4**.

Churchill Thai Kitchen
Churchill Arms, 119 Kensington Church Street, W8 7LN (7792 1246). High Street Kensington or Notting Hill Gate tube.

Meals served noon-9.30pm daily. **Main courses** £5.85. **Credit** MC, V. *Babies and children admitted. Book evenings. No-smoking tables.* **Map 7 B7**.

Nid Ting
533 Holloway Road, N19 4BT (7263 0506). Archway or Holloway Road tube. **Dinner served** 6-11.15pm Mon-Sat; 6-10.15pm Sun. **Main courses** £4.25-£9.50. **Set dinner** £15 2 courses incl coffee. **Credit** AmEx, DC, JCB, MC, V. *Babies and children admitted. Booking essential Fri, Sat. Takeaway service. Vegetarian menu.* **Map 26 C2**.

Paolina
181 King's Cross Road, WC1X 9BZ (7278 8176). King's Cross tube/rail. **Lunch served** noon-3pm Mon-Fri. **Dinner served** 6-10pm Mon-Sat. **Main courses** £3.95-£7.90. **Set dinner** £11.95 2 courses. **Unlicensed. Corkage** 50p. **No credit cards.** *Babies and children admitted. Booking advisable dinner. Takeaway service. Vegetarian menu.* **Map 4 M3**.

Pepper Tree
19 Clapham Common Southside, SW4 7AB (7622 1758). Clapham Common tube. **Lunch served** noon-3pm Mon-Fri. **Dinner served** 6-10.30pm Mon; 6-11pm Tue-Fri. **Meals served** noon-11pm Sat; noon-10.30pm Sun. **Main courses** £4-£6. **Service** 10% for parties of 8 or more. **Credit** JCB, MC, V.
Babies and children welcome: high chairs. Bookings not accepted dinner. No smoking. Takeaway service. **Map 22 A2**.

Soho Thai
27-28 St Anne's Court, W1F 0BN (7287 2000). Tottenham Court Road tube. **Lunch served** noon-3pm, **dinner served** 6-11.30pm Mon-Sat. **Main courses** £5.95-£8.95. **Credit** AmEx, MC, V. *Booking essential weekends. No-smoking area. Takeaway service. Vegetarian menu.* **Map 17 K6**.

Talad Thai
320 Upper Richmond Road, SW15 6TL (8789 8084). Putney Bridge tube/Putney rail. **Lunch served** 11.30am-3pm, **dinner served** 5.30-10.30pm Mon-Sat. **Meals served** 12.30-8.30pm Sun. **Main courses** £4.50-£7.95. **Set lunch** £5.50 1 course. **Credit** MC, V.
Babies and children admitted. No-smoking tables. Separate room for parties, seats 50. Takeaway service.

Thai Metro
38 Charlotte Street, W1T 2NN (7436 4201/www.thaimetro-uk.com). Goodge Street tube. **Meals served** noon-11pm Mon-Thur; noon-11.30pm Fri; 1-11.30pm Sat; 1-10.30pm Sun. **Main courses** £5.50-£10.95. **Set lunch** £5.50 1 courses, £7.50 2 courses, £9.50 3 courses. **Service** 10%. **Credit** AmEx, MC, V. *Babies and children admitted. Booking advisable. Tables outdoors (7, pavement). Takeaway service. Vegetarian menu.* **Map 9 J5**.

Thai Café
12 Mason's Avenue, Harrow, Middx HA3 5AP (8427 5385). Harrow & Wealdstone tube/rail. **Dinner served** 6-11pm Tue-Sat. **Main courses** £4-£5. **Unlicensed. Corkage** no charge. **No credit cards.** *Babies and children admitted. Booking advisable Fri, Sat. No-smoking tables. Takeaway service. Vegetarian menu.*

such as red curry with chicken, and tom yum soup for just £3.95 for a starter and main course. In the evenings, the restaurant switches to a pricier menu highlighting food from the Esarn region, which borders Laos in north-east Thailand. It's worth sampling a few classic Esarn dishes like laab (hot and sour minced meat salad) and grilled fish with lemongrass. We joined the students at lunchtime for a bowl of chicken tom yum soup that was easily the match of anything on Bangkok's Khao San Road. This was followed by a convincing and satisfying plate of pad kraprao (chicken fried with fish sauce, chillies and holy basil), served on steamed rice. Food could have been spicier, but otherwise the flavours were spot-on. With speedy service, friendly staff and simple uncluttered decor, it all made for a relaxing lunch.
Babies and children admitted. Booking essential Fri, Sat. No smoking. Takeaway service; delivery service (within 3-mile radius). Vegetarian menu.

South Norwood SE25

★ ★ Mantanah
2 Orton Building, Portland Road, SE25 4UD (8771 1148/www.mantanah.co.uk). Norwood Junction rail. **Lunch served** noon-3pm, **dinner served** 6-11pm Tue-Sun. **Main courses** £5.75-£8.50. **Set dinner** £16 per person (minimum 2) 3 courses, £22 per person (minimum 2) 4 courses. **Credit** AmEx, DC, MC, V.
Hidden behind a modest façade on an ordinary suburban street, this looks like any other local Thai restaurant, but it has a rare culinary flair, particularly when it comes to vegetarian food. Familiar southern curries are joined by regional delicacies from northern and eastern Thailand and innovative vegetarian dishes made from aubergine, beancurd, green beans, jackfruit, mock chicken and banana blossom – all with quirky names. We plumped for a generous portion of chicken satay followed by 'pink lady', a sublime concoction of caramelised aubergine in a sweet curry sauce with intoxicating flavours of chilli, palm sugar and lime leaves. Presentation was delightful; dishes were garnished with fresh orchids and the tables were set with woven grass table mats, elegant Thai cutlery and embroidered silk napkins. You'd be lucky to find more interesting Thai vegetarian food anywhere else in London. To sample a range of what Mantanah has to offer, visit on Sunday for the dinner buffet.
Babies and children admitted. Booking advisable. Takeaway service; delivery service (within 2-mile radius). Vegetarian menu.

East
Docklands E14

Elephant Royale
Locke's Wharf, Westferry Road, E14 3AN (7987 7999/www.elephantroyale.com). Island Gardens DLR. **Lunch served** noon-3pm, **dinner served** 5.30-10.30pm Mon-Fri. **Meals served** noon-10.30pm Sat; noon-10pm Sun. **Main courses** £4.80-£19.50. **Set meal** £19.50-£27.50 4 courses. **Set buffet** (noon-4pm Sun) £14.50. **Service** 12.5%. **Credit** AmEx, DC, MC, V.
Looking out over the Thames at the tip of the Isle of Dogs, Elephant Royale could be accused of trading on its location, but the food is good and the dining room – full of Thai bronze sculptures and palms, with a gushing artificial stream – has a certain chintzy appeal. The restaurant offers a broad, pricey menu of familiar royal Thai dishes, with a few surprises like red scallop curry, and a good-value Sunday lunch buffet. Buffets don't always show restaurants at their best, but most dishes we tried were competently prepared. We kicked off with a decent mixed seafood tom yum and a pile of paper prawns: moist tiger prawns wrapped in thin pastry and deep fried. The chicken satay didn't excite, and the yellow curry was bland and oversweet, but the red duck curry and tangy chicken and mango salad were both exemplary. For dessert, fried bananas came in a light tempura batter dusted with coconut flakes, while the Thai sago was packed in a banana-leaf

Isarn

box topped with coconut cream. We served ourselves, but waiting staff seemed keen and alert.
Children admitted. Booking essential. Disabled: toilet. Entertainment: band 7pm Wed-Sat. No-smoking tables (Mon-Fri). Tables outdoors (19, patio). Takeaway service. Vegetarian menu.

North
Archway N19

★ Charuwan
110 Junction Road, N19 5LB (7263 1410). Archway or Tufnell Park tube. **Lunch served** noon-3pm Mon-Fri. **Dinner served** 6-11pm daily. **Main courses** £4.30-£8.95. **Set dinner** £18 per person (minimum 2) 4 courses. **Service** 10%. **Credit** AmEx, MC, V.
Charuwan is every inch the neighbourhood Thai, with gilded wood-carvings on the walls, faded posters from the Thai tourist board, and a tiny pagoda-roofed bar in the corner. It's undeniably cosy and the Thai family who run the place do their best to make diners welcome. They can be a bit overstretched at times – service is often very slow – but your patience will be rewarded with some extremely authentic-tasting Thai food. We

started with a bowl of intoxicatingly flavoursome tom yam soup, packed with lemongrass, straw mushrooms, chilli and lime. The Thai spare ribs were also well spiced; the bowl of lemon water for washing fingers was a nice touch. Mains kept up the pace; the massaman curry with new potatoes was mellow and delicious, with clearly defined flavours of roasted coconut and chilli. All else faded into insignificance with the arrival of the pla lad prik, deep-fried fillets of white fish topped with a sublime sweet chilli sauce, complemented by a pleasing house white. Enjoy, but allow plenty of time for the tardy service.
Booking advisable. Children over 5 years admitted. Takeaway service. Vegetarian menu. **Map 26 B2.**

Islington N1

★ Isarn NEW
2005 RUNNER-UP BEST CHEAP EATS
119 Upper Street, N1 1QP (7424 5153/ www.isarn.co.uk). Angel tube/Highbury & Islington tube/rail. **Lunch served** noon-3pm, **dinner served** 6-11pm Mon-Fri. **Meals served** noon-11pm Sat; noon-10.30pm Sun. **Main courses** £6-£12.50. **Service** 12.5%. **Credit** AmEx, MC, V.

The slight déjà vu you might experience when walking into this sexily designed new restaurant can be explained by the fact that it's owned by Alan Yau's sister – he's the man behind Hakkasan (*see p69*), Yauatcha (*see p72*) and the Busaba Eathai (*see p265*) restaurants. But that's not to say Isarn doesn't know its own mind. Every last detail, from the pink-clad staff and wonderfully stylised decor (witness the oversized lightshades that illuminate an immaculate tunnel of a room) to the tantalising pick 'n' mix approach to Thai food, is very much its own. How about the salad of soft-shell crab with mango, for example? Or a yellow curry of mussels with mangosteens? Although they might sound outlandish, the combinations of heat and sweet work a treat, and we especially like the chewy texture of the crab shells. Proper Thai ingredients are used too (morning glory, fresh peppercorn and the rest). Expect good versions of the usual curries (the green variety with monkfish is particularly impressive) and authentic spicing. Wonderful smoothies and a decent wine selection are on hand to put out any fires. Bound to be hit in N1.
Babies and children admitted. No smoking. Tables outdoors (2, garden). Takeaway service. **Map 5 O1.**

Turkish

Turkish cuisine is slowly but surely spreading throughout the capital as more and more people realise that this can be great food, unrelated to the greasy döners sold from vans to drunken pub-goers. In the cafés of Hackney and Green Lanes, ocakbaşı restaurants predominate – an ocakbaşı being a large open grill under an extractor hood. Grills are cooked in plain view in front of the diners. In London the term 'mangal', which traditionally refers to a smaller brazier, is used interchangeably with the word ocakbaşı.

The successful, modern-style **Tas** chain continues to expand, with new branches opening in the West End and Southwark, but the most recent developments seem to have occurred to the east around the edge of the City, where a cluster of restaurants such as **Dolma**, **Haz** and **Savarona** is pushing upmarket. Centres of excellence remain Dalston, Stoke Newington and Green Lanes for authentic food in the heart of London's Turkish and Kurdish communities, and nearby Islington with **İznik** and **Pasha**.

Central
Bloomsbury WC1

Tas

2005 RUNNER-UP BEST FAMILY RESTAURANT
22 Bloomsbury Street, WC1B 3QJ (7637 4555/ www.tasrestaurant.com). Holborn or Tottenham Court Road tube. **Meals served** noon-11pm Mon-Sat; noon-10.30pm Sun. **Main courses** £5.25-£14.45. **Set meal** £8.25-£9.95 per person (minimum 2) meze selection; £8.25 2 courses, £18.50 3 courses. **Service** 12.5%. **Credit** MC, V.
This large, bright new branch of the hit Anatolian mini chain is well placed for sustenance following a hike around the British Museum. Families love it. Like most other Tas branches, the furnishings are modern and rather chic (the exception being the Tas Pide outlets, which have a classically derived decor and specialise in Turkish pizza). Food is made for sharing, and baskets of own-made pide and pots of olives and houmous arrive as you sit down. There's a choice of four set menus, most of which include hot and cold meze: the likes of falafel, feta salad, börek, enginar, cacik, tabouleh and manca (spinach with yoghurt). Lamb or chicken shish kebabs can follow. At the Borough branch we've enjoyed a plentiful portion of midye corbasi (mussels with celery, coriander and ginger) and tasty grilled hellim; at the new EV in Southwark (a bar/restaurant/deli combo that includes some odd fusion dishes) we liked the main courses of 'oven-cooked lamb', served with smoky grilled aubergine and cheese purée, and a stew-like mixed seafood broth. Staff are friendly and happy to explain each dish. They're also generous with the puddings, such as baklava or mousse-filled chocolate cake.
Babies and children welcome: high chairs. Disabled: toilet. No smoking. Separate room for parties, seats 70. Tables outdoors (12, pavement). Takeaway service. **Map 10 K5.**
For branches (Tas, Tas Café, Tas Pide, EV Restaurant) see index.

City E1

Dolma NEW

157 Commercial Street, E1 6BJ (7456 1006/ www.dolmalondon.com). Liverpool Street tube/rail. **Meals served** noon-midnight Mon-Fri, Sun;

6pm-midnight Sat. **Main courses** £7.95-£13.95. **Set lunch** £7.95 2 courses. **Set meze** £7.95 8 dishes. **Set meal** (Sun) £13.95 3 courses. **Service** 12.5%. **Credit** MC, V.
Located not far from Brick Lane, Dolma seems to be aiming to attract an office crowd. In the currently fashionable style, walls and tablecloths are white, floorboards are stripped. The venue shows its upmarket ambitions in the form of leather chairs and fancy silver wall lamps with flame patterns. Despite the somewhat gushing menu, it retains many of the best features of local Turkish restaurants. Fine pide bread is replenished without customers having to ask. Starters of houmous kavurma (smooth houmous with oil, diced lamb and pine kernels) and sucuk (good spicy sausage with salad) couldn't be faulted. The list of main courses included well-rendered versions of standard dishes like kuzu guveç (stewed lamb with mixed peppers) along with slightly more unusual options such as kuskonmazli piliç (chicken breast with asparagus). The place has yet to develop much character of its own, but Dolma has the potential to shine in this area as one of a number of newish Turkish restaurants heading south towards the City and upmarket from Hackney.
Babies and children admitted. No-smoking tables. Tables outdoors (2, pavement). Takeaway service. **Map 12 R5.**

Haz NEW

9 Cutler Street, E1 7DJ (7929 7923/ www.hazrestaurant.com). Liverpool Street tube/rail. **Meals served** 11.30am-11.30pm daily. **Main courses** £7-£13. **Set meal** £7.95 2 courses, £17.95 3 courses incl coffee. **Set meze** £12.95. **Service** 12.5%. **Credit** MC, V.
In line with many modern City restaurants, Haz appears very impersonal. It resembles a well-appointed canteen, with lots of glass, wood and white paint, and large communal tables in rows across the room. A high white ceiling contains a bank of small spotlights. This is no place for an intimate date. Nevertheless, service was efficient and the food of an exceptional standard. High-quality bread and olives were brought instantly to our table. Zeytinyagli dolma (rice and pine nuts wrapped in a vine leaf) made a gloriously fresh and tasty starter, while houmous kavurma combined an over-smooth houmous with well-done strips of

lamb. To follow, kül basti, a tender lamb escalope with oregano and basmati rice, was excellent. We also relished the fener baligi (monkfish with pear): rich, beautiful and worth the indulgence. The house vegetables, spinach and potato, were lightly cooked to maintain their flavour. A wide variety of desserts includes the decadent Turkish favourite, armut tatlısı, and the less common variant, fig tatlısı. Haz is often busy, with a noisy, upmarket, City crowd. We recommend it.
Babies and children welcome: high chair. Booking advisable. Takeaway service. **Map 12 R6.**

Edgware Road W1

Safa

22-23 Nutford Place, W1H 5YH (7723 8331). Edgware Road or Marble Arch tube. **Meals served** noon-midnight daily. **Main courses** £7.50-£16. **Set meal** £10.50, £14.50 meat, £19.50 fish, 2 courses. **Service** 10%. **Credit** MC, V.
In an area famed for Middle Eastern restaurants, Safa combines Turkish and Iranian cuisine. Mirrors at the back make this relatively small restaurant appear larger, and there's a burbling water feature. Arayes was a pleasantly different starter: own-made pitta filled with minced lamb, pine nuts and spices. Patlıcan salad (grilled aubergine, with green pepper, onion and garlic) was also enjoyable. The outstanding feature of the starters, however, was the crispy, wafer-thin Iranian bread, cooked in an oven by the entrance. A main-course order for ucler kebab produced a mixed grill of lamb chops, chicken and lamb. The portion was large, but the meat could have been more moist. Ghormeh sabzi, an Iranian lamb stew with kidney beans, chives, parsley, spring onion and lime, is worth trying, but has a strong sour taste that won't suit everyone. Slightly too much saffron had been used in the saffron rice, taking the subtle edge off the flavour. An unequivocally wonderful dessert of muhallabia (milk pudding with pistachio and rosewater) made a fine end to the meal. Service was friendly and helpful. In general, Safa succeeds as a Turkish restaurant – and its Iranian dishes add variety.
Babies and children welcome: high chair. Booking advisable weekends. Restaurant available for hire. Tables outdoors (5, pavement). Takeaway service; delivery service. **Map 8 F5.**

Fitzrovia W1

Istanbul Meze

100 Cleveland Street, W1P 5DP (7387 0785/ www.istanbulmeze.co.uk). Great Portland Street or Warren Street tube. **Meals served** noon-11pm Mon-Thur; noon-midnight Fri, Sat. **Dinner served** 5-11pm Sun. **Main courses** £7-£12. **Set lunch** £7.90 2 courses. **Set dinner** £10.90 2 courses. **Set meal** £15 4 courses. **Credit** AmEx, MC, V.
As we were seated in the ground-floor restaurant, a large plate loaded with olives and pickled chillies arrived. Our meal proper began with soup of the day, mercimek, which had just the right thickness and slightly nutty lentil texture. We also sampled a börek, but this had a mismatch of texture between the ideal crisp exterior and the liquefied feta within. A main course of vegetarian melemen (vegetables with egg, tomato and a fair number of green chillies) is an unusual offering in London restaurants, and this was a fine rendition. Karni yarik presented chunks of finely diced lamb (rather than mince) within a meltingly soft aubergine. It was a pity, however, that these dishes were accompanied by dry pitta rather than soft pide. Service, from a Slovak waitress, was friendly and chatty. A few tables nestle on the pavement outside for warm-weather eating. In an area otherwise lacking good authentic Turkish locals, Istanbul Meze stands out.
Babies and children admitted. Booking advisable weekends. Separate room for parties, seats 40. Tables outdoors (4, pavement). Takeaway service. Vegetarian menu. **Map 3 J4.**

RESTAURANTS

★ Özer

5 Langham Place, W1B 3DG (7323 0505/
www.sofra.co.uk). Oxford Circus tube.
Bar **Open** noon-11pm daily.
Restaurant **Meals served** noon-midnight daily.
Main courses £8.70-£15.70. **Set lunch** (noon-6pm) £7.95 2 courses. **Set dinner** (6-11pm) £10.95-£16.45 2 courses. **Service** 12.5%.
Both **Credit** AmEx, DC, MC, V.

Spacious and busy, with a bar at the front, Özer remains one of the premier Turkish restaurants in central London. The back wall is copper, the sides crimson, and a complicated metal lampshade sculpture dominates the ceiling. The menu is varied enough to suit a wide range of tastes, incorporating grills and stews, meat, fish and vegetarian dishes. The wine list includes French, Italian, New World and Turkish bottles. Good plump olives are brought to the table as you deliberate. To start, lentil köfte was outstanding. The selection in the mixed börek platter was very pleasing too, though in appearance looked, oddly, like Chinese spring rolls. For mains, we couldn't fault the sea bream steak with salad. The unusual beef shish is well worth trying; it is served with rice, though you don't really need it – our basket of hot pide was replenished throughout the meal. Service is distant, but quick and efficient.
Babies and children welcome: children's menu; high chairs. Disabled: toilet. Tables outdoors (5, pavement). Takeaway service. **Map 9 H5**.

Marylebone W1

Grand Bazaar

42 James Street, W1N 5HS (7224 1544/
www.grand-bazaar.co.uk). Bond Street tube.
Meals served noon-11pm Mon-Thur, Sun; noon-midnight Fri, Sat. **Main courses** £9-£10.
Set lunch £6.50 2 courses. **Set dinner** £8.95 mixed meze. **Credit** AmEx, MC, V.

On a street where the pavement has been colonised by tables from various restaurants, Grand Bazaar has its own outside area next to its distinctive purple frontage. Venture into the dark interior and you're confronted by a sparkling vista of lamps and incense burners hanging from the ceiling. Starters of houmous kavurma (houmous with pine nuts and shards of lamb) and sucuk izgara (grilled slices of spicy sausage) are both worth trying. Cheekily, pide bread is charged as an extra, even with a dip starter such as houmous; this would be seen as bizarre in most Turkish cafés. A good range of grills and stews, including vegetarian dishes, is offered for main courses. Grand Bazaar also serves both standard pizza and Turkish pizza. The '42 James Street special' contained a decent selection of meat, while the iskender was hearty and filling. Service was boisterous rather than efficient, and our request for water was forgotten. Tables are too small and the atmosphere too smoky, but Grand Bazaar brings some of the bustle of a local restaurant to the West End.
Babies and children welcome: high chairs. Booking advisable. Tables outdoors (16, pavement). Takeaway service. **Map 9 G6**.

Mayfair W1

Sofra

18 Shepherd Street, W1Y 7HU (7493 3320/
www.sofra.co.uk). Green Park tube. **Meals served** noon-11pm daily. **Main courses** £8.45-£15.95. **Set meze** (noon-6pm) £9.95; (6-11pm) £12.95. **Set lunch** (noon-6pm) £6.95-£8.95 2 courses. **Set dinner** (6-11pm) £9.95-£11.95 2 courses. **Cover** £1.50. **Service** 12.5%.
Credit AmEx, MC, V.

White decor is favoured at Sofra (in the paintwork, tiles and tablecloths). Wide windows look out over Shepherd Market, but if the place gets busy you might find yourself in the less salubrious basement. Complimentary houmous and high-quality olives arrive with a basket of fresh pide. A starter of baba ganoush (puréed aubergine) was well textured and smoky. Unusually, but fittingly, a crisp börek came with sweet 'Thai' sauce. For mains, mixed kebab gives a flavour of the grills offered, including köfte, lamb shish and tavuk

EV, part of the **Tas** chain

"Our main courses were both excellent. We shared a perfectly tender 'oven cooked lamb', served on a bed of very smoky grilled aubergine and cheese puree, and a stew like mixed seafood broth"

"It isn't what you'd expect from a traditional Turkish restaurant... it has many adventurous dishes, even oriental ingredients."

"It's beautifully run, thoroughly professional and the inventive modern Turkish food is delicious. imaginative and keenly priced"
- *Time Out Eating & Drinking Guide*

"A simple formula well executed is the consensus on this vibrant Turkish spot in Waterloo that's something of a jewel, with friendly staff serving interesting cooking (including a great vegetarian selection) at reasonable prices. Best of all, despite being very popular, it manages to keep it's feet on the ground"
- *Zagat Survey*

Tas Restaurant
72 Borough High Street,
SE1 1XF

Tel : 020 7403 7200
Tel : 020 7403 7277
Fax : 020 7403 7022

Tas Café
76 Borough High Street
SE1 1QF

Tel : 020 7403 8557
Fax : 020 7403 8559

Tas Restaurant
37 Farringdon Road
EC1M 3JB

Tel : 020 7430 9721
Tel : 020 7430 9722
Fax : 020 7430 9723

Tas Restaurant
22 Bloomsbury
WC1 B 3QJ

Tel : 020 7637 4555
Tel : 020 7637 1333
Fax : 020 7637 2226

Tas Restaurant
33 The Cut, Waterloo
SE1 8LF

Tel : 020 7928 1444
Tel : 020 7928 2111
Fax : 020 7633 9686

Tas Pide
20-22 New Globe Walk
SE1 9DR

Tel : 020 7928 3300
Tel : 020 7633 977
Fax : 020 7261 1166

EV Restaurant/Bar/Delicatessen

97/98 Isabella Street
London SE1 8DA

Tel: 020 7620 6191
020 7620 6192
Fax: 020 7620 6193

shish. All the meat is tender, and served with salad and rice. By contrast, a vegetarian dish of 'Silk Road vegetables' verged on the underdone. Nevertheless, all the ingredients are of a high standard. The selection of Turkish desserts is also worth noting. The once unstoppable expansion of the chain has halted, but there are still four branches, very similar to this original. Sofra deserves its reputation, but currently appears to be treading water. A little more direction would be appreciated.
Babies and children welcome: high chairs. Booking advisable. Separate room for parties, seats 14. Tables outdoors (10, pavement). Takeaway service. Vegetarian menu. **Map 9 H8.**
For branches see index.

West

Bayswater W2

Shish

71-75 Bishops Bridge Road, W2 6BG (7229 7300/www.shish.com). Bayswater or Royal Oak tube. **Meals served** 11.30am-11.30pm Mon-Fri; 10.30am-10.30pm Sat, Sun. **Main courses** £3.95-£8.45. **Set meal** (until 7pm) £7.95 2 courses incl glass of wine or beer. **Service** 12.5%. **Credit** MC, V.
This is the third branch of Shish, which terms itself a Silk Road restaurant and covers food from Turkey to Indonesia. It's very much like the others in Willesden and Shoreditch. The standard menu is augmented by a changing seasonal list that highlights a particular cuisine, Turkish on our visit. There's a sensible kids' menu and also an excellent juice bar; try the striped mixed fruit juice. Water pumps (£1.25 a head for unlimited still or sparkling water) dominate the long bar. Onion in pomegranate sauce (from the Turkish menu) was a bland first course; conversely, duck börek was too strongly flavoured. A tray with four types of bread was brought, but there's an extra charge for this and, like much here, you get the feeling Shish is trying too hard for diversity. For mains, we enjoyed an excellent apricot chicken with ginger on an enormous bed of basmati rice. The daily fish special (also from the seasonal menu) was a tasty tilapia. However, the waiter's 'Are you enjoying the meal?' was somewhat perfunctory. While much of the food is interesting and worth sampling, large, jolly photos of street vendors along the Silk Road only add to the impersonal, canteen-like feel.
Babies and children welcome: children's menu; crayons; high chairs. Disabled: toilet. Tables outdoors (4, pavement). Takeaway service. **Map 7 C6.**
For branches see index.

Notting Hill W11

Manzara

24 Pembridge Road, W11 3HL (7727 3062). Notting Hill Gate tube. **Breakfast served** 9am-noon, **lunch served** noon-6pm, **dinner served** 6-11.30pm daily. **Main courses** £6.75-£9.85. **No credit cards.**
Though it calls itself Mediterranean, the core of Manzara's menu is Turkish. That doesn't stop it serving organic beefburgers or a wide range of cakes and gateaux. A small wine list is also provided (organic wine is still promised, as it has been for more than a year). A very spicy aubergine dip got our meal off to a good start, though the aubergine chunks were cut too large for the dish to work as a dip (they went down very well with a fork, however). A main course of spicy lamb with yoghurt mixed shish with adana in a spicy but rather Italian-influenced tomato sauce. There is room for improvement: bright turquoise cloths cover fast-food-style tables, which are uncomfortable for a long stay; and pitta is served instead of pide bread (although a fine selection of pide pizzas is offered too). Although not worth a long journey, Manzara is a reliable neighbourhood restaurant.
Babies and children welcome: high chairs. Restaurant available for hire. Tables outside (2, pavement). Takeaway service. **Map 7 A7.**

West Kensington W14

★ Best Mangal

104 North End Road, W14 9EX (7610 1050/ www.londraturk.com). West Kensington tube. **Meals served** noon-midnight daily. **Main courses** £7.50-£16.50. **Set meal** £16 2 courses, £18 3 courses, incl soft drink. **Credit** MC, V.
Behind the narrow entrance of a busy takeaway, a fine ocakbaşı restaurant does brisk business. It's popular with locals, who like the friendly service and hearty, no-nonsense Turkish food. Best Mangal is good at the basics, and in this case that means grills. For example, the çöp şiş provides three skewers of small tender lamb cubes and a pleasing salad, with lots of lettuce and red cabbage. Yet the emphasis on grills doesn't mean that other dishes should be ignored. A starter of ıspanak tarator consisted of deliciously thick yoghurt combined with very fresh spinach. This is served with saç bread as well as fresh pide. Desserts are limited, but the baklava is a fine example of the genre. The staff are friendly and seem to know the regular customers. Another branch of Best Mangal sits further along the street at No.66: it's slightly plusher, but cast from the same mould.
Babies and children welcome: high chairs. Booking advisable. Takeaway service. Vegetarian menu. **For branch see index.**

South West

Southfields SW18

★ Kazans

607-609 Garratt Lane, SW18 4SU (8739 0055/ www.kazans.com). Earlsfield rail/44, 77, 270 bus. **Dinner served** 6-11pm Mon-Fri. **Meals served** 11am-11pm Sat, Sun. **Main courses** £6.50-£12.95. **Credit** AmEx, MC, V.
When it opened, Kazans seemed as if it was positively embarrassed about being a Turkish restaurant. Thankfully, it has overcome this shyness and now proudly displays its Turkish dishes. It is right to do so, as the cooking too has become more confident. Enginar made a beautiful opening to our meal, the lemon and broad beans complementing the artichoke nicely. Shaktuka looked like tuna salad, but was a delicious, light mix of aubergine and tomato. A main course of adana kebab was delightfully fresh and spicy, served with rice. İncik lamb knuckle fell off the bone on to its soft, tasty bed of mashed potato. Though pitta rather than pide is served, Kazans provides more adventurous Turkish wines than the average, such as Angora cabernet sauvignon. The front opens on to Garratt Lane, which is noisy and not ideal for outside dining. Our only complaint concerned our forgetful, rather confused waiter, but with reminders we got everything requested. Well worth visiting.
Babies and children welcome: high chairs. Booking advisable weekends. Disabled: toilet. Separate rooms for parties, seating 30 and 50. Tables outdoors (4, pavement). Takeaway service.

South

Battersea SW11

Adalar

50 Battersea Park Road, SW11 4GP (7627 2052). Battersea Park or Queenstown Road rail. **Meals served** noon-11.30pm Mon-Sat. **Main courses** £7.50-£8.50. **Set dinner** £14.25 per person (minimum 2) 3 courses incl coffee. **Credit** MC, V.
Adalar was very quiet on our evening visit. The name means archipelago, but the restaurant remains very much on its own in this area of London. Our starters were delicious: kavun (half a ripe galia melon) and dolma (freshly made, thick vine leaves stuffed with rice and lamb mince). Perhaps it is Adalar's isolation from other Turkish restaurants that means pitta is served rather than pide. A vegetarian moussaka made an excellent main course, coming with a fine selection of vegetables – but as the only vegetarian choice it needed to be good. For omnivores, kuzu shish is well worth trying; though this is a standard dish,

the lightly cooked herby taste of the lamb was a pleasure to savour. A selection of desserts is displayed on a trolley; we can recommend the baklava. Adalar has an enjoyable atmosphere for a quiet night out, and we're always surprised that it isn't busier. Though the restaurant is not cheap for a local, meals are currently half-price on Thursday, Friday and Saturday.
Babies and children welcome: high chairs. Booking advisable weekends. Separate room for parties, seats 30.

South East

Lewisham SE4

★ Meze Mangal **NEW**

245 Lewisham Way, SE4 1XF (8694 8099). Lewisham or St John's rail. **Meals served** noon-2am daily. **Main courses** £7-£14. **Set meze** £10 per person (minimum 2), £14.50 per person (minimum 4). **Credit** MC, V.
The menu at Meze Mangal is relatively limited, but contains a fair range of basic Turkish grills, alongside pide pizzas and vegetarian dishes. A generous portion of houmous made an enjoyable starter, especially as it is served here with hot sliced pide. Pirzola (lamb chops) came with a tasty, large chopped salad, dominated by fresh red cabbage; the meat consisted of four perfectly done chops, with a rich grilled flavour. They were accompanied by saç bread, but no rice. However, considering the plentiful supply of bread (which, pleasingly, is replenished whenever needed), and the accompanying salad, rice is not missed. The restaurant has simply decorated walls, thick pink tablecloths and a wooden ceiling. It obviously aims at being a cut above the average caff: somewhere to linger and savour a meal. This is a Turkish local in a district that's something of a wasteland for good Turkish food. It deserves to thrive.
Babies and children welcome: high chair. Takeaway service.

East

Shoreditch EC2

★ Savarona **NEW**

68 Great Eastern Street, EC2A 3JT (7739 2888/ www.savarona.co.uk). Old Street tube/rail. **Meals served** 11am-midnight daily. **Set lunch** £11.95 2 courses, £13.95 3 courses. **Set meal** £12.99-£20.99 10 dishes. **Service** 12.5%. **Credit** AmEx, MC, V.
Walk into this smart newcomer in the heart of Shoreditch and you're in the bar, which offers a wide array of spirits (including superior Tekirdig raki), cocktails and cigars. Leather seats with metallic screens, suggesting Ottoman opulence, decorate both the bar and the basement restaurant. Once you're seated at your table, a porcelain 'boat' filled with fat olives arrives, along with small loaves of warm, plump pide. The Turkish wine list includes much smoother varieties than you'll find elsewhere in Britain; try a Kave special reserve red. For starters, patlıcan salatası (grilled aubergine with tahini, yoghurt and lemon) was quite beautiful. Karisik sigara böregi (filo pastry with feta cheese) was also perfectly done, with a light, crisp, crumbling exterior. Some less well-known dishes figure among the main courses. Nar eksili karisik dolma comprised aubergine, courgette and pepper stuffed with rice and minced lamb, in a richly flavoured gravy, including sour pomegranate sauce. For an intense taste sensation, try uskumru dolmasi: mackerel stuffed with onions, walnuts, pine nuts and blackcurrants, deep-fried in breadcrumbs. Service is, if anything, over-attentive.
Babies and children admitted. Disabled: toilet. No-smoking tables. **Map 6 Q4.**

North East

From Dalston Kingsland rail station up the A10 to Stoke Newington Church Street, you are in the Turkish and Kurdish heart of Hackney. The food available on this strip is more authentic and varied than anywhere else in London. Intense competition means that restaurants and cafés come and go at dizzying speed, and there's a constant race to provide different services and dishes. A few years ago the bread with your meal would usually be bought in from Turkish bakers; now many of the best restaurants cook their own varieties in-house.

None of the following gets a full review, but only because the area is a cornucopia of choice: **Çitir Tantuni** (23 Stoke Newington Road), for tantuni, currently fashionable fried lamb in saç; **Dervish Bistro** (15 Stoke Newington Church Street); **Sölen** (84 Stoke Newington High Street); **Tava** (17 Stoke Newington Road), for guveç; **Testi** (36 Stoke Newington High Street); and **Turku** (79 Stoke Newington Road), for meze with folk music. Also, keep an eye open for the ever-popular **Best Turkish Kebab** (125 Stoke Newington Road), and the longer-established **Ali Baba** (144 Kingsland High Street), both superior versions of the English Turkish takeaway, and the pâtisserie **Öz Antepliler** (30 Stoke Newington Road), which sells perfect baklava.

Dalston E8, N16

Istanbul Iskembecisi
9 Stoke Newington Road, N16 8BH (7254 7291). Dalston Kingsland rail/76, 149, 243 bus. **Meals served** noon-5am daily. **Main courses** £6.50-£9.95. **Set lunch** (noon-5pm) £5 2 courses. **Set meal** (5pm-5am) £9.50 2 courses. **Credit** MC, V.
The lengthy menu ranges from the tripe soup that gives the restaurant its name (which translates as Istanbul Tripe House) through to a varied choice of vegetarian dishes. A starter of dolma looked soggy, which is usually a bad sign, but it had a fine flavour. Yoğhurtlu patlıcan (aubergine paste) was excellent, and came with wonderful pide. To follow, try the islim kebab. Chunks of lamb are wrapped in strips of aubergine and baked; the result resembles a mini Christmas pudding. Mücver, usually a starter, is also offered as a main course; though it is accompanied by an enormous green salad, it is still just mücver, which is fine if you like courgette patties (and these are commendable versions). Istanbul Iskembecisi's vaguely Regency look remains, along with the very late-night opening hours, but the place is not as far ahead of the pack as it once was. Other local eateries now have more consistently executed if less varied menus.
Babies and children welcome: high chairs. Book Fri, Sat. Takeaway service. **Map 25 B4**.

★ Mangal II
4 Stoke Newington Road, N16 8BH (7254 7888). Stoke Newington rail/76, 149, 243 bus. **Meals served** noon-1am daily. **Main courses** £7-£12. **Set meal** £14.50 per person (minimum 2) 2 courses. **No credit cards**.
A step upmarket from the rather spartan original Mangal café round the corner, and the Mangal Turkish pizza shop across the way (No.27 Stoke Newington Road) – which each remain excellent in their way – Mangal II is one of the area's favourite local restaurants. It remains casual enough to be filled with Turkish families eating out on a Sunday afternoon. To start, we can vouch for both the tender arnavut ciğeri (served with onion), and the well-textured, richly flavoured patlıcan esme. Starters are accompanied by two kinds of bread, pide and saç. Unusually for Mangal, the pide on this visit was slightly lacklustre and not warmed; a few years ago this would have passed without comment, but in the current Dalston climate excellent pide has become de rigueur. To follow, the distinctive gamey taste of bıldırcın (quail) made it worth braving the fiddly bones. Lokma kebab also stood out: very tender medallions of fillet lamb held together with a cocktail stick. Mangal II is

Savarona. See p275.

Menu

It's useful to know that in Turkish 'ç' and 'ş' are pronounced 'ch' and 'sh'. So şiş is correct Turkish, shish is English and sis is common on menus. Menu spelling is rarely consistent, so expect wild variations on everything given here. See also the menu boxes in **Middle Eastern** and **North African**.

COOKING EQUIPMENT
Mangal: brazier.
Ocakbaşı: an open grill under an extractor hood. A metal dome is put over the charcoal for making paper-thin bread.

SOUPS
İşkembe: finely chopped tripe soup, an infallible hangover cure.
Mercimek çorbar: red lentil soup.
Yayla: yoghurt and rice soup (usually) with a chicken stock base.

MEZE DISHES
Arnavut ciğeri: 'albanian liver' – cubed or sliced lamb's liver, fried then baked.
Barbunya: spicy kidney bean stew.
Börek or **böreği:** fried or baked filo pastry parcels with a savoury filling, usually cheese, spinach or meat. Commonest are **muska** or **peynirli** (cheese) and **sigara** ('cigarette', so long and thin).
Cacik: diced cucumber with garlic in yoghurt.
Çoban salatası: 'shepherd's' salad of finely diced tomatoes, cucumbers, onions, perhaps green peppers and parsley, sometimes with a little feta cheese.
Dolma: stuffed vegetables (usually with rice and pine kernels).
Enginar: artichokes, usually with vegetables in olive oil.
Haydari: yoghurt, infused with garlic and mixed with finely chopped mint leaves.
Hellim: Cypriot halloumi cheese.
Houmous: creamy paste of chickpeas, crushed sesame seeds, oil, garlic and lemon juice.
Houmous kavurma: houmous topped with strips of lamb and pine nuts.
İmam bayıldı: literally 'the imam fainted'; aubergine stuffed with onions, tomatoes and garlic in olive oil.
Ispanak: spinach.
Kalamar: fried squid.
Karides: prawns.

Kısır: usually a mix of chopped parsley, tomatoes, onions, crushed wheat, olive oil and lemon juice.
Kizartma: lightly fried vegetables.
Köy ekmeği: literally 'village bread'; another term for saç (qv).
Lahmacun: 'pizza' of minced lamb on thin pide (qv).
Midye tava: mussels in batter, in a garlic sauce.
Mücver: courgette and feta fritters.
Patlıcan: aubergine, variously served.
Patlıcan esme: grilled aubergine puréed with garlic and olive oil.
Pide: a term encompassing many varieties of Turkish flatbread. It also refers to Turkish pizzas (heavier and more filling than lahmacun, qv).
Pilaki: usually haricot beans in olive oil, but the name refers to the method of cooking not the content.
Piyaz: white bean salad with onions.
Saç: paper-thin, chewy bread prepared on a metal dome (also called saç) over a charcoal grill.
Sucuk: spicy sausage, usually beef, less often lamb.
Tarama: cod's roe paste.
Tarator: a bread, garlic and walnut mixture; **havuç tarator** adds carrot; **ıspanak tarator** adds spinach.
Yaprak dolması: stuffed vine leaves.
Zeytin: olive.

MAIN COURSES
Alabalik: trout.
Balik: fish.
Güveç: stew, which is traditionally cooked in an earthenware pot.
Hünkar beğendi: cubes of lamb, braised with onions and tomatoes, served on an aubergine and cheese purée.
İçli köfte: balls of cracked bulgar wheat filled with spicy mince.
İncik: knuckle of lamb, slow-roasted in its own juices. Also called kléftico.
Karni yarik: aubergine stuffed with minced lamb and vegetables.
Kléftico: see íncik.
Mitite köfte: chilli meatballs.
Sote: meat (usually), sautéed in tomato, onion and pepper (and sometimes wine).
Uskumru: mackerel.

KEBABS
Usually made with grilled lamb (those labelled **tavuk** or **piliç** are chicken), served with bread or rice and salad.

Common varieties include:
Adana: spicy mince.
Beyti: usually spicy mince and garlic, but sometimes best-end fillet.
Bıldırcın: quail.
Böbrek: kidneys.
Çöp şiş: small cubes of lamb.
Döner: slices of marinated lamb (sometimes mince) packed tightly with pieces of fat on a vertical rotisserie.
Halep: usually döner (qv) served over bread with a buttery tomato sauce.
İskender: a combination of döner (qv), tomato sauce, yoghurt and melted butter on bread.
Kaburga: spare ribs.
Kanat: chicken wings.
Köfte: mince mixed with spices, eggs and onions.
Külbastı: char-grilled fillet.
Lokma: 'mouthful' (beware, there's a dessert that has a similar name!) – boned fillet of lamb.
Patlıcan: mince and sliced aubergine.
Pirzola: lamb chops.
Şeftali: seasoned mince, wrapped in caul fat.
Şiş: cubes of marinated lamb.
Uykuluk: sweetbread.
Yoğhurtlu: meat over bread and yoghurt.

DESSERTS
Armut tatlısı: baked pears.
Ayva tatlısı: quince in syrup.
Baklava: filo pastry interleaved with minced pistachio nuts, almonds or walnuts, and covered in sugary syrup.
Kadayıf: cake made from shredded pastry dough, filled with syrup and nuts or cream.
Kazandibi: milk pudding, traditionally with very finely chopped chicken breast.
Kemel pasha: small round cakes soaked in honey.
Keşkül: milk pudding with almonds and coconut, topped with pistachios.
Lokum: turkish delight.
Sütlaç: rice pudding.

DRINKS
Ayran: a refreshing drink made with yoghurt.
Çay: tea.
Kahve (aka Turkish coffee): a tiny cup half full of sediment, half full of strong, rich, bitter coffee. Offered without sugar, medium or sweet.
Rakı: a spirit with an aniseed flavour.

usually busy with a mixed local crowd. Prices remain very reasonable, and the restaurant holds its own despite stiff competition.
Babies and children welcome: high chairs. Book weekends. No-smoking tables. Takeaway service. **Map 25 C4**.

Mangal Ocakbaşı
10 Arcola Street, E8 2DJ (7275 8981/ www.mangal1.com). Dalston Kingsland rail/76, 149, 243 bus. **Meals served** noon-midnight daily. **Main courses** £7-£12.50. **No credit cards.**
Mangal's legendary reputation is built on providing great grills. So, the drab surroundings, the workmanlike houmous offered as a starter, and the fact that it was only brought as a side dish with the main course – all can be forgiven. Pirzola

comprised beautiful lamb chops with some saç bread and a fresh mixed salad (a new development is the inclusion of gherkins). Tavuk beyti was fresh and garlicky (our only complaint being that we had ordered lamb, not chicken). The meal was served with good hot pide. Behind his grill, the cook was forming a great mountain of beyti ingredients into kebabs, giving some idea of how many orders this place gets through in a day. Mangal knows its role and performs it well, but service could be less confused (as well as a delayed starter and one wrong dish for mains, our tea was forgotten). The fact that the restaurant was packed suggests that punters are prepared to forget these shortcomings to enjoy the plentiful, authentic food.
Babies and children admitted. Book weekends. Takeaway service. **Map 25 C4**.

Hackney E8

★ Anatolia Ocakbaşı
253 Mare Street, E8 3NS (8986 2223). Hackney Central rail/48, 55, 253, 277, D6 bus. **Meals served** 11am-midnight daily. **Main courses** £4.50-£9.80. **Corkage** £3.50. **Credit** (£1.50 charge) MC, V.
The restaurant resembles a big open-plan café, with a popular takeaway at the front. It is worth visiting for the mixed cold meze alone, which offers 14 selections, all freshly made. Houmous and tarama are average, but the other meze are great. The only problem is that all the constituent parts are served on the same plate, so there's a tendency for them to blend into each other as warm pide bread is dipped and delicacies shared. Large portions continued

with the mains. A lamb külbasti consisted of an enormous slice of shoulder of lamb, prepared with herbs and grilled over charcoal. The meat was very tasty, but could have been more tender. The meat-oriented menu also contains steaks and burgers, as well as fish and Turkish pizzas; options for vegetarians are limited. It's pleasing to see a decent Turkish restaurant thriving in Hackney, away from the cluster in Dalston and Stoke Newington.
Babies and children admitted. Booking advisable weekends. Takeaway service. Vegetarian menu.

Newington Green N16

★ Beyti

113 Green Lanes, N16 9DA (7704 3165). Manor House tube then 141, 341 bus. **Meals served** noon-midnight daily. **Main courses** £4.50-£10. **No credit cards**.
At a time when many Turkish restaurants are losing any regional feel, Beyti keeps its own identity with a slightly different northern Anatolian selection. You'll also find beautiful hot bread here. Kalamar made a pleasantly tender starter, while mücver (courgette fritters) came bathed in yoghurt, accompanied by a chilli sauce. As with all of Beyti's dishes, the freshness is immediately noticeable. To follow, we sampled akçabat köfte (a delicately spiced Black Sea meatball speciality) and chicken yörük (chunks of chicken in a spicy 'devil's sauce'). The name means nomads' chicken, referring to the Turkomen of the northern region. The mustard-based sauce was good, but calling it 'devil's sauce' was something of an exaggeration. A selection of stews is available daily, and there's a good range of fish dishes too. Staff members are friendly and chatty. For aficionados jaded with the uniform menus of many otherwise excellent cafés, Beyti offers an intriguing alternative.
Babies and children admitted. Booking advisable. Restaurant available for hire. Tables outdoors (2, pavement). **Map 25 A3**.

★ Sariyer Balik

56 Green Lanes, N16 9NH (7275 7681). Manor House tube then 141, 341 bus. **Meals served** 5pm-1am daily. **Main courses** £6.50-£10. **No credit cards**.
Though easily missed, this fish restaurant has developed a wonderful reputation among those in the know. The tiny, black-painted interior gets ever more intimate as more dried fish and nautical

paintings are added to the mix; there are already fishing nets hanging from the ceiling. The mixed hot starters give a sense of the quality to come. Prawns in a rich chilli sauce accompany deep-fried mussels marinated in beer, and kalamar softened in vodka. The main course menu isn't long, and the fish listed are only available if the restaurant can get them fresh. Never mind: what is offered is always so well prepared that any worry about lack of choice is soon forgotten. Most dishes are char-grilled, but a wide range of flavours is achieved from the melt-in-the-mouth hamsi (anchovies), through the subtlety of sea bass to the rich taste of enormous tuna steaks. All are served with great chunks of warm bread and a large fresh salad. Nothing was over-fancy or pretentious; the food was simply perfect.
Babies and children welcome: high chairs. Booking advisable. Separate room for parties, seats 60. Takeaway service. **Map 25 A3**.

Stoke Newington N16

★ Bodrum Café

61 Stoke Newington High Street, N16 8EL (7254 6464). Stoke Newington rail/73, 76, 149, 243 bus. **Meals served** 7am-11pm daily. **Main courses** £5-£7.50. **Set lunch** £4.99 2 courses incl coffee. **No credit cards**.
A café known for its reliable English, Turkish and vegetarian breakfasts, Bodrum also serves full Turkish meals and excellent meze. A starter of kalamar arrived in a crisp coating, but was a bit chewy; patlıcan esme was wonderful and well-textured. For mains, manti – tiny meat parcels (like mini ravioli) in garlic yoghurt – is one of the newer dishes that have been added to the menu in recent months. It's a pleasing addition, but should be less salty. Izgara köfte was perfectly spiced, and served with a big salad. The café is yellow, the walls decorated with moody monochrome photos of Turkish scenes. Service can be slow when the place is busy, but the atmosphere is always enjoyable. The clientele is very mixed, from diehard Stoke Newington lefties and shoppers who've popped in to read the papers to police officers from the station a few doors down.
Babies and children welcome: high chairs. Booking advisable. Separate room for parties, seats 30. Tables outdoors (4, pavement). Takeaway service; delivery service (within 3-mile radius). Vegetarian menu. **Map 25 B2**.

★ Café Z Bar

58 Stoke Newington High Street, N16 7PB (7275 7523). Stoke Newington rail/73, 76, 149, 243 bus. **Meals served** 8am-9pm daily. **Main courses** £4.50-£7.50. **Set meal** £4.95 2 courses. **No credit cards**.
Mixing elements of café, bar, gallery and restaurant, Z Bar is something of a cultural centre. A central staircase leads down to a basement where concerts and events are held some evenings. Shifting exhibitions of photos or paintings decorate the walls of the light, airy ground floor. As you browse the menu, complimentary olives and steaming fresh bread are supplied. The menu is enticing, and incorporates a range of vegetarian and fish dishes, a batch of Turkish pizzas, and a short wine list. Freshly squeezed apple, orange or carrot juice costs £1.90 a glass. Mixed hot meze gives a good impression of the starters available, including a nicely spicy sucuk, sigara börek (with a particularly tasty filling), mitite köfte, hellim and kalamar. As a main course, we can recommend the alabalik (trout with potato). A moist çöp şiş (cubed lamb) was served on little wooden skewers, with rice and red cabbage. Finish with a well-made, hearty Turkish coffee. Z Bar continues to impress.
Babies and children welcome: high chairs. Book weekends. Entertainment: jazz workshop 8pm Thur. Separate room for parties, seats 50. Tables outdoors (2, pavement). Takeaway service. **Map 25 C2**.

★ ★ 19 Numara Bos Cirrik II

194 Stoke Newington High Street, N16 7JD (7249 9111). Stoke Newington rail/73, 76, 149, 243 bus. **Meals served** noon-midnight Mon-Thur, Sun; noon-1am Fri, Sat. **Main courses** £6.50-£9.50. **Credit** AmEx, MC, V.
The well-deserved success of the original down the road in Dalston has led to the opening of this second branch in the heart of Stoke Newington. The features that made the Dalston restaurant a classic are all in place here too, though at this branch the decor is more restaurant than café. A full range of starters is offered, and they are well made, but only the truly starving should indulge. Once a grill is ordered, a large salad and cold starters will be brought without any need to order extra: usually onion in chilli, and onion in pomegranate and turnip sauce. These are accompanied by endlessly replenished supplies of warm pide bread. Service is quick, efficient, and

friendly. The grills are exceptional. A portion of kaburga lamb ribs was generous, with the fat richly flavoured from the grill. Turkish pizzas are also available. Continuing to stand out in this outstanding area, both branches of this business are unreservedly recommended.
Babies and children welcome: high chairs. Booking advisable Fri, Sat. Disabled: toilet. Takeaway service. **Map 25 C1.**
For branch see index.

North
Finchley N3

Other decent, and long-established, Turkish restaurants in Finchley include **Izgara** (11 Hendon Lane, N3 1RT, 8371 8282); **Durum** (119 Ballards Lane, N3 1LJ, 8346 8977); and **Divan** (163 Ballards Lane, N3 1LJ, 8346 4414).

★ The Ottomans
118 Ballards Lane, N3 2DN (8349 9968). Finchley Central tube. **Meals served** noon-10.30pm daily. **Main courses** £6.90-£10.50. **Set lunch** £5.95 2 courses. **Set dinner** (Mon-Thur, Sun) £13.50-£14.75 3 courses incl coffee. **Credit** JCB, MC, V.
An enormous mural of nautical Bosphorus scenes taking up one wall effectively establishes the Turkish ambience here, while the glazed frontage gives a feeling of space. As well as serving a standard café menu, Ottomans offers an alluring collection of Turkish dishes. Starters include surprisingly tender kalamar, served with rich tartar sauce. Authentically smoky patlıcan esme (puréed aubergine), with an appetisingly rough texture, came with plentiful hot pide. Our main course, tavuk şiş, was accompanied by paper-thin saç bread, rice and salad. Another main, 'Ottomans bosfor', combined salmon, prawns and mussels in a rich sauce, which – unusually for Turkish cooking – included brandy. Traditional Turkish music played unobtrusively in the background, and service was friendly and efficient. Ottomans continues to improve and is the most interesting of a collection of perfectly acceptable Turkish restaurants in the area.
Babies and children welcome: children's portions; high chairs. Book weekends. No-smoking tables. Takeaway service. Vegetarian menu.

Gem. See p280.

Finsbury Park N4
★ Yildiz
163 Blackstock Road, N4 2JS (7354 3899). Arsenal tube. **Meals served** noon-11.30pm daily. **Main courses** £4-£12.65. **Set lunch** £6 1 course incl soft drink. **Credit** MC, V.
This narrow restaurant is tucked behind a takeaway. Furnishings include heavy red tablecloths, yellow walls and shell lampshades, creating a rather dark space. The menu is not exclusively Turkish, but Anatolian food remains very much its focus. A basket of good warm, slender pide arrived swiftly. A starter of small mitite köfte meatballs was over-fried, but this was quickly forgiven. Yildiz is one of a growing number of Turkish eateries (we believe Dalston's 19 Numara – *see 278* – was first), where starters are supplied as part of the meal, making it unnecessary to order your own. An excellent grilled onion in pomegranate and turnip sauce appeared (claimed as a house speciality). It was followed by a tomato salad and a chilli onion salad. Finally, a beautiful char-grilled kaburga (lamb ribs) with chunky rice made an appearance; the smoky, tender meat was cooked to perfection. The excellence of Yildiz's core dishes overcomes any worries we may have about the peripherals.
Babies and children admitted. Takeaway service.

Harringay N4

Green Lanes in Harringay developed as a Cypriot area, with a mix of Greek and Turkish Cypriots (that remains to this day). However, the area's character is shifting with the coming of newer arrivals from Turkey, many being Kurds from the south-east. These changes are gradually being reflected in Green Lanes' restaurants. Numerous cheap and vibrant ocakbaşı cafés line the street, several open 24 hours. Few are licensed for alcohol, but most will let you bring your own.

There's not much to distinguish most of these places from each other, but the following are worth a look (street numbers are given in brackets, numbers under 100 are on Green Lanes Grand Parade): **Bingöl** (No.551); **Damak** (395); **Diyarbakır** (69); **Gaziantep** (52); **Gökyüzü** (27); **Harran** (399); **Mangal** (443), with a wonderful psychedelic sign; **Mersin** (337), which follows a current fashion for tantuni, meat fried on an open hob and wrapped in saç; **Mizgin** (485); **Öz Sofra** (421); **Roj** (64), which is licensed; **Selale** (2 Salisbury Promenade); **Serhat** (403); and **Tara** (6), which has a more Middle Eastern feel.

★ Antepliler [NEW]
46 Grand Parade, Green Lanes, N4 1AG (8802 5588). Manor House tube/29 bus. **Meals served** 11.30am-11.30pm daily. **Main courses** £5-£8.50. **Credit** MC, V.
Another Turkish café in a parade of Turkish cafés, Antepliler has some advantages over the competition: it's larger, the decor (round the domed brick oven in the entrance) is more interesting, and the menu is more varied. For example, try the sögürme starter – oven-cooked aubergine mash, garnished with fresh mint leaves and with an interesting criss-cross pattern on top. Its texture was uneven, which is not a complaint, though less oil could certainly have been used. Another starter, the currently ubiquitous grilled onion, came in a flower pattern and contained far too much chilli, but a tomato and cucumber salad was suitably refreshing. Frenk kebab (which means European kebab) is a main course worth trying for a change; unspiced meatballs are grilled on a skewer interspersed with six medium-sized tomatoes - tasty, but too large to finish. In all, Antepliler is an interesting café worth a visit.
Babies and children welcome: high chairs. Takeaway service.

★ Yayla [NEW]
429 Green Lanes, N4 1HA (8348 9515). Manor House or Turnpike Lane tube/Harringay rail. **Breakfast served** 6am-noon, **meals served** noon-midnight daily. **Main courses** £5.50-£8. **No credit cards.**
You're likely to find a warming welcome at this café, which sports a bright green and orange colour scheme. To start, we enjoyed a lamb and yoghurt soup that arrived brimming with big chunks of tender meat; a garlic and chilli sauce had been mixed in with the stock. With pide, this soup was a meal in itself. A portion of esme salatası (a salad with olives and onions) also came in an impressively large portion, but was a tad oily. As our main course, we chose iskender. It was a very large (that word again) kebab and arrived bubbling hot, but was made with fillet lamb that was surprisingly dry. In contrast, an order for kaburga produced enormous quantities of juicy ribs served with basmati rice (but no salad). For a café, Yayla is very good at what it does. Nevertheless, this establishment isn't notably different from many others on the Green Lanes strip.
Babies and children welcome: high chair. Takeaway service.

Highbury N5
★ İznik
19 Highbury Park, N5 1QJ (7354 5697). Highbury & Islington tube/rail/4, 19, 236 bus. **Meals served** 10am-4pm Mon-Fri. **Dinner served** 6.30pm-midnight daily. **Main courses** £7.50-£9.50. **Service** 10%. **Credit** MC, V.
It's worth remembering that much of Turkish cuisine is not grill-based; İznik offers a wide choice of the alternatives. Carved wooden screens divide up the large, cluttered interior. The warm orange walls are decorated with blue patterned tiles typical of the city of İznik (a famous ceramics centre in the Ottoman era), and a mass of lamps and candles add to the welcoming, relaxing vibe. The ambience helps, but it's the food that keeps the punters coming in. For starters, patate köfte were perfectly fried potato balls, with a crisp outside collapsing into a soft interior; mücver was very moist and came with a fresh kısır. Kuzu fırında is a perennial main course favourite: a great hunk of lamb, tender to the point of disintegration. İznik's hünkar beğendi (aubergine with chunks of tender lamb) is also outstanding. Each dish is served with a portion of good basmati rice. We also shared a large salad (including sweet peppers and olives), which had been put together with loving care. Save space for the mouth-watering and extremely sweet desserts – we particularly like the gloriously decadent armut tatlısı (baked pear stuffed with pistachio, bathed in chocolate and cream). An excellent restaurant.
Babies and children admitted. Booking essential weekends. Takeaway service.

Islington N1
Gallipoli Again
120 Upper Street, N1 1QP (7359 1578/ www.gallipolicafe.co.uk). Angel tube. **Meals served** 10.30am-11pm Mon-Thur, Sun; 10.30am-midnight Fri, Sat. **Main courses** £4.95-£9.95. **Set lunch** £11.95 3 courses. **Set dinner** £14.95 3 courses incl coffee. **Service** 10% for parties of 10 or more. **Credit** MC, V.
There are three branches of Gallipoli spread along Upper Street: the original at No.102, North African-themed Gallipoli Bazaar at No.107, and this one. Together, they are the most popular Turkish restaurants in Islington. Gallipoli Again's front window opens on to the street in good weather, but the interior is always in shadow. Sit as close to the front as possible; the back section is cramped and uncomfortable, with a corrugated plastic roof. Reasonable prices and a party atmosphere draw in an enthusiastic young crowd. 'Mixed Gallipoli' is a selection of cold starters with a couple of hot ones. Despite most of these dishes being dips, the restaurant charges extra for pide; the bread,

though decent, is not as good as that which any Stoke Newington Turkish café would provide for free (and happily replenish). For mains, both incik and iskender are of good quality. Yet it's a pity that while Gallipoli is packed to the rafters every night, Angel Mangal (just up the road at No.139), which offers fine food from an authentic ocakbaşı grill, is often only half full.
Babies and children welcome: high chairs. Booking advisable. Tables outdoors (5, pavement). Takeaway service. Map 5 O1.
For branches see index.

★ Gem
265 Upper Street, N1 2UQ (7359 0405). Angel tube/Highbury & Islington tube/rail. Meals served noon-11pm Mon-Sat; noon-10.30pm Sun. Main courses £5.95-£8.50. Set lunch £5.95 3 courses, £7.95 4 courses. Set dinner £8.50 3 courses, £11.45 4 courses, £22.45 5 courses incl house wine or beer. Service 10% for parties of 6 or more. Credit MC, V.
This Kurdish restaurant towards the less fashionable end of Upper Street is often unjustly overlooked. Try the qatme bread, often seen being prepared just inside the door. Hot pitta and a dish of pickled vegetables appear on the table as you sit down. Our first course, kalamar, was served with crunchy tabouleh, while nicely spiced köfte came with fresh chilli. Next, iskender was offered with a choice of lamb or chicken, shish or beyti. We ordered the lamb shish, which was served on a plate (rather than the more usual bowl) with tomato sauce and yoghurt on a bed of pitta. Vegetarian kizartma was a stew of aubergine, mushroom, potato and courgette in tomato sauce, accompanied by yoghurt. We finished with complimentary portions of baklava and ice-cream. The atmosphere is enjoyable, and staff are attentive and helpful. Diners eat at heavy wooden tables, and look at large agricultural implements that hang from burnt orange walls. There's an additional eating area in the basement. Gem remains an excellent venue for good food at very reasonable prices.
Babies and children welcome: high chairs. Booking advisable weekends. Separate room for parties, seats 80. Takeaway service. Vegetarian menu. Map 5 O1.

★ Pasha
301 Upper Street, N1 2TU (7226 1454). Angel tube/Highbury & Islington tube/rail. Lunch served noon-3pm Mon-Fri. Dinner served 6-11.30pm Mon-Thur; 6pm-midnight Fri. Meals served noon-midnight Sat; noon-11pm Sun. Main courses £7.50-£13.95. Set meals £13.95 per person (minimum 2) meze selection, £19.95 3 courses incl dessert & coffee. Cover £1. Service 10% for parties of 6 or more. Credit AmEx, DC, MC, V.
Pasha maintains its supremacy among Islington's Turkish restaurants with quiet confidence. In summer the front opens on to busy Upper Street, offering outside seating. Inside, artily distressed yellow walls, with a burgundy wall at the rear, give a degree of warm intimacy. Black-clad waiters hover between the white tablecloths. The likes of Nitin Sawhney take the place of Turkish music on the restaurant's sound system. The wine list contains a fair selection of Turkish and European bottles. The food doesn't disappoint either. A first course of cızbız köfte meatball was pleasingly light in flavour and texture, while enginar subtly mixed artichoke with lemon, dill and broad beans. To follow, a range of dolma offered aubergine, pepper, courgette and vine leaves stuffed with mince and rice; the taste and the texture of the different vegetables was complementary (although the vine leaf was rather oversalted). The 'Pasha special' comprised medallions of exquisitely tender lamb, served with rice and a large succulent mushroom. Finally, the fırın sütlaç (rice pudding with the aroma and flavour of rosewater) remains the perfect dessert. Highly recommended.
Babies and children admitted. Booking advisable weekends. Tables outdoors (3, pavement). Takeaway service. Map 5 O1.

Sedir
4 Theberton Street, N1 0QX (7226 5489). Angel tube/Highbury & Islington tube/rail. Meals served 11am-11.30pm Mon-Thur; 11.30am-midnight Fri, Sat; 11.30am-11.30pm Sun. Main courses £7.95-£11.95. Set lunch £7.95 2 courses incl coffee. Set meze £16.50 per person (minimum 2) 8 dishes. Service 10% for parties of 6 or more. Credit AmEx, JCB, MC, V.
Sedir spreads across two floors, with an ever-increasing number of tables lined up along the street outside. Pastel-coloured walls lighten what is a rather crowded interior. Enormous prints of European paintings of the Ottoman bazaars and harems dominate. The waiter asked if we wanted bread with our mixed cold meze starter. An unusual question in a Turkish restaurant, but one that allows the pide to be charged as an extra dish rather than being an integral part of the meze. We tried houmous and tarama – both were nondescript, in contrast to the excellent, firm, own-made dolma. For mains, güveç had a well-rounded flavour, and non-standard ingredients including courgette. It would have been better with longer cooking – a good güveç takes a while to stew. Sedir's 'beyti' is not the spiced minced lamb kebab that might be expected, but medallions of fillet lamb, aka lokma. It's tasty, but slightly chewy. Such minor criticisms are less easily overlooked in what is a smart restaurant. Sedir is an 'evening-out' venue and acceptable as such, but in this intensely competitive district, it needs to keep an eye on the details.
Babies and children welcome: high chair. Booking essential dinner. Separate room for parties, seats 50. Tables outdoors (4, pavement). Takeaway service. Map 5 O1.

Muswell Hill N10

★ Bakko
172-174 Muswell Hill Broadway, N10 3SA (8883 1111/www.bakko.co.uk). Highgate tube then 43, 134 bus. Meals served 11.30am-10.30pm daily. Main courses £6.90-£15.50. Set lunch (11.30am-4pm Mon-Fri) £6.90 3 courses. Set meal £14.90 per person (minimum 2) 3 courses. Credit MC, V.
In summer, the glass front of this Muswell Hill restaurant opens on to the noisy Broadway. Bakko is a Kurdish term for village elder, and Kurdish artefacts decorate the brick-effect walls here, as do pictures of Kurdish women baking flatbread – but, unfortunately, what accompanies your meal is very ordinary pitta. A dish of good chunky olives is placed on each table. As well as the standard grills, the menu contains fish and vegetarian dishes and a selection of steaks. There's also a fabulous desserts trolley, with fruit salads and lots of chocolatey cakes. Patlıcan soslu was a ridiculously tasty concoction of diced aubergine with green pepper and tomato. The excellent iskender is recommended too: a mix of noticeably superior adana and tavuk shish in rich tomato and chilli sauce with yoghurt. Staff offered friendly, helpful service. Busy, and with a growing reputation as the standard of food has improved, Bakko has hit its stride. It's now an excellent local. But at the very least, a restaurant proclaiming its Kurdish roots should be serving fresh Kurdish bread.
Babies and children welcome: high chairs. Book weekends. No smoking. Vegetarian menu.

North West
Golders Green NW11

Beyoglu
1031 Finchley Road, NW11 7ES (8455 4884). Golders Green tube/82, 160, 260 bus. Meals served noon-midnight daily. Main courses £6.50-£10. Set dinner £12-£13.75 3 courses incl coffee. Credit MC, V.
The Turkish wall mats and old Ottoman photos that are typical of many a Turkish restaurant in London are accompanied at Beyoglu by mock-Tudor beams. We chose starters of kalamar and arnavut ciğeri; both were palatable, though the squid had been fried a little too long. The juicy liver was accompanied by a balancing, light kısır. For a main course, kilic baligi is recommended: meltingly tender grilled swordfish, served with a big salad. The house special is aubergine with adana (spicy mince) and tomato; ours was very good, but would have been even better if it had also come with salad. The olives and pide that accompanied our meal were both excellent. Service is friendly, but rather slow on this visit, even though the restaurant wasn't that busy. Beyoglu remains the best of the little cluster of Turkish restaurants in Temple Fortune, near Golders Green. Despite the odd niggle, we can still recommend it.
Babies and children welcome: high chairs. Book weekends. No-smoking tables. Tables outdoors (2, pavement). Takeaway service. Vegetarian menu.

Hampstead NW3

★ Zara
11 South End Road, NW3 2PT (7794 5498). Belsize Park tube/Hampstead Heath rail. Meals served 11.30am-11.30pm daily. Main courses £6.50-£9.50. Service 12.5%. Credit MC, V.
In warm weather, Zara's glass frontage opens up and a few tables are placed on the wide pavement. On our visit, two customers were playing backgammon over Turkish coffee. Cushioned benches run along the walls of the compact interior, which is divided into smoking and no-smoking areas. The mixed cold meze provides a good spread of starters, including houmous, tarama, börek, cacik and kısır. Each was nicely textured and notably fresh. The freshness continued with our main courses, which arrived on large oval plates. Islim kebab (aubergine strips baked around lamb and green pepper) was beautifully tender. We can also vouch for the firin kebab (flattened meatballs with potato and green peppers in rich gravy), which is rarely found in London. Both mains were accompanied by a fresh green salad served (unusually) with a dressing. Staff provided a jug of cold water on request, and service was hard to fault throughout our meal. A commendable range of Turkish desserts is available, as well as Italian-style ice-creams. Unpretentious and efficient, Zara isn't far from being the ideal restaurant.
Babies and children welcome: high chairs. Book weekends. No-smoking tables. Tables outdoors (3, pavement). Takeaway service. Vegetarian menu. Map 28 C3.

Willesden NW2

★ Mezerama
76 Walm Lane, NW2 4RA (8459 3311). Willesden Green tube. Dinner served 5pm-midnight Mon-Fri. Meals served 12.30pm-midnight Sat, Sun. Main courses £6.50-£11.95. Set lunch £6 1 course incl glass of wine or soft drink. Credit MC, V.
Every effort is made to make diners new to Turkish food feel at home at Mezerama, with dishes named in English and fully described on the menu. The furnishings – purple and green chairs, lilac walls and a giant distorting mirror – help to create a relaxed atmosphere. Despite the restaurant being removed from the main Turkish districts of the city, the menu is adventurous. It maintains its Turkish roots, but strays beyond the standard London Turkish repertoire. Try badadez köfte as a starter: loosely textured beef is mixed with onion into gloriously crispy meatballs, which are served with fresh lemon juice on a bed of lettuce. For a main course, chicken stuffed with spinach and feta in a creamy sauce, with sweet peppers and salad, was ideal. Both courses were served with cubed, almost toasted pide. Mezerama goes from strength to strength; we recommend that Turkish food fans from other parts of London pay it a visit.
Babies and children welcome: high chairs. Booking advisable; essential Fri, Sat. Restaurant available for hire. Takeaway service. Vegetarian menu.

RESTAURANTS

Vegetarian

The vegetarian dining scene in London is still lacking a little zip. True, there are a couple of newcomers this year – **222 Veggie Vegan** and **Little Earth Café** (one of the nominees for Best Vegetarian Meal in the 2005 *Time Out* Eating & Drinking awards) – but the rest of our award finalists will be found listed under other cuisines: **Kathiyawadi** (Indian), **Mangosteen** (Oriental), **Noura Central** (Middle Eastern) and **Salt Yard** (Spanish). Indeed, non-meat eaters still do well to look to other cuisines, notably vegetarian Gujarati and South Indian restaurants (see the **Indian** section, starting on p131). For more restaurants that make a special effort for vegetarians and vegans, look under **vegetarian food** in the **Subject index**, starting on p394.

Central

Barbican EC1

Carnevale
135 Whitecross Street, EC1Y 8JL (7250 3452/ www.carnevalerestaurant.co.uk). Barbican tube/Old Street tube/rail/55 bus. **Lunch served** noon-3pm Mon-Fri. **Dinner served** 5.30-10.30pm Mon-Sat. **Main courses** £11.50. **Minimum** (noon-2.30pm Mon-Fri) £5.50. **Set meal** (noon-3pm Mon-Fri, 5.30-7pm Mon-Sat) £13.50 3 courses. **Service** 12.5% for parties of 5 or more. **Credit** MC, V.
The name derives from the Latin phrase 'carne vale', meaning 'goodbye to meat' (in other words, the beginning of Lent), and this small restaurant and deli surely offers a carnival of Mediterranean flavours. The place is immensely popular with nearby office workers during the day and a Barbican-going crowd in the evenings, making it busy at all times. There are only about a dozen seats, so it gets extremely cramped; however, diners can spill out into the small courtyard with exposed brick walls and trailing plants at the back. We were brought good bread and olive oil to dip into, followed by a spirited rocket, caper, piquillo pepper and canellini bean salad made with very fresh ingredients. Another lovely starter was fried egg with soft, milky buffalo mozzarella, lively tomato-flavoured chilli jam and more peppery rocket. Mains included flageolet bean, fennel and red pepper stew, and fritedda (Italian spring vegetable casserole) with delicious chilli-flecked polenta fritters. Both dishes were hearty without being heavy, and packed with flavour. If Nigel Slater was vegetarian, this is the sort of food he would cook.
Babies and children admitted. Booking advisable. Tables outdoors (3, conservatory). Takeaway service. Vegan dishes. **Map 5 P4**.

City EC2

★ The Place Below
St Mary-le-Bow, Cheapside, EC2V 6AU (7329 0789/www.theplacebelow.co.uk). St Paul's tube/ Bank tube/DLR. **Breakfast served** 7.30-11am, **lunch served** 11.30am-2.30pm, **snacks served** 2.30-3pm Mon-Fri. **Main courses** £5.50-£7.50. **Unlicensed. Corkage** no charge. **Credit** MC, V.
Located in the Norman crypt of St Mary-le-Bow church, this smart canteen is owned by Bill Sewell, author of two excellent cookery books. The dining room, atmospheric with its high domed ceiling, columns and alcoves, is an unlikely hit with the area's stockbrokers. Individual tables are decorated with fresh flowers, and there's also a

222 Veggie Vegan. See p285.

communal table; in fine weather, it's possible to sit in the churchyard. A cauliflower soup was somewhat insipid, but barley salad with dates, pecan nuts, asparagus and roasted red peppers was an effortless marriage of textures. A potato bake would have been a veggie restaurant cliché, were it not for the addition of sharp shropshire blue cheese and celeriac. Red pepper, parmesan, thyme and caramelised onion quiche was superb – wobbly, flavoursome custard, encased within light, crumbly pastry. There's a good breakfast menu, offering pastries from the excellent French deli Comptoir Gascon and own-made Bircher muesli with honey and apples. Don't miss the freshly ground Illy coffee and headily perfumed valencia orange juice, squeezed on the premises.
Babies and children admitted. No smoking. Tables outdoors (24, churchyard). Takeaway service (7.30am-3pm). Vegan dishes. **Map 11 P6**.

Covent Garden WC2

★ Food for Thought
31 Neal Street, WC2H 9PR (7836 9072). Covent Garden tube. **Breakfast served** 9.30-11.30am, **dinner served** 5-8.30pm Mon-Sat. **Lunch served** noon-5pm Mon-Sat; noon-5.30pm Sun. **Main courses** £3-£6.50. **Minimum** (noon-3pm, 6-7.30pm) £2.50. **Unlicensed. Corkage** no charge. **No credit cards**.
Housed inside a listed 18th-century building that was once a banana-ripening warehouse, this Covent Garden institution attracts a worldwide following: it's almost unfathomably popular with students, tourists, local workers and Hollywood celebrities treading the boards in the West End. The dining room, crammed with rustic tables, is in the tiny basement; there's a takeaway counter upstairs; and enormous queues on the snaking staircase are part of the scenery. So why is it so popular? Because the prices are low, the portions are enormous and the service is friendly. The food isn't wildly adventurous, but it takes vegetarian standards (bakes, salads, quiches, soups, stir-fries, and numerous rice- and bean-based dishes) and offers them with masses of flavour and sometimes a slight twist. Vegetable veneziana (mushrooms, spinach, baby potatoes and tomatoes in a delicious red pepper sauce, topped with herb-flecked cheese and polenta mash) and creamy wild mushroom goulash with crisp potato pancakes, sour cream and beetroot were both very tasty. Desserts are scrumptious: don't miss the strawberry and banana scrunch – it's a legend in its own lunchtime.
Babies and children admitted. Bookings not accepted. No smoking. Takeaway service. Vegan dishes. **Map 18 L6**.

★ Neal's Yard Salad Bar
1, 2, 8 & 10 Neal's Yard, WC2H 9DP (7836 3233/www.nealsyardsaladbar.co.uk). Covent Garden tube. **Meals served** 8.30am-9pm daily. **Main courses** £8.25-£10.50. **No credit cards**.
Ensconced within the new age enclave that is Neal's Yard, this eccentric eaterie with alfresco seating is definitely a one-off. The eclectic Brazilian-influenced menu offers breakfasts (including a vegan one with spicy soy mince and cassava), soups and somewhat insipid, uninspiring salads – despite the restaurant's name, they are not the kitchen's strong point. Somewhat stodgy hot dishes include pizzas, burgers, pies, quiches, risottos, pastas, stuffed vegetables, couscous and polenta. Spicy Brazilian feijoada (here made with rice, turtle beans, soya mince, cassava, pumpkin and green banana) was heavy, lacking in flavour and sloppy. Much more successful were an array of flavoursome Brazilian cheese breads and the desserts, which included fig and walnut pudding. There are interesting Portuguese wines and beers on offer, alongside a variety of lovely Brazilian juices like guava. Service is chaotic but friendly. Our waiter, not a native English speaker, brought us vegan ice-cream to try (the kitchen was developing a range of flavours and wanted to gauge our reaction), then explained that they 'try to satisfy one's oddest tastes'. Indeed.

RESTAURANTS

Babies and children admitted. Tables outdoors (11, courtyard). Takeaway service. Vegan dishes. **Map 18 L6.**

★ World Food Café

First floor, 14 Neal's Yard, WC2H 9DP (7379 0298/www.worldfoodcafe.com). Covent Garden tube. **Meals served** 11.30am-4.30pm Mon-Fri; 11.30am-5pm Sat. **Main courses** £4.85-£7.95. **Minimum** (noon-2pm Mon-Fri; 11.30am-5pm Sat) £6. **Credit** MC, V.

Owned by Chris Caldicott, a freelance travel writer and photographer, this new age eaterie offers platters of popular international classics gathered from his various journeys. So you will find, for instance, African, Turkish and Thai meals alongside Indian thalis and Middle Eastern meze. We liked the Mexican platter, comprising crisp nachos with spicy refried beans, which had a deep, lusty flavour; a zippy, creamy guacamole; and crunchy tortilla chips. Large portions of light Egyptian falafel, served with good houmous and pitta, were also appreciated. Seating is on high stools at a horseshoe-shaped bar that partly surrounds the open kitchen – you can watch the chefs preparing your food. There are also tables by the window (which you may have to share) overlooking Neal's Yard. Otherwise, despite its framed prints and colourful window boxes, this white-walled café is rather sparse; the world music soundtrack offers welcome distraction.
Babies and children welcome: high chairs. No smoking. Takeaway service. Vegan dishes. **Map 18 L6.**

Marylebone W1

Eat & Two Veg

50 Marylebone High Street, W1U 5HN (7258 8595/www.eatandtwoveg.com). Baker Street tube. **Meals served** 9am-11pm Mon-Sat; 10am-10pm Sun. **Main courses** £6.50-£9. **Credit** AmEx, MC, V.

Billed as 'the world's first meat free diner', this funky restaurant divides opinion: like Marmite, you'll either love it or hate it. The bone of contention is not its penchant for bad puns (aside from the name, there's an item called 'crispy aromatic luck' on the English-nursery-food-goes-international menu), but the fact that almost every dish is cooked using meat substitutes. Whereas most veggie restaurants let vegetables and pulses shine, here soya protein reigns supreme. So the restaurant appeals mainly to omnivores, demi-vegetarians and meat-reducers rather than, say, vegans. In terms of its design too, it looks like no other veggie restaurant. There are sexy lipstick red leather banquettes, turquoise Formica tables and a cute cocktail bar. A rich, hearty lancashire hot-pot was a little salty and tepid, but schnitzel with creamy wine and watercress sauce was excellent – it would have given any meat counterpart a run for its money. Also on offer are breakfasts, sandwiches and salads. Another branch opened in Notting Hill in late 2004, but closed within a few months; plans remain to roll out more branches.
Babies and children welcome: high chairs. Booking advisable. Disabled: toilet. No-smoking tables. Takeaway service. Vegan dishes. **Map 3 G4.**

Soho W1

★ Beatroot

92 Berwick Street, W1F 0QD (7437 8591). Oxford Circus, Piccadilly Circus or Tottenham Court Road tube. **Meals served** 9.15am-9.30pm Mon-Sat; noon-7.30pm Sun. **Main courses** £3.15-£5.15. **No credit cards.**

Beatroot is a small, somewhat cluttered eaterie in the heart of Soho, decorated in earthy tones. Although there's bench seating inside and a few circular tables outside, takeaway is really the point of this place. Wholesome, mostly vegan dishes fill small, medium or large containers to the brim. Comforting daily hot specials include shepherd's pie, lasagne, quiche, moroccan vegetable tagine, and lentil and spinach curry. There are also salads, snacks (such as sausage rolls), organic juices and smoothies, and vegan cakes (such as cheesecake). We had a hefty portion of moussaka, served with brown rice and broccoli, alongside greek, carrot and beetroot salads. The flavours weren't particularly memorable – the moussaka was too herby, the rice too dry and the broccoli overcooked – but the salads were made with good ingredients. Soy mango smoothie was lovely, and the vegan chocolate dream cake also a delight. Staff are very friendly.
Babies and children admitted. No smoking. Tables outdoors (2, pavement). Takeaway service. Vegan dishes. **Map 17 J/K6.**

Mildred's

45 Lexington Street, W1F 9AN (7494 1634/ www.mildreds.co.uk). Oxford Circus or Piccadilly Circus tube. **Meals served** noon-11pm Mon-Sat. **Main courses** £6.50-£7.95. **Service** 12.5%. **No credit cards.**

Small and somewhat cramped (the tables are too close together), this down-to-earth restaurant is nonetheless always packed. Probably because the

Little Earth Café. See p285.

Interview
ADRIAN DANIEL

Who are you?
Chef-owner of the **Gate** (*see p284*) and co-author of *The Gate Vegetarian Restaurant Cookbook*.
Eating in London: what's good about it?
The variety of ingredients and cooking styles. The only other place that could be compared to it on that basis is New York.
What's bad about it?
You might call it the English disease – a lack of passion or quality. It's hard to find places that are really on the ball all the time, but that's probably true of all businesses. Also, it is really expensive in London, but we live and die by that sword, don't we?
What single thing would improve London's restaurant scene?
Better vegetarian choices. It can be quite limiting. Often there is a vegetarian choice, but it's an unappealing one. Sometimes I order something else and ask them to leave the meat out. I find a lot of vegetarian options are just very large starters: big portions of one thing, no mix of flavours and textures.
Any hot tips for the coming year?
What I'd love to see is more raw food restaurants. The trend is quite big in the US and I've been to some wonderful raw food restaurants there.
Should smoking in restaurants be banned?
You're talking to a smoker with a non-smoking restaurant. I do think smokers are being hounded out of restaurants. Having smoking and non-smoking areas doesn't work because the smoke does go beyond table three.
Anything to declare?
Food has become more fashionable and a lot more children are drawn to it now. The kind of food we give kids to eat in our establishments and in the home needs to be thought about and developed.

cooking is generally good. We started with a smooth carrot and coriander soup made with flavoursome stock, and an invigorating lentil, sprouted bean, carrot and sultana salad. Succulent beanburgers made with pinto beans were served with a tasty selection of relishes and amazing chunky chips. Mushroom and ale pie had an intense, muscular flavour and was accompanied by perfect mushy peas and mint sauce. Vegan cheesecake was sharp and luxurious, but a stodgy rhubarb and apple crumble was a disappointment. Vegan and wheat-free options on the menu also included baba ganoush, stir-fried vegetables and tofu with satay sauce, and vegan double chocolate pudding. Portions are huge and service is efficient. The interesting drinks list includes organic wines, smoothies, Fairtrade coffee, fresh fruit juices and 'health' juices such as wheatgrass and cranberry.
Babies and children admitted. No smoking. Tables outdoors (2, pavement). Takeaway service. Vegan dishes. **Map 17 J6.**

★ Red Veg

95 Dean Street, W1V 5RB (7437 3109/ www.redveg.com). Tottenham Court Road tube. **Meals served** noon-10pm Mon-Sat; noon-7pm Sun. **Main courses** £2.85-£3.55. **No credit cards.**
A notice inside this small takeaway and fast-food joint reads: 'To ensure freshness, all Red Veg food is cooked to order. Therefore, please allow up to 5 minutes to receive your food order.' Erm, does this mean it only takes five minutes to cook the food? Never mind. Falafels and hot dogs have been introduced to the menu, alongside the ever-popular burgers. Our veggie hot dog was tasty, but too small; the waitress confided that they had started off serving two dogs per person, but were told to cut down the portion size to just one – this has apparently led to complaints from customers. NoName nuggets were more like NoFlavour nuggets, as they didn't taste of anything. Next time we will stick to the fabulous chilli burger and

sesame falafels. This communist-themed eaterie has its heart in the right place, but the concept is no longer revolutionary. In the last few years, healthy fast-food joints serving superior food have started popping up in the capital, so Red Veg will have to try much harder.
Babies and children admitted. Takeaway service. Vegan dishes. **Map 17 K6.**

West

Hammersmith W6

★ The Gate

51 Queen Caroline Street, W6 9QL (8748 6932/www.thegate.tv). Hammersmith tube. **Lunch served** noon-2.45pm Mon-Fri. **Dinner served** 6-10.45pm Mon-Sat. **Main courses** £8.50-£13.50. **Service** 12.5%. **Credit** AmEx, MC, V.
Popular with the sort of people who holiday in Tuscany rather than stereotypical sandal-wearing, PETA-supporting hardcore veggies, this leading vegetarian restaurant poses more questions than it answers. Chief among these are: why has no other veggie restaurant in London managed to emulate its success and challenge its status, and why is the Gate enduringly popular? We think we know the answer to the last one. Chef-proprietors Adrian and Michael Daniel, who hail from Indo-Iraqi Jewish backgrounds, draw from their cultural heritage to create eclectic dishes where vegetables are truly allowed to shine. You won't find too many meat substitutes or pulses on the menu, but you will find an amazing array of exotic and everyday vegetables in their party frocks. Of the dishes we tried, the three that stood out were spicy green banana fritters laced with ginger, lime, chilli and garlic; roasted vegetable involtini with gubbeen cheese and puy lentils; and thyme-flecked potato galette with mixed wild mushrooms. A bright yellow interior filled with contemporary art and candlelight, a pretty courtyard perfect

for alfresco dining, and informed service complete the experience. A lovely place.
Babies and children welcome: high chairs. Booking essential. No smoking. Tables outdoors (15, courtyard). Vegan dishes. **Map 20 B4.**

Shepherd's Bush W12

★ Blah Blah Blah

78 Goldhawk Road, W12 8HA (8746 1337). Goldhawk Road tube/94 bus. **Lunch served** 12.30-2.30pm, **dinner served** 7-11pm Mon-Sat. **Main courses** £9.95. **Unlicensed. Corkage** £1.25 per person. **No credit cards.**
Situated in the shabby-chic environs of Goldhawk Road, this boho BYO restaurant is celeb central – a favourite haunt of Sir Paul McCartney, Boy George, Gwyneth Paltrow and Chris Martin. Owned by an ex-hairdresser from Australia, it's a vibrant place, with dusky lilac walls, moody lighting, an open-view kitchen, crayons on tables (well, we said it was boho), a party room in the basement and top-notch service. Food is elaborately made and beautifully presented – with particular care taken over the preparation of sauces and relishes. Leek and potato soup was gorgeously flavoured and served with light courgette fritters flecked with fresh mint and dill. Delicious grilled halloumi was served warm on salad leaves with roasted peppers, toasted ciabatta and own-made pesto. Perfectly cooked tagliatelle came with green beans, broccoli, sun-dried tomatoes, pine nuts and roasted chilli in a creamy basil sauce. Other tempting items on an eclectic, regularly changing menu include saffron crespellini, california sushi rolls, roasted vegetable tart, Indian coconut kashmiri, courgette and pumpkin fritters with blackeye beans, vegetable tempura, ricotta pie, and white chocolate cheesecake.
Babies and children admitted. Booking advisable. Separate room for parties, seats 35. Vegan dishes. **Map 20 B2.**

Manna. See p286.

West Kensington W14

222 Veggie Vegan NEW

222 North End Road, W14 9NU (7483 3344/ www.222veggievegan.com). West Kensington tube/28, 391 bus. **Lunch served** noon-3.30pm, **dinner served** 5.30-10.30pm daily. **Main courses** £7.50-£12.50. **Credit** MC, V.

Soho restaurant Plant closed in 2004, but the staff – including the Ghanaian chef, who has also worked at other vegan outfits – swiftly moved to this new venture. The nondescript decor (cream walls, wooden furniture) gives little clue to the fact that the place is wholly vegan: it could just as easily be a gastropub or even an Indian restaurant. The food, though by no means stunning, is some of the best vegan fare you'll find in London. We enjoyed baked avocados with tomatoes and vegan cream – if you're not convinced by the idea of warm avocados, try this dish and you'll be converted. Pancakes, which feature a lot on the menu, are unfortunately not the chef's strong point; it's difficult to make successful vegan pancakes, so the leathery wholemeal disc, stuffed with blackeye beans, was perhaps not a good choice. Things improved with a dish of spaghetti with tofu medallions, a perfectly tasty alternative to meatballs. There's a self-service buffet for lunch and à la carte in the evenings; in addition to its food, the menu is also notable for its imaginative drinks list.
Babies and children welcome: high chairs. Booking advisable. No smoking. Takeaway service. Vegan dishes. **Map 13 A12**.

South West
Wimbledon SW19

★ Service-Heart-Joy

191 Hartfield Road, SW19 3TH (8542 9912/ www.serviceheartjoy.com). South Wimbledon tube/ Wimbledon tube/rail. **Meals served** 8am-3.30pm Mon-Thur; 8am-5.30pm Fri; 9am-5.30pm Sat. **Main courses** £1.95-£6.95. **Credit** MC, V.

Run by followers of Sri Chinmoy (an Indian-born spiritual leader), the name of this café is effectively its mission statement. Shaped like a cheese wedge, it has a garish yellow exterior but a tranquil blue interior, filled with potted plants. With its deeply peaceful ambience and chatty, cheerful service, it seems to be forever poised in a 1960s timewarp – the scary modern world of chavs and ASBOs could be light years away. The menu offers a wide range of breakfast dishes, including pancakes (try the Balinese with coconut, banana and maple syrup), interesting sandwiches and salads. Drinks include smoothies, lassis, ice-cream floats and a good selection of coffee. Also on offer are hot dishes: we tried a meaty veggie burger served in a good bun, and a lasagne with garlic bread and mixed salad that proved to be heavy going. A refreshing mango sundae came with mango sorbet, fresh mangoes and dark chocolate pieces. A banana split with multi-flavoured ice-cream, chocolate sauce, whipped cream and jelly beans underlined the fact that, despite its worthy philosophy, this place retains a twinkle-in-the-eye frivolity.

Babies and children admitted. No smoking. Tables outdoors (2, pavement). Takeaway service. Vegan dishes.

East
Bethnal Green E2

★ Gallery Café

21 Old Ford Road, E2 9PL (8983 3624). Bethnal Green tube/8, 388 bus. **Meals served** 8.30am-3.30pm Mon, Wed-Fri; 8.30am-3pm Tue; 10.30am-5pm Sat. **Main courses** £3-£5.50. **Credit** MC, V.

Run by men from the nearby London Buddhist Centre, this plain, spacious, airy café is tucked into the basement of a Victorian building. A daily changing menu is chalked on a blackboard: one soup, two pastas, a daily special, and sandwiches made from baguettes and bagels from Brick Lane. We liked the creamy, mildly spiced Indonesian spinach and pumpkin soup, and pasta served with vegetarian puttanesca sauce was equally full-bodied in flavour. Other dishes may include quiche with new potatoes and salad, spaghetti with spinach and feta sauce, Spanish tortilla and (delicious and justly popular) Turkish meze. Fresh juices and organic Fairtrade coffee are also available, and there's a good selection of cakes and pastries (including gluten- and dairy-free options) such as apricot and polenta cake, cherry and almond cake, vegan mandarin and chocolate cake, and – despite this being a Buddhist operation – a scandalously sinful 'chocolate nemesis'.
Babies and children welcome: high chairs. No smoking (indoors). Tables outdoors (14, patio and conservatory). Takeaway service. Vegan dishes.

★ Wild Cherry

241-245 Globe Road, E2 0JD (8980 6678). Bethnal Green tube/8 bus. **Meals served** 11am-4pm Mon; 11am-7pm Tue-Fri; 10am-4pm Sat. **Main courses** £2.90-£5.50. **Unlicensed**. **Corkage** £1. **Credit** MC, V.

A hit with locals, this sparsely decorated canteen is run by women from the London Buddhist Centre, located next door. Queue at the self-service counter then eat your food in the ramshackle back garden. We liked the herbal, mineral flavours of watercress soup, although it was a little thin. A chilli bean casserole, packed with kidney beans and sweet potatoes, was hefty but well flavoured. Spaghetti with creamy mushroom, pea and mint sauce featured a tired tangle of pasta and flavourless sauce, but the roasted vegetable pie topped with polenta was tasty and surprising light. Other items on the daily changing menu may include baked potatoes, lasagne, risotto, filo pie, quiche, curries and salads. Avoid peak times if you don't like queueing – and it's best to turn up early, as the kitchen sometimes runs out of popular dishes.
Babies and children welcome: high chairs. No smoking. Tables outdoors (9, garden). Takeaway service. Vegan dishes.

North
Camden Town & Chalk Farm NW3

★ Little Earth Café NEW

2005 RUNNER-UP BEST VEGETARIAN MEAL

6 Erskine Road, NW3 3AJ (7449 0700). Chalk Farm tube/bus C11, 31. **Meals served** 10am-8pm Mon-Fri; 10am-6pm Sat; 11am-5pm Sun. **Main courses** £5.50-£6.50. **Credit** AmEx, MC, V.

During a yoga class, the focused mind is supposed to be in perfect harmony with the body. Most of us, though, find thoughts wandering – often to after-workout food. And this new café, located in the highly regarded Triyoga centre, is good enough to be very distracting. Everything is organic, vegan and, in the main, raw. Raw food is relatively new to this country, but is hugely popular in New York and California, where chefs of Gordon Ramsay calibre conjure up highly elaborate uncooked dishes designed to mimic cooked flavours. Here you could try warm quinoa topped with butternut squash,

RESTAURANTS

courgette and a creamy cashew sauce; a spectacular wooden platter piled with a pyramid of shredded hijiki salad (beetroot, avocado, cucumber and mixed seeds) and two giant pink 'sushi' (nori rolls bursting with alfalfa sprouts and raw veg in beetroot pâté); or bruschetta made from almond-based crackers, topped with tapenade, sun-dried tomato pâté and avocados. To finish, the ginger raw biscuits – a spicy date, almond and molasses blend – resembled a healthy refrigerator cake. Service was austere, but the place itself is a shoes-off sanctuary of mood music and water features. It's so tranquil and energising, you could even skip that yoga class. *Babies and children admitted. No smoking. Takeaway service. Vegan dishes.* **Map 27 A1.**

★ Manna
4 Erskine Road, NW3 3AJ (7722 8028/ www.manna-veg.com). Chalk Farm tube. **Brunch served** 12.30-3pm Sun. **Dinner served** 6.30-11pm daily. **Main courses** £9.50-£12.75 **Credit** MC, V.
Owned by two of its former customers, Manna seems to have gone from strength to strength since it was refurbished a few years ago. Opened in the 1960s, it's the capital's oldest vegetarian restaurant, and is edging towards its 40th birthday with self-assurance intact. In a lovely residential area, Manna's interior looks like a smart café, with pine tables, candles, framed pictures and a relaxed, new age vibe. Courgette flower and blue cheese tart (note: fashionable 'tart', not the much-derided 'quiche') turned a veggie cliché on its head: instead of indistinct Mediterranean vegetables and cheese, this was a stylish little number made with good pastry. The earthy, piquant flavours of organic beetroot and sorrel gazpacho were lifted by a mirepoix of peppery radish. We also adored a gratin of artichokes stuffed with olives, pine nuts and capers, served on a slab of roast polenta with cavolo nero and a sunny drizzle of yellow pepper sauce. The changing menu can occasionally be overambitious, too many ingredients competing for attention, but this time we found the flavours sophisticated, imaginative and harmonious. *Babies and children welcome: high chairs. Booking advisable. No smoking. Tables outdoors (2, pavement; 2, conservatory). Takeaway service. Vegan dishes.* **Map 27 A1.**

Outer London
Kingston, Surrey

Riverside Vegetaria
64 High Street, Kingston upon Thames, Surrey KT1 1HN (8546 0609/www.rsveg.plus.com). Kingston rail. **Meals served** noon-11pm Mon-Sat; noon-10.30pm Sun. **Main courses** £6.95-£8.50. **Credit** MC, V.
This bustling, two-floor restaurant overlooks the Thames and affords a beautiful view of swans, water and greenery – grab one of the outside tables when the weather allows. The interior too is pretty, with fresh flowers on every table, candlelight and colourful prints. The global, Sri Lankan-influenced menu has been informed by the Sri Lankan proprietor's religious beliefs – hence the many organic, vegan and gluten-free options. Sadly, the food isn't quite up to the mark. Cauliflower and almond soup had lovely, nutty undertones, but was otherwise bland. Avocado stuffed with mushrooms, beans, tomatoes and olives and drizzled in vinaigrette boasted good ingredients, but was too heavy for a starter. Next, the soft, crispy pancakes stuffed with well-flavoured potatoes and mixed beans were too substantial. Spicy Jamaican stew with mixed peppers, beans and sweet potatoes in a chilli-spiked coconut gravy was delicious, though. The extensive menu (with many more daily specials chalked on a blackboard) is filled with spicy, carbohydrate-heavy, old-school veggie fare, served in generous portions with lots of salad. We weren't bowled over by the food, but the place is well worth a visit for the view. *Babies and children welcome: children's portions; high chairs. Book weekends. No smoking. Tables outdoors (7, riverside terrace). Takeaway service. Vegan dishes.*

Vietnamese

There's no escaping the fact: most Londoners will need to head east for the best Vietnamese food. Fortunately, though, a bus pass should cover the travel expense. Before touching down in Hanoi, before even reaching Paris (where there's a sizeable and long-established Vietnamese restaurant scene), you'll get to Hackney, home to one of the largest Vietnamese communities in Britain: up to 4,000 at the last count. The majority of this contingent arrived in Britain in 1979, when the Conservative government offered homes to 20,000 Vietnamese boat people from Hong Kong. Some are ethnic Chinese who left northern Vietnam after the 1979 Sino-Vietnamese war; others are southern Vietnamese who fled the communist takeover in 1975.

It took some 15 years after their arrival for a Vietnamese culinary enclave to become established in Hackney. The seeds were sown when the An-Viet Foundation, a charity helping the boat people adjust to their new lives in London, opened a very basic canteen in a residential street in Dalston; **Huong-Viet** quickly became known for its fresh, authentic food. Some of the staff at Huong-Viet later opened **Viet Hoa** (at the southern end of Kingsland Road), which first appeared in this guide a decade ago. Nowadays, Viet Hoa is surrounded by Vietnamese restaurants of varying quality; of these, **Sông Quê** and **Loong Kee** are particularly recommended, as is the newer **Cây Tre** (not far away on Old Street). **West Lake** in Deptford is a notable outpost, and it's good to see newcomers **Saigon Saigon** (in Hammersmith) and **Pho** (in Clerkenwell). Restaurants in more salubrious areas may be more upmarket, but they tend to be Chinese-run and are seen as less authentic by the Vietnamese themselves.

Central
Clerkenwell & Farringdon EC1

★ Pho NEW
86 St John Street, EC1M 4EH (7253 7624). Farringdon tube/rail. **Lunch served** noon-3pm, **dinner served** 6-10pm Mon-Fri. **Main courses** £5.95-£7.45. **Credit** MC, V.
Correctly pronounced 'fur' or 'fer', Pho is the beef noodle soup that sustains Vietnam. Beef shinbones, oxtail and scraps of meat are simmered for half a day to make the consommé. Spices including star anise, ginger and cinnamon add complexity. Wide rice noodles are put in a big soup bowl and topped with beef or other meats, before the hot stock is poured over them to make the pho. Beef stock is central to a good pho, and the version at this modern café is the real thing; the noodles are also the right consistency, and our thin slices of beef steak, brisket and meatballs (one of several versions of pho on offer, this one £7.45) were succulent. Less successful was that Indochinese fusion dish, a supermarket-style baguette (bahn mi) with a filling of beansprouts and chicken (£3.50). And bun, a cold salad of rice vermicelli (prawn version: £6.95), was still bland despite stirring in a generous amount of nuoc cham, a dip containing chilli, garlic and fish sauce. Although the dishes could have had more kick, we liked Pho; with its huge portions and fair prices, plus friendly service from the English owners, it's like finding a new friend. *Babies and children admitted. No smoking. Takeaway service.* **Map 5 O4.**

Soho W1

Saigon
45 Frith Street, W1D 4SD (7437 7109). Leicester Square tube. **Meals served** noon-11.30pm Mon-Sat. **Main courses** £5-£13.75. **Set meal** £16.80-£20.05 per person (minimum 2). **Service** 10%. **Credit** AmEx, DC, MC, V.
The nostalgic name of this restaurant, its straw hut decor and the staff's traditional Vietnamese gowns are all evocative of Indochina. Although Saigon's menu suggests culinary authenticity, it doesn't quite live up to the promise. While the green papaya and cucumber salad certainly looked like the real thing, it lacked the unfolding of aromas and the complexity of traditional Vietnamese salads. Key flavours were missing – namely fresh herbs. Pho noodle soup, a northern Vietnamese speciality, was over-seasoned with fish sauce, which dominated the delicate star anise and cinnamon flavours. Goi cuon (cold summer roll wrapped in rice paper) at least provided us with entertainment, as the beef was barbecued at the table on a little gas stove, but again, vital components were missing. Staff didn't bring us rice vermicelli, an essential component for filling the rolls. At least the succulent, tender squid with mam ruoc (a dark purple/greyish fermented shrimp paste) gave some joy despite its pungent and truly authentic odour. Saigon looks shabby, and feels tired too; it's time the proprietors started looking forward, instead of back. *Babies and children admitted. Separate rooms for parties, seating 40 and 50. Vegetarian menu.* **Map 17 K6.**

West
Hammersmith W6

Saigon Saigon NEW
313-317 King Street, W6 9NH (0870 220 1398/ www.saigon-saigon.co.uk). Ravenscourt Park or Stamford Brook tube. **Bar Open/snacks served** 6-11.30pm Thur-Sun. *Restaurant* **Lunch served** 12.30-3pm, **dinner served** 6-11.30pm daily. **Main courses** £6-£13. *Both* **Service** 10%. **Credit** MC, V.

Run by a Vietnamese family, this newcomer is simply but attractively decorated in 1940s colonial style. It's a great place to sit outside and sip a Vietnamese coffee – espresso-style poured over condensed milk, with ice. The dishes transport you to Vietnam just as effectively. Mekong catfish is a bony fish that's slightly fatty under the skin, but slowly braised with pepper and fish sauce it becomes very tender, with a slightly caramelised sauce filling its clay serving pot. Pork stewed with quail eggs in coconut water was another winning dish, the pork tender but the broth remarkably light. A delicate beef pho was a good rendition; the accompanying herbs, in this case holy basil and the seldom-seen ngo gai (saw-leaf herb), were all present and correct. Precision of presentation seems to be a strong point. Banh xeo, a turmeric-yellow pancake of rice flour and coconut milk, was folded and perfectly sealed around the edges. Goi cuon were tightly rolled and as precisely arranged as any sushi, as pretty and perfect as any you'll find. If we have any criticism, it's that the food tends towards the bland; maybe they're scared of scaring off their mainly non-Vietnamese diners. *Babies and children welcome: high chairs. Bar available for hire. Booking advisable. No smoking. Tables outdoors (2, pavement).* **Map 20 A4**.

South East
Deptford SE8

★ ★ West Lake
207 Deptford High Street, SE8 3NT (8465 9408). Deptford rail. **Meals served** 11.30am-10pm daily. **Main courses** £3-£6. **Unlicensed. Corkage** no charge. **No credit cards.**

If you've ever visited Vietnam and want to recapture the feeling, head for this tiny Deptford café. We were the only non-Vietnamese present, but felt instantly drawn into the family atmosphere. A red Buddhist shrine can be glimpsed through the kitchen door, and there was something suitably divine about the food that emerged into the simple, peach-walled dining area. 'Grilled bird' proved to be a tender quail, whose salty segments we dipped into a delicious lemongrass and chilli sauce. Another snack perfect for sharing with a group over a beer (but remember to bring your own alcohol) is the crisp shrimp pastry, with whole shrimps staring out from their little pizza-type bases of deep-fried sweet potato and rice-flour. A fresh, tangy lotus and prawn salad provided a welcome contrast in texture. Morning glory was sublimely fresh and simple: a spinach-like vegetable stir-fried with garlic. And noodle soup with minced fish was a subtle blend of dill, basil and a compendium of other herbs. All in all, a hidden gem, however humble. *Babies and children admitted. Book weekends. Takeaway service.*

East
Shoreditch E2, EC1

★ Au Lac
104 Kingsland Road, E2 8DP (7033 0588/ www.aulac.co.uk). Old Street tube/rail/26, 48, 55, 67, 149, 242, 243 bus. **Lunch served** noon-3pm Mon-Fri. **Dinner served** 5.30-11.30pm Mon-Thur; 5.30pm-midnight Fri. **Meals served** noon-midnight Sat; noon-11.30pm Sun. **Main courses** £3.50-£7.80. **Set dinner** £10-£14.50 per person (minimum 2) 6 courses. **Credit** AmEx, MC, V.

Au Lac Shoreditch is less intimate than the original branch in Highbury, but yellow paint, hanging red lanterns and a mix of Vietnamese artworks bring warmth to the large space. The food is consistently good, with fresh, tangy flavours. Our char-grilled fish, deliciously caramelised at the edges, was eloquent with turmeric and lemongrass. We ate it as instructed, wrapping it with herbs and noodles in translucent sheets of rice starch, which we softened ourselves in a bowl of water: a typically Vietnamese adventure in layered tastes and textures. Steamed prawns were fresh and crisp, but the 'Au Lac sauce' of minced pork, tomato and peanut wasn't as titillating as we'd hoped. Spicy seafood soup was seductively hot and sour, with a

Cây Tre. See p288.

RESTAURANTS

bit of fruity pineapple – perfect for a damp London night. The menu contains several intriguing vegetarian options, and a highly drinkable house red wine. The slightly naff pop music soundtrack made us wince, though. Service was a little dozy, but good-natured enough.
Babies and children welcome: high chairs. Entertainment: pianist 8-10pm Fri. Takeaway service. **Map 6 R3.**

★ ★ Cây Tre NEW

301 Old Street, EC1V 9LA (7729 8662). Old Street tube/rail. **Lunch served** noon-3pm Mon-Sat. **Dinner served** 5.30-11pm Mon-Thur; 5.30-11.30pm Fri. **Meals served** noon-10.30pm Sun. **Main courses** £5-£9. **Set dinner** £16 per person (minimum 2) 3 courses. **Service** 10%. **Credit** MC, V.

This newcomer to the Shoreditch Vietnamese village has been the darling of restaurant critics over the past year. It's not surprising. Intense local competition has clearly raised standards, and encouraged restaurateurs to offer more and more interesting menus. Our dinner was delightful. To start: a ravishing soup of monkfish, streaked with fresh dill and juicy taro stems; refreshing and gently sour on a hot summer's evening. Then the waiter brought a barbecue plate to the table and we cooked our own beef. Thin slices of meat (rather tough on this occasion) were wrapped with rice vermicelli, shredded kohlrabi and pickled veg in thin rice wrappers: messy finger food. We couldn't resist another monkfish dish, and it was fabulous: the fish marinated in galangal and turmeric, sizzled in a pan at the tableside and then tossed with rice vermicelli, shrimp sauce, chilli and peanuts. Catfish in a sleek caramelised sauce was wonderful soaked up with plain steamed rice. Aside from the sinewy beef and a disappointing chicken salad, this was a revelatory meal. Service was excellent too.
Babies and children welcome: high chairs. Booking advisable. Takeaway service.

★ Hanoi Café

98 Kingsland Road, E2 8DP (7729 5610/ www.hanoicafe.co.uk). Old Street tube/rail/26, 48, 55, 67, 149, 242, 243 bus. **Meals served** noon-11.30pm daily. **Main courses** £3.50-£6.90. **Set lunch** £3.80 1 course. **Service** 10% dinner. **Credit** AmEx, MC, V.

From the outside, there's little to distinguish the Hanoi Café from its Vietnamese neighbours. Once you're inside, though, the light, contemporary space (decorated with black-and-white portraits and Vietnamese street scenes) stands out for its laid-back friendliness. The pleasingly varied menu ranges from street snacks to roll-your-own summer rolls and all-in-one dishes such as the buns – grilled meat of your choice served with vermicelli, salad and a tangy dipping sauce. Our bun was a mixed success; meat minced to a paste was dry, but the accompanying noodles were cooked perfectly, the salad fresh and crisp and the dipping sauce a treat. The rest of the meal was consistently better. A chicken and prawn vermicelli noodle soup featured ingredients with flavour and bite in a delicate stock; it scored points for presentation too, as did the side dishes of stir-fried water spinach with yellow beans and chilli, and stir-fried spicy okra with tomatoes. We left the friendly staff having their supper and felt like we hadn't intruded at all.
Babies and children welcome: high chairs. Restaurant available for hire. Takeaway service; delivery service (within 3-mile radius). **Map 6 R3.**

★ Loong Kee

134G Kingsland Road, E2 8DY (7729 8344). Old Street tube/rail/26, 48, 55, 67, 149, 242, 243 bus. **Lunch served** noon-3pm Mon-Fri. **Dinner served** 5-11pm Mon-Thur; 5pm-midnight Fri. **Meals served** noon-midnight Sat; noon-11pm Sun. **Main courses** £3.50-£5.50. **Unlicensed. Corkage** no charge. **No credit cards.**

Kingsland Road is packed with Vietnamese restaurants, each claiming to offer the best food on the block, but Loong Kee sticks to what it knows best – banh cuon (steamed spring rolls) and pho (rice noodle soup) – and does so brilliantly. This unassuming canteen by the Geffrye Museum has been serving authentic, home-style Vietnamese food for years. Diners run the gamut from Vietnamese families to City gents taking a break from the boardroom. Don't be put off by the simple surroundings; what Loong Kee lacks in style, it makes up for in taste and value. We were blown away by the house speciality: steamed spring rolls stuffed with morsels of black mushroom and ground pork, served with a fragrant vinegar dip. Equally impressive was the robust and filling pho soup, packed with fresh mint and coriander, shredded spring onions, rice noodles and tender hunks of beef. Service was prompt and attentive considering the lunchtime crowds. The restaurant is BYO, but designated drivers can sip on fresh fruit juices and own-made lemonade.
Babies and children welcome: high chairs. Booking advisable. Separate room for parties, seats 20. Takeaway service. **Map 6 R3.**

★ ★ Sông Quê

134 Kingsland Road, E2 8DY (7613 3222). Old Street tube/rail/26, 48, 55, 67, 149, 242, 243 bus. **Lunch served** noon-3pm, **dinner served** 5.30-11pm Mon-Sat. **Meals served** noon-11pm Sun. **Main courses** £4.40-£5.60. **Set meal** £8.50-£14.50 per person (minimum 2). **Credit** AmEx, MC, V.

With fake ivy and plastic lobsters on its mint-green walls, Sông Quê might not look a likely venue for exquisite food. Just as its name 'rustic river' implies, the surroundings are a little rough and ready. Nevertheless, the menu offers true Vietnamese cuisine. Like a culinary excursion through Vietnam, the assortment of dishes covers specialities from all regions – the aromatic pho from Hanoi, the chao tom (minced shrimp on sugar cane) from Hue and the southern Vietnamese banh xeo (pancake filled with pork, prawns and beansprouts). The food is delicious. Cold goi cuon were appetising, handy rice-paper rolls bearing little aromatic surprises inside, in the form of mint, coriander and chives. Ca kho to, a sizzling snapper cooked in brine and chillies, was tender and soft inside with just the right crunch on the outside. To finish, there's an excellent selection of desserts, including che ba mau, the 'three-colour pudding' (a jelly-like concoction of red beans, mung beans, tapioca and coconut milk) or the French-Vietnamese ca phe sua da, an ice-cold white coffee.
Babies and children welcome: high chairs. Booking advisable. No-smoking tables. Takeaway service. **Map 6 R3.**

★ Tay Do Café

65 Kingsland Road, E2 8AG (7729 7223). Old Street tube/rail/26, 48, 55, 67, 149, 242, 243 bus. **Lunch served** 11.30am-3pm, **dinner served** 5-11.30pm daily. **Main courses** £4-£8.50. **Unlicensed. Corkage** 50p. **Credit** (over £10) MC, V.

Khoai Café

A popular café in the heart of the Hoxton party district, Tay Do is perfect for those heading for a night on the razz. On weekend nights the place heaves, meaning long waits for tables and a decibel level that prohibits quiet conversation. Too few waiters struggle to service too many tables, but the lively atmosphere will put you in a good mood for the rest of the night. Lunchtimes are more low-key. The food is highly regarded by the Vietnamese community. Our char-grilled lamb with chilli and lemongrass was rich and succulent, and a Vietnamese pancake was delectably scrunchy with handfuls of fresh herbs and a sharp nuoc cham sauce (though somewhat meanly stuffed with chicken and prawn). We loved the Tay Do special noodles: cold rice vermicelli tossed with shredded vegetables, delicious grilled pork and crisp spring rolls in classic Viet style. The special southern rice noodles, with sliced pork and other goodies, came in an invigorating chilli-laced broth; fried water-spinach was seriously tasty with its fermented beancurd sauce. Prices are absurdly low. The place isn't licensed, so bring your own booze.
Babies and children welcome: high chairs. Takeaway service. **Map 6 R4.**

★ Viet Hoa
70-72 Kingsland Road, E2 8DP (7729 8293). Old Street tube/rail/26, 48, 55, 67, 149, 242, 243 bus. **Lunch served** noon-3.30pm Mon-Fri; 12.30-4pm Sat, Sun. **Dinner served** 5.30-11pm Mon-Fri; 5.30-11.30pm Sat, Sun. **Main courses** £3.50-£8.50. **Service** 12.5%. **Credit** MC, V.
The original Vietnamese canteen is still going strong in this enclave on Kingsland Road. Spread over two floors and with high ceilings, it's a big place. Decoration is limited, but the many and varied customers provide more than enough visual stimulation. Start with a range of soups (some available in bigger sizes for one-dish dining) or old favourites banh xeo (crispy pancake with either vegetables or prawns and pork, served with salad and herbs – although, on this occasion, not quite enough of the green stuff) or salted chilli squid (also available with prawns, tofu or ribs) or menu stalwarts spring rolls or crispy duck pancakes. Mains are divided by seafood, beef, pork, vegetables and so on. Wade through the list to unearth stir-fried tofu (or beef or chicken) with pickled greens, or one of the vibrant salads, or grilled minced pork meatballs with rice vermicelli. Drink tea or one of several Asian beers. Other Vietnamese restaurants hit higher culinary standards than Viet Hoa, but this place remains popular with pretty much everyone.
Babies and children welcome: high chairs. Booking advisable; essential dinner. No-smoking tables. Takeaway service. **Map 6 R3.**

Wanstead E11

★ Nam An
157 High Street, E11 2RL (8532 2845). Wanstead tube. **Lunch served** noon-2.30pm Wed-Sun. **Dinner served** 6-11.30pm daily. **Main courses** £5-£6.50. **Set meal** £20-£35 per person (minimum 2). **Service** 10%. **Credit** AmEx, JCB, MC, V.
Wanstead is an unlikely setting for Nam An's exotic re-creation of colonial Saigon (complete with carved teak furniture, a curving bridge over a fishpond and an antique cycle-rickshaw). On a slow weekday lunchtime, the restaurant has the air of an abandoned film set. But if the waiters seemed surprised to see us, they soon stirred themselves and the kitchen into action – with very pleasing results. Prawn paste on sugar cane sometimes tastes like pink sludge on a stick, but here the paste is genuinely prawny and the sugar cane sweet and juicy. Scallops with garlic couldn't have been more tender, and minced seafood made a succulent filling for a lettuce wrap. With the carp and goldfish in the pond inspiring us to splash out further, we then ordered a sea bass, and didn't regret it. Steamed in simple Cantonese style with ginger and spring onion, it was beautifully fresh. Let's hope more people pause for a spot of oriental indulgence at the busy junction of Wanstead High Street and the A12 and help keep this place going.

Babies and children welcome: high chairs. Booking advisable. Disabled: toilet. No-smoking tables. Separate room for parties, seats 26. Takeaway service. Vegetarian menu. **For branch see index.**

North East
Dalston N1

★ Huong-Viet
An Viet House, 12-14 Englefield Road, N1 4LS (7249 0877). Bus 67, 149, 236, 242, 243. **Lunch served** noon-3.30pm Mon-Fri; noon-4pm Sat. **Dinner served** 5.30-11pm Mon-Sat. **Main courses** £4.20-£6.90. **Set lunch** £6 2 courses incl soft drink. **Service** 10% (12.5% for parties of 5 or more). **Credit** JCB, MC, V.
This trusty grandfather to the gaggle of Vietnamese restaurants on nearby Kingsland Road and Mare Street has retained its simple, casual Asian feel and friendly, family-run atmosphere. It is housed in the same old community centre where it was originally set up as a canteen for Vietnamese refugees. True, the spring rolls did seem a trifle tired on this visit, but the prawns in crispy pancakes, and the tofu and egg fresh rolls with herbs in rice paper more than made up for them in terms of taste, texture and general zinginess. What the menu called tilapia and the waitress described as catfish was equally fresh by either name, and came in a rich dark broth of gingery galangal, black pepper and spring onion. And the vegetable curry, while by no means the most typically Vietnamese of dishes on the menu, was a delicious blend of aubergines, tomatoes, beans and peppers in a creamy coconut sauce. The customers may have changed over the years (clued-up Islingtonians now dine here), but the place continues to be special and the food excellent value.
Babies and children welcome: high chairs. Booking advisable; essential weekends. Disabled: toilet. Separate room for parties, seats 25. Takeaway service. Vegetarian menu.

Hackney E8

★ Green Papaya
191 Mare Street, E8 3QE (8985 5486/www. greenpapaya.co.uk). Bus 48, 55, 253, 277, D6. **Meals served** 5-11pm Tue-Sun. **Main courses** £5-£8. **Credit** DC, JCB, MC, V.
More bistro than canteen, Green Papaya has a lovely local feel fostered by bright, engaged staff and lots of contented regulars, including a laid-back Anglo-Vietnamese crowd. The food has a similarly personal feel. Distinctly non-production line, it comes over as enthusiastic home cooking, rough-chopped and varying noticeably depending on who's wielding the knife. There's not a starter on the list we wouldn't recommend, though the light, tasty deep-fried squid and big, bold banh tom (prawn and sweet-potato patties, for wrapping in lettuce) are our regular orders. By contrast, the main-course list needs some navigation to avoid the sauced and stir-fried dishes, which tend to be a tasteless, flaccid disappointment – even the interesting-sounding specials. Best to stick with dry dishes, notably the excellent barbecue chicken, or the noodles and soups. Desserts sound lovely (sweet pancake stacks, chocolate puddle pudding), but seem to be seldom available. The glassed-over garden area at the back is a light, bright space for non-smokers year-round; there's a tiny but valued covered courtyard for summer too.
Babies and children welcome: high chairs. Booking advisable. No-smoking tables. Tables outdoors (5, courtyard). Takeaway service.

★ Tre Viet
251 Mare Street, E8 3NS (8533 7390). Hackney Central rail/48, 55, 253, 277, D6 bus. **Meals served** 11.30am-11pm daily. **Main courses** £4-£10. **Unlicensed. Corkage** no charge. **No credit cards.**
A short walk from the Hackney Empire, this cheery corner restaurant is doing well. You're more likely to share one of the long tables with members of the local Vietnamese community than with

theatre-goers. Atmosphere, service and decor are bright and basic, the only frills being the bamboo cages housing the overhead lights. Sour soup with pickled vegetables – a vast bowl of shimmering greens and reds – had a kick to it more often associated with Thailand, but a host of more subtle flavours soon emerged to soothe and tantalise the back of the throat. Equally good were cubes of lean beef tossed in a dressing of garlic, soy and chilli and then dipped in salt and pepper with a squeeze of lemon. The mekong fish had been well salted and then braised in a delicious rich dark sauce. Its flesh fell away at the touch of a chopstick and melted wonderfully in the mouth. Steamed stuffed snails and lemongrass were unavailable and we couldn't bring ourselves to order raw goat. But we were full anyway: with some of the best Vietnamese food in London.
Babies and children welcome: high chairs. Booking advisable weekends. Disabled: toilet. Separate room for parties, seats 30. Takeaway service.

North
Crouch End N8

★ ★ Khoai Café NEW
6 Topsfield Parade, N8 8PR (8341 2120). Finsbury Park tube/rail then W3, W7 bus or Archway tube then 41, W5 bus. **Lunch served** noon-3.30pm, **dinner served** 5.30-11.30pm daily. **Main courses** £3.60-£8.50. **Set lunch** £6.95 3 courses. **Set meal** £12.85 4 courses. **Service** 12%. **Credit** MC, V .
In an area that has a reputation for going over the top, Khoai Café is an understated breath of fresh air. This simple restaurant looks more like an Italian bistro than a gourmet Vietnamese, but the atmosphere is laid-back, service fast and the food exemplary. Like many Vietnamese restaurants, Khoai serves plenty of Chinese dishes, but it's the Vietnamese cooking that steals the show. To start, grilled beef wrapped in wild betel leaves was deliciously moist and tender, with hints of chilli and lemongrass and a strange, other-worldly flavour from the betel leaves. For mains, we opted for one of Khoai's signature dishes, chao tom (prawn mince wrapped around spears of sugar cane) – a sublime experience. Rice vermicelli fried with chicken, chilli and lemongrass was also well judged, with crisp beansprouts and deep-fried garlic hidden among the noodles. Other popular options include fried tilapia, and pho (rice noodle soup). Diners can douse the spicier dishes with a range of imported Asian beers; Hue lager seems to be the beverage of choice. Overall, a great neighbourhood Vietnamese: lucky Crouch End.
Babies and children welcome: booster seats. No bookings taken 8-10pm Fri, Sat. Takeaway service.

Camden Town & Chalk Farm NW1

★ Bluu Grass
6 Plender Street, NW1 0JT (7380 1196). Mornington Crescent tube. **Lunch served** 11am-3pm Mon-Fri. **Dinner served** 5-11pm Mon-Sat. **Main courses** £4.90-£5.60. **Set lunch** £4.30-£5 2 courses. **Credit** MC, V.
It was a shame that the charming Korean waitress in this spruce, stylish restaurant was unable to tell us more about what we were eating, since Bluu Grass is unusual in stressing the French side of Vietnam's heritage. Casseroles, for instance, are offered with crusty bread. We duly began with frogs' legs, which came in a light, crispy tempura batter coated with a mild, sweetish curry sauce – and, like many dishes here, lots of onions. The more standard Vietnamese food was excellent. Chicken salad, light and fresh, arrived packed with beansprouts, peanuts and herbs (mainly mint). The prawns with lemongrass and chilli were fresh and firm. Pho was a meal in itself: a huge bowl of fragrant, delicious stock and thin noodles with an equally large side-dish piled with fresh green herbs and fiery red chillies for

RESTAURANTS

stirring into the soup. Not so very French after all, then, but Bluu Grass makes a nice change from all the Greek places around it. (The background music was more Simon & Garfunkel than bluegrass; perhaps the name refers to the concealed blue lighting overhead.)
Babies and children welcome: high chair. No-smoking tables. Separate room for parties, seats 25. Takeaway service; delivery service (within 2-mile radius). **Map 27 D3.**

★ Viet Anh
41 Parkway, NW1 7PN (7284 4082). Camden Town tube. **Lunch served** noon-4pm, **dinner served** 5.30-11pm daily. **Main courses** £3.95-£7.95. **Service** 10% (over £15, dinner only). **Credit** MC, V.
The food in this small, cheery café is a good match for the decor – fresh, clean and pleasingly wholesome. Asparagus and ginger made for a crunchy, colourful appetiser, the asparagus fresh and cooked to a turn. Pancakes bursting with beansprouts and shredded lettuce were fragrant and filling, if somewhat bland (even when dipped in the accompanying fish sauce: a slightly sweet and mild version). Star among the starters were the prawns in 'hawaii leaf': succulent prawns wrapped in what looked like vine leaves and scattered with toasted sesame seeds. The crispy-skinned roast duck may have been based on a Chinese idea, but its flesh proved far more moist and lean than you'd find in an average takeaway. Galangal eel came in a sauce thick with gingery, almost chocolatey fruitiness, while pho with tofu was quietly satisfying. There are no desserts, but you won't need them. Service is fast but friendly; Viet Anh is not somewhere to linger, but it's a good choice for a healthy meal with a difference.
Babies and children admitted. Booking advisable. No-smoking tables. Tables outdoors (2, pavement). Takeaway service. **Map 27 C2.**

Islington N1

★ Viet Garden
207 Liverpool Road, N1 1LX (7700 6040/ www.vietgarden.co.uk). Angel tube. **Lunch served** noon-3.30pm daily. **Dinner served** 5.30-11pm Mon-Thur, Sun; 5.30-11.30pm Fri, Sat. **Main courses** £4.50-£6.90. **Set lunch** (Mon-Fri) £6 2 courses. **Set dinner** £15 2 courses. **Service** 12.5%. **Credit** MC, V.
Only just out of earshot of the 21st-century buzz of Upper Street, this quiet, unassuming Vietnamese restaurant has something of a staid 1950s feel to it. On a weekday lunchtime it was almost eerily empty, and only the airy spaciousness of the dining area and the friendliness of the waitress managed to keep a sense of gloom at bay. Spirits rose with the arrival of summer rolls: the sauce dark, warm and peanutty, the rolls fresh, cool and translucent. The only disappointment came when we found crabsticks instead of prawns inside. But then came a sure-fire hit – hot and intensely herby minced beef packed into betel leaves, for dipping in a fish sauce that sparkled with red chillies. A highlight among the main courses was pomfret, the fish being liberally strewn with dill and turmeric and presented on an intoxicatingly sizzling platter. The waitress told us that her mother had discovered the recipe on a recent trip to northern Vietnam. Another house special, tiger prawns with coconut, was pleasant in a Malaysian sort of way, but less exciting.
Babies and children welcome: high chairs. Book weekends. Takeaway service. **Map 5 N1.**

Menu

Although most of London's Vietnamese restaurants offer a range of Chinese dishes, it's best to ignore these and head for the Vietnamese specialities. These contain fresh, piquant seasonings and raw vegetable ingredients that create a taste experience entirely different from Chinese cuisine. Vietnamese cookery makes abundant use of fresh, fragrant herbs such as mint and Asian basil, and refreshing, sweet-sour dipping sauces known generically as nuoc cham. Look out also for spices such as chilli, ginger and lemongrass, and crisp root vegetables pickled in sweetened vinegar.

Some dishes are steamed or stir-fried in the Chinese manner; others are assembled at the table in a way that is distinctively Vietnamese. Order a steaming bowl of pho (rice noodles and beef or chicken in an aromatic broth), and you'll be invited to add raw herbs, chilli and citrus juice as you eat. Crisp pancakes and grilled meats are served with herb sprigs, lettuce-leaf wraps and piquant dipping sauces. Toss your cold rice vermicelli with salad leaves, herbs and hot meat or seafood fresh from the grill. All these dishes offer an intriguing mix of tastes, temperatures and textures.

Aside from the pronounced Chinese influence on Vietnamese culinary culture, there are hints of the French colonial era (in sweet iced coffee, for example, and the use of beef), and echoes of neighbouring South-east Asian cuisines. Within Vietnamese cooking itself there are several regional styles; the mix of immigrants in London means you can sample some of them here. The food of Hanoi and the north – try **West Lake** and **Loong Kee** – is known for its plain, no-nonsense flavours and presentation. The former imperial capital Hue and its surrounding region are famed for a royal cuisine and robustly spicy soups; look out for Hue noodle soups (bun bo hue) on some menus. The food of Saigon (officially Ho Chi Minh City) and the south is more elegant and colourful in style, and makes great use of fresh herbs and vegetables.

Below are some specialities and culinary terms; spellings can vary. For recipes and info about Vietnamese food culture, look for *Pleasures of the Vietnamese Table* by Mai Pham, a Californian restaurateur of Vietnamese origin. It's published in the US by HarperCollins, but is available in the UK.

Banh cuon: pancake-like steamed rolls of translucent fresh rice pasta, sometimes stuffed with minced pork or shrimp (reminiscent in style of Chinese cheung fun, a dim sum speciality).
Banh pho: flat rice noodles used in soups and stir-fries, usually with beef.
Banh xeo: a large pancake made from a batter of rice flour and coconut milk, coloured bright yellow with turmeric and traditionally filled with prawns, pork, beansprouts and onion. To eat it, tear the pancake apart with your chopsticks, roll the pieces with sprigs of herbs in a lettuce leaf, and dip in nuoc cham (qv).
Bun: rice vermicelli, served in soups and stir-fries. These are also eaten cold, with raw salad vegetables and herbs, with a nuoc cham (qv) sauce poured over, and a topping such as grilled beef or pork, all of which are tossed together at the table.
Cha gio: deep-fried spring rolls. Unlike their Chinese counterparts, the wrappers are made from rice paper rather than sheets of wheat flour, and pucker up deliciously after cooking.
Chao tom: grilled minced prawn on a baton of sugar cane.
Goi: salad. There are many types in Vietnam, but they often contain raw, crunchy vegetables and herbs, perhaps accompanied by chicken or prawns, with a sharp, perky dressing.

Goi cuon (literally 'rolled salad', often translated as 'fresh rolls' or 'salad rolls'): cool, soft, rice-paper rolls usually containing prawns, pork, fresh herbs and rice vermicelli, served with a thick sauce similar to satay sauce but made from hoi sin mixed with peanut butter, scattered with roasted peanuts.
Nem: the north Vietnamese name for cha gio (qv).
Nom: the north Vietnamese term for goi (qv).
Nuoc cham: the generic name for a wide range of dipping sauces, based on a paste of fresh chillies, sugar and garlic that is diluted with water, lime juice and the ubiquitous fish sauce, nuoc mam (qv).
Nuoc mam: a brown or pale liquid derived from fish that have been salted and left to ferment. It's the essential Vietnamese seasoning, used in dips and as a cooking ingredient.
Pho: the most famous and best-loved of all Vietnamese dishes, a soup of rice noodles and beef or chicken in a rich, clear broth flavoured with aromatics. It is served with a dish of fresh beansprouts, red chilli and herbs, and a squeeze of lime; these are added to the soup at the table. Though now regarded as quintessentially Vietnamese, pho seems to have developed as late as the 19th century in northern Vietnam, and may owe its origins to French or Chinese influences. Some restaurants, such as Sông Quê, offer many versions of this delicious, substantial dish.
Rau thom: aromatic herbs, which might include Asian basil (rau que), mint (rau hung), red or purple perilla (rau tia to), lemony Vietnamese balm (rau kinh gioi) or saw-leaf herb (ngo gai).
Tuong: a general term for a thick sauce. One common tuong is a dipping sauce based on fermented soy beans, enlivened with hints of sweet and sour, and often garnished with crushed roasted peanuts.

RESTAURANTS

Cheap Eats

TABLE (AS BEFORE)
COFFEE CUP AND SAUCER FROM VILLEROY & BOCH
(020 8875 6060, WWW.VILLEROY-BOCH.COM)
COFFEE MAKER FROM HEALS (AS BEFORE)

Budget

Few people in London seem to think beyond the local greasy spoon or curry house when they're feeling short of pennies but need to get out of the house for a feed. But it doesn't have to be this way – you can demand more when you want to eat for less.

For cooking tied to a particular country, turn to the relevant chapter elsewhere in this guide (not just Indian, but Thai, Chinese, Turkish, Korean…) where you'll find cheap options indicated by a ★. All the places listed below serve food into the evening; for cheap eats in the daytime, see **Cafés**, starting on p298. Of particular note in the past couple of years has been the growth of the gourmet burger bar (blessed relief, at last, from McEverywhere), which inspired us to introduce a Best Burger Bar category to the 2005 *Time Out* Eating & Drinking Awards.

For even more choice, *Time Out*'s *Cheap Eats in London* is the most comprehensive guide to wallet-friendly dining in the capital, covering more than 700 eateries where you can eat for under £20 a head.

Central

Bloomsbury WC1

Ultimate Burger NEW

2005 RUNNER-UP BEST BURGER BAR
334 New Oxford Street, WC1A 1AP (7436 6641/ www.ultimateburger.co.uk). Holborn tube. **Meals served** 10am-11.30pm daily. **Main courses** £5.45-£6.95. **Credit** MC, V.
'Excuse me, do you think it's good?' asked the waitress, moments into the first bite of our burger. Just one example of the rather bizarre service at this New Oxford Street burger joint, where the chairs seemed to be constantly dragged around, just about drowning out the dreadful soft-rock soundtrack, and our plates were snatched away before we had quite finished. But Ultimate Burger otherwise proved another likeable, easy-going burger joint to add to the capital's collection. The thoroughfare location means the usual central London mixture of tourists, students and suits, but the clash doesn't dampen a bubbly vibe provided by keen and smiley staff. Burgers are portly little fellows – slightly smaller and, at £5.45, more expensive than at other patty shacks – but the menu includes some rarities (the 'surf and turf' contains spicy battered prawns and cheese, the 'tortilla burger' is topped with jalapeños and comes in a flour wrap) as well as a good assortment of chicken, lamb and veggie options. Sides were adequate, with American-style chilli fries impressing the most. Not quite the ultimate burger experience, but a welcome contender nonetheless.
Babies and children welcome: children's menu; high chairs. Disabled: toilet. No smoking. Takeaway service. **Map 18 L5.**
For branches see index.

Clerkenwell & Farringdon EC1

Little Bay

171 Farringdon Road, EC1R 3AL (7278 1234). Farringdon tube/rail. **Meals served** 10am-midnight Mon-Sat; 10am-11pm Sun. **Main courses** £5.95-£7.95. **Credit** MC, V.
An essential for the miser, Little Bay's same-across-the-board pricing policy means the Scrooges out there can say 'Order anything you like!' safe in the knowledge that – tee hee – everything costs the same. Mains are all £7.95 and starters all £2.95 (at lunchtime, there is a delightful reduction to £5.95 and £1.95 respectively), which makes for very good value indeed. A starter bowl of garlic-drizzled mussels or a trio of crab choux, followed by cod, mash and greens or an aubergine stuffed with veg and goat's cheese? Yes, please. There are occasional misses (in our experience, the steak is rarely a decent cut), but when three courses literally can't break the £15 barrier (unless you deviate and order from the often-disappointing specials board) it would be churlish to moan too much. The deep red interior is tightly packed and has a bizarrely realised sea theme (an enormous Neptune carving surveys all from the wall), but such craziness contributes to a fun atmosphere.
Babies and children admitted. Booking advisable. Disabled: toilet. Separate room for parties, seats 120. **Map 5 N4.**
For branches see index.

Covent Garden WC2

Canela NEW

33 Earlham Street, WC2H 9LS (7240 6926/ www.canelacafe.com). Covent Garden tube. **Meals served** 9.30am-10pm Mon-Sat; 10am-8pm Sun. **Main courses** £6.50-£7.90. **Credit** MC, V.
This friendly Portuguese and Brazilian café, carved into a corner of the Thomas Neal Building, has a converted warehouse feel. The dining area is dominated by a chiller cabinet over which the food is served; within it you'll find a wide range of rustic, savoury dishes. The Portuguese snacks, including chicken-stuffed coxinha (a pointed, deep-fried parcel resembling a drumstick), were priced at an enticingly low £2, with main courses such as chorizo tart and vegetable lasagne for a very reasonable £6-£7. The lasagne was delicious – topped with chopped cashew nuts and flavoured with blue cheese, it had a surprising texture and excellent flavour. There's also an impressive selection of gluten- and wheat-free cakes. Large glasses of fresh berry and apple juice are as popular as the strong black coffee. Customers get table service, whether they opt for the black wooden benches inside or the red metal furniture on the pavement.
Babies and children admitted. No smoking. Tables outdoors (4, pavement). Takeaway service. **Map 18 K6.**

Hamburger Union

2005 RUNNER-UP BEST BURGER BAR
4-6 Garrick Street, WC2E 9BH (7379 0412/ www.hamburgerunion.com). Covent Garden tube. **Meals served** 11.30am-9.30pm Mon, Sun; 11.30am-10.30pm Tue-Sat. **Main courses** £3.95-£9.95. **Credit** MC, V.
With two popular, sleekly designed central outlets in Covent Garden and Soho, Hamburger Union seems to be doing very well for itself. Deservedly so, as they churn out mighty good burgers: oozing juice and served in robust buns (with a cute teat), well padded with salad and relish. A decent menu includes chicken, steak, vegetarian and sausage options (go for the chorizo, avoid the 'vegetable sausage pattie'). The burgers aren't the best in London, but they're probably the cheapest at this top end of the market (at £3.95 the plain Union Burger costs barely a pound more than its superchain equivalent and tastes far, far better). Sides of fries, salad and coleslaw – served in funky, 1980s-style square bowls – also went down well. Our big gripe with the Union is as it's always been: staff still don't ask how you want your burger cooked. To make a claim for true gourmet status, punters must be allowed to specify whether they want their burgers (in Tarantino-speak) bloody as hell or burnt to a crisp. Is someone there going to listen or do we need to start chopping off ears?
Babies and children welcome: high chairs. Bookings not accepted. No smoking. Takeaway service. **Map 18 L7.**
For branch see index.

Leicester Square WC2

Gaby's

30 Charing Cross Road, WC2H 0DB (7836 4233). Leicester Square tube. **Meals served** 11am-midnight Mon-Sat; noon-10pm Sun. **Main courses** £3.80-£9. **No credit cards.**
Come hungry, that's all we advise. A towering salt beef sandwich platter from Gaby's could floor a mountain bear, should the beast be able to get its jaws around the sandwich's almighty height. Part New York-Jewish diner, part Mediterranean café, Gaby's has been serving and satisfying Leicester Square's lunch crowd for years. Primarily a takeaway joint, sandwiches and salads are turfed out at lightning speed from a counter at the front; an eat-in area at the back of the deep interior is not particularly pretty, but it is always jammed with customers: big menu, big portions and big flavour has proved a winning combination. A platter of smoked salmon (the real, meaty, dill-tickled, greasy kind) was served in the same criminally generous quantity as the salt beef equivalent, and was just as lip-smacking. Pick 'n' mix salads (we went for okra in a tomato sauce with whole mushrooms chucked in) made the perfect accompaniment; the falafel is justly renowned. Just don't expect to clear your plate.
Babies and children admitted. No-smoking tables. Takeaway service. **Map 18 K7.**

Soho W1

Burger Shack NEW

14-16 Foubert's Place, W1F 7BH (7287 6983/ www.burgershack.co.uk). Oxford Circus tube. **Meals served** noon-9pm Mon-Wed; noon-10pm Thur-Sat; noon-6pm Sun. **Main courses** £5.45-£7.40. **Credit** MC, V.
In summer, the Burger Shack's doors fold back to reveal a slick, spacious dining area with dark wooden furniture and red leather seats. Weather permitting, it's worth trying for one of the few seats on the street, where you can enjoy a glass of wine, bottle of beer or a milkshake at your leisure. Like most other new-wave burger joints, Burger Shack offers much more than the classic beefburger: burger options include chicken satay, falafel, chorizo and even duck, plus an interesting selection of salads. All orders are taken at the bar. The burgers are huge and satisfyingly messy to eat, with the beef of good quality. However, though requested medium, our beefburger came well done, as did the venison burger, making it too dry. The

skinny chips had a good bite, but were oversalted. Still, the grub is satisfying and filling, proving popular with families, tourists and groups of mates, and staff are friendly and efficient.
Babies and children welcome: children's menu; high chairs. Disabled: toilet. No smoking. Tables outdoors (30, pavement). Takeaway service. **Map 17 J6.**

Maoz NEW

43 Old Compton Street, W1D 6HG (7851 1586/ www.maoz.nl). Leicester Square or Tottenham Court Road tube. **Open** 11am-1am Mon-Thur; 11am-2am Fri, Sat; 11am-midnight Sun. **Main courses** £2.50-£3.50. **Unlicensed.** No alcohol allowed. **No credit cards.**
The Maoz logo will be familiar to anyone who's ever hungrily roamed the streets of central Amsterdam. The small chain is now expanding into territory outside its native Netherlands: along with branches in Spain, France and even the US, it's opened this plain but surprisingly large takeout operation right on ever-buzzing Old Compton Street. The menu is perfectly simple: freshly made falafel (from £3), served in pitta with or without houmous or tahini, and topped with as much or as little salad as you like. Service is fast and the vegetarian food is filling as well as healthy – though some prefer the falafel at nearby Gaby's (*see p292*). There are a few tables should you wish to eat in.
Babies and children admitted. No smoking. Tables outdoors (2, pavement). Takeaway service. **Map 17 K6.**

Stockpot

18 Old Compton Street, W1D 4TN (7287 1066). Leicester Square or Tottenham Court Road tube. **Meals served** 11.30am-11.30pm Mon, Tue; 11.30am-midnight Wed-Sat; noon-11pm Sun. **Main courses** £3.40-£5.50. **Set meal** (Mon-Sat) £5.65 2 courses; (Sun) £5.95 2 courses. **No credit cards.**

The hand-scrawled menu changes a little every day, but meals at the Stockpot always conform to the same litany: plated British favourites, served quickly, cheaply and generously. You're not going to come away wowed, but you're not going to come away hungry or broke or dissatisfied. Mains like grilled lamb cutlets, beef stroganoff (with rice *and* chips, by god), liver and onions, and gammon steak all caress the £5 mark; starters are absurdly cheap (where else can you sit down for a bowl of soup for less than £1.50?). Pasta dishes all ring in at under £4.20 and a selection of salads and omelettes round out the menu at a similar price. The canteen-look decor hasn't changed for years, though the shopfront has recently been spruced up with a fresh-made sign, making the Stockpot even easier to spot. Ever popular, ever reliable, we love it.
Babies and children admitted. Tables outdoors (2, pavement). Takeaway service. **Map 17 K6.**

Strand WC2

Exotika NEW

7 Villiers Street, WC2N 6NA (7930 6133). Charing Cross tube/rail or Embankment tube. **Open** 8am-11pm Mon-Wed; 8am-midnight Thur, Fri; noon-midnight Sat; noon-9pm Sun. **Main courses** £4.50-£7.20. **Set dinner** (5-8.30pm Fri, Sat) £5.50 1 course. **Credit** AmEx, MC, V.
Laid out like a café, this smallish restaurant has a sleek metallic and red interior, with high stools towards the counter and more comfortable seating at the window. On our lunchtime visit the place was rather empty, which, with the modern decor, left it feeling rather sterile, but the friendly staff, light music and abstract floral paintings were cheering. The menu offers a fusion of foreign flavours, such as lemongrass chicken, sweet chilli cod, and penne with tomato, basil and mascarpone. The last dish was delicious, full of fresh tomatoes

and wonderfully creamy. Great emphasis is put on healthy eating: many of the ingredients are non-GM and additive-free, and food is often cooked by steaming. There's also a good selection of salads and dishes to share, plus beer, wine, soft drinks, fruit juices and Innocent smoothies on offer. Orders are taken up at the bar and service is amazingly speedy. The sign outside Exotika says it all: fast quality eaterie.
Babies and children admitted. No-smoking tables. Takeaway service; delivery service (within half-mile radius). **Map 18 L7.**

Trafalgar Square WC2

Café in the Crypt

Crypt of St Martin-in-the-Fields, Duncannon Street, WC2N 4JJ (7839 4342/www.stmartin-in-the-fields.org). Embankment tube/Charing Cross tube/rail. **Lunch served** 11.30am-3pm Mon-Sat; noon-3pm Sun. **Dinner served** 5-7.30pm Mon-Wed, Sun; 5-10.15pm Thur-Sat. **Main courses** £5.25 soup and pudding. **Credit** MC, V.
Deep below the church of St Martin-in-the-Fields, in an ancient vault beneath Trafalgar Square, lies… a rather average canteen. In look, it fascinates: high arched ceiling, thick stone pillars, a dull echo of chattering sightseers and suits, and spooky low-lighting, kept so even in the middle of the day by an absence of windows or skylights (those 18th-century architects really weren't thinking ahead). But the food is a let-down. Hot-plate mains (think fish and meat with boiled potatoes and veg, ladled soup with a roll) and salad platters (chicken, fish or quiche) are too expensive and boring. £6.75 for half a papaya topped with a lump of chicken salad is pricing for tourists and no one else. The Café in the Crypt is worth a visit for the atmosphere, though; a note on each table informs diners that proceeds from the café go to 'the work of the church', if you need more encouragement.

Le Mercury. See p297.

Caffs with class

New Piccadilly

CHEAP EATS

The handful of British working men's cafés still left in London that retain some or all of their mid 20th-century Formica fixtures and fittings are often dismissed as mere greasy spoons. But for a country that emerged from World War II facing the collapse of long-held social and political certainties, these cafés became forcing houses for the cultural advance guard active in London at the time.

Within a decade of the Moka, Soho's first espresso bar, opening at 29 Frith Street in 1953, London became the world's hippest city: a ferment of music, fashion, film, photography, sex, crime, scandal and avant-gardism. The of-the-moment design of the cafés and their Populuxe youth appeal galvanised British cultural life and incubated a generation of writers, artists, musicians, crime lords and sexual interlopers.

Most of these cafés are now vanishing in a flurry of redevelopment and refitting, and the architecture and ambience of those that remain is fast being levelled by mega-coffee combines. But for their cultural impact on modern Britain, we owe these old classic cafés an immense debt of gratitude and a serious duty of care. And for their decently priced menus and hearty fare, we also owe them our custom. Help keep 'em classic by visiting the following fine survivors.
Adrian Maddox

Alpino
97 Chapel Market , N1 9EY (7837 8330). Angel tube. **Meals served** 6.30am-4pm Mon-Sat. **Main courses** £4-£5. **No credit cards**.

Founded in 1959, this popular local has held on to every ounce of its character. The plum-patterned cup and saucer sets alone are ceramic perfection, but the fine booth seating, teak-veneer Formica and glorious lamp holders make the place a stone classic. All the liver/bacon/sausage combinations come highly recommended, especially in an area that's been Starbucked in particularly comprehensive fashion. *Babies and children admitted. Disabled: toilet. Takeaway service.* **Map 5 N2**.

Frank's
Addison Bridge Place , W14 8XP (7603 4121). Kensington (Olympia) tube/rail. **Meals served** 6am-3pm Mon-Fri; 6-11am Sat. **Main courses** £2-£4.50. **No credit cards**.
Constructed out of an abandoned signal box, this is a superb old diner-style place with a crumbling interior, single-stool seating and a picturesque art deco counter area. Nosh-wise, it's probably best to stick with the bacon roll variants favoured by the rambunctious cabbies who fill the place. One of only two cafés featured in Jonathan Routh's *Good Cuppa Guide* of 1966 that survive today. *Babies and children admitted. Tables outdoors (2, pavement). Takeaway service.*

Gambardella
47-48 Vanbrugh Park, SE3 7JQ (8858 0327). North Greenwich tube. **Meals served** 7.30am-5.30pm Mon-Fri; 7.30am-2.30pm Sat. **Main courses** £2.50-£5. **No credit cards**.
The building that houses Gambardella dates from the 1930s, but the unique moulded plywood revolving chairs were only installed during the 1960s. Other fine features include the amazing

flesh-coloured Vitrolite and chrome front section, the red and black Formica back room, and the 100-year-old fridge and antique wall heaters. The chunky chip dishes are enduringly popular. *Babies and children welcome: high chairs. No smoking. Takeaway service.*

Harris' Café Rest
39 Goldhawk Road, W12 8QQ (8743 1753). Shepherd's Bush tube. **Meals served** 11.30am-9.45pm Mon-Sat; 11.30am-8.45pm Sun. **Main courses** £3-£7. **No credit cards**.
This is the dowager on Goldhawk Road. In 1951 Loizos Prodromou came to London from Cyprus to take over Harris'. The same Greek Cypriots have been running the place ever since. The beautiful signage, fluted wall panelling, net curtains, sun-ray relief designs and solicitous waitresses make this a real home from home. The immense portions and solid Sunday roast options are a big draw with the locals. *Babies and children admitted. Takeaway service.* **Map 20 B2**.

New Piccadilly
8 Denman Street, W1D 7HQ (7437 8530). Piccadilly Circus tube. **Meals served** noon-8.30pm daily. **Main courses** £4-£7.50. **No credit cards**.
This cathedral among caffs has to be experienced in all its Festival of Britain glory. Despite criticism of its 'tinned' dishes, the kitchen serves up pretty good house risottos and canellonis. Great tea is served in proper Pyrex cups underneath wall-to-wall yellow Formica; the menus have even become collector's items. Cravated proprietor Lorenzo Marioni is fast passing into Soho legend as a character composite of Muriel Belcher and Norman Balon. *Babies and children admitted. No-smoking tables. Takeaway service.* **Map 17 J7**.

E Pellicci
332 Bethnal Green Road, E2 0AG (7739 4873). Bethnal Green tube/rail/8 bus. **Meals served** 6.30am-5pm Mon-Sat. **Main courses** £4.20-£7.40. **Unlicensed. Corkage** no charge. **No credit cards**.
This 105-year-old East End masterpiece, with a primrose Vitrolite frontage and a rich, art deco-style interior, now has grade II listed status. Owner Nevio was born above the shop; his mother Elide supervised the marquetry Empire State-style panelling, crafted by Achille Capocci in 1946. These days, Maria Pellicci makes the grub, and her range of own-cooked Italian specials is unrivalled. Sample the liver and bacon butties and own-made steak pie with fresh veg. If you're lucky, you'll get a piece of Pellicci's rock cake, often given away free as a treat. *Babies and children admitted.*

● Adrian Maddox's **Classic Cafés** (Black Dog, £19.95) is the definitive study of British cafés. His website www.classiccafés.co.uk has five years' worth of archive material on the subject.

Babies and children welcome: high chairs. No-smoking tables. Restaurant available for hire. Separate room for parties, seats 70. **Map 18 L7**.

West
Ladbroke Grove, W11

Babes 'n' Burgers NEW
275 Portobello Road, W11 1LR (7229 2704). Ladbroke Grove tube. **Meals served** 10am-11pm daily. **Main courses** £3.50-£8.95. **Credit** MC, V.

Opened in September 2004, Babes 'n' Burgers still displays features from gushing west London mummy/journos, even a recommendation from Daniel Bedingfield, but the initial excitement has died down and it's easy to find a seat. Children get a playroom at the back, which has soft banquettes, books, crayons and toddler toys to smear ketchup over. The menu lists organic burgers, chicken breast, vegetarian alternatives, substantial breakfasts and a long list of healthful smoothies and wheatgrass-based sustainers, as well as hot drinks and fizzy pop. 'Healthy' cola, to the disgust of the children in our party, turned out to be a rather watery imitation of the real thing, but the juices are lovely. The burgers for kids are lean and flavoursome, but appear insubstantial, probably because the pleasantly doughy sesame seed bun also packs in mountains of leaves, tomato, onion and relish. The juicy tofu, bean and veg patty was delicious, with little crunchy burnt bits giving a barbecue flavour, but it could have been hotter. Chips are golden, crisp, a bit oily but tasty. Sweet things include chocolate brownies, cheesecake and a sugar-free banana cake.
Babies and children welcome: children's menu; crayons; high chairs; toys. Disabled: toilet. No smoking. Separate room for parties, seats 30. Tables outdoors (2, pavement). Takeaway service. **Map 19 B2**.

Notting Hill W11

Notting Hill Café & Bar NEW
19-21 Notting Hill Gate, W11 3JQ (7792 2521). Notting Hill Gate tube. **Meals served** 9am-9pm daily. **Main courses** £5.55-£10.50. **Service** (over £25) 10%. **Credit** MC, V.

Formerly a branch of Le Piaf, this is now a smart all-day diner. With its curvaceous maple bar counter, stirrup bar stools and flame-orange and bare-brick walls, the Notting Hill Café & Bar looks like a style bar; indeed, turn up in the evening and you'll find most of the punters downing glasses of wine and spirits. But earlier in the day, the emphasis is firmly on the food, a varied menu of breakfasts (including full English), sweet and savoury crêpes, paninis, pastas, salads, baked potatoes and grills. The keenly priced food is a good deal better than the café average, attracting a varied mix of Notting Hill daytime folk: single mothers with twin prams, estate agents from across the road and ragga boys. The blue-shirted staff are sweet and smiley; however, we thought that 30 minutes was a long time to wait for a burger, even if it was own-made and came with sautéed vegetables.
Babies and children admitted. No-smoking tables. Takeaway service. **Map 7 B7**.

South
Battersea SW11

★ Fish in a Tie ✓
105 Falcon Road, SW11 2PF (7924 1913). Clapham Junction rail. **Lunch served** noon-3pm, **dinner served** 6pm-midnight Mon-Sat. **Meals served** noon-11pm Sun. **Main courses** £5.95-£8.95. **Set meal** £6 3 courses. **Service** 10% for parties of 5 or more. **Credit** MC, V.

What's in an exterior? This quirkily named, quirkily designed bistro – with its purple paint, faded sign and darkened windows – hardly invites the casual stroller in. Not that the proprietors need worry too much about passing business: Fish in a

Tie has a huge (and deserved) fan following, with the close, cluttered interior always seeming full of happy diners. Perhaps they're pleased about being in on Clapham's best-kept secret. Fish dominates the menu (keenly priced at £3.45 for starters, £5.95 for mains, up to £8.95 for specials) but there's plenty of red meat too. On our visit, ostrich steaks intrigued, but a cavalcade of sliced duck in a rich sauce satisfied instead. And the fish? A starter of mussels came drowned in the most moreish cream and garlic sauce we've come across (it was swiftly mopped dry with bread) and a main of fleshy sea bass was about as good as it gets, budget-priced or not. Join the fan club.
Babies and children welcome: high chairs. Booking advisable. Separate rooms for parties, seating 25 and 40. **Map 21 C3**.

★ Gourmet Burger Kitchen ✓
2005 RUNNER-UP BEST BURGER BAR
44 Northcote Road, SW11 1NZ (7228 3309/ www.gbkinfo.co.uk). Clapham Junction rail/49, 77, 219, 345 bus. **Meals served** noon-11pm Mon-Fri; 11am-11pm Sat; 11am-10pm Sun. **Main courses** £5.45-£7.40. **Credit** MC, V.

What does it take for a burger bar to brand itself 'gourmet' these days? Knives and napkins, no McPrefixes, a slice of real cheese instead of the processed stuff? The Wimpy Bar almost qualifies. Gourmet Burger Kitchen, though, has a genuine claim to the tag: their imaginative selection of blimp-sized burgers are superb, and with this arsenal they have dominated the high-quality fast food market for the past few years, deservedly garnering positive reviews and foodie awards aplenty. The range of imaginative burger varieties (a 'Kiwiburger' comes with beetroot, egg and pineapple) means the adventurous need never tire of the menu. But be warned: at a staggering height of six inches, GBK burgers require a big mouth. The restaurant is a buzzy stop-and-go shack, with orders made at the front and food dished out lightning quick (though diners who want to linger will be more than happy with the stylish decor and friendly service). The fries are rather a disappointment: the delicious own-made sauces deserve better. Although recently bettered by newcomer Haché (*see p296*), GBK still remains a great favourite.
Babies and children welcome: children's portions; high chairs. No smoking. Tables outdoors (4, pavement). Takeaway service. **Map 21 C4**. **For branches see index.**

East
Brick Lane E1

★ Story Deli
3 Dray Walk, The Old Truman Brewery, 91 Brick Lane, E1 6QL (7247 3137). Liverpool Street tube/rail. **Meals served** 8am-7pm daily. **Main courses** £5-£7.50. **Unlicensed. Corkage** no charge. **Credit** AmEx, MC, V.

BEST BUDGET

For burgers
All the contenders for our 2005 Best Burger Bar award: **Fine Burger Company** (*see p296*), **Gourmet Burger Kitchen** (*see above*), **Haché** (*see p296*), **Hamburger Union** (*see p292*), **Ultimate Burger** (*see p292*).

For gut-busting portions
Gaby's (*see p292*), **Harris' Café Rest** (*see p294*), **Stockpot** (*see p293*).

For romantic encounters
LMNT (*see right*), **Le Mercury** (*see p297*).

For gastronomy on the cheap
Fish in a Tie (*see left*), **LMNT** (*see right*), **Small & Beautiful** (*see p297*).

This airy, child-friendly place in the ex-Truman Brewery just off Brick Lane is a pleasant spot in which to while away a lazy Saturday morning or a casual weekday afternoon. A cluster of rustic tables dot the airy room. The mezzanine kitchen is up the stairs at the back; spare a thought for the poor staff, who, while having to deal with a near-constant stream of customers, also have to traipse up and down some fairly steep steps just to get the grub. Perhaps because of this, service is a shambles (if you think staff may have forgotten your order, they almost certainly have), but your food will get there in the end. When it does, it'll be excellent, whether you pick from the breakfast menu (scrambled eggs, salmon, chunky hunks of toast) or the list of pizzas (thin, crispy, slightly undertopped but otherwise exceptional). Plates of brownies and other sweet things are left lying around the place like apples in the Garden of Eden, and are just as impossible to resist.
Babies and children welcome: high chairs; toys. No smoking. Tables outdoors (10, pavement). Takeaway service; delivery service. Vegan dishes. Vegetarian menu. **Map 6 S5**.

Shoreditch E2

Premises Café NEW
201-209 Hackney Road, E2 8JL (7684 2230/ www.premises.demon.co.uk). Old Street tube/ rail/26, 48, 55 bus. **Open** 8am-11pm Mon, Wed, Thur, Sun; 8am-6pm Tue; 8am-midnight Fri, Sat. **Main courses** £4.99-£9.95. **Credit** (over £10) MC, V.

How about breakfast with Billy Cobham, lunch with Lonnie Liston Smith and dinner with Django? They are just some of the jazz greats who have recorded at the Premises studios and now look down from the photographs on the otherwise unadorned walls of this bright little café. Otherwise, the decor extends no further than a spiral staircase in the corner, a fireplace (for decorative purposes only) and a drinks cabinet beside the counter. You can choose from myriad excellent breakfasts, including full English with black pudding and double cumberland sausage, or perhaps the veggie version's hash browns and bubble and squeak. There are also jacket potatoes, mediterranean salad or sandwiches with, say, houmous and grilled veg. The atmosphere is fun and buzzy, especially on a Sunday morning when the Columbia Road flower market is in full swing. Service is exceptionally friendly.
Babies and children welcome: high chairs. Tables outdoors (4, pavement). Takeaway service. **Map 6 S3**.

North East
Hackney E8

★ LMNT
316 Queensbridge Road, E8 3NH (7249 6727/ www.lmnt.co.uk). Dalston Kingsland rail/236 bus. **Open** noon-11pm Mon-Sat; noon-10.30pm Sun. **Main courses** £5.45-£7.95. **Credit** MC, V.

Egyptian, Italian, or Greek? The menu is European, but from the decor you'd never be able to tell. A hotchpotch of styles (woven canvas blinds, carvings of mythical Greeks, an enormous Tutankhamen bust) makes for an intriguing space, particularly when you factor in the variety of tables. We were seated in a giant kiln-shaped alcove (delightfully lit by only flickering candles) but there are also raised tables (almost like treehouses) far away in the corners. Despite its unattractive location – on a competition-free stretch of road in Hackney – this is perhaps one of the most romantic spots in London. The food is excellent, and wonderfully cheap at the blanket price of £2.95 for starters and £7.95 for mains. Highlights came at the latter stage of our meal: an enormous piece of sea bass with paprika-flavoured mash, and a delicate fillet of halibut in creamy prawn sauce. Meat-lovers will also find plenty to satisfy, and the specials board is extensive.
Babies and children admitted. Entertainment: opera 8pm Sun. Tables outdoors (6, garden). **Map 25 C5**.

CHEAP EATS

North

Camden Town & Chalk Farm NW1, NW3

★ Haché NEW

2005 WINNER BEST BURGER BAR

24 Inverness Street, NW1 7HJ (7485 9100/ www.hacheburgers.com). Camden Town tube. **Meals served** noon-10.30pm Mon-Sat; noon-10pm Sun. **Main courses** £4.95-£9.95. **Service** 12.5%. **Credit** AmEx, DC, MC, V.
Deftly stealing the crown long held by GBK (*see p295*), Haché is London's new burger-bar-to-beat. You'll even forgive the slightly pretentious names (steak au naturel, steak le grand) as all the burgers here are made with the French steak haché in mind: high-quality chopped Aberdeen Angus and an emphasis on flavour prevails over gimmicky toppings. Our plain burger came a perfect medium-rare as requested – red on the inside, juicy and pregnant with flavour. Neither toasted ciabatta bun nor side dishes let the order down: plump and tasty chips, choice green salad and a zesty fruit smoothie were all excellent. The wine list too is ample. Presentation is prioritised: of particular note was the beautifully constructed salad garnishing, as carefully laid as any nouvelle cuisine. The restaurant itself is just as tasteful; the cosy cabin with peaked, mirrored ceiling and well-judged low lighting makes for an ideal hideaway on grimy Inverness Street. Family-run and friendly as hell (the bill comes with Smarties) you'll fall hard for Haché. Plenty of joints ascribe gourmet status to their burgers. Finally, here's a restaurant that has earned the distinction.
Babies and children welcome: high chairs. No smoking. Tables outdoors (4, pavement). Takeaway service. **Map 3 H1.**

Marine Ices

8 Haverstock Hill, NW3 2BL (7482 9003). Chalk Farm tube. **Lunch served** noon-3pm, **dinner served** 6-11pm Mon-Fri. **Meals served** noon-11pm Sat; noon-10pm Sun. **Main courses** £6.10-£11.35. **Credit** MC, V.
A lovely place, this, both family-run and family-friendly. Located at the top of Chalk Farm Road, it's split into two parts: a twee, traditional gelateria in the back, specifically for those ordering from the (fantastic) ice-cream menu, and a more modern restaurant in the front, serving pizza, pasta and a few meatier Italian mains. We've never visited when there hasn't been at least one large family group, and the kids always seem to be having a wild time. The menu – with its sketched pictures of the different pasta shapes – is designed with them in mind, but the food is no kid's business. A bowl of enormous mussels and a platter of bresaola made excellent starters on our visit; paper-thin veal milanese was as good as it gets. The real treat, though, was our pasta dish: a creamy, rather unique scampi spaghetti that had us smiling like, well, children.
Babies and children welcome: high chairs. No smoking. Takeaway service. **Map 27 B1.**

Islington N1

Fine Burger Company

2005 RUNNER-UP BEST BURGER BAR

330 Upper Street, N1 2XQ (7359 3026/ www.fineburger.co.uk). Angel tube. **Meals served** noon-11pm Mon-Sat; noon-10pm Sun. **Main courses** £4.95-£8.95. **Credit** MC, V.
Let's get this straight: FBC does a lot right. The milkshakes are fantastic: thick, rich and served American-style with the extra container of leftover malt for mixing. Golden, hand-cut chips are even better, actually having an identifiable FBC taste (other burger operations take note). Even the basic side salad is spruced up with croutons and a tangy

---

Pie and mash

As London's working-class communities continue to sell up and shift out to outer boroughs, so the eateries that nourished them must transform, relocate or die. London's boozers have in the main trodden the transformation route, making the most of their Victorian interiors, yet jettisoning their pickled eggs for parma ham, their Ben Truman for Bourgogne Aligoté.

No such compromise has, and perhaps can, be made by London's time-honoured caterers to the workers: the pie and mash shops. They stick resolutely to providing food that has altered little since the middle of the 19th century: potatoes (a wedge of glutinous mash), pies (minced beef and gravy in a watertight crust), eels (jellied and cold, or warm and stewed) and liquor (an unfathomable lubricant loosely based on parsley sauce). Escalating eel prices mean that many places only serve pie and mash. Vinegar and pepper are the preferred condiments, a fork and spoon the tools of choice.

A choice bunch of these establishments remains as handsome bulwarks to the process, resplendent with tiled interiors, marble-topped tables and worn wooden benches. The oldest and most beautiful pie and mash shop is **Manze's** on Tower Bridge Road, established in 1902, though **F Cooke** of Broadway Market, the **Kellys'** and the **Harrington's** shops all date from the early 20th century. Visit these family-run businesses while you can, for each year another one closes, and with it vanishes a slice of old London. Relish the food, the surroundings, the prices (you'll rarely pay more than a fiver) and also your dining companions: Londoners to the core, not yet seduced by the trashy allure of the international burger chains.

None of these shops serves alcohol or accepts payment by credit card; all offer takeaways.

WJ Arment

7 & 9 Westmoreland Road, SE17 2AX (7703 4974). Elephant & Castle tube/ rail/12, 35, 40, 45, 68A, 171, 176, 468 bus. **Open** 10.30am-5pm Tue, Wed; 10.30am-4pm Thur; 10.30am-6.15pm Fri; 10.30am-6pm Sat.

Bert's

3 Peckham Park Road, SE15 6TR (7639 4598). Bus 21, 53, 78, 172, 177, 381. **Open** 11.30am-1.30pm, 4.30-6.30pm Tue, Thur, Fri; 11.30am-1.30pm Wed; 11.30am-1.30pm, 4.30-6pm Sat.
Babies and children admitted.

Castle's

229 Royal College Street, NW1 9LT (7485 2196). Camden Town tube/ Camden Road rail. **Open** 10.30am-3.30pm Tue-Fri; 10.30am-4pm Sat.
No credit cards.
Babies and children admitted.
Map 27 D1.

Clark's

46 Exmouth Market, EC1R 4QE (7837 1974). Farringdon tube/rail. **Open** 10.30am-4pm Mon-Thur; 10.30am-5.30pm Fri; 10.30am-5pm Sat.
Babies and children welcome: high chairs.
Map 5 N4.

Cockneys Pie & Mash

314 Portobello Road, W10 5RU (8960 9409). Ladbroke Grove tube. **Open** 11.30am-5.30pm Tue-Thur, Sat; 11.30am-6pm Fri.
Babies and children admitted.
Map 19 B1.

F Cooke

9 Broadway Market, E8 4PH (7254 6458). Bus 55, 106, 236. **Open** 10am-7pm Mon-Thur; 10am-8pm Fri, Sat.
Babies and children admitted. Delivery service.

F Cooke

150 Hoxton Street, N1 6SH (7729 7718). Old Street or Liverpool Street tube/rail/ 48, 55, 149, 242, 243 bus. **Open** 10am-7pm Mon-Thur; 9.30am-8pm Fri, Sat.
Babies and children admitted. Delivery service. **Map 4 R2.**

AJ Goddard

203 Deptford High Street, SE8 3NT (8692 3601). Deptford rail/Deptford Bridge DLR/1, 47 bus. **Open** 9.30am-3pm Mon-Fri; 9am-3pm Sat.
Babies and children admitted.

Harrington's

3 Selkirk Road, SW17 0ER (8672 1877). Tooting Bec or Tooting Broadway tube. **Open** 11am-9pm Tue, Thur, Fri; 11am-2pm Wed; 11am-7.30pm Sat.
Babies and children admitted.

G Kelly

414 Bethnal Green Road, E2 0DJ (7739 3603). Bethnal Green tube/rail/ 8 bus. **Open** 10am-3pm Mon-Thur; 10am-6.30pm Fri; 9.30am-4.30pm Sat.
Babies and children admitted.

G Kelly

600 Roman Road, E3 2RW (8983 3552). Mile End tube. **Meals served** 10am-2pm Mon, Wed; 10am-2.30pm Tue, Thur; 10am-4pm Fri; 10am-5.30pm Sat.

S&R Kelly

284 Bethnal Green Road, E2 0AG (7739 8676). Bethnal Green tube/rail/ 8 bus. **Open** 9am-2.30pm Mon-Thur; 9am-5.30pm Fri; 10am-3.30pm Sat.
Babies and children admitted.

Manze's

204 Deptford High Street, SE8 3PR (8692 2375). Deptford rail/Deptford Bridge DLR/1, 47 bus. **Open** 9.30am-1.30pm Mon, Thur; 9.30am-3pm Tue, Wed, Fri, Sat.
Babies and children admitted. No-smoking tables.

L Manze

76 Walthamstow High Street, E17 7LD (8520 2855). Walthamstow Central tube/ rail. **Open** 10am-4pm Mon-Wed; 10am-5pm Thur-Sat.
Babies and children admitted.

M Manze's

87 Tower Bridge Road, SE1 4TW (7407 2985/www.manze.co.uk). Bus 1, 42, 188. **Open** 11am-2pm Mon; 10.30am-2pm Tue-Thur; 10am-2.15pm Fri; 10am-2.45pm Sat.
Babies and children welcome: high chairs.

choose your mash from a smaller list. Done. The result is a hefty plate of ultra-comforting bosom-food: you'll want to smile and rub your tummy, it's all so happy and wholesome. Breakfasts – stretching from boiled egg and soldiers (a bargain at £1.50) to the full English – are also very popular, especially at weekends when hungover Londoners most lament the closure of almost all the capital's old-style caffs. The S&M chain may not have much history behind it, but it makes a worthy attempt at filling the gap left by those dear departed greasy spoons. The Islington S&M, in particular, has close links to the legacy: here they've preserved the 1920s blue-and-chrome interior of the previous occupant, Alfredo's, a much-loved caff in its day.
Babies and children welcome; children's menu; high chair. Tables outdoors (3, pavement). Takeaway service. Vegetarian menu. **Map 5 O1.**
For branches see index.

North West
Kilburn NW6

★ Small & Beautiful
351-353 Kilburn High Road, NW6 2QJ (7328 2637). Kilburn tube/Brondesbury rail/ 16, 32 bus. **Lunch served** noon-3pm, **dinner served** 6pm-midnight Mon-Fri. **Meals served** noon-midnight Sat; noon-11pm Sun. **Main courses** £4.25-£8.85. **Set meal** (Mon-Thur, Sun; noon-7pm Fri, Sat) £5.50 2 courses. **Service** 10% for parties of 7 or more. **Credit** MC, V.
A 'Tiger Island', as defined by this clean and cute (though not particularly small or beautiful) Kilburn restaurant, is an enormous bowl of perfectly prepared tiger prawns and mussels, thickly covered with a garlicky, tomato sauce. It was divine and, although the bistro's most expensive dish at £7.25, worth the visit alone. Elsewhere on the menu, a tidy wellington parcel of julienned vegetables in a mushroom sauce (£5.25) was rich and delicious, as were starters of feta-stuffed red peppers and a plate of asparagus (both under £3). The value, then, is superb – even more so when you order from the less exciting but just as competently prepared set menu, costing only £5 for two courses. Decor is of the stripped-wood variety, but with the occasional flourish (a snappily tiled entranceway catches the eye); a healthy selection of wine specials keeps the drinks menu fresh. In all, an absolute treasure of a cheap chomper: we only wish we could relocate it to the centre of town.
Babies and children welcome: high chair. Booking advisable weekends. No-smoking tables. Restaurant available for hire.

Outer London
Richmond, Surrey

Stein's NEW
Richmond Towpath, west of Richmond Bridge, Richmond, Surrey, TW10 6UX (8948 8189/ www.stein-s.com). Richmond tube/rail then 20-minute walk or 65 bus. **Meals served** *Easter-Christmas* 11am-dusk Mon-Fri; 10am-dusk Sat, Sun. **Closed** Christmas-Easter. **Main courses** £3.30-£7.60. **Set lunch** (noon-3pm Mon-Fri) £4.99 1 course and soft drink. **Credit** MC, V.
Fancy a little lederhosen-slapping fun and happen to be visiting Richmond? Stroll along the riverside past Richmond Bridge and you'll find yourself at Stein's. Little more than a kiosk and some outdoor tables (with heaters), Stein's sells Bavarian dishes to families from the German school in nearby Petersham. It's a real German snack bar, serving various styles of bratwurst (pork sausage), weisswurst (white veal sausage), side orders of tangy sauerkraut and potato salads, and, of course, apple strudel and Black Forest gateau. There's even Erdinger wheat beer on tap. The location, right beside the river, can't be bettered, and there are high chairs and a tiny playground if you've brought the children. Wunderbar. Note that Stein's is a summer-only operation.
Babies and children welcome: high chairs. Tables outdoors (30, towpath). Takeaway service.

Hamburger Union. See p292.

dressing. The decor is well pitched too: light, airy and very clean, without the stickiness of many fast-food joints. It was an enormous disappointment, then, to find the poorest feature of this burger bar were the burgers themselves. The selection is decent (beef, chicken, lamb and veggie), but the £4.95 'original' burger on our visit was very weak indeed. A rubbery, dumpy patty, nowhere near the medium-rare we ordered – it was barely better than the supermarket equivalent. What happened, we wanted to cry. Your burgers used to be so good! Another complaint: on more than one occasion, surly staff have made our meal an uncomfortable affair. With so much going for the place, it's an enormous shame that FBC seem to have forgotten the basics.
Babies and children admitted: children's menu; crayons; high chairs. No smoking. Tables outdoors (2, pavement). Takeaway service. **Map 5 O2.**

Flaming Nora NEW
177 Upper Street, N1 1RG (0845 835 6672/ www.flamingnora.com). Highbury & Islington tube/rail. **Meals served** 11am-midnight Mon-Thur, Sun; 11am-2am Fri, Sat. **Main courses** £3.75-£7.75. **Credit** MC, V.
Quality kebab fare on a stretch of road otherwise known for doner disasters: a great idea that could nonetheless be improved with gentle tweaking. The food works flaming well: burgers, chicken, lamb and fish are char-grilled to order by the always friendly chefs and literally drip with flavour. The menu is so vast you'll need a couple of trips to get to grips with it (the flour tortilla kebabs, a speciality, are worth trying first – the tidy parcel of lean, charred lamb with cooling cucumber and yoghurt was excellent). The flaw in the operation? The dining space. Flaming Nora is really a takeaway with some tables; those who eat-in will find themselves too close to the grills, with the otherwise attractive white counters way too hot for comfort. The situation isn't improved any by thumping dance music. As you'd expect from the

name, Flaming Nora has a good sense of humour (condoms with your meal, anyone?), but it's harder to smile while sweating over your food.
Babies and children welcome: children's menu; high chairs; toys. Disabled: toilet. No smoking Takeaway service. **Map 5 O1.**

Le Mercury
140A Upper Street, N1 1QY (7354 4088). Angel tube/Highbury & Islington tube/rail. **Meals served** noon-1am Mon-Sat; noon-11.30pm Sun. **Main courses** £5.95. **Service** 10% for parties of 5 or more. **Credit** AmEx, JCB, MC, V.
Useful as much for its proximity to the Almeida theatre as for its low prices, the triple-floored Le Mercury has the further bonus of being a very romantic spot, if you don't mind the couple on the neighbouring (practically adjoining) table hearing your avowals just as clearly as your beloved. The broad windows, which look on to Islington's busy Upper Street, ensure the restaurant is frequently peered into: not for the private-minded, then, nor the adulterous. The menu follows the same all-one-price policy employed by Little Bay (*see p292*) and LMNT (*see p295*), though the French-ish food here is a notch below both: on our visit, dishes were either too rich (a main of steak au jus, seared plaice with far too much crème fraîche) or served at fridge temperature (a crab-and-seafood-stick starter). Still, with starters at £3.45 and main courses at £5.95, the tidy bill eliminates most complaints.
Babies and children admitted. Book weekends. Separate room for parties, seats 52. **Map 5 O1.**

★ S&M Café
4-6 Essex Road, N1 8LN (7359 5361). Angel tube. **Meals served** 7.30am-11.30pm Mon-Thur; 7.30am-midnight Fri; 8.30am-midnight Sat; 8.30am-10.30pm Sun. **Main courses** £5.95-£6.95. **Service** 12.5% for parties of 6 or more. **Credit** DC, MC, V.
This couldn't be simpler. Choose your sausages from a big list (some butcher's classics, some gourmet experiments, some veggie variants), then

Cafés

There's no need to default to the cookie-cutter mega chains when it comes to finding a coffee in the capital. For quality food and drink, and a more individual, characterful experience, head to one of these outfits. There's plenty of choice, whether you're after posh pâtisserie, a homely breakfast fry-up, superior sandwiches, organic produce, global teas or somewhere that caters properly for children – **Crumpet**, **Eddie Catz** and **Gracelands** were all nominated for Best Family Restaurant in the 2005 *Time Out* Eating & Drinking Awards. Notable new arrivals include the elegant **Tea Palace** in Notting Hill, and two outdoor options: the **Garden Cafe** in Regent's Park and **Petersham Nurseries Café** in Richmond – both contenders for the Best Alfresco Dining award. Most of the places listed below are daytime-only operations, though some continue serving into the evening – and that Soho stalwart **Bar Italia** is open 24 hours.

Central

City E1

Market Coffee House NEW
50-52 Brushfield Street, E1 6AG (7247 4110). Liverpool Street tube/rail. **Open** 8am-5pm Mon-Fri; 9am-6pm Sat; 8am-6pm Sun. **Unlicensed.** **No credit cards.**
This lovely corner café on the edge of Spitalfields Market and within sight of Hawksmoor's looming masterpiece, Christ Church, is an ode to wood. None of your modern pine malarkey, though; from the weathered floorboards to the slatted walls lined with old *Spectator* covers, long serving counter and battered chairs and tables, it has a homely, old-fashioned air. As does the food and drink. Good coffees, fantastic hot chocolate (made with Charbonnel et Walker chocolate), loose-leaf teas and ginger beer are matched by high-quality tucker. At breakfast, try buttery crumpets or a fat smoked salmon and cream cheese bagel; at lunch there are hot soups (two daily), salads (ploughman's, crab and avocado) and freshly made sandwiches (roast beef and horseradish, say). A glass case atop the counter houses own-made cakes (lemon and poppyseed, perhaps, or banana and date) that the WI would be proud of. Radio 4 plays in the background. Rammed on Sundays when the market is in full flood, it's much quieter on Saturdays or during the week.
Babies and children admitted. Disabled: toilet. Tables outdoors (7, pavement). Takeaway service. **Map 12 B5.**

Clerkenwell & Farringdon EC1

De Santis
11-13 Old Street, EC1V 9HL (7689 5577). Barbican tube/Farringdon tube/rail/55 bus. **Open** 8.30am-11pm Mon-Fri. **Main courses** £5-£10. **Licensed.** **Credit** AmEx, MC, V.
Paninis with panache are the speciality at this modish offshoot of the original De Santis in Milan. Modest in size, decked out with glossy rosewood tables and high stools, this softly lit café apes the pared-down design ethos of a style bar. No surprise, then, that it's big on wine, mostly Italian. Plates of stuzzichini (panini morsels with tuna, tomato and mortadella – in £3, £5 and £8 sizes), add an authentically Italian spin to your aperitivos. The paninis themselves – wafer-light, own-baked, sliced on the diagonal and snugly bundled into finger-friendly napkins – form the mainstay of a perfect grazing menu. The simple parmigianino is the Milanese favourite; with its silky crudo ham, melting fontina cheese, black pepper and twist of lemon, we can see why. Only groups will find the pizzas a steal: a 'chairman' (mozzarella, tomato, gorgonzola and sliced apple), for example, serves six to eight, and rolls in at £28.
Babies and children admitted. Restaurant available for hire. Separate room for parties, seats 45. Tables outdoors (14, courtyard). Takeaway service; delivery service (within 3-mile radius). **Map 5 O4.**

Covent Garden WC2

Café at Foyles NEW
Foyles, 113-119 Charing Cross Road , WC2H 0EB (7440 3205/www.foyles.co.uk). Leicester Square, Piccadilly Circus or Tottenham Court Road tube. **Open** 8am-Mon-Sat; 11am-6pm Sun. **Main courses** £3-£5. **Unlicensed.** **Credit** MC, V.
Venerable jazz shop Ray's was saved from extinction when it found a new home a few years ago in revamped independent bookshop Foyles. This small, charming café, which has the air and looks of a laid-back San Francisco coffee house, is located on the first floor. From behind a chunky wooden counter affable staff dispense high-quality filled baguettes (cheese, avocado and cucumber, say), cakes and savoury and sweet pastries. There's also excellent coffee and assorted cold drinks, including old-fashioned 'botanically brewed' (and medicinal-tasting) dandelion and burdock cordial. Seating is limited, with a few chunky wooden tables squeezed in among the CD racks, and a counter along the window – from where you can stare smugly across Charing Cross Road to the hapless souls in the Starbucks concession inside Borders. Free music events – jazz, what else? – are held weekly.
Babies and children admitted. Disabled: toilet. No smoking. Takeaway service. **Map 17 K6.**

Kastner & Ovens
52 Floral Street, WC2E 9DA (7836 2700). Covent Garden tube. **Open** 8am-5pm Mon-Fri. **Main courses** £4-£4.50. **Unlicensed.** **No credit cards.**
Set just round the corner from Covent Garden tube station, bright and well-presented Kastner & Ovens does what is expected from a takeaway cafe in the bustling heart of London. Smiley staff serve fresh, organic, daily changing dishes with a sense of personal satisfaction and – most importantly – quickly. Before noon, take your pick from pastries, cute salads and organic juices (perhaps apple and ginger). After noon, simple but tasty hot dishes appear from the in-house kitchen in the basement, along with a large selection of top-class sandwiches. Vegetable curry was beautifully cooked, overflowing with cauliflower, carrots, potatoes and creamy rice. There are no tables, though staff are happy to bring one out from the back in off-peak hours.
Babies and children admitted. No smoking. Takeaway service. **Map 17 L6.**

Fitzrovia W1

Apostrophe
216 Tottenham Court Road, entrance in 20/20 optical shop or 9 Alfred Place, W1T 7PT (7436 6688/www.apostropheuk.com). Goodge Street or Tottenham Court Road tube. **Open** 7.30am-6pm Mon-Fri; 8.30am-5pm Sat, Sun. **Main courses** £3.50-£5. **Unlicensed.** **Credit** MC, V.
The small Apostrophe chain has grown steadily in the past few years and now has six outlets in London, so it's obviously doing something right. The aim is to create a modern version of the traditional boulangerie-pâtissiere, and in general it succeeds. This branch is housed, rather bizarrely, at the back of an optican's/beauty parlour. It's a small, clean-lined space with large communal wooden tables and stools along one wall facing a glass-topped counter, from where staff produce posh cakes and upmarket sarnies made with artisan breads. Savoury fillings include the likes of tuna, green beans and roasted pepper, or salami, rocket and chilli jam; assorted croissants and danish are among the sweet choices. Prices are on the high side, but then this is lovingly crafted, high-quality fare. This is one of the smaller branches; larger outlets also sell a full range of classy loaves, including the Rolls-Royce of breads, Poilâne sourdough at £9 a go.
Babies and children admitted. No smoking. Takeaway service. Tables outdoors (3, pavement). **Map 4 K5.**
For branches see index.

Marylebone W1, NW1

★ La Fromagerie
2-4 Moxon Street, W1U 4EW (7935 0341/ www.lafromagerie.co.uk). Baker Street or Bond Street tube. **Open** 10.30am-7.30pm Mon; 8am-7.30pm Tue-Fri; 9am-7pm Sat; 10am-6pm Sun. **Main courses** £6.50-£13.50. **Licensed.** **Credit** AmEx, MC, V.
This well-known cheese and deli shop has done well from its rustic-styled café, which positively heaves with customers at lunchtime. Marylebone ladies like it here, unfazed by the communal dining arrangements (basic benches alongside chunky tables). Cooking is of a consistently high standard: expect earthy soups, exquisite cheese platters and hunks of excellent bread (we especially liked the walnut and raisin version). Voluminous bowls of Mediterranean-style salads, dressed in fruity olive oil, are temptingly perched at the end of the table. It's hard to fault the produce or the cook's execution of dishes; however, the slack service does rather let the side down. For a more relaxing experience, visit for breakfast or pop in after 5pm, when you can linger over a cuppa and a slice of moist lemon polenta cake. The branch has no café, by the way.
Babies and children welcome. Bookings not accepted. Café available for hire (evenings only). No smoking. **Map 3 G5.**
For branch see index.

★ Garden Café NEW
2005 RUNNER-UP BEST ALFRESCO DINING
Inner Circle Regents Park, NW1 4NU (7935 5729/www.thegardencafe.co.uk). Baker Street or Regents Park tube. **Open** 10am-dusk daily. **Main courses** £4.25-£12.50. **Licensed.** **Credit** MC, V.
The spacious interior of the 40-year-old Garden Café in Regent's Park has recently been given a smart retro-chic look. A family-friendly spot,

there's enough space inside for little tots to run around with wobbly ice-creams in hand. However, if it's sunny, head outdoors to one of the tables surrounded by soft foliage, rosebeds and attractive pots of fuchsias. The tasteful Modern European menu celebrates great British produce with understatement and style. Try 'mum's-own' prawn cocktail, or mellow wisps of smoked salmon with tart capers and soda bread slices. Our ploughman's lunch included a weighty wedge of wholesome montgomery cheddar and spicy apricot chutney flecked with peppery mustard seeds; more adventurous palates are directed to the roasted carrot and softened red onion salad, drizzled with a cooling, cumin yogurt dressing. Finish with a fruity rosewater jelly or a decadent pavlova, and walk it off in the rose garden. Besides a full menu, there's also a take-away counter for picnickers. Great service too.
Babies and children welcome: children's menu; high chairs. Bookings not accepted. Disabled: toilet. No smoking. Takeaway service. **Map 3 G3**.

Le Pain Quotidien `NEW`
72-75 Marylebone High Street, W1U 5JW (7486 6154/www.lepainquotidien.com). Bond Street tube. **Meals served** 7am-7pm Mon-Fri; 8am-6pm Sat; 9am-6pm Sun. **Main courses** £5.75-£7.95. **Unlicensed. Service** 12.5%. **Credit** MC, V.
Already a hit in Europe and the US, this Belgian bakery/café chain opened its first UK outpost in Marylebone in early 2005. With exposed brick, a central communal table (surrounded by numerous smaller ones) and floor-to-ceiling windows, the spacious interior exudes sunlit warmth even in foul weather – an ambience enhanced by the smell of fresh sourdough and rustic baguettes from the shop at the front. At breakfast, authentic croissants are served on mini china breadboards, and excellent organic coffees come in white bowls of varying sizes. The lunchtime speciality is tartines (from around £5), the French version of open sandwiches , supplemented by salads, soup of the day, cakes and tarts. Everything is beautifully presented, even the salt and pepper: mills of sel gris l'Atlantique and poivre noir de la Côte de Malabar (for sale, along with the stylish crockery, preserves, Belgian chocolates and other gourmet foodstuffs). The place is very child-friendly; nippers will adore the own-label chocolate and hazelnut spread.
Babies and children welcome: high chairs. No-smoking tables. Takeaway service. **Map 9 G5**.

Paul
115 Marylebone High Street, W1U 4SB (7224 5615/www.paul.fr). Baker Street or Bond Street tube. **Open** 7.30am-8pm Mon-Fri; 8pm-8pm Sat, Sun. **Main courses** £3.50-£7.50. **Unlicensed. Credit** MC, V.
With its elegant cake counter, dark wood panelling and black and white prints on the walls, Paul embodies the old-fashioned, understated style so prevalent around this part of town. Popular with well-heeled shoppers, the menu focuses on light bites by way of salads, omelettes and crisp toast topped with regional French specialities (goat's cheese and cured ham, for example). However, our gold star goes to the buttery croissants and crusty walnut bread. A quiche-style landaise flan studded with ham, peppers and tomatoes was satisfyingly creamy, but the portion size was stingy and the plate was bulked up with a jungle of leafy greens. For a real treat, order a supremely frothy mug of latte and deliciously chewy assorted macaroons. Lunchtime sees a serpentine queue of office types snapping up the filled baguettes sold as takeaway. At peak times, service gets harried.
Babies and children welcome: high chairs. Bookings not accepted. No smoking. Takeaway service. **Map 9 G5**.
For branches see index.

Quiet Revolution
28-29 Marylebone High Street, W1V 4PL (7487 5683). Baker Street or Bond Street tube/ Marylebone tube/rail. **Open** 9am-6pm Mon-Sat; 11am-5pm Sun. **Main courses** £5.95-£9.95. **Unlicensed. No credit cards.**

The café in the back of Marylebone's Aveda shop is one of many in this chi-chi area – but it's probably the healthiest. The organic menu of salads, soups and hot dishes is chalked behind the till, while a selection of cakes in a chilled cabinet opposite offers the chance to diverge from your macrobiotic diet. Seating is at two communal wooden tables and a bar along the window; there are also a few outside tables on quiet Weymouth Street. While the food is fresh and wholesome, it could do with a bit more oomph. A salad of camargue rice, beetroot and feta was dressed with little more than the lemon provided to squeeze over it, and £6.95 seemed a high price to pay for a plate of leaves, cheese and rice. Feta and roasted veg frittata was tastier, but at £8.95 (including salad), we would hope so. Freshly squeezed juices (£4) were worthy, but on the warm side. Some staff could be friendlier.
Babies and children welcome: children's menu. No smoking. Tables outdoors (4, pavement). Takeaway service. **Map 9 G5**.

Mayfair W1

★ Parlour at Sketch
9 Conduit Street, W1S 2XZ (0870 777 4488/ www.sketch.uk.com). Oxford Circus tube. **Breakfast served** 8am-noon, **lunch served** noon-2.30pm, **afternoon tea/snacks served** 3-10.30pm Mon-Sat. **Main courses** £7-£10. **Licensed. Credit** AmEx, DC, MC, V.
With its expansive Georgian-style windows, droplet chandeliers and wispy drapes, all housed in a grade II listed building, Parlour feels like an elegant sitting room. Although there is an adventurous café menu, it's overshadowed by the selection of picture-perfect pâtisserie, which tastes as good as it looks. On recent visits, we've worked our way through a dozen or so delectable morsels: tonka bean and milk chocolate mousse fillings, red pepper marmalades and Chinese tea creams have all been terrific. Shot-glass treats have included strawberry panna cotta, layered with chunky strawberries; we especially liked the barely set wobbly strawberry jelly skidding across the surface of cool mascarpone cheese. Service can be slow, but the affluent clientele don't seem in any hurry to leave. Not as expensive as the other dining areas in Sketch (*see p129 and p226*), but every bit as special. As we went to press, there were plans to slim down the pâtisserie side, so best to call before you go.
Babies and children admitted. Bookings accepted lunch only. Café available for hire, seats 35. Takeaway service. **Map 9 J6**.

Piccadilly W1

★ The Wolseley
160 Piccadilly, W1J 9EB (7499 6996/ www.thewolseley.com). Green Park tube. **Breakfast served** 7-11.30am Mon-Fri; 9-11.30am Sat, Sun. **Lunch served** noon-2.30pm Mon-Fri; noon-3pm Sat, Sun. **Tea served** 3-5.30pm Mon-Fri; 3.30-6pm Sat, Sun. **Dinner served** 5.30pm-midnight Mon-Sat; 5.30-11pm Sun. **Main courses** £9.50-£23. **Cover charge** £2. **Credit** AmEx, DC, JCB, MC, V.

Garden Café

CHEAP EATS

Housed in a former car showroom, the Wolseley is lent an air of grand opulence by its high ceilings and sweeping art deco style. The main dinner menu may prove out of reach for many, but there's an accessible all-day café selection, which gives customers a chance to soak in the atmosphere, enjoy a light bite and perhaps spot a few celebs. The café snacks lean towards east European specialities (chicken soup with dumplings, salt beef sandwiches, bagels), but all are overshadowed by the lavish afternoon tea spreads. A tiered stand, laden with perfectly crafted finger sandwiches, freshly baked scones and a winsome pâtisserie selection, was a real treat. Cakes are perfectly proportioned, and light enough that they disappear in a jiffy. Service is well attuned to the needs of a discerning clientele without being in the least bit stuffy. *See also p226.*
Babies and children welcome; crayons; high chairs. Disabled: toilet. Takeaway service. **Map 9 J7.**

Soho W1

★ Amato

14 Old Compton Street, W1D 4TH (7734 5733/ www.amato.co.uk). Leicester Square, Piccadilly Circus or Tottenham Court Road tube. **Open** 8am-10pm Mon-Sat; 10am-8pm Sun. **Main courses** £3.95-£8.25. **Licensed. Credit** AmEx, DC, MC, V.
Amato's art deco posters and dark wood furnishings are an impressive backdrop to its lush pastry and cake display. In addition to a feast of towering cakes topped with chocolate fans, you can choose from an array of glistening lemon tarts and creamy, calorie-laden treats. There's also a good choice of hearty pasta dishes, soups and salads: we were bowled over by a vast helping of spaghetti puttanesca – perfectly cooked pasta in a rich tomato sauce, spiked with red chillies and toasted garlic. To follow: a first-class chocolate cake, crowned with summer fruit sitting pretty over masses of cream. Service is reassuringly homely; newspapers are available for those who'd like to linger over one more crisp pastry tart. We'll be back for more.
Babies and children welcome: high chairs. Takeaway service. **Map 17 K6.**

Bar Italia

22 Frith Street, W1D 4RT (7437 4520/ www.baritaliasoho.co.uk). Leicester Square, Piccadilly Circus or Tottenham Court Road tube. **Open** 24hrs Mon-Sat; 7am-4am Sun. **Main courses** £3.20-£8. **Licensed. Credit** (noon-3am) AmEx, DC, MC, V.
Now into its sixth decade, this Soho landmark coasts on; a little complacently, perhaps, but not so that many of its casual visitors notice. Inside, it's much as it's always been: red leatherette stools, Formica surfaces, chrome fittings, a big TV screen (good when there's Italian football on it, otherwise a blight) and the famous Rocky Marciano poster. Outside, the green neon sign glows around the clock. Like the coffee (we had a cappuccino, creamy if slightly cold), the food isn't too bad: a coppa and mozzarella panini was solid enough, while the house-speciality Bar Italia pizza (loads of parma ham, not much rosemary, pricey) was improved by the liberal addition of chilli oil. Still, it's really all about the atmosphere. You'll be dodging the ghosts of Soho past if you choose to sup inside at the long counter; ensconce yourself at one of the coveted outside tables, though, and everyone you know will eventually walk past.
Babies and children welcome: high chairs. Tables outdoors (4, pavement). Takeaway service. **Map 17 K6.**

★ Maison Bertaux

28 Greek Street, W1D 5DQ (7437 6007). Leicester Square, Piccadilly Circus or Tottenham Court Road tube. **Open** 8.30am-11pm daily. **Main courses** £1.50-£4.50. **Unlicensed. No credit cards.**
A true Soho landmark, Maison Bertaux cobbles together a delightful mix of wobbly tables, mismatched chairs and quirky artefacts, all of which adds up to a sight that's more akin to a theatre set than a French café. Ask for a menu and

you'll draw a blank: the house specials are whatever's come out of the oven. It's terribly endearing, unless you're unfortunate enough to roll up when there's a half-hour wait before the next batch of goodies are ready. The cakes are gloriously indulgent, especially the sumptuous, crammed-with-cream éclairs. Paris Brest, two choux pastry rings sandwiched with vanilla cream and hazelnut praline, and the glossy, silky-smooth lemon tarts are just two of the naughty-but-nice treats. Puff pastry slices, spread with Dijon mustard and white sauce, topped with peppers and melted cheese, are best enjoyed fresh from the oven. Service is utterly charming.
Babies and children admitted. No-smoking tables (ground floor). Tables outdoors (5, pavement). Takeaway service. **Map 17 K6.**

Pâtisserie Valerie

44 Old Compton Street, W1D 4TY (7437 3466/ www.patisserie-valerie.co.uk). Leicester Square, Piccadilly Circus or Tottenham Court Road tube. **Open** 7.30am-8.30pm Mon, Tue; 7.30am-9pm Wed-Fri; 8am-9pm Sat; 9.30am-7pm Sun. **Main courses** £3.75-£8.25. **Licensed. Credit** (over £5) AmEx, DC, MC, V.
Walk into this branch of Pâtisserie Valerie and step back in time to the 1950s: Formica tables, an old-fashioned pastry counter and, more to the point, a selection of classic French pâtisserie, such as éclairs, babas and mousse cakes. Most cakes are a shade too sweet for our liking; the layered sponge

wedges, filled with whipped cream and fruit, are better bets. Although the main menu offers a selection of pastas, salads and all-day breakfasts, we recommend playing safe and sticking with sandwiches: woefully overcooked omelette and a rubbery spinach, potato and egg tortilla came as serious disappointments. Service is chaotic, but it's a little easier to take if you manage to grab a window table upstairs, a cheerier, lighter and airier space than the hemmed-in café downstairs.
Babies and children admitted: high chairs. No-smoking tables. Takeaway service. **Map 17 K6.** **For branches see index.**

★ Yauatcha

15 Broadwick Street, W1F 0DE (7494 8888). Leicester Square, Oxford Circus or Piccadilly Circus tube. Tea house **Tea/snacks served** 10am-11pm Mon-Sat; 10am-10.30pm Sun. **Dim sum served** noon-11pm Mon-Fri; 11am-11pm Sat; 11am-10.30pm Sun. **Dim sum** £3-£14.50. **Set tea** £19. **Service** 12.5%. **Credit** AmEx, MC, V.
Although less well known than its basement dim sum restaurant (*see p72*), the spacious, strikingly sleek café on the ground floor at Yauatcha remains a popular meeting place for Soho media types. The low seating is surrounded by blue-glass opaque windows, offering customers a surreal, shadowy sight of chefs at work behind a glass divide. You can now partake of the dim sum menu here, as well as oriental-inspired French pastries and an

Le Pain Quotidien. See p299.

astonishing number of speciality teas (almost 60 varieties). The perfectly aligned cakes and mousses are a visual feast: Shibuya Casual, a miniature pear liqueur mousse topped with pineapple and pear matchsticks and encased in a border of sponge fingers, was a winsome medley of subtle fruity flavours. More adventurous combinations didn't always deliver the goods: matcha pamplemousse, a green tea mousse cake spiked with ginger and topped with grapefruit, was overwhelmed by thick, syrup-soaked lemon sponge. Service is slow, but charming.
Babies and children admitted. Booking advisable (restaurant). Disabled: toilet. No smoking. Takeaway service (tea house). **Map 17 J6.**

West

Chiswick W4

Classic Image
Café Gallery NEW
15 Devonshire Road, W4 2EU (8995 9977). Turnham Green tube. **Open** 9am-5pm Mon-Sat; 10am-3pm Sun. **Main courses** £3.95-£8. **Unlicensed. Credit** MC, V.
A café and a mini gallery? What a smart idea. Tucking into a snack, you can't stop your eyes roaming around the classic black and white photos, willing you to make a purchase while you're at your most vulnerable, which is to say content from all the nourishment. The small menu offers unchallenging sarnies, as well as more enticing options. A hearty bowl of delicious, freshly made carrot and coriander soup, followed by smoked salmon latkes with salad, made for a decent meal. Even if you're just popping in for a cuppa (teas and coffees are all organic) or one of the heavenly fresh smoothies, don't pass on a hefty slice of the café's fine own-made carrot cake. An ideal spot after a punishing shopping session, or to simply chill out with the papers.
Babies and children welcome: high chairs. No smoking. Tables outdoors (4, terrace). Takeaway service.

Ladbroke Grove W10, W11

Armadillo Café NEW
11 Bramley Road, W10 6SZ (7727 9799). Latimer Road tube. **Open** 8am-4.30pm Mon-Fri. **Main courses** £2-£6. **Unlicensed. No credit cards.**
A café serving decent coffee shouldn't be big news, but given the weak, watery, milky gunk that often passes for the stuff in London, anywhere that treats its java properly deserves applause. Armadillo takes its coffee very seriously indeed: there are only four varieties, among them a strong, smooth and lovely americano. The menu also offers salads, sandwiches, snacks, pastries and breakfast goodies made from artisanal ingredients, sourced mainly from farmers in Wiltshire and the West Country. A dense, mixed-pepper savoury muffin was delicious, as was a sandwich made with bread from Predor in Brittany, Ashmore Farmhouse cheese and tangy own-made chutney. Service is brisk, and seating is limited to bar stools, some of them in the dingy basement – so you might be better off using Armadillo as a takeaway.
Babies and children admitted. No smoking. Tables outdoors (10, pavement). Takeaway service. Vegetarian menu.

Books for Cooks
4 Blenheim Crescent, W11 1NN (7221 1992/ www.booksforcooks.com). Ladbroke Grove tube. **Open** 10am-6pm Tue-Sat. **Unlicensed. Credit** MC, V.
As famed for its tiny café as it is for its literary stock, Books for Cooks is a popular destination with affluent shoppers and tourists. A casually arranged assortment of tables, located at the rear of the shop, look on to a remarkably light and airy open kitchen. Yes, it's a squeeze to get seated, and during lunchtimes, the wait for a table can be tedious. However, the rustic cooking makes it all worthwhile, as does the temptation of the homely cakes. On our Saturday morning visit, the only

main course on offer was a peasant-style tomato broth, simmered with crunchy sugar snaps, diced carrots and butter beans, it proved a great medley of garden veggies and cooked-down tomatoes. During the week there's a choice of two, more substantial menus: expect hearty soups, flans and own-brewed wine. For cookery courses, *see p353. Bookings not accepted. Disabled: toilet. No smoking.* **Map 19 B3.**

Maida Vale W9

Raoul's
13 Clifton Road, W9 1SZ (7289 7313). Warwick Avenue tube/6 bus. **Open** 8.30am-10.15pm Mon-Sat; 9am-10pm Sun. **Main courses** £8.50-£15. **Minimum** £3.95. **Licensed. Service** 10%. **Credit** MC, V.
This Maida Vale fixture is a popular weekend hangout. The classic café interior – long mirror, brown banquettes – is looking worn round the edges, but that just adds to its neighbourhood vibe, and there's plenty of outside seating. A broad, brunchy menu of bagels, egg dishes, filled focaccia, salads and burgers is served until 6pm – a godsend for hangover-sufferers. Trouble is, staff can't seem to cope with the traffic; seated outside, we had to go in search of service twice. Food was fine if unmemorable. Croque madame appeared to have been done in a sandwich maker, and organic salmon burger with own-made tartare sauce bordered on bland. A smaller, Mediterranean-accented menu is served in the evening; excellent coffee accompanies a tempting display of desserts. Raoul's double-fronted deli across the road sells a wide array of fresh and packaged gastronomic goodies, plus salads, sandwiches and cakes to take away or consume at limited outside seating.
Babies and children welcome; high chairs. No smoking. Tables outdoors (13, pavement and patio). Takeaway service (6-10pm). **Map 2 D4. For branches see index.**

Notting Hill W11

Fresh & Wild NEW
210 Westbourne Grove, W11 2RH (7229 1063/ www.freshandwild.com). Notting Hill Gate tube. **Open** 8am-9pm Mon-Fri; 8am-8pm Sat; 10am-7pm Sun. **Unlicensed. Credit** AmEx, MC, V.
This great in-store café is housed in the Westbourne Grove branch of the organic 'real food' chain (motto: 'Whole Foods, Whole People, Whole Planet'). Beyond the store is a self-service eaterie with a terrific salad bar offering a great array of quiches, salads, couscous and pilau, individually weighed and priced. Adjacent is the hot food counter, where the dishes of the day could be anything from chilli con carne to Thai chicken curry or Sicilian meatballs. Staff pulp carrots and berries to make organic cocktails and protein shakes. Prices are surprisingly reasonable, and the sole drawback is the cramped space and the limited table room, making seating battles with pushchair-wielding young mothers a near inevitability.
Babies and children welcome: high chairs. No smoking. Tables outdoors (4, pavement). Takeaway service. **Map 19 C3. For branches see index.**

★ Tea Palace NEW
175 Westbourne Grove, W11 2SB (7727 2600/ www.teapalace.co.uk). Bayswater or Notting Hill Gate tube. **Open** 10am-7pm, **tea served** 3-7pm daily. **Main courses** £12.50-£15. **Set tea** £15-£22. **Licensed. Service** 12.5%. **Credit** AmEx, MC, V.
Look closely at the sumptuous grey and cream wallpaper and you'll see the pattern is based on paper doilies; tea caddies are printed in tones of amethyst and mulberry. Although the serene, ladylike Tea Palace offers echoes of the elegant tearooms of the 1930s, it avoids nostalgic clichés, thanks to founder Tara Calcraft's astute sense of style. Only loose leaf teas are available from the traditional tea counter by the entrance, weighed to order from decorative drums. Also for sale are various gadgets such as filter papers, teapots and infusers. On the left, with full-length windows giving pleasing views of the leafy residences

Interview
MIKE LUCY

Who are you?
Owner of Company of Cooks, which specialises in food operations run in public spaces. I am involved in the **Brew House** at Kenwood (*see p302*), Regent Park's **Garden Café** (*see p298*), the **Pavilion Tea House** in Greenwich (*see p303*), the Honest Sausage and the ICA café.
Eating in London: what's good about it?
Increased competition. Restaurants offering poor food or little value are being ruled out, and the divas of the 1990s are being challenged. There is much more professionalism and better management. Also, there is better food locally.
What's bad about it?
It's overly focused on the top end. There are not enough midmarket choices beyond the chains, and not enough recognition given to midmarket dining by the rest of the industry.
Which are your favourite London restaurants?
Eating at **Racine** (*see p93*) is like going to 60 square metres of grass and watching a couple of international football players doing their juggling skills. The CVs of the two patrons cover much bigger restaurants, and you get that kind of experience in a small, intimate way. **Gourmet Burger Kitchen** (*see p295*) has resurrected good burgers in London and is the best chain operation since Pizza Express.
What single thing would improve London's restaurant scene?
If New York restaurateur Danny Meyer opened something. In my opinion, he's the best restaurateur in the world.
Any hot tips for the coming year?
Wine bars. Also: independently run cafes, such as Bread in New York's Soho. And, eventually, movement in the right direction on street food.
Anything to declare?
I really enjoy a glass of chardonnay with a cheeseburger.

Park cafés

The popular image of park cafés – sticky seats, curled-up sandwiches, weak tea – is becoming a thing of the past, at least in London. While a handful of the capital's cafés have always bucked the trend, several others have spruced themselves up in recent years. Below are some of the best; for more alfresco dining, visit the **Garden Café** (*see p298*) in Regent's Park, **Inn The Park** (*see p56*) in St James's Park, and **Petersham Nurseries Café** (*see p306*).

Brew House

Kenwood, Hampstead Lane, NW3 7JR (8341 5384). Archway or Golders Green tube then 210 bus. **Open** *Apr-Sept* 9am-6pm (7.30pm on concert nights) daily. *Oct-Mar* 9am-4pm daily. **Main courses** £2.95-£9.95. **Licensed**. **Credit** MC, V.

Occupying part of the basement and terrace of neo-classical Kenwood House, this café is understandably popular on a sunny afternoon. Inside, it's light and airy, although the room is dominated by the counters, hotplates and chill-cabinets that are the bane of self-service museum establishments. Still, the food is fresh, free-range and made on the premises. The daily choices include three hot dishes and above-average sandwiches. Sausages are made to a house recipe (try the pork and red cabbage version). From the wide range of cakes and pastries, we can particularly recommend both the apple and thyme cake and the treacle tart with lemon zest.

Green factor The lavender-filled terrace, which has plenty of tables shaded by large umbrellas, gets packed at weekends.
Kid factor Children have a special menu, and are welcome inside and on the terrace.
Best for A mellow summer's lunch after a stroll around Hampstead Heath.
Babies and children welcome: children's menu; high chairs; nappy-changing facilities. Disabled: toilet. No smoking. Restaurant available for hire. Separate room for parties, seats 100. Tables outdoors (100, garden and terrace). Takeaway service. **Map 28 C1**.

Chumleigh Gardens Café [NEW]

Chumleigh Gardens, Burgess Park, SE5 0RJ (7525 1070). Elephant & Castle tube/ rail then 12, 42, 63, 68, 171, 343, P3 bus. **Open** 9am-5pm Mon-Fri; 10am-5pm Sat, Sun. **Main courses** £3-£5. **Licensed**. **No credit cards**.

This café, in the only attractive bit of Burgess Park, occupies two large rooms in a mellow enclave of almshouses set around carefully tended lawns. The chaotic-looking kitchen turns out big, wholesome meals on old china plates: delicious, light quiches, full breakfasts, generous sandwiches and a rib-sticking lasagne-and-chips combo. The place has a bohemian air; there's jazz on Sundays.

Green factor Outdoor seating is in the Islamic section of Chumleigh Park's globally themed gardens, with views of the Mediterranean and English country gardens through pretty arches and pergolas.

Kid factor There's no specific children's menu, but the range of sandwiches should please most young appetites, and there are crisps, confectionery, fizzy pop and ice-creams to keep them fuelled. Boxes of toys and high chairs sing out the child-friendliness.
Best for A budget meal surrounded by the buzzing of bees, the tweet of birds and the occasional parp of tenor sax.
Babies and children welcome: high chairs. Disabled: toilet. No smoking. Tables outdoors (10, garden). Takeaway service.

Common Ground

Wandsworth Common, off Dorlcote Road, SW18 3RT (8874 9386). Wandsworth Common rail. **Open** 9am-5.30pm Tue-Fri; 10am-5.30pm Sat, Sun. **Main courses** £3.50-£9. **Licensed**. **Credit** MC, V.

Common Ground is a happy place to idle away an hour or two. Warm, friendly staff skilfully avoid treading on contented toddlers (there are many well-cuddled toys), and effortlessly maintain a relaxed atmosphere. Eclectic antique furniture fills the sunny conservatory, and the cosy back room is a heavenly retreat on a winter's day. The food is reassuringly own-made: a goat's cheese, baby spinach, spring onion and pine nut tart was moist and tasty. There are also breakfasts and fresh sandwiches, along with a great selection of cakes.

Green factor The café is set a little away from the park itself; the large patio area is shaded by trees.
Kid factor The selection of 'mini-meals' is great (pasta, chicken goujons, jam, Marmite or ham sandwiches); treat them with cookies and fairy cakes or a sophisticated 'babycino'. A large section of the back room doubles as a play area.
Best for A relaxed ambience and the unobtrusive patter of happy little feet.
Babies and children welcome: children's menu; high chairs; nappy-changing facilities. No-smoking tables. Separate room for parties, seats 100. Tables outside (15, patio). Takeaway service.

Golders Hill Park Refreshment House

Off North End Road, NW3 7HD (8455 8010). Golders Green tube. **Open** *Summer* 10am-7pm daily. *Winter* 10am-4.30pm daily. **Main courses** £6-£7. **Licensed**. **No credit cards**.

This park café gets better every year. On a summer's day we were greeted with huge bunches of fresh lilies, and a large selection of interesting salads, rolls, sandwiches and pastas. Cakes and pies are also popular, and children love the bowls of strawberries and big wedges of watermelon. The interior feels spacious and clean (though there's no room for buggies); the lovely terrace is decorated with giant hanging baskets. Service could be friendlier.

Green factor The terrace offers lovely views of the park, though food can't be taken on to the grass.
Kid factor Children are very welcome, and older ones playing on the grass can be safely monitored.

Best for Own-made Italian ice-cream and sorbets served from a little kiosk.
Babies and children welcome: children's menu; high chairs. Disabled: toilet. Entertainment: brass band 2.30-5pm Sun (May-Sept); jazz & folk Tue evenings (June-Aug); children's entertainers weekly (Aug). No smoking. Tables outdoors (60, terrace). Takeaway service.

Kensington Palace Orangery

Kensington Palace, Kensington Gardens, W8 4PX (7376 0239/www.digbytrout.co.uk). High Street Kensington or Queensway tube. **Open** *Mar-Oct* 10am-6pm daily. *Nov-Feb* 10am-5pm daily. **Main courses** £5.95-£10.95. **Set teas** £6.95-£14.95. **Licensed**. **Service** 12.5%. **Credit** MC, V.

A popular tourist spot, the Orangery's ornate, airy interior makes for a pleasant afternoon's indulgence. All is white, crisp and clean: the tables are dressed with fresh flowers, and an enormous vase of lilies tops a huge table that's spread with mounds of sweet delights. Most visitors veer towards the cream cheese and cucumber finger sandwiches, the warm scones with jam and cream, the orange blossomtea, and the huge chunks of 'Orangery' cake. Savoury options – soup, pâté, beef, salmon – are offered at lunch. Staff were cool and calm despite the 30-minute queues.

Green factor Look, don't touch. Tall windows give a wonderful view of carefully manicured gardens, but there were no tables on the terrace on a recent summer visit.
Kid factor Definitely somewhere you'd take your mum, not your kids.
Best for An extravagant afternoon tea (champagne optional).
Babies and children welcome: children's menu; high chairs. Disabled: toilet. No smoking. Tables outdoors (10, terrace). **Map 7 C8**.

Pavilion Café

Dulwich Park, SE21 7BQ (8299 1383). West Dulwich rail/P4 bus. **Open** *Summer* 8.30am-6pm Mon-Fri; 9am-6pm Sat, Sun. *Winter* 8.30am-4.30pm Mon-Fri; 9am-4.30pm Sat, Sun. **Main courses** £4.50-£6.50. **Licensed**. **No credit cards**.

The slightly militant signage and 15-strong queue (being served by one rather hot and bothered waitress) made this popular park café feel a little unwelcoming on our visit. The food includes fresh sandwiches (there weren't many left by mid-afternoon), various all-day breakfasts and some very tasty cakes: a cherry and almond slice was sticky and delicious. A large selection of ice-creams and lollies ought to keep the little ones happy. The decor is simple and showcases the colourful work of local artists.

Green factor Food cannot be taken on to the grass, but there are big picnic tables on a large patio.
Kid factor Mini breakfasts and pasta bakes are filling and inexpensive. A dedicated children's corner is filled with toys and books.
Best for The secluded 'adults-only' area.

Pavilion Café NEW

Highgate Woods, Muswell Hill Road, N10 3JN (8444 4777). **Open** *Summer* 8am-8pm daily. *Winter* 9am-dusk daily. **Main courses** £5.75-£8.95. **Licensed. Credit** AmEx, MC, V.
This treasure deserves to be as popular as Oshobasho, its predecessor on this site. The menu isn't extensive, but the food is tasty and beautifully presented. A platter of houmous, baba ganoush, smoked mackerel, spiced pumpkin, white bean and garlic dips with organic bread was tempting, but lost out to a tasty penne puttanesca. Char-grilled free-range steak (sourced from a local butcher) with melted onions and fresh horseradish was excellent. Along with the intriguing likes of 'chocolate tea', there's a decent selection of alcoholic drinks. The only grumble is that the toilets are poorly maintained and the staff are just on the slow side of relaxed.
Green factor The eating area is enclosed by a mass of flowers and shrubbery, slightly set apart from the rest of the park.
Kid factor Youngsters are made very welcome into the evening; pasta, fish fingers, chicken goujons and ice-cream are available.
Best for Jazz on a Thursday or Friday evening (booking advisable).
Babies and children welcome: children's menu; high chairs. Entertainment: jazz 6pm Thur, Fri. No smoking. Tables outdoors (27, terrace; 8, veranda). Takeaway service.

Pavilion Tea House

Greenwich Park, Blackheath Gate, SE10 8QY (8858 9695). Blackheath rail/ Greenwich rail/DLR. **Open** 9am-6pm Mon-Fri; 9am-7pm Sat, Sun. **Main courses** £2.50-£7.25. **Licensed. Credit** MC, V.
Real care goes into the food at this lovely spot. Soup is accompanied by doorstop-wedges of fresh wholemeal bread; salads such as poached chicken and asparagus are huge, fresh and healthy; sandwiches are crammed with top-quality ingredients; and sweets range from rock cakes and bread and butter pudding to raspberry fool and ice-cream. Staff are polite, friendly and unruffled, and the interior is light and comfortable. The only downside is that to reach the café from central Greenwich, you'll have to negotiate a rather steep hill.
Green factor The fantastic garden is safely enclosed by a hedge; flowerbeds are beautifully kept and dotted around large tables shaded by umbrellas. If you're lucky, you can lunch in the company of a friendly squirrel.
Kid factor There's a small selection of children's options.
Best for Fabulous views over London.

Babies and children welcome; high chairs. Disabled: toilet. No smoking. Tables outdoors (20, garden). Takeaway service.

Ravenscourt Park Café NEW

Paddenswick Road, W6 0UL (8748 1945). Ravenscourt Park tube. **Open** *Summer* 9am-5.30 daily. *Winter* 9am-4pm daily. **Main courses** £5.50-£7.50. **Unlicensed. No credit cards.**
This pleasant park café caters for all appetites, whether you're after tea and cake or a full-blown meal. The food's much better than it needs to be; superior home-cooking that uses fresh ingredients. As well as sandwiches and Italian ice-cream, there's a good choice of light meals: chunky red lentil soup; cumberland sausages with puy lentils; field mushrooms on ciabatta with two (properly) poached eggs, salad and grilled toms; or jacket potatoes. For pud, try the ace lemon curd bread and butter pudding. There's a handful of pine tables in the small but bright interior.
Green factor The café is on the edge of the park, but feels bucolic enough, with lawns, pond and majestic trees in view.
Kid factor The outside picnic tables are popular with boisterous children and their weary mums. The healthy kids' menu includes pasta, free-range chicken nuggets and fish fingers.
Best for Watching the rollerbladers and fitness freaks from a safe distance.
Babies and children welcome: children's menu; high chairs; toys. Disabled: toilet. No smoking. Tables outdoors (10, patio). Takeaway service. **Map 20 A3.**

Springfield Park Café NEW

White Lodge Mansion, Springfield Park, E5 9EF (8806 0444/www.sparkcafe.co.uk). Stamford Hill or Stoke Newington rail. **Open** *Apr-Oct* 10am-6pm daily. *Nov-Mar* 10am-4pm daily. **Main courses** £3.90-£5.90. **Unlicensed. No credit cards.**
The Ikea knives and forks, easy-listening soundtrack and family-size packs of cyclists suggest a clientele of resolutely bourgeois families, but there's a warm, friendly hubbub among the peeling mustardy-orange walls of this relatively new café. Order at the counter, beside a big sculpture of a dog, from a pretty fabulous menu: Springfield Special sandwiches (roasted veg and grilled halloumi, perhaps), own-made soups, solid and tasty cakes, shakes and organic juices. The cooking was pretty casual on our visit (our full breakfast came with barely warm mushrooms and beans), but a tower of quality toast kept us quiet.
Green factor The lawn out front rolls down towards Lea River and the Springfield Marina.
Kid factor Children are very much welcomed: 'smiley potato waffles' come in at an eminently affordable £2.
Best for Own-made soups in winter; cheery family atmosphere all year round.
Babies and children welcome: children's menu; high chairs. Disabled: toilet. No smoking. Tables outdoors (20, garden; 6, pavement). Takeaway service.

opposite, is the tearoom. A brunch menu offers scrambled eggs, buttermilk pancakes, and fresh fruit salad, while lunchtime mains may include herb-crusted halibut with crunchy baby vegetables and truffle tapenade. Most importantly, however, this is a place for afternoon tea: hot scones with strawberry jam and organic clotted cream, own-made crumpets with honeycomb, and tempting cakes. You may find yourself musing as to how badly London's grand hotels compare.
Babies and children welcome: high chairs. Bookings advisable for parties of 6 or more. Disabled: toilet. No smoking. **Map 19 C3.**

Shepherd's Bush W12

Bush Garden Café

59 Goldhawk Road, W12 8EG (8743 6372). Goldhawk Road tube. **Open** 8am-5pm Mon-Sat. **Main courses** £4-£5. **Licensed. Credit** (over £10) AmEx, MC, V.
The health-conscious of Shepherd's Bush have taken to this higgledy-piggledy café and food shop next to the tube station. A popular spot for lunch, the local yummies like it because their children can play in the garden while they linger over the £7 quiche and salad special, with glass of wine included. The menu is chalked up on a big board over the counter, where cheerful young staff whisk up smoothies, warm pastries and advise on the contents of the impressive salad display. Daily specials usually involve a couple of nutritious soups (chicken, pumpkin and jalapeño chilli, or vegetarian chowder on our visit), and there are also tortillas, pies and tarts. We could have drunk a gallon of the acerola (a orangey Brazilian fruit) smoothie. A huge plate of mixed salad – beetroot and mixed bean, greek, carrot and courgette – was satisfying. More calories are crammed into the own-made cakes, including great fruit flapjacks and a syrupy Tunisian orange cake that is finger-licking good.
Babies and children welcome: children's menu; high chairs; toys. No smoking. Tables outdoors (6, garden). Takeaway service. Vegetarian menu. **Map 20 B2.**

Westbourne Grove W11

Tom's Delicatessen

226 Westbourne Grove, W11 2RH (7221 8818). Notting Hill Gate tube. **Open** 8am-6pm Mon-Sat; 9am-5pm Sun. **Main courses** £6.95-£9.75. **Unlicensed. Credit** MC, V.
Tom Conran's well-established café/deli is a hub of Notting Hill life, attracting tourists, local celebs and affluent mothers. You're greeted by a mouth-watering display of brightly coloured novelty sweets from around the world, racks of organic juices, and the enticing smell of freshly baked cheesecake and pecan pie. For a tasty start to the day, try delicious pancakes with apple, pear, cinnamon and crème fraîche or the full works of Tom's Big Breakfast (served all day). At noon, the lunch menu kicks in, full of grilled sandwiches, salads and freshly squeezed juices. Wall mirrors and Pop Art-style posters celebrating design classics such as HP sauce provide a homely, relaxed feel. It's small, cramped (though there are a few tables in the garden and on the rear terrace), and early breakfast and lunchtime are extremely busy, so expect to wait.
Babies and children welcome: high chairs. No smoking. Tables outdoors (4, garden; 2, terrace). Takeaway service. **Map 19 C3.**

South West
Putney SW15

Eddie Catz NEW
2005 RUNNER-UP BEST FAMILY RESTAURANT
68-70 Putney High Street, SW15 1SF (0845 201 1268/www.eddiecatz.com). Putney Bridge tube/ Putney rail/14, 39, 93, 424, 430 bus. **Open** 9.30am-6.30pm Mon-Sat; 10am-5pm Sun. **Admission** £5 3-12s; £4.50 under-3s; £3.50 under-2s, under 6 mths; free under 6 mths if with paying sibling. **Main courses** £2-£5. **Licensed. Credit** MC, V.

CHEAP EATS

'Edutainment' is an ugly word; so, for that matter, is 'downtime'. Nonetheless, they've been chosen by the good people of Eddie Catz to describe what goes on at this first-floor play centre and café, a big, bright, clean space bordered by windows and mirrors. A fiver buys children access to interactive video games, internet access, table ice-hockey and a themed adventure play-frame. However, none of these edutainments is allowed to dominate the central café area, where adults can take some downtime with the newspapers. Food is fresh, light and simple: pots of carrot and cucumber sticks, children's portions of pasta in tomato sauce, slices of pizza, generously stuffed paninis. Salad bowls – feta and olive, mozzarella and tomato, chicken, niçoise – come with a variety of dressings. Desserts include own-made biscuits, fairy cakes, frozen yoghurts and smoothies; the full complement of beverages includes babycinos (milk foam with chocolate powder). Everything we tried was tasty, although the reheating of the pasta rendered it starchy. Staff are friendly and fun.
Babies and children welcome: children's menu; high chairs; nappy-changing facilities; toys. No smoking. Vegetarian menu.

South

Battersea SW11

Boiled Egg & Soldiers
63 Northcote Road, SW11 1NP (7223 4894). Clapham Junction rail. **Open** 9am-6pm Mon-Sat; 9am-4pm Sun. **Main courses** £4.95-£9.95. **Licensed. No credit cards.**
Two types of Nappy Valley resident love this tiny café: bright young things in need of a hangover breakfast, and much younger things in need of a nursery tea. It's basically a well-to-do caff with added child-friendliness. Very hungry customers should make the most of the great-value, all-day breakfast – a massive plate of egg, bacon, black sausage, ordinary sausage, a slightly below par steak, mushrooms and beans, served with either a squeezed orange juice, Bloody Mary or Virgin Mary. Simpler brunches, such as scrambled eggs with toast, omelettes or filled baked potatoes all do the trick. The same, alas, cannot be said of the mediterranean vegetable quiche served with 'heaps of salad'. The pastry was rock-like and the egg filling rubbery: inedible. We complained and were not charged for it. We also made a bad choice with the chocolate brownie, a crumbly, mean affair. We should have stuck with own-made ice-cream, or perhaps the signature toast fingers and boiled eggs, served in jaunty egg cups.
Babies and children welcome: children's menu; high chairs. Tables outdoors (3, pavement; 8, garden). Takeaway service. **Map 21 C4.**

★ Crumpet NEW
2005 RUNNER-UP BEST FAMILY RESTAURANT
66 Northcote Road, SW11 6QL (7924 1117). Clapham Junction rail. **Open** 9am-6pm Mon-Sat; 10am-6pm Sun. **Main courses** £3.95-£14.95. **Licensed. Credit** AmEx, MC, V.
Crumpet takes the biscuit for child-friendliness. On our visit, it was so full of toddlers, crawlers, mewlers and pukers that our seven-year-old companion felt over the hill. The room has enough space for a fleet of buggies, and there's a jolly sort of raised play area at the back. Staff are saints in the face of awkward requests from fussy customers and cake-lobbing toddlers. The menu offers wholesome lunches and proper teas (22 varieties). The sarnies are made with real butter and fresh ingredients: our roasted salmon and salad version, in a granary doorstep with root vegetable chips on the side, was perfection, as was a club sandwich that came loaded with ham and chicken. An expertly assembled quiche of the day is served with salad in generous proportions. For the kids, cheese toasted fingers were golden and oozy, and there are also great pasta dishes. Cakes made by local mummies are typically yummy. You could stay here all afternoon if it weren't so busy.
Babies and children welcome: children's menu; high chairs; toys. No smoking. Tables outdoors (2, pavement). Takeaway service. **Map 21 C5.**

Parlour at Sketch. See p299.

South East

Blackheath SE3

Handmade Food NEW
40 Tranquil Vale, SE3 0BD (8297 9966/ www.handmadefood.com). Blackheath rail. **Open** 9am-6pm Mon-Fri; 9am-5.30pm Sat; 10am-3pm Sun. **Main courses** £5.25-£6.25. **Unlicensed. Corkage** no charge. **Credit** MC, V.
This is a friendly, organic deli-café with a large refrigerated display of imaginatively assembled meat and vegetarian dishes, and a wide range of salads. Chicken breasts stuffed with mushrooms and leeks with a cheesy risotto, golden salmon and herb fish cakes, and polenta cakes piled with tomatoes and aubergine all caught our eye, but we eventually chose the spicy beetroot and red cabbage ensemble, Spanish-style potato salad, colourful pad Thai noodles and well-seasoned fried chicken wings. All were excellent. Cakes cost from £1.40 – for a flapjack that's so large and buttery you can't pretend it's virtuous – to £2.75, which buys you a chocolate cake so rich and dark you get a massive endorphin surge just looking at it. There are plenty of bar stools, and the welcoming staff will make sure your stay is a pleasant one.
Babies and children admitted. No smoking. Tables outdoors (2, pavement). Takeaway service; delivery service.

Dulwich SE21

Au Ciel NEW
1A Carlton Avenue, SE21 7DE (8488 1111). North Dulwich rail/37 bus. **Open** 8.30am-5.30pm Mon-Sat; 10am-5.30pm Sun. **Main courses** £1.50-£2.95. **Unlicensed. Credit** MC, V.
Formerly an expensive pâtisserie and chocolaterie for the well-heeled doyennes of Dulwich Village, Au Ciel has recently been transformed into a French café. As a result, it's become deliriously popular with resident mums, who drop in to administer the afternoon feed (both baby's and their own). We recommend one of the sinfully pleasurable house hot chocolates, perhaps partnered by a slice of excellent cake, but there are also French chocolates from Valrhona, fresh pâtisserie from Didier (French bakery) and De Baere (Belgian), and organic bread and pastries from Sally Clarke. In fact, the whole operation is unashamedly indulgent (there are only two savoury dishes), providing a welcome touch of class and character in an area otherwise beset by pedestrian chain outlets.
Babies and children welcome: high chairs. Disabled: toilet. No smoking. Tables outdoors (2, pavement). Takeaway service. **Map 23 B5.**

Greenwich SE10

Buenos Aires Café & Deli NEW
86 Royal Hill, SE10 8RT (8488 6764). Greenwich rail/DLR. **Open** 8am-7pm Mon-Fri; 9am-6pm Sat; 9am-5pm Sun. **Main courses** £2.50-£8.50. **Corkage** £1 (beer), £2.50 (wine). **Unlicensed. Credit** AmEx, MC, V.
Set slightly apart from the chaos that is Greenwich during high season, Buenos Aires is a bit of a find. Its air is redolent with classy smells: wonderful arabica coffee, Italian cheeses and salamis, rustic loaves, croissants and pastries, freshly baked in Blackheath that morning. The shop section of the operation, run by former professional tango dancer and photojournalist Reinaldo Vargas and his wife Kate Dunford, has specialities from France, Italy and Vargas's native Argentina. Cooking equipment and foodie gifts sit alongside a wide selection of antipasti, such as own-made pesto, roasted vegetables in olive oil and sliced-to-order hams. The café offers coffees, teas and pastries, which you can consume while reading a newspaper on one of the big leather sofas, or sitting at a table. There are also filled-to-order baguettes: our pesto, goat's cheese and tomato ensemble was excellent. Fans of cured meats and exotic cheeses will be spoiled for choice by the range of deli sandwiches.
Babies and children welcome: crayons; toys. No smoking. Takeaway service.

London Bridge & Borough SE1

★ Konditor & Cook

10 Stoney Street, SE1 9AD (7407 5100/ www.konditorandcook.com). London Bridge tube/ rail. **Open** *7.30am-6pm Mon-Fri; 8.30am-4pm Sat.* **Main courses** £2.10-£4.75. **Unlicensed.** **Credit** AmEx, MC, V.

This delightful four-strong chain is a one-stop spot for sheer indulgence. It's famed for its cakes and classic tray bakes, but the kitchen also gets creative with chocolates and bags of spiced nuts, and serves up some great savouries. The takeaway lunches are a hit with office types: we appreciated our thin, crispy-based pizza squares topped with juicy olives, bacon strips and oodles of melted mozzarella cheese. Poached salmon flakes, flecked through herby pasta, also looked tempting. A slab of orange sponge topped with frosted lavender petals is our current favourite, but the seriously gorgeous banoffi slices, savoury muffins and chocolate chip brownies aren't far behind. A lemon meringue pie was marvellous, the crisp, buttery pastry encasing a deliciously tart lemon filling, all crowned with a heap of chewy meringue. Good old-fashioned baking at its best.

Babies and children admitted. No smoking. Tables outdoors (1, pavement). Takeaway service. **Map 11 P8.**
For branches see index.

Peckham SE15

Petitou NEW

63 Choumert Road, SE15 4AR (7639 2613). Peckham Rye rail. **Open** *9am-6pm Wed-Sat; 10am-6pm Sun.* **Main courses** £5.95-£6.45. **Licensed.** **Credit** AmEx, DC, MC, V.

By far the nicest of the brasseries, bars and cafés clustered in this little enclave of SE15, Petitou manages somehow to combine the qualities of homeliness and sophistication. Big windows allow plenty of daylight into an unfussy interior of bare floorboards, simple furniture and cosy lamplit corners. Blackboards dotted around the walls announce an ever-changing roster of quality food, encompassing soups, salads and sarnies, tart or quiche of the day, and tons of breakfast options, as well as heartier dishes (we relished the smoked mackerel pâté with warm pitta and salad). Most people, though, seem to come here for one of the excellent coffees or teas, a slice of any number of superb cakes (someone in this outfit could bake for Britain) and to relax and chat to the rhythm of the laid-back jazz that often burbles away in the background.

Babies and children welcome: children's portions; high chairs. No smoking. Takeaway service. **Map 23 C3.**

East

Shoreditch E2

★ Frizzante@City Farm

Hackney City Farm, 1A Goldsmith's Row, E2 8QA (7739 2266/www.frizzanteltd.co.uk). Liverpool Street tube/rail then 26, 48 bus/ Old Street tube/rail then 55 bus. **Meals served** *10am-4.30pm Tue-Sun.* **Main courses** £5-£7. **Unlicensed.** **Corkage** no charge. **Credit** MC, V.

Porky breakfast fry-ups with free-range eggs are an obvious star turn on the menu at this bucolic corner of Hackney, winner of *Time Out*'s award for Best Family Restaurant in 2004. The daily changing specials boards are less predictable, but demonstrate Mediterranean flair for colour and flavour as well as catering creatively for vegetarians. Diners put in their orders at the café/ deli counter, where own-made cakes and snacks are displayed, then sit down to wait at big communal dining tables inside the spacious eating area, or outside where there is limited seating next to simple play equipment. The farm location means minor diners make up much of the clientele, and the inexpensive child-sized pizzas and pastas are delicious, especially a loaded cheese and tomato pizza with a crust as thin as a matzo cracker. We can recommend the lamb moussaka; lean, roasted poussin; and a feta, chickpea and roasted vegetable salad so fabulously flavoured with a minty oil dressing that it couldn't have been healthy. A slice of raspberry cheesecake left us full enough to join Bella the saddleback sow for a snooze.

Babies and children welcome: children's menu; high chairs; toys. Booking not accepted Sun. Disabled: toilet. No smoking. Separate room for parties, seats 40. Tables outdoors (8, garden). Takeaway service. Vegetarian menu. Vegan dishes. **Map 6 S3.**

Jones Dairy Café

23 Ezra Street, E2 7RH (7739 5372/ www.jonesdairy.co.uk). Liverpool Street tube/ rail then 26, 48 bus/Old Street tube/rail then 55 bus. **Open** *9am-3pm Fri, Sat; 8am-3pm Sun.* **Main courses** £2-£5. **Unlicensed.** **No credit cards.**

You may have seen Ezra Street in a number of films: its cobbled stones and old lamps are occasionally called upon to cover for Victorian London. Indeed, you may even recognise the century-old façade of the old Jones Dairy on the corner. Although cows were last milked here in 1939, you can still buy all manner of British and continental cheeses, as well as breads, organic fruit and other delicious comestibles. On Sundays, the café does a roaring trade with shoppers stopping off for a well-filled smoked salmon and cream cheese bagel and a mug of organic Nicaraguan coffee on their way to or from Columbia Road flower market. Better still, though, pop down on a Friday or Saturday, when the market is closed and the menu is longer: poached or scrambled eggs on toast, kippers, salads with quality lettuce, tomatoes and cucumber, and spectacularly good cheesecake. If it's sunny, snaffle a wobbly old table outside.

Babies and children welcome: high chair. No smoking. Tables outdoors (2, pavement). Takeaway service. **Map 6 S3.**

Hotel teas

For a quintessential English experience, head to one of London's posher hotels to indulge in the ritual of a formal afternoon tea. It can be an expensive business, and you'll have to dress smartly, but when everything is as it should be – fresh and interesting sandwiches, hot crumpets, rivers of refreshing teas, and extravagant cakes – this is a great way to spend an afternoon. Just don't expect to want any supper, and book well in advance.

Basil Street Hotel

8 Basil Street, SW3 1AH (7581 3311/ www.thebasil.com). Knightsbridge tube. **Tea served** *3.30-5.30pm daily.* **Set teas** £10.50-£16.50. **Credit** AmEx, DC, MC, V. *Babies and children admitted. No-smoking tables.* **Map 8 F9.**

Claridge's

55 Brook Street, W1K 4HA (7409 6307/ www.claridges.co.uk). Bond Street tube. **Tea served** *3-5.30pm daily.* **Set teas** £30.25; £38.50 incl glass of champagne. **Cover** (if not taking set tea) £3. **Service** 10%. **Credit** AmEx, DC, MC, V. *Babies and children welcome: high chairs. Disabled: toilet. Entertainment: musicians 3-6pm daily.* **Map 9 H6.**

The Connaught

16 Carlos Place, W1K 2AL (7499 7070/ www.theconnaught.com). Bond Street or Green Park tube. **Tea served** *3-5.30pm daily.* **Set teas** £18-£24. **Credit** AmEx, JCB, MC, V. *Babies and children welcome: high chairs.* **Map 9 H6.**

The Dorchester

53 Park Lane, W1A 2HJ (7629 8888/ www.dorchesterhotel.com). Hyde Park Corner tube. **Tea served** *3-6pm,* **high tea served** *3-8pm daily.* **Set teas** £28.50; £34.50 incl glass of champagne; £38.50 high tea. **Credit** AmEx, DC, JCB, MC, V. *Babies and children welcome: high chairs. Disabled: toilet. Entertainment: pianist 3-11pm Mon-Sat; 3-7pm Sun.* **Map 9 G7.**

Fortnum & Mason

181 Piccadilly, W1A 1ER (7734 8040/ www.fortnumandmason.co.uk). Green Park or Piccadilly Circus tube. **Tea served** *10am-5.15pm Mon; 3-5.15pm Tue-Sat; noon-5pm Sun.* **Set teas** £19.50; £21.50 high tea. **Minimum** £19.50. **Service** 12.5%. **Credit** AmEx, DC, JCB, MC, V. *Babies and children welcome: high chairs. Disabled: lift; toilet. Dress: smart casual; no shorts.* **Map 17 J7.**

The Lanesborough

Hyde Park Corner, SW1X 7TA (7259 5599/ www.lanesborough.com). Hyde Park Corner tube. **Tea served** *3.30-6pm Mon-Sat; 4-6.30pm Sun.* **Set teas** £28-£37. **Minimum** £9.50. **Credit** AmEx, DC, MC, V. *Babies and children welcome: high chairs. Disabled: toilet.* **Map 9 G8.**

Le Meridien Piccadilly

21 Piccadilly, W1J 0BH (7734 8000/ www.lemeridien.com). Piccadilly Circus tube. **Tea served** *3-6pm daily.* **Set teas** £12.50; £25; £30 incl glass of champagne. **Minimum** £12.50. **Credit** AmEx, DC, JCB, MC, V. *Babies and children admitted. Booking advisable. Disabled: lift; toilet.* **Map 17 J7.**

The Ritz

150 Piccadilly, W1J 9BR (7493 8181/ www.theritzhotel.co.uk). Green Park tube. **Tea served** (reserved sittings) *11.30am, 1.30pm, 3.30pm, 5.30pm, 7.30pm daily.* **Set tea** £34. **Credit** AmEx, MC, V. *Babies and children welcome: high chairs. Disabled: toilet. Booking essential. Dress: jacket and tie; no jeans or trainers.* **Map 9 J7.**

The Savoy ✓

Strand, WC2R 0EU (7836 4343/ www.the-savoy.com). Covent Garden or Embankment tube/Charing Cross tube/ rail. **Tea served** *2-5.30pm Mon-Fri; noon-5.30pm Sat, Sun.* **Set teas** (Mon-Fri) £24; (Sat, Sun) £27. **Credit** AmEx, DC, JCB, MC, V. *Babies and children welcome: high chairs.* **Map 18 L7.**

Threadneedles

5 Threadneedle Street, EC2R 8AY (7657 8080). Bank tube/DLR. **Tea served** *3-5.30pm Mon-Fri.* **Set teas** £21.50-£29. **Service** 12.5%. **Credit** AmEx, MC, V. *Booking advisable. Disabled: toilet. Dress: smart casual.* **Map 12 Q6.**

Waldorf Hilton NEW

22 Aldwych, WC2B 4DD (7759 4080). Covent Garden or Holborn tube. **Tea served** *2.30-5.30pm daily.* **Set teas** £19-£23. **Service** 10%. **Credit** MC, V. *Babies and children welcome: high chairs; nappy-changing facilities (hotel). Disabled: lift; toilet. No-smoking tables.* **Map 18 M6.**

Petitou. See p305.

North East
Stoke Newington N16

Blue Legume
*101 Stoke Newington Church Street, N16 0UD
(7923 1303). Stoke Newington rail/73 bus.*
Open 9.30am-6.30pm daily. **Main courses**
£4.95-£6.95. **Licensed**. **No credit cards**.
In the heart of Stoke Newington's hippy/trendy
scene sits this exceedingly popular café. It's a pretty
spot – with Mediterranean colours, mosaic-inlaid
tables and a light-filled, no-smoking conservatory
to the rear – but very cramped, with elbows and
backs constantly in danger of being bumped.
Parked pushchairs and wandering toddlers don't
help the space constraints. From behind a high
wooden counter, staff dispense creamy coffees,
smoothies, juices and an array of all-day dishes,
from veggie breakfasts (with sausage, egg, tangy,
crumbly feta and salad garnish) to lasagne,
burgers, full-blown salads, calorific cakes and
pastries. Portions are on the small side, and the food
can look better than it actually tastes – but for a
slice of alternative Stokey life, you can't do better.
*Babies and children welcome; high chairs.
No-smoking tables. Tables outdoors (4, pavement).
Takeaway service.* **Map 25 B1**.

North
Highgate N6

Kalendar NEW
*15A Swains Lane, N6 6QX (8348 8300). Gospel
Oak rail/214, C2, C11, C12 bus.* **Open** 8am-10pm
Mon-Fri; 9am-10pm Sat, Sun. **Main courses** £7-
£12. **Licensed**. **Credit** AmEx, DC, JCB, MC, V.
There's an appealing Mediterranean atmosphere
to this new kid on the Highgate block, enhanced
by the outdoor tables and relaxed clientele. The
eclectic main menu features all-day breakfasts,
sunshine salads, sandwiches, indulgent puds and
substantial main courses, with blackboards
advertising daily specials that emphasise fresh
produce and organic breads. A reasonably priced
chicken liver pâté excelled with its delicious
buttery texture and subtle, brandy-infused flavour.
Main courses can be a touch heavy: better bets are
lighter bites such as a leafy Spanish salad studded
with chorizo sausage. If you're in for breakfast, try
the french toast, topped with bananas and lashings
of maple syrup, perhaps with one of the made-
from-scratch fruit and veggie juices; we loved the
refreshing sweet beetroot, spiked with tart orange
juice. Take-home treats included cheeses from a
well-stocked counter and tempting Konditor &
Cook cakes. Service could use a tweak to smoothen
the rough edges.
*Babies and children welcome: high chairs.
Bookings not accepted lunch. No smoking. Tables
outdoors (10, pavement). Takeaway service.*

North West
Kensal Green NW10

★ Gracelands NEW
2005 WINNER BEST FAMILY RESTAURANT
*118 College Road, NW10 5HD (8964 9161).
Kensal Green tube.* **Open** 8am-5pm Mon-Fri; 9am-
3pm Sat; 10am-2pm Sun. **Main courses** £2.50-£5.
Unlicensed. **Corkage** no charge. **Credit** MC, V.
Relaxed and friendly, Gracelands is big enough to
satisfy Kensal Green's organically-fed toddlers and
their dishevelled parents, as well as lunch-breakers
who can't resist the excellent quiches. Eating goes
on at scrubbed wooden tables; playing is confined
to a well-equipped play area at the front, which has
a book corner, a home corner and a big squashy
sofa (usually taken up by exhausted mothers).
Food is all made on the day: the hot dish on our
visit was chicken provençale served with rice,
which sold out fast. The salad selection, which may
include greek, mixed leaf or roasted vegetables,
can be served with a variety of breads or one of
the quiches. For afters, there's organic ice-cream,
the yoghurt and honey option from the popular

breakfast menu, own-baked cakes (the moist,
gluten-free chocolate and orange variety we tried
was not in the least worthy) or, if you're lucky,
excellent banoffi pie. The coffee is terrific, which
might explain why no one ever seems to go home;
children can have a 'babycino'.
*Babies and children welcome: children's menu;
high chairs; toys. No smoking. Tables outdoors
(4, pavement; 3, garden). Takeaway service.*

Kilburn NW6

Baker & Spice
*75 Salusbury Road, NW6 6NH (7604 3636/
www.bakerandspice.com). Queen's Park tube.*
Open 7am-7pm Mon-Sat; 8.30am-5pm Sun.
Licensed. **Credit** MC, V.
There's an earthy, chunky look to the decor of this
neighbourhood café. It's clearly a locals' place; the
communal dining table in the centre of the room,
laden with weighty slabs of butter and open jars
of fruity conserves, is large enough to seat ten.
Besides the regular choices of Danish pastries,
cakes, tarts and cookies, there are also tempting
salads, daily specials and classic snacks (try a
croque monsieur). On our visit, the more
substantial bites went down better than the lighter
munchies. Our almond croissant was let down by
a heavy sponge filling and dense texture, and
simple scones were just too stodgy. Although the
brisk Sunday morning takeaway trade ensures a
quick turnover, we weren't convinced that all the
breads were being sold at their freshest. Coffees are
excellent, and service remains bright and breezy
even when the place fills up.
*Babies and children admitted. No smoking. Tables
outdoors (3, pavement). Takeaway service.*
For branches see index.

St John's Wood NW8

Maison Blanc
*37 St John's Wood High Street, NW8 7NG (7586
1982/www.maisonblanc.co.uk). St John's Wood tube.*
Open 8am-7pm Mon-Sat; 9am-6.30pm Sun. **Main
courses** £5-£8. **Unlicensed**. **Credit** MC, V.
This informal, family-friendly café is more of a
meeting place than a refuelling stop. Expansive
prints of lush-looking cakes adorn the walls, but
the real eye-candy lies within the pastry counter
by the entrance. The café menu features savoury
tarts, posh sandwiches, salads and stuffed breads.
Tarte provençale, an open pastry flan filled with
emmental, sliced tomatoes and dijon mustard, won
our approval for its simple combination of

flavours. However, fougasse paysanne, a brioche
turnover filled with chicken, mushrooms and white
sauce was little more than a glorified pasty and did
little to endear itself. Cakes are hit or miss – our
mango and praline sponge was way too sweet – so
you're probably better off with the chocolate and
coffee éclairs. Service needs to be more enthusiastic
and quicker off the mark.
*Babies and children welcome; high chairs.
No smoking. Tables outdoors (3, pavement).
Takeaway service.* **Map 2 E2**.
For branches see index.

Outer London
Richmond, Surrey

★ Petersham Nurseries Café NEW
2005 WINNER BEST ALFRESCO DINING
*Off Petersham Road, Petersham, nr Richmond,
Surrey TW10 7AG (8605 3627/www.petersham
nurseries.com). Richmond tube/rail then 30min
walk or 65 bus.* **Open** noon-3pm Thur-Sun. **Main
courses** £11-£22. **Licensed**. **Credit** MC, V.
Rustic, recently revamped Petersham Nurseries
sits near the Thames, surrounded by meadows and
paddocks. Flanked by glasshouses, the garden
centre's café is furnished with reclaimed outdoor
furniture, wonky tables and heaps of blooms and
garden greenery. The kitchen, sited in an old shed,
has a homely, cottage-like charm, but don't be
fooled: the food, overseen by former Sugar Club
chef Skye Gyngell, is delivered with panache nnd
professionalism, using quality produce, often
grown on-site. Chilled gazpacho soup, thick with
peppers, puréed tomatoes and lashings of fruity
olive oil, had an appealing rustic chunkiness,
accented by its intense garlicky flavour. A main of
lightly fried wild salmon fillet, slathered with
herby salsa verde, also satisfied with its fresh
flavours and simple presentation. The daily-
changing menu is an added attraction: here's
hoping the strawberry-topped chocolate pots get
another look-in soon. To drink, expect thirst-
quenching jugs of mint-infused lemonade made
with Amalfi lemons, or sophisticated, rose-scented
Bellinis. A seriously busy Sunday lunchtime didn't
faze the staff, who remained attentive and
courteous throughout. The only downside: it's only
open for lunch three days a week.
*Babies and children welcome: high chairs; toys.
Booking advisable. Disabled: toilet. No-smoking
tables. Tables outdoors (12, garden).*

Fish & Chips

Golden brown, finger-thick chips; grease-free batter that is crunchy yet fragile; flaky-fresh fish, brilliant white and lightly steamed within its coating; mushy peas the consistency of the best porridge, soaked in-house and without lurid-green food colouring – together these amount to the Holy Grail for the seeker after the perfect chip shop. Sad to say, in our great city of some seven million souls, only around a score of establishments get fish and chips right – and even then not always. Yet pilgrims in search of this British national treasure should usually find redemption (not to mention girth-widening satisfaction) at any of the choice chippies listed below.

A welcome addition this year is **Fish Club** – winner of the Best Cheap Eats gong in the 2005 *Time Out* Eating & Drinking Awards – which continues the more modern approach to the business of selling fish and chips set by **Sea Cow** (now with two branches). For more high-falutin' restaurants, specialising in all manner of marine life, *see p85* **Fish**.

Central
Barbican EC1

★ Fish Central
149-151 Central Street, EC1V 8AP (7253 4970). Old Street tube/rail/55 bus. **Lunch served** 11am-2.30pm, **dinner served** 4.45-10.30pm Mon-Sat. **Main courses** £4.95-£10.90. **Credit** AmEx, MC, V.
Modern-looking, with bare wooden flooring, off-white walls and space-age serving area, Fish Central sits among the corporation flats of Central Street like an iMac in a sports shop. The stock in trade is still fish and chips; cabbies and locals remain the core clientele. But now this Hellenic-run business is more than just the local chippie. Head chef Azeddine Tachour has added extra quality to the menu. Starters of flapping but delicately flavoured spinach and ricotta ravioli, and mussels à la tarrantina (with a reduced sauce of white wine and tomato) sit next to a robust and finely judged dark brown fish soup, and prawn cocktail. Steaks, sausages, grilled dover sole and seared tuna are alternatives to good old haddock or cod in a crisp coating of golden batter. Despite the calibre of the extras, the fresh fish and chips remain supreme and that's what most locals choose. On our visit a batch of City types had wandered in and were hammering the chardonnay, char-grilled scallops and lamb chops, but no one seemed to mind.
Babies and children welcome: children's portions; high chairs. Booking advisable. Takeaway service. **Map 5 P3**.

Bloomsbury WC1

North Sea Fish Restaurant
7-8 Leigh Street, WC1H 9EW (7387 5892). Russell Square tube/King's Cross tube/rail/68, 168 bus. **Lunch served** noon-2.30pm, **dinner served** 5.30-10.30pm Mon-Sat. **Main courses** £7.90-£16.95. **Credit** AmEx, MC, V.
North Sea's location just south of King's Cross and the British Library makes it the natural choice for fish-loving academics, tourists and office workers to congregate in praise of the battered one. The decor of red velvet seats, dark wooden furniture and off-white paintwork may be reminiscent of an upmarket 1970s cafeteria, but it suits us. Culinary standards are high. Matronly waitresses will tempt you to starters of fish soup, own-made fish cakes

and scampi – all recommended – but we advise abstention. Main courses are large, teetering on the enormous. Fish comes grilled or fried in batter and in two sizes: jumbo and standard. Forget jumbo: standard would feed a couple of boxers in training. Chips arrive in a basket and are exactly what chips should be. Feast on your main course (the mushy peas are good enough to be practically compulsory) but leave room for 'afters'. Apple crumble is the size of a small drum, oozing juice and served with a pot of custard. Trifle is similarly sized and boozy enough to do for George Best once and for all. Yum.
Babies and children welcome: high chairs. Booking essential weekends. No-smoking tables. Separate room for parties, seats 35. Takeaway service (until 11pm). **Map 4 K4**.

Covent Garden WC2

Rock & Sole Plaice
47 Endell Street, WC2H 9AJ (7836 3785). Covent Garden tube. **Meals served** 11.30am-11pm Mon-Sat; noon-10pm Sun. **Main courses** £8-£14. **Credit** JCB, MC, V.
London's oldest surviving fish and chip shop has been through a few fish fingers since 1871 and continues to thrive under its current Turkish-extraction ownership. The decor of white tiling, potted plants, theatrical posters, piscine basement mural and chunky outside benches attracts a curious mix of local businessmen, tourists, luvvies, low-rent wide boys and tourists. There are far worse places for visitors to sample our national dish than in this bustling, friendly chippie. As long as you avoid Sundays and bank holidays, the fish will invariably be fresh, well prepared and succulent. Chips are chunky and among the best in town. As well as the usual battered fish, the likes of sardine and dover sole are available for the adventurous sailor.
Babies and children admitted. Booking advisable. Separate room for parties, seats 36. Tables outdoors (20, pavement). Takeaway service. **Map 18 L6**.

Fitzrovia W1

★ Fish Bone **NEW**
82 Cleveland Street, W1T 6NF (7580 2672). Great Portland Street or Warren Street tube. **Meals served** 11am-11pm Mon-Fri; 5-11pm Sat. **Main courses** £6-£10. **Credit** MC, V.

A change of ownership in June 2005 has seen standards soar at this chippie. All the fish are fresh (not frozen) and cooked to order. The two options are grilled, or breaded in matzo meal then fried in groundnut (ie peanut) oil. Our haddock in matzo was grease-free, in a batter that was crunchy yet fragile, and was too large a portion to finish. Sea bream was also a generous portion, perfectly grilled. The chips were hand-cut, and the size of fat fingers. The mushy marrowfat peas had just the right texture and didn't appear to be adulterated with food colouring, as so many other versions are. Service was solicitous on our visit, and when the sun's out, the tiny outdoor tables are appealing.
Babies and children admitted. No-smoking tables. Tables outdoors (3, pavement). Takeaway service. **Map 3 J4**.

Holborn WC1

★ Fryer's Delight
19 Theobald's Road, WC1X 8SL (7405 4114). Holborn tube/19, 38, 55 bus. **Meals served** noon-10pm Mon-Sat. **Main courses** £2.10-£5.70. **Minimum** £2.10. **Unlicensed. Corkage** no charge. **No credit cards**.
No need to dress up for this basic 1950s-style chippie, which is a haunt of cabbies, blue-collar workers and pre-club doormen. Avoid the standard array of sausages, pies, saveloys and suchlike, and choose between three types of fish: cod, haddock and plaice, all encased in chunky batter and fried in beef dripping. In fact, everything aside from the buttered bread (thick enough to vote UKIP) is fried. Chips come in large gangs, big and burly, but crisp and charming enough to get away with it. No frills, no healthy options – just oodles of what you fancy in an atmosphere redolent of a London of 60 years ago. Sample it while you can.
Babies and children admitted. Takeaway service (until 11pm). **Map 4 M5**.

Marylebone W1, NW1

Golden Hind
73 Marylebone Lane, W1U 2PN (7486 3644). Bond Street tube. **Lunch served** noon-3pm Mon-Fri. **Dinner served** 6-10pm Mon-Sat. **Main courses** £5-£10.70. **Minimum** (lunch) £4, (dinner) £5. **Unlicensed. Corkage** no charge. **Credit** AmEx, JCB, MC, V.
Since opening in 1914 – not a good year for fishing fleets, you'd imagine – the Hind has seen several skippers. It has been Greek-run since 1994, but aside from Greek pickles and calamares and a friendly if frenetic serving style, the Hellenic influence is minimal. The small ground floor features a decommissioned art deco fryer by F Ford of Halifax, and traditional dark-wood dining furniture set out in neat rows. In the basement is a slightly dingy overspill area and toilets. Certain dishes on the already short menu are invariably 'off', so those hankering after deep-fried mussels and own-made fish cakes are usually disappointed. We've had brilliant meals here and slightly disappointing meals, the last one being on the negative side. Although undoubtedly fresh, our fish verged on being undercooked and was rather slim; chips were good but few, and we received little more than a dollop of mushy peas. Oddly, the next table ordered exactly the same and the portion arrived falling off the plate; it might have come from a different kitchen. Serves us right for requesting fried mussels.
Babies and children welcome: children's portions. Booking advisable weekends. No smoking. Separate room for parties, seats 28. Takeaway service. **Map 9 G5**.

★ Sea Shell
49-51 Lisson Grove, NW1 6UH (7224 9000/ www.seashellrestaurant.co.uk). Marylebone tube/rail. **Lunch served** noon-2.30pm, **dinner served** 5-10.30pm Mon-Fri. **Meals served** noon-10.30pm Sat. **Main courses** £6.75-£16. **Credit** AmEx, JCB, MC, V.
Our recent experiences at Sea Shell haven't all been positive, but on our last visit we found a return to

the form that made this Lisson Grove outpost famous and a favourite with cabbies, the Old Bill and tourists alike. The black and white marble-effect wall tiles, light salmon walls and faux gilt-framed Renaissance prints aim for a classy classical vibe and seem to do the trick; the place was packed on an early Thursday evening. Salmon fish cakes (though more fish balls, really) and devilled whitebait served with aïoli are worth seeking out, but we went for a special of own-made vegetable soup, which was tip-top and came with three 'craft' breads. Fish can be poached, pan-fried or battered. We chose the latter and received textbook golden haddock, served with crisp chips that had recently formed part of a genuine potato, and nicely non-industrial mushy peas – a condition rarer than one might suppose.
Babies and children welcome: children's menu; high chairs. Booking advisable Thur-Sat. Disabled: toilet. No-smoking tables. Separate room for parties, seats 25. Takeaway service. **Map 2 F4**.

Victoria SW1

Seafresh Fish Restaurant
80-81 Wilton Road, SW1V 1DL (7828 0747). Victoria tube/rail/24 bus. **Lunch served** noon-3pm, **dinner served** 5-10.30pm Mon-Fri. **Meals served** noon-10.30pm Sat. **Main courses** £5.50-£16.95. **Credit** AmEx, DC, MC, V.
Seafresh was founded in 1965 by Greek immigrant Anastasis Leonidou and 40 years later is run by his son, Marius Leonidou, and extended family. To celebrate the jubilee, a fresh new look has banished the former dark wood panelling and fishing-net decor. Now we find a brightly lit, white-painted dining room with light wood tables and picture windows. The menu and the prices are pretty much unchanged, with starters such as well-packed own-made fish soup and deep fried king prawns leading on to the regulation fish and chip mains. There's little to fault when it comes to traditional main courses, with large, chunky chips battling for plate space with expertly fried or grilled deep golden battered fish. The only downer is the grossly overcooked peas. Stick to mushy and you'll be fine. Fish pie, stuffed with chunky fish pieces and generous dollops of prawns under a crispy cheese and potato topping, is a tempting alternative. The clientele is a reflection of London life and comes in all shapes and sizes, with a leaning towards cabbies, coppers and crinklies.
Babies and children welcome: high chairs. Booking advisable. No-smoking tables. Restaurant available for hire. Takeaway service. **Map 15 J10**.

West

Bayswater W2

★ Mr Fish
9 Porchester Road, W2 5DP (7229 4161/ www.mrfish.uk.com). Bayswater or Queensway tube. **Meals served** 11am-11pm daily. **Main courses** £5.95-£11.95. **Set lunch** £4.99 soup & chips incl soft drink, tea or coffee. **Credit** AmEx, MC, V.
We were delighted to discover veteran Jamaican DJ and club-owner Count Suckle tucking into chips on our last visit to this unpromising-looking chippie just off Westbourne Grove. Mr Fish took over what used to be a branch of the unremarkable Micky's Fish Bar chain, and it resembles a cross between a Wimpy Bar and a budget hotel coffee shop. Nonetheless, the fryers here come up with the goods. Eschewing the more basic fare of pies and saveloys, we chose a starter of fish chowder that proved to be suitably concentrated and flavoursome. To follow, a main course of cod and chips was just what the skipper ordered. We could have had haddock, plaice or a number of other options: grilled, poached, fried in breadcrumbs, in matzo or in batter. Our batter was pleasingly crisp and golden, the fish flaky white and fresh. Even the peas were good enough to mush for England.
Babies and children welcome: children's menu; high chair. No-smoking tables. Takeaway service (11am-midnight). Vegetarian menu. **Map 7 C5**.

Notting Hill W8

Costas Fish Restaurant
18 Hillgate Street, W8 7SR (7727 4310). Notting Hill Gate tube. **Lunch served** noon-2.30pm, **dinner served** 5.30-10.30pm Tue-Sat. **Main courses** £4.70-£7.40. **No credit cards.**
Costas offers an unassuming but sunnily decorated little eating area on the other side of its steaming fryers. The Greek-Cypriot background of the owners is reflected by the likes of retsina, houmous and calamares on the short but to the point menu. All is exactly as you'd expect from a chippie, in fact. Steer away from what is clearly bought-in, and you'll not go far wrong. Fish can be grilled or fried, normal-sized or large. 'Normal' cod was more than enough for us and came with a mountain of just-right chips and a smile from the waitress. Mushy peas were as good as you'd get in Guiseley, and a side salad was all you'd expect without turning into Brian Sewell. For those with giant appetites, puds include apple pie and baklava.
Babies and children admitted. Booking advisable dinner. Tables outdoors (2, pavement). Takeaway service. **Map 7 A7**.

Geales
2 Farmer Street, W8 7SN (7727 7528). Notting Hill Gate tube. **Lunch served** noon-3pm Mon-Fri. **Dinner served** 6-11pm Mon-Fri; 6-10.30pm Sun. **Meals served** noon-11pm Sat. **Main courses** £8.50-£11.50. **Cover** 50p. **Service** 12.5% for parties of 5 or more. **Credit** AmEx, MC, V.
This understated but decidedly upmarket fish-and-chipperie aims towards Notting Hill's better-heeled citizens, all of whom are no doubt careful to avoid Peter Mandelson's much-reported faux pas of mistaking mushy peas for guacamole. Starters include the non-traditional, such as crab and leek tart (wonderful, but not much over standard jam tart size and costing just under a fiver) and genuinely vegetarian soup, plus the likes of fish soup, smoked salmon, caviar and oysters. But it's the main option that takes the prizes. The battered fish is usually faultless, the chips rustic and well turned out, with grilled skate wing and grilled goat's cheese salad for dissenters. The Major can happily tuck into organic steak of the day with tomatoes, everyone can have a side order of broccoli and there's even London Pride on draught. Just leave room for the own-made tarts and puds.
Babies and children welcome: children's menu; high chairs. Booking advisable. No-smoking tables. Tables outdoors (4, pavement). Takeaway service. **Map 7 A7**.

South

Battersea SW11

★ Fish Club NEW
2005 WINNER BEST CHEAP EATS
189 St John's Hill, SW11 1TH (7978 7115/ www.thefishclub.com). Clapham Junction rail. **Meals served** noon-10pm Tue-Sat; noon-9pm Sun. **Main courses** £7.50-£12. **Credit** JCB, MC, V.
Usually it's the cuisines of other cultures that awaken the entrepreneurial beast in London's would-be restaurateurs, so it's a refreshing change to find a restaurant like Fish Club, where good-quality fish and chips are the dish of choice. The first and, visually, the most striking element that differentiates this slimline modern restaurant from your common or garden chippie is its wet fish counter. Make your choice (fresh mackerel, say, or tuna or red mullet), then just tell the obliging staff how you'd like it cooked (delicious smells are permanently wafting from the gleaming ranges behind the counter). There's a nicely varied choice of accompaniments too: potatoes come boiled, chipped or mashed; sweet potatoes are made into perfect, double-fried chips. Standouts from our most recent meal were gorgeously smoky grilled sardines, and whole grilled sea bass with chips and baby leaf salad. Among the sides and starters you'll find such delights as own-made potted shrimps or beetroot, onion and caper salad; among the sauces, own-made mayo and tartar. Quaffable house plonk helps the meal along, Illy coffee rounds it off.

Babies and children welcome: children's menu; high chairs. Bookings not accepted. Disabled: toilet. No smoking. Tables outdoors (4, courtyard; 3, pavement). Takeaway service. **Map 21 B4**.

Clapham SW4

★ Sea Cow ✓
57 Clapham High Street, SW4 7TG (7622 1537). Clapham Common or Clapham North tube. **Meals served** noon-11pm Tue-Sat; noon-9pm Sun. **Main courses** £7-£9. **Credit** JCB, MC, V.
This newish branch of the Dulwich original adopts the same clean-lined modern style, with pastel shades, flagstone flooring and a small iced wet-fish counter. The restaurant area is reached up a few stairs, but for us the bench seating at the front of the shop (courtesy of the wonderfully named Valentine Pine) with regularly changing artwork and picture windows looking out over life on Clapham High Street are what it's all about. The menu is compact, offering the usual deep-fried cod, plaice and haddock triumvirate, with the option of swordfish, red snapper and a daily special. Everything we tried was fresh and zingy, from the crisp-coated, white-fleshed haddock to the crab cakes with lime mayonnaise, and the mushy peas with fresh mint. Service was pleasant: not intrusive, but there when needed. We left feeling we'd witnessed the future of fish and chips.
Babies and children welcome: children's menu. Bookings not accepted for parties of fewer than 6. Disabled: toilet. No smoking. Takeaway service. **Map 22 B1.**
For branch see index.

Wandsworth SW18

★ ★ Brady's
513 Old York Road, SW18 1TF (8877 9599). Wandsworth Town rail/28, 44 bus. **Dinner served** 6.30-10pm Mon-Sat. **Main courses** £6.60-£8.75. **Service** 10%. **Credit** MC, V.
Potted shrimps are a welcome if rarely found starter these days and at Brady's come soft and flavoursome, encased in savoury butter and served with three corners of toast. We might have started with cockles, whole prawns, smoked salmon or cod's roe pâté – all of which have their followers at this slightly genteel Wandsworth eaterie. The menus are written on boards scattered around the room. Service is friendly and amateurish (we say this kindly), but good enough to get the food on to the table in a comely fashion. Mains include salmon fish cakes and the usual selection of fish (plus a few oddball specials), fried or grilled. Our small cod came as a golden-battered steak: fresh, perfectly cooked and sitting on a bed of robust chips. We've always found Brady's mushy peas a bit too sweet, but we're slowly acquiring the taste. Puddings include outstanding treacle tart and a toothsome apple crumble. Though well-behaved children are encouraged, you get the idea that Brady's is all about fish and chips for grown-ups.
Babies and children welcome: children's portions. Bookings not accepted. Takeaway service. **Map 21 A4.**

Waterloo SE1

Masters Super Fish
191 Waterloo Road, SE1 8UX (7928 6924). Waterloo tube/rail. **Lunch served** noon-3pm Tue-Sat. **Dinner served** 5.30-10.30pm Mon; 4.30-10.30pm Tue-Thur, Sat; 4.30-11pm Fri. **Main courses** £7-£16.50. **Credit** JCB, MC, V.
From the plate of whole cooked prawns that arrives when you do, via the complimentary french bread and the own-made pickled onions and gherkins, Masters exudes 'class'. Just ask any of the legion of cabbies and Old Vic regulars who make up the stock trade of this green-edged brick-and-dark-wood café. Starters for which you have to stump up include a hefty Cromer crab cocktail (in the shell) and grilled sardines. Main course alternatives to the standard cod in batter include grilled skate and tuna. But don't disregard the haddock, cod, plaice and chips. The fish comes large and perfectly cooked, with more chips than

Masters Super Fish

you'd need for two and a flurry of free pickles and own-concocted sauces. You'll probably find enough on your plate to make the idea of one of the apple pie-type puddings unthinkable.
Babies and children welcome: high chair. Booking advisable Fri, Sat. Takeaway service.
Map 11 N9.

South East
Herne Hill SE24

★ Olley's
65-69 Norwood Road, SE24 9AA (8671 8259/ www.olleys.info). Herne Hill rail/3, 68, 196 bus.
Dinner served 5-10.30pm Mon. **Meals served** noon-10.30pm Tue-Sun. **Main courses** £7.65-£18.25. **Credit** AmEx, MC, V.
One of the best reasons to live in SE24, Olley's is perpetually winning awards. Now the restaurant has been expanded to cut down queues. The interior remains the same: a kind of 'rancho deluxe' of rough plaster, beams and bare brick intended to look Dickensian. Still, once inside you'd never guess you were in a couple of knocked together railway arches. Neptune's punchbowl is a rich, creamy house fish soup that's bursting with the title devils, and rightly different every time you come. Owner Harry Niazi reckons the secret to proper batter is to chill it before frying, and the perfect chip has been blanched before the coup de grâce. It seems to work – you wonder why everyone doesn't achieve the same high standards. The main courses are arranged around jokey titles, such as *Time Out*'s own 'Guy Dimond Experience' (lemon sole fillet and chips) and 'Lord Archer's Experience' (cod and chips, 'tart not included'), but the cooking is serious enough. Whether fried, steamed or grilled, fish is the thing; you'd be hard-pressed to find better this side of Scarborough.
Babies and children welcome: children's menu; high chairs. Disabled: toilet. No-smoking tables. Tables outdoors (6, pavement). Takeaway service.
Map 23 A5.

Lewisham SE13

★ Something Fishy
117-119 Lewisham High Street, SE13 6AT (8852 7075). Lewisham rail/DLR. **Meals served** 9am-5.30pm Mon-Sat. **Main courses** £4.95-£5.95. **No credit cards**.
A self-service caff with plastic bucket seats attached to Formica tables ('they'd nick anything round here'), Something Fishy also has a posher, more general restaurant upstairs that lacks the atmosphere. Your fellow customers are likely to be shoppers and stall-holders from Lewisham Market, noshing some of London's best fish and chips at prices that make pound shops look swanky. It's

difficult to spend seven quid for a two-course meal that includes the freshest of fresh fish in a textbook crisp golden batter. Expect chunky chips capable of laying out a regiment of McDonald's Freedom Fries, and mushy peas that actually taste of pea. Other options include pie and mash, saveloys, sausages, and proper puds of the jam roll, apple pie and knickerbocker glory variety. Just don't ask for guacamole.
Babies and children welcome: children's menu; high chairs. Bookings not accepted. No-smoking tables. Tables outdoors (4, pavement). Takeaway service.

North East
Dalston E8

Faulkner's
424-426 Kingsland Road, E8 4AA (7254 6152). Dalston Kingsland rail/67, 76, 149, 242, 243 bus. **Lunch served** noon-2.30pm Mon-Fri. **Dinner served** 5-10pm Mon-Thur; 4.30-10pm Fri. **Meals served** 11.30am-10pm Sat; noon-9pm Sun. **Main courses** £8.50-£13. **Minimum** £4. **Credit** AmEx, JCB, MC, V.
A recent takeover (by owners of Turkish origin) hasn't affected the quality of food at this destination East End diner – just added crisper, whiter linen to the tables, and dishes like taramasalata and houmous to the otherwise traditional menu. Starters include the likes of whitebait, Cromer dressed crab, jellied eels and fish soup; own-made puds are of the cherry tart/jam roll variety. In between is fish. Most fish can be grilled, battered or crusted in matzo meal. Our portion of brilliant white, juicy haddock in thick but crisp batter was huge. It arrived with well-mushed mushy peas and chunky chips that were a little soft but eminently edible. Faulkner's had built up a strong following that could be typified as middle-aged Jewish couples, and they appear to be sticking with the new owners. The decor's certainly not changed, with sepia prints of old fishing and market scenes, a well-stocked fish tank and plenty of dark wood.
Babies and children welcome: children's menu; high chairs. Bookings not accepted. Disabled: toilet. No-smoking tables. Separate room for parties, seats 25. Takeaway service.
Map 6 R1.

North
Finchley N3

★ Two Brothers Fish Restaurant
297-303 Regent's Park Road, N3 1DP (8346 0469). Finchley Central tube. **Lunch served** noon-2.30pm, **dinner served** 5.30-10.15pm Tue-Sat. **Main courses** £9-£18.15. **Credit** AmEx, MC, V.
Jamie Oliver has bestowed his blessing by recommending this large, light, airy, modern-looking restaurant. When we visited it was packed – and on a Tuesday lunchtime too – with locals out for a good, reasonably priced meal. Brothers Leon and Tony Manzi run a tight ship, offering traditional fish and chips, grilled specials and firm local favourites like jellied eels, Tony's arbroath smokies (smoked haddock in a divine cream, tomato and cheese sauce) and plump and very fishy salmon fish cakes. Our fish soup was good, though with a touch more reduction could have been great, and the haddock that followed was near faultless. You can get your fish steamed, battered or coated in matzo. Think perfectly golden and crisp batter around firm, white and flaky fish and you'll have the idea. Families and minor celebrities flock to Two Brothers in droves. We dream that one day we'll spot Jamie, Maureen Lipman or Linda 'Mrs Oxo Mum' Bellingham, instead of that dreadful tabloid columnist we keep sitting next to.
Babies and children welcome: high chairs. Bookings accepted lunch only. No-smoking tables (daytime); no smoking (evenings). Takeaway service (until 10pm).

Muswell Hill N10

★ Toff's
38 Muswell Hill Broadway, N10 3RT (8883 8656). Highgate tube then 43, 134 bus. **Meals served** 11.30am-10pm Mon-Sat. **Main courses** £8.95-£17.50. **Set meal** (11.30am-5.30pm Mon-Sat) £7.95 2 courses. **Credit** AmEx, DC, JCB, MC, V.
Named after founding owner Andreas Toffalli, Toff's compact little restaurant is a dark-panelled space entered through saloon-style swing doors behind a bustling takeaway counter. Signed celebrity portraits and pictures of old Muswell Hill and Billingsgate Fish Market line the walls, set the tone and contrast with the wooden panels. Service is friendly and attentive. There's a well thought-out and executed kids' menu, and drawing materials are offered. Own-made fish soup comes thick and with plenty of fish pieces. Stand by for huge portions of fried battered fish – grilled or coated in matzo are alternatives. Chips come big and plentiful and look as if they've been lent out for a foodie photo shoot. If you've not eaten for a week you might be able to handle three courses at Toff's, otherwise settle for two.
Babies and children welcome: children's menu; high chairs. Bookings not accepted. No-smoking tables. Takeaway service.

North West
Golders Green NW11

Sam's
68-70 Golders Green Road, NW11 8LM (8455 9898). Golders Green tube. **Meals served** noon-10pm daily. **Main courses** £6.50-£15. **Credit** MC, V.
Although not kosher-supervised, this large, spacious fish and chip palace with its gold-painted chairs, walnut floor, chandeliers and uniformed waitresses includes a selection of Middle Eastern dishes within the otherwise traditional fish and chip menu. Sam's is a big hit with local families, especially couples of a certain age, and three-generation outings are common. After the complimentary chopped salad – practically a meal in itself – starters include crisp and delicious gefilte fish balls, cracked wheat and falafel. Fish can be steamed or fried in matzo or batter, and comes fresher than a first-year student. Portions are big, complaints are rare and it's a big belly that can even contemplate three courses. Even so, who can resist gloopy lockshen pudding (egg noodles baked with sugar and cinnamon) for afters?
Babies and children welcome: children's menu; high chairs. Booking advisable. Disabled: toilet. No-smoking tables. Takeaway service.

West Hampstead NW6

Nautilus
27-29 Fortune Green Road, NW6 1DT (7435 2532). West Hampstead tube/rail then 328 bus. **Lunch served** 11.30am-2.30pm, **dinner served** 5-10pm Mon-Sat. **Main courses** £8.50-£17.50. **Credit** JCB, MC, V.
There has been a recent change of ownership at Nautilus, but the combination of good fried fish and a menu with a Greek-Cypriot flavour still goes down well with locals. Most diners seem to be over 40, smartly dressed and regular enough not to need menus. Starters include throwbacks like grapefruit halves, prawn cocktail and smoked salmon, but we tend to jump straight in with main-course fish (expect the usual roster and more), most of which can be grilled. If fried the batter is hard to fault, but the fish is even better when cooked in matzo meal (staff have the matzo formula just right). Portions are plentiful, if not vast, and our middle-aged waitress was pleasantly on the ball. Three slight disappointments irritated rather than ruined our otherwise decent meal: nicely prepared mushy peas (a welcome addition to the menu) were cold and had to be returned to be reheated; there was no freshly made tartare sauce; and bought-in ice-cream novelty dishes predominated over own-made sweets. Still, you can't have everything.
Babies and children welcome: high chairs. Takeaway service.

Pizza & Pasta

Pizza and pasta restaurants are probably the capital's favourite option when it comes to budget eating. The scene is invariably dominated by the chains – which we've rounded up this year into a box to make it easier to compare what each one has to offer. But if you're after a more individual dining out experience, there are plenty of independent operations too. For more restaurants serving pizza and pasta, see **Italian**, starting on p166, and **The Americas**, starting on p35.

Central

Clerkenwell & Farringdon EC1

★ Epicurean Pizza Lounge NEW
10 Clerkenwell Green, EC1R 0DP (7490 5577). Farringdon tube/rail. **Meals served** noon-11pm Mon-Sat. **Main courses** £8.80-£16.50. **Set lunch** £7.50 incl pizza, 2 sides & soft drink (minimum 2); £12.50 2 courses incl glass of wine. **Credit** AmEx, DC, MC, V.
The phrase 'gourmet pizza' can set alarm bells ringing. But the Epicurean Pizza Lounge dodges the excesses of garlic with pineapple chunks, and uses interesting toppings that keep (just) within the bounds of decency. We intentionally chose two of the daftest options – the poseidon, complete with grilled lobster tail; and the elizabethan, topped with smoked chicken and an apricot sauce. And guess what: they worked well, especially the elizabethan, which included pine nuts, sultanas and cream cheese. At £19.50 the poseidon must be one of London's most expensive pizzas, but if you must order lobster tail on pizza, what do you expect? The pizza bases were OK, though we'd have preferred them a bit thinner and more elastic, in the traditional Napoli way. The front half of Epicurean blends seamlessly into a smart lounge bar, with glossy black surfaces, low Barcelona chairs and good lighting. The drinks list, which is as fine as those of the area's many presentable bars, covers cocktails, some decent wines, bottles of Mac's Gold beer from New Zealand and even Savannah, a dry South African cider.
Babies and children admitted. Disabled: toilet. Entertainment: DJ or jazz 8pm Fri, Sat. Takeaway service; delivery service. **Map 5 N4.**

Euston NW1

Pasta Plus
62 Eversholt Street, NW1 1DA (7383 4943/ www.pastaplus.co.uk). Euston Square tube/ Euston tube/rail. **Lunch served** noon-3pm Mon-Fri. **Dinner served** 5.30-11pm Mon-Sat. **Main courses** £6.50-£15.50. **Credit** AmEx, DC, MC, V.
Situated on an insalubrious Euston side street, first impressions of Pasta Plus aren't positive. But don't be deterred. It's a good pit stop when meeting or boarding a train. The bright, well-lit interior distracts from the grimy traffic out front, and tables in the conservatory overlook verdant neighbouring gardens. A pasta-centric menu also offers meat and fish (veal milanese, monkfish escalopes) and salad options. We started with tasty fat olives and bruschetta, followed by tagliatelle with prawns (chunks of roasted garlic with large, well-cooked and very fresh crustaceans topping olive oil-dressed pasta) and gorgonzola-filled tortelloni. The flavour of the latter was somewhat lost in a too-heavy parmesan and cream sauce. To end, chocolate mousse with rum and espresso was an indulgent blend of rich flavours and texture –

too good to share. Very much a local restaurant, with regulars enjoying lingering meals and chatting to the efficient, unobtrusive staff, Pasta Plus has the odd quirk too (a bucket of cosmetic products in the ladies' loo).
Babies and children welcome: high chairs. No-smoking tables. Tables outdoors (26, conservatory). Takeaway service. **Map 4 K3.**

Fitzrovia W1

Cleveland Kitchen NEW
145 Cleveland Street, W1T 6QH (7387 5966). Great Portland Street or Warren Street tube. **Lunch served** noon-3pm Mon-Fri. **Dinner served** 6-10.30pm daily. **Main courses** £9.50-£14. **Set lunch** £5 1 course incl drink, £10 2 courses. **Credit** AmEx, MC, V.
At first glance this tiny restaurant appears to hold only a handful of crammed tables, but there's more space for your elbows in the basement. Lunchtimes see both areas packed with diners attracted by the great-value, daily-changing set-price menu. Start with excellent bruschetta or perhaps pan-fried scallops with a mixed leaf salad; ingredients are notably fresh, and servings generous. For mains, our pan-fried cod literally melted in the mouth and was served with crisp mangetout and sautéed potatoes. The pasta is own-made and wonderfully fresh; aubergine and taleggio ravioli in a simple chunky tomato sauce was delicious and satisfying. Heartier à la carte mains might feature veal escalope in a lemon and white wine sauce or pan-fried duck breast. A dozen classic pizzas – napoli, margherita, quattro stagioni – are also offered, and the £5 pizza lunch special even includes a glass of wine, beer or a soft drink. Nice staff, friendly atmosphere, good food – you'd eat here all the time if you worked locally.
Babies and children admitted. Booking advisable lunch. No-smoking tables. Tables outdoors (2, pavement). Takeaway service. **Map 3 J4.**

Marylebone W1

Spighetta
43 Blandford Street, W1U 7HF (7486 7340/ www.spighetta.co.uk). Baker Street or Bond Street tube. **Lunch served** noon-3pm daily. **Dinner served** 6.30-11pm Mon-Sat; 6.30-10.30pm Sun. **Main courses** £10.30-£14. **Service** 12.5%. **Credit** AmEx, MC, V.
Visiting midweek, there was a noticeable lack of atmosphere in Spighetta's cavernous basement – perhaps because only two other tables were occupied. Highlights of the interesting Sardinian menu include malloreddus (wheat flour gnocchi) with sausage, and own-made ravioli filled with potato and pecorino cheese. Our calzone and pizza duo with ricotta, spinach, mushroom and asparagus was nicely presented, with a good crisp base, though toppings were rather thin. Linguine with baby clams and garlic was excellent, chilli strips adding heat and colour. It's a pity that the service failed to match these standards. Generally

ignored after our order was perfunctorily taken, we overheard other diners being offered a choice of interesting-sounding specials not mentioned to us, and had to repeatedly attract the attention of chatting staff for condiments, a bowl for empty clam shells, sugar for coffee, then – finally – the bill. Good food and location, but lazy and disappointing service.
Babies and children admitted. No-smoking tables. Takeaway service. **Map 9 G5.**

Mayfair W1

★ Rocket
4-6 Lancashire Court, off New Bond Street, W1Y 9AD (7629 2889). Bond Street or Oxford Circus tube. **Lunch served** noon-3pm, **dinner served** 6-11pm Mon-Sat. **Main courses** £7.50-£14. **Credit** AmEx, MC, V.
Tucked away in a tiny, lovely courtyard off New Bond Street, with a sleek downstairs bar and an airy upstairs restaurant, this stylish modern pizzeria is a real find. Considering its location, prices are reasonable. Fennel fritters with orange salad was a zestily moreish starter; aubergine purée and greek yoghurt with olive and tomato (sun-dried and fresh) salad was bursting with ripe Mediterranean flavours. Of the dozen pizzas, our generously topped pancetta, goat's cheese and basil version was spot-on: quality ingredients, perfect thin base. Well-composed mains include a few exotic-sounding options such as swordfish with roasted pineapple, asparagus and sweet plum with chilli dressing, or more conventional fare such as sage-stuffed chicken wrapped in pancetta with a warm new potato and green bean salad. Desserts are wipe-the-plate-clean gorgeous. Ladies who lunch make up the majority of diners, but you could just as easily visit with a group of friends or bring your kids and in-laws. We've heard mixed reports about the level of service, but during our visit staff were attentive and efficient, especially given the presence of two large birthday parties.
Babies and children welcome: high chairs. Booking advisable. No-smoking tables. Separate rooms for parties, seating 10 and 28. **Map 9 H6. For branch (Rocket Riverside) see index.**

Soho W1

★ Italian Graffiti
163-165 Wardour Street, W1F 8WN (7439 4668/www.italiangraffiti.co.uk). Oxford Circus tube. **Lunch served** 11.45am-3pm, **dinner served** 5.45-11.30pm Mon-Fri. **Meals served** 11.45am-11.30pm Sat. **Main courses** £6-£14. **Credit** AmEx, DC, MC, V.
With a central open kitchen, colourful 1960s film posters on bare brick walls, and two cosy fireplaces, this laid-back restaurant is the antithesis of pretentious Soho dining – and it serves generous portions of great food too. Starters are large enough to share; camembert fritto was deliciously crispy on the outside, gorgeously gooey within, and served with moreish gooseberry jam. Wood-fired oven-baked pizzas are a speciality and include a cheese-free pescatora, laden with tomato, clams, prawns, anchovies, mussels and garlic. The pasta is fresh, served precisely al dente and with optimum quantities of flavoursome – but not overpowering – sauces; ravioloni ai porcini was spot-on. Other options include chicken breast stuffed with spinach and ricotta cheese in a white wine sauce, and grilled swordfish with garlic and herbs. If you've room left for dessert, a wonderfully wobbly vanilla panna cotta makes a satisfying conclusion. Book at peak times; this place has many fans.
Babies and children welcome: high chairs. Booking advisable. Takeaway service. **Map 17 K6.**

Kettners ✓
29 Romilly Street, W1D 5HP (7734 6112/ www.kettners.com). Leicester Square or Piccadilly Circus tube.
Bar **Open** 11am-midnight Mon-Wed; 11am-1am Thur-Sat; 11am-10.30pm Sun. **Snacks** £6.95.

Restaurant **Meals served** noon-midnight Mon-Wed, Sun; noon-1am Thur-Sat. **Main courses** £7.95-£18.90. *Both* **Service** 12.5% for parties of 7 or more. **Credit** AmEx, DC, MC, V.

Founded in 1867, this Soho stalwart (now part of the Pizza Express group) is where to go for such favourites as baked dough balls and an American Hot pizza – but served in glamorous surroundings. Start (or finish) in the attractive champagne bar (choose from over 100, some very pricey). Tuck into a reliably good pizza (our flavour-packed boscaiola came with wild mushrooms, spring onions and parsley) or pasta dish (siciliana with aubergine, bolognese and béchamel sauce was satisfyingly creamy), or opt for good-quality steak or burgers from the grill. The all-day breakfasts and cured Italian meats are great for a posh but relaxed weekend brunch, and children are welcome too. The diverse dining areas, period features, plush banquettes, resident pianist, great service and relaxed atmosphere combine to make Kettner's a special but enjoyably informal place to eat or meet for drinks before an evening out.
Babies and children welcome: high chairs (restaurant only). Booking advisable for parties of 7 or more. Entertainment: pianist daily. No-smoking tables. Separate rooms for parties, seating 12, 16, 20, 40, 55 and 85. **Map 17 K6**.

Spiga
84-86 Wardour Street, W1V 3LF (7734 3444). Leicester Square, Piccadilly Circus or Tottenham Court Road tube. **Lunch served** noon-3pm Mon-Sat. **Dinner served** 6-11pm Mon, Tue, Sun; 6pm-midnight Wed-Sat. **Main courses** £8-£14. **Service** 12.5%. **Credit** AmEx, MC, V.

Spiga's modish good looks (warm ochres, atmospheric lighting) draw a young crowd attracted by the Italian menu and Soho setting. An appetising starter of grilled asparagus with quail's eggs and parmesan was followed by a faultless fiorentina – one of a dozen pizzas on the menu – with a perfect thin base, good toppings and a just-so runny egg. Among the own-made pasta dishes you'll find baby lasagne with duck ragoût and wild mushrooms, or linguine with lobster; a meatier main could be wrapped pork escalopes or sea bass with vernaccia sauce. Our pan-fried duck breast (precisely cooked to order) topped a moreish cake of asiago cheese, new potatoes and girolle mushrooms – an attractively presented and richly flavoursome dish. At full capacity, Spiga's tables seem rather too closely spaced, and noise levels could be considered too high – but this can also translate as buzzy. On our visit, the service, while seasoned with certain pretensions, was efficient and professional.
Babies and children welcome: high chairs. Booking advisable. Disabled: toilet. Restaurant available for hire. Takeaway service. **Map 17 K6**.

West
Maida Vale W9

★ Red Pepper
8 Formosa Street, W9 1EE (7266 2708). Warwick Avenue tube. **Lunch served** noon-3pm Mon-Fri. **Dinner served** 6.30-11pm Mon-Fri. **Meals served** noon-11pm Sat; noon-10.30pm Sun. **Main courses** £10-£15.50. **Service** 12.5%. **Credit** JCB, MC, V.

This cramped eaterie is very popular and the two-hour dining slots are highly coveted among Maida Vale's well-heeled inhabitants. You get a better class of pizza here; the rest of the menu is similarly upmarket, and features a good selection of daily specials as well as regulars. Linguini with clams was spot-on, with a good ratio of clams (the small, sweet variety) to pasta. Oven-baked kid goat with smoked aubergines arrived minus the aubergines, though they were produced when we pointed out their omission (albeit so subtly smoked that it was hard to tell the difference from the standard version). Finally, panna cotta with cooked peaches was blissfully smooth. We would have enjoyed our meal more if our table hadn't been blocking the main gangway and subject to a lot of bumping.

There's enough demand here to fill a site twice the size and, understandably, the owners have tried to squeeze in as many tables as possible, but ours was the one too many. The lively vibe and food provided some compensation for these hitches in space and service. Be sure to book.
Babies and children admitted. Booking advisable. Separate room for parties, seats 25. Tables outdoors (5, pavement). Takeaway service. **Map 1 C4**.

Westbourne Park W2

Oak
137 Westbourne Park Road, W2 5QL (7221 3599). Royal Oak or Westbourne Park tube. **Open** 6.30pm-midnight Mon; noon-midnight Tue-Sat; noon-11pm Sun. **Dinner served** 6.30-10.30pm Mon-Fri. **Meals served** noon-10.30pm Sat; noon-10pm Sun. **Main courses** £10-£14. **Service** 12.5%. **Credit** AmEx, DC, MC, V.

This former pub is very much a restaurant now, stylishly decorated with shiny tiles and simple wooden furniture, and packed every night with beautiful people unafraid of expensive pizza. There's no booking, so you'll have to squeeze into the bar area while you wait for a table, and then overcome the hurdle of getting served. The food's simple but good. Starters of roasted beetroot and mozzarella salad and deep-fried squid were both elegant, fresh and tasty. Pizzas are big and crispy, and topped with classy ingredients, though pricey at around the £12 mark. Staff are friendly if a bit overworked (our starters arrived well before our wine) and the candlelit semi-darkness is atmospheric but makes menu-reading slightly tricky. In summer, an animated crowd spills out on to a few pavement tables. An informal and very popular Notting Hill spot.
Babies and children admitted (until 6.30pm). Bookings not accepted. Tables outdoors (3, pavement). Takeaway service. **Map 7 A5**.

South West
Fulham SW6

Napulé
585 Fulham Road, SW6 5UA (7381 1122). Fulham Broadway tube. **Lunch served** 1.30-3.30pm Sat, Sun. **Dinner served** 6.30-11.30pm Mon-Sat; 6.30-10.30pm Sun. **Main courses** £8-£16. **Service** 12.5%. **Credit** MC, V.

Chequered tablecloths and lots of Italian voices lend an authentic feel to this bustling pizzeria on the Fulham Road. It's an informal space, with exposed brick walls, simple furniture, a display of antipasti, and a big pizza oven that produces large rectangular pizzas designed for sharing (the bigger the group, the bigger the pizza). We started with a selection of mainly meaty antipasti – rabbit and bean stew, sausages, marinated mushrooms and grilled carrots. Pizzas come on special wooden shelves designed for the middle of the table, with different toppings at either end of a single crispy base. Cherry tomatoes, mozzarella, wild porcini and Italian speck was a fine combination, made with seriously tasty mushrooms, while parma ham and rocket was less generous on the ingredients but still good. Service is a bit erratic and the rear conservatory can get very smoky.
Babies and children welcome: high chairs. Booking advisable. Separate room for parties, seats 40. Takeaway service. **Map 13 A13**.
For branches (Luna Rossa, Made in Italy, Mare Chiaro, Santa Lucia) see index.

Putney SW15

Il Peperone NEW
26 Putney High Street, SW15 1SL (8788 3303). Putney Bridge tube/Putney rail. **Open** 11am-4pm, 6-11.30pm Tue-Sun. **Main courses** £6.50-£10.95. **Set lunch** £5 1 course. **Set dinner** £10 3 courses. **Credit** AmEx, DC, MC, V.

An unassuming rustic pizza place opposite the Odeon cinema on Putney High Street, Il Peperone is a hidden gem, a class act run by a family from Oporto. Maybe the Portuguese have some secret knowledge of the arcane art of pizza-making, because the wood-fired examples here are amazing: thin and crispy bases with beautifully judged toppings – the ideal pizza and certainly the best in Putney. We shared spaghetti bolognese as a starter: the pasta was nothing special, but the sauce was authentic home-cooking – rich and beefy. The pizzas are the star, though, with 16 regular options plus half a dozen specials: fiorentina (mozzarella, wild spinach, organic egg and tomato) and formaggio di capra (goat's cheese and oven-roasted aubergine) were both superb. To drink, there's a handful of wines, as well as Portugal's lovely Sagrès beer.
Babies and children welcome: high chairs. Booking advisable. Tables outdoors (6, pavement). Takeaway service.

Italian Graffiti

CHEAP EATS

StringRay Globe Café, Bar & Pizzeria. See p316.

South

Balham SW12

Ciullo NEW

31 Balham High Road, SW12 9AL (8675 3072). Clapham South tube/Balham tube/rail. **Dinner served** 6-11pm Mon-Thur; 6-11.30pm Fri, Sat. **Meals served** 1-10.30pm Sun. **Main courses** £5.50-£12.50. **Credit** MC, V.
The Ciullo family has brought a taste of southern Italy to Balham. At night their restaurant catches the eye with twinkling fairylights – a little tacky, but very friendly, just like the helpful staff. In summer they fold back the doors and let the light stream into the cosy dining room. There are also a few pavement tables if you don't mind the roar of Balham High Road. The food is a tad inconsistent, perhaps because it's over-ambitious. A starter of steamed asparagus arrived swimming in butter, but the bresaola was terrific. More disappointing, a main course of gnocchi with tomato, basil and mozzarella was bland and not as fresh as it might have been. The pizzas, on the other hand, are good, with huge, crispy bases and generous toppings – and excellent value at around £6.50. For dessert, try some Italian ice-cream or own-made tiramisu. The wine list is more than adequate and, like the entire menu, reasonably priced. Ciullo has only been open for a year and deserves some success – especially if it concentrates on what it does best. *Babies and children welcome: high chairs. Booking advisable. Tables outdoors (3, terrace).*

Battersea SW11

Donna Margherita NEW

183 Lavender Hill, SW11 1EQ (7228 2660/ www.donna-margherita.com). Clapham Junction rail. **Lunch served** noon-2.30pm Fri, Sat. **Dinner served** 6-10.30pm Mon-Thur; 6-11pm Fri, Sat. **Meals served** 12.30-10.30pm Sun. **Main courses** £6.90-£16. **Service** 12.5%. **Credit** AmEx, DC, JCB, MC, V.
Well known locally for quality pizza and a friendly family vibe, Donna Margherita is an unpretentious and welcoming spot. The food is seriously good too, with pasta made on site and a proper pizza oven. We started with smoked scamorza cheese with garlic, toast and rocket: grilled but not quite melted cheese with garlicky bruschetta. There's a good selection of pizzas, all with perfect crispy bases. These include (inexplicably) 'lesbian' and 'gay' pizzas – both, for reasons beyond us, with combinations of ham, rocket and mushrooms. We liked the own-made pasta: thick noodles served with cherry tomatoes, prawns, calamari, cuttlefish, garlic and a touch of chilli was excellent, infused with fishy flavours. Gnocchi with clams, cherry tomatoes, radicchio, rocket and chilli was taste-packed too. The Sicilian house wine is reasonably priced, and puddings include capri almond and chocolate cake. *Babies and children welcome: high chairs. Booking essential. Separate room for parties, seats 6-18. Tables outdoors (18, terrace). Takeaway service; delivery service (within 1-mile radius on orders over £10).* **Map 21 C3.**

Pizza Metro NEW

64 Battersea Rise, SW11 1EQ (7228 3812/www. pizzametro.com). Clapham Junction rail. **Lunch served** noon-3pm Mon-Fri, **dinner served** 6-11pm Mon-Fri. **Meals served** noon-11pm Sat; noon-10.30pm Sun. **Main courses** £5.50-£17.50. **Service** 12.5%. **Credit** AmEx, MC, V.
A breezy yellow paint job has transformed Pizza Metro, adding extra lustre to the white tablecloths, customised crockery and brass cookware. Italian film posters add a moody note, but essentially this is a good-time Italian trattoria. The lively Italian waiters wield a mighty pepper pot and look like they're itching to pinch a bottom or two; a fish tank keeps younger family members amused; and the cooking, while a cut above the norm, revolves around immense strips of pizza, measured by the metre, and laid down the centre of the table on a scorching hot-plate. The crusts are thin, toppings are fresh. There's plenty of pasta on offer too (the gnocchi's especially good), a few meat dishes and cream-laden puddings. So a decent party venue, then, but also worth a visit at weekend lunchtimes. *Babies and children welcome: high chairs. Booking advisable. No-smoking tables. Tables outdoors (10, pavement). Takeaway service: delivery service (within 1-mile radius).* **Map 21 C4.**

Brixton SW9

Neon ✓

71 Atlantic Road, SW9 8PU (7738 6576/ www.neonbrixton.co.uk). Brixton tube/rail. **Dinner served** 6-11pm Tue-Sat; 4-10.30pm Sun. **Main courses** £9.95-£14.75. **Service** 12.5%. **Credit** DC, MC, V.
A self-styled 'modern Italian dining room and Martini bar', Neon considers itself a hip addition to the burgeoning Brixton bar and dining scene – and its minimalist red and black interior certainly delivers the look. The menu descriptions may be peppered with effusive ejaculations ('sexy!' 'lush!'), but our bruschetta starter arrived fridge-cold and soggy, various menu items were unavailable, and service was overly relaxed. Capelli d'angelo (angel's hair pasta) was well presented, though with a scarcity of the advertised courgettes and peppers, its creamy saffron sauce disappointingly bland. Pizzas were better; a just-so thin-crust diavola (chorizo, marinated peppers, rocket, chilli and garlic) was delicious. Heartier mains – such as pork parcels filled with pecorino and prunes, or pan-braised beef fillet – are also offered. Desserts included two tiny, disappointing scoops of 'probably the best home-made ice-cream outside Italy'; we tried a lip-puckeringly sharp lemon sorbet, the paucity of the serving emphasised by the enormity of the crockery. Perhaps we arrived too early in the evening to experience Neon at its best; a late licence and DJ lounge bar hint that buzzier times may be had later on. *Babies and children admitted. Restaurant available for hire. Separate area for parties, seats 35. Takeaway service; delivery service.* **Map 22 E2.**

Clapham SW4

★ Eco ✓

162 Clapham High Street, SW4 7UJ (7978 1108/www.ecorestaurants.com). Clapham Common tube. **Lunch served** noon-4pm, **dinner served** 6.30-11pm Mon-Fri. **Meals served** noon-11.30pm Sat; noon-11pm Sun. **Main courses** £5.40-£10.50. **Service** 12.5% for parties of 5 or more. **Credit** AmEx, MC, V.

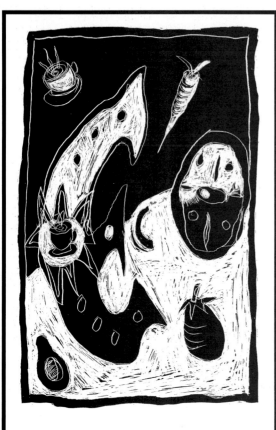

The archetypal Clapham eaterie, Eco – much like its High Street location – is a relaxed mix of trendy and comfortably worn. The interior is colourful, with twisted metal ceiling lights and a busy open kitchen. It's friendly, familiar and equally popular for an after-work pizza with mates or Sunday lunch with the kids. Pizzas range from the conventional (fiorentina, quattro stagioni) to the unusual (swordfish and spring onion), and if you opt for calzone, don't bother with a starter – portions are large and fillings generous. Asparagus and roast red pepper calzone with mushrooms and spinach was a delicious combination, oozing mozzarella and dolcelatte. Seafood pasta would have benefited from more of the advertised scallops, king prawns, mussels, squid and cuttlefish, but everything tasted fresh and the tomato sauce packed a good punch. Eco's extensive menu also features chunky pizza bread sandwiches and huge salads. Service was admirably attentive, despite the staff shortages on our visit.
Babies and children welcome: high chairs. Booking advisable; essential weekends. No-smoking tables (daytime). Takeaway service. **Map 22 A2**.
For branch (Eco Brixton) see index.

Verso
84 Clapham Park Road, SW4 7BX (7720 1515). Clapham Common tube. **Dinner served** 6-11.30pm Mon-Fri; 4-11.30pm Sun. **Meals served** noon-11.30pm Sat. **Main courses** £5.90-£12. **Credit** MC, V.
A quintessential neighbourhood restaurant, Clapham's Verso has a bright interior and a less hectic atmosphere than many other eateries on the nearby main drag. The seafood-strong Italian menu includes starters such as raw swordfish with baby spinach and lemon juice, and smoked duck's breast with quails' eggs and lentils. A pizza imperiale (with spinach, pancetta and egg) had a good crisp base and tasty tomato

sauce, although not enough spinach and too much fatty bacon made it rather greasy. Main courses include squid's ink risotto, monkfish with asparagus in a walnut and caper sauce, and spinach-stuffed chicken breast wrapped in parma ham. From the pasta choices, our tagliolini and rocket came with large, fresh prawns; staff thoughtfully brought a water bowl for mucky fingers and discarded shells. Service was helpful and brisk; they were happy to replace a spaghetti dish's advertised cream sauce with a vegan-friendly olive oil-based one.
Babies and children admitted. Disabled: toilet. Restaurant available for hire. Tables outdoors (6, pavement). Takeaway service; delivery service (within 2-mile radius on orders over £7.50). **Map 22 B2**.

South East
Camberwell SE5

★ Mozzarella e Pomodoro
21-22 Camberwell Green, SE5 7AA (7277 2020). Elephant & Castle tube/rail then 12, 35, 45, 68, 176, 185 bus. **Lunch served** noon-3pm Mon-Fri. **Dinner served** 6-11.30pm Mon-Sat. **Meals served** noon-11pm Sun. **Main courses** £5.25-£23.95. **Set lunch** (Mon-Fri) £7.50 2 courses. **Credit** AmEx, JCB, MC, V.
A wonderful escape from perpetually busy Camberwell Green, Mozzarella e Pomodoro has a relaxing and cosmopolitan airiness that is only enhanced by its charming waiting staff. The extensive menu features a great many fish options, a high point being the seafood spaghetti cooked in a paper bag, which is opened at the table to an applause of steam. The fairly small selection of pizzas includes the rather naff tropicale (ham and pineapple) and a goat's cheese pizza with roast peppers and fresh herbs. Alternatively, for a

delectable and rather traditional English dinner, char-grilled lamb cutlets with fresh mint sauce and rosemary was perfect. Thanks, at least in part, to the lack of decent competition nearby, this is a popular spot: the tables are squeezed quite closely and it is wise to book, especially at weekends when the place is full to the brim.
Babies and children welcome: high chairs. Booking advisable Fri, Sat. Separate room for parties, seats 120. Takeaway service. **Map 23 A2**.

East Dulwich SE22

Upstairs at the EDT
First floor, East Dulwich Tavern, 1 Lordship Lane, SE22 8EW (8693 1817). East Dulwich rail/40, 176, 185 bus. **Dinner served** 7-10.30pm Tue-Sat. **Meals served** noon-10pm Sun. **Main courses** £6.95-£11.95. **Credit** MC, V.
The restaurant at the East Dulwich Tavern is surprisingly serene after the busy vibe of the bar downstairs, and makes it a pleasant spot to which to retire for a quiet meal. A choice of seven stone-baked pizzas forms the backbone of the menu. We tried the rosso, with sweet caramelised onion, goat's cheese and sun-dried tomato pesto, a good combination of flavours; our only criticism was that the base could have been crisper. There are also a few vegetarian pasta dishes: one of them, agnolotti, consisted of mushroom-filled pasta parcels served with rather an excess of sage butter. Other main courses cover British classics such as steak and chips, lamb chump and sea bass. Own-made chocolate truffles made an indulgent end to our meal. On Sundays, pizzas give way to roast dinners, but the standards remain high. Staff are knowledgeable and helpful.
Babies and children welcome: high chairs. Booking advisable. Restaurant available for hire. Vegan dishes. **Map 23 C4**.

Chain gang

Think that one pizza chain restaurant is like any other? Think again. Here's the lowdown on the strengths and weaknesses of the main London chains.

★ ASK ✓
48 Grafton Way, W1T 5DZ (7388 8108/ www.askcentral.co.uk). Warren Street tube. **Meals served** noon-11.30pm daily. **Main courses** £4.95-£7.70. **Service** 10% for parties of 8 or more. **Credit** AmEx, DC, JCB, MC, V.
Started by brothers Adam and Samuel Kaye, the first ASK opened in Belsize Park in 1993. The chain (which also owns Zizzi) expanded rapidly across the capital and then the UK. There are now two dozen or so branches in London, sensibly scattered in prominent locations and offering a decent alternative to the ubiquity of the similarly styled Pizza Express. There's a huge selection of pizzas (including the inferno of double pepperoni and green chillies) and also a wider choice of pastas than that offered by most of the chains, including a satisfyingly decadent ravioli burro e pesce (large ravioli filled with crayfish, crab, smoked salmon and mascarpone with white wine and rocket).
What's available? 21 pizzas, 18 pastas, 6 salads.
How does the pizza rate? Pretty good, with large bases and decent toppings.
Number of branches 25.
Best for Lunchtime with family or a quick dinner with pals.

Babies and children welcome: high chairs. Booking advisable lunch. Disabled: toilet. Tables outdoors (5, pavement). Takeaway service. **Map 3 J4**.
For branches see index.

Café Pasta
184 Shaftesbury Avenue, WC2H 8JB (7379 0198/www.pizzaexpress.com). Covent Garden tube. **Meals served** noon-11.30pm Mon-Sat; noon-11pm Sun. **Main courses** £5.75-£12.95. **Service** 10% for parties of 7 or more. **Credit** AmEx, DC, MC, V.
Owned by the Pizza Express chain, Café Pasta can sometimes seem like a poor relation to that giant. The Shaftesbury Avenue branch is a case in point: although the location is good, the restaurant itself is far too small, with cramped tables, and service wasn't the best. Food can also be a disappointment. The emphasis is more on pasta than pizza (although there's a moderate choice of the latter, covering most of the classics). There is the odd speciality – linguine with Bantry Bay mussels, for instance, or fettuccine with chicken, tarragon, chilli, lemon and garlic. Average at best.
What's available? 10 pizzas, 13 pastas, 5 salads.
How does the pizza rate? Unspectacular. Chewy base and unimpressive toppings.
Number of branches 4.
Best for Flying visits with relatives.

Babies and children welcome: children's portions; high chairs. Bookings accepted for parties of 6 or more. Tables outdoors (4, pavement). Takeaway service.
Map 17 K6.
For branches (Café Pasta, Pizza al Rollo) see index.

★ Pizza Express ✓
The White House, 9A Belvedere Road, SE1 8YT (7928 4091/www.pizzaexpress.co.uk). Waterloo tube/rail. **Meals served** 11.30am-11.30pm daily. **Main courses** £4.95-£7.95. **Service** 10% for parties of 7 or more. **Credit** AmEx, DC, JCB, MC, V.
The first and biggest of the pizza chains, Pizza Express has an outlet on every street corner, or so it seems. It struggled in the face of newer opposition (Strada, Zizzi) in the 1990s, but has come back with a vengeance in the past couple of years, thanks to a revamped menu and a brighter, more modern design approach. The first branch opened in Wardour Street in 1965 and the company added new dishes in 2005 to celebrate its 40th birthday. The pizzas are definitely better than the pasta dishes: favourites include the soho (olive and garlic with rocket and parmesan shavings) and the veneziana (onions, capers, olives, sultanas and pine kernels), which includes a discretionary 25p to the Veneziana Fund to help protect Venice from the sea.
What's available? 21 pizzas, 6 pastas, 6 salads.

Elephant & Castle SE1

★ Pizzeria Castello

*20 Walworth Road, SE1 6SP (7703 2556).
Elephant & Castle tube/rail.* **Dinner served**
5-11.30pm Sat. **Meals served** noon-11pm
Mon-Thur; noon-11.30pm Fri. **Main courses**
£5-£12. **Credit** AmEx, MC, V.
Elephant and Castle may not be the first place that
springs to mind when you fancy eating out, but the
eyesore outside is forgotten once you're inside this
welcoming restaurant. The decor is stylish and
uncluttered, with black and white photographs
lining the walls. This place is all about pizza: thin
or thick crust, with a large choice of toppings. And
they're great; the hot green chillies certainly
packed a punch on our salami pizza. In addition, a
range of sauces can be matched with a choice of
pastas. We enjoyed the signature seafood dish
(linguine castello), as recommended by our waiter;
it arrived at the table steaming, a heap of linguine
entangled with a generous assortment of king
prawns and mussels, topped with lobster. Service
seemed slightly haphazard, the sound of dropped
cutlery punctuating the meal, but this is a warm-
hearted restaurant, with many satisfied customers.
*Babies and children welcome: high chairs.
Booking advisable. No-smoking tables. Separate
room for parties, seats 100. Tables outdoors
(4, pavement). Takeaway service.* **Map 24 O11.**

East
Bethnal Green E2

StringRay Globe Café, Bar & Pizzeria NEW

*109 Columbia Road, E2 7RL (7613 1141/
www.stringraycafe.co.uk). Bethnal Green tube/rail.*
Meals served 11am-11pm daily. **Main courses**
£4.50-£9.95. **Credit** MC, V.
StringRay is housed in a converted pub, with a
Spanish flavour to the decor and an open kitchen
at one end. Pizza forms the core of the long menu:
there are 18 cheap and cheerful options, including
the stringray, topped with tomato, mozzarella,
smoked salmon, avocado and mushrooms.
Alternatively, there are pasta dishes and plenty of
other reasonably priced, Mediterranean-slanted
options. You could start with the three-salmon
starter (marinated in beetroot, whisky and 'Thai
pesto'), perhaps followed by an excellent, firm-
fleshed sea bass, or the lucanica (pork sausage
marinated in rosemary and lemon, grilled and
served with leek mash and green peppercorn
sauce). Drinks are well priced and include a range
of cocktails. You can see why StringRay is always
packed – particularly on Sunday mornings when
Columbia Road's flower market is in full swing.
*Babies and children welcome: children's menu;
high chairs. Booking advisable. Disabled: toilet.
Tables outdoors (7, pavement). Takeaway service.*
Map 6 S3.
**For branches (Shakespeare's, StringRay
Café) see index.**

Wapping E1

Il Bordello

*81 Wapping High Street, E1W 2YN (7481 9950).
Wapping tube/100 bus.* **Lunch served** noon-3pm
Mon-Fri. **Dinner served** 6-11pm Mon-Sat.
Meals served 1-10.30pm Sun. **Main courses**
£7.75-£22.95. **Credit** AmEx, DC, MC, V.
Beaten copper and exposed brickwork are the
perfect backdrop for food locked into an
ostentatious 1980s sensibility. The emphasis is on
style over content; attentive and charming Italian
waiters serve a nicely mixed clientele what we
quickly labelled big-hair food. A starter of
carpaccio and shaved parmesan on rocket was
huge, with overly chilled beef and watery rocket,
though a broccoli and dolcelatte soup was tart and
delicious. The big guns are brought out for the
mains; from a good range of pastas, pizzas and
carni we opted for the specials – crab ravioli in an
aurora cream sauce of tomatoes and shrimp, and
monkfish tagliatelle with langoustine and scallops.
Both looked sumptuous, but both disappointed.
The ravioli's delicate crab was overwhelmed by the
rich sauce, and the tagliatelle was undone by the
quality of the fish, which lacked strength of
flavour. But all around us happy, relaxed diners
polished off fine-looking fish dishes and pizzas
with gusto, while a table of girls shared a
margherita pizza that looked exactly as it should.
We wished we'd chosen as wisely.
*Babies and children admitted. Booking essential.
Disabled: toilet. Takeaway service.*

North East
Stoke Newington N16

Il Bacio

*61 Stoke Newington Church Street, N16 0AR
(7249 3833). Stoke Newington rail/73 bus.*
Lunch served noon-2.30pm Tue-Fri; 12.45-
4.30pm Sat, Sun. **Dinner served** 6-11.15pm
daily. **Main courses** £6.50-£15.95. **Service**
12.5% for parties of 6 or more. **Credit** MC, V.
Family-owned and enthusiastically staffed, Il Bacio
is the sort of neighbourhood restaurant where
every tenth passer-by is a waving regular and even
an early Monday evening visit found a constant
flow of diners. Plants frame the entrance and the
cosy interior is strewn with colourful, eclectic
art. Service is genuinely friendly, the cooking
competent, portions generous, prices competitive.
This agreeable formula, combined with an interior
layout that separates noisy parties from cosy
couples and families with infants, attracts a
wide-ranging clientele. The menu encompasses

► **Chain gang (continued)**

How does the pizza rate? Pretty
impressive. Crisp and skinny base,
with good toppings; quality remains
consistently high given the chain's size.
Number of branches 97.
Best for Families. There can hardly be
a child in London who hasn't eaten at
Pizza Express at some point.
Anything else? The Pizza Express Jazz
Club on Dean Street is one of the
capital's top jazz clubs: Norah Jones,
Amy Winehouse and Jamie Cullum have
all played there in recent years.
*Babies and children welcome: high chairs.
Bookings accepted for parties 7 or more.
Disabled: toilet. Entertainment: pianist
7.30pm Mon. No-smoking tables. Takeaway
service.* **Map 10 M8.**
For branches see index.

Pizza Paradiso

*61 The Cut, SE1 8LL (7261 1221/
www.pizzaparadiso.co.uk). Waterloo tube/
rail.* **Meals served** noon-midnight Mon-Sat;
noon-11pm Sun. **Main courses** £6-£15.95.
Credit AmEx, DC, JCB, MC, V.
The original branch in Store Street
(called Ristorante Olivelli Paradiso) was
founded as a Sicilian-run restaurant in
1934, and has only really started to
expand into a chain in the past few
years. There are still only a handful of
restaurants, and they've all managed to
retain the original's cosy, boho, Italian
bistro atmosphere, with signed pictures
of celebrities and Italian legends on the
walls. Food is a cut above standard pizza

chain fare: gnocchi with sun-dried
tomato and calamari is a typical pasta
choice, and there's a proper selection
of *secondi*, including an expensive steak
and good fish options.
What's available? 16 pizzas, 14 pastas,
6 salads.
How does the pizza rate? Excellent.
Thin, crispy base and a good choice
of toppings.
Number of branches? 5.
Best for Casual dates and lazy lunches.
Anything else? The Marx brothers
insisted on eating at the original
restaurant on their one and only visit
to England. Other famous diners have
included Mae West, Danny Kaye, Bob
Hope and Liberace.
*Babies and children welcome: children's
menu; high chairs. Booking advisable
Wed-Fri. Tables outdoors (4, pavement).
Takeaway service.* **Map 11 N8.**
For branches see index.

★ La Porchetta

*33 Boswell Street, WC1N 3BP (7242
2434/www.laporchetta.co.uk). Holborn
or Russell Square tube.* **Lunch served**
noon-3pm Mon-Fri. **Dinner served** 6-11pm
Mon-Sat. **Main courses** £6.50-£7. **Service**
10% for parties of 5 or more. **Credit** MC, V.
Cheap and cheerful, La Porchetta has
spread its trotters (the pig theme is
inescapable) from its north London
base, offering budget bites at a select
number of locations (the Stroud Green
Road branch still gets the most praise).

We tried the Holborn branch, which had
far too many tables crammed into its
tiny, dimly lit interior, leading to one
unfortunate waiter clumping one of us
over the head with his elbow not once,
but twice. The reason they try to fit in
so many people is obvious once you see
the prices; this is the cheapest of the
chains, and clearly gets by on as a high
a turnover as possible. There's a huge
amount of choice whether you go for
pizza or pasta, but it's probably wisest to
stick with the classics rather than trying
anything more adventurous. Quality?
Well, you get what you pay for...
What's available? 26 pizzas, 35 pastas,
5 salads.
How does the pizza rate? Satisfactory,
but it's hard to complain at these prices.
Number of branches 4.
Best for Anybody who doesn't mind
getting assaulted by waiters during their
hunt for a bargain.
*Babies and children welcome: high chairs.
Booking advisable. Takeaway service.*
Map 4 L5.
For branches see index.

★ Prezzo

*161 Euston Road, NW1 2BD (7387 5587/
www.prezzoplc.co.uk). Euston tube/rail.*
Meals served noon-11.30pm Mon-Sat;
noon-11pm Sun. **Main courses** £5.45-
£8.50. **Credit** AmEx, DC, MC, V.
The original Prezzo opened in New
Oxford Street in 2000 and has since
expanded at a solid rate throughout

such favourites as spaghetti with clams, risotto funghi, gnocchi and dover sole. Enormous pizzas that overhang plates cost £5.50 to £8.50. At these prices, and with 24 choices, there's an element of quality being sacrificed for size, but while they're not quite top class, ingredients taste fresh and an additional £2.50 buys your pizza a buffalo mozzarella upgrade. Il Bacio is about enjoying a meal with friends, not winning a Michelin star. A café and deli up the road and a branch in Finsbury Park are testaments to its popularity in the area.
Babies and children welcome: high chairs. Booking advisable. Separate room for parties, seats 50. Tables outdoors (3, pavement). Takeaway service; delivery service (on orders over £10). Map 25 B1. For branch see index.

North West
Hampstead NW3

Fratelli la Bufala NEW
45A South End Road, NW3 2QB (7435 7814/ www.fratellilabufala.com). Belsize Park tube/ Hampstead Heath rail. **Lunch served** noon-3pm, **dinner served** 6-11pm Mon-Fri. **Meals served** noon-11pm Sat; noon-10pm Sun. **Main courses** £6-£13.50. **Set lunch** (Mon-Fri) £10 2 courses. **Credit** AmEx, MC, V.
This new restaurant on the former site of Cucina near Hampstead Heath is part of a family-owned international chain with branches in Milan, Naples and Rio de Janeiro, among others. We're used to seeing restaurants boasting about their fresh mozzarella di bufala, but the twist here is that most of the cheeses and meats are derived from buffalo – yep, even the piquant sausages. We loved the salentina pizza, topped with cream, mozzarella, scamorza, ricotta and caciotta, all made with buffalo milk. You'll also find buffalo steaks,

hamburgers and regional dishes from Campania, plus some rich desserts such as cannoli and ricotta cheesecake. Gourmet grub or naff novelty? The fact is buffalo meat, being very low in fat, can be tough. Even the minced sausage mixture is prone to chewiness. With cheeses forming so much of the savoury and sweet menu, you may find (as we did) that one or two courses are enough. But this is a cleverly positioned site and the friendly, casual atmosphere, with vivid modern paintings, is well-suited to family dining.
Babies and children welcome: children's menu, high chairs. Booking advisable. No-smoking tables. Tables outdoors (2, pavement). Takeaway service. Map 28 C3.

West Hampstead NW6

La Brocca
273 West End Lane, NW6 1QS (7433 1989). West Hampstead tube/rail/139, C11 bus. **Bar Open** noon-11pm daily. **Lunch served** noon-4pm Mon-Fri; noon-4.30pm Sat, Sun. **Main courses** £5.95-£10.95. **Restaurant Dinner served** 6.30-10.30pm Mon, Sun; 6.30-11pm Tue-Sat. **Main courses** £7.95-£14.50. **Service** 12.5% for parties of 6 or more. **Both Credit** AmEx, JCB, MC, V.
Located beneath noisy Bar Brocca, this small restaurant is popular with young locals. Exposed brickwork, gingham tablecloths and walls lined with wooden wine racks create a rustic Italian feel; there's also a leafy conservatory. Starters include a variety of bruschetta and antipasti dishes; antipasto nostra was a flavoursome selection served on a crisp pizza base. Main courses don't expand much beyond pizza, pasta and a few salads – take a look at the specials if you want something more unusual. Our main courses were disappointing; monkfish wrapped in parma ham served with roasted vegetables was fine, but spinach and ricotta ravioli was undercooked. An

excellent tiramisu finished our meal on a more positive note. Service is relaxed and friendly and there's a good choice of wines.
Babies and children welcome: high chairs. Booking advisable. Entertainment: jazz duo 8.30-11pm Thur (bar). Tables outdoors (5, patio). Map 28 A2.

Outer London
Kingston, Surrey

★ Terra Mia
138 London Road, Kingston upon Thames, Surrey KT2 6QJ (8546 4888/www.terra-mia. co.uk). Kingston rail. **Lunch served** noon-2.30pm, **dinner served** 6-11.30pm Mon-Sat. **Main courses** £4.20-£8.50. **Service** 10% for parties of 5 or more. **Credit** MC, V.
The cheery sounding La La Pizza may have changed its name but little else seems different – the rustic wall mural remains and staff are as friendly and accommodating as ever. Saturday lunchtime sees a steady influx of families and couples who barely need to cast their eyes over the familiar menu. The long list of daily specials features a great deal of seafood. From a typical assortment of pastas, we chose the lasagne, which arrived steaming and topped with fresh herbs. The accompanying garlic bread was more of a crispy flatbread, but delicious just the same. Pizzas seem the most popular choice among diners. We tried a firenze: the base had just the right bite and toppings of tomato, mozzarella and spinach were generously scattered; we weren't so keen on the rather rubbery-textured egg. The dessert menu presents an array of freezer favourites; it's probably better to opt for the cheesecake or tiramisu if you have the space.
Babies and children welcome: high chairs. Booking advisable. Tables outdoors (6, garden). Takeaway service.

England (though there are only a couple of branches in the capital). Aimed a notch above Pizza Express, but still offering more of a standardised chain experience than somewhere like Pizza Paradiso, Prezzo might not look anything special, but the food was some of the best of all the chains. The pizzas, in particular, were excellent – the reine came with plump mushrooms and tasty ham, while the tre gusti (pepperoni, seasoned chicken, bacon, mozzarella) is recommended for anybody with a healthy appetite. Prezzo is proof that when it comes to toppings, chains don't have to choose quantity over quality. The pasta was also very good, and there's a decent selection of grilled food.
What's available? 12 pizzas, 14 pastas, 6 salads.
How does the pizza rate? Very good: perfect base and some excellent quality toppings.
Number of branches 2.
Best for Couples on a quiet night out and business lunchers.
Babies and children welcome: high chairs. Booking advisable. Disabled: toilet. No-smoking tables. Takeaway service.
Map 4 K3.
For branches see index.

Strada
31 Marylebone High Street, W1U 4PP (7935 1004/www.strada.co.uk). Baker Street or Bond Street tube. **Meals served** noon-11pm Mon-Sat; noon-10.30pm Sun.

Main courses £6.95-£14.95. **Set meal** (3-6.30pm Mon-Fri) £5.95 1 pizza. **Service** 12.5%. **Credit** AmEx, MC, V.
The much praised Strada chain can be found anywhere that's reasonably trendy in an upscale urban sort of way – Clapham, Marylebone High Street, Exmouth Market – but our latest visit suggested that it might be expanding too fast for standards to keep up. Stylish and modern interiors are centred around the wood-fired oven, from which piping hot pizzas emerge. There is also a good range of pastas, risottos, grilled meat and fish dishes. One nice touch is the free water at each table – a habit that every restaurant in London should be encouraged to follow. Regulars swear by the pizzas, but we weren't particularly impressed by the quality of base or topping.
What's available? 12 pizzas, 8 pastas.
How does the pizza rate? Very disappointing; sloppy bases and not particularly tasty toppings.
Number of branches 20.
Best for All sorts: couples, tourists, gossiping friends.
Anything else? The wood for the ovens all comes from environmentally managed forests.
Babies and children welcome: high chairs. Booking advisable. Disabled: toilet. No-smoking tables. Separate rooms for parties, seating 12 and 20. Takeaway service. **Map 3 G5.**
For branches see index.

Zizzi
33-41 Charlotte Street, W1T 1RR (7436 9440/www.zizzi.co.uk). Goodge Street or Tottenham Court Road tube. **Meals served** noon-11.30pm daily. **Main courses** £8-£10. **Set meal** £14.95 2 courses. **Service** 10% for parties of 8 or more. **Credit** AmEx, DC, JCB, MC, V.
It might be part of the ASK empire (see p315), but Zizzi offers a rather different experience to the original chain. Restaurants tend to cater for groups or tourists, with large, open-plan interiors and plenty of tables that can be slung together in case of emergency. Although the wood-fired pizza oven is given much exposure in the open kitchen, the food itself is of a more variable quality than at ASK, and can sometimes be downright disappointing: our fiorentina pizza, for example, was flaccid, and the salad unimaginative. However, service is friendly and if you're with a crowd and the wine is kept flowing at a decent rate, you ought to have a pleasant enough experience.
What's available? 16 pizzas, 14 pastas, 5 salads.
How does the pizza rate? Disappointing. Tired toppings and a soft base.
Number of branches 18.
Best for Office parties and big groups.
Babies and children welcome: high chairs. Booking advisable. Disabled: toilet. No-smoking tables. Tables outdoors (4, pavement). Takeaway service. Map 9 J5.
For branches see index.

CHEAP EATS

TO

15% DISCOUNT
off your final food bill
Offer valid seven days a week.
Maximum party size of 6.

A WILD PLACE TO SHOP AND EAT®

Rainforest Cafe is a unique venue
bringing to life the sights and sounds
of the rainforest.
Come and try our fantastic menu with a
re-launched healthy kids menu, including
gluten free, dairy free and organic options.

020 7434 3111
20 Shaftesbury Avenue, Piccadilly Circus,
London W1D 7EU
www.therainforestcafe.co.uk
'Please show this advert to your safari guide when seated.
Cannot be used in conjunction with any other offer.

Octave

Casual Jazz
with
fabulous food

Octave is Covent Garden's hottest new Jazz haven.

Perfect for an intimate drinks date, a cocktail
evening with friends or a work party where
a tasty meal and plenty of drinks are
required!

With contemporary jazz artists
setting the mood, Octave
guarantees a fantastic
experience no matter
what the occasion.

27-29 Endell Street • Covent Garden
London WC2H 9BA
T: 020 7836 4616 • F: 020 7836 2608
www.octave8.com

Drinking

TABLE (AS BEFORE)
COCKTAIL SET FROM HEALS (AS BEFORE)
MARTINI GLASS FROM URBANBAR (0870 200 7020, WWW.URBANBAR.COM)

Bars

Here we list a few of our favourites from London's ever-growing, ever-changing bar scene. For pubs serving good food, see **Gastropubs**, starting on p105. For the best boozers, see **Pubs**, starting on p328. And for hundreds and hundreds of drinking options across the capital, see the annual *Time Out Bars, Pubs & Clubs* guide.

Central

Bloomsbury WC1

AKA
18 West Central Street, WC1A 1JJ (7836 0110/ www.akalondon.com). Holborn or Tottenham Court Road tube. **Open** 6pm-3am Tue-Thur; 6pm-4am Fri; 7pm-5am Sat; 10pm-4am Sun. **Snacks served** 6-11pm Tue-Fri; 7pm-11.30pm Sat. **Snacks** £2.50-£10. **Admission** £3 after 11pm Tue; £5 after 10pm Thur; £5 after 9pm, £7 after 10pm Fri; £10 after 9pm Sat; varies Sun. **Credit** AmEx, DC, JCB, MC, V.
A clubbing vibe throbs out of the main downstairs bar at AKA. With a long shiny zinc counter, curved-back seats and candlelit tables, this is the partner operation to adjoining nightclub the End. Renowned DJ nights are staged in the expansive, two-floor industrial space, a former Victorian sorting office. 'Dress up, dress down, but no suits' is the rule. Cocktails (£6.50-£8.50) are categorised by premium base spirits such as Ketel One vodka, Germana cachaça and Appleton white rum, but pride of place goes to the champagne varieties. Try a Lost in Translation (Devaux champagne, saké, passionfruit purée and marmalade) or perhaps an 18 West (Zubrowka Bison vodka, passionfruit, pear and lemon juice topped with Devaux champagne). Bottled beers include Russian Baltika and Belgian Grimbergen.
Bar available for hire. Disabled: toilet. Entertainment: DJs 10pm daily; quiz 8pm 1st Tue of mth. **Map 18 L6.**

Covent Garden WC2

Detroit
35 Earlham Street, WC2H 9LD (7240 2662/ www.detroit-bar.com). Covent Garden or Leicester Square tube. **Open** 5pm-midnight Mon-Sat. **Dinner served** 5-10.30pm Mon-Sat. **Main courses** £9.75-£13.50. **Set meal** (5-8pm) £13.50 2 courses, £17 3 courses. **Service** 12.5%. **Credit** AmEx, DC, MC, V.
Detroit celebrated its tenth anniversary in 2005, but this cool and cosy spot remains one of London's most revered style bars. The retro sci-fi decor (Tardis doors leading to a warren of alcoves, curved forms meeting the eye as it adjusts to the changing floor and ceiling heights) hasn't dated, and neither has the expert cocktail-making. The three dozen Martinis, short and long drinks (£6.80-£7.50) are created with flair: try the house Detroit (Wyborowa vodka, mint leaves and sugar syrup) for a fine example. Wreckless spendthrifts might also be enticed by the 'super premium' cocktails at £19.50. Bottled beers include Estonian Le Coq, Asahi Dry and Duvel, while bar snacks encompass parma ham and honey crostini, or samosas and sour cream.
Booking advisable. No-smoking tables. Separate room for parties, seats 27. Tables outdoors (5, pavement). **Map 18 L6.**

Lowlander ✓
36 Drury Lane, WC2B 5RR (7379 7446/ www.lowlander.com). Covent Garden or Holborn tube. **Open** noon-11pm Mon-Sat; noon-10pm Sun. **Meals served** noon-10.30pm Mon-Sat; noon-

9.30pm Sun. **Main courses** £8.95-£12.95. **Set meal** £12.95 2 courses, £16.95 3 courses. **Credit** AmEx, MC, V.
This superior gastrobar promises the best of Benelux. This means a varied choice of draught beers (De Koninck, Floris Apple, De Prael Andre, among others), poured from neatly logoed pumps into half-pint or two-pint logoed glasses, and more than 40 bottles, split into categories such as Trappist, fruit, pilsner, wheat, amber/dark and champagne. The all-day deli selections (Dutch and Belgian cheeses, charcuterie platters), the mains (Indonesian poached cod, Lowlander burger) and the set menu (roast pumpkin, pine nut and sage risotto) get the white napkin treatment from efficient waiting staff. The main bar is decorated with retro beer ads and the Lowlander logo of a skimmed beer head; it's overlooked by a mezzanine (newly kitted out in banquette seating) that's often hired out for private bashes. As good as it gets, on either side of the Hook or the North Sea.
Babies and children admitted. No-smoking area. Separate area for parties, seats 20. Tables outside (4, pavement). **Map 18 L6.**

Edgware Road W2

Salt Whisky Bar
82 Seymour Street, W2 2JB (7402 1155/ www.saltbar.com). Marble Arch tube. **Open** 5pm-1am Mon-Sat; 5pm-midnight Sun. **Meals served** 6-10.30pm daily. **Main courses** £7.50-£8.95. **Service** 12.5%. **Credit** MC, V.
This cosy, lounge-style bar is a favourite haunt of staff from Broadcasting House, and maintains a certain highbrow media chic. The vibe is more Radio 4 than Radio 1, so it was something of a shame that the club-style piped music was turned up so loud on our visit: like techno on the *Today* programme, it just didn't fit. That aside, the bar is a place of sanctity for acolytes of the whisky bottle: the 200-strong selection is nothing short of spectacular. Prices vary from around £5 for an average dram to an eye-watering £12,000 for a bottle of 1937 Glenfiddich. Our money-to-sense ratio held firm, but we couldn't resist a shot of Pappa Van Winkle's 20-year-old Bourbon: a little steep at £15, but still a discovery this side of the Mason-Dixon.
Entertainment: DJs 8pm Mon-Wed, Sun; 9pm Thur-Sat. Separate rooms for parties, seating 40 and 60. Tables outdoors (7, terrace). **Map 8 F6.**

Fitzrovia W1

Crazy Bear
26-28 Whitfield Street, W1T 2RG (7631 0088/ www.crazybeargroup.co.uk). Goodge Street or Tottenham Court Road tube. **Bar Open** noon-11pm Mon-Fri; 6-11pm Sat. **Restaurant Meals served** noon-10.45pm Mon-Fri. **Dinner served** 6-10.45pm Sat. **Dim sum** £2.50-£3.50. **Main courses** £7-£18.50. **Set lunch** £7.50 1 course. **Set meal** (tasting menus) £25 8 dishes, £30 10 dishes. **Service** 12.5%. *Both* **Credit** AmEx, MC, V.
Named after the Oxfordshire pub, hotel and restaurant of which it is an offshoot, Crazy Bear

features a ground-floor oriental restaurant (*see p244*) and a basement bar down an ornate staircase. The hospitable hostess leads you to a spot – on a swivelling cowhide bar stool, in a red padded alcove or on a low leather armchair – in a mirrored art deco wonderland. Drinks (around £7.50) include impeccable long, 'short and muddled', champagne, Martini and non-alcoholic cocktails, created with such ingredients as fresh tomatoes, raspberry purées, chilli-infused vodkas and Buffalo Trace bourbons. Six quality wines of both colours (plus two of rosé) are available by the glass, and there's an extensive choice by the bottle. Paulaner wheat beer and Timothy Taylor Landlord are two of the brews. Top-quality pan-Asian food, steamed, satayed or deep-fried, comes in canapé and snackform. We couldn't fault it.
Babies and children admitted (restaurant, lunch only). Booking advisable. **Map 4 K5.**

Hakkasan
8 Hanway Place, W1T 1HD (7907 1888). Tottenham Court Road tube. **Bar Open** noon-12.30am Mon, Tue; noon-1.30am Wed-Sat; noon-midnight Sun. **Restaurant Lunch/dim sum** served noon-2.45pm Mon-Fri; noon-4.30pm Sat, Sun. **Dinner served** 6-11.30pm Mon, Tue, Sun; 6pm-12.30am Wed-Sat. **Dim sum** £3.50-£16. **Main courses** £11.50-£68. *Both* **Service** 13%. **Credit** AmEx, MC, V.
The bar at Alan Yau's first-rate Chinese restaurant (*see p69*) has expanded to fill a decent side space of the exquisite basement premises, with button stools and candlelit tables. The bar is named Ling Ling, though bar-hoppers still call it the Hakkasan. The focal point is a long cocktail counter: pay £9.61 (including service) and you'll get a Hakkatini (Grey Goose l'Orange, Campari, Grand Marnier) or Saketini (saké, Hendrick's gin, Rain vodka) of such class you'll wonder why you bothered sipping cocktails elsewhere. Long and short drinks match the price and quality of the customised Martinis: a cornucopia of Ketel One and Rain vodkas, sakés, fresh fruits and ginseng spirits. Saké comes cold or hot, the beer is Yebisu. To eat, there are bar nibbles (prawn crackers, nuts, olives).
Disabled: toilet. Entertainment: DJs 9pm daily. Restaurant available for hire. Separate room for parties, seats 65. **Map 17 K5.**

Long Bar
The Sanderson, 50 Berners Street, W1T 3NG (7300 1400/www.spoon-restaurant.com). Oxford Circus or Tottenham Court Road tube. **Open** noon-12.30am Mon-Sat; noon-10.30pm Sun. **Lunch served** noon-2.30pm daily. **Dinner served** 6-11pm Mon-Sat; 6-10pm Sun. **Service** 12.5%. **Credit** AmEx, DC, MC, V.
The long bar in question is a thin rectangle of a silver, white and glass counter dotted with eyeball-embellished stools. It's the main attraction of this sleek space, sited beside the lobby of the ultra-stylish Sanderson hotel. Even though the decor, the drinks menu and the Japanese garden have hardly changed since the place opened in 1999, it remains a landmark rendezvous spot for urban shakers. The dozen Martinis include a Picasso (Wyborowa apple, crème de cassis and blueberries) and a Citroen (Ketel One citron stirred with limoncello, elderflower water and lemon zest). There are also champagne cocktails, such as Bubbles & Bling (Hennessey, caramel and cinnamon charged with Laurent Perrier), and highballs, such as Sweet Thing (crushed strawberries and Cariel vanilla vodka). Cocktails cost about £10; wines start at £6.50 a glass. The finger food matches the setting for style and price.
Babies and children welcome (terrace); high chairs. Disabled: toilet. Entertainment: DJs 7pm-12.30am Wed-Fri. Tables outdoors (20, terrace). **Map 17 J5.**

Shochu Lounge `NEW`
2005 WINNER BEST BAR
Basement, Roka, 37 Charlotte Street, W1T 1RR (7580 6464/www.rokarestaurant.com). Goodge Street or Tottenham Court Road tube.

DRINKING

Bar **Open** 5pm-midnight daily. **Meals served** 5.30pm-midnight daily. **Main courses** £3.60-£21.
Restaurant **Lunch served** noon-2.30pm, tea served 2.30-5.30pm Mon-Sat. **Dinner served** 5.30-11.30pm Mon-Sat; 5.30-10.30pm Sun. **Main courses** £3.60-£21.
Both **Service** 12.5%. **Credit** AmEx, DC, MC, V.
A sumptuous basement beneath the equally stylish Japanese restaurant Roka (*see p182*), Shochu Lounge is wonderfully original. Shochu, a vodka-like spirit made of buckwheat, barley, sweet potato or rice, has been around in Japan since the 14th century, but has only come to the attention of Londoners in the 21st. Here, it is mixed with fresh fruits and spices to create cocktails (£6-£7.50) both chilled (Tanuki Peach: shochu, peach purée and sugar) and hot (shochu, cinnamon and pear), in Martini, short, long, flute and goblet forms. Rows of preserving jars are part of the semi-rustic, semi-boutique decor. A table heaving with old kitchen utensils almost seems part of the island bar counter, except it's lined with customers. There's also a raised, red-shaded lounge to the rear. Saké and Sapporo beer are also available, and the bar snacks and mains (brought down from the restaurant) are superb.
Booking advisable. Disabled: toilet. No smoking (restaurant). **Map 9 J5**.

Holborn WC1

Guanabara NEW ✓

New London Theatre, Parker Street, corner of Drury Lane, WC2B 5PW (7242 8600/ www.guanabara.co.uk). Covent Garden or Holborn tube. **Open** 5.30pm-2.30am Mon-Sat; 5pm-midnight Sun. **Snacks served** 5.30pm-midnight daily. **Snacks** £3-£10. **Credit** AmEx, MC, V.
Housed in an externally nondescript wing of the New London Theatre, Guanabara warms to its theme immediately. Brazilian TV covers one wall; ahead is a Rio beach mural (Guanabara is the bay of Rio); and further on is a fiery nightspot. A dozen long wooden tables radiate from a central dancefloor and stage. There are 24 varieties of cachaça, eight fruit Caipirinhas and some classic cocktails, plus some South American wines and beers (Brahma, Palma Louca). Food is equally exotic, encompassing 'combinado' sharing platters (the vegetarian one contains cheese, rice croquettes, vegetable tortilla, olives, cheesebread and cassava chips), starters such as feijoada and desserts including chocolate cachaça cake.
Disabled: toilet. Entertainment: DJ 5.30pm daily; occasional bands. **Map 18 L6**.

Pearl Bar & Restaurant NEW

Chancery Court Hotel, 252 High Holborn, WC1V 7EN (7829 7000/www.pearl-restaurant.com). Holborn tube.
Bar **Open** 11am-11pm Mon-Fri; 6-11pm Sat.
Restaurant **Lunch served** noon-2.30pm Mon-Fri. **Dinner served** 7-10pm Mon-Sat. **Set lunch** £23.50 2 courses, £26.50 3 courses. **Set dinner** £45 3 courses, £55 5 courses (£100 incl wine).
Both **Service** 12.5%. **Credit** AmEx, JCB, MC, V.
Even within the swish five-star Chancery Court business hotel, Pearl shines. Past the courtyard entrance and a revolving door, a narrow bar drips and sways with strings of pearls: from huge, tubular brown lights, over the windows and dividing the groups of armless chairs and banquettes. The thick menu lists 44 cocktails (£9-£10.50), including a Pink Pearl of Rémy Martin VSOP and spiced berry cordials, topped with pink champagne; Zubrowkas and flavoured Absoluts inform the Martinis. Wine, though, is where Pearl really sings. Aided by a back-bar Cruvinet nitrogen machine that keeps bottles fresh, a clear cold room in the adjoining restaurant and switched-on staff, Pearl can provide 450 types by the bottle and 54 by the glass. For the restaurant, *see p126*.
Disabled: toilet. Entertainment: pianist 6pm daily. **Map 10 M5**.

Shochu Lounge

DRINKING

Knightsbridge SW1

Blue Bar

The Berkeley, Wilton Place, SW1X 7RL (7235 6000/www.the-berkeley.co.uk). Hyde Park Corner tube. **Open** 4pm-1am Mon-Sat; 4pm-midnight Sun. **Tapas served** 4pm-midnight Mon-Sat; 5pm-midnight Sun. **Tapas** £6.50. **Service** 12.5%. **Credit** AmEx, DC, JCB, MC, V.
The Blue Bar is located beside the lobby of the Berkeley hotel, and is just as stylish, discreet and expensive as you might expect. Onion-flavoured crostini, a bowl of warmed, glazed nuts, another of marinated black olives, a blue drinks menu, a napkin and a leather coaster were yet to arrive. Sit at the scented bar, or in the sunken side area, or simply enveloped by the original Lutyens panelling, while you muse over a Berkeley cocktail classic (£10) – say, a Lotus of green Chartreuse and fresh mint. Dom Pérignons (costing three-figure sums), vintage Cristals, 50ml malts at £59 a shot, Cohiba cigars and Beluga caviar, a thimble of Achille Musetti espresso – all arrive with optimum grace. Hungry? Try modish 'tapas' such as scallops with wasabi and lime vinaigrette, or nori-wrapped vegetable rolls marinated in mirin. Impeccable.
Bookings not accepted. Disabled: toilet. Dress: smart casual. **Map 9 G9.**

Mayfair W1

43 NEW

43 South Molton Street, W1K 5RS (7647 4343/ www.43southmolton.com). Bond Street tube. **Open** 11.30pm-3am Mon-Sat; 11.30am-midnight Sun. **Meals/snacks served** 11am-2.30am Mon-Sat; 11.30am-11.30pm Sun. **Main courses** £7-£14. **Snacks** £4-£12. **Credit** AmEx, MC, V.
Understatement of the year: you need to get here early. Jasper Tay, formerly of Milk & Honey (*see below*), has created a four-bar establishment run along similar phone-ahead-or-members-only lines. Its faceless frontage and name is part of the gag, as is the retro retail decor (by interior designer Russell Sage) in the intimate bar/diner at street level, the only space easily accessible to the general public. Larders full of Scottish porridge oats boxes, Listerine, Brasso and old *Beano* annuals form the decorative punchline. More eccentrica looms in the clubby basement ('Claridge's on acid!' says Jasper), while the private dining and drinking rooms upstairs, accessible next door, are boho clad and comfortable. The inventive drinks include a house Bloody Mary featuring horseradish-infused vodka, and a Silver Coin Margarita with Cointreau. The bar menu is in suitably good taste.
Babies and children welcome (lunch): high chairs. Entertainment: bands/DJs 7pm daily. Separate room for parties, holds 120. Tables outdoors (5, pavement). **Map 9 H6.**

Trader Vic's

The London Hilton on Park Lane, 22 Park Lane, W1K 4BE (7208 4113/www.tradervics.com). Hyde Park Corner tube .
Bar **Open/meals served** noon-1am Mon-Thur; noon-3am Fri; 5pm-3am Sat; 5-11.30pm Sun. **Main courses** £8-£11.
Restaurant **Lunch served** noon-5pm Mon-Fri. **Dinner served** 6pm-12.30am Mon-Sat; 6-11.30pm Sun. **Main courses** £18-£22.
Both **Service** 15%. **Credit** AmEx, DC, MC, V.
First, greatest and silliest of the international theme bars. It's been seven decades since Victor Bergeron established the first tiki bar in Oakland, California, and yet this Americo-Polynesian establishment never fails to both baffle (why?) and delight (who cares?). There's nothing authentic about it at all; indeed, as we all travel more and the world grows smaller, the already over-the-top theme seems even more preposterous – and, if you look closely in the dim light, a little shabby. Still, it's a hard heart that stays uninspired by this cheerily unsophisticated spot, especially after a couple of the good-value atomic cocktails. The Mai Tai, invented by Bergeron himself, is always a wise choice; other good bets include the rum-rich Samoan Fog Cutter, served in an absurd ceramic vase, and Doctor Funk of Tahiti, purely because it's such fun asking for one.

Babies and children welcome; high chairs. Booking advisable (restaurant). Disabled: toilet (hotel). Entertainment: musicians 10.30pm daily. No-smoking (restaurant). Separate room for parties, seats 30. **Map 9 G8.**

Piccadilly W1

Cocoon NEW

65 Regent Street, W1B 4EA (7494 7609/ www.cocoon-restaurants.com). Piccadilly Circus tube. **Lunch served** noon-3pm Mon-Fri. **Dinner served** 5.30pm-1am Mon-Sat; 5.30-10.30pm Sun. **Main courses** £7.50-£18.50. **Set meal** (lunch, 5.30-7pm daily) £12.50-£24 2 courses (minimum 2). **Service** 12.5%. **Credit** AmEx, MC, V.
Stephane Dupoux's ground-breaking design at this oriental bar/restaurant is laid out in step with the six-stage life cycle of the butterfly, but do the cocktails make it worth the effort of getting to the pretty, winged expanse of lounge bar at the end? Of course. A Jerry Collins features 42 Below Feijoa vodka shaken with kiwi fruit and apple juice, then mixed with ginger beer; an Espresso Martini has Wyborowa almond shaken with espresso, cognac and vanilla. Of the oriental mixes, an Asayake comprises crushed red grapes shaken with plum wine, cloudy apple juice and Bombay Sapphire, decorated with rose petals. The 'Luxury' items are absurdly decadent, though most are only in the £12 range. There is saké and shochu too, and dim sum bar food. From autumn 2005, Cocoon plans to open until 3am, and the space will really spread its wings. For the restaurant, *see p245.*
Babies and children admitted. Booking advisable; essential weekends. Disabled: toilet. No smoking. Separate room for parties, seats 14. **Map 17 7J.**

Soho W1

Alphabet

61-63 Beak Street, W1F 9SS (7439 2190/ www.alphabetbar.com). Oxford Circus or Piccadilly Circus tube. **Open** noon-11pm Mon-Fri; 5-11pm Sat. **Lunch served** noon-4pm, **dinner served** 5-9pm Mon-Sat. **Main courses** £6.90-£8.50. **Service** 12.5%. **Credit** AmEx, JCB, MC, V.
A recent refit has robbed Alphabet of one of London's most notable examples of cool bar design – the *A-Z* street-plan basement floor. Nevertheless, this remains a popular west Soho landmark; from lunchtime to mid-evening, the ground-floor bar is well populated with chatty diners. The menu is pretty much unchanged: eight whites, eight reds and a rosé on the wine list, with half a dozen or so available by the glass. Beer is bottled and includes Asahi, Hoegaarden, Negra Modelo, Cruzcampo and San Miguel. Cocktails are split into 'sparklers' (champagne, all at £7.80), 'slightly twisted' (£6.30; the Lotus Martini of mint leaves, Plymouth gin, grenadine, Blue Bols and lychee is a notable example), 'long & lush', 'los latinos' and 'something for the weekend'. Come evening, the DJs on the decks downstairs kick ass.
Babies and children admitted (until 5pm). Entertainment: DJs 7.30pm Thur-Sat. **Map 17 J6.**

Floridita NEW

2005 RUNNER-UP BEST BAR
100 Wardour Street, W1F 0TN (7314 4000). Leicester Square, Piccadilly Circus or Tottenham Court Road tube. **Meals served** 5.30pm-2.30am Mon-Sat. **Main courses** £16-£36. **Service** 12.5%. **Credit** AmEx, DC, JCB, MC, V.
Terence Conran has teamed up with Cuba's renowned (if tourist-pitched) Floridita bar to open this outpost: a bar/restaurant in the huge space formerly occupied by Mezzo. Glitzy couples gaze at the film-set scene of hot waitresses swaying past with clanking trays of exotic drinks, to the rhythms of the house band. It's all a little forced; the sooner a hipper (and ideally Latin) crowd latches on, the better. The quality of the cocktails, though, cannot be gainsaid. Fairly priced (£7-£8) and categorised as Cuban or international, old or new, they're flawless. Pride of place goes to the Daiquiri, invented at the venue's Havana counterpart and here offered in five varieties, with Havana Club Añejo Blanco as the base. Churchill

(with fresh lime and Earl Grey tea syrup) or Pomegranate may be inventive, but you can't beat the old-timers. It's all in the maraschino. For the restaurant, *see p44.*
Babies and children admitted. Booking advisable. Disabled: toilet. Entertainment: Cuban band/DJ 7.30pm Mon-Sat. Separate room for parties, seats 56. **Map 17 K6.**

Lab

12 Old Compton Street, W1D 4TQ (7437 7820/ www.lab-townhouse.com). Leicester Square or Tottenham Court Road tube. **Open** 4pm-midnight Mon-Sat; 6-10.30pm Sun. **Snacks served** 6-11pm Mon-Sat; 6-10.30pm Sun. **Snacks** £5.50-£13.50. **Credit** AmEx, MC, V.
A recent revarnish has brightened up this landmark cocktail bar, which has trained and nurtured some of the best mixers in the business. Its glossy drinks menu, where alchemy meets urban cool, is a treat. Set amid striking images of Soho, the cocktail categorisation of Streets Ahead (for instance, Big Apple with Jameson's and apple schnapps), Respect (Dick Bradsell Bramble with Plymouth gin and crème de mûre) and Hall of Fame (15 classics) is, well, streets ahead of nearly all the competition, and reasonably priced too (most are around £7). And therein lies the problem. This two-level bar is at best petite and at worst pokey, especially upstairs, and the chances of finding any space amid the moderately retro decor on a Friday night are slim indeed. That apart, Lab is a thoroughly commendable operation.
Entertainment: DJs 9pm Mon-Sat. **Map 17 K6.**

Milk & Honey

61 Poland Street, W1F 7NU (7292 9949/0700 655 469/www.mlkhny.com). Oxford Circus tube. **Open** *Non-members* 6-11pm Mon-Fri; 7-11pm Sat. *Members* 6pm-3am Mon-Fri; 7pm-3am Sat. **Snacks served** 6pm-2am Mon-Sat. **Snacks** £5-£15. **Credit** AmEx, DC, MC, V.
Winner of the Best Bar gong in the 2004 *Time Out* Awards, Milk & Honey oozes exclusivity, with the unmarked door and ring-for-entry arrangement of a Prohibition-era speakeasy. The interior is fantastic: a jazz age affair of dim booths, with a low ceiling covered in diner-style aluminium, and a corner bar area lit like a Hopper painting. Staff are the very model of professionalism, and the cocktails they prepare are sublime (and not too expensive at £7-£8.50). Discounting the caviar and oysters, bar snacks barely add up to half a dozen choices, but they're great, particularly the spicy fish cakes. But the best thing of all? Although it's essentially a members bar, anyone can visit: just phone ahead and make a reservation for a two-hour slot. It's a simple caveat, but it keeps the tourists at bay. Non-members will be asked to leave at 11pm, but members can linger smugly until 3am.
Booking essential. Separate room for parties, seating 20 and 60. **Map 17 J6.**

22 Below NEW

22 Great Marlborough Street, W1F 7HU (7437 4106/www.22below.co.uk). Oxford Circus tube. **Open** 5pm-midnight Mon-Fri; 7.30pm-midnight Sat. **Meals/snacks served** 5-10.30pm Mon-Fri; 7.30-10.30pm Sat. **Main courses** £6.95-£12.50. **Snacks** £2-£4.95. **Credit** AmEx, DC, MC, V.
Opened in 2004, this fresh, frisky cocktail basement is hidden beside street-level Café Libre opposite the Carnaby Street estuary. The neat interior combines photo gallery, aka the Dark Room (where Rosa Lykiardopoulos' provoking prints are strung up by clothes pegs), mini-cinema (short-film showcases, Kurosawa), public iPod (with cherry-picked tunes nightly) and comedy stage. Most of all, it offers good cocktails. Previously hired by some of the most prestigious bars of South-east Asia, South Africa and Soho, the bar manager has devised a menu of wit and verve. Named after mates, muses and musical memories, it's a crazy scrapbook (with a pulp fiction cover) of inventive mixology, in which fresh-fruit Martinis take centre stage. To eat, there are Asian bar snacks.
Bar available for hire. Booking advisable. Entertainment: comedy 8pm Mon; DJ 8pm Fri; jazz 1st Thur of mth. **Map 17 J6.**

Strand WC2

American Bar

The Savoy, Strand, WC2R 0EU (7836 4343/
www.fairmont.com/savoy). Covent Garden or
Embankment tube/Charing Cross tube/rail.
Open noon-1am Mon-Sat; noon-10.30pm Sun.
Meals served noon-11pm Mon-Sat; noon-
10.30pm Sun. **Main courses** £9-£14. **Credit**
AmEx, DC, JCB, MC, V.
The American Bar is trapped in time, but what a
time it was. Harry Craddock (of the seminal *Savoy*
Cocktail Book, brought the concept of cool mixed
drinks from Prohibition-era America to London
(today's maestro is Salim Khoury). As the black
and white portraits of celebrity drinkers – Lee
Marvin, Richard Burton – silently testify, the
American Bar was the talk of the town. In
deference, you dress smartly and wait to be seated
before a dish of fat olives and salted nuts arrives.
Today's menu nods to the modern, with cocktails
such as savoy.com (absinthe, Cointreau and lime
juice) and Martinis made with Ketel One, Grey
Goose or Plymouth. You're paying for the linen-
jacket-and-dickie-bow service, the art deco decor
and the memories. Find a table overlooking the
Thames, and you'll regret ever spending money at
any standard mid 1990s designer bar.
Babies and children admitted (until 5pm).
Disabled: toilet. Entertainment: pianist/singer
7pm-midnight Mon-Thur; 7pm-1am Fri, Sat.
No-smoking tables. **Map 18 L7**.

Lobby Bar

One Aldwych, 1 Aldwych, WC2B 4RH (7300
1070/www.onealdwych.com). Covent Garden
or Embankment tube/Charing Cross tube/rail.
Open 9am-midnight Mon-Sat; 9am-10.30pm
Sun. **Snacks served** 5.30pm-midnight Mon-
Sat. **Snacks** £6.95-£13.25. **Service** 12.5%.
Credit AmEx, DC, JCB, MC, V.
Hotel One Aldwych is blessed with a peach of a
bar: brilliantly conceived, with high-back chairs,
bizarre rowing sculpture and vast windows (for
viewing a moving tableau of London buses).
Warmed, spiced nuts arrive as you peruse the
enormous list of cocktails. Martinis (£9.10) come
in Apple Strudel (apple schnapps, crème de cacao),
Hazelnut (Potocki vodka, Frangelico) and Thai
(ginger-infused Wyborowa, fresh coriander,
lemongrass) flavours, to name but three of 22
varieties, not to mention the 22 high-end gins and
vodkas available for the simple vermouth version.
Passing over pear and rosemary Bellinis and
Number Ones of Wyborowa and De Venoge
champagne, you'll also encounter tempting
seasonal cocktails such as a mango and apricot
Martini. To eat, there's sushi on weekdays – fish
and veggie versions – plus continental breakfasts,
sandwiches and cakes. Staff are impeccable.
Babies and children welcome; nappy-changing
facilities (hotel). Disabled: toilet. Separate room
for parties, seats 30. **Map 18 M7**.

Trafalgar Square WC2

Albannach NEW

66 Trafalgar Square, WC2N 5DS (7930 0066/
www.albannach.co.uk). Charing Cross tube/rail.
Bar **Open/food served** noon-1am Mon-Sat;
noon-midnight Sun.
Restaurant **Lunch served** noon-3pm Mon-Sat.
Dinner served 5-10pm Mon-Thur; 5-10.30pm
Fri, Sat. **Main courses** (lunch) £9-£17.50.
Set dinner £27.50 2 courses, £32.50 3 courses.
Service 12.50%.
Both **Credit** AmEx, DC, MC, V.
A fantastic Trafalgar Square location, striking
design, postmodern Scottish theme, Caledonian-
inspired cocktails from Tony Conigliaro: this
newcomer is geared for success. The main ground-
floor bar is spacious; above is a small mezzanine
restaurant (*see p59*), while below is a stylish
cocktail lounge. Cocktails (around £7.50) include a
Rob Roy (Balvenie Double Wood, angostura,
Martini Rosso) and a Liquorice Whisky Sour
(Bailie Nicol Jarvie with fresh lemon and liquorice).
The whisky menu, as you might expect, is
encyclopaedic, with malts from the Lowlands to
Islay and everywhere in between. Snacks include

Guanabara. See p321.

oak-smoked salmon and smoked venison. Nothing
has been left to chance; even the polemically
ancient name – meaning 'he of Alba', as opposed
to Sassenach – is a beauty.
Disabled: toilet. Separate room for parties, seats
20. Tables outdoors (3, pavement). **Map 17 K7**.

West

Maida Vale W9

Graze NEW

2005 RUNNER-UP BEST BAR
215 Sutherland Avenue, W9 1RU (7266 3131/
www.graze.co.uk). Maida Vale tube. **Open** 6pm-
1am Tue-Sun. **Meals served** 6pm-12.30am Tue-
Sun. **Main courses** £6.50-£16. **Service** 12%.
Credit AmEx, DC, MC, V.
From the people responsible for making 1
Lombard Street (*see p92*) such a treasure, Graze
brings a touch of style to Maida Vale. The roomy
bar acts mainly as a holding operation for the
restaurant opposite, but is an increasingly buzzy
space on its own account. The main base on the
shortish cocktails list is Wyborowa vodka, put to
excellent use in a zingy, zesty long drink such as a
Gimp of Wyborowa, fresh pineapple purée, lime
juice, fresh ginger and topped with ginger beer.

Fruit Martinis (apple, pineapple, raspberry) are
another speciality; wines come £5 to the glass, £15
to the bottle.
Babies and children admitted (restaurant).
Bar available for hire. No smoking (restaurant).
Map 1 C3.

Notting Hill W11

Lonsdale

44-48 Lonsdale Road, W11 2DE (7727 4080/
www.thelonsdale.co.uk). Ladbroke Grove or
Notting Hill Gate tube. **Open** 6pm-midnight
Mon-Sat; 6pm-11.30pm Sun. **Dinner served**
6.30-11.30pm Mon-Sat; 6.30-11pm Sun. **Main**
courses £7-£12. **Service** 12.5%. **Credit** AmEx,
MC, V.
There's a plethora of bars in this almost
unbearably trendy neighbourhood, but the sassy
little Lonsdale manages to outshine the lot. The
decor is an explosion of post-space-age chic, a kind
of 1970s vision of how we would be living in the
21st century. Glinting bronze hemispheres
protrude from metallic walls, and an enormous
skylight spirals above the bar, as if preparing to
suck everybody out through the roof. The long
cocktail list (devised by Dick Bradsell and Henry
Besant) is suitably imaginative: a Thyme Daiquiri

was earthy and unusual, while the New York Sour was tart and perfectly mixed. Food is based around starter-size courses and is split into three sections: 'knife and fork', 'fingers' and desserts.
Booking advisable. Disabled: toilet. Entertainment: DJs 9pm Wed-Sat. Separate room for parties, seats 25. **Map 7 A6.**

Trailer Happiness
177 Portobello Road, W11 2DY (7727 2700/ www.trailerhappiness.com). Ladbroke Grove or Notting Hill tube. **Open** 5-10pm 1st Mon of mth; 5-11pm Tue-Fri; 6-11pm Sat; 6-10.30pm Sun. **Snacks served** 6-10.30pm Tue-Sat. **Snacks** £3-£8. **Credit** AmEx, MC, V.
Tongue firmly wedged in its groovy cheek, Trailer H describes itself as a 'retro-sexual haven of cosmopolitan kitsch and faded trailer park glamour – cork tiles and shag pile, love songs and vol-au-vents, Lynch prints and Tiki drinks'. The reality is a small basement bar on Portobello Road, but otherwise, the PR blurb isn't too wide of the mark. The decor is fairly negligible (brown, brown and brown, with some of those 1970s doe-eyed dusky lady portraits). All the attention falls on the spotlit bar, stocked with dozens of Caribbean rums. The cocktail menu has a section of international bar creations, 'house favourites' (£6) – and, best of all, Tiki specials (£6-£20), some of the fruitiest, frothiest and most lurid knockout concoctions going. The Zombie is so evil that it's limited to two per person per night. Food includes a pick 'n' mix section of international snack platters (crispy roast duck, marinated cuttlefish, satay chicken).
Entertainment: DJs 8pm Thur-Sun. **Map 19 B3.**

South
Battersea SW11

Dusk
339 Battersea Park Road, SW11 4LF (7622 2112/www.duskbar.co.uk). Battersea Park rail. **Open** 6pm-12.30am Mon-Wed; 6pm-1.30am Thur-Sat. **Snacks served** 6-10.30pm Mon-Sat. **Snacks** £6-£13.50. **Credit** AmEx, MC, V.
Runner-up for Best Bar in *Time Out's* 2004 Awards, the much-lauded Dusk continues to impress, pulling in the crowds from Battersea and beyond. A luscious red ceiling canopies three distinct areas: the lounge, bordered by hand-stitched leather cube chairs and low tables; the members' section, a diminutive space which, despite being roped off, is more crowded than anywhere else; and the glowing space towards the back, which has a little more room in which to move to the sounds of the DJ. Outside is a patio. Cocktails are the thing, and all are made with premium spirits. The attention to detail can, however, make for long waits on busy nights.
Dress code: smart casual. Entertainment: DJs 9pm Wed-Sat. Tables outdoors (10, terrace). Separate room for parties, seats 90. **Map 15 H13.**

Waterloo SE1

Baltic
74 Blackfriars Road, SE1 8HA (7928 1111/ www.balticrestaurant.co.uk). Southwark tube. *Bar* **Open/snacks served** noon-11pm Mon-Sat; noon-10.30pm Sun. **Snacks** £4-£10. *Restaurant* **Lunch served** noon-3pm Mon-Sat. **Dinner served** 6-11.15pm Mon-Sat. **Meals served** noon-10.30pm Sun. **Main courses** £9.50-£15. **Set meal** (noon-3pm, 6-7pm) £11.50 2 courses, £13.50 3 courses. **Service** 12.5%. *Both* **Credit** AmEx, DC, MC, V.
Baltic occupies the ground floor of a frost-white townhouse. Its lofty, wood-beamed east European restaurant (*see p83*) is its real raison d'être, but early each evening the long, granite-hued bar to the front of the premises goes into cocktail-making overdrive for the Old Vic pre-theatre crowd. It's a classy but relaxed venue, enhanced by a fabulous cocktail menu that changes every few months, always drawing on an impressive arsenal of Russian and Polish spirits. Baltic Martinis (£6.25) include the feisty Polish Passion, a blend of 42

Below passionfruit, champagne and fresh chilli. The fizzy Baltic flutes are sublime: try the Pasja Royale with vodka, strawberries, passionfruit and champagne. Beer includes Lapin Kulta, Okocim, Lech and Le Coq. Bar food is pricey but tempting: herring fish cakes with pickled vegetable salad, blinis with assorted caviars.
Babies and children welcome; high chair. Disabled: toilet. Entertainment: jazz 7pm Sun. Separate room for parties, seats 30. Tables outdoors (6, terrace). **Map 11 N8.**

South East
East Dulwich SE22

Liquorish NEW
123 Lordship Lane, SE22 8HU (8693 7744/ www.liquorish.com). East Dulwich rail/P13, 40, 176 bus. **Open** 11am-midnight Mon-Thur; 11am-1am Fri, Sat; 11am-11.30pm Sun. **Meals/snacks served** noon-5pm, 6-10.30pm daily. **Main courses** £7-£10. **Snacks** £3-£5. **Credit** MC, V.
From the moment Liquorish wriggled into its tunnel-like premises on Lordship Lane, it's been regularly packed to the rafters. The formula is simple: one part sleek cocktail bar, one part simple diner, with some discreetly positioned decks for after-dark vibe control. But the place is more sophisticated than most DJ bars, and nor is it exactly a gastropub (no farmhouse tables or Sunday papers). Take, for example, English Summer, one of the cocktails we selected from a long and impressively diverse list: its combination of gin, Campari, grapefruit juice, coriander and cucumber had the pleasantly dreamy effect of evoking sunlit lawns and the sound of leather on willow, as if the whole PG Wodehouse canon had been distilled in a single drink. The wine list also has an excellent selection by the glass.
Babies and children welcome (lunch): high chairs. Booking advisable Fri, Sat. Entertainment: DJs 9pm Fri, Sat. Tables outdoors (3, terrace). **Map 23 C4.**

Greenwich SE10

Polar Bar NEW
13 Blackheath Road, SE10 8PE (8691 1555). Deptford Bridge DLR. **Open** noon-1am Mon-Thur; noon-2am Fri, Sat; noon-10.30pm Sun. **Snacks served** noon-10pm daily. **Admission** £5 after 9pm Fri, Sat. **Credit** MC, V.
The party-oriented Polar Bar, the newest late-opening DJ bar on the burgeoning scene where Deptford and Greenwich meet, takes cool seriously. The air-conditioning is switched to 'chill', the beer (Grolsch) comes in frozen glasses, and blue is the colour of choice. Cocktails (£5.50 a glass, £12 a jug) are similarly themed, although made of unspecified base spirits: try an Arctic Summer (gin, apricot brandy and bitter lemon) or a Polar Bar Cooler (dark rum, port and orange juice). The food and music are suitably hot, with peri-peri chicken and spicy tapas available daily. There's occasional salsa on Sunday, R&B on Thursday and funky house (with live percussion) on Saturday. Club nights incur a door charge and a mild dress code (no caps or tracksuits), but the salsa is free. Greenwich Magistrates' Court is next door, so don't go overboard on the large shooters.
Babies and children welcome (before 8pm). Entertainment: DJs 9pm Wed-Sat. Tables outdoors (15, garden).

East
Bethnal Green E2

Napoleon Bar NEW
2005 RUNNER-UP BEST LOCAL RESTAURANT
Bistrotheque, 23-27 Wadeson Street, E2 9DR (8983 7900/www.bistrotheque.com). Bethnal Green tube/Cambridge Heath rail/26, 48, 55 bus. *Bar* **Open** 5.30pm-midnight Mon-Sat; 5.30-10.30pm Sun. *Restaurant* **Dinner served** 6.30-10.30pm Mon-Sat. **Meals served** 1-9pm Sun. **Main courses** £8-£25. **Service** 12.5%. *Both* **Credit** AmEx, MC, V.

Down a deserted-looking alley off Mare Street, Bistrotheque combines a cool bar on the ground floor with a great French restaurant (*see p100*) on the first floor. The bar is small, with bare brick walls, twinkling chandeliers and glass wall sconces; an etched-glass mirror hangs on dark wood panelling behind the bar – and it offers a great, laid-back drinking experience for Hackney folk who can't be bothered to schlep down to Hoxton. Service is friendly and efficient, bar staff serving anything from pints of draught Kronenbourg to bottles of wine. But cocktails are the thing: a short list includes the ubiquitous Bramble (Dick Bradsell's masterpiece) as well as old faves Negroni, Mojito and Sidecar. Beside the bar there's a cabaret venue where we noticed a man fiddling with a wax torso.
Babies and children welcome (restaurant): high chairs. Booking advisable (restaurant). Disabled: toilet. Entertainment: cabaret 9pm Wed-Sat. Separate room for parties, seats 50.

Brick Lane E1

Big Chill Bar NEW
2005 RUNNER-UP BEST BAR
Old Truman Brewery, off Brick Lane, E1 6QL (7392 9180/www.bigchill.net). Aldgate East tube/ Liverpool Street tube/rail. **Open** noon-midnight Mon-Sat; noon-11.30pm Sun. **Meals served** noon-11pm Mon-Sat; noon-10.30pm Sun. **Credit** DC, MC, V.
The flagship outlet of the earnest Big Chill multimedia group, 'dedicated to transforming the spirit of our times', is as relaxing as its name suggests. Comprising a terrace and a spacious main bar with a long counter and banquette opposite, the Big Chill gives deck space to all kinds of DJs, some of whom might appear at one of the festivals it organises in the summer. A bison's head and lone chandelier deflect from the functionality of the main room. Drinks include draught Budvar, Weston's press cider and König Ludwig wheat beer, with Voll-Damm, Sagres and Moretti by the bottle. Wines run from a glass of Viña Rey tempranillo to a bottle of Brocard Chablis; a Big Chill punch of Finlandia vodka, fresh lemon juice and peach purée brightens up the £6 standard cocktail list. Global tapas and platters comprise the bulk of the edible offerings, while Sunday meals include the Big Vegan breakfast. It's all very worthy, but not painfully so.
Babies and children admitted. Disabled: toilet. Entertainment: DJs 7pm daily. Tables outdoors (4, patio). **Map 6 S5.**

Shoreditch E1, E2, EC2

Bar Kick
127 Shoreditch High Street, E1 6JE (7739 8700/ www.cafekick.co.uk). Liverpool Street tube/rail then 149, 242 bus/Old Street tube/rail then 55, 243 bus. **Open** noon-11pm Mon-Wed, Sun; noon-midnight Thur-Sat. **Lunch served** noon-3.30pm Mon-Fri. **Dinner served** 5-10pm Mon-Wed; 5-11pm Thur, Fri. **Meals served** noon-11pm Sat; noon-10pm Sun. **Main courses** £4-£12. **Credit** MC, V.
Beneath flags from around the world, there's a truly continental feel to Bar Kick that goes beyond the authentic *fut* (table football) tables. The zinc bar and mismatched tables, chairs and battered sofas give the place a cosy retro vibe. There's a great range of bottled beers (almost as varied as the flags), including Früli, Belgian Duvel, clean-tasting Italian Peroni and malty Portuguese Superbock. Then there's the food, made with top ingredients: serrano ham from Aragón, Campagna mozzarella cheese, Helsett Farm organic Cornish ice-cream. The crowd is mixed too: from suits to Shoreditch locals to those from further afield looking for a bar that does everything right. This is it. Sister venue Café Kick is in Exmouth Market.
Babies and children admitted (lunch). Disabled: toilet. Entertainment: table football tournaments 7pm last Thur of mth. No-smoking tables. Separate room for parties, seats 50. Tables outdoors (4, pavement). **Map 6 R4.**
For branch (Café Kick) see index.

DRINKING

Loungelover

1 Whitby Street, E2 7DP (7012 1234/ www.loungelover.co.uk). Liverpool Street tube/ rail then 8, 388 bus. **Open** 6pm-midnight Mon-Thur; 6pm-1am Fri; 7pm-1am Sat. **Snacks served** 6.30-10.30pm Tue-Fri; 7-11pm Sat. **Snacks** £6.50. **Service** 12.5%. **Credit** AmEx, MC, V.

Bringing glorious camp to a barren Shoreditch backstreet earned Loungelover the Best Design gong at *Time Out*'s 2004 Eating & Drinking awards. It's an eye-popping riot of colour and gaudy styling – stuffed hippo's head, grandfather clock, revolving dummy, 1960s chairs, Victorian gas lamps, Japanese lanterns, coloured Perspex lights, glass-fronted cases displaying the wine, big gold letters spelling out 'lover' over the bar, and some fabulous chandeliers – but success seems to have gone to their heads. Those who don't bag a seat in any of the nooks (bookings are required at weekends) are corralled into a tiny space by the bar and given orders not to wander or distract the bar staff. The cocktails (divided into Current Obsession, Moment of Madness and Old Flame) are great, but at £11 you'd expect as much, and a dash of courtesy to go with them.
Booking advisable. Disabled: toilet. Entertainment: musician/singer 10.30pm Fri, Sat. **Map 6 S4.**

Smersh

5 Ravey Street, EC2A 4QW (7739 0092/ www.smersh.co.uk). Liverpool Street or Old Street tube/rail. **Open** 5pm-midnight Mon-Sat. **Credit** (over £10) AmEx, DC, MC, V.

You have to like a place that names itself after a counter-espionage wing of the KGB, as described in early Bond novels. Add a slap of red paint in the tiny basement space, Cold War newspaper cuttings in the loos, and eastern European booze – Polish beers, excellent vodkas – and we like it even more. Bar staff are friendly, happy to suggest drinks to the uninitiated (they were spot-on with the Soplica vodka), though most of the good folk who crowd in seem happy to raise their spirits on the more common pepper- or honey-flavoured variants. Full marks for the enthusiastic musical mix; regular nights range from Northern soul to a Norwegian female DJ spinning honky-tonk and country swing. A venue for vodka aficionados to add to Baltic (*see p83*) and Na Zdrowie (*see p79*).
Bar available for hire (Sat). Entertainment: DJs 7pm Mon-Sat. **Map 6 Q4.**

Sosho

2 Tabernacle Street, EC2A 4LU (7920 0701/ www.sosho3am.com). Moorgate or Old Street tube/rail. **Open** noon-10pm Mon; noon-midnight Tue; noon-1am Wed, Thur; noon-3am Fri; noon-3am Sat. **Snacks served** noon 10pm Tue-Fri; noon-10.30pm Sat. **Credit** AmEx, DC, JCB, MC, V.

The zeal of the amiable and informative Argentine barman is appropriate, since, as part of the Match chain, Sosho is indeed on a mission: to enhance the reputation of the cocktail. Walk past the 14 eyes of the Pop Art *Magnificent Seven* prints on the wall, and you get to a space of industrial brickwork and leather settees, where the bar benevolently looms. A massive, kitsch, plastic chandelier overhangs a staircase leading to a cosy low-seating alcove, and ultimately to a discreetly lit lounge bar, where a range of DJs has boosted the establishment's reputation. Bottled beers from the Meantime micro-brewery, along with wines and cocktails from the imagination of the celebrated Dale DeGroff, testify to Sosho's insistence on quality, and should ensure that the joint continues to buzz.
Babies and children welcome (daytime). Disabled: toilet. Entertainment: DJs 9pm Wed-Sat. Separate room for parties, seats 120. **Map 6 Q4.**

T Bar

The Tea Building, 56 Shoreditch High Street, E1 6JJ (7729 2973/www.tbarlondon.com). Liverpool Street tube/rail/8, 35, 47, 242, 344, 388 bus. **Open** 9am-11pm Mon-Thur; 9am-2am Fri; 8pm-2am Sat. **Meals served** 9am-9pm Mon-Fri; 8-9pm Sat. **Main courses** £5.50-£8. **Service** 12%. **Credit** MC, V.

Part of the huge Tea Building (home to a design agencies and a gallery, among many other commercial ventures), T Bar is a behemoth of a drinking venue. What it lacks in atmosphere it makes up for in space, space and space. The Brave New World interior is part warehouse, part chi-chi bar with colour-coded areas: black and white retro furniture, black leather sofas, odd 1970s-style jungle murals, luxurious red-curtained areas and velvet couches. There's beer and wine, but the main line is cocktails (around £5.50): along with the classics, the menu includes such concoctions as the Bethnal Green Tea (five spirits) or the East End Sour (scotch, orgeat syrup, lemon juice and egg white). If you're hungry, there are sandwiches and bar snacks, plus breakfast, brunch and lunch on Sunday. Nothing out of the ordinary, really, but it's the only venue in Shoreditch with room to shake a leg on a Friday night.
Booking advisable. Disabled: toilet. Entertainment: 8.30pm Thur-Sat. Separate room for parties, seats 50. **Map 6 R4.**

22 Below. See p322.

Camden Town & Chalk Farm NW1

Bullet NEW

147 Kentish Town Road, NW1 8PB (7485 6040/ www.bulletbar.co.uk). Camden Town or Kentish Town tube. **Open/snacks served** 5.30pm-midnight Mon-Wed, Sun; 5.30pm-1am Thur; 5.30pm-2am Fri, Sat. **Snacks** £3.50-£5.50. **Admission** £3 after 10pm. **Credit** MC, V.

A revamp has transformed a grungy rockin' dive into Bullet, a swanky cocktail hangout – and there aren't many of those between Camden and Kentish Town. Many of the stylistic details are familiar – retro leather sofas, wine-red walls, bare bricks, table football – but, taken together, they create an easy-going, warm and comfortable vibe; there are fine cocktails and tapas bar snacks too. Owner Adam Marshall clearly wants a creative space, not another joint to get wasted in: there's artwork on the walls, salsa sessions on Tuesday and comedy on Wednesday. It bills itself as 'a cocktail bar and live music venue', but it's DJs that drive the party action on Friday and Saturday nights.
Disabled: toilet. Entertainment: open mic 7.30pm Mon; salsa 7pm Tue; comedy 7.30pm Wed; bands 7pm Thur; DJs 7pm Fri, Sat. Tables outdoors (25, garden). **Map 27 D1.**

Islington N1

Anam NEW

2005 RUNNER-UP BEST BAR
3 Chapel Market, N1 9EZ (7278 1001/ www.anambar.com). Angel tube. **Open** 6pm-midnight Mon, Tue; 6pm-2am Wed-Sat. **Snacks served** 6-11pm Mon-Sat. **Snacks** £2.50-£10. **Credit** AmEx, MC, V.

Opening as Chapel Market traders are packing up their boxes, Anam should have little right to stake any great pretensions. And yet this Celtic-themed cocktail bar does lay it on thick. 'Anam (Life, Soul)' is splattered over the retro mural and matchboxes, coupled with Spirit, Essence, Sparkle, Enthusiasm, Vivacity, Zest and so on. Despite all this twaddle, it's an enjoyable – if small – space. The street-level area has modest window seating, and a handful of stools by the dog-leg bar. Ten's company, twelve's a crowd. Downstairs is more spacious, but the space also has to house a back area decked out in Chinese lanterns (invariably booked a fortnight in advance), DJ decks and a dancefloor. The cocktails (£6.50) are spiffing: the list isn't long, but it's crafted and occasionally themed (a Craic Cosmo with Ketel One Citron, for example). Dolmades and chicken yakitori are typical snacks – what, no eggs and soda bread?
Booking essential Wed-Sat after midnight. Disabled: toilet. Dress: no tracksuits. Entertainment: DJs 8pm Wed-Sat. Separate room for parties, seats 35. **Map 5 N2.**

Embassy Bar

119 Essex Road, N1 2SN (7226 7901/ www.embassybar.com). Angel tube/38, 56, 73 bus. **Open** 4pm-midnight Mon-Thur, Sun; 4pm-2am Fri, Sat. **Admission** £3-£4 after 9pm Fri, Sat. **Credit** MC, V.

Although it would never be so gauche as to boast about it, the Embassy might be the coolest bar in Islington. The whole proposition – from the leather swivel high chairs to the softly glowing red wall-lights, the miniature palms, the art deco mirrors, the unapologetic flock wallpaper and the impeccable soundtrack – speaks of an effortlessly low-temperature sensibility that's louche, loungey and loveable all at once. Downstairs, well-chosen DJs do their thing for a tightly packed but ample dancefloor. The draught beer selection isn't up to much (the likes of Carlsberg, Carling and Guinness), and a handful of red and white wines supplement the modest cocktail and shooter menu.
Bar available for hire. Entertainment: DJs 8pm Thur, Sun; 9pm Fri, Sat. **Map 5 P1.**

DRINKING

Pubs

Things could be much worse. London is still blessed with two venerable real ale brewers (Fuller's in Chiswick, Young's in Wandsworth), the odd new microbrewery, and hundreds upon hundreds of pubs. But ideal hostelries are getting harder to find. More often you're faced with chain-owned replicas selling industrially made beer amid ersatz surroundings dreamed up by corporate head office. Yet gems remain. You'll find several of the city's best drinking establishments below; for more, grab a copy of the latest edition of *Time Out Bars, Pubs & Clubs*.

For pubs that specialise in food, see **Gastropubs**, starting on p105.

Central

Aldwych WC2

Seven Stars
53 Carey Street, WC2A 2JB (7242 8521).
Chancery Lane, Holborn or Temple tube.
Open 11am-11pm Mon-Fri; noon-11pm Sat, Sun.
Lunch served noon-3pm, **dinner served**
5-9pm Mon-Fri. **Meals served** 1-10pm Sat, Sun.
Credit AmEx, MC, V.
Gastropub queen Roxy Beaujolais – a boho Aussie Sohoite and passionate authoress on innkeeping food – is the force behind this outstanding little place. Well-sourced meat and fish are the mainstay of the blackboard menu, which might range from charcuterie to char-grilled ribeye steak, via warm goat's cheese salad or red snapper. Lawyers from the nearby Royal Courts of Justice snap up these exquisite lunches, accompanying them with decent (and decently priced) wines, Aspall's Suffolk Cyder and Bitburger lager, or perhaps Adnams, Harveys Sussex Best or London Pride bitter. The Seven Stars was built as a pub in 1602, hence the wooden front and wonky beamed interior. The green-and-white checked tableclothed dining areas at either end of the narrow bar give it a rustic, French appeal. The eccentric furnishings, though, are Anglo: feathers and skull in the window, and Boulting Brothers movie posters with a legal slant. **Map 10 M6**.

Bloomsbury WC1

Lamb ✓
94 Lamb's Conduit Street, WC1N 3LZ (7405 0713/www.youngs.co.uk). Holborn or Russell Square tube. **Open** 11am-11pm Mon-Sat; noon-4pm, 7-10.30pm Sun. **Lunch served** noon-2.30pm daily. **Dinner served** 6-9pm Mon-Thur, Sat. **Credit** AmEx, MC, V.
Local office workers sup happily alongside students and academics from the nearby halls of London University at this handsome old pub. The Lamb, a Grade II listed structure, was built around 1730 over William Lamb's river dam (conduit). Thanks to a sympathetic restoration in the 1960s, the ornate Victorian interior has been left largely intact. The mahogany island bar is edged with rotating etched-glass snob screens, complemented by matching mirrors and windows and racing-green upholstery. Walls are heavy with pictures of Victorian thespians, and the round-topped tables have funny little brass balustrades. The partitioned non-smoking section (more of a cubicle) is a nice idea but completely ineffective. The complete range of Young's beers is on tap, including seasonal ales. Food is of the routine pub grub variety: fish and chips, steak and ale pie, vegetable curry with rice. *No-smoking tables. Separate room for parties, seats 25. Tables outdoors (3, patio; 3, pavement).* **Map 4 M4**.

Clerkenwell & Farringdon EC1, WC1

Jerusalem Tavern ✓
55 Britton Street, EC1M 5UQ (7490 4281/ www.stpetersbrewery.co.uk). Farringdon tube/ rail. **Open** 11am-11pm Mon-Fri. **Lunch served** noon-3pm Mon-Fri. **Credit** MC, V.
Occupying an 18th-century building, but only a pub since 1996, the Jerusalem is the solitary London representative of Suffolk's St Peter's Brewery. The list of beers on tap changes weekly but always includes Golden Ale and Organic Best; others might be Honey Ale, Strong Ale or even Grapefruit Ale. Still more beers are dispensed in marsh-green bottles: combinations such as lemon and ginger, cinnamon and apple or, in the case of King Cnut Ale, supposedly a typical beer of the first millennium, barley, nettles and juniper. Lunch from the daily changing menu might include duck breast and butternut squash, or salmon and asparagus. The pub itself is a marvellously mad affair composed entirely of niches, nooks and crannies, with a tiny front room leading to a squeezed corridor between bar counter and tiny raised gallery, and, beyond that, a minuscule backroom adorned with stuffed fox and fowl. Floors are warped, flat surfaces scarce. A modern reconstruction, yes, but an eccentric little hostelry and a thing to be cherished. *Babies and children admitted. Bar available for hire (Sat, Sun only). Tables outdoors (2, pavement).* **Map 5 O4**.

Pakenham Arms
1 Pakenham Street, WC1X 0LA (7837 6933). Russell Square tube/King's Cross tube/rail. **Open** 9am-1am Mon-Sat; 9am-10.30pm Sun. **Breakfast served** 9.30-11.30am, **lunch served** noon-2pm, **dinner served** 6-9pm Mon-Fri. **Meals served** 10am-6pm Sat, Sun. **Credit** MC, V.
Under new management since autumn 2004, this large, single-bar, old-school local has widened its appeal beyond the posties from the Mount Pleasant sorting office across the road. In the evening, the daytime stragglers are joined by darts players, sports fans (served by two TVs and several big pull-down screens) and real ale freaks. The Pakenham takes its beer very seriously indeed. A regular fixture in the North London Camra newsletter, it offers six or seven different ales on draught including four regulars: London Pride, Timothy Taylor Landlord, Adnams Broadside and Greene King IPA. You might also encounter Fuller's ESB and Harveys Sussex Best. In winter, the pub opens for weekend breakfasts – the usual infarction-inducers – then it's simple lunches (irish stew, cumberland sausage and champ, haddock and chips, with filled baguettes or chicken caesar salad in summer). Similar nosh is served in the evenings, when the pub remains open until 1am. *Tables outdoors (6, pavement).* **Map 5 M4**.

Covent Garden WC2

Lamb & Flag
33 Rose Street, WC2E 9EB (7497 9504). Covent Garden tube. **Open** 11am-11pm Mon-Sat; noon-10.30pm Sun. **Lunch served** noon-3pm Mon-Fri, Sun; noon-4.30pm Sat. **Credit** MC, V.
Arrive after 5pm and you'll find little but standing room in either of the two downstairs bars of this famous and ancient inn. Historians disagree about the Lamb & Flag. Conflicting accounts mounted beneath the original wooden frames and low ceilings recall the 'Bucket of Blood' and bare-knuckle fighting days – but John Stow's *Survey of London* (1603) doesn't mention it at all. Still, millions of customers have imbibed here, a few earning a name plaque. Today's are treated to Young's and Courage Best and a changing line-up that might include Courage Directors, Ridleys IPA and Adnams Bitter. Löwenbräu and Hoegaarden are also on tap. There are ploughman's lunches and doorstep sandwiches downstairs, full pub grub (pies, roasts and chicken curry) on red checked tablecloths in the Dryden room upstairs. It's said that the poet John Dryden was beaten up outside, on still-eerie Rose Street, in 1679. *Babies and children admitted (lunch only). Entertainment: jazz 7.30-10.15pm Sun. No piped music or jukebox.* **Map 18 L7**.

Holborn EC1, WC1

Princess Louise
208 High Holborn, WC1V 7EP (7405 8816). Holborn tube. **Open** 11am-11pm Mon-Fri; noon-11pm Sat; noon-10.30pm Sun. **Lunch served** noon-2.30pm, **dinner served** 6-8.30pm Mon-Fri. **Meals served** noon-10pm Sat, Sun. **Credit** AmEx, MC, V.
It was built in 1872 and named after Queen Victoria's fourth daughter, yet the Princess Louise owes its fame to the spectacular refurbishment carried out in 1891 by WH Lascalles & Co. The centrepiece is a magnificent horseshoe wooden bar, long enough to race dogs on, and complete with its original clock, mirrors and spidery globe lamps. You're also treated to an elaborately moulded ceiling, tall engraved mirrors and intricately carved woodwork. Even the loos are awe-inspiring. All the place lacks are the partitions that separated the various drinking areas until Watney's saw fit to rip them out in the 1960s. Now, the Princess is under the benevolent control of Samuel Smith (so although you get the brewery's own-brand bitter and lager, at least the prices are low). Standard bar food is served, but there's usually little space to eat it; come 5pm (and often before), the place is packed with the after-work mob; staff have little time for chit-chat. *No piped music or jukebox.* **Map 18 L5**.

Ye Old Mitre
1 Ely Court, Ely Place, at the side of 8 Hatton Gardens, EC1N 6SJ (7405 4751). Chancery Lane tube/Farringdon tube/rail. **Open** 11am-11pm Mon-Fri. **Meals served** 11am-9.30pm Mon-Fri. **Credit** AmEx, MC, V.
Clearly folk were shorter in 1546, when this pub was founded. So mind your head (the low ceilings are deadly after a couple of pints) and settle yourself in one of the tiny rooms. The basic finger food ranges from cheese toasties to sausages on sticks, but further nourishment is supplied by a selection of real ales that includes Adnams Best, Adnams Broadside, Tetley's and a monthly changing beer from a guest brewery. The Mitre's name derives from its use as quarters for the retainers of the Bishops of Ely, on whose land it stands and whose church is still next door. The building was reconstructed in the 18th century using the original plans and materials. The decor is an eccentric hotchpotch of wood panelling, exposed stonework, low doorways and comfy chairs. Oliver Cromwell once owned the property, which he is said to have converted into a hospital and then a prison during the Civil War. Customers are a mix of legal types and tourists. *Separate room for parties, seats 30. Tables outdoors (10 barrels, pavement).* **Map 11 N5**.

Princess Louise

DRINKING

West
Hammersmith W6

Dove
19 Upper Mall, W6 9TA (8748 5405).
Hammersmith or Ravenscourt Park tube.
Open 11am-11pm Mon-Sat; noon-10.30pm Sun.
Lunch served noon-2.30pm Mon-Sat; noon-4pm
Sun. **Dinner served** 5-9pm Mon-Sat. **Credit**
AmEx, MC, V.
If you're lucky enough to bag a seat at this peerless example of an old Thameside boozer, treat yourself to a pint of Fuller's (there's ESB, London Pride and Discovery on draught, all brewed up the road in Chiswick) and celebrate. The Dove ticks all the boxes: dangerously low-beamed ceiling, dark panelled walls, rickety furniture, terrace overlooking the river (an excellent spot to view the University Boat Race) and history oozing from every pore. It even has a record-breaking tiny bar room, measuring a mere four feet by seven – though there is another, much larger room as well. AP Herbert put the Dove into his 1930s novel *The Water Gypsies*, as the Pigeon; William Morris lived and died within a stone's throw at 26 Upper Mall. Today, the food menu stretches from sandwiches to the likes of peppered mackerel niçoise, steak and ale pie, or penne arrabbiata. Impress foreign friends by taking them to this beautiful slice of old London – preferably before the evening crowds swamp the place.
No piped music or jukebox. Tables outdoors
(15, riverside terrace). **Map 20 A4.**

Ladbroke Grove W11

Elgin
96 Ladbroke Grove, W11 1PY (7229 5663).
Ladbroke Grove tube. **Open** 11am-11pm Mon-
Sat; noon-10.30pm Sun. **Meals served** noon-
9pm daily. **Credit** AmEx, MC, V.
When the Elgin was built in 1853 – by Dr Samuel Walker, a property-speculating clergyman – it was the only structure in Ladbroke Grove aside from a convent. Today this is undoubtedly W11's best-looking pub. For the treasure trove of spectacular stained-glass screens, wall tiles and delicious carved mahogany, we owe thanks to William Dickinson, who acquired the pub in 1892 and decorated it in opulent style. In the 1970s the Elgin became famous as a centre for the *Time Out*-wielding 'alternative' society. The 101ers (precursors to the Clash) performed here every Thursday; Alexei Sayle and Keith Allen launched their careers in the back room. More recent additions to admire at this three-bar, high-ceilinged boozer include three rotating real ales (Greene King IPA is a regular), draught Hoegaarden and a decent supply of Belgian bottled beers. There's also good-value pub food (pies and sausages of the day, fish and chips, £4-£8), outdoor bench seating for warmer weather, two pool tables, big-screen sports and an on-site ATM: a pub for all seasons, no less.
Babies and children admitted (before 6pm).
Separate room for parties, seats 25. Tables
outdoors (12, pavement). **Map 19 B2.**

South West
Colliers Wood SW19

Sultan
78 Norman Road, SW19 1BT (8542 4532).
Colliers Wood tube. **Open** noon-11pm Mon-Sat;
noon-10.30pm Sun. **Credit** MC, V.
Its backstreet location is unassuming, but the Sultan is truly a prince among pubs and has been crowned with laurels (including winning the Best Pub category in *Time Out*'s 2004 Eating & Drinking awards). This is the only London pub of Salisbury's Hop Back brewery, so springing from its taps are Summer Lightning, Entire Stout and the wonderful GFB. You can even take a polypin or minipin of draught beer home with you. Ale lovers will also appreciate the beer club every Wednesday evening (6-9pm), when real ale is just £1.70 a pint; they'll also be reassured by the many Camra award certificates around one of the pub's several open fires. New pine tables and bar stools furnish the interior, with unobtrusive piped radio providing the backing track. Outside, there's an appealing beer garden, which comes complete with barbecue for the summer months – otherwise, no food is served. Despite its name, the Sultan has no eastern connections, being named after a great racehorse of the 1830s.
Disabled: toilet. Tables outdoors (13, patio).

Parsons Green SW6

White Horse
1-3 Parsons Green, SW6 4UL (7736 2115/
www.whitehorsesw6.com). Parsons Green tube.
Open 11am-11pm Mon-Sat; 11am-10.30pm Sun.
Meals served noon-10pm Mon-Fri; 11am-10pm
Sat, Sun. **Credit** AmEx, MC, V.
Yes, it's also known as the Sloaney Pony (posh locals have long favoured the pub), but don't let that put you off. At the apex of the Green, this is a lovely old Victorian hostelry. Down one side of the horseshoe bar, polished flagstones extend past a huge fireplace into a small, formal dining room looking on to a tiny courtyard. Pink walls on one side add a merry note, and elsewhere tightly bound chesterfields sit beside long wooden tables. Beer is treated with great respect, with draught ales such as Harveys, Adnams Broadside and Oakham Ales' JHB being joined by continental stars like Chimay and De Koninck. There's also a list of 75 bottled beers and 120 wines. Gastropub food on the ground floor might include roast pumpkin salad with pine nuts, goat's cheese, red onion and rosemary, or pan-fried mullet on saffron rice, while in the classy new upstairs restaurant drunken

DRINKING

risotto (with organic pork sausage, Amarone wine and beetroot) could be followed by a whole sea bass in a salt and herb crust.
Babies and children admitted. Disabled: toilet. No piped music or jukebox. No-smoking area (restaurant). Separate room for parties, seats 55. Tables outdoors (30, garden).

South

Waterloo SE1

White Hart

29 Cornwall Road, SE1 8TJ (7401 7151). Waterloo tube/rail. **Open** noon-11pm Mon-Sat; noon-10.30pm Sun. **Meals served** noon-10pm Mon-Sat; noon-9.30pm Sun. **Credit** AmEx, MC, V.
A remarkable conversion has transformed what was once a decrepit backstreet boozer into this smart little Fulhamesque venue. Thanks to pub company Mitchell & Butler, the current owner, you'll find wispy parlour palms and brasserie-style seating on the pavement, and bottled Chimay, Duvel and Frambozenbier (wrapped in its own logoed paper) on the back bar shelves. With sofas, kitchen chairs and benches, beaded curtains and candles, the feel is part lounge bar, part gastropub (the food menu offers light bites, standard sandwiches, salads and mains such as smoked haddock fish cakes, gnocchi with wilted spinach and Aberdeen Angus burger, all at around £6-£8). Draught beers include regularly changing real ales (the likes of Bateman's Miss Saucy and Hop Back's Summer Lightning) and boutique lagers Leffe, Hoegaarden, Früli and Küppers Kölsch. Staff are young, smiley and female; customers are equally youthful, which gives the place a buzzy, charged vibe. Really not bad at all.
Disabled: toilet. Tables outdoors (4, pavement). **Map 11 N8.**

South East

Deptford SE8

Dog & Bell

116 Prince Street, SE8 3JD (8692 5664). New Cross tube/rail/Deptford rail. **Open** noon-11pm Mon-Sat; noon-10.30pm Sun. **Lunch served** noon-2.30pm Mon-Fri; 2-4pm Sun. **Dinner served** 6-9pm Mon-Fri. **No credit cards.**
A classic pub, and easily the best Deptford has to offer, the Dog & Bell is situated down a dark sidestreet beyond the creek end of the High Street. It was the Camra London Pub of the Year in 2004, no doubt due to its superb ales sold at fair prices (£1.80-£2.50 a pint). As well as Fuller's London Pride and ESB, there are three regularly changing guests, perhaps including Dark Star's Sunburst, or Barnstormer from Bath. You'll also find immoderate quantities of communal warmth and local character here, all within a cheery, intimate two-lounge space. The best lager to be had is bottled and Belgian, starting with Kriek, and there's decent pub grub available in two daily servings: from sandwiches or cod and chips to stuffed vine leaves and Sunday roasts. Local bohos tend to congregate here, happy amid the offbeat furnishings of arty photos and chefs' heads on plates. Further entertainment comes by dint of the bar billiards table.
Tables outdoors (6, garden).

Greenwich SE10

Greenwich Union

56 Royal Hill, SE10 8RT (8692 6258/ www.greenwichunion.co.uk). Greenwich rail/ DLR. **Open** 11am-11pm Mon-Fri; 10am-11pm Sat; 10am-10.30pm Sun. **Meals served** noon-9.30pm Mon-Fri; 10am-9pm Sat, Sun. **Credit** MC, V.
The flagship outlet of Alastair Hook's Meantime Brewing Company deserves its many garlands. Hook's beer apprenticeship began in Munich, where techniques are age-old and authenticity is sacrosanct. Thus the house Blonde is cask-

preserved in the traditional way and, as with the other draught lagers – Union, Golden, Pilsner, Raspberry, Chocolate Stout, White and a rather excellent Kölsch – it can be tasted in miniature in a handy try-before-you-buy exercise. Staff are friendly and knowledgeable, swiftly manning a bar that divides the beerhall-like front area from the loungey back, all done out in orange and brown, with a solid flagstone floor. A back patio opens in summer. Food is notable too, with daily specials augmenting such classy main courses as pork stuffed with pistachio, spinach and dry speck with a parmesan crisp; and spring vegetable risotto. Musicians play every Monday.
Babies and children admitted (before 9pm). Tables outdoors (12, garden).

London Bridge & Borough SE1

Royal Oak

44 Tabard Street, SE1 4JU (7357 7173). Borough tube. **Open** 11.30am-11pm Mon-Fri; 6-11pm Sat; noon-6pm Sun. **Lunch served** noon-3pm Mon-Fri; noon-5pm Sun. **Dinner served** 5-9.30pm Mon-Fri; 6-9.30pm Sat. **Credit** AmEx, DC, MC, V.
Very much a locals' pub, the handsome and wonderfully maintained Royal Oak also draws in an assorted crowd of demanding beer lovers. It is the only pub in the capital tied to excellent Lewes brewer Harveys. The ales are in tip-top condition, the line-up comprising Sussex Best, Long Man Pale Ale, Armada, a seasonal and, wonder of wonders, Mild (rare, indeed, to find in London). Food includes the likes of stuffed aubergine, steak and kidney pudding, grilled halibut steak, braised lamb shank, and roast Sunday lunches, and is of a high standard and fairly priced. There's no music, and service is sharp and witty whenever co-landlord Frank is around the bar. Sadly, the sign that read 'Lager drinkers will be served only if accompanied by a responsible adult' is gone.
Disabled: toilet. No piped music or jukebox. Separate room for parties, seats 20. **Map 11 P9.**

East

Limehouse E14

Grapes

76 Narrow Street, E14 8BP (7987 4396). Westferry DLR. **Open** noon-3pm, 5.30-11pm Mon-Fri; noon-11pm Sat; noon-10.30pm Sun. **Lunch served** noon-2pm Mon-Sat; noon-3.30pm Sun. **Dinner served** 7-9pm Mon-Sat. **Credit** AmEx, MC, V.
Its history is longer than a yard of ale, and the Grapes has all the off-kilter floorboards, creaking staircases and cramped little rooms to prove it. Charles Dickens supposedly had this place in mind when he wrote *Our Mutual Friend*, imagining it as the Six Jolly Fellowship Porters. There has been a pub here since 1583, though the current building dates back to 1720. The back bar features an open fire and steps leading to a deck over the Thames. Fish is the speciality, both in the bar (where battered haddock or cod comes with hand-cut chips, and salmon fish cakes with caper sauce) and in the venerable, pricier upstairs restaurant (where you can sample potted shrimps or scallops in bacon while pondering the river view). In Dickens' day, the Grapes was a hard-bitten working-class boozer; today, most punters are well-off denizens of this riverside neighbourhood. Beers run from the standards (Carlsberg, Stella) to a clutch of decent real ales (Adnams Bitter, Timothy Taylor Landlord, Marston's Pedigree). If this was your local, you'd never leave Limehouse.
No piped music or jukebox. No smoking.

Shoreditch E2

George & Dragon

2 Hackney Road, E2 7NS (7012 1100). Old Street tube/rail/26, 48, 55 bus. **Open** 4-11pm Mon-Thur; noon-11pm Fri, Sat; noon-10.30pm Sun. **Credit** MC, V.

Just near the junction of Old Street and Kingsland Road, the George & Dragon is a fine little corner bar wrought from a classic boozer. Its old, dark-wood tables, nicotine-stained wallpaper and splashes of brick-red paintwork have been taken straight from the pub-design box. To this has been added skeins of red heart-shaped lights, vintage cowboy and cowgirl signs, and a few oil paintings of chaps in hunting gear enjoying bucolic pleasures. The look has been topped off with a fabulous modern light, a gorgeous centrepiece of glowing glass circles. A chatty, friendly gay crowd (both sexes) comes to show its appreciation and enjoy DJ nights, with plenty of louche classics throbbing through the air. The choice of beer is mundane in comparison (John Smith's is the only bitter), with San Miguel lager and Scrumpy Jack cider the best of a routine bunch. Note that food is no longer served.
Disabled: toilet. Entertainment: DJs 8pm daily. **Map 6 R3.**

North

Harringay N4

Salisbury Hotel

1 Grand Parade, Green Lanes, N4 1JX (8800 9617). Manor House tube then 29 bus. **Open** 2pm-1am Mon-Wed; noon-2am Thur-Sat; noon-midnight Sun. **Dinner served** 5-11pm Tue, Wed. **Meals served** noon-11pm Thur-Sat; noon-6pm Sun. **Credit** MC, V.
A remarkable visual treat, the Grade II listed Salisbury features an imposing, bulging Victorian exterior together with a main entrance replete with decorative ironwork and intricate mosaics. The interior is better still. There are long marble bars, pillars, alcoves and carved woodwork. The scale and attention to detail are exquisite, the fixtures and fittings varying from one area to the next like the different rooms of a stately home. Thankfully, the beer's great too: draught Fuller's Chiswick, London Pride, ESB and Discovery, plus Litovel, Zubr, Leffe Blonde and Hoegaarden lagers also on tap. The menu changes regularly, but there's a fair choice of snacks as well as such main courses as osso bucco, vegetable pasta and grilled swordfish, along with well-reputed Sunday roasts. Monday is quiz night, while jazz bands play most Sunday evenings – all this in the middle of Green Lanes. Rather special.
Babies and children admitted (restaurant). Disabled: toilet. Entertainment: jazz 8.30pm Sun. No-smoking area. Separate room for parties, seats 75.

Holloway N7

Swimmer at The Grafton Arms

13 Eburne Road, N7 6AR (7281 4632). Holloway Road tube/Finsbury Park tube/rail. **Open** noon-2.30pm, 5-11pm Mon-Thur; noon-11pm Fri, Sat; noon-10.30pm Sun. **Lunch served** noon-2pm Mon; noon-4pm Sun. **Dinner served** 6-9.30pm Mon-Fri. **Meals served** noon-9.30pm Sat. **Credit** MC, V.
Making headway against the tide of lacklustre boozers in the vicinity, the Swimmer is an enjoyable little place (with a rather long name) hidden down a backstreet. The array of beers on tap is especially appealing, whether you're fond of real ale (the choice includes Adnams as well as ESB, London Pride and a seasonal ale from Fuller's) or lager (Leffe, Erdinger and Zubr are all on draught). The modern decor is fetching and well judged. Wooden benches and endearingly shabby sofas flank the cream-coloured walls, while an open recess gives a goldfish-bowl view of the adjoining kitchen, from which a spot-on range of upper-class bar food is dispensed to appreciative punters. Starters such as char-grilled prawns or penne arrabbiata might be followed by the likes of sun-dried tomato and asparagus risotto, or chicken and mushroom pie. Somewhere to savour.
Babies and children welcome (garden). No-smoking tables. Tables outdoors (15, garden).

Wine Bars

We may be drinking ever more wine, but the standard of wine bars in London remains static. Many conform to the stereotype of dark, dingy basements full of men in suits drinking claret amid scatterings of sawdust – and their owners seem happy for them to stay that way. Chains such as **Balls Brothers** and **Davy's** are better examples of this type. Wine merchant Brinkley's – owner of **Putney Station** and the **Oratory** – has been following the lead of City chain **Corney & Barrow** in providing more modern places to drink. To be fair to these outfits, local authorities don't help. When staff at the **Jamies** chain attempted to serve a line-up of six small glasses of wine, giving people a taste of lots of different wines – known as 'flights' – the powers that be raised objections. But with many pub chains too reliant on wine brands, and bar personnel in gastropubs devoid of any real wine knowledge, such creativity is much needed.

At present, only **Wine Wharf** at London Bridge and two bars in the Farringdon area – **Bleeding Heart Bistro & Tavern** and **Cellar Gascon** – offer genuinely interesting lists, coupled with enthusiastic, well-trained staff. The owners of Cellar Gascon haven't tried to compile an all-encompassing list, but have focused on the south-west of France – showing that it's worth trying something different.

London's best wine bars are listed below, but **Kettners** (see p310) in Soho, which has a great champagne bar, shouldn't be forgotten. For further options, consult the latest edition of the *Time Out Bars, Pubs & Clubs* guide. For where to buy wine, see **Drink Shops**, starting on p357.

Central
Bloomsbury WC1, WC2

Grape Street Wine Bar
222-224A Shaftesbury Avenue, WC2H 8EB (7240 0686). Holborn or Tottenham Court Road tube.
Bar **Open** noon-11pm Mon-Fri.
Restaurant **Lunch served** noon-3.30pm, **dinner served** 5-10pm Mon-Fri. **Main courses** £6.95-£12.95.
Both **House wine** £10.95 bottle, £2.75 glass. **Credit** AmEx, MC, V.
Despite being largely rebuilt in 1997, this warm, friendly bar is something of a 1980s throwback with its salmon-pink walls, wood-look shelving and collection of corks in framed boxes. The effect is cosy and atmospheric, if not altogether stylish. A calm, after-office crowd collects in groups at the well-spaced tables: couples in their late thirties and older men reading the paper over a few glasses of claret. The wine list is very good indeed, strong in aromatic styles such as the excellent 2003 Mantineia from Domaine Tselepos in Greece (£18.95) and with an acceptable total of 13 wines by the glass. Prices are keen, although who would order 2003 Sauvignon de Touraine (£11.95) – described on the list as 'the poor man's Sancerre'? Food is eclectic, encompassing tandoori chicken, grilled ribeye with cabernet sauvignon butter, and roast mediterranean vegetables with chickpea couscous topped with grilled goat's cheese. Look for the bar wedged into the corner where Shaftesbury Avenue meets Grape Street.
Babies and children admitted. Separate room for parties, seats 20. Tables outdoors (2, pavement). **Map 18 L6.**

Truckles of Pied Bull Yard
Off Bury Place, WC1A 2JR (7404 5338/ www.davy.co.uk). Holborn or Tottenham Court Road tube.
Café/bar **Open** 11am-10pm Mon-Fri. **Snacks served** noon-9pm Mon-Fri.
Restaurant **Lunch served** noon-3pm, **dinner served** 5-9pm Mon-Fri. **Main courses** £7.95-£13.95. **Set dinner** £10.95 2 courses, £13.95 3 courses.
Both **House wine** £13.65 bottle, £3.65 glass. **Credit** AmEx, DC, MC, V.
A refit may have given a Harvester-style tinge to Truckles' ground-floor bar – yellow walls, pine floors, a couple of leather sofas – but it seems to have widened the appeal. You'll now find literary types from the neighbouring London Review Bookshop as well as old regulars in pinstriped shirts and patterned ties. In summer the sunny, characterful courtyard is the prime spot. The bar is one of 40-plus owned by Davy's the wine merchants. The wine list includes a healthy 29 by the glass, but is a little patchy, full of Davy's own-label tipples. Try the 2003 Domaine des Billards Saint-Amour instead or Delaforce's 1985 port. There are just three beers, by the bottle, but they're all good – Beck's, Budvar and Bishop's Finger – and five Cuban cigars, including an excellent Cohiba at £8.95. Bar snacks include sandwiches and salads, while the basement restaurant (aka Ale & Port House) serves the likes of char-grilled sirloin steak, bangers and mash, or wild mushroom risotto – it's à la carte at lunchtime, with a set price menu in the evening.
Babies and children admitted. Bar/restaurant available for hire. Booking advisable. Tables outdoors (20, courtyard). **Map 10 L5.**
For branches (Davy's) see index.

Vats Wine Bar
51 Lamb's Conduit Street, WC1N 3NB (7242 8963). Holborn or Russell Square tube.
Bar **Open** noon-11pm Mon-Fri.
Bar & Restaurant **Lunch served** noon-2.30pm, **dinner served** 6-9.30pm Mon-Fri. **Main courses** £9.95-£15.95. **House wine** £13.95 bottle, £3.75. **Service** 12.5%. **Credit** AmEx, DC, MC, V.
Local solicitors and media types (including the odd boisterous *Spectator* party) have long frequented this well-established watering hole. They help make up a crowd of mainly forties-plus men and women who are fond of a drink or ten. Panelled walls, wooden benches and large sash windows lend a Dickensian feel to the place. The Rhône and Bordeaux are highlighted on a wine list that includes a dozen options by the glass and around 20 half bottles. Avoid the obvious temptations of 1997 Château Bastor-Lamontagne from Sauternes (£22.50) and try something new – Bual Madeira, perhaps, or Moscatel Superior from Lustau. Domaine de Grangeneuve's 2000 Vieilles Vignes from the Rhône is the best tipple outside of the sweet wines. There's no beer. The monthly changing food menu shows the owners' Sussex origins, with Ashdown Forest venison and lamb making appearances; porcini and spinach lasagne might be a vegetarian alternative. At lunchtime, drinkers are confined to the bar or two small benches by the fire.
Babies and children admitted. Booking advisable restaurant. Separate room for parties, seats 40. Tables outdoors (4, pavement). **Map 4 M5.**

City EC2, EC4

Corney & Barrow
111 Old Broad Street, EC2N 1AP (7638 9308/ www.corney-barrow.co.uk). Liverpool Street tube/ rail. **Open** 7.30am-11pm Mon-Fri. **Breakfast served** 7.30am-noon, **meals served** noon-10pm Mon-Fri. **Main courses** £6.25-£13.95. **House wine** £12.95 bottle, £3.75 glass. **Credit** AmEx, DC, MC, V.
You'd think that after work the last place corporate lawyers and investment bankers would want to head to is somewhere that looks like an office. The large plate-glass windows and hard stone floors of Corney & Barrow's outlets must seem horribly familiar, although they have a sports bar feel too. Bloomberg blinks away on multiple TV screens, men in suits perch on suede banquettes and groups in shirt sleeves take a finger buffet in the corner. C&B are keen for you to know how modern and different their wine bars are compared to the older type of City bar – even the walls have been painted to look like concrete. Staff are different from the surly norm too, offering good advice on a wine list that improves with price – though the Côtes du Ventoux from Perrin is a good buy at £16.95. Cape Mentelle's semillon/sauvignon blanc blend from Western Australia is one of many good wines over £20. A modern-style listing by grape rather than region hides the large amounts of mediocre French vin de pays, but a total of 77 wines by the glass is to be applauded. The array of snacks is almost as vast, including mixed platters, burgers and steaks.
Booking advisable. Disabled: ramp; toilet. Restaurant and bar available for hire.
Map 12 Q6.
For branches see index.

El Vino
47 Fleet Street, EC4Y 1BJ (7353 6786/ www.elvino.co.uk). Chancery Lane or Temple tube/Blackfriars tube/rail.
Bar **Open** 8.30am-9pm Mon; 8.30am-10pm Tue-Fri.
Restaurant **Lunch served** noon-3pm Mon-Fri. **Main courses** £8.50-£12. **Service** 12.5%.
Both **House wine** £14.75 bottle, £3.50 glass. **Credit** AmEx, MC, V.
Today, El Vino has no dress code and is keen to welcome women. It has been nearly quarter of a century since females were barred from being served at the bar, but the image has been hard to shift. Otherwise, tradition is to the fore. The firm

started trading in 1879 and is now run by the fourth generation of the same family; these premises opened in 1923. Lawyers account for much of the clientele, populating the slightly dingy, wooden interior, which is bathed in rather harsh lighting. The wine list is long (running to 200-plus labels) and largely European, with claret to the fore. Come here too for a glass of sherry, port or Madeira. The New World isn't overlooked, though; try the Marlborough sauvignon blanc from New Zealand's Greenstone Point. The food menu is unswervingly traditional, including pâté starters, egg and mayo sandwiches, and mains such as fish and chips or beef bourguignon. The bar empties out later in the evening – as is the City norm.

Booking advisable. Dress: smart casual; no trainers. Separate room for parties, seats 40. Tables outdoors (4, pavement). **Map 11 O6. For branches see index.**

Chain gang

There are four main wine bar chains in London, together responsible for almost 100 outlets. Each chain offers its own approach to the pleasures of the grape – but which to choose? Read on.

Balls Brothers

Smaller than Davy's, but just as traditional, this chain is shaping up well in the City and West End. The Balls family founded a wine merchant in the mid 19th century, opened its first bar in 1960, and has stuck with yellow wall lamps, dark wood panelled walls and small etchings ever since. But new venues in Victoria and Cheapside with high ceilings, big windows and plain painted walls signal a move to keep up with the times.

What's the wine list like? An impressive array of older vintages from Bordeaux and Burgundy – too often wines are listed too young. The 1996 Château Haut-Bailly, Pessac-Léognan (£38.50) has fine cherry and red fruit notes. However, the choice from Italy and Spain is poor and the south of France even more so.

Number of branches 18.

Best for The decent food in next-door restaurants at seven of their City bars; dishes such as sea bass with tomatoes, basil and chorizo or best end of lamb with herb crust, pancetta and beans.

Anything else? Try Strangford Lough oysters at the Balls Brothers-owned Mulligans of Mayfair bar.

Corney & Barrow

Proof that not every wine bar has to look like ye olde dusty tavern. In 1983 Corney & Barrow decided to follow the route of other wine merchants in opening wine bars – but they did so with a difference. Style bar looks have been melded with extensive wine lists and decent, near restaurant-standard food. The Broadgate branch, curving around an open space that becomes an ice rink in winter, is particularly striking. Punters in these glass and concrete-look venues tend to be pumped-up and suited, so steer clear if you want to relax somewhere with a glass of wine and a good book.

What's the wine list like? Balanced between the New and Old World. The list is divided according to grape variety, as is the modern way, and in keeping with the bars' sleek looks. There's a particularly strong sauvignon blanc line-up that includes the acid zip of Nelson's Creek 2004 from Paarl, South Africa.

Number of branches 12.

Best for Drinking by the glass: a total of 77 choices, including the tasty 2004 pouilly fumé from Les Chaumiennes, puts other wine bars to shame.

Anything else? Corney & Barrow's newest bar, in Paternoster Square, has a terrace that offers a view of St Paul's Cathedral.

Davy's

With its first outlet opening in 1870, this unashamedly old-fashioned chain has sawdust scattered on the floor of most of its dark basement sites and 'English Fayre' (grilled meats and fish) to eat. Silly names such as Skinkers, Chopper Lump and City Flogger accompany the more regular Davy's moniker. Some places, such as the Heeltap & Bumper in Borough, have a more modern, café-like feel.

What's the wine list like? Highly traditional, with lots from the expected areas of France, including the pleasant spice- and vanilla-scented Chasse Spleen 1997 (£39.95), as well as some inferior own-label bottles. Some recognition of the increasing quality emerging from Chile and South Africa wouldn't go amiss.

Number of branches 42.

Best for Claret – the wine merchant side of Davy's can buy Bordeaux for you, prior to bottling, making it much cheaper. This is known as purchasing 'en primeur'.

Anything else? You can down a pint of Old Wallop in a pewter tankard at Davy's Creed Lane.

Jamies

If Radio 2 opened a themed bar, it would look like a Jamies. Having lacked success with a chain of restaurants, the Hartford Group bought the bars in 2002 and have done rather better since. The soft furnishings and hard edges have impinged on the traditional wine bar market, and they've got the funny names too, like Heads & Tails and Willys Wine Bar. Heads & Tails in Smithfield shows the rather confused nature of some outlets, being half DJ-bar, half-restaurant.

What's the wine list like? There's plenty from the New World to fit the group's pretensions to innovation, although actual choices, Knappstein's 2004 white blend 'Trio' apart, are fairly standard. Lists in City bars are twice as long and give France more of a look-in.

Number of branches 21.

Best for? The dense, spicy 2002 Catena Malbec from Argentina on City bar lists (£33).

Anything else? Every Wednesday night in summer you can bowl on Finsbury Circus Gardens, outside the Pavilion branch (*see right*).

La Grande Marque

47 Ludgate Hill, EC4M 7JU (7329 6709/ www.lagrandemarque.com). St Paul's tube/ Blackfriars tube/rail. **Open** 11.30am-11pm Mon-Fri. **Lunch served** 11.30am-3pm, **snacks served** 5-8pm Mon-Fri. **Main courses** £4.70-£6.50. **House wine** £14 bottle, £4 glass. **Credit** AmEx, DC, JCB, MC, V.

Look for an elaborate 'M' engraved in the glass on the doorway; that's the main clue as to the location of this subtle, sophisticated and gorgeous champagne bar. Inside you'll find a stunning, intricately carved Victorian ceiling. The premises, dating from 1891, were once a banking headquarters; the marble-topped bar stands precisely where the bank counter used to be (try to spot the outline marked in the original mosaic floor). Walls are wood-panelled, seats are wooden – and buttock-bruisingly hard. The operation, presided over by charismatic French manager Olivier, is focused on champagne (La Grande Marque is an old French term signifying a brand of superior quality). The stuff dominates what is a first-rate wine list. Prices are high, though you'd expect that in these parts. A bottle of the house champers (Canard Duchêne) will set you back £28. Food is limited to sandwiches. There's no music, but conversation is plentiful.

Separate room for parties, holds 50. **Map 11 O6.**

Jamies at the Pavilion

Finsbury Circus Gardens, EC2M 7AB (7628 8224/www.jamiesbars.co.uk). Liverpool Street or Moorgate tube/rail. *Bar* **Open** 11am-11pm Mon-Fri. **Lunch served** 11am-3pm, **dinner served** 6.30-9pm Mon-Fri. **Main courses** £7.95-£14.95. *Restaurant* **Lunch served** 11am-3pm Mon-Fri. **Main courses** £9.95-£16.95. *Both* **House wine** £13 bottle, £3.25-£4.50 glass. **Service** 12.5%. **Credit** AmEx, JCB, MC, V.

At its best in summer, this branch of the Jamies chain occupies a pavilion that's also the clubhouse for the City of London Bowling Club. Outside is a neat bowling green and a circle of trees and shrubbery – bucolic relief indeed in the concrete confines of the City. Willie Lebus of Bibendum advises on the wine list, which changes three times a year. It's a measured choice, sensibly ordered by grape variety, with Old World and New just about equally represented. Over 30 wines are available by the glass, making this a good place to experiment. Several bottles cost less than £20: 2003 San Rafael Reserva syrah from Chile; and 2003/4 Pierre Sparr pinot blanc from Alsace, for instance. To eat there are shared snack plates, sandwiches and more substantial main courses such as oven-baked whole rainbow trout with salsa verde, or sirloin steak with a blue cheese and butter crust.

Bookings not accepted for parties of fewer than 6 (bar). Dress: smart casual. Restaurant and bar available for hire. **Map 12 Q5. For branches see index.**

Clerkenwell & Farringdon EC1

★ Bleeding Heart Bistro & Tavern

Bleeding Heart Yard, off Greville Street, EC1N 8SJ (7242 8238/www.bleedingheart.co.uk). Farringdon tube/rail. *Tavern* **Open** 7.30am-11pm Mon-Fri. **Lunch served** noon-3pm, **snacks served** 3-6pm, **dinner served** 6-10pm Mon-Fri. **Main courses** £7.95-£12.95. **House red** £11.75 bottle, £2.95 glass. **House white** £14.45 bottle, £3.65 glass.

Bistro **Lunch served** noon-3pm, **dinner served** 6-10.30pm Mon-Fri. **Main courses** £7.45-£14.95. **House red** £13.50 bottle, £3.40 glass. **House white** £14.25 bottle, £3.60 glass. *Restaurant* **Lunch served** noon-2.30pm, **dinner served** 6-10.30pm Mon-Fri. **Main courses** £11.95-£21.50. **House red** £19.95 bottle, £4.95 glass. **House white** £16.45 bottle, £4.15 glass. *All* **Service** 12.5% for parties of 6 or more. **Credit** AmEx, DC, MC, V.

There's been a pub on this site since 1746, but today you'll find an altogether more upmarket enterprise. Three distinct venues are incorporated. The Tavern is a restored version of the pub and oozes a rich history of bloody murders and royal weddings, celebrated in the publicity literature. It does good beers (Adnams Best, Broadside and, recently, Explorer), but of greater note is the wine list, which runs to 450 varieties – including bottles from the firm's own vineyard in Hawkes Bay, New Zealand – and reads like a who's who of viticulture. Open early for breakfasts, the Tavern takes on the appearance of a boardroom at lunch. Every table seems to be surrounded by suits and spreadsheets piled between plates of spit-roasted, ale-fed suckling pig with black pudding and apple stuffing or grilled salmon on leeks. The smart cellar restaurant serves more elaborate concoctions (grilled sea bass on a fennel brochette with fennel confit and asparagus, for instance). Further into the yard, the Bistro keeps up the good work with French cuisine and yet more fine wines.
Booking advisable. Dress: smart; no shorts, jeans or trainers (restaurant). Separate rooms for parties, seating 30-40. Tables outdoors (15, terrace). **Map 11 N5.**

★ Cellar Gascon
59 West Smithfield, EC1A 9DS (7796 0600). Barbican tube/Farringdon tube/rail. **Open** noon-midnight Mon-Fri. **Tapas** £5-£6. **House wine** £15.70 bottle, £4 glass. **Service** 12.5% (food). **Credit** AmEx, JCB, MC, V.

Along with its neighbouring French restaurant, Club Gascon, this stylish little wine bar is dedicated to educating Londoners in the vinous and culinary treasures of Gascony. There's a wine list of around 120 bottles, all from south-west France. Explore it with the help of the black-clad,

chic and knowledgeable staff who can guide you to lesser-known districts such as Pacherenc and Irouléguy. Food comprises addictive 'dégustations' (in other words, fancy bar snacks) that range from slippery, rich foie gras (a house speciality) to rarely found treats such as andouille de Benejac. Slick design rather than space is what characterises the interior, which is furnished with leather scoop bar stools, banquettes and stylish copper hanging lamps; get here early to bag a seat. If you must, you can stray from the wine list and try a regional aperitif – perhaps a glass of Floc de Gascoigne – but if it's a beer you're after, you really have come to the wrong place.
Bar available for hire. Tables outdoors (3, pavement). **Map 11 O5.**

Covent Garden WC2

Café des Amis
11-14 Hanover Place, WC2E 9JP (7379 3444/ www.cafedesamis.co.uk). Covent Garden tube. *Bar* **Open** 11.30am-1am Mon-Sat. *Restaurant* **Meals served** 11.30am-11.30pm Mon-Sat; 11.30am-4pm Sun. **Main courses** £13.50-£20.50. **Set meal** (11.30am-7pm, 10-11.30pm Mon-Sat) £14.50 2 courses, £16.50 3 courses. **Service** 12.5%. *Both* **House wine** £14.50 bottle, £3.50-£4.90 glass. **Credit** AmEx, DC, MC, V.

This bustling basement bar (and its sister restaurant upstairs – *see p48*) changed ownership in January 2005, though modifications to the decor have been few so far. Metal spotlights still guide you into a small, minimalist room that's more business-class airport lounge than sexy style bar: full of Habitatesque fittings and blokes in Thomas Pink shirts. A large wine rack is in full view behind the central bar, showing off an impressive array of bottles that's divided (how French) into 'vins français' and 'les étrangers' on the wine list. There's the odd gem, such as Rolly Gassmann's 2001 Alsace riesling (£30.50), and an impressively large selection of 21 wines by the glass (though you should steer clear of Michel Laroche's merlot-grenache and a soupy De Loach pinot noir). A prix-fixe menu (written in franglais) is served, including the likes of smoked fish terrine, pan-fried guinea fowl with polenta, and butternut squash ravioli in cep sauce. Among 'les desserts' there's tiramisu with coffee sauce.

Babies and children welcome: high chairs. Booking advisable Thur-Sat. No-smoking tables. Separate room for parties, seats 80. Tables outdoors (12, terrace). **Map 18 L6.**

Leicester Square WC2

Cork & Bottle
44-46 Cranbourn Street, WC2H 7AN (7734 7807). Leicester Square tube. **Meals served** 11am-11.30pm Mon-Sat; noon-10.30pm Sun. **Main courses** £4.50-£12.95. **House wine** £15 bottle, £3.50 glass. **Credit** AmEx, DC, JCB, MC, V.

It may be just off Leicester Square, but this old-fashioned basement wine bar is a world away from its neighbours: a sex shop and a purveyor of kebabs. Beyond a discreet glass door, a narrow spiral staircase winds down into two small rooms, heavily decorated with art nouveau posters for Moët & Chandon and Mumm. It's a gorgeous space: small tables sit on a battered red tiled floor, and an alcove dives under the street into a blue-painted space for six. Owner Don Hewitson loves his wine, and has compiled a list that has top choices from the Rhône, California and his native New Zealand. Te Mata's 2002 'Gravitas' sauvignon blanc from New Zealand is a must-try at £29.50 a bottle, and wines by the glass – such as the 2003 Domaine L'Aulnay from St Nicholas de Bourgueil – have improved since Hewitson installed a Verre de Vin preservation system. Food includes the house burger that combines beef and pork, and an interesting array of fish: grilled moonfish with new potatoes and salad being a recent option.
Bookings accepted until 6.30pm. Children admitted. No-smoking area (daytime). Separate room for parties, seats 10. **Map 18 K7.**

Mayfair W1

Balls Brothers
34 Brook Street, W1Y 1YA (7499 4567/ www.ballsbrothers.co.uk). Bond Street tube. **Open** 11am-11pm, **meals served** 11am-9pm Mon-Fri. **Main courses** £6.95-£11.95. **House wine** £15.50 bottle, £4 glass. **Credit** AmEx, DC, JCB, MC, V.

This outlet of the Balls Brothers chain is in something of a quandary. It backs on to the fashion mecca of South Molton Street, while also facing the squat Georgian houses of Mayfair. A blackboard invites you to 'Come in and chill out',

Cellar Gascon

but don't expect blue neon lights or DJs in this dark basement bar. Walls are painted to look like old panelled wood, head-high windows are barred and prison-like, and pictures of Regent's Street arcade adorn the walls. The staff wouldn't be out of place in a bar or club, however. Young and wearing lots of black, they offer good advice on a 100-strong list that majors in Burgundy. Good choices include the leafy, ripe 2002 cabernet sauvignon/merlot blend from Pask's Hawkes Bay winery in New Zealand or, if you're drinking by the glass, the 2003 Gavi di Gavi La Chiara, from Piedmont, which has good grapefruit and melon flavours. The tables are just big enough for snacks, but a bit squeezed if you eat a two-course meal, such as Welsh rarebit followed by mussels, fish, leek and cider pie. *Separate rooms for parties, seating 8 and 10.* **Map 17 J8.** **For branches see index.**

Soho W1

Shampers

4 Kingly Street, W1B 5PE (7437 1692). Oxford Circus or Piccadilly Circus tube. **Open** 11am-11pm Mon-Sat (*Aug* closed Sat). **Food served** noon-11pm Mon-Sat. **Main courses** £8.75-£13.50. **House wine** £11.50 bottle, £3.25 glass. **Service** 12.5%. **Credit** AmEx, DC, JCB, MC, V.
Older rugby-loving men (plus the occasional duo of young women) are drawn to Shampers; it's an odd mix that only works later on at night, when this dark oblong space (racing-green walls and ceiling) fills up. If you just want a drink, prepare to squeeze around three tables at the back (though in summer there's a few more outside). Otherwise, there are plenty of tables for diners beneath wine racks attached to the walls, with service from friendly French waitresses. The look is trad-flimsy, but the wine list more than compensates, thanks to choices such as the eccentric Josmeyer's 1997 pinot gris Vieilles Vignes (£28.50) and a half-bottle of Heidsieck Dry Monopole, a bargain at £14.50.

The 31-strong by-the-glass selection includes Lustau manzanilla sherry – worth a try. The food menu changes regularly, but usually includes grilled calf's liver with bacon, mash and spinach; several fish of the day (perhaps grilled monkfish with lentils and roast tomatoes); and a couple of vegetarian choices (grilled aubergine salad with avocado, roast peppers and mozzarella, say). *Babies and children admitted. Booking advisable. Restaurant and bar available for hire. Separate room for parties, seats 50. Tables outdoors (3, courtyard).* **Map 17 J6.**

Strand WC2

Gordon's ✓

47 Villiers Street, WC2N 6NE (7930 1408/ www.gordonswinebar.com). Embankment tube/ Charing Cross tube/rail. **Open** 11am-11pm Mon-Sat; noon-10pm Sun. **Food served** noon-10pm Mon-Sat; noon-9pm Sun. **Main courses** £6.95-£8.95. **House wine** £11.70 bottle, £3.30 glass. **Credit** AmEx, MC, V.
If ever a London wine bar deserved to be called a classic, this is it. Gordon's has been conducting subterranean dealings in alcohol since 1890. A crumbling, candlelit cavern, it seems unchanged since *Brief Encounter* and makes an ideal venue for trysts. Press cuttings cover the walls, detailing Britannia's proud rule from the time when the *Mail* and *Express* were broadsheets. Madeira (blended by Gordon's) is served from the wood in dock glasses; Graham's LBV port comes by the schooner, beaker or bottle. The main wine list is admirable: well priced (virtually everything under £20), global in scope, and containing nearly 30 options by the glass. Food consists of unfussy pub grub, including ploughman's, pies, salads and hot specials such as turkey fillet with mushroom sauce, or spinach and potato gratin. If the cramped basement is too crowded – and getting a table is near impossible, more often than not – try the tables outside, overlooking Embankment Gardens.

Babies and children admitted. Bookings not accepted. Tables outdoors (10, terrace). **Map 18 L7.**

Victoria SW1

Tiles

36 Buckingham Palace Road, SW1W 0RE (7834 7761/www.tilesrestaurant.co.uk). Victoria tube/rail.
Bar **Open** noon-11pm Mon-Fri. **Snacks served** noon-2.30pm, 5.30-10pm Mon-Fri. *Restaurant* **Lunch served** noon-2.30pm, **dinner served** 5.30-10pm Mon-Fri. **Main courses** £7.95-£14.75.
Both **House wine** £12.50 bottle, £3.50-£4.50 glass. **Service** 12.5%. **Credit** AmEx, DC, JCB, MC, V.
The tone is romantic – no, resolutely smoochy – on the ground floor of this charming bar, helped by tables for two, candles, low lighting and large bowls of flowers. Named after its blue and white diamond-patterned ceramic floor, Tiles also has room in the basement (pine floor here, plus modern lamps, the odd sofa and trendy pictures of wine bottles) for those who want to hang out with mates. There are 22 wines by the glass, but few catch the eye. Antares' 2003 chardonnay (£3.75 a glass, £13.50 a bottle) confirms the view that most entry-level Chilean whites should be avoided; try instead the Santa Carolina Reservado 2004 sauvignon blanc (£16.95 a bottle) from the same country – or, if you have the cash, sample Léoville-Barton's second-growth Bordeaux wine, 'La Réserve de' from the cracking 2000 vintage (£42). Food is of decent quality, encompassing risotto of roquefort, leeks and pine nuts; fish cakes with horseradish caper mayonnaise; and organic duck breast with rosemary and honey, sautéed new potatoes, spinach and toasted almonds.
Babies and children admitted. Booking advisable. Restaurant available for hire. Separate room for parties, seats 60. Tables outdoors (6, pavement). **Map 15 H10.**

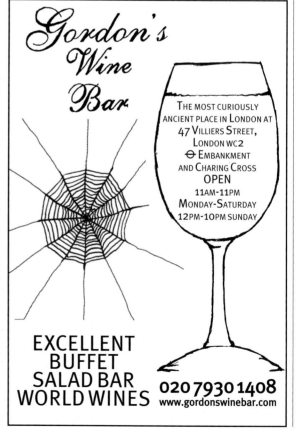

West

Holland Park W11

Julie's

*135 Portland Road, W11 4LW (7229 8331/
www.juliesrestaurant.com). Holland Park tube.*
Bar **Open** 9am-11pm Mon-Sat; noon-10pm Sun.
Lunch served noon-2.45pm Mon-Sat; 12.30-
3.30pm Sun. **Afternoon tea served** 3-6.30pm
daily. **Dinner served** 7-10.45pm Mon-Sat;
7-10pm Sun.
Restaurant **Lunch served** 12.30-3pm Sun.
Dinner served 7-11.30pm Mon-Sat.
Both **Main courses** £10-£17. **House wine**
£17 bottle, £4 glass. **Service** 12.5%. **Credit**
AmEx, JCB, MC, V.
Baroque Julie's still attracts the haut monde of
west London; it was the scene of Prince Charles'
first engagement party and remains familiar
territory for familiar faces. An exceptionally well-
chosen wine list includes Chassagne-Montrachet
blanc 2001 Domaine Colin-Deleger for £50, should
you be feeling flush; more economical options
include a Coldstream Hills cabernet merlot 2000
from Australia (£18) and a Santa Rita Reserva
sauvignon blanc 2004 from Chile (£17).
Alternatively, there's 14-year-old Oban malt (£8 a
measure). The bar food is ambitious, with separate
menus for breakfast, lunch, afternoon and dinner.
So you could start the day with smoked salmon
and scrambled egg, then lunch on grilled sardines,
slip-in some goat's cheese wrapped in vine leaves
with beetroot and lentil salad in the mid-afternoon,
before dinner of pan-roasted guinea fowl with
baked fig, spinach and soft parmesan polenta.
*Babies and children welcome: children's set meal
Sun; crèche (1-4pm Sun); high chairs. Booking
advisable. Separate rooms for parties, seating 12,
16, 24, 35 and 45. Tables outdoors (10, pavement).*
Map 19 B5.

Kensington W8

Whits

*21 Abingdon Road, W8 6AH (7938 1122/
www.whits.co.uk). High Street Kensington tube.*
Bar **Open** noon-11pm Tue-Sat.
Restaurant **Lunch served** 12.30-2.30pm
Tue-Fri. **Dinner served** 7-10.30pm Tue-Sat.
Main courses £11.50-£17.95. **Service** 12.5%.
Both **House wine** £12.75 bottle, £3.25 glass.
Credit AmEx, MC, V.
Under new management and a new name (Goolies
having been kicked into touch), Whits is
concentrating more on food. A former chef from
Le Gavroche has been hired as consultant; tables
that were once for drinking in the front bar area
now have tablecloths. Lunch might be a cassoulet
of duck confit or piquillo peppers with goat's
cheese, aubergine ganoush, pine nuts and tabouleh.
Dinner includes such elaborate concoctions as fillet
steak with escargots gratin and frogs' legs
provençale. But eating is not compulsory; sit at the
bar on spindly metal chairs and sip a cocktail or
Champagne, preferably a half bottle of the
excellent Billecart-Salmon rosé (£35). The excellent
collection of liqueurs includes Guyot cassis for a
superior Kir Royale. The wine list is strong too,
from a Clos L'Abeilley (£3.50 a glass, £13.50 a
bottle) to a Gevrey-Chambertin 'Le Poissenot'
premier cru 2001 at £67. Fine dessert wines include
a Sauternes 1999 at £8 a glass.
Children admitted (restaurant). Booking advisable.
Map 7 9A.

Shepherd's Bush W12

Albertine

*1 Wood Lane, W12 7DP (8743 9593). Shepherd's
Bush tube.* **Open** 11am-11pm Mon-Fri; 6.30-11pm
Sat. **Meals served** noon-10.30pm Mon-Fri; 6.30-
10.30pm Sat. **Main courses** £5.50-£7.50. **House
wine** £11 bottle, £2.90 glass. **Credit** MC, V.
This gorgeous, unaffected little wine bar is
furnished with an appealingly mismatched array
of furniture. Enormous blackboards stretch down
half the length of the walls, detailing the
outstanding choice to be had. The wine list runs to
150 different labels, popular options being the

Oratory. See p336.

Alsace pinot blanc (£3.95 a glass, £15.80 a bottle)
and a Chilean pinot noir (£3.80/£15.30). Food is of
the bistro ilk, so ostrich sausage and mash, spinach
and ricotta tortellini, and fish pie might grace the
regularly changing menu. Bar snacks include an
excellent cheeseboard. Albertine is more suited to
the backstreets of Montmartre than the debatable
charms of Wood Lane. When we entered the tiny,
slightly scruffy bar-cum-dining room (the first
floor has recently been redecorated along the same
lines), an elegantly dishevelled older gentleman
was perched behind the bar, patiently going over
the wine list with a couple of punters, while the
gentle strains of Marvin Gaye played on the stereo.
They don't make places like this any more.
*Booking advisable for large parties. Separate room
for parties, seats 28.* **Map 20 B2.**

South West

Earlsfield SW18

Willie Gunn

*422 Garratt Lane, SW18 4HW (8946 7773).
Earlsfield rail.* **Open** 11am-11pm Mon-Sat;
11am-10.30pm Sun. **Meals served** 11am-
10.30pm Mon-Sat; 11am-10pm Sun. **Main
courses** £9.50-£15. **Set lunch** £6.50 1 course.
House wine £12 bottle, £3.25 glass. **Service**
12.5%. **Credit** AmEx, MC, V.
Willie Gunn has the tricky task of attracting the
first-time buyers that populate Earlsfield. On a
street that majors in banks and furniture shops,
many an operation has gone bust, but new owner
Barry Rutter has so far carried on in the same
fairly nondescript vein. The open, knocked-
through bar and restaurant has grey-painted
walls, stripped wood floors and repro Picasso
prints. Staff frantically polish cutlery, middle-aged
men watch racing on the corner telly and large
shutters flap in the breeze. Come evening, the real
action begins as PR execs slide off the train from
Waterloo, enjoying gems such as Domaine du
Salvard's 2003 sauvignon blanc from Cheverny –
a cheaper version of next-door Sancerre. Or there's
Geoff Merrill's well-balanced, strawberry-scented
grenache rosé from the Owens Estate – just avoid
the many, mediocre Hispanic whites. The
restaurant at the back serves simple dishes
such as burgers and fish cakes, or bream with
crushed potato.
Babies and children welcome: high chairs.
Booking advisable. Tables outdoors (4, pavement).

Putney SW15

Putney Station

94-98 Upper Richmond Road, SW15 2SP (8780 0242/www.brinkleys.com). East Putney tube. **Bar Open/snacks served** noon-11pm Mon-Sat; noon-10.30pm Sun. *Restaurant* **Meals served** noon-11pm Mon-Sat; noon-10.30pm Sun. **Main courses** £6.50-£14.50. *Both* **House wine** £7.50 bottle, £3-£4 glass. **Service** 10%. **Credit** MC, V.

Opened by Brinkley's the wine merchants in 2004, this modern-looking venue has a wine list that is both adventurous and accessible. As with all Brinkley's sites, prices are pretty pleasing too: you pay near-off licence rates. You could snap up a pinot grigio (Terre del Noce, 2004) for £9 or splash out on a bottle of Trinity Hill 2003, from New Zealand's Hawkes Bay (£17.50). Food ranges from lamb burgers to roast cod or spinach and ricotta ravioli, via a varied choice of pizzas. The bar advertises itself with a groovy sign outside, but within, its interior exudes the air of a would-be sophisticated wine bar circa 1982: strip lighting, metal blinds and a distressingly Sadé-like soundtrack. On our visit, most of the weary commuters pouring out of East Putney station in the early evening seemed to be giving the place a miss, but it can get pretty packed too. Brinkley's other venues include the Oratory (*see below*) near Brompton Oratory. Wine lists at all are similar.

Babies and children welcome: high chairs. Booking advisable. Disabled: toilet. No-smoking tables. Separate rooms for parties, each seating 30. Tables outdoors (3, pavement). Takeaway service.

South Kensington SW3

Oratory

234 Brompton Road, SW3 2BB (7584 3493/ www.brinkleys.com). South Kensington tube. **Bar Open** noon-11pm daily. *Restaurant* **Meals served** noon-11pm Mon-Sat; noon-10.30pm Sun. **Main courses** £8-£15. *Both* **House wine** £7.50 bottle, £3.50 glass. **Service** 10%. **Credit** AmEx, MC, V.

This rather funky little brasserie not far from the Michelin Building is part of the Brinkley's chain, so wines are supplied at retail price. A lunchtime crowd of chatty shoppers and mums gives way to a more buzzy atmosphere in the evening. Baubled chandeliers, tangled vine patterns over light blue walls, and pinkish banquettes down the sides help create a bright space, but the room can feel a little cramped, not least if you find yourself parked on the wrought-iron seats at the tiny bar. The menu is eclectic in the modern brasserie style, so you might order sausages and mash with onion gravy; or seared tuna with warm niçoise vegetables, pesto and aïoli; or even Thai chicken curry. Wine, though, is what you come here for, and there are four whites and four reds by the glass, plus several half bottles. For £7.50 you can purchase a humble bottle of Caliterra (red or white). More illustrious labels include a 2002 Vergisson Pouilly-Fuissé (£27.50) and a Hamilton Russell pinot noir 2002 from South Africa (£25).

Babies and children admitted (restaurant). Booking advisable. No smoking. Tables outdoors (9, pavement). **Map 14 E10.**

South

Waterloo SE1

Archduke

Concert Hall Approach, SE1 8XU (7928 9370). Waterloo tube/rail. **Bar Open** 8.30am-11pm Mon-Fri; 11am-11pm Sat. **Meals served** 11am-11pm Mon-Sat. **Main courses** £4.70-£7.75. *Restaurant* **Lunch served** noon-2.15pm Mon-Fri. **Dinner served** 5.30-11pm Mon-Sat. **Main courses** £10-£14.95. **Set meal** (noon-2.15pm, 5.30-7.30pm Mon-Fri, 5.30-7.30pm Sat) £13.50 2 courses, £16.75 3 courses incl unlimited bread and coffee. *Both* **House wine** £11.85 bottle, £2.95 glass. **Service** 12.5%. **Credit** AmEx, DC, MC, V.

During the day, the Archduke is like an art gallery tea room, populated by tourists, harassed parents and large groups in their forties discussing the latest exhibition at the nearby Hayward. It's a two-storey glass-fronted affair set beneath dark Victorian railway arches, with a split-level bar and upstairs restaurant. Large, fake plastic plants hang down from baskets, competing with heavy metal lamps as trains boom overhead. At night, the bar gleams with coloured lights and rings to the sound of jazz. Salads, sandwiches and two hot dishes daily are served, with brunch on Saturdays. In the restaurant, targeted at the Royal Festival Hall crowd, you'll find jazz-themed sketches hanging from the arch, an outside conservatory and food such as duck breast with dauphinois potatoes, or whole grilled plaice. The wine list covers all the right bases. New Zealand sauvignon blanc? Check. Good-value southern Italian red? Check. And the examples are fine ones – respectively, the up-and-coming Waipara Estate's 2003 bottle (£26.15) and Madonne della Grazie's 2002 primitivo di Puglia 'A Mano' (£20.75).

Babies and children admitted. Bar available for hire. Booking advisable: restaurant. Entertainment: jazz 8.30-11pm Mon-Fri; 8.30-11.30pm Sat. No-smoking areas. Separate rooms for parties, seating 35 and 45. Tables outdoors (11, pavement). **Map 10 M9.**

South East

East Dulwich SE22

Green & Blue NEW

38 Lordship Lane, SE22 8HJ (8693 9250/www. greenandbluewines.com). East Dulwich rail/ 40, 176, 185 bus. **Open** 11am-11pm Mon-Sat; noon-10.30pm Sun. **Snacks** £2-£5. **House wine** £10.50 bottle, £3 glass. **Credit** MC, V.

So, is it a wine bar or a wine shop? The answer is 'yes'. The Italians have a word for a wine shop-cum-casual-wine-bar like this: an enoteca. At the front is a wine shop, all clean lines and remarkable wines. If you want your usual branded stuff, look elsewhere, because owner Kate Thal is a proponent of small, artisanal producers (many of the wines are also organic) and there are bottles here you'll be hard-pressed to find elsewhere. If you want to drink on the premises, you can do so at the back, for a modest (about 60%) mark-up on the off-licence price. Or you can drink a small but well-

---

BEST WINE BARS

Oak-aged
Wood panelling, old gents and lots of claret at **Balls Brothers St James's Street, Davy's at Creed Lane** (for both, *see index*) and **El Vino** (*see p331*).

Young and fruity
Keen staff and New World wines at **Jamies Charlotte Street** (*see index*) and **Wine Wharf** (*see above*).

Drinking à deux
Romantic corners at **Café des Amis** (*see p333*), **Gordon's** (*see p334*) and **Vats** (*see p331*).

Wining and dining
Eat and drink well at **Bleeding Heart** (*see p332*), **Cellar Gascon** (*see p333*) and **Wine Wharf** (*see above*) – all have good restaurants attached.

Footballers' wives
Chardonnay, pinot grigio and the blonde and wealthy are to be found at **Balls Brothers, Victoria** (*see index*); **Julie's** (*see p335*) and **Whits** (*see p335*).

Champagne Charlies
Great fizz at **Cork & Bottle** (*see p333*), **La Grande Marque** (*see p332*) and **Kettners** (*see p310*).

---

chosen selection of wines by the glass. About a half-dozen bottles are open at any time and customers are able to taste before they commit themselves to the likes of raspberry-scented Pinot Noir from Luxembourg or gutsy, savoury Chilean Carmenere. There's no kitchen, so food is of the nibbly sort: a selection of Neal's Yard cheeses, some dolmades, a plate of Spanish cured meats and so on – simple food made for sharing. On Monday evenings G&B also runs tutored tasting sessions on subjects like 'how to taste' or 'organic wines'; prices are reasonable at about £12 per person , but you should book ahead.

Babies and children welcome (before 7pm): toys. Booking advisable Fri, Sat. No smoking. Takeaway service. Vegan dishes. Vegetarian menu. **Map 23 C4.**

London Bridge & Borough SE1

★ Wine Wharf

Stoney Street, Borough Market, SE1 9AD (7940 8335/www.vinopolis.co.uk). London Bridge tube/rail. **Open** 11.30am-11pm Mon-Fri; 11am-11pm Sat. **Meals served** noon-9.30pm Mon-Sat. **Main courses** £4.50-£9.95. **House white** £13.75 bottle, £3-£3.75 glass. **House red** £15.25 bottle, £3.50-£4.25 glass. **Credit** AmEx, DC, MC, V.

There can scarcely be a better place than this in London for oenophiles to experiment. Wine Wharf is the bar attached to Vinopolis the wine museum, and it offers an impressive and global selection of interesting wines. You can wander from a Château Musar from Lebanon's Bekaa Valley (£42.75 a bottle for the 1997 vintage) to a £65.75 bottle of 2001 Ata Rangi pinot noir from Martinborough, New Zealand. Options by the glass are strewn all over the menu, meaning choice is exceptional. This is a good-looking place: a modish wharf-style interior of bare bricks, beams and metal, softened by sofas and low lighting. The young, friendly staff are wine-savvy and always let you try before you buy. For those with the nerve to ask for them, the bar also stocks a few brands of bottled beers like Heineken and Budweiser. Bar food includes cheese platters, as well as more substantial dishes like chorizo with sun-dried tomatoes and new potatoes, and snacks such as welsh rarebit. Mod Euro restaurant Cantina Vinopolis is housed in the same complex.

Babies and children admitted (until 8pm). Disabled: toilet. Restaurant and bar available for hire. **Map 11 P8.**

North West

West Hampstead NW6

No.77 Wine Bar

77 Mill Lane, NW6 1NB (7435 7787). West Hampstead tube/rail. **Meals served** 6-11pm Mon, Tue; 6pm-midnight Wed; noon-midnight Thur-Sat; noon-10.30pm Sun. **Main courses** £7.25-£13.50. **House wine** £11.45 bottle, £2.75 glass. **Service** 12.5%. **Credit** MC, V.

Punters often spill out on to the pavement during No.77's regular events (morris dancing on St George's Day being one of them). Rugger types of both sexes and hemispheres like to hang out here, and one section of the labyrinthine network of little spaces is decked out with framed rugby shirts. Ethnographic art provides further decoration, as do palm trees and pine tables. Wine is taken seriously enough to include a list of 17 whites and 15 reds, many of which are available by the glass. A Château Senailhac is a nice find at £3.95 a glass, as is a Rooiberg Winery sauvignon blanc (£3.30). A solitary Budvar beer tap is backed up by bottles of Hahn, Steinlager and, from Australia, Tooheys New. On the menu, 'the sexiest food in West Hampstead' features pan-fried scallops; prawns sautéed in citrus herb butter; mushroom, courgette and blue cheese gateau; and assorted 'bits on the side' – olives, chorizo, and the like.

Babies and children admitted. Booking advisable. Separate room for parties, seats 40. Tables outdoors (8, pavement). **Map 28 A1.**

Eating & Entertainment

Comedy

It's difficult to find a comedy venue that serves food and laughs of equal standard. There are, however, a few places that offer dishes of a higher quality than standard old-style pub grub. In south London, **Up the Creek** (302 Creek Road, SE10 9SW, 8858 4581, www.up-the-creek.com) is well worth a visit. Over in Maida Vale there's the **Canal Café Theatre** (first floor, The Bridge House, on the corner of Westbourne Terrace Road and Delamere Terrace, W2 6ND, 7289 6056, www.canalcafetheatre.com; map 1 C5), while Shoreditch boasts the popular **Comedy Café** (66-68 Rivington Street, EC2A 3AY, 7739 5706, www.comedycafe.co.uk; map 6 R4).

The best-known comedy club in London is probably Leicester Square's **Comedy Store** (1A Oxendon Street, W1Y 4EE, information 0870 060 2340, bookings Ticketmaster 7344 4444, www.thecomedystore.co.uk; map 17 K7). Another favourite is **Jongleurs Camden Lock** (Middle Yard, Camden Lock, Chalk Farm Road, NW1 8AD, 0870 787 0707, www.jongleurs.com; map 27 C1) – which has two other London branches, in Battersea and Bow.

For up-to-date information on the capital's comedy clubs, see the Comedy section in the weekly *Time Out* magazine.

Dining afloat

Vessels for hire include canal cruisers from the **Floating Boater** (Waterside, Little Venice, Warwick Crescent, W2 6NE, 7266 1066, www.floatingboater.co.uk; map 1 C5); the **Leven is Strijd** (West India Quay, Hertsmere Road, West India Docks, E14 6AL, 7987 4002, www.theleven.co.uk), a classic Dutch barge, for views of Canary Wharf; and the **Elizabethan** (8780 1562, www.thamesluxurycharters.co.uk), which is a replica of a 19th-century Mississippi paddle steamer that cruises from Putney to beyond the Thames Barrier.

The **Sunborn Yacht Hotel ExCeL** (Royal Victoria Dock, E16 1SL, 0870 040 4100, www.sunbornhotels.com) has good food, but a conference-centre vibe, while the **RS Hispaniola** next to Hungerford Bridge (Victoria Embankment, WC2N 5DJ, 7839 3011, www.hispaniola.co.uk; map 10 L8) is a popular party venue with tapas bar, cocktail lounge and a large restaurant. There's also Danish-oriented restaurant **Lightship Ten** (see p163).

Dinner & dance

Some of London's swankiest hotels still provide the opportunity for an evening bursting with glitz, glamour and gourmet food. Weekend dinner dances are offered at the **Ritz** (see p129; £75 4 courses Fri, Sat), at the Park Lane Hilton's **Windows** (see p129; £59.50 5 courses plus £7.50 cover charge per person, Fri, Sat), and at the Conservatory restaurant inside the **Lanesborough** (see p305 **Hotel teas**; £48 3 courses Fri, Sat).

DIY

Blue Hawaii

2 Richmond Road, Kingston upon Thames, Surrey, KT2 5EB (8549 6989/www.bluehawaii.co.uk). Kingston rail. **Lunch served** noon-3pm, dinner served 6pm-1am Mon-Sat. **Meals served** noon-1am Sun. **Set meal** £8.95-£11.95 unlimited barbecue. **Set dinner** (8pm-1am Fri) £19.50 3 courses; (8pm-1am Sat) £21.50 3 courses. **Service** 10%. **Credit** AmEx, DC, MC, V.
The Blue Hawaii experience is a mix of light-hearted entertainment, provided by both the waiters and Hawaiian-styled musicians and an all-you-can-eat barbecue. There are themed fancy dress parties on the last Saturday of each month. Weekend lunchtimes see a children's menu and supervised play area. Popular with party groups. *Babies and children welcome: children's menu; high chairs; supervised play area (noon-3pm Sat, Sun). Booking essential weekends. Disabled: toilet. Entertainment: musicians 8.30pm Fri, Sat, occasional weekdays.*

Mongolian Barbeque

12 Maiden Lane, WC2E 7NA (7379 7722/www.themongolianbarbeque.co.uk). Covent Garden tube. **Meals served** noon-11pm Mon-Fri, Sun; noon-11.30pm Sat. **Set meal** £7.95 1 bowl, £9.95 starter & 1 bowl, £12.95 unlimited buffet. **Service** 12.5%. **Credit** AmEx, MC, V.
This venue has a fun, relaxed vibe even on busy nights, with pitchers of beer and cheap wine to help things along. You create your own meal, choosing the meat, fish and vegetables you fancy, adding a sauce along the way (there are recipe cards to guide you) and then the chef does his magic on the griddle. Add to your meal with ready-made starters, side orders of rice, noodles and flatbreads and, if you have space, a dessert. *Babies and children welcome: children's menu; high chairs. Booking advisable. Tables outdoors (7, patio). Map 18 L7.*

Tiger Lil's

270 Upper Street, N1 2UQ (7226 1118/www.tigerlils.com). Highbury & Islington tube/rail/4, 19 bus. **Lunch served** Oct-June noon-3pm Fri; noon-4pm Sat, Sun. **Dinner served** 6-11pm daily. **Set lunch** £5.35 1 course. **Set dinner** £11.90 3 courses, £12.65 unlimited buffet. **Credit** AmEx, MC, V.
The procedure at this modern, friendly restaurant is simple: first, a range of raw ingredients are selected from the huge range available, then a sauce is chosen (teriyaki or black bean are mild; hot tomato and garlic add zing) and finally you hand the lot over to the chefs in the central cooking area, where it's stir-fried. The place is child-friendly (one under-five per adult eats free, for example). *Babies and children welcome: children's menu; high chairs. Disabled: toilet. Separate room for hire, seats 40.*
For branch see index.

Dogs' dinners

Walthamstow Stadium

Chingford Road, E4 8SJ (8531 4255/www.wsgreyhound.co.uk). Walthamstow Central tube/rail then 97, 97A, 215, 357 bus. **Meals served** 6.30-9.30pm Tue, Thur, Sat. **Set meal** £18 3 courses. **Admission** *Popular enclosure* free Tue; £3 Thur, Sat. *Main enclosure* £6 Tue, Thur, Sat. Free under-15s. **Credit** MC, V.
There's no threat of going hungry here, although what you eat may depend on your winnings. There's a classic diner area offering either scampi or chicken with chips, two drinks, a couple of £1 bets and a programme, all for £14.50. The Stowaway restaurant offers a similar deal with three courses, admission and a programme for £18. Alternatively, for a pricier sit-down meal with great views over the track, opt for the Paddock Grill. Free lunchtime races (with half-price drinks) are held on Monday and Friday each week; call ahead for details. *Booking advisable. Disabled: toilet. Private boxes for hire, seating 25-200.*

Wimbledon Stadium

Plough Lane, SW17 0BL (8946 8000/www.wimbledonstadium.co.uk). Tooting Broadway tube/Earlsfield rail/44, 270, 272 bus. **Meals served** 7-9.30pm Tue, Fri, Sat. **Set meal** *Broadway* £14 2 courses (Tue); £16-£24 3 courses. *Star Attraction* £16 2 courses (Tue); £19-£28 3 courses. **Admission** £5.50 grandstand. **Credit** AmEx, MC, V.
Both restaurants at the stadium offer a welcome alternative to the usual takeaway outlets. The Star Attraction is the larger and more luxurious of the two, and has a perfect view of the finishing line. The set meal package includes admission, a three-course menu (a two-courser is also offered on Tuesdays), a race card and a service that means waiters can place bets for you. The menu offers international standards such as steak, tagliatelle carbonara and Thai red curry. *Babies and children admitted. Disabled: lift; toilet. Separate rooms for parties, seating 28-120.*

Jazz & soul

Dorchester Bar

The Dorchester, 53 Park Lane, W1K 1QA (7629 8888/www.dorchesterhotel.com). Hyde Park Corner tube. **Open** noon-11pm Mon-Sat; noon-10.30pm Sun. **Meals served** noon-11.30pm Mon-Sat; noon-10.30pm Sun. **Main courses** £19-£28. **Music** 6.30pm-midnight Mon-Sat; 7-11pm Sun. **Credit** AmEx, DC, JCB, MC, V.
During the evenings, the Dorchester Bar becomes a relaxed jazz venue, with a variety of musicians playing throughout the week (on Sunday there's a soothing background pianist, for example). The menu is traditional Italian fare. *Disabled: toilet. Entertainment: musicians 6.30pm-midnight Mon-Wed; jazz band 6.30pm-midnight Thur-Sat; pianist 7-11pm Sun.* **Map 9 G7.**

Dover Street

8-10 Dover Street, W1S 4LQ (7629 9813/www.doverst.co.uk). Green Park or Piccadilly Circus tube. **Open** noon-3.30pm, 5.30pm-3am Mon-Thur; noon-3.30pm, 7pm-3am Fri; 7pm-3am Sat. **Main courses** £13.75-£21.95. **Set lunch** £17.95 2 courses. **Music** *Bands* 9.30pm Mon; 10.30pm Tue-Sat. *DJs* until 3am Mon-Sat. **Admission** £6 after 10pm Mon; £7 after 10pm Tue; £8 after 10pm Wed; £12 after 10pm Thur; diners only until 10pm, then £15 Fri, Sat. **Credit** AmEx, DC, MC, V.
Now in it's 26th year, Dover Street is a favourite for upmarket parties. The three bars and the restaurant host jazz bands as well as blues, swing, soul and funk, with DJs playing late into the night. The menu – Modern European meets French – features the likes of fillet steak with foie gras, and char-grilled sea bass. Check the website for up-to-date band listings. *Booking advisable. Dress: no jeans or trainers. No-smoking tables.* **Map 9 G7.**

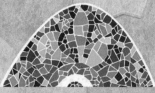

Jazz After Dark

9 Greek Street, W1D 4DQ (7734 0545/
www.jazzafterdark.co.uk). Leicester Square tube.
Open 2pm-2am Mon Thur; 2pm 3am Fri, Sat.
Meals served 2pm-midnight Mon-Sat. **Main**
courses £5-£10. **Set menu** £10.95 3 courses.
Tapas £3.95 per dish. **Music** 9pm-1.30am Mon-
Thur; 10.30pm-2.30am Fri, Sat. **Admission** £3
Mon-Wed; £5 Thur; £10 Fri, Sat. **Credit** AmEx,
DC, JCB, MC, V.
This Soho haunt attracts twentysomethings with
a passion for jazz and blues. The menu lists fish
and chips for a fiver. and mint and rosemary lamb
at £10.95. A large choice of tapas is also available,
as are steak or chicken pitta sandwiches. An
impressive cocktail list helps to prolong the night's
entertainment for post-pub party people.
Booking essential Fri, Sat. Dress: smart casual;
no trainers. Entertainment: musicians 9pm Mon-
Thur; 10.30pm Fri, Sat. Bar available for hire.
Tables outdoors (2, pavement). **Map 17 K6.**

Jazz Café ✓

5-7 Parkway, NW1 7PG (7916 6060/
www.jazzcafe.co.uk). Camden Town tube. **Open**
7pm-1am Mon-Thur; 7pm-2am Fri, Sat; noon-
4pm, 7pm-midnight Sun. **Meals served** 7.30-
9.30pm daily. **Main courses** £15.50. **Set meal**
£25 3 courses. **Music** 8.30-11.30pm Mon-Thur,
Sun; 8.30-11pm Fri, Sat. **Club nights** 11pm-2am
Fri, Sat. **Admission** £12.50-£25. **Credit** MC, V.
The impressive line-up of contemporary soul,
R&B, jazz and acoustic rock acts attracts slightly
more mature music connoisseurs. If you want to
eat in the balcony restaurant overlooking the stage,
reserve a table when buying your ticket. At
weekends, club nights start when the musicians
stop, and continue on into the early hours. Check
the website for listings.
Booking advisable; essential weekends. Disabled:
toilet. **Map 25 D2.**

Pizza Express Jazz Club ✓

10 Dean Street, W1D 3RW (7439 8722/
www.pizzaexpress.com/jazz). Tottenham Court Road
tube. **Meals served** noon-midnight daily. **Main**
courses £4.95-£8.25. **Music** 9pm-11.30pm daily.
Admission £15-£20. **Credit** AmEx, DC, MC, V.
With appearances from legends such as Van
Morrison and new stars like Amy Winehouse and
Jamie Cullen, this basement club and restaurant is
usually well attended. The menu of Pizza Express
standards rarely lets you down, and the atmosphere
is upbeat. Musicians play nightly; check the
website for details.
Babies and children welcome: high chairs. Booking
advisable. Disabled: toilet. No-smoking tables.
Takeaway service. **Map 17 K6.**

Ronnie Scott's

47 Frith Street, W1D 4HT (7439 0747/
www.ronniescotts.co.uk). Leicester Square tube.
Open 8.30pm-3am Mon-Sat. **Meals served**
8.30pm-1am Mon-Sat. **Main courses** £3.80-
£14.80. **Music** 9.30pm-2am Mon-Sat. **Admission**
(non-members) £20 Mon-Thur; £25 Fri, Sat.
Membership £60/yr. **Credit** AmEx, DC, MC, V.
Ronnie Scott's has been showcasing top musicians
since the 1960s. Food at this Soho institution is
comfort fare, such as bangers with mash or steak
and chips. On Friday and Saturday from 9.30pm
there are salsa classes in the upstairs bar (£7
entry). Check the website for forthcoming acts.
Booking advisable. Entertainment: bands daily;
salsa classes 9.30pm Fri, Sat (upstairs bar).
No-smoking tables. **Map 17 K6.**

606 Club

90 Lots Road, SW10 0QD (7352 5953/
www.606club.co.uk). Earl's Court tube.
Open 7.30pm-1am Mon-Wed; 8pm-1.30am
Thur; 8pm-2am Fri, Sat; 8pm-midnight Sun.
Meals served 7.30-11.30pm Mon-Wed; 8-
11.30pm Thur; 8pm-12.30am Fri, Sat; 8-10.30pm
Sun. **Main courses** £8.45-£16.25. **Music** 8pm-
1am Mon-Wed; 9.30pm-1am Thur-Sat; 9pm-
11.30pm Sun. **Admission** *Non-members*
£7 Mon-Thur; £9 Fri, Sat; £8 Sun. *Members*
(if dining) £6 Mon-Thur; £8 Fri, Sat; £7 Sun.
Membership £95 first yr; £60 subsequent yrs.
Service 12.5%. **Credit** MC, V.

This Chelsea members club is a focal point during
the London Jazz Festival (usually November),
presenting musicians as established as pianist Stan
Tracey, as well as newcomers like vocalist Polly
Gibbons. Around ten bands play nightly, with
double bills scheduled from Monday to Wednesday.
Non-members are admitted, but can only purchase
alcohol with a full meal. The global-accented menu
changes daily, and offers the likes of grilled lemon
sole with cherry tomatoes alongside steak and
chips. Drop in towards the end of the evening and
you may witness an impromptu jam session.
Map 13 C13.

Latin

There's also Cuban food and music at
Conran restaurant **Floridita** (*see p44*).

Cuba ✓

11-13 Kensington High Street, W8 5NP
(7938 4137/www.barlondon.co.uk). High Street
Kensington tube. **Open** *Club* 9.30pm-2am Mon-
Sat; 8.30pm-12.30am Sun. *Restaurant & bar* 5pm-
2am Mon-Thur; noon-2am Fri, Sat; 5pm-12.30am
Sun. **Admission** £3-£5 after 9.30pm Mon-Thur;
£3-£8 after 8pm Fri, Sat. **Credit** AmEx, MC, V.
Musicans, a happy hour (jugs of cocktails for a
tenner), and a tapas-style, South American menu
pulls an enthusiastic crowd to this venue. Every
evening salsa lessons are offered in the basement
club, followed by DJs spinning Latin grooves until
the early hours.
Babies and children admitted (noon-5pm Fri, Sat).
Entertainment: salsa classes 7.30-9.30pm Mon-
Sat, 6.30-8.30pm Sun; Latin singer 8.30pm Wed;
jazz 8.30pm Sun; DJs 9.30pm daily; occasional
bands (call for details). **Map 7 C8.**

Havana

17 Hanover Square, W1S 1HU (7629 2552/
www.fiestahavana.com). Oxford Circus tube.
Bar **Open** 5pm-2am Mon-Thur; 5pm-3am Fri,
Sat; 6pm-1am Sun. **Admission** £3-£6 Mon-Thur;
£5-£10 Fri, Sat; free for diners.
Restaurant **Meals served** 5pm-2am Mon-Sat;

Pizza Express Jazz Club

DRINKING

6pm-midnight Sun. **Main courses** £10-£18.
Set dinner (incl free entry to club) £23.95
3 courses. **Service** 12.5%.
Both **Credit** AmEx, MC, V.
Cocktails and free dance classes (except on Sunday,
when lessons cost £5) are the attractions here.
Havana's lengthy menus cover the usual bar
snacks and tapas, alongside more substantial
dishes such as cajun-seasoned salmon and spicy
mussels with chorizo (in the restaurant).
*Booking essential weekends. Dress: smart casual;
no trainers. Entertainment: DJs/bands 7pm daily;
dance classes (phone for details). Restaurant
available for hire.* **Map 9 H6.**
For branch see index.

Salsa! *Greasy!*
*96 Charing Cross Road, WC2H 0JG (7379
3277/www.barsalsa.info). Leicester Square or
Tottenham Court Road tube.*
Bar **Open** 5.30pm-2am Mon-Sat; 6pm-12.30am
Sun.
Café **Open** 9am-5.30pm Mon-Sat. **Snacks
served** noon-5.30pm Mon-Sat. **Snacks** £1.30-£5.
Set buffet (noon-6pm Mon-Sun) 89p/kilo.
Restaurant **Meals served** 5.30-11pm daily.
Main courses £4.75-£11.50. **Tapas** £3.50-£4.50.
Bar & Restaurant **Music** *Dance classes* 7-9pm
daily. **Admission** £4 after 9pm Mon-Thur; £2
after 7pm, £4 after 8pm, £8 after 9pm, £10 after
11pm Fri, Sat; £3 after 7pm, £4 after 8pm Sun.
All **Credit** AmEx, MC, V.
For 2004's tenth anniversary celebrations, Salsa!
got a new café and dancefloor. Classes are held in
the bar, followed by DJs, so you can carry on
practising your moves into the night. Latin
American fare (fajitas, enchiladas, nachos) and a
substantial cocktail list add to the spirit of the
place. During the week the Brazil café offers a
South American buffet, charged by weight.
*Booking advisable. Dress: no sportswear or
trainers. Entertainment: DJs 9.30pm daily; dance
classes 7pm Mon, Wed-Sun; bands 9.30pm Tue,
Thur-Sat. Tables outdoors (10, pavement).
Takeaway service (café).* **Map 17 K6.**

Music & dancing
Costa Dorada
*47-55 Hanway Street, W1T 1UK (7636 7139).
Tottenham Court Road tube.*
Restaurant **Dinner served** 7pm-2.30am Mon-
Sat. **Main courses** £8.75-£18.50.
Tapas bar **Open** 6pm-3am Mon-Sat. **Tapas**
£3-£12.50.
Both **Service** 10%. **Credit** AmEx, DC, MC, V.
With its twice nightly flamenco shows (Thursday
through Saturday), cheerful decor and a late-night
licence, an evening at Costa Dorada can be a fun
night out. The place was beginning to look a bit
tired; a takeover and makeover in autumn 2005
means a fresh look and more emphasis placed on
the cocktail bar. Food remains Spanish.
*Booking advisable Fri, Sat. Entertainment:
DJ 8.30pm Tue-Sat; flamenco shows 9.30pm,
11.30pm Thur; 10pm, 12.30am Fri, Sat.*
Map 17 K6.

Roadhouse
*35 The Piazza, WC2E 8BE (7240 6001/
www.roadhouse.co.uk). Covent Garden tube.*
Open 5.30pm-3am Mon-Sat; 3pm-3am last Sun
of mth. **Meals served** 5.30pm-1.30am Mon-Sat.
Main courses £6.50-£13.90. **Admission** £3
after 10.30pm Mon-Wed; £5 after 10pm Thur; £5
after 9pm, £10 after 10pm Fri; £10 after 9pm Sat;
£5 after 7pm Sun. **Service** 12.5%. **Credit**
AmEx, MC, V.
Roadhouse's Covent Garden location makes it a
prime target for beery lads and riotous hen bashes,
with the attractions of happy-hour cocktails,
nightly DJs and rock/pop cover bands playing
party favourites. There's also an open mic session
on Mondays. To eat, there are grills, barbecue
chicken wings, wraps and burgers, plus calorific
desserts like banoffi pie.
*Booking advisable. Dress: smart casual.
Entertainment: bands/DJ 10.30pm Mon-Sat;
cocktail flair competition 3pm last Sun of mth.*
Map 18 L7.

One-offs
Drag artistes perform on Thursdays at
international restaurant **Globe** (*see p165*).

Elvis Gracelands Palace
*881-883 Old Kent Road, SE15 1NL (7639 3961/
www.gracelandspalace.com). New Cross Gate tube.*
Open 6pm-midnight Mon-Thur, Sun; noon-3pm,
6pm-midnight Fri, Sat. **Shows** 10pm-late daily;
also by arrangement. **Set meal** £16.50-£19;
£15 vegetarian. **Service** 10%. **Credit** AmEx,
DC, MC, V.
The Chinese food served here includes the likes of
crispy aromatic duck as well as a decent vegetarian
selection. The main attraction to the restaurant
though is Paul 'Elvis' Chan and his well-rehearsed
tribute act. The relaxed mood, friendly staff and
catchy tunes will soon have you singing along too.
*Babies and children welcome (lunch): high chairs.
Booking advisable. Entertainment: Elvis
impersonator 10pm daily. No-smoking tables.
Vegetarian menu.*

La Pergola
*66 Streatham High Road, SW16 1DA (8769
2646/www.lapergola.co.uk). Streatham Hill rail/
109, 159 bus.* **Lunch served** noon-3pm Mon-Sat.
Dinner served 6-11pm Tue, Wed; 6pm-2am
Thur-Sat. **Shows** 9pm-1am Fri, Sat; also by
arrangement. **Set dinner** (Fri) £20 3 courses;
(Sat) £22 3 courses. **Service** 10%. **Credit** AmEx,
MC, V.
Every weekend, La Pergola welcomes Streatham
locals for a night of eating, drinking and spirited
entertainment, care of resident Elvis impersonator
Kim Bridges. A three-course dinner is included in
the price; most customers arrive early, eat up and
then get down to the serious business of singing
and hip swivelling.
*Babies and children welcome: high chairs.
Booking advisable. Entertainment: DJs/Elvis
impersonator 9pm Fri, Sat. No-smoking tables.
Restaurant available for hire.*

DRINKING

Just Around the Corner

446 Finchley Road, NW2 2HY (7431 3300).
Finchley Road or Golders Green tube.
Open/meals served 6pm-midnight Mon-Sat;
noon-midnight Sun. **Credit** AmEx, MC, V.
An unusual concept, maybe, but this restaurant's
'pay what you like' policy seems be to be a winning
formula. Lamb wellington and duck à l'orange are
typical of the main courses offered.
Babies and children welcome: high chairs.
Booking advisable. Disabled: toilet. No-smoking
tables. Separate room for parties, seats 40.

Rainforest Café

20 Shaftesbury Avenue, W1D 7EU (7434 3111/
www.therainforestcafe.co.uk). Leicester Square or
Piccadilly Circus tube. **Meals served** noon-10pm
Mon-Thur, Sun; noon-7.30pm Fri, Sat. **Main**
courses £10.25-£16. **Service** 12.5% for parties
of 6 or more. **Credit** AmEx, DC, MC, V.
Designed with kids in mind, this full-on restaurant
has animatronic apes and elephants, cascading
waterfalls and thunderstorm sound effects. Most
of the menu is aimed at younger tastes, but
alongside burgers and fries you'll find such dishes
as spaghetti with sun-ripened tomatoes and herbs;
food intolerances are also considered.
Babies and children welcome: bottle-warmers;
children's menu; crayons; high chairs; nappy-
changing facilities. No smoking. Separate rooms
for parties, seating 11-100. **Map 17 K7**.

Sound

Swiss Centre, Leicester Square, W1D 6QF
(7287 1010/www.soundlondon.com). Leicester
Square tube.
Café **Open** 10am-2am Mon-Sat; 10am-1am Sun.
Meals served noon-1am Mon-Sat; 10am-
midnight Sun. **Set lunch** £10.50 2 courses,
£13.50 3 courses.
Bar & restaurant **Open** 5pm-3am Mon-Sat;
5pm-2am Sun. **Set menu** £18.50 2 courses,
£22.50 3 courses. **Admission** £10 after 9pm,
£12 after 11pm Fri; £10 after 9pm, £15 after
11pm Sat. **Service** 12.5%.
All **Main courses** £4.50-£7.80. **Credit** AmEx,
MC, V.
Sound is the perfect stomping ground for herds of
girls and boys looking for cocktails, a touch of
West End decadence (the blue room is a haven of
velvet and diamante) and DJs. The upstairs café
serves pizza, pasta and burgers, while the restaurant
offers a grill menu, steaks and seafood.
Booking advisable. Disabled: toilet. Dress: smart
casual. Entertainment: DJs 9pm daily. Separate
rooms for parties, holding 40, 80 and 150.
Tables outdoors (6, pavement). **Map 17 K7**.

The Spitz

109 Commercial Street, E1 6BG (7392 9032/
www.spitz.co.uk). Aldgate East tube/Liverpool
Street tube/rail. **Open** *Bar/Bistro* 10am-midnight
daily. *Gallery* noon-7pm Mon-Fri; noon-5pm Sat;
11am-5pm Sun. **Meals served** 10am-10.30pm
Mon-Sat; 10am-9pm Sun. **Main courses** £7-
£14.95. **Credit** MC, V.
The Spitz has the perfect combination of a chilled
bar/bistro serving a decent international menu,
and an equally diverse music programme covering
all genres in the venue upstairs. The bar area has
a pleasant terrace overlooking the market. The
bistro menu offers wild mushroom ravioli, moules
marinère, sausage and mash, and various salads.
Check the website for listings, including photo
exhibitions at the Spitz gallery.
Babies and children welcome (bistro): high
chairs. Booking advisable Fri, Sat; bookings
not accepted lunch Sun. Disabled: toilet.
Entertainment: harpist 8pm Mon (bistro); jazz
8pm Tue, Fri (bistro); blues 8pm Sat (bistro);
bands 7pm daily (venue). Gallery and venue
available for hire. Tables outdoors (12, terrace).
Vegetarian menu.
Map 12 R5.

Twelfth House

35 Pembridge Road, W11 3HG (7727 9620/
www.twelfth-house.co.uk). Notting Hill Gate tube.
Bar **Open/snacks served** noon-11pm Mon-Fri;
10am-11pm Sat; 10am-10.30pm Sun.
Restaurant **Meals served** noon-10pm Mon-Fri;

10am-10pm Sat, Sun. **Main courses** £10-£15.
Service 12.5%.
Both **Credit** MC, V.
This mystical and magical-themed café/restaurant
offers astrological chart sessions with owner
Priscilla for £30. You can also just have your basic
chart printed for £5, or select a 'tarot card of the
day' for £3. The restaurant upstairs serves an
international mix of ribeyes, smoked haddock,
salmon teriyaki and meze platters.
Babies and children admitted (restaurant).
Booking advisable. Restaurant available for hire,
seats 25. **Map 7 A7**.

Opera

Mamma Amalfi's

45 The Mall, W5 3TJ (8840 5888). Ealing
Broadway tube/rail. **Meals served** 11.30am-
11pm Mon-Thur; 11.30am-11.30pm Fri, Sat;
noon-10.30pm Sun. **Main courses** £4.95-£12.95.
Service 12.5%. **Credit** AmEx, MC, V.
Drink or dine at this family-friendly trattoria on
Thursdays or Sundays around 8.30pm and you can
enjoy a free operatic performance. The traditional
Italian menu includes thin-crust pizzas from a
wood-fired oven, pastas and salads. The Croydon
branch offers operatic recitals on Friday evenings.
Babies and children welcome: children's menu;
high chairs. Entertainment: opera 8.30pm
Thur, Sun. No-smoking tables. Tables outdoors
(8, pavement). Takeaway service.
For branches (Amalfi's, Mamma Amalfi's)
see index.

Sarastro

126 Drury Lane, WC2B 5QG (7836 0101/
www.sarastro-restaurant.com). Covent Garden or
Holborn tube. **Meals served** noon-11.30pm daily.
Main courses £8.50-£17.50. **Set lunch** (noon-
6pm Mon-Fri) £12.50 2 courses. **Set dinner**
(from 6pm Tue-Sat) £23.50 3 courses incl coffee.
Service 12.5%. **Credit** AmEx, DC, MC, V.
Individually styled opera boxes line the sides of
this flamboyantly designed restaurant; velvet
drapes, statues and knick-knacks provide the
finishing touch. All this provides the backdrop for
opera-based entertainment performed by singers
from the nearby opera houses. The cuisine is
Turkish/Mediterranean fare. Sister establishment
Papageno is similarly colourful.
Babies and children welcome: high chairs.
Booking advisable. Disabled: toilet. Entertainment:
opera 1.30pm, 8.30pm Sun; 8.30pm Mon.
No-smoking tables. **Map 18 M6**.
For branch (Papageno) see index.

Sports bars

American barbecue restaurant **Bodean's**
(*see p37*) has become the venue of choice
for expat Yanks catching up on baseball,
hockey and American football. The TV
screens are constantly tuned to NASN, the
North American Sports Network.

Elbow Room

89-91 Chapel Market, N1 9EX (7278 3244/
www.theelbowroom.co.uk). Angel tube. **Open**
5pm-2am Mon; noon-2am Tue-Thur; noon-3am
Fri, Sat; noon-midnight Sun. **Meals served**
5-11pm Mon; noon-11pm Tue-Sun. **Main courses**
£5-£8. **Admission** £5 after 8pm Thur; £2
9-10pm, £5 after 10pm Fri, Sat. **Credit** MC, V.
A popular pool bar and lounge with six sport
screens and a late-night DJ. There are burgers and
sandwiches to nibble on while shooting a few balls
or watching from the curved leather booths. Friday
and Saturday nights get extremely busy.
Disabled: toilet. Entertainment: DJs 9pm Wed-Sat;
bands 9pm Thur, Sun. Separate room for parties,
seats 30. **Map 5 N2**.
For branches see index.

Sports Café

80 Haymarket, SW1Y 4TE (7839 8300/
www.thesportscafe.com). Piccadilly Circus tube/
Charing Cross tube/rail. **Open** noon-3am Mon,
Tue, Sat; noon-2am Wed, Thur; noon-12.30am
Sun. **Meals served** noon-midnight daily.

Main courses £8.45-£15.95. **Admission** £5
after 11pm Mon, Tue, Fri, Sat; £3 after 11pm
Wed, Thur. **Credit** AmEx, DC, JCB, MC, V.
More than 100 TV screens at this US-styled bar
present a string of competitive activities, from
football and rugby league to Formula One and
tennis. During big matches or tournaments it can
get uncomfortably busy and loud. Escape comes
in the shape of dining areas, where buffalo wings,
ribs, steaks and burgers are the backbone of the
menu. After 10pm most days, DJs appear and the
dancefloor becomes the focus of attention.
Children admitted (until 6pm, dining only).
Entertainment: DJs 10pm Mon, Tue, Fri, Sat.
Restaurant available for hire. Takeaway service.
Map 17 K7.

24-hour eats

Tinseltown

44-46 St John Street, EC1M 4DT (7689 2424/
www.tinseltown.co.uk). Farringdon tube/rail.
Open 24hrs daily. **Main courses** £3.50-£27.50.
Set lunch £5 2 courses incl soft drink. **Credit**
AmEx, DC, MC, V.
Late-night clubbers in need of refuelling, cabbies
and general stop-outs frequent this US-styled
basement diner. Booth seating, music-TV and
milkshakes with intriguing flavours (Oreo biscuit,
Maltesers or pear) should help to keep you going.
Babies and children welcome: children's menu;
high chair. Takeaway service. **Map 5 O5**.

Vingt-Quatre

325 Fulham Road, SW10 9QL (7376 7224).
South Kensington tube. **Meals served** 24hrs
daily. **Main courses** £5.75-£14. **Service** 12.5%.
Credit AmEx, MC, V.
V-Q is licensed until midnight, and as befitting its
Chelsea location, offers a classy alternative to more
typical 24-hour joints. Here you'll find King's Road
clubbers filling up on double eggs benedict at 3am.
There are salads and steaks, all-day (and all-night)
brunches, club sandwiches piled high with french
fries, and fish and chips.
Map 14 D12.

Views & victuals

The Tenth

Royal Garden Hotel, 2-24 Kensington High Street,
W8 4PT (7361 1910/www.royalgardenhotel.co.uk).
High Street Kensington tube. **Lunch served**
noon-2.30pm Mon-Fri. **Dinner served** 5.30-
10.45pm Mon-Sat. **Main courses** £15-£42.
Credit AmEx, DC, MC, V.
For stunning views over Hyde Park, the Tenth is
ideal – but at a price. The last Saturday of the
month is Manhattan Night, when Gary Williams
Orchestra evokes the glitz and glamour of the New
York dinner-dance scene, playing 1950s big band
classics (the evening costs £60 per person). The
everyday carte includes dishes such as lobster
cannelloni with champagne and vanilla sauce.
Babies and children welcome: high chairs.
Disabled: lift; toilet. Dress: smart casual.
Entertainment: pianist 8.30pm Sat. No-smoking
tables. **Map 7 B8**.

Vertigo 42

Tower 42, 25 Old Broad Street, EC2N 1PB
(7877 7842/www.vertigo42.co.uk). Bank tube/
DLR/Liverpool Street tube/rail. **Open** noon-3pm,
5-11pm Mon-Fri. **Lunch served** noon-3pm,
dinner served 5-9.30pm Mon-Fri. **Set lunch**
(noon-3pm Mon-Fri) £15 3 courses. **Main**
courses £9.80-£28. **Service** 12.5%. **Credit**
AmEx, DC, JCB, MC, V.
Situated on the 42nd floor, this bar has a truly
stunning panorama; the seating lines the windows,
so everyone gets a view. The interior has the feel
of an upmarket airport lounge. Some 18 floors
down, Gary Rhodes' restaurant, Rhodes Twenty
Four (*see p54*), serves classic British fare. Security
arrangements mean that prior booking is essential
for both bar and restaurant; diners must obtain a
pass and walk through an X-ray machine. And the
last admission time – 9.45pm – is strictly followed.
Bar available for hire. Booking essential. Dress:
smart casual. No cigars or pipes. **Map 12 Q6**.

Shops & Courses

TABLE (AS BEFORE)
OTHER ITEMS FROM THE WOLSELEY
(020 7499 6996, WWW.THEWOLSELEY.COM)

Food Shops

When you're eating out in London, you can't help stumbling across a world of new regional cuisines. The capital's multicultural population ensures your culinary adventure can continue when you eat at home: food ranges from top-quality British cheeses (**Neal's Yard Dairy**) through Japanese sweets (**Minamoto Kitchoan**) to African and Caribbean staples at **Brixton Market**. **Borough Market** remains a favourite weekend jaunt for London's gourmets, but the capital is well served throughout with farmers' markets. And, given our continuing love affair with the curry, it's no surprise that London's range of Indian food shops is unparalleled beyond the subcontinent.

Lack of space has prevented us giving any more than a taste of what's available. You'll find more comprehensive listings in the latest *Time Out Shopping Guide*.

Food halls

Fortnum & Mason
181 Piccadilly, W1A 1ER (7734 8040/ www.fortnumandmason.co.uk). Green Park or Piccadilly Circus tube. **Open** 10am-6.30pm Mon-Sat; noon-6pm Sun. **Credit** AmEx, DC, JCB, MC, V.
A decline in company fortunes has recently led F&M to make their popular food hall a focus of their business: there are ambitious plans to expand the entire food range over the next few years. Justly famous for its teas (such as rose pouching, Russian caravan), Fortnum & Mason also sells excellent biscuits (like Lancashire flips) and condiments (picnic pickle, say, or Polish silver fir honey). There are fabulous meat, fish and cheese counters (also offering fresh sevruga and beluga caviars), and confectionery, oils, vinegars and seasonal fruit and vegetables. Shopping in these lavish surroundings remains a quintessentially English experience.

Harrods
87-135 Brompton Road, SW1X 7XL (7730 1234/www.harrods.com). Knightsbridge tube. **Open** 10am-7pm Mon-Sat; noon-6pm Sun. **Credit** AmEx, DC, MC, V.
Harrods has one of London's most famous, beautiful and spacious food halls. This sumptuous venue, with painted tiles and tall columns, incorporates meat, cheese and fish counters, a bakery, a sushi bar, an oyster bar, an ice-cream parlour (where you can place an order for bespoke ice-cream) and a Krispy Kreme doughnut outlet. Also on offer are coffees (try Colombian San Augustin coffee beans), condiments (like pickled quail's eggs), the Green Cuisine range of herbs and spices, biscuits, cakes, chocolates and a full range of wines, spirits and Champagnes. Food orders (including the famous hampers) are particularly popular with British expats.

Harvey Nichols
109-125 Knightsbridge, SW1X 7RJ (7235 5000/ www.harveynichols.com). Knightsbridge tube. **Open** 10am-8pm Mon-Fri; 10am-7pm Sat; noon-6pm Sun. **Credit** AmEx, DC, MC, V.
The stylish, modern design of this bijou food market incorporates a lovely wine shop. Also on sale are biscuits (including a delectable blueberry variety); oils, vinegars and dressings (try the wasabi and ginger dressing); confectionery (the espresso chocolate bar is irresistible); teas and coffees; condiments and fresh fruit and veg. There are particularly good ranges of Italian ingredients and American products. Butchers, bakers, greengrocers, fishmongers and cheesemongers are on hand to give specialist advice. Packaging is trendily monochrome. Specialist events such as tastings and cookery book launches also occur.

Selfridges
400 Oxford Street, W1A 1AB (0870 837 7377/ www.selfridges.com). Bond Street or Marble Arch tube. **Open** 10am-8pm Mon-Fri; 9.30am-8pm Sat; noon-6pm Sun. **Credit** AmEx, DC, MC, V.
Offering an outstanding selection of global ingredients, this popular food hall also sells ready-prepared dishes at its numerous international food counters (Lebanese, Indian, Japanese, Moroccan and kosher). Other sections offer fresh and cooked meat, fish, cheese, freshly baked pretzels, pies from the Square Pie Company, and caviar from Caviar Kaspia. There's a wonderful bakery, a fresh juice counter and a notable selection of unusual fruits and vegetables (including organic varieties). Our favourites are fresh, handmade Machiavelli pasta from Italy and the Oddono's Italian ice-cream parlour (the hazelnut, green apple, and ginger and fig ice-cream flavours are to die for). Look out for demonstrations, tastings, food and wine events, and food-themed festivals.

Markets

Borough Market
Between Borough High Street, Bedale Street, Stoney Street & Winchester Walk, SE1 1TL (www.boroughmarket.org.uk). London Bridge tube/rail. **Open** noon-6pm Fri; 9am-4pm Sat. **No credit cards.**
Borough Market could be taken as an index of the importance food – both the eating and the buying of it – has taken as a leisure activity. Regularly polling well as a favourite day out (*see p8* **SE Wonderful**), it brings together an exciting mix of food from all over the world. Many stalls offer tasters and quality is high – although prices are too. If you can't make it here in person, you can always order from Food Ferry (*see p347*).

Farmers' markets

Shopping at farmers' markets enables you to discover the joys of seasonal produce while supporting the south-east's farmers. All produce at London's accredited farmers' markets comes from within 100 miles of the M25, bringing the industry a welcome £3 million a year. For further information, get in touch with the **National Association of Farmers Markets** (0845 458 8420, www.farmersmarkets.net), the umbrella outfit for farmers' markets across the country. **London Farmers Markets** (7704 9659, www.lfm.org.uk) covers all the true farmers' markets in the capital – each one independently certified by FARMA – except those in Barnes and Richmond. Beware the handful of places labelling themselves 'farmers' markets' that are nothing of the sort.

Wednesday market
Finchley Road O_2 Centre car park, Finchley Road, NW3.

Thursday market
Paddington Central Sheldon Square, W2.

Saturday markets
Barnes Essex House, Station Road, SW13; **Ealing** Leeland Road, W13; **Notting Hill** car park on the corner of Kensington Church Street, W8; **Pimlico** Orange Square, SW1; **Richmond** Heron Square, off Hill Street; **Stoke Newington** William Patten School, Stoke Newington Church Street, N16; **Twickenham** Holly Road car park, off King Street, TW1; **Wimbledon Park** Wimbledon Park First School, Havana Road, SW19.

Sunday markets
Blackheath Blackheath railway station car park, SE3; **Islington** Essex Road, N1; **Marylebone** Cramer Street car park, W1; **Peckham** Peckham Square, SE15; **Pinner** Queen's Head pub, Pinner High Street, HA5; **Queen's Park** Salusbury Road, NW6.

Bakeries & pâtisseries

Many places listed in the **Cafés** chapter (starting on p298) specialise in posh pâtisserie, while British restaurant **St John** (*see p55*) has a fabulous bakery created with the input of master baker Dan Lepard.

& Clarke's
122 Kensington Church Street, W8 4BU (7229 2190/www.sallyclarke.com). Notting Hill Gate tube. **Open** 8am-8pm Mon-Fri; 8am-4pm Sat. **Credit** AmEx, MC, V.
Located next to her acclaimed restaurant (*see p229*), Sally Clarke's bakery sells a vast range of freshly baked breads, pastries and cakes, many of which are supplied to restaurants and delis. The range encompasses fig and fennel, and rosemary and raisin breads, jewel-like redcurrant and nectarine tarts, and citrus peel and almond croissants made with unsalted Normandy butter. The shop also sells over 40 British and Irish cheeses from Neal's Yard (*see p347*), coffee from Monmouth Coffee House (*see p358*), fresh soups, condiments, olive oils and chocolates. The seasonal fruits, vegetables, herbs and salad leaves include New Forest wild mushrooms, new season Egyptian garlic and pumpkins from Sunnyfields Organic Farm.

De Gustibus   NEW
53 Blandford Street, W1U 7HL (7486 6608). Baker Street tube. **Open** 7am-4pm Mon-Fri. **No credit cards.**
This multiple-award-winning company started life as a home-baking business before becoming one of the most acclaimed artisan bakers in Britain. Set up by Dan and Annette de Gustibus in Oxfordshire in 1990, it now supplies restaurants and offers day courses in bread-making. The bread range changes regularly, but usually incorporates American varieties (old milwaukee rye, chestnut wholemeal, honey and lavender, and the famous boston brown – the original bread used in baked beans on toast) and British (spelt, cotswold cobbler). Other varieties include continental (Portuguese cornbread, Swiss cantonese), Mediterranean (porcini, sage and bay) and East European (potato and courgette, cossack sour). All breads are made with natural ingredients, including naturally occurring yeasts.

Borough Market

Lighthouse Bakery

64 Northcote Road, SW11 6QL (7228 4537/ www.lighthousebakery.co.uk). Clapham Junction rail. **Open** 8.30am-5pm Tue-Sat. **Credit** MC, V.
Owned by Rachel Duffield (front of house) and Elizabeth Weisberg (one of the few female commercial bakers), this small artisan bakery sells American, British and continental breads, cakes and pastries. The range encompasses speciality breads (gloucester rye, dark salt-free tuscan), traditional English wheat breads (coburg), wholemeal and malted (geordie brown), seasonal varieties (hot cross buns) and pastries (gingerbread critters, chinois). Breads are baked on the premises in small batches, using Shipton Mill flour. Each loaf is hand-moulded, and long fermentation methods are used, resulting in a fuller flavour. The shop also stocks a good selection of American treats (like blueberry cobbler), plus bread crocks and bespoke hand tools for bakers.

Poilâne

46 Elizabeth Street, SW1W 9PA (7808 4910/ www.poilane.fr). Sloane Square tube/Victoria tube/rail. **Open** 7.30am-7.30pm Mon-Fri; 7.30am-6pm Sat. **Credit** MC, V.
This popular company's sourdoughs are some of the most famous breads in the world – they're

ubiquitous in delis and restaurants, as well as at upscale dinner parties. The bread is made using a modernised version of an ancestral recipe. Pesticide-free wheat and spelt flour is mixed with salt from the salt marshes of Guérande in western France, which is scented with seaside violets; after fermentation, the loaves are baked in wood-fired ovens for an hour. Other than sourdough, the bakery produces such varieties as rye and walnut, currant and raisin, mixed nut, and milk bread.

Cheese

Not just an exemplary café, **La Fromagerie** (*see p298*) is a superlative cheese shop, selling more than 100 French, Spanish, Italian and British varieties.

The Cheeseboard NEW

26 Royal Hill, SE10 8RT (8305 0401/ www.cheese-board.co.uk). Greenwich rail/DLR. **Open** 9am-5pm Mon, Wed, Sat; 9am-4.30pm Tue; 9am-1pm Thur; 9am-5.30pm Fri. **Credit** AmEx, MC, V.
Owned by the British Cheese Board – whose aim is to encourage the use of British cheeses and promote their health benefits – this shop sells over 400 varieties of English (as well as French

and Italian) cheese. The range includes popular varieties like sage derby, dovedale, buxton blue, and cornish yarg. Breads, wine and relishes to go with your cheese are also available, and there are educational material for parents and teachers.

Cheeses NEW

13 Fortis Green Road, N10 3HP (8444 9141). East Finchley tube. **Open** 9.30am-5.30pm Tue-Fri; 9.30am-6pm Sat. **Credit** MC, V.
Vanessa Wiley's tiny shop is packed with mainly British and French cheeses, plus a few Italian, Spanish and Dutch varieties. The selection includes manchego, emmenthal, aged gouda and somerset goat's cheese. Also on offer are olives, meats, relishes and organic bread (on Saturdays). Cheeseboards and knives are sold too.

Hamish Johnston

48 Northcote Road, SW11 1PA (7738 0741). Clapham Junction rail. **Open** 9am-6pm Mon-Sat. **Credit** MC, V.
There is a huge selection of goat's and sheep's milk cheeses at this friendly cheesemonger's, which stocks approximately 150 cheeses. Most are British or French, but there are some Spanish and Italian varieties too. You'll also find terrines, preserves, oils and vinegars.

Neal's Yard Dairy

17 Shorts Gardens, WC2H 9UP (7240 5700). Covent Garden tube. **Open** 11am-6.30pm Mon-Thur; 10am-6.30pm Fri, Sat. **Credit** MC, V.
Dozens of restaurants and delis in London offer Neal's Yard cheeses, which are, quite simply, shorthand for quality. They're sourced from artisan producers in Britain and Ireland and matured in the company's own cellars. The range includes coolea, berkswell, extra-mature stilton, goat's cheeses and wash-rind cheeses – depending on season. Staff are exceptionally knowledgeable, and encourage you to taste before buying. Related items – breads and relishes, for example – are also on sale here.

Paxton & Whitfield

93 Jermyn Street, SW1Y 6JE (7930 0259/ www.paxtonandwhitfield.co.uk). Green Park tube. **Open** 9.30am-6pm Mon-Sat. **Credit** MC, V.
Set up in 1797, Britain's oldest cheesemonger has been endorsed by everyone from the royal family and Winston Churchill to Sophie Grigson and Nigella Lawson. Artisan cheeses are sourced from the UK, France and Italy, and allowed to mature. Varieties include British (shires farmhouse), soft (cornish capra) and blue (caradon blue). Biscuits, cakes, relishes, preserves, pâtés, terrines, wines and ales are also available; as are cheese knives, cheeseboards and tableware. There is a monthly cheese club for those who want cheeses delivered to their home in peak condition. The friendly staff's knowledge of their subject is second to none.

Rippon Cheese Stores

26 Upper Tachbrook Street, SW1V 1SW (7931 0628). Pimlico tube/Victoria tube/rail. **Open** 8am-5.15pm Mon-Sat. **Credit** MC, V.
Around 550 varieties of mainly British and French cheeses are stocked here, including epoisses, roquefort, bleu de cours, beaufort, wensleydale,

comte and stilton. Look for regional and seasonal specialities, such as assorted goat's cheeses, stinking bishop and vacherin.

Confectioners
Chocolates

L'Artisan du Chocolat

89 Lower Sloane Street, SW1W 8DA (7824 8365/ www.artisanduchocolat.com). Sloane Square tube. **Open** 10am-7pm Mon-Sat. **Credit** MC, V.
This glass-fronted shop with enticing chocolate sculptures is a small-scale, London-based business, set up by Belgium-trained ex-pastry chef Gerard Coleman. He makes small quantities of very fresh chocolates (to be eaten within two weeks), using natural ingredients, judicious quantities of sugar and a variety of ganache. They are acclaimed by food writers and triple-Michelin-starred chefs, with flavours that are imaginative and original, including green cardamom, lemon verbena, lapsang souchong, basil and lime, Moroccan mint, Sichuan pepper, banana and thyme, lavender bud, red wine and tobacco. The salt caramels are delectable. Chocolate-tasting evenings are also held.

La Maison du Chocolat

45-46 Piccadilly, W1J 0DS (7287 8500/ www.lamaisonduchocolat.co.uk). Piccadilly Circus tube. **Open** 10am-7pm Mon-Sat. **Credit** AmEx, MC, V.
Legendary Parisian chocolatier Robert Linx's sophisticated handmade chocolates are available in two London stores – here and at Harrods. The Piccadilly shop is handsome and spacious, with black-suited staff on hand to ease you around Linx's trademark assorted ganache (Spanish lemon or fresh mint), pralines and champagne truffles. No preservatives are used, so the ganache's shelf-life is just four weeks. Other treats include

jewel-like pâtisserie, candied peel and classic French fruit jellies. Expect elegant packaging and formidable prices (£32 for 400g).

Pierre Marcolini

6 Lancer Square, W8 4EH (7795 6611/ www.pierremarcolini.co.uk). High Street Kensington tube. **Open** 10am-7pm Mon-Sat. **Credit** AmEx, MC, V.
This glamorous chocolate boutique, with smart wooden floors and judiciously placed spotlights, displays chocolates like precious jewellery on hand-crafted wooden counters. Pierre Marcolini is one of only four master chocolatiers in Europe. He sources natural ingredients from around the world, and selects his own chocolate beans. Fabergé-like sculptured eggs at Easter, pretty 'handbags' of chocolates inspired by couture collections, jasmine tea ganache and raspberry hearts are packaged in stylish designer boxes. The on-site café serves hot chocolate, coffee and pastries. There's a service offering personalised chocolates, chocolate fountains are available for hire, and chocolate-tasting evenings are held.

Rococo

321 King's Road, SW3 5EP (7352 5857/ www.rococochocolates.com). Sloane Square tube then 11, 19, 22 bus. **Open** 10am-6.30pm Mon-Sat; noon-5pm Sun. **Credit** MC, V.
Chantal Coady co-founded the Chocolate Society (36 Elizabeth Street, 7259 9222, www.chocolate.co.uk) to promote the consumption and enjoyment of chocolate. Founding this beautiful shop was another step in the same direction. Rococo offers fruit and flower fondants, caramels and gingers. Chilli- and passion-fruit-flavoured chocolates are great for adventurous palates, as are saffron and ginger fudge or truffles filled with Islay single malt whisky. Chocolate bars come in flavours like orange and geranium, rosemary, lavender, and Arabic spices. Cuban chocolate cigars and cinnamon granduja almonds are other popular choices; sugar-free, dairy-free and organic varieties are also sold.

International

For Indian dainties, *see p156* **Sweets menu**.

Minamoto Kitchoan NEW

44 Piccadilly , W1J 0DS (7437 3135/ www.kitchoan.com). Piccadilly Circus tube. **Open** 10am-7pm Mon-Fri, Sun; 10am-8pm Sat. **Credit** AmEx, MC, V.
Specialising in wagashi (traditional Japanese confectionery made from rice flour, aduki bean paste and seasonal fruit and nuts), this beguiling confectioner has branches in many major cities. Choose from saisaika (Japanese loquat marzipan), tousenka (white peach stuffed with baby green peach, covered in jelly), oribenishiki (pastry stuffed with red bean and chestnuts), kohakukanume (whole plum encased in plum wine jelly, decorated with gold powder), and honey and green tea sponge cakes.

Reza Pâtisseries NEW

345 Kensington High Street, W8 6NW (7603 0924). High Street Kensington tube. **Open** 9am-10pm daily. **Credit** MC, V.
We can't understand why this aromatic shop isn't better known: the quality and variety of freshly made Iranian sweets, pastries and confectionary is astonishing. Flours, doughs and filo pastry sheets are pummelled into shapes, dipped in flower waters and honeys, flavoured with saffron, fresh fruit and nuts, and topped with edible gold and silver leaf. The result resembles a cross between Indian and Mediterranean flavours. There's also a small selection of groceries, fresh fruit and veg.

Delicatessens

The following restaurants, reviewed in full elsewhere in the guide, all have great delis attached: **Flâneur Food Hall** (*see p48*), **Villandry** (*see p225*), **Ottolenghi** (*see p165*) and **Le Pont de la Tour** (*see p236*).

Home delivery

The boom in supermarket online shopping means that the weekly trudge down the aisles is no longer a necessity. Supermarkets offering online shopping include **Sainsbury's** (www.sainsburys.com), **Tesco** (www.tesco.com) and **Waitrose** (www.ocado.com). For organic box schemes and gastronomic treats delivered to your door, try the outfits below.

Abel & Cole

8-15 MGI Estate, Milkwood Road, SE24 0JF (7737 3648/www.abel-cole.co.uk). **Open** phone enquiries 9am-7pm Mon-Thur; 9am-6pm Fri. **Credit** MC, V.
From succulent lamb and rosemary sausages to biodynamic pasta and Ecover cleaning products, this environmentally conscious and ethically minded enterprise delivers Soil Association-certified organic fruit and vegetables, meat, fish and dairy goods right to your door.

Food Ferry Co

Units B24-27, New Covent Garden Market, 9 Elms Lane, SW8 5HH (7498 0827/www.foodferry.com). **Open** phone enquiries 8am-6pm Mon-Fri. **Credit** AmEx, MC, V.
This long-established, award-winning outfit, based at New Covent Garden Market, delivers an impressive range of foodstuffs. Having merged recently with Swaddles Organic Farms, it now deals in a full range of organic produce,

including ready meals and wines, as well as bakery-fresh breads, larder essentials and luxurious hampers.

Forman & Field

30A Marshgate Lane, E15 2NH (8221 3939/www.formanandfield.com). **Open** phone enquiries 9am-5pm Mon-Fri. **Credit** MC, V.
Britain's oldest salmon smokers (celebrating their centenary in 2005), Forman & Field supply to top hotels and restaurants around the world, including the Savoy Grill and Nobu. The company also offers a variety of upmarket foodstuffs, from traditional condiments and preserves to rare-breed sausages, game and suckling pigs. Unfortunately, as its factory site has been chosen as the location of the Olympic Stadium, its future is under threat.

Fresh Food Co

The Orchard, 50 Wormholt Road, W12 0LS (8749 8778/www.freshfood.co.uk). **Open** phone enquiries 24hrs daily. **Credit** AmEx, MC, V.
This company lays claim to being Britain's first online organic food retailer, supplying fresh produce direct to customers' doors since 1989. Boxes, delivered weekly or fortnightly, contain fruit, vegetables, herbs and salad ingredients; you can also order meat, farmed or wild fish, plus wine and beer – all of it organic.

Leila's

East Dulwich Deli

15-17 Lordship Lane, SE22 8EW (8693 2525).
East Dulwich rail. **Open** 9am-6pm Mon-Sat;
10am-4pm Sun. **Credit** MC, V.
Specialising in Italian and Spanish artisan
products, this friendly deli sells pastas, olives,
cheeses, charcuterie and cooked dishes like tarts,
pies and stuffed vegetables. There is also a
selection of Born and Bread breads, including
wholemeal, white, ciabatta, black olive and the
absolutely amazing kentish flute, which has to be
tasted to be believed.

The Grocer on Elgin NEW

6 Elgin Crescent, W11 2HX (7221 3844/
www.thegroceron.com). Ladbroke Grove or
Notting Hill Gate tube. **Open** 8am-8pm Mon-Fri;
8am-6pm Sat, Sun. **Credit** MC, V.
Owned by Vivienne Hayman and Ashley Sumner,
this spacious, trendy shrine to good food is famous
for seasonal, hand-made ready meals in distinctive
vacuum-packed pouches. Saffron and asparagus
risotto or rabbit with bayonne ham are examples
of a range of starters, mains, sides and desserts
that can be assembled to create a complete meal.
An enticing selection of groceries from around
the world is also available, among them smoked
garlic from Arleux, artisan pasta from Abruzzo,
piquillo peppers, sweet chilli sambal, sashimi
dressing, slow-roast tamarillos, and spices and
dukkahs from the Sugar Club collection. The new
branch, the Grocer on Warwick (*see p245*), is more
restaurant than deli.

Korona NEW

30 Streatham High Road, SW16 1DB (8769
6647). Streatham Hill rail. **Open** 9am-7pm
Mon-Fri; 9am-6pm Sat; 9.30am-3pm Sun.
Credit MC, V.
Groceries from around the world (France, Italy,
eastern Europe and even South Africa) are stocked
at this continental store in Streatham. Alongside
deli staples such as cheese and charcuterie, there
is a notable range of breads (from over a dozen
bakeries) and drinks.

Leila's NEW

17 Calvert Avenue, E2 7JP (7729 9789).
Liverpool Street or Old Street tube/rail/
26, 48, 55, 242 bus. **Open** 10am-6pm Thur-Sat;
10am-4pm Sun. **Credit** AmEx, MC, V.
This small shop has a lot of charm. It's run by
Leila McAlister, who stocks the place with a
selection of things she likes. Always available
are breads from St John, classy dried goods
(Southern Alps muesli), preserves and seasonal
fruit and veg. McAlister also runs Polish stall
Topolski in Borough Market (*see p344*), plus
she and her crew cater for parties, film shoots and
the like.

Melrose & Morgan NEW

42 Gloucester Avenue, NW1 85D (7722 0011/
www.melroseandmorgan.com). Chalk Farm tube.
Open 9am-8pm Tue-Sat; 10am-4pm Sun.
Opposite Primrose Hill's ever-popular gastropub,
the Engineer (*see p115*), this beautifully presented
deli champions quality produce from small British
suppliers and farmers. Standout items include
jams and jellies in nostalgic flavours like medlar
and crab apple; hand-made Madame Oiseau
chocolates from a French confectioner based in
Canterbury; organic meats; and seasonal fruit and
veg. Pâtés, fish pie and even ketchup are made on
the premises by the house chefs, and the honey is
produced on nearby Hampstead Heath.

Mise-en-Place

53 Battersea Rise, SW11 1HH (7228 4329/
www.thefoodstore.co.uk). Clapham Junction rail.
Open 8am-8pm daily. **Credit** AmEx, MC, V.
This attractive deli has a small café at the back and
outside seating in fine weather. Amazing
charcuterie, cheeses, salads, antipasti and freshly
cooked dishes are displayed at the counter, and
shelves are laden with pickles, chutneys, pasta
sauces, oils, vinegars, herbs and spices. Also on
offer is a small selection of artisan breads, and top-
notch ice-creams and frozen desserts.

Mortimer & Bennett

33 Turnham Green Terrace, W4 1RG (8995
4145/www.mortimerandbennett.com). Turnham
Green tube. **Open** 8.30am-6pm Mon-Fri; 8.30am-
5.30pm Sat. **Credit** MC, V.
One of London's most acclaimed delis, M&B
sources exclusive speciality products from small
family suppliers around the world, particularly
France. Here you'll find Lebanese fruit syrups,
mulberry or wild rose jams, verjuice (very
fashionable right now), Terre Exotique brown cane
sugar with vanilla, the award-winning Mas Pares
Spanish foie gras, barrel-aged feta, New Zealand
extra virgin olive oil, and charcuterie including
Tuscan prosciutto, and mini wild boar and venison
salamis in oil. Also on sale are Kama Sutra jam
(billed as 'the world's most expensive jam'), and
unusual fruit and flower vinegars and fruit
dressings from Womersley Foods (try the golden
raspberry dressing with geranium).

Mr Christian's

11 Elgin Crescent, W11 2JA (7229 0501/
www.mrchristians.co.uk). Ladbroke Grove tube.
Open 6am-7pm Mon-Fri; 5.30am-6.30pm Sat;
7am-5pm Sun. **Credit** AmEx, MC, V.
Now part of the Jeroboams group (*see p357*),
Mr Christian's opened a wine shop at 13 Elgin
Crescent in October 2004. Friendly, unpretentious
and well established, the original deli is still busy

with local customers taking their pick from the
huge variety of cheese (up to 120 varieties), hams,
fresh pasta, olives, own-made chutneys and
preserves. The range of up to two dozen traiteur
dishes changes daily, but might run from char-
grilled lamb kebabs to asparagus risotto. Sempre
Viva frozen yoghurt has proved a huge hit with the
calorie-conscious. On Saturdays and Sundays, a
bread stall is set up outside the shop.

North Street Deli NEW

26 North Street, SW4 0HB (7978 1555).
Clapham Common tube. **Open** 10am-6pm
Mon-Sat. **Credit** MC, V.
Co-owned by chef Maddalena Bonino and
Nathan Middlemiss, this popular deli boasts
friendly, knowledgeable staff – it won *Time Out*'s
award for Best Food Shop in 2004. It offers
top-quality charcuterie, breads from Marcus Miller,
cakes like carrot gateau and layered chocolate
fudge cake, preserves, pickles and oils. Lovely
sandwiches and snacks are available for eating in
or to take away.

Panzer's

13-19 Circus Road, NW8 6PB (7722 8596/
www.panzers.co.uk). St John's Wood tube.
Open 8am-7pm Mon-Fri; 8am-6pm Sat; 8am-2pm
Sun. **Credit** MC, V.
Established more than 50 years ago, this large,
family-run deli is chock-a-block with items from
France, Germany, Greece, Italy, Spain, South
Africa and the US. Famous for exceptional rare
fruits, herbs and vegetables, the shop also has a
good kosher range (including cakes and foie gras),
more than 50 types of bread, South African dried
fruit and nuts, a vast selection of US products
(marshmallow fluff, instant grits) and an organic
line. The counter at the back stocks charcuterie
(bresaola, biltong), cheeses (vacherin, English
varieties from Neal's Yard), freshly made salads,
olives, smoked salmon and caviar.

Rosslyn Delicatessen

56 Rosslyn Hill, NW3 1ND (7794 9210/
www.delirosslyn.co.uk). Hampstead tube.
Open 8.30am-8.30pm Mon-Sat; 8.30am-8pm Sun.
Credit AmEx, MC, V.
Owned by Helen Sherman, this deli is one of
the best-loved in London. It's crammed with
chocolates (Charbonnel & Walker, Neuhaus) and
confectionery (hand-made burnt sugar fudge);
caviar, including the cheaper trout version;
American classics (Froot Loops, Aunt Jemima
cornbread mix); biscuits; British, Irish, French,
Italian, Swiss, German, Spanish and Danish
cheeses; meats (sausages, beef, ham, salami,
rillettes, terrines); pastas and sauces; rice and
polenta; and oils and vinegars. The range of
preserves, condiments, dried herbs and spices is

particularly impressive. Other attractions include regular food tastings, picnic hampers and foodie gifts for festivals and special occasions.

Spice Shop NEW
1 Blenheim Crescent, W11 2EE (7221 4448/ www.thespiceshop.co.uk). Ladbroke Grove tube. **Open** 9.30am-6pm Mon-Sat; 11am-4pm Sun. **Credit** MC, V.
Domestic and professional cooks in the capital would be at a loss without this iconic shop. It's owned by Birgit Erath, who sources hundreds of spices and authentic spice-mixes from her travels around the world. The tiny, intensely aromatic space is packed with fresh and dried herbs and spices (from anise myrtle to zedoary medieval ginger), a large variety of dried chillies, curry blends, condiments, roots and barks, Japanese seasonings, flower waters and essential oils. No gluten, starch, nuts, salt or animal products are used in the products; neither are artificial flavours or colourings.

Verde & Co NEW
4 Brushfield Street, E1 6AG (7247 1924). Liverpool Street tube/rail. **Open** 8am-8pm Mon-Fri; 11am-5pm Sat, Sun. **Credit** MC, V.
Next door to A Gold (see p350), and in an equally lovely restored Georgian building, this exquisite shop is owned by author Jeanette Winterson (who also lives above it) and run by ex-chef Harvey Cabannis. In contrast to its neighbour's British specialism, many of the goods are Italian, supplied by importer Machiavelli, including fresh pasta flown in twice a week and charcuterie. Pierre Marcolini chocolates are arrayed like trinkets in a jewel case in a refrigerated cabinet. Fruit and veg are displayed outside with a window dresser's art, alongside a selection of orchids. As well as organic produce, you'll find such delicacies as French white peaches, courgette flowers and chanterelles from Scotland. Prices reflect the rarefied mood. Sandwiches made on the premises, cakes and good espresso-based coffees are sold to take away.

International

The bustling Thai foodshop near and run by **Talad Thai** restaurant (see p270 **Local Thais**) sells mangosteen and toddy palm seed, as well as hosting popular cookery classes; and the **Maroush** mini chain (see p213) runs a Lebanese deli. For French delicacies, trot along to **Truc Vert** (see p49); for Italian goods, visit the **Carluccio's Caffè** chain (see p168).

For **Oriental City**, a large complex in Colindale, north London, containing a huge supermarket selling mainly Japanese ingredients, plus a Japanese confectioner, Japanese bakery and a bustling pan-oriental food court, see p247 **Oriental City**. There's more information on the capital's subcontinental heartlands in the **Indian** section, starting on p131.

Arigato Japanese Supermarket
48-50 Brewer Street, W1R 3HN (7287 1722). Piccadilly Circus tube. **Open** 10am-9pm Mon-Sat; 11am-8pm Sun. **Credit** MC, V. Japanese
This bright shop is neatly stacked with Japanese and Korean staples, such as rice, noodles, sauces, kimchis, miso pastes, Hello Kitty confectionery, drinks such as Blendy and Pulpy, and snacks like rice crackers and wasabi peas. There are chiller cabinets filled with baked wheat balls with octopus or fried fish cakes with green soybean. Sushi and bento boxes are also available, and prices are surprisingly low.

Athenian Grocery
16A Moscow Road, W2 4BT (7229 6280). Bayswater tube. **Open** 8.30am-7pm Mon-Sat; 8.30am-1pm Sun. **No credit cards.** Greek
Imported fresh fruit and vegetables (including fresh nuts in season) are laid out at the entrance of this small, family-run shop. Inside you'll find a

counter stacked with cheese, meat, olives and pastries. Oils, pickles, preserves, honeys and (pre-packed) breads line the shelves.

Blue Mountain Peak NEW
2A-8 Craven Park Road, NW10 4AB (8965 3859). Willesden Junction tube. **Open** 7am-6pm Mon, Thur; 7.15am-6pm Tue, Wed; 6.30-6pm Fri, Sat. **Credit** MC, V. African & Caribbean
This large shop is packed with Jamaican and West African groceries. There's a huge variety, encompassing everything from Caribbean hardough breads to herbal tonics and roots drinks. Other items include spices, seasonings and condiments; beans and flours; dried fish; different types of rice; and tropical fruit and veg, such as African mangoes, purple 'elephant' yam, coo coo, and fresh sugarcane.

La Bodeguita NEW
Unit 256, Upper Level, Elephant & Castle Shopping Centre, SE1 6TE (7708 5826). Elephant & Castle tube/rail. **Open** 8am-8pm Mon-Sat. **Credit** MC, V. Latin American
Who would have thought that the eyesore that is Elephant & Castle shopping centre would house a charming little Colombian food shop? But London is full of such surprises. Here you'll find masa harina flour, a range of Mexican chillies, spices, cakes and drinking chocolate. Tortillas, cheese breads, chilli rellenos and other hot snacks are available to take away.

Brick Lane, E1
Aldgate East tube. Indian
Interspersed with Bangladeshi restaurants, characterful Brick Lane is strewn with small Indian groceries selling rare Bangladeshi veg, fruit and authentic Bengali sweets. The best of the bunch is the huge **Taj Stores** (No.112, E1 0RL, 7377 0061), which has an amazing array of fresh vegetables and fruit rarely seen outside Bangladesh (and, sadly, as rarely seen on Brick Lane menus), plus spices, pickles, rice and snacks. A smaller selection of these items can also be found at **Zaman Brothers** (Nos.17-19, E1 6BU, 7247 1009), which offers a good variety of breads. Don't leave Brick Lane without a box or two of famous Bengali sweets: **Alludin Sweets** (No.72, E1 6RL, 7377 0896) and **Bangladeshi Banoful Mishti** (No.108, E1 6RL, 7247 3465) both offer rosagulla and sondesh (the best-known varieties).

Brindisa
32 Exmouth Market, EC1R 4QE (7713 1666/ www.brindisa.com). Farringdon tube/rail. **Open** 10am-6pm Mon-Sat. **Credit** MC, V. Spanish
Owned by Monika Linton, this fabulous importer of top-quality Spanish foods enjoys a cult following among food lovers. Items are sourced from the best-known Spanish producers (including organic ones), and tastings are available. Charcuterie is a strong point – try cecina (cured beef), morcilla (black pudding), lomo (pork loin), Ibérico ham or a dozen varieties of chorizo. Fishy delights include boquerones (marinated fresh white anchovies), bacalao and the ever-popular Ortiz anchovies. Or there are cheeses, such as cabrales (made with a blend of cow's, goat's and sheep's milk), preserves (bitter-sweet green figs), confectionery (turrón, chocolate cigarillos), rice, beans, honey, nuts, herbs and spices, pickles, olives and dried vegetables. You can even buy paella pans and ham-carving sets. Brindisa also runs a stall at Borough Market and a new eaterie nearby, Tapas Brindisa (see p260).

Brixton, SW9
Brixton tube/rail. African & Caribbean
Inside the bustling Brixton Village indoor market, you'll find everything you need to assemble African and Caribbean meals. **Back Home Foods** sells imported spices, pulses, fruit and veg, such as callaloo, yams, breadfruit and mangoes. On nearby Atlantic Road, **First Choice** offers a wide range of Jamaican patties, including lamb and peas, chicken and sweetcorn, salt fish, beef and mixed vegetables.

I Camisa & Son
61 Old Compton Street, W1D 6HS (7437 7610). Leicester Square or Piccadilly Circus tube. **Open** 8.30am-6pm Mon-Sat. **Credit** MC, V. Italian
A great place to pick up fresh pumpkin and sage ravioli, this homely, rustic deli is crammed with an exquisite selection of fresh and dried pastas and olive oils. There's also cured meat, cheese, wild mushrooms, polenta, wine, bread and antipasti.

Chinatown, WC2
Leicester Square or Piccadilly Circus tube. Chinese
Just off Leicester Square, Chinatown remains the place to buy Chinese and South-east Asian ingredients. You'll find fresh produce such as leafy greens, herbs and exotic fruit, as well as noodles, myriad condiments and other staples. At **Golden Gate Grocers** (100 Shaftesbury Avenue, W1D 5EE, 7437 0014) goods are labelled in English, clearly priced and cover all kinds of exotica, from red date tea to pig maw (stomach). There's even a greengrocer out back who sells everything from miniature pak choi to sticky brown yam beans. Loon Fung, once the area's largest Chinese foodstore, has closed, but **New Loon Moon Supermarket** (9 Gerrard Street, W1D 5PN, 7734 3887) remains strong on fresh fruit, vegetables and herbs. Other worthwhile shops are **Good Harvest Fish & Meat** (65 Shaftesbury Avenue, W1B 6LH, 7437 0712), **Golden Gate Hong Supermarket** (700 Shaftesbury Avenue, WC2 7PR, 7437 0014) and **See Woo** (19 Lisle Street, WC2 7P, 7439 8325), which is particularly strong on South-east Asian ingredients. Chinatown is in the process of (controversial) redevelopment, so expect changes.

Ealing Road, Wembley
Alperton tube. Indian
After a lull (when affluent Gujaratis and Gujarati businesses moved out to places like Harrow and Kingsbury), Ealing Road seems to be enjoying a renaissance: lots of new Gujarati restaurants and snack shops have opened, alongside Sri Lankan, Tamil and Somali places. **Wembley Exotics** (Nos.133-135, HA0 4BP, 8900 2607) remains iconic: its colourful displays of imported fruit and veg are second to none, and if you get midnight munchies for Alphonso mangoes, it's open till late. The compact **Prashad Sweets** (No.222, HA0 4QL, 8902 1704) is as popular for its sweets and snacks as it is for its rock-bottom prices (most items cost less than £1). Sri Lankan **Bismillah Butchers** (Nos.19 & 33, HA0 4YA, 8903 4922) is perhaps better for tropical fish than meat, and **Ganapathy Cash & Carry** (Nos.34-38, HA0 5YD, 8795 4627) is a trove of Sri Lankan breads, pickles, rice, frozen ready meals, and fruit and vegetables.

L'Eau à la Bouche
49 Broadway Market, E8 4PH (7923 0600/ www.labouche.com). Liverpool Street tube then 48 or 55 bus/London Fields rail/26, 55, 106, 277, 394 bus. **Open** 9am-7pm Mon-Fri; 9am-5pm Sat; 10am-4pm Sun. **Credit** MC, V. French
A newcomer to increasingly gentrifying Broadway Market, this lovely, mainly French deli has a few tables for eating in. On offer are cold meats, cheeses, coffees, and ready-prepared food such as pizza, quiches and sandwiches. A small selection of breads includes sourdough, rye and sunflower.

R García & Sons
248-250 Portobello Road, W11 1LL (7221 6119). Ladbroke Grove tube. **Open** 9am-6.30pm Mon-Sat; 11am-7pm Sun. **Credit** AmEx, MC, V. Spanish
There's a good selection of Spanish bread at this lovely family-run shop, which also sells Spanish pasta, pickles, nuts, saffron, smoked pimentón and other groceries imported from Spain. The owners have recently opened a great tapas bar next door, Café Garcia (see p258).

German Wurst & Delicatessen
127 Central Street, EC1V 8AP (7250 1322/ www.germandeli.co.uk). Barbican tube/Old Street tube/rail. **Open** 10am-7pm Mon-Fri; 10am-6pm Sat. **No credit cards.** German

Specialising in imported wurst and other meats from Germany, this tiny deli also has a small selection of cheeses, pickles and groceries. However, it's the meat that's the real draw – you'll find an excellent selection of frankfurters and other sausages, as well as pâtés and hams. Loaves include the fashionable 'bread of Westphalia' – a style of rye bread that's a speciality of central and eastern Europe.

A Gold, Traditional Foods of Britain

42 Brushfield Street, E1 6AG (7247 2487/ www.agold.co.uk). Liverpool Street tube/rail. **Open** 11am-8pm Mon-Fri; 10am-6pm Sat; 11am-6pm Sun. **Credit** AmEx, MC, V. British
Can you still buy Vimto lollies and Scottish clootie dumplings in the capital? Indeed you can. This charming shop would be at home in a 1950s village, but the nostalgia-inducing ingredients are carefully sourced from artisan producers all over the UK, with regional products a speciality. How about biscuits such as currant shrewsburys or oat bannocks? Or Cornish saffron cake and ginger brack? Other items include gravy salts, smoked Cornish pilchard fillets, cheeses (cooleeney, cashel blue), teas, preserves, condiments, mustards, cured meats and smoked fish. In the popular confectionery range, you'll find liquorice torpedos, pontefract cakes, sugar mice and chocolate coins that contain real farthings and sixpences. A notable range of soft drinks features dandelion and burdock; the alcoholic drinks run to mead and damson gin.

Green Lanes, N4, N8

Manor House or Turnpike Lane tube.
Turkish/Middle Eastern
Best-known for pastries, breads and seasonal fruits, vegetables, herbs and fresh nuts of notable quality, Green Lanes is a mecca for lovers of Turkish and Middle Eastern food. For Syrian confectionery and pastries, aromatic **Nasrullah Pâtisserie** (No.483, N4 1AJ, 8342 9794) is a delight, with helpful staff on hand to assist. Turkish staples like pickles, beans, lentils, yoghurt and olives can be found at **Turkish Food Market** (Nos.385-387, N4 1EU, 8340 4547), and halal meat and chicken is sold at **Salah Eddine** (51 Grand Parade, N4 1AG, 8800 4333). The enormous **Yasar Halim** (No.495, N4 1AL, 8340 8090) is packed with nuts, dried fruit, preserves, rice, halal meat, dips, cheese and fresh, own-baked bread, pastries and biscuits.

Green Street, E7

Indian
Disembark from Upton Park tube, and you'd be forgiven for thinking you have arrived at an Indian bazaar. The long, bustling, colourful street is lined with scores of Indian restaurants and food shops (run by Indians of every hue, region and religion), plus a few Afro-Caribbean ones. **Green Street Supermarket** (No. 414-416, E13 9JJ, 8503 4422) is good for grocery, greengrocery and butchery. Pop into **Super Save** (No. 343, 8471 1593) and **Rana Food Store** (No.367, 8471 7523) for low-cost Indian, African and Caribbean spices, grains and pulses. **Bharat Food Store** (No.5, 8472 6393), **Green Village** (No.10A, 8503 4809), and **Variety Foods** (No.20, 8471 0008) are all located at Carlton Terrace (a part of Green Street), and stock everything from snake-like striped marrows to yam flour. For meatier options, head to **United Halal Meat** (3 Carlton Terrace, 8586 0545), **Iman** (319 Green Street, 8472 3308), **Humza Halal Meat** (No.389, 8470 9093) and **Kaz's Halal Meat** (No.397, 8470 1009). **Green Street Fresh Fish** (No.3, 8472 8918) is an old-fashioned East End operation, where the quality of tuna, salmon and haddock is sparklingly fresh.

Green Valley

36-37 Upper Berkeley Street, W1H 5QF (7402 7385). Marble Arch tube. **Open** 8am-midnight daily. **Credit** MC, V. Middle Eastern
The splendid array of pastries in the window is a compelling lure to passers-by, but there's far more to be found inside this spacious Lebanese

supermarket in Mayfair. Stock is extensive, ranging from store-cupboard staples, fresh fruit and veg to Middle Eastern traiteur dishes and a delectable assortment of nuts. There a bakery, a halal meat section and an ice-cream counter.

Huong-Nam Supermarket

185-187 Mare Street, E8 3RD (8985 8050). Hackney Central or London Fields rail/48, 55, 106, 253 bus. **Open** 9.30am-8.30pm Mon-Fri; 10am-9pm Sat, Sun. **No credit cards.** Vietnamese
This Vietnamese supermarket also sells Chinese and Thai goods. The shop is proud of its selection of fruit from Vietnam, while fresh shellfish (crab, mussels and the like) is available on Thursdays. The chiller cabinets hold fresh goods (egg noodles, tofu, fish balls and pigs' trotters), while at the back of the shop a tightly packed freezer stores fish, meat and dim sum. Although there is sometimes an English speaker on hand to help and give recipe advice, most imported goods are labelled in French and/or Vietnamese, so it helps if you know what you're after.

Japan Centre

212 Piccadilly, W1J 9HG (7255 8255/ www.japancentre.com). Piccadilly Circus tube. **Open** 10am-7pm Mon-Fri; 10.30am-8pm Sat; 11am-7pm Sun. **Credit** JCB, MC, V. Japanese
Offering London's Japanese community numerous services, this building houses a restaurant (*see p185* **Bargain central**), and a food shop that incorporates delicatessen Yoshino. The shop stocks hundreds of items imported from Japan, Korea and the US, among them seaweed, sauces, confectionery, snacks, tofu, edamame, koshihikari rice, fresh Japanese vegetables, organic meats, bento boxes (from the restaurant), freshly baked bread such as an-pan, and teas. The delicatessen sells wonderfully fresh sushi and sashimi, and organic sushi rice milled on-site. Recommended for hard-to-find Japanese items at reasonable prices.

Lina Stores

18 Brewer Street, W1R 3FS (7437 6482). Piccadilly Circus tube. **Open** 9am-6.30pm Mon-Fri; 9am-5.30pm Sat. **Credit** AmEx, MC, V. Italian
This old-fashioned, long-established deli is crammed with a wide range of pasta (stored in charming wooden crates), rice, polenta, dried mushrooms, beans and lentils, confectionery and preserves. There's also a counter stacked with antipasti, cured meat and fresh pasta. Staff are polite and helpful.

Lisboa

54 Golborne Road, W10 5NR (8969 1052). Ladbroke Grove tube. **Open** 9.30am-7.30pm Mon-Sat; 10am-1pm Sun. **Credit** MC, V. Portuguese
Owned by Mr and Mrs Gomes (also also have the buzzy Lisboa pâtisserie opposite; *see p250*) and run by their children, this friendly shop is notable for its meat counter, which houses an enormous range of Portuguese sausages and cured meats, plus a few cheeses. Freshly baked bread is another plus. The interior is charmingly old-fashioned, and the two Lisboa outlets provide something of a focal point for the local Portuguese community.

Luigi's Delicatessen

349 Fulham Road, SW10 9TW (7352 7739). Fulham Broadway or South Kensington tube/ bus 14. **Open** 9am-9.30pm Mon-Fri; 9am-7pm Sat. **Credit** MC, V. Italian
A large array of wines and spirits line the shelves of this friendly, scarlet-hued deli, which is popular for its excellent selection of own-cooked dishes. These include salads, fresh pasta, stuffed risotto balls, lasagne, tarts and a tiramisu that's so popular it's sold in three sizes. There is a good variety of biscuits, olive oil, balsamic vinegar, sauces and meat, includingly the increasingly fashionable lardo di colonnata.

Manila Supermarket

11-12 Hogarth Place, SW5 0QT (7373 8305). Earl's Court tube. **Open** 9am-9pm daily. **Credit** AmEx, MC, V. Filipino

This spacious, friendly shop is packed with imported jars, tins, packets and frozen food from the Philippines. There's a wide selection of fresh fruit and vegetables, pickles, seasonings, sauces, instant mixes, pastries and frozen foods. Unless you know what you are looking for, the items may be unfamiliar even to those who are well versed in oriental cuisines; many are based on coconut, yams, tropical fruits, eggs and rice.

Le Maroc

94 Golborne Road, W10 5PS (8968 9783). Ladbroke Grove or Westbourne Park tube. **Open** 9am-7pm Mon-Sat. **No credit cards.** Moroccan
This vibrant shop has a halal butcher who offers prepared meat, kibbeh and merguez sausages. Beans, lentils, cracked wheat, coffee, tea, preserves and pickled fruit are also available.

Platters

10 Hallswelle Parade, Finchley Road, NW11 0DL (8455 7345). Golders Green tube then 82, 102, 260 bus. **Open** 8.30am-4.30pm Mon-Fri; 8.30am-4pm Sat; 8.30am-2pm Sun. **Credit** AmEx, MC, V. Jewish
This small deli isn't flash, but it does have understated cool: organic spelt flour bagels are sold ('to cater for all these young people on faddy diets,' we were told), alongside a great selection of pickles and cold meats that would make a perfect New York-style picnic. Tempting own-cooked dishes, sandwiches, cheese and grocery items like Israeli couscous are also available.

St Marcus Fine Foods

1 Rockingham Close, SW15 5RW (8878 1898/ www.stmarcus.equology.com). Barnes rail/337 bus. **Open** 9am-6pm daily. **Credit** MC, V. South African
Ever tried Monkey Gland Sauce? It's a spicy fruit sauce that goes well with cheese and coriander flavoured boerewors. This leading supplier of South African food (to hotels, restaurants, pubs and delis) also sells an award-winning range of droewors, sosaties and biltong. Other products include spicy chakalaka sauce, youngberry jam, guava fruit rolls, spice rubs, cane spirit liqueurs, fruit ales, Rose Kola tonic drink and cooking equipment. Iconic items like Castle Lager and Ouma Muesli Rusk are also available.

I Sapori di Stefano Cavallini

146 Northcote Road, SW11 6RD (7228 2017). Clapham South tube/Clapham Junction rail. **Open** 9.30am-7pm Mon-Fri; 9.30am-6.30pm Sat. **Credit** MC, V. Italian
%Michelin-starred Stefano Cavallini's venture is notable for amazing food cooked on the premises. The fresh pasta (mushroom, asparagus, butternut squash, spinach and ricotta, and goat's cheese and mixed pepper ravioli, plus cuttlefish ink spaghetti) is particularly appealing. Groceries include oils, preserves and antipasti; chocolates are also on sale.

Southall

Southall rail. Indian
Home to Punjabi and Sindhi communities, the first thing that hits you about Southall are the sights (garishly embroidered salwar kameez that makes everyone look like they're going to an Indian wedding), sounds (loud Punjabi rap blaring out of shops and car windows) and smells (sizzling samosas or freshly cooked 'naan kebabs'). Having thus whetted your appetite, head to the enormous **Quality Foods** (Witley Gardens Industrial Estate, UB2 4ES, 8571 4893), where you can pick up ingredients to assemble your own Indian meal; the variety of fresh fruit and veg displayed outside is staggering. On the Broadway, family-run **Dokal & Sons** (Nos.133-135, UB1 1LW, 8574 1647) and **Sira Cash & Carry** (No.128, UB1 1QF, 8574 2280) stock rice, bread, pulses, canned food and imported vegetables like yellow baby aubergines and gigantic marrows.

Sri Thai

56 Shepherd's Bush Road, W6 7PH (7602 0621). Goldhawk Road tube. **Open** 9am-6.30pm Mon-Sat; 10am-5pm Sun. **No credit cards.** Thai

Verde & Co. See p349.

This wonderful family-run shop sells most ingredients required for a Thai meal: seasonings, bottled sauces, canned and frozen meat and fish, and fresh herbs and spices. Rarely seen fruit and vegetables are delivered from Thailand once a week, and the small, daily changing selection of takeaway meals cooked by the owner's wife (such as barbecued pork, and sticky rice with jackfruit) are delicious. Fresh, own-made curry pastes are also noteworthy.

Super Bahar
349A Kensington High Street, W8 6NW (7603 5083). High Street Kensington tube.
Open 9am-9pm daily. **Credit** AmEx, MC, V.
Middle Eastern
Iranian caviar, top-notch nuts and spices, super-sweet confectionery, and stacks of prepared, ready-to-eat fresh fruits are the greatest hits at this Iranian shop on Kensington High Street. Service is helpful and easy-going.

Tawana Oriental Supermarket
18-20 Chepstow Road, W2 5BD (7221 6316). Notting Hill Gate tube. **Open** 9.30am-8pm daily. **Credit** MC, V. Thai
For more than two decades, Tawana has been a temple for those after Thai food. Its freezers offer great bulk buys in squid, shrimps, prawns and scallops, alongside bags of purple yam, jute leaves and grated coconut, but you'll also find food from across South-east Asia – frozen dim sum, for example, and wun tun wrappers. Ready-made meals include pad Thai and green and red curries.

L Terroni & Sons
138-140 Clerkenwell Road, EC1R 5DL (7837 1712). Farringdon tube/rail. **Open** 9am-5.45pm Tue-Fri; 9am-3pm Sat; 9.30am-1.45pm Sun. **Credit** MC, V. Italian
Since being sold to Foodhouse UK at the end of 2003, Terroni & Sons has been able to import an even wider selection of Italian goods – as well as opening a café next door. Charcuterie, cheese, fresh pasta and antipasti sit alongside olive oil, vinegar, pasta sauces, preserves and confectionery.

Tooting, SW17
Tooting Broadway or Tooting Bec tube.
South Asian
People from all over the Indian subcontinent – Pakistan, Sri Lanka and both north and south India – have made their home in Tooting, making it a great place to eat out or to get provisions. Try **Deepak** (953-959 Garratt Lane, SW17 0LW, 8767 7819), a good generalist, or **Shiv Darshan** (169 Upper Tooting Road, SW17 7TJ, 8682 5173) and **Pooja** (168 Upper Tooting Road, SW17 7EN, 8682 5148) for Indian sweets. **Nature Fresh** (126-128 Upper Tooting Road, SW17 7EN, 8682 4988) and **Daily Fresh Foods** (152 Upper Tooting Road, SW17 7ER, 8767 7856) stock Asian fruit and veg.

Wing Yip NEW
395 Edgware Road, NW2 6LN (8450 0422/ www.wingyip.com). Cricklewood rail/16, 32, 316 bus. **Open** 9.30am-7pm Mon-Sat; 11.30am-5pm Sun. **Credit** MC, V. Chinese
Well respected in the Chinese community (its own-label products are a standard-bearer of quality), Wing Yip is the main supplier to Chinese restaurants. The range of imported Chinese, Thai, Malaysian, Japanese and Indonesian products is vast; many come in catering packs. The selection includes frozen foods, oriental sauces and marinades (extra hot Maysan curry sauce concentrate, perhaps), herbs and spices (dried angelica root, liquorice powder), snacks, meat, fish, veg, rice, noodles and cooking utensils. Popular staples include Chinese instant cereal, yellow rock sugar and black sesame dessert mix.

Health food & organic

Alara Wholefoods
58-60 Marchmont Street, WC1N 1AB (7837 1172). Russell Square tube. **Open** 9am-6pm Mon-Wed, Fri; 9am-7pm Thur; 10am-6pm Sat. **Credit** MC, V.
Friendly, family-run Alara combines a shop and a café. The latter serves daily changing hot specials that range from lasagne to the ever-popular sweet curry; dishes can be taken away. Much of the stock, which runs to groceries, grains, pulses, cereals, fruit and vegetables, is organic. Prices are keen.

Bumblebee
30, 32 & 33 Brecknock Road, N7 0DD (7607 1936/www.bumblebee.co.uk). Kentish Town tube/ rail/29 bus. **Open** 9am-6.30pm Mon-Wed, Fri, Sat; 9am-7.30pm Thur. **Credit** AmEx, MC, V.
The Bumblebee hive consists of three shops: two neighbours and one opposite. You'll find deli food (including freshly baked bread), grains, loose nuts and pulses, an impressive range of miso and dried seaweed, and fresh produce, including seasonal organic fruit and veg, eggs and an enticing cheese counter (the only stock that isn't vegetarian, though it is organic). The organic booze range mainly covers wine, but also features saké, cider and Champagne. They run a delivery service throughout London.

SHOPS & COURSES

Bushwacker Wholefoods

*132 King Street, W6 0QU (8748 2061).
Hammersmith tube.* **Open** 9.30am-6pm Mon,
Wed-Sat; 10am-6pm Tue. **Credit** MC, V.
Bushwhacker makes a valiant effort to source
organic, fair trade and sugar-free goods wherever
possible; it's Soil Association-certified, GM-free
and even bags its own goods on the premises,
thereby creating employment opportunities and
reducing waste. The shop itself has an old wooden
counter by the door, packed with herbs and spices.
Vitamins, supplements and homeopathic remedies
are another focus, as well as macrobiotics. Fridges
stock organic milk, non-dairy alternatives and
vegetarian lunchtime treats.

Fresh & Wild

*210 Westbourne Grove, W11 2RH (7229
1063/www.freshandwild.com). Notting Hill Gate
tube.* **Open** 8am-9pm Mon-Fri; 8am-8pm Sat;
10am-7pm Sun. **Credit** AmEx, MC, V.
The Fresh & Wild chain, already the biggest
organic and natural foods retailer in Britain, joined
forces with Whole Food Market, the biggest in the
world, in January 2004. Prices may not be the
cheapest, but the range is outstanding, with more
than 5,000 different products covering organic fruit
and veg, supplements, frozen and chilled food and
pet care, plus a select library of books. The design
cleverly combines an earthy wholefood-shop ethic
with a supermarket layout for easy navigation.
This branch has a café (*see p301*).

Here

*Chelsea Farmers' Market, 125 Sydney Street,
SW3 6NR (7351 4321). Sloane Square or South
Kensington tube.* **Open** 9.30am-8pm Mon-Sat;
10am-6.30pm Sun. **Credit** MC, V.
The concept of supermarket-style health food
shops is no longer new, but Here was a pioneer –
and it's still slick enough to match its location just
off the swanky King's Road. Stock is 100%
organic, comprising fruit, vegetables, meat and
fish, as well as supplements and beauty products.
Staff are a helpful lot.

Oliver's Wholefoods Store

*5 Station Approach, Kew, Surrey TW9 3QB
(8948 3990). Kew Gardens tube/rail.* **Open**
9am-7pm Mon-Sat; 10am-7pm Sun. **Credit** MC, V.
Oliver's is a lovely shop with a good local buzz. As
well as a great range of groceries (organic poultry,
sausages, tofu), there are regular deliveries from
quality bakers (Cranks, Authentic Bakery, All
Natural Bakery), plus Dr Hauschka products,
including make-up. Treatment rooms next door
(about to open as we went to press) offer clients a
variety of therapies and organic beauty
treatments; those looking to cheer themselves in
less healthy ways might be interested in the range
of organic wines, beer, cider and spirits.

Planet Organic

*42 Westbourne Grove, W2 5SH (7221 7171/
www.planetorganic.com). Bayswater tube.*
Open 9.30am-8.30pm Mon-Sat; noon-6pm Sun.
Credit AmEx, MC, V.
Established nearly a decade ago, Planet Organic
has three branches, all in London, all following the
same approach. All produce is organic, and the
popular lunchtime takeaway counters adopt a
simple approach: choose a size of container and
they'll keep filling it up with tasty, wholesome
tucker for as long as they can still get the lid on
top. The Westbourne Grove branch has a meat
counter and fishmonger, excellent fresh fruit and
veg, and a bakery for croissants, pastries, cakes
and speciality loaves. The health and beauty
section is enhanced by a treatment room (you'll
need to book to see the nutritionist or the
homeopath), and carries a great range of products
– Dr Hauschka and REN remain very popular.
For branches see index.

Total Organics [NEW]

*6 Moxon Street, W1U 4ER (7935 8626).
Baker Street tube.* **Open** 10am-5.30pm Mon,
Fri; 10am-6.30pm Tue-Thur; 10am-5pm Sat;
10am-3pm Sun. **Credit** MV, V.

The popularity of their vegetarian stall in Borough
Market led the owners – two cousins – to set up
shop in the midst of Marylebone. Beans, grains,
lentils, cereal, bread and condiments are all sold –
along with lots of non-gluten and dairy-free items.
Highlights include the Nomato range of tomato-
free products (ketchup, baked beans), fresh fruit
and veg that are cheaper than at the supermarket,
an olive oil refill service, and a juice bar that offers
free bags of juice pulp to those who want to make
their own compost. Freshly made salads and
snacks are available to take away – try the
delicious Spanish tortilla if it's on the menu.

Meat, fish & game

A Dove & Son

*71 Northcote Road, SW11 6PJ (7223 5191/
www.doves.co.uk). Clapham Junction rail.* **Open**
8am-4pm Mon; 8am-5.30pm Tue-Sat. **Credit** MC,
V.
In business since 1889, Dove's sells prime Scottish
beef, grass-fed English lamb, pedigree pork and
own-made sausages. Free-range bronze turkeys are
available at Christmas.

Allen & Co

*117 Mount Street, W1K 3LA (7499 5831). Bond
Street or Green Park tube.* **Open** 4am-4pm Mon-
Fri; 5am-noon Sat. **Credit** (over £20) MC, V.
With its beautifully tiled interior, this venerable
Mayfair butcher's is a rare 19th-century survivor.
Order a prime cut at Le Gavroche (*see p128*) or the
Wolseley (*see p226*) and chances are it came from
this purveyor of top-class meat, notably beef and
game when in season.

Fishy business

Decent displays of fresh fish can be
found at many London **food halls**
(*see p344*), and there are also
several outstanding stalls at **Borough
Market** (*see p344*). Mini chain
FishWorks (*see p87*) combines a
fishmonger and a fish restaurant.
The following shops are all reliable:

B&M Seafood *258 Kentish Town Road,
NW5 2AA (7485 0346). Kentish Town
tube/rail.* **Open** 7.30am-9.30pm Mon-
Sat. **Credit** MC, V.
Chalmers & Gray *67 Notting Hill Gate,
W11 3JS (7221 6177). Notting Hill
Gate tube.* **Open** 8am-5pm Mon-Fri;
8am-4pm Sat. **Credit** MC, V.
Copes Seafood Company *700 Fulham
Road, SW6 5SA (7371 7300). Parsons
Green tube.* **Open** 10am-8pm Mon-Fri;
9am-6pm Sat. **Credit** AmEx, DC, MC, V.
Covent Garden Fishmongers
*37 Turnham Green Terrace, W4 1RG
(8995 9273). Turnham Green tube.*
Open 8am-5pm Tue, Sat; 8am-5.30pm
Wed-Fri. **Credit** MC, V.
France Fresh Fish *99 Stroud Green
Road, N4 3PX (7263 9767). Finsbury
Park tube/rail.* **Open** 9am-6.45pm Mon-
Sat; 11am-5pm Sun. **No credit cards.**
Golborne Fisheries *75 Golborne Road,
W10 5NP (8960 3100). Ladbroke
Grove tube.* **Open** 8am-6pm Mon-Sat.
No credit cards.
Sandy's *56 King Street, Twickenham,
Middx TW1 3SH (8892 5788/
www.sandysfish.net). Twickenham rail.*
Open 8am-6pm Mon-Sat. **Credit** MC, V.
Steve Hatt *88-90 Essex Road, N1 8LU
(7226 3963). Angel tube.* **Open** 7am-
5pm Tue-Sat. **No credit cards.**
Walter Purkis & Sons *17 The Broadway,
N8 8DU (8340 6281/www.purkis4fish.
co.uk). Finsbury Park tube/rail then
W7 bus.* **Open** 8am-5pm Tue-Sat.
Credit AmEx, MC, V.

Frank Godfrey

*7 Highbury Park, N5 1QJ (7226 2425).
Highbury & Islington tube/rail.* **Open** 8am-6pm
Mon-Fri; 8am-5pm Sat. **Credit** MC, V.
This friendly, family-run butcher sells only the best
free-range meat and poultry, some of which is
organic. Orkney Island Gold beef and lamb are a
particular speciality, plus award-winning own-
made sausages and bronze turkeys at Christmas.

Ginger Pig

*8-10 Moxon Street, W1U 4EW (7935 7788).
Bond Street or Baker Street tube/Marylebone
tube/rail.* **Open** 8.30am-6.30pm Mon-Sat; 9am-
3pm Sun. **Credit** MC, V.
A carnivore's paradise, Ginger Pig sells beef, pork
and lamb from the owners' Yorkshire Moors farm,
which boasts the largest herd of rare-breed pigs in
the country. There is also superb bacon, a range of
over 25 bangers, plus pâtés, terrines and pies made
on the premises. Ginger Pig also has a stall at
Borough Market (*see p344*).

Kingsland, the Edwardian Butchers

*140 Portobello Road, W11 2DZ (7727 6067).
Notting Hill Gate tube.* **Open** 7.30am-6pm
Mon-Sat. **Credit** AmEx, MC, V.
Despite the name, this picturesque shop was
established in 1848. It's known for its free-range
and organic meats: beef is pure-bred Aberdeen
Angus, while most of the pork, sausages and
bacon comes from Old Spot and Tamworth pigs.
There's also a good range of deli-style cooked
meats, black puddings and own-made pies.

Lidgate

*110 Holland Park Avenue, W11 4UA (7727
8243). Holland Park tube.* **Open** 7am-6pm
Mon-Fri; 7am-5pm Sat. **Credit** MC, V.
For free-range and organic meat and poultry fit for
a prince, head to this select butcher; its stock comes
from farms including Highgrove Estate, and rare
breeds are well represented. Customers flock here
at Christmas for free-range bronze and black
turkeys and geese, plus award-winning, own-made
pies, oven-ready dishes and sausages.

Macken Bros

*44 Turnham Green Terrace, W4 1QP (8994
2646). Turnham Green tube.* **Open** 7am-6pm
Mon-Fri; 7am-5.30pm Sat. **Credit** AmEx, MC, V.
This shop has a loyal local following for its prime
Scottish beef, free-range pork, lamb and poultry.
Free-range turkeys are available at Christmas, as
well as geese and game in season.

M Moen & Sons

*24 The Pavement, SW4 0JA (7622 1624/
www.moen.co.uk). Clapham Common tube.*
Open 8am-6.30pm Mon-Fri; 8am-5pm Sat.
Credit MC, V.
Only free-range and additive-free or organic meat
is sold at this family butcher's, including prime
Scottish beef, lamb and pork. Game, from snipe to
wild venison, is available in season. Marinated
meats (using own-made marinades) and sausages
(more than 20 types) are also popular.

Randalls Butchers

*113 Wandsworth Bridge Road, SW6 2TE
(7736 3426). Fulham Broadway tube.*
Open 7am-5.30pm Mon-Fri; 7am-4pm Sat.
Credit MC, V.
In addition to its top-class selection of free-range
meat, poultry and rare-breed pork, ever-popular
Randalls does a roaring trade in marinated meats
such as spiced Moroccan lamb or lemon and
coriander chicken kebabs.

Simply Sausages

*Harts Corner, 341 Central Markets, EC1A 9NB
(7329 3227). Farringdon tube/rail.* **Open** 8.30am-
6pm Mon-Fri; 9am-2.30pm Sat. **Credit** MC, V.
The name says it all: here you'll find a peerless
selection of bangers, from traditional lincolnshire
and cumberland to more exotic combinations such
as thai chilli and lemongrass; duck, apricot and
orange; or the fiery 'Lucifer'.

Courses

Cookery

Almeida Cookery Demonstrations NEW
30 Almeida Street, N1 1AD (7354 4777/ www.conran.com). Angel tube/Highbury & Islington tube/rail. **Open** phone enquiries/ bookings 9am-5pm Mon-Fri. **Credit** MC, V.
Almeida's head chef Ian Wood has developed quite a reputation for regional French cooking at Conran's Islington restaurant, and his personal enthusiasm for the subject has led to the creation of a popular series of cookery demonstrations. Held around once a month, they tend to focus on a particular region such as the Pyrenees, Burgundy or Normandy, taking the form of a one-hour demonstration followed by lunch or dinner. Prices start at £55 per person, including meal and matching wines.

Art of Hospitality
St James Schools, Earsby Street, W14 8SH (7348 1755/www.artofhospitality.co.uk). Kensington (Olympia) tube/rail. **Open** 8.30am-4pm Mon-Fri. **No credit cards.**
Guest experts such as highly regarded food writer Anissa Helou on Lebanese dishes often feature at the practical cookery demonstrations, held on Thursday mornings. A light lunch of the dishes shown, a glass of wine and copies of the recipes are included in the £35 price. On Saturdays, six- to 12-year-olds are taught practical skills with seasonal ingredients, such as bread-making or creating pasta from scratch. These cost £20 per place, with a discount offered for booking a whole term. Check the website for other options, including summer holiday courses.

Billingsgate Seafood Training School NEW
28 Billingsgate Market, Trafalgar Way, E14 5ST (7517 3548/www.seafoodtraining.org). Blackwall DLR. **Open** phone enquiries 9am-4pm Mon-Fri. **No credit cards.**
Fish fans, be warned: the bad news is that you'll probably have to get up around 5am, but a masterclass (£175) at Fishmongers' Hall is a luxurious indulgence for any lover of seafood or history. After a guided tour of Billingsgate Market, participants head to the City headquarters of the Worshipful Company of Fishmongers for breakfast, a cookery class, a tour of the building, and a gourmet lunch, served by liveried staff and accompanied by top-notch wines (always reds, by the way, and you'll find out why on the day). Billingsgate Market also has a teaching facility, with classes (£150) for the general public led by food writer CJ Jackson, covering themes such as global fish cookery and shellfish.

Books for Cooks
4 Blenheim Crescent, W11 1NN (7221 1992/ www.booksforcooks.com). Ladbroke Grove tube. **Open** 10am-6pm Tue-Sat. **Credit** MC, V.
Arrive early for the best seats at this popular, informal cooking school set above the long-established Notting Hill bookshop/café. Prices (from £30) reflect the cramped premises, and with so many expat American regulars talking through the demonstrations, the atmosphere, while friendly, sometimes borders on the chaotic. Early booking is advised too, as places are limited. Regular demonstrators include Celia Brooks-Brown on vegetarian cooking, Ursula Ferrigno on Italian, and Kimiko Barber on Japanese. Hands-on workshops (£75-£90) are also available on subjects such as knife skills, fresh pasta and chefs' secrets.

Cookery School
15B Little Portland Street, W1W 8BW (7631 4590/www.cookeryschool.co.uk). Oxford Circus tube. **Open** phone enquiries 9am-5pm Mon-Fri. **Credit** MC, V.
Boost your culinary confidence with Rosalind Rathouse's six-part evening courses (£300), which aim to show that cooking is fun as well as satisfying. Condensed three-day courses are run in summer, ideal for uni students and home-leavers. One-off hands-on workshops are held on Wednesday evenings and during Saturdays. Guest experts include renowned artisan baker Dan Lepard on bread, and chocolatier Paul Young. Evening classes cost £60, day workshops £125.

Le Cordon Bleu
114 Marylebone Lane, W1M 6HH (7935 3503/ www.lcblondon.com). Bond Street tube. **Open** phone enquiries 8.30am-7.30pm Mon-Fri. **Credit** MC, V.
You don't have to be an aspiring chef to benefit from the classical tuition at the world-famous Cordon Bleu. A limited number of places are available at the daily demonstrations, sitting in with the certificate and diploma students for a mere £15. Guest chef demos occur on occasional weekday evenings. Short courses vary from single days on a theme such as vegetarian dinner party menus (£160) to three-day daytime courses (£265-£395). There are also eight-week evening courses on basic techniques (£335), or a four-week full-time course for complete novices (£1,940).

La Cucina Caldesi NEW
118 Marylebone Lane, W1U 2QF (7487 0750/ 0759/www.caffecaldesi.com). Bond Street tube. **Open** phone enquiries 9am-5pm Mon-Fri. **Credit** AmEx, MC, V.
Tucked in the quaint mews behind Marylebone's Caffè Caldesi restaurant, this new cooking studio specialises in Italian cuisine. Friendly owner Giancarlo Caldesi and wife Katie are particularly known for Tuscan fare, and teaching children. Tutors include pâtisserie specialist Stefano Borella (a chef at the restaurant), TV cook Sophie Grigson and Franco Taruschio, formerly of the Walnut Tree Inn near Abergavenny and godfather of the gastropub movement. Prices start at £45 for a two-hour session and hit £120 for a five-hour fish class including four-course meal with wine.

La Cuisine de Pierre
29 College Cross, N1 1PT (7700 1349/ www.lacuisinedepierre.com). Angel tube/Highbury & Islington tube/rail. **Open** phone enquiries 3-10.30pm Mon-Fri. **No credit cards.**
Pierre Béghin and Stephane Martin aim to give clients the confidence to entertain friends at home, and to enjoy doing it. While the two hail from France, Italian, low-cal and vegetarian cuisines are also covered, and Fridays focus on fish. The hands-on sessions (£70) cover at least three seasonal recipes which students prepare and then eat.

Denise's Kitchen NEW
PO Box 83, Northwood, Middx HA6 2HD (01923 836456/www.jewishcookery.com). **Open** phone enquiries 9.30am-10pm Mon-Fri, Sun. **No credit cards.**
According to food writer and tutor Denise Phillips, being strictly kosher should not restrict enjoyment of food or demand the sacrifice of culinary trends. Themed hands-on classes (£50) include Chinese and Italian cuisines, healthy entertaining, new ways with salmon, and Jewish classics made easy. Singles should check out her monthly 'Date on a Plate' evening classes (also £50) for those in their mid 30s to late 40s.

Divertimenti
33-34 Marylebone High Street, W1U 4PT (7935 0689/www.divertimenti.co.uk). Baker Street or Bond Street tube. **Open** 9.30am-6pm Mon-Wed, Fri; 9.30am-7pm Thur; 10am-6pm Sat; 11am-5pm Sun. **Credit** AmEx, DC, MC, V.
Demonstration sessions (£30-£60) at Divertimenti's shops in Marylebone and Knightsbridge benefit from modern, spacious premises and high-tech facilities such as TV relay of countertop action. Add a generous supply of food and wine, and it makes for an entertaining day or night out. If we have a criticism, it's that there have at times been too many similarities between the range of classes and teachers offered here and at Books for Cooks (*see above*). But Divertimenti is developing its own, more upmarket niche, attracting such impressive food names as Bill Granger, Peter Gordon, Antonio Carluccio and David Thompson. Lunchtime classes (£25), workshops (£90-£150) and six-week skills courses for beginners and intermediates (£395) are also available. Divertimenti's handy new online booking facility is another key advantage over competitors.

The Kids' Cookery School NEW
107 Gunnersbury Lane, W3 8HQ (8992 8882/ www.kidscookeryschool.co.uk). Acton Town tube. **Open** phone enquiries 9am-5.30pm Mon-Fri. **No credit cards.**
The first children's cookery school to achieve charitable status, this not-for-profit organisation

La Cucina Caldesi

encourages children to learn about the need for a healthy, balanced diet while giving them a fun time preparing and eating a wide range of tasty dishes from around the world. Three professionally qualified cookery teachers and occasional guest chefs are on hand to ensure all goes well, and happily take into account any dietary requirements for health or religious grounds. Holiday courses and an after-school club are also available. All proceeds go to providing assisted places and equal opportunities for children most in need. Students in wheelchairs are welcome to attend.

Leiths School of Food & Wine
21 St Alban's Grove, W8 5BP (7729 0177/ www.leiths.com). High Street Kensington tube. **Open** phone enquiries 9am-5pm Mon-Fri. **Credit** MC, V.
Enthusiastic amateurs can attend this world-renowned professional catering school for evening classes, Saturday morning sessions, intensive one- or two-week holiday courses, or one-off workshops focusing on a special interest such as fish or game cookery, chocolate or Christmas food. The useful online booking facility allows you to see which sessions still have places available. Expect to pay £540-£555 for a ten-week evening class, or £90 for a half-day practical in which you work with a partner to prepare a three-course lunch with wine.

Mosimann's Academy NEW
5 William Blake House, Bridge Lane, SW11 3AD (7326 8344/www.mosimann.com). Clapham Junction rail. **Open** phone enquiries 9am-5pm Mon-Fri. **Credit** MC, V.
The facilities in this Battersea teaching studio are as classy as Anton Mosimann's celebrated cuisine. Half-day courses on topics such as vegetarian cookery or various Asian cuisines are often followed by lunch at the chef's private dining club in Belgravia. Some full-day courses are available, as well as guided shopping and cooking tours of Borough Market.

Sophie's Cookery Cube NEW
22 Parkside, SW19 5NA (8946 4000/ www.sophiescookerycube.co.uk). Wimbledon tube/ rail. **Open** phone enquiries 9am-6pm Mon-Fri. **No credit cards.**
Chef and writer Sophie Baimbridge has worked at prestige restaurants including the River Café, Chez Panisse, Sally Clarke's and with the Roux Brothers, with whom she first trained. She's a great demonstrator too, with an extensive knowledge of Italian cuisine and healthy cooking. Her 'cookery cube' is near the war memorial in Wimbledon Village, though bookings can be made through local kitchenware shop Estilo. £45 will get you a two-hour demonstration with food and wine served afterwards and recipes to take home.
Bookings also available at Estilo Kitchen, 38 High Street, SW19 5BY (8944 6868).

À Table
7 Arlington Road, Richmond, Surrey TW10 7BZ (8940 9910/www.atable.info). Richmond tube/rail. **Open** phone enquiries 9am-5pm Mon-Fri. **No credit cards.**
With everything prepared in advance, Austrian-born chef Martina Lessing believes, you are free to relax with your dinner guests. This is the guiding principle of her cooking 'seminars', which tend to be based on three-course menus (seasonal or regional), or topics such as starters, vegetable side dishes and sushi. Morning or evening classes (90 minutes) followed by a meal cost £28, with a discount if you book more than three sessions.

Tasting Places
Unit 108, Buspace Studios, Conlan Street, W10 5AP (8964 5333/www.tastingplaces.com). **Open** phone enquiries 10am-5pm Mon-Fri. **Credit** AmEx, DC, MC, V.
Masterclasses held in the kitchens of top restaurants such as Chutney Mary, Racine and the Connaught are the speciality of this culinary holiday agency. Restaurant sessions are pricey (£140-£220), but usually include lunch or dinner with wine at the venue. Alternatively, take a look

at the 'Hands-on in Holland Park' schedule, which starts at £120 per person for a two-hour daytime class in an elegant designer kitchen with informal lunch to follow.

Vegetarian Society NEW
Citrus House, Mews entrance, 70 Fortune Green Road, NW6 1DS (bookings 0161 925 2014/ www.vegsoc.org). West Hampstead tube. **Open** phone enquiries 9am-5pm Mon-Fri. **Credit** MC, V.
Cordon Vert, the Vegetarian Society cookery school based in Altrincham, Cheshire, has a London offshoot at a studio in West Hampstead. Demonstration sessions followed by lunch cover themes such as Lebanese, Indian and Thai cuisines. Recipes are meat-free, of course. Expect to pay around £93 for a demonstration/lunch.

Wine & beer

Leiths (*see above*) and **La Cucina Caldesi** (*see p353*) also run wine courses.

The Beer Academy NEW
01276 417855/www.beeracademy.org. **Open** phone enquiries 9am-5pm Mon-Fri. **No credit cards.**
This not-for-profit organisation aims to help people deepen their understanding and appreciation of beer. Its courses are run at various venues around the UK, including the estimable White Horse pub (*see p329*) in Parsons Green, and the George IV in Chiswick. How to taste beer, how to match it with food (a fascinating field), plus the effects of different ingredients and brewing processes on the styles produced are all covered. It's meant to be fun, and it is, but you may find there is a little examination at the end.

Better Tasting NEW
8767 0027/www.bettertasting.co.uk. **Open** phone enquiries 9am-5pm Mon-Fri. **No credit cards.**
Oenologist and winemaker Richard More models his Better Tasting course on the diploma course of Bordeaux University, where he first trained. The £125 one-day masterclass, suitable for many levels of experience, teaches wine tasting through theory and practice, covering white wines in the morning and reds in the afternoon, with plenty of tips and tests. Former chief winemaker for Sandeman in Oporto, More feels that people need to know not only how to evaluate wine, but how to assess their own tasting skills.

Connoisseur
Marlborough Hotel, 9-13 Bloomsbury Street, WC1B 3QE (07956 870772/www.connoisseur. org). Tottenham Court Road tube. **Open** phone enquiries 9am-6pm Mon-Fri. **No credit cards.**
These informal tasting classes for groups of ten to 25 are run by Margaret Silbermann, who has over 15 years' experience in the wine import trade. Each class examines at least seven good-quality, readily available wines, from classic regions as well as lesser-known areas. The five-session introductory course (£169) focuses on major grape varieties and how they differ from Old to New World; a condensed one-day version (£75) is also offered. Intermediates move on to studying regional wine styles of the major wine-producing countries, and wine trends. Check the website for other classes, such as matching food and wine.

Sotheby's
34-35 New Bond Street, W1A 2AA (7293 5727/www.sothebys.com). Bond Street tube. **Open** phone enquiries 9am-5pm Mon-Fri. **Credit** MC, V.
Places on Sotheby's prestigious six-week wine courses are much sought after. As befits the company's position as auctioneers, fine wines are the main focus, yet the 90-minute classes aim to be informal and friendly. The Varietal course (held on Monday evenings in January/February and September/October) looks at major grape varieties, including cabernet sauvignon, merlot, pinot noir, shiraz, chardonnay, riesling and sauvignon blanc. The Regional course (May/June and November/ December), emphasises French territories, but also

touches on Spain, Italy and the New World. If you take the courses consecutively, you pay £450 for both, instead of £240 per course.

Tim Atkin's Wine 'Uncorked' Series
Bank Aldwych, 1 Kingsway, WC2B 6XF (7379 5088/www.bankrestaurants.com). Holborn or Temple tube. **Credit** AmEx, DC, MC, V.
Master of Wine and *Observer* newspaper columnist Tim Atkin runs six-week courses for beginners and intermediates at Bank Aldwych restaurant from September to November. The courses, both entertaining and instructive, are designed to be taken one after the other, but those with a basic knowledge of tasting and major wine styles can sign straight up for the intermediate course. Classes can also be taken individually. You'll learn how to navigate supermarket wines, as well as how to decipher restaurant wine lists. Cost is £270 per course or £45 per session.

Vinopolis, City of Wine
1 Bank End, SE1 9BU (0870 241 4040/ www.vinopolis.co.uk). London Bridge tube/rail. **Open** noon-9pm (last tour 7pm) Mon, Fri, Sat; noon-6pm (last tour 4pm) Tue, Wed, Thur, Sun. **Credit** MC, V.
Although it is a tourist attraction that's open daily, Vinopolis also runs private one-hour wine tasting sessions (3pm Sunday) designed for enthusiastic beginners. Six wines introduce you to wine regions, grape varieties and tasting technique. The £25 price also gives access to the standard Vinopolis Tour, which includes a further five wine tastings plus a cocktail. Check the website for details of other events and classes – such as a 'Contemporary Choice' tasting session (£35, 1pm last Sunday of the month), which takes a more in-depth look at the world's best-known wines, vineyards and production methods.

Wine & Food Academy NEW
93 Hazelbourne Road, SW12 9NT (8675 6172/ www.winefoodacademy.com). Clapham South tube. **Open** phone enquiries 8.30am-6pm Mon-Sat. **Credit** AmEx, MC, V.
Past and present students are able to buy all wines tasted at wholesale prices from of the Wine & Food Academy, which hosts workshops at various London venues, including Clerkenwell Clapham, and Barons Court. 'Harmonising Wines & Food' (£285) is an informal ten-week evening course with supper included. The academy is also a certified training centre for the Wine & Spirit Education Trust (*see below*), offering the Intermediate (£325) and Advanced (£570) certificates.

Wine & Spirit Education Trust
39-45 Bermondsey Street, SE1 3XF (7089 3800/ www.wset.co.uk). London Bridge tube/rail. **Open** phone enquiries 9-5pm Mon-Fri. **Credit** MC, V.
You don't have to aspire to Master of Wine status to take classes with the WSET. Prices start at £35-£40 for after-work tutored tastings and food matching sessions. Typical tastings cover pinot noir; Champagne; port; New Zealand wines; and 'Chardonnay Around the World'. The matching workshop explains the theory before delving into practical sampling with various food components such as spice, smokiness and sweetness.

WineWise
107 Culford Road, N1 4HL (7254 9734/ www.michaelschusterwine.com). Highbury & Islington tube/rail/30, 38, 73, 76, 141 bus. **Open** phone enquiries 8.30am-8.30pm Mon-Fri. **No credit cards.**
Michael Schuster is one of Britain's best wine educators, with long experience in the wine retail trade. He now focuses on writing and teaching, with Sotheby's (*see above*) among his clients. His WineWise school runs beginners' and fine wine courses, as well as tutored tastings for those with more experience. On the beginners' course (£175 for six sessions, two hours each), you can expect to sample wines costing from £4 to £25 per bottle, while learning the basics of tasting techniques, grape varieties and food matching.

Open all hours

Looking for the perfect after-work cocktail bar or cosy local?
With more than 1,000 bar & pub reviews literally at your fingertips,
you'll never be stuck for ideas again.

NEW WEBSITE timeout.com/bars

Drink Shops

Beer

For some fine establishments in which to drink beer, see **Pubs**, starting on p328.

The Beer Shop
14 Pitfield Street, N1 6EY (7739 3701/www. pitfieldbeershop.co.uk). Old Street tube/rail. **Open** 11am-7pm Tue-Fri; 10am-4pm Sat. **Credit** MC, V.
A smell of fermenting malt greets you at this Shoreditch shop, seeping in from the organic brewery next door. The beers brewed there go under the Pitfield name, and include Shoreditch Stout and vegan Eco Warrior. The shop is packed with beers from Belgium, Germany and elsewhere, including plenty of organic brands and a few lovely ciders, such as a range with an apple varietal name from Mr Whitehead's Cider Company in Hampshire. Helpful pony-tailed owner Martin Kemp has just added the floral, delicate Swiss Appenzeller beers, complementing beers at the other end of the weight spectrum, such as the fantastic, smoky Guinness brewed in Dublin for the Belgium market. Home-brewing and wine-making equipment is also on sale, should you fancy a go yourself.

Wine

Wine merchants

Some retailers also have wine bars; for details, see **Wine Bars**, starting on p331. If you want to learn more about wine, see **Courses**, starting on p353.

Balls Brothers
313 Cambridge Heath Road, E2 9LQ (7739 1642/www.ballsbrothers.co.uk). Bethnal Green tube. **Open** 9am-5.30pm Mon-Fri. **Credit** AmEx, DC, MC, V.
Far away from the hub of its bars in the City and the West End, the Balls Bros head office and cellars sit amid Victorian railway arches under the main Liverpool Street to Cambridge line. There's enough cellarage to allow for a fine selection of older Bordeaux and Burgundy, but this extensive listing of classic areas is at the expense of Spain and Italy, where the selection is poor. The New World needs work too, with only Grant Burge's range from Australia really drinkable. If you wish to try the wines, the bars hold occasional tastings, which anyone can attend for a small fee.

Berry Bros & Rudd
3 St James's Street, SW1A 1EG (7396 9600/ www.bbr.com). Green Park tube. **Open** 10am-6pm Mon-Fri; 10am-4pm Sat. **Credit** AmEx, DC, MC, V.
More like the reception area of a country house hotel than a shop, the large wood-panelled main room is gorgeous, rickety – and intimidating. Dodge into one of the three rooms showing part of the company's vast selection if you need to get away from the friendly, but slightly pompous staff. Traditional areas rule, with a moderate amount of 2004 Bordeaux en primeur (to be bought before it's been aged – it's cheaper, but more risky), not a great deal of vodka or gin, but decent cognac, armagnac, calvados and whisky. The fortified selection is one of the best in London, with good sherries, port and Madeira. The company's website is also excellent.

Corney & Barrow
194 Kensington Park Road, W11 2ES (7221 5122/head office 7265 2400/ www.corneyandbarrow.com). Ladbroke Grove tube. **Open** 10.30am-9pm Mon-Fri; 10.30am-8pm Sat. **Credit** AmEx, MC, V.

Wedged in between pavement cafés and restaurants, this small shop offers a mere selection of the overall Corney & Barrow range. Bordeaux is passed down piecemeal from the broking division, which explains the fantastic, if erratic, array of older vintages in the mid-price range. C&B tends to concentrate on medium-sized winemakers, rather than hand-picking tiny growers, with mixed results. A separate catalogue is devoted to Burgundy producer Oliver Leflaive – his 2000 Puligny-Montrachet 'Champ Grain' is one of the better wines in a good-to-middling range. Gosset magnum Champagne is also good value.

Green & Blue [NEW]
38 Lordship Lane, SE22 8HJ (8693 9250/ www.greenandbluewines.com). East Dulwich rail/ 40, 176, 185 bus. **Open** 11am-11pm Mon-Sat; noon-10.30pm Sun. **Snacks** £2-£5. **House wine** £10.50 bottle, £3 glass. **Credit** MC, V.
Run by Kate Thal (former sommelier at now-defunct Pharmacy and Dakota), who has always harboured a distaste for large brands, this shop is a compilation of the unusual and delicious. It's definitely worth putting some time aside to browse this small, minimalist shop. You can't miss the loud lime green shopfront, and there's a lovely bar at the back. Barrie Smith and Judi Cullam are renowned for their rieslings, made in Western Australia's Frankland River estate; the 2004 Rocky Gully has gorgeous, exotic honeysuckle flavours. Muscadet, which is often undistinguished, is represented by the fabulously concentrated Sur Lie, 2002 Semper Excelsior from Pierre Luneau.

Handford Wines
105 Old Brompton Road, SW7 3LE (7589 6113/ www.handford.net). South Kensington tube. **Open** 10am-8.30pm Mon-Sat. **Credit** AmEx, MC, V.
Highly personable James Handford has assembled a list of smaller growers in his tiny shop, often shipping them direct rather than relying on intermediary importers. His best discoveries include the excellent premier cru Champagne producer Brochet-Hervieux, which provides 500 cases a year for Handford. There are also some lovely Bordeaux blends from South Africa. Handford has another outlet at 12 Portland Road, W11 4LE (7221 9614).

Jeroboams
6 Pont Street, SW1X 9EL (7235 1612/ www.jeroboams.co.uk). Knightsbridge or Sloane Square tube. **Open** 10am-8pm Mon-Fri; 10am-7pm Sat. **Credit** AmEx, MC, V.
Jeroboams has become a small chain in the past year, taking on the La Réserve shops, including Milroy's of Soho (see p358). The company closed La Réserve in Fulham, but it still has seven wine outlets, and has kept the old Victorian-style cornershop look in many, with large windows and awnings. Although Mark Reynier has left La Réserve in Knightsbridge, he still works as a consultant to Jeroboams, maintaining the standard of Burgundy with good but lesser-known producers such as Didier Chevillon at Domaine Dupont-Tisserandot. Look too for the wines of up-and-coming Burgundy producer David Duband.

Majestic Wine Warehouse
63 Chalk Farm Road, NW1 8AN (7485 0478/ www.majestic.co.uk). Chalk Farm tube. **Open** 10am-8pm Mon-Fri; 9am-7pm Sat; 10am-5pm Sun. **Credit** AmEx, MC, V.
Although there's less room than in many other Majestic car parks (you could get in about a dozen vehicles), you can still load cases of wine into your parked motor in the garage-like forecourt. Which

is important when the minimum sale is 12 bottles. The format is working well for Majestic, which is one of the few high-street chains to be showing a steady sales climb. People are attracted by an OK range and some really good prices. Choose two bottles of the fine 2004 sauvignon blanc Drylands from New Zealand in a case of 12, and they become £7.99 each, rather than the standard price of £9.99. Chile's 2004 Casillero del Diablo shiraz is available in every supermarket, but not at £4.67, the price for which multiple bottles can be bought here. Check the website for the branch nearest you.

Nicolas
157 Great Portland Street, W1W 6QR (7580 1622/www.nicolas-wines.com). Great Portland Street or Oxford Circus tube. **Open** 9am-7.30pm Mon-Fri; 11am-6pm Sat. **Credit** AmEx, MC, V.
This French-owned shop makes a pleasant change. With most high-street chains having gone New World-mad, the sight of shelf after shelf of wines from France is unusual indeed. Avoid the average selections from classic regions and consider the excellent AC Beaujolais Saint-Armour 2004 Domaine des Billards or René Muré's 2003 pinot noir from Alsace, worth trying for its fruit and refreshing acidity. Other pluses are helpful French staff and clean, bright, well-laid-out premises. Nicolas has 475 shops around Europe, including 21 in London; check the website for details.

Oddbins
57 Lombard Road, SW11 3RX (7738 1029/ www.oddbins.com). Clapham Junction rail. **Open** 10am-9pm Mon-Thur; 10am-10pm Fri, Sat; 10am-8pm Sun. **Credit** AmEx, MC, V.
Many people walk past this flagship store of the Oddbins chain, tucked beneath Holborn Viaduct. But it's worth a peek, if only to inhale the dank fumes of water seeping through brick arches. The fine wine room is not quite the delight it was, with too much 2003 Burgundy from a deal done for the 2002 vintage. The range from Greece has been wound down of late, and the selection from Italy and Spain, aside from Alejandro Fernandez's wines, needs some attention. The obsession with Aussie producers D'Arenburg and South African Bruce Jack continues, and there is a great array of 2004 New Zealand sauvignon blanc. Oddbins was taken over in 2002 by French company Castel (which also owns the Nicolas chain), and many key staff, including star buyer Steve Daniel, have now left. Check the website for the branch nearest you – there are more than 50 within the M25.

Philglas & Swiggot
21 Northcote Road, SW11 1NG (7924 4494/ www.philglas-swiggot.co.uk). Clapham Junction rail. **Open** 11am-7pm Mon-Sat; noon-5pm Sun. **Credit** AmEx, MC, V.
A branch in Marylebone has recently been added to those in Richmond and Battersea, but it hasn't diluted the quality of this outstanding outfit, which is still the place to go for top New World wines. The line-up of Australian rieslings from cool climate regions in Victoria is exemplary; there are some crackers from the other side of the country too. The Italian selection is mostly made from the local grape sangiovese; it's good, even if it isn't quite Super ('Super-Tuscans' tend to major in French varietals like merlot and cabernet sauvignon). Wood floors, spare white walls and spotlights provide pleasant surroundings in which to survey some great wines.

Wine of Course
216 Archway Road, N6 5AX (8347 9006/ www.wineofcourse.com). Highgate tube. **Open** 10am-9pm Mon-Sat; noon-9pm Sun. **Credit** AmEx, MC, V.
This super selection of the world's wines largely avoids Bordeaux and Burgundy, but has a good spread from Australia, Italy, Spain, Germany and New Zealand. You can park outside the shop between 10am and 4pm, and after 7pm. Delivery within the M25 costs a very reasonable £8 for up to ten cases, and free if you live in certain north or east postcodes.

Mail order & internet

Adnams Wines
East Green, Southwold, Suffolk IP18 6JW (01502 727222/www.adnamswines.co.uk). **Open** phone enquiries 9am-8pm Mon-Fri; 9am-5pm Sat. **Credit** MC, V.
This excellent regional merchant began as a brewery in the 14th century, and its Adnams ale is available throughout the South-east. Now the company owns two hotels in Southwold, as well as a wine shop: the Wine Cellar & Kitchen Store. The merchant business delivers wines anywhere in the UK, whether you want the 2003 en primeur port, the 2001 chardonnay from Viña Leyda in Chile or the 2002 Sur from Bodegas Inurrieta in Spain. There's also plenty of good southern Burgundy 'away from the region of premier cru egos,' as senior wine-buyer Alastair Marshall puts it.

Domaine Direct NEW
6-9 Cynthia Street, N1 9JF (7837 1142/www.domainedirect.co.uk). **Open** phone enquiries 8.30am-6pm Mon-Fri. **Credit** MC, V.
In business since 1981, Domaine Direct offers an outstanding selection of wines from Burgundy, as well as a few good buys from the New World, on a very well-designed website. Jean-Marc Boillot's 1999 premier cru Montrevenots, Beaune, stands out as good value at £19.98.

Farr Vintners
220 Queenstown Road, SW8 4LP (7821 2000/www.farr-vintners.com). **Open** phone enquiries 9am-6pm Mon-Fri. **Credit** MC, V.
This highly renowned Bordeaux specialist also lists some fine producers from Burgundy and the Rhône, plus a few more from around the globe. There's still plenty of 2000 claret, including the sublime Ausone (£375), which Alain Vauthier has taken to a new, inspired level. Minimum order is £500; delivery for up to 14 cases costs £14 in London and £15-£25 in the rest of the UK.

Justerini & Brooks
61 St James's Street, SW1A 1LZ (7493 8721/www.justerinis.com). **Open** phone enquiries 9am-5.30pm Mon-Fri. **Credit** AmEx, MC, V.
Up the road from competitor Berry Bros & Rudd (*see p357*), this retail outlet is more office than shop, with computers and curvy desks where staff wheel and deal premium wines. Much of their sales come from broking, and on-site they will only sell wines by the case. Beware the vintage reports, which can be overly positive. Tasting notes – a 'summer fruit core encircled by bracingly fresh acids' – are also a bit ripe, but the website is easy to use. Great wines include those by maverick Loire producer Didier Dagueneau, who looks like Björn Borg.

Lay & Wheeler
Holton Park, Holton St Mary, Suffolk CO7 6NN (01206 764446/www.laywheeler.com). **Open** phone enquiries 9am-6pm Mon-Fri; 9am-1pm Sat. **Credit** MC, V.
This well-respected East Anglian company has recently followed the trend of wine merchants opening wine bars in London, with two new outlets in the City (details on the website). The merchant list has good offerings from New Zealand, supplemented by plenty from Bordeaux and Burgundy. Unfortunately, you can't view the full list on the website.

Stone, Vine & Sun NEW
13 Humphreys Far, Hazeley Road, Twyford, Winchester, Hants SO21 1QA (01962 712351/www.stonevine.co.uk). **Open** 9am-6pm Mon-Fri; 9.30am-4pm Sat. **Credit** MC, V.
This new outfit has a name that fashionably suggests an emphasis on the growing rather than the making of wine. The inclusion of the lovely 2002 'Les Caillerets' Chassagne-Montrachet from René Lequin-Colin confirms that individuals and not factories are behind most of the list; it has real intensity and is one to lay down. Credit is due for the extensive range from the Loire, overlooked by so many UK wine merchants, and especially for the examples from Chinon.

Vinceremos Wines & Spirits
74 Kirkgate, Leeds LS2 7DJ (0113 244 0002/www.vinceremos.co.uk). **Open** phone enquiries 9am-5.30pm Mon-Fri. **Credit** AmEx, MC, V.
Organic specialist Vinceremos offers 300 wines from across the globe, as well as beer, cider, spirits, cordials and olive oil. From the US, the Fetzer sub-brand Bonterra is a good starting point. It's a reliable, aromatic, peach-flavoured take on the unusual southern French grape roussanne. France has led the way with organics and, while it's a shame not to see pioneers like Nicolas Joly from the Loire or Jean Meyer from Alsace here (due to their deals with other importers), biodynamic producer Huet's luscious, honeyed 2002 Vouvray Le Haut Lieu Sec is present and correct.

Vintage Roots
Farley Farms, Reading Road, Arborfield, Berks RG2 9HT (0118 976 1999/www.vintageroots.co.uk). **Open** phone enquiries 8.30am-5.30pm Mon-Fri. **Credit** MC, V.
The best-known organic wine merchant is owned by Neil Palmer, a man committed to the cause of more naturally made wine. Many top organic winemakers are stocked at other merchants without being flagged up as such, but at least Vintage Roots guarantees that you won't be drinking a concoction of chemicals. It's an odd fact that many wines are filtered using gelatine or cow's bladder; Vintage Roots has wines that have used neither of these during the winemaking process, which means that certain bottles are suitable for vegetarians and vegans.

The Wine Society
Gunnels Wood Road, Stevenage, Herts SG1 2BG (01438 740222 /www.thewinesociety.com). **Open** phone enquiries 8.30am-9pm Mon-Fri; 9am-5pm Sat. **Credit** MC, V.
'The Society buys direct from suppliers, shipping wine from all over the world to Stevenage,' states the web page. It's hardly the most romantic image, but the storage facilities are extensive and some of the wines really impressive. Membership costs £40, which might seem steep, but this gives access to wines like Gaston Huet's Vouvrays dating back to 1921 – yes, white wine can age if it's well made and there's enough residual sugar. The good-to-average 2004 Burgundy vintage is on offer in bond, so you can buy it without paying VAT, have it stored, then pay up when it comes out of the warehouse.

Yapp Bros
The Old Brewery, Mere, Wilts BA12 6DY (01747 860423/www.yapp.co.uk). **Open** phone enquiries 9am-6pm Mon-Sat. **Credit** MC, V.
Praise is due to Robin Yapp for majoring in two areas of France that the British wine trade once so neglected – the Loire and the Rhone. The latter has gained in popularity in recent years, but few can match the outstanding selections here from Jean-Louis Chave, including his exceptional 1997 Hermitage (to be kept for ten years), as well as the best of Auguste Clape. From the Loire, Domaine du Closel's 2000 'La Jalousie', Cuvée Classique, is a superb chenin blanc and Domaine Filliatreau's 2003 an excellent Saumur-Champigny.

Spirits

Gerry's
74 Old Compton Street, W1D 4UW (7734 4215). Leicester Square or Piccadilly Circus tube. **Open** 9am-6.30pm Mon-Fri; 9am-5.30pm Sat. **No credit cards.**
There's an incredible range of spirits in this quirky, label-infested shop (handwritten – someone had fun penning all those). The great range of tequilas includes Herradura's excellent Blanco, and J Bally's white version from Martinique is among the rarely found rums. You'll find a choice of 160 vodkas, five cachaças, four piscos, plus limoncello for dainty drinkers and absinthe for the decadents. A terrific range of miniatures enables you to find out what quality Madeira tastes like with a tiny sample of Blandy's or to experiment with a measure of De Kuyper's cherry brandy in a cocktail. Note: no credit cards are accepted.

Milroy's of Soho
3 Greek Street, W1V 6NX (7437 9311/www.milroys.co.uk). Tottenham Court Road tube. **Open** 10am-8pm Mon-Fri; 10am-7pm Sun. **Credit** AmEx, MC, V.
Having been bought by La Réserve, Milroy's has now fallen under the Jeroboams (*see p357*) umbrella. Although you can take advantage of some good deals on wine, as Jeroboams sells through old La Réserve stock, it is the phenomenal range of whiskies that catches the eye: there are some 700 single malts (with about a dozen available to taste or, in the tasting cellar, purchase by the dram), as well as bourbon, and Canadian Irish, even Japanese whiskies.

Tea & coffee
Piccadilly store **Fortnum & Mason** (*see p344*) is renowned for its collection of fine teas from around the world.

Algerian Coffee Stores
52 Old Compton Street, W1V 6PB (7437 2480/www.algcoffee.co.uk). Leicester Square or Piccadilly Circus tube. **Open** 9am-7pm Mon-Sat. **Credit** AmEx, MC, V.
Founded in 1887, this little Soho shop is one of the oldest coffee establishments in the UK. It sells more than 140 different kinds of coffee, with beans carefully selected from all corners of the world, including estate coffees from Colombia and Hawaii. Variations include terrific espresso coffees – should you wish, you can also buy liveried espresso cups. Nor should you overlook a fantastic range of 200 teas, including herbal, Chinese (white and black), Japanese green, fruit infusions and Argentinian maté – with handsome gourds and bombillas to drink it from. There are special offers each month and a mail order service.

HR Higgins
79 Duke Street, W1K 5AS (7629 3913/www.hrhiggins.co.uk). Bond Street tube. **Open** 9.30am-5.30pm Mon-Fri; 10am-5pm Sat. **Credit** AmEx, MC, V.
Grandson David is the third Higgins generation to take charge of this traditional shop, run by friendly and knowledgeable staff. In addition to an exemplary range of coffee, freshly roasted at its Waltham Abbey premises and ground on-site, Higgins brooks innovation in the form of decaffeinated Colombian and Costa Rican varieties. There are also teas from Ceylon, China, Taiwan and India, and fruit varieties (try the grapefruit-flavoured Blue Lady). The revamped website has improved mail order services.

Monmouth Coffee House
27 Monmouth Street, WC2H 9EU (7379 3516/www.monmouthcoffee.co.uk). Covent Garden tube. **Open** 8am-6.30pm Mon-Sat. **Credit** MC, V.
At the Monmouth Coffee House, a lot of care goes into choosing ethically sourced, top-quality beans, as suggested by their involvement in the laudable Cup of Excellence project. You may still be able to catch the Colombian Cup of Excellence; if not, the El Salvadorian should arrive in late September 2005. The discerning selection of coffees changes each year, and staff are hugely well informed. This branch has a cosy tasting area at the back, so you can sample a brew with a pastry before you buy; there is also a shop and a stall at Borough Market.

The Tea House
15A Neal Street, WC2H 9PU (7240 7539). Covent Garden tube. **Open** 10am-7pm Mon-Sat; 11am-6pm Sun. **Credit** AmEx, MC, V.
A location in Covent Garden isn't generally a good advert for gourmets, but this shop pretty much avoids the tacky souvenir accessories. Instead there are more than 100 types of loose-leaf and bagged tea, including a good range of fruit blends and specialist green teas (white monkey and pai mun tan are among the Chinese rarities), Argentinian maté, even a powdered Japanese variety complete with whisk. Mail order is also available.

SHOPS & COURSES

Maps

The following maps highlight London's key restaurant areas – the districts with the highest density of good places to eat and drink. The maps show precisely where each restaurant is located, as well as major landmarks and underground stations. For an overview of every area, see **Key to Maps** below; this shows which areas are covered, and places them in context.

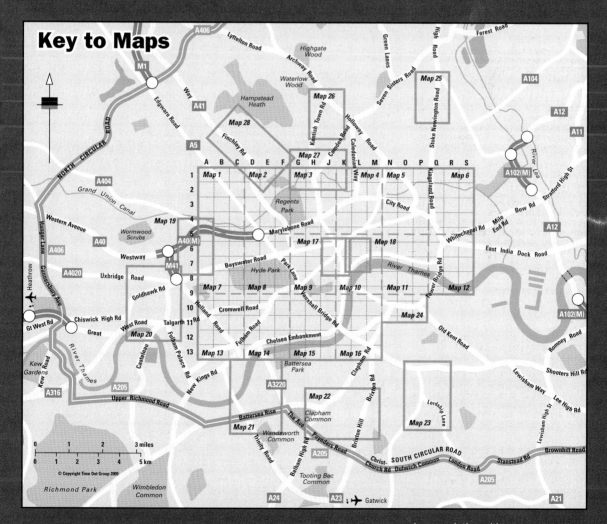

Key to Maps

In association with

Gordon's

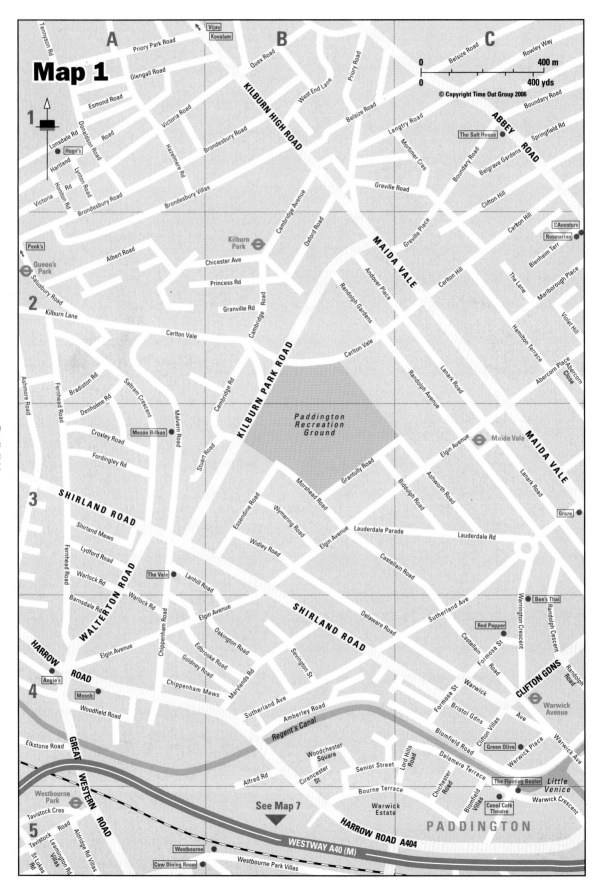

Map 1

MAPS

A   B   C

Vijay
Kovalam

Tennyson Rd
Priory Park Road
Glengall Road
Esmond Road
Road
Donaldson Road
Victoria Road
Brondesbury Road
KILBURN HIGH ROAD
Quex Road
West End Lane
Priory Road
Belsize Road
Belsize Road
Langtry Road
Mortimer Cres
Boundary Road
The Salt House
ABBEY ROAD
Springfield Rd
Boundary Road
Rowley Way
400 m
400 yds
© Copyright Time Out Group 2006

Lonsdale Rd
Hartland Rd
Lynton Road
Hazelmere Rd
Hugo's
Victoria Rd
Hemlon Rd
Brondesbury Road
Brondesbury Villas
Cambridge Avenue
Oxford Road
Greville Road
Greville Place
MAIDA VALE
Carlton Hill
Clifton Hill
Carlton Hill
Belgrave Gardens
Carlton Hill
The Lane
Blenheim Terr
Marlborough Place
L'Aventure
Rosmarino
Violet Hill
Abercorn Place
Abercorn Close

Penk's
Queen's Park
Salusbury Road
Albert Road
Chicester Ave
Princess Rd
Kilburn Park
Randolph Gardens
Andover Place
Hamilton Terrace

Kilburn Lane
Carlton Vale
Granville Rd
Cambridge Road
Cambridge Ave
Carlton Vale
Randolph Avenue
Lanark Road

Ashmore Road
Fernhead Road
Bradiston Rd
Denholme Rd
Saltram Crescent
Malvern Road
Mesón Bilbao
Stuart Road
Cambridge Rd
KILBURN PARK ROAD
Paddington Recreation Ground
Morshead Road
Grantully Road
Elgin Avenue
Maida Vale
MAIDA VALE
Lanark Road
Graze

Croxley Road
Fordingley Rd

3 SHIRLAND ROAD
Shirland Mews
Lydford Road
Fernhead Road
WALTERTON ROAD
Warlock Rd
Barnsdale Rd
Warlock Rd
The Vale
Lanhill Road
Elgin Avenue
Chippenham Road
Oakington Road
Edbrooke Road
Goldney Road
Chippenham Mews
Essendine Road
Wymering Road
Widley Road
Elgin Avenue
Lauderdale Parade
Lauderdale Rd
Castellain Road
SHIRLAND ROAD
Delaware Road
Sevington St
Maryland's Rd
Sutherland Ave
Amberley Road
Biddulph Road
Ashworth Road
Sutherland Ave
Castellain
Formosa St
Warrington Crescent
Randolph Crescent
Ben's Thai
Red Pepper
Warwick
Bristol Gdns
Formosa St
CLIFTON GDNS
Randolph Road
Clifton Villas
Green Olive
Warwick Place
Warwick Avenue
Warwick Ave

HARROW ROAD
Angie's
Mosob
Woodfield Road
Sutherland Ave
Regent's Canal
Woodchester Square
Cirencester St
Senior Street
Lord Hills Road
Chichester Road
Blomfield Road
Delamere Terrace
The Floating Boater
Little Venice
Warwick Crescent

Elkstone Road
GREAT WESTERN ROAD
Westbourne Park
Tavistock Cres
Tavistock Road
Aldridge Rd Villas
Leamington Rd
St Lukes Rd
Alfred Rd
See Map 7
Bourne Terrace
Warwick Estate
Blomfield Villas
Canal Café Theatre
PADDINGTON

Westbourne
WESTWAY A40 (M)
HARROW ROAD A404
Cow Dining Room
Westbourne Park Villas

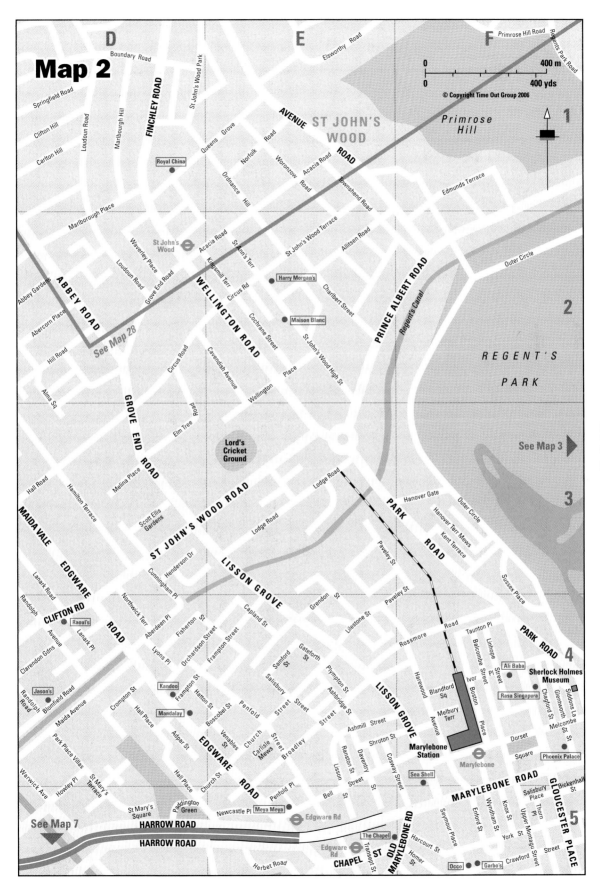

Map 2

D   **E**   **F**

Boundary Road

Springfield Road

Clifton Hill

Carlton Hill

Loudoun Road

Marlborough Hill

FINCHLEY ROAD

St John's Wood Park

AVENUE   ROAD

Elsworthy   Road

Primrose Hill Road

Regents Park Road

ST JOHN'S WOOD

Primrose Hill

0   400 m

0   400 yds

© Copyright Time Out Group 2006

1

Queens Grove

Norfolk Road

Woronzow Road

Acacia Road

Townshend Road

Ordnance Hill

Royal China

Edmunds Terrace

Marlborough Place

St John's Wood

Waverley Place

Loudoun Road

Acacia Road

Kingsmill Terr

St Ann's Terr

Circus Rd

Circus Road

St John's Wood Terrace

Allitsen Road

Charlbert Street

Outer Circle

Abbey Gardens

Abercorn Place

Hill Road

ABBEY ROAD

See Map 28

WELLINGTON ROAD

Harry Morgan's

Cochrane Street

St John's Wood High St

Maison Blanc

PRINCE ALBERT ROAD

Regent's Canal

2

REGENT'S PARK

Alma Sq

GROVE END ROAD

Circus Road

Cavendish Avenue

Road

Wellington Place

Elm Tree

Hamilton Terrace

Hall Road

Melina Place

Scott Ellis Gardens

Lord's Cricket Ground

Lodge Road

Hanover Gate

Hanover Terr Mews

Outer Circle

See Map 3 ▶

3

MAIDA VALE

EDGWARE

Lanark Road

Randolph

Lanark Pl

CLIFTON RD

Raoul's

ST JOHN'S WOOD ROAD

Henderson Dr

Cunningham Pl

Aberdeen Pl

LISSON GROVE

Lodge Road

Paveley St

PARK ROAD

Kent Terrace

Hanover Terr Mews

Sussex Place

Northwick Terr

Lyons Pl

Fisherton St

Orchardson Street

Frampton Street

Capland St

Grendon St

Lilestone St

Paveley St

Rossmore Road

Taunton Pl

Linhope St

Balcombe Street

PARK ROAD

4

Ali Baba

Sherlock Holmes Museum

Clarendon Gdns

Avenue

Randolph Road

Blomfield Road

Jason's

Maida Avenue

Park Place Villas

Crompton St

Hall Place

Kandoo

Frampton St

Hatton St

Boscobel St

Mandalay

Penfold Street

Samford St

Gateforth St

Salisbury Street

Plympton St

Ashbridge St

Street

Ashmill Street

Shroton St

LISSON GROVE

Harewood Avenue

Blandford Sq

Ivor Boston Place

Melbury Terr

Dorset Square

Balcombe Street

Rasa Singapura

Glentworth Chagford St St

Siddons La

Melcombe St

Phoenix Palace

Warwick Ave

Howley Pl

St Mary's Terrace

EDGWARE ROAD

Adpar St

Hall Place

Church Street

Carlisle Mews

Venables Street

Broadley Street

Ranston St

Daventry St

Lisson Street

Cosway Street

Marylebone Station

Marylebone

Dorset

Square

Phoenix Palace

Bickenhall

See Map 7

St Mary's Square

Paddington Green

Newcastle Pl

Meya Meya

Edgware Rd

Penfold Pl

Bell Street

Sea Shell

MARYLEBONE ROAD

Salisbury Place

Wyndham St

Enford St

Knox St

Thorn Pl

Upper Montagu Street

GLOUCESTER PLACE

5

HARROW ROAD

HARROW ROAD

Edgware Rd

Transept St

The Chapel

OLD MARYLEBONE RD

CHAPEL ST

Harcourt St

Homer St

Seymour Place

Occo   **Garbo's**

York St

Crawford Street

Herbet Road

MAPS

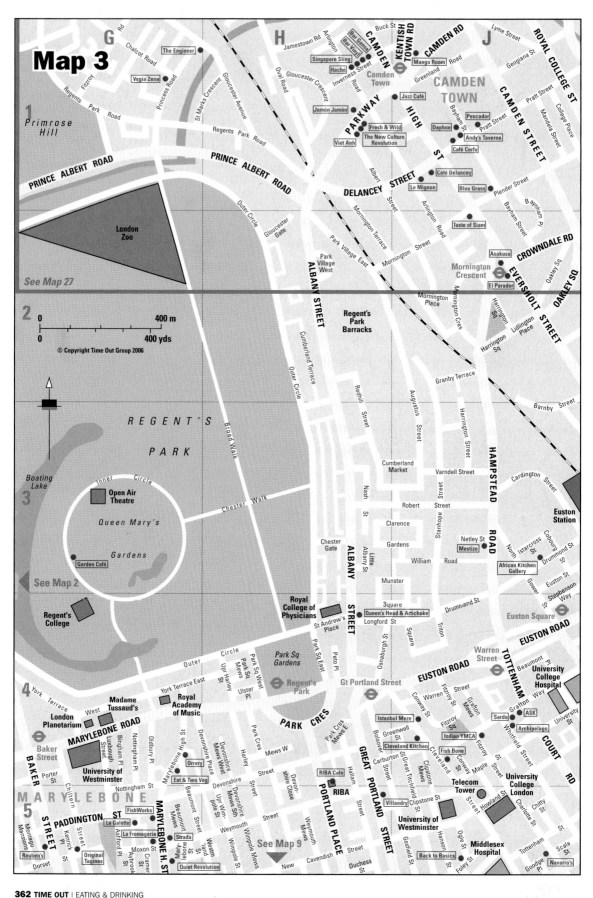

Map 3

Primrose Hill

The Engineer

Vegia Zena

PRINCE ALBERT ROAD

PRINCE ALBERT ROAD

London Zoo

See Map 27

Bar Gansa
Bar Vinyl
Singapore Sling
Haché
CAMDEN TOWN
Buck St
KENTISH TOWN RD
CAMDEN RD
Lyme Street
Geogiana St
ROYAL COLLEGE ST

Mango Room
Greenland Road
CAMDEN TOWN
Pratt Mews
College Place
Mandela Street

Jazz Café
Jamón Jamón
Fresh & Wild
Viet Anh
The New Culture Revolution
PARKWAY
HIGH
Pescador
Daphne
Andy's Taverna
Café Corfu
Bayham St
Pratt Street
CAMDEN STREET

Café Delancey
DELANCEY
STREET
Le Mignon
Bluu Grass
Plender Street
Bayham Pl

Taste of Siam
Arlington Road
Bayham Street
CROWNDALE RD

Asakusa
Mornington Crescent
El Parador
Mornington Street
EVERSHOLT STREET
Oakley Sq
OAKLEY SQ

Regent's Park Barracks

Harrington Sq
Lidlington Place

ALBANY STREET

Park Village West
Park Village East
Mornington Terrace
Mornington Road
Mornington Place
Mornington Cres

Granby Terrace

Barnby Street

2
0 ———— 400 m
0 ———— 400 yds
© Copyright Time Out Group 2006

Cumberland Terrace
Outer Circle
Gloucester Gate

Augustus Street
Redhill Street
Harrington Street
Cardington Street

REGENT'S PARK

Broad Walk

Cumberland Market
Varndell Street
HAMPSTEAD ROAD

Boating Lake

Open Air Theatre

Chester Walk

Nash St
Robert Street
Clarence Gardens
Stanhope Street
William Road

Netley St
Mestizo
North Istarcross
Cobourg St
Drummond St

Euston Station

3
Queen Mary's
Gardens
Garden Café
See Map 2

Inner Circle

Chester Gate
Little Albany St
Munster Square
Drummond St

African Kitchen Gallery
Euston St
Gower St
Stephenson Way

Regent's College

Royal College of Physicians
St Andrew's Place
ALBANY STREET
Queen's Head & Artichoke
Longford St
Triton Square

Euston Square

Outer Circle
Park Sq West
Park Sq Mews
Upr Harley St
Ulster Pl
Park Sq Gardens
Park Sq East
Peto Pl

Osnaburgh Street
EUSTON ROAD
Warren Street
TOTTENHAM
EUSTON ROAD
University College Hospital

4
York Terrace
West
Madame Tussaud's
London Planetarium
Royal Academy of Music
York Terrace East
Regent's Park
Gt Portland Street
Warren St
Conway St
Fitzroy St
Grafton Mews
Grafton Way
Warren St
Beaumont Pl
Istanbul Meze
Sardo
ASK
Archipelago
University St

MARYLEBONE ROAD
Nottingham Pl
Luxbough Street
Bingham Pl
Oldbury Pl
Devonshire Mews West
Harley Street
Greenwell St
Bolsover St
Fitzroy Sq
Cleveland St
Whitfield Street
COURT RD

Baker Street
BAKER STREET
Porter St
University of Westminster
Orrery
Eat & Two Veg
Devonshire St
Devonshire Place
Devonshire Mews Sth
Clipstone Mews
Clipstone
Indian YMCA
Cleveland Kitchen
Fish Bone
Maple St
University College London

5
MARYLEBONE
PADDINGTON STREET
FishWorks
La Galette
La Fromagerie
Strada
Reuben's
Original Tagines
Quiet Revolution
Nottingham St
MARYLEBONE H. ST
Ashford Pl
Moxon St
Cramer St
Aybrook
Beaumont Mews
Beaumont Street
Upr Wimpole Mews
Devonshire Mews
Upr Wimpole St
See Map 9
Weymouth Mews
Wimpole Mews
Wimpole Street
Hallam Street
PORTLAND PLACE
RIBA Café
RIBA
GREAT PORTLAND STREET
Villandry
Clipstone Street
Telecom Tower
University of Westminster
Howland Street
Charlotte St
Chitty St
University College London

Montagu Mansions
Dorset St
Kenrick Pl
Weymouth Street
New Cavendish Street
Duchess St
Back to Basics
Gosfield St
Middlesex Hospital
Foley St
Ogle St
Goodge St
Tottenham St
Scala St
Navarro's

MAPS

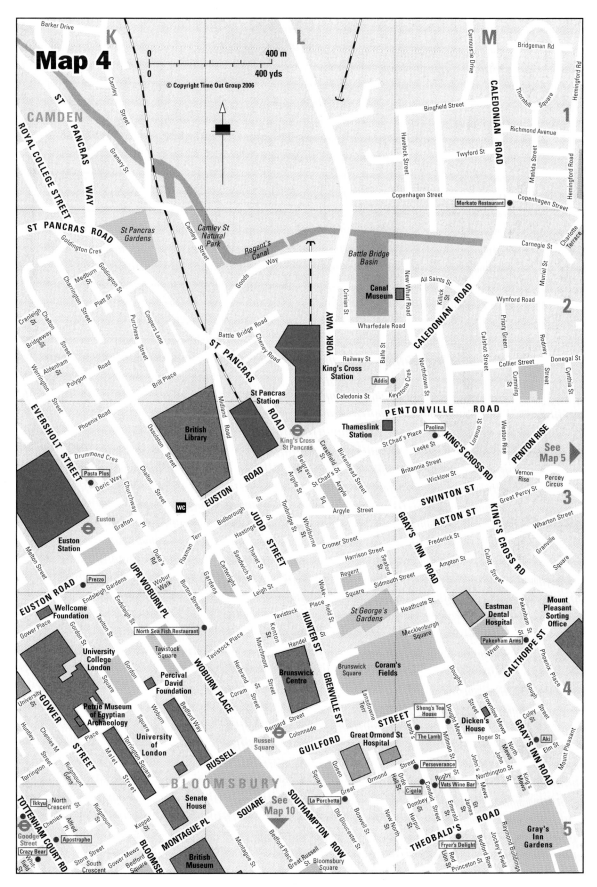

Map 4

K   L   M

Barker Drive

400 m
400 yds

© Copyright Time Out Group 2006

CAMDEN

ST PANCRAS WAY

ROYAL COLLEGE STREET

Camley Street

Granary St

Bridgeman Rd

Carnoustie Drive

CALEDONIAN ROAD

Bingfield Street

Thornhill Square

Hemingford Rd

Hemingford Road

1

Richmond Avenue

Twyford St

Matilda Street

ST PANCRAS ROAD

St Pancras Gardens

Goldington Cres

Medburn St

Goldington St

Charrington Street

Platt St

Purchese Street

Coopers Lane

Brill Place

Camley Street

Regent's Canal

Camley St Natural Park

Goods Way

Battle Bridge Basin

Canal Museum

Havelock Street

Copenhagen Street   Merkato Restaurant   Copenhagen Street

Charlotte Terrace

Carnegie St

All Saints St

Killick St

New Wharf Road

Wharfedale Road

Crinan St

Muriel St

Wynford Road

CALEDONIAN ROAD

Priory Green

Collier Street

Rodney Street

Donegal St

Calshot Street

Cynthia St

2

Cranleigh St   Chalton St   Bridgeway

Aldenham St   Polygon Road

Phoenix Road

Werrington Street

Osulston Street

Chalton Street

Midland Road

St Pancras Station

Battle Bridge Road

Cheney Road

ST PANCRAS ROAD

YORK WAY

Railway St

King's Cross Station

Balfe St

Addis

Caledonia St

Keystone Cres

Northdown St

Cumming St

EVERSHOLT STREET

Drummond Cres

Pasta Plus

Doric Way

Churchway

British Library

Euston Road

WC

Grafton Pl

Duke's Rd

Wobur Walk

King's Cross St Pancras

Thameslink Station

St Chad's Place

Paolina

Belgrave St

Argyle St

Crestfield St

Birkenhead Street

Leeke St

Britannia Street

Wicklow St

PENTONVILLE ROAD

KING'S CROSS RD

Weston Rise

Penton St

PENTON RISE

See Map 5

Vernon Rise

Percey Circus

Great Percy St

Wharton Street

3

Euston Station

Melton Street

Euston Road   Prezzo

Endsleigh Gardens

Wellcome Foundation

Gordon St

Taviton St

Endsleigh St

UPR WOBURN PL

North Sea Fish Restaurant

Flaxman Terr

Cartwright Gardens

Bidborough St

Hastings St

Thanet St

Sandwich St

Leigh St

St Chad's St

Argyle Sq

Argyle   Street

Whidborne St

Tonbridge St

Cromer Street

Harrison Street

Regent Square

Sidmouth Street

Seaford Street

Wakefield St

Ampton St

GRAY'S INN ROAD

SWINTON ST

ACTON ST

Frederick St

Cubitt Street

KING'S CROSS RD

Granville Square

4

University College London

Gower Place

Gordon Square

Percival David Foundation

Petrie Museum of Egyptian Archaeology

Tavistock St

Tavistock Square

Woburn Square

WOBURN PLACE

Bedford Way

University of London

Torrington Square

Tavistock Place

Marchmont Street

Herbrand Street

Coram St

Handel St

HUNTER ST

Kenton St

Bernard Street

Colonnade

Russell Square

Brunswick Centre

Brunswick Square

Coram's Fields

Lansdowne Terr

St George's Gardens

Mecklenburgh Square

Heathcote St

Doughty Mews

Doughty Street

Sheng's Tea House

Dicken's House

Roger St

Eastman Dental Hospital

Pakenham St

Pakenham Arms

Wren St

Mount Pleasant Sorting Office

CALTHORPE ST

Phoenix Place

Gough St

Brownlow Mews

North Mews

Elm St

GRAY'S INN ROAD

Coley St

Aki

Mount Pleasant

Huntley Street

Chenies M

Ridgmount Gdns

University St

GOWER STREET

Malet Street

Torrington Place

Ridgmount Street

Ridgmount Pl

Alfred Pl

BLOOMSBURY

Keppel Street

Montague St

Bedford Way

Russell Square

SOUTHAMPTON ROW

See Map 10

GUILFORD   STREET

Guilford Street

Queen Square

Great Ormond St Hospital

Orde Hall St

Ormond

Lamb's Conduit Street

The Lamb

Perseverance

Cigala

Vats Wine Bar

Great James Street

Millman St

John's Mews

Northington St

John St

Dombey Street

Emerald St

Harpur Street

Dombey St

King's Mews

GRAY'S INN ROAD

James M

5

Ikkyu

North Crescent

Apostrophe

Goodge Street

TOTTENHAM COURT RD

Crazy Bear

Windmill St

Chenies St

Store Street

South Crescent

Gower Mews

Bedford Avenue

BLOOMSBURY

MONTAGUE PL

Montague Street

British Museum

Bedford Square

Great Russell St

Bloomsbury Square

La Porchetta

New North Street

Boswell Street

Old Gloucester Street

Great Ormond St

THEOBALD'S   ROAD

Fryer's Delight

Red Lion St

Bedford Row

Princeton St

Jockey's Field

Raymond Buildings

Gray's Inn Gardens

MAPS

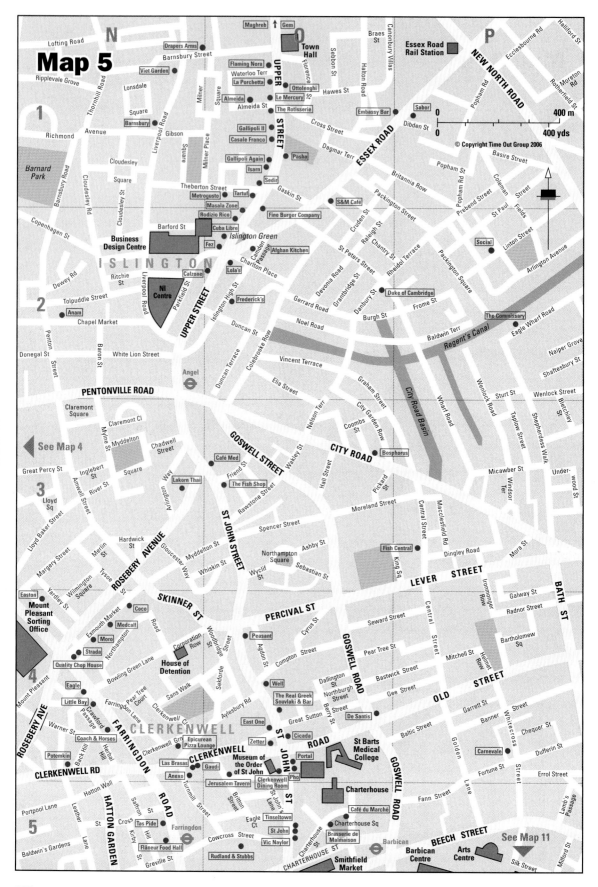

Map 5

N

Lofting Road
Ripplevale Grove
Richmond
Barnard Park
Thornhill Road
Lonsdale
Square
Avenue
Barnsbury Road
Cloudesley
Square
Cloudesley Rd
Copenhagen St
Dewey Rd
Ritchie St
Tolpuddle Street
Chapel Market
Penton Street
Donegal St
White Lion Street
Baron St

ISLINGTON

Barnsbury Street
Drapers Arms
Maghreb Gem
Town Hall
Braes
St
Canonbury Villas
Halton Road
Florence St
Hawes St
Sebbon St
Cross Street
Dagmar Terr
Britannia Row
Embassy Bar Sabor
Dibden St

NEW NORTH ROAD   **P**
Eccleshourne Rd
Halliford St
Popham Rd
Moreton Rd
Rotherfield St
Basire Street
Popham St
Popham Rd
Prebend Street
St Paul
Coleman
Street
Linton Street
Arlington Avenue
Social
© Copyright Time Out Group 2006

0   400 m
0   400 yds

Essex Road Rail Station

ESSEX ROAD

Flaming Nora
Waterloo Terr
La Porchetta
Almeida
Le Mercury
Ottolenghi
Almeida St
The Rotisserie
Viet Garden
Barnsbury
Gallipoli II
Casale Franco
Pasha
Gallipoli Again
Isarn
Sedir
Theberton Street
Metrogusto Tartuf
Gaskin St
Masala Zone
Rodizio Rico
Cuba Libre
Islington Green
Fez
Afghan Kitchen
S&M Café
Fine Burger Company
Cruden St
Raleigh St
Chantry St
Rheidol Terrace
Packington Street
Packington Square
Business Design Centre
Barford St
Camden Passage
Charlton Place
Devonia Road
St Peters Street
Grantbridge St
Danbury St
Duke of Cambridge
Frome St
The Commissary
Eagle Wharf Road
Naiper Grove
Shaftesbury St
Wenlock Road
Calzone
Lola's
NI Centre
Frederick's
Duncan St
Duncan Terrace
Colebrooke Row
Gerrard Road
Noel Road
Burgh St
Baldwin Terr
Regent's Canal
Anam
Angel
Vincent Terrace
Elia Street
Graham Street
City Road Basin
Wharf Road
Sturt St
Wenlock Street
Bletchley St
Taplow Road
Shepherdess Walk
Micawber St
Windsor Ter
Under-wood St

PENTONVILLE ROAD

Claremont Square
Claremont Cl
Great Percy St
Mylne St
Inglebert St
River St
Chadwell Street
Square
Way

See Map 4

Lloyd Sq
Lloyd Baker Street
Amwell Street
Margery Street
Merlin St
Hardwick St
Gloucester Way
Myddelton St
Whiskin St
Wyclif St

GOSWELL STREET
Café Med
Friend St
Wakley St
Lakorn Thai
The Fish Shop
Rawstone Street
Spencer Street
Northampton Square
Ashby St
Sebastian St
CITY ROAD
Bosphorus
Nelson Terr
City Garden Row
Coombs St
Hall Street
Pickard St
Moreland Street
Central Street
Macclesfield Rd
Dingley Road
King Sq
Fish Central

ROSEBERY AVENUE

ST JOHN STREET

LEVER   STREET

BATH ST

Mount Pleasant Sorting Office
Easton
Yardley St
Wilmington Square
Tysoe St
Exmouth Market
Coco
Medcalf
Moro
Strada
Quality Chop House
Northampton St
Bowling Green Lane
Corporation Row
Woodbridge Street
Sekforde St

SKINNER   ST
PERCIVAL ST
Cyrus St
Agdon St
Compton Street
Seward Street
Pear Tree St
Mitchell St
Helmet Row
Ironmonger Row
Galway St
Radnor Street
Bartholomew Sq
Peasant

GOSWELL ROAD
Dallington St
Northburgh Street
Bastwick Street
Gee Street
Garrett St
Banner
Whitecross
Chequer St
Dufferin St
Errol Street
Bastwick Street

OLD   STREET

House of Detention
Well
Eagle
Little Bay
Pear Tree Court
Sans Walk
Aylesbury Rd
The Real Greek Souvlaki & Bar
Great Sutton St
Berry St
De Santis
Baltic Street
Golden
Lane
Carnevale

FARRINGDON   **ROAD**

CLERKENWELL

Coach & Horses
Potemkin
Crawford Passage
Herbal Hill
Warner St
Beech Hill
CLERKENWELL RD
Las Brasas
Anexo
Epicurean Pizza Lounge
Gaudi
Clerkenwell Grn
Zetter
East One
Cicada
Zetter
Portal
Pho
Museum of the Order of St John
Clerkenwell Dining Room
Jerusalem Tavern
St Barts Medical College
Charterhouse
Café du Marché
De Santis
Fortune St
Fann Street
Lamb's Passage

ROSEBERY AVE
Mount Pleasant
Hatton Wall
Portpool Lane
Leather Lane
Hatton Garden
Saffron St
Cross St
Kirby St
Hill
Farringdon
Tas Pide
Flâneur Food Hall
Baldwin's Gardens
Greville St

CLERKENWELL
ST JOHN ST
Britton Street
St John's Lane
St John's St
Eagle Ct
Tinseltown
St John
Vic Naylor
Cowcross Street
Rudland & Stubbs
CHARTERHOUSE ST
Charterhouse Sq
Brasserie de Malmaison
Smithfield Market
Charterhouse
Barbican

BEECH   STREET
See Map 11
Barbican Centre
Arts Centre
Silk Street
Milford St

MAPS

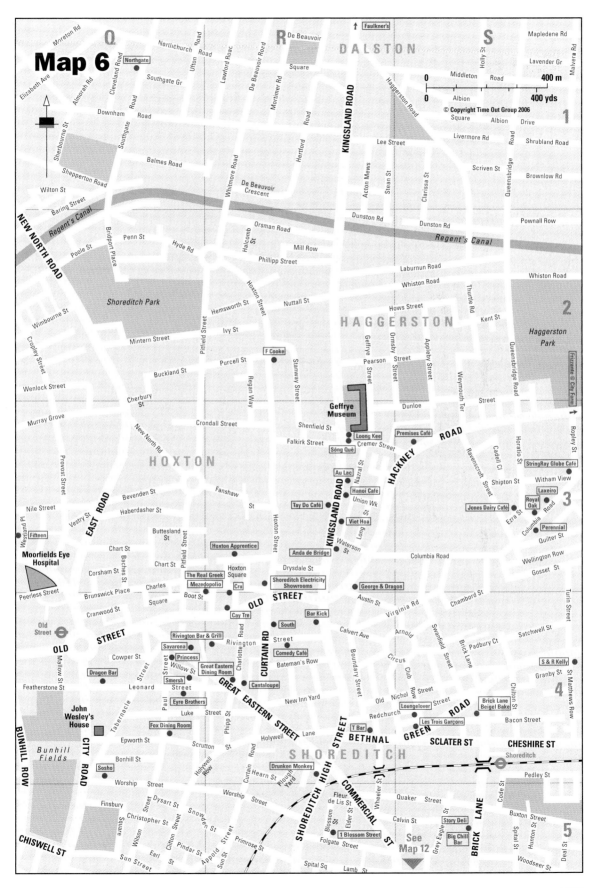

Map 6

DALSTON

HAGGERSTON

Haggerston
Park

Regent's Canal

Shoreditch Park

HOXTON

Geffrye
Museum

Moorfields Eye
Hospital

Old
Street

John
Wesley's
House

Bunhill
Fields

SHOREDITCH

BETHNAL GREEN

See
Map 12

© Copyright Time Out Group 2006

400 m
400 yds

Northgate
Faulkner's
Fifteen
F Cooke
Loong Kee
Premises Café
Söng Quê
StringRay Globe Café
Au Lac
Laxeiro
Hanoi Café
Royal Oak
Tay Do Café
Jones Dairy Café
Perennial
Viet Hoa
Anda de Bridge
Hoxton Apprentice
George & Dragon
The Real Greek
Shoreditch Electricity Showrooms
Mezedopolio
Cru
Cay Tre
Bar Kick
South
Rivington Bar & Grill
Comedy Café
Savarona
S & R Kelly
Princess
Great Eastern Dining Room
Loungelover
Dragon Bar
Smersh
Cantaloupe
Brick Lane Beigel Bake
Eyre Brothers
Les Trois Garçons
Fox Dining Room
T Bar
Sosho
Drunken Monkey
Story Deli
1 Blossom Street
Big Chill Bar
Frizzante @ City Farm

MAPS

TIME OUT | EATING & DRINKING **365**

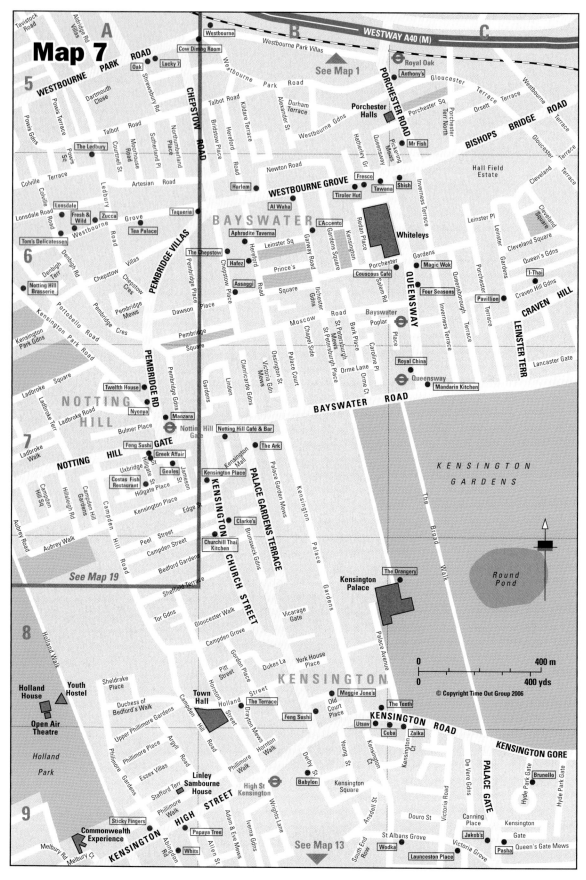

Map 7

A · B · C

WESTWAY A40 (M)

5

Westbourne
Cow Dining Room
Oak · Lucky 7
Royal Oak
Anthony's

WESTBOURNE PARK ROAD

Westbourne Park Villas
Gloucester
Terrace
Terrace
Westbourne
ROAD

Dartmouth Close
Talbot Road
Westbourne
Park Road
Porchester Sq
Porchester Terr North
Orsett Terrace
Gloucester Terrace
BISHOPS BRIDGE

Powis Terrace
Powis Gdns
Kildare Terrace
Durham Terrace
Alexander St
PORCHESTER ROAD
Porchester Sq
Terrace

Talbot Road
Bridstow Place
Hereford Road
Westbourne Gdns
Mr Fish
Hatherley Gr
Queensway
Pickering Mews
Hall Field Estate
Cleveland Terrace

The Ledbury
Colville Terrace
Newton Road
Harlem
WESTBOURNE GROVE
Fresco
Tawana · Shish
Inverness Terrace
Leinster Pl
Cleveland Square
Cleveland Square

Colville Road
Lonsdale
Fresh & Wild · Zucca
Taqueria
Al Waha
Tiroler Hut
L'Accento
Redan Place
Kensington
Gardens Square
Whiteleys
Gardens
Leinster Gardens
Queen's Gdns
I-Thai

BAYSWATER

Lonsdale Road
Grove
Tea Palace
Aphrodite Taverna
Leinster Sq
Garway Road
Gardens Square
Porchester
Gardens
Magic Wok
Porchester Terrace
Craven Hill Gdns

Tom's Delicatessen
Westbourne Grove
The Chepstow
Hereford Rd
Prince's Square
Couscous Café · Salem Rd
Four Seasons
Pavillion
CRAVEN HILL

6

Notting Hill Brasserie
Denbigh Terr
Denbigh Rd
Chepstow Villas
Hafez
Assaggi
Chepstow Place
QUEENSWAY
Ilchester Gdns
Moscow Road
Bayswater
Poplar
LEINSTER TERR

Portobello Road
Pembridge Villas
Pembridge Place
Chepstow Cres
Dawson Place
Ossington St
St Petersburgh Mews
St Petersburgh Place
Orme Lane
Orme Ct
Caroline Pl
Place
Lancaster Gate

Kensington Park Gdns
Pembridge Mews
Pembridge Square
Victoria Gdn Mews
Palace Court
Bark Place
Royal China
Queensway
Mandarin Kitchen

Kensington Park Road
Pembridge Gdns
Clanricarde Gdns
Linden Gardens
BAYSWATER ROAD

7

Ladbroke Square
PEMBRIDGE RD
Twelfth House
Nyonya
Manzara
Notting Hill Gate
Notting Hill Café & Bar
The Ark

NOTTING HILL
Ladbroke Road
Bulmer Place
Feng Sushi GATE
Greek Affair
Geales
Kensington Mall
Kensington Place
Palace Gardens Mews
KENSINGTON GARDENS

Ladbroke Walk
Uxbridge St
Jameson St
Hillgate St
Costas Fish Restaurant
Kensington Place
The Broad Walk
Round Pond

Campden Hill Gardens
Hillsleigh Rd
Hillgate Place
Edge St
Clarke's
PALACE GARDENS TERRACE
Kensington Palace Gardens

Aubrey Road
Peel Street
Campden Street
Churchill Thai Kitchen
Brunswick Gdns
Kensington Palace
The Orangery

Aubrey Walk
Camden Hill Road
Bedford Gardens
CHURCH STREET
Palace Avenue

See Map 19
Sheffield Terrace
Tor Gdns
Gloucester Walk
Vicarage Gate

8

Holland Walk
Campden Grove
Gardens

Holland House
Youth Hostel
Sheldrake Place
Pitt Street
Gordon Place
Dukes La
York House Place
KENSINGTON

Open Air Theatre
Duchess of Bedford's Walk
Town Hall
Hornton Street
Holland Street
Maggie Jones's
The Tenth
0 · 400 m
0 · 400 yds
© Copyright Time Out Group 2006

Holland Park
Upper Phillimore Gardens
The Terrace
Drayton Mews
Feng Sushi
Old Court Place
KENSINGTON ROAD
KENSINGTON GORE

Phillimore Gardens
Argyll Road
Phillimore Place
Campden Hill Road
Hornton Walk
Derby St
Young St
Utsav
Cuba · Zaika
Kensington Ct
De Vere Gdns
PALACE GATE
Brunello

9

Phillimore Walk
Babylon
Kensington Square
Kensington Gate
Jakob's
Pasha
Hyde Park Gate

Commonwealth Experience
Sticky Fingers
Linley Sambourne House
High St Kensington
Canning Place
Queen's Gate Mews

Melbury Rd
Melbury Ct
Papaya Tree
KENSINGTON HIGH STREET
Stafford Terr
Phillimore Walk
Adam & Eve Mews
Allen St
Whits
Iverna Gdns
Wrights Lane
St Albans Grove
Wodka
Victoria Grove
Launceston Place
Ansdell St
Douro St
Victoria Road
South End Row

See Map 13
See Map 1

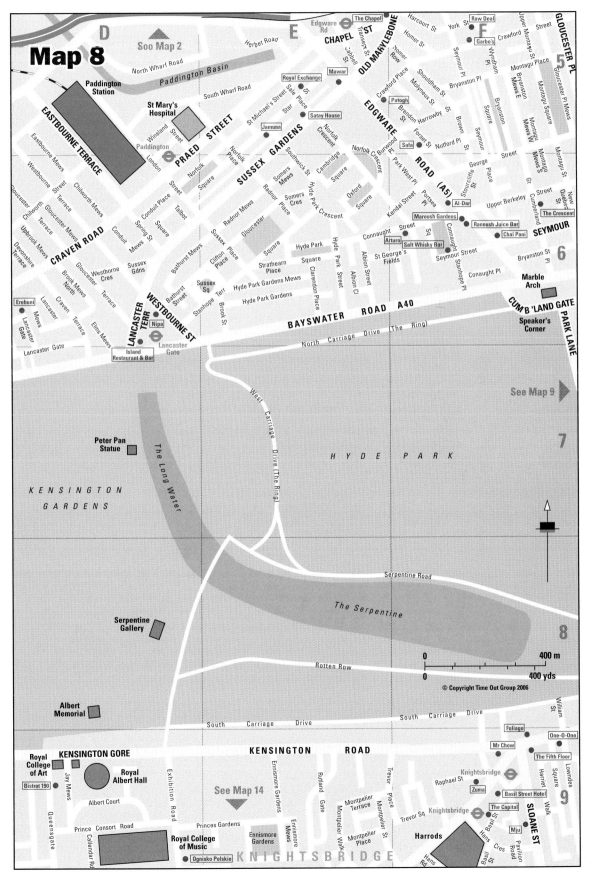

Map 8

D · **E** · **F**

Soo Map 2

North Wharf Road

Herbet Road

Paddington Basin

South Wharf Road

Paddington Station

St Mary's Hospital

EASTBOURNE TERRACE

PRAED STREET

Winsland Street

Paddington

London Street

The Chapel

Edgware Rd

CHAPEL ST

Transen St

Jabbell St

CHAPEL ST

OLD MARYLEBONE

Harcourt St

Homer St

York St

Raw Deal

Garbo's

Crawford Street

Upper Montagu St

GLOUCESTER PL

Somer Row

Seymour St

Wyndham Pl

Montagu Pl

Gloucester Pl Mews

5

Royal Exchange

Mawar

St Michael's Street

Sale Place

Star St

EDGWARE

Crawford Place

Shouldham St

Molyneux St

Bryanston Pl

Montagu Mews E

Montagu Square

Montagu St

Satay House

Patogh

Brendon St

Harrowby St

Brown St

Seymour

Bryanston Square

Montagu Mews W

Jamuna

Norfolk Crescent

Burwood Pl

Safa

Forset St

Nutford Pl

Montagu Mews S

SUSSEX GARDENS

Norfolk Place

Southwick St

Cambridge Square

Norfolk Crescent

ROAD (A5)

Park West Pl

George Street

Great Cumberland St

New Quebec St

Conduit Place

Talbot Square

Norfolk Square

Somers Mews

Radnor Place

Hyde Park Crescent

Oxford Square

Kendal Street

Portsea Pl

Al-Dar

Stourcliffe St

Upper Berkeley St

The Crescent

CRAVEN ROAD

Eastbourne Mews

Westbourne Street

Chilworth Mews

Spring St

Conduit Mews

Sussex Place

Gloucester Square

Hyde Park Square

Maroush Gardens

Ranoush Juice Bar

Chai Pani

SEYMOUR

Chilworth Terrace

Gloucester Mews

Sussex Mews

Clifton Place

Connaught Street

Arturo

Salt Whisky Bar

Connaught Sq

6

Upbrook Mews

Devonshire Terrace

Westborne Cres

Gloucester Terrace

Bathurst Mews

Strathearn Place

Hyde Park Street

St George's Fields

Seymour Street

Stanhope Pl

Conaught Pl

Bryanston St

Brook Mews North

Bathurst Street

Clarendon Place

Hyde Park Gardens Mews

Albion Street

Albion Cl

Marble Arch

Craven Terrace

Lancaster Mews

Sussex Sq

Stanhope Terr

Hyde Park Gardens

Brook St

CUM B 'LAND GATE

Erebuni

Lancaster Gate

Elms Mews

WESTBOURNE ST

LANCASTER TERR

Nipa

Lancaster Gate

BAYSWATER ROAD A40

North Carriage Drive (The Ring)

Speaker's Corner

PARK LANE

Island Restaurant & Bar

West Carriage Drive (The Ring)

See Map 9

7

Peter Pan Statue

The Long Water

HYDE PARK

KENSINGTON GARDENS

Serpentine Road

The Serpentine

Serpentine Gallery

8

Rotten Row

0   400 m
0   400 yds

© Copyright Time Out Group 2006

Albert Memorial

South   Carriage   Drive

South   Carriage   Drive

William St

Foliage

One-O-One

Royal College of Art

KENSINGTON GORE

Jay Mews

Bistrot 190

Royal Albert Hall

Albert Court

KENSINGTON   ROAD

Exhibition Road

See Map 14

Ennismore Gardens

Rutland Gate

Trevor Place

Mr Chow

The Fifth Floor

Knightsbridge

Raphael St

Zuma

Basil Street Hotel

Harriet Walk

Lowndes Square

9

Queensgate

Prince Consort Road

Calendar Rd

Royal College of Music

Ognisko Polskie

Princes Gardens

Ennismore Gardens

Ennismore Mews

Montpelier Terrace

Montpelier Walk

Montpelier St

Montpelier Place

Trevor Sq

Knightsbridge

Harrods

Hans Rd

Basil St

Hans Cres

The Capital

Mju

SLOANE ST

Pavilion Road

K N I G H T S B R I D G E

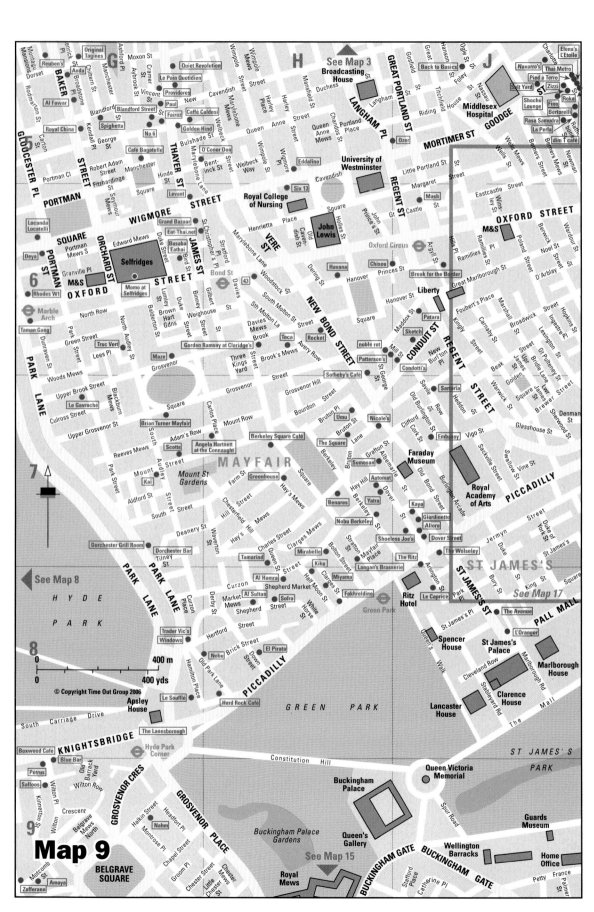

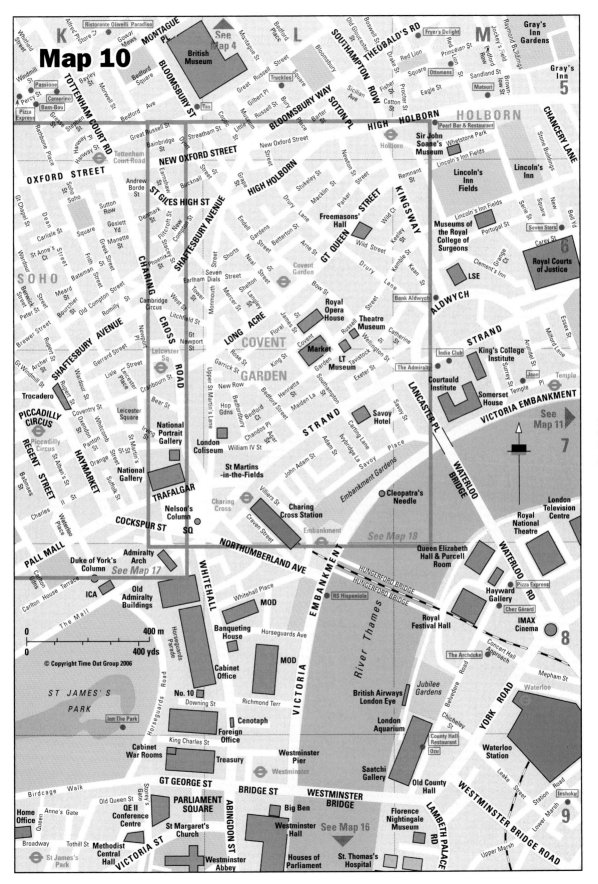

Map 10

MAPS

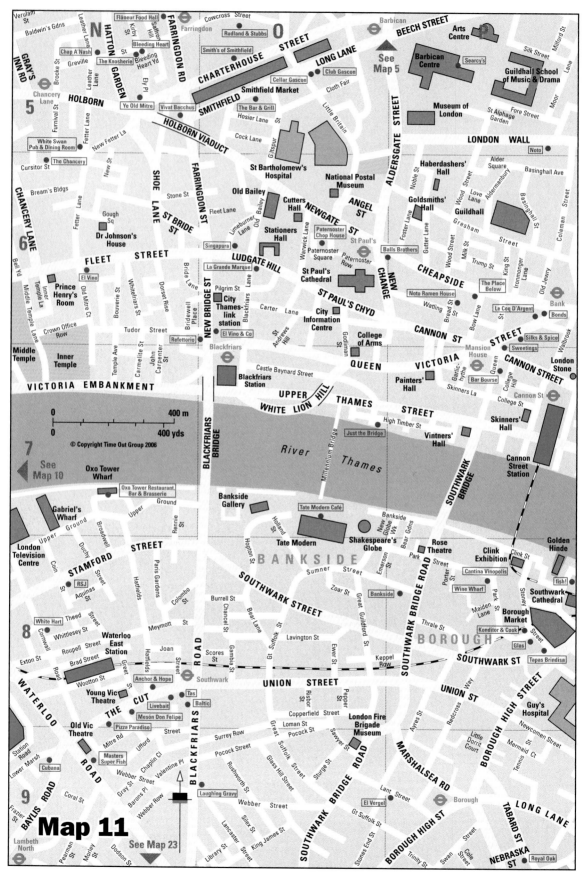

MAPS

Map 11

See Map 23

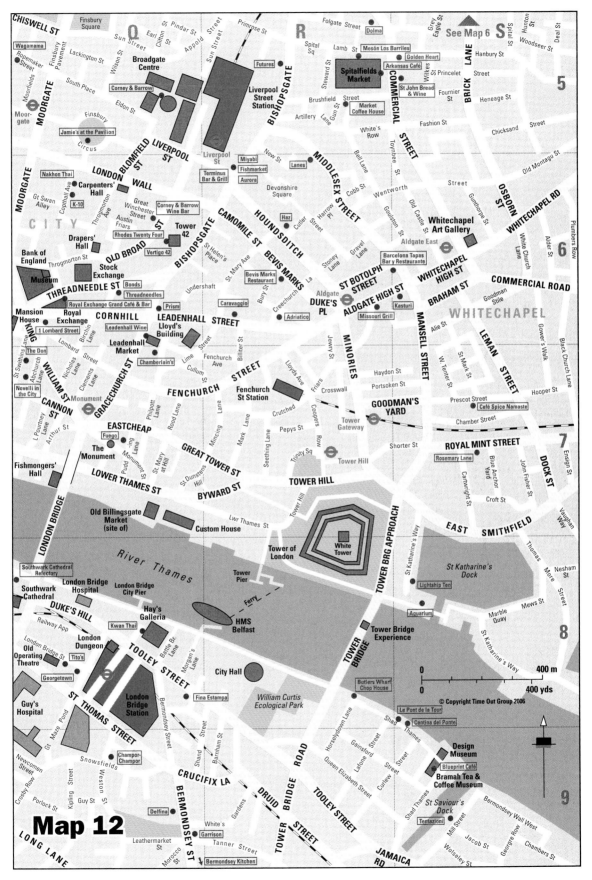

Map 12

MAPS

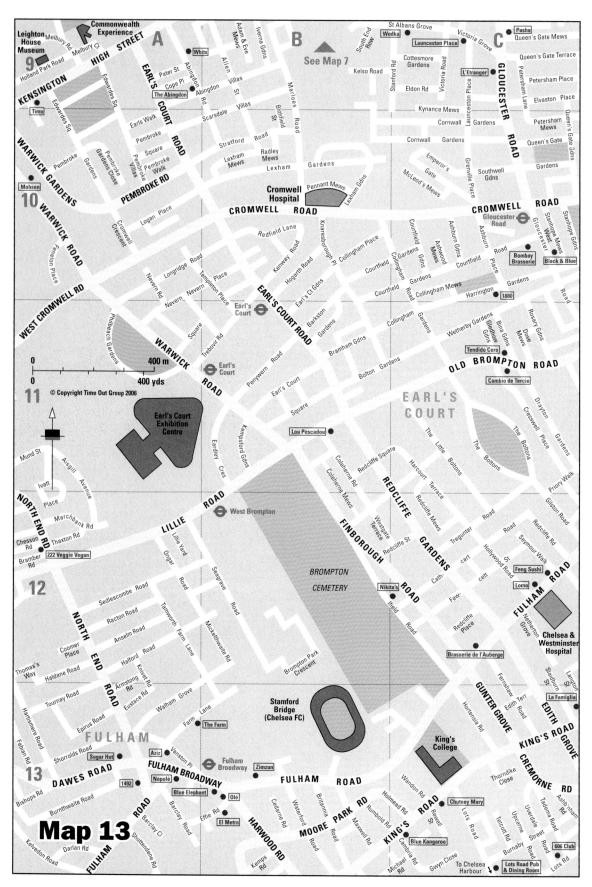

MAPS

Leighton House Museum

Commonwealth Experience

Melbury Rd Melbury Ct

A

Adam & Eve Mews

Iverna Gdns

St Albans Grove

South End Row

Wodka

B

See Map 7

Victoria Grove

Pasha

Queen's Gate Mews

C

Launceston Place

Queen's Gate Terrace

KENSINGTON HIGH STREET

Holland Park Road

Whits

Pater St

Cope Pl

The Abingdon

EARL'S COURT ROAD

Abingdon Rd

Allen St

Abingdon Villas

Scarsdale

Earls Walk

Pembroke Square

Pembroke Gardens

Pembroke Gardens Close

Pembroke Villas

Pembroke Walk

PEMBROKE RD

Stratford Road

Lexham Mews

Radley Mews

Lexham Gardens

Kelso Road

Stanford Rd

Cottesmore Gardens

Eldon Rd

Kynance Mews

Cornwall

Cornwall Gardens

L'Etranger

GLOUCESTER ROAD

Launceston Place

Petersham Lane

Petersham Place

Elvaston Place

Petersham Mews

Queen's Gate Gdns

Emperor's Gate

McLeod's Mews

Grenville Place

Southwell Gdns

Queen's Gate

Gardens

Timo

WARWICK GARDENS

Mohsen

10

WARWICK ROAD

WEST CROMWELL RD

Fenelon Place

Edwardes Sq

Edwardes Sq

Cromwell Crescent

Logan Place

Cromwell Hospital

Pennant Mews

Lexham Gdns

CROMWELL ROAD

CROMWELL ROAD

Gloucester Road

Courtfield Gardens

Ashworth Mews

Ashburn Gdns

Ashburn Place

Courtfield Road

Bombay Brasserie

Stanhope Mews West

Stanhope Gdns

Gloucester Road

Black & Blue

Redfield Lane

Longridge Road

Nevern Rd

Templeton Place

Kenway Road

Hogarth Road

Knaresborough Pl

Collingham Place

Courtfield Gdns

Collingham Road

Collingham Gardens

Courtfield

Gardens

Collingham Mews

Harrington

1880

Rosary Gdns

Rosary Gardens

Road

Nevern Place

Earl's Ct Gdns

Barkston Gardens

Bramham Gdns

Collingham

Gardens

Wetherby Gardens

Bina Gdns

Gledhow Gdns

Dove Mews

WARWICK ROAD

Nevern Square

Earl's Court

Trebovir Rd

Bolton Gardens

Tendido Cero

OLD BROMPTON ROAD

Earl's Court Road

Earl's Court

Earl's Court Square

Penywern Road

Cambio de Tercio

11

0   400 m

0   400 yds

© Copyright Time Out Group 2006

Earl's Court Exhibition Centre

Kempsford Gdns

Eardley Cres

Lou Pescadou

Coleherne Rd

Coleherne Mews

Redcliffe Square

The Little Boltons

The Boltons

EARL'S COURT

Drayton Gardens

Cresswell Place

Priory Walk

Gilston Road

Mund St

Aisgill Avenue

Ivatt Place

Marchbank Rd

Thaxton Rd

LILLIE ROAD

Lillie Yard

West Brompton

Westgate Terrace

Harcourt Terrace

Redcliffe Mews

REDCLIFFE GARDENS

Redcliffe St

Tregunter Road

Redcliffe Road

Seymour Walk

Hollywood Rd

FULHAM ROAD

Chesson Rd

Bramber Rd

NORTH END RD

222 Veggie Vegan

Ongar Road

Seagrave Road

FINBOROUGH ROAD

Redcliffe St

Cath-

cart

cett

Faw-

Feng Sushi

Lomo

12

Sedlescombe Road

Racton Road

Anselm Road

BROMPTON CEMETERY

Ifield Road

Nikita's

Redcliffe Place

Fernshaw

Stadburn St

FULHAM ROAD

NORTH END ROAD

Tamworth

Coomer Place

Halford Road

Micklethwaite Rd

Knivet Rd

Brasserie de l'Auberge

Chelsea & Westminster Hospital

Langton St

Thomas's Way

Haldane Road

Armstrong Rd

Eustace Rd

Farm Lane

Brompton Park Crescent

Stamford Bridge (Chelsea FC)

GUNTER GROVE

Edith Terr

EDITH GROVE

La Famiglia

Tournay Road

Walham Grove

The Farm

Hortensia Rd

King's College

KING'S ROAD

Epirus Road

Farm Lane

FULHAM

Hartismere Road

Shorrolds Road

Aziz

Vanston Pl

Wandon Rd

Thorndike Close

CREMORNE RD

Fabian Rd

Sugar Hut

Fulham Broadway

Zimzun

FULHAM ROAD

Holmead Rd

Ashburnham Rd

Tadema Road

Uverdale Road

Bishops Rd

13

DAWES ROAD

1492

Napulé

FULHAM BROADWAY

Blue Elephant

Olé

MOORE PARK RD

Britannia Rd

Rumbold Rd

Chutney Mary

Rewell St

Lots Road

Uverdale

Teicott Rd

Burnaby Street

606 Club

Burnthwaite Road

FULHAM ROAD

Barclay Cl

Barclay Road

Effie Rd

El Metro

HARWOOD RD

Cedarne Rd

Waterford Rd

Maxwell Rd

KING'S ROAD

Cambria St

Blue Kangaroo

Kelvedon Road

Darlan Rd

Shottendane Rd

Kemps Rd

Michael Rd

Gwyn Close

To Chelsea Harbour

Lots Road Pub & Dining Room

Lots Rd

Map 13

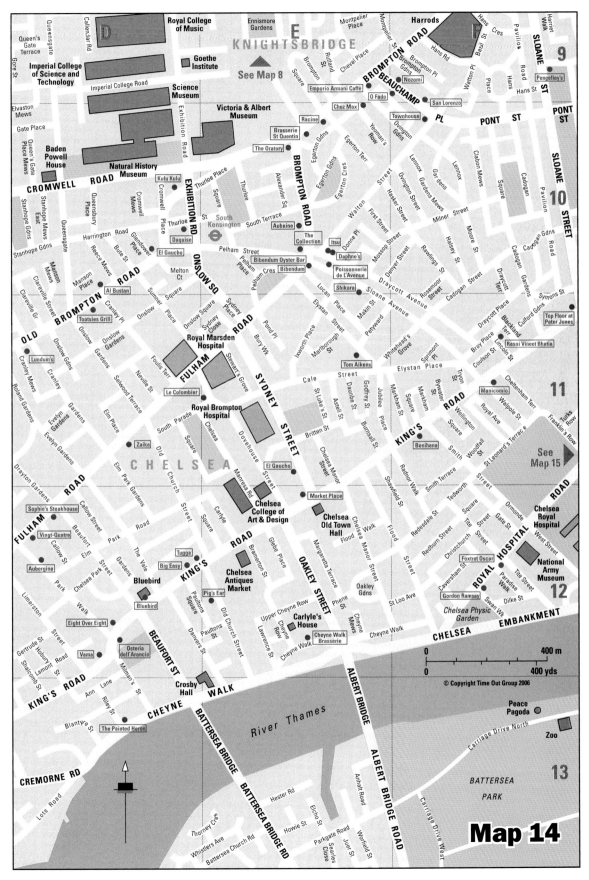

Map 14

MAPS

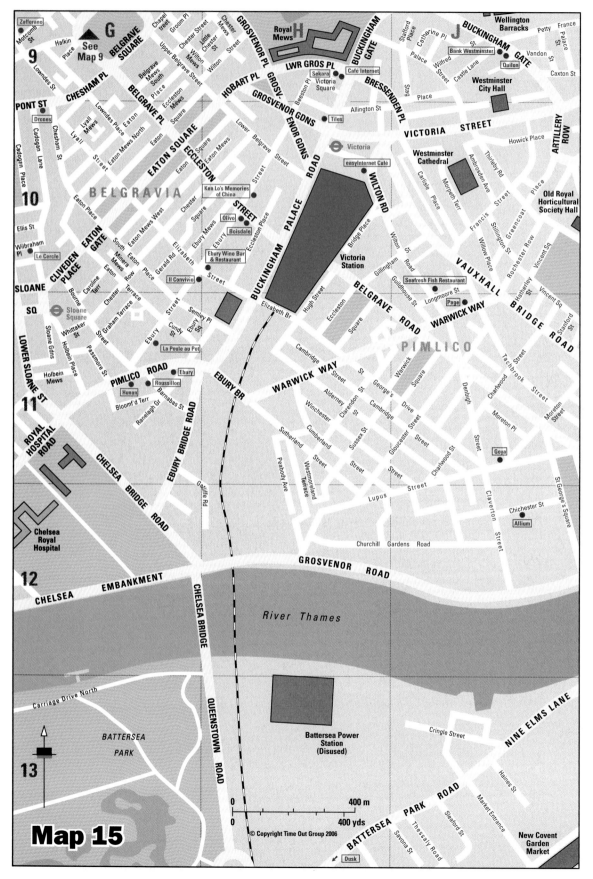

Map 15

MAPS

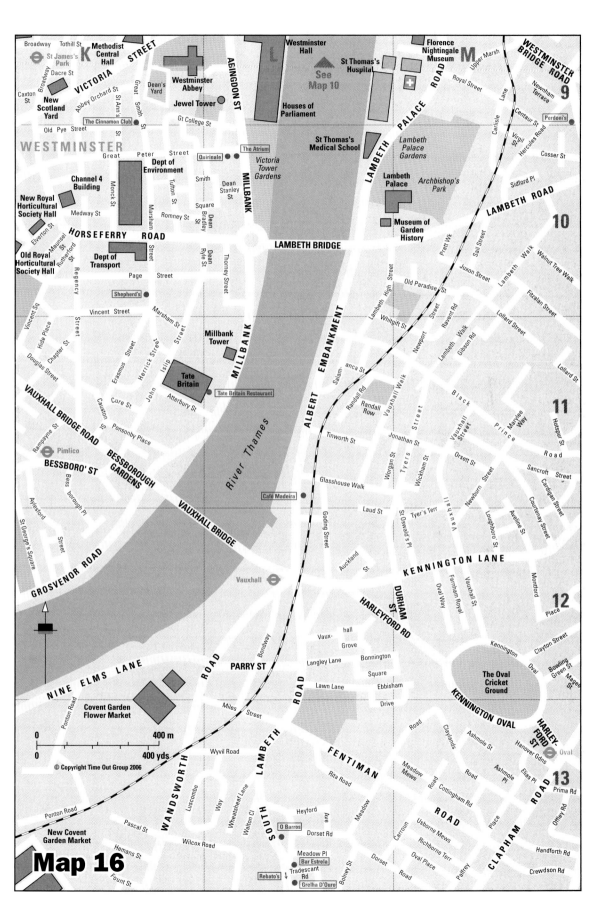

Map 16

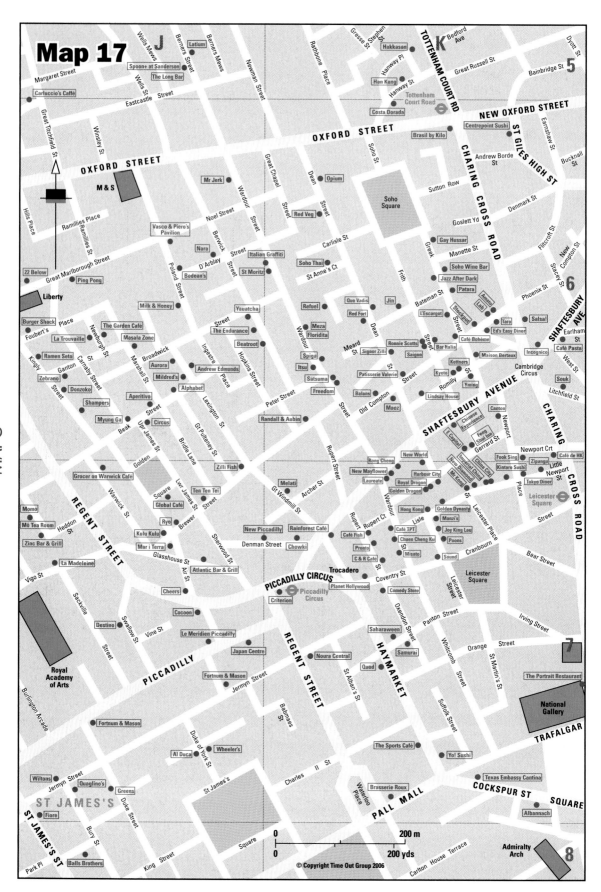

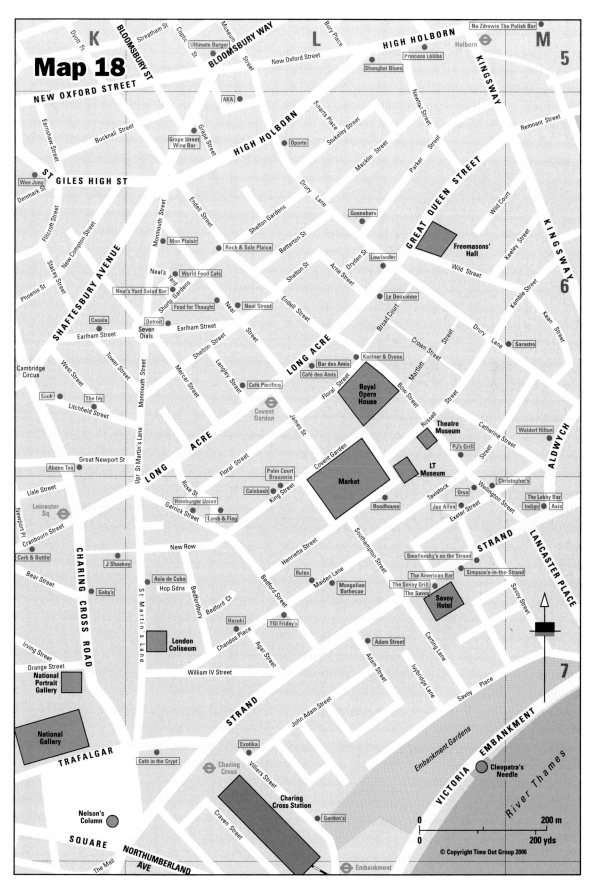

Map 18

CUT WITH LEMONGRASS AND GINGER.
GORDON'S® DISTILLER'S CUT.®

Gordon's
THE COLOURFUL GIN

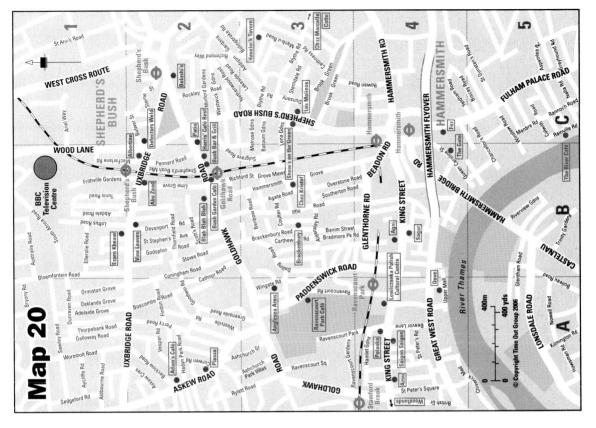

Map 20

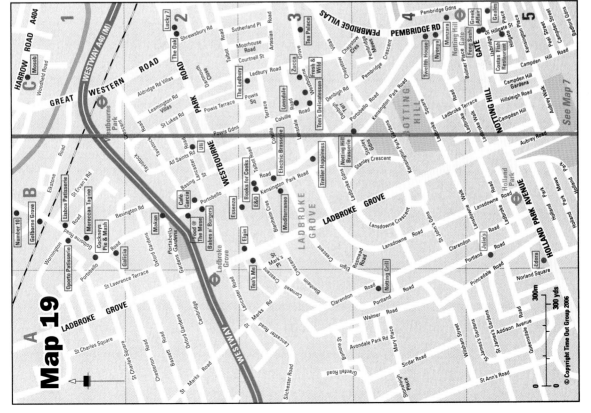

Map 19

MAPS

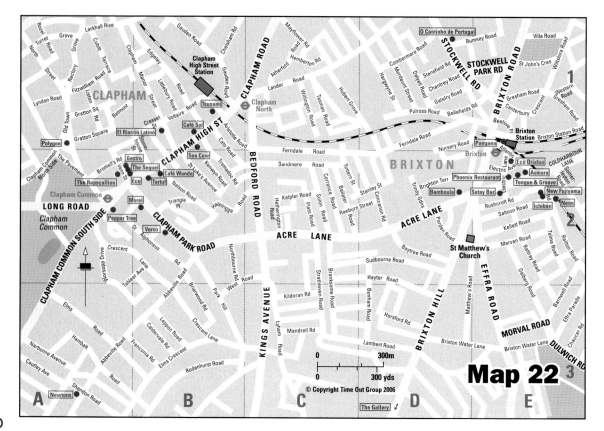

Map 22

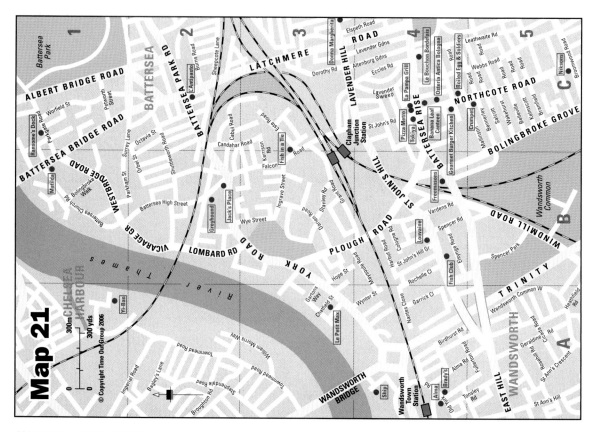

Map 21

MAPS

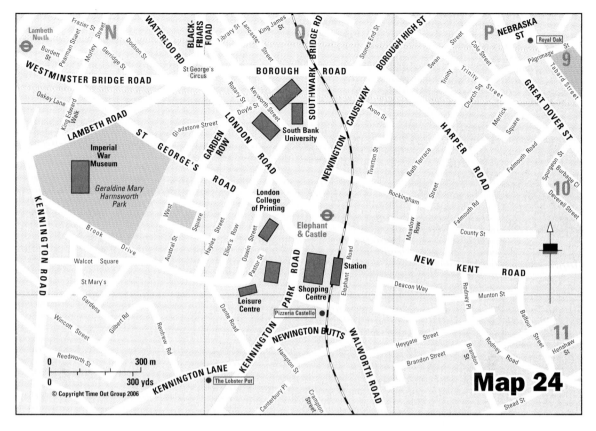

Map 24

N

Lambeth North

WATERLOO RD

BLACK-FRIARS ROAD

SOUTHWARK BRIDGE RD

BOROUGH HIGH ST

NEBRASKA ST

P

Royal Oak

Frazier St
Burdett St
Pearman Street
Morley St
Gerridge St
Dodson St

St George's Circus

Library St
Lancaster St
King James St

Stones End St

Swan
Street

Street

Cole Street

Pilgrimage

Tabard Street

9

WESTMINSTER BRIDGE ROAD

BOROUGH ROAD

Trinity

Trinity
Street

Church Sq

GREAT DOVER ST

Oakey Lane

King Edward Walk

LAMBETH ROAD

Gladstone Street

LONDON ROAD

Keyworth Street
Rotary St
Doyle St

South Bank University

NEWINGTON CAUSEWAY

Avon St

Bath Terrace

HARPER ROAD

Merrick
Square

Falmouth Road

Spurgeon St
Burbage Cl

Deverell Street

10

Imperial War Museum

ST GEORGE'S ROAD

GARDEN ROW

Tiverton St

Rockingham
Street

Falmouth Rd

KENNINGTON ROAD

Geraldine Mary Harmsworth Park

West

London College of Printing

Meadow
Row

County St

Brook
Drive

Walcot Square

St Mary's

Austral St

Hayles Street

Elliot's Row

Oswin

PARK ROAD

Elephant & Castle

Station

NEW KENT ROAD

Deacon Way

Rodney Pl

Munton St

Balfour Street

11

Square

Pastor St

Shopping Centre

Elephant Road

Gardens

Gilbert Rd

Renfrew Rd

Dante Road

Leisure Centre

Pizzeria Castello

Heygate Street

Brandon Street

Rodney Road

Henshaw St

Wincott Street

Reedworth St

KENNINGTON LANE

KENNINGTON

NEWINGTON BUTTS

Hampton St

WALWORTH ROAD

Crampton Street

Brandon St

Stead St

0   300 m
0   300 yds

© Copyright Time Out Group 2006

The Lobster Pot

Canterbury Pl

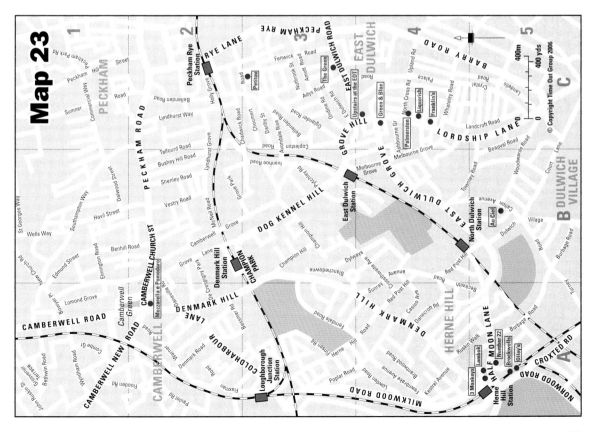

Map 23

1

PECKHAM

Peckham Park Rd
Peckham Hill
Street

Sumner
Road

Commercial Way

2

RYE LANE

PECKHAM ROAD

Peckham Rye Station

Holly Grove

Ballenden Road

Lyndhurst Way

Talfourd Road

Bushey Hill Road

Shenley Road

Vestry Road

3

PECKHAM RYE

Fenwick
Road

Nunhead
St

Adys Road

Petrou

Danby St

Chadwick Road

Choumert
Road

Copleston Rd

Bellenden Road

Avondale Rise

Ivanhoe Road

EAST DULWICH ROAD

4

EAST DULWICH

The Green

Upstairs at the EDT

Green & Blue

North Cross Rd

Palmerston

Liquorish

Franklin's

Whateley Road

Melbourne Grove

LORDSHIP LANE

BARRY ROAD

Crystal
Road

Landells

Upland Rd
Palace

Beauval Road

Woodwarde Road

Landcroft Road

5

Court
Lane

DULWICH VILLAGE

0   400m
0   400 yds

© Copyright Time Out Group 2006

C

St Georges Way

Wells Way

Southampton Way

Havil Street

Benhill Road

CAMBERWELL CHURCH ST

DENMARK HILL

Denmark Hill Station

Champion Park

CHAMPION PARK

Grove

DOG KENNEL HILL

Melbourne Grove

East Dulwich Station

EAST DULWICH GROVE

Townley Road

Calton Avenue

North Dulwich Station

Au Ciel

Dulwich
Village

Burbage Road

B

New Church Rd

Dawood Street

Edmund Street

Elmington Road

Camberwell
Grove

McNeil Road

Grove Park

Grove
Lane

Camberwell

Denmark Hill

Champion Hill

Champion Hill

Dylways
Sunray Ave

Red Post Hill

Red Post Hill

Dulwich

Red Post Hill

Road

DENMARK HILL

Beckwith
Road

HERNE HILL

Court

CAMBERWELL ROAD

CAMBERWELL

Jackson Rd

Lomond Grove

Camberwell Green

Warner
Road

Mozzarella e Pomodoro

CAMBERWELL NEW ROAD

DENMARK ROAD

COLDHARBOUR LANE

De Crespigny Park

Bessemer Rd

Flaxman Road

Blanchedowne

Casino Ave

Dalecroft Rd

Crosswaite Ave

Ferndale Road

Herne

Hill
Road

Finsen Rd

Brantwood Road

Ruskin Walk

Lombok

Number 22

Brockwells

Olley's

HALF MOON LANE

A

John Ruskin St

Grosvenor Terrace

Wyndham Road

Bethwin Road

Fleeden St

Combe Gr

Grove

Paulet Rd

Pauler Rd

Loughborough Junction Station

MILKWOOD ROAD

Lowden Road

Fawnbrake Avenue

Poplar Road

Kestral Avenue

3 Monkeys

Herne Hill Station

NORWOOD ROAD

CROXTED RD

TIME OUT | EATING & DRINKING 381

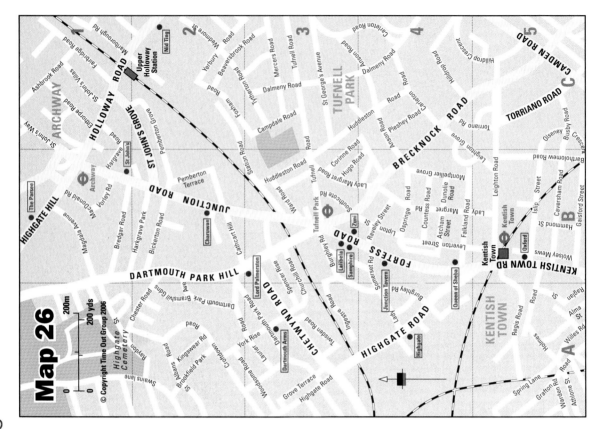

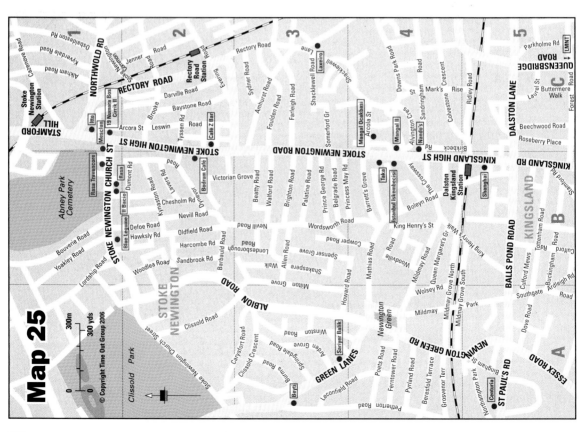

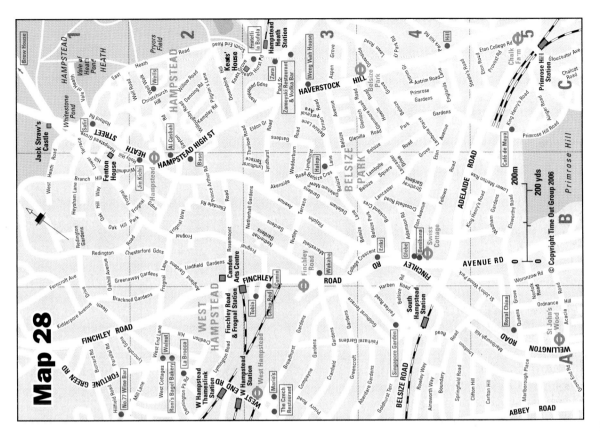

Map 28

Brew House

HAMPSTEAD HEATH

Whitestone Pond

Jack Straw's Castle

Fenton House

Vale of Health Pond

Pryors Field

Wells

Al Casbah

Base

Jin Kichi

HAMPSTEAD HIGH ST

HEATH STREET

Fratelli la Bufala

Keats' House

Hampstead Heath Station

Zara

Weng Wah House

HAVERSTOCK HILL

Safir

BELSIZE PARK

Haidepi

Eriki

Benihana

Café de Maya

Primrose Hill

ADELAIDE ROAD

AVENUE RD

Swiss Cottage

FINCHLEY ROAD

Camden Arts Centre

Finchley Road & Frognal Station

FINCHLEY

Cumin

Cafe Red

Tobia

FINCHLEY ROAD

WEST HAMPSTEAD

Wakaba

Globe

South Hampstead Station

Singapore Garden

BELSIZE ROAD

Royal China

St John's Wood

WELLINGTON ROAD

FORTUNE GREEN RD

No.77 Wine Bar

Walnut

La Brocca

Roni's Bagel Bakery

W Hampstead Thameslink Station

W Hampstead Station

WEST END RD

Mario's

The Czech Restaurant

ABBEY ROAD

© Copyright Time Out Group 2006

200m

200 yds

MAPS

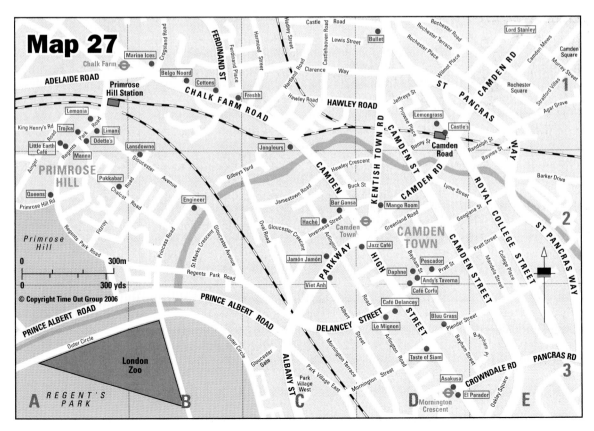

Map 27

Marine Ices

Chalk Farm

ADELAIDE ROAD

Primrose Hill Station

Belgo Noord

Cottons

Freshh

FERDINAND ST

CHALK FARM ROAD

Bullet

Lord Stanley

CAMDEN RD

ST PANCRAS

Lemonia

Trojka

Little Earth Café

Manna

Limani

Odette's

Lansdowne

Pukkabar

Engineer

Jongleurs

HAWLEY ROAD

KENTISH TOWN RD

CAMDEN ST

Lemongrass

Castle's

Camden Road

CAMDEN RD

ROYAL COLLEGE STREET

ST PANCRAS WAY

King Henry's Rd

PRIMROSE HILL

Airgrid

Queens

Primrose Hill Rd

Primrose Hill

CAMDEN

Bar Gansa

Mango Room

Haché

Camden Town

Jazz Café

Jamón Jamón

PARKWAY

Viet Anh

CAMDEN TOWN

CAMDEN STREET

HIGH STREET

Pescador

Daphne

Andy's Taverna

Café Corfu

Café Delancey

Bluu Grass

Le Mignon

Taste of Siam

Asakusa

El Parador

DELANCEY STREET

ALBANY ST

PRINCE ALBERT ROAD

CROWNDALE RD

PANCRAS RD

Mornington Crescent

London Zoo

REGENT'S PARK

Primrose Hill

0 300m
0 300 yds

© Copyright Time Out Group 2006

MAPS

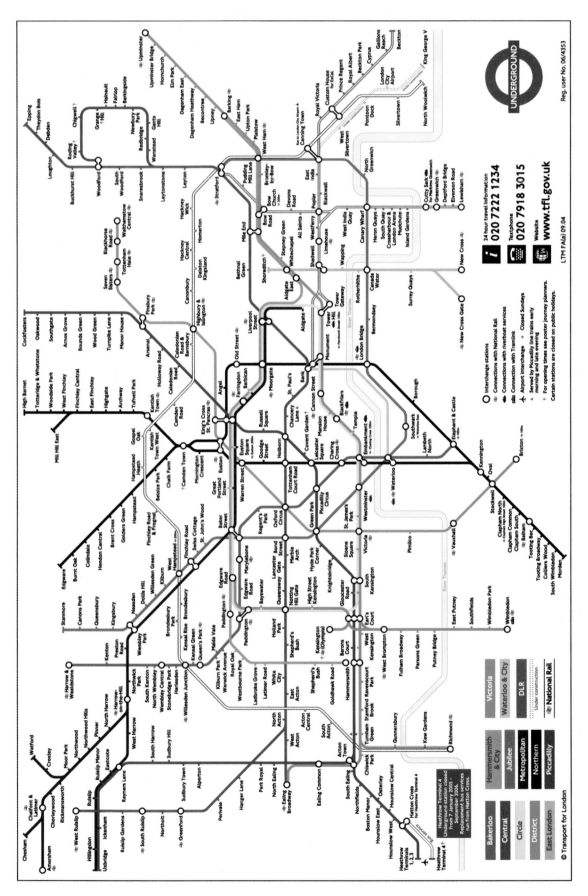

Street Index

Grid references not allocated to a specific map can be found on Maps 1-18, which are contiguous and cover central London. Maps 19-28 cover individual outlying areas. The areas covered by all the maps are shown on p359.

INDEX

INDEX

INDEX

Advertisers' Index

Please refer to relevant sections for addresses/telephone numbers

INDEX

Subject Index

INDEX

INDEX

Shops Index

INDEX

INDEX

Restaurant Area Index

INDEX

INDEX

INDEX

INDEX

INDEX

INDEX

INDEX

INDEX

Restaurants A-Z Index

INDEX

INDEX